D. McKee

W9-AJU-255

Cover, frontispiece (details), and title page: The Ebstorf world map, c. 1235, is probably the work of Gervase of Tilbury. Representing the medieval world view, the map shows Jerusalem at the center and is drawn on a background of the crucified Christ, with the head at the top (east), the feet at the bottom (west), and the arms pointing north and south. Preserved by Benedictine monks, who used it as an altar stone, the map was destroyed in World War II.

T. WALTER WALLBANK
Emeritus Professor of History, University of Southern California

ALASTAIR M. TAYLOR
Professor of Political Studies and Geography, Queen's University

NELS M. BAILKEY
Professor of History, Tulane University

MARK MANCALL
Associate Professor of History, Stanford University

Critical Readers
Michael Altschul, Case Western Reserve University
George M. Beckmann, Claremont Graduate School
John A. Brinkman, Oriental Institute, University of Chicago
Ainslie T. Embree, Columbia University
W. Creighton Gabel, Boston University
Martin J. Havran, University of Virginia
Tom B. Jones, University of Minnesota
Walter Emil Kaegi, Jr., University of Chicago
Archibald R. Lewis, University of Texas
Martin Deming Lewis, Sir George Williams University
Lauro Martines, University of California, Los Angeles
Duane H. D. Roller, University of Oklahoma
Franz Schulze, Lake Forest College
William R. Trimble, Loyola University, Chicago
Carl H. Trubschenck, Jr., Sacramento City College
G. E. von Grunebaum, University of California, Los Angeles
Gordon R. Willey, Harvard University

SCOTT, FORESMAN AND COMPANY

Civilization
past & present

VOLUME ONE SIXTH EDITION

Library of Congress Catalog Card No. 69-11738
Copyright © 1960, 1965, 1969 by Scott, Foresman and Company, Glenview, Illinois 60025
All rights reserved. Printed in the United States of America.
Regional offices of Scott, Foresman and Company are located in
Atlanta, Dallas, Glenview, Palo Alto, and Oakland, N.J.

Preface

For several thousand years men have passed down to posterity oral traditions and written records describing their own time and place. For the most part the place was where the scribe or historian lived; there was little concern about "the strange people" beyond the borders. In early modern times man's horizon began to expand, and a new genre of history was born. One of its first products was Voltaire's *Essay on the Manners and Spirit of Nations* (1769), called the first modern universal history. This innovation of the eighteenth century's Enlightenment gained few devotees, however. Following the French Revolution the mode of Clio was national history. The activities of mankind were written as a study of disparate and, unfortunately, often antagonistic parts.

The impact of World War I, however, encouraged a faint revival of universal history, as witness the appearance in 1919 of the well-known *Outline of History* by H. G. Wells. In 1926 the pioneer work, *A Short History of Civilization*, written by the late American historian Lynn Thorndike was published. Commenting on the lack of any text presenting "the main thread of the story of civilization," the author observed: "For college students who are preparing to enter, let us say, the medical profession, or to specialize in the natural or mathematical sciences, and any others who hardly have the time to pursue more than one course in history, a course in the history of civilization seems most fitting."[1]

This viewpoint became increasingly pertinent in the mid-1930's as the affairs of distinct peoples became caught up in the general affairs of mankind. The result was the publication in 1942 of the two-volume *Civilization: Past and Present,* the first text of its kind. Its objective was to present a survey of global cultural history treating the story of man not as a unique European experience but as a global one through which all the great culture systems have interacted to produce the present-day world.

Over the span of just more than a quarter of a century of revising *Civilization: Past and Present,* using it in the classroom, and benefiting from comments obtained from its many users, the authors from time to time have reviewed the text's objectives and modified its organization. In the main, however, the purposes of *Civilization,* as envisaged in the first edition, would seem to have even more relevance in this sixth edition. As Geoffrey Barraclough observed a little more than a decade ago, "an interpretation which surveys the background to the present almost exclusively from the point of view of western Europe has little relevance to our current problems."[2]

The increasingly interrelated and compressed affairs of mankind point up markedly the invalidity of any segmented approach in a general history survey course. A knowledge of western civilization is a rich and essential foundation for all college students, but this alone is no longer adequate. It is appropriate to note that some demographers estimate that within thirty years the population of Europe may be only 10 per cent of the world's total. Some historians, exaggeratedly, speak of the "end of European history." Perhaps the most significant happening in our times, and most disturbing to the European-centered position, is the emergence of the world's nonwestern peoples. They are going to be heard, they will play an increasing role in world affairs, and they must be understood.

In seeking to provide the general student with a broad survey of world civilization, the most obvious problem is how to mesh European and Afro-Asian history within a reasonable compass. The authors of this sixth edition believe it has been possible to present a meaningful continuum of universal history, related to significant seg-

[1]Lynn Thorndike, *A Short History of Civilization* (New York: F. S. Crofts Company, 1933), p. v.
[2]Geoffrey Barraclough, *History in a Changing World* (Oxford: Basil Blackwell & Mott, Ltd., 1957), p. 1.

ments of Afro-Asian tradition, but whose central core still continues to be western civilization.

By covering the full global story, *Civilization Past and Present* permits each instructor to follow his own desires and beliefs about how the course should be presented. The text has been structured for maximum flexibility: the nonwestern sections of the book, as well as many of the chapters on cultural history, are so placed that they can be covered in whole or in part, assigned as outside reading, or excluded without detracting from the western or political narrative. Thus the instructor can make several choices in emphasis, depending on the needs and backgrounds of his students, the time available, and his own special interests.

While the sixth edition is basically the same as its predecessor in organization and general approach, much of the book has been rewritten for greater clarity and for relevance to the latest scholarship. Historical minutiae have been reduced and more emphasis given to broad trends and interpretations. In keeping with this text's dual objective of describing the development of both western and nonwestern civilizations, the treatment of the latter, particularly Asia and Africa, has been revised and expanded. New material has been added on China, India, Japan, Africa, and pre-Columbian America. A noteworthy addition is a section on Southeast Asia presenting the historical antecedents of the present impasse in Vietnam. Technology and science, increasingly important in the twentieth century, are given expanded attention as significant factors in the history of civilization.

More specifically, turning to Volume I, the treatment of Hebrew history and religion has been recast and expanded. Much of the material on the ancient Near East and on Greece has been revised. Chapter 8, dealing with Byzantine and early Russian history, has been reshaped. Substantial segments of medieval political and economic history have been rewritten. The material on the Renaissance has been revised, and the last chapter in the fifth edition ("New Dimensions of the Mind") has been shifted back to Part V. This restructuring places all the scientific, artistic, and intellectual history of early modern Europe together. The concluding Part VI then deals exclusively with non-European civilizations and the impact of an expansive West. The format of the book has been completely redesigned. All the maps within the text have been completely redrawn in two colors; all the four-color maps in the reference sections are original; and many maps appear in relief. Color plates are mainly new and are more numerous; there are four additional pages in Volume I and eight in Volume II.

More than half of the black and white illustrations are new, and there are numerous one- and two-page picture spreads. The bibliographies have been updated, and the chronological charts have been shifted to the end of the book for more convenient reference. The Frontier Essays are replaced by a new series called Historical Critiques (twelve in all), each by a noted scholar. These brief essays provide an extra dimension of interpretation.

A distinguished group of historians have given invaluable advice in this revision; and whatever merit the text may have is due in no small measure to their painstaking cooperation and invaluable suggestions. Professor Carl H. Trubschenck, Jr., of Sacramento City College read the entire manuscript. Professor Ainslie T. Embree of Columbia University provided the scholarly expertise on all the material dealing with India; Professor George M. Beckmann of the Claremont Graduate School checked all the material on China and Japan; and Professor Martin Deming Lewis of Sir George Williams University read all the Asian material. Professor W. Creighton Gabel of Boston University commented on Chapter 1 and the African material in Chapter 19, while Professor Gordon R. Willey of Harvard University examined the discussion of pre-Columbian America. Chapter 2 was scrutinized by John A. Brinkman of the Oriental Institute, University of Chicago; the history of the West in classical times, Chapters 4, 5, and 7, were evaluated by Professor Tom B. Jones of the University of Minnesota; Professor Walter Emil Kaegi, Jr., of the University of Chicago provided scholarly assistance for Chapter 8; and Professor G. E. von Grunebaum of the University of California, Los Angeles, was consulted on Chapter 9. For medieval and early modern Europe the following scholars provided specialistic assistance: Professor Archibald R. Lewis of the University of Texas for Chapters 11 and 12; Professor Michael Altschul of Case Western Reserve University for 13 and 14; Professor Lauro Martines of the University of California, Los Angeles, for 15 through 18; Professor Duane H. D. Roller of the University of Oklahoma for science in Chapter 18; and Professor William R. Trimble of Loyola University, Chicago, for 20. The authors are under special obligation to Professor Martin J. Havran of the University of Virginia who initially provided a critical review of the previous edition and then perused all the western chapters. Franz Schulze, Professor of Art at Lake Forest College, supervised the full-color illustration program which, with its informative captions, provides a capsule history of world art.

Note to the Student

This book has been developed with the dual purpose of helping you acquire a solid knowledge of past events and, equally important, of helping you think more constructively about the significance of those events for the difficult times in which we live. In the Prologue to this volume you will learn more about studying the meaning of history. This Note is intended to acquaint you with the principal features of the text.

THE INTERCHAPTERS

Aid in the organization and review of your reading will be provided by the interchapters, which outline the material to be covered in each unit.

THE HISTORICAL CRITIQUES

Appearing in each unit is a Historical Critique contributed by a specialist. These brief essays are integrated with the text to provide an extra dimension of interpretation. Each relates to one or more of the following: (1) the philosophy of history; (2) the dynamics of the conceptualizing process, namely, how changing social conditions affect men's outlook toward the historical process; and (3) the methodology of history. The first category of critiques examines the role of the individual vis-à-vis "impersonal" forces; the validity of dividing the temporal continuum into specific periods, such as the "Renaissance"; and whether broad regularities of human behavior can be discerned in widely scattered societies. The second type of critique traces changing attitudes among historians from early to modern times and shows how different civilizations conceptualize the writing of history in terms of their respective culture patterns. The third type brings us up to date on the latest techniques used in gathering and analyzing evidence.

THE COLOR PLATES

Six folios of full-color art reproductions appear with the interchapters. The works of art have been carefully selected and faithfully reproduced to illustrate, in every case, some facet of a culture pattern discussed in the text.

SUGGESTIONS FOR READING

In addition to the general bibliography at the end of each volume, you will find in each unit an annotated bibliography, pertaining especially to that unit and listing special historical studies, biographies, reputable historical fiction, and some collections of source materials. As indicated in the listings, many of these works can be purchased in inexpensive paperbound editions. These bibliographies will provide you with ample readings from which to develop special reports or with which to improve your understanding of a given subject.

THE CHRONOLOGICAL CHARTS

At the end of each volume is a series of six chronological charts which show the sequence of events discussed within the six units of the text. By studying these charts, you can fix in your mind the relationship of events in the various parts of the world.

THE MAPS

Two-color maps are liberally distributed throughout these volumes. Some are designed to make clear the nature of a single distinctive event or idea discussed in the text; others illustrate larger trends, as, for example, the map showing trade and cultural interchange in the ancient world (see p. 166). At the end of each volume are sixteen pages of full-color reference maps, showing all the major areas of the world and virtually every town, political subdivision, and geographic feature mentioned in the text. Most of the reference maps and several of the two-color maps appear in relief.

THE PRONUNCIATION KEY

In the general index to each volume, the correct pronunciation is given for most proper names. Thus you will find it easy, as well as extremely helpful, to look up the correct pronunciation of the names of persons and places referred to in the text.

Contents VOLUME ONE

Prologue

Perspective on Man

If the time span of our planet—now estimated at some five billion years—were telescoped into a single year, the first eight months would be devoid of any life. The next two months would be taken up with plant and very primitive animal forms, and not until well into December would any mammals appear. In this "year" members of *Homo erectus,* the best known species of "near men," would mount the global stage only between 10 and 11 P.M. on December 31. And how has man spent that brief allotment? He has given over almost half of it—the equivalent of at least 500,000 years—to making tools and weapons out of stone. His revolutionary changeover from a food-hunting nomad to a farmer who raised grain and domesticated animals would occur in the last sixty seconds. And into that final minute would be crowded all of his other accomplishments: the use of metal, the creation of civilizations, the mastery of the oceans, the harnessing of steam, then gas, electricity, oil, and, finally, in our own lifetime, atomic energy. Thus, among man's greatest achievements on earth has been his development of tools, machines, and controlled power—in short, technology. Yet even this planet earth no longer satisfies man's technological ambitions, for he has at last succeeded in escaping the age-old bondage to the earth and is about to propel himself into the interplanetary age.

While human technology is at present moving ahead at supersonic speed, there has been no corresponding increase in man's own mental or physical capacity. He probably has no more native intelligence than his Stone Age ancestors —and undoubtedly less muscle! So we come to a fundamental question: how is twentieth-century man to cope with the ever widening disparity between what he *is* and what he *has*? How can he control and utilize his tremendous technological

powers for happiness and not for nuclear self-annihilation? Today he seeks to conquer other planets before he has learned to govern his own.

Surely an indispensable step toward solving contemporary man's dilemma—technology without the requisite control and power without adequate wisdom—must be a better understanding of how man and all his works became what they are today. Only by understanding the past can mankind assess both the perils and the opportunities of the present. This accumulated experience, the memory of the race, is available for study. We call it *history*.

THE USE OF HISTORY

Definition of history. History is the record of the past actions of mankind, based upon surviving evidence. The historian uses this evidence to reach conclusions which he believes are valid. In this way, he becomes an interpreter of the development of mankind. History shows that all patterns and problems in human affairs are the products of a complex process of growth. By throwing light on that process, history provides a means for profiting from human experience. There would be no landmarks, no points of reference, no foundations on which to build if the individual were bereft of the knowledge of his past. The system of government under which he lives, the frontiers of his country, and its economy—such factors are meaningful because of history. In our age of global interdependence and atomic propulsion, the neglect of history would be more than folly—it could prove suicidal.

In this connection it is salutary to recall the words of the philosopher George Santayana when he declared, "Those who cannot remember the past are condemned to repeat it." Actually, history is itself a way of looking at reality, and many cultures, particularly food-collecting societies, which tend to exist on a day-to-day basis, appear to be little aware of their own past, content to live more or less in the present. As economic, social, and political activities grow more complex, however, it becomes necessary to keep records— of the grain sown, or of battles waged over disputed land. A knowledge of the past then becomes indispensable to decisions that are relevant to contemporary needs and future prospects. In such literate societies, where knowledge can be written down and preserved for future use, we find the

birth and development of history and the historical method.

In this edition of *Civilization Past and Present* a number of experts have contributed special essays called Historical Critiques, concentrating on what is known as historiography—that is, the study of the philosophy and methodology of the writing of history. Some of the earliest attempts to use history for various purposes are discussed in the critiques, "The Birth of History in the West" and "Chinese and Indian Historiography." As these Historical Critiques will attest, the "use" of history means that the scribe or historian has to answer two related questions: "how" is his account to be written, and "why" has he undertaken the task?

THE "HOW" OF HISTORY

Is history a science? There is more than one way of treating the past. In dealing with the American Revolution, for example, the historian may describe its events in narrative form. Again, he may prefer to analyze its general causes or perhaps compare its stages of revolution with the patterns of revolutions in other countries. Because of these descriptive and analytical functions, historical writing has sometimes been regarded as a science. But the historian does not aim for or attain the same kind of results as the scientist. The latter can verify his conclusions by repeating his experiment under controlled conditions in his laboratory, and he also attempts to classify the phenomenon in a general group or category. The historian, on the other hand, has to pay much greater attention to the *uniqueness* of his data, because each event takes place at a particular time and in a particular place. And since that time is now past, he cannot verify his conclusions by duplicating the circumstances in which the event occurred. Moreover, since history is concerned fundamentally with the lives and actions of men, the search for causes is bound to be relatively subjective.

Nevertheless, historians insist that history be written as scientifically as possible and that evidence be analyzed with the same objective attitude employed by the scientist when he examines natural phenomena. This scientific spirit requires the historian to handle his evidence according to established rules of historical analysis, to recognize his own biases and attempt to eliminate their effects from his work, and to draw only such conclusions as the evidence seems to warrant.

Historical method. To meet these requirements, historians have evolved the "historical method." The first step is the search for what is called *sources,* without which there can be no history. These sources may consist of material remains such as bones, tools, weapons, and pottery; oral traditions such as myths, legends, and songs; pictorial data such as drawings and maps; and, of course, written records ranging from ancient manuscripts to treaties, diaries, books, and yesterday's newspaper. The Historical Critique "The Archaeologist's Spade" will give a clearer view of the extent to which the natural sciences, as well as archaeology, paleontology, and aerial photography, contribute to the historical method today.

Having acquired his sources, the historian must next infer from them the facts. This process has two parts. *External criticism* tests the genuineness of the source. The importance of external criticism was demonstrated dramatically in recent years by the unmasking of a hoax—Piltdown man—which had long duped scientists (see p. 16). Generally, however, the historian has to deal with less spectacular problems, such as checking ancient documents for errors that have crept into the text through faulty copying or translating.

The second step in the analytical process is called *internal criticism.* In evaluating written materials, the historian must ascertain the author's meaning and the accuracy of his work. To do so may require study of the language of the era or of the circumstances in which the author's statement was made. A politician's memoirs may be highly suspect because of an almost universal human tendency to present oneself in the most favorable light. Official documents must also be examined for what they may conceal as well as

reveal—especially if they are documents released by governments to explain or justify a change in foreign policy or their involvement in a war.

The final step in historical method is *synthesis.* Here the historian must determine which factors in a given situation are most relevant to his purpose, since obviously he cannot include everything that occurred in the period under review. This delicate process of selection underscores the role that subjectivity plays in the writing of history. "The more complex the events dealt with, the wider their spread in time and space, the greater are the calls made upon the historian's judgment."[1]

The problem of periodization. Can we really categorize history as "ancient," "medieval," and "modern"? When we reflect upon this question, it becomes obvious that what is "modern" in the twentieth century could conceivably be considered "medieval" in the twenty-fifth century, and ultimately "ancient" in the thirty-fifth or fortieth century A.D. Yet not to break up the account would be akin to reading this book (or any other) without the benefit of parts, chapters, paragraphs, or even separate sentences. Like time itself, history would then become a ceaseless flow of consciousness and events. To simplify his task and to manage his materials more easily, the historian divides time into periods. The divisions he chooses, the lines he draws, reveal the distinctive way the historian regards the past—namely, in terms of patterns which appear to him logical and meaningful. Needless to say, no two historians see the past in an identical pattern; thus the division of the past into periods is necessarily arbitrary and, like railway or airline timetables, subject to change without prior notice.

That periodization is far from being simply a theoretical problem of interest only to the specialist can be seen from an examination of several of the Historical Critiques in this volume and its companion. The authors of "Chinese and Indian Historiography" demonstrate that those two massive societies have held very different views both of the meaning of time as a philosophical concept and of the significance of chronology as a means of dividing their respective histories into meaningful periods. Even within our own western tradition, historians do not agree as to when "medieval" history ends and "modern" history begins. Or to raise a question discussed in one of the Historical Critiques (p. 477), "Was there really a Renaissance?" Obviously, the "how" of historical method and writing raises a number of difficult, but fascinating, problems.

THE "WHY" OF HISTORY

Historical analysis. The historian seeks to describe not only *what* has happened in the past and *how* it happened but also *why* society undergoes change. Any search of this kind raises a number of fundamental questions: the roles of Providence, the individual, and the group in history; the extent to which historical events are unique and the extent to which they fit into patterns; and the problem of progress in human affairs. The answers vary with the different philosophical views of mankind.

Providence or the individual. Those who hold the teleological view see in history the guidance of a Divine Will, directing human destinies according to a cosmic purpose. This concept was accepted as self-evident in ancient theocratic societies and remained prevalent in medieval thought, but it lost ground after the Renaissance, when the spread of rationalistic doctrines and scientific triumphs seemed to forecast unlimited progress in human affairs. Yet in our own day there has been a reaction against the nineteenth century's comfortable assumption that man is a completely free agent. One distinguished historian, for example, has asserted that the only tenable interpretation of the human drama is the religious one.[2]

Others have minimized the role of Providence while exalting the role of the individual in the historical process. The nineteenth-century historian Thomas Carlyle maintained that the Alexanders, Muhammads, and Cromwells were the "Great Men" whose leadership chiefly determined the course of human events. Later historians discounted this generalization by emphasizing the impact of economic and other "impersonal" forces. With the increasing centralized control of the twentieth century, however, especially as evidenced in recent dictatorships, the rise of a leader with a strong magnetic personality, projected and "amplified" by the mass media, again underscores the power of the individual, not only to involve himself in a nation's decision making but, as in the case of Hitler, Stalin, or Mao, to affect the direction of global events. This problem, central to our own age, is examined in the Historical Critique, "The Charismatic Figure in History."

"Laws" and "forces" in history. The opponents of Carlyle's approach often contend that history is determined by "forces" and "laws" and by the actions of entire societies. One geographer, for example, has even argued that a people's genius and progress are decided principally by climate. We can reject such an extreme claim but—as we shall see when we take up the earliest, or fluvial, civilizations—physical environment does play a significant part in the development of human societies.

Sociologists approach history primarily by analyzing the origins, institutions, and functions of groups. Some attach special importance to population factors as criteria for judging the evolution of a given society, while others analyze societies in terms of their division of labor.

Like the sociologist, the economist tends to look at the historical record from the standpoint of group action and especially the impact of economic forces such as that of, say, supply and demand or diminishing returns. Whereas historians have traditionally emphasized political and military events, sociologists and economists have brought a new dimension of interpretation to the study of history, since they are concerned with such areas as the interaction of various classes in a society, the ethics and political consequences of economic philosophies, and the impact of technology upon the living standard and economic well-being of a given society. Examples of the way in which socioeconomic interpretations of historical data can enrich our understanding of the past are found in two Historical Critiques, "Advances in Medieval Agriculture" and "Was There an 'Industrial Revolution'?"

Karl Marx's theory of history. The most explosive interpretation of history in modern times was made by Karl Marx. To him, irresistible economic forces governed men and determined the trend of events. Marx contended that the shift from one economic stage to another—such as from feudalism to capitalism—is attained by sporadic upheavals, or revolutions, occurring because the class controlling the methods of production eventually resists further progress in order to maintain its vested interests. Marx predicted that the proletariat would overthrow the exploiting capitalists and that the end result would be a classless society, followed by a gradual withering away of the state itself.

Many of Marx's basic assumptions, however, have been conclusively disproved by events. Contrary to his prediction, social legislation and higher productivity have enabled the living standards of the "exploited" masses in capitalist countries to become higher than ever before. And instead of the development of a classless society in the Soviet Union and other Marxist countries, the state controls all aspects of a stratified society

Scientific

Moon

War in V N.

Attica prison
riot

Wage-price freeze

Pol. Situation — res
cong. symp. out.

Ec. Side

Pol. Side

Draft

Arms race between two nations

Ecology

Rioter housing

Rel. with China

Emperor of Japan

Social

Cultural

Rel.

Ec.

what is a point of hist?

Do you have a phil. of hist.? what?

1. Do you think history does any good? Does his. repeat itself?

2. Patterns in history?

3. What ought to cover in history? Hist. of institutions?

4. The question of progress.

5. Cultural approach to hist.

A. Golden age in the past? When would you want to live? compful. a problem today — not before in most of world.

7. _____→

Men   Pol.
                                       Ec.
                                       Scientific
War, Japan, China, Berlin Treaty

Space
                                       Spiritual Rev
War in VN —

Spiritual rev.

G. B. in common market

in which a wage and privilege differential (greater than that in western societies) exists between the administrative and military elites on one hand and the masses of workers and peasants on the other. In short, although Marx claimed to have made history "scientific," events continue to attest to the presence of unpredictable factors in human affairs for which no ideological forces or laws have yet been able to account.

Theories of civilization. Numerous other attempts have been made to explain the rise and fall of civilizations according to a set of principles. The different views of modern historians are analyzed in the final Historical Critique, "Twentieth-Century Reinterpretations of History and Society" (Volume II). One of these historians, Oswald Spengler, a disillusioned German, maintained that civilizations were like organisms; each grew with the "superb aimlessness" of a flower and passed through a cycle of spring, summer, autumn, and winter. He declared that western civilization was in its winter period and had already entered a state of rapid decline.

Spengler influenced the English historian Arnold J. Toynbee, whose works became best sellers after World War II. To Toynbee, "challenge and response" explain the rise and fall of civilizations. Man achieves civilization "as a response to a challenge in a situation of special difficulty which rouses him to make a hitherto unprecedented effort."[3] The ancient Egyptians, for example, built their civilization by learning to control the Nile River. Toynbee holds that a civilization continues to grow as long as it is motivated by creative individuals; when they can no longer inspire the majority, social disunity brings about decline and disintegration.

Spengler was not unique in likening societies to organisms. Other thinkers have also sought to explain the life and behavior of human society in terms of biological growth and decay. In particular, the evolutionary hypothesis developed by Charles Darwin had a strong impact upon nineteenth-century intellectuals and gave rise to the concept that the principle of "survival of the fittest" must equally apply to human societies. This line of thought—known as Social Darwinism—raises social and ethical questions of major importance, as the Historical Critique on that subject attests (Volume II).

Is the course of history inevitable? Many eminent historians profess to find no recurring pattern in past events, seeing only, as one of them has put it, "the only safe rule for the historian [is] that he should recognize in the development of human destinies the play of the contingent and unforeseen."[4] These differences of view all lead to the question: Are men really free to choose or does history obey impersonal laws and forces—in short, is the course of history inevitable? We seem to have to accept either inevitable laws—which appear to leave no room for significant freedom of action—or the equally extreme alternative that makes every event a unique act and history merely the record of unrelated episodes.

Can this dilemma be avoided? We believe it can. Even though all events are in various respects unique, they also contain elements which invite comparison—as in the case of the origin and course of revolutions in different countries. The comparative approach permits us to seek relationships between historical phenomena and to group them into movements, or patterns, or civilizations.

The authors of this book eschew any single "theory" of history. They are eclectic in their approach because they see merit in a number of basic concepts. These include the important effects of physical environment on social organization and institutions; the powerful roles played not only by economic but also by political and religious factors; and the impact exerted upon events by various outstanding personalities occupying key positions in history.

The question of progress. Somewhere along the line, the student is likely to ask: "Are we making any progress? Is mankind getting better?" Nineteenth-century optimists confidently answered "Yes!" but our crisis-ridden century is by no means so sure. In any case, such questions are difficult to answer because of the difficulty of defining such terms as *progress* or *better*. (Better than what, for example?) Those who equate progress with material advancement might remember that the Athens of Socrates and Aristotle produced an unsurpassed galaxy of thinkers and artists without the benefit of electricity, television, or the Madison Avenue ad-man. Conversely, the advanced literacy and technology boasted by Nazi Germany did not prevent it from wallowing in the moral depravity which created concentration camps and gas chambers.

Nevertheless, our lawmakers, educators, and scientists do assume that progress can be both defined and defended on rational grounds. Various factors might be applied to test this proposition. *Material advancement* calls for improved living and health standards, increased economic production, and a distribution of goods so as to benefit the greatest number of people. *Intellectual and spiritual progress* includes educational opportunities for all and is measured in terms of creative achievements in science, the humanities, and arts. For example, Einstein's theory constitutes an advance over Newton's theory of gravitation because it can solve not only the same problems as the earlier theory but also problems that hitherto defied solution. *Social progress* covers the "pursuit of happiness" and includes such essentials as equal status for women, abolition of conditions of servitude, and enlightened treatment of prisoners and the insane.

Yet another significant factor is *political participation*. In a democracy progress can be tested by the opportunities for the individual to assume public responsibilities and by the protection of his right to hold views at variance with those held by others, especially in the case of minorities. Finally, the growth of *international cooperation* becomes basic in any meaningful discussion of progress. This growth depends on and contributes to the maintenance of peace and security, the peaceful settlement of international disputes, and world-wide improvement in economic and social standards.

THE CULTURAL APPROACH TO HISTORY

The universal culture pattern. In the interplay of man with his environment and with his fellowmen, of which history is the written record, men have always expressed certain fundamental needs. These form the basis of a "universal culture pattern" and deserve to be enumerated.

1. *The need to make a living.* Man must have food, shelter, clothing, and the means to provide for his offspring's survival.

2. *The need for law and order.* From the earliest times communities have had to keep peace among their members, defend themselves against external attack, and protect property.

3. *The need for social organization.* In order that people may make a living, raise families, and maintain law and order, a social structure is necessary. Ideologies may differ in their concepts of the relative importance of the group and the individual within any such social organization.

4. *The need for knowledge and learning.* Since earliest times mankind has transmitted the knowledge painfully acquired from experience, first orally and then by means of language and writing systems. As societies grow more complex, there is an increasing need to preserve knowledge and to make it available through education to as many people as possible.

5. *The need for self-expression.* Man has responded creatively to his environment even before the days when he decorated the walls of Paleolithic caves with paintings of the animals he hunted. The arts appear to have a lineage as old as man himself.

6. *The need for religious expression.* Equally as old is man's attempt to answer the "why" of his existence. What primitive peoples considered supernatural in their environment could at a later date often be explained by science in terms of natural phenomena. Yet today, no less than in prehistoric times, men continue to search for answers to the ultimate questions of existence.

These six briefly described needs have been common to men at all times and in all places. Taken together, they form the basis of a universal culture pattern. To carry this concept one step further: when a group of people behave similarly and share the same institutions and ways of life, they can be said to have a common culture. Each person born into that group will in turn derive from it his basic way of life. It follows that the basic differences between the farmers of ancient China and those of present-day Nebraska are due mainly to the fact that their culture traits are at different stages of development or that they have worked out different methods of solving the same problems of existence. In the succeeding chapters we shall be looking at a large number of different cultures, some of which are designated as *civilizations* (for a definition of this term see pp. 32 and 591).

Diffusion as a factor in culture change. Cultures are never static or wholly isolated. A particular culture may have an individuality which sets it off sharply from other cultures, but invariably it has been influenced by external contacts. Such contacts may be either peaceful or warlike, and they meet with varying degrees of resistance. The early American colonists took from the Indians the use of corn and tobacco, while the latter obtained the horse and firearms from the newcomers. On the other hand, the Second World War saw the Nazis and Japanese force their cultures upon subjugated peoples with no permanent results.

Environment and invention in culture change. While geography has profoundly influenced the development of cultures, we should not exaggerate its importance. Although riverine civilizations evolved along the Nile and the Tigris-Euphrates, for example, none emerged in the physically comparable valleys of the Jordan and the Rio Grande.[5] Moreover, environmental influences tend to become less marked as man gains increasing mastery over nature, as shown by the transformation of deserts in southwestern United States into rich citrus belts and the extension of the grain-growing belt in the Canadian prairies further north through the development of frost- and rust-resistant types of wheat.

Invention is therefore another important source of culture change. The automobile—which has revolutionized transportation, the growth of cities, and even home life—was made possible only by a host of earlier inventions, such as the internal-combustion engine and that most ancient and indispensable tool, the wheel. The study of the origins of certain basic inventions again underscores the fact that historical change is a continuous process at once dynamic and often unpredictable. The domestication of animals and grain, for example, took place in both the old and new worlds, albeit the animals and cereals were different because of the dissimilar ecological factors involved; yet so far as we know, there was no physical contact at the time between the two cultural heartlands. To what extent, then, is physical contact required in the process of invention? Or, is it possible for men in different times and places to hit upon similar solutions to the challenges posed by their respective environments —resulting in the phenomenon known as "parallel invention"? This intriguing question is examined in the Historical Critique entitled "The Question of Parallel Invention in the Old and New Worlds."

Is race a factor in culture change? Just as no pure culture was ever developed in isolation by one group, so there is no pure race of people. Ethnic types have intermingled along with the diffusion of cultures. *Race,* a much misused term, has value only in denoting the major human divisions, each with its own distinctive physical characteristics: Caucasian (white), Mongoloid (yellow), and Negroid (black). No race has ever monopolized culture, though for a specific period one race may produce an impressive record of cultural creativity.

Unfortunately, just as ignorance has all too often led to unscientific generalizations about the differences between the "races" of *Homo sapiens* —which in turn have been employed to justify discriminatory, and even brutal, behavior toward one people by another—so the factor of race has also been employed at different times and places to "explain" the superiority which groups perceive in their own cultures as compared with those of others. Thus Caucasian peoples have been all too guilty of assuming that their particular cultural patterns and activities must be superior to the cultures which they associate with Asian and African peoples. To hold such arrogant, and demonstrably fallacious, views was more understandable, if not pardonable, in the era of western colonialism. In today's world, how-

ever, to retain such stereotyped concepts of non-western peoples can be dangerously explosive. As the Historical Critique on western images of Africa (Volume II) demonstrates, new and scientifically valid images of the nonwestern world are required, and a study of history can do much to get rid of western cultural myopia.

Culture lag. Some parts of a culture pattern change more rapidly than others, so that one institution sometimes becomes outmoded in relation to others in a society. When different parts of a society fail to mesh harmoniously, the condition is often called *culture lag*. Numerous examples of this lag could be cited: the failure to enfranchise women until this century, the tragedy of hunger in the midst of plenty during the 1930's, or, in our own day, the repeated inability of the United Nations to limit atomic energy to peaceful use because of the insistence by national states to arm themselves as they wish.

In the view of some observers, culture lag has assumed its most dangerous form in the apparently widening gap in communications and outlook between science and the accelerating technological sector on the one hand and our traditional humanistic culture and values system on the other. These two major segments of our culture pattern appear to be advancing, and changing, at the speeds of a supersonic jet and of a horse and buggy respectively. Just what dynamic factors are at work which bring about different rates of speed in the processes of change? Because our modern age owes its particular world-outlook in ever growing measure to the discoveries and philosophy of science, and because the processes of change are today most apparent in our contemporary technological order, we have need to understand much more clearly than ever before the nature of the scientific revolution—not only in the way that it began in the sixteenth century, but also how it operates today and is already shaping the pattern of our culture for the decades ahead. It is upon this critical area that another Historical Critique, "Science in the Sixteenth and Seventeenth Centuries" (Volume II) is focused.

THE CHALLENGE

A century of conflict. The twentieth century has been phenomenally fruitful in raising economic, social, and health standards. But ours is also a century of conflict. It has been said that contemporary man is involved in three kinds of conflict: with nature, with his fellow man, and with himself. In some ways, the first can be richly rewarding. Thus the harnessing of atomic energy holds out hope for almost unlimited human advancement. But meanwhile we are depleting the earth's natural resources at an unprecedented rate, and vast areas of the globe are being ravaged by erosion.

These unresolved conflicts with nature in turn increase human tensions. Hundreds of millions in underdeveloped regions are hungry, a situation that breeds social unrest and political conflict. Today all Asia and Africa demand political freedom; but if chaos or new forms of aggression are not to follow the granting of independence, the emergent nations must be offered support in raising the living standards of the masses. This aid, however, must come from the more developed countries, which themselves are dangerously split into ideologically warring camps. Tensions abound among both the strong and the weak. Today's tensions find repercussions within man himself, as is shown by the increasing incidence of nervous and mental disorders, by the feelings of general insecurity among average people everywhere, and by a seemingly pervasive sense of rootlessness and restlessness among members of the young generation in all nations.

In short, ours is an age that is questioning all the accepted traditional concepts of what is good and permissible. The universe of Newton, with its emphasis on permanence and fixed principles, has given way to Einstein's model of a universe that is relativistic not only in its physical behavior but in the behavior of men and societies as well. Ours is an uncertain and obviously dangerous time in which to live, but at the same time it is exceedingly dynamic and challenging. In such a world it would be strange if the study of history itself were not to reflect this search for new concepts about the nature of man's involvement in his environment and his relationship to his fellow man. Understandably, then, the historians of our century have been updating the methodology of their discipline in order to take full advantage of the contributions of science and technology. Even more important, the final Historical Critique (Volume II) shows that twentieth-century historians are also engaged in subjecting the traditional philosophical postulates of their discipline to a searching reinterpretation in order to acquire a greater understanding of the human condition on this planet.

No time for defeatism. To many, it seems almost hopeless to try to rectify a world which, in Hamlet's phrase, seems so "out of joint." The authors disagree heartily with these prophets of doom. A study of history quickly proves that the "good old days" were actually not that good and that every age has had to bear its full burden of dire forebodings. Moreover, history teaches us that man has never yet given up his struggle for survival and the betterment of life. The authors agree with the scholar who wrote: "Others claim man will destroy himself, which is of course a political prediction. This seems to me a fate as unlikely as committing suicide by holding your breath. Man, for all his frailties, is now one of the toughest, most tenacious, most adaptable animals in the kingdom . . . and I am sure that he is here to stay."[6]

Part One

In the Beginning

In the beginning God created the heaven and the earth. And the earth was without form, and void; and darkness was upon the face of the deep. And the Spirit of God moved upon the face of the waters. . . . And God said, Let the waters bring forth abundantly the moving creature that hath life, and fowl that may fly above the earth. . . . And God said, Let us make man in our image, after our likeness. . . . So God created man in his own image, in the image of God created he him; male and female created he them. And God blessed them, and God said unto them, Be fruitful, and multiply, and replenish the earth, and subdue it: and have dominion over the fish of the sea, and over the fowl of the air, and over every living thing that moveth upon the earth. . . . And God saw every thing he had made, and, behold, it was very good.*

■ In these words the Old Testament accounts for the creation of the earth and the origin of man. Throughout this great collection of ancient writings, men struggle with life's profound mysteries, seeking the meaning of human existence. Since Biblical times mankind has continued the quest, earnestly attempting to reconcile the knowledge acquired since the days of Moses and the Prophets with the accounts handed down by these and other great religious figures. And always the search returns to life's origin. Thus, in our story of man's journey out of the primordial darkness, we, too, must go back to the beginning.

How old the universe is and how the planet earth came into being may never be known precisely, but modern scientists believe that our world has been circling the sun for four and one-half to five billion years. During that incredibly long time, the earth changed from a gaseous to a liquid state and finally solidified; waters formed on the earth's shell, and in their depths life took form. As one geological epoch succeeded another, first single-celled and then multicelled organisms evolved, and some of them learned to live on land. Eventually this ceaseless process of adaptation to environment brought forth the mammal class, of which man is a member.

Remains of the earliest manlike creatures, unearthed in Africa, may be nearly two million years old. The time span from those remote days to about 3500 B.C. is usually referred to as prehistoric, or preliterate, times. By far the greater part of that time span was taken up by man's relentless struggle for survival—a struggle in which he learned to shape crude weapons and tools from stone, make fire, and domesticate certain plants and animals. The latter achievement was of revolutionary consequence, for it freed man of the necessity to hunt the migrant beasts. And a measure of control over plants and animals meant that he could settle down in one place and become a farmer and herdsman.

The stage was now set for a progressively rapid extension of man's control over his environment. Life became more complex and more rewarding. The discovery of metallurgy, progress in arts and crafts, the organization of larger social and political units, and the invention of writing heralded a new era of existence. These momentous advances did not occur over the entire earth but were concentrated in a few great river valleys. There the well-watered, fertile soil produced abundant harvests and food surpluses supported increased populations. Villages and cities sprang up, inhabited by men with diverse talents and trades: priests, potters, basket weavers, tool makers, and merchants. The rivers provided the means for carrying the fruits of the field and the wares of the town from one locality to another. Trade, a potent force in the shaping of human destiny, fostered the exchange of ideas and inventions between different regions.

Along the banks of rivers, then, we must look for the first civilizations. We shall find them widely scattered: Mesopotamia straddled the Tigris and the Euphrates; Egypt stretched along the Nile; India arose along the Indus and the Ganges; and China expanded eastward from the region of the Wei and the Huang Ho. Prolific in their gifts to mankind and so dynamic that two of them have retained unbroken continuity to our own day, these civilizations possessed similarities at least as arresting as their differences. In all four, political systems were developed, crafts flourished and commerce expanded, calendars and systems of writing were invented, art and literature of extraordinary beauty were created, and religions and philosophies came into being to satisfy men's inner yearnings.

We are at the beginning of man's travels through the ages. When we first find him, he is almost completely at the mercy of a stern environment; today he is exploring the solar system.

*Holy Bible, Authorized King James Version, Genesis 1:1-31.

1. Prehistoric cave painting (c. 15,000-10,000 B.C.). Among the oldest known examples of pictorial art are the animal paintings found in caves near Altamira, Spain. They are products of the late Paleolithic age. The exact purpose of these works is not clear, but it is often presumed that they were part of a magic ritual intended to gain dominance over the animals' spirits and thus to assure success in the hunt. They reveal a remarkable visual and formal sensibility: the shapes and attitudes of the animals (note the wounded posture of the two bisons) have been keenly observed and conveyed with an assured elegance of pattern and line. At the same time the figures are often superimposed, with little apparent regard for their compositional relationships, suggesting that the act of painting them may have been more ritualistically important than the final images themselves.

2. Stonehenge (c. 1800-1400 B.C.). The organized social life of the Neolithic age engendered man's first attempts at a large-scale architectural ordering of space. The massive boulders of Stonehenge, on England's Salisbury Plain, were set in a huge circular plan of upright slabs capped with mammoth lintels. Their purpose was probably religious; since the entire structure is placed with reference to the exact point where the sun rises on the summer solstice, it may have been the setting of a sun-worshiping ceremony.

3. (below left) **Sumerian harp with bull's head** (3000-2700 B.C.). The vigor which pervades Mesopotamian art throughout its long history is already evident in the bold imagery and rich variety of materials (gold foil, lapis lazuli, wood, shell, red stone) of this very early work. Doubtless sustaining a practice of prehistoric times, Sumerian mythology was greatly preoccupied with sacred animals. The four panels under the bull's head depict a number of human activities which are acted out with notable vivacity by symbolic animals. (In the second scene from the bottom, an ass plays a bull's-head harp much like the one the panel decorates.) **4.** (below right) **Ritual vessel from Shang dynasty** (c. 1300-1028 B.C.). The artisans of the Shang dynasty produced bronze vessels by a casting process as sophisticated as any ever devised. These containers were designed for the water, wine, meat, or grain that was appropriate to certain sacrificial rites. The complex decorations, handsomely united with the vessel's overall form, were usually derived from animal motifs whose representation was rigidly governed by long-standing conventions.

5. Egypt: Tomb of Queen Nefertari (c. 1250 B.C.). Since Egyptians believed the soul to be the counterpart of the body and the hereafter a reflection of the here-and-now, elaborate material provision was made in the tombs to assure the safe voyage of the deceased into the life after death. The pictures and hieroglyphs which adorn the richly painted New Kingdom tomb of Nefertari associate her with such Egyptian deities as Osiris, god of the dead (the standing figure on the left) and Khepri, the sun god (the seated figure with the beetle's head).

Chapter 1

Out of Darkness

Origins of the Earth
and the Development of Man

INTRODUCTION. At one time it was believed that the earth had been created in 4004 B.C. Scientific evidence today would appear to indicate that the age of our planet antedates this figure by at least four to five billion years. Furthermore, some two million years ago parts of this earth were inhabited by our ancestors comprising the species known as genus *Homo*. How can we learn about the huge span of time which encompasses the life of the planet and in which the first steps in man's journey took place? To do so, we must rely on information painstakingly gathered by scientists in many fields. Early men left no written records tell of their progress in the business of living but archaeologists have unearthed remains of skeletons and tools and weapons which the story of human development be told. To piece together the account the physical and cultural development modern man, anthropologists have parts of the African savannah examination, while others have into the steaming hinterland of South America, the snowy wastes of the Arctic, the coral atolls of the Pacific, and the arid heartland of Australia to study present-day primitive cultures. Paleontologists have demonstrated how living matter evolved from one-celled organisms to the species of plant and animal life existing today. The geologists' investigations of fossils preserved in rock strata have penetrated to the dawn of life—about two billion years ago. Astronomers have learned about the mechanics of our universe and speculated about its origins. In our survey of civilization, then, let us begin at the beginning by considering the origins of this spinning planet.

PRELUDE TO HUMAN HISTORY

Theories of the earth's origin. Our solar system—comprising nine planets and a sun from which our earth is separated by some 93 million miles—is but a small part of a vast celestial disc called the Galaxy, strewn with billions of stars and producing that band of light across the heavens called the Milky Way. Employing as a basic unit of measurement the light-year—the distance that a beam of light will travel in one year—astronomers have calculated that while a man traveling at this speed would take less than one sixteenth of a second to go from Los Angeles to New York, another one and three-sixteenths seconds to pass the moon, and eleven hours to traverse the solar system, he would require 100,000 years to cross the Milky Way. Yet immense as it is, the Galaxy includes only a fraction of the matter in the universe. Astronomers estimate that outer space contains over a hundred million galaxies, each one comprising billions of stars. They have discovered, moreover, that the universe is constantly expanding, that each galaxy is receding from all others at ever increasing speeds.

The origin of the solar system, and hence of our own planet, has also given rise to conflicting hypotheses. Some astronomers have postulated a cataclysmic, or "dynamic encounter," theory, whereby a star wandering close to the sun pulled away large masses of flaming gases and vapor in its wake. Subsequently, these orphan masses condensed into bodies which later became the nuclei of the planets in the solar system. A more commonly accepted theory today holds that the sun and the planets condensed out of a vast cloud of primordial gas similar to the cosmic clouds visible within the Milky Way. In the process of condensation the material in the center of the swirling cloud contracted to form a large, incandescent mass, the sun, whose gravitational attraction held in orbit a number of smaller contracting masses—the protoplanets. In time these protoplanets condensed into planets, most of which developed satellites in the same way in which they themselves had been formed.

Both theories assume that the planet was originally in a gaseous state. After a time it cooled to a liquefied globe, and eventually it solidified to form a thick, uneven outer shell with large elevated surfaces and huge craters. Vast quantities of rain water held by the earth's force of gravity filled the craters. Mountain ranges and other topographical features were produced by volcanic action, weathering, and shifts in the bedrock. The formation of some of these features can be traced in the strata, or layers, of the earth.

A chart of the earth's strata constitutes what is commonly known as the geologic timetable. Since 1946 geologists have utilized a method measuring the degree of radioactivity found in certain elements in the earth's strata. Knowing that these radioactive elements disintegrate according to a definite time pattern, they have been able to date the lowest rock formations at about 3.5 billion years. The earth, still conceived to be a billion years older than these strata, would thus be some 4.5 billion years old. On the basis of this new evidence, the strata of the earth's crust have been redated and

Geological Time Chart and Development of Primates

Era	Epoch		Number of millions of years ago	First appearance of primates
Cenozoic		Holocene	Present	
	Quaternary Period	Pleistocene glacial phase 4 3 2 1	0.01 to 3*	Neanderthal man; *Homo sapiens* Java man; Peking man *Australopithecus; Homo habilis*
	Tertiary Period	Pliocene	3 to 12	
		Miocene	12 to 28	Apelike forms
		Oligocene	28 to 40	Monkeys
		Eocene	40 to 60	Tarsierlike and lemurlike types Earliest primates
Mesozoic			60 to 185	
Paleozoic			185 to 500	
Proterozoic			500 to 825	
Archeozoic			825 to 1550	

*The Pleistocene epoch probably lasted approximately two or three million years and ended about ten thousand years ago.

reclassified. The geologic time scale is divided into five major eras (see chart).

Earliest forms of life. Scientists have learned about the earliest forms of life and how they evolved through the study of fossils—petrified remains of organisms. In the early 1800's an English fossil collector, William Smith, noticed that certain strata always exhibited the same kinds of fossils. He theorized that those fossils found only in strata of a given geologic period represented the forms of life living in that period. This theory, self-evident to us today, proved revolutionary, because Smith's contemporaries believed that all plant and animal species had been simultaneously created (as set forth in Genesis) and that their descendants had remained unchanged thereafter. But Smith and other scientists were able to demonstrate that an unmistakable pattern of the evolution of life could be traced from the ancient to the most recent rock formations.

While no evidence of life remains from the Archeozoic era, scientists believe that pro-

tozoa—one-celled organisms such as the amoeba—existed at that time. In the strata of the next era, the Proterozoic, fossils of the simplest kind have been found, such as simple plants called algae and microscopic creatures known as radiolaria. The third era, the Paleozoic, abounds with evidence of increasingly complex plant and animal life. The water teemed with shellfish, crabs, and worms; and fish multiplied until they became the dominant form of animal life. Near the end of the era, amphibians—animals able to live both in the water and on land—appeared, and some species of plants capable of surviving without being surrounded by water developed. Increasingly, life was moving in the direction of the land, away from its oceanic origins.

The Mesozoic was the era of great reptiles. Some reptile species were able to walk on their hind legs, while others could fly. The largest reptiles were the dinosaurs; some species were over fifty feet long, with massive heads towering some twenty feet above the ground. During this era the earliest mammals began to appear—and were to supersede the reptiles which for millions of years had dominated the environment. Many reptile species had become highly specialized and could not cope with climatic and other environmental changes. Mammals, on the other hand, proved more adaptable, exhibiting such biological innovations as warm-bloodedness, the production of living young (instead of eggs) from within the body, mammary glands for nursing their young, enlarged brains, hair, two sets of clearly differentiated teeth, and limbs capable of efficient locomotion.

Cenozoic era of mammals and man. By the beginning of the most recent geological era, the Cenozoic, the natural world had largely acquired its present appearance. The era is divided into two periods, of which the Tertiary lasted about sixty million years. The earliest primates—the order of mammals to which apes, monkeys, and man belong by reason of their similar anatomic structure—developed during this time. The second period, the Quaternary, has covered a span of at least two million years and is significant for the appearance of *Homo sapiens,* or modern man. The subdivisions of this period are the Pleistocene, or Glacial, epoch, which ended between ten and fifteen thousand years ago, and the Holocene, or Recent, epoch, in which we now live.

Until recently it was believed that the Pleistocene lasted about one million years and was characterized in the Northern Hemisphere by four great advances of ice. It would now appear to have begun much earlier, at least two million years ago. At present geologists speak of a "Basal Pleistocene," a period of more than two million years of gradual cooling but with increasing fluctuation from cool to warm climates. This was followed by a number of glacial and interglacial periods; great ice sheets advanced from the polar regions down over much of Europe, northern Asia, and North America.

The glaciers locked a large amount of the earth's moisture in their icy masses so that the sea level fell. This phenomenon permitted land bridges to emerge across the Bering Strait, the English Channel, and

elsewhere, thereby facilitating the movement of animals and people (see Reference Map 1). In intervals between glaciers the climate in Europe was subtropical to temperate. In Africa and other areas where glaciers did not penetrate, the Pleistocene epoch witnessed alternating dry and rainy phases. The Pleistocene must be regarded as central to the evolution of human technology and society. It created the landscape and soils familiar today in the Northern Hemisphere and, above all, presented environmental challenges and opportunities which stimulated the movement of peoples from the lower to the higher latitudes and their invention of appropriate tools and forms of social organization to cope successfully with those new environments.

THE DEVELOPMENT OF MAN

Evolution, a controversial issue. Had God created man "in His own image," or was *Homo sapiens* himself no less than the rocks, plants, and animals the product of physical change and adaptation? This question—so basic in nineteenth-century thought that it caused the deepest soul-searching among theologians and scientists alike and engendered bitter controversy—was in effect posed by the French biologist Jean Baptiste de Lamarck in 1801 when he declared that mankind had evolved by a series of progressive changes from an apelike ancestor. This concept was slow to win converts during the first half of the century. In 1830, however, Sir Charles Lyell's *The Principles of Geology* provided evidence that the earth was a product of a long period of evolution. His followers reconciled their religious beliefs with the scientific discoveries by arguing that the six-day Creation story should be interpreted not literally but rather in the spirit of the Ninetieth Psalm: "For a thousand years in thy sight are but as yesterday when it is past, and as a watch in the night."

The issue became critical with the appearance of Charles Darwin's two scientific treatises, *The Origin of Species* (1859) and *Descent of Man* (1871). The controversy surrounding the theory of man's evolution has raged on into the twentieth century—although with decreasing intensity as fossil evidence has come to light. Of course, the fossil record can probably never be complete, and paleontologists have only skeletal remains (usually partial ones) to analyze. To many contemporary scientists, while the evidence for evolution appears overwhelming, the theory by no means precludes the presence of a guiding intelligence ultimately responsible for a progressive development of organic life from simple to more complex forms, culminating thus far in the intelligence and creativity of man himself.

The earliest primates. According to the theory of evolution, man belongs to the primate order, which also includes the lemurs, tarsiers, monkeys, and apes. The primates possess a similar skeletal structure, their hands and feet can grasp and retain objects, and, compared with other creatures, they have a relatively large brain, excellent stereoscopic vision, and a mediocre sense of smell. The earliest primates, living perhaps sixty million years ago, were small mouselike creatures resembling the modern tree shrew which lived in trees and hunted insects at night. Their way of life encouraged the development of mobile thumbs, flexible forelimbs, keen eyesight, and eye-hand coordination. Many species of these first primates became extinct, but tarsierlike and lemurlike types survived and became the ancestors of higher forms of primates.

During the Tertiary period important developments occurred among the primates. In the Oligocene epoch different lines of monkeys evolved, as well as primitive forms of anthropoid apes, while in the next epoch, the Miocene, the ape family grew in size and variety and spread over much of Africa, Asia, and Europe. Before the end of this epoch (that is, no later than 28 million years ago), a development of the first magnitude occurred when the ape family became differentiated. One line evolved into the tree-dwelling apes, while the second led to ground-dwelling types known as *hominids*, or what we may arbitrarily call "prehumans" or "protohumans." In time these prehumans learned to walk upright, their legs grew longer than their arms, and their hands—no longer required for locomotion—became more dexterous. Most important of all, the head gradually shifted toward a more upright position, rendering superfluous much of the muscle at the back of the neck. This development favored the progressive expansion of the brain, which in turn ultimately led to modern "thinking man" (*Homo sapiens*), the only survivor on the many-branched *hominid* family tree.

Development of genus Homo. No conclusive fossil evidence bearing on prehuman evolution during the Pliocene epoch, which followed the Miocene, has yet been found. On the other hand, the Pleistocene epoch

The ape, primitive man, and modern man all developed as separate branches from a common, very ancient, primate source. A comparison of these four skulls indicates that while structural similarities exist, there are also pronounced differences, the most marked of which are the larger size of the cranium and the humanizing of the facial features in *Homo sapiens*.

GORILLA   SINANTHROPUS (*HOMO ERECTUS*)   EARLY *HOMO SAPIENS*   MODERN *HOMO SAPIENS*

provides us with increasing data of the dynamic development of genus *Homo*—a process that we might divide into four stages. The first is that of the Australopithecines (Southern Apes) who lived in Africa. Possessing a fully erect posture but apelike brains, they were about the size of present-day pygmies. *Australopithecus* belongs to an extinct genus and may not be in modern man's line of descent. In 1964 the British anthropologist L. S. B. Leakey discovered at Olduvai Gorge in Tanzania what he claimed was the earliest representative of the genus *Homo*. If Leakey's claim is accepted it will push back man's age to approximately two million years. *Homo habilis* (mentally skillful man), as Leakey called his find, was about four feet tall, walked erect, had a well-developed thumb and the teeth of a meat eater, and his remains were found in association with crude tools. Was *Homo habilis* an advanced form of *Australopithecus*, or a different genus from which modern man is descended? Scientists are not agreed—but *Homo habilis* in any case deserves notice because of his apparent tool-making capability.

The second stage in man's development relates to the primate known as *Pithecanthropus*. In 1891 a Dutch army surgeon, Dr. Eugene Dubois, found in Java several fossil fragments of a primate which he designated *Pithecanthropus erectus* (erect ape-man), or Java man. In the 1930's more fossil discoveries were made of these creatures, whose brain size varied from 700 to 1000 cubic centimeters—placing the Pithecanthropines at a point on the evolutionary scale between the Australopithecines and modern man, whose brain capacity averages between 1300 and 1600 cubic centimeters. A somewhat younger member of this group—often referred to as *Homo erectus*—was *Sinanthropus*, or Peking man, who possessed a larger brain than his Javanese counterpart. *Homo erectus* was about five feet tall, had heavy brows, a receding forehead, and—by modern standards—possessed relatively low intelligence. With their pronounced apelike characteristics, the *Pithecanthropus* group died out before the end of the Pleistocene epoch.

The third stage is that of Neanderthal man and his contemporaries during the earlier Upper Pleistocene, possibly as early as 250 thousand years ago. From late in the third interglacial phase until after the middle of the fourth glaciation, *Homo neanderthalensis* was the principal inhabitant of Europe and adjacent parts of Africa and Asia. About five feet tall, Neanderthal man possessed a thick-set body, short forearms, and a slouching posture. He was a powerful hunter, and he adapted himself to cold weather by using fire and by living in caves and rock shelters.

The fourth stage occurs in the later Upper Pleistocene, when Neanderthal man in Europe is displaced by *Homo sapiens*—who has been described as the forerunner of a "modern European type." *Homo sapiens* may have been living in France and England as early as the third interglacial phase (or about seventy thousand years ago), probably as a contemporary of Neanderthal. It seems probable that Neanderthal man constituted a specialized line of development in man's evolution rather than, as was formerly supposed, an intermediate stage between *Pithecanthropus* and *Homo sapiens*. Since his appearance in the later Upper Pleistocene, the latter has migrated into every continent and comprises the only member extant of the genus *Homo* today.

Piltdown, a hoax with a moral. Fascinating to scientists and laymen alike during the past century has been the search for a "missing link"—that is, for some intermediate or transitional form between an outright simian type on the one hand, and a recognizable human type on the other. In 1912, and again in 1915, fragmentary remains of creatures perhaps half a million years old were discovered at Piltdown in Sussex, England. Most startling and intriguing to the scientific community was the fact that in both discoveries the cranial pieces were essentially human while the lower jaws were distinctly apelike. Here, it appeared, was irrefutable confirmation of the theory that man had evolved from apelike ancestors.

Yet the Piltdown man puzzled scientists. In the following decades many new discoveries from other parts of the world pointed to the evolution of man from a prehuman stage—but in a manner the reverse of Piltdown. The newer discoveries indicated that man had acquired a human jaw and teeth early in his development but that his large brain had evolved slowly.

To resolve the seeming disparity, in 1949 and 1953 British scientists subjected the Piltdown remains to a battery of sophisticated tests. The amount of fluorine found in the bones proved that these could be no older than fifty thousand years and that the jaw and teeth were much younger than the cranium. The remains were also subjected to radiocarbon dating tests. Carbon[14], a radioactive form of carbon, is created in the upper atmosphere and subsequently enters the earth's carbon cycle, where it is absorbed by all living matter. After an organism's death, it ceases to be assimilated, and the existing content diminishes at a known rate. As a result, carbon[14] has proved an excellent means of measuring the age of once living matter as old as thirty thousand years. Carbon[14] and other tests all proved that no relation existed between the skull and the jaw of the Piltdown man. Microscopic examination of the teeth showed that they had been artificially ground down to assume human appearance; the jaw in fact must have belonged to an orang-utan. Also, Piltdown man's famous clublike implement had been shaped with a metal knife—which Piltdown man obviously could not have possessed. Science had proved conclusively that the Piltdown "men" were fakes and had demonstrated brilliantly an arsenal of new tools and techniques which are now at the disposal of the research in preliterate history (see the Historical Critique on p. 57).

But why the hoax in the first place? Its perpetrator evidently sought to "prove" the evolutionary theory in spectacular fashion and to make it appear that the Piltdown man constituted the actual "missing link" between ape and man. Conceivably it could have started as a prank which in turn became too involved to permit its author to turn back, but in any case we should recognize that Piltdown man with its accompanying animal fossils and tools all tallied with what scientists had long expected to find. They were already predisposed to accept the evidence placed before their eyes. And herein lies the moral. The hoax—which fooled a large part of the academic and scientific world for some forty years—shows clearly how meticulous and objective must be the gathering of evidence. Also, and this may be the most important lesson for the student of history to acquire, the Piltdown forgery and its aftermath warn us of the danger of attempting to make the "facts" fit the theory —in this case, that man would develop a human cranium while retaining an apelike jaw. This theory was not only erroneous but, ironically, damaging to the acceptance of the evolutionary hypothesis, a result undoubtedly opposite to that intended by the perpetrator.

MAN THE CULTURE BUILDER

Man's physical and mental endowments. In strength, speed, vision, hearing, and other physical endowments, man is eclipsed by numerous creatures. Yet he possesses certain attributes that have enabled him to forge far ahead of all other species. Erect posture is one characteristic; another is the opposable thumb, which is longer and more powerful than the thumb of other primates and gives man greater manual skill. Although apes and monkeys have eyes capable of stereoscopic and color vision, only man has the capacity for close visual attention. Again, his finely attuned central nervous system—in which the brain is the vital hub—has enabled him to outdo all other creatures in both adjusting to his immediate environment and, in turn, progressively modifying it to his own needs and goals.

Human intelligence is unique not only because of the physical size of man's brain but also because of the quality which that intelligence displays. It enables him to reason and apply imagination and to make tools to "a set and regular pattern." At the same time, we should recognize that many of the higher animals are also capable of solving problems in adjusting to their environment and they display considerable imagination in the process. Furthermore, some nonhuman primates are occasional tool-users or even engage in patterned tool manufacture. For example, chimpanzee bands in East Africa have been observed to make more than five types of tools—with the young learning how to fashion them by copying from their mothers.[1] Yet while these primates can make tools, they lack what seems to be unique to man, namely, a type of intelligence and imagination that functions by means of symbols.

Like other creatures, man possesses a practical intelligence by which he makes meaningful responses to his environment. But in addition, he has the capability of both thinking and communicating symbolically. The principle of symbolism operates so as to give everything a name and to make its functioning universally applicable rather than to restrict it to local or particular cases. A symbol is not only universal but versatile, since the same meaning can be expressed in various languages or, again, in different contexts within the same language. By means of this capability to engage in symbolic thought and communication, man has created patterns of behavior and learning which can be termed "cultures."

Man has, as it were, discovered a new method of adapting himself to his environment. Between the receptor system and the effector system, which are to be found in all animal species, we find in man a third link which we may describe as the *symbolic system*. This new acquisition transforms the whole of human life. As compared with the other animals man lives not merely in a broader reality; he lives . . . in a new *dimension* of reality. . . . No longer in a merely physical universe, man lives in a symbolic universe. Language, myth, art, and religion are parts of this universe. They are the varied threads which weave the symbolic net, the tangled web of human experience. All human progress in thought and experience refines upon and strengthens this net.[2]

The dawn of Paleolithic culture. During the course of the Pleistocene epoch a distinct evolution in the use and manufacture of tools among the *hominids* can be perceived. Australopithecine sites in South Africa would indicate that while man's early Pleistocene ancestors perhaps did not fashion tools, they

at least occasionally made use of objects as improvised tools and weapons. Improvisation probably continued to play an important part among the first men—even as today some Australian aborigines carve wooden implements with naturally fractured stone pieces. Progressively, however, men developed the ability to fashion tools by striking pieces of rocks with other stones. Since this method of making implements was the most distinctive feature of man's earliest culture, the first stage in his cultural development is known as the Paleolithic, or Old Stone, Age. Strictly speaking, Paleolithic is a cultural and not a chronological term, and indeed "Paleolithic" methods and customs survived among some peoples into modern times. From an economic standpoint, the Paleolithic is also a food-*collecting* stage, when men hunted, fished, and collected wild fruits, nuts, and berries on which to survive.

Occasional tool making is associated with the dawn of early Paleolithic, while regular tool making, but with little or no standardization, was engaged in by Peking man, in whose cave deposits have been found thousands of artificially broken pieces of stone. Sometimes he would use the core of the stone, at other times the resulting flakes which might be trimmed into points or scrapers. The caves in which he lived contain evidence that he was an excellent hunter, possibly ate human as well as animal flesh, and knew how to use fire and keep it burning, but probably not how to kindle it. Perhaps man first knew fire when he found it started by lightning, by volcanic eruption, or by dry branches rubbed together by the wind.

The next technological stage takes the form of regular tool making, with marked standardization but little specialization. We are still in the early Paleolithic stage, where in Africa—such as at Olduvai in Tanzania—there occurs a clear progression from the simplest core tools to finely flaked hand-axes with carefully shaped cutting edges. These hand-axes, which for hundreds of thousands of years were employed to kill prey and cut and scrape hides, comprised the first standardized implements. They have been found over nearly one fifth of the land surface of the globe and possess such uniformity of design that specimens from sites as distant as London, the Cape of Good Hope, and Madras are indistinguishable from each other as regards form.

Middle and late Paleolithic cultures. From the third interglacial phase until after the middle of the fourth glaciation—that is, from about 70,000 to 35,000 years ago—the European and western Asian landscape was inhabited by Neanderthal man who, as we have mentioned, learned to adapt himself to colder climatic conditions by living in caves and rock shelters and also probably by wearing animal pelts in severe weather. His tool-making industries (known as Mousterian) involved the rudimentary beginnings of

specialized tools and weapons. For example, the Neanderthalers made side-scrapers, small heart-shaped hand-axes, and invented stone-tipped wooden spears to hunt their quarry.

About 35,000 B.C. the middle Paleolithic in Europe gave way to late Paleolithic cultures, a development accompanied by the displacement of Neanderthal man by *Homo sapiens*. By the end of the glacial phases *Homo sapiens* inhabited Europe, western Asia, Africa, and Australia—and subsequently migrated into the New World as well. *Homo sapiens'* technology was marked by a wide range of new specialized tools and weapons. They included blade tools—narrow, parallel-sided flakes—as well as tool-making tools, such as the burin, shaped like a chisel, which

Although no one ancient tool tradition existed exclusive of all others at any one time, the tools shown here represent a progression from rudimentary to more sophisticated. Pebble tools (top left), frequently indistinguishable from naturally occurring stones, have been found associated with Australopithecine remains. The core hand-ax (top center) was formed by using a wooden club to remove chips from a stone. The Mousterian side scraper (top right) represents an initial step toward specialization and gave rise to a gradual transition to such complex tools as the backed blade and the two burins (bottom left), shown with approximately equivalent modern tools. Microliths, the most specialized Stone Age tools, were used for various purposes. This one (bottom right) was inserted into a wooden spear and acted like a barb, catching and ripping at the flesh of a victim animal.

SOUTH AFRICAN PEBBLE TOOL

ACHEULEAN BIFACE

MOUSTERIAN SIDE SCRAPER

TWO BURINS

BACKED BLADE

BLADE FRAGMENT

was employed for working bone, antlers, ivory, and wood into implements for particular purposes. The fashioning of small, specialized flints—known as microliths—represented a compact and sophisticated use of materials somewhat analogous to the emphasis upon miniaturization which we associate with today's electronics and space technology. In late Paleolithic cultures, too, we find man "taking to the air" by applying mechanical principles to the movement of tools and weapons.

Spears were launched with throwers which, working on the lever principle, increase the effective propelling power of a man's arm. The bow was invented late in this period, probably in north Africa. It was the first means of concentrating muscular energy for the propulsion of an arrow, but it was soon discovered that it also provided a means of twirling a stick, and this led to the invention of the rotary drill.[3]

To withstand the cold weather, late Paleolithic peoples fashioned garments from sewn skins—bone needles with eyes, belt-fasteners, and even buttons have been found in their sites—and they erected the first man-made buildings in areas where natural caves did not exist. Thus the reindeer and mammoth hunters of present-day Russia and Czechoslovakia lived in tents and huts made of hides and brush or in communal houses partially sunk into the ground with a mammoth's ribs for roof supports. There is also evidence that coal was used for fuel.

The first artists. A special achievement of late Paleolithic cultures was their aesthetic expression. In 1879 Sautuola, a Spanish nobleman, discovered a long procession of magnificently drawn bison on the ceiling of a cave on his Altamira estate in northern Spain (see Color Plate 1). Archaeologists scoffed at Sautuola's discovery: the paintings were "too modern" and "too realistic." In a few years, however, other caves in northern Spain and southern France yielded many examples of prehistoric art, and Sautuola was vindicated.

In the Altamira murals skillfully drawn animals were outlined in black and shaded with a mixture of red, black, and yellow. It is generally believed that by drawing pictures of food animals, man thought he could wield magical power over his prey. Occasionally he drew arrows piercing the animals he presumably hoped to kill. Paleolithic man also chiseled pictures on rock and bone, modeled in clay, and made bas-relief friezes on cave walls.

Mesolithic, or Transitional, cultures. Climatic changes which ended the fourth glacial phase initiated in turn the Holocene, or Recent, epoch. As the vast ice sheets melted, changes in the sea level greatly altered coastlines, dense forests replaced areas in Europe marked hitherto by sparse vegetation, or tundra, while regions of the Near East and North Africa had their savannas transformed into deserts, with occasional oases. Because of their highly specialized adaptation to cold weather, the mammoth and other animals hunted by late Paleolithic peoples became extinct.

Man himself, however, proved able to adjust to the conditions of postglacial times by developing new cultures called Mesolithic, or Transitional. Many of these Mesolithic groups lived along the coast, fishing, sealing, and gathering shellfish. Whereas Paleolithic man was a hunter and lived a largely nomadic life, Mesolithic man followed a semi-sedentary existence—as attested by the large mounds of sea shells and other debris, known as kitchen middens, found in Denmark and elsewhere along the Baltic seacoast. Other Mesolithic groups lived inland, where in the plentiful forests they chopped wood with stone axes equipped with handles, made bows and arrows for hunting, and devised such forms of transport as skis, sleds, and dugout canoes. To provide propulsion for these sleds, our Mesolithic forebears quite possibly domesticated the dog—the first of the many animals brought into this special relationship with man.

Mesolithic peoples were not able to produce their own food supply, but while they retained the traditional food-gathering pattern of existence in Europe, Africa, and Australia, groups in southwest Asia began to augment their food resources with edible grasses which they found growing seasonally. Here we see a significant transition taking place: the shift from a food-gathering to a food-producing economy, which we associate with the Neolithic Age. Paleolithic and Mesolithic men were hunters and fishermen; our Neolithic ancestors were also farmers and herdsmen. The overall result comprised what has been described as the "first economic revolution" in the history of man —and, in the view of some scholars, perhaps the most far-reaching breakthrough in the dynamic relationship of man to his external environment.

Neolithic cultures and the advent of agriculture. Neolithic cultures are usually characterized by the cultivation of grains, domestication of animals, pottery making, and the use of polished stone tools (hence the use of Neolithic, or New Stone, Age to describe these cultures). Actually, all four characteristics are not always present in a given Neolithic culture. Furthermore, as we have seen, certain advances usually associated with the Neolithic had been anticipated by Mesolithic groups. Again we would do well to remember that the Neolithic is a technological and economic "stage" and not an "age," i.e., chronological period. While Neolithic settlements in Palestine date back some nine thousand years, the domestication of animals in Britain did not occur until many millennia later.

Remains of a community dated between 8000 and 6000 B.C.—older than any previously known settlement—have been unearthed at Jericho in Jordan. Farming was possible because wild grains grew well there and a spring provided a continuous source of water, creating an oasis. Some authorities hold, however, that agriculture originated not on oases but in sites, such as Jarmo and Hassuna, in the mountainous uplands of what is now Iraq. The wild ancestors of wheat and barley are thought to be highland forms; rainfall was greater there than on the arid lowlands; and wildlife was abundant. Neolithic farmers generally settled near a reliable water supply and combined agriculture with hunting to furnish themselves with sufficient food. They also domesticated animals to provide ready food, clothing, and transport. Tending herds instead of hunting them made possible a more settled life. In southern Asia, in turn, water buffalo

and elephants were domesticated, as were the llama and alpaca in the Peruvian highlands.

Developments in the ancient Near East. Because the ancient Near East represents the heartland not only of the Neolithic revolution but of the breakthrough to the next cultural stage—riverine civilizations—we might set forth a rough chronology of cultural progress for this region. Scholars believe that the eighth millennium B.C. witnessed a gradual move from caves to open-air sites, accompanied by the establishment of the first villages (such as at Jericho). These primitive settlements contained huts and storage space for wild grain; their inhabitants had domesticated the dog and goat, but hunting and fishing remained important economic activities. Agriculture proper may have begun between 7000 and 6500 B.C., although hunting still continued. Some of the villages grew into small towns (such as prepottery Jericho), defended by walls, and this progressive urbanization attests to a more complex societal organization, including perhaps the presence of local rulers.

In the millennium following 6500 B.C. pottery was invented, notable improvements occurred in architecture, and towns appeared on the South Anatolian plateau. In parts of the region grain was cultivated, but elsewhere the economy remained unchanged. In the period 5500–5000 B.C. pottery was in general use, while metal working had begun in Iran and Anatolia. Probably the first irrigation works were constructed in southern Mesopotamia, together with the advent of an efficient farming economy. The beginnings of religious architecture—such as at Eridu—date from the fifth millenium B.C.; during this same period metallurgy gradually spread to Mesopotamia. In the following millennium the Ubaid period in Mesopotamia is associated with the rise of towns. The arrival of new elements—probably the Sumerians— during the Uruk period initiated a protoliterate stage of culture; writing and cylinder seals were invented, and an impressive advance occurred in representational art. Finally, as of 3000 B.C., we come to the beginning of the historical period in Sumer and Egypt, with the rise of dynastic states and national civilizations along the banks of the Tigris-Euphrates and the Nile.[4]

Neolithic domestic arts. Neolithic artisans ground and polished stones to produce axes, adzes, and chisels with strong and sharp cutting edges. They devised methods for drilling holes in stone, used boulders for grinding grain, and stone bowls for storage. These stone artifacts show a much greater interest in design than had previously been the case. Moreover, when Neolithic peoples ceased to roam in search of food, they were better able to make pottery in quantity and to decorate it with geometric designs. Clothing and baskets had been fashioned in pre-Neolithic cultures, but the pattern of Neolithic life gave women more time to develop skills in the domestic arts. Similarly, Neolithic man paid more attention to the art of constructing shelter than did his semisedentary Mesolithic forebears. In Europe, where wood was abundant, rectangular timber houses were constructed; some had two rooms, a gabled roof, and walls of split saplings. Remains found near Swiss lakes show that even on soft swampy earth the builders could erect houses by placing them on wooden foundations or on piles sunk into the ground.

Neolithic cultures bring economic and social changes. While Paleolithic and Mesolithic peoples could not develop any permanent settlements or accumulate an excess of food, a food-producing economy was radically different. By cultivating plants or by stock breeding, men could now add to the food acquired by hunting. As a consequence, they greatly increased their control over the external environment. A food-producing way of life required permanent settlements and also enabled larger populations to be sustained. Any food surplus could be put aside for planting the following year's crops or, alternatively, was available as barter to obtain various commodities not locally produced.

Within the community, a division of labor existed between the sexes. While the men made the tools and weapons, tended the herds, hunted, and built the dwellings, the women grew and prepared the food, wove baskets, and fashioned clothing and pottery —in addition to their traditional role of rearing the young. Each Neolithic village was largely self-supporting, growing its own food and using local materials for its tools, weapons, and houses. Because the people in Neo-

This drawing of a reconstructed Neolithic village in the Rhineland district shows, at the right, the long semisubterranean dwellings; to the left, the palisaded area containing small granaries on posts, rectangular structures probably used as communal working areas, and pasturage for cattle; and the cultivated fields surrounding the village. The two concentric circles are a common feature of Neolithic villages (see top lefthand corner of photograph on p. 23).

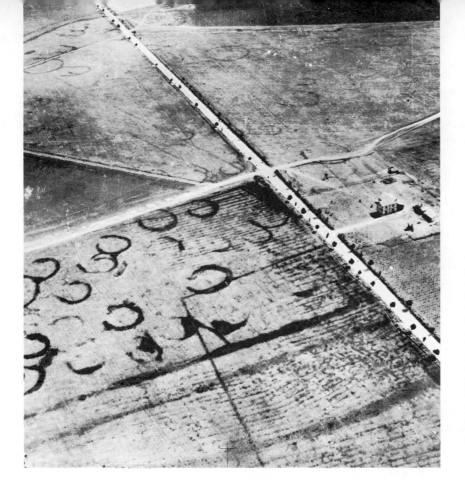

The site of a Neolithic village near Foggia, Italy, is revealed by an aerial photograph in which the ditches surrounding both the village and the individual huts are outlined by the extra growth of corn over the buried earth-works. Measuring fifteen hundred yards across, this village is among the largest discovered in Europe. During World War II the Royal Air Force took thousands of aerial reconnaissance photographs, similar to this one, which have proved invaluable to archaeologists.

lithic settlements had only limited contacts with the outside world, each village tended to develop its own localized culture. This condition of isolation permitted two settlements, a Mesolithic and a Neolithic, for example, to coexist for centuries with little interchange of culture and consequently few modifications in their respective patterns of living.

PRIMITIVE THOUGHT AND CUSTOM

Analysis of primitive societies. Perhaps it is natural for most of us, living as we do in a highly complex machine-age society, to assume that primitive men, prehistoric or modern, would possess few laws, little education, and only the simplest codes of conduct. But this is far from true. The organization of a primitive society may be as complex as our own. Rules regarding the role of parents, the treatment of children, the punish-

ment of the evildoer, the conduct of business, the worship of the gods, and the conventions of eating and recreation have existed for thousands of years, along with methods to compel the individual to do "the correct thing."

We cannot know with certainty about those features of the culture of early man which are not apparent from the remains of tools and other objects, but we can speculate about these prehistoric cultures by applying the conclusions anthropologists have drawn from studies of the cultures of present-day primitive societies. But here a word of caution is necessary. Because the general level of technological development in a modern-day primitive society appears to be similar to the level of achievement reached in a prehistoric society, it does not mean that all aspects of the two cultures are comparable. Furthermore, it is often difficult to measure in what degree modern primitive societies have been affected by the impact of advanced civilizations like our own.

Forms of social organization. Among all

peoples, past and present, the basic social unit appears to be the elementary family group—parents and their offspring. Anthropologists do not know what marriage customs were prevalent in the earliest societies, but monogamy—one husband and one wife—was probably most common.

The extended family—an individual family together with a circle of related persons who usually trace their descent through their mothers and are bound together by mutual loyalty—is often found in primitive social groupings. The extended family strengthens the elementary unit both in obtaining food and in protecting its members against other groups. Because of its social and economic advantages, this form of organization may have existed in ancient times.

A third primitive social unit is the clan—a group of individuals within a community who believe that they have a common ancestor and therefore are "of one blood, of one soul." A clan is patrilineal if its members trace their relationship through the male line, and matrilineal if through the female. Many primitive peoples identify their clans by a totem—an animal or some natural object—which is revered and is made the subject for amulets of various sorts. Nearly everyone is acquainted with the totem poles and masks made by the Indians of British Columbia and Alaska. Forms of totemism in modern-day society include the insignia worn by a particular military unit, the emblems of such organizations as the Elks and Moose, and animal mascots used by college football teams.

A fourth grouping among some primitive peoples is the tribe. This term lacks a precise definition, but it may be thought of as applying to a community characterized by a common speech or distinctive dialect, a common cultural heritage, and a specific inhabited territory. Group loyalty is a strong trait among members of a tribe and is often accompanied by a contempt for the peoples and customs of other communities. Some Eskimos, for example, speak of neighboring Indians as "children of a louse's egg."

Collective responsibility in law and government. In primitive societies ethical behavior consists in not violating custom. The close relationships that exist in extended families and clans encourage conformity.

The concept of justice among the individuals of a primitive group is synonymous with maintaining equilibrium. Thus, if one man steals another's property, the economic equilibrium has been unjustly disturbed. Such a theft constitutes a wrong against the individual; and, where modern legal procedure calls for punishment of the thief, in primitive societies justice is achieved by a settlement between the injured man and the thief. If the thief restores what has been stolen or its equivalent, the victim is satisfied and the thief is not punished. On the other hand, certain acts are considered dangerous to the whole group and require punishment by the entire community. Treason, witchcraft, and incest are typical offenses in this category. Such acts are not settled by the payment of compensation; the punishment meted out is usually death. If a member of a clan gets into trouble too often, his fellows will regard him as a social nuisance and an economic liability; thus they may outlaw him from the group or execute him.

Scholars theorize that in food-gathering societies and the earliest food-producing societies, as in primitive societies of today, the governing political body was small and of a democratic character. The adults participated in the decisions of the group, with special deference being paid to the views of the older tribal members because of their greater experience and knowledge of the group's traditions and ceremonies. In the more advanced food-producing communities, however, government tended to fall increasingly under the control of the richest members. In time there emerged strong individuals claiming political and religious leadership; we shall encounter them in the following chapters on early civilized societies.

Religion and magic. Perhaps the strongest single force in the life of primitive people is religion. Man's religious sensibilities apparently originated in the feeling of awe that came over him when he first became conscious of the universe about him. Awe and wonder led to the belief, usually called animism, that all things in nature—winds, stones, trees, animals, and man himself—were inhabited by spirits. Many spirits became objects of reverence, with man's own spirit being one of the first. Neanderthal man placed food and implements alongside his carefully buried dead, an indication that he believed in an afterlife and held his ancestors in awe. We know also that late Paleolithic man revered the spirits of the animals he hunted for food as well as the spirit of fertility upon which both human and animal life depended. This led to totemism and to the worship of a fertility goddess who is known to us from many carved and modeled female figurines with grossly exaggerated sexual features. Neolithic farmers developed a special reverence for this embodiment of fertility in the form of the Earth Mother (or Mother Goddess).

Closely associated with primitive religion is the practice of magic. In addition to revering the spirits, primitive man wants to compel them to favor him. For this purpose he employs magic of the kind previously described in the discussion of late Paleolithic art. Primitive man also turns to medicine men to ward off droughts, famines, floods, and plagues through magical powers of communication with the spirits.

SUMMARY

The birth of our planet occurred in an incomparably distant past. Although geologists who have dated the earth's rock strata believe it to be between four and five billion years old, the genesis of the earth has given rise to numerous conflicting theories, some based upon an evolutionary concept and others upon the occurrence of a cataclysmic event. During vast geologic ages organic life developed from single-celled protozoa to multicelled organisms of extraordinary complexity. The world acquired much of its present appearance in the Cenozoic era, and the earliest primates appeared during the Tertiary period. During the Oligocene epoch different lines of monkeys and primitive forms of anthropoid apes evolved. Before the end of the Miocene epoch one line of apes developed into tree-dwelling apes; another led to the ground-dwelling *hominids,* or prehumans. A great gap exists in our knowledge of prehuman development during the following Pliocene epoch.

The Pleistocene epoch provides us with rich data on the evolution of genus *Homo.* In Africa emerged an apelike hominid, *Australopithecus,* who may not be in modern man's line of descent. There was also *Homo habilis,* who poses the problem of whether he was an advanced form of *Australopithecus* or instead the earliest known representative of genus *Homo.* Next appeared the *Pithecanthropus* group of primates, including Java man and Peking man, followed by Neanderthal man and *Homo sapiens.* With his ability to think and communicate in symbolic terms, coupled with a tool-making capability, early man began to acquire slowly but progressively, control over his terrestrial environment—and, in so doing, to lay the foundations for the technological order so dominant in our lives today.

Thus, paralleling his biological evolution, began the first great period of man's cultural evolution, called the Paleolithic, or Old Stone, Age. We have seen how his tool-making capability advanced from reliance upon a standardized, all-purpose hand-ax—in use for hundreds of thousands of years—to ever more specialized and sophisticated tools and techniques of operation. This technological evolution enabled *Homo* in turn to move into and adapt himself to different environments, whether in the higher latitudes of Eurasia and North America, or again in the rain forests of southeast Asia and the deserts of Australia. By the end of the last glacial phase man had spread over most of the world, while in the postglacial period he developed a semisedentary form of existence as found in the Mesolithic, or Transitional, cultures.

Paleolithic and Mesolithic cultures had food-gathering economies. Then, perhaps some eight thousand years ago, the Neolithic, or New Stone, stage was initiated with the appearance of food-producing communities in western Asia. Neolithic cultures are usually characterized by the cultivation of grains, the domestication of animals, pottery making, and the fashioning of polished stone tools. These advances probably occurred in various places at different chronological times. Agriculture, for example, may have originated in the high-lands of Iraq or in oasis settlements such as at Jericho. Again, wheat may have been domesticated in one area, sheep and cattle in yet others. What is most important, however, is to realize that the revolutionary change from a food-gathering to a food-producing economy made possible the next stage in man's cultural evolution—riverine civilizations.

Chapter 2

Along the Banks of Rivers

The Ancient Near East

INTRODUCTION. In early Egyptian picture writing, a town is shown as a cross within a circle—the intersection of two roads enclosed by a wall. The symbol is an appropriate one, for in the history of mankind the town— ⊗ —marks the spot where civilization as we know it began.

The first towns were farming villages, built by men who could raise enough food to support themselves and their families. Thus they were freed of the necessity of endlessly moving on in search of food, as their ancestors had done for countless generations. Where the land was good, these ancient farmers were able to produce more food than they needed for survival—surpluses to tide them over seasons of cold and drought. Thus, in green oases, along the banks of rivers, and on fertile plateaus, farming villages sprang up.

Within these settlements, the business of living took new turns. Communal effort remained essential—all the men in a village might help erect a wall of brick or wood to protect the inhabitants against marauding nomads—but it was no longer necessary for each man to concentrate solely on farming or hunting. True, the majority farmed, but others turned out specialized wares, traded with friendly neighbors, and conducted religious ceremonies. While contributing to the well-being of the community, each person performed a distinct function. As life became more stable, time could be found for such intellectual and artistic pastimes as storytelling, clay modeling, wood carving, painting, singing, and dancing, which developed a cultural heritage.

A culture can endure only if it is passed on from generation to generation. Early people relied solely on information transmitted by word of mouth—an undependable means of communication. But as towns grew larger and cultures became increasingly complex, methods for keeping records were devised and systems of writing were created. To most authorities, the development of writing is a prerequisite to civilization.

The rise of the four earliest civilizations—the Sumerian, the Egyptian, the Indian, and the Chinese—between c. 3500 B.C. and c. 1500 B.C., took place, in each case, in the valley of a great river system. In this chapter we shall trace the progress of civilization, including man's earliest advances in technology and his creation of written languages, in Mesopotamia and Egypt. In Chapter 3 we shall see the stirrings of civilization far to the east, in India and in China.

THE DAWN OF CIVILIZATION

The metallurgical revolution. By discovering how to use metals to make tools and weapons, Neolithic man effected a revolution as far-reaching as that wrought in agriculture. Neolithic artisans ingeniously discovered how to extract copper from oxide ores by heating them with charcoal. At first they worked the copper by hammering, but by 3000 B.C. they had discovered how to cast it as well. Unlike those made of stone or bone, copper implements could be formed into any desired shape, and they were less likely to break—an important factor, especially in time of combat. Moreover, a stone tool had to be discarded when broken; a damaged copper implement could be recast. Early metalworkers in time discovered that copper was improved by the addition of tin. The resulting alloy, bronze, was more fusible than copper and therefore could be cast more easily; also, bronze was harder, less malleable, and provided a sharper cutting edge.

Metal ousted stone slowly in the Near East and still more slowly elsewhere. Bronze implements did not supersede stone ones in Assyria until about 3000 B.C., in Egypt until 2000 B.C., and in the Aegean until five hundred years later, while in barbaric Europe stone tools continued to be used for many hundreds of years.[1]

Other inventions. The fourth millennium was momentous for other basic inventions. The farmer's first plow was probably a stick which he pulled through the soil with a rope. In time, however, the cattle that his forebears had domesticated for food and milk were harnessed to drag the hoe in place of his mate or himself. Yoked, harnessed animals pulled plows in the fields of western Asia and Egypt by 3000 B.C. and in India somewhat later. As a result, farming advanced from the cultivation of small plots to the tilling of extensive fields. "By harnessing the ox man began to control and use a motive power other than that furnished by his own muscular energy. The ox was the first step to the steam engine and gasoline motor."[2]

Our Mesolithic forebears had used sleds to transport goods; a great advance in transport took place when some enterprising inventor saw the value of a wheel. Archaeologists have unearthed ancient wheels made of three carved wooden planks clamped to-gether by wooden struts, the rims of the wheels studded with copper nails as pro-tection against wear. Soon after 3500 B.C. men were turning out wheeled wagons in Sumer, and by the end of that millennium their use had extended as far up the Tigris as Assyria. Wheeled vehicles dating from 2000 B.C. have been found in areas as far apart as India and Crete. They did not appear in Egypt, however, until about 1700 B.C. or in Britain until about 500 B.C.—and in fact did not appear in the New World until the coming of the Europeans (see the Historical Critique, p. 57).

Improvements in water transport paral-leled developments on land. Dugout canoes had been used since Mesolithic times, and the oldest sailing boat known is represented by a model found in a Mesopotamian grave of about 3500 B.C.

Another important invention was the potter's wheel. Earlier, men had fashioned pots by molding or coiling clay by hand, but with the potter's wheel a symmetrical product could be produced in a much shorter time. Although none of the ancient wooden potter's wheels have survived, examples made of clay and stone have been excavated. The oldest, found at Ur in the lower Eu-phrates valley, dates from about 3250 B.C. Potter's wheels were used in Syria and Pales-tine about 3000 B.C., in Egypt some 250 years later, in India before 2500 B.C., and in Greece about 1800 B.C. On the other hand, they did not appear in England until ap-proximately 50 B.C. and in the Americas until 1550 A.D.

Effect of the new discoveries. During the millennium preceding 3000 B.C. some of the most significant discoveries and inven-tions in human history had been achieved. They laid the foundations for a type of an economy and social order markedly differ-ent from anything previously known. Be-cause full-time specialists such as potters, metalworkers, and wheelwrights did not raise their own food, a surplus had to be produced by the rest of the community. Around settlements like those in the Syrian steppes and the Iranian plateaus, however, there was insufficient arable land to accumu-late substantial surpluses. A more congen-ial physical environment was necessary. It was found in the alluvial valleys of certain great rivers.

These river valleys (except for those in China) lie in a broad steppe and mountain region stretching from North Africa across the Arabian peninsula and the Iranian plateau to the northwest section of the Indian subcontinent. Within this region is found the Fertile Crescent, a narrow strip of land connecting the Persian Gulf with the eastern Mediterranean coast (see map, p. 33). Into this area at various times came peoples who represented two of the great language families of mankind—Semites and Indo-Europeans. The original home of the Semitic-speaking peoples is thought to have been the Arabian peninsula, while the Indo-Europeans migrated from the region north of the Black and Caspian seas. A third, much smaller, language family was the Hamitic, which included the Egyptians and other peoples of northeastern Africa. The Sumerians, however, who founded man's first civilization at the eastern tip of the Fertile Crescent, spoke an agglutinative language unrelated to any now known. (In an agglutinative language words are altered not by inflection but by the addition of prefixes and suffixes.) The cradle of Sumerian civilization was the delta of the Tigris and Euphrates rivers.

MESOPOTAMIA: THE FIRST CIVILIZATION

Potential of the Tigris-Euphrates delta. The broad plain watered by the Tigris and Euphrates rivers—in what is now Iraq—was known in ancient days as Mesopotamia (Greek for "between the rivers"). The lower reaches of this plain, beginning near the point where the two rivers nearly converge, was called Babylonia. Babylonia in turn encompassed two geographical areas—Akkad in the north and Sumer, the delta of this river system, in the south. Broken by river channels teeming with fish and re-

The economies of the ancient river valley civilizations were primarily based on agriculture, which occupied a central position in both the daily lives of the people and in their religions. The Sumerian cylinder seal impression depicts an offering bearer carrying stalks of wheat; the detail from an Egyptian mural shows the reaping and threshing of grain. All the river valley civilizations depended on relatively sophisticated irrigation systems for water during the dry seasons. The cuneiform map and translated diagram of fields and canals near Nippur, in Sumer, show the complexity of these systems.

fertilized every year by alluvial silt, this delta had a splendid agricultural potential—but one which could be developed only by large-scale cooperative efforts. "Arable land had literally to be created out of a chaos of swamps and sandbanks by a 'separation' of land from water; the swamps . . . drained; the floods controlled; and lifegiving waters led to the rainless desert by artificial canals."[3] Provided these steps were taken, the fertile soil could produce more than a hundred times the amount of grain sown. In this way food surpluses could be accumulated, making possible a diversified economy that would support tradesmen and craftsmen as well as farmers. On the other hand, the plain had no stone, no metals, and no timber except that available from its palm trees.

The emergence of civilization in Sumer. The earliest inhabitants of Sumer emigrated from the highlands east of the Tigris about 4000 B.C. when the delta swamps had begun to dry out. These Neolithic farmers built an irrigation system and villages of mud-plastered reed huts. They fashioned a few of their tools and weapons of copper, but most were still made of stone. In honor of their local deity they erected shrines and staffed them with priests. Most of the land in each community belonged to the temple, where the communal food surplus was stored. In this way the temple assumed a central role in the economy, a distinctive feature of this Ubaid culture, as it is called, that was carried over into later Sumerian society.

About 3500 B.C. the Ubaid culture in Sumer gave way to a more complex and advanced culture—the Uruk. (It is named for the ancient city of Uruk—the present-day Warka, also known in the Bible as Erech.) New settlers appeared in Sumer at the beginning of the Uruk period, and another migration occurred shortly before 3000 B.C. Scholars cannot agree on which, if either, of these newcomers were the Sumerians. It may be that the historical Sumerians were an amalgam of all the racial stocks that entered the land during prehistoric times.

How would the advanced Uruk culture have appeared to a visitor seeing it for the first time? As he approached the city of Uruk, situated on the lower Euphrates, he would pass farmers working in their fields with wheeled carts and plows drawn by oxen. He might see some of the workers using bronze sickles. The river would be dotted by boats with high prows and sterns, carrying produce to and from the city. Dominating the flat countryside would be the great ziggurat at Uruk, a lofty, terraced tower, built in the shape of a pyramid and crowned by a sanctuary, or "high place." For the people of Uruk, this was the "holy of holies," sacred to the local god. Leaving the farmers in the fields and the river fishermen who resided with them in nearby towns, the visitor would see, upon entering the city, a large number of specialists pursuing their appointed tasks as agents of the community—some craftsmen casting bronze tools and weapons, others fashioning their wares on the potter's wheel, and still others, merchants, arranging to trade grain and manufactures for the metals, stone, lumber, and other essentials not available in Sumer. Scribes would be at work incising thin tablets of clay with picture signs. Some tablets might bear the impressions of cylinder seals, small stone cylinders engraved with a design (see illustration, p. 30). Examining the clay tablets, the visitor would find that they were memoranda used in administering the temple, which was at once the warehouse and workshop of the entire community. Some of the scribes might be making an inventory of the goats and sheep received that day for sacrificial use, others might be drawing up wage lists. They would be using a system of counting based on the unit 60, still used over five thousand years later in our modern world in computing divisions of time and angles.

Can this advanced and complex culture be termed a *civilization*? Many authorities agree that "a civilization is a culture which has attained a degree of complexity usually characterized by urban life"[4]—that it is capable, in other words, of sustaining a substantial number of specialists to cope with the economic, social, political, and religious needs of a populous society. Other characteristics usually present in a civilization include a system of writing to keep records, monumental architecture in place of simple buildings, and an art that is no longer merely decorative but representational of man and his activities. Moreover, an urban environment is important because of the self-consciousness and pride which it generates. If we accept the view that the advent of all or most of these characteristics distinguishes the emergence of civilization, the people of the Uruk period in Sumer deserve the credit for having created the first civilization in world history.

It should be clearly understood, however, that *civilization* is defined here as a technical term to emphasize a societal structure embracing an urban element and requiring the performance of specialized social and economic functions. Hence the authors reject any value judgment implied by such terms as *savagery*, which they equate with a food-gathering economy—or *barbarism*, the food-producing stage. At the same time *civilization* for its part can claim no moral superiority. Global history makes clear that many so-called "primitive" societies have moral and ethical systems that compare favorably with the behavior of numerous "civilized" peoples (see p. 591).

Diffusion of Sumerian culture traits. The Uruk culture, which lasted until about 3000 B.C., influenced the development of other riverine cultures. Certain technical inventions of the Uruk period eventually made their way to both the Nile and the Indus valleys. Chief among these were the wheeled vehicle and the potter's wheel. The discovery in Egypt of cylinder seals similar in shape to those used in Sumer attests to contact between the two areas toward the end of the fourth millennium B.C. Later the Egyptians replaced the cylindrical seal with a stamp seal in the form of a scarab, a beetle they considered sacred. Certain early Egyptian art motifs and architectural forms are also thought to be of Sumerian origin. And it is probable that the example of Sumerian writing stimulated the Egyptians to develop a script of their own. Whereas the Sumerian script evolved in the direction of abstract symbols, the Egyptian script retained its pictorial images. These are examples of how cultures during their most formative stages

may influence one another yet continue to develop unique features which stamp them as distinctive civilizations.

Sumerian writing. As we have noted, the symbols on the oldest Sumerian tablets were primarily pictures. However, many matters, including thought processes, cannot be depicted conveniently by pictures. Sumerian scribes overcame this problem by arbitrarily adding marks to the picture signs to denote new meanings. During the Uruk period some two thousand signs were in use. This cumbersome system could have been still further enlarged and complicated by the creation of more pictures and modifying marks. Fortunately, the Sumerians adopted an alternative solution whereby the signs represented sounds rather than objects or ideas. By giving the signs a phonetic value, the Sumerians could spell out names and compound words instead of inventing new signs. The use of syllabic signs reduced the number of signs to some six hundred by 2800 B.C.

In writing, a scribe used a reed stylus to make impressions in soft clay tablets. The impressions took on a wedge shape, hence the term *cuneiform* (Latin *cuneus*, "wedge"). The cuneiform system of writing was adopted by many other peoples of the Near East, including the Babylonians, Assyrians, Hittites, and Persians.

The Old Sumerian period. A sufficient number of decipherable Sumerian documents have been recovered to permit historians to re-create the political, economic, and social life in Sumer as it was after 2800 B.C. This first historical age in Sumer, called the Old Sumerian (or Early Dynastic) period, was characterized by continual rivalry and fighting among the dozen or more city-states, each seeking to enlarge its territory or prevent one state from dominating the rest. The boundary dispute between Lagash and Umma, for example, can be traced in detail over more than two centuries. The Old Sumerian period ended about 2370 B.C., when the failure of the Sumerians to unite led to their conquest by Semites from neighboring Akkad.

Like life in medieval Europe, early Sumerian society was highly collectivized. "Each temple owned lands which formed the estate

THE ANCIENT NEAR EAST

Fertile Crescent

of its divine owners. Each citizen belonged to one of the temples, and the whole of a temple community—the officials and priests, herdsmen and fishermen, gardeners, craftsmen, stonecutters, merchants, and even slaves—was referred to as 'the people of the god X.' "[5] That part of the temple land called "common" was worked by all members of the community, while the remaining land was divided among the citizens for their support at a rental of from one third to one sixth of the crop. Priests and temple administrators, however, held rent-free lands.

Recent scholarship has revealed that a considerable part of a city's territory originally consisted of collectively owned clan lands which in time became the property of great landowners called *lugals* (literally, "great men"). Deeds of sale record the transfer of clan lands to private owners in return for substantial payments in copper to a few community leaders and insignificant grants of food to the humbler folk. These private estates were worked by "clients" whose status resembled that of the dependents of the temples.

The Sumerian city-state experienced a constitutional development that parallels, in part, that of the more famous Greek city-state (see p. 97).[6] Epic tales reveal that the earliest type of government in Sumer was a form of primitive monarchy in which the actions of the ruler, essentially a war leader, were limited by a council of his fellow aristocrats and by an assembly of all the male citizens. In time the aristocratic council gained full control and imposed an oppressive oligarchy upon the mass of the people. Oligarchy in turn was followed by the rule of a despot who rode to power on a wave of popular discontent. Since these despots were *lugals* (great landowners), *lugal* became a political title and is generally translated "king." The Sumerian *lugals,* as well as their Akkadian and Babylonian successors, were enlightened despots who made the general welfare their major concern. Best known is Urukagina, who usurped power at Lagash at the end of the Old Sumerian period. His reform inscriptions state that when he "had received the lugalship . . . he removed from the inhabitants of Lagash usury, forestalling, famine, robbery, attacks; he established their freedom . . . [and] protected the widow and the orphan from the powerful man."[7]

Akkadian dominance. Immediately north of Sumer lay the narrow region of Akkad, inhabited by a Semitic-speaking people who had absorbed Sumerian culture. Appearing late in the fourth millennium B.C., the Akkadians were the earliest of the Semitic peoples who filtered into Mesopotamia from Arabia. A generation after Urukagina, Sargon I (2370-2315 B.C.), an energetic Akkadian ruler, conquered Sumer and went on to establish an empire which, he boasted, extended "from the lower sea to the upper sea" (the Persian Gulf to the Mediterranean Sea).

Very proud of his lower-class origins, Sargon boasted that his humble, unwed mother had been forced to abandon him: "She set me in a basket of rushes . . . [and] cast me into the river."[8] Rescued and brought up by a gardener, Sargon rose to power through the army. As *lugal,* Sargon looked after the welfare of the lower classes, distributing part of the temple lands among them. In addition, he aided the rising class of private merchants. At their request he once sent his army to far-off Asia Minor to protect a colony of merchants from interference by a local ruler. We are told that Sargon "did not sleep" in his efforts to promote prosperity; trade moved as freely "as the Tigris where it flows into the sea, . . . all lands lie in peace, their inhabitants prosperous and contented."[9]

Despite these innovations the successors of Sargon were unable either to withstand the attacks of semibarbaric invaders from the Iranian plateau or to overcome the deep-rooted desire for independence of the Sumerian cities. As a result, the house of Sargon collapsed about 2230 B.C.

The Neo-Sumerian period. Order and prosperity were restored a century later by the *lugals* of the Third Dynasty of Ur (c. 2113-2006 B.C.). By creating a highly centralized administration in Sumer and Akkad, these rulers solved the problem of internal rebellion that had plagued Sargon and his successors. The formerly temple-dominated cities became provinces administered by governors who were watched closely by a corps of "messengers." The "church" became an arm of the state; the high priests were state appointees, and the temple economic organization was retained and used as the state's agent in rigidly controlling the economy.

At the head of this bureaucratic state stood the now-deified ruler, celebrated in hymns as a heaven-sent messiah who "brings splendor to the land, . . . savior of orphans whose misery he relieves, . . . the vigilant shepherd who conducts the people unto cooling shade."[10] Much of what we now call social legislation was passed by these "vigilant shepherds." Such laws were called "rightings" (Sumerian *nig-si-sa,* usually translated "equity"), since their object was the righting of wrongs that were not covered by the old customary law (*nig-ge-na,* "truth"). The prologue to the law code of Ur-Nammu, founder of the dynasty, declared that it was the king's purpose to see that "the orphan did not fall a prey to the wealthy" and that "the man of one shekel did not fall a prey to the man of one mina (sixty shekels)."[11]

Disaster struck Ur about 2006 B.C., when Elamites from the highlands to the east destroyed the city. Henceforth the Sumerians never again figured politically in history, but their culture persisted as the foundation for all subsequent civilizations in the Tigris-Euphrates valley.

For more than two centuries following the destruction of Ur, disunity and warfare again plagued Mesopotamia, along with depression, inflation, and acute hardship for the lower classes. Merchants, however, utilized the lack of state controls to become full-fledged capitalists who amassed fortunes which they invested in banking operations and in land. (These merchants used a form of double-entry bookkeeping which they called "balanced accounts." Their word for capital, *qaqqadum,* meaning "head," influenced later peoples; our word *capital* is derived from the Latin form, *caput.*[12]) The stronger local rulers of the period freed the poor from debt slavery and issued a variety of reform laws which are best illustrated by the legislation of Hammurabi.

Hammurabi and the Babylonian empire. Semitic Amorites (from *Amurru,* the "West"), under the rule of their capable king, Hammurabi (c. 1792-1750 B.C.), again brought most of Mesopotamia under one rule by 1760 B.C. Hammurabi's empire had its capital in Babylon, previously an obscure village on the Euphrates.

Hammurabi is best known for his code of nearly three hundred laws touching on economic, social, and moral life. Hammurabi's stated objective was "to cause justice to prevail in the land, to destroy the wicked and the evil, to prevent the strong from oppressing the weak . . . and to further the welfare of the people."[13] His legislation reestablished a state-controlled economy in which merchants were required to obtain a "royal permit," interest was limited to 20 per cent, and prices were set for basic commodities and for fees charged by physicians, veterinarians, and builders. Minimum wages were set, and debt slavery was limited to three years.

In family life various provisions protected wives and children, although a wife who had "set her face to go out and play the part of a fool, neglect her house, belittle her husband"[14] could be divorced without alimony, or the husband could take another wife and compel the first to remain as a servant. Punishments were graded in their severity; the higher the culprit in the social scale, the more severe the penalty.

In the epilogue to the code, Hammurabi eloquently summed up his efforts to provide social justice for his people:

Let any oppressed man, who has a cause, come before my image as king of righteousness! Let him read the inscription on my monument! Let him give heed to my weighty words! And may my monument enlighten him as to his cause and may he understand his case! May he set his heart at ease! (and he will exclaim): "Hammurabi indeed is a ruler who is like a real father to his people. . . ."[15]

Mathematics, science, and technology. Carrying on the work of the Sumerians, the Babylonians made advances in arithmetic, geometry, and algebra. For ease of computation with both whole numbers and fractions, they compiled tables for multiplication and division and for square and cube roots. They knew how to solve linear and quadratic equations, and their knowledge of geometry included the theorem later made famous by the Greek philosopher Pythagoras: the square of the hypotenuse of a right-angled triangle is equal to the sum of the squares of the other two sides. Perhaps their greatest achievement was the principle of place-value notation which gave numbers a value according to their position in a series. It has been said that Babylonian "mathematical methods can well stand comparison with the accomplishments of all other civilizations up to the middle of the second millennium A.D., i.e., for more than three thousand years."[16]

The Babylonians achieved little that today deserves to be called science. They did observe nature and collect data, which is the first requirement of science; but in seeking intelligible explanations of natural phenomena, they did not go beyond the formulation of myths which explained things in terms of the unpredictable whims of the gods. The sun, the moon, and the five visible planets were thought to be gods who were able to influence men's lives; accordingly, their movements were watched, recorded, and interpreted.

By using the scientific and mathematical knowledge they had to master their environment and to increase their productivity, the Mesopotamians (and, as we shall see later, the Egyptians) reached an impressive level of technological accomplishment. Yet various historians of science see the need to differentiate between "necessary" or "hard-core" technology and science on the one hand and the emergence of a truly scientific method on the other. Mesopotamian mathematical texts, for instance, dealt with a large group of practical problems—such as the work quotas and food requirements for men constructing irrigation canals, the volume of earth to be moved, the number of bricks required, and so forth. Yet though the Mesopotamians could comprehend the properties of numbers and account arithmetically for the motions of the sun and planets, they employed only "strictly numerical methods of predicting dates and positions of the phenomena in question. We have no indication of the underlying ideas concerning the mechanism which was thought to bring about these phenomena. . . ."[17]

Here would appear to be the dividing line between "hard-core" technology and science on the one hand and a "scientific revolution" on the other. In the first we find the compilation and use of disparate data to cope with specific problems; in the second there must occur a fundamental breakthrough so as to conceptualize natural phenomena in terms of general hypotheses to which the observable data can in turn be related. As we shall see, this breakthrough occurred with the Greeks —and the resulting "Greek miracle" was to lay the foundations for the science and technology which are revolutionizing our lives today.

Babylonian literature. The dependence of the Babylonians upon Sumerian culture is clearly evident in the field of literature. They produced a variety of literary types ranging from heroic epics that compare favorably with the *Iliad* and the *Odyssey* to wisdom writings that have their counterparts in the Old Testament books of Job, Proverbs, and Ecclesiastes. Longest and most famous is the *Epic of Gilgamesh,* which recounts the exploits of a heroic ruler of Uruk who lived about 2700 B.C. The central theme of the epic is Gilgamesh's hope of immortality. This leads him to seek out and question Ut-napishtim, the Babylonian Noah who was granted eternal life because he saved all living creatures from the flood. Ut-napishtim's story has many remarkable similarities with the Hebrew account of the flood. But Gilgamesh's quest is hopeless, and he is so informed on several occasions:

Gilgamesh, whither are you wandering?
Life, which you look for, you will never find.
For when the gods created man, they let death be his share, and life withheld in their own hands.
Gilgamesh, fill your belly—day and night make merry, let days be full of joy, dance and make music day and night.
And wear fresh clothes, and wash your head and bathe.
Look at the child that is holding your hand, and let your wife delight in your embrace.
These things alone are the concern of men.[18]

And here are a few lines from the lamentation of the Babylonian Job:

I look about me: evil upon evil!
My affliction grows, I cannot find justice. . .
Yet I thought only of prayer and supplication,
Invocation was my care, sacrifice my rule;
The day of the worship of the gods was my delight. . .
Who can comprehend the counsel of the gods in heaven?
The plan of a god is deep waters, who can fathom it?
Where has befuddled mankind ever learned what is a god's conduct?[19]

Fall of the Babylonian empire. The pattern of disunity and warfare, all too familiar in Mesopotamia, reasserted itself following Hammurabi's death. In 1595 B.C. the Hittites, an Indo-European people who had established themselves in Asia Minor (see p.45), mounted a daring raid down the Euphrates, capturing and plundering Babylon. The next five centuries is a dark age about which little is known; yet it did preserve the cultural heritage left by the Sumerians and Babylonians. Meanwhile, in a neighboring river valley, another civilization had emerged.

EGYPT: GIFT OF THE NILE

Early developments along the Nile. In Paleolithic times most of North Africa was covered with vegetation. As the glacial period ended, the decrease in rainfall forced men to search for food in the Nile valley, which up to the second millennium was covered with marshes. There, papyrus and rushes grew to heights taller than a man, and animal life abounded.

The valley was dominated by the Nile River, which rises and falls with unusual precision. The rise begins early in July and continues until the banks are overrun, reaching its crest in September. By the end of October the river is once more contained within its banks. Vegetation thrives in the moist, fertile soil, and crops are harvested in April or early May.

According to archaeologists, the first farmers in the Nile valley cultivated emmer wheat and barley, ground stone axes for felling the trees that grew in the swamps, made pottery, and wove linen. By the fifth millennium Neolithic peoples had undertaken the systematic cultivation of the Nile's flood plain. Proficient in carving and in working flint, these people also made small tools and pins out of copper, although they did not know how to cast it or how to make bronze. Egypt did not acquire bronze metallurgy until about 2000 B.C.

During the last centuries of the fourth millennium farmers may have begun to reclaim the marshland in southern Egypt. Population grew and social organization advanced. The valley below Aswan was dotted with farming villages populated by related families. Warfare among neighboring clans seems to have been common, and the settlements were fortified. Flint blades of excellent quality were produced, and artisans cast copper into various shapes for daggers, knives, harpoons, and axes. Copper ore was imported, as were lead, lapis lazuli, and silver—evidence of substantial trade with western Asia. Certain features of Sumerian culture also appear to have been borrowed (see p. 32).

The period prior to the unification of Egypt in 3100 B.C. is known as the Predynastic period. Toward its end, two distinct kingdoms came into existence: Lower Egypt included Memphis and the broad Nile delta, while Upper Egypt extended southward along the narrow river valley as far as Aswan. Each kingdom contained about a score of districts, or *nomes*, which had formerly been ruled by independent chieftains.

About 3100 B.C. Menes, a dynamic leader in Upper Egypt, united the two kingdoms and established his capital at Memphis. This event marks the beginning of the Dynastic period, so called because Manetho, an Egyptian priest of the third century B.C., compiled a history of Egypt in which he grouped the reigns of the kings into thirty dynasties. With the First Dynasty appear a few examples of Egyptian writing, already in a state of advanced development, but because little is known of the first two dynasties, the period is called Egypt's archaic age.

The Old Kingdom (c. 2700-2200 B.C.). The pharaohs of the Third through the Sixth Dynasties—the period called the Old Kingdom or Pyramid Age—firmly established order and stability and the essential elements of Egyptian civilization. The nobility lost its independence, and all power was centered in the pharaoh (*Per-ao*, "Great House"). In theory, the pharaoh owned all the land, decided when the fields should be sown, controlled the irrigation system, and received the surplus from crops produced by laborers on the huge royal estates. This surplus supported a large corps of specialists—administrators, priests, scribes, artists, and artisans—who worked continuously in the service of the pharaoh.

Like the Mesopotamian states, Egypt was a theocracy—that is, its ruler combined religious and political functions. But in Egypt the pharaoh was considered a god who returned to the heavens after death rather than the human agent of a god, as was the rule in Mesopotamia. The people's welfare was thought to rest on absolute fidelity to the god-king. "If you want to know what to do in life," advised one Egyptian writer, "cling to the pharaoh and be loyal. . . ."[20]

The belief that the pharaoh was a god led to the practice of mummification and the construction of colossal tombs—the pyramids—to preserve the pharaoh's mummy for eternity. The mummy was thought to house the spirit of the dead pharaoh during the daytime when it communicated with the living and enjoyed their offerings. At sunset the spirit left the tomb on a solar boat and accompanied the sun through the underworld. The pyramid tombs, in particular those of the Fourth Dynasty at Gizeh near Memphis which are the most celebrated of all ancient monuments, reflect the great power and prestige of the Old Kingdom pharaohs.

Toward the end of the Sixth Dynasty the centralized authority of the pharaohs was undermined by a resurgent nobility. The nobles assumed the prerogatives of the pharaohs, including the claim to immortality, and the *nomes* again became independent. For about a century and a half, known as the First Intermediate Period (c. 2200-2050 B.C.), civil war raged, and outsiders raided and infiltrated the land. The lot of the common people became unbearable as they faced famine, robbery, and oppression by petty tyrants. "The land trembled," wrote a contemporary, "all the people were in terror, the villages were in panic, fear entered into their limbs."[21]

The Middle Kingdom (c. 2050-1800 B.C.). Egypt was rescued from anarchy by a prince from the south who reunited the country, established his capital at Thebes, and founded the Eleventh Dynasty. The nobility remained powerful but paid tribute to the pharaoh. With the accession of the Twelfth Dynasty, vigorous rulers regained the power and splendor enjoyed by the pharaohs in the Old Kingdom.

Stressing their role as watchful shepherds of the people, the pharaohs of this dynasty promoted the welfare of the downtrodden. One of them claimed: "I gave to the destitute and brought up the orphan. I caused him who was nothing to reach [his goal], like him who was [somebody]."[22] No longer was the nation's wealth expended on pyramids, but on public works. The largest of these, a drainage and irrigation project in the marshy Fayum district south of Memphis, resulted in the reclamation of 27,000 acres of arable land. Moreover, a concession

that has been called "the democratization of the hereafter" gave the lower classes the right to have their bodies mummified and thereby to enjoy immortality.

The prosperous Twelfth Dynasty was succeeded by a less competent one, which lost control of the country. Once more Egypt was racked by civil war as provincial governors fought for the pharaoh's throne. During the last century of this Second Intermediate Period (c. 1800-1570 B.C.), the Hyksos, a mixed but preponderantly Semitic people, easily conquered the delta and made the rest of Egypt tributary. It was probably at this time that the Hebrews entered Egypt, led by the patriarch Joseph, who rose to high position under a friendly Hyksos king.

The New Kingdom or Empire (c. 1570-1090 B.C.). The Hyksos conquest was viewed by the Egyptians as a great humiliation imposed on them by detestable, ruthless barbarians. An aggressive nationalism emerged, promoted by the prince of Thebes who renounced paying tribute to the Hyksos and proclaimed: "No man can settle down, when despoiled by the taxes of the Asiatics. I will grapple with him, that I may rip open his belly! My wish is to save Egypt and to smite the Asiatics!"[23] Adopting the new weapons introduced by their conquerors—horse-drawn chariots, the composite bow, and swords and daggers of bronze rather than copper—the Egyptians expelled the Hyksos and pursued them into Palestine. The pharaohs of the Eighteenth Dynasty, who reunited Egypt and founded the New Kingdom, made Palestine the nucleus of an Egyptian empire in western Asia.

The outstanding representative of the aggressive state that Egypt now became was Thutmose III (c. 1490-1436 B.C.). This "Napoleon of Egypt" led his professional standing army on seventeen campaigns into Syria, where he set up his boundary markers on the banks of the Euphrates. Nubia and northern Sudan were also brought under his sway. The native princes of Palestine, Phoenicia, and Syria were left on their thrones, but their sons were taken to Egypt as hostages. Here they were brought up and, thoroughly Egyptianized, eventually sent home to rule as loyal vassals. Thutmose III erected obelisks—tall, pointed shafts of stone —to commemorate his reign and to record his wish that "his name might endure throughout the future forever and ever." Four of his obelisks now adorn the cities of Istanbul, Rome, London, and New York.

Under Amenhotep III (c. 1398-1361 B.C.) the Empire reached a dazzling height. Tribute flowed in from conquered lands; and Thebes, with its temples built for the god Amon across the Nile at Luxor and Karnak, became the most magnificent city in the world. The Hittites of Asia Minor and the rulers of Babylonia and Crete, among others, sent gifts, including princesses for the pharaoh's harem. In return, they asked the pharaoh for gold, "for gold is as common as dust in your land."

During the reign of the succeeding pharaoh, Amenhotep IV (c. 1369-1353 B.C.), however, the Empire went into sharp decline as the result of an internal struggle between the pharaoh and the powerful and wealthy priests of Amon. The pharaoh undertook to revolutionize Egypt's religion by proclaiming the worship of the sun god Aton in place of Amon and all the other deities. One of the first men to attempt to introduce monotheism, Amenhotep changed his name to Akhenaton ("He who is devoted to Aton"), left Amon's city to found a new capital (Akhetaton), and passed the rest of his life in worshiping Aton and in composing hymns (see p. 45). Most of Egypt's vassal princes in Asia defected when their appeals for aid against invaders went unheeded. Prominent among these invaders were groups of people called the Habiru, whose possible identification with the Hebrews of the Old Testament has interested modern scholars. At home the army leaders joined with the Amon priesthood to encourage dissension. When Akhenaton died, his weak successor, Tutankhamen (c. 1352-1344 B.C.) —famed for his small but richly furnished tomb discovered in 1922—returned to Thebes and the worship of Amon.

One of the army leaders who succeeded Tutankhamen founded the Nineteenth Dynasty (c. 1305-1200 B.C.), which sought to reestablish Egyptian control over Palestine and Syria. The result was a long struggle with the Hittites, who in the meantime had pushed south from Asia Minor into Syria. This struggle reached a climax in the reign of Ramses II (c. 1290-1224 B.C.), the pharaoh of the Hebrew Exodus from Egypt. Ramses II regained Palestine, but when he failed to dislodge the Hittites from Syria, he agreed to a treaty. Its strikingly modern character is revealed in clauses providing for nonaggression, mutual assistance, and extradition of fugitives.

The long reign of Ramses II was Egypt's last period of national grandeur. The number and size of Ramses' monuments (see p. 44) rival those of the Pyramid Age. Outstanding among them are the great Hypostyle Hall, built for Amon at Karnak, and the temple at Abu Simbel, with its four colossal statues of Ramses, which has recently been raised to save it from inundation by the waters of the new High Dam at Aswan. After Ramses II, royal authority grad-

THE EGYPTIAN EMPIRE

ually declined as the power of the priests of Amon rose.

Period of Decadence (1090-332 B.C.). During the early part of the Period of Decadence the Amon priesthood at Thebes became so strong that the high priest was able to found his own dynasty and to rule over Upper Egypt. Meanwhile another monarch ruled the Nile delta. Civil war grew increasingly common, and Egypt became, in the words of the Old Testament, a "broken reed" and ceased to be a factor in international affairs except as the object of foreign conquest.

Libyan mercenaries revolted and established a dynasty; next came a dynasty of Ethiopians; then in 671 B.C. the Assyrians made Egypt a province of their empire. With the aid of Greek mercenaries the Assyrians were expelled by a native Egyptian prince who established the Twenty-Sixth Dynasty (663-525 B.C.), and Egypt enjoyed a short Indian summer of revived glory. These rulers sought to revive the arts and literature of the bygone Old and Middle Kingdoms, but their efforts were imitative and the results sterile. Their attempts to regain Palestine were crushed by the Chaldean ruler Nebuchadnezzar (605-562 B.C.), "and the king of Egypt came not again any more out of his land" (II Kings 24:7). Only the commercial policies of these rulers were successful. Egyptian ports were opened to Greek and Phoenician traders, who settled in Egypt and made it the middleman between the Mediterranean and the East. In about 600 B.C., to facilitate this trade, Pharaoh Necho ordered a canal dug between the Nile mouth and the Red Sea (it was later completed by the Persians), and he commissioned a Phoenician expedition which circumnavigated Africa in three years —a feat not to be duplicated until 1497 A.D.

In the long run all attempts to restore the greatness of the past failed. Egypt passed under Persian rule in 525 B.C.; two hundred years later this ancient land came within the domain of Alexander the Great. Greek rule marked the end of the thirty Egyptian dynasties which had existed for nearly three thousand years.

Egyptian society. In Egypt, as elsewhere, the growth of population, the development of specialized vocations, and the increase of wealth resulted in the emergence of social classes. Three main divisions can be distinguished: (1) the upper class, including the priests, the court nobility, and the landed aristocracy; (2) the middle class, composed of merchants and craftsmen; and (3) the lower class, made up of laborers. Stratification was not rigid, and people of merit could rise to a higher rank.

The best avenue of advancement was education. The pharaoh's administration needed many scribes, and young men were urged to attend a scribal school: "Be a scribe, who is freed from forced labor, and protected from all work. . . . he directeth every work that is in this land." Yet then as now the education of a young man was beset with pitfalls: "I am told thou forsakest writing, that thou givest thyself up to pleasures; thou goest from street to street, where it smelleth of beer, to destruction. Beer, it scareth men from thee, it sendeth thy soul to perdition."[24]

In the days of the Empire, Egypt proper, excluding the subject peoples, had a population of about seven million. The great bulk of people were serfs, who were subject to forced labor—working on the roads, tilling the royal fields, or hauling huge stones for temples, statues, and obelisks. They lived in squalid villages made up of small mud and thatch houses with only a few crude jars, boxes, and stools as furnishings. Merchants and craftsmen had more comfortable homes, and the nobility lived in luxuriously furnished dwellings with beautiful gardens.

Women dressed with great care, used cosmetics lavishly, stained their nails with henna, and attempted to beautify and strengthen their hair with such brews as this: "Paws of a dog, one part; kernels of dates, one part; hoof of a donkey, one part. Cook very thoroughly with oil in an earthen pot, and anoint therewith."[25]

Largely because all landed property descended from mother to daughter, the status of Egyptian women was exceptionally favorable. Upon the death of his wife a husband lost the use of the property, which was then inherited by the daughter and her husband. Brother and sister marriages often took place within the Egyptian ruling family to ensure the right of succession to the throne, which

In this relief from Queen Hatshepsut's temple at Deir el-Bahri (c. 1500 B.C.), live baboons and such rare African flora as incense trees are loaded on boats which will return to Egypt from Punt, a land probably located on the Somali coast of eastern Africa. Hatshepsut considered the successful expedition to Punt one of the major events of her reign, and it was depicted conspicuously on the temple walls.

was always through the female line.

Economic life. The economy of Egypt has been called "theocratic socialism" because the state, in the person of the divine pharaoh, owned the land and monopolized commerce and industry. Although agriculture remained basic, industry developed rapidly after the early days of the Old Kingdom. The process of fusing copper and tin to make bronze was introduced during the Middle Kingdom; and tanning, weaving, glass blowing, and enameling became highly specialized crafts.

Because of the Nile and the proximity to the Mediterranean and Red seas, most of Egypt's trade was carried on by ships. During the Old Kingdom boats plied regularly up and down the Nile River, which, unlike the Tigris and the Euphrates, is easily navigable in both directions down to the first cataract. (Ships are carried downstream by the current, and the almost constant north wind enables them to sail upstream without difficulty.) During the same period Egyptian ships were sailing to Phoenicia and trade relations existed with Crete. Trade reached its height during the Empire, when Egypt controlled the trade routes of the Near East. Imperial commerce traveled along four main routes: the Nile River; the Red Sea, which was connected by caravan to the Nile bend

near Thebes; a caravan route to Mesopotamia and southern Syria; and the Mediterranean Sea, connecting northern Syria, Greece, and Crete and other islands with the delta of the Nile. Egypt's indispensable imports were lumber, copper, tin, and olive oil, paid for with gold from its rich mines, linens, wheat, and papyrus rolls—the material that revolutionized the development of writing in the ancient world.

Mathematics and science. The Egyptians were much less skilled in mathematical theory than were the Mesopotamians. Their arithmetic was limited to addition and subtraction, which also served them when they needed to multiply and divide. They could cope with only simple algebra, but they did have considerable knowledge of practical geometry. The obliteration of field boundaries by the annual flooding of the Nile made land measurement a necessity. Similarly, a knowledge of geometry was essential in computing the dimensions of ramps for raising stones during the construction of pyramids. In these and other engineering projects—the building of dams and irrigation systems, the erection of heavy obelisks, the construction of walls and ceilings of temples—the Egyptians were superior to their Mesopotamian contemporaries. Like the Mesopotamians, the Egyptians had acquired a "necessary" technology without effecting a conceptual breakthrough to a truly scientific method.

The Egyptians were familiar with the practical uses of medicinal herbs, but their knowledge of anatomy, derived from the practice of embalming, was far more advanced and scientific. Indeed, the oldest known scientific treatise was composed during the Old Kingdom. Its author described forty-eight cases requiring surgery, drawing conclusions solely from observation and rejecting supernatural causes and treatments. In advising the physician to "measure for the heart" which speaks in various parts of the body, he recognized the importance of the pulse and approached the concept of the circulation of the blood. This text remained unique, however, for in Egypt as elsewhere in the ancient Near East, thought failed to free itself permanently from bondage to religion.

The Old Kingdom also produced the world's first known solar calendar, the direct ancestor of our own. In order to plan their farming operations in accordance with the annual flooding of the Nile, the Egyptians kept records and discovered that the average period between inundations was 365 days. They also noted that the Nile flood coincided with the annual appearance of the Dog Star (Sirius) on the eastern horizon at dawn, and they soon associated the two phenomena. (Since the Egyptian year was six hours short of the true year, Julius Caesar in Roman times corrected the error by adding an extra day every four years.)

Egyptian religion. As in most other ancient societies, religion saturated Egyptian life and influenced every aspect of its culture. "The kings of Egypt were gods; its pyramids were an 'act of faith'; its art was rooted in religious symbolism; its literature began as religious decoration of tombs, temples, and pyramids; its science centered in the temple; its gods were conceived to be in intimate touch with men and alive as men; a vast part of its wealth and energy was spent in the effort to secure the continuance of the physical life after death."[26]

Early Egyptian religion had no strong ethical character; relations between men and gods were based largely on material considerations, and the gods were thought to reward those who brought them gifts of sacrifice. But widespread suffering during the First Intermediate Period led to a revolution in religious thought. It was now believed that instead of propitiatory offerings the gods were interested in good character and love for one's fellow man: "More acceptable [to the gods] is the character of one upright of heart than the ox of the evildoer . . . . Give the love of thyself to the whole world; a good character is a remembrance."[27]

The cult of Osiris became very popular when it combined the new emphasis on moral character with the supreme reward of an attractive afterlife. "Do justice whilst thou endurest upon earth," men were told. "A man remains over after death, and his deeds are placed beside him in heaps. However, existence yonder is for eternity. . . . He who reaches it without wrongdoing shall exist yonder like a god."[28] Osiris, according to an ancient myth, was the god of the Nile, and the rise and fall of the river symbolized his death and resurrection. The myth recounted that Osiris had been murdered by Seth, his evil brother, who cut the victim's body into many pieces. When Isis, the bereaved widow, collected all the pieces and put them together, Osiris was resurrected and became immortal. Osiris was thus the first mummy, and every mummified Egyptian was another Osiris.

But only a soul free of sin would be permitted to live forever in the "Field of the Blessed, an ideal land where there is no wailing and nothing evil; where barley grows four cubits high, and emmer wheat seven ells high; where, even better, one has to do no work in the field oneself, but can let others take care of it."[29] At the time of soul testing, Osiris weighed the candidate's heart against the Feather of Truth. If the ordeal was not passed, a horrible creature devoured the rejected heart. During the Empire the priesthood of Osiris became corrupt and claimed that it knew clever methods of surviving the soul testing, even though a man's heart were heavy with sin. Charms and magical prayers and formulas were sold to the living as insurance policies guaranteeing them a happy outcome in the judgment before Osiris. They constitute much of what is known as the Book of the Dead, which was placed in the tomb.

Akhenaton's religious reformation was directed against the venal priests of Osiris as well as those of the supreme god Amon. As we have seen, Akhenaton failed to replace Amon and the multiplicity of lesser gods with a single cosmic force (Aton, symbolized by the sun's disk); his monotheism was too cold and intellectual to attract the masses who yearned for a blessed hereafter.

Monumentalism in architecture. Because of their impressive and enduring tombs and temples, the Egyptians have been called the greatest builders in history. The earliest tomb was the mud-brick mastaba, so called because of its resemblance to a low bench. By the beginning of the Third Dynasty stone began to replace brick, and an architectural genius named Imhotep constructed the first pyramid by piling six huge stone mastabas one on top of the other. Adjoining this Step Pyramid was a temple complex whose stone columns were not free standing but attached to a wall, as though the architect was still feeling his way in the use of the new medium.

The most celebrated of the true pyramids were built for the Fourth Dynasty pharaohs Khufu, Khafre, and Menkaure. Khufu's pyramid, the largest of the three, covers thirteen acres and originally rose 481 feet. It is composed of 2,300,000 limestone blocks, some weighing fifteen tons, and all pushed and pulled into place by human muscle. This stupendous monument was built without mortar, yet some of the stones were so perfectly fitted that a knife cannot be inserted in the joint. The Old Kingdom's eighty pyramids are a striking expression of Egyptian civilization. In their dignity, massiveness, and repose, they reflect the religion-motivated character of Egyptian society.

As the glory and serenity of the Old Kingdom can be seen in its pyramids, constructed as an act of faith by its subjects, so the power and wealth of the Empire survives in the temples at Thebes, made possible by the booty and tribute of conquest. On the east side of the Nile stand the ruins of the magnificent temples of Karnak and Luxor. The Hypostyle Hall of the temple of Karnak, built by Ramses II, is larger than the cathedral of Notre Dame. Its forest of 134 columns is arranged in sixteen rows, with the roof over the two broader central aisles (the nave) raised to allow the entry of light. This technique of providing a clerestory over a central nave was later used in Roman basilicas and Christian churches.

Sculpture and painting. Egyptian art was essentially religious. Tomb interiors have been found to contain paintings and relief sculpture depicting the everyday activities which the deceased wished to continue enjoying in the afterlife. Statues glorify the god-kings in all their serenity and eternity. And since religious art is inherently conservative, Egyptian art seldom departed from the traditions established during the vigorous and self-assured Old Kingdom. Sculptors from this period idealized and standardized their subjects. The human figure is always shown looking directly ahead (see illustration, p. 44), with a rigidity very much in keeping with the austere architectural settings of the statues. So that they would not be dwarfed by their massive backdrops, many of the statues were made colossal in size. The ear of the sphinx—the recumbent lion with the head of Pharaoh Khafre which lies before the great pyramids at Gizeh—measures four and a half feet.

On two occasions an unprecedented naturalism appeared in Egyptian sculpture. The faces of some of the Middle Kingdom rulers appear drawn and weary, as though they were weighed down by the burden of reconstructing Egypt after the collapse of the Old Kingdom. An even greater naturalism is seen in the portraits of Akhenaton and his beautiful queen, Nefertete. The pharaoh's brooding countenance is realistically portrayed, as is his ungainly paunch and his happy but far from godlike family life as he holds one of his young daughters on his knee or munches on a bone. The "heretic" pharaoh, who insisted on what he called "truth" in religion, seems also to have insisted on truth in art.

Painting in Egypt shows the same precision and mastery of technique that are evident in sculpture. No attempt was made to show objects in perspective, and the scenes give an appearance of flatness. The effect of distance was conveyed by making objects in a series or by putting one object above another. Another convention employed was to depict everything from its most characteristic angle. Often the head, arms, and legs were shown in side view and the eye, shoulders, and chest in front view. Certain colors—rich reds and yellows with black and blue-green for contrast— were generally used in all paintings (see Color Plate 5).

Writing and literature. In Egypt, as in Sumer, writing began with pictures. But

unlike the Mesopotamian signs, Egyptian hieroglyphs ("sacred signs") remained primarily pictorial although it was much easier for Egyptian scribes to draw on papyrus than it had been for the Sumerians to incise their clay tablets. At first the hieroglyphs represented only objects, but later they came to stand for ideas and syllables. Early in the Old Kingdom the Egyptians began to use alphabetic characters for twenty-four consonant sounds. Although they also continued to use the old pictographic and syllabic signs, this discovery was of far-reaching consequence. It led to the development of the Semitic alphabet, from which our present alphabet is derived.

Egypt's oldest literature is the Pyramid

The temple at Luxor, dedicated to Amon, was built by several New Kingdom pharaohs over a period of about two hundred years and testifies to the characteristic Egyptian love of grandiose monuments. The massive statues were built by Ramses II, who was responsible for numerous other huge testimonials to his own power and grandeur.

Texts, a body of religious writing found inscribed on the walls of the burial chambers of the Fifth and Sixth Dynasty pharaohs. Their recurrent theme is a monotonous insistence that the dead pharaoh is a god and no obstacle can prevent him from joining his fellow gods in the heavens.

The troubled life that followed the collapse of the Old Kingdom produced the highly personal literature of the First Intermediate Period and Middle Kingdom. It contains protests against the ills of the day, demands for social justice, and praise for the romantic excitements of wine, women, and song. The universal appeal of this literature is illustrated by the following lines from a love poem, in which the beloved is called "sister":

I behold how my sister cometh, and my heart is in gladness.
Mine arms open wide to embrace her; my heart exulteth within me: for my lady has come to me. . . .
She kisseth me, she openeth her lips to me: then am I joyful even without beer.[30]

A classic of Egyptian literature is Akhenaton's *Hymn to the Sun*, which is similar in spirit to Psalm 104. A few lines will indicate its lyric beauty and its conception of one omnipotent and beneficent Creator.

Thy dawning is beautiful in the horizon of the sky,
O living Aton, beginning of life!
When thou risest in the eastern horizon,
Thou fillest every land with thy beauty.
Thou art beautiful, great, glittering, high above every land,
Thy rays, they encompass the lands, even all that thou hast made.
How manifold are thy works!
They are hidden from before us,
O sole god, whose powers no other possesseth.
Thou didst create the earth according to thy heart
While thou wast alone.[31]

By the fifth century A.D. the ability to read ancient Egyptian writing had been lost. Not until fourteen hundred years later, when the Rosetta Stone was deciphered by Jean François Champollion (1790-1832), could modern man appreciate this ancient literature.

The Rosetta Stone, discovered in Egypt in 1799 by an officer in Napoleon's army, supplied the means by which Jean Champollion was able in 1822 to decipher Egyptian writing. On the stone a decree is inscribed in three different languages, as is shown by the section reproduced here. The bottom layer of writing is Greek, which Champollion could read. Working from the Greek he was able to figure out the other inscriptions. The middle layer is Egyptian demotic, and the top layer is the more formal system of hieroglyphic writing.

THE HITTITES

The Hittite empire. Except for brief mention in the Bible, very little was known about the Hittites until archaeologists began to unearth the remains of their civilization in Asia Minor in 1906. By 1920 their language had been deciphered, and it proved to be the earliest example of a written Indo-European language. The Hittites are thought to have entered Asia Minor about 2000 B.C., coming from the north by way of the Caucasus. They conquered the native people and adopted the name of their country (Hatti) and many of their gods. (For the extent of the Hittite Kingdom, see Reference Map 2.)

About 1450 B.C. a series of energetic Hittite kings, effectively employing light horse-drawn chariots, created an empire that included Syria, lost by the Egyptian pharaoh Akhenaton. Pharaoh Ramses II moved north from Palestine in a vain attempt to reconquer Syria. Ambushed and forced back to Palestine after a bloody battle, Ramses agreed to a treaty of "good peace and good brotherhood" in 1269 B.C. (see p. 39). The Hittite and Egyptian versions of the treaty show how each of the rival kings sought to save face by claiming to have assented to the other's appeal for peace. The Hittites may have been eager for peace with Egypt because of the threat posed by a new movement of Indo-European peoples. Shortly after 1200 B.C. these barbarians crossed the Hellespont from Europe and destroyed the Hittite empire. Darkness settled over Asia Minor until after 800 B.C.

Hittite civilization. The Hittite state under the empire was modeled after the older oriental monarchies of the Near East. The king claimed to represent the sun god and was deified after death. Although the homeland was now governed by appointed officials rather than noble vassals, the nobles held large estates from the king and in return provided weapons and men for war. The masses worked the land as peasants, and the towns were populated by numerous craftsmen. The Hittites are credited with being the first people to work iron, although copper and bronze remained their common metals. That they had begun to produce hard iron weapons and to hoard them is revealed in a letter written by a thirteenth-century Hittite king to a neighboring ruler:

As for the good iron which you wrote about to me, good iron is not available in my seal-house in Kizzuwatna. . . . They will produce good iron, but as yet they will not have finished. When they have finished I shall send it to you. Today now I am dispatching an iron dagger blade to you.[32]

After 1200 B.C. the production of iron implements spread throughout the Near East.

The Hittites adopted the Mesopotamian cuneiform script together with many Sumerian and Babylonian words as well as some works of Babylonian literature. While their law code shows some similarity to the code of Hammurabi, it differed in prescribing more humane punishments. Instead of retaliation ("an eye for an eye"), the Hittite code made greater use of restitution and compensation.

The chief importance of Hittite culture lies in the legacy it left to the Phrygians and Lydians and, through them, to the Greeks who settled along the Aegean coast of Asia Minor. The Hittite goddess Kubaba, for example, became the great Phrygian goddess Cybele, the "Great Mother" whose worship became widespread in Roman times.

After 1200 B.C., with the Hittite empire destroyed and Egypt in decline, the Semitic peoples of Syria and Palestine ceased being pawns in a struggle between rival imperialisms. For nearly five hundred years, until they were conquered by the Assyrians, these peoples were able to play an independent and significant role in history.

THE ERA OF SMALL STATES

The Phoenicians. *Phoenician* is the name the Greeks gave to those Canaanites who dwelt along the Mediterranean coast of Syria, an area that is today the state of Lebanon. Hemmed in by the Lebanon Mountains to the east, the Phoenicians turned to the sea and by the eleventh century B.C. had become the greatest traders, shipbuilders, navigators, and colonizers before the Greeks. To obtain silver and copper from Spain and tin from Britain, Gades (Cadiz) was founded on the Atlantic coast of Spain. Carthage, one of a number of Phoenician trading posts around the shores of the Mediterranean, was destined to become Rome's chief rival in the third century B.C.

Although the Phoenicians were essentially traders, their home cities—notably Tyre, Sidon, and Byblos—also produced manufactured goods. Their most famous export was woolen cloth dyed with the purple dye obtained from shellfish found along their coast. They were also skilled makers of furniture (made from the famous cedars of Lebanon), metalware, glassware, and jewelry.

Culturally the Phoenicians were not creative. They left behind no literature and little art. Yet they made one of the greatest contributions to human progress, the perfection of the alphabet, which, along with the Babylonian sexagesimal system of notation, they carried westward. The origin of the alphabet is still a moot question. Perhaps between 1800 and 1600 B.C. certain western Semitic peoples, influenced by Egypt's semialphabetical writing, started to evolve a simplified method of writing. Carrying on the experiment, the Phoenicians developed an alphabet of twenty-two consonant symbols (the vowel signs were introduced later by the Greeks). The first two symbols of the Phoenician alphabet were *aleph* and *beth*, which mean "ox" and "house" respectively.

The half dozen Phoenician cities never united to form a strong state, and in the last half of the eighth century B.C. all but Tyre were conquered by the Assyrians. When Tyre finally fell to the Chaldeans in 571 B.C., the Hebrew prophet Ezekiel spoke what reads like an epitaph to the once great role played by the Phoenicians:

"When your wares came from the seas, you satisfied many peoples; with your abundant wealth and merchandise you enriched the kings of the earth. Now you are wrecked by the seas, in the depths of the waters; your merchandise and all your crew have sunk with you."[33]

The Arameans. Closely related to the Hebrews were the Arameans, who settled in Syria east of the Lebanon Mountains during the twelfth century B.C. The most important of their little kingdoms was centered on Damascus, one of the oldest continuously inhabited cities of the world. Situated at the head of the camel caravan route to Babylon, Damascus controlled the trade between Phoenicia, Mesopotamia, and Egypt. The Arameans have therefore been called the Phoenicians of inner Asia. Damascus was conquered by the Assyrians in 732 B.C., but the Arameans continued to dominate the trade of western Asia. The

Aramaic language, which used an alphabet very similar to the Phoenician, became the international language of the Near East. In Judea it displaced Hebrew as the spoken language and was used by Jesus and his disciples.

The Hebrew kingdoms. In war, diplomacy, inventions, and art, the Hebrews made little splash in the stream of history. In ethics and religion, however, their contribution to world civilization was tremendous, even though they were few in number and generally weak in political power. Out of their experience grew three great religions: Judaism, Christianity, and Islam.

The Biblical account of the history of the Hebrews (later called Israelites and then Jews) begins with the patriarchal clan leader Abraham. About 1800 B.C. Abraham led his people out of Ur in Sumer, where they had settled for a time in their wanderings, and eventually they arrived in the land of Canaan, later called Palestine. Tucked between the desert and the sea, Canaan was only 150 miles long and very narrow, about the size of the state of Vermont.

About 1700 B.C., driven by famine, some Hebrews followed Abraham's great-grandson Joseph, the son of Israel (also called Jacob), into Egypt. Joseph's rise to power in Egypt, and the hospitable reception of his people there, is attributed to the presence of the largely Semitic Hyksos, who had conquered Egypt about 1710 B.C. (see p. 38). Following the expulsion of the Hyksos by the pharaohs of the Eighteenth Dynasty, the Hebrews were enslaved by the Egyptians. Shortly after 1300 B.C. Moses led them out of bondage and into the wilderness of Sinai, where they entered into a pact or covenant with Yahweh, as the God of their fathers was hereafter called. The Sinai Covenant bound the people as a whole—the nation of Israel, as they now called themselves— to worship Yahweh before all other gods and to obey his Law. In return, Yahweh made the Israelites his chosen people whom he would protect and to whom he granted Canaan, "a land flowing with milk and honey." The history of Israel from this time on is the story of the working out of this covenant.

Yahweh's Law is recorded in the Five Books of Moses; its core is embodied in the Ten Commandments and the Covenant Code (Exodus 21-23). The latter consists largely of case law: if such-and-such occurs, then such-and-such will be the legal consequences. Since most of these laws represent an agricultural rather than a nomadic way of life, the Covenant Code reflects later settled life in Palestine and is thus several centuries more recent than Moses and the Ten Commandments. Contact with the Canaanites in Palestine, where Babylonian cultural influences had long been felt, may also explain certain similarities between the Covenant Code and the Code of Hammurabi.

The Israelites had to contend for Palestine against the Canaanites, whose Semitic ancestors had migrated from Arabia early in the third millennium B.C. Joined by other Hebrew tribes already in Palestine, the Israelites formed a confederacy of twelve tribes (clans of the twelve sons of Israel) and, led by war leaders called judges, in time succeeded in subjugating the Canaanites. In the meantime, however, a far more formidable foe had appeared. The Philistines, from whom we get the word *Palestine,* settled along the coast about 1175 B.C., having been uprooted from Asia Minor by the invasions that destroyed the Hittite empire (see p. 46). Aided by the use of iron weapons, which were new to Palestine, the Philistines by the middle of the eleventh century were well on their way to dominating the entire land.

It became apparent that the loose twelve-tribe confederacy, held together by allegiance to Yahweh rather than by a centralized government, could not cope with the Philistine danger. "Give us a king to govern us," the people demanded, "that we also may be like all the nations, and that our king may govern us and go before us and fight our battles."[34] Saul, the first king of Israel (1020-1000 B.C.), died while fighting the Philistines, but his successor David (1000-961 B.C.) not only restricted the Philistines to a narrow coastal strip but became the ruler of an empire that stretched from the Euphrates to the Gulf of Aqaba and from the Mediterranean to the Arabian Desert.

The work of David was completed by his son Solomon, in whose long reign (961-922 B.C.) Israel reached a pinnacle of worldly power and splendor as an oriental-style monarchy. In the words of the Bible:

Solomon ruled over all the kingdoms from the Euphrates to the land of the Philistines and to the border of Egypt; they brought tribute and served Solomon all the days of his life. . . . And Judah and Israel dwelt in safety, from Dan even to Beer-sheba, every man under his vine and under his fig tree, all the days of Solomon. . . . And God gave Solomon wisdom and understanding beyond measure, and largeness of mind. . . . Now the weight of gold that came to Solomon in one year was six hundred and sixty-six talents of gold, besides that which came from the traders and from the traffic of the merchants, and from all the kings of Arabia and from the governors of the land. . . . The king also made a great ivory throne, and overlaid it with the finest gold. . . .[35]

ANCIENT ISRAEL
8TH CENTURY B.C.

Damascus

Tyre

PHOENICIA

Kadesh

KINGDOM OF ARAM

MEDITERRANEAN SEA

Sea of Galilee

Megiddo

KINGDOM OF ISRAEL

Samaria

Joppa

Shiloh

Bethel

Jordan R.

Jericho

AMMON

Jerusalem

Bethlehem

PHILISTIA

KINGDOM OF JUDAH

Gaza

Hebron

DEAD SEA

MOAB

Beersheba

NEGEV (DESERT)

EDOM

Uncertain   Boundary

But the price of Solomon's vast bureaucracy, building projects (especially the palace complex and temple at Jerusalem), standing army (1400 chariots and 12,000 horses), and harem (700 wives and 300 concubines) was great. High taxes, forced labor, and the loss of tribal independence led to dissension, and on the death of Solomon in 922 B.C., the realm was split into two kingdoms—Israel in the north and Judah in the south. These two weak kingdoms were in no position to defend themselves when new, powerful empires rose again in Mesopotamia. In 721 B.C. the Assyrians captured Samaria, the capital of the northern kingdom, taking 27,900 Israelites into captivity and settling foreign peoples in their place. The resulting mixed population, called Samaritans, made no further contribution to Hebrew history or religion.

The southern kingdom of Judah held out until 586 B.C. when Nebuchadnezzar, the Chaldean ruler of Babylonia, destroyed Jerusalem and "carried away all Jerusalem, and all the princes, and all the mighty men of valor, ten thousand captives, and all the craftsmen and the smiths; none remained, except the poorest people of the land."[36] Thus began the famous Babylonian Exile of the Jews (Judeans), which lasted until 538 B.C. when Cyrus the Persian, having conquered Babylon, allowed them to return to Jerusalem where they rebuilt the temple destroyed by Nebuchadnezzar.

Persian rule was followed by that of the Hellenistic Greeks and Romans. In 66-70 A.D. the Jews rebelled against Rome, and Jerusalem was totally destroyed in the savage fighting that ensued. The Jews were again driven into exile, and the Diaspora—the "scattering"—was at its height.

Hebrew religion. From the time of Abraham the Hebrews worshiped one god, a stern, warlike tribal deity whose name Yahweh (Jehovah) was first revealed to Moses. Yet they also recognized the existence of other gods—a concept that is called *monolatry* and needs to be distinguished from *monotheism*, which denies the existence of more than one god. Yahweh differed from the many Near Eastern sun gods, storm gods, and so on, who were immanent in nature.

This mural from the synagogue in Dura Europus, showing Moses leading the twelve tribes through the Red Sea, dates from about 240 A.D. Although it portrays events of approximately a millennium earlier, both the Egyptians and Hebrews are anachronistically clad in Roman dress and armor.

Yahweh was completely separate from the physical universe which He had created; according to the Nineteenth Psalm, "The heavens declare the glory of God, and the firmament showeth his handiwork." This view of Yahweh as the Creator of all things everywhere was inevitably to lead to the belief that He was the sole God in the universe.

Although the matter is much debated, Moses may have been the first Hebrew monotheist. After their entrance into Palestine, however, many Hebrews adopted the fertility deities of the Canaanites as well as the more sophisticated and luxurious Canaanite manner of living. This was especially true of the northern Hebrews. As a result prophets arose who "spoke for" (from the Greek word *prophetes*) Yahweh in insisting on strict adherence to the Sinai Covenant and in condemning the "whoring" after other gods, the selfish pursuit of wealth, and the growth of social injustice.

Between roughly 750 and 550 B.C. appeared the great "literary" prophets, so called because they, unlike their predecessors, wrote down their messages. They sought to purge the religion of Israel of all corrupting influences and to elevate and dignify the concept of Yahweh. As summed up by Micah in a statement often cited as the essence of all higher religion, "He has shown you, O man, what is good; and what does the Lord require of you but to do justice, and to love kindness, and to walk humbly with your God?"[37] The prophets viewed the course of Hebrew history as being governed by the sovereign will of Yahweh, seeing the Assyrians and the Chaldeans as "the rod of Yahweh's anger" to chastise His stubborn, wayward people. They also developed the idea of a coming Messiah, the "anointed one" from the family of King David, who would inaugurate a reign of peace and justice.

Considered the greatest of the prophets are Jeremiah and the anonymous Second Isaiah, so called because his message was incorporated in the Book of Isaiah (chapters 40-55). Jeremiah witnessed the events that led to Nebuchadnezzar's destruction of Jerusalem and the temple and to the Babylonian Captivity of the Jews. He prepared the people for these calamities by affirming that Yahweh would forgive their sins and restore "a remnant" of his people and by proclaiming a "new covenant." The old covenant had been between Yahweh and the nation, which no longer existed, and it had become overlaid with ritual and ceremony and centered in the temple, which had been destroyed. The new covenant was between Yahweh and each individual; religion was now a matter of a man's own heart and conscience, and both the nation and the temple were considered superfluous. Second Isaiah, who lived at the end of the Babylonian Captivity, capped the work of his predecessors by proclaiming Israel to be Yahweh's "righteous servant," purified and enlightened by suffering and ready to guide the world to the worship of the one, eternal, supreme God. Thus were the Jews who returned from the Exile provided with a renewed faith in their destiny and a new comprehension of their religion which would sustain them through the centuries to come.

LATER EMPIRES OF WESTERN ASIA

Assyrian expansion. By 700 B.C. the era of small states was practically at an end. For two hundred years the Assyrians had been bidding to translate the growing economic unity of the Near East—evidenced by Solomon's trading operations and even more by the activities of Aramean merchants —into political unity. The Assyrian push toward the Mediterranean began in the ninth century and, after a lapse, was resumed in the eighth century, during which Babylon was also subdued. By 721 B.C. the Assyrians were the masters of the Fertile Crescent.

Racially the Assyrians were a mixed stock, predominantly Semitic. Reared in the invigorating climate of a hilly, upland region and schooled for a thousand years by constant war, the Assyrians, mostly peasants, became formidable soldiers. The secret of Assyria's creation of an empire was fourfold: a matchless, well-equipped army, the terrorization of all people who resisted Assyrian rule, the most advanced system of political administration developed up to that time, and the support of the commercial classes that wanted political stability and unrestricted trade over large areas.

The Assyrian empire existed by and for its army. Assyrian soldiers were the first to be fully outfitted with iron weapons. The bow, with vicious iron-tipped arrows, was their principal weapon. After a stream of well-directed arrows had weakened the enemy, the Assyrian heavy cavalry and chariots smashed the ranks of their foes, driving them headlong from the field. All the ancient world dreaded their fighters.

The second factor in the success of the Assyrians was their use of systematic terrorization. In boasting of his exploits one Assyrian emperor inscribed on a monument:

Their booty and possessions, cattle, sheep, I carried away; many captives I burned with fire. I reared a column of the living and a column of heads. I hung up on high their heads on trees in the vicinity of their city. Their boys and girls I burned up in flame. I devastated the city, dug it up, in fire burned it; I annihilated it.[38]

Sometimes the lives of the vanquished were spared, but many were then forced to leave their homelands. In the long run the transplanting of conquered peoples made the Near East more cosmopolitan and brought the inventions and customs of one people more quickly to the attention of others.

The breadth of the Assyrian empire also stimulated trade, which the Assyrian rulers openly encouraged. For example, when Babylon was taken, its merchants were granted the privilege of unrestricted trade throughout the empire. And Sargon II (d. 705 B.C.) proudly recorded the fact that he forced Egypt to abandon its "sealed-off frontiers" and to trade with other lands.

The well-coordinated Assyrian system of political administration was another factor in the success of the empire. Theoretically, the Assyrian king himself drew up the laws, made all decisions concerning war and peace, and fixed tax rates. In practice, however, much of the work was performed by court officials, assisted by scribes. The officials formed a kind of council which advised the king, but he alone usually bore the responsibility for the most important state decisions and policies. Communication between the ruler and his provincial governors required roads, and thus the earliest system of nation-wide highways, as well as a postal system, was inaugurated.

The Assyrian rulers "thus laid secure administrative foundations for central rule of the entire Near East from Mesopotamia to Egypt. It was these secure foundations . . . which made first the Persian, later Alexander's, empire possible and which are therefore a—perhaps the—major conditioning factor behind all of the following Hellenistic and Roman history. . . ."[39]

Assyrian art and architecture. In order to glorify themselves and enhance their prestige, Assyrian rulers built imposing and luxurious palaces. The royal palace at Khorsabad, built into the wall of the city on a high platform, had thick, heavy walls like those of a fortress. The palace contained not only the king's living quarters and the royal stables but also a temple and a ziggurat.

The arch, borrowed from Babylonia, became an impressive feature in Assyrian palace gates. To guard the gateways the Assyrians installed huge human-headed, winged lions and bulls carved from imported stone. The palaces were decorated with splendid relief sculptures that glorified the king as warrior and hunter. Assyrian sculptors were especially skilled in portraying realistically the ferocity and agony of charging and dying animals.

Assyrian kings were interested in preserving records of the past, and the royal annals were kept with great care. At immense cost and effort the knowledge of the Near East was gathered for King Ashurbanipal's library, which contained over 22,000 clay tablets. Hymns, temple rituals, myths of creation and the deluge, grammars, and medical texts all found their way to his library. These tablets provided modern scholars with their first knowledge of Sumero-Babylonian literature.

THE ASSYRIAN EMPIRE
ABOUT 670 B.C.

The Assyrian king, Sennacherib (705-681 B.C.), reviews a procession of fettered prisoners as he sits in front of the palace of a conquered city. In the six small tents or huts workers engage in their trades. Their prominence in this record of a military victory indicates the importance of artisans in the ancient world.

Downfall of the Assyrian empire. The Assyrian empire obtained its main resources from booty and conquest, and the collapse of such a system was inevitable when Assyria's strength waned and effective opposition arose. By the middle of the seventh century B.C. the sturdy Assyrian stock had been decimated by wars, and the Assyrian kings had to rely heavily on mercenary troops. To the north and northeast the vigorous Indo-European Medes and Persians were on the march, and a new group of Semites, the Chaldeans, had filtered into Babylonia. The Chaldeans successfully revolted in 626 B.C., and in 612 they joined the Medes in destroying Nineveh, the Assyrian capital. From one end of the Fertile Crescent to the other people rejoiced: "Nineveh is laid waste: who will bemoan her?"[40]

With the exception of their sculpture, their innovations in military science, and their ability as imperial administrators, the Assyrians made few original contributions to civilization. Their role was rather one of borrowing from the cultures of other peoples, unifying the best elements into a new product, and assisting in its dissemination over the Fertile Crescent.

The Lydians and the Medes. The destruction of the Assyrian empire in 612 B.C. left the following powers to struggle over the crumbs of empire: the Medes and Persians, the Chaldeans, the Egyptians, and the Lydians.

After the collapse of the Hittite empire about 1200 B.C., the Lydians had followed the Phrygians, whose last king was the semilegendary Midas (d. c. 680 B.C.), in establishing a kingdom in western Asia Minor. Lydia profited from being astride the commercial land route between Mesopotamia and the Aegean and from the possession of valuable gold-bearing streams. As a result, the Lydians invented coinage (about 675 B.C.), which replaced the silver bars hitherto in general use. The most famous king of this wealthy state was Croesus, and the phrase "rich as Croesus" is a reminder of Lydian opulence. With the defeat of Croesus by the Persians (see p. 54), Lydia ceased to exist.

This clay tablet map of the Mesopotamian temple city of Nippur, dating from about 1500 B.C., is the oldest known cartographic city plan. The Euphrates River appears at the far left, the famous temple complex is at the far right, and a canal divides the city in the middle from north to south. The map is unusual because it depicts an actual city plan rather than a stylized representation and because the buildings are apparently drawn to scale.

THE CHALDEAN AND
PERSIAN EMPIRES

Chaldean Empire
About 586 B.C.

Persian Empire
About 500 B.C.

0 100 200 300 400 500

1" = 430 MILES

The Medes were an Indo-European people who by 1000 B.C. had established themselves just east of Assyria and in the eighth century B.C. had created a strong kingdom with Ecbatana as capital. Two hundred years later, the Medes extended their overlordship to the Persians, who lived south of them. The Persians were of the same racial ancestry as the Medes and for a time were content to be their vassals.

The Chaldean empire. While the Median kingdom controlled the highland region, the Chaldeans, with their capital at Babylon, were masters of the Fertile Crescent. Nebuchadnezzar, becoming king of the Chaldeans in 604 B.C., raised Babylonia to another epoch of brilliance after more than a thousand years of eclipse. By defeating the Egyptians in Syria, Nebuchadnezzar ended their hopes of re-creating their empire. As we have seen earlier (p. 49), he destroyed Jerusalem in 586 B.C. and carried

several thousand Jews captive to Babylon.

Babylon was rebuilt and became one of the greatest cities of its day. The tremendous city walls were wide enough at the top to have rows of small houses on either side; between the rows of houses was a space wide enough for the passage of a chariot. In the center of the city of Babylon ran the famous Procession Street, which passed through the Ishtar Gate. This arch, which was adorned with brilliant tile animals, is the best remaining example of Babylonian architecture. The immense palace of Nebuchadnezzar towered terrace upon terrace, each resplendent with masses of ferns, flowers, and trees. These roof gardens, the famous Hanging Gardens of Babylon, were so beautiful that they were regarded by the Greeks as one of the seven wonders of the ancient world.

Continuing the work of the Mesopotamians in mathematics and astronomy, the

Chaldeans observed the heavens and, without any telescopes or accurate time-recording instruments, worked out detailed tables of the movements of the sun, moon, and planets, using mathematics to figure the velocity, acceleration, and positions of these bodies. Their astronomy was scientific in that it was based upon recorded observations and involved the use of mathematics. One astronomer computed the length of the year to within twenty-six minutes. Like their predecessors, however, the Chaldean astronomers failed to search for or find the governing principles that would enable them to draw general conclusions about the universe. Their computations were later utilized by the Greeks of the Hellenistic era with more promising results (see p. 122).

The Chaldeans also observed the movements of celestial bodies in order to foretell the future by interpreting their supposed influence on human affairs. These early astrologers identified groups of stars with the twelve signs of the zodiac, an imaginary belt in the heavens in which each sign covered 30 degrees of a full circle. Chaldean astrology later spread among the Greeks with the result that by the end of the second century B.C. it had largely killed astronomy.

Persian imperialism. During the long reign of Nebuchadnezzar the Chaldean empire flourished; but after his death in 562 B.C. Chaldean power quickly crumbled. Meanwhile the Persians suddenly rose to prominence and soon eclipsed all the great states of the ancient world. Within twenty years the vigorous Cyrus the Great created a vast Persian empire. He threw off the Median yoke and captured Ecbatana in 550 B.C. Apparently the Medes readily accepted their new ruler. When King Croesus of Lydia moved across the Halys River in 546 B.C. to pick up some of the pieces of the Median empire, Cyrus defeated him and annexed Lydia, including those Greek cities on the coast of Asia Minor which were under the nominal control of Lydia. Then he turned east, establishing his power as far as the frontier of India. Babylon was next on his list; with little resistance, the city capitulated to the Persians in 539 B.C. Following the death of Cyrus, his son

Cambyses conquered Egypt. At the beginning of the fifth century B.C. the next ruler, Darius I (522-486 B.C.), began a series of campaigns against the Greek mainland. The struggle between the Greeks and the Persians ended about 150 years later with the resounding defeat of the Persians by the youthful Alexander the Great (see Chapter 4).

Persian government. The governmental structure of Persia was built upon the Assyrian model but was far more efficient than its predecessor. The imperial system, first designed by Cyrus the Great to administer his extensive dominions, was carried to completion by Darius. Four capitals—Susa, Ecbatana, Babylon, and Persepolis—were established in various parts of the empire; and the total empire was divided into twenty-one provinces, or satrapies, each governed by a provincial governor called a satrap. To check the satraps, a secretary and a military official representing the king were installed in every province. Also, special inspectors, "the Eyes and Ears of the King," traveled throughout the realm.

Realizing the need for good communications, the Persians built great imperial post roads, which in the thoroughness of their construction rivaled the later Roman roads. The main highways connected the important cities of the empire. Along the Royal Road between Sardis and Susa there was a post station every fourteen miles, where the king's messengers could obtain fresh horses. By means of this ancient pony express, royal messengers could cover a distance of fifteen hundred miles in a little more than seven days; ordinary travelers, however, took three months.

The Persian empire was the first to attempt governing many different racial groups on the principle of equal responsibilities and rights for all peoples. In the Persians' treatment of subject peoples there was a humaneness and consideration that had been completely absent in the Assyrian government. So long as his conquered subjects paid their taxes and kept the peace, the king allowed religious freedom and encouraged trade and commerce. The introduction of a uniform system of coinage also served to weld the empire together.

Persian religion and art. The humaneness of the Persian rulers may have stemmed from the ethical religion founded by the prophet Zoroaster, who lived in the early sixth century B.C. Zoroaster sought to replace what he called "the lie"—ritualistic, idol-worshiping cults and their Magi priests—with a religion centered on the sole god Ahura-Mazda ("Wise Lord"), who demanded "good thoughts of the mind, good deeds of the hand, and good words of the tongue" from those who would attain paradise (a Persian word). The new religion made little progress until first Darius and then the Magi adopted it. The Magi revived many old gods as lesser deities, added much ritual, and replaced monotheism with dualism by transforming what Zoroaster had called the principle or spirit of evil into the powerful god Ahriman, rival of Ahura-Mazda. The complicated evolution of Zoroastrianism is revealed in its holy writ, the *Avesta* ("The Law"), assembled in its present form between the fourth and the sixth centuries A.D. Zoroastrian eschatology—"the doctrine of final things" such as the resurrection of the dead and a last judgment—influenced Judaism. Following the Muslim conquest of Persia in the seventh century A.D., Zoroastrianism gradually died out in

A double staircase, decorated with reliefs, led to the magnificent audience hall where the Persian emperors received foreign envoys and visiting dignitaries. Persepolis was constructed during the reigns of Darius and Xerxes.

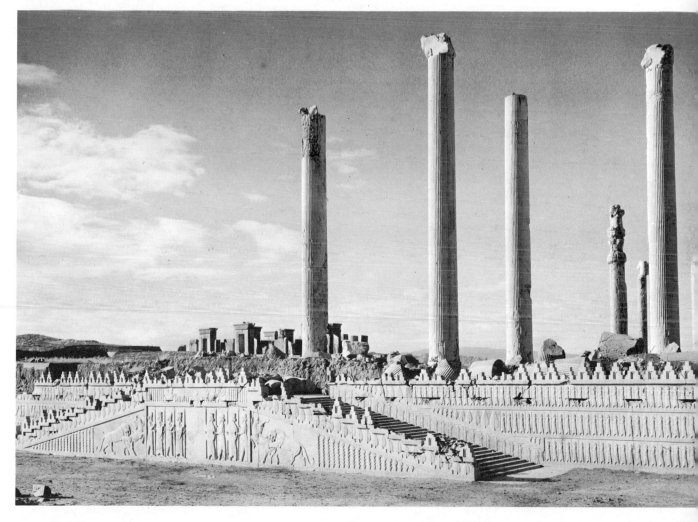

its homeland. It exists today among the Parsees in India.

In art the Persians borrowed largely from their predecessors in the Fertile Crescent, especially the Assyrians. Their most important work was in palace architecture, the best remains of which are at Persepolis. Built on a high terrace, the royal residences were reached by a grand stairway faced with beautiful reliefs. Instead of the warfare and violence that characterized Assyrian sculpture, these reliefs depict hundreds of soldiers, courtiers, and representatives of twenty-three nations of the empire bringing gifts to the king for the festival of the new year.

SUMMARY

Civilization rose about the same time in Mesopotamia and in Egypt. Both these civilizations were river-made, one by the Nile, the other by the Tigris and Euphrates. In each case their respective inhabitants made the transition from a food-gathering to a food-producing economy and thus achieved a way of life in which new forms of economic, political, and social organization developed.

Perhaps the words *monumental* and *timeless* best describe Egyptian culture. The Egyptians built colossal statues, huge tombs, and gigantic irrigation works. Because they believed in an afterlife, their burial customs were designed to outwit time itself. The state centered upon the absolute rule of the pharaohs; economic life was patterned on the seasonal ebb and flow of the Nile.

The story of ancient Mesopotamia is primarily concerned with the achievements of the Sumerians and the later adoption of their civilization by various invaders. The most important of these new states was the Babylonian empire, created by Hammurabi. Following an era of brilliant Babylonian civilization, the Hittites expanded southward from Asia Minor. In Syria the duel between Egyptians and Hittites, which

weakened both contestants, gave small nations—for example, Phoenicia and the Hebrew kingdoms—a chance to enjoy a brief period of independence. Political diversity was ended by the rise of the Assyrian empire, which lasted about three hundred years (900-600 B.C.). After the fall of Assyria, a new Babylonian empire arose—the creation of the Chaldean ruler Nebuchadnezzar—but the expansion of Persia soon terminated its independence. Persia, in its turn, became one of the greatest empires the world had seen.

Peoples in the ancient Near East and Egypt contributed many institutions and technological inventions to civilization. There, metals were first used on an extensive scale, and the wheeled vehicle, the potter's wheel, and the sailboat were introduced. In Egypt, as in Mesopotamia, scientific advances were limited to the "hard-core" technology needed to solve specific problems. Political administration became increasingly centralized and well coordinated but never developed beyond the benevolent despotism of a god-king, as in Egypt, or a divine-right monarch, as was customary in the Near East. While the economy of Egypt remained largely collectivized, an individualistic, capitalistic economy flourished for a time in Mesopotamia.

These first civilizations also established artistic, literary, and religious patterns for subsequent cultures. Writing was evolved about 3200 B.C.; later the Phoenicians perfected an alphabet and transmitted it to the West. In literature and religion the greatest gifts to our civilization were the Hebrew scriptures. Among the basic architectural accomplishments developed by these people, the Sumerians contributed the arch and the Egyptians the basilica. Justly famous also are the sculpture and palace architecture of the Assyrians and Persians.

We have examined a large and complex canvas of human history. At a glance, it may seem that, like the Sphinx and the Hanging Gardens of Babylon, the peoples and events depicted there belong to the long-dead past. Yet features of our own civilization can be traced back to cultural elements of those bygone days.

Historical Critique

THE ARCHAEOLOGIST'S SPADE
by Froelich Rainey

Froelich Rainey, Director of the University Museum and Professor of Anthropology at the University of Pennsylvania, has spent more than thirty years in archaeological research and is currently interested in developing new scientific techniques for archaeological discovery and interpretation. His most recent publication, with Carlo Lerici, is *The Search for Sybaris* (1968).

When the undergraduate students assemble for their first session in my general course in archaeology, I ask what history they have read. Most are well versed in the history of western civilization since 1500, very few have read ancient history, and only one or two may know something about Asia, Africa, or precolonial America. Surely, this is a measure of the ethnocentric attitudes in our educational system. History for the majority apparently means the last five hundred years of the latest great civilization. To the archaeologist, on the other hand, it means the record of many civilizations over a period of five thousand years and the reconstruction of human events for about two million years.

Archaeology, as a specific intellectual discipline, is little more than a century old. We can now recognize its origin in Egypt with the French scholars who accompanied Napoleon's invasion early in the nineteenth century, but only after the discovery of other lost civilizations in the Mediterranean and the Near East during the last half of the nineteenth century did it crystalize as a particular study within the broad field of the humanities. Today it has become a rare combination of history, anthropology, art, paleontology, and science. It attempts to discover, on a world-wide basis throughout all of human history, what happened, how it happened, and what this may mean in terms of understanding the nature of human affairs. Undoubtedly archaeology's greatest contribution to modern thought is its effect upon historic perspective; with anthropology, it has enabled modern man to escape the intellectual confines of one civilization and one period and to see his own particular age with fresh objectivity.

There is no clear distinction between archaeology and paleontology. When Leakey excavates the fossil remains of extinct animals from Pleis-tocene beds in Olduvai Gorge, he is a paleontologist; when he finds and describes the bones of *Homo habilis,* he is an anthropologist; but when he describes what he believes to be stone implements from Bed I in those deposits, he is an archaeologist. Today archaeologists are excavating fossil bones and human artifacts dating from many hundreds of thousands of years ago, deciphering inscriptions in Sumer which tell of religious beliefs two thousand years before Christ, and excavating the foundations of buildings destroyed only in the last century.

Because the archaeologist deals with things and not men, his view of human history tends to be materialistic and technological. He excavates and translates clay tablets, and he orders and classifies fragments of pottery, stone tools, art objects, pollen grains, coins, and the bones of men and animals. But as a professional archaeologist, his overriding concern remains with the people who left behind all these bits and pieces. He is interested in people, rather than in things per se.

The twentieth century has seen a remarkable refinement in the techniques of digging, recording, and interpreting relics of the past, together with thoughtful commentaries on the objectives of the discipline. Like many other studies, archaeology has been dramatically affected, since World War II, by discoveries in atomic-nuclear research. Radiocarbon dating of ancient organic materials (see Chapter 1) is a convenient means to establish a firm historic chronology of man's affairs during the past forty or fifty thousand years. It is well to remember that the earliest date in recorded history that has been fixed by correlation with our present calendar through an observation in Egypt of the simultaneous rising of Sirius and the sun is 1829 B.C. Moreover, all dating of events recorded in various inscriptions in Egypt and the Near East prior to the eighth century B.C. is, at best, uncertain. Thus recorded historical time is very brief indeed when compared to the total life of humans on this planet. Unless handed down orally, no names of a people or of an individual can be known to us prior to the invention of writing, presumably by the Sumerians about 3000 B.C.; but with carbon dating, an event such as the construction of a Neolithic town at what is now Jericho in Jordan can be fixed in time thousands of years before any written record. From a historical point of view, this provides a very different perspective than the relative chronologies worked out by archaeologists prior to the radiocarbon technique.

Greater precision in dating prehistoric events

has also altered many of our ideas about the sequence of human events. Urban living is now known to have developed before, not after, the invention of pottery manufacture; the end of the Ice Age and the beginning of a new economic order in human existence took place some ten to twelve thousand years ago, not twenty thousand years as once believed; the development of agriculture is now known to be almost as early in Central America as in the Near East. Precision in dating by the radiocarbon method applies to events in most of the world prior to about 1500 A.D. and to all of the world prior to about 800 B.C.

Radiocarbon was only the first of many dating techniques derived from atomic-nuclear research. Thermoluminescence, recently developed for archaeological dating at the University Museum in Philadelphia, now makes it possible to date fragments of fired clay (pottery) made during the last eight to nine thousand years. Again, a number of new methods—involving potassium-argon, rubidium-strontium, and uranium-lead isotope ratios—which enable geological phenomena to be dated accurately for many million years, have also proved their worth in establishing a precise chronology of very ancient man and his artifacts. They confirm that the oldest known human remains come from Africa and also indicate that true *Homo sapiens* may well have been at one time contemporaries of more primitive forms of man.

Atomic-nuclear research is also producing new archaeological tools. Experiments with sensing apparatus to seek out buried remains began with resistance instruments which measure electrical conductivity in surface soils. These are useful in detecting archaeological remains of shallow depth in limited areas. Two types of magnetometers, relying upon an atomic-nuclear principle, measure very slight variations in magnetic intensity in surface soils. They are now capable of locating buried remains up to five or six meters in depth and of exploring as many as ten acres per day.

Aerial photography has been employed in archaeology for more than thirty years. However, the development of aerial cameras and film during World War II led to such discoveries as the extensive Etruscan cemeteries in Italy, Roman settlement patterns in England, and curious stone-marked figures in the deserts of Peru. This, in turn, led to systematic archaeological surveys, such as those now being made in Italy. Today archaeologists' interest is turning to a new order of aerial search based upon a number of remote sensing devices utilized in high-flying aircraft. Recently it has been suggested that archaeological surveys on a grand scale will be made from satellites. Satellites such as "Eros," using remote sensing instruments to survey world-wide natural resources, may one day be programed to record ancient settlement patterns, evidence of which lies outside the visual bands of the spectrum. With the present development of exploration instrumentation, archaeologists should eventually be working in hitherto completely unknown field sites and also recording broad areas of ancient agriculture, canal systems, and underground water supplies. All this is part of the new scope of archaeology.

The interpretation of what archaeologists find is at once the most difficult and most rapidly changing part of the discipline. Today, research involves physicists, chemists, geologists, paleobotanists, zoologists, climatologists, medical researchers, and even computer centers. One of the most impressive techniques is the analysis of pollen grains in ancient lake beds or other sedimentary deposits which guide the archaeologist to conclusions about the changing environment during and since the Ice Age. This study not only provides time markers but demonstrates the connection between cultural change and symbiotic relationships among men, animals, and plants over the ages. Historians, in the time-limited sense, are perhaps less conscious of these forces in human affairs than modern archaeologists who, equipped with the latest techniques, seek to understand long-range influences upon the history of man.

The analysis of fluorine content in very ancient bones of animals and men is another of these interpretative techniques. It is now well known to the general public because it was utilized in exposing the famous Piltdown hoax (see Chapter 1). But there are now many new methods of analyzing materials which explain the time relation of objects, methods of manufacture, the local origin of the raw material used, and hence much about trade relations in ancient times. The number and rate of development of these new techniques emphasize their probable future effect upon archaeology in general.

One result of the application of scientific techniques in archaeology is the return effect. Probably in no other study do the sciences and the humanities work in closer collaboration to solve technical problems of mutual interest. Here are a few examples. Several radiocarbon laboratories located in different parts of the world have been working to improve archaeological and geological methods. From this research has come the discovery that the amount of radiocarbon in the atmosphere has not remained constant as originally supposed. Also it has been demonstrated that carbon dioxide in the atmosphere is increasing. These basic phenomena of the earth's biosphere are of fundamental interest to earth sciences. For many years archaeologists have been working out the history of plant domestication, which has had such a vital effect upon human cultures and populations. This has naturally involved botanists, paleobotanists, and geneticists. The discovery of ancient and primitive maize, wheat, beans, and so on in archaeological sites has not only contributed to our knowledge of plant genetics but has made it possible to recreate species which have long since disappeared. A recent study of the Harrapan civilization in the Indus valley (see Chapter 3) made by archaeologists and hydrologists promises to lead to a clearer understanding of the mechanics of river deposits and river systems.

In recent years undersea research, involving many different sciences, has reached massive proportions. Archaeologists have begun systematically searching for and excavating ancient wrecks, submerged ports, and other human remains on the floor of the sea. Such work, made possible by the surge of postwar technology, at the same time stimulates the development of new techniques. For example, a minute two-man submarine has been used successfully not only for archaeology but for all kinds of undersea search—the investigation of lobster beds, the search for military equipment lost at sea, and general oceanographic work. Archaeologists with several years of experience in undersea Mediterranean research are testing various types of side-scanning sonar, new undersea cameras, magnetometers, metal detectors, and undersea televisions.

Modern archaeology not only establishes a fresh, long-range view of human history but effectively alters the ethnocentric, progress-oriented philosophy which has dominated western society. Like the cultural anthropologist who, through a study of living primitive people, opens our eyes to societies with a wholly different philosophy and orientation, the archaeologist rediscovers lost civilizations, forgotten or historically unknown epochs. His tools comprise both the spade and an elaborate set of scientific techniques. Thus archaeology is obliterating the traditional distinction between history and prehistory. It is demonstrating that even without written records the whole vista of mankind's past is history.

SUGGESTED READINGS

The interested student may wish to consult George F. Bass, *Archaeology Underwater*, Praeger, 1966; Don Brothwell and Eric Higgs, eds., *Science in Archaeology*, Basic Books, 1963; *Archaeology: Horizons New and Old*, proceedings of the American Philosophical Society, 1966; and Froelich Rainey and Carlo Lerici, *The Search for Sybaris*, Lerici Press, 1968.

Chapter 3

The Asian Way of Life

Ancient India and China

INTRODUCTION. Civilization had its genesis in four Afro-Asian regions: Egypt, Mesopotamia, and the valleys of the Indus and the Huang Ho. For some two thousand years these areas charted the path for mankind's onward march of civilization. By 500 B.C. western peoples began to join this procession, making rapid progress in the civilized arts of life; and for a thousand years both great segments of the human race were roughly in equilibrium.

One of the basic themes of world history, therefore, may be called the Afro-Asian strand. The chapters in Volume I relating to this theme are largely concerned with the origins, growth, and flowering of the Afro-Asian cultures from the fifth century B.C. to the fifteenth A.D. During their classical period great civilizations emerged in Asia and northern Africa. Imbued with massive political power and economic opulence and graced with cultural magnificence, these civilizations of the East were not only comparable to those of the West, but from time to time, in important respects, superior. During this period isolated sub-Saharan

Africa suffered from inertia and a certain amount of cultural stagnation. Yet the accomplishments of her peoples were not trivial, and their worth has recently been rediscovered and truly appreciated.

This period of creativity, during which Afro-Asians had no doubts about the basic worth of their civilizations and possessed a proud and clear sense of their identities, began to ebb after 1500 A.D. Hereafter, Africa and Asia came increasingly into contact with the West; their life patterns became progressively modified by intrusive, dynamic occidental forces. By the end of the nineteenth century this encounter had brought most of the non-West, directly or indirectly, under western imperialist control. Volume II will treat two main facets of this phase of Afro-Asian history: the imposition of alien colonial rule and the resultant penetration of nonindigenous traits of culture into the non-West; and, finally, the overthrow of this colonial rule within very recent times and the advent of a large number of independent Afro-Asian states.

This latest chapter in nonwestern history is presently characterized by a complex inner struggle that can be described as a Crisis in Identity. It springs from the fact that for some three hundred years there has been a massive intrusion of western ideas in religion, technology, and government. The recipients have found much of the new appealing. But independence, and with it the right and duty of free choice, has brought a deep-seated ambivalence. How much of the old cultural heritage should be jettisoned; and what elements of the historic past should be jealously guarded and perpetuated? Can some kind of harmonious meld be achieved that will retain treasured and distinctive elements side by side with nonindigenous culture traits considered essential in this modern age?

Conceivably, nonwestern cultures could attempt one of several solutions—complete rejection of western culture, its complete acceptance, or some kind of synthesis. The last alternative, it would seem, is the most likely.

INDIA: UNITY IN DIVERSITY

Geography of India. We can think of India* as a gigantic triangle bounded on two sides by ocean and on the third by the mountain wall of the Himalayas. In ancient times, when travel by sea was limited, the significant approach to India lay through the mountain passes of the rugged Kirthar and Sulaiman Mountains to the northwest. Through these passes swarmed the armed conquerors, restless tribes, and merchants and travelers who did much to shape the turbulent history of this land.

For purposes of discussion, the land can be divided into four major parts: Baluchistan, Hindustan, the Deccan, and Tamil Land (see map, p. 65). In this chapter our interest lies principally in the events that took place in Hindustan, for in the alluvial plain watered by the upper Indus and its tributaries (called the Punjab, or Land of the Five Rivers) and in the territory along the lower Indus (called Sind), India's earliest civilization developed.

Ancient communities in western India. In recent years scholars have come to believe that the ancient Near East should not be considered as isolated from the Asian lands to the east. Rather, we should conceive of a "Greater Near East" which extended beyond the Fertile Crescent through Iran and Baluchistan to the Indus valley. By taking this larger western Asian setting as the subject for investigations, archaeologists are discovering significant cultural links between Mesopotamia, Iran, and prehistoric India. Scholars now emphasize that the transition from food gathering to food production, the all-important agricultural revolution, did not emerge inde-

*Until the text deals with the creation of the separate states of India and Pakistan in 1947, the word *India* will refer to the *entire* subcontinent.

pendently in India. Food production began in Mesopotamia, then radiating in several directions, diffused eastward across the Iranian plateau into Baluchistan and hence into the Indus valley. In this northwestern area of India the new farming became the economic basis for India's first civilization.

Excavations have indicated that the Quetta valley, lying in the now semiarid upland region of Baluchistan, had many farming communities in early times. On the basis of radiocarbon dating, one of the farming communities in the Quetta valley is known to have existed in 3000 B.C., and it is possible that its beginnings extended back more than a thousand years before that. If this were true, the oldest Indian settlements would be placed "closer in time to such early village complexes as those at Jarmo and Jericho."[1]

The prehistoric inhabitants of the Quetta valley were herdsmen who lived in mud huts and used primitive bone and stone tools. Later they learned the rudiments of agriculture and acquired the ability to make copper implements and wheel-made pottery which strongly resembles the pottery of ancient Mesopotamia and Iran. Meanwhile, other localized cultures had developed elsewhere in Baluchistan and in Sind; archaeologists distinguish among the different groups primarily by their varying types of pottery.

Prehistoric agricultural communities in western India shared various cultural features: the people adhered to a fertility cult and the worship of a mother goddess— practices also common to agricultural communities in other lands of the Greater Near East. Their later development was marked by contact with the great riverine civilization that arose in the Indus valley.

The Indus civilization. The first culture in this region to achieve a level that can be described as civilization was the Indus valley culture. The very existence of this culture was generally unsuspected and unknown until its remains were archaeologically excavated during the past fifty years. Its script cannot yet be read; its historical development remains unknown; but its widespread material remains show striking similarities to those of contemporary Egypt and Sumer. It may have extended in time from about 2500 to 1500 B.C.

The Indus civilization eventually extended some 950 miles along the valley from the Himalayan foothills in the north to the coast, embracing an area estimated as twice the size of the Old Kingdom in Egypt and some four times the size of Sumer and Akkad. Harappa and Mohenjo-Daro, the two largest cities that have been excavated, were the political capitals and commercial centers of this region.

The Indus civilization comprised numerous cities and small towns, and although Harappa and Mohenjo-Daro were 350 miles apart, the Indus River made possible the maintenance of a strictly organized and uniform administration and economy over the large area. In this stretch of territory, containing some three dozen settlement sites, houses were built of uniform-sized baked bricks. The people used stamp-seals, engraved with a uniform script, and a standard system of weights. They cultivated grains, domesticated cattle and sheep, worked metals, made textiles, and carried on trade. The agricultural communities of Baluchistan had been in contact with Sumer since the Old Sumerian period, and there is evidence that considerable trade also existed between the Indus cities and those of Sumer. Indus valley crafts and techniques were similar to those of Sumer and Egypt; thus some direct borrowing perhaps took place across or around the Iranian plateau.

Harappa and Mohenjo-Daro were similar in plan and layout and impressive in their functional excellence. Excavations at the latter site reveal straight streets, a great public bath, houses with private wells and baths, and an elaborate drainage system consisting of horizontal and vertical drains. In these respects the two Indian cities were much more advanced than cities of similar size which appeared in Europe thousands of years later. The construction of the streets and houses indicates considerable skill in surveying and a rudimentary knowledge of geometry. In architecture, however, the efforts of the inhabitants were prosaic. Whereas the members of other advanced

In the center of the ancient city of Mohenjo-Daro stands this great bath, with a pool eight feet deep and walls six feet thick. On one side are a row of chambers and a large well from which the pool could be filled. It is thought that people visited the pool to wash away their sins and sufferings, a ritual still practiced by Hindus today. Excavations at Mohenjo-Daro have unearthed mother-goddess figurines and seals which may also have had religious significance. The seals bear Indus writing, essentially a pictographic script employing about 250 symbols and 400 characters, which is still undeciphered. Such seals have been found along the Iranian plateau trade routes and on an island in the Persian Gulf, indicating that trade existed between the Indus civilization and western civilizations. This seven-inch-high statue of a man also suggests contacts between the Mesopotamian and Indus valley civilizations because of its heavy beard, a common feature of contemporaneous Sumerian sculpture.

civilizations constructed great royal palaces and massive religious edifices, the inhabitants of Harappa and Mohenjo-Daro erected efficiently designed but artistically dull buildings. They were apparently a practical, conservative people with austere tastes.

There were, however, imaginative artists and artisans among the citizens of Harappa and Mohenjo-Daro. Archaeologists have found many seals and amulets, ornamented by tigers, elephants, crocodiles, and other animals, as well as pottery of highly burnished red ochre, ingenious toys, and bird and animal forms.

Like the inhabitants of the village cultures in Baluchistan and Sind, these people of the Indus valley worshiped a mother goddess. Also, some seals depict a three-faced male god, surrounded by four symbolic beasts. Scholars believe that this is the prototype of Shiva, the later Hindu god of destruction.

For centuries the people of the Indus valley pursued a meticulously regulated, efficient, but relatively static way of life. At Mohenjo-Daro, however, excavations show clearly the decline of the city in its latter days. Street frontages were no longer strictly observed, the brickwork became shoddy, and residential areas degenerated into slums. Finally, groups of skeletons huddled together in their dwellings suggest that this city, and perhaps the entire civilization, came to a sudden end. We can only speculate on what great common disaster— a plague or a flood, perhaps—may have overtaken these unfortunate people. Alternatively, the city may have fallen to barbarian attack. Though some unexplained disaster overwhelmed Mohenjo-Daro, elements of its culture lived on to become an integral part of the modern pattern of Indian life, especially in the sphere of religion. An Indian historian writes: "We must hold that there is an organic relationship between the ancient culture of the Indus valley and the Hinduism of today."[2] With the exception of China, no part of the world possesses a civilization so unbroken and durable as that of India.

The Aryan invasions. Sometime around 1500 B.C. a group of Aryans migrating from the shores of the Black and Caspian seas began to invade India. These newcomers came in conflict with the Dravidians, described as short and dark people, who were the first important ethnic stock to enter India, and who were perhaps the people whose forebears had originated the Indus civilization. In a few hundred years these Aryan invaders conquered and settled the upper Indus valley and began penetrating the Ganges region. A tall people with fair skins and long heads, the Aryans ate and drank heartily, fought readily, and lived simple lives. They knew nothing of writing or of city life. The number of cattle a man owned was the measure of his wealth, and the word for war meant "a desire for more cows." Each tribe was headed by a rajah ruler, women had a high social status, and marriage was monogamous and confined to the group.

The languages spoken by the Aryan invaders of India and by those who, in the same period, migrated from the steppes into the Fertile Crescent, belonged to the great family of languages linguists call Indo-European. Various dialects of the invading bands, mixed with the speech of pre-Aryan natives, gradually developed into Sanskrit, the classical language of India. By the fourth century B.C., however, vernacular languages had evolved which were much different from the traditional Sanskrit of the priests and bards. Hindi, the chief modern language of northern India, was finally derived from the speech of this period.

At first the Aryans referred contemptuously to the people they conquered as *Dasyu*, or slaves, because of their different physical type and color and because of their religious conduct, which seemed strange and damnable to the Aryans. Some of the *Dasyu* were enslaved and relegated to the bottom rung of the socioeconomic ladder. Others were driven southward. Even today, the inhabitants of south India are mainly the darker Dravidian stocks which have remained fairly pure ethnically and speak non-Aryan languages.

It is thought that in important essentials the culture of the Dravidians was at a higher level than that of the Aryans. It was natural, therefore, that a fusion of cultures between conquerors and vanquished should have taken place. This process, in which the Aryans borrowed Dravidian systems of land tenure and taxation, religious ideas, and the institution of the village community and added linguistic elements to classic Sanskrit, is referred to as the Aryo-Dravidian synthesis.

Little tangible evidence exists regarding the Aryan invasions. Our knowledge of the period after the Aryan conquest is more complete, however, as the result of Aryan literature that has survived to this day. Using complex poetic techniques, priests composed hymns to accompany sacrifices to tribal gods. This earliest Aryan literature, transmitted orally through countless generations by highly developed memorization techniques, was called the *Vedas*.

Early Vedic Age (c. 1500-900 B.C.). Aside from the rajah, his tribal assembly, and the common tribesmen, there were few social gradations in the Aryan tribal structure prior

to the invasion of India. In the process of subjugating and settling among the dark-skinned natives, the Indo-Aryans realized that they would be absorbed racially unless they took steps to prohibit intermarriage. Class division now took on a new purpose—that of preserving purity of race. This concept is intrinsic in the Vedic Sanskrit word for class, *varna*, which means "color." (It was translated later by Portuguese travelers as *casta*, from the Latin *castus*, meaning "pure.") We shall soon see that while the earliest caste division separated the Indo-Aryans from the dark-skinned peoples, caste later involved social stratification within the Aryan group itself.

The Aryan collections of religious hymns, the *Vedas*, provide us with a picture of the times in which they were composed. After the Aryan invaders had conquered the land, they settled down to a rural life, tilling and irrigating the soil and raising grains. In many ways village life was similar to that of

ANCIENT INDIA

Indus Valley Civilization

modern India, although complexities of later Indian life such as the restriction of women's rights and the prohibition against eating cattle did not exist at this time. The most important figure of the village was the headman, sometimes elected and at other times holding his position by hereditary right. The village was composed of a group of families, and the villagers worked as farmers or artisans or both. Their houses were made with mud walls, clay floors, and thatched roofs. Clothing consisted principally of a shawl worn over the shoulders and a skirt. Among the popular amusements were gambling, dancing, chariot racing, and listening to tribal bards.

Later Vedic Age (c. 900-500 B.C.). About the beginning of the ninth century B.C., the center of power and culture shifted eastward from the upper Indus valley to the upper Ganges valley. There the Aryans created small, isolated territorial states, each sovereign unto itself. The great epic poems that describe the life of these times tell of constant warfare and shifting military alliances among these states.

The cities of the Later Vedic Age were surrounded by moats and walls, and their streets were well planned. The rajah, usually occupying a palace located at the center of a city, possessed powers greater than those of the village headman of the Vedic Age. He had his own retinue of followers and was advised by a royal council composed of his relatives and nobles. He received taxes and was probably, in theory at least, the owner of all land. In cities a tradesman class existed, and unskilled, menial tasks were performed by slaves.

Earlier we noted the existence of trade contacts between the Indus valley civilization and Mesopotamia. These contacts were renewed during this period, and merchants may have brought back from the West the use of coinage and the notion of an alphabetic system of writing that was eventually adapted to Sanskrit.

The village, caste, and family. In the Later Vedic period the three pillars of traditional Indian society—the autonomous village, caste, and the joint-family—were established. India has always been primarily agricultural, and its countryside is still a patchwork of thousands of villages, as in each fluvial primary civilization. The village in early times was made up of family groups who possessed certain rights and duties and were governed by the headman. An elected council of villagers distributed the land and collected taxes. Women were allowed to serve on the council. Villages within a city-state enjoyed considerable autonomy, with the rajah's government hardly interfering at all as long as it received its quota of taxes. This system of self-governing villages continued until government became more centralized under British rule.

If the earliest caste division had been inaugurated to separate the Aryans from the *Dasyu,* by the Later Vedic period caste became more sharply defined and complex as the Aryans themselves split into castes. The four castes recognized at this time were ultimately ranked: (1) the Brahmins, or priests; (2) the Kshatriyas, or warriors; (3) the Vaisyas, or traders, merchants, and bankers; and (4) the Sudras, or farm workers and serfs. In addition there was a group of outcastes, or Pariahs, called "untouchables" because their touch was considered defiling to the upper castes. The non-Aryan population remained at the bottom of the social scale, as Sudras and outcastes.

At first the Kshatriyas had a higher social rank than the Brahmins; but as time went on warfare declined while religion increased in importance. As educators, historians, and intermediaries between the gods and men, the priests assumed the dominant position which they have successfully maintained into the twentieth century. Eventually the four castes were subdivided into thousands of groups with special social, occupational, and religious significance. The definition and order of importance of the four castes have remained much the same, however, throughout India's history.

The third pillar of Indian society was the joint-family. "Joint in food, worship, and estate," the family was made up of descendants of a common ancestor. The joint-family was governed by the patriarch during his lifetime; after his death, authority was transferred to the eldest son. All males of the group had to be consulted on serious matters, since the property belonged to the family as a whole. Everything earned by individuals in the group went into a common fund, from which was drawn what was needed to supply each member. It was possible for a man to acquire property and to live in his own residence, but he had to show that his holdings had been obtained without use of the family patrimony.

The joint-family was not only a cooperative economic unit but also a powerful instrument for social cohesion. It has been appropriately alluded to as the "constituent atom of the social order."[3] It encouraged a strong family life in which the individual was made to feel his subordination to the group. Marriage was all-important in protecting family ties, and the individual member's desires were considered less important than the maintenance of the family interests. For thousands of years the joint-family concept dominated the socioeconomic life of the large majority of India's people.

The emphasis placed on the interests and security of the group rather than on the individual is a common denominator of the three pillars of Indian society—the autonomous village, the caste system, and the joint-family. Thus Indian society has always been concerned with stability rather than with progress in the western sense, and the individual Indian has tended to acquire a more passive outlook toward life than his western counterpart. This traditional emphasis upon the group also helps explain the socialistic approach of Nehru and his successors toward contemporary economic and social issues.

Literature. The oldest Sanskrit literature, the *Vedas* (meaning "knowledge") consisted of thoughts concerning religion, philosophy, and magic. The earliest was the *Rig-Veda,* a peculiar combination of childlike questions (such as why white milk should come from red cows) and religious concepts of deep insight. Ultimately the *Vedas* became so sacred that no changes were allowed. Even long after writing was in common use, these sacred poems, and the prose and secular epics associated with them, continued to be transmitted principally—if not entirely—by oral tradition.

After the *Vedas* had been composed, a series of prose commentaries on them began to be produced, including the famous *Upanishads* (from the term which means "a session," at which a teacher gives instruction in philosophical doctrine). Written between 800 and 600 B.C., the *Upanishads* extend and replace the old Vedic concepts with profound speculations about the ultimate truths of creation and life. The teachings of the *Upanishads* are discussed later in this chapter.

A different, and originally secular, Indian tradition produced two great epic poems. The *Mahabharata,* with more than ninety thousand stanzas, is certainly the world's longest poem; it glorifies the ideals of aristocratic warriors and ostensibly celebrates a titanic struggle between two Aryan tribes (which, if it has a factual basis, may have occurred in the tenth century B.C.). The *Mahabharata* may be compared to the Homeric *Iliad.*

The most famous section of the *Mahabharata* is a philosophical poem called the *Bhagavad-Gita (The Lord's Song).* Famous for its poetic and philosophical content, this anonymous poem has been revised often and is still the most treasured piece in Hindu literature. The *Bhagavad-Gita* emphasizes that men must never shirk their duty but must perceive it clearly so that their actions will be free from selfishness and passion. Death is no cause for unbridled grief because the soul is indestructible. In modern times Indian leaders have often based their actions on their interpretations of this ancient poem. Some have found in it a justification for what they consider to be righteous warfare; others have used the *Bhagavad-Gita* to evolve the remarkable political technique of nonviolence and passive resistance.

The other magnificent epic, the *Ramayana,* has been likened to the Greek *Odyssey* because it tells of a hero's wanderings and his faithful wife's long vigil. Where the *Mahabharata* is a vigorous glorification of war and adventure, the *Ramayana* shows the growth of chivalric ideals among the Indo-Aryans. Its main characters, Rama and Sita, are the Hindu ideals of perfect manhood and womanhood. Their mutual loyalty, devotion, truthfulness, and self-abnegation are tenderly lauded. When Sita's husband is banished to the jungle, she remarks:

My mother often taught me and my father
  often spoke
That her home the wedded woman doth beside
  her husband make,
As the shadow to the substance, to her lord
  the faithful wife,
And she parts not from her consort till she
  parts with fleeting life.
Therefore let me seek the jungle where the
  rangers rove,
Dearer than the royal palace, where I share
  my husband's love.[4]

Perhaps no other pieces of literature have influenced so many people for so long a time as have these Indian epics. In a sense they are what the Bible, *Pilgrim's Progress,* Milton, and Shakespeare have been to the English-speaking people. Everywhere in India their characters are sculptured in the temples, carved in the woodwork of houses, or painted on the walls. Common people all over the land know and love the old plots and characters of these epics.

Nightly to listening millions are the stories of the *Ramayana* and *Mahabharata* told all over India. They are sung at all large assemblies of the people, at marriage feasts and temple services, at village festivals and the receptions of chiefs and princes. Then, when all the gods have been duly worshipped a reverend Brahman steps upon the scene and sitting down, slow and lowly begins his antique chant [of the epics], and late into the starry night holds his hearers, young and old, spellbound.[5]

The Kailasa Temple at Ellora, the largest and most elaborate of the Indian temples carved out of solid rock, contains intricate carvings of incidents and characters from the great epics, the *Mahabharata* and the *Ramayana.*

Religion in India. The power of religion in Indian life has always been extraordinarily strong. From this ancient land have come some of the most novel and complex religious ideas. These concepts constitute one of India's unique contributions to world civilization. Its religious values and philosophical tradition were not fully known to western scholars until the late eighteenth and mid-nineteenth century. In 1848 the *Rig-Veda* was translated from the Sanskrit and edited by Max Muller, a famous pioneer orientalist at Oxford University. Another unexcelled interpreter of Hindu thought was Sir Edwin Arnold; his *Song Celestial* is a magnificent translation into English of the *Bhagavad-Gita.* Throughout the nineteenth century Hindu philosophical and spiritual thought intrigued numerous literary and intellectual circles in the western world. Thoreau, Emerson, Goethe, Wordsworth, Tolstoi, and many other figures attest to this influence, and the founding of the famous Theosophical Society in the 1870's was a mark of the wide appreciation of the Hindu spiritual tradition. In the twentieth century a champion and a practitioner of the Hindu way of life became world famous. Mohandas K. Gandhi castigated western materialism, espoused reverence for life and nonviolence, and championed self-denial.

What was to become one of the world's most complex religious and philosophical systems, touching upon all facets of life, had the most simple beginnings. The early Aryans had unsophisticated religious views; they worshiped various gods with sacrificial rites. The most popular deity was Indra, a boisterous god who wielded the thunderbolt, ate bulls by the score, and quaffed lakes of wine. The earliest Vedic philosophy was not complicated. After death the human soul experienced either eternal punishment or everlasting bliss. Gradually, however, there evolved the idea that Something existed beyond the everyday acts of both gods and men, Something which underlay all life, a Moral Law governing even the gods themselves. The *Vedas* show the evolution of Indian religion from a simple belief in many gods toward a complete pantheism, a conception of the universe and everything in it as God. This pantheism can be seen in the "Creation Hymn" found in the *Rig-Veda:*

Nor Aught nor Naught existed; yon bright sky
Was not, nor heaven's broad roof outstretched
    above.
What covered all? what sheltered? what con-
    cealed?
Was it the water's fathomless abyss?
There was not death—yet was there naught im-
    mortal,
There was no confine betwixt day and night;
The only One breathed breathless by itself,
Other than It there nothing since has been.
Darkness there was, and all at first was veiled
In gloom profound—an ocean without light—
The germ that still lay covered in the husk
Burst forth, one nature, from the fervent heat. . . .
Who knows the secret? who proclaimed it here,
Whence, whence this manifold creation sprang?
The gods themselves came later into being—
Who knows from whence this great creation
    sprang?
He from whom all this great creation came,
Whether his will created or was mute,
The Most High Seer that is in highest heaven,
He knows it—or perchance even He knows not.[6]

The Upanishads: core of Indian theology.
The pantheistic conception was subsequently developed with great subtlety in the *Upanishads,* which form the core of all subsequent Indian religious thought and are the foundation on which Hinduism was built. The main teachings of the *Upanishads* may be summarized as follows:

1) Brahman or, to use another term, God, is the Absolute, the eternal universal essence, the all-pervading force permeating the universe.

2) As part of this world stuff is its Atman, the Universal Soul, to which all individuals belong.

3) As individual souls living in a world of the senses, we think we exist apart from the One Soul—but this is *maya,* or illusion. As long as individuals exist in this world, they are kept from the desired goal of absorption into the Absolute, into Brahman.

4) While living in this state of illusion, of separateness from the One Soul, the individual places his faith in things that are meaningless, transitory, and unsatisfying. As long as such earthly goals as pride, power, and material success are sought, the result must be pain and sorrow. Deliverance and emancipation can only be attained by *moksha,* the ultimate absorption and loss of self into Brahman. The essence of *Upanishadic* thought is escape from illusion.

5) This release from the meaningless state of earthly existence and its attendant *maya* is part of a cosmic and complicated process of reincarnation. The individual soul must go through a long series of wanderings—of earthly reincarnations from one body to another. A man's status at any particular point in time is not the result of fortuitous lot but depends on his soul's actions in previous existences.

6) Gradually Hinduism gave the caste system a religious significance by linking it to the process of reincarnation. In effect, caste became the essential machinery for the educative process of the soul as it went through the infinitely long succession of rebirths from the lowest categories in caste to that of the Brahmin, who presumably is near the end of the cycle.

Life in the universe is seen as being something like a school, in which, if one performs his duties properly, he mounts from class to class till at last he graduates, each class being a lifetime, and promotion being by rebirth as determined by Karma.[7]

Found in Sind and dated at about 600 A.D., this gilt bronze statue of Brahma has four faces, three of which are visible here. The serene and meditative pose of the creator god conveys a strong sense of both his power and his remoteness from mundane affairs.

7) *Karma* is the inexorable law of caste and salvation. A man must accept whatever caste he is born into. There is no favoritism in the universe, for a man brings his *karma* into the world and everything that happens to him springs from this fact. "Just as he acts, just as he behaves, so he becomes." If and as long as *karma* is defied, the soul is condemned to an infinite number of earthly existences and denied escape from the sufferings of *maya*. Central to *Upanishadic* teaching is the belief that death is only a single, essential incident in the foreordained cycle of rebirths. In the *Bhagavad-Gita* the Lord loftily proclaims:

You grieve for those who should not be mourned, and yet you speak words of wisdom! The learned do not grieve for the dead or for the living.
Never, indeed, was there a time when I was not, nor when you were not, nor these lords of men. Never, too, will there be a time, hereafter, when we shall not be.
As in this body, there are for the embodied one [i.e., the soul] childhood, youth, and old age, even so there is the taking on of another body. The wise sage is not perplexed thereby.

    · · ·

He is not born, nor does he die at any time; nor, having once come to be will he again come not to be. He is unborn, eternal, permanent, and primeval; he is not slain when the body is slain.

    · · ·

Just as a man, having cast off old garments, puts on other, new ones, even so does the embodied one, having cast off old bodies, take on other, new ones.[8]

Hinduism: a religious synthesis. The philosophy of the *Upanishads* permeates Hinduism. Although the main tenets of Hinduism can be summarized, as in the preceding section, it has been said that it is less a religion than a way of life because it possesses no canon, such as the Bible or the Koran, or a single personal founder, such as Christ or Muhammad, or a precise body of authoritative doctrine of belief. In short, "Hinduism is a complete rule of life, arising from a distinctive outlook on the universe, and the term covers not merely creed and worship, but law, both public and private, and practically the whole of social and economic life."[9]

In time literally thousands of deities, demigods, and lesser spirits came to be added to Indra and the early Aryan gods, forming the Hindu pantheon. Early Indo-Aryan and Dravidian gods merged, evolved, and acquired new characteristics and new names for many centuries. This process of accretion and evolution—bewildering to the outsider—is explained by an outstanding Indian philosopher:

Every God accepted by Hinduism is elevated and ultimately identified with the central Reality which is one with the deeper self of man. The addition of new gods to the Hindu pantheon does not endanger it. . . . Differences in name become immaterial for the Hindu, since every name, at its best, connotes the same metaphysical and moral perfections.[10]

Hindus, therefore, do not think of their religion as polytheistic, for all gods and various spirits are manifestations of the Absolute Reality, Brahman, which pervades everything.

Gradually Hinduism acquired a trinity consisting of Brahma, the creator; Vishnu, the preserver; and Shiva, the destroyer. These names and others have often been used interchangeably for the Absolute Reality. In popular worship Vishnu and Shiva, two deities evolved from Vedic and Dravidian origins, achieved special importance, a position they continue to maintain. Vishnu is a benevolent deity, working continually for the welfare of the world; his followers believe that he has appeared in some ten incarnations to save the world from disaster. The other great god is Shiva, who personifies the Life Force. As such, Shiva is worshiped by his devotees as embodying power, in both its constructive and destructive aspects. Some representations of Shiva portray him in terrifying guise, garlanded with skulls, while others show him as the Lord of Dancers, whose activities are the source of all movement within the cosmos. Although the basic teachings of the *Upanishads* remained constant, Hinduism from its earliest origins exhibited an unusual organic quality of growth and adaptation (see Chapter 10).

The simplicity of Gautama Buddha. During the time of the later *Vedas* and the *Upani-shads* (900-500 B.C.), religious rites were supervised by the Brahmins. They kept strict control over the people and stressed religious ceremonies, costly sacrifices, and the passive acceptance of Brahmin dogmas. But many individuals criticized or even rejected Brahminic caste requirements and claims for special prerogatives. Some would-be religious reformers sought to make the goals of *Upanishadic* thought available without priestly apparatus and sacrificial ritual. None did this more simply and effectively than Gautama of the Siddhartha clan of the Shakya tribe, who became the Buddha ("The Enlightened One"). The Buddha (563?-483 B.C.) stands out as one of the most profound influences in the history of mankind because of two principal factors: the beauty and simplicity of his own life and the philosophical depth and ethical purity of his teaching.

Gautama was the son of the ruler of a kingdom located at the foot of the Himalayas. As a privileged youth, he led a happy life and married his beautiful cousin, who bore him a son. One day, according to traditional Indian literature, Gautama was deeply shocked by the misery, disease, and sorrow that he saw was the lot of other men as he walked

A temple wall painting shows the many-armed Hindu god Shiva as the Lord of the Dancers. In his hands he holds symbols of the various aspects of his divine power.

through the streets of his native city. The happiness that his wife and son offered him only made the world's suffering appear more unbearable by contrast. He determined to abandon palace life and seek in the outside world an answer to his questions about life and death. For seven years he dwelt in a forest, practicing the self-mortification rites of the ascetics he found there. Gautama almost died from fasting and self-torture and at last concluded that these practices did not lead to wisdom.

One day, while sitting beneath a large tree meditating on the problem of human suffering, he received "enlightenment." From this insight, he constructed a religious philosophy that has affected the lives of millions of people for 2500 years. He soon attracted disciples, the most devoted being the faithful Ananda, who occupies the same position in Buddhist stories as the disciple John in the New Testament. Dressed always in a simple yellow robe, with begging bowl in hand, the Buddha wandered through the plains of the Ganges, preaching to the villagers who flocked to hear him. He spoke with everyone, regardless of caste, and, like Jesus, who congregated with sinners and publicans instead of the "respectable" Pharisees, he would decline the sumptuous banquets of nobles to partake of the simple hospitality of peasants and social outcasts.

At last, when eighty years old and enfeebled by his constant travels, the Buddha was invited by a poor blacksmith to a meal. According to legend, the food was tainted, but Gautama ate it rather than offend his host, although he forbade his disciples to follow his example. Later in the day the Buddha was taken with severe pains, and he knew death was near. Calling his disciples together, he bade them farewell. Ananda burst into tears, and the master gently reproved him, saying, "Enough, Ananda! Do not let yourself be troubled; do not weep!" After telling his disciples to inform the poor blacksmith that he should not reproach himself for the food, the Buddha addressed the group: "Behold now, brethren, I exhort you saying, 'Decay is inherent in all component things! Work out your salvation with diligence!'"[11]

Buddhist teachings. The fundamental teachings of the Buddha, briefly stated, consist of the Four Noble Truths, which were revealed to the Buddha in the Great Enlightenment:

"1. 'the truth of pain,' as manifest in 'birth, old age, sickness, death, sorrow, lamentation, dejection, and despair';

"2. 'the truth of the cause of pain,' viz., craving for existence, passion, pleasure, leading to rebirth;

"3. 'the truth of cessation of pain,' by ceasing of craving, by renunciation; and

"4. 'the truth of the way that leads to the cessation of pain,' viz., the Middle Path, which is the Eight-fold Path consisting of 'right views, intention, speech, action, livelihood, effort, mindfulness, and concentration'."[12]

In addition to these teachings, the Buddha set forth certain moral injunctions: not to kill, not to steal, not to speak falsely, not to be unchaste, and not to drink intoxicating liquors. Nonviolence and respect for all life were strongly enjoined.

Buddhism should not be thought of as a completely new religion. Its founder has been termed the Martin Luther of Hinduism. His teachings were aimed at reforming an existing system, not at completely repudiating it. He accepted such concepts as *karma, maya,* and reincarnation, subject to his own interpretation.

Although a definite relationship exists between Buddhist and *Upanishadic* philosophies, they differ in important aspects. The Buddha sought to strip the *Upanishadic* teachings of the encumbrances and superstitions which, with the passage of time, had enveloped them. Gautama taught that a man's caste, whether Brahmin or Sudra, had no bearing on his spiritual stature. Only by living the true philosophy could one win deliverance from illusion *(maya).* Nor was the Buddha interested in rituals or ceremonies or priestly mediation between gods and man. "Buddhism is personal and individual to the end. One holds fast to one's own personality until one's final beatitude is attained."[13] As a consequence, Buddhism (unlike Hinduism) has no trinity, nor does it even postulate the existence of a God or

First Cause. When the whole cosmos attains its ideal state, all beings will be in perfect harmony.

According to the Buddha, the individual cannot hope to attain an ideal state so long as he remains attached by transitory desires to the wheel of birth and rebirth. Reincarnation is a necessary doctrine in Buddhism, for only by repeated lives can the individual come to realize that the world of the senses is but a spiritual illusion. Once this is learned, the path by which sorrow is removed opens to the seeker. The strict rules of the Eightfold Path will free him from the bondage of rebirth and make possible a reabsorption into the Universal Soul, the "slipping of the dewdrip into the Silent Sea"—the entry into *nirvana.* And unlike Hinduism, the process of rebirth could be long or short, not in the control of some unapproachable and unchangeable cosmic process, but dependent upon the degree of morality of an individual's everyday life. Man, therefore, was essentially a free agent despite *karma.*

What is *nirvana*? Does it constitute the total annihilation of the individual or rather the end of the illusion of separateness from the One Soul? According to one Indian scholar, "*nirvana* is incommunicable, for the Infinite cannot be described by finite words. The utmost that we can do is to throw some light on it by recourse to negative terms. *Nirvana* is the final result of the extinction of the desire or thirst for rebirth. . . . it is the incomparable and highest goal. . . . [The] Buddha purposely discouraged questions about the reabsorption of the individual soul, as being of no practical value in the quest for salvation."[14]

The Buddha and later Buddhism. The Buddha reformed Indian religion. He censured the rites and dogmas of the Brahmins, broke with the rules of caste, taught that all men are equal, and gave the world a code of morals whose purity is universally recognized. He founded orders of monks, and the monasteries gradually developed into important academic centers. During his lifetime his teachings were disseminated through central India. The beauty and nobility of his thought can be appreciated from the following excerpts from Buddhist literature:

Hatred does not cease by hatred at any time; hatred ceases by love.

Let a man overcome anger by love, let him overcome evil by good. Let him overcome the greedy by liberality, the liar by truth.

All men trouble at punishment, all men love life. Remember that you are like unto them, and do not cause slaughter.

Not by birth does one become an outcaste, not by birth does one become a Brahmin. By deeds one becomes an outcaste, by deeds one becomes a Brahmin.[15]

Though the Buddha was a reformer, after his death many of the evils that he had attacked crept, ironically enough, into Buddhism itself. In spite of the Buddha's denigration and rejection of deities, in time men prayed to him as a god who could assure their salvation. Subsequently his teachings were elaborated into metaphysical beliefs, and Buddhism in its new form spread throughout eastern Asia.

In this chapter we have seen how, five centuries before the coming of Christ, a major civilization had developed on the great Indian subcontinent and two of the world's major religions had been founded. In Chapter 6 we shall continue the story of India and see how its civilization flourished and came into contact with other cultures to the east and west. Meanwhile, far to the east, another great fluvial civilization had arisen in the secluded land of China.

CHINA: THE FORMATIVE CENTURIES

The checkerboard land. Chinese civilization arose and developed in a vast land of over four million square miles which was for centuries almost completely isolated from the other centers of civilization by mountains, deserts, and ocean. This isolation helps explain the great originality of China's culture. For example, of all the world's writing systems today, only the Chinese and its derivatives are not based ultimately on the alphabet developed in West Asia.

Geographically, China looks like a vast checkerboard divided by mountain ranges and river systems. Internal communications were more difficult than in India or the eastern Mediterranean. Two mountain ranges cross the country from the southwest to the northeast, one inland and the other along the coast. Three more mountain chains extend from west to east, forming the great river valleys.

Three great river systems cross China from Central Asia in the west to the Pacific in the east. In the north, the Yellow River (Huang Ho), traditionally known as China's Sorrow because of the misery caused by its periodic flooding, traverses the great North China Plain, the largest area of level terrain in East Asia. Here was the original homeland of Chinese culture.

The Yangtze River, longer than the Yellow, is 3200 miles in length and is navigable for more than 1500 miles from the coast. The Yangtze valley, with its great cities like Shanghai and Hankow, is the heartland of Central China, and eventually it superseded the Yellow River valley as the most important economic and cultural region in the country. The shorter rivers and valleys converging on present-day Canton and entering the sea at Hong Kong form the third major river system in China.

These rivers were of crucial importance in the development of Chinese civilization. They provided water for irrigation and served as a cheap and efficient transportation system. As in Egypt, the beginning of political organization was linked with geography: governing bodies were needed to construct and control irrigation systems and to prevent ruinous flooding. The complex system of mountain ranges and river systems has, throughout China's history, created problems of political and military unity. At the same time, the great river valleys were suited to the growth of a homogeneous civilization extending over a greater land area than any other culture in the world.

China's prehistoric origins. As we saw in Chapter 1, the discovery of Peking man in 1927 made it evident that very ancient man-like creatures with an early Paleolithic culture had dwelt in China. Certain physical characteristics of Peking man, such as the conformation of the jawbone and teeth, are distinctive marks of the Mongoloid branch of the human race. Skulls of *Homo sapiens* have also been found, providing evidence that later Paleolithic culture flourished in China between 100,000 and 20,000 years ago.

Neolithic culture sites are found in all parts of China. Two distinctive but sequentially related subcultures existed in North China in the Yellow River valley toward the end of the Neolithic period, before 2000 B.C. The people of the Yang Shao culture, named for an important archaeological site (see map), domesticated dogs and pigs for food, engaged in farming, and produced a striking red pottery decorated boldly in black. Remains of similar pottery have been found in both Russia and Chinese Turkestan (Sinkiang), leading to disagreement among scholars, some of whom believe the resemblance proves that Yang Shao culture derived from the Near East.[16]

The people of a later Neolithic farming culture, the Lung Shan, domesticated more varieties of animals than their Yang Shao predecessors, and produced a thin, lustrous, wheel-made black pottery. They also used pounded-earth techniques for building walls; the remains of one of these measures thirty feet thick and a mile long and resembles the town walls of modern North China. Some scholars believe that the Lung Shan culture is the link between earlier Neolithic culture and the people of the Shang period, which began about 1500 B.C.

The Shang dynasty: China enters history. The first Chinese state for which we possess written historical evidence, the Shang dynasty, flourished in the region of An-yang, a site in the Yellow River valley, from about 1500 to 1027 B.C. An-yang was a crossroads of influence from North and Southeast Asia as well as from West Asia. It had long been a culture center, and Shang sites are found on top of remains of black pottery culture sites, which in turn overlie red pottery culture sites. Archaeological discoveries show that the Shang civilization was remarkably advanced; it was distinguished from its predecessors by three important developments: bronze metallurgy, a writing system, and the emergence of a state organization in an urban environment.

The Shang people carried bronze metallurgy, probably originating in West Asia, to heights never surpassed in world history. Bronze was used to cast elaborate ceremonial vessels and weapons which were intricately decorated with precisely incised or high-relief designs (see Color Plate 4). While the shapes of bronze vessels were often derived from Neolithic clay and wooden forms, the Shang artistic style is different from anything found in prehistoric China or the West. Its patterns resemble, instead, those found in other parts of East Asia, the Pacific Northwest, and the South Seas. Shang design may be the earliest example of a unique Pacific Basin style, characterized by frontal views of animal heads, in contrast to animal profiles which predominated in the West. The elaborate ceremonial bronze vessels were required for religious rituals, which also fostered sacred dancing and music. Various in-

struments introduced in these early centuries—drums, cymbals, bells, stone chimes, and ocarinas—are still in use. Stringed instruments may also have appeared in this period.

The Shang people invented or perfected a distinctive writing system, unquestionably Chinese in both language and form. They possessed sufficient written words, over two thousand, to express themselves with considerable facility. Some are still in use today. These characters, or glyphs, representing individual words, rather than sounds, consisted of three types: pictographs, recognizable as pictures of observable objects; ideographs, representing ideas; and characters, formed in part on the basis of phonetic principles.

Although some inscriptions were made on bronzes, most were written on "oracle bones," fragments of animal bones and tortoise shells, on which were inscribed questions put to the gods and ancestors. For

Oracle bone inscriptions usually contained questions, the answers to which were determined by various rituals. The writing on this bone, however, demonstrates Chinese scientific sophistication. It reads: "On the seventh day of the month . . . a great new star appeared in company with Antares." Note that the script is markedly pictographic.

example, the diviner would ask a god or a family's ancestor whether a particular member of the family would recover from his illness. The diviner would then heat the shell or bone and interpret the resulting cracks as a revelation answering the question. This system of divination was similar to that used by the black pottery culture and, in recent times, by various primitive peoples in other parts of the Far East. The Shang "oracle bones" are unique because they sometimes contain written descriptions of answers and the outcome of the situation in question. Consequently, they are important material for the study of Shang culture.

Shang society appears to have centered on a city-state and its surrounding settlements, ruled by hereditary kings. These kings probably were originally prominent shamans who communicated between the people on the one hand and the ancestral spirits and various natural phenomena on the other. Shang kings and aristocrats lived in imposing buildings, went to battle in horse-drawn chariots resembling those of Homer's Greece, conducted human sacrifices, and buried live servants with their dead masters. In contrast,

the common people lived in primitive pit dwellings like their Neolithic ancestors and went to war on foot. Warfare was frequent in Shang times, and the chariot, a new military weapon, facilitated the spread of Shang power through large parts of the Yellow River valley and its tributaries. Both military and administrative inventions made possible the emergence of a recognizable state by the late Shang period. Political and social authority rested on the aristocrats' monopoly of bronze metallurgy, their possession of expensive war chariots, and the king's religious functions.

Shang religion centered around the worship of deities, spirits, ancestors, natural phenomena such as the wind and the earth, and the cardinal points of the compass. Animal sacrifices were usual, and sometimes libations of a beerlike liquor were poured on the ground. One of the deities worshiped was Shang Ti (Supreme Ti). In Chinese mythology the Five Ti were early Chinese rulers, and Shang Ti was probably worshiped as a "supreme ancestor."

In the nascent urban centers of the period, people made a living in specialized occupations, such as bronze casting, and trade. The majority of the population, however, consisted of peasants who grew wheat, millet, and rice and raised cattle, sheep, pigs, and horses. Farming methods were primitive; farmers used a stick for a plow; it was held by one laborer and dragged through the soil by another, who bound it to himself with a rope.

Chou: the classical period. In 1027 B.C. (or 1122 B.C., according to some sources), the Chou people conquered the Shang. With their capital at Hao, near modern Sian, the Chou lived on the edge of Shang civilization and authority, sharing its culture and language. A frontier people, probably partly Turkish in origin, the Chou undoubtedly benefited from their proximity to nomadic tribes in the north and west, from whom they may have learned some of the martial skills that made their conquest of Shang possible.

The Chou kings conquered most of the North China Plain, but the lack of efficient communications made the development of a unified state impossible. Consequently, the kings delegated local authority, particularly in the eastern parts of their lands, to relatives or to military chieftains and social magnates. These vassal lords, whose power was hereditary, recognized the suzerainty of the Chou kings, who retained direct control only over their original homeland. The vassals, while all-powerful in their own lands, were responsible for supplying the kings with military aid, particularly against the northern and western "barbarians." The vassals resided in walled towns and controlled the surrounding communities and countryside. At various times they numbered between seventy and two hundred. With the passage of time the power of the vassals vis-à-vis the Chou kings increased, and by the eighth century B.C. the vassals no longer went to the capital for investiture, as had previously been the custom. As the vassal states grew in size and developed their own bureaucratic and military organizations, they became virtually independent, and the Chou kings continued to reign only on the sufferance of the feudal lords.

The remnants of Chou royal power disappeared completely in 771 B.C., when an alliance of dissident vassal states and "barbarians" seized the capital and killed the king. Part of the royal family managed to escape eastward to Lo-yang, however, where the dynasty survived for another five centuries and was known as the Eastern Chou. Lo-yang, in the province of Honan, was the center of the most heavily populated and economically important region in China and was therefore considered safer from attack than the old western capital.

At Lo-yang, Chou royal functions were largely confined to performing state religious rituals and arbitrating differences among the feudal lords. As power became delicately balanced among the rulers of the more vigorous feudal states, the stronger principalities gradually absorbed their weaker neighbors, and the domains of the Chou kings themselves diminished in size and strength in comparison with their vassals'.

Warfare between the feudal states was incessant, particularly in the "Period of Warring States" (403-221 B.C.), and the struggle for power eventually lay between two. In 256 B.C. the Chou ruler was overthrown by the ruler of Ch'in, the most aggressive of the warring states, possessed of superior military force and a new political credo resembling modern totalitarianism. By 221 B.C. the Ch'in united all of China for the first time in its history.

The Chou destruction of Shang did not result in any sharp break in the development of Chinese culture. The writing system became more complex and sophisticated, and the Chou continued to produce bronze vessels, often with long inscriptions but with less elaborate designs than the Shang. Although in the eighth century B.C. China was still behind West Asia technologically, during the sixth century iron was introduced and came into general use by the end of the Chou, when China had drawn abreast, if not ahead, of technological developments in the rest of the world. Iron weapons made warfare more efficient, and iron plows contributed to the expansion of agriculture.

The Eastern Chou is unrivaled by any later period in Chinese history for its energy and dynamic creativity. The ox-drawn iron-tipped plow, together with the growth of large-scale irrigation and water-control projects, led to population growth based on increased agricultural yields. Canals were constructed to facilitate the moving of commodities over long distances. Commerce and wealth grew rapidly, and a merchant and artisan class emerged in towns that became commercial centers. Cowrie shells, bolts of silk, and ingots of precious metals were the media of exchange, and by the end of the Chou period copper cash, small round coins with square holes, were being minted and used in general circulation. They remained the basic coinage of China into the late nineteenth century. Chopsticks and lacquer, today universally considered as symbols of Chinese and East Asian culture, were also in use by the end of the period.

The art of horseback riding, which was developing among the nomads of Central and West Asia, deeply influenced Chou China because it contributed to the ease and growth of communications between east and west. Technological and intellectual developments in the Indian and West Asian regions were gradually carried to China. In design, for instance, the typical western profile replaced the Shang highly stylized frontal view. Central Asian horsemen threatened China militarily, and in response the Chinese began constructing defensive walls, later joined together to become the Great Wall of China. Inside China itself, cavalry replaced the chariot in warfare, and the use of the horse improved internal communications, contributing to the process of political centralization that was to reach a climax under the Ch'in dynasty, successor to the Chou. All these developments led to a growing self-consciousness on the part of the Chinese who, while divided into states fighting among themselves, began to distinguish between their own high civilization and the barbarian peasants and nomads. This sense of the unique superiority of their own civilization became a lasting characteristic of Chinese culture.

The classes. Class divisions and consciousness were highly developed during the Chou and have remained so to the present. The king and the aristocracy were sharply separated from the mass of the people on the basis of land ownership and family descent. The nobility were members of a territorially dispersed clan system, and the clans in turn were divided into families, each with a male head possessing authority over the other members. Until the later stages of Chou, the nobility held the chief posts in the army and administration. The fact that the aristocrats' inherited privileges depended on proof of their noble ancestry was at least partly responsible for the great emphasis which the Chinese placed on ancestor worship and its rituals. The wide gulf between the nobles and the masses is reflected in this aphorism from the classic *Book of Rites:* "The ritual does not descend down to the common people; punishments do not extend up to the nobles."

Village life. Agriculture, of course, was the occupation of the overwhelming proportion of the population. Large-scale irrigation, fertilizer, and the ox-drawn iron-tipped plow modified the traditional feudal land system, stimulating a gradual changeover to private land ownership based on in-creased productivity.[17] But the masses generally had no political rights and, until the end of the Chou, little or no land. The peasants cultivated their fields as the tenants of nobles or landlords, paid taxes, and served as common soldiers. Families lived together in villages often situated on heights overlooking the fields and out of the reach of floods. These hamlets clustered about the residence of a noble or, after feudal times, a landlord. Eventually, the village community included members not related by blood to the original family groups.

Although private property and landlord-tenant relationships gradually replaced feudalism, this basic communal pattern continued down to the Communist victory in 1949. A study conducted before World War II of a typical village in Shantung province showed that village organization was based on clan relationships and that local affairs were dominated by clan heads and official leaders. Moreover, the attitude of these leaders was conservative, often so conservative as to prohibit the introduction of any new ideas.[18]

Despite increased agricultural productivity and changes in property structure, the farm population still had difficulty eking out an existence. A major problem in the Chinese economy has been that the majority of farmers worked fields so small that they could not produce a crop surplus to tide them over periods of scarcity. This is evident as early as 400 B.C., in the "first family-budget study in China," and as late as the twentieth century, in studies of modern Chinese peasant family budgets. This problem became especially acute from the eighteenth century on, when population pressures led to a marked decline in the size of peasant holdings.

Ancient Chinese chivalry, custom, and fashion. The feudal nobles lived a far different life from that of the farmers. Their customs can be compared in a general way to those of Europe's feudal nobility (see Chapter 12). Underlying the feudal structure was a code of chivalry, practiced in both war and peace. The intricate and complex code became so important to the nobility as a symbol of gentility that nobles devoted years to its mastery. Arrayed in breastplate and helmet, the Chinese noble waged war from his chariot and, to display his martial skill and social grace, "would come to the court of his seigneur to take part in tournaments of the noble sport of archery which was accompanied by musical airs and interspersed with elegant salutations, the whole regulated like a ballet."[19] Chou courtiers spent their leisure time playing checkers, gambling with dice, hunting, fencing, and training horses and dogs.

Life was luxurious and refined among the wealthy classes, in sharp contrast to the poverty prevailing among the peasants and unskilled laborers. The houses of the poor were hovels of earth with thatched roofs, while the abodes of the rich had tiled roofs and were laid out in groups of buildings separated by courts and gardens. Food was served in dishes of bamboo, bronze, or earthenware. While the peasants lived largely on millet in the north and rice in the Yangtze valley, the rich had sumptuous banquets involving the "five flavors," sweet and sour, salty and spicy, and bitter.

The basic male costume of the period was a long gown over which a shorter coat was worn. Ornaments of gold, jade, and precious stones decorated women's ears and fingers, and some ladies of the seventh century B.C. wore wigs.

Social and political change in ancient China. Chou technological and economic advances stimulated and were accompanied by important social and political changes. Because they had room to expand territorially, and because they were in almost constant contact with non-Chinese "barbarians" and therefore were less bound by tradition than the states in the heartland of Chou China, the frontier states were more innovative than those in the central region.

The state of Ch'in, located in the far northwestern part of China in the area of what is now Kansu and Shensi provinces, is an excellent example of an innovative frontier state. The other Chinese states considered Ch'in a country of barbarians, uncivilized and ignorant. Gradually, however, Ch'in was more and more influenced by Chou culture, and in 352 B.C. Shang Yang, a scion of the ruling house of a small Chou state, became chancellor of Ch'in, ruling until 338 B.C. Only five of the eighteen chancellors of Ch'in known to history were members of ruling houses. Of the rest, many were of humble origins and rose to their high positions by virtue of merit and ability.

Shang Yang instituted far-reaching changes in Ch'in government and society, and these were maintained or further developed by his successors. Recognizing that the growth of Ch'in's strength and power depended on a more efficient and centralized bureaucratic structure than could exist under feudalism, Shang Yang suppressed the old nobility and created a new aristocracy based on military merit. He divided the population into five- and ten-family units ruled directly by officials of the state and introduced a universal draft beginning at approximately age fifteen. Soldiers distinguishing themselves in battle were awarded with the services of five peasant families, and all noble ranks and access to a life of luxury were based on military accomplishment. Based on this new system, Ch'in eventually fielded and supported an army of one million men.

Economic changes accompanied the transformation of the Ch'in military and administrative system. Shang Yang encouraged agricultural development and for the first time in the state's history levied direct state taxes on land in the place of the older system of communal work. (Private ownership of land, however, appears to have developed before Shang Yang arrived in Ch'in, and his reforms simply recognized an already existing fact.) Commerce, too, was encouraged, under a system of laws that protected merchants and their property.

These reforms made Ch'in the most powerful state of the time; and after Shang Yang's death Ch'in began to conquer the other states of Chou China. By 221 B.C. Ch'in had established the first really unified empire in Chinese history, extending to the entire country the institutional innovations and social changes that had taken place in Ch'in as well as those that had occurred in the states it had conquered—for example, regulation of weights and measures, price control, state monopolies in the salt and iron industries, and a uniform agricultural tax system.

The peripheral states brought more and more non-Chinese "barbarians" under the influence of Chinese culture. The spoken languages in the newly incorporated areas gave rise to the great variety of dialects that survive in spoken Chinese to the present day. But the Chinese written language, so important for bureaucratic administration, provided a standard means of communication for all educated people. Even now, a man from Canton in the southwest and a man from Peking in the north may understand each other's writing perfectly though their spoken languages are mutually unintelligible. This also contributed to the strong sense of regionalism which is an important characteristic of Chinese society.

The interstate system. The disappearance of Chou influence over the vassal states during the Eastern Chou period led to rapidly increasing interstate warfare and a decline in adherence to the rules for the proper conduct of warfare and the establishment of legitimacy. Particularly in the fourth and third centuries B.C., many state rulers took the title *wang*, or king, formerly reserved for the Chou ruler alone. Enemy states sought to exterminate each other and to annex each other's territory. As the states grew in size, the scale of warfare grew too. In the latter years of the Chou some states could throw thousands of chariots and tens of thousands of peasant foot soldiers into battle. Interstate conferences were held to consider and conclude treaties and alliances and to develop disarmament proposals. Alliances were established and cemented through royal marriages, and hostages were exchanged to ensure loyalty.

The older, more traditional states of the North China Plain sought to defend themselves from the rising powers on the periphery of the Chinese culture area by the formation of leagues of alliance. The first was established in 651 B.C., when the ruler of one state was recognized by the other central states as *pa*, or hegemon, of a Chinese confederation. This attempt ended in utter failure by the first part of the fifth century B.C., however.

The formation of leagues and alliances, the exchange of ambassadors, political marriages, and the holding of interstate conferences all resemble the interstate system that developed in Europe in late medieval and early modern times. By 221 B.C., however, the state of Ch'in had conquered all its rivals, and while Europe, after the fall of the Roman empire, was never again to achieve political or administrative unity, China was never again permanently disunited.

The rise of philosophical schools. By the fifth century B.C. rapid economic, social, political, and technological change, coupled with increasing warfare between the states, destroyed the apparent stability that had characterized Chinese society internally during the Shang, Western Chou, and early Eastern Chou dynasties. Educated Chinese became aware of the great disparity between the traditions inherited from their ancestors and the reality in which they themselves lived. Moreover, the nascent bureaucratic class had no place in the traditional scheme of Chinese society, with its two classes: the aristocracy and the peasants.

The tension between inherited tradition and existing reality led directly to the birth of social and personal consciousness in China on the eve of the Period of Warring States. Many scholars have noted with excitement the parallel between the flourishing intellectual life of fifth-century B.C. China and the Golden Ages of Greek philosophy and Indian religious thought at the same time. Some have gone so far as to suggest that improved communications made it possible for these three great centers of world civilization to stimulate and influence each other, but little or no historical evidence exists to support such suggestions. The birth of consciousness in China, at least, isolated as she was from the other centers of civilization, must be understood in terms of internal developments rather than external influences. More than Indian and Mediterranean thinkers, Chinese philosophers concerned themselves primarily with man's control of himself and his society in an age when it appeared that he could no longer control either. The social and political orientation of Chinese thinkers was reinforced by the fact that most of them were members of the new class of educated bureaucrats. Because education was the basis of this new class, the politician-administrators were often teachers as well, gathering disciples who founded schools of thought to pass on the teachings of their masters.

Although they often disagreed violently among themselves, most of the schools of Chinese philosophy in the Eastern Chou shared certain characteristics. Dismayed with the present state of man and society, they looked to the past for models on which to base their programs for the construction of a meaningful ethical system for man and for the reconstruction of Chinese society. This led to a greater consciousness of history in China than in other world cultures. From this time on, the writing of history was a major literary activity among educated Chinese, and down to the end of the nineteenth century all intellectual innovations sought their justification in historical examples and classical writings (see the Historical Critique, p. 308). These influences are even present in Communist China today. All schools of Chinese thought also shared a common interest in the achievement of order in society and of a proper balance between man and man and man and nature. The rules for social conduct developed by the various schools all emphasized the value of order and balance, though they did not necessarily agree on how these should be achieved.

Master K'ung, the sage. The first, most famous, and certainly most influential professional Chinese philosopher and teacher was K'ung-fu-tzu, Master K'ung, known in the West by the Latinized form of his name, Confucius (551-479 B.C.). His teachings had a greater and longer-lasting influence in China and the rest of East Asia than those of any other philosopher and became the official school of thought in Japan, Korea, the Ryukyu Islands, and Vietnam, as well as in China. He is still venerated as the official philosopher of the Nationalist Chinese government on Taiwan. The teachings of the sage and his most famous disciple, Mencius, are written down in a group of books known as the Thirteen Classics. In the West the best known of these is the *Analects*, a collection of Confucius' responses to his disciples' questions. In this work, each of Confucius' statements begins with the phrase, "The Master said," the original of the English expression, "Confucius say. . . . "

Confucius was born in the small state of Lu, in modern Shantung province, into what was evidently a family of the lower aristocracy that had sunk into poverty. Orphaned as a child, he obtained an education and became a member of the new bureaucratic class. Tradition has it that he found employment for a while as an official in his native state, but he never achieved the prominent public position he sought. Dissatisfied with the conditions of Chinese social and moral life, he spent at least ten years wandering around the country advising princes and teaching young men who, he hoped, might succeed where he had failed. Confucius was evidently a teacher of rare ability, and it is said that he had more than three thousand students. Seventy-two of these became his close disciples and were known for their remarkable virtue. Toward the end of his life, again according to tradition, he retired from teaching and devoted his remaining years to the editing of some of the works that were later included in what became known as the Confucian Classics.

It is fitting that Confucius, the first historical figure in China consciously to consider the human condition, should also have been the author of the first Chinese autobiography of which we have record, short as it is:

At fifteen, I set my heart on learning. At thirty, I was firmly established. At forty, I had no more doubts. At fifty, I knew the will of Heaven. At sixty, I was ready to listen to it. At seventy, I could follow my heart's desire without transgressing what was right.[20]

Confucius said of himself, "I am a transmitter and not a creator. I believe in and have a passion for the ancients." Living in an age of social, political, and moral turmoil, Confucius was probably the first Chinese to be conscious of tradition as tradition, and he sought to revive it by organizing it into a system of thought.

Confucianism is a social and moral philosophy, not a religion. While accepting the existence of Heaven *(T'ien)* and spirits, Confucius was fundamentally an agnostic who believed that the basic concern of man is man. "We don't know yet how to serve men, how can we know about serving the spirits?" he said. And, "We don't know yet about life, how can we know about death?" "Devote yourself to the proper demands of the people, respect the ghosts and spirits but keep them at a distance—this may be called wisdom."[21]

Confucius' home state of Lu was known for its conservatism, and the Master believed that the social and political problems of his day could be solved only if men would return to the traditions of the founders of the Chou dynasty. Society would be stable if only each man would play his assigned role: "Let the ruler be a ruler and the subject a subject; let the father be a father and the son a son."[22] He advocated a paternalistic form of government in which the ruler made himself responsible for the welfare of his people and the family was the model for the state.

Government, according to Confucius, was primarily a problem of ethics. While he did not challenge the hereditary rights of the rulers, he insisted that their primary responsibility was to serve as an example of correct ethical conduct for the people. The cultivation of virtue depended on *li*, or "propriety," which characterized proper conduct for those in a ruler's court; *li*, in turn, depended on education. Each man would play his proper role in society if he performed the rituals proper to his station. "By nature men are pretty much alike; it is learning and practice that set them apart."

The ideal man, according to Confucius, was the *chün-tzu*, the "ruler's son," "aristocrat," or "gentleman," the cultivated man. The primary virtues, he taught, were integrity, righteousness, conscientiousness or loyalty toward others, altruism, and love for one's fellow man. Etiquette or decorum were essential expressions of virtue. Confucius said, "Courtesy without decorum becomes tiresome. Cautiousness without decorum becomes timidity, daring becomes insubordination, frankness becomes effrontery."[23] The ruler who possessed the essential virtues and behaved with decorum, Confucius insisted, would be able to rule by example rather than through force.

Taoism: intuitive mysticism. While Confucianism stressed reason and social cohesiveness, Taoism, the most important school of Chinese thought next to Confucianism, emphasized the individual man and insisted that man's greatest problem was to conform to nature, not to society. Taoism often represented the revolt of the man of sensibilities and the common man against the social and moral rigidity of orthodox Confucianism.

The origins of Taoism are lost in myth. Some scholars have suggested that it derived from pre-Confucian Chinese or barbarian culture, and its mysticism may have been a legacy from popular shamans or medicine men. The *Tao te ching*, or the *Classic of the Way and Power*, is the most important Taoist work, and though attributed to Lao-tzu, who tradition says was slightly older than Confucius, it probably dates only to the third century B.C. Lao-tzu himself appears to be a mythical figure, but he is typical of the antisocial recluses mentioned in the Confucian *Analects*, who may have been precursors or early representatives of Taoism. Because the style of the *Tao te ching* is cryptic and overly concise, it has been subject to many different interpretations, and no two western translations agree on its precise meaning. Taoism's second most important book, the *Chuang-tzu*, was also written in the third century B.C., though it is attributed to a fourth-century philosopher of the same name. It is one of the most beautiful works of Chinese literature, containing stories and passages of great poetic delight and philosophical insight, as the following example indicates:

Once Chuang Tzu was fishing in the P'u River when the King of Ch'u sent two of his ministers to announce that he wished to entrust to Chuang Tzu the care of his entire domain.

Chuang Tzu held his fishing pole and, without turning his head, said: "I have heard that Ch'u possesses a sacred tortoise which has been dead for three thousand years and which the king keeps wrapped up in a box and stored in his ancestral temple. Is this tortoise better off dead and with its bones venerated, or would it be better off alive with its tail dragging in the mud?"

Courtesy, Museum of Fine Arts, Boston, Bigelow Collection

Buddha, Lao-tzu, and Confucius were three of the great leaders of East Asian thought. In this Japanese painting from the Kano period (1336-1558) they are depicted conversing together. Although the three philosophers were not contemporaries, their discussion symbolically represents the interaction of the three philosophical schools. The portrait of Confucius, a stone engraving dating from the eighteenth century, shows the sage in the traditional garb of a scholar. This portrait stood in a temple dedicated to the thinker and illustrates a later dynasty's—the Manchu's—acceptance of Confucius as the empire's official philosopher. On this Sung period incense burner Lao-tzu, whose name means "the old one" or "the old philosopher," sits placidly on a water buffalo. Chinese artists frequently portrayed sages as old men because age was highly revered by the Chinese as a source of wisdom.

"It would be better off alive and dragging its tail in the mud," the two ministers replied.

"Then go away!" said Chuang Tzu, "and I will drag my tail in the mud!" [24]

Popular Taoism quickly degenerated into a religion of spirits and magic, but philosophical Taoism sought to define the "true nature" of man in abstract terms. The word *tao*, meaning "road" or "way," in Confucianism stood for the ideal society which that school advocated. The Taoists defined it to mean the scheme of nature to which man should conform. Man could live in harmony with nature only if he turned his attention inward and experienced oneness between himself and the universe. In the Tao there are no distinctions. Everything is relative. The Taoists' highest ideal was the state of original and complete simplicity, and they advocated a society in which man lived simply, without law or machinery, without striving to be more than a harmonious part of nature. Some even suggested that the Chinese writing system should be done away with in favor of the more primitive method of communication by means of knotted ropes. This state of primitive simplicity was frequently symbolized in Taoist writing by an uncarved block of wood, as in the following passage from the *Tao te ching:*

He who knows glory but keeps to disgrace,
  Becomes the valley of the world.
Being the valley of the world,
  He finds contentment in constant virtue,
  He returns to the uncarved block.
The cutting up of the uncarved block results in vessels,
  Which, in the hands of the sage, become officers.
Truly, "A great cutter does not cut."[25]

The Taoists believed that the only way to achieve union with nature was through inaction, doing nothing: "Do nothing and nothing will not be done." Spontaneity, not conscious planning, was the key to correct behavior. The ideal political system, according to Taoism, would be "a small country with a few inhabitants."[26] In the early history of Chinese thought Taoism represented a strain of romanticism in contrast to Confucian rationalism.

The Hundred Schools. Philosophical disputation flourished in the latter years of the Eastern Chou, and numerous schools of thought rose to compete with Confucianism and Taoism, though few left a really lasting mark on Chinese philosophy. The *Naturalists* believed that nature was based on certain cosmic principles, chief among them the dualistic concept of *yin* and *yang*. Whereas in western dualism light and dark, good and evil, were thought to be in constant conflict, the Chinese Naturalists taught that the universe was derived from the harmony of balanced and complementary opposites. The *Dialecticians*, like the Greek Sophists, tried to create a system of logic based on the analysis of the meaning of words. Confucianism itself developed its own offshoots, such as the school of the philosopher Motzu, who advocated a strict and extreme form of social utilitarianism.

Mencius and the "Mandate of Heaven." The most significant transmitter of Confucian doctrine was Mencius (372-289 B.C.), who was born in a small state on the border of Confucius' home state of Lu. Like Confucius, Mencius failed to achieve a high position in government and became a wandering teacher, followed by his disciples.

Mencius added important new dimensions to Confucian thought. He taught that man's nature was fundamentally good and could be developed by self-cultivation through education and a kind of spontaneous inner search resembling Taoist mystical experiences. Government should be guided not by opportunism but by ethical standards, he claimed. A moral ruler will behave benevolently toward his people, providing for their well-being. A true king must have the support of his people. Heaven manifests itself through the people, and if the people accept and support their ruler, Mencius taught, he has the "Mandate of Heaven" to rule over them. If they overthrow their ruler, he has lost Heaven's mandate and has lost his right to leadership. This rationalization of revolution had originally been used by the Chou to justify their revolt against the Shang, but Mencius now developed it into a full justification of revolution.

Modern commentators, both Chinese and western, have seen in Mencius' concept of the Mandate of Heaven a form of protodemocratic thought. Mencius evidently believed that all men were morally equal and that the good ruler needed the consent of his people. But it would perhaps be more accurate to define Mencius' political theories as advocating benevolent autocracy rather than popular democracy.

The school of law. Hsün-tzu (c. 300-237 B.C.), who was also a Confucianist, attacked Mencius' concept that man is basically good and taught that human nature is evil because man's desires and emotions lead to conflict. He advocated a society organized on strict hierarchical principles and maintained by ritual. The ruler should use discipline and punishment, as well as education, to control the people and improve their nature.

Hsün-tzu's ideas were developed further by a non-Confucian school of philosophy, the School of Law or the Legalists, which became closely identified with the state of Ch'in. The Legalists taught that man is by nature selfish and evil and that moralists like the Confucians contributed to evil by encouraging human desires. According to the Legalists, people primarily want security and social order, and this can be achieved only in a society where the uneducated citizen, living in a kind of Taoist primitive state, blindly follows an absolute ruler and is subordinate to the state. To achieve this kind of society, harsh punishments and the strictest laws would be necessary. People were to be mutually responsible for the enforcement of the law, and anyone who had knowledge of a crime but did not report it was considered as guilty as the criminal himself. The ruler, by nature, would seek to create a strong and secure state, and therefore only his desires would be right.

Bearing strong resemblances to modern totalitarian thought, Legalism contributed greatly to Ch'in's eventual success in conquering and unifying all China. Although it disappeared as a legitimate philosophical school with the fall of the Ch'in empire about 206 B.C., its advocacy of a strong ruler and a universal criminal code were important additions to Chinese statecraft and strongly influenced the orthodox philosophy, founded on the teachings of Confucius and Mencius, that was to dominate China for over two thousand years.

Chinese art and literature. In general the Chinese arts are marked by restraint, a quality probably derived from Chinese conservatism and serenity. For example, a poem seldom employs a great deal of highly ornate language, nor is it effusive in its effect. The following love poem is timeless in spirit and typically Chinese in restraint and expression:

The morning glory climbs above my head,
Pale flowers of white and purple, blue and red.
I am disquieted.

Down in the withered grasses something stirred,
I thought it was his footfall that I heard.
Then a grasshopper chirred.

I climbed the hill just as the new moon showed,
I saw him coming on the southern road.
My heart lays down its load.[27]

During the Shang and Chou periods the Chinese were already skillful craftsmen and sensitive artists. Jade ornaments have been found in the earliest Chinese graves. From Shang times the Chinese cut jade into forms of fishes to use as "sound stones" which, when struck, emitted a clear tone for a considerable length of time. The ancient Chinese considered jade so sacred that it alone was used in fashioning ritualistic objects. Strikingly beautiful ceremonial bronzes were produced during the Shang period and for the next 1500 years (see Color Plate 4). The bronzes served as sacrificial jars or libation cups in family ancestor worship.

Taoism made a profound impression upon Chinese art. The Taoist and the Chinese artist alike are deeply introspective and intuitive in approach, seeking to understand the processes of nature that create the landscape. Painting to express his reaction to a scene is more important to the Chinese artist than depicting the landscape realistically. Unfortunately almost no examples survive of the earliest Chinese painting, but literary references indicate that it was an established art centuries before the birth of Christ. Confucius speaks of temple frescoes which he thought were admirable in quality and design.

In the Chinese spoken language, differences in meaning are achieved through the use of tones, of which there are from four to nine for each word sound depending on the dialect. While the spoken language has split into various dialects the written language has remained comparatively unchanged. Under the Chou dynasty it assumed the form which, with some modifications, it possesses today. The historic continuity of the written language has advantages, for a literate Chinese today can read works written twenty centuries ago. The difficulty, however, is to become a literate Chinese; the language never developed beyond a primitive form expressing each idea with a different character, so that today it includes forty thousand separate characters, rather than the small alphabet of letters used in other languages.

During China's formative centuries, literature flourished. Although most poetry written prior to the age of Confucius has unfortunately been lost, 305 poems have been preserved in the *Shih Ching,* or *Book of Odes.* These poems were supposedly selected by Confucius from the poetry that was in existence in his time. From the *Shih Ching* we see that human nature has changed little and that the age-old problems of living affected the ancient Chinese much as they affect us. In our own age we can sympathize deeply with soldiers engaged in a conflict which they did not create:

How free are the wild geese on their wings,
And the rest they find on the bushy Yu trees!
But we, ceaseless toilers in the king's services,
Cannot even plant our millet and rice.

What will our parents have to rely on?
O thou distant and azure Heaven!
When shall all this end? . . .
What leaves have not turned purple?
What man is not torn from his wife?
Mercy be on us soldiers—
Are we not also men?[28]

SUMMARY

The earliest settlements in India were farming villages located in what are now Baluchistan and Sind. From about 2500 to 1500 B.C. the Indian counterpart of the Nile and Tigris-Euphrates cultures existed in the Indus valley. With its two capital cities, Harappa and Mohenjo-Daro, this civilization possessed a well-regulated government and economy.

About 1500 B.C. Indo-Aryan nomads began to invade India, and as a result a new culture developed. The Indian language of Sanskrit evolved, and the oldest Sanskrit literature, the *Vedas,* was composed. The *Upanishads* form the core of Hinduism, the pantheistic religion which has had an extraordinarily strong influence on Indian life. During the Later Vedic period the three pillars of Indian society—the autonomous village, the joint-family, and the caste system—evolved. In the sixth century B.C. Gautama Buddha gave India and the world a philosophy which has endured for centuries.

Human beings have lived in China since the early Pleistocene epoch, and in the second millennium B.C. advanced Neolithic cultures, the Yang Shao and the Lung Shan, appeared. The Shang civilization began around 1500 B.C. in the Huang Ho valley. During this period a system of writing evolved on which later Chinese script was based. The next dynasty—the Chou—had the longest existence of any dynasty in China's history. Chou times are considered China's classical period, for social customs, economic organization, philosophy, literature, and art which have endured to modern times originated during that dynasty.

The greatest glory of the Chou was its contribution to philosophy. Such Chinese philosophers as Confucius and Mencius sought to show men how to live rational, ethical lives on earth. The ideas of these philosophers and of Lao-tzu, who developed an intuitive, mystical approach to life (Taoism), have strongly influenced Chinese culture for over two thousand years.

Suggestions for Reading

ASPECTS OF PREHISTORY

G. Gamow, **A Planet Called Earth,*** Bantam. Presents the newest theories of the origin of the earth and the planets, the evolution of the solar system, and the successive changes of the earth's surface. **The Creation of the Universe,*** Bantam, by the same author, analyzes the varying modern theories of the origin of the universe. Also recommended are **The Universe,** Time, Inc., 1962, by D. Birgamini and the editors of **Life;** A. Broms, **Our Emerging Universe,*** Dell; Thornton Page, ed., **Stars and Galaxies: Birth, Aging, and Death in the Universe,*** Spectrum.

Gabriel W. Lasker, **The Evolution of Man: A Brief Introduction to Physical Anthropology,** Holt, Rinehart and Winston, 1961. This useful survey contains an account of the radiocarbon and other scientific methods of dating the past. See also W. E. LeGros Clark, **The Antecedents of Man: An Introduction to the Evolution of the Primates,*** Torchbooks; C. S. Coon, **The Origin of Races,** Knopf, 1962; G. G. Simpson, **The Meaning of Evolution,*** Yale; R. Ardrey, **African Genesis,*** Dell.

R. Linton, **The Tree of Culture,*** Vintage. An esteemed introduction to cultural anthropology. See also M. F. Ashley Montagu, ed., **Culture and the Evolution of Man,** Oxford, 1962; L. S. B. Leakey, **Adam's Ancestors: The Evolution of Man and His Culture,*** Torchbooks; K. P. Oakley, **Man the Tool-Maker,*** Phoenix; R. J. Braidwood, **Prehistoric Men,** 7th ed., Scott, Foresman.

Jacquetta Hawkes, **Prehistory*** (**History of Mankind, Cultural and Scientific Development,** Vol. I, Pt. 1), Mentor. A comprehensive account. See also Grahame Clark, **World Prehistory: An Outline,*** Cambridge; and **The Epic of Man,** Time, Inc., 1961, by the editors of **Life.** Also recommended are A. Radcliffe-Brown, **Structure and Function in Primitive Society,*** Free Press; F. Boaz, **The Mind of Primitive Man,*** Free Press; B. Malinowski, **Magic, Science and Religion and Other Essays,*** Anchor; M. Mead, ed., **Cultural Patterns and Technical Change,*** Mentor.

H. R. Hays, **From Ape to Angel,*** Capricorn. Describes the fascinating story of the great anthropologists—Mead, Malinowski, Benedict, Boas. L. Cottrell, **Digs and Diggers: A Book of World Archaeology,** World, 1964, is a lively general survey. **Lost Cities,*** Universal Library, by the same author, and C. W. Ceram, **Gods, Graves and Scholars,** Knopf, 1951, are also popular surveys. K. Kenyon, **Beginning in Archaeology,*** Praeger, and S. Piggott, **Approach to Archaeology,*** McGraw-Hill, describe the techniques and contributions of the archaeologist.

H. Bandi et al., **The Art of the Stone Age: Forty Thousand Years of Rock Art,** Methuen, 1961; A. Leroi-Gourhan, **Treasures of Prehistoric Art,** Abrams, 1967. Lavishly illustrated.

THE ANCIENT NEAR EAST

M. Covensky, **The Ancient Near Eastern Tradition,*** Harper & Row, 1966. A very brief but perceptive overview. More detailed general surveys are S. Piggott, ed., **The Dawn of Civilization,** McGraw-Hill, 1962; Sir L. Woolley, **The Beginnings of Civilization*** (**History of Mankind, Culture and Scientific Development,** Vol. I, Pt. 2), Mentor; H. Frankfort, **The Birth of Civilization in the Near East,*** Anchor; S. Moscati, **The Face of the Ancient Orient,*** Anchor; Cyrus H. Gordon, **The Ancient Near East,*** Norton.

H. Frankfort et al., **Before Philosophy,*** Penguin. A notable interpretation of Mesopotamian and Egyptian thought. J. B. Pritchard, **The Ancient Near East: An Anthology of Texts and Pictures,*** Princeton, is an abridgment of the best collection of translated ancient Near Eastern texts.

P. Cleator, **Lost Languages,** Mentor;* E. Chiera, **They Wrote on Clay,*** Phoenix. Deal vividly with hieroglyphic and cuneiform writing. See also I. J. Gelb, **A Study of Writing,** rev. ed., Univ. of Chicago, 1964.

G. Roux, **Ancient Iraq,*** Penguin. An excellent detailed history of Mesopotamia from prehistoric times to the Christian era. See also A. Oppenheim, **Ancient Mesopotamia: Portrait of a Dead Civilization,** Univ. of Chicago, 1964; S. N. Kramer, **The Sumerians: Their History, Culture, and Character,** Univ. of Chicago, 1963; and the same author's popular **History Begins at Sumer,*** Anchor.

C. Aldred, **The Egyptians,*** Praeger; L. Casson, **Ancient Egypt,** Time, Inc., 1965. Two brief topical surveys. Alan Gardiner, **Egypt of the Pharaohs,*** Galaxy, is a recent political history by a noted authority. The outstanding work on the Empire period is G. Steindorff and K. Seele, **When Egypt Ruled the East,*** Phoenix. L. Cottrell, **Life Under the Pharaohs,*** Grosset & Dunlap, and C. Desroches-Noblecourt, **Tutankhamen,*** Doubleday, engrossingly portray life in the imperial age.

John A. Wilson, **The Culture of Ancient Egypt,** Phoenix* (originally published as **The Burden of Egypt,** Univ. of Chicago, 1951). Highly recommended. See also J. H. Breasted, **The Dawn of Conscience,*** Scribner.

O. R. Gurney, **The Hittites,*** Penguin; D. Harden, **The Phoenicians,*** Praeger; S. Moscati, **Ancient Semitic Civilizations,*** Capricorn. Authoritative surveys.

J. A. Hexter, **The Judaeo-Christian Tradition,*** Harper & Row, 1966. A succinct overview of Hebrew history and religion. Excellent longer surveys are H. M. Orlinsky, **Ancient Israel,*** Cornell; W. F. Albright, **The Biblical Period from Abraham to Ezra,*** Torchbooks; John Bright, **A History of Israel,** Westminster Press, 1959.

Bernhard W. Anderson, **Understanding the Old Testament,** Prentice-Hall, 1957. Skillfully blends religious and political history. See also M. Buber, **Moses: The Revelation and the Covenant,*** Torchbooks; H. Rowley, **The Growth of the Old Testament,*** Torchbooks; S. R. Driver, **Introduction to the Literature of the Old Testament,*** Meridian; Mary Ellen Chase, **Life and Language in the Old Testament,*** Norton.

A. Olmstead, **History of Assyria,** Scribner, 1923; and **History of the Persian Empire,*** Phoenix. The standard accounts. See also R. N. Frye, **The Heritage of Persia,** World, 1963; G. Contenau, **Everyday Life in Babylon and Assyria,*** Norton; R. Zaehner, **The Dawn and Twilight of Zoroastrianism,** Putnam, 1961.

Seton Lloyd, **Art of the Ancient Near East,*** Praeger. See also H. Frankfort, **The Art and Architecture of the Ancient Orient,** Penguin, 1954; W. S. Smith, **The Art and Architecture of Ancient Egypt,** Penguin, 1958; I. E. S. Edwards, **The Pyramids of Egypt,*** Penguin.

*Indicates an inexpensive paperbound edition.

O. Neugebauer, **The Exact Sciences in Antiquity,*** Torchbooks. The authoritative work on Mesopotamian and Egyptian achievements in science and mathematics. See also Charles Singer *et al.*, eds., **A History of Technology, Vol. I: From Early Times to Fall of Ancient Empires,** Oxford, 1957.

Recommended historical fiction: H. Treece, **The Golden Strangers,** Random House, 1957 (Stone-Age Britain); M. Waltari, **The Egyptian,*** Pocket Books (Egypt under Akhenaton); D. C. Wilson, **Prince of Egypt,*** Pocket Books (Moses in Egypt); Thomas Mann, **Joseph and His Brothers,** Knopf, 1948; I. Fineman, **Ruth,** Harper, 1949.

INDIA

S. Piggott, **Prehistoric India,*** Penguin. Describes the Indus valley civilization and points out the relationship of western India to the whole of western Asia. See also Sir Mortimer Wheeler, **The Indus Civilization,** Cambridge, 1953, and **Early India and Pakistan to Asoka,** Praeger, 1962.

G. E. Sen, **The Pageant of Indian History,** Longmans, 1948; and R. Thapar, **A History of India,** Vol. I., Penguin,* 1966. Nonspecialistic surveys of early Indian history.

A. L. Basham, **The Wonder That Was India,*** Evergreen. A comprehensive, well-organized study of Indian culture prior to the coming of the Muslims in the eleventh century. Beatrice Pitnery Lamb, **India: A World in Transition,** Praeger, 1963, is a good introduction to Indian culture, especially Hinduism. J. Auboyer, **Daily Life in Ancient India,** Macmillan, 1965. Excellent on caste, religion, and family life.

Excellent translations of Hindu religious texts are S. Prabhavananda and F. Manchester, trans., **The Upanishads: Breath of the Eternal,*** Mentor; and S. Prabhavananda and C. Isherwood, trans., **The Song of God—the Bhagavad-Gita,*** Mentor.

S. Radhakrishnan, **The Hindu View of Life,** Macmillan, 1927. Today's foremost Indian philosopher compares Hinduism with western philosophy. Recommended for an account of the origins and tenets of Hinduism is A. C. Bouqet, **Hinduism,** Longmans, 1950.

W. T. de Bary *et al.*, ed., **Sources of Indian Tradition,** Columbia, 1958. Invaluable anthology of source material on Jainism, Buddhism, and Hinduism.

E. A. Burtt, ed., **The Teachings of the Compassionate Buddha,*** Mentor. Book I: selections from early scriptures of Buddhism; Book II: excerpts from Chinese and Japanese Buddhist works.

C. Humphreys, **Buddhism,*** Penguin. Describes the life of the Buddha and the rise of the major branches of Buddhism. A. de Silva-Viger, **The Life of the Buddha in Art,** Doubleday, 1955. The Buddha legend, handsomely illustrated by 160 works of Asian Art, showing varying interpretations of his story.

A. Foucher, **The Beginnings of Buddhist Art,** Oxford, 1918. A classic on the relationship of Indian and Greek art. For other opinions see A. Coomaraswamy, **Christian and Oriental Philosophy of Art,*** Dover; B. Rowland, **The Art and Architecture of India,** Penguin, 1953; H. Ingholt, **Gandharan Art in Pakistan,** Pantheon, 1957.

CHINA

W. Watson, **China Before the Han Dynasty,** Praeger, 1962. A valuable survey by a leading Sinologist; contains numerous illustrations and a full bibliography. See also W. Watson, **Early Civilizations in China,** McGraw-Hill, 1966. L. Cottrell, **The Tiger of Ch'in,** Holt, Rinehart and Winston, 1962, is a rapid history to the third century B.C., with stress on leading personalities.

J. G. Andersson, **Children of the Yellow Earth,** Macmillan, 1934. Considered the standard work on the Neolithic Age in China.

For information about pre-Shang and Shang periods, see H. G. Creel, **The Birth of China,** Ungar, 1954; and Chi Li, **The Beginnings of Chinese Civilization,** Univ. of Wash., 1957.

T. Chêng, **Chou China,** Univ. of Toronto, 1964. An intensive study of the development of Chou culture based on the latest archaeological findings.

Yu-lan Fêng, ed., **History of Chinese Philosophy,** 2 vols., trans. by D. Bodde, Princeton, 1952-1953. Probably the most authoritative work on the subject. Vol. 1 follows developments to 100 B.C.

Wu-Chi Liu, **A Short History of Confucian Philosophy,*** Dell. A systematic presentation of Confucianism in nontechnical language which correlates the major philosophical systems and defines the place of Confucianism in present-day China.

Leonard Shih-lien Hsü, **The Political Philosophy of Confucianism,** Dutton, 1932. Deals with the political thought of Confucius and Mencius. See also J. R. Ware, trans., **The Sayings of Confucius,*** Mentor; and H. G. Creel, **Confucius: The Man and the Myth,** Day, 1949. A. Waley, **Three Ways of Thought in Ancient China,*** Anchor, 1956. A concise introduction to Confucianism, Taoism, and Legalism, by the greatest western translator of Chinese and Japanese literature.

Lao-tzu, **The Way of Life: Tao Te Ching,*** trans. by R. B. Blakney, Mentor. Complete text of this famous work. A. Waley, ed. and trans., **The Way and Its Power; A Study of the Tao Tê Ching and Its Place in Chinese Thought,*** Grove, is an interpretation of Lao-tzu's classic. Chuang Tzu, **Basic Writings,** trans. by Burton Watson, Columbia, 1964, provides a delightful introduction to Taoist thought and literature. H. Welch, **Taoism: The Parting of the Way,*** Beacon, is a superb and fascinating history of Taoism and its development.

J. Needham, **Science and Civilization in China,** 4 vols., Cambridge. Vol I: **Introductory Orientations,** 1954; Vol. II: **History of Scientific Thought,** 1956; Vol. III: **Mathematics and the Science of the Heavens and the Earth,** 1960; Vol. IV, **Physics and Physical Technology,** Pt. 1, **Physics,** 1962; Pt. 2, with Wang Ling, **Mechanical Engineering,** 1965. Students interested in correcting misconceptions prevalent in the West regarding Chinese civilization should consult these volumes, first of a projected sevenvolume study. In Vol. I Needham examines the structure of the Chinese language, reviews the geography of China, and discusses scientific contacts between East and West. In Vol. II he discusses the relationship of the major philosophical systems to Chinese science.

W. T. de Bary, *et al.*, eds., **Sources of Chinese Tradition,** Columbia, 1964, 2 vols. An invaluable anthology of source materials covering the entire range of Chinese thought, with valuable introductions and commentaries on each period and school.

Chapters 1-5 of D. Carter, **Four Thousand Years of Chinese Art,** Ronald, 1951, treat the art of the Shang and Chou periods. See also B. Gray, **Early Chinese Pottery and Porcelain,** Pitman, 1952; and P. Ackerman, **Ritual Bronzes of Ancient China,** Dryden, 1945.

For surveys of Chinese and Indian history with chapters pertinent to Chapter 3 text material, see *List of Readings,* p. 656.

Part Two

The World in Classical Times

■ Thus far we have watched man advance from a Paleolithic savage to a Neolithic herdsman-farmer and finally to a builder of towns and cities who was able to support a new form of society, sufficiently stable and complex to merit the term *civilization.* We have also seen that, in some cases, the life spans of these fluvial civilizations have been in keeping with the magnitude of the original accomplishment. Thus the inhabitants of ancient India and China created societies which have never lost their cultural continuity, so that many of the most fundamental characteristics of their social organization, government, art, and philosophy in the twentieth century are far more than twenty centuries old.

Meanwhile, in the regions sustained by the Tigris-Euphrates and Nile river valleys, one civilization after another contributed to the enrichment of mankind. From the ancient Near East came the calendar, the alphabet, coinage, advances in science, technology, and mathematics, as well as splendid painting and sculpture, imposing architecture, the inspired writings of the Hebrew prophets, the Zoroastrian *Avesta,* and magnificent epic poetry. But the creative genius of the Near East was ultimately sterilized by royal autocracy and the rigid conformity imposed by despotic priests. For the next great cultural breakthrough in human progress, we must shift our focus to the northern shores and hinterland of the Mediterranean basin.

Acting as an intermediary in this transition was the civilization that flourished around the Aegean Sea. Indebted to the Egyptians and Mesopotamians, the inhabitants of Crete and Mycenaean Greece fashioned a wealthy, sophisticated, commercial culture. Much of this Aegean civilization —the first advanced culture to appear in Europe— was destroyed by the end of the second millennium B.C., but enough remained to serve as the foundation for Hellenic civilization.

The chapters making up this unit are to a great degree a record of the achievements of a relative handful of extraordinary people—the Greeks. Insatiably curious about man and man's world, the Greeks enjoyed a freedom of thought and expression unknown in earlier societies. Their fierce passion to remain untrammeled, however, was too often unrestrained. Thus, in the promising democracy of Athens, the citizens proved unable to achieve long-term stability along with liberty, while in the larger sphere the failure of the Greek city-states to find a workable basis for cooperation doomed them to political disaster. Although the conquest of the city-states by King Philip of Macedonia ended the Hellenic Age, the influence of the Greeks was destined to increase. The establishment of a vast empire in the Near East by Philip's talented son, Alexander the Great, ushered in the Hellenistic Age and the widespread diffusion of Greek culture.

Meanwhile, a new power—Rome—had been evolving on the Italian peninsula. After five centuries of modest growth, this city-state embarked upon a career of unprecedented expansion. The splendor of Roman arms was matched by skill in administration, wisdom in law, and ingenuity in the practical arts of engineering and communication. Upon these foundations was erected a Mediterranean empire which survived for so many centuries that its eventual disappearance in the West left a void which medieval Europeans struggled for centuries to fill. Despite the failure of their attempts to re-create the past, the Europeans of the Middle Ages and all their descendants benefited from the legacy of Graeco-Roman culture, which created the foundations of western civilization.

The civilization of the Greeks and Romans was essentially a product of the Mediterranean area. Yet the very impetus of their expansion carried adventurers and traders from the West far eastward where, following the trails blazed by Alexander the Great and others, they braved the vast stretches separating the Mediterranean empire from the two other massive civilizations of the age, India and China. In the first centuries of the Christian era, we enter a brief but fascinating period in which the principal civilizations of West and East were in contact, engaged in a mutually beneficial exchange of wares and ideas.

Unhappily, this process of culture contact and diffusion—which, had it been allowed to continue, might have had incalculable effects for good on world history—was brought to an untimely halt, largely as a result of a crisis in the West. The Graeco-Roman world was subjected to a series of shattering invasions which will be described in Chapter 7 of the next unit. Before we turn our attention to the ensuing political and social upheavals of that time, let us for the present enjoy the world in classical times—a period which must always remain one of the glorious epochs in human achievement.

An undeciphered Minoan pictographic script, more primitive than Linear A or Linear B, appears on the terra-cotta Phaistos Disk. Although the disk cannot be read, the position of the pictographs indicates that the inscription probably reads from the outer rim in toward the middle.

the English archaeologist Sir Arthur Evans that first brought to light this civilization, whose existence had previously only been hinted at in Greek legends and the epics of Homer. Between 1900 and 1905 Evans unearthed the ruins of a great palace at Knossos, the dominant city in Crete after 1700 B.C. Rising at least three stories high and sprawling over nearly six acres, this "Palace of Minos," built of brick and limestone and employing unusual downward-tapering columns of wood, was a maze of royal apartments, storerooms, corridors, open courtyards, and broad stairways. Walls were painted with elaborate frescoes in which the Minoans appear as a gay, peaceful people with a pronounced liking for dancing, festivals, and athletic contests. Women are shown enjoying a freedom and dignity un-

known elsewhere in the ancient Orient or classical Greece. Furnished with running water, the palace had a sanitation system surpassing anything constructed in Europe until Roman times and, after that, until the nineteenth century. The palace was linked to other parts of Crete by well-paved roads lined with the luxurious dwellings of the nobility.

The glory of Minoan culture was its art —gay, spontaneous, and full of rhythmic motion. Art was an essential part of everyday life and not, as in the ancient Orient, an adjunct to religion and the state. What little is known of Minoan religion also contrasts sharply with conditions in the Near East: there were no great temples, powerful priesthoods, or large cult statues of the gods. The principal deity seems to have been the Mother Goddess, and a number of recovered statuettes show her dressed like a fashionable Cretan lady with flounced skirts, a tightly laced, low-cut bodice, and an elaborate coiffure. It is also noteworthy that the later classical Greeks believed that Zeus and other deities came from Crete.

Mycenaean civilization. In time a second center of Aegean civilization arose on the Greek mainland. About 2000 B.C., or shortly thereafter, the first Indo-European Greek tribes, collectively called Achaeans, entered Greece, where they absorbed the earlier settlers and ruled from strongly fortified citadels at Mycenae, Pylos, Thebes, and other sites. By 1600 B.C. the Achaeans had evolved their own civilization, based largely on borrowings from Crete and even the Near East, and were plying the seas both as pirates and as traders.

Some of the wealth accumulated by the kings of Mycenae—the greatest single hoard of gold, silver, and ivory objects found anywhere before the discovery of Tutankhamen's tomb—was unearthed in 1876 by Heinrich Schliemann, fresh from his even more sensational discoveries at Troy (see p. 96). The royal palace on the acropolis, or citadel, of Mycenae had well-proportioned audience rooms and apartments, fresco-lined walls, floors of painted stucco, and large storerooms.

A striking feature of Mycenaean culture

Today the Acropolis bears the heavy "injury of time"; yet for us no less than for Plutarch, ancient Athens has retained a "flourishing freshness." This quality, together with a refined sense of symmetry and proportion, is characteristic of the Greek spirit and the dazzling achievements of Greek civilization. The ancient Greeks repeatedly demonstrated an ability to regard the world about them from a "young and fresh" perspective and to inject a love of proportion not only into their architecture but into almost everything they attempted. Yet in the crucial sphere of politics, their sense of proportion failed them. Instead of compromising their differences, the city-states quarreled continually, and that fervid individualism which moved them to brilliant creative efforts blinded them to the necessity of cooperation. Thus the political life of the Greeks was marked by conflicts between the city-states until they were at last subjugated by King Philip of Macedonia, the father of Alexander the Great.

Yet the Macedonian conquerors, out of genuine admiration of the Greek cultural achievement, strove to perpetuate the learning of the city-states as they set forth to forge a world-state. The Greek accomplishment was indeed to prove so enduring that her magnificent legacy of knowledge and art would provide much of the cultural heritage of the West and, to a lesser extent, of the East. Thus the English poet Shelley could say with justification that "We are all Greeks." Probably no other people has made so lasting an impression upon man's intellectual history.

BACKGROUND FOR GREEK CULTURE

Aegean civilization. Greek civilization was unique in so many ways that a student of history might infer that Greek culture developed in a vacuum or, free from outside influences, sprang full-blown from the rocky hills of this small land. The Greek achievement, however, was preceded by an advanced civilization located on the lands surrounding the Aegean Sea. This Aegean civilization, which came into full flower about 2000 B.C. and collapsed suddenly following 1200 B.C., developed through two major periods. The first and longer period, which ended about 1400 B.C., is called "Minoan" after the legendary Cretan King Minos. Crete was the center of Minoan civilization, which spread also to the Aegean Islands, to Troy in Asia Minor, and to Greece. The last period of Aegean civilization, the two centuries following 1400 B.C. when the center of Aegean political power and culture lay on the Greek mainland, is called "Mycenaean" after its most important site at Mycenae.

Minoan civilization. The narrow, 160-mile-long island of Crete was a stepping stone between Europe, Asia, and Africa. Stimulated by contacts with Mesopotamia and Egypt, a brilliant civilization emerged here.

Minoan prosperity was based on large-scale trade that ranged from Troy to Egypt and from Sicily to Syria and employed the first ships capable of long voyages over the open sea. (According to one theory, the technical skill that produced the famous prehistoric shrine at Stonehenge in England—see Color Plate 2—may have been the result of contact with the Minoans.) Chief exports were olive oil, wine, metalware, and magnificent pottery. This trade was the monopoly of an efficient bureaucratic government under a powerful ruler whose administrative records were written on clay tablets, first in a form of picture writing and later in a syllabic script known as Linear A. Neither script can be read, but Linear A appears to contain some borrowed Semitic words, the result of Cretan trade with the coastal cities of Syria. Our knowledge of Minoan civilization is therefore scanty and imprecise; most of it is derived from the material remains uncovered by archaeologists.

It was the epoch-making discoveries of

THRACE

Byzantium

SEA OF
MARMARA

Hellespont

PHRYGIA

MYSIA

Pergamum

Ilium (Troy)

LYDIA

Hermus R.

Sardis

Maeander R.

Ephesus

Miletus

Halicarnassus

RHODES

LESBOS

CHIOS

SAMOS

SPORADES

SEA

AEGEAN

NAXOS

PAROS

SEA

CYCLADES

THERA

CRETAN SEA

Knossos

CRETE

SEA

MELOS

MACEDONIA

OLYMPUS

THESSALY

EPIRUS

AETOLIA

ACHAEA

Delphi Thebes

BOEOTIA

EUBOEA

ATTICA

Athens
Piraeus

Corinth

Mycenae

Argos

ARCADIA

PELOPONNESUS

Sparta

LACONIA

MESSENIA

Olympia

Pylos

CYTHERA

MEDITERRANEAN

LEUCAS

CEPHALLENIA

ZACYNTHUS

CORCYRA

SAMOTHRACE

LEMNOS

75

50

25

0

THE AEGEAN WORLD

Chapter 4

The Glory That Was Greece

The Aegean Culture, the Hellenic and Hellenistic Ages

INTRODUCTION. Scarred by time and weather, the ruins of the Athenian Acropolis stand against a vivid blue sky and overlook the trees and buildings of a modern city sprawled beneath. These ruins are striking symbols of a departed civilization—the democracy of Athens at its height.

In the fifth century B.C. the temples and statuary of the Acropolis were gleaming and new, fresh from the hands of builders and sculptors. Five hundred years later Plutarch wrote:

The works are . . . wonderful: because they were perfectly made in so short a time, and have continued so long a season. . . . [The Acropolis looks] at this day as if it were but newly done and finished, there is such a certain kind of flourishing freshness in it . . . that the injury of time cannot impair the sight thereof. As if every one of those . . . works had some living spirit in it, to make it seem young and fresh: and a soul that lived ever, which kept them in their good continuing state.[1]

10. Room in a villa at Boscoreale, near Pompeii (first century B.C.). Rome's singular accomplishment in architecture included an attention to domestic buildings that reflected a traditional concern for home and family. Since the Roman country house had few doors and windows, a large amount of wall space was available for the lavish decoration that is a mark of so much Roman art. Wall paintings were often intended to create the illusion of space beyond the room and, as is evident here, the realistic Roman style achieved the illusion quite convincingly.

7. (above) **Toreador Fresco, Knossos** (c. 1500 B.C.). Considering the animation of this Cretan work, one begins to discern some of the sources of the vitality and freedom that marked Greek civilization a millennium later. It is enough to cite the remarkable ritual game so forcefully represented here: a light-skinned girl grasps a bull's horns, while a darker youth vaults over the animal's back. 8. (above right) **Three figures from the east pediment of the Parthenon** (c. 445-440 B.C.). The Greeks' massive contribution to the ancient world, and finally to western civilization, is graphically evident in their figure sculpture, a genre which claims no finer examples than the pedimental remains from the Parthenon. This group—probably a trio of goddesses—is treated by the Greek sculptor in so naturalistic a manner that the relative abstractness of Egyptian and Mesopotamian figures is supplanted with a vigorous immediacy and freedom of action. 9. (right) **The Seven Steps of Buddha** (c. 500-200 B.C.). The influence of Greek culture extended not only west to Rome but east as far as Gandhara in India, where artists often echoed Alexandrian styles in the faces and clothing of their figures. In this Gandharan relief the Buddha is shown being born miraculously from his mother's right side; then, reappearing below, he immediately walks, taking seven steps in all.

6. The Arena at Leptis Magna in North Africa (third century A.D.). The far-flung reaches of the Roman empire were united in a complex, efficient network which infused even the cities of the provinces with the reflected glory of the capital itself. In turn, much of Rome's own splendor—at least artistically speaking—was a reflection of Greece. If the order, scale, and ambition of the buildings at Leptis Magna are Roman, their stylistic grace has its roots in the earlier Hellenic civilization which the Romans so eagerly emulated.

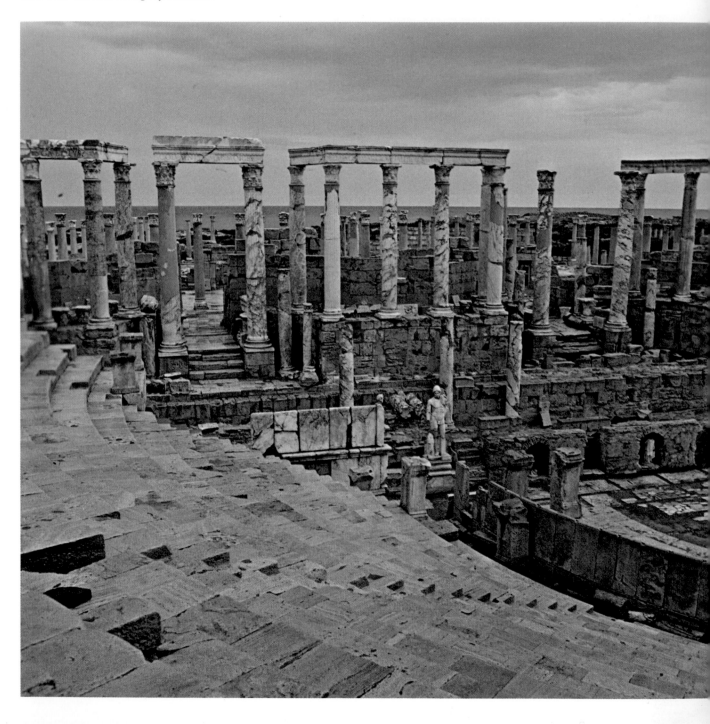

was its beehivelike tombs. Dug out of the sloping hillsides and approached by an unroofed entrance passage cut horizontally into the hill, these tombs were conical, with walls made of successive courses of cut stone. The most famous of these royal tombs, called by Schliemann the "Treasury of Atreus," has a splendidly proportioned interior chamber, fifty feet in diameter and forty-five feet high. It has been called "the first great architectural monument on the mainland of Europe."[2]

The expansive force of this hitherto unimagined Mycenaean civilization led to the planting of colonies in the eastern Mediterranean (Hittite sources refer to Achaeans in Asia Minor) and to the conquest of Knossos early in the fifteenth century B.C. Later, about 1400 B.C., the labyrinthian palace at Knossos was destroyed by fire—the aftereffect, it is now conjectured, of a great tidal wave caused by the eruption of the small volcanic island of Santorini (Thera) eighty miles north of Crete. The palace at Knossos was never rebuilt, and the center of Aegean civilization shifted to the Greek mainland.

This story of Achaean-Cretan relations was unclear until after 1952 when a young English architect, Michael Ventris, startled the scholarly world by deciphering a type of Cretan script known as Linear B, many examples of which had been found by Evans at Knossos and by later archaeologists at Pylos, Mycenae, and Thebes. When Linear B turned out to be an early form of Greek written in syllabic characters, it followed that the rulers of Knossos in the fifteenth century B.C. must have been Achaean Greeks who had adopted the Cretan script to write their own language.

The Linear B texts, which are administrative documents and inventories, greatly add to our knowledge of Mycenaean life. The Mycenaean centers were fortified palaces and administrative centers and not, as in Crete, true cities. The bulk of the population lived in scattered villages where they worked either communal land or land held by nobles or kings. The titles of the nobility correspond to those used later in medieval Europe: duke (literally "war leader"), baron ("man of the burden"), and count ("companion"). The Mycenaean nobles, however, were under the close control of the kings. Prominent in their administrative records, which were kept daily by a large number of scribes, are details of the disbursement of grain and wine as wages and the collection of taxes in kind. The most important item of income was olive oil, the major article in the wide-ranging Mycenaean trade which was operated as a royal monopoly. The discovery at Thebes in 1964 of more than thirty inscribed Babylonian cylinder seals, dating from the fourteenth century B.C., attests to the extent of Mycenaean trade. Perhaps it was their role as merchant-monopolists that led the Achaean kings late in the thirteenth century B.C. to launch the famous expedition against Troy in order to eliminate a powerful commercial rival.

Troy, site of the Homeric epics. The city of Troy occupied a strategic position on the Hellespont (the straits between the Black and Aegean seas now known as the Dardanelles). From there, Troy could command both the sea traffic through the straits and the land caravans between Asia and Europe. For many years scholars thought this city existed only in the epic poems of Homer. Heinrich Schliemann (1822-1890), a German romantic dreamer and amateur archaeologist, believed otherwise. As a boy, he had read Homer's *Iliad*, and thereafter he remained firmly con-

This vase, with its six helmeted soldiers carrying lances and round shields, shows both the adventurous and martial nature of the Mycenaeans.

vinced that Troy had actually existed. At the age of forty-eight, having amassed a fortune in the California gold rush and in worldwide trade, Schliemann retired from business to put his persistent dream of ancient Troy to the test.

In 1870 Schliemann began excavations at the legendary site of Troy, where he unearthed several cities, built one on top of the other. He discovered a treasure of golden earrings, hairpins, and bracelets in the second city, which led him to believe that this was the city of Homer's epics. Excavations in the 1930's, however, showed that the seventh city, more than a thousand years later than the second, was the one made famous by Homer.

Neither the view that Troy was the victim of commercial rivalry nor the other widely held theory that it was destroyed by Achaean pirates seeking booty corresponds to Homer's view that the Trojan War was caused by the abduction of the beauteous Helen, queen of Sparta, by the Trojan prince Paris. Led by Agamemnon, king of Mycenae, the wrathful Achaeans besieged Troy for ten long years. Homer's *Iliad* deals only with a few weeks during the tenth year of the siege.

The fall of Mycenaean civilization. Around 1200 B.C., not long after the fall of Troy, a new wave of Indo-Europeans, the Dorian Greeks, materially aided by weapons made of iron instead of bronze, burst upon Greece. First of the Mycenaean strongholds to fall was Pylos, whose Linear B archives contain numerous references to hastily undertaken preparations to repel the invaders.[3] We find orders directing women and children to places of safety; instructions to armorers, "rowers," and food-suppliers; and a report entitled "how the watchers are guarding the coastal regions." The preparations were in vain, however. Pylos was sacked and burned, and the destruction of the other major Mycenaean citadels soon followed, with Mycenae itself probably the last to fall about 1120 B.C.

The next four centuries—the Greek Dark Ages—were marked by the disappearance of the major characteristics of the relatively advanced Mycenaean civilization—political centralization, wide-ranging commerce, so-

phisticated art forms (including monumental architecture), and writing. Yet while the Dorian invasion was an undoubted catastrophe, it was also vital to the ultimate rise of a unique Hellenic (from *Hellas*, the Greek name for Greece) civilization that was not largely an offshoot of the Near East, as was Aegean civilization.

Greek civilization could never have arisen if that disruption had not occurred and had not shaken the old conventions. In the dull, repetitive cases of [late] Mycenaean pottery which can be seen in modern museums, in the palace tablets which now show the centralizing drive of royal masters, we can sense that the Mycenaean world was far too attached to outside models ever to develop an independent outlook of its own. These links were broken by the barbarian invasions . . . ; men were set free to create new political and intellectual views, once the worst of the chaos was over.[4]

THE RISE OF HELLENIC CIVILIZATION

The influence of geography. The Greek peninsula is a jagged piece of land comprising some 45,000 square miles of mountain ranges and narrow plains. Geographical factors not only determined the maritime character of Greek civilization but also played an important part in shaping the events of Greek history. The numerous islands and indented coastlines of the Greek peninsula and of Asia Minor stimulated seagoing trade. The Greeks had every incentive to go down to the sea in ships. The climate was warm and the winds favorable to sailing; the rocky soil (less than a fifth of Greece is arable) and limited natural resources encouraged the Greeks to establish colonies abroad; and the numerous mountain ranges which crisscross the peninsula severely hampered internal communications and led to the development of fiercely independent, autonomous political units—the city-states.

The Homeric Age. Most of our information about the Greek Dark Ages (c. 1150-750 B.C.) which followed the Dorian invasion is derived from the epics composed during the last century of this period and attributed to the blind poet Homer. Controversy surrounds the problem of Homer's existence and whether he or several poets composed the *Iliad* and the *Odyssey*. Nevertheless, the last century of this period can conveniently be called the Homeric Age. The Homeric epics retain something of the material side of the bygone Mycenaean age; yet in filling in the details of political, economic, and social life, the religious beliefs and practices, and the ideals that gave meaning to life, the poet could only describe what was familiar to him in his own environment.

The values that gave meaning to life in the Homeric Age and, it can safely be assumed, to the whole Greek Dark Ages, were predominantly heroic values—the strength, skill, and valor of the preëminent warrior. Such was the early Greek meaning of *aretē*, "excellence" or "virtue," a key term throughout the course of Greek culture. (The Greeks redefined *aretē* whenever changing conditions forced them to formulate new and different human ideals.) To obtain *aretē*—defined by one Homeric hero as "to fight ever in the forefront and outvie my peers"—and the imperishable fame that was its reward, men welcomed hardship, struggle, and even death. Honor, like fame, was a measure of *aretē*, and the greatest of human tragedies was the denial of honor due to a great warrior. Homer makes such a denial a theme of the *Iliad*: "The ruinous wrath of Achilles that brought countless ills upon the Achaeans" when Achilles, insulted by Agamemnon, withdraws from battle.

Today the heroes of the age appear splendid in many respects but far from praiseworthy in others. The hero of the *Odyssey*, Odysseus, is commended by Homer for his untruthfulness; and in the *Iliad* the great Achilles carried his revenge against the slain Hector to savage extremes:

In both of his feet at the back he made holes by
　the tendons
in the space between ankle and heel, and drew
　thongs of ox-hide through them,
and fastened them to the chariot so as to let the
　head drag,
and mounted the chariot, and lifted the glorious
　armour inside it,

then whipped the horses to a run, and they
　winged their way unreluctant.
A cloud of dust rose where Hektor was dragged,
　his dark hair was falling
about him, and all that head that was once so
　handsome was tumbled in the dust. . . .[5]

To the Homeric Greeks, the gods were plainly human: Zeus, the king of the gods, was often the undignified victim of the plots of his wife Hera and other deities, and he asserted his authority through threats of violence. Hades, the abode of the dead, was a subterranean land of dust and darkness, and Achilles, as Homer tells us in the *Odyssey*, would have preferred to be a slave on earth than a king in Hades.

Society was clearly aristocratic—only the *aristoi* ("aristocrats") possessed *aretē*—and the common man was reviled and beaten when he dared to question his betters. Yet the common man had certain political rights as a member of the assembly that was summoned whenever a crisis, such as war, required his participation. Two other instruments of government described by Homer were the tribal king and his council. The king was hardly more than a chief among his peers, his fellow nobles, who sat in his council to advise him and to check any attempt he might make to exercise arbitrary power. Economic conditions were those of a simple, self-sufficient agricultural system much like that of the early Middle Ages in western Europe.

The city-state: origin and political evolution. The *polis*, or city-state, the famed Greek political unit consisting of a city and its surrounding plains and valleys, did not exist in the Greek Dark Ages. The nucleus of the *polis* was the elevated, fortified site—the *acropolis* —where people could take refuge from attack. With the revival of commerce in the eighth and seventh centuries B.C., another center developed below the acropolis, called the *asty*, where people lived and traded. In time the two parts combined, forming the city-state, or *polis*. Our word *politics* is derived from *polis*.

Since the city-state was large neither in area (generally ranging from fifty to five hundred square miles) nor in population, most of its citizens knew one another by sight. In marked contrast to the ordinary people in the absolute monarchies of Egypt and the Near East, no vast social gulf separated citizens from their leaders. The compact size of the *polis* also encouraged men to participate directly in political life. Little wonder, then, that Aristotle should commence his *Politics* with the statements that the city-state "is a natural growth," "it exists for the good life," "man is by nature a political animal," and "the city-state is prior in nature to the household and to each of us individually."[6]

Physically and intellectually, the citizen's horizons were bounded by his *polis*, and its distinctive tone wielded a profound influence upon him. Complete independence was the keynote of the city-state, and their overweening desire for freedom prevented the Greeks from cooperating for their own mutual benefit (except on rare occasions) or from uniting in a permanent confederacy. This weakness one day proved fatal.

The political development of the city-state was so rich and varied that it is difficult to think of a form of government not experienced—and given a lasting name—by the Greeks. Four major types of government evolved in most of the city-states: (1) monarchy of a limited sort, like that described in the Homeric epics; (2) oligarchy (rule of the few), arising when the aristocratic council ousted the king and abolished or restricted the popular assembly; (3) tyranny, imposed by one man who rode to power on the discontent of the lower classes; (4) democracy (rule of the people), occurring after the tyrant was deposed and the popular assembly was revived and made the chief organ of government. Democracy, the outstanding political achievement of the Greeks, did not represent the final stage, however. After dissatisfaction with democratic government became widespread, many of the city-states returned either to oligarchy or to one-man rule.

The Age of Oligarchy. By the middle of the eighth century B.C. the nobles, who resented the power wielded by the tribal kings, had taken over the government, ushering in the Age of Oligarchy. Ruthlessly exercising their superior power, the nobles acquired a monopoly of the best land, reducing many commoners to virtual serfdom and forcing others to seek a living on rocky, barren soil.

The hard lot of the common man under oligarchy produced the anguished protest of Hesiod's *Works and Days* (c. 700 B.C.). A commoner who had been cheated out of his parcel of land by his evil brother in league with "bribe-swallowing" aristocratic judges, Hesiod was the prophet of a more exalted conception of the gods and a new age of social justice. To establish a just society, Hesiod argued, men must learn to pursue moderation (*sophrosynē*) in all things—apparently the first expression of this famous Greek ideal—and realize that "far-seeing" Zeus and the other gods punish evildoers and reward the righteous. He redefined human excellence, or *aretē*, in a way to make it attainable for the common man. Its essential ingredients were righteousness and work—honest work in competition with one's fellows being a form of strife in moderation. "Gods and men hate him who lives without work," Hesiod insisted. "His nature is like the drones who sit idle and eat the labor of the bees." Furthermore, "work is no shame, but idleness is a shame," and "esteem," "glory," and "riches" follow work.[7]

Hesiod's new ideals of moderation and justice took root slowly, and the poor found relief only by emigrating to new lands overseas. As Plato later noted, the wealthy promoted colonization as a safety valve to ward off a threatened political and economic explosion:

When men who have nothing, and are in want of food, show a disposition to follow their leaders in an attack on the property of the rich—these, who are the natural plague of the state, are sent away by the legislator in a friendly spirit as far as he is able; and this dismissal of them is euphemistically termed a colony.[8]

From 750 to 550 B.C. the Greeks planted colonies throughout much of the Mediterranean world, a development often compared with the expansion of Europe in modern times. The colonies were planned in detail before the emigrants left the mother city, and although each colony was politically independent, sentimental and economic ties with the homeland usually persisted.

Settlements sprang up along the northern coast of the Aegean and around the Black Sea. So many Greeks migrated to southern Italy and eastern Sicily that the region became known as *Magna Graecia,* or Great Greece. (The word *Greek* was originally derived by the Romans from the obscure Graeans who were among those who settled around the Bay of Naples.) Colonies were also founded as far west as present-day France—at Massilia, modern Marseilles—and Spain and on parts of the African coast. Unique was Naucratis in Egypt, not a true colony but a trading post whose residents gained extraterritorial rights (their own magistrates and law courts) from the Egyptians.

In time colonization ameliorated Greece's economic and social problems. By 600 B.C. the use of coined money, learned from the Lydians, had created a new class of enterprising merchants—the beginnings of a middle class. The Greek home states gradually became "industrialized" as a result of concentrating upon the production of specialized wares—vases, metal goods, textiles, olive oil, and wine—for export in exchange for foodstuffs and raw materials. But before this economic revolution was completed, the continuing land hunger of the peasants contributed to a political revolution. After 650 B.C. tyrants arose in many Greek states and, supported by the aggrieved peasantry and the rising merchant class, seized the reins of government from the nobility. These tyrants (the word meant simply "master" and did not at first have the unfavorable meaning it now possesses) not only distributed land to the peasants but, by promoting further colonization, trade, and industry, accelerated the rise of a mercantile class and the completion of the Greek economic revolution.

Athens to 500 B.C. Athens and Sparta, the city-states destined to dominate the history of Greece during the classical period (the fifth century and most of the fourth), underwent markedly different developments during the period prior to 500 B.C. While Athens' political, economic, and social evolution was typical of most other Greek states, Sparta's development produced a unique way of life that elicited the wonder and often the admiration of other Greeks.

During the course of the seventh century B.C. at Athens, the council of nobles became supreme. The popular assembly no longer met, and the king was replaced by nine aristocratic magistrates, called archons, chosen annually by the council to exercise the king's civil, military, and religious powers. The nobility acquired the good land on the plain; the peasants either stayed on as sharecroppers, who were often reduced to debt slavery, or took to the hills.

When the Athenian nobles finally realized that their failure to heed the cry for reform would result in the rise of a tyrant, they agreed to the policy of compromise advocated by the liberal aristocrat Solon. In 594 B.C. Solon was made sole archon with broad authority to reconcile the lower classes. Inspired by the new ideals of moderation and justice, Solon instituted middle-of-the-road reforms that have made his name a byword for wise statesmanship.

Solon provided a new start for the lower classes by canceling all debts and forbidding future debt bondage, but he rejected as too radical their demand for the redivision of the land. His long-range solution to the economic problem was to seek full employment by stimulating trade and industry. To achieve this goal, Solon required fathers to teach their sons a trade, granted citizenship to foreign artisans who settled in Athens, and encouraged the intensive production of olive oil for export.

Moderation also characterized Solon's political reforms—the common people were granted important political rights, but not equality. While laws continued to originate in the new aristocratic Council of Four Hundred (one hundred from each of the four Athenian tribes), they now had to be ratified by the popular assembly, which Solon revived. And since property, not birth, became the qualification for membership in the Council and for the archonships, wealthy commoners acquired full political equality. Furthermore, the assembly could now act as a court to hear appeals from the decisions of the archons and to try them for misdeeds in office.

Unfortunately, Solon's moderate reforms satisfied neither party. The poor had received neither land nor political equality, while the nobles thought Solon a radical who had betrayed his class. Deeply discouraged, Solon described what is too often the lot of moderate reformers:

Formerly they boasted of me vainly; with averted eyes
Now they look askance upon me; friends no more, but enemies.[9]

Solon had warned the Athenians to accept his reforms lest "the people in its ignorance comes into the power of a tyrant." He lived to see his prediction fulfilled. In 560 B.C., after a period of civil strife, Pisistratus, a military hero and champion of the commoners, usurped power as tyrant. He solved the economic problem by banishing many nobles and distributing their lands among the poor and by promoting commerce and industry. Together with extensive public works and the patronage of culture—thus starting Athens on the road to cultural leadership in Greece—these reforms gave rise to a popular saying that "Life under Pisistratus was paradise on earth."

Pisistratus was succeeded by his two sons, one of whom was assassinated and the other exiled. When the nobles, aided by a Spartan army, took this opportunity to restore oligarchy, Cleisthenes temporarily seized power in 508 B.C. and put through constitutional reforms that destroyed the remaining power of the nobility. He disregarded the old noble-dominated tribes and created ten new ones, each embracing citizens of all classes from widely scattered districts. The popular assembly acquired the right to initiate legislation, while the new and democratic Council of Five Hundred, selected by lot from the ten tribes, advised the assembly and supervised the administrative actions of the archons. A final reform of Cleisthenes was the peculiar institution of *ostracism*, an annual referendum in which a quorum of six thousand citizens could vote to exile for ten years any individual thought to be a threat to the new Athenian democracy.

Sparta to 500 B.C. In sharp contrast to Athens was the rival city-state Sparta. Sparta had not joined the other Greek cities in trade and colonization but had expanded instead by conquering and enslaving its neighbors. To guard against revolts by the state slaves (helots), who worked the land for their conquerors, Sparta was forced to deviate from the normal course of Greek political development and transform itself into a militaristic totalitarian state. Aristotle called the government of Sparta a "mixed constitution"; for the small minority of ruling Spartans, it was a democracy, but for the great mass of subjected people, it was an oligarchy. The government included two kings, a small Council of Elders, and a popular assembly. True power resided in five overseers, the ephors, who were elected by the assembly and wielded more influence than the dual monarchs.

The state enforced absolute subordination of the individual to its will. Throughout his life every Spartan was first of all a soldier. Sickly infants were left to die on lonely mountaintops; boys were taken from their families when they were seven years old to live under rigorous military discipline for the rest of their lives; girls were trained to become healthy mothers of warrior sons. As their men marched off to war, Spartan women bid them a laconic farewell: "Come back with your shield or on it."

While Sparta fostered the physical fitness of its citizens and developed the finest military machine in Greece, it remained backward culturally and economically. Trade and travel were prohibited because the city fathers feared that alien ideas might disturb the status quo. Sparta's self-imposed isolation forbade those cultural contacts without which no balanced civilization can develop. Individual expression and creative thinking were effectively suppressed. Sparta is a classic example of how intellectual stagnation accompanies rigid social conformity and military regimentation.

To provide additional assurance that its helots remain uncontaminated by democratic ideas, Sparta allied itself with oligarchic parties in other Peloponnesian states and aided them in suppressing their democratic opponents. The resulting Spartan League of oligarchic states, in operation by the end of the sixth century B.C., was shortly to be faced by an Athenian-led union of democratic states (see map, p. 105).

UNITY AND STRIFE IN THE HELLENIC WORLD

The Persian Wars. The leaders of the Greek economic and cultural revival after 750 B.C. were the Ionian Greeks living along the Aegean coast of Asia Minor and its offshore islands. The Ionians were descendants of Mycenaean peoples who had fled eastward seeking refuge from the savage Dorians. Influenced by contacts with Phoenician traders (from whom they borrowed the alphabet in the eighth century), neighboring Lydia, and Egypt, the Ionians "first kindled the torch of Hellenism."

We have seen in Chapter 2 that when the Persians conquered Lydia in 547 B.C., they also annexed Ionia, which had been under nominal Lydian rule. Chafing under Persian-appointed tyrants, the Ionian cities revolted in 499 B.C., established democratic regimes, and asked the mainland Greeks for aid. The Athenians, who were also Ionians, sent twenty ships to defend their kinsmen. By 494 B.C., however, Darius I had crushed the revolt, burning Miletus in revenge.

The battle of Marathon. Darius knew that Ionia was insecure as long as Athens remained free to incite her kinsmen to revolt, and thus in 490 B.C. a Persian force of about twenty thousand men sailed across the Aegean and debarked on the plain of Marathon near Athens. Darius' aim of forcing the Athenians to accept the exiled son of Pisistratus as a pro-Persian tyrant was frustrated when the Athenian army, half the size of the Persian, won an overwhelming victory, killing 6400 of the foe while losing only 192. Describing the battle of Marathon, the Greek historian Herodotus wrote:

So when the battle was set in array, and the victims showed themselves favorable, instantly the Athenians . . . charged the barbarians at a run. Now the distance between the two armies was a little short of a mile. The Persians, therefore, when they saw the Greeks coming on at speed, made ready to receive them, although it seemed to them that the Athenians were bereft of their senses, and bent upon their own destruction; for they saw a mere handful of men coming on at a run without either horsemen or archers . . . the Athenians in close array fell upon them, and fought in a manner worthy of being recorded. They were the first of the Greeks, so far as I know, who introduced the custom of charging the enemy at a run, and they were likewise the first who dared to look upon the Median garb, and to face men clad in that fashion. Until this time the very name of the Medes had been a terror to the Greeks to hear.[10]

The battle of Marathon was one of the most decisive in history. It destroyed the belief in Persian invincibility and demonstrated, in the words of Herodotus, that "free men fight better than slaves." The victory also gave the Athenians the self-confidence that would soon make their city the leading Greek state.

End of the Persian Wars. Ten years later the Greeks were well prepared for a new Persian invasion under Xerxes, Darius' successor, whose objective was the subjection of all of Greece. Athens now had two hundred ships, the largest fleet in Greece, and Sparta had agreed to head a defensive alliance of thirty-one states.

The Persian army—reckoned by Herodotus at 1,700,000 but more likely 150,000 or so—was too huge to be transported by ship. Crossing the swift-flowing, mile-wide Hellespont on two pontoon bridges—a notable feat of engineering—the army marched along the Aegean coast accompanied by a great fleet carrying provisions. The Spartans insisted on abandoning all of Greece except the Peloponnesus to the invaders but finally agreed to a holding action at the narrow pass of Thermopylae. Here three hundred Spartans and a few thousand other Greeks held back the Persians for three days, until a Greek traitor led them over a mountain path to the rear of the Greek position. The Spartans fought magnificently until all were slain, together with seven hundred other Greeks. The Spartan dead were immortalized on a monument erected at the pass:

Go tell the Spartans, thou that passeth by,
That here, obedient to their laws, we lie.

The Persians then burned Athens, whose inhabitants had fled, for they placed their faith in "wooden walls"—their fleet. Their faith was not misplaced; in the Bay of Salamis the Greek fleet, largely Athenian, destroyed 200 of Xerxes' 350 ships, thereby turning the tide of victory. The following account of the start of this decisive battle is from *The Persians*, written by the Athenian tragedian Aeschylus, who probably witnessed the action. The speaker is a Persian messenger who reports to Xerxes' mother that the Greeks first sang

the deep-toned hymn, *Apollo, Saving Lord,* that cheers the Hellene armies into battle.

Then trumpets over there set all on fire; then the sea foamed as oars struck all together, and swiftly, there they were! The right wing first led on the ordered line, then all the rest came on, came out, and now was to be heard a mighty shouting: "On, sons of the Greeks! Set free your country, set your children free, your wives, the temples of your country's gods, your fathers' tombs; now they are all at stake." And from our side the Persian battle-cry roared back the answer; and the time was come.[11]

With his lines of communication cut, Xerxes had no alternative but to retreat to Asia, although he left a strong force in Greece. The following summer (479 B.C.) the Greek army, with the Spartan contingent in the van, routed the Persian force at Plataea, and Greece was for the time being safe from invasion.

Culmination of Athenian democracy. Following the expulsion of the Persians, the Athenians "felt themselves suddenly to be 'on the top of the world,'" and from this in a large measure sprang the reckless confidence and boundless energy which now carried them forward to the greatest phase of their history. Athens' heyday lasted less than eighty years, and the number of her adult male citizens scarcely exceeded fifty thousand. Yet this handful of men attempted more and achieved more in a wider variety of fields than any nation great or small has ever attempted or achieved in a similar space of time."[12]

For more than thirty years (461-429 B.C.) during this Golden Age of Greece, the great statesman Pericles guided Athenian policy. In Pericles' time the actual executive power no longer resided in the archonship, which was filled by lot, but in a board of ten elected generals. This board operated much like a modern-day governmental cabinet. The generals urged the popular assembly to adopt specific measures, and the success or failure of their policies determined whether or not they would be reëlected at the end of their annual term. Pericles failed of reëlection only once, and so great was his influence on the Athenians that, in the words of the contemporary historian Thucydides, "what was in name a democracy was virtually a government by its greatest citizen."[13]

To enable even the poorest citizen to participate in government, Pericles extended payment to jurors (a panel of six thousand citizens chosen annually by lot) and to members of the Council. While his conservative opponents called this opportunism, Pericles insisted that it was essential to the success of democracy:

Our constitution is named a democracy, because it is in the hands not of the few but of the many. But our laws secure equal justice for all in their private disputes, and our public opinion welcomes and honours talent in every branch of achievement, not as a matter of privilege but on grounds of excellence alone. . . . [Athenians] do not allow absorption in their own various affairs to interfere with their knowledge of the city's. We differ from other states in regarding the man who holds aloof from public life not as "quiet" but as useless; we decide or debate, carefully and in person, all matters of policy, holding, not that words and deeds go ill together, but that acts are foredoomed to failure when undertaken undiscussed.[14]

Such payments to jurors, together with a slave population of about 100,000, are thought to have made possible what is called the Hellenic concept of leisure, in which citi-

Greek pottery painting, which depicted sacred and profane scenes of many kinds, provides an invaluable source of information about everyday life in Greece. The vase at the top portrays various aspects of the art of weaving, from preparing the yarn to folding the finished product. In the detail from a cup, center, youths are learning to play the harp and to read while the *paidogogos*, a slave responsible for attending them to and from class, sits at the far right. At the bottom left, a shoemaker places his customer's foot on a piece of leather which he cuts to measure. The tools of the shoemaking trade hang to the far left, above the cobbler's head. The painting at the bottom right shows the gusto with which the Greeks engaged in athletics. Greek states provided carefully structured courses in athletics and military training, which included learning to run both unclothed and in full armor.

zens had time to cultivate their minds and beautify their environment.

The majority of the inhabitants of Athens, however, were not recognized as citizens. Women, slaves, and resident aliens were denied citizenship and had no voice in the government. Nor did they have any standing in the law courts. If a woman desired the protection of the law, she had to seek out a citizen to plead for her in court.

Social life in Athens. Athenian democracy demanded active participation by its citizens. But during their leisure hours Athenians attended drama festivals, held long discussions on politics, art, and philosophy, and relaxed at gambling houses.

Believing firmly in the words of Homer that "a sound mind in a manly body" was one of the greatest blessings in life, all Greeks gave sports a key role in their culture. They frequented the numerous gymnasiums and wrestling schools for exercise and recreation. Every four years the finest athletes from the city-states gathered at Olympia for the Olympic games held in honor of Zeus. According to tradition, the first Olympic games were held in 776 B.C., and this date marked the beginning of the first Olympiad, a chronological period of four years used for dating historical events. For the duration of the games, a sacred truce was proclaimed and wars were put aside. Chariot racing, foot racing, leaping, wrestling, boxing, throwing the discus, and casting the javelin were the chief events. Women were forbidden to watch the Olympics or to participate in them, so they organized games of their own. The glory of the Olympic games was heightened by the splendid introductory procession and the banquets and religious rites which accompanied the athletic activities.

Athenian society was predominantly masculine. The prevailing attitude toward women can be discerned in the cold comfort shown by Pericles to a group of widows:

If I am to speak of womanly virtues . . . let me sum them up in one short admonition: to a woman not to show more weakness than is natural to her sex is a great glory, and not to be talked about for good or for evil among men.[15]

Aristotle wrote: "the male is by nature better fitted to command than the female."[16] In Periclean Athens, women did not participate in public life: their sphere of influence was restricted to the kitchen and the nursery.

The Athenians led a daily existence which frowned on extravagant display. As Pericles declared:

For we are lovers of the beautiful yet simple in our tastes, and we cultivate the mind without loss of manliness. Wealth we employ, not for talk and ostentation, but when there is a real use for it. To avow poverty with us is no disgrace; the true disgrace is in doing nothing to avoid it.[17]

Athenian imperialism. The victory over Persia had been made possible by the unity of Hellenic arms; but with victory assured, unity quickly dissolved. Fearful of helot rebellion at home, Sparta recalled its troops and resumed its policy of isolation. Because the Persians still ruled the Ionian cities and another invasion of Greece seemed probable, Athens in 478 B.C. invited the city-states bordering on the Aegean to form a defensive alliance called the Delian League. To maintain a two-hundred-ship navy that would police the seas, each state was assessed ships or money in proportion to its wealth. From the beginning, Athens dominated the League. Since almost all of the 173 member states paid their assessments in money, which Athens was empowered to collect, the Athenians furnished the necessary ships.

By 468 B.C., after the Ionian cities had been liberated and the Persian fleet destroyed, various League members thought it unnecessary to continue the confederacy. In suppressing all attempts to secede, the Athenians were motivated by the fear that the Persian danger still existed and by the need to maintain and protect the large free-trade area so necessary for Greek—and especially Athenian—commerce and industry. The Athenians created an empire because they dared not unmake a confederation. By aiding in the suppression of local aristocratic factions within its subject states, Athens both eased the task of controlling its em-

GREEK POLITICAL ALLIANCES
ABOUT 431 B. C.

Athens and Allies
Sparta and Allies
Neutral Greek States

pire and emerged as the leader of a union of democratic states.

To many Greeks—above all to the members of the oligarchic Spartan League and the suppressed aristocratic factions within the Athenian empire—Athens was a "tyrant city" and an "enslaver of Greek liberties." Pericles, on the other hand, justified Athenian imperialism on the ground that it brought "freedom" from fear and want to the Greek world:

We secure our friends not by accepting favours but by doing them. . . . We are alone among mankind in doing men benefits, not on calculations of self-interest, but in the fearless confidence of freedom. In a word I claim that our city as a whole is an education to Hellas. . . .[18]

The Peloponnesian War. In 431 B.C. the Peloponnesian War broke out between the Spartan League and the Athenian empire. While commercial rivalry between Athens and Sparta's ally Corinth was an important factor, the conflict is a classic example of

how fear can generate a war unwanted by either side. According to Thucydides:

The real but unavowed cause I consider to have been the growth of the power of Athens, and the alarm which it inspired in Lacedaemon [Sparta]; this made war inevitable.[19]

Several incidents served to ignite the underlying tension, and Sparta declared war on the "aggressors."

At the beginning of the war, Athens possessed a large empire, an unrivaled navy, and a rich treasury. Against this power Sparta raised a strong army, invaded Attica, and besieged Athens. Pericles depended on the navy's ability to maintain a food supply for Athens and to harass its enemies' coasts. Fate took a hand in this game, however. In the second year of the war a plague carried off a third of the Athenian population, including Pericles. His death was a great blow to the Athenians. Leadership of the government passed to demagogues. In the words of Thucydides:

Pericles, by his rank, ability, and known integrity, was able to exercise an independent control over the masses—to lead them instead of being led by them. . . . With his successors it was different. More on a level with one another, and each grasping at supremacy, they ended by committing even the conduct of state affairs to the whims of the multitude. This, as might have been expected in a great imperial state, produced a host of blunders. . . .[20]

Eight more years of indecisive warfare ended in 421 B.C. with a compromise peace. During the succeeding period Athenian imperialism manifested itself in its worst form through the actions of Pericles' unworthy successors. In 416 B.C. an expedition embarked for Melos, a neutral Aegean island, to force it to join the Athenian empire. According to Thucydides, this displayed the tragic transformation of Athenian democracy into naked imperialism and the specious logic employed by the Athenians to justify it:

We believe that Heaven, and we know that men, by a natural law, always rule where they are stronger. We did not make that law nor were we the first to act on it; we found it existing, and it will exist forever, after we are gone; and we know that you and anyone else as strong as we are would do as we do.[21]

The Athenians put all Melians of military age to death and sold the women and children into slavery.

The war was resumed in 415 B.C. with an Athenian expedition against Syracuse that was destined to end in despair. Acting on the invitation of states that feared Syracusan expansion, the Athenians hoped to add Sicily to their empire and so become powerful enough "to rule the whole of the Greek world."[22] After two years of fighting, two great Athenian fleets and a large army were destroyed by the Syracusans, who were advised by a Spartan general. The war dragged on until 404 B.C., when Athens capitulated after its last fleet was destroyed by a Spartan fleet built with money received from Persia in exchange for possession of the Greek cities in Ionia. At home, Athens had been weakened by the plots of oligarchic elements to whom Sparta now turned over

the government. The once great city was also stripped of its possessions and demilitarized.

Aftermath of the war. Anarchy and depression were the political and economic legacies of the Peloponnesian War. Having ended the "tyranny" of Athens over Greece, the Spartans substituted their own form of rule which made the Athenian empire seem mild in comparison. Everywhere democracies were replaced by oligarchies supported by Spartan troops. The bloody excesses of these oligarchs soon led to revolutions which Sparta could not suppress. As one of their generals admitted, the Spartans did not know how to govern free men. Incessant warfare filled the early fourth century as a bewildering series of shifting alliances, usually financed by Persia which wanted to keep Greece disunited and weak, sought to keep any state from predominating.

Political disintegration in turn caused the economic and social ills that plagued Greece during the fourth century B.C. Commerce and industry languished, and the unemployed who did not go abroad as soldiers of fortune supported demagogues and their radical schemes for the redivision of wealth. The wealthy, for their part, became increasingly reactionary and uncompromising. Class hatred was so deep and bitter that the Athenian orator Isocrates wrote:

Instead of securing general conditions of well-being by means of mutual understanding, the antisocial spirit has reached such a pitch, that the wealthy would rather throw their money into the sea than relieve the lot of the indigent, while the very poorest of the poor would get less satisfaction from appropriating to their own use the property of the rich than from depriving them of it.[23]

Isocrates believed that economic depression was the underlying cause of Greece's ills. To solve this economic problem, he urged the Greeks to unite in war against Persia in order to open Asia to Greek colonization and trade:

We cannot enjoy a sure peace unless we join together in a war against the barbarians, nor can the Greeks achieve concord until we wrest our material advantages from the same source. . . . when we have been freed from the poverty surrounding our lives—which breaks up friendships, perverts to enmity the ties of kindred, and throws all mankind into wars and seditions—then surely we shall enjoy a spirit of concord and our mutual good will will be real.[24]

When Isocrates later realized that the individual states were too jealous of their sovereignty to form a voluntary union, he openly urged King Philip of Macedonia to unify Greece by force and then undertake a joint Greek-Macedonian invasion of Asia.

The Macedonian unification of Greece. To the north of Greece lay Macedonia, inhabited by hardy peasants and nobles who were related to the Greeks but were culturally inferior to them. Macedonia became a centralized, powerful state under the able and crafty Philip II (359-336 B.C.), who created the most formidable army yet known by joining the crack Macedonian cavalry of nobles with the infantry phalanx used by the Greeks. In his youth, Philip had been a hostage at Thebes where he acquired an appreciation of Greek culture, an understanding of Greek political weakness, and a desire to win for Macedonia a place in the Hellenic world.

After unifying Macedonia—including a string of Greek colonies that had been established along its coast during the earlier centuries of Macedonia's weakness—Philip turned to the Greek city-states, whose wars afforded him the opportunity first to intervene, then to dominate. In vain did Demosthenes, the great Athenian orator and political opponent of Isocrates, warn that "democracies and dictators cannot exist together" and urge the Athenians and other Greeks to stop Philip before it was too late. Belatedly, Athens and Thebes acted, but their combined forces were shattered at Chaeronea in 338 B.C. Philip then forced the Greeks into a federal league in which each state, while retaining self-government, swore to "make war upon him who violates the general peace" and to furnish Philip with men and supplies for a campaign against Persia. On the eve of setting out for Asia Minor, Philip was assassinated by a noble with a personal grudge, leaving the war against Persia as a legacy for his brilliant son Alexander.

The battle of Chaeronea marks the end of the Hellenic Age. Incapable of finding a solution to the anarchy that tore their world to shreds, the Greeks ended as political failures and at the mercy of a great outside power, first Macedonia and then Rome. Despite the loss of their political independence, however, the Greeks retained their cultural leadership. The culture of the new Hellenistic Age and its successor, the world of Rome, was to be largely Greek.

THE GREEK GENIUS

The Greek character. The Greeks were the first to formulate many of the western world's fundamental concepts in philosophy, science, and art. How was it that a relative handful of people could bequeath such a legacy to civilization? The definitive answer may always elude the historian, but a good part of the explanation lies in environmental and social factors.

The Greeks were separated geographically from the Near East with its traditions of absolutism, priestcraft, and supernaturalism. Thus they had a unique opportunity to sidestep the bondage of the past. The isolation of the city-states accentuated the growth of individualistic cultures, the easy access to the seas made the Greeks adventurous seafarers into unknown lands, and military successes stimulated pride and self-confidence.

To a large extent, the *polis* shaped Greek character. Because the city-states were modest in size, their citizens neither sought to build vast empires nor suffered from delusions of grandeur which might have warped their reasoning faculties and aesthetic standards. Thus the *polis* fostered moderation and a sense of proportion. In the more enlightened city-states, an alert, informed electorate was required to perform various civic duties and to take an active part in the discussions of the assembly. The Greeks relished debate and argument, and one of their most striking characteristics was a fondness for good talk. The nature of the universe and of man, man's duty to the state and to his fellow citizens, law and freedom, the purpose of art and poetry, the standards of a good life—these problems they discussed brilliantly and with pertinence for our times as much as for theirs.

The Greek character was one of energy and bold experimentation tempered by the exercise of reason and clear judgment. The Greeks' curiosity about the natural world led them to an appreciation of the simplicity and balance in nature. They believed that an ideal life based on a harmony of interests and abilities should include a healthy balance of action and thought. The life of Sophocles offers an excellent example: an Athenian general and chief treasurer of the city, he also wrote such deeply moving tragedies as *Antigone* and *Oedipus Rex.*

To obtain this harmony and balance, it was essential to avoid *hubris.* Just as the terms *karma* and *tao* provide clues to an understanding of the Indian and Chinese ways of life (see Chapter 3), *hubris,* meaning "pride" or "insolence," is a key to fathoming the Greek character. Resulting from human excesses and lying at the root of personal misfortune and social injustice, *hubris* invariably provoked *nemesis,* or retribution, as the result of an inexorable moral law. Greek mythology offers many stories of *hubris* resulting in *nemesis,* and Athenian dramatists often employed this theme in poetic tragedies, as did historians.

An Egyptian priest told Solon, the law-giver, that the Greeks were perennially children. That they were all too often immature in their political relationships was demonstrated by their failure to cooperate for their mutual benefit. But the Greeks also possessed such childlike virtues as boundless curiosity, an instinctive response to nature, and a refreshingly direct and candid approach to life. In their enthusiasm for athletics and exercise and in their frank delight in physical satisfactions, they manifested a zest for earthly pleasures. In the words of a Greek orator: "Rejoice in what is delightful, and be not overvexed at ill: and recognize what a balance our life maintains."[25]

The Greeks exhibited human frailties and failings—they could be suspicious, vindictive, and cruel. But at their best they were guided by the ideals that permeate their intellectual and artistic legacy. Their philosophy was profound; their art sublime. The philosopher Protagoras is credited with the statement, "Man is the measure of all things" —a saying which sums up the Greek attitude toward themselves and the world of men. In short, the Greeks were humanists.

Greek religion. Early Greek religion abounded in gods and goddesses who personified physical elements. Thus Demeter was the earth and giver of grain, Apollo, the sun and giver of light, and Poseidon, who dwelled in the sea, was the ruler of the waters. Other deities had special functions, such as Aphrodite, the goddess of love, Dionysus, the god of fertility and wine, and Athena, the goddess of wisdom and the guardian of Athens. The Greeks of Homeric times believed in manlike deities, capable of malice, favoritism, and jealousy, and differing from ordinary men only in their immortality and their possession of supernatural powers. Zeus, the king of sky, earth, and men, supposedly ruled the world from Mount Olympus with the aid of lesser deities.

By the time of Hesiod, as we have seen (p. 98), a religious reformation had begun which changed the vengeful and capricious gods of Homer into austere arbiters of justice who rewarded the good and punished the wicked. Demeter and Dionysus gained prominence as the central figures of "mystery" cults whose initiates *(mystae)* were promised an afterlife of bliss in the Elysian fields—formerly the abode of heroes only. And from the famous oracle at Delphi the voice of Zeus' son Apollo urged all Greeks to follow the ideals of moderation and reasonableness: "Nothing in excess."

Early Greek philosophy and science. Philosophy arose from the insatiable Greek curiosity about nature. The early Greek philosophers—or scientists, as we would call them—proceeded on the assumption, which has remained basic to all science since the classical age, that the universe is an orderly and intelligible whole. In this the Greek outlook differed from that of the older Near Eastern cultures. As we noted in Chapter 2, the Mesopotamians were skilled observers of astronomical phenomena such as eclipses, but they attributed these to magical and supernatural causes instead of searching for an underlying reason within the natural order. In a different environment—the Mediterranean—and under different social and economic conditions, a new concept about the nature of reality emerged. This more rational and practical view evolved first in the Ionian cities on the western coast of Asia Minor and was stimulated by various developments. The cheaper production of tools and weapons, made possible by the new Iron Age technology, enabled these smaller Greek city-states to compete successfully with the monarchies of the Near East. Moreover, the Phoenician alphabet gave wider distribution to learning; and finally, large-scale trade, carried on by Miletus and other Ionian cities also stimulated a practical mentality and encouraged a progressive shift of emphasis among the Ionian Greeks from a mythological cosmology to a natural "philosophy" with a strongly utilitarian bent.

The first philosopher of importance is Thales of Miletus (c. 636-546 B.C.), often called the "father of philosophy." This highly original thinker speculated on the nature of the basic substance from which all else in the universe is composed. Thales concluded that it was water, which exists in different states or forms and is indispensable to the maintenance and growth of organisms. Thales was thus the first western philosopher to offer a rational explanation of life in terms of natural causes.

By the beginning of the fifth century B.C. some Greeks were criticizing the views of Thales. Water, they reasoned, could not change into a multitude of things absolutely unlike water. The problem of change thus became of paramount importance. Existence alone was real, they argued, and it was impossible for it to be other than eternal, immovable, and indivisible. Therefore, movement and change were logically impossible and only illusions of the mind. The contrary view held by Heraclitus of Ephesus

(c. 540-475 B.C.) was that life was change and change alone. "Everything changes except change," declared Heraclitus. The entire universe is in flux; human bodies and minds are always changing.

Some thinkers concluded that the universe was composed of earth, water, fire, and air rather than a single substance, water, as Thales believed. Democritus (c. 460-370 B.C.) developed a theory that the universe was composed of indivisible atoms, which differed in shape, size, position, and arrangement but not in quality. Moving about continuously, atoms combined to create objects. To Democritus, reality was the mechanical motion of atoms. Scientists have used this theory to the present day, although we are now aware that the atom is neither indivisible nor indestructible.

As ideas developed about the composition of the physical universe, questions arose as to the place of man in the scheme of things. Hence Greek philosophers interested themselves in problems of ethics, logic, and political theory. The view of an objective, impersonal universe arose along with the belief that the key to understanding it lay in the application of *logos*, or man's reasoning powers. Late in the fifth century B.C. and early in the fourth, three Hellenic philosophers employed logic to lay down the most important lines of Greek thought.

Socrates, a martyr to truth. During the last half of the fifth century B.C., the Sophists —"men of wisdom" who taught public speaking and prepared men for public life— submitted all conventional beliefs to the test of rational criticism. Concluding that truth was relative, they denied the existence of universal standards to guide human actions.

The outstanding opponent of the Sophists was the Athenian-born Socrates (c. 470-399 B.C.), a snub-nosed, plain man but a fascinating conversationalist. In the words of the Roman statesman Cicero, Socrates was "the first to call philosophy down from the heavens and to set her in the cities of men, bringing her into their homes and compelling her to ask questions about life and morality and things good and evil."[26] Socrates believed that by asking salient questions and by subjecting the answers to logical analysis, agreement could be reached about ethical standards and rules of conduct. And so he would question passers-by in his function of midwife assisting in the birth of correct ideas (to use his own figure of speech). He might ask them, for example, the difference between piety and impiety, the beautiful and the ugly, or the noble and the base. Taking as his motto the famous inscription on the temple of Apollo at Delphi, "Know thyself," he insisted that "the unexamined life is not worth living." To Socrates, human excellence or virtue *(aretē)* is knowledge, and evil and error are the result of ignorance.

In time Socrates' quest for truth led to his undoing, for the Athenians, unnerved by the Peloponnesian War, arrested him on the charge of impiety and corrupting youth. By a slim majority a jury of citizens condemned Socrates to die, a fate which he accepted without rancor and with a last request:

When my sons are grown up, I would ask you, my friends, to punish them, and I would have you trouble them, as I have troubled you, if they seem to care about riches, or anything, more than about virtue; or if they pretend to be something when they are really nothing, then reprove them, as I have reproved you, for not caring about that for which they ought to care, and thinking that they are something when they are really nothing. And if you do this, both I and my sons will have received justice at your hands.

The hour of departure has arrived, and we go our ways—I to die, and you to live. Which is better God only knows.[27]

After Socrates' death, philosophical leadership passed to his most famous disciple, Plato (427-347 B.C.), and later to Plato's best student, Aristotle (384-322 B.C.). These two men represented the high points of two divergent strains in classical philosophy, two antithetical views of ultimate reality.

Plato and his Theory of Ideas. Like Socrates, Plato believed that truth exists and, furthermore, that it is eternal and fixed. Yet Plato saw that nothing experienced by the senses is permanent. Permanence, he asserted, could be found only in the realm of thought, the spiritual world of Ideas or

Forms. According to Plato, an Idea has a real existence apart from the material world. In the world of Ideas, certain universals such as Beauty, Truth, Justice, and the greatest of all—Good—exist. The concepts of justice, beauty, or truth in the world of the senses are only imperfect reflections of eternal and changeless Ideas. Man's task is to come to know the True Reality—the eternal Ideas—behind these imperfect reflections. Only the soul, and the "soul's pilot," reason, can accomplish this, for the human soul is spiritual and immortal, and in its prenatal state it existed "beyond the heavens" where "true Being dwells."[28]

Plato expounded his concepts of an ideal state in the *Republic,* the first systematic treatise on political science. The state's basic function, founded on the Idea of Justice, was the satisfaction of the common good. In the ideal state, Plato contended, there should be three classes of people: workers to produce the necessities of life; warriors to guard the state; and philosophers to rule in the best interests of all the people. "Until philosophers are kings," wrote Plato in a famous statement,

or the kings and princes of this world have the spirit and power of philosophy, and political greatness and wisdom meet in one, and those commoner natures who pursue either to the exclusion of the other are compelled to stand aside, cities will never have rest from their evils—no, nor the human race. . . .[29]

The society Plato favored was a kind of "spirtualized Sparta," in which the state would vigorously regulate every aspect of a man's life. He believed that the family and private property should be abolished on the grounds that both institutions bred selfishness, and that marriage should be controlled in order to produce strong, healthy children. Although much of the *Republic* has proved unpalatable to ancient and present-day readers alike, it was man's first attempt to devise a planned human society.

Plato founded the Academy in Athens, the famous school which existed from about 388 B.C. until 529 A.D. Here he taught and encouraged his students, whom he expected

Renaissance man's interest in classical learning is reflected in Raphael's *"School of Athens,"* which portrays many of the greatest Greek philosophers and scientists grouped together as if they had all lived contemporaneously. In this detail from the painting, Plato (left) is carrying a copy of one of his most metaphysical works, the *Timaeus,* while Aristotle carries his *Ethics.* The two philosophers, Plato pointing toward heaven and Aristotle holding his hand parallel to the earth, seem to be disputing about the differences between their philosophies.

to become the intellectual elite who would go forth and reform society. His best known student, Aristotle, later set up his own school, the Lyceum. Because Aristotle would walk up and down while lecturing to his pupils, the group came to be known as "peripatetic" (from the Greek *peripatein,* to walk around), a term afterwards applied to the Aristotelian system.

Aristotle and concrete reality. Reacting against the other-worldly tendencies of Plato's thought, Aristotle differed from his teacher on the question of the existence of Ideas or Forms. For Aristotle, Real Being was found not in universal Ideas but in the particular fact, the individual thing, and the concrete object. Furthermore, he believed every concrete object to be composed of Form and Matter. In a marble statue the marble is the Matter, while the shape conferred by the sculptor is the Form. In opposition to Plato, who separated Form from Matter, Aristotle claimed that neither Form nor Matter had any existence apart from the other.

Aristotle's most influential treatises, the

Ethics and the *Politics,* deal with what he called the "philosophy of human affairs," whose object is the acquisition and maintenance of human happiness. Two kinds of virtue *(aretē),* intellectual and moral, which produce two types of happiness, are described in the *Ethics.* Intellectual virtue is the product of reason, and only such men as philosophers and scientists ever attain it. Much more important for the good of society is moral virtue—for example, liberality and temperance—which is the product less of reason than of habit and thus can be acquired by all. In this connection Aristotle introduced his Doctrine of the Mean as a guide for good conduct. He considered all virtues to be means between extremes; thus courage, for example, is the mean between cowardice and rashness.

In the *Politics* Aristotle viewed the state as necessary "for the sake of the good life," because its laws and educational system provide the most effective training needed for the attainment of moral virtue and hence happiness. Thus to Aristotle the viewpoint that the state stands in opposition to the individual would be unthinkable. He formulated no concept of a planned ideal state, such as Plato's *Republic*, but wrote only about the small *polis* of his own age. Again in contrast to Plato, Aristotle contended that property and family are valuable incentives for the achievement of a good life. Because democracy had degenerated in Greece during his lifetime, Aristotle agreed with Plato in favoring the rule of a single strong man.

Aristotle's writings on formal logic, collectively known as the *Organon* ("Instrument"), describe two ways in which new truth can be acquired. The first, induction, moves from particular facts to general truths. Deductive logic, on the other hand, moves from the general to the particular. To facilitate deductive reasoning from general truths, Aristotle devised the syllogism, a logical structure requiring a trio of propositions. The first two propositions (the major and minor premises) must be plainly valid and logically related so that the third proposition, the conclusion, inevitably follows. For example, (1) all Greeks are human; (2) Socrates is a Greek; (3) therefore Socrates is human.

There has probably never been another man whose interests were so widespread or whose knowledge was so encyclopedic as Aristotle's. He investigated and wrote brilliantly in such diverse fields as art, biology, mathematics, astronomy, physics, psychology, rhetoric, logic, politics, ethics, and metaphysics. His accomplishments won him renown, and he was ultimately requested to tutor the young prince of Macedonia, who became his most famous pupil— Alexander the Great. In ancient times, however, Aristotle was considered second to Plato, and only during the Middle Ages in Europe did he take precedence (see Chapter 13).

The "Greek miracle." The evolution of Greek science can be discussed in terms of four main chronological divisions: (1) the formative, or pre-Socratic period, c. 600-400 B.C.; (2) the period of Plato and Aristotle c. 400-300 B.C.; (3) the Hellenistic period, the high point of Euclid and Archimedes, c. 300-100 B.C.; and (4) the Graeco-Roman period, c. 100 B.C.-600 A.D., when Greek science was affected by nonrational currents partly responsible for the rise of Christianity, after which it passed to the Arabs and through them to the Latin West in the Middle Ages.[30]

We have already seen that early Ionian scientists and philosophers departed from the Mesopotamian and Egyptian system of data collecting to seek out the fundamental principles of the universe. When Thales and other pre-Socratic thinkers asked questions about the nature of reality, they reflected a distinctive feature of Greek mentality that emerged during this formative period. This was a shift of interest away from purely empirical data and rules, which had characterized Mesopotamian and Egyptian thinking, towards a generalized science based on certain fundamental principles that must apply throughout the whole universe of matter. This significant development led to what has been called the "Greek miracle."[31]

In the first stage of the evolution of Greek science, the formulation of generalized rules was particularly evident in the fields of mathematics and geometry. Pythagoras of Samos (c. 582-500 B.C.) believed that the universe was founded on mathematical principles. To analyze these principles he devised theorems, the most famous of which is known to every geometry student. (He went so far as to maintain that everything had a numerical value and that, to obtain the principal characteristics of an object, one must "get its number.") As we saw previously, the Egyptians had been proficient at solving individual problems, such as finding the area of a particular field, but they had left unexpressed the theoretical geometry behind these empirical operations. The pre-Socratic Greeks, and particularly Pythagoras, transformed geometry, seeking its basic principles and setting them forth as abstract theorems. In this way they established a general procedure for the solution of *any* triangle.

Along similar lines, the application to science of the reason and logic so important to the philosophers brought further advances during the second stage in the evolution of

Greek science. Through the deductive and inductive processes so brilliantly exemplified by such thinkers as Plato and Aristotle, this period abounded with new discoveries in the abstract and physical sciences. Aristotle, for example, made many advances in biology. From keen observation, the use of dissection, and data gathered by fishermen, travelers, and scholars, he concluded that over a period of time an organism evolves from a simple to a more complex form, with a parallel increase in intelligence.

Still another factor assisted in developing Greek science during this second period. In the pre-Socratic era an individual scientist worked in almost complete isolation and on his own, with the result that there was little if any scientific dialogue. But by the time of Plato and Aristotle this situation had changed significantly. Thus, in Plato's Academy, abstract subjects such as astronomy and mathematics seem to have been pursued vigorously, while, not surprisingly, Aristotle's Lyceum became an institution for concrete scientific research.

As we shall see later in this chapter, Greek science reached a zenith in the Hellenistic period at Alexandria, the third stage in the evolution of Greek scientific thought. In this era we can discern a synthesis of the pre-Socratic Ionian approach—namely, the employment of science largely in order to *do* things, with the Hellenic ideal of pursuing science in order to *know* things. As a result, we find the Hellenistic scientists making signal contributions to both pure and applied science. Research was actively pursued, and Alexandria boasted outstanding facilities, chief among which was the Museum, a state-sponsored center of scientific research. Connected with the Museum was the famous Alexandrian library, until modern times the largest in the world with more than half a million books.

The final main division in the evolution of Greek science deals with the Graeco-Roman period extending from about 100 B.C. to 600 A.D. (which we shall examine in a later chapter). Meanwhile, there had occurred in the western world what has been aptly described as the "Greek miracle"—a special way of regarding reality. A tremendous breakthrough had occurred in man's ability to view his external environment in objective terms and to recognize his proper place within it; he had acquired the capacity, by vigorous application of reason and logic, to discern universal principles in nature. The "Greek miracle" led men to the threshold of today's world of science and technology.

Medicine. Preconceived and false ideas about the human body blocked the development of medical science until 420 B.C., when Hippocrates, the "father of medicine," founded a school in which he emphasized the value of observation and the careful interpretation of symptoms. After conducting practical experiments, the members of this school were firmly convinced that disease resulted from natural, not supernatural, causes.

Hippocrates set forth a high code of professional ethics still sworn to by doctors today. In abridged form this oath is still administered to most graduates in medicine:

I will look upon him who shall have taught me this Art even as one of my parents. I will share my substance with him, and I will supply his necessities, if he be in need. I will regard his offspring even as my own brethren, and I will teach them this Art, if they would learn it, without fee or covenant. I will impart this Art by precept, by lecture and by every mode of teaching, not only to my own sons but to the sons of him who has taught me, and to disciples bound by covenant and oath, according to the Law of Medicine.

The regimen I adopt shall be for the benefit of my patients according to my ability and judgment, and not for their hurt or for any wrong. . . . Whatsoever things I see or hear concerning the life of men, in my attendance on the sick or even apart therefrom, which ought not to be noised abroad, I will keep silence thereon, counting such things to be as sacred secrets.[32]

The writing of history. History for the Hellenic Greeks was not an account of legendary events and mythical figures, nor were the forces of history attributable simply to the whims of the gods. The Greeks viewed history as a humanistic study by which historians sought to learn about the actions and characters of men. As such, history could be subjected to rational standards and critical judgment.

If history be defined as an "honest attempt first to find out what happened, then to explain why it happened," Herodotus of Halicarnassus (484?-425? B.C.) deserves to be called the "father of history" (but see the Historical Critique on p. 160). In his history of the Persian Wars he discerned the clash of two distinct civilizations, the Hellenic and the Near Eastern. His portrayal of both the Greeks and the Persians was eminently impartial, but his fondness for a good story often led him to include tall tales in his work.

Although Herodotus emphasized the effects of climate and geography upon social customs, the first truly scientific historian was Thucydides (460-400? B.C.), who wrote a notably objective chronicle of the Peloponnesian War. To appreciate the extent of his objectivity, we must keep in mind that he was a contemporary of the events and, moreover, a staunch Athenian himself. Yet a reader can scarcely detect whether the historian favored Athens or Sparta. Thucydides describes his approach to his subject matter in this way:

With reference to the narrative of events, far from permitting myself to derive it from the first source that came to hand, I did not even trust my own impressions, but it rests partly on what I saw myself, partly on what others saw for me, the accuracy of the report being always tried by the most severe and detailed tests possible. My conclusions have cost me some labour from the want of coincidence between accounts of the same occurrences by different eyewitnesses, arising sometimes from imperfect memory, sometimes from undue partiality for one side or the other. The absence of romance in my history will, I fear, detract somewhat from its interest; but I shall be content if it is judged useful by those inquirers who desire an exact knowledge of the past as an aid to the interpretation of the future, which in the course of human things must resemble if it does not reflect it. My history has been composed to be an everlasting possession, not the show-piece of an hour.[33]

Hellenic poetry and drama. Greek literary periods can be classified according to dominant poetic forms which reflected particular stages of social evolution in Greece. First

came the time of great epics, followed by periods in which lyric poetry and drama flourished.

Sometime during the eighth century B.C. in Ionia, the *Iliad* and the *Odyssey*, the two great epics attributed to Homer, were set down in their present form. The *Iliad*, describing the clash of arms between the Greeks and the Trojans "on the ringing plains of windy Troy," glorifies heroic valor and physical prowess against a background of divine intervention in human affairs. The *Odyssey*, relating the adventure-filled wanderings of Odysseus on his return to Greece after Troy's fall, gives a detailed picture of everyday life and underscores the Greeks' attachment to the sea at the time when they were engaged in their first wave of maritime exploration and colonization. These stirring epics provided inspiration and source material for generations of poets in the western world.

As Greek society became more sophisticated, a new type of poetry, written to be sung to the accompaniment of the lyre, arose among the Ionian Greeks. Its authors sang not of legendary events but of present delights and sorrows. This new note, personal and passionate, can be seen in the following examples, in which the contrast between the new values of what is called the Greek Renaissance and those of Homer's heroic age is sharply clear. Unlike Homer's heroes, Archilochus of Paros (seventh century B.C.) unashamedly throws away his shield and runs from the battlefield:

My trusty shield adorns some Thracian foe;
I left it in a bush—not as I would!
But I have saved my life; so let it go.
Soon I will get another just as good.[34]

And in contrast to the older view of an unromantic, purely physical attraction between Paris and Helen, Sappho of Lesbos (sixth century B.C.), the first and one of the greatest of all woman poets, sees Helen as the helpless victim of romantic love:

She, who the beauty of mankind
Excelled, fair Helen, all for love
The noblest husband left behind;
Afar, to Troy she sailed away,

Sophocles, on whose *Oedipus* plays Aristotle based his theory of tragedy, explored the nature of man's involvement with fate.

Her child, her parents, clean forgot;
The Cyprian* led her far astray
Out of the way, resisting not.[35]

Drama, which developed from the religious rites of the Dionysian mystery cult, filled a civic-religious function in Greek society. In Athens, by the fifth century B.C., two distinct forms—tragedy and comedy—had evolved. The plays were performed in an open-air theater on the slope of the Acropolis; the actors wore thick-soled boots to increase their stature and prominence and held to their faces masks characteristic of the roles they portrayed. The masks were equipped with speaking tubes to increase the volume of the actor's voices.

Plato had condemned poetry as irrational, but Aristotle, in his *Poetics*, recognized the value of the poet in refining human passions. Aristotle defined tragedy as an imitation of a painful action or event (usually resulting in the death of the hero) which, by arousing pity and fear in the audience, effects a cleansing of those emotions. Drama critics today often use his aesthetic theories when evaluating plays.

By depicting man in conflict with destiny, the tragedies expressed the Greek concern for achieving harmony and avoiding the excesses of passion or the intellect. Borrowing the familiar legends of gods and Homeric heroes for their plots, playwrights followed rigorous canons of form to arouse in the audience the pity and fear which Aristotle taught were essential to the purification of these emotions.

Most of the Greek plays have been lost; but of the writers of tragedies whose works survive, all were giants of their art. The plays of Aeschylus (525-456 B.C.) were imbued with his deeply religious spirit. In his trilogy, the *Oresteia*, for example, he concerns himself with *hubris*, as applied to the murder of the hero Agamemnon by his false queen, and then proceeds to work out its ramifications—murder piled on murder until men through suffering learn to substitute the moral law of Zeus for the primitive law of the blood feud. Like the prophets of Israel, Aeschylus taught that while "sin brings misery," misery in turn leads to wisdom:

Zeus the Guide, who made man turn
Thought-ward, Zeus, who did ordain
Man by Suffering shall Learn.
So the heart of him, again
Aching with remembered pain,
Bleeds and sleepeth not, until
Wisdom comes against his will.[36]

A generation later, Sophocles (c. 496-406 B.C.) largely abandoned the problem of how to justify the ways of god to man and concentrated upon character. To Sophocles, a

*Aphrodite, the goddess of love, who was thought to have been born on the island of Cyprus.

certain amount of suffering was inevitable in life. No man is perfect; there is a tragic flaw in the character of the best of men which causes them to make mistakes. Sophocles dwelled mainly on the way in which men react to suffering. Like his contemporary, the sculptor Phidias, Sophocles viewed man as an ideal creature—"Many are the wonders of the world, and none so wonderful as Man"—and he displayed man's greatness by depicting him experiencing great tragedy without whimpering.

Euripides (c. 480-406 B.C.), the last of the great Athenian tragedians, reflects the rationalism and critical spirit of the late fifth century. To him, the life of man is pathetic, the ways of the gods ridiculous. His recurrent theme is "Since life began, hath there in God's eye stood one happy man?" and for this he has been called "the poet of the world's grief." Euripides has also been called the first psychologist, for he looked deep into the human soul and with intense realism described what he saw. Far more than Aeschylus or even Sophocles, Euripides strikes home to modern man.

Comedies were bawdy and spirited. There were no libel laws in Athens, and Aristophanes (c. 445-385 B.C.), the famous comic-dramatist and a conservative in outlook, brilliantly satirized Athenian democracy as a mob led by demagogues, the Sophists (among whom he included Socrates) as subversive, and Euripides as an underminer of civic spirit and traditional faith.

The Greeks as builders. In the sixth century B.C. architecture flourished in Ionia and Greece with the construction of large temples of stone, the form having developed from earlier wooden structures which had been influenced by the surviving remains of Mycenaean palaces. The Persian invasion made Athens a heap of ruins, but the withdrawal of the invaders left the Athenians free to reconstruct the Acropolis into a treasury of temples and statues. Architecture reached its zenith in the Athens of the fifth century B.C.

The Parthenon, the Erechtheum, and the other temples on the Acropolis exhibit the highly developed features characteristic of Greek architecture (see photo, p. 117).

Here the post and lintel construction, gable roof, marble colonnade, statues, and carved reliefs were subtly and precisely combined to attain the harmony that makes Greek structure so pleasing to the eye. All relationships, such as column spacing and height and the curvature of floor and roof lines, were calculated and executed with remarkable precision to achieve a perfect balance, both structurally and visually. The three orders, or styles, usually identified by the characteristics of the columns, were the Doric, which was used in the Parthenon; the Ionic, seen in the Erechtheum; and the later and more ornate Corinthian. Later, the Romans used the ostentatious Corinthian style in their massive public buildings.

Located where all men could see and enjoy them, the Greek temples afford an interesting comparison with those of Egypt. Whereas the Egyptian temple was enclosed and mysterious, the Greek temple was open, with a colonnade porch and single inside room which contained the statue of the god. Sacrifice and ritual took place outside the temple, where the altar was placed.

Other types of buildings, notably the theaters, stadiums, and gymnasiums, also express the Greek spirit and way of life. In the open-air theaters the circular shape of the spectators' sections and the plan of the orchestra section set a style which has survived in principle to the present day.

Sculpture and pottery. Greek sculpture of the archaic period (c. 625-480 B.C.), although crude in its representation of human anatomy, has the freshness and vigor of youth. Influenced partly by Egyptian models, the statues of nude youths and draped maidens usually stand stiffly with clenched fists and with one foot thrust awkwardly forward (see photo, p. 123). The fixed smile and formalized treatment of hair and drapery also reveal how the sculptor is struggling to master the technique of his art.

The achievement of mastery of technique by 480 B.C. ushered in the classical period of fifth-century Greek sculpture whose "classic" principles of harmony and proportion have shaped the course of western art. Sculpture from this period displays both the end of technical immaturity and the begin-

In the Parthenon, which housed Phidias' huge gold and ivory statue of Athena, great care was taken to design a structurally and visually perfect building. The tops of the Doric columns lean toward the center of each colonnade, the steps curve upward at the center, and the columns are more widely spaced in the middle of each row than at the ends—all these refinements create an illusion of perfect regularity which would be lacking if the parts were actually perfectly proportioned. The Parthenon was originally brightly painted, and painted sculpture adorned the gables and parts of the frieze, while another sculptured and painted frieze ran around the walls inside the colonnade. A reconstruction of the entire Acropolis appears at the right.

ning of idealization of the human form which reached its culmination in the dignity and poise of Phidias' figures in the Parthenon frieze and pediments (see Color Plate 8). Carved with restraint and "calm exaltation," the frieze depicts the citizens of Athens participating in the Panathenaic procession in honor of Athena which took place every four years.

The more relaxed character of fourth century B.C. Hellenic sculpture contrasts with the grandeur and dignity of fifth-century art. Charm, grace, and individuality characterize the work of Praxiteles, the most famous sculptor of the century. These qualities can be seen in his supple statues of the god Hermes holding the young Dionysus and of Aphrodite stepping into her bath. The latter statue, called the Aphrodite of Cnidus, is known only from inferior copies.

The making of pottery was a highly developed art in Greece. The earliest vases were decorated with abstract geometric designs, then came paintings of scenes from mythology and daily life. From the surviving Greek pottery, we can get an inkling of what Greek painting, now lost, was like (see illustrations, p. 103).

THE HELLENISTIC AGE

Alexander the Great. When Philip of Macedonia was assassinated in 336 B.C., his crown fell to his gifted twenty-year-old son, Alexander, who crushed unrest and rebellion in Greece and proved himself a resolute, ambitious king from the beginning of his reign.

Like his father, the youthful Alexander was alive to the glories of Hellenic culture, having as a youth been tutored by Aristotle. Reveling in the heroic deeds of the *Iliad*, Alexander may have seen himself as a second Achilles waging war against barbarians when he planned to revenge the Persian attacks on Greece. Two years after Philip's death, he set out with an army of 35,000 soldiers recruited from Macedonia and the Greek League that his father had

organized (see p. 107). In quick succession he subdued Asia Minor, Syria, Palestine, and Egypt. Then the young leader marched into Mesopotamia and there, in 331 B.C., defeated the last powerful army of Darius III, the Persian monarch. Alexander was now master of Persia, the proud empire that had controlled the Near East. He ventured as far east as the rich river valleys of India (see Chapter 6); but at last his weary soldiers forced him to turn back. In 323 B.C., while he was planning the circumnavigation and conquest of Arabia, Alexander died at the age of thirty-two, the victim of malaria. Although his many military successes were due largely to the superb army his father had created and to the disorganization that had existed within the Persian empire, Alexander in his own right was an outstanding general and a gallant leader of men.

Alexander's legacy to political thought was the vision of a unified world and the brotherhood of mankind. Various of his military and administrative policies sought to unify the lands he conquered and to promote what he himself called "concord and partnership in the empire" between orientals and westerners. He blended orientals with Greeks and Macedonians in his army and administration; he founded numerous cities—seventy, according to tradition—in the East and settled many of his veterans in them; and he married two oriental princesses and encouraged his officers and men to take foreign wives. Alexander also promoted empire-wide trade by opening new trade routes, founding port cities, and minting a standard coinage. Finally, to complete the unification of the empire and strengthen his authority, Alexander ordered the Greek city-states to accord him "divine honors" in the manner of an oriental monarch.

The division of Alexander's empire. Alexander's sudden death destroyed his plans for bringing about the "marriage of Europe and Asia." Since his heirs were a feeble-minded brother and a yet unborn son, a struggle for power among his generals ensued. The empire was roughly divided among those controlling the African, Asian, and European segments: Egypt was ruled by Ptolemy; Alexander's conquered lands in Asia were governed by Seleucus; and Macedonia and Greece constituted a separate power under Antigonus Gonatas. This three-part division of Alexander's empire constituted the Hellenistic world and, somewhat modified under their heirs, lasted for three centuries, dating from Alexander's death in 323 B.C. to the Roman defeat of the last Ptolemy in 30 B.C. (see p. 140).

Some of the city-states in Greece continued to exist as independent political entities, however, and much of Asia Minor did not fall under the sway of the Seleucids. One important kingdom in Asia Minor was Pergamum (see Reference Map 2), which became an independent state after 280 B.C. This small but wealthy state boasted luxurious palaces and baths, a theater, and a library, second only to Alexandria's in size. Its scholars enjoyed a high reputation; Pergamum's fame has been perpetuated in the word *parchment,* derived from its name.

How did Alexander's successors try to resolve the crucial problem of creating workable political organizations in their sizable empires? Although absolutism was tempered in the empire ruled by Antigonus and his successors, the rulers in the Seleucid and Ptolemaic domains adopted undisguised absolutisms, founded upon the theory of the divine right of kings. Political administration was centralized in a bureaucracy staffed by Greeks and Macedonians, an arrangement which created a vast gulf between a ruler and his subjects. A fairly large measure of self-government was conceded to the cities, however. This pattern of semiautonomy for cities influenced the Romans when they organized their rule over a far-flung empire.

Such a political organization did not free the Hellenistic monarchies from internal dissension. Plagued by divisive tendencies, dynastic troubles, and civil wars, the king-

THE HELLENISTIC EMPIRES ABOUT 300 B.C.

Claimed by Macedonia
Claimed by Seleucids

founded in the East, thus creating new markets. An economic union between East and West hitherto unknown in the ancient world came into existence. Prosperity was also stimulated when Alexander put into circulation huge hoards of Persian gold and silver and introduced a uniform coinage.

By the third century B.C. the center of trade had shifted from Greece to Egypt, Rhodes, and the coast of Asia Minor. Largest of the Hellenistic cities, and much larger than any cities in Greece itself, were Antioch in northern Syria, Seleucia-on-the-Tigris, and Alexandria in Egypt. The riches of India, Persia, Arabia, and the Fertile Crescent were brought by sea and land to the Mediterranean ports, particularly Alexandria and Antioch.

Many industries were royal monopolies, and the state exercised close control over economic life. Industrial development was accompanied by greater specialization of workers and the organization of the apprentice system. Because free labor was plentiful and cheap, slave labor declined in industry and agriculture.

Despite the wealth of such cities as Alexandria and Antioch, discontent was rife. Harsh social and economic differences separated the rich from the poor, and the exploited workers, having formed associations for mutual aid, frequently went on strike. Political power, land, money, and trading privileges increasingly fell to royal favorites, and the majority of the population had neither political rights nor economic security. To keep the masses from revolting, various cities furnished them with cheap or free grain—a practice subsequently adopted by the Romans.

Alexandria. Alexandria outdistanced all other Hellenistic cities as a commercial and cultural center. Its merchants imported metals, wool, marble, wines, spices, and horses and supplied the ancient world with linen, paper, glass, and jewelry. Boasting a population of about a million, the city had a double harbor in which a great lighthouse, judged one of the wonders of the ancient world, rose to a height estimated at 370 feet. Two wide boulevards laid out at right angles led to the four gates, with porticoes

doms soon began to crumble. Macedonia lost control of Greece when Athens asserted its independence and most of the other Greek states formed two federal leagues—the Aetolian in the north and the Achaean in the Peloponnesus—which successfully resisted Macedonian domination. The eastern reaches of Alexander's empire—India, Bactria, and Parthia—gradually drifted out of the Seleucid sphere of influence (see pp. 165-167). In the year 200 B.C. the new power of Rome entered upon the scene, and by 30 B.C. an expanding Rome had annexed the last remaining Hellenistic state, Egypt. While Roman expansion was in some measure responsible for the demise of the Hellenistic empires, it only accelerated the process of destruction already initiated by trouble within the empires.

Economic growth and expansion. The Hellenistic Age was a time of great economic growth. In the wake of Alexander's conquests, a network of Greek cities was which were illuminated at night. With its great library and museum, both founded by Ptolemy I, Alexandria was the intellectual capital of the Hellenistic world. Other striking features of the city were an arena for chariot races, a zoo, the tombs of the Ptolemies, a mausoleum built for Alexander's body, and the magnificent royal palace with its spacious gardens.

The busy streets were filled with a mixture of peoples—Greeks and Macedonians, plus Egyptians, Jews, and other Asiatics and Africans. In the Greek sense, Alexandria was not a city but a great collection of many peoples, the privileged Greeks and Macedonians at the top of the social scale and the mass of Egyptians at the bottom.

Skepticism, Epicureanism, and Stoicism. Developments in philosophy reflected the political and psychological changes which took place as a result of Alexander's conquests. With the growing loss of freedom and the prevalence of internal disorder, philosophers ceased to speculate about fundamental substances or to formulate plans for the reform of existing society; they shifted instead to the consideration of individual happiness. This emphasis on peace of mind in a chaotic world led to the rise of three principal schools of thought—Skepticism, Epicureanism, and Stoicism.

The Skeptics reflected most clearly the doubts and misgivings of the times. According to this school, not only is it impossible to know anything outside the physical senses, but no two people can agree as to what is pleasurable or painful; pleasure for one is pain for another; one person feels cold when another feels warm. If no one can state what is true, the wise man, so the Skeptics argued, does not pretend to hold any opinions of his own but follows the customs of the region where he happens to live.

The Athenian Epicurus (c. 342-270 B.C.) taught that the wise man could achieve happiness simply by freeing his body from pain and his mind from fear—particularly the fear of death. To reach this goal, men must avoid bodily excesses, including those of pleasure, and accept the scientific teaching of Democritus that both body and soul are composed of atoms which fall apart at death. Thus, beyond death there is no existence and nothing to fear. Epicurus maintained that the finest pleasures were intellectual, but many of his followers later distorted his teachings so that Epicureanism appeared to be concerned only with the gratification of sensual desires.

The Stoics, followers of Zeno (c. 336-c. 264 B.C.), a Semite from Cyprus, argued in contrast to Epicureanism that the universe is controlled by some power—variously called Reason, World Soul, Fortune, and God—which determines everything that happens. Fortified by this knowledge, the Stoic

This mosaic from Pompeii is a copy of a fourth-century B.C. Greek painting depicting the defeat of Darius, at the right, by Alexander, at the left, at the Battle of Issus. While this mosaic can only be an imperfect realization of the original painting, the intricacy and vitality of the composition attest to the skill of the Greeks at painting, an art at which they themselves believed they excelled.

wise man conforms his will to the World Will and "stoically" accepts whatever part fortune allots him in the drama of life. Far more than Epicureanism, Stoicism with its insistence on duty and on the brotherhood of man in One Great City was attractive to the Romans.

Discoveries in science and mathematics. Hellenistic scientists were essentially practical in their aims, and their methodology emphasized specialization and experimentation. The expansion of geographical knowledge incited scientists to make accurate maps and to estimate the size of the earth, which had been identified as a globe through observation of its shadow in a lunar eclipse. Eratosthenes of Alexandria (276?-195? B.C.) calculated the circumference of the globe by measuring the difference in the angles of the noonday sun at Aswan and Alexandria during the summer solstice and estimating the distance between the two cities. According to some authorities, he computed the earth's circumference at 24,662 miles, or less than 200 miles short of the actual figure by modern calculations. Actually, interpretations vary concerning the modern equivalent of his unit of measure, the *stade,* and Eratosthenes may have been as much as 11 or 12 per cent off. Yet he made the only sound attempt to measure the globe up to his time, and his calculations remained the most accurate measurement available until a few centuries ago. Eratosthenes also drew a map of the world which was both more accurate and more extensive than any previous map.

In this period astronomy also made rapid advances, so that one Alexandrian astronomer was able to compute the solar year correctly to within five minutes and the lunar month to within one second. In the third century B.C. Aristarchus put forward the radical theory that the earth rotates on its axis and moves in an orbit around the sun. Most of his contemporaries adhered, however, to the prevailing geocentric theory, which stated that the earth was stationary and the sun revolved around it. This view not only was supported by the powerful authority of Aristotle, but it also seemed to explain all the known facts of celestial motion. This was particularly true after Hipparchus in the next century added the new idea of epicycles—each planet revolves in its own small orbit while moving around the earth. It was not until the sixteenth century A.D. that scientists were again to espouse the views of Aristarchus.

Euclid, the most famous mathematician of Alexandria (c. 300 B.C.), developed the forms and theorems of plane geometry which are still taught today. Archimedes of Syracuse (287?-212 B.C.) contributed to higher mathematics by calculating the value of π. He also invented a terminology for expressing numbers up to any magnitude and laid the foundations of calculus. But it was in the field of physics that Archimedes excelled. He invented a compound pulley, the windlass, and an endless screw for pumping out ships and draining flooded fields, and he improved such military weapons as catapults.

The Hellenistic Greeks extended the advances in medicine made earlier by Hippocrates and his school. By dissecting bodies of dead criminals, they were able to trace the outlines of the nervous system, to understand the principle of the circulation of the blood, and to ascertain that the brain, not the heart, was the true center of consciousness.

Architecture, sculpture, and literature. The host of new cities which sprang up in Hellenistic times served as a tremendous impetus to architecture. The new cities benefited from town planning: the streets were laid out according to a rectangular plan. The great public edifices were elaborate and highly ornamented; this was an age which preferred the more ornate Corinthian to the simple Doric order.

Hellenistic sculptors continued and intensified the realistic, dramatic, and emotional approach that began to appear in Hellenic sculpture during the fourth century B.C. Supported by rulers and other rich patrons in Alexandria, Antioch, Rhodes, and Pergamum, they displayed their technical virtuosity by depicting violent scenes, writhing forms, and dramatic poses—all with a realism which could make stone simulate flesh (see illustration, p. 123). Little

Between the sixth and the fourth centuries B.C., Greek art developed from the rigid stylization, reminiscent of Egyptian art, of the *Kourai* figure (top left) to the more complex and realistic, yet obviously idealized, Ephebe of Marathon (top right), probably an original bronze representation of Hermes by Praxiteles. The trend toward realism and increased complexity culminated in the art of the Hellenistic period, which produced such intricate sculptures as the contorted Laocoön group and, finally, the naturalistic and even grotesque drunken old woman (bottom), a work created during the "Baroque" period of Hellenistic art.

evidence remained of the balance and restraint of classical Greek sculpture. The famous Laocoön group and the frieze from the altar of Zeus at Pergamum, with their twisted poses, contorted faces, and swollen muscles, remind one of the Baroque sculpture of seventeenth-century Europe which replaced the classical art of the Italian Renaissance.

The quality of literature from the Hellenistic Age was generally inferior to that of the Hellenic Age. Like the sculptors, the writers of the period exhibited an extraordinary technical virtuosity, and their works generally were modeled after those of the classical age. Scholarship flourished, and the literature of the earlier Hellenic Age was edited and commented upon. We are indebted for the preservation of much of Greek classical literature to the subsidized scholars at the Alexandrine library—"fatted fowls in a coop," as a Skeptic philosopher called them. Yet, paradoxically, these sophisticated scholars produced superb pastoral poetry extolling the simple life of shepherds. The best of such poetry was written by Theocritus at Alexandria in the third century B.C.; the following short example, written by a contemporary, well illustrates its character and appeal:

Would that my father had taught me the craft
   of a keeper of sheep,
For so in the shade of the elm-tree, or under the
   rocks on the steep,
Piping on reeds I had sat, and had lulled my
   sorrow to sleep.[37]

The Hellenistic contribution. Apart from its splendid advances in science, the greatest contribution of the Hellenistic Age was undoubtedly the diffusion of Greek culture throughout the ancient East and, in time, the newly rising Roman West. Only because the Hellenistic world possessed a common language (a simplified form of Greek called *koine*, "common") and experienced socioeconomic and, to a lesser degree, political unity was this achievement possible. Although, in retrospect, the Hellenistic world may appear confused and frustrated, with warring empires and heterogeneous peoples, the men of this age were not without aspirations. In the words of a modern scholar, the Hellenistic world, and its Stoic philosophers in particular,

aimed at . . . humanizing . . . the brutal world; it longed and strove for *Homonoia,* Concord, between man and man; lastly, it proclaimed a conception of the world as One Great City . . . which should on the one hand supersede all local allegiances and on the other should, like Plato's imagined Republic, be in itself an organization of the righteous life.[38]

This outlook was taken over by the Romans.

SUMMARY

The two most important centers of the Aegean maritime civilization were Knossos on the island of Crete and Mycenae on the Greek mainland. Aegean civilization reached its zenith first in Crete (2000-1400 B.C.), where the island dwellers fashioned a sophisticated urban culture, synthesizing cultural elements from the Near East and Egypt. By the fourteenth century B.C. the center of Aegean culture had shifted to Mycenae on the Greek mainland, where another zenith was attained. The Mycenaean civilization endured until the warlike Dorians invaded the Peloponnesus and forced the Mycenaeans to flee eastward to Athens in Attica and Ionia in Asia Minor. There, by the eighth century B.C., fiercely independent city-states evolved a distinctly Hellenic culture which was to come to fruition in the Hellenic Age (the eighth to fourth centuries B.C.).

Achilles, the hero of Homer's *Iliad*, would have lived forever had not a Trojan arrow pierced him fatally in the heel, the only vulnerable part of his body. Like Achilles, the Greek city-states of the Hellenic period had one fatal defect—in their case, an inability to submerge individual differences for the sake of common survival. The city-states failed to adapt themselves to the political realities of the fifth century B.C., which had resulted from the colonial expansion and economic revolution of previous centuries and which linked the destinies of Athens and other Greek cities with those of a larger Mediterranean community. Instead of developing the Delian League into a true Greek federation, Athens placed its own interests first and converted the League into an Athenian maritime empire, thus plunging the Greeks into the disastrous Peloponnesian War.

Fortunately for the Greeks, Philip II, the Macedonian ruler who conquered the city-states sixty years after the Peloponnesian War, sincerely admired Hellenic culture—an admiration which was shared by his son, Alexander the Great. It was the ambitious and gallant Alexander who conquered the Near East and laid the boundaries for three large empires carved from his conquered lands. The Hellenistic Age, which began after Alexander's death, was primarily a period of economic expansion, but it was also an age of growing cosmopolitanism, of striking intellectual and artistic achievements, and of the wide diffusion of Greek culture.

Perhaps the greatest Greek contribution to western political thought was a body of theory which included the concepts of a democratic government responsible to the governed, of trial by jury, and of civil liberties. From the Greeks have come also the ideals of public service and the concept of the responsibilities and privileges of being a good citizen.

In the nonpolitical fields, our debt to the Greeks is almost unlimited. They were the first to emancipate thought from myth and religion and to search after a rational explanation of the universe. Many of the philosophical problems they posed are still questions for which we are seeking answers. Especially important among Greek contributions to science was the atomic theory, while Plato's Theory of Ideas and Aristotle's system of logic have been of tremendous influence upon western philosophy.

We are indebted to Aristotle for classifying the main divisions of scientific knowledge and to Hippocrates for searching after the causes of disease. In physics the work of Archimedes has proved invaluable, as has that of Pythagoras and Euclid in geometry, Aristarchus in astronomy, and Eratosthenes in geography.

We still find delight and food for thought in the epic poems of Homer, the lyrics of Sappho, the tragedies of Aeschylus, Sophocles, and Euripides, and the brilliant comedies of Aristophanes. The basis of modern historical writing was established by Herodotus, while Thucydides is noteworthy for his scientific objectivity and brilliant interpretation. In architecture, sculpture, and minor arts, the work of Phidias and other Greeks is a fresh and constant source of inspiration to both artists and laymen.

What is it about Greece that leads us to speak so admiringly? The secret lies in the originality with which the Greeks met every situation. Free of Near Eastern superstitions and traditions, they examined each problem in a spirit of critical inquiry and sought for an explanation that accorded with the natural world rather than supernatural law. Thus their view of life, something entirely new in the world's history, tended to be secular rather than religious, rational instead of credulous. This clear-cut, straightforward approach to life may have been the most lasting contribution of the Greeks to human history.

Chapter 5

The Grandeur That Was Rome

The Roman World: 509 B.C. to 180 A.D.

INTRODUCTION. As the Athenian saw the symbol of his city-state's democracy and culture in the rock-jutting Acropolis, so the Roman viewed the Forum as the symbol of imperial grandeur. Temples were to be found there, but in contrast to the Acropolis, the Forum was dominated by secular buildings —basilicas, the nearby Colosseum, and the great palaces of the emperors rising on the neighboring Palatine Hill. Long vistas contributed to the effect of massiveness and opulence. While the Acropolis was crowned with statues to Athena, the Forum gloried in triumphal arches and columns commemorating military conquests. Rome was the capital of a world-state, extending from the Rhine to the Euphrates, and its citizens were proud of their imperial mission.

Although the buildings in the Forum appear fundamentally Greek in style, they are more monumental and sumptuous. The Hellenic architect most often employed the simple Doric order in his columns, but the Roman preferred the ornate Corinthian. Here, then, are two clues to an understanding of the Romans: they borrowed profusely from the Greeks, and they modified what they took. *Adoption* and *adaptation* are key words in the study of Roman civilization.

Rome was the great intermediary—the bridge over which passed the rich contributions of the Fertile Crescent, Egypt, and especially Greece to form the basis of modern western civilization. The Romans replaced the anarchy of the Hellenistic Age with law and order and embraced the intellectual and artistic legacy of the conquered Greeks. As the Roman empire expanded, Hellenistic civilization was spread westward throughout Europe.

Yet Rome was more than an intermediary. It had greatness in its own right and made many important and original contributions to our western culture. Throughout a history which led from a simple farming community in the plain of Latium to a strong state which became the master of the Mediterranean and finally of the entire known western world, the Romans met one challenge after another with practicality and efficiency. In the shadows of its marching legions went engineers and architects, so that today, scattered throughout the lands which once were part of the Roman empire, the remains of roads, walls, baths, basilicas, amphitheaters, and aqueducts offer convincing evidence of the Romans' technical prowess (see Color Plate 6). Most lasting and far-reaching of all, their administrative institutions—the legal codes and governmental systems which they developed and modified to meet changing needs—have served as the framework of western political life.

ROME TO 509 B.C.

Early settlers of Italy. The Greeks and Romans were offshoots of a common Indo-European stock, and settlement of the Greek and Italian peninsulas followed broadly parallel stages. Between 2000 and 1000 B.C., when Indo-European peoples invaded the Aegean world, a western wing of this nomadic migration filtered into the Italian peninsula, then inhabited by indigenous Neolithic tribes. The first invaders, skilled in the use of copper and bronze, settled in the Po valley. Another wave of Indo-Europeans, equipped with iron weapons and tools, followed; and, in time, the newer and older settlers intermingled and spread throughout the peninsula. One group, the Latins, settled in the lower valley of the Tiber River, a region which became known as the plain of Latium.

For ages history had by-passed the western Mediterranean, but it was henceforth to become an increasingly significant area. By the ninth century B.C. the Etruscans, a non-Indo-European people who probably came from Asia Minor, brought the first city-state civilization to Italy. Expanding from the west coast north to the Po valley and south to the Bay of Naples, the Etruscans organized the backward Italic peoples into a loose confederation of Etruscan-dominated city-states. After 750 B.C. Greek colonists migrated to southern Italy and Sicily, where they served as a protective buffer against powerful and prosperous Carthage, a Phoenician colony established in North Africa around 750 B.C. No one then would have believed that the future of the entire Mediterranean basin belonged to an insignificant village on the Tiber River, then in the shadow of Etruscan expansion. Here was Rome, destined to be ruler of the ancient world.

Rome's origins. According to ancient legend, Rome was founded by the twin brothers Romulus and Remus, who were saved from death in their infancy by a she-wolf who sheltered and suckled them. Virgil's *Aeneid* preserves a different tradition that the founder of the Roman race was Aeneas, a Trojan who after the fall of Troy founded a settlement in Latium. Turning from fable to fact, modern scholars believe that early in the eighth century B.C. the occupants of some small Latin settlements on hills in the Tiber valley united and established a common meeting place, the Forum, around which the city of Rome grew. Situated at a convenient place for fording the river and protected by the hills and marshes from invaders, Rome was strategically located. Nevertheless, the Etruscans conquered Rome and during the sixth century ruled the city and the surrounding plain. Under Etruscan tutelage, Rome expanded into an important commercial center.

Some aspects of Etruscan culture had been borrowed from the Greek colonies in southern Italy, and much of this, including the alphabet, was passed on to the conquered Romans. (Etruscan writing can be read phonetically but not understood.) From their Etruscan overlords, the Romans probably acquired some of their gods and goddesses and the practice of prophesying by examining animal entrails. From the conquerors, too, the conquered learned to build arches and vaults. Even the name *Roma* appears to be derived from the Etruscan word *ruma.* But, although they were culturally indebted to the Etruscans, the Romans retained their own language and kept some of their Latin tribal customs intact.

The Roman monarchy. Rome's political growth followed a line of development similar to that of the Greek city-states: limited monarchy of the sort described by Homer, oligarchy, democracy and, finally, the permanent dictatorship of the Roman emperors. We shall see that in moving from oligarchy to democracy, the Romans, unlike the Greeks, succeeded in avoiding the intermediate stage of tyranny.

According to tradition, early Rome was ruled by kings elected by the people. After the Etruscan conquest, this elective system continued, although the kings chosen were, naturally enough, of Etruscan origin. The king's executive power was called the *imperium,* which was symbolized by an eagle-headed scepter and an ax bound in a bundle of rods *(fasces).* The *fasces* symbol is found on the United States dime. In the 1930's this device also provided both the symbol and the name for Mussolini's political creed of fascism, which glorified the authority of the state.

Cheerful artwork frequently adorned Etruscan tombs. In this painting the youth at the far right is playing a lyre, while the performer in the center blows on a double lute, an instrument the music-loving Etruscans particularly enjoyed.

Although the *imperium* was conferred by a popular assembly made up of all arms-bearing citizens, the king turned for advice to a council of nobles called the Senate. Each senator had lifelong tenure, and the members of this group and their families constituted the patrician class. The other class of Romans, the plebeians, were mostly small farmers and artisans, who, except at the infrequent assemblies, exercised little influence in government at this time.

THE EARLY REPUBLIC, 509-133 B.C.: DOMESTIC AFFAIRS

Establishment of the republic. In 509 B.C., according to tradition, the patricians expelled the last Etruscan king, claiming that he had acted despotically, and established what they called a republic (from *res publica,* literally "public affairs"), in which they held the reins of power. The *imperium* was now transferred to two new officials, called consuls. Elected annually from the patrician class, the consuls invariably exercised their power in its interest. When the consular offices were first established, their powers were very broad: the consuls commanded the army and acted as high priests and supreme magistrates in Rome. In the event of war or serious domestic emergency, a dictator could be substituted for the two consuls, but he was given absolute power for six months only.

Demand for political equality. For two centuries following the establishment of the republic, the plebeians struggled for political and social equality. Although violence often accompanied their bitter conflict with the patricians, outright civil war was averted by the willingness, however reluctant and delayed, of the patricians to compromise. This largely explains why it was unnecessary for the plebeians to have recourse to tyrants to assist them in gaining their goals, as had happened in the Greek city-states. Much of the success of the plebeians in this struggle was due also to their tactics of collective action and to their having

organized a corporate group within the state. This unofficial body, a sort of state within a state, was known as the *Concilium Plebis* and was presided over by ten plebeian officials called tribunes. (The persons of the tribunes were considered sacrosanct—whoever injured one of them could be put to death. They had the job of safeguarding the interests of the plebeians and of negotiating with the consuls.) Finally, the wars of conquest in which Rome presently found itself engaged gave the plebeians, indispensable in filling the ranks of the Roman army, greater bargaining power.

The advancement of the plebeians during the early republic took two main lines: the safeguarding of their fundamental rights and the progressive enlargement of their share of political power. Feeling that the laws of Rome were often interpreted to suit patrician interests, the plebeians demanded that the laws be written down and made available for all to see. As a result, about 450 B.C. the laws were written on twelve tablets of bronze and set up publicly in the Forum. The Law of the Twelve Tables was the first landmark in the long history of Roman law, and Cicero tells us that their memorization was required of Roman school children.

The plebeians in time acquired other fundamental rights and safeguards: they secured the right to appeal a death sentence imposed by a consul and to be retried before the popular assembly; the tribunes gained a veto power over any legislation or executive act that threatened the rights of the plebeians; and marriage between patricians and plebeians, prohibited by the Law of the Twelve Tables, was legalized. Important also was the abolition of the enslavement of citizens for debt, which had been permitted by the Law of the Twelve Tables (with the stipulation, however, that a debt-slave could not be bound with weights of more than fifteen pounds).

Little by little the plebeian class acquired more power in the functioning of the government. In 367 B.C. one consulship was reserved for the plebeians, and before the end of the century plebeians were eligible to hold other important magistracies which the patricians had in the meantime created.

Among these magistracies, whose powers originally had been held by the consuls, were the praetor (in charge of the law courts), quaestor (treasurer), and censor (supervisor of public morals and the letting of state contracts). The right to hold high political offices proved to be a stepping stone to the Senate, and some plebeians succeeded in gaining entry to that august body.

The long struggle for equality ended in 287 B.C. when the *Concilium Plebis* was recognized as a constitutional body, henceforth known as the Tribal Assembly, with the right to pass laws that were binding on all citizens, patricians as well as plebeians. The plebeians demanded this right because of the undemocratic organization and procedure of the older popular assemblies, which the patricians had been able to control. The Roman republic was now technically a democracy, although in actual practice the senatorial aristocracy of patricians and rich plebeians continued to control the state. Having gained political and social equality, the plebeians were willing to allow the more experienced Senate to run the government during the remainder of this period of almost constant warfare down to 133 B.C.

After 287 B.C. conflict in Roman society gradually assumed a new form. Heretofore, the issue had been primarily social and political between hereditary classes, as the plebeians sought to gain equality with the patricians. When this goal was achieved, many plebeians were able to profit from new opportunities and to amass prestige and wealth in the state's expanding economy. As a result, wealth instead of aristocratic descent was most important, and the old distinction between patrician and plebeian became much less fundamental than the new conflict between the wealthy minority and the underprivileged—including the landless and dispossessed in the countryside and a growing proletariat in the cities.

The Roman citizen. The fundamental unit of early Roman society was the family, where the father's power was absolute, and strict discipline was imposed to instill in children those virtues to which the Romans attached particular importance—loyalty, courage, self-control, and respect for laws and ancestral customs. The father taught his sons at home what we would call the "three R's." Although young Romans in this period were not exposed to the intellectual stimulation that Greek youths enjoyed, the strong influence of home and family life undoubtedly provided the early Romans with a stability which the brilliant but erratic Greeks sometimes lacked.

The strength and simplicity of the Romans in the days of the republic have perhaps been overromanticized, but it is generally accepted that they were stern, hard-working, and practical. Man's relationship to the universe and the possibilities of immortal life did not concern them unduly. Religious practices were confined to placating supernatural powers and enlisting divine support for the family and the state. The most important gods were Jupiter, who controlled the universe; Mars, the god of war; Janus, the guardian of the gateway to Rome; Juno, the patron saint of women; and Minerva, the goddess of war, skill, and wisdom. But these official state deities were of less importance to the Roman than the spirits of his household.

THE EARLY REPUBLIC, 509-133 B.C.: FOREIGN AFFAIRS

Roman conquest of Italy. The growth of Rome from a small city-state to the dominant power in the Mediterranean world in less than four hundred years (509-133 B.C.) is a remarkable story. By 270 B.C. Rome had conquered both the Etruscans in the north and the Greeks in the south of Italy and was master of all the peninsula south of the Po valley.

Rome's position was favored by geography. While the Italian peninsula has a great mountainous backbone, the Apennines, running down most of its length, the country is not so rugged as in Greece. Consequently the mountains did not constitute a barrier to political unification. Also, the Alps in the north kept all but the most intrepid barbarian tribes from entering the Italian peninsula. In addition, the Latins occupied a central position on the peninsula.

Thus Rome was marked out by Nature to be the capital of a unified Italy, just as Italy, by virtue of its large manpower and relatively central situation within the Mediterranean lands, was the natural seat of a Mediterranean empire. Rome's lordship over the ancient Mediterranean world was in accordance with the basic facts of Mediterranean geography.[1]

In 493 B.C. Rome and the Latin League, composed of Latin peoples in the vicinity of Rome, entered into a defensive league against the Etruscans. This new combination was so successful that by the beginning of the fourth century B.C. it had become the chief power in central Italy. But the members of the Latin League grew alarmed at Rome's increasing strength, and war broke out between the former allies. With the victory of Rome in 338 B.C., the League was dissolved, and the Latin cities were forced to sign individual treaties with Rome. Thus the same year which saw the rise of Macedonia over Greece (see p. 107) also saw the rise of a new power in Italy.

Border clashes with aggressive highland Samnite tribes led to three fiercely fought Samnite wars and the extension of Rome's frontiers southward to the Greek colonies in Great Greece. Fearing Roman conquest, the Greeks prepared for war and called in the Hellenistic Greek king, Pyrrhus of Epirus, who dreamed of becoming a second Alexander the Great. With 20,000 infantry, 3000 cavalry, and a force of Indian elephants, Pyrrhus defeated the Romans in two encounters but at so heavy a cost that such a triumph is still called a "Pyrrhic victory."

During an interlude in this struggle a Roman ambassador met with Pyrrhus to negotiate the release of Roman prisoners. The Greek biographer Plutarch described the scene in a way which points up the gulf that then existed between the stern, unaffected Romans and the sophisticated Greeks. Pyrrhus first sought to bribe the Roman, whose name was Fabricius, and then to upset him by secreting an elephant which suddenly thrust its trunk through some hang-

ings and emitted "a horrid and ugly noise." Whereupon, according to Plutarch,

Fabricius calmly turned and said with a smile to Pyrrhus: "Your gold made no impression on me yesterday, neither does your beast to-day." Again, at supper, where all sorts of topics were discussed, and particularly that of Greece and her philosophers, Cineas [an Epicurean philosopher and close friend of Pyrrhus] happened somehow to mention Epicurus, and set forth the doctrines of that school concerning the gods, civil government, and the highest good, explaining that they made pleasure the highest good, but would have nothing to do with civil government on the ground that it was injurious and the ruin of felicity, and that they removed the Deity as far as possible from feelings of kindness or anger or concern for us, into a life that knew no care and was filled with ease and comfort. But before Cineas was done, Fabricius cried out and said: "O Hercules, may Pyrrhus and the [Greeks] cherish these doctrines, as long as they are at war with us."[2]

When a third battle failed to induce the Romans to make peace, Pyrrhus is reported to have remarked, "We are waging a war against a hydra," and returned to his homeland. The Roman army then moved into southern Italy and conquered all the Greek cities there. By 270 B.C. Rome had mastered all Italy south of the Rubicon, a river in the Po valley of northeastern Italy.

Roman expansion had not been deliberately planned; rather, it was the result of dealing with successive crises, caused by unsettled conditions in Italy, which the Romans considered to be threats to their security. Although exaggerated, the Roman claim that their wars were always defensive contains at least a kernel of truth.

The Roman legions. The efficiency of the Roman military forces was a significant factor in the conquest of the peninsula. The basic military unit, the legion, was composed of 3000 heavily armed men, supplemented by a group of 1200 light-armed soldiers and a cavalry squadron of 300. In contrast to the gradual crushing power of the Greek and Macedonian phalanx, the Roman legion was like a pack of lions, incredibly swift and mobile. To achieve maximum maneuverability, a legion was divided into companies of

Rhine R.

Rhone

Drava

Sava

Danube R.

R.

VENETIA

TRANSPADANE GAUL

LIGURIA

CISPADANE GAUL

Po R.

Parma

Genoa

A P E N N I N E

Pisa

Arno

Florentia

Rubicon R.

U M B R I A

M O U N T A I N S

A L P S

A D R I A T I C

S E A

E T R U R I A

Spoletium

Tiber R.

Rome

Ostia

L A T I U M

S A M N I U M

CAMPANIA

A P U L I A

MT. VESUVIUS

Pompeii

Brundisium

Tarentum

C O R S I C A

S A R D I N I A

T Y R R H E N I A N   S E A

L U C A N I A

B R U T T I U M

Messina

M E D I T E R R A N E A N

MT. ETNA

S I C I L Y

S E A

Syracuse

Carthage

A F R I C A

ROMAN ITALY BEFORE AUGUSTUS

0   50   100

120 men, each company capable of rapid and independent action. The sturdy peasants who made up the bulk of the legions were superb soldiers.

Treatment of conquered peoples. Instead of slaughtering or enslaving their defeated foes, the Romans usually treated them justly, in time creating a strong loyalty to Rome throughout the peninsula. Each defeated state was required to sign a treaty of alliance with Rome which bound it to adhere to Rome's foreign policy and to supply troops for the Roman army. No tribute was required, and each state retained local self-government. Rome did, however, annex about one third of the conquered lands, on parts of which Roman colonies were established.

Roman citizenship was a prized possession and was granted sparingly. In fact, where citizenship was granted, it was not always full citizenship; those people with partial citizenship had the property and marriage rights of citizens but could not vote or hold office in Rome.

In time, the term *Italia* came to be applied to the whole peninsula, indicating its military unity under the protection of Rome and anticipating the growth of national unity. Actual political and cultural unity, however, was still a long way off; the language and customs of Rome were not widely adopted in other parts of Italy for another two centuries.

The First Punic War. With the elimination in the third century B.C. of the Greek cities of Italy as a threat to Roman supremacy in the West, only Carthage remained as Rome's rival. Much more wealthy and populous than Rome, with a magnificent navy that controlled the western Mediterranean and with a domain that included the northern coast of Africa, Sardinia, western Sicily, and parts of Spain and Corsica, Carthage seemed more than a match for Rome. But Carthage was governed by a commercial aristocracy which hired mercenaries to do the fighting. In the long run, the lack of a loyal body of free citizens and allies, such as Rome had for its army, proved to be Carthage's fatal weakness.

The First Punic War (from *punicus*, Latin for "Phoenician") broke out in 264 B.C. when Rome sought to oust a Carthaginian force that had occupied Messina on the northeastern tip of Sicily just across from Roman Italy. According to Polybius (a Hellenistic Greek historian who is discussed in the Historical Critique on p. 160), the Romans "felt it was absolutely necessary not to let Messina fall, or allow the Carthaginians to secure what would be like a bridge to enable them to cross into Italy."[3] This conflict cost the Romans 200,000 men in disastrous naval engagements. Although they were not a seafaring people like the Carthaginians, the Romans nevertheless persisted in the conflict, raised money for new ships, trained their crews on land, and finally defeated their foes. In 241 B.C. the Carthaginians sued for peace, and Rome annexed Sicily and Sardinia-Corsica as the first two provinces of an overseas empire, governed and taxed (in contrast to Rome's Italian allies) by Roman officials.

The contest with Hannibal. Thwarted by this defeat, Carthage concentrated upon enlarging its empire in Spain. But the Romans were determined to restrict the Carthaginian sphere of influence. While both powers jockeyed for position, a young Carthaginian general, Hannibal, precipitated the Second Punic War by attacking a Spanish town allied to Rome. Then, seizing the initiative again, Hannibal in 218 B.C. led an army of about 40,000 men, 9000 cavalry troops, and a detachment of African elephants across the Alps into Italy. Although the crossing had cost him nearly half of his men and almost all of his elephants, Hannibal defeated the Romans three times within three years.

Hannibal's forces never matched those of the Romans in numbers. At Cannae, for example, where Hannibal won his greatest victory, some 70,000 Romans were wiped out by barely 50,000 Carthaginians. From time to time Hannibal obtained additional recruits from Spain and from among the wild Celtic tribes of Gaul, but the reinforcements were untrained and totaled no more than 10,000 men. On the whole Rome's allies remained loyal—a testimony to the generous and statesmanlike character of Rome's treatment of her Italian subjects—and because the Romans controlled the seas, Hannibal received little aid from Carthage. Thus, although never decisively defeated in Italy, Hannibal was unable to inflict a mortal blow against the Romans. The Second Punic War has been described as a "colossal contest between the nation Rome and the man Hannibal."[4]

Like Alexander the Great, Hannibal was a military genius and an inspiring leader who maintained the high morale of his army through many ordeals. He was never too tired to mingle with his men after a bloody battle or to cheer the wounded and disconsolate. In the words of the Roman historian Livy:

> . . . [Hannibal] was fearless in undertaking dangerous enterprises, he was prudent in discharging them. Toil could not weary his body or subdue his spirit. Heat and cold he endured alike. He ate and drank to satisfy nature, not pleasure. Hours for sleeping and waking were not determined by the clock; whatever time was left after work was done he devoted to sleep. Nor was sleep wooed by soft couches and stillness; often he could be seen lying on the ground among the sentries and pickets, covered with a soldier's cape . . . he was the first to engage in a battle, the last to leave the engagement.[5]

The Romans finally found a general, Scipio, who was Hannibal's match in military strategy and who was bold enough to invade Africa. Forced to return home after fifteen years spent on Italian soil, Hannibal clashed with Scipio's legions at Zama, where the Carthaginians suffered a complete defeat (see map, p. 137). The power of Carthage was broken forever by a harsh treaty imposed in 201 B.C. Carthage was forced to pay a huge indemnity, disarm its forces, and turn Spain over to the Romans. Hannibal sought asylum in the kingdom of the Seleucids where he stirred up anti-Roman sentiment. He committed suicide in 182 B.C. to prevent capture by the Romans, and his last words were reputed to have been: "Let us relieve the Romans of their anxiety; they are too impatient to wait for an old man to die."[6]

Roman intervention in the East. The defeat of Carthage left Rome free to turn eastward and settle a score with Philip v of Macedonia who, fearing Roman expansion, had allied himself with Hannibal during the darkest days of the war. Now, in 200 B.C., Rome was ready to act, following an appeal for aid in protecting the smaller Hellenistic states from Philip, who was advancing in the Aegean, and the Seleucid emperor, who was moving into Asia Minor. The heavy Macedonian phalanxes were no match for the mobile Roman legions, and in 197 B.C. Philip was soundly defeated and his dreams of empire were ended when Rome deprived him of his warships and military bases in Greece. The Romans then proclaimed the independence of Greece and were eulogized by the grateful Greeks:

> There was one people in the world which would fight for others' liberties at its own cost, to its own peril, and with its own toil, not limiting its guaranties of freedom to its neighbours, to men of the immediate vicinity, or to countries that lay close at hand, but ready to cross the sea that there might be no unjust empire anywhere and that everywhere justice, right, and law might prevail.[7]

A few years later Rome declared war on the Seleucid emperor who had moved from Asia Minor into Greece. The Romans forced him to vacate Greece and Asia Minor, pay a huge indemnity, and give up his warships and war elephants. The Seleucids were checked again in 168 B.C. when a Roman ultimatum halted their invasion of Egypt, which became a Roman protectorate, and a year later Rome supported the Jews in their successful revolt against the Seleucids (see p. 197).

Most of the East was now a Roman protectorate, the result of a policy in which Roman self-interest was mingled with idealism. But the behavior of the Greeks soon soured the Romans and turned their idealism into harsh realism. Anti-Romanism became widespread in Greece, particularly among the radical masses who resented Rome's support of conservative governments and the status quo in general. (A Roman army, for example, was used to crush a revolution in Sparta.) The new policy was revealed in 146 B.C. when, after many Greeks had supported an attempted Macedonian revival, Rome destroyed Corinth as an object lesson, set up oligarchic governments in all Greek states, and placed Greece under the watchful eye of the governor of Macedonia, which was made a Roman province.

Destruction of Carthage. In the West, Rome's hardening policy led to suspicion of Carthage's reviving prosperity and to a demand by extremists for war—*Carthago delenda est* ("Carthage must be destroyed"). Treacherously provoking the Third Punic War, the Romans besieged Carthage, which resisted heroically for three years, destroyed the city in 146 B.C.—the same year of Corinth's destruction—and annexed the territory as a province.

Rome, supreme in the ancient world. In 133 B.C. the king of Pergamum, dying without heir, bequeathed his kingdom to Rome. Apparently he feared that the discontented masses would revolt after his death unless Rome, with its reputation for maintaining law and order in the interest of the propertied classes, took over. Rome accepted the bequest and then spent the next three years suppressing a proletarian revolution in its first province in Asia.

With provinces on three continents—Europe, Africa, and Asia (see map, p. 137)—the once obscure Roman republic was now supreme in the ancient world. But the next century, during which Rome's frontiers reached the Euphrates and the Rhine, would witness the failure of the republic to solve the problems that were the by-products of empire.

THE LATE REPUBLIC, 133-30 B.C.

Economic and social conditions in the republic. The political history of Rome thus far consists of two dominant themes: the gradual liberalization of the government and the expansion of the Roman dominion over the Mediterranean world. Now let us examine some of the most important social and economic problems which Rome faced by roughly the midpoint of the second century B.C. The historian Appian described the times thus:

. . . the powerful ones became enormously rich and the race of slaves multiplied throughout the country, while the Italian people dwindled in numbers and strength, being oppressed by penury, taxes, and military service.[8]

One of the most pressing problems facing the state was the growing tendency of the wealthy to control the land at the expense of the small farmers. Improved farming methods learned from Greeks and Carthaginians encouraged rich aristocrats to buy up tracts of land and introduce large-scale farming. This trend was especially profitable because thousands of slaves from the conquered areas were available to work on the estates. The large slave plantations, called *latifundia,* had become common in Italy by about 200 B.C., while small farms were the exception.

When Sicily was conquered, its inhabitants were required to pay an annual tax of one tenth of their wheat crop. Cheap grain was also imported into Italy from Africa. Finding it impossible to compete with imported produce and large-scale farming methods, the small farmers flocked to Rome and created a city mob of unemployed malcontents. The disappearance of the small landowner was one of the basic causes of the degeneration of the Roman republic.

The land problem was further complicated by the government's earlier practice of leasing part of the territory acquired in the conquest of the Italian peninsula (known as public land) to anyone willing to pay a percentage of the crop or animals raised on it. Only the wealthy plebeians or patricians could afford to lease large tracts of land, and in time they treated it as if it were their own property. In the fourth century B.C. plebeian protests had led to an attempt to limit the holdings of a single individual to 320 acres of public land, but the law devised for that purpose was never enforced. The illegal disposition of the public lands remained a blot upon the record of the republic.

Corruption in the government was another mark of the growing degeneracy of the Roman republic. Provincial officials seized opportunities for lucrative graft, and a new class of Roman businessmen scrambled selfishly for the profitable war contracts which supplied the army with wheat, meat, clothing, and weapons. The opulent living of the wealthy hastened the decay of the old Roman traits of discipline, simplicity, and respect for authority.

The government and many of the people suffered as a result of these economic and social conditions. The political gains of the plebeians, achieved only after a long struggle, were nullified by the many wars of conquest. During the war against Hannibal the people had allowed the Senate to run the state. Although in theory the government remained a democracy, in practice it was now an oligarchy. The tribunes, guardians of the people's rights, became mere yes-men of the Senate.

Thus by the middle of the second century B.C., the government was in the hands of the wealthy, self-seeking Senate, which was unable to cope with the problems of governing a world-state. Ordinary citizens were for the most part impoverished and landless; and Rome swarmed with fortune hunters, imported slaves, unemployed farmers, and discontented war veterans.

The next century (133-30 B.C.) saw Rome convulsed by civil war, even while engaged in occasional foreign wars. The Senate was noticeably inefficient in carrying on foreign conflicts, but its most serious weakness was its inability to solve the economic and social problems following in the wake of Rome's conquests. This led to the establishment of a dictatorship and the end of the republic.

Reform movements of the Gracchi. While a majority of the senators opposed any basic reforms, some citizens demanded drastic action, especially in regard to the land problem. Such a reformer was Tiberius Gracchus, who was elected tribune in 133 B.C. at the age of twenty-nine. A scion of one of Rome's finest families, he was also a grandson of the Scipio who had defeated Hannibal. His reforming zeal was the product of the liberal learning of Greece, newly imported and popular among the younger Roman aristocrats, and an awareness that the old Roman character and way of life was fast slipping away. He sought to arrest Roman decline by restoring the backbone of the old Roman society—the peasant landowner.

Tiberius proposed to the Tribal Assembly that the act limiting the holding of public land to 320 acres per person be reënacted. Much of the public land would in the future be held by the present occupants and their descendants as private property, but the surplus was to be confiscated and allotted to landless Roman citizens. "The wild beasts that roam over Italy," Tiberius noted in his address to the assembly,

have every one of them a cave or lair to lurk in; but the men who fight and die for Italy enjoy the common air and light, indeed, but nothing else; houseless and homeless they wander about with their wives and children. And it is with lying lips that their commanders exhort the soldiers in their battles to defend sepulchres and shrines from the enemy; . . . they fight and die to support others in wealth and luxury, and though they are styled masters of the world, they have not a single clod of earth that is their own.[9]

Although the Tribal Assembly adopted Tiberius' proposal by a wide majority, the Senate induced one of the other tribunes to veto the measure. On the ground that a tribune who opposed the will of the people thereby forfeited his office, Tiberius took a fateful—and, the patricians claimed, unconstitutional—step by having the assembly depose the tribune in question. The agrarian bill was then passed.

To ensure the implementation of his agrarian reform, Tiberius again violated custom by standing for reëlection after completing his one-year term. During the election, however, partisans of the Senate murdered Tiberius and three hundred of his followers and threw their bodies into the Tiber. The republic's failure at this point to solve its problems without bloodshed stands in striking contrast to its previous development by peaceful means.

Tiberius' work was taken up by his younger brother, Gaius Gracchus, who was elected tribune in 124 B.C. Gaius' program included an extension of the policy of reallocating public land. He also wanted to establish colonies in southern Italy and northern Africa as outlets for Rome's surplus population and to extend the Roman franchise to the Latin cities and to the Italian allies. To protect the poor against speculation in the grain market (especially in times of famine), Gaius committed the government to the purchase and storage of wheat and to its subsequent distribution to the urban masses at about half the former market price. Unfortunately, what was intended as a relief measure later became a dole, whereby free food was distributed—all too often for the advancement of astute politicians—to the entire proletariat.

In order to carry out his program, Gaius, like Tiberius, had revived the power of the Tribal Assembly at the expense of the hitherto dominant Senate. The senators' hired thugs again retaliated. In 121 B.C. three thousand of Gaius' followers were killed and Gaius committed suicide.

The Gracchi were inspired by idealistic motives, but it is doubtful whether their policies, even if fully implemented, could have solved Rome's dilemma. Rome had now developed into a world-wide power, and either a high caliber of statesmanship

or new forms of government were required to cope with its far-flung political commitments and the drastic changes that had taken place in its economy and society. The Senate had shown that it had no intention of initiating needed domestic reforms, or of allowing others to do so, and the Gracchi's deaths were ominous portents of the manner in which the Romans were to decide their internal disputes. In foreign affairs, also, the Senate was soon to demonstrate its incapability.

Civil war—first stage: Marius and Sulla. Between 111 and 105 B.C. Roman armies, despatched by the Senate and commanded by senators, failed to protect Roman capitalists in North Africa and to prevent Germanic and Celtic tribes from overrunning southern Gaul, now a Roman province, and threatening Italy itself. Accusing the Senate of lethargy and incompetence in directing Rome's foreign affairs, the people elected Gaius Marius (155-86 B.C.) to the consulship in 107 B.C., and the Tribal Assembly commissioned him to raise an army and deal with the foreign danger. Marius first pacified North Africa and then crushed the northern invaders. In the process he created a new-style Roman army that was destined to play a major role in the turbulent history of the late republic.

In contrast to the old Roman army, which was composed of conscripts who owned their own land and who thought of themselves as loyal citizens of the republic, the new army created by Marius was recruited from landless citizens for long terms of service. These professional soldiers identified their own interests with those of their commanders, to whom they looked for bonuses of land or money, and were ready to follow them in any undertaking. Thus the character of the army changed from a militia to a career service in which loyalty to the state was no longer paramount. Marius was loyal to the republic, but later generals were to use their military power to overthrow the government.

In 88 B.C. the ambitious king of Pontus in Asia Minor, encouraged by the growing anti-Roman sentiment in Greece and Asia Minor, declared war on Rome. This declaration of war raised the question of the choice of a general to oppose him. It was customary to select one of the consuls then in office, and the Senate ordered Cornelius Sulla (138-78 B.C.), an able general and a staunch supporter of the Senate's prerogatives, to go east. However, those who opposed the Senate contended that important decisions in foreign affairs rested with the Tribal Assembly. As a countermove, this group chose Marius for the eastern command.

Thus the rivalry between Sulla and Marius exposed a fundamental weakness in the existing governmental machinery. In effect both the Senate and the Tribal Assembly claimed to be the ultimate authority in the state. The result of this conflict was disastrous: civil war broke out between the rival generals, each of whom in turn captured Rome, and thousands of people on either side were slain in the attending reigns of terror. The first stage of civil war ended in a complete victory for Sulla, who in 82 B.C. had himself appointed dictator for an unlimited period with power to "issue edicts and reorganize the republic."

Sulla could have abolished the republic had he so desired. Instead he set out to restore the preëminence of the Senate in order to protect the state from demagogues, ambitious generals, and civil disturbances. To this end, he increased the powers of the Senate and drastically curtailed those of the tribunes and the Tribal Assembly. A measure was enacted stating that no proposal could be brought before the Tribal Assembly without the consent of the Senate. This gave the Senate the complete power over legislation which it had enjoyed two hundred years before. With the conviction that his work would be permanent, Sulla voluntarily resigned his dictatorship in 79 B.C.; he died in the following year. Sulla was hardly in his grave before the government he had established began to totter. Sulla's changes, which had set the clock back two centuries, were not to last.

Civil war—second stage: Pompey and Caesar. The years of civil war had increased factionalism and discontent and had nursed the ambitions of individuals eager for personal power. Even with its increased powers, the Senate proved unable to cope with the foreign entanglements and domestic disturbances facing the state, and the people looked for new strong men to lead them. The first to come forward was Pompey (106-48 B.C.), who had won fame as a military leader. In 70 B.C. Pompey was elected a consul, and, though he was a former partisan of Sulla, courted the populace by repealing Sulla's laws against the tribunes and the Tribal Assembly. Pompey then put an end to anarchy in the East caused by piracy, the protracted ambitions of the king of Pontus, and the death throes of the Seleucid empire. New Roman provinces and client states brought order eastward to the Euphrates and southward through Palestine.

Still another strong man made his appearance in 59 B.C., when Julius Caesar (102?-44 B.C.) allied himself politically with Pompey and was elected consul. Caesar conquered Gaul, extended Roman frontiers to the Rhine, and even crossed the English Channel into Britain, though the Roman conquest of Britain was not effected until one hundred years later. When absent from Rome, Caesar cannily kept his name before the citizens by reporting his experiences in the lucidly written account of his military conquests, *Commentaries on the Gallic War.*

Caesar's conquest of Gaul was to have tremendous consequences for the course of western civilization, for its inhabitants quickly assimilated Roman culture. Consequently, when the Roman empire collapsed in the West in the fifth century A.D., Romanized Gaul—or France—emerged before long as the center of medieval civilization.

Jealous of Caesar's achievements in Gaul and fearful of his ultimate aims, Pompey conspired with the Senate to ruin him. When the Senate demanded in 49 B.C. that Caesar disband his army, he crossed the Rubicon—the river which formed the boundary between Italy and Cisalpine Gaul, therefore marking the limit of Caesar's province. By crossing the Rubicon—a phrase which we employ today for any step which commits a person to a given course of action—Caesar in effect declared war on Pompey and the Senate. He marched with his forces to Rome, and within a short time the senatorial opposition had been crushed, Pompey was dead, and Caesar was absolute master of Rome.

Caesar assumed the office of dictator "for the administration of public affairs," and during his brief rule (46-44 B.C.) he initiated far-reaching reforms. He packed the Senate with many new provincial members, thus making it a more truly representative body as well as a rubber stamp for his policies. He provided a model system of local self-government for the municipalities of Italy and reformed the administration of the provinces. In the interest of the poorer citizens, he reduced debts, inaugurated a public works program, established colonies outside Italy, and decreed that one third of the laborers on the slave-worked estates in Italy be persons of free birth. As a result, he was able to reduce greatly the number of people receiving free grain. One of his most enduring acts was the reform of the calendar in the light of Egyptian knowledge; with minor changes, this calendar of 365¼ days is still in use today.

In the early first century B.C. Roman citizenship had been extended to Rome's Italian allies after the Senate's failure to deal with their grievances had goaded them into revolt (99-88 B.C.). One of Caesar's most constructive acts of statesmanship was the extension of Roman citizenship to Cisalpine Gaul and to many provincials outside Italy, "the starting-point of a process that transformed the Roman Empire from a military dominion into a commonwealth of equal partners."[10]

Caesar was one of the few leaders of his day who realized that the old republic was, in fact, dead. In his own words, "The republic is merely a name, without form or substance." He believed that benevolent despotism alone could save Rome from continued civil war and the collapse of the state. But Caesar incurred the enmity of two very different groups of people: those who sought wealth for their own ends at the expense of the state and those who still believed that the republic should be retained and who saw Caesar only as a dangerous tyrant. On the Ides (the fifteenth) of March, 44 B.C., a group of conspirators stabbed Caesar to death in the Senate, and Rome was once more plunged into conflict.

Caesar's assassins had been offended by his trappings of monarchy—his purple robe, the statues erected in his honor, and the coins bearing his portrait—and they assumed that with his death the republic would be restored to its traditional status. But the people of Rome remained unmoved by the conspirators' cry of "Liberty! Freedom! Tyranny is dead!" The majority of them were prepared to accept a successor to Caesar in power and in a position that stopped just short of a royal title. The real question was: Who was to be Caesar's successor?

Civil war—third stage: Antony and Octavian. Following Caesar's death, his eighteen-year-old heir, Octavian (63 B.C.-14 A.D.), allied himself with Caesar's chief lieutenant, Mark Antony, against the conspirators and the Senate. Although he was not a conspirator, Cicero, the renowned orator and champion of the Senate, was put to death, and the conspirators' armies were routed. Then for more than a decade Octavian and Antony exercised complete autocracy, thanks to their control over the armed forces.

But the ambitions of each man proved too great for the alliance to endure. Antony, who took charge of the eastern half of the empire, became infatuated with Cleopatra, the last of the Egyptian Ptolemies. He even went so far as to transfer Roman territories to her dominions. Octavian took advantage of this high-handedness to arouse Rome and Italy against him. When Octavian's fleet met Antony's at Actium in Greece, first Cleopatra and then Antony deserted the battle and fled to Egypt. There Antony committed suicide, as did Cleopatra soon afterwards when Alexandria was captured in 30 B.C. At the end of a century of civil violence Rome was at last united under one ruler, and the republic gave way to the empire. Two centuries of imperial greatness followed: this period, known as the *Pax Romana* (the Roman peace), lasted approximately two centuries, until 180 A.D.

THE PAX ROMANA: 30 B.C. TO 180 A.D.

Augustus initiates the Pax Romana. Following his triumphal return to Rome in 29 B.C., Octavian announced that he would "restore the republic." But he neither took this step nor established an outright monarchy. Instead he provided the Senate with considerable authority, consulted it on important issues, allowed it to retain control over about half of the provinces, and gave it the legislative functions of the nearly defunct Tribal Assembly. The Senate in return bestowed upon Octavian the title *Augustus* ("The Revered," a title previously used for gods), by which he was known thereafter.

After 23 B.C. Augustus held the consulship only twice, and then for only a short part of the year. Where, then, did his strength lie? Throughout his career he kept the power of a tribune (which gave him control of legislation) and the power over the frontier provinces where the imperial armies were stationed. The chief source of Augustus'

strength lay in the fact that the army, whose soldiers paid allegiance to him personally, was under his direction. As supreme leader of the army he held the title *imperator*, from which the modern term *emperor* is derived. Thus Augustus effected a compromise "between the need for a monarchical head of the empire and the sentiment which enshrined Rome's republican constitution in the minds of his contemporaries."[11] He summed up his position as that of *princeps*, or first among equals, and his form of government is therefore known as the principate. At the beginning of the empire, then, political power was divided between the Senate and the *princeps* (Augustus). For over two hundred years (the period known as the *Pax Romana*) this form of government endured, although the Senate slowly faded into the background. After 235 A.D. (as we shall see in Chapter 7) the *Pax Romana* was followed by fifty years of military anarchy, at the end of which the Senate had lost any appearance of being an effective arm of the government and there emerged an absolute monarchy which had no constitutional basis but was backed by the power of the legions.

At the outset of his reign as *princeps*, Augustus faced the problems of curing a sick society and removing the scars resulting from a century of civil strife. The aristocracy was too decadent to be patriotic, and the common people had lost confidence in their government and in the destiny of the state. In the cities an unemployed mob favored with free bread and circuses had long since lost interest in hard work. Some of the provinces had been depopulated by the ravages of war, and on the frontiers large armies of professional soldiers toyed with the idea of setting their own leaders on the imperial throne.

Wisely, Augustus concentrated on internal problems. Although he extended Roman control as far as the Danube as a defense against barbarian invasions and also made a vain attempt to penetrate beyond the Rhine, expansion of the empire was not one of his major concerns. His thorough reconstruction of the whole imperial administration laid the foundation for two centuries of prosperity and good government. By means of legislation and propaganda, Augustus also sought with some success to check moral and social decline and to revive the old Roman ideals and traditions.

The Julio-Claudian and the Flavian emperors. Augustus was followed by four descendants of his family, the line of the Julio-Claudians, who ruled from 14 to 68 A.D. Tiberius, Augustus' stepson whom the Senate accepted as his successor, and Claudius were fairly efficient and devoted rulers. In Claudius' reign the Roman occupation of Britain began in 43 A.D. with an invasion which crushed the resistance of the Celtic inhabitants. The other two rulers of this imperial line were of a different stripe: Caligula was a madman, who on one occasion made his favorite horse a consul; Nero was infamous for his immorality, the murder of his wife and his mother, and his persecution of Christians in Rome.

During Nero's reign, in 64 A.D., a great fire devastated the capital. The Roman historian Tacitus has left us a vivid description of this catastrophe:

Whether the disaster was accidental or the wicked doing of the emperor is uncertain . . . but the fire was the most violent and destructive that had ever befallen the city. It began in the part of the circus adjacent to the Palatine and Caelian hills. It started in shops stacked with combustibles, was sped by the wind, and at once seized the whole length of the circus. There was no masonry of houses or walls of temples to retard it. First the blaze ran through the level areas, then rose to the hills and devastated the hollows. Its velocity outstripped preventive measures, for old Rome with its winding streets and irregular plan was vulnerable. Aggravating the evil were terrified and shrieking women, the feeble old and inexperienced young, people saving themselves or others, dragging the infirm or waiting for them, hurrying or delaying.[12]

We are again indebted to Tacitus for his account of how Nero made the Christians in the capital the scapegoats for the great fire:

Mockery was added to . . . [the Christians'] deaths. They were covered with animal skins and torn to pieces by dogs, many were crucified or burned, and some were set afire at nightfall to serve for illumination. For the spectacle Nero offered his gardens, and he presented horse

The Gemma Augustea, showing Augustus as the father of an imperial line, celebrates some of the great events of Augustus' reign. Holding the imperial staff, Augustus and Roma rest their feet on the weapons of conquered peoples. The emperor is receiving a laurel crown, the symbol of civilization. Tiberius, Augustus' successor, steps from a chariot at the left, while Caligula appears as a small child, at the right. Victorious Roman soldiers occupy the lower panel.

races in addition. In the dress of a charioteer he himself mingled with the crowd or stood up in his sulky. Hence . . . [the victims] aroused compassion, for it was not for the public good but for one man's savagery that they were being destroyed.[13]

The Julio-Claudian line ended in 68 A.D. when Nero, faced by army revolts, committed suicide. In the following year four emperors were proclaimed by rival armies, with Vespasian the final victor. For nearly thirty years (69-96 A.D.) the Flavian dynasty (Vespasian followed by his two sons) provided the empire with effective, if autocratic, rule. The fiction of republican institutions gave way to a scarcely veiled monarchy as the Flavians openly treated the office of emperor as theirs by right of conquest and inheritance.

The Antonines: "five good emperors." An end to autocracy and a return to the Augustan principle of an administration of equals—emperor and Senate—characterized the rule of the Antonine emperors (96-180 A.D.), under whom the Roman empire reached the height of its prosperity and power. Selected on the basis of proven ability, these "good emperors" succeeded, according to the Roman historian Tacitus, in "reconciling things long incompatible, supreme power and liberty." Two of these emperors are especially worthy of notice.

Hadrian reigned from 117 to 138 A.D. His first important act was to stabilize the boundaries of the empire, as Augustus had done before him. In order to avoid foreign wars and be free to concentrate on domestic affairs, Hadrian gave such recently conquered territories as Mesopotamia and Assyria back to the Parthian kingdom (see p. 165). In Germany he erected protective walls, and in Britain he raised Hadrian's Wall, a structure running across a narrow part of the island to protect the northern frontier.

Hadrian traveled extensively throughout the empire and devoted his talents to its interests. New towns were founded, old ones restored, and many public works were constructed. To correct the unequal distribution of governmental powers between Italy and the provinces, he saw to it that provincial governors were strictly supervised, special officials appointed to control finances, and the postal service throughout the empire placed under the control of the state. Hadrian's other reforms included humane regulations for the treatment of slaves. No longer was it legal for a master to put a slave to death or to sell him for immoral or gladiatorial purposes.

The last of the "good emperors," Marcus Aurelius, who ruled from 161 to 180 A.D., approached Plato's ideal of the "philosopher king" and preferred the quiet contemplation of his books to the blood and brutality of the battlefield. Yet, ironically, he was repeatedly troubled by the invasions of Germanic tribes along the northern frontier. While engaged in his Germanic campaigns, he wrote his *Meditations,* a philosophical work notable for its lofty Stoic idealism and love of humanity.

The "immense majesty of the Roman peace." In the finest period of the empire, a vast area stretching from Britain to the Euphrates and from the North Sea to the Sahara was welded together into what a Roman author, Pliny the Elder, termed the "immense majesty of the Roman peace."

Others were equally conscious of the rich benefits derived from Roman rule. To a writer of the late second century, it was

a world every day better known, better cultivated, and more civilized than before. Everywhere roads are traced, every district is known, every country opened to commerce. Smiling fields have invaded the forests; flocks and herds have routed the wild beasts; the very sands are sown; the rocks are planted; the marshes drained. There are now as many cities as there were once solitary cottages. Reefs and shoals have lost their terrors. Wherever there is a trace of life there are houses and human habitations, well-ordered governments and civilized life.[14]

This quotation throws significant light upon the period known as the *Pax Romana.* First of all, the *Pax Romana* applied to a vast area and population; by the reign of Hadrian, the empire comprised more than one and a quarter million square miles containing upwards of one hundred million people—Italians, Greeks, Egyptians, Germans, Celts, and others.

Second, this period witnessed the rapid increase of cities, particularly in frontier provinces; for example, some 160 towns were to be found in the frontier zone across the Rhine and another 120 north of the Danube in what is now Rumania. While the economy remained predominantly agricultural, the empire became progressively more urban in character, with towns and cities forming vital nerve centers linked together by a vast network of roads and waterways. Traveling along one of the great imperial trunk roads, one would see soldiers marching to the frontier, merchants making their way from village to village, caravans bringing oriental luxuries into the empire, horse-drawn coaches of wealthy travelers, and mounted imperial messengers bearing dispatches to the emperor from distant provincial governors. A rich and varied commerce, the lifeblood of the empire, passed over the Roman roads. The empire lay secure behind natural frontiers guarded by well-trained armies, while within the confines of the empire the roads had been cleared of brigands, and the seas of pirates.

Third, the *Pax Romana* saw the creation of a cosmopolitan world-state where races

THE GROWTH OF THE ROMAN EMPIRE
44 B.C. TO 180 A.D.

Acquired before the Death of Caesar, 44 B.C.
Acquired before the Death of Augustus, 14 A.D.
Acquired before the Death of Marcus Aurelius,
180 A.D.

and cultures intermingled freely. What were the ties that held this vast empire together?

The Graeco-Roman cultural synthesis. Writing during the rule of Augustus, the Roman poet Virgil was the spokesman for what enlightened Romans felt to be the "mission" of the empire:

Others shall beat out the breathing bronze to softer lines . . . shall draw living lineaments from the marble; the cause shall be more eloquent on their lips; their pencils shall portray the pathways of heaven, and tell the stars in their arising: be thy charge, O Roman, to rule the nations in thine empire; this shall be thine art, to ordain the law of peace, to be merciful to the conquered and beat the haughty down.[15]

By "others," Virgil was referring to the Greeks, to whom the Romans willingly acknowledged a cultural debt. The Roman world-state, while enriched by many cultural strains, was predominantly a synthesis of Greek and Latin cultures. The Romans learned the Greek language, copied Greek architecture, employed Greek sculptors, and identified their gods with Greek deities. Although Greek ways of life introduced sophisticated habits which were often corrupting to the Roman virtues of self-reliance, personal integrity, family cohesion, and discipline, Greek influences made the Romans on the whole less harsh and insensitive.

Largely because of their admiration for Greek culture and their belief in maintaining a diversity of cultures within a political unity, the Romans succeeded in establishing a world-state instead of a narrow national empire. While Latin was used in official circles and always in the law, Greek and other native tongues were permitted for everyday conversation in the provinces which had been the Hellenistic states. The Romans spread Greek knowledge, in addition to their own, throughout the world-state, and a synthesis of cultures took place among the diverse peoples. By assimilating and spreading Hellenic elements and preserving Hellenistic culture in the eastern provinces, the Romans helped to perpetuate the Greek legacy. The *Pax Romana* was the acme of Graeco-Roman civilization.

Governing the diverse state. At the head of this huge world-state stood the emperor, at once the chief defender and the symbol of unity, and an object of veneration. The empire was divided into two groups of provinces in accord with the system established by Augustus. Certain provinces were governed by the Senate, acting through proconsuls appointed annually, while the imperial provinces were under the direct administration of the emperor, who delegated powers to magistrates serving under his direction.

The provinces possessed their own councils of deputies sent from towns and districts; these councils usually convened once a year. By reporting back to Rome on the activities of the provincial governors, the councils helped greatly to provide a more efficient provincial administration than had existed under the republic. A strong feature of the early period of imperial administration was the large measure of local self-government enjoyed by both provinces and cities. Hundreds of cities even issued their own coins. It was generally believed that such local autonomy contributed to imperial unity. Expressing this view, a Greek orator from the East told his listeners in Rome:

There are no satraps fighting one another as though they had no king; no cities lining up on one side or the other, or garrisons being introduced into some cities and expelled from others . . . the whole world speaks in unison, more distinctly than a chorus; and so well does it harmonize under this director-in-chief [Rome] that it joins in praying this empire may last for all time.[16]

The Roman empire, however, lacked organic unity because it failed to work out means for the ordinary citizens to participate directly in political affairs. True, Roman citizenship had been granted to provincials beyond the Italian peninsula, but no machinery based on representative government had been devised. The interests and loyalties of the provincial peoples centered on their cities, so that patriotism was never sufficiently channeled into the service of the empire. The imperial structure functioned for centuries because the administrative and military machinery remained basically healthy and effective, but the failure to develop institutions which could have bridged the chasm between the imperial government and the governed meant that no popular force could revitalize the central machinery once it started to slow down.

Political theorists have lamented the failure of the Romans to develop an effective system of representative government, whereby regional assemblies could have sent representatives to a central council. However, when one considers that most people had neither the basic education nor the current information necessary to form intelligent opinions about imperial affairs, it is doubtful that an adequate public policy could have been established through representative government.

Prosperity in trade and industry. Rome's unification of the eastern and western segments of the empire had far-reaching economic consequences. The *Pax Romana* was responsible for the creation of new tastes in the West, the elimination of tolls and other artificial barriers, the suppression of piracy and brigandage, and the establishment of relatively good communications and a reliable coinage. All of these factors, in addition to improved methods of banking and credit, explain in large measure the vast economic expansion that occurred in the first and second centuries A.D., probably reaching its height during the reign of Hadrian. (See also pp. 164, 165-167, 177-178, 184-185.)

Although the city was the dominant influence in Roman life, agriculture remained the basic economic activity in the empire. Huge estates, often belonging to absentee owners, prospered. On these tracts large numbers of *coloni,* free tenants, tilled the soil. The *coloni* were gradually replacing slave labor, which was becoming increasingly hard to secure with the disappearance of the flow of captives from major wars.

The most important commercial center of the empire was Alexandria, hub of the rich trade with the East. Rome itself exported comparatively little. However, so much revenue poured into the capital from the provinces that its citizens had the necessary purchasing power to buy immense quantities of goods from other parts of the empire and even from regions far to the east of the imperial frontiers. Grain was one of the most important Roman imports, which also included textiles, papyrus, and a variety of luxury goods.

The growth of industry kept pace with the expansion of trade. Extensive mining operations were carried on in Spain, Britain, and north of the Danube. The Gauls excelled in pottery making, and in the eastern Mediterranean provinces, industry continued to flourish. Asia Minor produced purple dyes, carpets, and tents; Syria exported glassware and leather goods; and Alexandria dealt in perfumes, embroideries, gems, and cosmetics.

As with commerce, the advances made by industry were due to such general factors as the expansion of markets and demand rather than to any fundamental improvements in organization or technology. Industry in the Roman empire was organized on a small-shop basis, and the producers were widely scattered, partly because of the difficulty and cost of distributing goods across such a wide empire, even with the comparatively good Roman transportation system.

Despite the general prosperity, the empire under the Antonines had already entered upon its "Indian summer." Once the empire had ceased to expand geographically, its economy in turn became progressively more static. Late in the first century A.D. Italian agriculture began to suffer from the loss of its markets in the western provinces, which were becoming self-sufficient in the production of wine and olive oil. To aid the wine producers by creating an artificial scarcity, the Flavian emperor Domitian forbade the planting of new vineyards in Italy and ordered the plowing under of half the existing vineyards in the provinces. This was followed by a program of state subsidies, inaugurated by the Antonine emperors. Loans at 5 per cent interest were made to ailing landowners, with the interest to be paid into the treasuries of declining Italian municipalities and earmarked "for girls and boys of needy parents to be supported at public expense." This system of state subsidies to both producers and consumers was soon extended to the provinces. Also contributing to Roman economic stagnation was the continuing drain of money into the oriental luxury trade (see p. 185).

This early evidence of declining prosperity foreshadowed the economic crisis of the third century A.D., when political anarchy and monetary inflation caused the economy of the empire to decline rapidly (see Chapter 7).

Rome, imperial capital. At the hub of the sprawling empire was Rome, a kaleidoscopic cross section of society during the *Pax Romana*. About a million inhabitants crowded into an area of a few square miles around the Forum, the center of public and private life.

Augustus boasted that he had found a city of brick and had left one of marble. Nonetheless, Rome presented a striking contrast of magnificence and tawdriness, of splendid public buildings and squalid tenements. The crowded narrow streets, lined with apartment houses and swarming with all manner of people, are described by the satirist Juvenal:

> Hurry as I may, I am blocked
> By a surging crowd in front, while a vast mass
> Of people crushes onto me from behind.
> One with his elbow punches me, another
> With a hard litter-pole; one bangs a beam
> Against my head, a wine-cask someone else.
> With mud my legs are plastered; from all sides
> Huge feet trample upon me, and a soldier's
> Hobnails are firmly planted on my toes.[17]

Rome possessed a large police force to keep order. Nevertheless, at night few honest citizens dared venture down the winding streets without proper guard. Juvenal attests to other hazards encountered by the passer-by at night:

> . . . That roof, from which
> A tile may crash down on my skull, how high

A passion for detailed artistic realism produced these horses, which are so anatomically precise that the wrinkles in their skin and even the veins under the skin are evident. Aristocratic Romans enjoyed racing in such richly ornamented chariots or *bigas*.

It seems above us! How many times are cracked
Or broken crocks flung from the window! Look
With what a heavy blow they dint and bruise
The pavement! It may well be you'll be deemed
An easy-going fool, improvident
Of sudden accidents, if you should go out
To dinner intestate; for you have indeed
As many dangers to your life to fear,
As at night there are wakeful windows open
Beneath which you must pass. You can but hope,
And silently put up this piteous prayer
That they may be content to pour down on you
Nothing worse than great pailfuls of their
    slops.[18]

For the inmates, meanwhile, the apartment houses held two special terrors. Their flimsy construction often caused them to collapse, and fires were constantly trapping tenants in the upper floors.

Roman social classes. The living conditions of slaves throughout the empire varied greatly. Those in domestic service were often treated humanely, and their years of efficient service perhaps rewarded by emancipation. Nor was it uncommon for freed slaves to rise to places of eminence in business and letters. On the other hand, conditions among slaves on the large estates could be indescribably harsh.

While a large proportion of the capital's populace was dependent upon state support in whole or in part, others made a fairly good living as artisans. These workers usually belonged to *collegia,* or guilds, of which there were about eighty, each comprising the workers of one trade. The *collegia* provided a hall for their members, cared for the sick, and arranged for feasts and celebrations. As in Hellenistic times, guild artisans could often bargain successfully for higher wages. Where working conditions were harsh, unorganized labor might be driven to strike or even riot before its demands for improvement were met.

In contrast to the tenements of the poor, the homes of the rich were palatial, containing courts and gardens with elaborate fountains, rooms furnished with marble walls, mosaics on the floors, and numerous frescoes and other works of art. An interesting feature of Roman furniture was the abundance of couches and the scarcity of chairs. People usually reclined, even at meals—a custom which may have had its value during the sumptuous dinners served by the wealthy gourmands, who were not above administering emetics to permit disgorging and starting afresh on more food and wine.

Public entertainment. Recreation played a key role in Roman social life. Both rich and poor were exceedingly fond of their public baths, which in the capital alone numbered eight hundred during the early days of the empire. The baths served the same purpose as our modern-day athletic clubs. In Rome the famous baths of Diocletian and Caracalla contained enclosed gardens, promenades, gymnasiums, libraries, and famous works of art as well as a wide variety of types of baths. An old Roman inscription expresses an interesting philosophy: "The bath, wine, and love ruin one's health but make life worth living."

Foot races, boxing, and wrestling were minor sports; chariot racing and gladiatorial contests were the chief amusements. The cry for "bread and circuses" reached such proportions that by the first century A.D. the Román calendar had 159 days set aside as holidays, 93 of which were given over to games furnished at public expense. The most spectacular sport was chariot racing. The largest of six race courses at Rome was the Circus Maximus, a huge marble-faced structure measuring some 600 by 200 yards and seating at least 150,000 spectators. The games, which included upwards of twenty-four races each day, were presided over by the emperor or his representative. The crowds bet furiously on their favorite charioteers, whose fame equaled that of the all-American football heroes of our own day.

Scarcely less popular, but infinitely less civilized, the gladiatorial contests were also organized by the emperors as a regular feature on the amusement calendar. These cruel spectacles, which have no exact counterpart in any other civilization, were held in arenas, the largest and most famous of which was the Colosseum. The contests took various forms. Ferocious animals were pitted against armed combatants or occasionally even against unarmed men and women who had been condemned to death. Another type of contest was the fight to the death between gladiators, generally equipped with different types of weapons but matched on equal terms. It was not uncommon for the life of a defeated gladiator who had fought courageously to be spared at the request of the spectators. Although many Romans decried these bloodletting contests, there persisted a streak of cruelty in Roman public amusements which can scarcely be comprehended, far less condoned, today.

Social life in Rome was duplicated on a smaller scale by the towns in the provinces. They, too, had their circuses and chariot races, their arenas and gladiatorial contests, their theaters and baths.

THE ROMAN CONTRIBUTION

The Roman spirit. The Roman spirit was compounded of many factors. Never completely lost was the tradition of plain living and serious thinking that stemmed from their background as a nation of farmers. Geography was another factor, for the Romans lived in the middle of a peninsula, and Italy itself was in the middle of the Mediterranean. For centuries the Romans were faced with the need to conquer or be conquered, and they had to stress discipline and duty to the state. Their geographical and political growth in turn demanded the practical solution of new administrative and legal problems. The Romans provided a practical response to a complex and ceaseless challenge; and the result was not only a workable world-state but the development of a strong sense of duty and a skill in administration, law, and practical affairs.

But the Roman spirit also had another side. It could be arrogant and cruel, and its deep-rooted sense of justice was too often untempered with mercy. Where the Greeks had worshiped reason, the Romans enshrined authority; where the former had demanded self-expression and personal freedom to the point of anarchy, the latter emphasized self-control and discipline.

Although the Romans lacked the brilliance of the Greeks as theorists and creative artists, they excelled in the arts of government and administration. If it is said that the Romans constructed no original system of philosophy, invented no new art forms, and made no outstanding scientific discoveries, it should be added that they made unique and lasting contributions in the fields of jurisprudence and political theory. By and large, the Romans lacked the creative fire of the Greeks, but they knew superbly well how to preserve, adapt, and disseminate civilization. Therefore we might characterize the Romans as synthesists rather than innovators—and at the same time pay respect to their recognition of cultural indebtedness. For all their limitations, the Romans had greatness as a people. The *Pax Romana* could have been fashioned and maintained only by a people grave in nature, mature in judgment, and conscious of their responsibilities to others.

Contributions in government. Roman political thinkers such as Cicero contributed the germinal ideas for many governmental theories destined to be influential in later centuries. Some of these deserve mention:

the social-contract theory (that government originated as a voluntary agreement among citizens); the idea of popular sovereignty (that all power ultimately resides with the people); the principle of the separation of powers (that the legislative, executive, and judicial branches of the government should be kept separate); and the concept that law must be the paramount rule in government. The despotism of the Roman emperors in the last phases of the empire corroded many of these theories and in their place substituted the eastern concept of the divine ruler, which began in the West with divine honors paid to Augustus. Yet the older concepts were never lost sight of; they were transmitted to early modern times to form the theoretical basis of contemporary constitutional governments in the West.

The Romans laid the foundations for the political framework of modern Europe in still other ways. Many current administrative divisions, such as the county and province, are derived from Roman practice. In some instances European boundaries are little altered from those existing under the Caesars. The medieval Church also modeled its organization, administrative units, and much of its law after that of the empire (see map, p. 209). In addition, both the eastern Roman emperors who ruled at Constantinople until 1453 and the German kings of western Europe retained Roman imperial titles and symbols of authority, a Roman system of public finances, and Roman law. The lasting influence of the Romans in government is further illustrated by such present-day political terms as *fiscal, senate, consul, plebiscite, citizens, municipal,* and *census.*

Evolution of Roman law. Of the contributions made by the Romans in government and politics, Roman law is preëminent. Two great legal systems, Roman law and English common law, are the foundation of jurisprudence in most modern western nations. Roman law is the basis for the law codes of Italy, France, Scotland, and the Latin American countries. Where English common law is used, as in the United States, there is also a basic heritage of great legal principles originated by ancient Roman jurists. In addition, Roman legal principles have strongly affected the development of the canon law of the Roman Catholic Church; and international law has borrowed principles inherent in the Roman system.

Roman law evolved slowly over a period of about one thousand years. At first, when Rome was a struggling city-state, the law was unwritten, mixed with religious custom, narrow in its point of view, and harsh in its judgments. In the fifth century B.C., as we have seen (p. 129), the law was written down in the Law of the Twelve Tables. During the remainder of the republic the body of Roman law (*jus civile,* "law of the citizen") was enlarged by legislation passed by the Senate and the assembly and, equally important, by judicial interpretation of existing law to meet new conditions. By the second century A.D. the emperor had become the sole source of law, a responsibility he entrusted to scholars "skilled in the law" (*jurisprudentes*). Holding to the idea of equity ("follow the beneficial interpretation"), and influenced by Stoic philosophy with its concept of a "law of nature" common to all men and ascertainable by means of human reason, these jurists humanized and rationalized Roman law to meet the needs of a world-state. Finally, in the sixth century A.D., the enormous bulk of Roman law from all sources was codified (see p. 227). This work of codification and systematization, which took seven years, enabled the Roman law to be condensed in a few volumes and thus easily preserved for posterity.

Roman engineering and architecture. The empire's administrative needs required a communication system of paved roads and bridges as well as huge public buildings and aqueducts for the cities. Pride in the empire led also to the erection of ostentatious monuments symbolizing Rome's dignity and might.

As road builders, the Romans surpassed all previous peoples. Constructed of layers of stone according to sound engineering principles, their roads were planned for the use of armies and messengers and were kept in constant repair. One of the earliest main Roman highways was the Appian Way, a heavily traveled route to the southeastern

Italian ports, from which the Romans sailed for Greece and the eastern Mediterranean. Later the Flaminian Way, running northeast from Rome to the Adriatic Sea and connected with other roads to the northern provinces, was built. It has been said that the speed of travel possible on Roman highways was not surpassed until the early nineteenth century.

In designing their bridges, the Romans placed a series of arches next to one another to provide mutual support. The aqueducts consisted of several tiers of arches, one above the other, which provided a tall base for a water channel. Fourteen aqueducts, stretching a total of 265 miles, supplied some fifty gallons of water daily for each inhabitant of Rome. The practical nature of the Romans and their skill and initiative in engineering were demonstrated also in the many dams, reservoirs, and harbors they constructed.

At first the Romans copied Etruscan architectural models, but later they combined basic Greek elements with distinctly Roman developments. The structural simplicity of Hellenic buildings was too restrained for

First used by Neolithic men and brought to perfection in classical Athens, post and lintel construction (left) is a simple solution to the problem of supporting weight above an opening. Because the one-piece lintel carries the weight, the strength of the material determines the width of the aperture. Since the large stones necessary for one-piece lintels were not available in Sumer as they were in Egypt, Crete, and Greece, the Sumerians sometimes used mud bricks to form arches, although arch and vault construction (right) was not used extensively until Roman times. Instead of supporting the direct down-thrust of weight as in post and lintel construction, the wedge-shaped bricks pressing against each other transfer the weight outward and down to the ground.

From the Etruscans, the Romans learned how to build the barrel vault—a continuous series of arches forming a tunnellike structure. The walls of the vault had to be thick and strong to support the sideways and downward pressure of the material above. An advance in technique was made when Roman engineers joined two barrel vaults at right angles to form an intersecting vault. Because the weight of the material was then spread over a larger area, the walls did not need to be as thick as those of a barrel vault. Also, openings in the supporting walls furnished window space.

the Romans, who developed new concepts for enclosing space. The static post and lintel system of the Greeks was replaced with the more dynamic structural system of the arch and vault (see illustration, p. 152).

The arch was used extensively to provide openings in walls, and the basic Greek orders of columns were used as part of the wall to add the strength needed to bear the thrust of the arch. The barrel vault, basically a series of adjoining arches forming a structure resembling a tunnel, was a new method of enclosing space. In the barrel vault, the piers, or supports, of the arches became heavy masonry walls to bear the weight of the vaulted roof. The Romans then proceeded further to achieve the intersecting of two barrel vaults.

Another important advance in architectural engineering was the Romans' success in constructing concrete domes large enough to roof a substantial span. The weight of the dome was transferred directly to the walls, and since there was no sidewise thrust, no other support was necessary. The largest of the domed structures was a Roman temple, the Pantheon, which still stands.

The basilica, an important Roman civic building, was a colonnaded building. It had a central nave with side aisles. To permit clerestory windows like those found in such Egyptian temples as Karnak, the

Roman skill at portraiture is illustrated by the individuality of these busts of various emperors and their families (Augustus, crowned with laurel, appears in the foreground). Roman artists did not hesitate to portray even their deified emperors in a realistic manner.

central roof was elevated above the side walls. Beginning in the fourth century A.D. Christian architects commonly modeled their churches after the Roman basilica (see illustration, p. 204).

Perhaps the most famous Roman edifice is the Colosseum (see illustration, p. 153), a huge structure about one quarter of a mile around on the outside and with a seating capacity estimated to have been at least 45,000. The Colosseum utilized three stories of arches; for ornamental effect, columns were "engaged," which means that they were applied flat to the wall with only about half of their diameter protruding. In the Colosseum the three orders of columns—Doric, Ionic, and Corinthian—were arranged with the heaviest (the Doric) at the bottom and the most ornate (the Corinthian) at the top.

Two basic characteristics of Roman construction were solidity and magnificence. Roman buildings were built to last, and their size, grandeur, and decorative richness aptly symbolized the proud imperial spirit of Rome. Whereas the Greeks evolved the temple, theater, and stadium, the Romans contributed the triumphal arch, bath, basilica, amphitheater, and multistoried apartment house. Many modern public buildings show the influence of Roman models.

Realism in sculpture and painting. After the conquest of Greece thousands of statues and other art pieces were brought to Rome. Many Romans acquired a passion for art, and the homes of the wealthy were filled with all kinds of Greek art.

Although they were strongly influenced by Greek models, the Romans developed a distinctive sculpture of their own which tended to be realistic, secular, and individualistic. Perhaps the earlier Etruscan art had exerted a strong influence on the Romans in this regard. Whereas the Greeks idealized their subject matter and portrayed types rather than individuals, the Romans were at their best when producing lifelike busts of administrators, soldiers, and emperors. Roman coins with relief portraits of emperors served to glorify the Roman empire, and they were also effective propaganda for particular emperors. Equestrian statues, sculptured coffins, or sarcophagi, and the reliefs found on Roman imperial monuments were also exceptionally fine works of art. The Romans developed a great fund of decorative motifs, such as cupids, garlands of flowers, and scrolls of various patterns, which are still used today. Stucco wall decoration was distinctive and much more fanciful than the Greek.

In painting the Romans were technically far advanced; they relied to some extent on Greek models, adapting and embellishing Greek style according to their own tastes. The Romans were particularly skilled in painting frescoes; those still to be seen in Pompeii and elsewhere show that the artist drew the human figure accurately and showed objects in clear though imperfect perspective (see Color Plate 10).

Literary Rome. In literature as in art the Romans turned to the Greeks for their models. Roman epic, dramatic, and lyric poetry forms were usually written in conscious imitation of Greek masterpieces. Compared with Greek literature, however, Latin writing was more moralistic and less speculative and imaginative. But it remains one of the world's great literatures largely because of its influence upon medieval, Renaissance, and modern culture.

The most important development in early Latin literature was the drama. In Rome as in Athens, plays were presented during religious and civic festivals, and the female roles were taken by men. Tragic drama was not popular in Rome; but the people delighted in bawdy comedies, most of which were adapted from Hellenistic Greek originals. Plautus (c. 254-184 B.C.) wrote comedies that were ribald and vigorously humorous. His rollicking plots of illicit love and his stock characters of the shrewish wife, henpecked husband, lovelorn youth, clever slave, and swashbuckling soldier appealed to the common man. The works of Plautus suggest many of the types that modern comedy has assumed—the farce, burlesque, and the comedy of manners. From him Shakespeare got ideas for his *Comedy of Errors* and *The Merry Wives of Windsor*, and Molière, the seventeenth-century French dramatist, was also influenced by Plautus.

Another type of comic dramatist was Terence (c. 190-159 B.C.), whose subtle and sophisticated plays were written in polished Latin. Terence's plays never enjoyed the popular acclaim accorded Plautus' works: the people preferred slapstick to wit and vulgarity to subtlety. However,

Terence has been acclaimed for molding the Latin language into a literary instrument that would make possible the prose of Cicero and the poetry of Virgil.

The Golden Age of Latin literature. Although Latin literature had its beginnings before the Punic Wars, it entered its first great period of creative activity in the first century B.C. An outpouring of splendid intellectual effort coincided with the last stages of the republic. This period marks the first half of the Golden Age of Latin literature, known as the Ciceronian period because of the stature of Marcus Tullius Cicero (106-43 B.C.), the greatest master of Latin prose and perhaps the outstanding intellectual influence in Roman history. The Ciceronian period was also marked by the excellent historical narrative of Julius Caesar, *Commentaries on the Gallic War.*

Acclaimed as the greatest orator of his day, Cicero found time during his busy public life to write extensively on philosophy, political theory, rhetoric, and literary criticism. Some nine hundred of his letters still exist and these, together with his other numerous writings, give us insight into Cicero's personality, as well as into the problems and manners of republican Rome. Much of the value of Cicero's letters lies precisely in the fact that they were not intended for publication and thus he spoke his mind freely. Cicero also made a rich contribution to knowledge by passing on to later ages much of Greek thought—especially that of Plato and the Stoics—and at the same time interpreting it from the standpoint of a Roman intellectual and practical man of affairs. He did more than any other Roman to make Latin a great literary language, and his influence extended through the Italian Renaissance and the "classical" period of English thought and literature which began in the late seventeenth century.

The Ciceronian period also witnessed the writing of exuberant lyrical poetry, the best of which was composed by Catullus (c. 87-54 B.C.), a young man about town who wrote intensely of his loves and hates:

I hate and love—the why I cannot tell,
But by my tortures know the fact too well.[19]

Perhaps the greatest architectural contribution of the Romans was the enclosure of vast interior spaces. Arch construction, which the Romans did not invent but which they resourcefully developed, provided a means of freeing interiors of columnar support. The Pantheon, shown in an eighteenth-century painting by the Italian Giovanni Paolo Pannini, is the most impressive surviving example of the Roman dome, which is a variation of the arch principle. Arches were also employed in building aqueducts, such as this one at Segovia, Spain, which is still in use. Roman engineers were aware that water always seeks its own level, and using this principle, they were able to bring water to cities from many miles away by maintaining a slight but consistent fall in the height of the ducts. Amphitheaters, unknown to the Greeks, are another characteristically Roman form of architecture. The Colosseum, largest of such structures, uses arch construction both to light the interior and to disperse weight. It was used for gladiatorial combats, animal fights, and even for naval exhibitions —water pipes for flooding still exist in some arenas. Corresponding to the Greek *agora*, the Forum Romanum centered around a rectangular open space which was used for political demonstrations or as a general meeting place. Designed as the center of Roman public life, the Forum included important government offices and temples, as well as numerous triumphal columns.

At the other end of the personality spectrum was Catullus' contemporary, Lucretius (99-55 B.C.), who found in the philosophy of Epicurus an antidote to his profound disillusionment with his fellow citizens who, he wrote, "in their greed of gain . . . amass a fortune out of civil bloodshed: piling wealth on wealth, they heap carnage on carnage. With heartless glee they welcome a brother's tragic death."[20]

Augustus provided the Roman world with a stability that was conducive to a further outpouring of poetry and prose. The second phase of the Golden Age of Latin literature, the Augustan Age, was notable particularly for its excellent poetry. Virgil (70-19 B.C.) was probably the greatest of all Roman poets. His masterpiece, a great national epic called the *Aeneid,* glorifies the work of Augustus and eloquently asserts Rome's destiny to conquer and rule the world (see quotation, p. 143). Using Homer's *Iliad* and *Odyssey* as his models, Virgil recounted the fortunes of Aeneas, the legendary founder of the Latin people, who came from his home in Troy to Italy. The *Aeneid* breathes Virgil's deep and enthusiastic patriotism and is as much a piece of imperial symbolism as Rome's triumphal arches.

Horace (65-8 B.C.) was famous for both lyrical odes and satirical verse. Succeeding generations have turned to Horace because of his urbane viewpoint and polished style. Modeled on Aristotle's Doctrine of the Mean, Horace's philosophy stipulated a constant equanimity, even to the point of being indifferent to death. This belief is evident in "To Leuconoë":

It is not right for you to know, so do not ask,
    Leuconoë,
How long a life the gods may give or ever we are
    gone away;
Try not to read the Final Page, the ending colo-
    phonian,
Trust not the gypsy's tea-leaves, nor the prophets
    Babylonian.
Better to have what is to come enshrouded in
    obscurity
Than to be certain of the sort and length of our
    futurity.
Why, even as I monologue on wisdom and
    longevity

How Time has flown! Spear some of it! The longest life is brevity.[21]

Quite a different sort was Ovid (43 B.C.-17 A.D.), a poet akin to Catullus in spirit and personal life, who combined a predilection for themes on sensual love with first-rate storytelling. In fact, it is largely through his *Metamorphoses,* a collection of Greek stories about the life of the gods, that classical mythology was transmitted to the modern world.

The Silver Age. The period following Augustus' death in 14 A.D. was one of continuing prosperity and stability. Interest in literature remained high, the theater flourished, and writers both in Rome and in the provinces produced a large volume of original work in poetry and prose. In the main, the quality of this production did not measure up to the superlative standard set during the Augustan period. Nevertheless, it was excellent enough to merit the title "The Silver Age of Latin Literature," a period of time which comprised the century and a quarter from the death of Augustus to the death of Hadrian (14-138 A.D.). The Silver Age was marked by a more critical and negative spirit than that of its predecessor. Whereas the Augustan period had evoked lyrical odes and a majestic epic, the Silver Age was memorable for its brilliant satirical poetry.

With Juvenal (55?-130 A.D.), satire in Latin poetry reached its peak. This master of poetic invective flayed the shortcomings of contemporary Roman society (see also quotations, pp. 145-146):

Whatever passions have the soul possessed,
Whatever wild desires inflamed the breast
(Joy, Sorrow, Fear, Love, Hatred, Transport, Rage),
Shall form the motley subject of my page.
For when could Satire boast so fair a field?[22]

His brilliant epigrammatic phrases were destined to influence the writings of the famous Neoclassical English satirists John Dryden, Jonathan Swift, and Alexander Pope.

Juvenal had an older friend, Martial (c. 40-102 A.D.), who was also a close observer and caustic critic of his age. Martial's fame rests on his epigrams, brief poems of which he wrote over fifteen hundred. The following example is typical of Martial's wit:

The golden hair that Galla wears
  Is hers: who would have thought it?
She swears 'tis hers, and true she swears,
  For I know where she bought it.[23]

And here he jibes at a type of tradesman who had a reputation no less in Roman days than in our own for being talkative:

By the time the barber Eurus
  Had circled Lupo's face
A second beard had sprouted
  In the first one's place.[24]

The writing of history. Two Roman historians produced notable works during the Golden and Silver Ages. The first, Livy (59 B.C.-17 A.D.), was a contemporary of Virgil; his immense *History of Rome,* like the latter's *Aeneid,* is of epic proportions and glorifies Rome's conquests and ancestral ways. By assembling the legends and traditions of early Roman history and welding them into a continuous narrative, Livy, like Virgil, sought to advance Augustus' program of moral and social regeneration. He glorified the virtues of the ancient Romans—their heroism, patriotism, and piety—and sought to draw moral lessons from an idealized past. "What chiefly makes the study of history wholesome and profitable," he wrote in his preface,

is this, that you behold the lessons of every kind of experience set forth as on a conspicuous monument; from these you may choose for yourself and for your own state what to imitate, from these mark for avoidance what is shameful in the conception and shameful in the result.[25]

In the Silver Age, historians did not attempt to emulate the wide range of Livy's *History* but confined their efforts to writing about shorter and more contemporary periods. Tacitus (55-117 A.D.), like his contemporary Juvenal, was concerned with improving society, but he used history rather than poetry to serve his ends. In his *Germania*

This detail from a mosaic found in Africa shows Virgil reading from his masterwork, the *Aeneid.* Commissioned by Augustus, the *Aeneid* glorifies both the emperor and the Roman state, the founding of which is described as a direct result of the fall of Troy. Virgil intentionally imitated Homer in both style and content.

Tacitus contrasted the life of the idealized, simple Germanic tribes with the corrupt and immoral existence of the Roman upper classes. In the *Annals* and *Histories* he used his vivid, epigrammatic prose to depict the shortcomings of the emperors and their courts from the death of Augustus to 96 A.D. Some of his brief, trenchant statements have been quoted for centuries; for example, "Tyrants merely procure infamy for themselves and glory for their victims"; "The more corrupt the state, the more numerous the laws"; and (in his description of Roman conquest) "They make a solitude and call it peace." Critical in his use of source materials, Tacitus nevertheless suffered from the bias of his own senatorial class; he looked upon the emperors as tyrants and thus could not do justice in his writing to the positive contributions of imperial government.

The most famous Greek author in the Roman empire was Plutarch (46?-120? A.D.). Holding a governmental office under the Roman authority in his local city, he used his leisure time to carry out research on the outstanding figures in Roman and Greek history in order to discover what qualities make men great or ignoble. His best known work, *The Parallel Lives,* contains forty-six biographies of famous Greeks and Romans, arranged in pairs for the purpose of comparison. Plutarch's *Lives* is a mine of invaluable information for the classical historian. Shakespeare used this work to obtain facts and historical background for such tragic dramas as *Julius Caesar* and *Antony and Cleopatra.*

Latin, the standard language for Rome's successors. After the second century A.D. chaotic conditions discouraged the creation of great works, either in art or in literature. But the decline and fall of Rome did not mean oblivion for the language of the Romans. Its influence upon western thought and letters had been so strong that for more than a thousand years after the collapse of the Roman empire educated men wrote in Latin.

Latin literature was also the dominant influence in the development of vernacular languages and literature in much of Europe. Out of the Latin spoken by the common people in the Roman empire there gradually evolved during the Middle Ages the Romance languages, of which Italian, Spanish, Portuguese, French, and Rumanian are the major examples. It is estimated, moreover, that more than half of our English words are of Latin origin. By early modern times the vernacular languages had largely displaced Latin as a literary medium. But even today Ciceronian Latin remains a regular part of many educational curriculums, while the style of Latin used by Christian writers of the late empire is still employed by the Roman Catholic Church.

Stoicism and Epicureanism. Neither in science nor in philosophy did the Romans approach the Greeks. They contributed no original philosophical theories but preferred to adapt existing Greek systems of thought to suit their needs. As men of action with grave governmental responsibilities, the Romans paid scant attention to such abstract problems as the nature of the universe and of human knowledge. Instead, they concentrated on Hellenistic Greek ethics, which had an obvious bearing on questions of politics and personal behavior. As a consequence, the two main Hellenistic Greek ethical systems, Epicureanism and Stoicism, attracted far more interest in Rome than the speculations of Plato and Aristotle.

Epicureanism made its greatest impact during the last days of the republic, since men found its tenets comforting in a period of political upheavel when no one knew what the morrow would bring. As young men, Virgil and Horace embraced Epicureanism, but the poet-philosopher Lucretius was perhaps the most important Roman interpreter of this philosophy. In his work *On the Nature of Things,* Lucretius based his explanation of the "nature of things" on materialism and atomism. He called on men to free themselves from superstition and to rely instead upon their own resources, since the gods had nothing to do with the fate of human beings. Interpreting the views of Epicurus, Lucretius exhorted his readers to "make the most of today," to seek pleasure not in sensuous gratification but in philosophical serenity, and to have no fear of death since souls, like bodies, are composed of atoms that fall apart when death comes:

What has this bugbear Death to frighten man,
If souls can die, as well as bodies can? . . .
So, when our mortal frame shall be disjoin'd,
The lifeless lump uncoupled from the mind,
From sense of grief and pain we shall be free;
We shall not feel, because we shall not be.[26]

More enduring, especially in the days of the empire, was the appeal of Stoicism as modified to suit the Roman temperament. It has been said that the Romans gave Stoicism "a dose of common sense," for they aimed at controlling rather than stifling their emotions. The Roman Stoic sought to remain poised in a world full of uncertainty, pain, and sorrow through resignation and self-sufficiency. Man must not question the operation of natural law but, if wise, should accept whatever fate nature has in store for him, remaining in full control of his emotions and impervious to pleasure and pain alike.

Stoicism was too intellectual and austere to appeal to the Roman populace, but its influence was far-reaching nonetheless. It had a humanizing effect on Roman law, for example, by introducing the concept that a man is innocent until proved guilty. Also, it stressed the dignity and worth of men, irrespective of their social status, and advocated a way of life embracing service to humanity, constancy to duty, and courage in adversity.

One of the most outstanding Stoics was Seneca (4 B.C.-65 A.D.), Nero's tutor, a major writer of tragic drama, and a significant essayist. He was regarded with high favor by the leaders of the early Christian Church for, like the other late Roman Stoics—the ex-slave Epictetus (d. 135 A.D.) and the emperor Marcus Aurelius—he stressed "Providence" and the immortality of the soul. In addition, like all Roman Stoics, he emphasized the virtue of service to mankind and the concept of human brotherhood. Seneca occupies an important place in the development of moral theory in Europe because his essays enjoyed a wide reputation among thinkers during the Middle Ages and the Renaissance.

Science in the Roman empire. The Romans had little scientific curiosity, and they preferred to put the findings of Hellenistic science to their own practical uses. They became masters in applied medicine, public health, and engineering.

The Romans pioneered in public health service and developed the extensive practice of hydrotherapy—the use of mineral baths for healing. Beginning in the early empire, doctors were employed in infirmaries where soldiers, officials, and the poor could obtain free medical care. Great aqueducts and admirable drainage systems indicate Roman concern for public health.

Characteristic of their utilitarian approach to science was the Romans' predilection for amassing immense encyclopedias. The most important of these was the *Natural History* compiled by Pliny the Elder (23-79 A.D.), an enthusiastic collector of all kinds of scientific odds and ends. In writing his massive work, Pliny is reputed to have read more than two thousand books. The result is an intriguing mixture of fact and fable thrown together with scarcely any method of classification. Aside from such fanciful observations as the descriptions of men whose feet point the wrong way, other men with heads directly on their shoulders, and one man whose keen sight enabled him to see objects more than a hundred miles distant, the *Natural History* contains many valuable facts regarding science, geography, and various other subjects. It was the most widely read book on science during the empire and much of the Middle Ages. Pliny himself was suffocated by a rain of hot ashes while he was studiously observing the eruption of Mount Vesuvius at Pompeii.

If the Romans themselves were seldom preoccupied with scientific investigation, others in the empire were engaged in serious research. During the *Pax Romana* the Greeks at Alexandria continued their mathematical and geographical studies. Roman legions in Europe and Greek traders traveling to distant Asian lands provided geographers with important data for new maps of the world. The most famous geographer and astronomer was an Alexandrian scholar named Ptolemy, who lived in the middle of the second century A.D. His maps show a comparatively accurate knowledge of a broad section of the Old World, and he used an excellent projection system (see p. 608).

Unfortunately for his reputation in centuries to come, Ptolemy is often remembered for some of his serious errors. He exaggerated the size of Asia, an error which influenced Columbus to underestimate the width of the Atlantic and to set sail from Spain in search of Asia. Later explorers were also eager to find the *terra australis incognita* —a strip of land extending from Africa to Asia which Ptolemy had drawn on his maps —and by chance they stumbled upon the continent of Australia. In astronomy Ptolemy's researches resulted in the work entitled *Syntaxis* (known also by the Arabic term *Almagest*). This work includes the usual Hellenistic proofs that the world is round but accepts a theory already discarded by the Greek Aristarchus—that the world is at rest in the middle of the universe. As a result of Ptolemy's views, the geocentric theory was generally accepted in western Europe until the sixteenth century.

Still another Greek in the Roman empire advanced the scope of scientific knowledge. Born in Pergamum in Asia Minor, Galen (139?-200? A.D.) was a physician for a school of gladiators. His fame spread and he was called to Rome where he became physician to Marcus Aurelius. Galen was responsible for notable advances in physiology and anatomy; for example, he was the first to explain the mechanism of respiration. Forbidden by the Roman government to dissect human bodies, Galen experimented with animals and demonstrated that an excised heart can continue to beat outside the body and that injuries to one side of the brain produce disorders in the opposite side of the body. The most experimental-minded of ancient physicians, he once wrote: "I confess the disease from which I have suffered all my life—to trust . . . no statements until, so far as possible, I have tested them for myself."[27] His medical encyclopedia, in which he summarized the medical knowledge of his time, remained the standard authority for medical men until well into the Renaissance.

Limitations and achievements of classical science. By observing nature objectively, applying reason and deductive logic to the problems at hand, engaging in systematic research, and extracting *generalities*—that is, universal underlying concepts—from the available evidence, the Greeks and Romans brought science to the threshold of the modern world. Not until the sixteenth century did science move forward from where they left off. The student may indeed wonder why classical thought itself did not cross that threshold and why a millennium elapsed before pure and applied science could again surge forward dynamically.

One scholar finds the answer in social factors. Instead of being applied to the needs of society, science came to be viewed as a study for the privileged few, an "adornment, a subject of contemplation." Ironically, this educated elite, who could have utilized science to good purpose, were members of a society that precluded any effective use of power other than the muscles of slaves. The universal social cleavage between free man and slave produced a "mischievous separation of the logic from the practice of science. . . . This was not good either for practice or for theory. As Francis Bacon put it, . . . if you make a vestal virgin of science you must not expect her to bear fruit."[28]

Other scholars look to different factors, such as the limited use of mathematical, observational, and experimental techniques. The Greeks had developed these techniques to some extent in mechanics, astronomy, and zoology, but before they were recognized as necessary methods in *all* fields of natural investigation, the scientific method was stultified by various social and political developments. In latter-day Rome, for example, political upheavals, social tensions, and the rise of Christianity with its struggles against competing faiths and traditional attitudes created an environment more conducive to polemics than detached scientific inquiry.

Yet if it has required the past four centuries to bring their scientific labors to fulfillment, our classical ancestors deserve to be applauded for their accomplishments. To the Greeks' trust in reason and their insistence on probing beyond the appearance of things to the underlying principles, the Romans in turn brought a practical bent. By making results conveniently accessible—for example, by writing encyclopedias—they helped develop the concept of the unity of science. Moreover, the Greeks and Romans had dedication and enthusiasm, essential components of the true scientific spirit. Thus we can rejoice with Ptolemy when he declared:

I know that I am mortal, a creature of a day; but when I search into the multitudinous revolving spiral of the stars, my feet no longer rest on the earth, but, standing by Zeus himself, I take my fill of ambrosia, the food of the gods.[29]

SUMMARY

The story of how Rome rose from the insignificant status of a muddy village along the banks of the Tiber River to the mighty position of ruler of the Mediterranean world will always remain one of the most fascinating epics in world history. Emerging from obscurity about the middle of the eighth century before Christ, the Latin people who clustered about Rome and its seven hills succeeded in 509 B.C. in ousting their Etruscan overlords and establishing a republic. Two themes are dominant in the next four hundred years of Roman history: the gradual democratization of the government and the conquest of the Mediterranean.

During the first two centuries the plebeians succeeded in breaking down the privileged position of the patricians by obtaining recognition of their fundamental rights as citizens and by acquiring a progressively more important share of political power. Despite these gains, the rank and file of citizens seldom exercised full control of the government of the republic and saw it eventually transformed into the principate and then into an undisguised monarchy. But the influence of the democratic tradition is seen in the development of Roman law and political theory. Roman law was a basic influence upon subsequent legal thought in the West. The Romans left us the concepts of the supremacy of the law, the social contract, the sovereignty of the people, and the separation of governmental powers.

The other theme in the early history of Rome was the conquest of the Mediterranean. Between the years 509 and 270 B.C. the Romans crushed all resistance to their rule in Italy. They then turned their attention to Carthage, and after a herculean struggle, Carthage surrendered in 201 B.C. Having conquered the West, the Romans turned toward the East and in short order defeated the successors of Alexander the Great. But as the Mediterranean world succumbed to the Roman legions, Rome itself faced civil war and degeneration.

Several patriotic reformers, such as the Gracchi brothers, tried to persuade the Senate to enact necessary reforms, but to no avail. Marius, Sulla, Pompey, and Julius Caesar mark the appearance of one-man rule and the end of the republic. Augustus, the heir of Caesar, ruled Rome wisely and well. On the surface the old republican characteristics of government, such as the Senate, were preserved, but Augustus wielded the real power in the new government, which is called the principate. For two hundred years, during the *Pax Romana,* many millions of people in Italy and the empire's provinces enjoyed peace and prosperity.

Through the Roman achievement of a single empire and a cosmopolitan culture, the Greek legacy was preserved, synthesized, and disseminated—and the Romans were able in their own right to make important contributions. For the first time in the western world, secular architecture on a monumental scale evolved with the erection of baths, government buildings, stadiums, and triumphal arches throughout the empire. The Romans also contributed realistic portrait sculpture and painting. Although they accomplished little in pure science, they developed Hellenistic science on a new scale to meet their practical need for such things as hospitals, public medical service, efficient sewage systems, and a workable calendar. The Romans evolved few new literary forms, but they produced some masterpieces, and their sonorous prose set a standard for later centuries. The Latin language, which throughout the Middle Ages was the vehicle of law, the Church, and much of literature, is the foundation of modern languages spoken by hundreds of millions of people.

The Romans excelled in political theory, governmental administration, and jurisprudence. While the Greeks were individualistic, the Romans put a higher value on conformity, and their essentially conservative and judicious attitude of mind compensated for their lack of creativity. Primarily synthesists rather than innovators, the Romans willingly admitted their cultural indebtedness and by doing so exhibited a magnanimity characteristic of the Roman spirit at its best.

Historical Critique

THE BIRTH OF HISTORY IN THE WEST
by Thomas W. Africa

Thomas W. Africa, currently Professor of History at the University of Southern California, is the author of *Phylarchus and the Spartan Revolution* (1961), *Rome of the Caesars* (1965), and *Science and the State in Greece and Rome* (1968).

Although Herodotus is called the father of history, the label is not accurate even for Greek history. The writing of history seems to have begun in the ancient Near East with official reports to the gods. Kings boasted of military victories and the construction of temples and often inscribed their letters to Heaven in inaccessible places where only the gods would see them. Successful rulers also made public reports of their deeds to awe posterity; but, of course, these brief annals did not explore the problems of causation. Priestly scribes, however, saw men and events in a broader perspective and sought lessons in history. The author of the Sumerian King List claimed that "universal kingship" (control over Mesopotamia) had been "lowered from Heaven" and bestowed in turn on various cities in the primeval past. Nonetheless, in dealing with more recent events "after the flood," the Sumerian historian dispensed with the Mandate of Heaven and attributed shifts in imperial fortune to warfare. In Mesopotamian historiography religious and realistic concepts existed side by side, and the scholars of Babylon carefully recorded the sins (usually impiety) which brought about the fall of great kingdoms. The Hittites, too, were concerned with sin and retribution as causal factors in history, and Hittite kings confessed their own errors in remarkably frank autobiographies. The realism of the Hittites was in sharp contrast to the boastful annals of the Egyptians, who were unable to raise history above the level of propaganda for the reigning dynasty. Yet all Near Eastern peoples agreed that the gods would not tolerate undue wickedness.

The most impressive remains of Near Eastern historiography are the historical books of the Old Testament. Like their neighbors, the Hebrews drew upon legends and sagas for their notions of prehistory and antiquity. However, an anonymous contemporary wrote a vivid account of David's career, filled with admiration for the king but forthrightly depicting his crimes and follies as well. This historical masterpiece (the "Early Source") may be found in parts of the Books of Samuel and Kings. Later Hebrew historians idealized the image of David; but they had little sympathy with most of the kings of Israel and Judah, and the general tone of the Old Testament is hostile to monarchy. The authors of the Book of Kings explained the successes and failures of the Hebrew states as rewards or punishments dealt out by the national god, Yahweh, who made his servants prosper and handed sinners over to their enemies. When the Jews returned to Palestine after the Babylonian Captivity, Jerusalem became a temple state ruled by priests, who assembled the body of literature which is the Old Testament. In their pious hands, even secular history was edited to follow the religious theme of a constantly unfolding covenant between Yahweh and Israel. Accordingly, the post-exilic historians of the Book of Chronicles revised the national past from a theocratic point of view with great emphasis on priests and ritual. Later, the Hellenistic Book of Daniel added a scheme of history which was probably borrowed from Iranian sources. According to Daniel, a series of four great monarchies would be followed by a universal empire, the Messianic kingdom. In every era history was to Hebrew historians a record of Yahweh's acts, usually in the interest of Israel.

In contrast to the Near Eastern traditions, there was no Hellenic point of view on history—only the views of individual Greeks. About 700 B.C. the poet Hesiod saw history as a grim pattern of decline, in which mankind degenerated from a utopian primal age of gold through eras of silver and bronze into the warlike present, an age of iron. At best, Hesiod's notions were poetic insights. Two centuries later Ionian intellectuals replaced imagery with facts and wrote history in prose. Unlike poets who relied on intuition, historians wrote only after investigation (*historia* in Greek), and some, like Hecataeus, were openly skeptical of the legends of the past. Herodotus, too, was a rationalist and enjoyed debunking pious tales, but he also believed that man was morally accountable for his sins and that the gods particularly punished the sin of arrogance. His great history of the Persian invasions of Greece centered on the theme: Pride goes before a fall. Like other Asian Greeks, Herodotus was interested in foreign peoples and wrote sympathetic accounts of their folkways. For the most part, he was broad-minded and freely conceded the merits of Persians, the enemies of Hellas. With his wide interests and general fairness, Herodotus was the first universal historian.

The Athenian historian Thucydides had narrower notions of men and history. He was contemptuous of the past and exaggerated the importance of the war between Athens and Sparta in which he had participated. Exiled from Athens because of his failure as a military commander, Thucydides filled his account of the war with bitter criticism of his political enemies, the democratic leaders of the city. In general, he was a pessimist and believed that most men were motivated by a lust for power. Unlike Herodotus, Thucydides did not view the gods as active agents in history, but he was a fervent moralist and felt that Attic arrogance brought about the war and Athens' ultimate defeat. A keen student of international relations, Thucydides distinguished between the immediate causes of the conflict and the underlying psychological conditions which made men willing to fight. Though scrupulous in collecting and assessing evidence, Thucydides had no qualms about putting appropriate speeches in the mouths of historical figures. This practice set a disastrous precedent for succeeding historians in Greece and Rome, who filled their works with pompous artificial speeches. Both Herodotus and Thucydides display the moralistic tendencies of Greek historiography, and both consciously composed works of literature.

In the fourth century lesser authors followed the examples of the two great historians. Like Thucydides, Xenophon wrote about contemporary events, but Ephorus saw history on a broader scale and wrote a general history of Hellas beginning with the Dorian invasions. Many Greek historians inflated their works with rhetoric, and the exploits of Alexander the Great soon gave such writers an opportunity to describe sensational events. There was also a growing concern over the role of the unpredictable in human affairs, and historians often personified the factor of chance as Fortune. In the Hellenistic Age some historians sought to recapture the vitality of the past by writing in a highly dramatic style, emphasizing emotion and pathos and even inventing episodes to enliven their narratives. Hellenistic historians also loved to moralize, particularly on the whims of Fortune and the corrupting effects of luxury. As a result of these tendencies, history became popular among general readers, but truth was often sacrificed for dramatic effect.

However, one major Greek historian, Polybius (c. 200-117 B.C.), protested against dramatic history in the name of science. He scoffed at sensationalism and demanded that historians be able to validate their accounts of the past. Yet Polybius was equally critical of scholars who never left their libraries. In his view, history should only be written by former politicians and ex-generals, who are familiar with public affairs. The historian should also travel and investigate the scenes where history took place, and he must consult original documents whenever possible. Above all, the historian must be impartial and overcome the biases of his sources and informants. In effect, Polybius expressed the ideal of scientific history which is often associated with the nineteenth century A.D. He was a diligent researcher and composed an impressive history of the Mediterranean world from 220 to 145 B.C. Characteristically, Polybius distinguished between the pretexts over which nations fought and the underlying causes of war (such as national rivalries and resentment over past injuries). However, like his contemporaries, Polybius retained the concept of Fortune as a major factor in history.

On most matters Polybius was more reliable than other Greeks or those Romans who wrote on the same topics, but he failed to attain his own ideal of scientific objectivity. In discussing Hellenic affairs Polybius was blindly prejudiced against opponents of his own city, and in regard to Roman politics he embraced the biases of his friends in the Roman aristocracy. He was also unscientific in employing the concept of historical cycles. Continual linear progress was too optimistic a notion for the pessimistic Greeks, and the spectacle of the rise, decline, and fall of both Persia and Macedon may have suggested the idea of fixed cycles. Some Greeks believed that decay and collapse were implicit in any society, however flourishing it might appear to be. Polybius was the most famous historian to embrace the concept of predictable patterns of growth and decline, but he modified the "laws of history" to account for the Roman experience. Thus Rome conquered the Mediterranean world because of the superiority of its "mixed constitution," and as long as Rome retained this constitutional balance in its political life, the cycle of decay would be arrested. (In reality, the "mixed constitution" was a thin veil for oligarchy, and Polybius was hostile to democracy.) Should the balance ever be upset—that is, if the senatorial nobles lost control and Rome became more democratic—the cycle would turn again, and the Roman state would soon decline and perish. Though he was sure that he was being scientific, Polybius' law of "cyclic arrest" was an expression of his own political conservatism. Nevertheless, Polybius was the greatest Hellenistic historian and a devoted exponent of the ideal of scientific history.

At Rome, the writings of Polybius were highly regarded, for he was an apologist for Roman dominion, but his pleas for science and objectivity had little effect. Among the Romans, history was a political weapon with which to attack enemies while glorifying one's own family and faction. Roman historians were hopelessly partisan and constantly revised the past to fit the preconceptions of their friends in the present. New nobles discovered previously unknown glories for their ancestors, and the constitutional evolution of the republic was freely rewritten to justify the political biases of historians. In addition, Roman writers aped the bad habits of Greek historians, inventing speeches and dramatizing episodes beyond recognition. A typical republican historian was the gloomy Sallust, who moralized about corruption, maligned his opponents, and often lapsed into melodrama. The most famous historian of the republic was Livy, who composed a long but highly dramatic epic history of Rome's divinely ordained and very manifest destiny. As a patriot, Livy defamed Hannibal and the enemies of Rome; as a moralist, he deplored "modern godlessness" and depicted the early republic as a golden age of simple virtue and rustic valor. According to Livy, the empire had brought luxury and laxity, and struggles for power among Roman leaders had led to the greatest of evils, civil war. Happily for Livy, his views of the Roman past coincided with the aims of his patron, the emperor Augustus, who planned to restore patriotism and piety. Propaganda is most effective when the author himself believes it, and Livy's history was a great literary success, still worth reading today.

Under the emperors, many Roman historians were mere apologists for the men in power; others were hostile to the regime but feared to speak openly. In the second century A.D. Tacitus recounted the crimes and follies of the rulers of the first century, but he failed to do justice to their merits. Tacitus had loyally served the despot Domitian, and he later relieved his guilt by portraying all emperors, except Vespasian, as tyrants. Obsessed with abuses of power, Tacitus dis-

torted the image of an entire era with his grim epigrams and sly innuendos. To the last days of the empire, Roman historiography remained warped by political partisanship. Accordingly, even accounts of able emperors were marred by sensational reports of vice and crime, which modern readers should view with suspicion.

Modern readers will search the classical historians in vain for more than passing comments on economic causation in history. Class conflict was a commonplace to them, but their orientation was political, not economic. The ancients were interested in individuals, their interactions in factions and groups, their personal virtues (e.g., courage) and failings (e.g., the lust for power), and the major roles played by great men for good or ill. Except for two centuries at Athens, history was made by the few, not the many, and the history of the Roman republic was essentially that of an oligarchy. Accordingly, history was written by the few for the few, and the illiterate masses could not even read it. Ancient historians made only brief mention of economic factors and sociological changes; instead, they concentrated on the intricacies of politics, the psychology of leaders, and the disturbing element of Fortune.

The distinguishing features of classical historiography, its overemphasis upon politics, personalities, and even melodrama, do not diminish its positive contributions to the discipline of history. The great historians of Greece and Rome—Herodotus, Thucydides, Polybius, Livy, and Tacitus—were men of intelligence and perception who rescued the past from oblivion and tried to enlighten their readers with pungent comments on human nature. Since they felt too strongly about men and events, objectivity was beyond their grasp; but this is a failing not confined to ancient writers.

SUGGESTED READINGS

Penguin Books has published excellent modern translations of Herodotus, Thucydides, Xenophon, Livy, Tacitus, and Plutarch. A. J. Toynbee's *Greek Historical Thought*, Mentor, 1952, is a very useful anthology. The scholarly literature on ancient historiography is vast, but interested students should sample J. L. Myres, *Herodotus: Father of History*, Oxford, 1953; F. E. Adcock, *Thucydides and His History*, Cambridge, 1963; or P. G. Walsh, *Livy: His Historical Aims and Methods*, Cambridge, 1961.

Chapter 6

The Meeting of East and West

**The West, India, and China:
334 B.C. to 220 A.D.**

INTRODUCTION. To visualize the known world in classical times, we would have to gain sufficient distance to take in with one sweeping glance the giant land mass of Eurasia and North Africa, which together formed the homeland for the three inter-communicating civilizations of the ancient world. To the west we would look down on the hurly-burly of the Graeco-Roman empire, a conglomeration of diverse peoples living for the most part around the Mediterranean but all united under the *Pax Romana*. Next, we might see ships plowing through the Arabian Sea to reach a second dynamic center of civilization—India. Still farther east in the Eurasian land mass, we could perceive caravans trekking across the wastes of Central Asia into Chinese Turkestan and reaching their destination in the mighty Han empire of China proper.

The centuries immediately preceding and following the birth of Jesus were marked by cultural developments in India and China which, to a striking degree, paralleled those in the Roman world. The thousand years ending in the fifth century A.D. might be considered the formative period of the great world civilizations. This millennium spanned the evolution of the Graeco-Roman culture and the Judaic-Christian tradition, from which much of present-day western culture is derived; and in India and China it witnessed the development of religious movements, philosophical systems, and intellectual and artistic achievements which continue to play a vital role in the contemporary cultures of these Asian lands.

At this time each of the great areas of civilization—Graeco-Roman, Indian, and Chinese—was developing its own way of life, yet they were also connected by tenuous, sprawling routes of mutual commercial and cultural exchange. Let us visualize three scenes that were possible in any decade of the second century A.D.: in a Roman palace on the Palatine Hill, an empress admires priceless silks from China; at a southern Indian seaport, Greek sailors buy cinnamon

with Roman coins; and near a stone tower in the wastes of Turkestan, traders from the West and East exchange their wares. Although the contact between East and West was eventually severed, it continued long enough to establish a durable tradition in both the Orient and the Occident that beyond the mountains and deserts to the east or to the west lay other great civilizations. This tradition incited adventurous spirits many centuries later to bring the great "halves" of world civilization together once again.

Nurtured by centuries of stability and prosperity, the Graeco-Roman world-state constituted one of the crests of human endeavor. The tremendous influence of this civilization on the course of western history has been discussed; this chapter will trace the penetration of western culture into Asia and the cultural countermovement which resulted. These exchanges provide us with our first view of historical development on a global scale.

MONSOONS AND SILK ROUTES

Beyond the Roman frontiers. During its period of greatest prosperity, the Graeco-Roman world-state, centered in the Mediterranean basin, maintained trade contacts extending far beyond the imperial boundaries. Then, as now, in Seneca's words, "desire of trafficking [dragged] a man headlong over every land and sea in the hope of making gain."[1] In Europe, traders pushed north into the territories of the Germans and the peoples of Scandinavia, carrying with them glass, pottery, metalware, and Roman coins and receiving in exchange livestock, hides, furs, dried fish, amber, and slaves. In the southernmost parts of the Mediterranean world, other traders led their caravans across the Sahara or steered their vessels through the Red Sea and along the east coast of Africa. From Africa they returned to Europe with cargoes of ivory, gold dust, ostrich feathers, slaves, precious stones,

palm oil, and wild beasts for the amphitheaters of Rome and the provincial cities.

It was to the east, however, that the most important transfrontier penetrations were made, resulting in direct or indirect contacts with two other great civilizations: India and China. In the market quarter of imperial Rome, Chinese silk was sold, and Indian merchants frequented the streets of Alexandria. Strabo, the Greek geographer, stated that 120 ships sailed to India every year from Egyptian ports. During the four centuries which began after 334 B.C. (the year when Alexander the Great entered Asia), the frontiers of civilization were progressively enlarged until finally a great chain of intercommunicating states stretched across Eurasia from the Atlantic to the Pacific.

The impact of Hellenism. Alexander the Great's outstanding contribution to cultural history was to extend the influence of Greek culture eastward by conquering Asia as far as the Indus valley. The cities which Alexander and his successors built became the chief agents for spreading Hellenistic culture from the Aegean Sea to India and from the Caspian Sea to the cataracts of the Nile (see map, p. 119). Literate Asians learned Greek to facilitate trade, to become a part of the ruling circles of the Hellenistic states, and to read Hellenic classics. Let us now focus upon the conquered areas to understand the impact of Hellenism upon Asia.

After the death of Alexander (as we recall from Chapter 4), Seleucus acquired domains in Asia extending from the Mediterranean to the borders of India. For a time the Seleucid empire provided the peace and economic stability necessary to ensure the partial Hellenization of a vast area. However, there were not enough Greeks to colonize so large an area as the Near East. The Greek city-states remained only islands in an Asian ocean, and as time elapsed this ocean encroached more and more upon the Hellenized areas.

Emergence of Bactria and Parthia. The gradual weakening of the loosely knit Seleucid empire eventually resulted in the creation of independent kingdoms on the edge of the Hellenistic world. The Seleucid province of Bactria achieved independence in the middle of the third century B.C. and was soon recognized as a kingdom (see Reference Map 5). Located high on the western watershed of the great Pamir divide in what would now be northern Afghanistan and Soviet Turkestan, Bactria can be described as a "mark," or "march"—a state situated on the boundary of a larger community to which it belongs by race and culture. Under its third king—a Greek who had married into the Seleucid royal family—Bactria became a strong state. For over a century the Bactrian kingdom was to shield the Greek and Iranian peoples to the west from fierce nomads.

At the same time that Bactria was achieving independence, the kingdom of Parthia, situated between the Seleucid kingdom to the west and the emerging Bactrian kingdom to the east, was founded by a tribe of nomads who had thrust south from beyond the Caspian. After a century the Parthian rulers wrested Babylonia and Media from the Seleucids; Persia and parts of Bactria were added to these conquests to form the Parthian empire, which was destined to endure for almost five centuries. Because of their strategic position between East and West, the Parthians dominated the rich trans-Asian caravan trade. Although the Parthian empire included a number of Greek cities and absorbed some Hellenistic culture, it was essentially a native Iranian state, not a Hellenistic one.

For centuries the Parthians were the dogged enemies of the Romans. The overlordship of Armenia was the chief bone of contention, but Roman conquests in the Near East also contributed to the enmity between the two empires. A tale has come down to us about a notoriously avaricious Roman consul who was captured in the first century B.C. by the Parthians and killed by having molten gold poured down his throat. Although the story is probably false, it is indicative of the frightening reputation the Parthians had among Roman merchants and travelers.

The eastward drive of Hellenism was accompanied by a marked increase in economic activity throughout western Asia and in the exchange of goods between East and West. The trade between India and the West took several routes (see map, p. 165). From northern India caravans proceeded across Parthia, while ships from southern Indian ports sailed to meet overland routes across Mesopotamia, Arabia, and Egypt. In particular, Seleucia and Alexandria and the "caravan cities" of Petra and Palmyra enjoyed the prosperity of this commerce.

Trade and intercommunicating states. After Egypt and other Hellenistic areas had succumbed to Roman conquest, the Romans took over the rich trade with the East. From the Roman standpoint, the routes from India that centered on Seleucia had serious disadvantages: they led through Parthian territory, and the caravans were subject to heavy tolls by the Parthian government. The high profits which caravan merchants made as middlemen also boosted costs. Therefore Augustus and his successors encouraged the use of the southern sea route to India.

Meanwhile, a most important discovery in navigation was made when mariners found how to use the monsoon winds which blow from the southwest across the Arabian Sea from May to October. Eliminating the tedious journey along the coasts, sailors could now voyage from Aden to the west coast of India across the open sea. Furthermore, ships could return from India by using the counter-monsoon blowing from the northeast between November and March. Round-trip voyages required less than a year; the open-sea route lessened the danger from the pirates infesting the coasts of Arabia; and the costs of shipping were greatly reduced by the swifter voyages and the elimination of the tolls paid to Arab officials on the land routes.

The improvement in the sailing route encouraged western merchants to strike still farther east by ship, and they subsequently rounded the southern points of India and Ceylon. It is even possible that westerners may have crossed the Bay of Bengal to southeast Asia during these times. Gold coins and other Roman artifacts dating from the reigns of Antoninus Pius and Marcus Aurelius have been unearthed in excavations of an ancient town site in the Mekong River delta of Vietnam.

The first move to pierce the land barrier separating China from the West was made by the Chinese rather than the Europeans. In 138 B.C. the Chinese emperor Wu Ti dispatched an ambassador into west Central Asia to seek allies. Although the ambassador was unable to secure diplomatic alliances, he aroused Wu Ti's curiosity by describing the lands beyond the Pamirs and by showing his ruler the alfalfa and grape seeds he had carried back with him to China. Wu Ti resolved to open up trade relations with the peoples to the west. Thus, as a result of Chinese initiative, the use of silk spread to the Mediterranean during the early part of the first century B.C.

TRADE AND CULTURAL INTERCHANGE
ABOUT 50 B.C.

The World As Known To The Classical West
Land Routes
Water Routes

The silk caravans from northwest China which passed through Turkestan and Parthia before reaching the Roman dominions were also subject to heavy tolls. By diverting the caravans around Parthia to Indian ports and by transporting goods in Roman ships from there to the Red Sea and Egypt, the price of silk was reduced. As a result of this sea-borne competition, the silk trade became highly developed; the reduction of prices made this commodity available for more than just the wealthiest people in the West.

Chinese historical annals include an account of the arrival at Lo-yang in 166 A.D. of an "embassy" from the Roman empire:

[The Romans] . . . make coins of gold and silver. . . . They traffic by sea with . . . India, the profit of which trade is ten-fold. They are honest in their transactions, and there are no double prices. . . . Their kings always desired to send embassies to China, but the . . . Parthians wished to carry on trade with them in Chinese silks, and it is for this reason that they were cut off from communications . . . .[2]

The Roman "embassy" was probably not a governmental mission but rather a group of merchants who had sold their cargoes in India and then traveled farther eastward with Indian goods.

Thus, a series of impacts—political, cultural, and commercial—occurred during classical times, affecting in varying degrees the three major civilizations. In some instances, the contacts were direct, such as Alexander's conquests in western Asia and northern India. On the other hand, contacts between China and the West were tenuous and depended almost entirely upon intermediaries. Although Roman merchants reached China by ship in 166 A.D.—and ancient records mention other visits in the third century as well—we do not know whether any Roman subject ever arrived in China by means of the overland route. Nevertheless, the world in classical times was linked by intercommunicating states.

Having seen this contact of East and West, let us now examine the development of the characteristic culture patterns of India and China and explore further the cultural impact between the Eurasian civilizations.

INDIA UNDER THE MAURYAS AND THE KUSHANS

Alexander the Great in India. Nearly a score of royal states or tribal republics had been established in northern India by the sixth century B.C. Of these the most important was Magadha, along the lower Ganges (see map, p. 173). Its kings expanded their power by absorbing neighboring states; thus enlarged, Magadha was to become the nucleus of India's first empire.

In 326 B.C. Alexander of Macedon, continuing his conquest of the former Persian empire, brought his phalanxes into the easternmost Persian satrapy in the Indus valley, defeating local Punjab rulers. He turned back from a contemplated attack into the Ganges valley because of the near mutiny of his travel-weary troops. After Alexander died, the empire he had built in such meteoric fashion quickly disintegrated; by 321 B.C. his domain in the Punjab had completely disappeared. But from the towns he had founded in Bactria, beyond the northwest passes, were to come important Hellenistic influences on India in later times.

Chandragupta Maurya. By 322 B.C. a new era was at hand for India. In that year Chandragupta Maurya, whose origins are obscure but who apparently had served as a Magadhan soldier, gathered an army and seized the Magadha state from an unpopular sovereign. In the next twenty-four years Chandragupta conquered much of north India and founded the Maurya dynasty, which endured until about 185 B.C. At its height the empire included Afghanistan, the Punjab, much of the Gangetic plain—practically all of the Indian subcontinent north of the Narbada River (see Reference Map 5).

India's first empire was a vast realm reflecting the imperial vision of its founder. In many ways its governmental efficiency was not duplicated in other contemporary civilizations. And in India it was not surpassed until the advent of British colonial rule in the nineteenth century. The success

The caravan route between China and the Mediterranean coast, known as the Silk Road, was approximately four thousand miles from end to end and traversed some of the most difficult terrain in the world. Caravans leaving China would skirt the Taklamakan Desert, cross the Pamir Mountains, travel through Samarkand, Baghdad, and Palmyra, and eventually reach Antioch at the northern corner of the Mediterranean (see map, p. 166). No one caravan ever made the whole trip; instead the silk was carried by several merchants, each making a stage of the journey and each adding his profit to the final cost of the silk. These pottery figures and model houses (top left), taken from Chinese tombs where they were intended to serve the dead in the spirit world, have been arranged to show a village street. A caravan has just passed around the "ghost screen" (far left) which keeps evil spirits out of the village. Drummers on horseback, announcing the caravan's arrival, ride at the head of the procession. The oasis of Tunhuang at the edge of the Gobi Desert was an important stopping place along the Silk Road. Arriving there in the fourth century A.D., Buddhist monks carved hundreds of grottos out of solid cliffs and decorated them with paintings and statues of Buddha (bottom left). Although Buddha was a suitable subject for art, the caravans themselves apparently were not, and this hastily sketched graffito (top right) from a wall at Dura-Europus is the only existing caravan picture. Palmyra, a Syrian oasis, became a wealthy and magnificent city as a result of levying high duties on the goods which passed through it. The city was destroyed by the Romans in 273 A.D., but its ruins still testify to its former grandeur (middle right). This relief of a caravan leader with his camel (bottom right), which comes from Palmyra, is an interesting synthesis of Hellenistic and oriental artistic traditions. The flowing robes are typically Graeco-Roman, while the direct frontal view and formalized hair and beard are characteristically oriental.

of this Mauryan empire stemmed from three significant factors, the first economic. By the sixth century B.C. north India witnessed important advances in agriculture, trade, and general prosperity. Forests were cleared, areas of arable land extended, and new cities founded. The use of currency also spread rapidly. A new merchant class emerged whose interests were menaced by constant feuds and wars between numerous petty kingdoms. This middle class sought law and order and naturally favored the creation of large stable governments. The second factor behind the emergence of the Mauryan state was foreign intrusion. Alexander's invasion had broken the power of numerous small Indian kingdoms leaving behind a debris of weakness and confusion. Into this vacuum intruded the third factor: a new type of ruler who by force and craft created the "new kingship in India." The power of these rulers was based upon a large professional army, an incredibly large force of some 700,000 men.

Chandragupta may be considered the first emperor of India, though his power did not extend to the southern regions of the subcontinent. He was a brilliant general and administrator, an alert thinker, and a colorful figure. Whether or not there is truth to a Greek historian's report that Chandragupta had once visited Alexander's camp in the Punjab, the Magadhan did maintain contacts with the Greeks after he became emperor and fostered a friendly exchange of information between the Seleucid empire and his own. He lived in great splendor; his court included Greek courtiers and was run according to Persian ceremonial, factors which scarcely endeared him to his Indian subjects. So great was the danger of conspiracy that Chandragupta lived in strict seclusion, surrounded by a bodyguard of women who cooked his food, served his wine, and in the evening carried him to his apartment where they lulled him to sleep with music. He would even change bedrooms at night to thwart possible attempts on his life by enemies who are said to have gone so far as to dig tunnels under the palace walls.

Life in the Mauryan empire. Meanwhile, after an unsuccessful attempt to restore Greek control over the Indus valley, Seleucus established friendly relations with the Mauryan empire and sent an envoy, Megasthenes, to the court of Chandragupta at Pataliputra, the splendid capital city. Thanks to this ambassador's reports, we have a fascinating picture of these early times. Pataliputra, known today as Patna, covered eighteen square miles and boasted massive wooden city walls containing 64 gates and 570 towers. The streets were well planned and lined with inns, theaters, gambling houses, bazaars, and two- and three-story houses. In the center of the city stood the royal palace surrounded by a walled park containing tame peacocks, fish ponds, and ornamental trees.

In its structure and the hierarchy of administrative divisions, the Mauryan empire was remarkably advanced. It was divided into a small number of provinces, each of which was governed by a viceroy and a staff of officials. The emperor was not limited by any law, and the central government over which he presided maintained a tight rein over the distant provinces. Excellent roads, marked by milestones, connected the many villages and towns; and a postal service was maintained by royal couriers, who could rest at inns placed along the highways.

A picture of the government has been left for us by Chandragupta's able chief minister, Kautilya. His book, *The Arthasastra,* is practically the only work on statecraft in India which has survived from ancient times. From it we learn that justice was dispensed sternly but with fairness in both civil and criminal cases. Under the supervision of a well-organized war office the large army was fed, trained, and led. Apparently like the later Renaissance Italian author on statecraft, Machiavelli, Kautilya believed in deception or unscrupulous means to attain any desired end. *The Arthasastra* comments that "intrigue, spies, winning over the enemy's people, siege and assault" are the five means of capturing a fort. The main pillar of the government was the pervasive and dreaded secret service employing a large number of spies and secret agents.

Over all, there were some thirty imperial departments overseeing such affairs as markets, canal irrigation, public works, and revenues. The municipal organization of the capital was amazingly comprehensive. Comprising six boards, it provided for the treatment of foreigners, birth and death statistics, retail trade, manufacturing, and the collection of a sales tax. The British Indologist, Vincent Smith, comments: "Many readers probably will be surprised to learn of the existence at such an early date of a government so thoroughly organized which anticipated in many respects the institutions of modern times. The dark spots on the picture are the appalling wickedness of the statecraft taught in *The Arthasastra* and the hateful espionage which tainted the whole administration."[3]

All land belonged to the state, and agriculture was the chief source of wealth. Irrigation and crop rotation were practiced, and Megasthenes tells us that famines were almost unknown. Trade was cosmopolitan; in the bazaars of Pataliputra were displayed goods from southern India, China, Mesopotamia, and Asia Minor. Indian ships sailed the Indian Ocean to the head of the Persian Gulf and to Arabia, and from these points caravans carried Indian goods overland toward markets as distant as the cities of Greece. Manufacturing was also important in the Mauryan empire. Greek accounts refer to the making of arms and agricultural implements and the building of ships; northwestern India was famous for cotton cloth and silk yarn.

Weavers and other craftsmen were often organized into guilds, and slaves were treated humanely and could in many instances purchase their freedom. On the other hand, the caste system was becoming more rigid. Violations of caste rules resulted in fines being imposed by the council or even the outcasting of an erring member.

Popular amusements included dice playing and an early form of chess, as well as dancing, wrestling, and chariot racing. State feasts, caste festivals, entertainments by strolling players, and gay processions through the illuminated streets of the capital added to the excitement and pleasure of living.

About 297 B.C. Chandragupta was succeeded by his son Bindusara. A charming story about Bindusara indicates the close cultural relations which existed at this time between the Mauryan and Seleucid rulers. Writing to Antiochus, Bindusara asked for a sample of Greek wine, some raisins, and a Sophist. In his reply Antiochus stated that he was sending the wine with pleasure, but that "it isn't good form among the Greeks to trade in philosophers."[4]

Ashoka, propagator of Buddhism. Ashoka, a son of Bindusara, reigned from 273 B.C. to 232 B.C. He was one of the few early kings who pursued the arts of peace more diligently than the arts of war; his first military campaign was also his last.

In 262 B.C. Ashoka attacked the state of Kalinga to the south, whose inhabitants stubbornly resisted his invasion. In the war of extermination which followed, victory fell to Ashoka, and at least 200,000 Kalingans were killed or captured. Thus Ashoka extended his empire so that it included nearly all of India to the edge of Tamil Land. But the cruelty of the campaign horrified him, and he resolved never again to permit such acts of butchery. Soon after this war, Ashoka was converted to Buddhism, whose gentle teachings increased his aversion to warfare. In Ashoka's own words:

When an unconquered country is conquered, people are killed, they die, or are made captive. . . . Today, if a hundredth or a thousandth part of those who suffered in Kalinga were to be killed, to die, or to be taken captive, it would be very grievous to the Beloved of the Gods. If anyone does him wrong it will be forgiven as far as it can be forgiven. . . . For the Beloved of the Gods desires safety, self-control, justice and happiness for all beings. The Beloved of the Gods considers that the greatest of all victories is the victory of Righteousness. . . .[5]

As the years passed, Ashoka became even more deeply religious. Throughout his empire he had his imperial edicts carved on rocks and stone pillars. Some of the latter still stand today. These huge, polished sandstone pillars, thirty to forty feet high, together with a series of Rock Edicts, give little or no information concerning political events, but their inscriptions are invaluable for appreciating the spirit and purpose of

Ashokan rule. Stressing compassion, kindness to all living things, truth, purity, and liberality, the edicts were a practical application of the teachings of Buddha. For example, as an emperor guided by the Buddhist Law of Piety, Ashoka declared:

Thus saith His Majesty—
Father and Mother must be obeyed, similarly respect for living creatures must be enforced; truth must be spoken. These are the virtues of the Law of Duty. . . . Similarly a teacher must be reverenced by the pupil, and proper courtesy must be shown to relations.[6]

And regarding Ashoka's conception of the Duty of a Ruler—

He shall, therefore, personally attend to the business of gods, of heretics, of Brahmans . . . of earth, of sacred places, of minors, the aged, the afflicted, and the helpless, and of women. . . . In the happiness of his subjects lies his happiness; in their welfare his welfare; whatever pleases himself he shall not consider as good, but whatever pleases his subjects he shall consider as good.[7]

The inscriptions on Ashoka's pillars show not only that the art of calligraphy was highly developed but also that writing was commonly used for practical purposes throughout the empire.

Although he himself was a devout Buddhist, Ashoka believed in complete religious toleration; he did not persecute the Brahmins, who upheld Hindu tradition. A strong believer in the doctrine of *ahimsā*, or noninjury to men or animals, he forbade animals to be sacrificed in the capital, substituted royal pilgrimages to Buddhist shrines for hunting expeditions, and did away almost entirely with the slaughter of animals for meat at the palace. Ashoka ate no meat himself and probably encouraged vegetarianism among his subjects.

Termed "the first royal patron of Buddhism," Ashoka has been likened to St. Paul and Constantine—a successful propagator of his faith. Ashoka sent Buddhist missionaries to many lands—the Himalayan regions, the Tamil kingdoms, Ceylon, Burma, and even as far away as Syria, Egypt, and Macedonia—to teach the gospel of salvation and equality. Thus transformed from a small Indian sect to

a powerful religion, Buddhism began to make its influence felt beyond its homeland. Ashoka's missionary efforts had enduring success in neighboring Asiatic lands, particularly in Ceylon, where Buddhism is found today in nearly its original form.

Undoubtedly Ashoka deserves a place on the world's roster of illustrious rulers. Modern-day Indians revere his memory, and the famous lion capital of Sarnath (see illustration, p. 176) has been adopted as the national seal of the present Indian republic. As H. G. Wells wrote:

Amidst the tens of thousands of names of monarchs that crowd the columns of history, the name of Ashoka shines and shines almost alone, a star. From the Volga to Japan his name is still honoured. China, Tibet, and even India, though it has left his doctrine, preserve the tradition of his greatness.[8]

Fall of the Mauryan empire. Almost immediately after Ashoka's death in 232 B.C., his empire began to disintegrate. The last Mauryan emperor was assassinated in about 185 B.C., and the state was then invaded by a ruler from southern India and also by Demetrius, the fourth Bactrian king who swept into northwest India and overran the Punjab.

Although the Mauryan state had once been powerful, it crumbled almost overnight. So dramatic was the collapse and so grave the consequences that, like the decline and fall of the Roman empire, it has provoked much scholarly speculation. Some historians have felt that the fall of the Mauryans can be traced to a hostile Brahmin reaction against Ashoka's patronage of Buddhism. However, Ashoka had treated this group with marked respect, and there is no evidence of Brahmin hostility. Other scholars believe that Ashoka's doctrine of nonviolence curbed the military ardor of his people and left them easy prey for invaders. Still other possible explanations for the fall of the Mauryan state take into account the communications problems facing this widespread empire, the growth of local autonomy in outlying provinces, and the intrigue and oppression by various members of the royal family—all of which contributed to a weakening of central control. Whatever the circumstances of the sudden collapse of the Mauryan empire, its contribution to world civilization survived, for "the moral ascendancy of Indian culture over a large part of the civilized world, which Ashoka was mainly instrumental in bringing about, remained for centuries as a monument to . . . [India's] glory. . . ."[9]

The Graeco-Bactrian kingdom. When Demetrius invaded northern India (c. 185 B.C.) he occupied Gandhara—an area whose inhabitants had been converted to Buddhism by Ashoka. The Bactrians organized the chief Gandharan town as a Hellenistic city and even fashioned an acropolis there. The blending of Greek and Buddhist influences at Gandhara later resulted in a remarkable artistic development (see p. 176). Demetrius also acquired Taxila (an administrative center of the Mauryan empire and the site of a famous university, whose buildings have recently been excavated) and Pataliputra,

the Mauryan capital. Thus Demetrius ruled an area stretching from the Persian desert to the middle of the Ganges valley.

Demetrius organized his domain much as a Seleucid kingdom. In keeping with Alexander's ideal of bringing East and West together on a basis of equality, Demetrius issued a bilingual coinage bearing Greek inscriptions on one side and Indian on the other. "His realm was to be a partnership of Greek and Indian; he was not to be a Greek king of Indian subjects, but an Indian king no less than a Greek one, head of both races."[10]

His general, Menander, who subsequently ascended the throne (180-160 B.C.), continued the concept of partnership. Whereas in the West, the Seleucid rulers had endeavored to create a basically Greek empire filled with Greek settlements, it was not possible to found Greek cities on any such scale in India. Thus Menander's kingdom was essentially Indian with a small Greek

ASHOKA'S EMPIRE
• Cities △ Rock Edicts ▲ Pillar Edicts

ruling class; its continuance depended upon an absence of national feelings among the Indian people. Menander was a wise ruler and, according to some legends, even became a Buddhist before he died in the middle of the second century B.C. The kingdom of Bactria attained a high state of culture before being crushed by the nomadic tribes which swept out of Central Asia in the second century B.C. and seized Bactria, the Kabul valley, and adjoining regions. In India, the last remnants of Greek rule were extinguished about 30 B.C.—one year after the battle of Actium, in which Augustus defeated Anthony and Cleopatra and gained the supremacy of the Mediterranean world.

The Kushan empire. A turbulent period followed the fall of the Bactrian kingdom. But, by the first century A.D., the most important of the invading clans, the Kushans, had established themselves as masters of a large part of northwestern India.

Kanishka, the most outstanding of the Kushan rulers, became king sometime between 78 and 128 A.D. (probably closer to the former date). All of northwest India, perhaps as far south as the Narbada River, and much of present Afghanistan to the north were under his sway. This enlightened monarch took over the religion of the people he conquered. During his reign the arts and sciences flourished, imposing buildings were constructed, and advances were made in the field of medicine.

By the end of the first century A.D., little culture remained in India which could be called distinctively Greek. The few Greek cities had been either destroyed or completely Indianized, Greek inscriptions ceased to appear on coins, and all traces of Greek script vanished from India.

Varieties of Mahayana and Hinayana Buddhism. Following the Buddha's death, some Buddhists had maintained the spirit and practice of the founder, but other followers began to make his doctrines increasingly complex. Whereas Gautama had been concerned primarily with the removal of individual suffering by a life of purity and self-denial, later Buddhists added to this central doctrine more emotional and metaphysical concepts, together with myths and rituals. To some Buddhists, this development was a corruption of the original Buddhism, but the more mystical approach had great appeal and in Kanishka's reign showed its strength.

An important systematization of Buddhist doctrine took place when Kanishka convened a great council of five hundred monks; from their work arose the *Mahayana,* or "Great Vehicle," school of Buddhism. The *Mahayanists* conceived of the Buddha as a Bodhisattva, an exalted being who renounced *nirvana* to save mankind. They claimed that their belief was the great vehicle for carrying men to salvation and that the earlier form of Buddhism represented the *Hinayana,* or "Lesser Vehicle." These terms were invented by the *Mahayanists;* the members of the rival school called themselves *Theravadins*—that is, followers of the Doctrine of the Elders. While the *Hinayana* remained primarily a moral philosophy, austere and rational, the more emotional *Mahayana* approach offered faith as a road to salvation.

Rapidly becoming popular in much of India, *Mahayana* Buddhism spread along the trade routes to the northeast as its believers converted the people of Nepal, Tibet, China, Korea, and Japan to the Buddhist faith. But *Mahayana* Buddhism did not obliterate the simpler *Hinayana* Buddhism of the *Theravadins.* Geographically speaking, the *Hinayana* may be considered the southern branch of Buddhism, for it was that form of Buddhism which spread from India and Ceylon to Burma, Thailand, Cambodia, the Malay peninsula, and Indonesia.

Like Ashoka, Kanishka was a Buddhist convert who was instrumental in helping to make Buddhism a world religion. Hinduism, however, still had a strong hold on the Indian people. While the Buddhists had disregarded caste and accepted both the Greeks and the Kushans, the Hindus rejected the foreign invaders as outcastes. Gradually the Indians came to consider Hinduism a more characteristically Indian movement than Buddhism. Therefore, although Kanishka helped to spread Buddhism to other countries, in the long run his support probably lessened its popularity within India.

Evolution of Buddhist temple architecture. Indian art undoubtedly had a rich history prior to Ashoka, for the remains of the artistic works produced in his reign display advanced techniques. Sculpture especially achieved a high degree of excellence in the Mauryan period. The skill of the stonecutter was superb, and it is said that the Mauryan art of polishing the hardest stone has never been excelled. Stone instead of wood was gradually introduced in monumental building, but most edifices were constructed of wood. The magnificent buildings of the Mauryan emperors have all disappeared; excavations, as at Pataliputra, have unearthed few remains.

Of particular interest are Ashoka's *stupas*, dome-shaped monuments which were used as funeral mounds to enshrine the relics of Buddhist saints or to mark a holy spot. Originally of earth, the mounds were later made of earth faced with brick and surrounded by railing and four richly carved gateways of stone. On top of the dome was a boxlike structure surmounted by a carved umbrella, the Indian emblem of sovereignty which symbolizes the Buddha's princely birth. As centuries passed, the low dome was heightened into a tall, tapered structure more like a tower. Later, when Buddhism spread to other countries, the *stupa* type of architecture went along; its gateway was widely copied, and the *stupa* itself inspired magnificent temple architecture.

Graeco-Roman Buddhist art. In a previous section we noted the intermingling of Greek and Buddhist elements in Gandhara during the period of the Graeco-Bactrian kingdom. From this fusion evolved a prolific Graeco-Roman Buddhist school of art—as early as the first century B.C. in the view of some scholars, in the Kushan period according to others. Prior to the emergence of this school, Indian artists had refrained, because of the Buddha's prohibitions against idolatry, from portraying the Buddha in human form. Instead they depicted certain symbols associated with his life and teachings— the lotus, the symbol of Gautama's miraculous birth; the tree, under which he received illumination; and the wheel, the symbol of birth and rebirth.

As the Gandhara area became progressively Indianized, and in closer touch with the culture of West Asia, after the first century B.C., Indo-Greek artists began to depict the Buddha in human form. This new style, influenced increasingly by Hellenistic rather than early Greek art forms, can best be termed Graeco-Roman. The Gandharan artists evolved a subtle blending of Hellenistic and Indian techniques; representations of the Buddha combined the Indian monastic robe and distended earlobe with such Graeco-Roman touches as the straight profile and supple folds of drapery. The results were artistically impressive, and the compassionate appearance and facial beauty of the images made them popular. Since *Mahayana* Buddhism accepted the worship of sacred images, the Gandharan school flourished through the support of Kanishka and his successors (see Color Plate 9).

Because the Kushan empire touched upon the Chinese empire to the north, Graeco-Roman Buddhist art penetrated into the heart of Central Asia; its influence was felt first in Chinese Turkestan, then in China proper, and finally in Japan. Thus we see that the *Mahayana* school of Buddhism and Graeco-Roman Buddhist art—both of which developed in the Kushan empire—spread together through eastern Asia.

The Andhra dynasty and the Tamil states. Contemporary with the Kushans but farther south was another important dynasty, the Andhra. From about 100 B.C. to 225 A.D. this dynasty dominated the region in central India known as the Deccan. The Andhra state was organized into administrative divisions, and local control was left to feudal rulers who were subject in turn to royal supervision. The Hindu rulers were tolerant toward all religions and foreigners, and the effects of cultural exchange can be seen in the Buddhist *stupa* of Amaravati, for example, whose sculpture reflects the influence of Graeco-Roman Buddhist motifs originating at Gandhara. Both the eastern and western coasts of the Deccan were dotted with busy trading ports. Like the Kushan empire, however, the Andhra domains broke up in the early part of the third century, and the Deccan again endured political disunity.

At the tip of the Indian peninsula lay the Tamil country, peopled by Dravidians whose

The development of Indian Buddhist art from the time of Ashoka through the Gupta period reflects changes in the Buddhist religion. At first the Buddha was symbolically represented as a lion or bull to suggest his majesty and power, as on this capital from one of Ashoka's pillars (left). The wheel underneath the lion is the Wheel of the Law which Buddha set in motion through his teachings. A fine example of Graeco-Roman Buddhist art, the head of Buddha from Gandhara (center) shows Hellenistic influence in the modeling of the features and hair, while the heavy-lidded eyes and expression of deep repose are typically Indian. Also Indian are such symbols of his virtue as the third eye of wisdom, between his brows, the protuberance of knowledge on top of his head, and his very long ear lobes. During the Gupta period, Indian artists, encouraged by their rulers, began to produce works of a more indigenous style, as is evident in the teaching Buddha (right) and the painting of the temptation of Buddha from the Ajanta caves (bottom).

civilization had long been absorbing Hindu culture from the lands to the north. The composite culture of Tamil Land is described in early Tamil literature dating from the first centuries of the Christian era.

The chief religion was Hinduism, the prevailing form of government was hereditary monarchy, and the kings maintained professional armies employing chariots, elephants, cavalry, and infantry. The wealthier classes lived in houses made of brick and mortar and decorated with wall paintings. Leisure time was given over to feasting, hunting, wrestling, boxing, dicing, and to the arts of music, dancing, and poetry. For poets it was an auspicious age; they might expect from their patrons such princely gifts as land, chariots, and golden lotuses—in one instance a poet received an elephant.

Here are two samples of Tamil poetry; in the first the poet describes his countrymen at work and in the second at play during a village festival.

The toiling fishermen catch the shoals
in their close-meshed nets, and the soft-headed
    prawn,
thin as the cassia bud in the forest.

Like hunters who chase the deer in the woods
young fishermen chase in the waste of the waters
the saw-toothed shark, and return with meat.

They return to the shore and unload on the
    sand,
where the wind plays wild across the salt
    pans . . .[11]

The farmers who harvest rice in the hot sun
now leap into the waves of the clear sea.
The sailors, captains of stout craft,
drink strong liquor and dance for joy,
as they clasp the bright-bangled hands of women
who wear garlands of clustering *punnai* . . .

In the cool woods, where the bees seek flowers,
women, bright-bangled and garlanded, drink
the juice of the palm and the pale sugar-cane,
and the juice of the coconut which grows in the
    sand,
then running they plunge into the sea.[12]

Trade with the West. Throughout the long period of the ascendancy of the Hellenistic kingdoms and then of the Roman empire, trade between India and the West was brisk and widespread. The Kushan rulers were on friendly terms with the Romans; spices and silks left Indian ports in exchange for Roman gold coins, Greek wines, and "choice girls for the royal harems."

The greatest part of Indian trade with the West, however, was carried on by the Tamil kingdoms. These states enjoyed prosperous commercial ties with the Hellenistic Greeks, particularly those in Egypt, and the vigor of the commercial contact is shown by some interesting examples of linguistic influences: the Hebrew term for peacock and the Greek words for ginger, cinnamon, and rice come from the Tamil language.

In Roman times trade with the Tamil kingdoms was expanded still further. Large hoards of western coins discovered in southern India attest to the vigor of East-West trade during this period. The scarceness of Hellenistic coins as compared with those of the Roman empire shows that commercial interchange reached its height in the first two centuries A.D.

When Augustus became head of the Roman world, the Tamil kingdoms sent him a congratulatory embassy, an honor never before paid a western prince. The ambassadors took about four years en route and bore such gifts as "a gigantic python, huge tortoises, and an armless boy who could shoot arrows and throw darts with his feet!"[13] In the period from Augustus' rule to the reign of the first Constantine, at least nine other embassies from India visited Roman emperors to arrange for the protection and well-being of Indian ships and traders at Roman ports.

Roman merchants, meanwhile, dwelt in Tamil seaports, and through them precious metals, coins, wine, pottery, glassware, silverware, and even craftsmen and masons were brought to India. In recent years a Roman trading post of the first century A.D. has been discovered at Arikamedu on the east coast of southern India. The excavation of Italian-made pottery in this remote site on the further side of the subcontinent attests to the extent of the commerce that "was reaching out eastwards to the sources of pearls and silk. The imagination of the modern enquirer kindles as he lifts from the alluvium of the Bay of Bengal sherds (fragments of pottery) bearing the names of craftsmen whose kilns lay on the outskirts of Arezzo...."[14] Tamil poets described Roman ships which carried a guard of archers to ward off pirates, while the Tamil kings employed bodyguards of Roman soldiers, whose long coats aroused much comment in a land where comparative nudity was the rule.

For its part, India was exporting drugs, pearls, silks, muslins, and spices. Sometimes works of art also left India for the West; a fine ivory statuette of Indian workmanship portraying the Indian goddess of luck, Lakshmi, was uncovered in the excavations of Pompeii. In view of the magnitude of Roman-Tamil trade, we can understand why Ptolemy shows considerable knowledge of the geography of southern India.

Northern and central India entered into a chaotic period after the fall of the Kushans and Andhras, to emerge later with a splendid Hindu civilization under the Guptas. In the third century A.D. the Tamil kingdoms also experienced a period of strife and decline. This story goes beyond the limits of the present chapter, so let us now follow the direction of the missionaries of *Mahayana* Buddhism and the silk merchants who plodded eastward through Central Asia toward China, the third great civilization of classical times.

CHINA: THE FIRST EMPIRES

Ch'in unites China. As we recall from Chapter 3, China was experiencing significant growth despite, or perhaps because of, its division into many petty, warring states. No state strove more for internal centralization and wielded increasingly autocratic power than the state of Ch'in, which embraced the ruthless philosophy of Legalism. As early as the middle of the fourth century B.C., a leading Ch'in statesman reportedly "instituted a strict system of rewards and punishments in Ch'in, forced all persons into 'productive' occupations, set up a system of

mutual responsibility and spying among the people, and attempted to replace the old hereditary families by a new, purely honorary aristocracy based on military exploits."[15]

In the middle of the third century B.C. the Legalist Li Ssu, a disciple of Hsün-tzu (see Chapter 3) and one of the most remarkable statesmen in Chinese history, helped the king of Ch'in prepare and carry out the conquest and unification of China, which was accomplished by 221 B.C. The king then assumed the title *Shih Huang-ti,* "First Emperor," taking for his title two terms that referred to the gods (Shang Ti) and the sage-emperors of the mythical age (the Three Huang and the Five Ti).[16] *Huang-ti* remained the title of Chinese emperors until the end of the imperial system in 1911.

Shih Huang-ti and Li Ssu were men of immense drive, skill, and imagination, and together they carried out a revolution in Chinese society that went far beyond the unification of the country through centralization of bureaucratic administration. In effect, they created a precursor of the modern totalitarian state, particularly its fascist variety, in a premodern society. They gathered the complete aristocratic class—some 120,000 families, according to tradition—at the capital and replaced them with their own bureaucratic administrators in the provinces. With the exception of the imperial soldiers, the entire population had to surrender its weapons to the state. Shih Huang-ti standardized weights, measures, coinage, and axle lengths throughout the empire. The latter was particularly important as it permitted the creation of a unified road system radiating out from the capital, thus contributing to the ease of imperial control. Roads in North China were often simply wheel ruts in the soft soil, and differences in axle lengths from region to region had inhibited the growth of communication.

A single harsh legal code replaced all local laws and went far toward shattering long-standing traditions; the entire realm was divided into provinces, administrative units drawn to obliterate traditional feudal units and to facilitate direct rule by the emperor's own centrally controlled civil and military appointees. To destroy the source of the aristocracy's power and to permit the emperor's agents to tax every farmer's harvest, private ownership of land by peasants was allowed.

Vast public works of both a civilian and a military nature were undertaken for the greater security of the state and glory of the emperor. Monuments lauding the emperor's works lined the new road system. Shih Huang-ti built a vast palace and a great tomb for himself; the latter was said to be a man-made mountain. His most spectacular public work was repairing the remnants of walls built in earlier times by the northern feudal states and joining them into the Great Wall, extending from the sea into Central Asia for a distance of over fourteen hundred miles. The wall was both a line of defense against the barbarians who habitually raided into China to obtain wealth and products they themselves did not make, and a symbol of the distinction between China's sedentary agricultural civilization and the nomadic animal-husbandry societies of Central Asia. It was meant to keep the nomads out and, at the same time, to keep the Chinese in. This wall remains today one of the greatest monuments to man's engineering skill in the pre-industrial age and one of the wonders of the world.

One of the most important keystones of Ch'in imperial policy was intellectual control and enforced conformity. Li Ssu standardized the Chinese writing system, giving it essentially its modern form, thus facilitating written communication and inhibiting heterodox thought by destroying regional scripts. Furthermore, he tried to enforce intellectual conformity and make the Ch'in imperial system appear to be the only natural political order by attempting to destroy the historical memory of the intellectuals. In 213 B.C. he instituted the first literary inquisition in history, known as the "Burning of the Books." The Confucian classics, all works of history that did not support the

THE CH'IN AND HAN EMPIRES
221 B.C. — 87 B.C.

Ch'in, and any other books that appeared to be of a subversive nature were destroyed, and scholars who protested were banished from the empire or killed. The only exceptions were works of a utilitarian nature, according to Legalist philosophy: books on medicine, agriculture, divination, Ch'in history, and certain government libraries and documents. These measures, strongly resembling Hitler's purge of German literature in the twentieth century, dealt a blow to Chinese thought from which it never fully recovered.

Organized, like many modern societies, on the basis of increasing authoritarian centralization, China, from Ch'in times on, could not tolerate much intellectual diversity and freedom. Intellectual conformity and orthodoxy appeared then, as it does now, to be a necessary support for bureaucratic centralization.

When Shih Huang-ti died in 210 B.C., an inept son succeeded to the throne with the title of Second Emperor. He was, however, unable to control the rivalry among the First Emperor's chief aides. Ch'in policies, harshly applied, had alienated large segments of society, especially the masses, who were continually subjected to harsh forced labor. As the court sank into intrigue, anarchic popular rebellion swept the land; by 206 B.C. the Ch'in dynasty, which claimed that it would endure for "ten thousand generations," had completely disappeared. But the Chinese empire, which Ch'in created, lasted for more than two thousand years, evolving eventually into Communist China today. Although Ch'in itself disappeared, it created the longest-lived political institution in world history.

The Han dynasty: the Legalist state survives. In 202 B.C., the year in which the Romans defeated the Carthaginians at the battle of Zama, Liu Pang, better known under his posthumous title Kao Tzu (High Ancestor), won control of China and established the Han dynasty, with its capital at Ch'ang-an (see map, p. 179). The Han dynasty is traditionally divided into two parts, the Earlier Han, from 206 B.C. to 8 A.D., and the Later Han, from 23 A.D. to 220 A.D. It was interrupted by the short-lived Hsin, or New, dynasty, under a usurper of the throne. The Han corresponded in the East to the Roman empire in the West in time, significance, power, and prestige. Chinese today still call themselves "Men of Han," and the Japanese call the Chinese characters they use in writing their own language "Han characters," much as we speak of the "Latin alphabet."

Although the anti-Ch'in rebellions were characterized in part by a nostalgia for Chou society, the Ch'in dynasty had changed China more profoundly than was realized at the time. The clock could not be turned back, and the Legalist imperial state had become a permanent feature of the Chinese political landscape. Kao Tzu himself was a peasant who had become a Ch'in general by virtue of his own abilities. The empire and power he sought were those of the Ch'in, and neither he nor his rivals would have been satisfied with the old Chou feudal multi-state system. Moreover, the Ch'in had completely destroyed the feudal aristocracy on which the Chou system had rested, and it could not be reconstituted.

Kao Tzu and his successors succeeded where the Ch'in had failed because they retained the Legalist state in all its essentials but tempered their approach to the intellectuals and the people with moderation. At first Kao Tzu and his immediate successors, faced with the problem of ruling a vast empire without efficient means of communications, reëstablished some of the vassal kingdoms and states in regions distant from the capital, but they spent the first century and a half of their rule subjugating their own creations, returning to Legalist political institutions. Although the dynasty constantly faced internal threats in the form of recalcitrant generals and peasant revolts and external danger from the Central Asian nomads, the population under its rule grew dramatically. A "census" of 2 A.D. listed the population of the empire as almost sixty million, a greater number of people than ever recognized Rome's rule.

In accord with Legalist principles, which were tempered by the Confucian ideas that had developed during the Chou period, the Han emperors established complex admin-

Built as a defense against the barbarians, the Great Wall symbolizes China's self-enforced and militant isolation.

istrative organs staffed by a salaried bureaucracy to rule their vast empire. Periodic searches were made for men of talent, chosen for government service through a primitive examination and recommendation system and promoted by merit. By the first century B.C. the government employed more than 130,000 bureaucrats, or one for every 400 to 500 people in the empire. Relatively small by modern standards, the Han bureaucracy set the pattern for all subsequent periods of Chinese history down to 1949.

The bureaucracy served the state, not the people, with whom it came into contact mainly as tax collectors and directors of public works projects. The masses were left alone in their villages to conduct their own internal affairs under the guidance of village elders or local landlords. The bureaucrats were, for the most part, men of substance themselves, drawn largely from the landlord class, because wealth was the only means to buy the leisure necessary to obtain the kind of education that would enable a man to pass the examinations. Consequently, the division of Chinese society between aristocrats and the peasant masses that had existed in the Shang and Chou was now transformed into a division between landowner-bureaucrats on the one hand and the peasants on the other. Theoretically, however, the examinations were open to all Chinese except merchants, who were socially disadvantaged under the official ideology much as they were in pre-Renaissance Europe.

Wu Ti, the "Martial Emperor." After sixty years of consolidation, the Han empire reached its greatest extent and development during the long reign of Wu Ti, from 141-87 B.C. With the growth of bureaucracy, the empire could manage itself when a weak emperor was on the throne, and often a weak emperor allowed greater flexibility in affairs of state than a strong emperor whom everyone had to obey. Wu Ti, however, was a strong personality who conducted the affairs of the state and empire.

As was often to be the case with strong Chinese emperors, Wu Ti embarked on a policy of territorial expansion. To accomplish this he made the laws and administration more severe than had his Han predecessors,

increased taxes, established state monopolies on such vital products as salt and iron, and used conscript and slave labor on such public works as a canal connecting his capital with the Yellow River, thus facilitating the transportation of grain from East China to Ch'ang-an.

The Martial Emperor justified his expansionist policies in terms of self-defense against the threat of attacks by nomads, but desire to control the trade routes of Central Asia may also have been a major factor. In the north, he drove the nomads into and beyond the Gobi Desert, hurling huge armies against them. In the west, he extended the Great Wall out into the desert of the Tarim Basin and settled some 700,000 Chinese on the borders of this barren region, conquering it for China forever. His armies conquered parts of what is now Russian Turkestan, and under one of his successors Han armies reached beyond this point, extending Chinese power farther from the capital than Roman power reached out from Rome at any time. In the east, Wu Ti conquered southern Manchuria and northern Korea, bringing these areas once and for all under the sway of Chinese culture. And to the south, he extended his empire along the coast beyond the modern city of Canton well into North Vietnam.

Wu Ti's great conquests were based on far-reaching economic and financial reforms aimed at providing the government with revenue to administer the growing empire. As costs increased, taxes increased, until the government's fiscal situation grew precarious and the peasants' burdens led to revolt. This in turn increased the government's need for revenue to pay for the suppression of the rebellions its policies had caused. Moreover, as the government at the center grew weaker because of rebellion in the provinces and increasing luxury at the court and capital, it had to rely more and more on local military commanders and magnates for control of the population, giving them great power and prestige at its own expense. This vicious circle of decline after an initial dynastic period of increasing prosperity and power has been the pattern of most Chinese dynasties since the Han; western historians of China call it "the dynastic cycle." In the Han this eventually led to a temporary usurpation of the throne, which divided the Earlier from the Later Han.

The Later Han dynasty never reached the heights of its predecessor. War lords in the provinces seized more and more power for themselves, and widespread peasant rebellions sapped the state's resources. Reduced to a political fiction for the last three decades of its reign, the dynasty finally collapsed completely in 220 A.D. when the throne was usurped by the son of a famous general. But China succeeded where Europe failed: after three and a half centuries of disunion, China once again was united under the Sui dynasty and, with minor exceptions, has remained united to this day. In Europe, unification remains, even now, a dream.

Han eclectic Confucianism. In his political style and policies, Wu Ti was almost as much a Legalist as the Ch'in First Emperor, and yet his court was strongly oriented toward Confucianism. Neither Wu Ti nor Kao Tzu, the founder of the dynasty, wasted much affection on scholars. But both recognized that a literate and educated bureaucracy was necessary for governing so vast an empire, and consequently the way was open for a revival of the intellectual life that had been suppressed under the Ch'in. In 191 B.C. the Han lifted the Ch'in ban on Chou literature, and some older men were apparently able to write down from memory texts they had memorized in their youth, before the Ch'in dynasty was established. Legend has it that other texts were found hidden in the walls of houses, where they had been put by scholars to escape the Ch'in book burning.

Han thought included ideas drawn from a variety of schools, which were woven into a new synthesis that was very different from Chou philosophy. Taoist magic, alchemy, the *yin-yang* concepts of the Naturalists, and popular religion all influenced the Han scholars, whose primary interest during the first century of Han was the recovery of Chou literature. Their understanding of the old texts was at times vague, however, and it was Confucius as the ideal image of the sage rather than Confucianism as a political and social philosophy that eventually triumphed

during the Han. The state and the scholar-bureaucracy existed in a symbiotic relationship; the state needed the scholars to staff the bureaucracy, and the scholars needed the financial aid of the state and wanted to benefit from its power. Consequently, while Legalism as a philosophical school was anathema to the Han scholars, Legalist statecraft was redefined in Confucian terms (as understood by the Han scholars), and Chou ethical concepts tempered the harshness of Legalist practice. The result was a philosophy of benevolent imperial despotism, a far cry from Confucius' feudal concept of the *chün-tzu* and Mencius' doctrine of the Mandate of Heaven (see Chapter 3).

The Han dynasty witnessed many other important intellectual developments. The Five Classics were established as the primary Confucian canon and the basis of education. In 124 B.C. an imperial university was established, and by the latter half of the first century B.C. it was said to have had three thousand students. In the Later Han this increased tenfold. By 1 A.D. one hundred men a year entered government service through official examinations based on the Confucian classics, and Han Confucianism became the orthodox philosophy of the state in 58 A.D., when regular sacrifices to Confucius were ordered performed in all government schools.[17]

In Wu Ti's reign, Ssu-ma Ch'ien, a court astrologer, wrote the *Shih chi,* or *Historical Records,* in 130 chapters and more than 700,000 characters. This work set the pattern for all subsequent Chinese historical writing up to the twentieth century. Ssu-ma Ch'ien was an unusually sophisticated historian, and his work includes annals, chronological tables, essays on such subjects as music, astronomy, rivers and canals, and economics; over half the book is made up of biographies (see the Historical Critique, p. 308). In the Later Han, Pan Ku wrote the *History of the [Earlier] Han,* and thereafter it was customary for each dynasty to write the official history of its immediate predecessor. Chiang Kaishek's Nationalist government has recently published the official history of the Manchu dynasty. It remains to be seen if the Chinese Communists will write an official history of

Chiang Kai-shek. The world's first modern dictionary, the *Shuo wen (Explanation of Writing),* was also published during Wu Ti's reign.

Technological advancement. During the Han period China equaled and even surpassed the level of scientific and technological development in the rest of the world. Advances were particularly notable in the fields of mineralogy, alchemy and chemistry, pharmacology, zoology, and botany.[18] The Han Chinese invented a primitive seismograph, knew of sunspots, invented the water-powered mill, paper, and porcelain, and reckoned accurately the length of the year as early as 28 B.C. In textiles they were far ahead of the West. Although little remains of it, tradition indicates that the capital at Ch'ang-an must have rivaled Rome in wealth, splendor, and the cosmopolitan nature of its population.

Buddhism and Buddhist art enter China. In Central Asia, where Wu Ti extended the *Pax Sinica,* the Chinese were in contact with the Kushan empire in northwest India. This contact facilitated the penetration of China by the first Buddhist missionaries, who made their way through the heart of Asia along the same protected routes as the silk caravans. Evidence indicates that Buddhist communities existed in China before the reign of Emperor Ming (58-75 A.D.). By the end of the Han dynasty Buddhist pagodas were beginning to appear. It is interesting to note that one of the most important missionaries was not an Indian but a Parthian prince who arrived at the Han capital about 148 A.D. He established a center for the translation of Buddhist works into Chinese, and he was assisted in this work by other foreigners, including a Scythian.

The Buddhists made some converts, but very few Chinese became monks. Han dynasty Chinese evidently considered Buddhism to be only another sect of Taoism, because in translation many of its precepts and customs apparently resembled those of the Taoists. Only toward the end of the Han dynasty did Buddhism begin to assert an independent spirit in China, and the period of its great attraction of converts and influence on Chinese culture came only after the fall of the Han, when social turmoil made Buddhism's emphasis on an other-worldly salvation appealing to the people.

The silk trade links China and the West. In addition to the introduction of Buddhism, Chinese control of the Central Asian trade routes permitted the development of commerce with West Asia and the Mediterranean region. While Roman subjects traded directly with India, the silk trade between Rome and China was carried on through middlemen. The Chinese were aware of the existence of Rome, which they called Ta Ch'in, or "Great Ch'in," and the Romans were aware of China, the source of Mediterranean silk imports. The Chinese obtained wool and linen and glass from the West, but more important was China's export of silk to Rome in such large amounts that the Roman economy was hurt by the outflow of precious metals required to pay for its Chinese imports. This pattern of an international balance of trade in favor of China continued down to the nineteenth century.

Contact with the West was also made by

During the Han dynasty, the wealthy classes lived luxuriously in houses similar to this model from that period. The graceful proportions and artful decorations are typical of Han architecture.

sea across the Malay peninsula and through the Indian Ocean. The Hanoi region in North Vietnam was the major Chinese center for seaborne contact with the West. In 120 A.D. the Han court was visited by a group of jugglers who claimed to come from Ta Ch'in, and in 166 A.D. some merchants arrived in South China, claiming to represent Marcus Aurelius Antoninus. The claims of both groups were probably false, but they indicate that China was aware of Rome's great prestige.

Trade with the West influenced China, particularly in the arts. Graeco-Roman Buddhist artistic techniques, which originated at Gandhara, stimulated important changes in Chinese design. The portrayal of the human figure, formerly comparatively rare in Chinese art, now became extremely popular. In the scientific realm Han achievements in mathematics and astronomy may well have been stimulated by the West. Alfalfa and grapes from Central Asia were also introduced into China during the Han period.

The decline of the Han dynasty. The *Pax Sinica* had brought to China new lands, a new religion, and new developments in the arts, sciences, and scholarship. But the Han dynasty lapsed into decadence, and in 220 A.D. the last of the Han rulers was deposed. Although Chinese civilization was again to rise to new heights, China first had to endure a long period of transition and strife. The centuries that followed the fall of the Han were filled with civil wars; the division of China into numerous petty kingdoms, some of which were controlled by Central Asian nomads; and external wars against such invaders as the Tatars and Turks. But what appeared on the surface to be a great civilization in collapse was in reality one in transition.

THE END OF AN EPOCH

Severance of East-West contacts. Unfortunately for the cause of international relations, commercial and cultural interchange among the three great civilizations of clas-

Constructed with remarkable precision, this Chinese sundial from the Han period was superior to any devised in the West until the thirteenth century A.D. The base and vertical shaft have been reconstructed for this photograph.

sical times was interrupted more and more frequently after the beginning of the third century A.D. With the overthrow of the Han dynasty in 220 A.D., China's power and prestige dwindled in Central Asia. By coincidence, in the same year, the Kushan empire in northeast India succumbed, and Indian civilization also underwent a process of change and transition. About the same time, and probably the most significant factor in the disruption of Eurasian relations, came profound changes in the Graeco-Roman world.

Soon after the death of Marcus Aurelius in 180 A.D., the Roman empire was beset by internal strife, foreign conflict, and economic stagnation. The decline of Roman strength and prestige was accompanied not only by a diminution of Roman purchasing power—so that the volume of trade with the East suffered—but by an increasing inability to carry on energetic commerce with the East and safeguard the trade routes. A severe blow came when the Abyssinians and Arabs, then in a position to dominate the important sea route to the East, intercepted Red Sea commerce. The powerful new Persian empire (see p. 220) established a stranglehold over the trans-Asian trade routes supplying silk, which had become by this time more of a necessity than a luxury among the upper classes in the West. In the fifth century the western half of the Roman world sank so far under barbarian invasion and general disruption that its capacity to purchase and transport oriental goods declined considerably. Even in the West, however, trading persisted on Mediterranean sea routes until the Arab conquests of the seventh and eighth centuries. While the western half of the Roman world was declining as a market, the still commercial eastern half made itself less dependent on Chinese silk by establishing its own silk industry. Thus the mutual trade of the *Pax Romana* and the *Pax Sinica* lost its vigor.

An economic consequence of East-West trade. The volume of the Graeco-Roman world's oriental trade had been surprisingly large. Because Roman exports to the East did not match in quantity or value the empire's imports of silk, spices, perfumes, gems, and other luxuries, the West had suffered seriously from an adverse balance of trade. Thus precious metals were continually being exported to Asia. Pliny declared that India, China, and Arabia drained away annually at least 100,000,000 sesterces (around $5,000,000 at a time when dollars had more purchasing value than today)—"that is the sum which our luxuries and our women cost us."[19] The discovery of vast hoards of Roman coins in India supports Pliny's statement, as does the reference in old Indian poems to western ships coming to Malabar with gold and leaving with pepper. Few Roman coins have been found in China, but this was probably because the Chinese sold their silk to Parthians, Kushans, and other middlemen in western Asia, who then resold it to Roman merchants.

One competent scholar has estimated that between 31 B.C. and 192 A.D. alone, Rome's trade with the Orient cost her a net money loss of about $500,000,000. This serious drain, which took place at a time when the empire's known sources of gold and silver

were being exhausted, was a prime cause of the deterioration of the imperial coinage and one of the factors in the general economic decline of the Roman world.

Geographical knowledge. East-West relations in classical times, along with Rome's other explorations and trade in Europe and Africa, resulted in a great increase in man's knowledge of his physical world. Mariners had explored not only the entire Mediterranean Sea and the coast of western Europe but also both coasts of Africa down to the equator or farther, as well as far-off Asia from Suez to Canton. On land, men had come to know all Europe south of the Rhine and Danube, much of North and East Africa, the lands lying between Asia Minor and the Indus River, and that part of the huge Eurasian hinterland traversed by the silk route to China.

This ancient knowledge of distant lands had a profound effect in medieval and early modern times. From the geographical data available in the Roman trading centers of his day, Ptolemy constructed a map of the world (see p. 157), which was to be used by explorers in the early modern period when Europe was again ready and eager to trade with distant peoples.

The influence of West upon East. Roman trade with India and China substantially increased the knowledge of West and East about each other. But Greek influence was even more consequential.

There is little doubt that the strongest Greek influence on Indian civilization was in the field of sculpture, as demonstrated by the results of the Graeco-Roman Buddhist school at Gandhara, which in turn affected art forms in China and even in Japan. For a time, Indian coinage also bore the strong imprint of Hellenistic influence.

It seems certain that Indian astronomy, which made significant advances in its own right, also benefited from Greek learning. On the other hand, the claim that the Greeks influenced Indian drama is debatable. It is also doubtful that Indian medical science was influenced by western thought. In the field of religion, there is no question that many of the Greek and Roman deities were known to the Indians, but there is no proof that they had any influence on Indian religious thought.

The influence of East upon West. The trade with both India and China made a powerful impact on the economy of the Graeco-Roman world, as we have pointed out, and those Romans and Greeks who could afford luxuries enjoyed a variety of imported spices, muslins, silks, and other goods. On the other hand, it is difficult to estimate the intangible imports from the East. One Indian scholar is of the view that there are numerous coincidences between Indian philosophy and the ideas of Pythagoras and other Greek philosophers. "Whether the doctrines of these Greek thinkers were derived from Indian philosophy, or were independently evolved, cannot, of course, be definitely decided." However, he points out that the Greek accounts which state that many Hellenic philosophers visited oriental countries to study "render the first alternative at least highly probable."[20] This scholar also states that when Christianity arose, Indian culture and religion were already important factors in the countries around the eastern Mediterranean, and that undoubtedly some of the early Christian mystics were profoundly influenced by Indian ideas.

Whatever the immediate impact upon the West may have been, the long-range consequences of its meeting with the East were quite significant. With the contact once established, cultural exchange would continue, even though sometimes at a slow pace and by indirect means. Medieval Europe was to benefit from the success of the classical civilizations in establishing contact with each other. For example, "Chinese technological inventions poured into Europe in a continuous stream during the first thirteen centuries of the Christian era, just as later on the technological current flowed the other way."[21] In later chapters such borrowed items as paper, silk-reeling machinery, and a host of major and minor inventions will be discussed. No longer can an educated westerner assume, as he once did, the attitude that the meeting of East and West has always demonstrated the superiority of the West.

GOALS AND PROBLEMS OF THE CLASSICAL EMPIRES

The growth of "universal" states. A distinctive feature of the centuries of cross-cultural contacts between the classical empires was the effort to establish a "world-state" in each of the old fluvial centers of India and China, in addition to the Graeco-Roman world-state bordering the Mediterranean. Although diffusion of many culture traits resulted from trade and missionary contacts between these three major centers, the classical empires did not normally establish direct and continuing relations with each other. Thus, to understand this period we cannot use the notion of a world of nation-states adapted to some regular pattern of international relations, as has characterized the modern era. Each of the classical empires was, in a sense, a world complete unto itself, with its own pattern of relations with its neighbors.

Despite the fact that each classical empire established a style of its own, it is useful to consider whether the Mauryan, Chinese, and Roman empires faced similar or identical problems; whether their objectives were similar; and whether their achievements were comparable.

Each of the empires could, first of all, be considered a political achievement; by use of a monopoly of power, a single political center sought to bring within one general framework many components that had not previously been territorially or culturally united. Their common problem was to reconstruct a stable and peaceful society after a long period of disruption, crisis, and revolutionary change.

In the political realm, each empire faced the problem of preserving absolute power in some systematic fashion. In terms of cultural values, each made a conscious, conservative effort to preserve, disseminate, and give relatively homogeneous expression to values that would serve as a unifying force throughout the empire. In the economic order, each attempted to sustain and enlarge the livelihood of the entire society by maintaining peace within its borders. Finally, infusing the total effort of each empire was an ecumenical ideal: that the whole of meaningful civilization be brought within one institutional framework.

Lack of unity in Mauryan empire. Of the three classical empires under consideration—Mauryan, Chinese, and Roman—the Mauryan empire emerged first and fell most swiftly. Why was this so? As we noted in Chapter 3, the Indian historical record is meager; yet we can make certain comments on its overall character and achievement.

In both the Mauryan state and the short-lived later efforts at building inclusive empires in India, there does not appear to have been a continuingly effective central administrative system (such as Roman and Chinese emperors devised) that could give character to the state in the absence of an able and masterful despot on the throne. In a sense, the system lacked integrity unless the personal loyalty of subordinate rulers could be maintained. Chandragupta's role can be compared to that of Julius Caesar or Shih Huang-ti: he destroyed tradition to acquire unique personal power, but he did not give his power permanent and systematic form.

On the other hand, Ashoka—quite apart from the sincerity of his personal commitment—saw in Buddhism a universal set of values by which the state might be justified beyond being the mere power mechanism brought into being in his grandfather's day. In this sense, Ashoka's political perception of his state's needs was like that of Augustus in Rome; yet in his relation to Buddhism his role resembled that of Constantine still later in the Roman story, as we shall see in the next chapter. His encouragement of Buddhism and his expenditures on its behalf contributed to the emergence of new Buddhist art and ideas and set a precedent for similar official status under later regimes such as the Kushan.

Ashoka, even while honoring Buddhism, tolerantly urged his non-Buddhist subjects to follow faithfully their own religions. Thus, in effect, the head of the state insisted that religious commitments were primary; this insistence was confirmation of the tendency of Indian society to be attentive to other-worldly rather than to this-worldly goals. The Mauryan state had been cosmopolitan to begin with; Ashoka was preparing the way for the state to dissolve in the vision of the more universal community conceived in religious rather than political terms.

Despite Chandragupta's empire building, and perhaps because of the way Ashoka tried to solve its problems, India in these centuries remained essentially a "federation of cultures." Later there emerged, periodically, a kind of union of kingdoms under the hegemony of one state or another. But it is clear that no tradition of central government, or of institutions to support it throughout the country, developed enough strength to counter the horizontal division of Indian society into the functional and religious groups we call castes.

Effective centralization in Chinese empire. In contrast to this failure to create a long-lived central state in India, the Chinese created a unified political form that dominated Chinese life and to which they returned again and again whenever the society was fragmented from within or without. The two-stage development of the Chinese state was more sharply marked than was the case with the emergence of the Roman empire. The Ch'in regime completely and dramatically destroyed the political forms of earlier days; then the Han dynasty's more conservative founders devised new ways to make despotism workable as an institution and to make it palatable by basing it on commonly accepted cultural values.

The Han empire continued the political and economic innovations of the Ch'in: a unitary despotism exercised through a centrally controlled administrative machinery, and a system of free peasant landholdings taxed directly by the state. But the Han drastically changed the rationale for this system: by turning for justification to the Confucian doctrine of a paternal form of government, the Han state enrolled the support of Confucian scholars, who possessed just the literate skills needed for administration. At the same time, Confucianism harmonized with the family-centered paternalism of

Chinese popular culture, providing a means for integrating most elements of the population into one society.

By deliberately disavowing the code of harsh punishments and extraordinary taxation of the Ch'in legalist regime, and by maintaining a simple, frugal court style for its first half-century, the Han state exhibited its acceptance of the Confucian doctrine that the sage-king ruler should pay primary attention to the well-being of his people. But Han state Confucianism not only displayed Legalist and Taoist elements; it incorporated popular magical notions as well. Like ancient Sons of Heaven, Han emperors conducted elaborate state sacrifices to Heaven and to the spirits of grain and soil, thereby displaying their desire to maintain a proper balance of natural forces for man's good. At the same time they much more effectively controlled the intellectual life of the land, not by banning books and spokesmen of dissident beliefs, but by selecting officials on the basis of their individual mastery of the Confucian tradition and its books alone and making this the path to preferment. Thus the Han civil service was loyal not merely to the person who was emperor but to the moral order of society his office symbolized.

This Han pattern of government was elastic enough to apply to Chinese relations with the outer world as well. At first glance the building of the Great Wall seems to symbolize—as did Augustus' definition of Roman frontiers—a sharp distinction between the civilized world within and the barbarian world outside. But, in reality, Chinese experience differed from the Roman. Wu Ti's imperialism pushed Han authority more than a thousand miles into the nomad and oasis world. It met none it could not subdue: it effectively destroyed the threat of Hunnish cavalry, and it established under Chinese control the trade routes along which the Chinese might obtain curious and useful commodities not produced in their own realm. But above all, Wu Ti's imperialism supported the Chinese notion that theirs was the "central realm" of highest civilizational achievement, to which all others were necessarily dependent and tributary. The appearance of tribute missions at the Han court

thus "proved" the claimed universal sway of the Son of Heaven.

The Chinese believed that the barbarians, if given a chance, would perceive the superiority of the Chinese way and be converted to it. (The Chinese world-state, however—like the great family it purported to be—sometimes had children and younger brethren whose undeveloped understanding necessitated the use of force to supplement the power of superior example.) Barbarians were thus considered capable of becoming a part, if a sometimes troublesome part, of the Chinese empire.

Roman unity through administration and law. The Mediterranean world to which Augustus sought to bring unity and peace included more diverse ethnic and cultural groups than either Mauryan or Han emperors sought to consolidate. The synthesis Augustus and his successors tried to establish seems to have had more built-in potential strains and tensions than the Chinese encountered. It did far more than the Mauryan state to find a means in institutions and in concepts to effect its goals. Roman practicality in administration and law was to be a model for centuries thereafter.

The Augustan solution, which was discussed in detail in Chapter 5, can be summarized as follows: Augustus and his successors sought to adapt the traditions of the city-state to a world-state. The office of *princeps* was legally a kind of supermagistracy of the Roman republic. "Old Roman" virtues were deliberately evoked by Augustan poets and publicists; colonies and towns were planted which, as in the Hellenistic tradition, might serve equally as administrative, cultural, and economic centers; and frontiers were defined (a new use of the older Greek sense of sharp distinction between Hellene and barbarian).

This Roman synthesis, however, was riddled with many paradoxes that were eventually to erode it and to change the entire system drastically. The most obvious paradox, of course, was that Augustus and his heirs did in fact wield absolute power just as the Mauryan and Han monarchs did, even while claiming to be magistrates of a restored republic.

In Chapter 7 we shall see how the Augustan balance and synthesis changed: central mechanisms of absolute power (the army and fiscal controls) submerged the city-state forms; empty "old Roman" virtues, already replaced by Hellenistic value systems (notably Stoicism and Epicureanism), gave way to other-worldly religious concerns; and internal economic and political crises deepened. Finally, just as in India and China, the integrity of the state's frontiers was sundered by ruder peoples from beyond the border.

SUMMARY

The hackneyed statement that "East is East and West is West, and never the twain shall meet"[22] has been disproved not only in our own day but also by centuries of contacts made during classical times. Alexander's soldiers followed their leader through remote waste lands into the Indus valley. Mariners braved the Arabian Sea in frail craft to reach the ports of southern India. Chinese envoys and generals struck westward across forbidding deserts and mountain ranges to make contact with other peoples. As a result, East and West were brought together in the Parthian empire and the mountain kingdom of Bactria and along the northwest frontiers of India; they met on the silk routes of Turkestan and in the market places of Rome and Alexandria.

The thousand years ending in the fifth century A.D. were the truly formative centuries of our modern world, for the Graeco-Roman civilization established intellectual, political, and artistic forms of expression for lands of the West. At the same time the Mauryan rulers, and especially the pious Ashoka, stimulated the progressive evolution of Indian culture and the dissemination of the civilizing tenets of Buddhism throughout southern and eastern Asia. In turn the great Kushan monarch Kanishka further stimulated Indian cultural trends and the missionary advance of Buddhism into Central Asia and China. One of China's greatest dynasties was the Han, under whose Confucian adaptation of Ch'in Legalism, the empire was enlarged and the *Pax Sinica* established, in which the arts and scholarship could flourish on a scale never before known in Far Eastern history.

In these centuries three world-states emerged in India, China, and Rome, and came into distant contact with each other. Each set its own style, suffered internal changes, and was violently beset by attacks from outside its main borders; then they passed from the historical stage in the order in which they had first appeared. But each world-state also left a marked imprint on the ages yet to come.

Suggestions for Reading

AEGEAN CIVILIZATION

L. Cottrell, **The Bull of Minos,*** Universal. A popular account of the great archaeological discoveries in the Aegean area. Other introductory surveys include C. W. Blegen, **Troy and the Trojans,** Thames and Hudson, 1963; Alan E. Samuel, **The Mycenaeans in History,*** Prentice-Hall, 1966; W. Taylour, **The Mycenaeans,** Thames and Hudson, 1964.

R. W. Hutchinson, **Prehistoric Crete,*** Penguin; E. Vermeule, **Greece in the Bronze Age,** Univ. of Chicago, 1964. Comprehensive accounts. See also G. Mylonas, **Ancient Mycenae,** Princeton, 1957; J. Alsop, **From the Silent Earth,** Harper & Row, 1964 (on Pylos); S. Marinatos and M. Hirmer, **Crete and Mycenae,** Abrams, 1960 (photographs of objects and ruins). John Chadwick, **The Decipherment of Linear B,*** Vintage, reads like a detective story.

M. Renault, **The King Must Die,*** Pocket Books. An absorbing novel which contrasts the vigor of Mycenaean Greece with the decadence of Minoan Crete.

GREECE

A. R. Burn, **The Pelican History of Greece,*** Penguin; M. I. Finley, **The Ancient Greeks,*** Compass; A. Andrewes, **The Greeks,** Knopf, 1967. Valuable fresh analyses. Other absorbing surveys include M. Bowra, **The Greek Experience,*** Mentor; H. Kitto, **The Greeks,*** Penguin; H. Lloyd-Jones, ed., **The Greek World,*** Penguin.

J. B. Bury, **A History of Greece to the Death of Alexander the Great,** 3rd ed., rev. by R. Meiggs, Macmillan, 1951; N. G. L. Hammond, **A History of Greece to 322 B.C.,** Oxford, 1959. Standard detailed histories.

Chester G. Starr, **The Origins of Greek Civilization, 1100-650 B.C.,** Knopf, 1961. An illuminating critical survey of the formative centuries of Greek civilization. See also T. B. L. Webster, **From Mycenae to Homer,*** Norton; G. S. Kirk, **The Songs of Homer** [paperback title: **Homer and the Epic**], Cambridge, 1962; D. L. Page, **History and the Homeric Iliad,*** Univ. of Cal.; M. I. Finley, **The World of Odysseus,*** Compass. A. R. Burn, **The World of Hesiod,** Dutton, 1937, and **The Lyric Age of Greece,** Arnold, 1960, treat in detail the Greek renaissance of the seventh and sixth centuries B.C. On Greek colonization see A. Woodhead, **The Greeks in the West,** Praeger, 1962; J. M. Cook, **The Greeks in Ionia and the East,** Praeger, 1963.

A. Andrewes, **The Greek Tyrants,*** Torchbooks; W. G. Forrest, **The Emergence of Greek Democracy, 800-400 B.C.,** McGraw-Hill, 1966. Excellent studies on the transition from oligarchy to democracy.

A. E. Zimmern, **The Greek Commonwealth: Politics and Economics in Fifth-Century Athens,*** Galaxy. A famous work about politics, economics, religion, and everyday life during the days of Pericles and the Athenian empire. See also G. Glotz, **The Greek City and Its Institutions,** Knopf, 1930; Victor Ehrenberg, **The Greek State,** Barnes and Noble, 1960; A. R. Burn, **Pericles and Athens,*** Collier; A. H. M. Jones, **Athenian Democracy,** Praeger, 1957. Rex Warner, **Pericles the Athenian,** Little, Brown, 1962, is an absorbing biographical novel. Athens' great rival is best described in H. Michell, **Sparta,*** Cambridge.

A. de Sélincourt, **The World of Herodotus,** Little, Brown, 1963. A brilliant book on the age of the Persian wars. A. R. Burn, **Persia and the Greeks: The Defense of the West, 546-478 B.C.,** St. Martin's, 1962, is a detailed account. B. W. Henderson, **The Great War Between Athens and Sparta,** Macmillan, 1927. See also W. S. Ferguson, **Greek Imperialism,** Houghton Mifflin, 1913; J. H. Finley, **Thucydides,** Harvard, 1942.

Edith Hamilton, **The Greek Way to Western Civilization,*** Mentor. A popular and enthusiastic appreciation of the beauty and values of Hellenic literature. A. Lesky, **A History of Greek Literature,** Crowell, 1966, and W. Jaeger, **Paideia: The Ideals of Greek Culture,** 3 vols., 2nd ed., Oxford, 1943-1945, are outstanding detailed treatments. See also P. D. Arnott, **An Introduction to the Greek Theatre,** Macmillan, 1959.

C. Seltman, **The Twelve Olympians,*** Apollo. The myths and gay stories about the Olympian gods and goddesses. See also Edith Hamilton, **Mythology,*** Mentor; W. K. C. Guthrie, **The Greeks and Their Gods,*** Beacon; E. R. Dodds, **The Greeks and the Irrational,*** Beacon.

Good introductions to Greek philosophy and science include W. K. C. Guthrie, **Greek Philosophers from Thales to Aristotle,*** Torchbooks; F. M. Cornford, **Before and After Socrates,*** Cambridge; R. Warner, **The Greek Philosophers,*** Mentor (contains many extracts); B. Farrington, **Greek Science,*** Penguin; T. L. Heath, **Manual of Greek Mathematics,*** Dover. See also A. E. Taylor, **Socrates: The Man and His Thought,*** Anchor, and **Plato: The Man and His Work,** Dial, 1929; W. D. Ross, **Aristotle,*** Barnes and Noble.

Recommended for the fine arts student are C. Seltman, **Approach to Greek Art,*** Dutton; G. Richter, **The Sculpture and Sculptors of the Greeks,** Yale, 1950; A. W. Lawrence, **Greek Architecture,** Penguin, 1957; G. Rodenwaldt, **The Acropolis,** Univ. of Okla., 1953; M. Robertson, **Greek Painting,** Skira, 1959.

THE HELLENISTIC WORLD

C. A. Robinson, Jr., **Alexander the Great; The Meeting of East and West in World Government and Brotherhood,** Dutton, 1947. Places special emphasis on Alexander's ideas about universalism. See also **Alexander the Great,*** Beacon, by W. W. Tarn, the British authority; A. R. Burn, **Alexander the Great and the Hellenistic Empire,*** Collier, which is short and lively. W. W. Tarn, **The Greeks in Bactria and India,** Cambridge, 1951, treats developments on the far edge of the Hellenistic world.

W. W. Tarn, **Hellenistic Civilization,*** 3rd ed., rev. by author and G. T. Griffith, Meridian. Government, society, economics, religion, philosophy, and literature—all are examined as parts of the Hellenistic culture pattern. See also M. Hadas, **Hellenistic Culture: Fusion and Diffusion,** Columbia, 1959; F. A. Wright, **History of Later Greek Literature,** Macmillan, 1932; R. D. Hicks, **Stoic and Epicurean,** Russell, 1962. M. Rostovtzev,

*Indicates an inexpensive paperbound edition.

The Social and Economic History of the Hellenistic World, 3 vols., Oxford (Clarendon Press), 1941, is a monumental achievement of scholarship.

ROME

H. Pallotino, **The Etruscans,*** Penguin; R. Bloch, **The Etruscans,** Praeger, 1958. Two books—the one scholarly, the other popular—which throw new light on Etruscan civilization. D. H. Lawrence's **Etruscan Places,*** Compass, is an enthusiastic appreciation. See also H. Scullard, **The Etruscan Cities and Rome,** Cornell Univ., 1967; Emeline Richardson, **The Etruscans: Their Art and Civilization,** Univ. of Chicago, 1964.

On Rome's other neighbors see T. Dunbabin, **Western Greeks,** Oxford, 1948; T. G. E. Powell, **The Celts,** Thames and Hudson, 1958; B. Warmington, **Carthage,*** Penguin.

R. Bloch, **The Origins of Rome,** Praeger, 1960. An examination of the archaeological, historical, and legendary evidence. See also A. Alföldi, **Early Rome and the Latins,** Univ. of Mich., 1965. For an instructive survey of archaeological discovery in Italy, see P. MacKendrick, **The Mute Stones Speak,*** Mentor.

Alexander H. McDonald, **Republican Rome,** Thames and Hudson, 1966. A good survey. For greater detail see H. Scullard, **History of the Roman World from 753 to 146 B.C.,** 3rd ed., Methuen, 1961; F. B. Marsh, **History of the Roman World from 1946 to 30 B.C.,** 2nd ed., Methuen, 1953; G. P. Baker, **Hannibal,** Dodd, 1936; R. E. Smith, **Cicero the Statesman,** Cambridge, 1966; G. Ferrero, **The Life of Caesar,*** Norton; Lily R. Taylor, **Party Politics in the Age of Caesar,*** Univ. of Cal.

H. H. Scullard, **From the Gracchi to Nero,** Methuen, 1959. An admirable survey of the transition from the late Republic to the early empire. Also recommended are R. E. Smith, **The Failure of the Roman Republic,** Cambridge, 1955; R. Syme, **The Roman Revolution,*** Oxford; F. B. Marsh, **The Founding of the Roman Empire,** Oxford, 1927.

E. Salmon, **A History of the Roman World from 30 B.C. to A.D. 138,** 4th ed., Methuen, 1963; H. M. D. Parker, **A History of the Roman World from A.D. 138 to A.D. 337,** 2nd ed., Methuen, 1958. Detail the history of the early empire. See also J. Buchan, **Augustus,** Houghton Mifflin, 1937; Mason Hammond, **Augustan Principate in·Theory and Practice,** Harvard, 1933; B. W. Henderson, **Five Roman Emperors: Vespasian, Titus, Domitian, Nerva, Trajan, A.D. 69-117,** Macmillan, 1927; T. Africa, **Rome of the Caesars,** Wiley, 1965.

D. R. Dudley, **The Civilization of Rome,*** Mentor; M. Grant, **The World of Rome,*** Mentor; R. Barrow, **The Romans,*** Penguin; H. Mattingly, **Roman Imperial Civilization,** Arnold, 1957. Excellent general surveys.

F. E. Adcock, **Roman Political Ideas and Practices,*** Univ. of Mich.; D. Earl, **The Moral and Political Traditions of Rome,** Cornell Univ., 1967; L. Homo, **Roman Political Institutions,** Knopf, 1930. Ideals and realities of Roman politics. On Roman law see H. Wolff, **Roman Law: An Historical Introduction,** Univ. of Okla., 1951; John Crook, **Law and Life of Rome,** Cornell Univ., 1967.

M. Johnston, **Roman Life,** Scott, Foresman, 1957. This lavishly illustrated work contains a wealth of information about every-day life in Rome. Also recommended are W. Fowler, **Social Life at Rome in the Age of Cicero,*** St. Martin's; S. Dill, **Roman Society from Nero to Marcus Aurelius,*** Meridian; H. Mattingly, **Man in the Roman Street,*** Norton; J. Balsdon, **Roman Women,** Day, 1963; H. J. Rose, **Ancient Roman Religion,*** Torchbooks; W. Stahl, **Roman Science,** Univ. of Wis., 1962.

M. Grant, **Roman Literature,*** Penguin. A good introduction. Also recommended are Edith Hamilton, **The Roman Way,*** Norton; M. Laistner, **The Greater Roman Historians,*** Univ. of Cal.; T. Frank, **Life and Literature in the Roman Republic,*** Univ. of Cal. G. Highet, **Poets in a Landscape;** Knopf, 1957, is a brilliant evocation of the time of Catullus, Virgil, Horace, Ovid, and Juvenal. The most useful collection of Roman sources, with valuable commentary, is N. Lewis and M. Reinhold, **Roman Civilization: Selected Readings,*** 2 vols., Torchbooks.

M. Wheeler, **Roman Art and Architecture,*** Praeger. A valuable survey, beautifully illustrated. See also A. Maiuri, **Roman Painting,** Skira, 1953; G. Rivoira, **Roman Architecture,** Oxford, 1925.

Historical novels which display both literary excellence and historical accuracy are Bryher (W. Ellerman), **The Coin of Carthage,*** Harvest, the Second Punic War as viewed by the common people of Italy; R. Warner, **The Young Caesar,*** Mentor, an account of Caesar's life as he himself might have told it; T. Wilder, **The Ides of March,*** Signet, a witty novel of Caesar's last days; R. Graves, **I, Claudius,*** Vintage, a vivid portrayal of imperial Rome, its intrigues and debaucheries; M. Yourcenar, **Memoirs of Hadrian,*** Noonday, a novel in the form of a memoir.

EAST MEETS WEST

G. F. Hudson, **Europe and China; A Survey of Their Relations from the Earliest Times to 1800,** Beacon.* Reviews the interplay of forces between China and Rome.

M. Wheeler, **Rome Beyond the Imperial Frontiers,*** Penguin. A well-illustrated study of Rome's foreign trade practices under the Empire and East-West cultural interchange. See also H. G. Rawlinson, **Intercourse Between India and the Western World from the Earliest Times to the Fall of Rome,** Cambridge, 1928; E. H. Warmington, **The Commerce Between the Roman Empire and India,** Macmillan, 1928; M. Seshadri, "Roman Contacts with South India," **Archaeology,** Oct. 1966.

A stimulating study of Indian-Chinese cultural relations is E. C. Bagchi's **India and China; A Thousand Years of Cultural Relations,** Philosophical Lib., 1951. C. Dawson, ed., **Mission to Asia: Narratives and Letters of the Franciscan Missionaries in Mongolia and China in the Thirteenth and Fourteenth Centuries,** Harper, 1966, is an anthology of the original records of early travelers who contributed to European knowledge and myths concerning the Far East.

For Ashoka and his dynasty see Romila Thapar, **Asoka and the Decline of the Mauryas,** Oxford, 1960; B. G. Gokhale, **Asoka Maurya,** Twayne, 1966. Sir Percival Spear, **India: A Modern History,** Univ. of Mich., 1961, presents an excellent picture of the Mauryan period.

For surveys of Chinese and Indian history with chapters pertinent to Chapter 6 text material, see *List of Readings,* p. 656.

Part Three

Decline
and
Resurgence

■ History may be likened to a wide loom in which the threads of man's activities, shuttling ceaselessly against the threads of his environment, are forever creating great tapestries—the most complex and splendid of which are his civilizations. In the period examined in the preceding unit, the loom operated on a vast rectangular frame extending from the Atlantic across the Eurasian land mass to the Pacific and from subarctic to equatorial latitudes. In one section of this frame, Greek and Roman patterns had merged to form a masterwork—classical civilization. On the other side of the frame, cultural patterns no less brilliant had been woven—the civilizations of India and China. The immense middle section of the frame still had to be filled in before the tapestry could reveal the design of a global civilization. Yet even there a pattern was slowly taking shape as merchants and others traveled back and forth between West and East.

But the tapestry was never completed. As the result of tensions in the West, the tenuous threads across the middle of the frame were snapped; the Graeco-Roman design was rudely torn by the rough hands of Germanic barbarians. Many men despaired of salvaging anything from the splendid pattern. The task, less of mending than of fashioning a whole new design, fell to the Church, the heir to the Caesars. The dynamic and expansive Christian Church spread its message of hope and salvation throughout Europe; it restrained and Christianized the crude Germanic invaders; and, by sheltering precious manuscripts in its monasteries, it endeavored to preserve the best of classical culture. Thus a new pattern began to emerge—a civilization combining the pagan culture of the Graeco-Roman world, the strength and virility of the German barbarians, and the spiritual beauty of the Christian faith.

It would indeed have been a calamity if, after the collapse of Rome, civilization elsewhere had also retrogressed. But thus far in world history, the decline of one civilization has been compensated for either by its resurgence or by the growth of another. In fact, only the western half of the Graeco-Roman world underwent a temporary eclipse. To the east at Constantinople, where the Roman emperor had erected a second capital, civilization was maintained on a high and even dazzling plane. When we speak of the "fall" of Rome, we perhaps forget that the great classical tradition was carried on for another thousand years without interruption in "New Rome." From the fifth to the fifteenth centuries the Byzantine empire acted as a buffer for western Europe, staving off attacks from the east and thereby enabling Europe to recover its shattered strength. When the citadel at last crumbled, the Byzantine influence among the Slavs was so great that the tsars in Russia claimed to be the true inheritors of the Graeco-Roman legacy and dubbed Moscow the "Third Rome."

Much of Byzantine strength was dissipated in warfare against the Persian Sassanids, whose empire enjoyed a brief period of splendor. Then both empires fell before the onslaught of the Muslims. Islam was a dynamic way of life developed by the followers of Muhammad, an eloquent prophet who instilled in his people a vital sense of their destiny to rule in the name of Allah. With unbelievable swiftness, the followers of the Prophet became the rulers of the Near East, swept across North Africa and surged into Spain, and expanded eastward to India and to the western frontiers of China. The Muslims became the great middlemen of medieval times, shuttling back and forth across vast expanses, trading the wares of East and West, and acting as the caretakers and conveyors of culture. The style of the figures which number these pages was brought from India by the followers of Islam and later given the name *Arabic*. Again, it was the Arabs who transmitted to the West the Greek learning which they had absorbed in the Near East.

Trekking still farther east, we shall find both India and China experiencing golden eras while Europe languished in its so-called "dark ages." In Gupta India, the government was stable and orderly, and science and the arts flourished. Under the rule of the T'ang dynasty, the Chinese created a magnificent pattern of culture. Later, the Mongols put together the largest empire in the world, stretching from China west as far as Russia and Mesopotamia. Indian and Chinese colonists and adventurers spread their native cultures throughout Southeast Asia and northward to Japan.

The chapters in this unit present a kaleidoscopic world tour—one which moves from the western Mediterranean progressively eastward. The tensions and tribulations of western Europe give way to the colorful flowering of the Byzantine empire, next to the fervor and vitality of the sprawling Muslim world, and finally to the development of the rich empires of India and China.

11. (preceding page) **Hagia Sophia, Istanbul** (532-537 A.D.). By the sixth century the gradual decline of the Roman empire had emptied the Graeco-Roman classical tradition of nearly all its strength. The imperial capital had been moved from Italy to Constantinople in 330. Christianity was now the state religion and already showing signs of becoming what it was destined to be: a primary force in shaping the world of the next 1000 years. Europe was on the brink of the Middle Ages. At this moment of climactic transition in western history, Hagia Sophia was erected, an immense stone symbol linking past and future. The grandeur of its construction —it is one of the greatest domed vaults of all time—recalls the glory of Rome, while its almost mystical illumination and spiritualized atmosphere prefigure the coming dominance of the Christian faith. After Constantinople was captured by the Turks in 1453, Hagia Sophia became an Islamic mosque, serving in this capacity until recently, when it was converted into a museum. **12.** (above) **Muhammad Ascending to Paradise** (sixteenth century). Islam's meteoric rise to power and subsequent hegemony in the whole Middle East were attended by notable, often superb, achievements in the arts. This manuscript page from Persia was executed at a time when influences from both Christianity and the Far East relaxed the abhorrence Muslims traditionally felt toward making images of Muhammad. Note, however, that the Prophet's face is blank.

13. A Temple on a Clear Day in the Mountains, by Li Ch'eng (c. 960-990 A.D.). Li Ch'eng was one of the greatest exponents of the monumental style in Chinese landscape painting. The twofold goal of this art is to discover the unity and harmony that underlie nature and to incorporate man—both artist and viewer—into that harmony. Li Ch'eng's landscapes are among the most exquisitely wrought and deeply felt objects from the whole vast range of Chinese art.

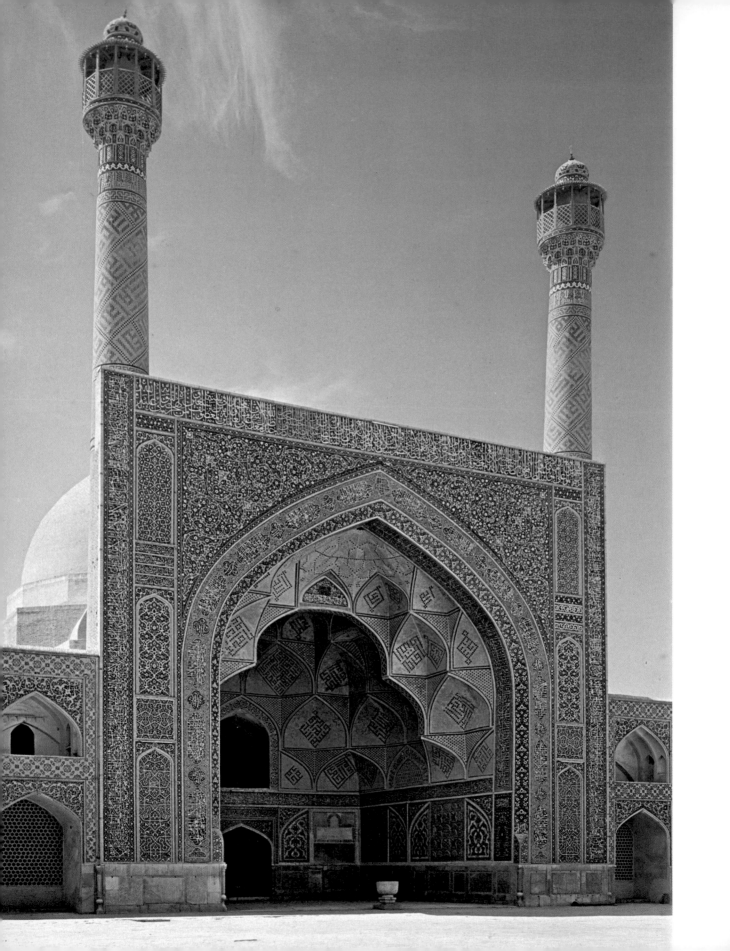

Chapter 7

The City of God

**The Rise of Christianity and the Fall of Rome,
Upheaval and Revival in the West,
Survival in the East**

14. School of Theology, Isfahan, Persia (sixteenth century). Muslim architecture sometimes features an extraordinary delicacy of decoration on structural forms which are themselves sturdy and powerful. Here the surface patterns of the façade, rendered in brilliant glazed tile, are derived from Persian script as well as from the floral motifs which are a constant reminder of that region's ancient love of gardens.

INTRODUCTION. To the inhabitants of the Graeco-Roman world, Rome was the "Eternal City"—a proud designation which is still used today. When, therefore, in 410 A.D. the barbarian Visigoths responded to its magnetic lure by entering Italy and sacking the city, a cry of anguish reverberated throughout the crumbling empire. In distant Bethlehem St. Jerome cried, "The lamp of the world is extinguished, and it is the whole world which has perished in the ruins of this one city."[1]

This chapter tells the story of the fall of the City of the Caesars and of the emergence, like the phoenix arising from the ashes, of the "City of God." It was St. Augustine who, in the wake of the Visigoths' capture of Rome, devised that phrase to represent the rise of a new Christian society on the ruins of paganism and a once invincible empire—and to assure Christians that the "community of the Most High" would endure, although the greatest city on earth had fallen.

This period in history has many facets. One concerns the national history of the

195

Jewish people, the coming of Jesus in the midst of their turbulent relations with the Romans, and the eventual triumph of His teachings. Another is the story of the progressive decline of the Roman empire during the time when Christianity was born and began to grow. A third element is the migration of barbarian peoples and their settlement in Europe—a movement which eventually broke down the imperial boundaries. A final aspect is the shift in civilization's center of gravity—from the West, overrun by barbarians, to the eastern shores of the Mediterranean and even beyond.

The period of devastation and decline in the West is of great historical significance. Graeco-Roman civilization, which inherited much from the older civilizations of the Near East, was slowly blended with Germanic institutions to produce a new historical compound. In this process, the catalytic agent was the Christian Church. It is a fascinating story—how elements from the ancient Near East, Greece, Rome, and the Germanic tribes were fashioned into a new culture, which in time produced outstanding intellectual, literary, and artistic achievements for the enrichment of civilization throughout the world.

THE TRIUMPH OF CHRISTIANITY

Rise of Jewish nationalism. At the very time when the principate of Augustus was laying the foundations of Rome's imperial greatness, events were taking place in the distant Roman province of Judea that would one day alter the course of western history. Following the conquests of Alexander the Great in the Near East, Palestine was ruled at different times by the Ptolemies and the Seleucids. Since their return from exile in Babylonia in 538 B.C. (see p. 49), the Jews in Palestine had created a theocratic community, based upon the Pentateuch—the five books said to have been revealed by Jehovah to Moses—and supplemented by the teachings of the prophets and the writings of scholars. Religious life centered on the great temple at Jerusalem, which echoed with the cry "Hallelujah" ("Praise ye Yahweh") in thanksgiving for Yahweh's gracious dealing with his people. The most powerful figure was the high priest, assisted by the Sanhedrin, the high court for the enforcement of the Law. Since there was no distinction between civil and religious law, the jurisdiction of the Sanhedrin covered all aspects of Jewish life.

The Hebrews, the "People of God," were tightly knit; even the Jewish groups outside Palestine were linked by spiritual bonds to the temple and to a law which they be-lieved to be divinely inspired. But, being unable to participate in the services of the temple at Jerusalem, the Jews of the Diaspora met in local synagogues (from the Greek word for "assembly") for informal worship and instruction in the scriptures. In the long run, the synagogue, which probably first arose during the Babylonian Exile, outlived the temple to become the heart of Judaism. It also influenced the forms of worship in the Christian church and the Muslim mosque.

During the Hellenistic Age, Greek influences were constantly at work among the Jews. Many learned to speak Greek, and Jerusalem itself acquired gymnasiums, temples, and Greek amusements. The translation at Alexandria in the third or second centuries B.C. of the Hebrew scriptures into Greek—called the Septuagint (Latin for "seventy") from the tradition that it was the work of seventy scholars whose independent translations miraculously were identical—not only stimulated the use of that language among Jewish intellectuals but also broadened Jewish thought. For example, *Yahweh,* the Hebraic name for God, was translated as "lord" or "sovereign," which had a universal rather than an exclusively Jewish connotation.

Greek influence might have become

stronger had it not stirred up factionalism within the Jewish community in Jerusalem. Eventually, one puritanical group came to blows with the aristocratic Sadducees, as they came to be called, who were favored by the Hellenistic Seleucid kings then ruling Palestine from Syria. The internal conflict gave the Seleucid king an opportunity to intervene, and in 168 B.C. he ordered the temple dedicated to the worship of Zeus. Viewing this decree as a blasphemous defilement, the Jews rebelled. Under their leader, Judas Maccabaeus, the Jews triumphed, secured religious freedom, and rededicated the temple to Yahweh.

Aspiring to political freedom, the Jews continued the conflict. Judas Maccabaeus was slain, but his brothers kept up the struggle until 142 B.C., when the Seleucid king was forced to recognize Jewish independence. A Maccabean dynasty was created which reigned over most of Palestine.

Although Judas and his immediate successors contented themselves with the title of high priest, later members of the family were known as kings. In time these rulers became worldly and corrupt, and factionalism again flared up, resulting in persecution and bloodshed. It was in the midst of a civil war that the Roman legions appeared on the scene.

Roman occupation of Palestine. Adopting the practice habitually followed by eastern Mediterranean states, one Jewish faction appealed to Rome for aid. Pompey, who was then completing his pacification of Asia Minor and Syria (see p. 138), ended the civil war in 63 B.C. by making Judea one of several Roman client kingdoms in the East.

Eventually, Herod the Great, a leader from a tribe that had long been enemies of the Jews, rose to power as a tool of the Romans. Appointed by Mark Antony, he served as king of Judea from 37 to 4 B.C. Of exceptional ability, Herod erected a magnificent palace, a theater, and a hippodrome. He also rebuilt the temple on a lavish scale. To the Jews, however, he remained a usurper who professed Judaism as a matter of expediency. Soon after Herod's death, Judea was made into a minor Roman province ruled by governors called procurators, the best

known of whom is Pontius Pilate (26-36 A.D.), under whom Jesus was crucified.

The Jews themselves remained unhappy and divided. During centuries of tribulation the Prophets had taught that God would one day create a new Israel when righteousness prevailed under a God-anointed leader, the Messiah. In time the Jews, with the notable exception of the Sadducees, conceived of the Messiah as a divine being whom God would send to lead the righteous and resurrected dead to a spiritual kingdom. But a group of ardent Jewish nationalists, called Zealots, favoring the use of force to drive the hated foreigner out of God's land, precipitated a fatal clash with Rome.

Destruction of Jerusalem. In 66 A.D. violence erupted. The Roman garrison at Jerusalem was massacred, and the revolt spread beyond the walls of the city. Rome met the challenge with a large army commanded by Vespasian. When in 69 A.D. Vespasian was proclaimed emperor and went to Rome (see p. 141), his son Titus completed the siege of Jerusalem. The siege was recorded in all its horror by an eyewitness, the Jewish historian Josephus:

While the [temple] was on fire, everything was plundered that came to hand, and ten thousand of those that were caught were slain: nor was there a commiseration of any age, or any reverence of gravity, but children, and old men . . . and priests, were all slain in the same manner . . . one would have thought that the hill itself, on which the temple stood, was seething hot . . . the blood was larger in quantity than the fire . . . the ground did nowhere appear visible, for the dead bodies that lay on it, but the soldiers went over heaps of those bodies, as they ran upon such as fled from them.[2]

What came to be called the "Wailing Wall," a small part of the temple complex, was left standing. The story is that it was protected by angels whose tears cemented the stones in place forever. It was later prophesied that the rest of the walls would be rebuilt and a third temple erected on the site when the Messiah came. (The Dome of the Rock, a mosque built by the Muslims, has occupied the site since the eighth century A.D.)

The partially unrolled Thanksgiving Scroll, one of the Dead Sea Scrolls preserved at the Hebrew University in Jerusalem, is composed of religious hymns which poetically develop the Essenes' theological doctrines.

Although other revolts erupted in 115 and 132 A.D. and Roman armies devastated Palestine even more completely, the wholesale destruction of Jerusalem in 70 A.D. spelled the end of the ancient Hebrew state. The Jewish dream of an independent political state was to remain unrealized for almost nineteen centuries, until the republic of Israel was proclaimed in 1948.

Development of Jewish religious thought. The destruction of Jerusalem did not destroy the most important single aspect of Jewish culture—its religion. Through centuries of suffering, captivity, and subjugation, the Jews had been taught by a succession of prophets to cleave to their covenant with Yahweh and to safeguard their religious inheritance.

In the centuries just preceding and following the birth of Christ, Judaism exhibited vigor and strength. Advocating unswerving fidelity to the traditional beliefs, the Pharisees made up the strongest and most learned of the religious factions. From their ranks came the rabbis, scholars who expounded the Law and applied it to existing conditions. In the Gospels many Pharisees are severely criticized for their arrogance and for concerning themselves with complicated rules of daily behavior based on the letter rather than the spirit of the Law. But from the second century B.C. to the second century A.D., it was the Pharisaic sect which provided Judaism with its greatest intellectual leaders. Moreover, by reëstablishing rabbinical schools following the fall of Jerusalem, the Pharisees did much to ensure that Judaism would endure.

Contemporary with the Pharisees was another sect, the Essenes. Josephus described these ascetics thus:

These Essen[e]s reject pleasures as an evil, but esteem continence and the conquest over our passions, to be virtue. . . . Nor is there any one to be found among them who hath more than another; for it is a law among them, that those who come to them must let what they have be common to the whole order, insomuch that among them all there is no appearance of poverty or excess of riches, but every one's possessions are intermingled with every other's possessions, and so there is, as it were, one patrimony among all the brethren. . . . And as for their piety towards God, it is very extraordinary. . . .[3]

In recent years the discovery of the Dead Sea Scrolls has helped substantiate Josephus' account, has added greatly to our knowledge of the Essenes, and most certainly has enhanced their importance.

The Dead Sea Scrolls. While exploring caves above the desolate western shore of the Dead Sea in 1947, two Bedouin boys came across several clay jars containing long manuscripts wrapped in linen. Later, scholars examined all the caves of the area and found more scrolls. Nearby were the ruins of an ancient building which most scholars believe was once a monastery inhabited by members of the Essene sect. The building had apparently been occupied between the second century B.C. and 68 A.D., when the Romans destroyed it during the great Jewish revolt. We do not know what became of this group of Essenes, but prior to their destruction or dispersal they managed to hide their manuscripts in the caves.

Some scrolls are portions of the Old Testament, centuries older than the earliest text previously known. The analysis of the script used on the scrolls and radioactive carbon dating of fragments would place their composition in the first century B.C. Jewish and Christian scholars alike have been thrilled to read the Book of Isaiah in such ancient manuscript and to discover that the version we have been using, although based on much later sources, has been accurate except in some details. This discovery has encouraged members of the Jewish and Christian faiths to believe that their sacred books survived centuries of copying with little error.

As for the history of Christianity itself, the Dead Sea Scrolls have been described as constituting "a whole missing chapter of the history of the growth of religious ideas between Judaism and Christianity."[4] This interpretation of their importance results from analysis of those scrolls which describe the Essene sect in the first century B.C.—that is, just prior to the appearance of Christianity. Some scholars have attached much significance to the possible influence of Essene belief on the founding of Christianity. This group considered itself the true remnant of God's people, preached a "new covenant," and waited patiently for the time when God would destroy the powers of evil and inaugurate His Kingdom. Its most important leader, known as the Teacher of Righteousness, suffered persecution and perhaps martyrdom. Scholars also suggest that the Christian monastic tradition may owe its origin to the Essenes and that the ritual of the Last Supper bears striking resemblances to procedures found in the Essenes' Manual of Discipline. Other scholars, however, have seen far less significance in the parallels between Essene and Christian belief.

The life of Jesus. Whatever its possible debt to the Essenes, Christianity bears the unmistakable imprint of the personality of its founder, Jesus Christ. According to the Biblical account, He was born in Bethlehem in the reign of Herod; therefore He may have been born by the time of Herod's death (4 B.C.) rather than in the year which traditionally begins the Christian era. After spending the first thirty years of His life as a carpenter in the village of Nazareth, Jesus began His brief mission, preaching a gospel of love for one's fellow man, condemning violence, and urging people to "Repent, for the kingdom of heaven is at hand" (Matthew 4:17).

The fame of Jesus' teaching and holiness spread among the Jews as He and His twelve disciples traveled from village to village in Palestine. When He came to Jerusalem to observe the feast of Passover, He was welcomed triumphantly by huge crowds as the promised Messiah. But Jesus was concerned with a spiritual, not an earthly, kingdom, and when the people saw that He had no intention of leading a nationalistic movement against the Romans, they turned against Him. His enemies then came forward—the moneylenders whom he had denounced, the Pharisees who resented His repudiation of their minute regulations of daily behavior, the people who considered Him a disturber of the status quo, and those who saw Him as a blasphemer of Yahweh. Betrayed by Judas, one of His disciples, Jesus was condemned by the Sanhedrin for blasphemy "because he claimed to be the Son of God" (John 19:7). Before the procurator Pontius Pilate, however, Jesus was charged with treason for claiming to be the king of Jews.

"Are you the king of Jews?" he [Pilate] asked him. Jesus answered, . . . "My kingdom does not belong to this world; if my kingdom belonged to this world, my followers would fight to keep me from being handed over to the Jews. No, my kingdom does not belong here. . . . You say that I am a king. I was born and came into the world for this one purpose, to speak about the truth. Whoever belongs to the truth listens to me." "And what is truth?" Pilate asked.[5]

Jesus was condemned to the death that Rome inflicted on criminals—crucifixion.

With His death it seemed as though His cause had been exterminated. No written message had been left behind, and His few loyal followers were disheartened. Yet in the wake of His martyrdom the Christian cause took on new impetus. Reports soon spread that Jesus had been seen after His

Crucifixion and had spoken to His disciples, instructing them to spread His teachings. At first there were few converts within Palestine itself, because of the strongly traditional and exclusive character of Judaism during this period of national trouble. But the Hellenized Jews living in foreign lands, in contact with new ideas and modes of living, were less firmly committed to traditional Jewish doctrines. The new religion first made real headway among the Jewish communities in such cities as Damascus, Antioch, Corinth, and Rome.

Paul's missionary work. As long as the followers of Jesus regarded Him exclusively as a Messiah in the traditional Jewish sense, with no message for the salvation of non-Jews, the new religion could have no universal appeal. Largely through the missionary efforts of Paul, this obstacle was removed.

Born Saul, of strict Jewish ancestry, and raised in a Hellenistic city in Asia Minor, this Christian saint possessed a wide knowledge of Greek ideas and Hellenistic literature. Saul was also a strict Pharisee who held it his first duty to uphold the Law of his people. He considered Jesus and His followers to be blasphemers against the Law and took an active part in the persecution of Christians. One day, on the road to Damascus—in Saul's own words:

And as I was traveling and coming near Damascus, about midday a bright light suddenly flashed from the sky around me. I fell to the ground and heard a voice saying to me, "Saul, Saul! Why do you persecute me?" "Who are you, Lord?" I asked. "I am Jesus of Nazareth, whom you persecute," he said to me. The men with me saw the light but did not hear the voice of the one who was speaking to me. I asked, "What shall I do, Lord?" and the Lord said to me, "Get up and go into Damascus, and there you will be told everything that God has determined for you."[6]

Saul, henceforth known as Paul, turned from being a persecutor into perhaps the greatest of Christian missionaries.

Perceiving that Christianity could grow only very slowly in Palestine, where the Jews were steeped in orthodox beliefs, Paul shrewdly concentrated his missionary efforts in the cosmopolitan cities of the eastern Mediterranean. Here lived not only many Hellenized Jews but also large numbers of non-Jews, or gentiles, dissatisfied with pagan cults and the state religion. Preaching the gospel (from the Greek word for "good news") throughout the eastern part of the Roman empire, he encouraged and inspired the small Christian communities by sending letters to his converts.

Some of these letters, or Epistles, became part of the New Testament—a series of books whose basic purpose was to tell the story of Jesus and to transmit His teachings. Paul was one of several outstanding followers of Christ whose writings make up this cornerstone of the Christian faith.

Paul also exercised great influence upon the shaping of Christian doctrine. He taught that Jesus was Christ (from *Christos,* Greek for "Messiah"), the Son of God, and that He had died to atone for the sins of mankind. Acceptance of this belief guaranteed life after death to Jews and gentiles alike if they observed His commandments and followed all of His teachings. Tradition states that after covering eight thousand miles teaching and preaching, Paul was beheaded at Rome about 65 A.D. (as was also Peter, founder of the church at Rome) during the reign of Nero. By this time Christian communities had already been established in all important cities of the Roman empire.

Government persecution of Christians. The Roman government tolerated any religion which did not threaten the safety or tranquillity of the state. While the worship of the emperor was considered an essential patriotic rite uniting all Roman subjects in common loyalty to the imperial government, Roman officials had no quarrel with a person's religious preference so long as he was willing to take part in the ceremonies of the state cult. But the Christians refused to participate in the ceremonies. To them there was only one God; no other could share their loyalty to Him. In the eyes of the Roman officials this attitude branded the Christians as traitors. In addition, many Christians refused to serve in the army or hold political office. Intolerant of other religious sects, they would not associate with pagans or take part in

From the time that Constantine legalized Christianity within the Roman empire, representations of Jesus became numerous throughout the empire and in converted barbarian areas. These images changed in accord with the temper of the times and the people creating them. A bas-relief from a late fourth-century sarcophagus shows a mild, youthful Jesus speaking with the bearded apostle, Peter. Both are dressed in traditional Roman robes. In the late fifth century, when the Church had gained considerable secular power, a mosaic from Ravenna portrays Jesus as a militant Roman legionary. Combining eastern and western influences, a frieze from a northern Italian altar is more abstract than the two Roman portraits and emphasizes the spiritual aspect of Jesus by showing him surrounded by angels. The transfigured Christ carved on a seventh-century Frankish tomb is extremely abstract, but the total halo surrounding Jesus is evident, as is the spear he carries. Even in a spiritual image, a militant rather than a meek Savior may have seemed most appropriate to the warlike Franks.

social functions which they considered sinful or degrading.

The emperors began to persecute the Christians not because of intolerance of belief but because they believed the Christians threatened the very existence of the state. During the first two centuries A.D. persecution was only sporadic and local, like that at Rome under Nero (see p. 141). But during the latter half of the third century, when, as we shall see, the empire was in danger of collapse, three organized empire-wide efforts were made to suppress Christianity. The first systematic campaign against the Christians, who now comprised perhaps one tenth of the population, was instigated by the emperor Decius in 250, and the last and greatest by Diocletian in 303. But they could not stamp out the new religion by force. In fact, the Christians seemed to welcome martyrdom, for, as a third-century Christian writer stated, "The blood of the martyrs is the seed of the Church."[7]

Official recognition and acceptance. In 311 the emperor Galerius saw the failure of the efforts at suppression and issued an edict of toleration making Christianity a legal religion in the East. In the following year the emperor Constantine was swayed toward Christianity during a desperate battle with the army of a rival for the throne. At the height of the conflict, tradition has it that:

A little after noon, as the sun began to decline, . . . [Constantine] declared that he saw with his own eyes in the sky beneath the sun a trophy in the shape of a cross made of light with the inscription "By this conquer." He was astounded by the spectacle, as were the soldiers who accompanied him on his march and saw the miraculous phenomenon. At first he was at a loss to know what the apparition meant, and when night fell he was still reflecting and puzzling over the matter. But when he fell asleep God's Christ appeared to him with the sign which he had seen in the sky and instructed him to fashion a likeness of the sign and to use it as a protection in the encounters of war.[8]

Constantine won the battle, and in 313 he issued the Edict of Milan, which legalized Christianity throughout the empire and put it on a par with all the pagan cults. Constantine favored Christianity but, probably for political reasons, waited until he was on his deathbed before becoming a convert. His successors (with the exception of Julian) were Christians.

To many sincere pagans, however, the depressing cultural, economic, and political conditions seemed evidence that the Rome which had abandoned its gods was suffering from the loss of those protecting deities. In his brief reign (361-363) the scholarly emperor Julian, who had been raised a Christian, renounced his faith and sought to revive paganism, as a result of which he was branded the Apostate. Julian did not persecute the Christians ("Those who are in the wrong in matters of supreme importance," he wrote, "are objects of pity rather than of hate"[9]), and his efforts to revive paganism failed dismally. On his deathbed he is supposed to have said, "Thou hast conquered, O Galilean."

The final step was taken during the reign of Theodosius I (379-395), who denounced the old religion as "a pagan superstition" and decreed the closing of temples, the prohibition of sacrifices, and even the end of the Olympic games. Thus, within less than four hundred years, in spite of all obstacles, Christianity had become the official religion of a world empire.

Reasons for the spread of Christianity. In its rise to preëminence Christianity had had to compete with the philosophies and religions of the day. Most Roman intellectuals had embraced Stoicism which, unlike Epicureanism with its unyielding materialism, had room for God (see p. 156). Other intellectuals had been attracted to Neo-Platonism, which taught that the only reality is spirit and that the soul's principal objective is to escape from the material world and get back to its spiritual home. There were also popular religions such as the worship of the Phrygian Great Mother (Cybele), the Egyptian Isis, the Greek Dionysus, and the Persian Mithras (see p. 222). All of these cults presented the comforting idea of a divine protector and the promise of everlasting life. They offered new hope to their followers and stirred their emotions with ritual pomp and ceremony.

Yet the need for a greater hope and a

deeper emotion had persisted. Even in the best years of the *Pax Romana* many men and women had sought solace in religion to escape the misery of their daily lives. In particular, there had been a gradual impoverishment of small farmers, the growth of an urban proletariat largely dependent upon government doles, together with a large slave population without dignity or hope.

The depressed and oppressed alike found consolation in Christianity. This religion upheld the equality of all men, taught that a loving Father had sent His only Son to atone for men's sins, and offered a vision of immortality and an opportunity to be "born again" and be cleansed of sin. Christian doctrines met the growing spiritual longing during a period when traditional standards were losing their value. During the late centuries of the empire, as the problems of a declining society became increasingly burdensome, the appeal of Christianity was felt more and more widely.

The cultural and administrative unity of the Roman empire made possible the rapid growth of Christianity into a world religion. Moreover, Christianity was a dynamic aggressive religion in its own right. Its teachings were definite, its converts displayed enthusiasm and zeal, and the courage with which the Christians faced death and persecution impressed even their bitterest enemies. In time, also, a Church organization was created that was far more united and efficient than any possessed by its competitors.

Early Church organization. The years immediately following Christ's death had passed with little organization in the Christian movement. Viewing the present world as something which would end quickly with the imminent Second Coming of their Lord, the earliest converts saw no necessity for organization. But Christ did not reappear, and the Christians gradually adjusted themselves to the practical fact that since hundreds of years might elapse before the Second Coming, it was essential to develop a definite Church organization.

At first there was little or no distinction between laity and clergy. Traveling teachers visited Christian communities, preaching and giving advice where it was needed. But this system soon proved inadequate. The steady growth in the number of Christians made necessary special Church officials who could devote all their time to religious work, clarify the body of Christian dogma, conduct services, and care for the funds. The earliest officials were called presbyters (elders) or bishops (overseers). By the second century the offices of bishop and presbyter had become distinct. Churches in the villages adjacent to the mother Church, which was usually located in a city, were administered by priests (a corruption of *presbyter*) responsible to a bishop. Thus the diocese evolved, a territorial administrative division under the jurisdiction of a bishop. The bishop had charge of all Church property in his diocese, had authority over the clergy, and was the official interpreter of Christian dogma.

A number of dioceses made up a province; the bishop of the most important city in each province enjoyed more prestige than his fellows and was known as an archbishop or metropolitan. The provinces were grouped into larger administrative divisions called patriarchates. The title of patriarch was applied to the bishop of such great cities as Rome, Constantinople, and Alexandria. Thus, in the evolution of an organized hierarchy, the Church adapted the administrative divisions of the Roman empire and borrowed much of its law. The title of bishop, for example, came from an important office of the Roman municipality.

Foundations of Christian doctrine and worship. While the administrative structure of the Church was being erected, Christian beliefs were being defined and systematized. Christians needed a theology which would clarify the nature of Christ, the role the Church should play in this world, and the course which man must follow to obtain salvation. As we have seen, this process of fixing the dogma began with Paul, who stressed the divinity of Christ and interpreted His death as an atonement for man's sins.

While the process of explaining the creed was going on, differences of opinion over doctrinal matters caused frequent clashes. One of the most important controversies

The Church of St. Apollinare in Classe, outside Ravenna, is an early basilica (from the Greek, *basilikos*, meaning "kingly") which Justinian erected on the site of a temple of Apollo. Strong Byzantine influence is especially apparent in the remarkable mosaics in the apse. The richly ornamented interior of the church is in sharp contrast to the austere brick exterior (the round bell-tower is a tenth-century addition). This juxtaposition, which is characteristic of early Christian architecture, may have been intended to emphasize the difference between the everyday world and the spiritual magnificence of the Kingdom of God.

was over Arianism. The basic issue in the Arian controversy was the relative position of the three persons of the Trinity. In the doctrine of the Trinity, Christ was regarded as one of three persons—God the Father, God the Son, and God the Holy Spirit. The common view of the equality of God the Father and the Son was vigorously denied by Arius (256-336), a presbyter of Alexandria, who believed that Christ was not God because He was not of a substance identical with God and was not coeternal with Him. The controversy became so serious that the emperor Constantine in 325 convened the first ecumenical Church council, the Council of Nicaea, to resolve the problem. With Constantine presiding, the council branded the Arian belief a heresy—an opinion or doctrine contrary to the official teachings of the Church—and Christ was declared to be of the same substance and coeternal with God the Father. Thus the creed of Christianity became more subtle and complex, and

the beliefs sustained at the Council of Nicaea were soon formulated into what is called the Nicene Creed.

The early Church also selected an official body of Christian literature. To be accepted into this official body—the Christian canon —a piece of writing must be ascribed to divine inspiration. Early churchmen used this criterion in reducing the contents of the New Testament to twenty-seven books. All major Christian churches today use essentially the same New Testament.

The liturgy in the early churches was plain and simple, consisting of prayer, Scripture reading, hymns, and preaching. Gradually the service became an elaborately beautiful ceremonial. In the early period of Christianity the believer worshiped God and sought salvation largely through his own efforts. Following the growth of Church organization and ritual and the crystallization of its dogma, the Church was believed to be the indispensable intermediary between God and man. Without the Church the individual could not hope to approach God.

Both the development of the Church's administrative hierarchy and the creation of a body of authoritative dogma owed much to the Church Fathers of the second through fifth centuries. Since most of them were intellectuals who came to Christianity by way of Neo-Platonism and Stoicism, they maintained that Greek philosophy and Christianity were compatible. Because both reason (*logos* in Greek) and truth come from God, "philosophy was a preparation," wrote Clement of Alexandria (d. 215), "paving the way towards perfection in Christ,"[10] the latest and most perfect manifestation of God's reason. Thus Christianity was viewed as a superior philosophy which could supersede all pagan philosophies and religions.

In the West the three greatest Church Fathers were St. Jerome (340-420), whose scholarship made possible the famous Vulgate translation of the Bible into Latin, which in a revised form is still the official translation of the Roman Catholic Church; St. Ambrose (340-397), who resigned his government post to become bishop of Milan where he employed his great administrative skills to establish a model bishopric; and St. Augustine (354-430), probably the most important of all the Fathers. At the age of thirty-two he finally found the meaning of life in Christianity, as he relates in his *Confessions*, one of the world's great spiritual autobiographies, and during the remainder of his life he wrote more than a hundred religious works which became the foundation of much of the Church's theology.

The bishop of Rome becomes leader of the Church. A development of outstanding importance in the Christian movement was the rise of the bishop of Rome to a position of preëminence in the hierarchy of the Church. At first Rome was only one of several patriarchates, no more important than Alexandria, Jerusalem, Antioch, or Constantinople. But gradually the bishop at Rome became recognized as the leader of the Church and assumed the title of pope— from the Greek word meaning "father." (The pope's claim to supremacy was dis-

puted in the East by the patriarch at Constantinople—a story which will be taken up in the next chapter.)

Perhaps the most important factor in the rise of the papacy was the Petrine doctrine, which taught that the Roman Church had been founded by Peter, the leader of Christ's disciples. This doctrine stated that the Savior had appointed Peter as His successor and that Peter came to Rome and established his headquarters there as bishop of Rome. Successors of St. Peter, the subsequent bishops of Rome, would govern all other dioceses.

There were many other factors explaining the development of the papacy at Rome. As the largest city in the West and the capital of the political world, Rome had a proud tradition. Rome had been the center of Christian persecution, and its Church was sanctified with an aura of martyrdom. Rome was also the hub of a strong Christian missionary movement. The churches founded by missionaries from Rome turned naturally to the mother Church and its bishop for help and guidance. Nor was the Church at Rome rent by the doctrinal disputes which divided and weakened Christians in the East. The Roman Church's reputation for purity of doctrine encouraged other churches engaged in theological disputes to bring their problems to the bishop at Rome for settlement, a practice which redounded to the prestige of the pope. Finally, the higher offices of the Church in the West were in the main filled by a series of outstanding administrators and theologians, whose efforts increased the power of the bishop of Rome.

The weakening of political power in the West and the transfer of the imperial authority from Rome to Constantinople in the fourth century resulted in the bishops there being overshadowed by the emperors, while in Rome the Church had almost no political competition. By the beginning of the seventh century the bishop of Rome had become the spiritual leader of the western world.

The regular clergy. So far we have discussed the secular clergy, who administered the Church's services and communicated its teachings to the laity. But another type of churchmen also arose—the regular clergy, so called because they lived by a rule (*regula*) within monasteries. These monks sought to lead lives of contemplation, simplicity, and seclusion from the world.

The monastic way of life actually originated before Christianity, having existed in Judaism, for example, among the Essenes, who sought isolation from worldly preoccupations (see p. 198). Christian ascetics, who had abandoned the worldly life and become hermits, could be found in the East as early as the third century A.D. Some ascetics went so far as to denounce even beauty as evil and, in pursuit of spiritual perfection by subordinating their flesh, tortured themselves and fasted to excess. In Syria, for example, St. Simeon Stylites lived for thirty years on top of a pillar sixty feet high, braving pain and harsh weather.

In time, however, such extreme asceticism brought a reaction. As a more moderate expression of asceticism, Christians in Egypt developed the monastic life, wherein men seeking a common spiritual goal lived together under a common set of regulations. St. Basil (330-379), a Greek from Asia Minor, pioneered in the monastic life by substituting hard labor, works of charity, and a communal life for the asceticism of the hermit. The Rule of St. Basil is still the standard guide for monasteries of the eastern Church.

In western monasticism the work of St. Benedict (c. 480-543) paralleled St. Basil's efforts in the East. About 529 St. Benedict led a band of followers to a hill between Rome and Naples, named Monte Cassino, where they erected a monastery. There he composed a set of rules which gave order and discipline to western monasticism. Under the Benedictine Rule, the monks took the three basic vows of poverty, chastity, and obedience to the abbot, the head of the monastery. Their daily activities were closely regulated: they participated in eight divine services, labored in field or workshop for six or seven hours, and spent about two hours studying and preserving the writings of Latin antiquity. The Church recognized the merits of St. Benedict's Rule by endorsing his system as a model monastic pattern.

DECLINE AND DIVISION IN THE ROMAN WORLD

A century of decline. Thus far in this chapter the rise and eventual triumph of Christianity in the Graeco-Roman world has been traced. Now it will be shown that, for the greater part, this ascendancy took place at the very time when the empire was in a process of progressive deterioration. True, Rome reached its peak of prosperity and good government during the second century A.D. But from then on, unhappily, the intellectual vigor and creative activity of classical culture began to flag, and more obvious distress signals—political unrest and economic hardship—quickly followed.

Upon the death of Marcus Aurelius in 180 A.D., his son, Commodus, succeeded him. Unlike his father and the other "good emperors," Commodus was an incompetent voluptuary who shocked the Romans with his dissipation and cruelties and neglected affairs of state. After he had reigned twelve years, a group of conspirators, motivated by shock and fear, had him strangled.

Following the murder of Commodus, civil war broke out briefly among the army leaders, who fought for the imperial throne. After much bloodshed, Septimius Severus became emperor in 193. His accession marks the approaching end of the principate.

Augustus' provision that the Senate should retain some governing power and also function as an advisory body had been steadily watered down during the *Pax Romana*. With the reign of Septimius Severus, the Senate lost all appearance of authority and began to lose its position as advisor to the emperor. From this time on the emperors made no attempt to hide the fact that they were "army made" and would not tolerate interference from the Senate. By the late third century the emperor was no longer addressed as *princeps,* meaning first among equals, but as *dominus et deus,* "lord and god." The principate had been replaced by absolute rule known as the dominate.

The army was now the real power in the empire, and many high government offices were filled with uncouth, rough-and-tumble soldiers to whom the emperor was indebted for support. On his deathbed, Septimius Severus is reputed to have told his sons, "Make the soldiers rich and don't trouble about the rest." This toadying to the soldiery was to have dire effects on the empire.

The line of Septimius Severus held the imperial office until 235, but after its extinction a long period of anarchy ensued. In the next fifty years there were twenty-six emperors; only one died a natural death. During this unhappy period Rome was lashed from without by foreign invaders and rent from within by bloody civil wars.

The end of the Pax Romana. The most obvious factor in the rapid decline of the empire after 235 was the near collapse of the central government's authority. No effective system of succession to the imperial throne had been worked out, and no one was ever certain who the next emperor would be. The imperial scepter was dragged in the gutter by generals who murdered emperors with no compunction, intimidated all opposition, and put themselves or their puppets on the throne. Unrestrained, irresponsible legions often pillaged the countryside, stripping the inhabitants of their possessions and carrying off or destroying vast amounts of wealth.

Another factor contributing to the decline of Rome in the third century was the onslaught of external enemies. The preoccupation of the Roman armies with civil warfare gave numerous Germanic tribes their chance to harass the imperial frontiers and raid deep into Gaul, northern Italy, and the Balkans. Meanwhile, Dacia, the territory held by Rome north of the Danube, was permanently abandoned to the Goths. In Asia a powerful new menace appeared during this century—a reinvigorated Persia under the rule of the Sassanid dynasty, which proceeded to attack Syria (see p. 220).

In the face of the central government's inability to cope with these attacks, the people on the frontiers began to carve out separate states and take measures for their own defense. One general ruled Gaul, Britain, and northern Spain as an independent unit; and the client ruler of Palmyra in Syria,

after repulsing the Persians, created an independent kingdom that included Egypt and part of Asia Minor. The energetic Emperor Aurelian (270-275), known as "Hand on Hilt," restored imperial authority throughout the empire, but it is a sign of the times that he felt it necessary to protect Rome with a twenty-foot wall, which still stands.

As deadly to the well-being of the empire as governmental weakness and foreign invasions was prolonged economic decline. The trend toward the concentration of land ownership in a few hands was greatly accelerated by the turbulent conditions of the third century. Small farmers abandoned their lands which were then bought up cheaply by large landowners, and the emperors added to their vast estates through confiscations. The number of tenant farmers, or *coloni* (see p. 144), increased as small farming decreased and men fled the insecurity of city life to find jobs and protection on the large estates with their fortified villas. There they cultivated their patches of land, paying rent to the landowner and providing him with free labor at sowing and reaping time. The condition of the *coloni* worsened as they fell behind in their rents and taxes and, by imperial order, were bound to their tenancies until they had discharged their debts. This was a first step toward serfdom and the social and economic pattern of the Middle Ages.

To make matters worse, the monetary system became extremely confused. In order to meet their military and administrative expenses, the emperors repeatedly devalued the coinage by reducing its silver content. Ultimately the amount of alloy reached 98 per cent, and prices soared as people gradually lost confidence in the debased currency. Even the government eventually refused to accept its own money for taxes and required payment in goods and services. Civil war also disturbed trade and thus helped undermine the prosperity of the cities, whose population decreased correspondingly.

Basically, the empire was a collection of city-states which were to the empire what cells are to the human body. As trade decreased and cities lost their vigor, the urban

Diocletian and his co-Augustus, each with his appointed Caesar, are shown in an embrace symbolic of the unity which Diocletian hoped to maintain despite administrative division of the empire. This sculpture now adorns St. Mark's Cathedral in Venice.

basis of the imperial structure was in danger of collapsing. During the third century, when evidence of serious decline began to be manifest, the western half of the empire appeared to be going downhill much faster than the eastern half. The absolute necessity for controlling, taxing, and defending the still productive eastern cities forced the emperors to spend more and more of their time in the eastern provinces.

Diocletian. A much-needed reconstruction and reorganization of the empire began during the reign of Diocletian (285-305) and was completed by Constantine (306-337). A strong and capable administrator, Diocletian immediately took drastic steps to prevent further civil wars over the succession, restore governmental efficiency, defend the frontiers, and stop economic deterioration. His reconstruction of the Roman world after a century of civil war and severe decline is often compared with Augustus' reorganization after a similar period of turmoil. But while Augustus had established a form of constitutional monarchy, Diocletian founded an undisguised oriental despotism.

To increase the strength of the govern-

ment, Diocletian completed the trend toward autocracy. The Senate was relegated to the status of a mere city council, while the person of the emperor was exalted. Adorned in robes laden with jewels, the emperor surrounded himself with all the splendor of an oriental despot. An imperial etiquette was established which transformed the emperor into a veritable god; rigid ceremonial demanded that men bow low before him and address him as "the most sacred lord."

The administration of the empire was modified drastically. First of all, Diocletian introduced what he hoped would be an orderly method of succession to the throne as well as a more efficient system of administration. Realizing that the empire had become too large for one man to govern, he divided it. He retained the eastern half for his own administration, while in the West he created a coemperor who, like himself, was designated an Augustus. Each Augustus in turn was to entrust the direct rule of half his realm to an assistant, termed Caesar. Each Caesar would succeed his Augustus when the senior official died or retired. A new Caesar would then be appointed. It was thought that this scheme would also solve the problem of succession.

Next, Diocletian greatly increased the number and variety of administrative units within the four divisions of the empire. The provinces were reduced in size and more than doubled in number. (Italy, incidentally, lost its hitherto favored position and was divided into provinces.) The 120 provinces were grouped into thirteen dioceses, each under a vicar. The dioceses in turn were grouped into four prefectures, each under a prefect who served directly under one of the four emperors. A large secret service was created to keep close watch over this vast bureaucracy. Even the Christian Church did not escape the spreading tentacles of the new regimented state, as Diocletian's ruthless persecution of Christianity demonstrates.

Diocletian also divided the civil and military functions, and a separate hierarchy of officials exercised military authority in the numerous new administrative units of the empire. The actual command of armies was in the hands of generals called *duces*, from which we got the term *dukes*. In this purely professional military establishment, in which cavalry was becoming more important than infantry, anyone, even the barbarians who were increasingly recruited, could rise to the top of the ladder.

Diocletian also made strenuous efforts to arrest economic decay in the empire. In order to pay their armies and other costs of government, the third-century emperors had debased the coinage to the point where bronze was merely coated with silver. Diocletian gradually restored confidence in the currency by issuing new standard silver and gold coins. In the meantime, in an effort to stem the runaway inflation, he issued an edict fixing maximum prices for all essential goods and services. These ranged from peas ("split" and "not split") to beer ("Gallic," "Pannonian," and "Egyptian"), and from haircuts to freight rates. The following selection from the preamble of the edict reflects the paternalistic social philosophy of the new age:

If the excesses perpetrated by persons of unlimited and frenzied avarice could be checked by some self-restraint—this avarice which rushes for gain and profit with no thought for mankind . . . ; or if the general welfare could endure without harm this riotous license by which, in its unfortunate state, it is being seriously injured every day, the situation could perhaps be faced with dissembling and silence. . . . But the only desire of these uncontrolled madmen is to have no thought for the common need. . . . Therefore we who are the protectors of the human race, are agreed, as we view the situation, that decisive legislation is necessary. . . .[11]

According to a hostile Christian witness, Diocletian's edict of prices proved unworkable—despite the death penalty for violators—and was therefore rescinded. It is more likely, however, that price fixing became unnecessary after Diocletian's new coinage finally replaced the old and after the econ-

**THE ROMAN EMPIRE AFTER DIOCLETIAN
ADMINISTRATIVE DIVISIONS**

omy had been stabilized further by a new system of taxation based upon clearly defined units of various types of land and labor.[12]

Constantine. After Diocletian and his fellow Augustus retired in 305, his scheme for the succession collapsed, and civil war broke out once again. Within a few years there were five rival emperors because no Caesar was willing to wait patiently for his turn to become an Augustus. Constantine, the only one of the rival emperors who favored Christianity (see p. 202), forged to the front, and after sharing the empire for a few years with an eastern rival, became sole emperor in 324.

Constantine carried on Diocletian's work of reconstructing and stabilizing the empire. We have already noted his solution of the Christian problem. To stabilize the manpower situation in the empire, necessary for the production of essential goods and services as well as the collection of taxes, Constantine issued a series of decrees which froze people to their occupations and places of origin. Henceforth no *colonus* could leave the soil, and the children of a *colonus* had to accept the same status as that of their father. In the cities the same restrictions were applied to members of those guilds whose activities were essential to the state, such as baking and transportation. Born into and bound to their occupations, members had to marry within the guild and see their sons carry on the same line of work. Thus, to serve the economic interests of the state, a veritable caste system was established.

Were the remedies instituted by Diocletian and Constantine effective, or were they worse than the disease itself? Can we accept the contemporary view, contained in an inscription found in North Africa, that Diocletian was a ruler "by whose virtue and foreseeing care all is being reshaped for the better"? It is generally held that the work of these emperors did not allay the decline of the western half of the empire, which collapsed in the fifth century, but it may have had much to do with the survival of the eastern half, which endured for another thousand years during which it adhered to the paternalistic and authoritarian pattern laid down by these reforming emperors.

Division of the empire. The Roman world's center of gravity shifted eastward during the age of Diocletian and Constantine. The administrative reforms swept away Italy's former primacy, and Rome even ceased to be a seat of imperial authority. Diocletian's coemperor in the West ruled from Milan, while Diocletian himself chose to govern the eastern half of the empire and set up his court at Nicomedia on the eastern coast of the Sea of Marmara. His was a logical choice; the East had declined less than the West, and the greatest dangers to the empire came from beyond the Danube River and from imperial Persia. But even more strategic than Nicomedia was the ancient site of Byzantium, across the water, selected by Constantine for a new capital city. This site could be reached only through a long narrow channel which could be made practically impregnable and which possessed a splendid harbor at the crossroads of Europe and Asia.

Constantine may have had another motive for establishing a new capital. Rome was associated with a pagan past, and its Senate was a bastion of paganism. Favoring Christianity, Constantine may have believed that the Roman world should have a new—and from the very beginning, a Christian—capital. He dubbed his capital New Rome, but it soon became known as Constantinople.

The establishment of an eastern capital foreshadowed the impending division of the empire into two completely separate states, the East and the West. For about fifty years following the death of Constantine in 337, the unity of the empire was preserved, although there were often two joint emperors, one in the East and the other in the West. But after Theodosius I divided it between his two sons in 395, the empire was never afterwards governed as a single unit. From this time on a definite separation between the two halves was acknowledged, even though the fiction of imperial unity continued long afterward. Henceforth we can speak of a western Roman empire, which soon fell, and of the eastern Roman empire, which in time achieved a splendid Byzantine culture.

UPHEAVAL IN THE WEST

Mounting pressures on the frontiers. More than once in its long history Rome had weathered critical situations. Now, weakened by economic, social, and political decline, it had turned to the most extreme forms of absolutism in an effort to ride out the storm that threatened to engulf it. But its internal crisis was compounded by mounting external pressures that threatened to stave in its far-flung frontiers.

In North Africa there was little to be feared from the Berber tribes; yet because of their marauding and plundering, garrisons were required to protect the imperial boundaries along the Sahara. On the easternmost flank of the empire stood a much more dangerous enemy, the Sassanid monarchy of Persia (see p. 220). The presence of aggressive Persian forces with their mounted archers and mail-clad heavy cavalry placed a heavy burden upon Roman military resources, even when the legionnaires were not actually engaged in hostilities on the eastern perimeter. But the greatest danger to Rome lay to the north, where restless bands of fierce barbarians the Germans—roamed close to the imperial frontiers.

The Germanic tribes. The Germans covered Europe from the Rhine to southern Russia and from the Baltic to the Danube. From the Franks on the Rhine to the Goths on the Black Sea, they were grouped into tribes (whose names will appear in the text as each makes its bid for the spoils of a tottering empire). Seminomads, the Germans were at a cultural stage midway between a pastoral and an agricultural economy. They engaged in so little commerce that cattle, rather than money, were sufficient as a measure of value. The Germans were notorious as heavy drinkers and gamblers. The Roman historian Tacitus recounted that:

For drink they extract a juice from barley or grain, which is fermented to make something not unlike wine. . . . Their food is plain—wild fruit, fresh game or curdled milk. They satisfy their hunger without any elaborate service or appetizers. But they show no corresponding self-control in drinking. . . .

. . . they go in for dicing, if you can believe it, in all seriousness and in their sober hours, and are so recklessly keen about winning or losing that, when everything else is gone, they stake their personal liberty on the last decisive throw. The loser goes into slavery without complaint. . . . Such is their perverse persistence, or to use their own word, their honour.[13]

On the other hand, Tacitus praised the Germans for their courage, respect for women, and freedom from many Roman vices. A favorite amusement was listening to the tribal bards; ancient tales of heroes and gods were often told at feasts on the eve of battle to instill courage into the warriors. The names of some of the Germanic deities (Wotan, the chief of the gods; Thiu and Thor, the gods of war and power; and Freya, goddess of fertility) have been perpetuated in the names of four days of the week: Wednesday, Tuesday, Thursday, and Friday.

Important Germanic institutions. Each warrior leader had a retinue of followers, who were linked to him by personal loyalty. According to Tacitus:

On the field of battle it is a disgrace to the chief to be surpassed in valour by his companions, to the companions not to come up to the valour of their chief. As for leaving a battle alive after your chief has fallen, *that* means lifelong infamy and shame. To defend and protect him, to put down one's own acts of heroism to his credit—that is what they really mean by "allegiance". The chiefs fight for victory, the companions for their chief.[14]

In return for their fighting services the chief gave his band of companions—called *comitatus* in Latin—food, weapons, and shelter. This institution had an important bearing on the origin of feudalism, the characteristic political system of the Middle Ages, which was based on the personal bond between knights and their feudal lords. The heroic virtues associated with the *comitatus* also continued into the Middle Ages where they formed the basis of the value system of the feudal nobility.

In order to eliminate blood feuds, the Germanic system of justice was based on the principle of compensation. For the infliction of specific injuries a stipulated payment termed a *bot* was required. The amount of compensation varied according to the se-

GERMANIC INVASIONS

Roman Empire 4th And 5th Century

- Angles, Saxon Jutes
- Vandals And Alans
- Suevi
- Lombards
- Huns
- Visigoths
- Ostrogoths
- Franks
- Burgundians

SLAVS

GOTHS After 100

GOTHS After 250

BLACK SEA

OSTROGOTHS

VISIGOTHS After 200

CARPATHIAN MTS.

HUNS

VANDALS

BALTIC SEA

Constantinople

Pergamum   Sardis   Miletus

AEGEAN SEA

CRETE

Adrianople 378

Athens

Sparta

Nicopolis

IONIAN SEA

MEDITERRANEAN SEA

JUTES   ANGLES

LOMBARDS

SAXONS   FRANKS

BURGUNDIANS to 436

LOMBARDS About 450

SUEVI About 403

BURGUNDIANS About 250

Mediolanum

Florentia

Rome

Benevento

ADRIATIC SEA

CORSICA

SARDINIA

SICILY

MALTA

Carthage

VANDALS 439-534

Hippo Regius

NORTH SEA

ANGLES

London   SAXONS

English Channel

Paris

Seine R.

Loire R.

Garonne R.

PYRENEES

Ebro R.

WEST GOTHS

WEST GOTHS

ATLANTIC OCEAN

BAY OF BISCAY

BALEARIC IS.

SUEVI From 411

VANDALS 411-421

ALANS 411-418

VANDALS 411-418

ALANS to 429

Catalaunian Plains 451

VANDALS 430-431

verity of the crime and the social position of the victim. For example, it cost forty times as much to kill a man of rank as a common man. Some crimes were botless—that is, so grave in character that compensation could not be paid. A person charged with such a crime had to stand trial and produce oath-helpers who would swear to his innocence. If unable to obtain oath-helpers, he was subjected to trial by ordeal, of which there were three kinds. In the first, the defendant had to lift a small stone out of a vessel of boiling water; unless his scalded arm had healed within a prescribed number of days, he was judged guilty. In the second, he had to walk blindfolded and barefooted across a floor on which lay pieces of red-hot metal; success in avoiding the metal was a sign of innocence. In the third, the bound defendant was thrown into a stream which had been blessed; only if the holy water accepted him and he sank was he believed innocent. Trial by ordeal, which was employed only where a strong presumption of guilt existed, lasted until the thirteenth century, when it was outlawed by Pope Innocent III and various secular rulers.

Germanic political and legal practices influenced the institutions of later western civilization. In medieval England parliamentary government owed something to the Germanic tribal assembly, composed of all freemen; the assembly elected the ruler and approved the major decisions of the ruler and his council of chiefs. Possessing no written law, the Germans meted out justice according to tribal custom—a practice similar to the workings of English common law, which is based not so much on enacted law as upon a developing body of custom.

The early Germanic invasions. Such were the people who began to press against the Roman bastions in the later days of the republic, only to be turned back by Marius in 101 B.C. (see p. 137). Their later attempt to drive into Gaul was frustrated by Julius Caesar. Augustus planned to conquer and incorporate into the empire all Germans living between the Rhine and the Elbe. But in 9 A.D. a Germanic leader named Hermann wiped out three Roman legions in an ambush, and from that time on the frontier remained at the Rhine-Danube line. For a century and a half the Germanic tribes caused little trouble; then, during the reign of Marcus Aurelius (161-180), they again made determined efforts to break into the empire. In the next century the Franks and Goths shook the defenses of the Rhine and the Danube, but after 300 the Germanic danger subsided for about seventy-five years.

During the many centuries that the Romans and Germans faced each other across the northern frontier, there was much contact—peaceful as well as belligerent—between the two peoples. Roman trade reached into Germany, and Germans entered the empire as slaves. In the course of the troubled third century many Germans were invited to settle on vacated lands within the empire or to serve in the Roman legions. While the use of barbarians in the army represented a short-term gain in men for the Romans, hard-pressed as they were on many fronts, by the end of the fourth century the Roman army in the West had become almost completely German. Its generals were also German, and it operated much like the Germanic war-bands described by Tacitus.

The Germans beyond the frontiers were kept in check by force of arms, by frontier walls, by diplomacy and gifts, and by employing the policy of "divide and rule"—playing off one tribe against another. In the last decades of the fourth century, however, these methods proved insufficient to prevent a series of great new invasions. A basic factor behind Germanic restlessness seems to have been land hunger. Their numbers were increasing, much of their land was forest and swamp, and their methods of tillage were inefficient. Another factor was their desire to enjoy the rich and promising life found in the empire. Still another impelling reason lay in the Germanic love of adventure and gain: the prospect of booty and riches was, for them, too enticing to ignore.

The Huns. Meanwhile, another restless people were on the move. The Huns, a Mongolian people, were nomads from central Asia who had for centuries plundered and slain their Asian neighbors.

In the fourth century the appearance of the Huns in eastern Europe struck terror into the Germans who were first in the path of this fierce horde. "Their swarthy aspect was fearful," wrote a Roman historian, "and they had a sort of shapeless lump, not a head, with pinholes rather than eyes." His description continues:

They all have compact and sturdy limbs and thick necks and are so monstrously ugly and misshapen that you might suppose they were two-legged animals or the roughhewn stumps on the parapets of bridges . . . their mode of life is savage. They need no fire or prepared food but live on wild roots and the flesh of any kind of animal, eaten half raw; they warm it a little by putting it between their thighs and the backs of their horses. . . . Their dress is linen or skins of field mice stitched together, and they have no change of clothing, indoors or out. Once they have put their necks in a dun tunic they never take it off or change it until rottenness has crumbled it to rags. They cover their heads with round caps and their hairy legs with goatskins. . . . Like unreasoning beasts, they are utterly ignorant of right and wrong . . . and they are bound by no reverence for religion or superstition. They burn with lust for gold.[15]

Superb horsemen and fighters, the Huns literally lived on horseback. Their favorite food was *kumitz* (fermented mare's milk).

Wholesale barbarian invasions. In 372 the Huns crossed the Volga and soon subjugated the easternmost Germanic tribe, the Ostrogoths. Terrified at the prospect of being conquered in turn by the advancing Huns, the Visigoths petitioned the Romans to allow them to settle as allies inside the empire. Permission was granted, and in 376 the entire tribe crossed the Danube into Roman territory. But soon corrupt Roman officials cheated and mistreated the Visigoths, and the proud barbarians went on a rampage. The inept East Roman emperor sought to quell them, but he lost both his army and his life in the battle of Adrianople in 378.

Adrianople has been described as one of history's decisive battles: it destroyed the legend of the invincibility of the Roman legions and ushered in a century and a half of chaos. Soon barbarian tribes moved almost at will within the empire and began to destroy the governmental structure in the West. For a few years the capable emperor Theodosius held them off, but after his death in 395 the Visigoths began to migrate and pillage under their leader, Alaric. He invaded Italy, and in 410 his followers sacked Rome. Peace was made with the Roman officials who ceded to the Visigoths a large tract of territory in southern Gaul. The Visigoths went on to create an extensive kingdom, which at its zenith covered most of Spain.

Alaric's march had triggered wholesale invasion by the Germans along the northern frontier. In 406 the Roman defenses on the Rhine collapsed, and a flood of Germanic tribes streamed into Gaul. The Vandals pushed their way through Gaul to Spain and, after pressure from the Visigoths, moved on to Africa, where they established a kingdom. In 455 the apex of Vandal power was reached when a raiding force sailed over from Africa and Rome was sacked a second time. Meanwhile, the Burgundians settled in the Rhone valley, and the Franks gradually spread across northern Gaul.

As the great German invasions penetrated the empire, Roman authorities began regrouping the western legions. After the last Roman troops left England in 407, the island was defenseless, and within a generation swarms of Angles, Saxons, and Jutes from the base of the Danish peninsula and the German lowlands invaded Britain and began to take possession of the country. The Germanic conquest in Britain seems to have been more devastating than in any other area of the empire; Roman civilization was almost completely obliterated. During the fifth and sixth centuries Romanized and Christianized Britons were driven to the western highlands of the island. Others escaped across the sea to Ireland or to Brittany in Gaul.

Each of several tribes which entered the confines of the Roman empire set up a German-ruled kingdom, although only the Franks in Gaul and the Angles and Saxons in England managed to perpetuate their kingdoms longer than a century or two.

As the Germans moved relentlessly through the western part of the empire, the

Huns pushed farther into Europe to menace both Germans and Romans. Led by Attila, the mounted nomads crossed the Rhine in 451. The Germans and Romans, fighting for common survival, joined forces to defeat the "scourge of God" near Troyes. Attila then plundered northern Italy and planned to take Rome, but disease, lack of supplies, and the dramatic appeal of Pope Leo I— which was to give the papacy great prestige —caused him to return to the plains of Hungary. The Hunnic hordes disintegrated after 453, when Attila died on the night of his marriage to a Germanic princess whom legend immortalized as Krimhild of the *Nibelungenlied* (see p. 401).

The fall of Rome. What was happening to the imperial throne in the West during this turbulent period? As we have mentioned, after the death of Theodosius in 395, the empire was divided between his two sons. Although Roman civilization did not perish with the sacking of Rome in 410 by the Visigoths and again in 455 by the Van-

dals, Roman rule in the West grew increasingly impotent and Roman emperors incompetent and decadent. The emperor was little more than a puppet. Leaders of the mercenary soldiers, whose ranks were now mainly German, wielded the real power.

In 475 Orestes, a Germanic commander of the troops, forced the Senate to elect his young son Romulus Augustus (satirically nicknamed *Augustulus*, meaning "Little Augustus") as emperor in the West. In the following year another Germanic commander, Odovacar, slew Orestes and, seeing no reason for continuing the sham of an imperial line, deposed Romulus Augustus and proclaimed himself head of the government. The deposition of the boy, who by a strange irony bore the names of the legendary founder of Rome and the founder of the empire, marks the traditional "fall" of the Roman empire.

Actually, no single date is accurate, for the fall of Rome was a long and complicated process. Yet 476 at least symbolizes the end of the Roman empire in the West, for in this year the long line of emperors inaugurated by Augustus ended and the outright control of Italy by Germanic leaders began. In theory Odovacar accepted the overlordship of the eastern emperor in Constantinople, who, now that the emperors in Rome were no more, considered Italy as one of his administrative divisions. But in reality the western part of the empire was in the hands of the Germans, and the emperors at Constantinople had little or no power there.

Theodoric's kingdom in Italy. While the Visigoths were creating a kingdom in southern Gaul and Spain, their kinfolk, the Ostrogoths, were suffering under the harsh rule of the Huns. Following the death of Attila, the Ostrogoths were free to migrate as other tribes were doing, and when Theodoric (c. 454-526) became their king, they were galvanized into action. This energetic and gifted Ostrogoth had grown to manhood at Constantinople, where he had been sent as a hostage when a child. Returning to the Ostrogoths, he determined to improve the lot of his people.

Reminiscent of the classical architecture which the Ostrogothic king admired, Theodoric's tomb in Ravenna is remarkable for its dome, which is one enormous slab of stone, 35 feet in diameter and weighing 470 tons.

Fearful of Theodoric's ambitions, the emperor in the East offered him the commission of reimposing imperial authority over Italy, now in Odovacar's hands. Theodoric accepted the offer and in 488 led an army of more than 100,000 Ostrogoths into the Italian peninsula. After hard fighting, Odovacar sued for peace and was treacherously murdered. Theodoric then established a strong Ostrogothic kingdom in Italy with its capital at Ravenna. Because he appreciated the culture he had seen at Constantinople, Theodoric made strenuous efforts to preserve classical civilization by retaining Roman law, supporting schools, and using Latin at his own court. Coins were issued in the name of the eastern emperor, for Theodoric took seriously his legal position of being an imperial official as well as king of the Ostrogoths. Following his death in 526, civil war and factionalism broke out in Italy, paving the way for its conquest in 554 by the armies of Justinian, the Roman emperor in the East (see p. 226).

The Lombards. A few years after the destruction of the Ostrogothic kingdom by Justinian's army, the last wave of Germanic invaders, the Lombards, poured into northern and central Italy. Reputed to have been the most brutal and fierce of all the Germans, by 568 these people had established a powerful kingdom in Italy which endured until 774, when it was conquered by the Franks (see Chapter 11).

The problem of the fall of Rome. The shock and dismay felt by contemporaries throughout the Roman world on learning of Alaric's sack of the Eternal City were to echo down the centuries, leaving the impression that the fall of Rome was a major calamity, one of the greatest in history.

Pagan writers attributed the sack of Rome in 410 and the other disasters overtaking the empire to the abandonment of the ancient gods. They charged that once the Romans turned to Christianity, all-powerful Jupiter no longer protected his people. In *The City of God* St. Augustine attempted to justify the new faith, to argue against the charge that the empire's adoption of Christianity resulted in the humiliation of the capital by the barbarians, and to direct attention from

Indicative of Theodoric's loyalty to the eastern emperor, this coin is inscribed *Rex Theodoricus Pius Princis,* but does not show Theodoric in the traditional Roman trappings of royalty, the diadem and the robe.

the ruinous condition of the classical world to the new goals of Christianity. St. Augustine contended that any calamities which had befallen Rome since the advent of Christianity were far less than those that had occurred in pagan societies. He put forth the theory that history unfolds according to God's design. Thus St. Augustine saw Rome's fall as part of the divine plan—"the necessary and fortunate preparation for the triumph of the heavenly city where man's destiny was to be attained."[16] Also, early Christians liked to dwell upon Roman vices and to interpret Rome's fall as divine judgment on its wickedness, including the persecution of Christians. This view was challenged by historians of the eighteenth-century Age of Reason, who were openly biased against Christianity. In particular, Edward Gibbon, author of the famous *Decline and Fall of the Roman Empire,* saw Rome's fall as the "triumph of barbarism and religion." Christianity, he argued, had played an important role in undermining the imperial structure: "The clergy successfully preached the doctrines of patience and pusillanimity; . . . the last remains of the military spirit were buried in the cloister."[17]

In our time some explanations of Rome's fall have been rooted in psychological theories. For example, the basic cause has been attributed to a weakening of morale in the face of difficulties, to a "loss of nerve." Or it has been argued that the ultimate failure of Rome came from its too complete success. The easy acquisition of power and wealth and the importing of ready-made cultures from conquered peoples led to "a changed attitude of men's minds" and indolence and self-gratification among the ruling classes. Such subjective theories can scarcely be proven, however, or even fairly assessed.

Meanwhile, other historians have examined natural phenomena in their attempt to find some major single cause for imperial decline. It has been argued that in its latter stages the empire suffered from soil exhaustion which depleted the food supply and drove farmers from the land. Social historians have examined the heavy incidence of malaria and other endemic diseases, and some have concluded that the primary exhaustion occurred in human resources.

Most historians account for Rome's decline in terms of a variety of interacting forces. On the political side, the failure of civil power to control the army following the death of Marcus Aurelius resulted in military anarchy, the disintegration of central authority, and the weakening of Rome's ability to withstand external pressures. In the area of economic causes, the small farmer class disappeared, and more and more land was consolidated into huge *latifundia;* civil war and barbarian attacks disturbed trade relations; a debased currency and a crushing tax burden undermined the confidence of the people. Eventually the rigid economic and social decrees of Diocletian and Constantine created a vast bureaucracy which only aggravated the existing ills in the western half of the empire, already far gone along the road to decline.

Case study: the man-power shortage. Among the numerous factors contributing to Rome's decline and collapse, we might single out the man-power shortage. A consideration of this problem illustrates how one factor affected and was in turn affected by a number of other contributory factors. Scholars have learned that by the time of Marcus Aurelius the population of the empire had begun to decline; in the troubled times that followed, the downward trend continued. The shortage of rural labor seriously diminished agricultural production. Furthermore, since the rural population constituted the chief source of military man power, its depletion meant a progressive enfeeblement of the imperial armies. During the third century the amount of abandoned land greatly increased and with it the amount of land taxes in arrears. Also, because of growing insecurity, the breakdown of communications, ruinous taxation, the decline in trade, and the resulting impoverishment of the merchant classes, the cities shrank in size. Consequently, the decline in urban population—attested by archaeological evidence—added to the tax burdens of the remaining citizens. Moreover, urban decline saddled them with administrative services which still had to be maintained. With imperial revenues falling, the government faced a fiscal crisis. The empire was no longer expanding; the economy had become static. Gold and silver were also being drained away because of the one-sided trade with India and China. In the past, military expansion had paid off in rich booty, and the tapping of new sources of wealth had justified a large army. Now, however, wars were defensive, and the army had become a financial liability rather than an asset.

Historians have argued as to what extent slavery contributed to Rome's decline, both morally and economically, and whether its presence prevented the invention of a machine technology. But here it should be noted that by the fourth century the empire suffered from a shortage of labor, free and slave alike. Having to engage now in defensive wars, the empire could no longer draw on its former convenient source of man power—slaves captured in campaigns of conquest.

With the frontiers either threatened or under attack from Persians and barbarians alike, Diocletian and his successors had to increase the military establishment despite the acute shortage of recruits. "Hence they found themselves on the horns of a dilemma. Either they could conscript Roman civilians for military service and so decrease still further production and the state revenues, or they could adopt and employ on a larger scale the policy initiated by Marcus Aurelius . . . to make up the deficit with barbarians."[18] The decision they felt called on to make led to the barbarization of the army and to wholesale barbarian colonization within the empire.

In the West by the fifth century, vast tracts of formerly cultivated land were left untilled. Meanwhile, the failure of communications and transportation, coupled with a drying up of the labor force in the cities, brought on progressive decentralization of the economy. Much industry had been transferred from cities to large country estates, and scores of once flourishing towns near the frontiers ceased to exist, while those closer to the Mediterranean shrank in size and importance. "Roman civilization had been essentially urban; medieval civilization was to be essentially rural. With the decline of the towns the general level of civilization was lowered and western Europe began to assume its medieval aspect."[19]

The fusion of cultures. Before the terrible chaos of the fifth century, a gradual process of culture fusion, or blending, was taking place. The menace of the Huns accelerated the onrush of the Germanic tribes into the empire, and what had formerly been a process of peaceful infiltration became a pell-mell attack on the frontier provinces.

The barbarian invasions must not, however, be regarded as cataclysmic. True, the invaders pillaged ruthlessly, and in certain sections of the empire, especially in Britain, Roman civilization was entirely wiped out. The Germans also seized a great deal of land, but most of this was either vacant or belonged to the emperors; few private landowners were displaced. In the main, the blending and fusing of the cultures and the blood of the two peoples continued without interruption.

In most areas of the empire the invaders still represented a minority of the population. Although the Germans viewed the Roman government as an enemy, they admired Roman civilization and continued to assimilate it. Thus the barbarians soon began to lose their Germanic speech, customs, and religion. Furthermore, most Germanic leaders kept Roman administrative agencies largely intact and employed members of the old civil service. In governmental affairs the use of Latin was perpetuated; that is why hardly a trace of the Germanic languages remains in Italy, France, and Spain.

The role of the Church. The eagerness of most of the barbarian invaders to imitate Roman civilization helps explain the preservation of much classical culture. But in addition there was at work a powerful and positive force—the Christian Church—which assisted the fusion between conqueror and conquered and cushioned the shock of the impact between German and Roman. By the time of the collapse of the empire in the West, the Church had already become sufficiently powerful to begin to fill the gap left by the vanished Caesars.

The Church believed and still maintains that, as a divine instrument, its survival and later successes were the inevitable result of God's will. Historians point out various other reasons why the Church did not collapse along with the Roman empire. In addition to the power of its ideology and the psychological appeal of its doctrines, it had at its service the outstanding minds of the time. Furthermore, the Church had developed an autonomous organization with its own hierarchy and landholdings, which provided both administrative and economic strength. It was therefore in a position to assert moral leadership and to assume many secular responsibilities in the West when the Roman empire collapsed.

From the time of the fall of Rome, then, the three elements which, interwoven, were to create the pattern of western civilization in the Middle Ages were already coexisting: Graeco-Roman culture, the Christian Church, and the Germanic peoples and their institutions. Here, in a sense, were the mind, spirit, and muscle which were to work together in western man during the next thousand years.

SURVIVAL IN THE EAST

Significance of the "survival in the East." We have reached a point where we should try to see events in broad historical perspective. In our study of history thus far it is apparent that the most westerly focus of civilization was Rome, from which in turn cultural forces had radiated still farther to the west and northwest until stopped by the Atlantic and the North Sea. In plotting the general movement of human advancement to the west, then, we can see that Rome was not only far removed from the "heartland" of civilization in the Fertile Crescent and Egypt but was also the cultural area most exposed at this time to counterforces. As a consequence, the western half of the Roman empire was overwhelmed by those forces, while the eastern half, though seriously threatened, managed to ride out the storm.

What was to survive in the East? First of all, it was here that the imperial tradition persisted. Until 1453, as we shall see, the eastern (later, Byzantine) rulers at Constantinople were to continue to call themselves *Basileus Rhomaion,* "King of the Romans." Not only the imperial tradition but also the administrative structure of the Roman state was preserved in the East—and with it Roman law and legal procedures. In addition, the Roman world-state had fallen heir to the Greek cultural legacy, and it was in the Byzantine empire that the Greek language and learning were carefully preserved.

The East also continued as the center of major importance to the growing Christian religion. Here the early ecumenical Church councils convened—the first at Nicaea in 325—to hammer out the fundamentals of Christian theology. Even in the West the language of the Church was Greek for the first two centuries, and as late as the seventh and eighth centuries half the popes in Rome had been born in Greece or Syria. Nor will it come as a surprise that an area so influential in the development of organized Christianity would in time evolve its own Orthodox Church with a vital role to play in shaping the course of civilization in Russia and the Slavic world.

For these reasons, we must redirect our steps toward the East, which has proved to be not only the originator but so often throughout history the arbiter of human affairs. For in this area once again the stage is being set for a new drama involving two neighboring but conflicting civilizations: one the last remaining citadel of Graeco-Roman civilization, the other the conquering faith of Islam storming out of the Arabian Desert. That the citadel was able to withstand the desert storm and endured for well-nigh a thousand years was to prove of incalculable consequence. It enabled the Graeco-Roman legacy to survive in the East and one day to be transmitted back to the West, which meanwhile had revived its depleted strength.

Meanwhile, also, a reinvigorated Persia under the brilliant Sassanid dynasty (226-641 A.D.) had emerged in the Near East. During more than four centuries the fervidly nationalistic and imperialistic Sassanids were the West's implacable foes.

The ruins of the White Palace at Ctesiphon are almost all that remain of the once flourishing center of the Sassanid empire. The brick vault, nearly one hundred feet across and over one hundred feet high, rivals the greatest works of Roman and Byzantine architecture.

Their earlier attacks hampered Old Rome's efforts to cope with the Germanic danger, and their later aggressions left New Rome and Persia itself exhausted and ill prepared to face the onslaught of the Muslim Arabs.

The heirs of Darius and Xerxes. Before the Germans shattered the northern and western defenses of the empire, Rome had for centuries believed that its most dangerous foe lay beyond the eastern frontier. For three centuries, the first century B.C. and the first and second centuries A.D., Parthia had been the only neighboring state at all worthy to compete with Rome in size and power. While they often fought on equal terms (see p. 165), in time a strongly centralized Rome prevailed over a Parthia unable to effectively control its many vassal principalities. Like Rome, Parthia had fallen heir to Hellenistic culture, but the native Iranian traditions soon revived and gradually swallowed up the legacy of Hellenism.

In 226 A.D. the Persian king, who was a vassal of the Parthians, ousted his Parthian overlord. As a member of the Sassanid family, he claimed direct descent from the ancient monarchs Darius and Xerxes, and he set out to weld together a new Persian empire. Eastward from their Iranian homeland, the Sassanids held sway as far as the Indus River. In attempting to annex all the western Asian lands which had belonged to the ancient Persian empire, the Sassanids embarked on frequent wars against Rome. During the third and fourth centuries clashes occurred largely over the possession of Mesopotamia, Syria, and Armenia. Affairs reached a humiliating low point for Rome in 259 when the emperor Valerian was captured and held prisoner for the remainder of his life.

Like the peoples of the West, the Persians suffered invasion from central Asia, but the outcome was remarkably different. During the fifth century, while Attila's Huns stormed through Europe, other Hunnish hordes invaded Persia only to be thrown back across the Oxus River. And in the next century an even more formidable Mongolian threat, that of the Turks, was held at bay.

Zenith of the Sassanids. During the reign of Chosroes I (531-579), the Sassanid empire reached its zenith. In external affairs, Chosroes extended Persian power both by force and by skillful diplomacy. His armies overwhelmed the east Romans and the Turks in nearly every engagement, and Persia established itself in a position it had not held since the days of Darius the Great. Little wonder that Chosroes' name was later used to designate all Sassanid rulers, just as Caesar was used for Roman emperors.

On the domestic scene, Chosroes was an equally dynamic ruler. At the time he ascended the throne, the empire was disordered and ill regulated, and the common folk were heavily taxed and oppressed by a powerful nobility whose intense individualism had long been the bane of Persia. Immediately, Chosroes set to work. He divided the empire into four administrative units, each headed by men whom he trusted and whose duty it was to control the nobility and direct the provincial satraps. In addition, he traveled throughout the land to check on his administrators and to deal out justice as he saw fit.

To finance his efficient administration, Chosroes instituted land and head taxes modeled after those established by Diocletian in the Roman empire. A heavier head tax was imposed on Christians and Jews, with the Christian bishop and the Jewish leader made responsible for its collection. This practice was later adopted by both Arabs and Turks and became a famed feature of Muslim administration.

Chosroes encouraged agriculture by urging the reclamation of waste lands, increasing the amount of land under irrigation, settling captives from foreign wars on farms, and distributing seed corn, cattle, and implements to the peasants. Bridges and dams were built, roads improved, and public works and palaces constructed. Today few structures remain, but the splendor of some Sassanid palaces can still be discerned. At Ctesiphon, the capital on the banks of the Tigris, Chosroes I built the White Palace, a huge building with a high vaulted audience hall.

Chosroes lived more luxuriously than any other monarch of the day. His golden throne had ruby-studded supports, and his

An ancient symbol of power, the killing of a fierce beast by the king himself, is depicted in silver relief work on the bottom of a Sassanid bowl. The full beard, tightly curled long hair, and long earring are characteristic of Sassanid representations of kings, as are the stylized flowing draperies, which suggest rapid motion.

priceless crown had to be suspended in the air because of its great weight. One of Chosroes' treasures was the "Paradise" carpet, 105 feet long and 90 feet wide. The design represented a garden, with the ground wrought in gold and the walks in silver; the meadows were of emeralds; the rivulets of pearls; and the trees, flowers, and fruits of sparkling diamonds, rubies, and other precious stones.

During the stately court ceremonies, the king sat remote on his throne behind curtains. No one, not even the highest born noble, was allowed to approach within thirty feet of him unless especially summoned. As we shall see in the next chapter, this formality influenced the court ceremonial of the Byzantine rulers.

Chosroes also was famed as a patron of learning. In 529, when the last pagan schools of philosophy at Athens were closed by the Byzantine emperor, the refugee philosophers were welcomed in Persia. They found Chosroes already acquainted with the writings of Plato and Aristotle, which he later had translated into Persian. Near Susa he established a medical school which gradually expanded its curriculum until it became a university where philosophy, rhetoric, and poetry could also be studied. Chosroes also fostered the study of Persian history and jurisprudence and encouraged the collection of the lays and legends of ancient Iran that formed a national epic and glorified the state.

Persian religions. Zoroastrianism, the dominant religion in the Persian empire of Darius, was revived during the era of the Sassanids and transformed into a state religion headed by a powerful priesthood. The ancient Zoroastrian literature was collected and canonized as a sacred book, the *Avesta*. Emphasis on religious orthodoxy resulted in frequent persecution of foreign religions, particularly Christianity, as well as Zoroastrian heresies. The most important heresy was Manicheism which, for a time, not only rivaled Zoroastrianism in the Sassanid territories but spread eastward as far as China and westward into the Roman empire where it became a strong rival of Christianity.

Founded by Mani, a new Persian prophet who was crucified in 276 at the instigation of the Zoroastrian priests, Manicheism borrowed elements from Zoroastrianism, Christianity, and Buddhism. Mani believed that the religious truths taught by Zoroaster, Jesus, and Buddha had been corrupted by their respective followers, and he claimed to be a messiah sent to restore the original truths and save mankind from sin and damnation. He taught that Light and Darkness (God and Satan, spirit and matter) were in eternal conflict and that the world was composed of both good and evil. The first man (Adam) was created in the image of Satan but possessed a spark of Light. The only way by which a man could rid himself of Darkness was to become an ascetic and avoid all sensual desires. The strong emphasis which Manicheism placed upon salvation by means of asceticism influenced the growth of asceticism in the Christian Church of the day. Although driven underground in late Roman times, Manicheism reappeared in the medieval West in the guise of the Albigensian heresy (see p. 388).

An earlier religion which grew out of Zoroastrianism and which became a more important rival to Christianity was Mithraism. Originally an ancient Persian sun god who had been repudiated by Zoroaster, Mithras was later revived by the Zoroastrian priests to become Ahura-Mazda's chief lieutenant in the battle against the powers of Darkness. In time Mithras was worshiped in his own right as an intermediary between suffering mankind and the austere, impersonal Ahura-Mazda. He destroyed evil men and rewarded those who were virtuous, conducting their souls to paradise. During the first century A.D. Mithraism was transmitted to the Roman empire and spread rapidly through the army, merchant class, and slave groups. As the militant Unconquerable Sun, Mithras was especially revered by soldiers, and during the critical third century various emperors identified themselves with Mithras in an effort to bolster their power by claims of divine right.

Mithraism had a number of similarities to Christianity, which helps explain why it was the latter's greatest rival. Important differences included Mithraism's compromise with polytheism, its worship of a mythical rather than a historical figure (Jesus), and its refusal to accept women into the cult.

Final struggle with East Rome. Despite its glittering court, efficient administration, and armies of skilled archers, mail-clad cavalry, and redoubtable war elephants, the Sassanid empire came to an untimely end after squandering its resources. From their beginnings in the third century, the Sassanids engaged in a dreary round of wars against the Romans—a practice which proved a fatal weakness. The experience of Chosroes II (590-628), the last famous Sassanid king, underscores the sudden vicissitudes of fortune which the empire underwent. In his struggle against the Romans in the East, his armies penetrated to within a mile of Constantinople itself, ravaged Syria, reduced Antioch, Damascus, and Jerusalem, and carried off what was believed to be the True Cross to Ctesiphon in 615. Yet within a few years the emperor Heraclius defeated Chosroes everywhere. He invaded Assyria and Mesopotamia, brought about the deposition and murder of Chosroes, restored the old frontiers, and recovered the True Cross.

The end of this long and fruitless struggle between the east Romans and the Sassanids left both empires enfeebled. Then in 633 there suddenly appeared a common enemy as Arab converts to the new faith of Islam penetrated Persian territory. By the middle of the seventh century the Arabs had occupied every province of the once great Sassanid empire, yet in the long run it was Persia that conquered Islam. As we shall see in Chapter 9, by the tenth century Persian influence had shorn Islam of its narrow Arabic and Bedouin background, thereby transforming it into a universal culture and faith. In the words of a noted scholar, "just as Greek civilisation served as a vehicle for Christianity, so did Iranian civilisation for Islam."[20] The core of the once mighty Sassanid empire still survives as the nation of Iran.

With the fall of the Sassanid empire in the seventh century, the stage had been set for a new and prolonged struggle for dominion over the Near East. The antagonists now were Islam and Byzantium.

SUMMARY

Christianity's roots extend back into Jewish history long before the birth of Christ, and it is there that we find the concept of the Messiah, the divinely appointed leader who would create a new Israel. Under the rule of the Hellenistic Seleucid empire and later of Rome, the Jews hoped for such a Messiah to lead them to political independence; and when Jesus attacked the shortcomings of the established religion and refused to head a political revolt against the Romans, His enemies brought about His condemnation and execution. But His teachings did not die with His Crucifixion. Interpreted largely through the efforts of St. Paul, they spread rapidly through the Roman empire. Despite persecution, converts flocked to the new faith, and finally, with the Edict of Milan in 313, the emperor Constantine made Christianity a legal religion. Thereafter the Church grew and flourished, with an organization based on the imperial Roman pattern and a hierarchy of officials culminating in the pope at Rome.

From the death of Marcus Aurelius in 180 A.D., the Roman empire declined as its rulers became pawns of the army. Only Diocletian and Constantine were able to check the downward trend, and in the long run their system of despotism failed to save the western half of the empire from further deterioration. When the Visigoths, pushed by the Huns, defeated Roman forces at the battle of Adrianople in 378, the gates of the empire burst open before the barbarian tribes. The date of the final collapse of Rome may be set at 476, when the last Roman emperor in the West was deposed and barbarian rulers assumed control.

The fall of Rome—one of the great dramatic developments in history—has been explained in a variety of ways by later historians. No single cause can be given: the collapse appears to have been the result of various interacting factors, such as a shortage of man power, economic decline, political breakdown, and loss of intellectual vigor. Following the devastating invasions which overwhelmed the western half of the empire, a powerful new agency moved into the gap left by the Caesars; this was the Christian Church, headed by popes like Leo i whose qualities of leadership were demonstrated when he assumed the role of protector of Italy from the Huns.

In the East, civilization did not crumble with Rome's fall. The Sassanids revived the old Persian empire and Zoroastrian religion and reached a peak of political power in the sixth century under Chosroes i. And as the Roman empire crumbled in the West, a new center of imperial strength arose in the East at Constantinople. To this brilliant, kaleidoscopic city we should now turn, for, as we shall see, a unique civilization developed in the Roman empire of the East—the Byzantine—which persisted for a thousand years.

Chapter 8

New Rome and The Third Rome

The Byzantine Empire and Early Russia

INTRODUCTION. On May 11, 330 A.D., the emperor Constantine formally dedicated his magnificent new capital in the eastern part of the Roman empire. Christened New Rome, it soon became known throughout the world as Constantinople, the city of Constantine. In 1453 another emperor Constantine—the eleventh of that name—met a heroic death in battle as the Turks smashed the empire that had stood as the successor to Roman sovereignty for over a thousand years. This chapter recounts the dramatic and tragic story of a civilization standing as an outpost of Europe, braving the strength of a hostile East, and protecting an unappreciative West slowly emerging from semibarbarism.

During the millennium that it endured, the Byzantine empire seemed close to collapse numerous times. But these periods of crisis were followed by resurgences of power and revivals of culture. The empire displayed in abundance the symptoms of its weakness—revolts and intrigues, despotism, theological disputes, and an overemphasis upon luxury and pleasure. But its aberrations were more than compensated for by its great contributions to civilization: Greek language and learning were preserved for posterity; the Roman imperial system was continued and Roman law codified; the Greek Orthodox Church converted the Slavic peoples and fostered the development of splendid forms of a new Graeco-oriental art which was dedicated to the glorification of the Christian religion. Moreover, situated at the crossroads of East and West, Constantinople acted as the disseminator of culture for all peoples who came in contact with the empire. Such contacts were numerous, because the merchants of the empire were extremely active in the ports of the Mediterranean and Black seas and had trade connections which reached far into Europe and the Near East.

For several centuries the Byzantine empire was the most magnificent civilization in Christendom. The splendor of Constantinople was proclaimed everywhere, for this rich and turbulent metropolis was to the early Middle Ages what Athens and Rome had been to classical times. Called with justification "The City," it was applauded and envied on three continents. But, like its namesake, New Rome aroused the cupidity of other peoples both to the West and to the East. After centuries of stout defense, the empire collapsed. In the meantime, its religious mission and political conceptions had borne fruit among the Slavs and especially among the Russians. The latter were to lay claim to the Byzantine tradition and to dub Moscow the "Third Rome."

THE PRECARIOUS FORTUNES OF THE EASTERN EMPIRE

Constantine's city. At the southern extremity of the Bosporus stands a promontory that juts out from Europe toward Asia, with the Sea of Marmora to the south and a long harbor known as the Golden Horn to the north. On this peninsula stood the ancient Greek city of Byzantium, which Constantine enlarged considerably to create a capital, New Rome. The English historian Gibbon describes the fixing of the city's limits by Constantine:

On foot, with a lance in his hand, the emperor himself led the solemn procession; and directed the line which was traced as the boundary of the destined capital; till the growing circumference was observed with astonishment by the assistants, who, at length, ventured to observe that he had already exceeded the most ample measure of a great city. "I shall still advance," replied Constantine, "till HE, the invisible guide who marches before me, thinks proper to stop."[1]

Even these wide boundaries, however, soon proved too small to encompass the new capital, which in size, population, and grandeur rivaled the first Rome.

Constantine had chosen his site carefully. The city commanded the waterway connecting the Mediterranean and the Black seas and separating Europe and Asia. Both commercially and politically, Constantinople was in a position to influence a rich region extending from the Adriatic to the Persian Gulf and as far north as the territory surrounding the Dnieper River. Moreover, the site favored defense. Enemies marching against Europe from Asia Minor could not attack the capital without crossing the straits linking the Mediterranean and Black seas, which in turn could be easily defended against hostile fleets. The addition of walls and fortifications on the inland side of the city enabled a fairly small force to hold off large numbers of attackers. This advantageous site enabled Constantinople not only to become the great warehouse for East-West commerce but above all to be a buffer protecting Europe from attack.

In Chapter 7 we saw how, during the fourth and fifth centuries, both the eastern and western provinces of the Roman empire were beset with dangers from beyond the northern frontier. Storming into the empire, Visigoths, Huns, and Ostrogoths pillaged the Balkans and threatened Constantinople.

This oldest known view of Constantinople, drawn in 1420, shows both its wealth of monumental architecture and its outstanding fortifications—two attributes which particularly impressed contemporaries. With the sea on two sides, a sixty-foot-wide moat on another, and thirteen miles of very thick triple walls, the city was impregnable for many centuries. The largest domed building on this map is Hagia Sophia.

But the more populous eastern provinces, with their greater military and economic strength, were saved from the fate which befell Rome.

As the western half of the Roman empire crumbled, Constantinople turned eastward for its livelihood and culture, becoming gradually less Roman and western and more Greek and oriental. A panorama of triumphs and defeats, Byzantine history for the next one thousand years can be divided into four main periods—expansion, peril, recovery, and disintegration.

Justinian expands the empire. The history of the empire in the sixth century focuses upon the reign of Justinian (527-565). Justinian was Roman in outlook and attitude, and he spoke and thought in Latin; his ambition was to restore the Roman empire to its ancient scope and grandeur.

Justinian owed much to his wife, Theodora. Because she had been a dancer and was said to be the daughter of a circus animal trainer, the court officials opposed the marriage. But Theodora proved to be a brave empress and a wise counselor. In 532, early in Justinian's reign, occurred the Nike rebellion (described later in this chapter), the most famous of many popular revolts which have led historians to characterize Byzantine history as a despotism tempered by revolution. Theodora's coolness and bravery inspired her hard-pressed husband to remain in the capital and crush the rebellion:

May I never be separated from this purple, and may I not live that day on which those who meet me shall not address me as mistress. If, now, it is your wish to save yourself, O Emperor, there is no difficulty. For we have much money, and there is the sea, here the boats. . . . as for myself, I approve a certain ancient saying that royalty is a good burial-shroud.[2]

To carry out his plan for recovering the lost half of the Roman empire from the semi-barbarians in the West, Justinian inaugurated an ambitious military program. His tactics were defensive in the East and offensive in the West; he bought off the Persian Sassanid kings, who threatened his possessions in the Near East, and devoted his attention to conquering the West. In 533 he seized North Africa and the islands of the western Mediterranean from the Vandals. After twenty years of exhausting warfare his generals took Italy from the Ostrogoths and drove the remnant back across the Alps. Rome and other great Italian cities lay in ruins, and the classical civilization that the Ostrogothic king Theodoric had taken care to preserve was virtually annihilated. Justinian also wrested the southeastern portion of Spain from the Visigoths. But Justinian's empire was still much smaller than the Roman empire at its height. Only a small part of Spain was his; nor had he recovered

Gaul, Britain, or southern Germany. Furthermore his reconquests had been accomplished at the price of exhausting the empire, both militarily and financially.

In domestic affairs as in warfare, Justinian sought to restore the dignity and splendor of the Roman empire. The artistic triumph of his reign was the erection in Constantinople of the huge Church of Hagia Sophia (meaning "Holy Wisdom"), whose architecture and decoration bore witness that a new and lustrous civilization had arisen (see p. 240). So imposing and splendid was this structure that men of the early Middle Ages called it "The Great Church."

Justinian's greatest accomplishment was the codification of Roman civil law. In 528 he convoked a commission to gather and classify the vast, disorganized, and often contradictory mass of law which had accumulated during centuries of Roman government. The result was a great legal work popularly known as the Justinian Code and formally titled the *Corpus Juris Civilis*. A modern edition of the *Corpus* fills three large volumes totaling more than 2200 closely printed pages. Its two main parts were the *Codex*, a collection of valid imperial edicts since the time of Hadrian, and the *Digest*, a harmonious ordering of the often contradictory rulings of Roman jurists. In addition,

the *Corpus* included the *Institutes*, a textbook for students of law, and the *Novels*, the new laws promulgated by Justinian and the only part written in Greek, now the dominant language of the empire.

By this codification, Rome's priceless legal heritage was preserved and passed on to posterity. In holding that the will of the emperor is the source of law, that the judge is the emperor's representative in interpreting law, and that equity is the basic principle of law, Justinian's Code stands in sharp contrast to Germanic folk law (see p. 211). The Code was unknown in the West during the early Middle Ages, but in the twelfth century it slowly began to have a notable influence on the improvement of medieval justice and the emergence of strong monarchs, who borrowed for their own use the Roman doctrine of imperial autocracy.

Three centuries of peril, 565-867. In his ambitious endeavor to reunite the two major segments of the old Roman empire and glorify the imperial capital, Justinian had exhausted his treasury. His successor's description of conditions, which tells of "the government treasury overburdened with many debts and reduced to extreme poverty" and of "an army so desperately in need of all necessaries that the empire was easily and frequently attacked and raided by the

In this late tenth-century mosiac over the south door of Hagia Sophia, Constantine is offering his city and Justinian is presenting his church to the Virgin. The combination of oriental style and Christian subject matter is characteristic of Byzantine art.

THE BYZANTINE EMPIRE
UNDER JUSTINIAN

Empire at his Accession 527
Empire at his Death 565

barbarians,"[3] is evidence of the state of affairs after Justinian died.

With Justinian's death, the first and perhaps the greatest period of Byzantine history ended. Now followed an era of peril lasting from the final decades of the sixth to the end of the eighth century. Justinian's successors concentrated increasingly upon saving the provinces in the East rather than fighting on both eastern and western fronts. In 568 the Lombards established a new kingdom in Italy, leaving the empire in control only of Sicily, southern Italy, and areas around Venice and Ravenna. Shortly thereafter the Visigoths regained the territory lost to Justinian in southern Spain. Fierce Slavic and Asiatic tribes invaded the Balkans; among them were the Avars, who established themselves along the Danube and between 591 and 626 menaced Constantinople itself three times.

When Heraclius (610-641) ascended the throne, the empire was in a desperate position. The Avars and Slavs still threatened from the north, and the Persian Sassanids had conquered Syria and Jerusalem. In the Holy City, Christian churches and sanctuaries were destroyed, thousands of Christians perished, and various sacred relics, including what was reputed to be the Holy Cross, were carried off to the Persian capital. While one Sassanid army conquered Egypt, other Persian forces advanced to a point in Asia Minor opposite Constantinople. In three brilliant campaigns (622-628) Hera-

clius defeated the Persians so decisively that he regained Syria, Palestine, and Egypt, along with the Holy Cross. The Sassanid empire disintegrated soon thereafter.

Although the centuries-old menace of the Persians had now been removed, the eastern empire was confronted with a new danger. The early part of the seventh century saw in Arabia the birth of a new faith—Islam (see Chapter 9). With fanatical zeal the Muslims began a wholesale conquest of the eastern and southern provinces of the empire. By the end of the century their armies had subjugated Palestine, Syria, Egypt, North Africa, and part of Asia Minor, while their navies seized Cyprus and Rhodes and harassed Byzantine shipping in the Aegean. An Arabian fleet and army even besieged Constantinople annually for several years, and the distracted empire was also losing its grip on the Balkans to a new Hunnish menace, the Bulgars, who in 680 settled in what is now Bulgaria.

By 700 the eastern empire stood on the brink of disintegration. The power of the emperor sometimes extended little farther than the environs of the capital and a fringe of ports in the eastern Mediterranean. In Asia Minor the emperor's hold was precarious, and in the western Mediterranean his power was disappearing altogether.

The rule of Leo III (717-741), founder of the Isaurian dynasty, restored order to the hard-pressed Byzantine empire. Defeating the Muslims on the sea in several engagements,

Leo also successfully repulsed their last great assault on Constantinople in 717 and 718. His internal reforms were extensive. He brought the law code abreast of developments since Justinian. The resulting code, the *Ekloga*, written in Greek, reflected Christian principles in addition to classical concepts. Leo also reorganized the administration of the empire by subdividing the large administrative districts, known as *themes* (see p. 235). This policy diminished the danger of revolt against the emperor by powerful governors; Leo himself had become emperor in precisely this manner. Although his centralization of government increased absolutism still further, he is credited with providing the empire with the necessary stability to withstand external aggression and internal disintegration for another three hundred years.

Last days of grandeur, 867-1057. The decline of the empire, brought to a halt by Leo III, began again after his death. Then in the ninth century, under the strong Macedonian dynasty (867-1057), the third period of Byzantine history began as the empire with renewed energy rode out the storm of external attack. The power of the Arabic Muslims was shattered as Byzantine armies entered Syria and regained Antioch, lost since the seventh century. Meanwhile, the powerful Bulgarians, now Christianized and seeking to possess all the Balkans, were held in check.

Under the dynamic leadership of Basil II (976-1025), the empire reached a high level of power and prosperity. Byzantine military forces finally crushed their Bulgarian foes with great severity. On one occasion fifteen thousand Bulgars were blinded and only a handful left with a single eye each to guide the rest home. The Bulgarian king is said to have died of shock when this sightless multitude returned. Basil the "Bulgar-slayer," as he was called, incorporated the Bulgarian kingdom into the empire and, after restoring Byzantine control over the Balkan peninsula, permitted the Bulgars to retain considerable autonomy.

Basil II was friendly with Vladimir, the prince of Kiev in southern Russia, and was instrumental in bringing about that ruler's conversion to Christianity. Other Russians also began to adopt Christian beliefs and gradually accepted various Byzantine customs and much of its learning. Trade augmented these friendly relations.

Because Basil II had fostered commerce and industry, a large surplus was built up in the imperial treasury by the time of his death. The empire stretched from the Danube into Syria, its once formidable Bulgarian and Arabic foes were shattered, and Byzantine influence reached deep into Russia. Unfortunately, Basil's demise was followed by that all too familiar phenomenon—a decline in Byzantine resources and initiative.

Four centuries of decline: Part I, 1057-1204.

At the end of the Macedonian dynasty in 1057, the Byzantine empire entered its last tempestuous period, one of decline, at times obvious and rapid, then again imperceptible and gradual. In this period, which lasted four centuries, imperial decline was due chiefly to the rise of commercial rivals and to invasions by both Muslims and Christians.

In the eleventh century Constantinople was still the richest and most active trading city in the Mediterranean world. Byzantine ships swarmed along the coasts of the Black Sea, the eastern Mediterranean, and the Adriatic. But within the orbit of Byzantine commerce a dangerous rival was emerging— the city of Venice in northeastern Italy.

In the fifth and sixth centuries Venice had been settled by refugees who fled the barbarian invasions of northern Italy and found safety on a cluster of small islands off the northern Adriatic coast. Because it was separated from the mainland by lagoons, the island city of Venice was relatively safe from the barbarian hordes and thus remained under Byzantine sovereignty when most of the Italian peninsula was overrun. As subjects of the Byzantine empire, the Venetians enjoyed access to the eastern Mediterranean trade, but they were far enough away from Constantinople to run their own affairs. By the eighth century Venetian merchants were transporting wine, wheat, wood, and slaves to Constantinople and returning with Byzantine fabrics and luxury goods and Asian spices. Soon the Venetians were trading actively with the Muslims, despite the deadly conflict between the Christians and the followers of Muhammad. By the eleventh century Venice had acquired undisputed supremacy in the Adriatic, and ambitious Venetian merchants were dreaming of supplanting Byzantine commercial supremacy over all the eastern Mediterranean.

In the eleventh century also, the Byzantine emperors were confronted with a rejuvenated Islam led by the formidable Seljuk Turks (see p. 264), who began to threaten Asia Minor. The Byzantines suffered a critical blow when their army was decisively defeated by the Turks at the battle of Manzikert in 1071, and all of Asia Minor, the main source of Byzantine man power, was soon lost.

With its main forces committed against the Seljuk Turks, the Byzantine government was unable to withstand the onslaught of a new enemy in the West. During the eleventh century hardy Norman adventurers, led by Robert Guiscard, began to carve out possessions for themselves in southern Italy. The Byzantine government did not abandon southern Italy without a struggle (see p. 355), but with the fall of Bari in 1071, in the same year as the battle of Manzikert, the empire lost its last stronghold in southern Italy. The empire's authority west of the Adriatic Sea was irretrievably lost and its prestige in the West irreparably damaged.

In 1081, when the empire stood deprived of rich possessions, sapped by growing commercial rivalry, and torn by the struggle of pretenders to the throne, a powerful landowner, Alexius Comnenus, became emperor by a coup d'état. To restore internal order, this remarkable ruler reformed imperial finances and the judicial system and won the support of other landed magnates by lavishing on them high honors and titles. He then turned to the problem of dealing with the empire's external enemies.

The first crisis of Alexius' reign occurred when the Normans, led by Guiscard, landed on the eastern Adriatic coast with the intention of conquering the Balkans. By granting commercial concessions to the Venetians, who also feared Norman control of the mouth of the Adriatic, the emperor enlisted their aid against the invaders. (These grants were subsequently to aid Venice in wresting control of trade in the eastern Mediterranean from the Byzantine empire.) The death of Robert Guiscard in 1085 weakened the Norman campaign, and the Byzantine and Venetian fleets combined to defeat the invaders. Alexius then repelled the nomadic tribes from beyond the Danube who had been raiding the peninsula, but he still faced the power of the Seljuk Turks in Asia Minor.

At this juncture, 1096, the first crusaders from the West appeared on the scene. Hoping to obtain some European mercenary forces to help defeat the Turks, Alexius had appealed to Pope Urban II for assistance, but he was dismayed to find a host of crusaders, including Normans, approaching the capital. The western response to Urban's appeal to save the eastern empire and the Holy Land from the Seljuks (see Chapter 12) was met with suspicion on the part of the Byzantines, who viewed the pope as heretical and the crusaders as potentially dangerous to the eastern empire. With his usual adroit diplomacy, Alexius encouraged the crusaders to forgo his hospitality as quickly as possible and attack his Seljuk enemies. The successful weakening of Muslim power by the First Crusade enabled Alexius to recover valuable portions of Asia Minor.

Among the successors of Alexius, who died in 1118, were some brilliant rulers who spread Constantinople's renown as a cultural center throughout the world. But the next century was also marked by external warfare and internal intrigue and violence. There were wars with Venice over trading privileges and with other western powers over Balkan territory, and there was even a futile Byzantine attempt to regain a footing in southern Italy. More crucial was the failure of a great effort to retrieve Byzantine supremacy in Asia Minor, which had been the empire's most valuable possession. Here, in 1176, the Turks overwhelmingly defeated the Byzantine forces and sent the emperor fleeing back to Constantinople.

Relations with western powers had been strained during the Second Crusade (1147-1149) and the Third (1189-1192), but in both cases the emperors had managed to avoid any serious clash. However, with the Fourth Crusade (1202-1204), the envy and enmity which had been building up for decades in the West against the Byzantine empire were converted into violence. The Venetians, upon whom the crusading army was dependent for ships and money, persuaded the crusaders to attack Constantinople. The crusaders could not withstand the lure of a campaign which would make their fortunes and at the same time would appear to be justified by the reunification of the Roman and Orthodox Churches. When the crusaders arrived at the environs of Constantinople, Alexius v, the Byzantine ruler, refused to pay the heavy tribute they demanded. In April 1204 Constantinople was attacked by land and sea.

A French noble who accompanied the Fourth Crusade described the city's downfall:

[I saw] . . . the great churches and the rich palaces melting and falling in, and the great streets filled with merchandise burning in the flames. . . . The booty gained was so great that none could tell you the end of it: gold and silver, and vessels and precious stones, and samite, and cloth of silk, and robes vair [squirrel] and grey, and ermine, and every choicest thing found upon the earth . . . never, since the world was created, had so much booty been won in any city.[4]

The booty was divided according to prior agreement: three eighths to the crusaders, and three eighths to the Venetians, while a quarter was reserved for an emperor who was to be selected from among the leading crusaders.

Many of the art treasures subsequently adorned churches in the West, but priceless works of art were destroyed, including the statue of Athena by Phidias. A judgment of modern times is:

There was never a greater crime against humanity than the Fourth Crusade. Not only did it cause the destruction or dispersal of all the treasures of the past that Byzantium had devotedly restored, and the mortal wounding of a civilization that was still active and great; but it was also an act of gigantic political folly. It brought no help to the Christians in Palestine. Instead it robbed them of potential helpers. And it upset the whole defence of Christendom.[5]

The empire had received a blow from which it never recovered, even though it retained a pathetic semblance of its former status for another two centuries.

Four centuries of decline: Part II, 1204-1453. Following the sack of Constantinople in 1204, a Latin empire was established at Constantinople with Count Baldwin of Flanders, a leader of the Fourth Crusade, as the first emperor and a Venetian as patriarch. Other crusading leaders carved out feudal principalities for themselves in Greece, while Venice took as its share of the spoils part of Constantinople, strategic coastal points, and islands in the Aegean and Ionian seas.

Meanwhile, various Byzantine leaders organized the unconquered remnants of the empire in Asia Minor and Greece as small, independent states. The most important of these, centered at Nicaea in Asia Minor, gradually consolidated its position. The Latin empire, on the other hand, faced continual crises, with the Greeks planning to regain Constantinople and the Bulgars also attacking. In 1261 Michael Palaeologus of Nicaea, allying himself with the Bulgarians and with Genoa, which was jealous of Venetian commercial supremacy in the eastern Mediterranean, reconquered Con-

stantinople from the Latin emperor. Amid the rejoicing of the populace, a Greek patriarch was reinstated in Hagia Sophia.

The rule of the Palaeologi lasted until the demise of the Byzantine empire—a span of two centuries of decline in imperial power. Internally, the empire lost strength and resiliency. A form of feudalism developed in which the great landed magnates resisted the authority of the emperor and the imperial bureaucracy. Bitter religious disputes arose between the clergy and the emperors who sought western aid by attempting to heal the rupture between the Orthodox and Roman churches. Taxes and customs duties diminished, coinage was debased, and the military and naval forces, composed increasingly of mercenaries, grew fatally weak.

Externally, the situation was critical. The empire held only a small portion of its former territory and was surrounded by ambitious rivals and foes. The Latins still retained southern Greece; the Venetians and Genoese each possessed coastal cities and island territories of the empire; and in the fourteenth century a powerful Serbian kingdom developed in the Balkans. While the Serbs weakened the empire by prolonged warfare, the Venetians and Genoese took advantage of Constantinople's troubles to strengthen their commercial positions at Byzantine expense.

During the fourteenth century, too, a new and ultimately fatal menace arose in Asia Minor. The Ottoman Turks, former subjects of the Seljuk sultans, became independent. In the struggle with the Slavs the Byzantines called the Ottomans to their support, but these allies, sensing their opportunity, quickly changed from rescuers to conquerors. Seizing Gallipoli, the Turks by-passed Constantinople and pushed into the Balkans.

With the Turks securely astride the straits, the destruction of the Byzantine empire was now only a matter of time. The end came in 1453. After a magnificent defense of Constantinople, in which Constantine XI confronted the Turkish army of nearly 160,000 soldiers with only 9000 fighting men (half of whom were foreign mercenaries), the great eastern bulwark of Christian civilization collapsed before the might of Islam. As the Turks stormed the walls of the city, the emperor rushed to meet them, crying out as he was cut down: "God forbid that I should live an Emperor without an Empire! As my city falls, I will fall with it."[6]

The significance of Constantinople's fall. Thus ended the tempestuous history of the Byzantine empire. It had lived perilously since its early days of greatness under Justinian. It had survived internal crises and invasions under Heraclius and Leo III and had enjoyed its last great period of splendor under Basil II. Then came the long twilight of decline and final oblivion.

Why was it that in the fifteenth century the West stood idly by and saw the Byzantine empire—long the buffer for western Europe against the Turk—smashed by the forces of Islam? The main reason was the implacable religious rivalry, even hatred, between Rome and Constantinople. A pope once commented that it was just as well for heretical Constantinople to come under Islam. To this remark, a high Byzantine official retorted: "I would rather see the Muslim turban in the midst of the city than the Latin mitre."[7]

The fall of Constantinople reverberated throughout the contemporary world. The last direct link with the classical era was shattered. First Rome had perished, now New Rome; and an epoch that had seemed eternal

had passed into history. In assessing the significance of this event, historians of a later period often regarded it as the beginning of a new era in the West, the era of early modern times. In support of this view, these historians claimed that the West fell heir to the learning of the Byzantines in their final hours and that this heritage formed the basis for the Renaissance. They further believed that the fall of Constantinople led to the closing of the principal trade routes to the East, thus providing the impetus for the age of exploration. Evidence has shown, however, that Greek learning had begun to penetrate the West long before the fifteenth century and that the fall of Constantinople in itself did not disrupt trade enough to necessitate the opening of new routes.

Reasons for endurance of the Byzantine empire. As the preceding résumé of Byzantine history attests, the empire's political life had always been stormy. During its thousand years of existence it experienced some sixty-five revolutions and the abdications or murders of more than sixty emperors. How did the empire manage to survive for such a long period?

One reason lay in its continuous use of a money economy, in contrast to the primitive barter economy then prevailing in the West. The money economy facilitated trade and the payment of taxes and enabled the empire to maintain standing military

As heirs of the Romans, the Byzantines were fierce and disciplined fighters. The Byzantine cavalry maneuvered in tight, intricate formations, and the navy coupled its battle prowess with a secret weapon, Greek fire. A complex network of turreted walls surrounding Constantinople was also of great value to the Byzantine defense system. Not until the Turks besieged the capital city with a new weapon, gunpowder, did Constantinople fall.

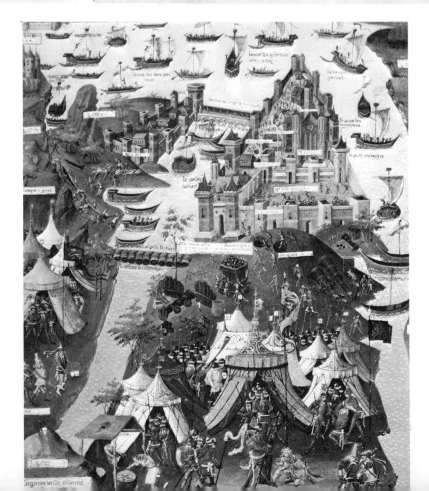

and naval forces. Until the latter days of the empire Byzantine military science was relatively advanced and the armed forces effective. Surviving military manuals indicate the efficiency of army organization, which included engineering and medical units. Also, the Byzantines had a secret weapon called "Greek fire," an inflammable chemical mixture whose main ingredient, saltpeter, made it a forerunner of gunpowder. As from a modern flame thrower, Greek fire was catapulted out of tubes onto the decks of enemy ships.

Of great significance for the endurance, as well as the character, of the empire was the wholesale loss of African, Italian, and eastern territory by the year 700. The lands still under the emperor's control were now more homogeneous; most of the population was Greek. Thus historians speak of the seventh century as the period when the eastern Roman empire was transformed into the "Byzantine" empire—that is, transformed into a Hellenized civilization taking its name appropriately from the original Greek settlement on which Constantinople had been built.

Another reason for the empire's endurance was the centralized system of administration. Where the West was broken up into numerous feudal principalities, the Byzantines were governed by a strong monarchy, aided by a well-trained bureaucracy. By providing continuity of administration, this bureaucracy helped the empire to ride out its political storms. The emperor was consecrated with holy oil by the patriarch and thus claimed to rule by divine right. He regulated Church, state, business, and military affairs with an iron hand; the individual had little voice in the government. So absolute was the control of the emperor that the early title *Autokrator* has been carried over into the English word *autocracy,* meaning "absolute supremacy." Only a successful revolution could depose him.

At first the empire was divided into provinces, ruled by governors, with the provinces being grouped into dioceses and these in turn into prefectures. In the seventh and eighth centuries, however, changes were instituted. The settlement of army corps in different areas led to the creation of *themes,* or military districts, which replaced the former provinces. Civil and military powers were united under the military commander of the *theme,* and these generals took their orders from the emperor. In the eighth century, as we have seen, Leo divided the *themes* into smaller districts which were not large enough to feel independent of the central government.

Another factor in the endurance of the empire was the Orthodox Church. Linked as it was to the state, the Church automatically claimed the loyalty of the people. But the Church claimed their loyalty in its own right; it satisfied the people's religious needs and at the same time gratified their love of pageantry by the splendor of its rituals. Although the Church has been accused of becoming progressively intolerant and rigid during the lifetime of the Byzantine empire, its orthodoxy and apparent imperviousness to change had its compensations. In later years, when the empire was beset by troubles from without and within, the Church, as the staunchest ally of the throne, stood firm in its resistance to political disintegration.

THE ORTHODOX CHURCH

Collaboration between Church and state. The Byzantine, or Orthodox, Church, not only dominated religious and cultural life in the empire but was also interwoven with the political fabric. Whereas the Roman Church did not identify itself with the Roman empire or any other state in the West but became an international body, the Orthodox Church was a state church closely allied with the policies and the administration of the Byzantine empire. In essence, the Church was a department of the state, and the emperor at times even intervened in spiritual matters. In many respects the patriarch of Constantinople had a position analogous to that of the pope in Rome, but with a significant difference—the patriarch was appointed by the emperor, who

ATLANTIC
OCEAN

NORWAY

SWEDEN

BALTIC
SEA

RUSSIA

ENGLAND

GERMANY

FRANCE

HUNGARY

BLACK   SEA

SPAIN

ITALY

BYZANTINE

EMPIRE

MEDITERRANEAN   SEA

AFRICA

**THE EASTERN AND WESTERN
CHURCHES ABOUT 1204**

The Eastern Church
The Western Church

tion was reconfirmed in 451 by the Council of Chalcedon, which stated that the patriarch of Constantinople was to be accorded equal privileges with the pope at Rome and should be considered second in honor only to the pope. In addition, the Council granted to Constantinople patriarchal jurisdiction over certain provinces of Asia Minor and the Balkans. Pope Leo I rejected this canon because it diminished the primacy and jurisdiction of the Apostolic See. Thus began the schism between the western and eastern Churches. In the years that followed, Rome and Constantinople were constantly at odds over doctrine. Justinian sought to reconcile these differences but failed.

The iconoclastic controversy. Relations between the eastern and western branches of the Church, continually undermined by what Constantinople viewed as Rome's excessive claims of primacy, deteriorated sharply in the eighth century as a result of the policies of the emperor Leo III. Although Leo had no use for Islam as a religion, he agreed with its contention that the employment of images and pictures in worship eventually led to idolatry. Therefore, Leo issued edicts in 726 and 730 forbidding image worship as superstitious and irreverent. It was decreed that religious statues be removed and that all church walls be whitewashed to cover pictures of the saints.

In Constantinople rioting in protest against the iconoclasm, or image breaking, broke out immediately; officials who were taking down the large figure of Christ Crucified from the palace gate were beaten to death by a fanatic mob. The demonstration was put down by troops, who killed some of the rioters. Leo then had a plain cross placed above the palace gate and explained that symbols of the Christian faith were to be substituted for pictures and statues. When the patriarch of Constantinople objected, he was replaced by another man more agreeable to the emperor's will. Riots continued to break out in Greece and Italy, and the pope at Rome, Gregory II, protested vehemently. The succeeding pope called a council of bishops who read out of the Church all those who had accepted the program of iconoclasm. Icon worship was temporarily

selected him from a list of candidates drawn up by a council of bishops. Such blending of authority over Church and state in the office of emperor has been termed *Caesaropapism* (combining the functions of Caesar and pope). We shall see that this political philosophy was later adopted by the Russian tsars.

Beginnings of the religious schism between East and West. In the fourth century a pope had described the Church at Rome as the Apostolic See—that is, the bishopric with authority derived directly from St. Peter. A Church council which was called by the emperor Theodosius at Constantinople in 381, however, rejected the claim that Rome's ecclesiastical privileges were due to apostolic authority as set forth in the Petrine doctrine. The council declared that Constantinople was the second see of Christendom because it was the New Rome, implying that Rome was the first see only because it was the older capital. This declararestored in 787, but in the early ninth century there was a resurgence of iconoclasm. The final victory of the icon worshipers occurred in 843. Meanwhile, relations between the Church of Rome and the Byzantine Church were strained for a hundred years.

Final separation of eastern and western branches of the Church. Although the controversy over iconoclasm had been settled by the restoration of images in the eastern Church, other sources of friction made permanent reunion impossible. Some of the eastern ecclesiastics accused the Latins of acting irregularly by eating eggs during Lent, making use of unleavened bread in the Mass, and permitting priests to shave their faces. The rivalry between Latin and Greek churchmen over the conversion of the Slavic peoples in eastern Europe was still another source of irritation and complaint.

Exactly when the final breaking point was reached is difficult for scholars to determine. The traditional date of 1054, when a papal legate quarreled violently with the patriarch of Constantinople, has been challenged in favor of the later date of 1204, when crusaders completely alienated the Orthodox people and clergy. One modern scholar has written: "[The Byzantines] . . . could not forget the Fourth Crusade . . . and henceforward . . . in the hearts of the East Christians the schism was complete, irremediable and final."[8] The important fact is that for centuries the papacy in the West and the Orthodox Church in the East steadily grew apart until they came to maintain distinctly separate existences, each viewing the other with suspicion and intolerance.

Missionary activity of the Church. The credit for converting many Slavic tribes to Christianity goes to the Orthodox Church. About 863 two missionaries, Cyril and Methodius, set out from Constantinople to bring the gospel to the pagan Moravians, a Slavic group living in what is now Czechoslovakia. They took with them translations of the Bible and the divine service written in an alphabet of modified Greek characters adapted to the Slavic languages. (The Cyrillic alphabet, used even now in many Slavic countries, is named after Cyril, although he may not have invented it.) Although the Moravians and others of the westernmost Slavs eventually came under the sway of the Roman Church, the work begun by the two brothers triumphed among the Slavs to the east and south, so that ultimately the Orthodox Church extended throughout eastern Europe. From the Orthodox Church sprang the Russian Church and an accompanying extension of Byzantine culture into Russia. Today, five hundred years after the final collapse of the Byzantine empire, the Orthodox Church still retains a great deal of importance and vitality in eastern Europe.

BYZANTINE ECONOMY, SOCIETY, AND CULTURE

Byzantine prosperity. During the early Middle Ages, Constantinople was called "The City"—with good reason. Sophisticated theologians from Alexandria, barbarian chieftains from the hinterland, merchants from Kiev, crusaders from the West—all were fascinated by the vitality of the citizens of this metropolis, the pomp and pageantry of the court and Church, the scholarly and artistic endeavors, and the wealth, which far surpassed anything to be found in the West. The complex urban civilization of the Byzantine world rested upon a foundation of strong and well-diversified economic activities.

For centuries a stable agricultural system provided city and country folk with adequate food. The emperors fixed the prices of foodstuffs and employed various methods to colonize the land: soldiers were furnished with farms, and barbarian tribes were given districts to colonize in various parts of the empire, especially in the Balkan peninsula. Finally, a diversified industrial and commercial economy successfully supported large urban populations. The decline of population which had contributed to the collapse of the Roman empire in the West did not occur in the East.

Geography was another major factor responsible for Byzantine prosperity. Constantinople stood at the crossroads of Europe and Asia at a time when the eastern Mediterranean was more populous and advanced than the western half. In an age when water provided the cheapest and often the only effective means of transport, Constantinople's site ensured its being a port of transit for a great marine trading basin extending from the Adriatic to southern Russia. The city remained for centuries the focal point of commerce in the eastern Mediterranean.

This great center of trade exported two main types of goods: products manufactured within the empire itself and products which came from the East and were reëxported from the empire's trading centers. The merchants of Constantinople exported luxury goods, wines, spices, and silks to Russia and in turn imported furs, fish, caviar, beeswax, honey, and amber. Metalwork, leather goods, and other products manufactured in the empire went to the East, while back to Constantinople came spices, precious stones, costly woods, and perfumes, some of which were transported on to the few western Europeans who could afford the luxuries of the Orient.

Prosperous trade supported, and was in turn stimulated by, the existence of a sound gold currency. In the West a decline in commerce had been attended by a shrinkage in the supply and use of money. The Byzantine empire, on the other hand, retained a currency of such excellence that its gold bezant was a medium of international exchange. Until the eleventh century the currency remained stable and free of debasement. The traffic of goods, stimulated by this stable currency, helped make possible an urban civilization which throve on the free exchange of ideas and customs.

A diversified industry. Besides being the greatest trading center of the early Middle Ages, Constantinople had industries which supplied Christendom with many products. The city specialized in luxury goods. The manufacture of armor, weapons, hardware, bronze pieces, and other metalwork also flourished. Gold caskets and cups were beautifully decorated by jewelers. Goldsmiths met the ecclesiastical demand for altars, crosses, censers, and reliquaries; and

religious needs also encouraged a large business in wax and tallow candles. Tapestries and hangings of unexcelled workmanship found a ready market outside the empire, as did enameled glasswork and mosaics. Perfumes, manuscripts, carpets, leather goods, and a variety of ornaments were also prized wherever they were sent.

Other important industrial centers such as Thessalonica added to the empire's prosperity. Byzantine industry was famous for its textiles. Until the time of Justinian, all raw silk necessary for manufacturing fabrics had been imported from China, but after silkworms had been smuggled out of China about 550 A.D., silk production began to flourish within the empire. Silken fabrics embroidered with gold and silver thread and fashioned into costly vestments for Church services or court attire were eagerly sought all over Europe. The silk industry was a profitable state monopoly.

At Constantinople tradesmen and members of the professions were organized into a system of guilds. The guilds were hereditary and resembled the Roman *collegia* in some respects. Although they were given monopolistic rights, governmental regulations controlled such matters as wages, prices, and working conditions. Employers were not allowed to exploit their laborers ruthlessly, but the craftsmen in turn were bound to their guilds. The state designated when and where goods manufactured by the guilds were to be sold and also fixed prices for purchasing raw materials.

The splendor of Byzantine civilization was derived from the wealth amassed from its extensive industry and commerce. With pardonable exaggeration the Byzantines maintained that three quarters of the world's wealth lay within their capital's confines. A twelfth-century traveler gives us a vivid picture of the wealth and bustle of Constantinople:

From every part of the Empire of Greece tribute is brought here every year, and they fill strongholds with garments of silk, purple, and gold. Like unto these storehouses and this wealth, there is nothing in the whole world to be found. It is said that the tribute of the city amounts every year to 20,000 gold pieces, derived both from the rents of shops and markets, and from the tribute of merchants who enter by sea or land. The Greek inhabitants are very rich in gold and precious stones, and they go clothed in garments of silk with gold embroidery, and they ride horses, and look like princes. Indeed, the land is very rich in all cloth stuffs, and in bread, meat, and wine. Wealth like that of Constantinople is not to be found in the whole world. Here also are men learned in all the books of the Greeks, and they eat and drink [,] every man under his vine and his fig tree.[9]

This perceptive traveler also wrote of streets teeming with merchants from such distant lands as Mesopotamia, Persia, Egypt, Russia, Hungary, Italy, and Spain.

Constantinople, city of contrasts. The colorful social life of the empire was concentrated in Constantinople. The city itself had three centers: the imperial palace, the Church of Hagia Sophia, and the giant Hippodrome.

Court ceremonial—some elements of which may have been borrowed from the glittering Sassanid rituals—was arranged to impress both foreigners and Byzantines with the emperor's exalted nature and his remoteness from mundane matters. An envoy to the palace was escorted through great lines of uniformed guards and dignitaries into a resplendent hall. At the appointed time a curtain was raised, disclosing the emperor clad in his imperial robes on his throne. Golden lions flanked the throne and golden birds perched in pomegranate trees. While the envoy prostrated himself, the throne would be raised aloft, symbolizing the unapproachability of the heir of the Caesars. During the audience the emperor remained motionless, silent, and aloof, while a court official spoke in his name. In all his public functions the emperor was the center of a magnificent ceremonial.

Byzantine social life encompassed striking contrasts. Genuine interest in theological problems and a strong vein of religious mysticism among the people existed side by side with an exceptional fondness for amusements. Seating eighty thousand spectators, the Hippodrome was the scene of hotly disputed chariot races. Like the chariot drivers of ancient Rome, each charioteer wore one of four colors; rival factions were named after

the colors, the most prominent of these groups being the Greens and the Blues. One historian has described these exciting spectacles and their aftermath:

Every reader will picture the scene for himself: the serried ranks of Greens and Blues in their thousands, the patricians and senators in their gorgeous robes of silk and flashing jewels seated on the terrace reserved for them; high above the course, connected with the palace and cut off from the Circus itself, the boxes of Empress and Emperor. The long suspense; then the arrival of the imperial guard; a movement: the Emperor enters his box; he raises his mantle, and makes the sign of the Cross. The choirs sing, and strangely mingled with praises to the Christ and the Virgin pour the passionate supplications for the victory of this or that charioteer. Then the cars burst away: Triumph! Defeat!—and later under cover of night in the dark passageway of the narrow street a knife gleams for an instant, and a body falls; a splash in the sea and the current sweeps something away. A "Green" has had his revenge on a victorious "Blue."[10]

A typically Byzantine combination of opulence and religiosity is evident in the *Pala d'Oro,* an altar screen at St. Mark's in Venice. One of the finest existing examples of Byzantine craftsmanship, it shows rich cloisonné enameling as well as gold and gem work.

The synthesis of Graeco-Roman and oriental styles is apparent in this ivory carving of a Byzantine empress. She is flanked by Roman eagles and degenerated Corinthian columns, but her stiff, frontal pose and jewels are oriental.

These antagonistic factions differed on religious and political, as well as sporting, grounds and were the source of the dangerous Nike rebellion which nearly overthrew Justinian in 532. On that occasion the Blues and the Greens united against the imperial government; rioters set fire to buildings and monuments, shouting "Nike" (meaning "conquer" or "vanquish"). By an ironic twist, after Justinian's troops had routed the mobs in the streets, the rebels made their last stand in the Hippodrome and were there slaughtered by the thousands.

The Byzantines coupled their love of beauty with a streak of cruelty and viciousness. Their sports were often bloody, their tortures horrible, and the lives of the aristocrats a mixture of luxury, intrigue, and studied vice. While some historians may have exaggerated this aspect of Byzantine life, it would seem that the Byzantines were "cultivated, charming, and talented sinners."[11]

Where the Greek ideal had been one of moderation, the Byzantines tended toward excess, a phenomenon that may be partly explained by their political situation. The empire was never free from the threat of invasion, and its inhabitants were constantly aware of their imminent danger. Because Byzantine civilization was a fusion of the oriental and Greek, the conflicting influences of different cultural forces may have contributed to this lack of balance. Perhaps we can ascribe to the oriental influence the Byzantine love of splendor and indulgence, and to the Greek the keen appreciation of intellect and art.

Byzantine art: a unique synthesis. While Byzantine art was basically Roman in character during the reigns of the first Constantine and his immediate successors, the new capital's eastern location could not fail to bring additional artistic forces into play. The Hellenistic tradition had persisted in Alexandria and Antioch, and Constantinople was exposed also to influences from the flourishing Sassanid culture in Persia. By the sixth century these elements were fused with the strong Christian spirit that had motivated New Rome since its inception; the result of this fusion was a new style of a uniquely Byzantine character.

Byzantine painting, for example, displays a synthesis of different—and even conflicting—cultural influences. The Greek tradition provided a graceful and idealistic approach; from Persia came a more abstract, highly decorative style; while Assyrian and other Semitic sources inspired a forceful, realistic approach to figure drawing. Art historians point out that while classical elements remained in Byzantine art, oriental influences—with their emphasis upon a formalized style, vivid coloring, and ornamentation—eventually predominated.

Church architecture. The first great age of Byzantine art was associated with Justinian, who commissioned the magnificent Church of Hagia Sophia, as well as many other churches and secular buildings. When Hagia Sophia—henceforth to be the spiritual capital of Orthodox Christendom—was dedicated in 537, Justinian is said to have exclaimed: "Glory be to God, who hath deemed me worthy to complete so great a work. I have outdone thee, O Solomon!"[12]

No other Byzantine church equaled Hagia Sophia in size or magnificence. According to Procopius, the historian of Justinian's reign, it was "a church, the like of which has never been seen since Adam, nor ever will be." The effect of light playing upon its multicolored marbles and bright mosaics moved Procopius to declare:

On entering the church to pray one feels at once that it is the work, not of man's effort or industry, but in truth the work of the Divine Power; and the spirit, mounting to heaven, realizes that here God is very near and that He delights in this dwelling that He has chosen for Himself.[13]

Hagia Sophia is rectangular in shape and surmounted by a huge dome, with forty windows piercing its base (see Color Plate 11). The effect was vividly described by Procopius as

marvellous in its grace, but by reason of the seeming insecurity of its composition altogether terrifying. For it seems somehow to float in the air on no firm basis, but to be poised aloft to the peril of those inside it.[14]

The dome is the crowning glory of Hagia Sophia both because of its beauty and because it represents a major advance in archi-

Although the Romans had attempted to construct a square building topped with a dome, the Byzantines were the first to succeed. They used pendentives—triangular, curved segments placed at each corner of the substructure and joined to form a continuous circle. The diameter of the circle determined the diameter of the dome. The weight of the dome was received by the pendentives, which distributed the thrust to the corners of the four supporting piers.

tecture. The Romans had been able to construct a huge dome in the Pantheon but had erected it upon massive circular walls which limited the shape of the building. The dome of Hagia Sophia was supported by pendentives, a method which permitted flexibility in the design of domed structures.

Over the centuries many other fine structures employed the pendentive principle. A favorite design, with symbolic appeal, was a church in the shape of a cross, surmounted by a dome. A still further development was the five-domed church, which was cross-shaped, with a central dome at the crossing and a smaller dome on each of the four arms. The most famous existing example of this design is St. Mark's in Venice, constructed in the eleventh century (see illustration, p. 242).

Vivid mosaics and decorative arts. The second outstanding period of Byzantine art lasted from the middle of the ninth century to the sack of Constantinople in 1204. This age is notable for producing the finest examples of Byzantine decorative art.

In the decoration of churches, Byzantine artists made extensive use of mosaics—small pieces of multicolored glass or stone cemented into patterns to form brilliant decorations. Not only did the rich colors of the mosaics increase the splendor of the church interiors and heighten the emotional appeal of the rituals, but the representations also served as useful teaching devices by presenting the viewer with scenes from the Bible and with images of Christ, the Virgin, and the saints.

With their penchant for vivid colors and elaborate detail, Byzantine artists excelled in a number of decorative arts, such as carving in ivory, the illumination of manuscripts, and the decoration of book covers, chests, thrones, and altars. Constantinople was renowned for its cloisonné technique, by which enamel was inlaid between thin gold bands to form the design. Byzantine designs and decorative motifs had a great influence on artists in the West.

Wall and panel painting. Although Constantinople never recovered political preeminence following the sack of the city in 1204, its art revived. The third important period of Byzantine artistic activity took place during the fourteenth and fifteenth centuries when Byzantium was no longer wealthy. This revival expressed itself in brilliant paintings on walls and panels, a form of art necessitated in some measure by the need to find cheaper substitutes for expensive mosaics and enamels.

Like mosaics, Byzantine wall paintings were employed to decorate churches. In addition, icons—panel paintings of sacred personages—were used in daily worship. At first icon subject matter tended to be restricted to a single figure, such as Christ; but later, panels often depicted a number of figures or a variety of subjects. Symbolic rather than realistic in its treatment of subject matter, the art has been described thus:

. . . the figures of the icon are not of everyday; they are themselves fundamentally religious, of the other world rather than of this, the aim being to exalt the spirit to a higher plane . . . like much of the art of today, which is not easy to understand at first glance, its significance lies below the surface; it is an art of the spirit rather than of the flesh, and must be approached from that point of view.[15]

Byzantine painting during this period wielded an influence far beyond the confines of the now diminutive empire. In contemporary Italy such masters as Giotto and Cimabue were directly affected by Byzantine iconography (see Chapter 15). Similarly, Russian painting at this time reflected many Byzantine developments. An important influence on the sixteenth-century artist El Greco was the Byzantine atmosphere of his native island of Crete (see p. 543).

The preservation of classical learning. The official adoption of the Greek language in the formative centuries of the Byzantine empire proved a stimulus to the preservation of classical works in philosophy, literature, and science. The scholars who perpetuated the Greek tradition were

The original appearance of St. Mark's Cathedral in Venice is preserved in a mosaic above one of the west doors. Inspired by Byzantine models, St. Mark's is in the form of a Greek cross, with a dome over each arm of the cross and a large dome at the central crossing. In this mosaic priests and laymen are assembled to honor the relics of St. Mark, which are being borne into the church.

not clerics, as in the West, but members of the civil service.

The principal school of higher learning in Constantinople appears to have been in existence as early as the fifth century. This university appointed both Latin and Greek teachers; the latter came to outnumber their colleagues, however, as Greek learning became the basis of education in the empire. In a capital beset by foreign wars and civil struggles, the university had an uncertain life and at various times fell inactive. After one of these periods of inertia, it was refounded in 1045 by Constantine IX and divided into two schools, law and philosophy.

Heading the school of philosophy in the university was Michael Psellus (1018-1079). This scholar had an inquisitive mind, and his admiration for Plato's philosophy did much to encourage the study of that subject. In range of knowledge, literary productivity, and mastery of style, he has been compared to Voltaire in eighteenth-century France. Psellus made contributions in many fields—politics, science, law, and history—and his is one of the greatest names in Byzantine scholarship.

Scholarship in the empire flourished particularly between the ninth and twelfth centuries, although one of the greatest single achievements of Byzantine scholarship, the codification of Roman law, occurred in the sixth century (see p. 227). Most of the scholars were concerned entirely with recovering and classifying Hellenic and Hellenistic learning. Greek contributions to mathematics, biology, medicine, and the physical sciences were recovered in large measure by Byzantine scholars, and from them in turn the Muslim scientists derived much of their knowledge. The preservation of Greek philosophy and literature kept alive the interest in classical culture which was to stimulate the flowering of scholarship centuries later in Italy—a movement known as humanism. Byzantine scholarship suffered, however, from being imitative rather than creative. Although scholars performed useful work in compiling and classifying the Greek classics, their own contributions tended to be only a rehash of classical works.

EARLY RUSSIA

The Slavs. While the fortunes of the Byzantine empire had been ebbing and flowing, its culture had exercised continuous and substantial influence upon the development of Russia in its formative centuries.

The ancestors of the Russians were the Slavic tribes, whose original home was the wooded area of the Pripet Marshes (see map). Moving into the lands vacated by the migrating Germans, in time three main groups developed. The Western Slavs—Poles and Bohemians—reached the Elbe and came under Latin Christian influences. Both the Southern Slavs, who moved into the Balkans, and the Eastern Slavs, the ancestors of the Russians who occupied the lands between the Carpathians and the Don, were subjected to Greek Christian influences.

The early Russians lived chiefly by agriculture, though hunting and fishing were also important. Most important, they established towns along the great rivers and lakes which form a natural commercial route connecting the Baltic and Black seas. The members of these communities sometimes were at war with each other or with roving tribesmen, but they also traded peacefully with each other and to some extent with the outside world.

Founding of a Russian state. About the time when their Viking brethren from Denmark and Norway were plundering and conquering throughout western Europe (see p. 326), Swedish Norsemen, combining piracy with trade, began to venture along the waterways from the eastern Baltic to the Black and Caspian seas. Evidence of the far-flung trading activities of these Varangians, as the Swedish adventurers were called, is indicated by the fact that more than 200,000 Arabic and Byzantine coins have been unearthed in Sweden.

The Slavic settlements along the rivers often hired the fierce Varangians as protectors. According to the earliest of the *Russian Chronicles,* written by a monk in Kiev about the beginning of the twelfth century, one such warrior, the half-legendary Rurik, was employed by the people of Novgorod. In about 862 he became the prince of the city. His brothers and companions established themselves in other cities, one being Kiev. On Rurik's death he was succeeded in Novgorod by a Varangian relative named Oleg, who seized Kiev in about 882 and thus extended his authority into south Russia.

The founding of the first Russian state dates back to the joining of these key centers along the river route, although Soviet Russian historians have recently sought to deny that early Russia owed anything to the activities of such foreigners. The early Norsemen soon merged with the Slavs, and later bands of Scandinavians, who continued to immigrate until the eleventh century, were in turn assimilated by the indigenous population. But the name *Rus* (meaning "seafarers"), by which the Slavs knew the Norse, persisted and came to be identified with the state which the Norse had founded and which was loosely centered upon Kiev; in the eleventh century the term *Rusin* became synonymous with Kievan. The extension of Kievan authority spread the name *Russia* until it was universally employed.

The Kievan state was a ramshackle affair. The prince of Kiev was considered to be the senior among his distant kinsmen who ruled the several other city-states of Russia, but only occasionally was his power equal to his prestige. When it was, Kievan Russia was more or less ruled as one political entity; when it was not, the Kievan state operated as a loose confederation of states.

Kievan Russia was less a political entity than a commercial entity, a coordinated group of princely states with a common interest in maintaining trade along the river routes. Kievan military expeditions against Constantinople itself began as early as 860, partly as typical Viking raids for plunder and partly to extort treaties which opened up a profitable Russian-Byzantine trade. Every spring after the ice had melted on the Dnieper, cargoes of furs, wax, honey, and slaves were floated down to Kiev. From there a great flotilla would descend the Dnieper

and proceed along the Black Sea shore to Constantinople. Returning with silks, spices, jewelry, wines, and metalwares, the Kievans would pass these goods on to northeastern Europe via Novgorod and the Baltic. This commercial interchange did not prevent the Kievan rulers from attempting unsuccessfully an occasional attack on the empire.

Christianity in Kievan Russia. The early Russians believed in ancestor worship and venerated the forces of nature. Their official conversion to Christianity took place about 989 under Prince Vladimir of Kiev.

According to the *Russian Chronicles,* Vladimir shopped around before making his choice of religions. He rejected Islam because of its injunctions against the use of strong drink; Judaism, because the God of the Jews could not be considered very powerful since He had allowed them to be ejected from their Holy Land; and Roman Christianity, because the pope entertained dangerous ideas about his superiority to all secular rulers. There remained the Orthodox Church of the Byzantines, which was presented to Vladimir's subjects as his choice.

Actually, Vladimir's choice was the most logical and natural one and continued a line of conversion that had already begun with his grandmother, who had been converted at Constantinople in 957. Although the Kievan state had contact on its various borders with the Roman Catholic Poles, with Muslims, and with a southeastern Russian tribe converted to Judaism, the strongest close influence on Kiev was Constantinople; and Russian merchants also had their main commercial contact with the Byzantines.

Meanwhile, the Byzantine emperor Basil II had offered his sister as a bride to the Kievan prince in exchange for troops needed to put down a rebellion. When the emperor later tried to withdraw his promise, military pressure applied by Vladimir changed his mind again. In 990 Vladimir and his bride returned to Kiev together with a number of priests, icons, and holy relics. Idols were destroyed, the whole population of Kiev was ordered to the Dnieper to be baptized en masse, Christian churches were quickly erected, and by the end of Vladimir's reign (1015) seven bishoprics had been established. From the outset the Kievan princes followed the Byzantine example and kept the Church dependent on them, even for its revenues, so that the Russian Church and state were always closely linked. The Russians also copied the Byzantines in Church ritual, theology, and such practices as monasticism.

Yaroslav the Wise, a scholarly monarch. Kiev reached its greatest splendor in the reign of Yaroslav the Wise (1019-1054 A.D.). He ensured the security of his provinces by defeating the barbaric Asiatic horsemen who were constantly threatening his southeastern borders and his trading vessels along the lower Dnieper. This scholarly monarch translated Greek works, beautified Kiev, and built churches, one of which was the cathedral he called Hagia Sophia. Yaroslav secured a place in the politics of all Europe by negotiating marriage alliances for his children with the royal families of Poland, Norway, Hungary, and France.

Following the death of Yaroslav, however, the princes of the various cities fought increasingly among themselves for possession of the Kievan state; and to these disruptions was added the devastation of the nomads who roamed uncomfortably close to the capital. The trading and farming population around Kiev could not sustain such hardships indefinitely. Long before Kiev had vacated its apparent primacy among the Russian city-states, it had lost much of its power, wealth, and population.

When the Mongols destroyed Kiev in 1240 (see p. 435), there was no longer any doubt that the supremacy of Kiev in Russia was ended. In Chapter 14 we shall trace the rise of the new center of Russian power—the grand duchy of Moscow.

Byzantine aspects of Kievan culture. The importance of commercial contacts between Constantinople and Kiev and the growth of

RUSSIA ABOUT 1000
--- Varangian Trade Route

In the Ostrominovo gospels, one of the earliest known Russian manuscripts, executed about 1056, St. Luke is depicted at the moment of inspiration. Although Byzantine influence is obvious, a characteristically Russian style has already begun to emerge. The curled hair, pointed beard, and intense facial expression are all more typical of Slavic than of Byzantine art.

the power of the Orthodox Church during the Kievan period were the chief factors responsible for the strength of Byzantine influences in Russia. Architecture, for example, came within the province of the Church. The cathedral built in Kiev by order of Prince Vladimir in the tenth century was designed by architects from Constantinople and was Byzantine in plan and style. The outstanding churches built in the eleventh and twelfth centuries at Kiev, Novgorod, and other cities also show strong Byzantine influence. In time architects developed a distinctly Russian style, including the characteristic "onion dome," which is merely a fanciful "helmet" covering the dome.

The decoration of churches also followed Byzantine models. In fact, the earliest mosaics, as well as mural and icon paintings, appear to have been the work of Byzantine artists who were brought to Russia. At Hagia Sophia in Kiev, some of these wall paintings still remain.

The adaptation of the Greek alphabet to the Slavic tongue and the translation of Church liturgy into Slavic stimulated the growth of Russian literature. Although at first Kieven literature consisted for the most part of translations of Byzantine works or of original material based on Byzantine models, in time a literature of the Russian people emerged, as epics of their fierce struggles to resist barbaric nomads from the steppes appeared. But the use of Slavic in the Church also had less beneficial effects on Russian cultural development. Many churchmen remained ignorant of Latin and sometimes lacked even a good knowledge of Greek; hence the majority of the learned had no direct contact with the literature in those two languages. Much of the cultural isolationism of the Russians in the past has been ascribed to this factor.

Broadly speaking, by the eleventh century and particularly during the reign of Yaroslav the Wise, Kievan Russia could boast of a culture and an economy which were probably superior to what then existed in western Europe; for these achievements Kiev was primarily obligated to the Byzantine empire, which at the time enjoyed the highest cultural level in Christendom. Yet the Kievans were not slavish imitators; although they accepted many features of Byzantine civilization, the Russians adapted them to their own needs and background.

"Two Romes have fallen, and the third stands." In the years following the fall of Constantinople to the Turks in 1453, the rising capital of Russia—Moscow—claimed to be its heir on two counts. First, Moscow had become the seat of the most important Orthodox Church not under Turkish rule; second, Ivan the Great of Russia in 1472 had married the niece of Constantine XI and adopted the double-headed imperial eagle of Byzantium as his coat of arms. The Russian rulers, claiming to be the legitimate successors of the Byzantine emperors and the protectors of Orthodox Christianity, took the title of *tsar*, or *czar*, meaning "Caesar."

Early in the sixteenth century Philotheos of Pskov, a Russian monk, addressed the tsar thus:

. . . the Old Rome fell because of its church's lack of faith . . . ; and of the second Rome, the city of Constantine, the pagans broke down the doors of the churches with their axes. . . . And now there is the Holy synodal Apostolic church of the reigning third Rome, of your tsardom, which shines like the sun in its orthodox Christian faith throughout the whole universe. . . . Listen and attend, pious tsar, that all Christian empires are gathered in your single one, that two Romes have fallen, and the third one stands, and a fourth one there shall not be.[16]

A chronicler of about a century later, Palytsin, referred to the "reigning city of Moscow" as "New Rome,"[17] using the same designation given by the original Constantine to his capital. On the basis of the belief that they were heirs of the Byzantine tradition, Russian rulers were later to press claims to the Dardanelles and parts of southeastern Europe. Moreover, as in the idea expressed by Philotheos when he said "you are the only tsar for Christians in the whole world,"[18] the Russian tradition would henceforth encompass a great imperial mission pointing toward universal domination.

Some historians see this Russian sense of destiny still operating in a new manifestation—Communism—with the same fervor of the earlier Russian dedication to Orthodox Christianity. "Five centuries ago the words of Philotheos of Pskov may have sounded arrogant and foolhardy; but for us today, in the new constellation of world-forces after 1945, they echo through the centuries as the prophetic expression of the most momentous consequence of the fall of Constantinople . . . . on the wider stage of world-history the effects of the events of 1453 are only now making themselves felt."[19]

SUMMARY

The ornate civilization that centered for a thousand years in Constantinople, crossroads of the world, was fascinatingly cosmopolitan, for its inhabitants came from diverse regions of Europe and Asia, enriching the city on the Golden Horn with a multitude of customs and ideas. The variegated social life of those who flocked to Hagia Sophia and the Hippodrome, the costly wares and the lively bickerings of merchants who traveled far up into Russia, the bejeweled splendor of Byzantine art— these factors, together with the energy exhibited by a people conditioned through historical and geographical circumstances to "live dangerously," mark this civilization as particularly kaleidoscopic.

When Constantine chose the site for New Rome, he picked a location that was geographically excellent from the point of view of protection and also of trade. Constantinople's tradition as the eastern capital of the Roman empire encouraged Justinian to attempt to recover the western territory which had been under Roman rule—but these efforts failed, and in the long run Byzantium had to fight continually against invasions that diminished its empire on all sides. Venice diverted the Fourth Crusade against Constantinople, and in 1204 the city was sacked. The capital was later regained by the Byzantines, but the final centuries saw the continual decline of the empire, battered by external attacks and internal strife. In 1453 the Ottoman Turks conquered "The City," and the empire of a thousand years was destroyed.

For a millennium the empire had acted as a buffer state, repulsing the attacks of Persians, Arabs, Turks, and barbarian tribes, while the weak, divided West grew in strength. And while learning was all but lost in medieval western Europe, the Byzantine world remained the custodian of classical knowledge and ideals until a resurgent West was able to appreciate and assimilate its classical inheritance.

Constantinople did much more than all this. In "The City," Roman, Greek, and oriental elements were fused into a distinct and original culture; in Byzantine art the lavish riches of the Orient were united with western elements in the glorification of Christianity. Other contributions of lasting value included the codification of Roman law, the conversion of the Slavic peoples to Christianity, and the bringing of the benefits of civilization to Russia and neighboring lands.

One wonders how this empire could persist for so long while constantly harassed by many foes. Perhaps the answer lies in its unity. But this was achieved only by despotism in government and rigid control of all facets of life by the state. The Byzantine structure was markedly autocratic and rigid. Its lack of freedom may well have contributed ultimately to its downfall.

In the wake of the fall of Constantinople, Russia appropriated much of the Byzantine tradition, dubbing Moscow the "Third Rome." From the beginning Russia had been influenced by the Byzantine empire. The Norsemen who founded a Russian state by joining Kiev and Novgorod also set up trade with Constantinople which continued for centuries. Through this medium, culture and religion were imported into Russia from the eastern empire. While Constantinople itself fell in 1453, its heritage was in many ways maintained in the new Slavic state that was spreading across the vast Russian plain.

Chapter 9

The Ascendancy of Islam

Muslim Expansion to About 1500

INTRODUCTION. Medieval Christian literature is filled with the word *Mahound,* a name given to the devil himself. The fact that *Mahound* is a corruption of *Muhammad* shows the horror that Europeans of the Middle Ages felt toward the founder of Islam, the militant faith which for a time threatened to engulf all Europe. To rid the Holy Land of the Prophet's followers, the "infidels," the pope organized European knights in a series of crusades. The failure of the crusades to achieve their purpose must have been a sore point in the mind of more than one devout theologian who could not understand how Mahound was able to triumph over the forces of Christianity. But it must have been even more disconcerting for the observant crusader to discover that his Muslim enemy was the product of an infinitely richer civilization than any in western Christendom.

The Islamic civilization is religious in its origin, for it springs from the teachings of the prophet Muhammad (or Mohammed). Muhammad lived in Arabia, then a crossroad between the Mediterranean area and eastern lands. The Prophet united the Arabian peninsula under the banner of his new religion, Islam, with its fundamental teachings of monotheism. The term *Islam,* meaning "submission to God," comes from the Muslim holy book, the Koran. The followers of Muhammad are known as Muslims. (This faith is often referred to as *Muhammadanism,* but Muslims have come to frown on this term, which implies the worship and deification of Muhammad.) Within a hundred years after the Prophet's death, his followers had conquered an area extending from Spain across North Africa and western Asia to Turkestan and India, carrying the dynamic new religion with them.

This breath-taking religious and political expansion was followed by a flowering of Islamic culture which rivaled the achievements of the Byzantine empire and far surpassed those of western Europe at this time. The Muslims share with the Byzantines chief credit for preserving and disseminating learning in the Middle Ages.

MUHAMMAD AND HIS FAITH

Pre-Islamic Arabia. Arabia is a quadrangular peninsula with an area of about 1,200,000 square miles. Much of it is desert, and rainfall is scarce in the rest of the peninsula. Thus, vegetation is scant and very little land is suitable for agriculture. On the other hand, Arabia from the earliest times had been an important trading area. Bordered by the Red Sea, the Arabian Sea, the Persian Gulf, and the valley of the Tigris and Euphrates, Arabia had ample access to the sea lanes. Caravans carried to the Mediterranean lands the products of Arabia and also the precious cargoes from eastern Asia which were unloaded at Arabian ports.

Although the racial origin of the Arabs is obscure, it is known that they belong to the Semitic language group. During the first millennium B.C. some Arab kingdoms in the south developed a high state of civilization, but the fourth to sixth centuries A.D. witnessed a decline of settled life in Arabia and an increase in nomadism. Throughout much of Arabia, particularly in the interior, nomadism was the only way of life. The nomads, or Bedouins, lived according to a tribal pattern; at the head of the tribe was the sheik, elected and advised by the heads of the related families comprising the tribe. Driven from place to place in their search for pastures to sustain their flocks, the Bedouins led a precarious existence. Aside from their flocks, they relied on booty from raids on settlements, on passing caravans, and on one another. Yet, if raiding became a way of life in the desert—where the fighting mood seems to be a chronic mental condition—its evils were partially offset by the Bedouin's strongly ingrained sense of hospitality.

Intensely fond of storytelling and poetry, the Bedouins have left evidence in verse of their way of life. They prized courage, strength, and loyalty, accorded women considerable freedom and dignity, and sang the praises of their nomadic existence:

Roast meat and wine: the swinging ride
On a camel sure and tried,
Which her master speeds amain
O'er low dale and level plain . . . .[1]

The Bedouins worshiped a large number of gods and spirits, many of whom were believed to inhabit trees, wells, and stones. Each tribe had its own god, symbolized generally by a sacred stone which served as an altar where communal sacrifices were offered. Various nontribal deities, representing the Sun, Venus, and Fortune, were also recognized.

Monotheistic influences. Although the Bedouins of the interior led a primitive and largely isolated existence, some parts of Arabia were influenced by neighboring—and more advanced—cultures. To the north, in Mesopotamia and Persia, lay the Sassanid empire (see p. 220), while to the west and north were Egypt, Palestine, and Syria, provinces of the Byzantine empire. From Ghassan and Hira, two Arab states sharing a common border with Syria and Mesopotamia, Arab mercenaries were enlisted to fight in the long series of wars between the Byzantine and Sassanid empires. These soldiers brought back to Arabia new military skills and weapons, as well as various cultural techniques, including, perhaps, writing.

Another result of outside contacts was the introduction of Christianity and Judaism into Arabia. Some areas in the Yemen and the Hejaz (regions along the Red Sea) had adopted Christianity. With the immigration of considerable numbers of Jews, Hebraic religious influences entered Arabia. In the first and second centuries A.D. Rome violently crushed a Jewish independence movement, and it may have been during the dispersal afterward that Jews came to Arabia. Many of them settled in the Yemen and in the Hejaz city of Medina, where it has been estimated that they accounted for a large share of the total population. By the latter half of the sixth century Christian and Jewish groups were found throughout the Arabian peninsula. Their religious convictions and moral principles had a strong effect on the indigenous population, and their monotheistic beliefs were later incorporated into Islamic doctrine.

Mecca. Several of the more advanced cities were in Hejaz, among them Mecca, destined to be the key city in the Islamic religion. Fifty miles inland from the port of Jiddah, Mecca was favorably located for trade. Its merchants carried on business with southern Arabia, with Abyssinia across the Red Sea, and with the Byzantine and Persian empires. Mecca was controlled by the Quraysh, an Arabian tribe whose members formed trading companies that cooperated in dispatching large caravans north and south. The government of the city was in the hands of a syndicate of Quraysh merchants.

These same businessmen were also concerned with protecting a source of income derived from the annual pilgrimage of tribes to a famous religious sanctuary at Mecca. Known as the Kaaba (cube), this square temple contained the sacred Black Stone, by legend brought to Abraham and his son Ishmael by Gabriel. According to tradition, the stone was originally white but had been blackened by the sins of those touching it. The Kaaba supposedly housed the images of some 360 local deities and fetishes.

Muhammad, founder of Islam. Into this environment at Mecca was born a man destined to transform completely the religious, political, and social organization of his people. Muhammad (570-632) came from a family belonging to the Quraysh tribe. Left an orphan in early life, he was brought up by an uncle and later engaged in the caravan trade. Muhammad's formative years are known to us by legend only, but his first biographer relates that he was influenced by a monotheist named Zayd, who may have been either a Jewish or a Christian convert. Originally a member of the Quraysh, Zayd had been expelled from the tribe for his religious views. Zayd was approached by Muhammad, who later described the incident:

I had a bag containing meat which we had sacrificed to our idols . . . and I offered it to Zayd b.'Amur—I was but a lad at the time—and I said, 'Eat some of this food . . .' He replied, 'Surely it is part of those sacrifices of theirs which they offer to their idols?' When I said that it was, he said '. . . I never eat of these sacrifices, and I have no desire to do so.' Then he upbraided me for idolatry and spoke disparagingly of those who worship idols and sacrifice to them, and said, 'They are worthless: they can neither harm nor profit anyone,' or words to that effect. The apostle [Muhammad] added, 'After that I never knowingly stroked one of their idols. . . .'[2]

When he was about twenty years old, Muhammad entered the service of a wealthy widow, Khadija, whose caravans traded with Syria. In his twenty-fifth year he married his employer, who was some fifteen years his senior. Despite the difference in their ages, the marriage was a happy one; and they had four daughters. Through his marriage Muhammad attained economic security and an important social position in Mecca. Yet

As these manuscript illuminations demonstrate, the life of Muhammad provided material for Muslim artists just as Biblical stories did for European medieval illuminators. In the miniature at top a Christian monk, Bahira, bows before the child, Muhammad, whom the monk and the other awed sages accompanying him recognize as a prophet. Even the camels kneel before Muhammad, while an angel anoints the child's head as a sign of divine inspiration. In the center picture Muhammad, now an adult, triumphantly enters a city and is again anointed by an angel who cries: "Thou art the prophet of God." The final illumination shows Muhammad preaching to a group of faithful disciples on the occasion of his last visit to Mecca.

he continued to live simply and abstemiously.

According to tradition, Muhammad frequently went into the foothills near Mecca to meditate. One night he dreamed that the archangel Gabriel appeared with the command, "Recite!" When Muhammad asked, "What shall I recite?" he was told:

Recite in the name of thy Lord who created
Man from blood coagulated.
Recite! Thy Lord is wondrous kind
Who by the pen has taught mankind
Things they knew not (being blind).[3]

This was the first of a series of visions and revelations.

Far from regarding himself as a prophet, Muhammad was at first afraid that he had been possessed by a spirit, and he even contemplated suicide. During his periods of doubt and anguish Muhammad was comforted by Khadija, and finally he became certain that he was a divinely appointed prophet of Allah, *"The* God," a deity in the pre-Islamic pantheon who had been recognized as the father of such nontribal deities as the Sun and Fortune. He became convinced that Allah was the one and only God and that Allah had commanded him to preach of men's duty to their Creator and of the need to repent their sins, for the judgment of God was at hand. These doctrines resemble the Christian and Jewish monotheistic concepts which were becoming increasingly prevalent in the peninsula.

At first Muhammad had little success in attracting followers. His first converts were his wife, his cousin Ali, and Abu Bakr, a leading merchant of the Quraysh tribe who was highly respected for his integrity. Abu Bakr remained the constant companion of the Prophet during his persecution and exile and eventually became the first caliph of Islam. Most other early converts were slaves or oppressed persons. Opposition came from the leading citizens ("Shall we forsake our gods for a mad poet?"), who either ridiculed Muhammad's doctrine of resurrection (pre-Islamic Arabs had only vague notions concerning the afterlife) or feared that his monotheistic teaching might harm the city's lucrative pilgrimage trade to the Kaaba. Muhammad's popularity reached its lowest ebb at the time of Khadija's death in 619. He was accused of being a sorcerer and fraud, and his converts were few.

The Hijra and triumphal return to Mecca. The first encouraging development occurred when a group of pilgrims from Medina, a prosperous town supported by agriculture and handicrafts, accepted the Prophet's teachings. Subsequently, the inhabitants of Medina, exhausted from a protracted war between rival tribes, invited Muhammad to their city to act as arbitrator and peacemaker. Meanwhile, the increased persecution of the Muslims in Mecca encouraged the Prophet to migrate with his band northward to Medina.

Carried out in secrecy, this move took place in 622 and is known as the *Hijra,* which means "emigration." The Hijra was such a turning point in Muhammad's career that the year in which it occurred is counted as the first in the Muslim calendar. In Mecca, Muhammad's own kinsmen had persecuted him, but in Medina he came to be acknowledged as a leader with divine authority in spiritual and temporal matters.

Muhammad's judgment and his codes of social, religious, and political conduct were accepted by his followers, and he proved himself an able and far-seeing political leader. He worked out a charter establishing a new type of community. In it, faith superseded kinship, so that its members gave up such tribal practices as the blood feud.

The large Jewish population of Medina, however, rejected Muhammad's initial conciliatory overtures, which included the adoption of such Jewish practices as praying in the direction of Jerusalem. The Jews could appreciate Muhammad's recognition of the divine mission of Abraham, Moses, and the prophets, but they resented his inclusion of Jesus and Ishmael among God's messengers and Muhammad's own claim to be His apostle. For his part, Muhammad regarded the presence of pockets of disaffected Jews as a source of political weakness, and their prosperity had earned the envy and dislike of the Arabs. Eventually, the Jews were expelled from Hejaz.

Adopting the Jewish practice for his own purposes, the Prophet commanded the Muslims to turn toward Mecca when praying. This practice served to recognize the city as the spiritual capital of Islam and at the same time emphasized the need for its conquest from the pagan trading oligarchy that governed it.

Muhammad took advantage of Medina's situation on the trade route leading north from Mecca to apply pressure on his native city to accept Islam. This pressure led to three battles with the Meccans—Badr, Uhud, and the "Ditch"—which were fought in the second, third, and fifth years of the Hijra. Then, in 628, Muhammad negotiated a ten-year truce which permitted the Muslims to make a pilgrimage to Mecca the following year. This development increased the number of converts, and Muhammad's prestige rose within Mecca itself. Two years later, when the Quraysh broke the truce, Muhammad marched on Mecca with an army. His old enemies were forced to surrender to the Prophet, who acted with magnanimity toward them. His first act was to cast out of the Kaaba its multitude of idols and fetishes; but the temple itself, together with the Black Stone, was preserved as the supreme center of Islam, the "Mecca" to which each devout Muslim should make a pilgrimage during his lifetime.

With Mecca and Medina both under his control, Muhammad became the undisputed master of the Hejaz. Tribe after tribe of Bedouins throughout Arabia offered him their loyalty. In the two remaining years of his life he consolidated Islam's position. Upon his death in 632 the Prophet left behind a faith which had united Arabia and which was to astound the world with its militant expansion.

The Koran, the Muslim bible. Muslims believe that the Koran contains the actual word of God as revealed to Muhammad. The Prophet's revelations occurred over a period of more than twenty years, and before his death many of the messages had been written down. Abu Bakr, Muhammad's successor as head of the community, ordered the compilation of all these materials, including the passages which had only been committed to memory by his followers. Twenty years after the death of the Prophet, an authorized version was promulgated, which has remained the official text to the present day.

As a language, Arabic has unusual force and beauty of sound, and the Arabs as a people have always been especially moved by the spoken word. Thus the Koran was designed particularly to be recited and heard. Anyone who has listened to its chant can attest to the Koran's cadence, melody, and power. It would be difficult to exaggerate the important role the Koran plays in the daily life and attitudes of Islamic people.

For the pious Muslim it is the holy of holies. It must never rest beneath other books, but always on the top of them; one must never drink or smoke when it is being read aloud, and it must be listened to in silence. It is a talisman against disease and disaster. . . . Some people never leave their homes without having a small copy of the Qurān [Koran] on their person. The bereaved find their great consolation in reading it. No event of consequence in family or public life passes without the reading of an appropriate passage.[4]

Because the Koran must never be used in translation for worship, the spread of Islam created a great deal of linguistic unity, which still remains today. Arabic supplanted many local languages as the language of daily use, and that part of the Muslim world which stretches from Morocco to Iraq is still Arabic-speaking. In addition, local languages which survived elsewhere in spoken usage were written in Arabic script. No matter what part of the world they live in, nearly all literate Muslims use the Koran as a basic primer from which to learn at least enough Arabic to recite the holy creed. Furthermore, this seventh-century book remains the last word on Muslim theology, law, and social institutions and is therefore still the most important textbook in Muslim universities.

Theology of Islamic faith. Within the Koran one finds the central tenet of Islam—monotheism. There is only one God, Allah; this is proclaimed five times daily from the minaret of the mosque as the faithful are called to prayer:

God is most great. I testify that there is no God but Allah. I testify that Muhammad is God's Apostle. Come to prayer, come to security. God is most great.[5]

While Allah is the only God, many other supernatural figures are acknowledged, as in Christianity. Islamic angels, for example, are similar to those described in the Bible. In addition, there exist jinn, who are spirits midway between angels and men. Some jinn are good, while others are evil. Islam recognizes the existence of prophets who preceded Muhammad. The Koran mentions twenty-eight, of whom four are Arabian, eighteen are found in the Old Testament, three in the New Testament (including Jesus), and one of the remainder has been identified as Alexander the Great. But to Muslims the greatest prophet is, of course, Muhammad. He is ascribed no superhuman status, although he was chosen to proclaim God's message of salvation, as revealed in the Koran.

That message called for the belief in the Last Judgment and the existence of paradise and hell. The Prophet pictured the cataclysmic last day in vivid and splendid imagery:

When the sun is overthrown,
And when the stars fall,
And when the hills are moved,
And when the camels big with young are abandoned,
And when the wild beasts are herded together,
And when the seas rise,
And when souls are reunited,
And when the girl-child that was buried alive is asked
For what sin she was slain,
And when the pages [of the Book] are laid open,
And when the sky is torn away,
And when hell is lighted,
And when the garden [paradise] is brought nigh,
[Then] every soul will know what it hath made ready.[6]

Geography played an important role in the Prophet's concepts of heaven and hell, even as it did in Hebrew literature. Both heaven and hell are described in terms that incite an immediate reaction in people who live in the desert. Those who have submitted to Allah's rule—the charitable, humble, and forgiving—and those who fought for His faith, shall dwell in a Garden of Paradise, reposing in cool shades, eating delectable foods, attended by "fair ones with wide, lovely eyes like unto hidden pearls," and hearing no vain speech

or recrimination but only "Peace! Peace!" This veritable oasis is far different from the agonies of a desert hell, which awaits the unbelievers, the covetous, and the erring. Cast into hell with its "scorching wind and shadow of black smoke," they will drink of boiling water.

Islam imposes on all Muslims five obligations, known as the "Pillars of Faith"—belief in only one God, Allah, and in Muhammad as His Prophet, prayer, almsgiving, fasting, and a pilgrimage to Mecca. Prayers are said five times a day, and each occasion calls for a sequence of recitations coordinated with a sequence of postures. The Muslim is required to give alms, a practice regarded as expressing piety and contributing to one's salvation. During the month of Ramadan, the ninth month of the lunar year, Muslims fast. Since food and drink are prohibited between sunrise and sunset, this is a very strenuous observance, although sick persons and travelers are exempted provid-

ISLAM UNDER MUHAMMAD 622-632 A.D.

ing they fast for an equal length of time later. The second chapter of the Koran commands Muslims to make a pilgrimage to Mecca, where they go through traditional ceremonies, such as kissing the Black Stone in the Kaaba. Each Muslim should make the pilgrimage to Mecca at least once during his lifetime if he has the means. Every year multitudes of pilgrims converge on the holy city —from which non-Muslims are barred— some coming overland from the interiors of Africa and Asia and others journeying by ship from such faraway places as Indonesia.

The Koran also provides the Muslims with a body of ethical teachings. Idolatry, infanticide, usury, gambling, the drinking of wine, and the eating of pork are all prohibited. Similarly, Islam encouraged the humane treatment of slaves and regulated such matters as the guardianship of orphans and divorce. Muslim men were allowed four wives (and an unspecified number of concubines), but if he could not treat them all with equal kindness and impartiality, a husband should retain but one.

Pervading Islam was the principle of religious equality. There was no priesthood. There were leaders of worship in the mosques as well as the ulema, who interpreted the sacred law; but they were all laymen. Muhammed stressed the essential unity of all true believers. In this way Islam was spared the priestly tyranny which arose in India, where the Brahmins considered themselves superior to all other classes in the rigid caste system.

Muhammad taught that all men within the confines of Islam were brothers. In one of his famous sermons, he urged:

Know ye that every Moslem is a brother to every other Moslem, and that ye are now one brotherhood. It is not legitimate for any one of you, therefore, to appropriate unto himself anything that belongs to his brother unless it is willingly given him by that brother.[7]

Islamic law. In addition to being a religion, Islam offered a system of government, law, and society. The Islamic community was an excellent example of a theocratic state, one in which all power resides in God in whose behalf political, religious, and other forms of authority are exercised.

Especially in the period of expansion after the Prophet's death, the Islamic state required detailed rules covering a variety of new situations. The code that was developed was based partly on pre-Islamic legal customs. Before Muhammad's time each tribe had its own Sunna, or body of custom, which served as a law code. By compiling the recollections of the Prophet's companions, his followers prepared a Sunna based on his life and teachings.

Using the Koran and the Sunna as their sources, Islamic jurists developed a body of religious law which regulated all aspects of Muslim life. Its development and interpretation were in the hands of the ulema. Agreement among these scholars set the seal of orthodoxy on questions of text and doctrine, with the result that Islamic law became progressively authoritarian and static.

THE SPREAD OF ISLAM

Expansion under the first four caliphs. Upon the Prophet's death in 632 the question arose as to who should direct the fortunes of Islam. This was a dangerous moment. Muhammad left no son to succeed him; and, even if he had, neither his unique position as the Prophet nor Arab custom permitted any such automatic succession. Acting swiftly, Muhammad's associates selected the Prophet's most trusted friend and advisor, Abu Bakr, as his official successor, the caliph. The title of caliph (from *khalifa,* meaning "deputy") carried with it the controlling power in political affairs. When the Muslim community later broke apart politically, more than one ruler claimed the title of caliph.

Since a number of tribes considered their religious and political allegiance to have ended with the Prophet's death, the new leader's first task was to prevent the disintegration of the Islamic community. Abu Bakr succeeded in reuniting Arabia under Muslim control before his death in 634, only two years after Muhammad had died. The fate of his immediate successors made clear the perils of the position of caliph—all three were murdered.

After Abu Bakr, the caliphate went to another of the Prophet's earliest companions, Umar, who ruled until his murder in 644. The next caliph, Uthman, fell under the control of his clan of rich Meccan merchants, who usurped for themselves the highest imperial posts. In 656 Uthman, too, was murdered and was replaced by Ali, a cousin of the Prophet who was married to Fatima, one of Muhammad's daughters. His accession was disputed by the governor of Syria, Muawiya, a member of Uthman's family. Ali was slowly losing a civil war when he was assassinated in 661. This event marked the end of a period known as that of the Rightly Guided Caliphs (632-661).

During the reigns of the first four caliphs Islam spread rapidly, partly as a result of the attitudes and aptitudes of the Muslim Arabs themselves. Their wars of conquest were aided by the Prophet's belief that any Muslim dying in battle for the faith was assured entrance into paradise. This sanctification of warfare bred in the Arabs, already a fierce fighting people, fanatical courage. The proud and tenacious Bedouins, who have been described as a "bundle of nerves, bones, and sinews," were particularly magnificent warriors. Their natural fighting ability was augmented by military techniques learned from the Byzantines and Persians and by their adroit use of the desert, from which they could strike the enemy and to which they could retreat. The Arabs were spurred on by economic as well as religious desires. The prospect of rich and fertile territory, as well as plunder, proved a strong incentive to a people who had been eking out a bare existence from the desert.

The Islamic cause was also aided by political upheavals occurring outside of Arabia. The Muslim triumphs in the Near East can be partly accounted for by the long series of wars between the Byzantine and Sassanid empires. The Byzantine victory in 628 had left both sides exhausted and open to conquest by a third party. The Arab soldiers who had fought in the wars as mercenaries were eager to revenge the shabby treatment they had received at the hands of both the Byzantines and the Persians. Moreover, the inhabitants of Syria and Egypt, alienated by religious dissent, were anxious to be free of Byzantine rule. Similarly, Iraq, with its largely Semitic population, welcomed the end of Persian control.

Abu Bakr's military action against the recalcitrant Arab tribes eventually developed into campaigns of conquest, and Syria was the first to fall. An expedition into that land captured the historic city of Damascus; one year later, in 636, Arab forces conquered Syria for good. The Muslims then wrested Iraq from the Sassanids and, within ten years after Muhammad's death, subdued Persia itself and destroyed the once mighty Sassanid empire. The greater part of Egypt, where Byzantine rule had proved harsh and corrupt, fell with little resistance in 640 and the rest shortly afterward. Thus, by the end of the reigns of the first four caliphs, Islam had vastly increased its territory (see map, p. 258).

While the conquerors did not drastically alter any existing social patterns, Islamic influence made itself felt. The Muslim garrison towns became centers for the spread of the Arabic language and the religion of Islam. The imposition of a head tax on all non-Muslims encouraged many to become converts to Islam. Contrary to exaggerated accounts in the West of the forceful infliction of Islam upon conquered peoples, the Jews and Christians outside of Arabia enjoyed Muslim protection. This was because they belonged to the "tolerated" religions—that is, religions based on a revealed book.

Islam is one of the most effective religions in removing barriers of race and nationality. Apart from a certain privileged position allowed the Arabs, distinctions were mostly those of class. The new religion converted and embraced peoples of many colors and cultures. This egalitarian feature of Islam undoubtedly aided its expansion.

Arab domination under the Umayyads. The reigns of the first four caliphs were followed by the Umayyad dynasty (661-750). Muawiya, the first caliph of this line,

**THE EXPANSION OF ISLAM
TO 750 A.D.**

Under Muhammad 622-632

Under The First Four Caliphs
632-661

Under the Umayyad Caliphs
661-750

0   200   400   600

established his capital at Damascus in Syria. Henceforth, the caliphate was to be in fact, although never in law, a hereditary office, not, as previously, a position filled by election.

Islam expanded with continued rapidity under the Umayyads. While still governor of Syria, Muawiya had constructed an Arab fleet which won a naval victory over the Byzantines, thereby gaining some islands in the eastern Mediterranean. As caliph, he organized a disciplined standing army, which the Muslims had lacked before. He carried on the war against the Byzantine empire, strengthening his forces by adding the former frontier guards of the Byzantines. The Umayyad armies pushed through Asia Minor and attacked Constantinople in 674, but that city withstood all Muslim sieges until 1453 (see Chapter 8).

The Muslims had even greater success in the west, where they subdued the North African coastal belt into eastern Morocco. At first the Berbers, a warlike Hamitic-speaking people inhabiting the land between the Mediterranean and the Sahara from Egypt to the Atlantic, resisted stubbornly. Eventually the Muslims won out, and the indigenous population was converted to Islam. The next logical jump was across the Strait of Gibraltar into the kingdom of the Visigoths in Spain. The governor of Muslim North Africa sent his general, Tarik, and an army across the Strait into Spain in 711. Seven years later the kingdom of the Visigoths had completely crumbled. The Muslims swept across the Pyrenees and gained a foothold in southwest France, where they carried out a major raid to explore the possibility of a further northward advance. However, they were defeated by Charles Martel near Tours in 732 (see p. 319), in a battle which proved decisive in halting their expansion, exactly one century after Muhammad's death.

Meanwhile the Muslims had been expanding eastward into central Asia, raiding and seizing lands held by the Turks, Afghans, Chinese, and Indians. By the eighth century Muslim warriors could claim for the caliph lands as far as Turkestan and the Indus valley.

During the caliphate of Walid (705-715) Umayyad power reached its peak. The caliphate controlled an empire extending from the Pyrenees and the Atlantic across North Africa and western Asia to the Indian province of Sind. The mainstay of Umayyad power was the privileged ruling class of the Arabs. The Arabs paid no taxes on the lands which they acquired by conquest, and Arab warriors received preferential treatment in the form of pay and booty. Though a minority within the empire, the Arabs provided its leaders and government officials and, in short, controlled millions of conquered people.

This state of affairs could not endure. Within the Muslim population itself, the Arabs were outnumbered by non-Arabic converts to Islam—Egyptians, Syrians, Persians, Berbers, and many others. Many of these possessed cultures much more advanced than that of the Arabs, and the economic and cultural life of the Arab empire depended on these people. But because they were not Arab by birth, they were treated as second-class Muslims. Though they fought in Muslim armies, they received less pay and booty than the Arabs and at the same time were subjected to high taxation. Resentment grew among the non-Arabic Muslims and eventually helped bring about the downfall of the Arab kingdom of the Umayyads.

Shia movement against the ruling group. This resentment also found expression in the religious sphere, where large numbers of the non-Arabic Muslims joined the sect known as the Shia. We will recall that Ali, the prophet's son-in-law and fourth caliph, had been assassinated. However, numerous Muslims continued to regard Ali and his descendants as the rightful rulers of the Islamic community. Later the Shia adopted a divine-right doctrine, which held that in every age an infallible leader of the Prophet's family must be obeyed as the only rightful caliph, whose every decision (including his interpretation of the Koran) had to be accepted. Though originally an Arab party, the

Shia in time became a general Islamic movement that stood for opposition to the ruling dynasty, and as such it attracted the non-Arabic Muslims and other disaffected groups. The Shia evolved into one of the two major groups in Islam. The majority, named Sunnites because they were the "orthodox" perpetuators of Muhammad's Sunna, or tradition, upheld the principle that the caliph owed his position to the consent of the Islamic community. The numerical superiority of the Sunnites has continued to this day.

The Abbasids, high tide of Islamic civilization. In 750 the Umayyad dynasty was crushed by rebels, and a new dynasty, the Abbasid, ruled most of the Muslim world from 750 to 1258. The city of Baghdad was built in 762 as the capital of the new dynasty. The Abbasids owed their success to the discord among the Arab tribes and also to the discontent of the non-Arabic Muslims, who were the chief elements in the towns and in the Shia.

The fall of the Umayyad dynasty marked the end of Arab predominance; henceforth, Persians and other non-Arabs were to create a new political order. The Arab aristocracy had led the forces of conquest during the great period of Islamic expansion, but with the advent of more stable political conditions, the important status thus far held by the Arab soldier was given to non-Arab soldiers and administrators. In the social and economic spheres, too, the change of dynasties reflected and also encouraged new forces. The traditional Arabic patterns of nomadism and tribal war were giving way before economic prosperity, the growth of town life, and the rise of a merchant class. The Abbasid caliph who built Baghdad forecast that it would become the "most flourishing city in the world"; and indeed it rivaled Constantinople for that honor, situated as it was on the trade routes linking West and East. At the same time, the Abbasids gave their patronage to the arts and scholarship.

The location of a new capital at Baghdad resulted in a shift of Islam's center of gravity to the province of Iraq, whose soil, watered by the Tigris and Euphrates, had nurtured man's earliest civilizations. The new capital, Baghdad, was built on the west bank of the

Tigris, not far from the ruins of the old Sassanid capital, Ctesiphon, which provided stones for the new city. In their new site the Abbasid caliphs set themselves up as potentates in the traditional style of the ancient East—and more particularly of Iran—so that they were surrounded by a lavish court that contrasted sharply with the simplicity of the Prophet. Baghdad was sufficiently removed from Mediterranean contacts to evolve a culture in which Persian influence predominated.

Abbasid government. From their headquarters at Baghdad the Abbasid caliphs ruled with the same absolute authority that had marked Persian monarchy since the days of Darius and Xerxes. In theory the caliph governed in accordance with Islamic law, but actually he based his position on military might. Whereas the Arab aristocracy had an important part in administering the Umayyad caliphate, the Abbasid administration was completely in the hands of a salaried bureaucracy analogous to that of the Byzantine government. The most powerful person next to the caliph was the vizier, who carried out the highest functions of government on behalf of his superior and, in fact, was often the power behind the throne when the caliph was weak-willed. The vizier appointed and removed governors of provinces and supervised the heads of the different bureaus (dîwân), of which the most important was the treasury. The "ministries" also included the war office, post office, bureau of expenditure, and the caliph's cabinet, which was concerned with petitions to the ruler.

The treasury derived its income from various sources: tribute from conquered lands; battle loot; agricultural tithes; taxes levied on non-Muslims; local and municipal sales taxes and tolls; and "sums extorted from fallen officials and confiscations of one sort or another."[8] The caliph used the revenue from these taxes for governmental administration as well as other purposes such as the payment of troops, upkeep of mosques, and construction and repair of roads and bridges.

The Abbasid dynasty marked the high tide of Islamic power and civilization. In the early years of the caliphate the empire was greater in size than the domain of the Roman Caesars; it was the product of an expansion during which the Muslims had assimilated peoples, customs, cultures, and inventions on an unprecedented scale. This Islamic state, in fact, drew on the resources of the entire known world.

Trade, industry, and agriculture. From the eighth to the twelfth centuries the Muslim world enjoyed a prosperity such as post-Roman Europe did not experience until early modern times. One reason for this success was the empire's geographical position. The trade among the numerous countries within the Muslim world itself accounted for most of the commerce, but in addition the Muslims traded beyond their borders and acted as middlemen for trade between lands around them. Being in close contact with three continents, the Muslims could shuttle goods back and forth from China to western Europe and from Russia to central Africa. Another reason for Islam's economic well-being lay in the tolerance of its rulers, who allowed non-Muslim merchants and craftsmen to reside in their territories and carry on commerce with their home countries. The presence of such important urban centers as Baghdad, Cairo, and Cordova stimulated trade and industry throughout the Muslim world.

The cosmopolitan nature of Baghdad was evident in its bazaars, which contained goods from all over the known world. There were spices, minerals, and dyes from India; gems and fabrics from central Asia; honey and wax from Scandinavia and Russia; and ivory and gold dust from Africa. One bazaar in the city specialized in goods from China, including silks, musk, and porcelain. The slave marts in turn attested to the far-flung activities of the Muslim traders, who bought and sold white-skinned Scandinavians, Mongolians from central Asia, and African Negroes.

The extent of the commerce between the Muslim world and other widely separated lands can be seen by the large number of Islamic coins which have been unearthed in such northern European countries as Sweden, Finland, Russia, and Norway. Proof also comes from a ninth-century Muslim geographer, who tells of Jewish merchants from southern France

who speak Arabic, Persian, Greek, Frankish, Spanish and Slavonic. They travel from west to east and from east to west, by land and by sea. From the west they bring eunuchs, slave-girls, boys, brocade, castor-skins [beaver-skins], marten and other furs, and swords. They take ship from Frank-land in the western Mediterranean sea and land at Farama [on the Mediterranean coast of Egypt], whence they take their merchandise on camel-back to Qulzum [on the Red Sea]. . . . Then they sail on the eastern (Red) sea from Qulzum to Al-Jar [on the Red Sea] and Jedda [Jiddah, see map on p. 255], and onward to Sind, India and China. From China they bring back musk, aloes, camphor, cinnamon, and other products of those parts and return to Qulzum. Then they transport them to Farama and sail again on the western sea. Some sail with their goods to Constantinople, and sell them to the Greeks, and some take them to the king of Franks and sell them there.[9]

Muslim textile industries turned out excellent muslins, silks, cottons, and linens. Metal, leather, enamel, pottery, and luxury goods similar to Byzantine products were also manufactured in abundance. As in the Byzantine empire, the workers in the large Islamic cities were organized into guilds and crafts. Despite governmental regulations, the guilds enjoyed a large measure of freedom.

The fact that the Muslims were skilled not only in trade and industry but also in agriculture provided them with a well-balanced economy—though it suffered from the exploitation of the countryside by the city. Under the Abbasids agriculture was both extensive and profitable. Vast irrigation projects in Iraq resulted in an increase of cultivable land which yielded large crops of fruits and cereals. Wheat came from the Nile valley, cotton from North Africa, olives and wine from Spain, wool from eastern Asia Minor, and horses from Persia. As in medieval Europe, the land was worked by serfs and by free peasants, whose lot was for the most part miserable. In some regions large estates employed slave labor.

The opulent reign of Harun al-Rashid. Just as the Abbasid was the most brilliant of Muslim dynasties, so the rule of Harun al-Rashid (786-809) was the most spectacular of the Abbasid reigns. He was the contemporary of Charlemagne, and there can be no doubt that Harun was the more powerful ruler of the two and the symbol of the more highly advanced culture. (As we will see in Chapter 11, Charlemagne was the first ruler in western Europe to establish an extensive empire after Rome's fall.) The two monarchs were on friendly terms, based on self-interest. Charlemagne wanted Harun as a possible ally against the Byzantine emperors. Harun, on the other hand, saw Charlemagne as an ally against the Umayyad rulers of Spain, who had broken away from Abbasid domination (see p. 264). The two rulers exchanged embassies and presents. The Muslim sent the Christian rich fabrics, aromatics, and even an elephant. An intricate clock from Baghdad seems to have been looked upon as a miracle in the West.

Relations between the Abbasid caliphate and the Byzantine empire were never very cordial, and conflicts often broke out along the constantly shifting border that separated Christian and Muslim territories. While still the heir to the throne, Harun in 782 commanded an expedition that reached the Bosporus and forced the Byzantines to conclude a peace involving the payment of a huge tribute. Later the Byzantine emperor repudiated the terms of the treaty and even sent a letter asking for the return of the tribute money already paid. Harun al-Rashid sent back the emperor's letter with the following penned on the back:

In the name of God, the Merciful, the Compassionate. From Haroun, Commander of the Faithful, to Nicephorus, the dog of the Greeks. I have read your letter, you son of a she-infidel, and you shall see the answer before you hear it.[10]

Whereupon the irate caliph sent forth expeditions to ravage Asia Minor. He captured several Byzantine cities and imposed a humiliating tax on the emperor himself and on each member of the royal household.

In the days of Harun al-Rashid, Baghdad's wealth and splendor equaled that of Constantinople, and its chief glory was the royal palace. With its annexes for eunuchs, officials, and a harem, the caliph's residence occupied a third of Baghdad. Resplendently furnished, the caliph's audience chamber was the setting for an elaborate ceremonial which continued that of the Byzantines and Sassanids down to minor details.

Some ceremonial occasions dramatized the extent of the caliph's riches. At the marriage of the daughter of one of Harun's viziers, the caliph had a thousand pearls of extraordinary size rained upon the couple, who stood upon a golden mat studded with sapphires and pearls. Balls of musk, each containing a ticket claiming an estate or splendid slave, were showered on the royal princes and guests. At one reception (held in the early tenth century) some Byzantine envoys mistook first the chief chamberlain's office and then the vizier's office for the royal audience hall. In the Hall of the Tree they saw an artificial tree of gold and silver, which had on its branches birds of the same metals that chirped by means of automatic devices. These marvels were only a few of many, and it is little wonder that the magnificence and lavishness of the Abbasid court created a legend of oriental romance and splendor which has persisted to our own times, particularly through the tales of the *Arabian Nights.*

The social order. Four major divisions made up the Muslim social order. These separated the Muslims from the nonbelievers; distinguished the various religious communities within Islam itself; differentiated the various Islamic nationalities; and delimited medieval society according to a hierarchy of professions and activities. The most rigid barrier was that separating Muslims from non-Muslims, since the faith taught that the world belonged to the believer by divine right. According to Muslim law, pagans and idolators could choose only between conversion and death. On the other hand, Jews, Christians, and Zoroastrians were entitled to legal recognition as organized minorities, since they possessed part of the divine revelations.[11]

As for class distinctions within Abbasid society, the highest level consisted of the caliph and his family, government officials, and prominent members of the army. The upper portion of the common people included scholars, artists, professional men, and merchants. Islam, which had developed in an urban environment, favored the city at the expense of the rural inhabitants, who for the most part possessed a lower social status, while the nomad was viewed with distrust as lacking in restraint and discipline and posing a threat to the settled and progressive life of the towns.

Slaves were brought from Africa and other countries by slave traders; many slaves were non-Muslim—Greeks, Slavs, and Armenians, for example—who had been captured in war. But though slavery was prevalent, it is

important to bear in mind that the slave was generally the body-servant or retainer of his master, and that slavery was in no sense the economic basis of Muslim society. Master and slave thus stood in a more humane relationship than did the slave cultivator to the Roman landed proprietor or the American planter. There was consequently less stigma attaching to slavery, and in no other society has there been anything resembling the system by which . . . the white slaves came to furnish the privileged cadres whence the high officers of state, commanders, governors, and at length even sultans, were almost exclusively drawn.[12]

Some of the slaves were eunuchs attached to the harems, while slave girls were often employed as dancers, singers, and concubines.

Islamic society in general has been much criticized in western literature for the low social and moral status assigned to women. It is true that the Prophet's permission of polygyny did not make for equality between the sexes. A woman's only life was to obey her father until she married, at which time she became obligated to obey her husband, care for his children, and manage his household. In judging Muslim standards, however, we must remember the task which Muhammad faced in dealing with illiterate, fetish-worshiping nomads, who used to abandon unwanted female infants. While Islam places women in an inferior position and forbids them to lead prayer when men are present, it secures their property rights and assigns them a definite religious role. During Mu-

The Islamic world enjoyed a rich and varied civilization. The few wealthy members of society lived in great luxury, spending leisurely hours conversing in well-tended gardens, waited on by servants and entertained by dancers and musicians (top left). Muslim scholars devoted themselves to the study of science and medicine. In an observatory in Constantinople (top right) some astronomers make mathematical computations with the assistance of a variety of instruments, while others gather around a globe showing Asia, Africa, and Europe. An Arabian doctor (bottom left) lectures on plants useful as antidotes to snake poison, and in the miniature (bottom right) a turbaned judge, seated on cushions, metes out punishments to criminals.

hammad's time women as well as men attended congregational prayers, although custom has since called for women praying at home.

Disintegration of the Abbasid empire. Despite the unprecedented prosperity of the far-flung Islamic world, the political unity of Islam began to disappear almost immediately after the Arab empire reached its full extent. With the accession of the Abbasid dynasty, the caliphs in the Near East, at the center of Islam, began to lose their hold on the Muslims in the west. The first sign of political disintegration appeared as early as 756 when a member of the deposed Umayyad family founded his own dynasty at Cordova in Spain; Muslim Spain became independent of the caliphs at Baghdad, and in 929 its ruler assumed the title of caliph. In 788 a great-great-grandson of the fourth caliph, Ali, founded a new dynasty in Morocco, and twelve years later the Abbasid governor of Tunisia in turn declared himself independent.

In 909, at a time when the Shia sentiment was growing strong in North Africa, the Abbasid dynasty was displaced by the Fatimids, who claimed descent from Ali and Fatima. Later in the same century the Fatimids conquered Egypt and transferred their capital to Cairo, which soon rivaled if not surpassed Baghdad as a center of Muslim culture. The Fatimid dynasty reached its zenith early in the eleventh century, when its domains comprised Morocco and the rest of North Africa, Egypt, Sicily, Syria, and western Arabia. In a short time, however, the Fatimids lost their control over the more distant portions of this large empire, and their strength in Egypt declined. In 1171 Saladin (see Chapter 12) did away with the Fatimid dynasty and restored the Sunnite rule at Cairo. This action was part of his program to unify the Near East against the crusaders.

An interesting description of the luxurious life of the Fatimid caliph Mustansir (1036-1094) has been left us by a Persian writer. The caliph's palace appears to have housed 30,000 people, including 1000 guards and 12,000 servants. Inheritor of vast riches and countless works of art, the elegant Mus-

tansir is supposed to have had erected in his palace a pavilion shaped like the Kaaba in Mecca. There he would drink wine to the accompaniment of song and maintain that: "This is pleasanter than staring at a black stone, listening to the drone of the mu•edhdhin [the crier who sounds the call to prayer], and drinking bad water."[13]

While the Abbasid empire was being reduced by the Fatimid state to the west, independent Muslim states appeared in Persia and central Asia to the east of Baghdad. The Abbasid caliphs not only were unable to stem the disintegration of their empire but became victims of rival political factions themselves. Imperial extravagance and a political system based upon tyranny and nepotism—and susceptible to intrigue, bribery, and rebellion—had paved the way for the progressive fragmentation of the Abbasid empire and eventually for disaster at the capital itself.

Seljuk and Mongol invaders. In the latter part of the tenth century Turkish nomads, called Seljuks, had migrated from central Asia into the Abbasid lands, where they accepted Islam. The Seljuks then began to seize land from the Abbasids and, after annexing most of Persia, gained control of Baghdad in 1055 and absorbed Iraq. Subsequently, the Seljuks conquered Syria and Palestine at the expense of the Fatimids and proceeded to annex most of Asia Minor from the Byzantines (see map, p. 231). It was the Seljuks' great advance that prompted the First Crusade in 1095. The Seljuks permitted the Abbasids to retain nominal rule, but a new and terrible enemy was now to appear and change everything.

Early in the thirteenth century Genghis Khan succeeded in uniting the nomads of Mongolia; he and his successors conquered eastern and central Asia (see Chapters 10 and 14) and swept into Persia and Iraq. In 1258 a grandson of Genghis Khan captured Baghdad and slew the caliph. "The city itself was given over to plunder and flames: the majority of its population, including the family of the caliph, were wiped out of existence. . . . For the first time in its history the Muslim world was left without a caliph whose name could be cited in the Friday prayers."[14] The conquerors also destroyed the embankments and headworks of the rivers and irrigation system, thereby converting large areas of Iraq into steppe or swamp. The inhabitants, decimated by massacre and then by malaria and famine, proved too weak to rebuild the canal system or to prevent nomads from terrorizing the countryside and its remnant areas of cultivation. Following an unremitting struggle between a few towns and pastoral tribes, Iraq fell into a state of collapse from which it was not to recover until modern times. The dynasty established by the Mongols survived for only a short time, and the Mongol ruling class was eventually absorbed into the Muslim culture of Persia and Iraq.

Meanwhile, in 1260, an army of foreign-born slaves in Egypt called Mamluks saved Muslim Egypt from the Mongol advance. The Mamluks revived the caliphate as a nominal office with its center at Cairo and made and deposed caliphs, chosen from among their own number, with brutal frequency. In spite of Mamluk control, however, Cairo retained its position as a center of Islamic culture. Mamluk power, corroded by civil wars and its refusal to modernize the army, fell before the onslaught of another offshoot of the once great Seljuk empire, the Ottomans.

The Ottoman Turks. Having settled in northwestern Asia Minor early in the thirteenth century as vassals of the Seljuks, the Ottoman Turks had organized their own aggressive state of Muslim frontier fighters by the end of the century. The Ottomans pitted their strength against the crumbling power of the Byzantines and about 1350 secured a foothold in Europe on the Gallipoli peninsula. As we saw in the preceding chapter, the Ottomans captured Constantinople in 1453 and then pressed on into southeastern Europe, driving as far as Vienna, where they were turned back with difficulty in 1529 and again in 1683. Meanwhile, in 1517, the Ottomans had conquered the Mamluk territories, and within a few years they had added to their possessions Syria, Iraq, much of Arabia, and all of the North African coastal belt to the borders of Morocco.

Far from being the "Sick Man of Europe," as it came to be called in the nineteenth century, the Ottoman empire from the fifteenth through the seventeenth centuries was outstandingly powerful and efficient. A perceptive British traveler wrote in 1634 that the Turks were "the only modern people great in action," and that "he who would behold these times in their greatest glory, could not find a better scene than in Turkey."[15]

We have reviewed the expansion of Islam into western Asia and areas around the Mediterranean. Here, as well as in other lands where Islam had spread by 1500, its influence was greater than the comparable later impact of the West. In Chapter 10 we shall trace its expansion as a missionary faith into South and Southeast Asia, and Chapter 19 will describe the medieval Afro-Muslim kingdoms of equatorial Africa. Although political solidarity was not maintained in the Islamic world, a form of unity was perpetuated by a common religion and culture. As a result, that world emerged in modern times as an almost solid ribbon of peoples stretching from Morocco in the west through Indonesia in the east. Today about one seventh of the world's population is composed of Muslim peoples, whose religious solidarity and cultural heritage provide the basis for a program of political resurgence.

ISLAMIC CULTURE

Borrowing the best from other cultures. The high attainment of the Muslims in the intellectual and artistic fields can be primarily attributed not to the Arabs, who as a group remained concerned with religion, politics, and commerce, but rather to those peoples who had embraced Islam in Persia, Mesopotamia, Syria, Egypt, North Africa, and Spain. Muslim learning benefited primarily from Islam's ability to synthesize the best in other cultures rather than from native genius. The cosmopolitan spirit which permeated the Abbasid dynasty supplied the tolerance necessary for a diversity of ideas, so that the philosophy and science of ancient Greece and India found a welcome in Baghdad. Under Harun al-Rashid and his successors the Greek nonliterary classics were translated into Arabic, thus making the writings of Aristotle, Euclid, Ptolemy, and Archimedes available to Muslim scholars. The period from 762 to 900 was an era of translation not only of Greek treatises but also of Indian medical, mathematical, and astronomical works together with materials from Sassanid Persia. Thus, from Greece, conquered Persia, and India came the basis of Muslim learning, which in turn was later transmitted to scholars in western Europe (see p. 395). The Muslims, however, were not only invaluable transmitters of learning but also made original contributions of their own to science.

Advances in medicine. The two hundred years between 900 and 1100 can be called the golden age of Muslim learning. This period was particularly significant for advances made in medicine; in this field one of the most outstanding translators was Hunain ibn-Ishaq (d. 877), a Christian. He and his associates translated works on medicine by Galen and Hippocrates and collected manuscripts to create a magnificent library in Baghdad.

Perhaps the greatest Muslim physician was al-Razi (c. 860-925), better known to the West as Rhazes. Among the greatest doctors of all time, Rhazes wrote more than two hundred works, of which one of the most famous is *On Smallpox and Measles,* the first clear description of the symptoms and treatment of these diseases. In his *Comprehensive Book,* a huge medical encyclopedia, Rhazes cites for each disease all Greek, Syrian, Arabian, Persian, and Indian authorities and includes his own experiences and opinions as well. Translations of the encyclopedia were later used by many European physicians, and by 1542 five separate editions had been printed in Europe. A man of varied talents, Rhazes also wrote copiously on theology, mathematics, astronomy, physics, meteorology, optics, and alchemy.

The most familiar name in Muslim medicine is that of Avicenna (980-1037), a great physicist, philosopher, and physician. In his vast *Canon of Medicine* he organized the legacy of Greek knowledge together with Arabic medical learning. In the twelfth century the *Canon* was translated into Latin and was so much in demand that it was issued sixteen times in the last half of the fifteenth century and more than twenty times in the sixteenth. It is still read and used in the Orient today.

Medical theory was augmented by practical application. Hospitals operating throughout the empire were divided into sections for men and women. The qualifications of physicians and druggists were subject to inspection.

In spite of a ban against the study of anatomy and a few other limitations imposed on Muslims by their religious scruples, their medical men were in many ways superior to their European contemporaries. Whereas the Muslims were skilled practitioners whose technique was at least sane, medieval Christian doctors were plagued with superstition. For proof we have an account by a Muslim physician in Syria at the time of the crusades:

They brought before me a knight in whose leg an abscess had grown. . . . To the knight I applied a small poultice until the abscess opened and became well. . . . Then a Frankish physician came to [the knight] and said, 'This man knows nothing. . . .' He then said to the knight, 'Which wouldst thou prefer, living with one leg or dying with two?' The latter replied, 'Living with one leg.' The physician said, 'Bring me a strong knight and a sharp ax.' A knight came with the ax. And I was standing by. Then the physician laid the leg of the patient on a block of wood and bade the knight strike his leg with the ax and chop it off at one blow. Accordingly he struck it—while I was looking on—one blow, but the leg was not severed. He dealt another blow, upon which the marrow of the leg flowed out and the patient died on the spot. . . . I returned home, having learned of their medicine what I knew not before.[16]

Progress in other sciences. Although other branches of science did not keep pace with medicine, they did make progress. Physics continued along the paths of inquiry laid down by Hellenistic thinkers, but Muslim scientists arose who were no mere copyists. Alhazen (965-1039?) developed optics to a remarkable degree and challenged the view of Ptolemy and Euclid that the eye sends visual rays to its object. The chief source of all medieval western writers on optics, he interested himself in optic reflections and illusions and examined the refraction of light rays through air and water.

The progress of both astronomy and chemistry was impeded because of confusion with pseudosciences. Even though Muslim astronomers accepted the views of Ptolemy, developed good instruments, and built observatories, they fell into the error of mixing astronomy with astrology. Chemistry started out as alchemy, the attempt to transmute base metals into precious ones and to find the magic elixir for the preservation of human life. Despite the dubious origins of the science, the experiments and investigations of Muslim chemists produced many new drugs and chemicals.

Significant advances were made in mathematics. In this field the Muslims were particularly indebted to the Greeks and Hindus, from whom they learned most of their arithmetic, geometry, and algebra. From the Greeks came the geometry of Euclid and the fundamentals of trigonometry which Ptolemy had worked out. From the Hindus came the nine signs now known as the Arabic numerals. It may be that the Muslims invented the all-important zero, although some scholars would assign this honor to the Indians (see p. 280). Two names deserve mention in connection with algebra: al-Khwarizmi (d. about 840) wrote treatises on astronomy, the Hindu method of calculation, algebra, and arithmetic, while the poet Omar Khayyám (d. 1123?) advanced even beyond al-Khwarizmi in equations. Where al-Khwarizmi dealt only with quadratics, Omar Khayyám devoted much of his treatise on algebra to cubic equations.

In an empire that straddled continents, where trade and administration made an accurate knowledge of lands imperative, the science of geography flourished. Certainly the geographical knowledge of the Muslims within their range of operations was far superior to that of any people in Christendom during the Middle Ages. From the ninth to the fourteenth century a voluminous geographical literature was written in Arabic. In the ninth century Greek treatises on geography were translated. In the next century maps of the world as known by the Muslims were made, the first of them showing Mecca in the center, just as early medieval Christian cartographers were inclined to allot this position of honor to Jerusalem. The tenth and eleventh centuries witnessed studies relating to climate and descriptive geography. In the eleventh century the mathematical aspect of geography was stressed when one scientist began to make tables of latitudes and longitudes. Another scientist, al-Idrisi (1099-1154), was a geographer at the court of the Christian ruler Roger II of Sicily. From information received from emissaries dispatched to various countries, this geographer compiled a detailed treatise in which he divided the "inhabited earth" into seven "climates" (extending north from the equator to the point where the earth was supposedly too cold for habitation), with each climate in turn being divided by perpendicular lines into eleven equal parts, extending from the western coast of Africa to the eastern coast of Asia. This world map has been described as perhaps the best product of Islamic cartography in the Middle Ages.

The surface of the earth was made more familiar by the reports of traders and travelers. Outstanding among Islamic travelers was ibn-Battuta, who between 1325 and 1354 visited Constantinople, Ceylon, Indonesia, and China, as well as the lands of every Muslim ruler in the vast Islamic regions in Asia and Africa. His account of his travels, in which he covered many thousands of miles, makes vivid and fascinating reading.

Islamic literature and scholarship. The importance of poetry to the early Bedouins carried over into Islamic times. To westerners, whose literary tastes have been largely formed by classical traditions, Arab literature may seem strange and alien. Where we are accustomed to restraint and simplicity, "the Muslim writer excels . . . in clothing the essential realism of his thought with the language of romance."[17] Consequently, Arabic poetry abounds in elegant expression, subtle combinations of words, fanciful and even extravagant imagery, and witty conceits.

Westerners' knowledge of Islamic literature tends to be limited to the *Arabian Nights* and to the hedonistic poetry of Omar Khayyám. The former is a collection of tales of mixed origin and datable to the eighth through the fourteenth centuries, often erotic and told with a wealth of local color; although it professedly covers different facets of life at the Abbasid capital, it is in fact often based on life in medieval Cairo. The fame of Omar Khayyám's *Rubáiyát* is partly due to the musical (though not overaccurate) translation of Edward Fitzgerald. The following stanzas indicate the poem's beautiful imagery and gentle pessimism:

We are no other than a moving row
Of Magic Shadow-shapes that come and go
  Round with the Sun-illumined Lantern held
In Midnight by the Master of the Show;

But helpless Pieces of the Game He plays
Upon this Checker-board of Nights and Days;
  Hither and thither moves, and checks, and slays,
And one by one back in the Closet lays. . . .

The Moving Finger writes; and, having writ,
Moves on: nor all your Piety nor Wit
  Shall lure it back to cancel half a Line,
Nor all your Tears wash out a Word of it.

And that inverted Bowl they call the Sky,
Whereunder crawling coop'd we live and die,
  Lift not your hands to *It* for help—for It
As impotently moves as you or I.[18]

The same rich use of imagery is found in much Islamic prose, the most highly regarded of which is more philosophical and scholarly than fictional. As the first important prose work in Arab literature, the Koran set the stylistic pattern for Arabic writers even down to modern times. Although Muhammad was not a poet in the technical sense, he was highly poetic in his utterance, and the early chapters of the Koran were modeled

This map, which al-Idrisi made for Roger II of Sicily (note the size of Sicily in comparison to the rest of Europe), represents a direct contact between medieval Arab and European cartography. Al-Idrisi placed Arabia near the top of the world; thus for clarity the map should be viewed upside down. Based on classical Ptolemaic models, the map uses a grid system of horizontal and vertical lines to divide the world into seventy geographical areas, thus producing a forerunner of the modern rendering of longitude and latitude.

upon the rhythmical prose of the pagan soothsayers. Commentaries on the Koran soon took their place in Islamic prose along with grammars and dictionaries to help explain the scriptures. The Sunna and the religious law gave rise to juridical works, while Greek philosophy and Syriac Christianity stimulated the writing of theological treatises.

Philosophy, a favorite Muslim subject, developed as a result of contacts with other cultures. Thus Muslim philosophy is essentially Greek in origin and structure, though it also contains some Indian elements. Avicenna, the physician with many talents, wrote commentaries on Aristotle as well as on Muslim philosophers. These studies were translated into Latin and had a far-reaching effect on European thought. Like the medieval Christian philosophers (see Chapter 13), Muslim thinkers were largely concerned with reconciling Aristotelian rationalism and religion. For example, Averroës (c. 1126-1198) attempted to harmonize faith and reason for Islam, while Moses Maimonides (1135-1204), his Jewish contemporary who, like Averroës, was born in Muslim Spain but avoided persecution by moving to Egypt, sought in his still influential *Guide for the Perplexed* to do the same for Judaism. When St. Thomas Aquinas in the next century undertook a similar project for Christianity, he was greatly influenced by the profound studies of these two philosophers.

The West owes a considerable debt of gratitude to the Muslim philosophers.

They kept alive the light of learning, and however small their contribution towards the advancement of purely philosophical thought may have been, their service to theology was of the greatest value. . . . The presence of doctrines of Islamic origin in the very citadel of Western Christianity, the *Summa* of Aquinas, is a sufficient refutation of the charge of lack of originality and sterility.[19]

Muslim scholars also made an outstanding contribution to historical writing and criticism. They wrote biographies of Muhammad and the caliphs, histories of Arabia and the expansion of Islam, tribal histories, and even histories of the world. A strong

Artistry and precise observation combine to make this illustration from a thirteenth-century Islamic natural history text both graceful and accurate. Not only the doe and stag but also the willow tree and the various small grasses and shrubs are carefully rendered.

point with Muslim scholars was historical criticism, a carry-over from their concern for the accuracy of Koranic texts and biographical stories about Muhammad and his companions.

Islamic historiography found its finest expression in the work of ibn-Khaldun (1332-1406), who has been judged "the first writer to treat history as the proper object of a special science."[20] Despite his busy life in public affairs, he found time to write a large general history, dealing particularly with the history of the Arabs in Spain and Africa. The book maintains that history should analyze man's social development, which ibn-Khaldun held to be the result of the interaction of society and physical environment. He defined the historian's function as follows:

It should be known that history, in matter of fact, is information about human social organization, which itself is identical with world civilization. It deals with such conditions affecting the nature of civilization as, for instance, savagery and socia-

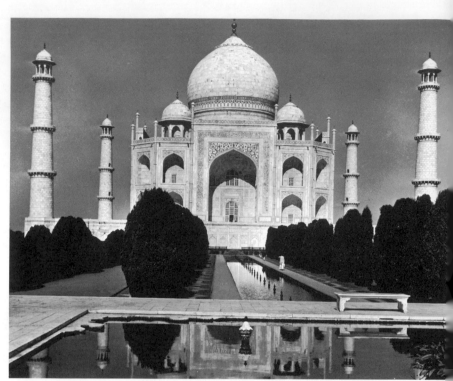

The Court of the Lions in the
Alhambra palace at Granada and
the Taj Mahal in India are fine
examples of Islamic architectural
traditions. The pervasive influence
of these traditions, which were
themselves influenced by
Byzantine conventions, is evident
in the Mosque of Selim I at Edirne
(Adrianople) in European Turkey.

bility, group feelings, and the different ways by which one group of human beings achieves superiority over another. It deals with royal authority and the dynasties that result (in this manner) and with the various ranks that exist within them. (It further deals) with the different kinds of gainful occupations and ways of making a living, with the sciences and crafts that human beings pursue as part of their activities and efforts, and with all the other institutions that originate in civilization through its very nature.[21]

Whereas Christian historians of the Middle Ages believed in a static concept of events, ibn-Khaldun conceived of history as an evolutionary process, in which societies and institutions change continually.

Art and architecture. As might be expected, religious attitudes played an important part in Muslim art. Because the Prophet inveighed strongly against idols and their worship, there was a prejudice against pictorial representation of human and animal figures. That such presentation was not prohibited absolutely, however, can be seen from the wealth of human and animal figures found in Islamic ornamentation. There seem to be fine distinctions in the ways in which figures could be portrayed. On the one hand, "realistic" portrayal, such as three-dimensional sculpture, was not permitted; on the other hand, two-dimensional carved reliefs with animals and people often appeared. In general, the effect of the prejudice against the representation of living things was to encourage the development of stylized and geometrical design.

Like Muslim learning, Muslim art borrowed from many sources. Islamic artists and craftsmen followed Byzantine, Persian, and Chinese models and eventually integrated what they had learned into a distinctive and original style. Islamic art was particularly indebted to Persian models. The brilliant Sassanid era had produced architecture, sculpture, and richly ornamented minor arts; and its love of decorative animal figures was carried over into Islamic art.

The Muslims excelled in two fields—architecture and the decorative arts. That Islamic architecture can boast of many large and imposing structures is not surprising, because it drew much of its inspiration from the Byzantines and Sassanids, who were monumental builders. In time an original style of building evolved; the great mosques embody such typical features as domes, arcades, and minarets, the slender towers from which the faithful are summoned to prayer. The horseshoe arch is another graceful and familiar feature of Muslim architecture. Different stylistic features characterize various types of Muslim architecture. This is the case, for example, with the dome, which was borrowed from the Byzantines. Except in North Africa and Spain, domes became a dominating feature of mosque architecture, and considerable variation is shown in their shape and in their place in the structure. Interestingly enough, the most direct borrowing from the early Byzantine dome at St. Sophia came very late, when the Ottoman Turks were making Constantinople the capital of their Muslim empire.

On the walls and ceilings of their buildings, the Muslims gave full rein to their love of ornamentation and beauty of detail. This

Muslim artists, discouraged from reproducing the human form, responded to the challenge of restricted subject matter by depicting and elaborating natural forms. The geometrization which grew from this process is apparent in the intricate carving of a wooden Koran stand and in the formal Arabic script on a page from the Koran.

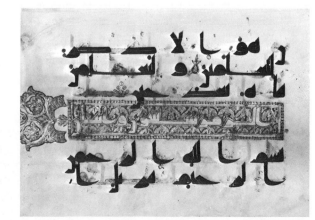

quality is shown to advantage in the School of Theology at Isfahan (see Color Plate 14), the walls of which are covered with intricate and beautiful mosaics. The Spanish interpretation of the Muslim tradition was particularly delicate and elegant. Other outstanding examples of Islamic architecture are to be found in India; the Taj Mahal, for example, is based largely on Persian motifs (see illustration, p. 270).

Being restricted in their subject matter, Muslim craftsmen conceived beautiful patterns from flowers and geometric figures. Even the graceful script made a delicate ornamentation on walls and the sides of urns. Tiles and mosaics were employed effectively to produce intricate and lavishly colored patterns. Muslim decorative skill also found expression in such fields as carpet and rug weaving, brass work, and the making of steel products inlaid with precious metals. And yet another highly successful field of expression was the Islamic art of producing lustrous pottery, a technique which spread from Persia as far west as Spain.

SUMMARY

Muhammad (570-632), the founder of the religion of Islam, was born in a desert area populated by nomadic Bedouins and a few scattered groups of townsmen. Inspired by a series of visions, Muhammad began to preach the new beliefs of Islam. Persecution and ridicule at Mecca caused the Prophet to flee to Medina, where public opinion was more receptive toward the new religion, and during his lifetime Islam spread through Arabia. Soon after Muhammad's death, his monotheistic teachings were compiled in the Koran, and from the Koran and the Sunna, a law code covering all aspects of Muslim life developed.

Muhammad had succeeded in organizing the fierce Arabs into a dynamic unit capable of astonishing expansion. During the reigns of the first four caliphs and the century of the Umayyad dynasty (661-750), great strides were made in annexing new territories and

people. But the Umayyad dynasty, whose source of strength was the privileged ruling class of the Arabs, incurred the enmity not only of the non-Arabic converts to Islam but also of many Arabs who resented the amount of power obtained by the Umayyads. This resentment was channeled into a revolution which set the Abbasid dynasty (750-1258) on a new throne in Baghdad.

During the early Abbasid period Islam attained its cultural zenith. Unparalleled prosperity evolved from a combination of successful trade, industry, and agriculture. But notwithstanding these great accomplishments, the Muslims were not able to maintain an integrated empire; and despite a religious unity, which still exists (though without formal organization), politically the empire broke up into smaller Muslim states.

The Muslims were especially interested in medicine, mathematics, and geography among the sciences; in poetry and historical writing in the field of literature; and in philosophy and theology. The unity of Muslim thought was preserved by using Arabic —a language which was at once clear, concise, poetic, and adaptable to the most technical scientific terminology—as the sole medium of expression. But we should not forget that Muslim intellectual life was in good part the product of a genius for synthesizing varying cultures rather than creating original contributions. The Muslims' broad diffusion of Greek and Arabic knowledge, more or less completed by 1300, was a tremendous factor in the revival of classical learning and the coming of the Renaissance in Europe.

Islamic contributions to western culture are both many and varied, ranging from new foods, beverages, and art forms to industrial, maritime, and commercial techniques and new terms and concepts in medicine and the sciences. Throughout the medieval period, the Muslim and Christian worlds experienced a "love-hate" relationship: although engaged in religious and territorial conflict, they continuously influenced each other by the exchange of both ideas and goods. For most of that period, the West was the chief cultural beneficiary, while retaining its spiritual independence. "From the fourteenth century onward the two civilizations grew more and more apart. The political and commercial ties with the heartlands of Islam slackened. Europe concentrated on itself, regaining its classical past in the process. Intellectual contact with the East, so long a need, became a luxury. From being the teacher Islamic civilization gradually changed into an object of study, and in this capacity its contribution to Western self-interpretation has been invaluable."[22]

As has been observed, western Europe owed much of its Renaissance to the Muslims, who had preserved and disseminated the best in ancient culture. Ironically, while the arts and learning were beginning to thrive in the West, Islamic civilization itself entered a period of cultural decline. Various reasons have been advanced for this phenomenon, including the influx of semibarbarous peoples into Islamic lands, intellectual stagnation resulting from too rigid interpretation of the Koran, and the despotic and eventually corrupt rule of such Muslim dynasties as the Ottomans in Turkey, who destroyed all progressive political and economic movements.

But the twentieth century has seen a new day dawn for Islam. The rejuvenation of Turkey after the First World War under the guidance of Mustafa Kemal Atatürk has shown the way for the modern followers of Muhammad; and like the Turks, other Muslim peoples have been on the march in recent times. The Arab peoples of North Africa and the Near East—Moroccans, Tunisians, Egyptians, Iraqis, and Syrians—not to mention other Muslims such as the Iranians, Pakistanis, and Indonesians, have experienced a dynamic awakening. This Muslim revival constitutes one of the major themes of the twentieth-century world.

Chapter *10*

The Guptas and the T'ang: Two Golden Ages

India, China, and Japan: 200-c. 1450 A.D.

Introduction. During the span of years covered in this chapter the great civilizations in Asia reached a high peak. In India the Gupta rulers came to power, and the sub-continent benefited from their enlightened government. Hindu culture entered a period of flourishing growth marked by important advances in mathematics, medicine, chemistry, textile production, and imaginative literature. In fact, in the realm of culture diffusion and creative thought, India played the major role in Eurasia during the four centuries from 200 to 600 A.D. In the following period, from the seventh through the tenth centuries, the T'ang dynasty held sway in China, reviving the greatness of Chinese civilization after a period of disorder and division. For the most part, the Chinese enjoyed prosperity and good government, and there was a flowering of scholarship and the arts. It was during the T'ang and Sung dynasties that such revolutionary inventions as printing, explosive powder, and the compass were devised.

The period of the Guptas and the T'ang is also notable for the cultural diffusion which took place in Asia. Indian civilization expanded throughout Southeast Asia and enriched indigenous societies in what are now Burma, Indochina, the Malay peninsula, and Indonesia. Similarly, there was a continous flow of Chinese culture eastward to the Korean peninsula and the islands off the Asian mainland, including Japan.

Both India and China suffered periodically from internal conflict and external aggression. In the latter part of the period covered in this chapter, Muslim conquest exerted an appreciable influence on Indian society, and repeated invasions by Mongols and other nomadic people wrought important political and social changes in China. But while China was able to assimilate foreign elements into its basic culture pattern, the synthesis of opposing cultures in India was incomplete and only partially successful. Nevertheless, in both countries basic modes of living evolved which have endured to modern times.

The events related in this chapter point up a significant theme in history—the important role played by restless, nomadic peoples in the rise and fall of civilizations.

In the decline of the Roman empire, as treated in Chapter 7, we witnessed a classic example of this recurring phenomenon—nomad tribes pressing and probing "softer," more civilized, less dynamic groups, discovering the weak spots in their defenses, and finally overwhelming them. Again, in Chapter 8, we saw Byzantium assailed continuously for a thousand years until it at last fell victim to inexorable outside pressures. Perhaps the most awesome of all the nomads were the Mongols ruled by Genghis Khan, who led his hordes into China in search of booty and went on to create the greatest empire the world had yet seen—a vast realm which extended all the way from the China Sea to eastern Europe. But if the assault of nomads is an important concern of this chapter, a corollary is how, once victorious, the predatory invader usually becomes respectable and sedentary, ceasing to be a menace to neighboring peoples.

The Japanese archipelago, after being occupied by ancestors of the present inhabitants, was never successfully invaded until the twentieth century. Influenced greatly by China, the proud and independent Japanese gradually developed a unique culture pattern best symbolized by the *samurai*, the knight, and *bushido*, the code of the warrior. Here, too, was a development which centuries later affected world history.

INDIA: THE IMPERIAL GUPTAS

The Gupta empire. As we recall from Chapter 6, the Kushan dynasty, which had witnessed one of the richest periods in Indian civilization, crumbled about 200 A.D. Subsequent events in northern India followed a pattern that has recurred time and time again in the history of the subcontinent: an epoch of distinction followed by an era of political disintegration and comparative cultural darkness.

With the advent of the Gupta empire in the fourth century, northern India came out of its dark era and entered upon another epoch of greatness. In about 320 A.D. the

first ruler of the Gupta dynasty, Chandragupta I (not related to Chandragupta Maurya, p. 167) established himself as monarch of the Ganges valley; and his successor extended the imperial boundaries in all directions. As a result, much of northern India from the Himalayas south to the Narbada River was included within the Gupta empire, thus making it the most extensive and powerful Indian state since the days of Ashoka six centuries earlier. Nor had its limits been reached. The grandson of the dynasty's founder, Chandragupta II, extended the empire still farther west until it stretched from sea to sea (see map, p. 279). During his reign (c. 380–c. 413) the Gupta empire reached its zenith. In all its long history before British rule India probably came closest to political unity during the reigns of Ashoka, Chandragupta II, and the Mughuls (see Chapter 19).

The Gupta monarchs "held all the levers and handles which worked the governmental machinery," with the king himself often administering justice. The king's revenues came principally from the earnings of crown lands and mines, from duties levied at ports and ferries, and from his one-sixth share of the land's produce.

The journal of Fa-hsien, a Chinese Buddhist pilgrim to India, contains a graphic account of conditions in the reign of Chandragupta II:

The people are numerous and happy. . . . The king governs without decapitation or other corporal punishment. Criminals are simply fined, lightly or heavily, according to the circumstances of each case. Even in cases of repeated attempts at wicked rebellion, they only have their right hands cut off [instead of undergoing execution, the typical punishment for revolutionists up to our own day]. . . .[1]

Fa-hsien's journal shows that Indian society had advanced considerably since the days of the Mauryan dynasty, thanks in large part to the elevated ethics and beneficent influence of Buddhism. In fact, India exhibited a state of cultural integration and social harmony such as it has never since achieved. By comparison with the Roman empire, which was nearing its demise, and China, enduring a troubled interim period between the two great eras of the Han and the T'ang, India was probably the most civilized region of the world at this time.

Dominance of Hinduism. During the Gupta age important religious developments took place. Ashoka and Kanishka had given Buddhism great impetus, but it lost ground in succeeding centuries and in time almost vanished from the land of its birth. Although religious tolerance was characteristic of the Gupta period, the Gupta rulers, for political reasons, preferred Hinduism to Buddhism, and the Brahmin caste enjoyed imperial patronage. While Buddhism as a distinct faith became practically extinct, certain of its teachings lived on. Its principle of *ahimsā*, for example, nonviolence and respect for life, became a strong element in Hinduism and later in the twentieth century gained world attention in the pacifism of Gandhi.

From about 185 B.C. to about 800 A.D., Hinduism not only became dominant in India but also gradually crystallized into its present form. In its philosophical aspects, the tenets of the *Upanishads* were developed and interpreted. Hindu thought developed into six orthodox philosophical systems, each a distinctive explanation of the world as well as a program for salvation. Probably the most important of the six systems is *Vedanta,* on which modern intellectual Hinduism is largely based. To *Vedanta,* "there is only one single Absolute Reality, the *Brahman,* and outside the *Brahman,* there is nothing which actually and genuinely exists. The entire world which we behold is a cosmic illusion. . . . It is not until we attain to true knowledge that we find salvation and deliverance from the deception in which we are entangled."[2]

The most important influence in this philosophical activity was the scholar Shankara (c. 788–828), who was also a philosopher, mystic, and poet. He founded religious orders and traveled throughout India debating and presenting his views. This philosophical dialogue carried on by Shankara and his colleagues has been likened to the vogue of Scholasticism in the universities of medieval Europe. His philosophy of *Vedanta* came to be the dominant school of Hindu thought.

Vedanta and allied religious thought constitutes what may be referred to as Higher or Philosophical Hinduism in contrast to the Lower or Popular faith followed by the masses. While intellectuals appreciated the subtleties of the former, the religion of the people was monopolized with the worship of such great deities as Vishnu and Shiva together with thousands of lesser deities represented by sacred stones and myriad images. The cow also came to be venerated as a symbol of the sanctity of life, and because of its gentleness, no orthodox

Shiva and Vishnu have long been two of the most popular Hindu deities. This fifteenth-century sculpture of Shiva (right) shows him as the divine dancer, a paradoxical figure symbolizing both the destructive and generative forces in the universe. Vishnu is represented in this seventeenth-century sculpture (far right) in his role as divine teacher and exponent of caste duty and fulfillment of one's *dharma*.

Hindu would countenance the slaughter of a cow or the eating of its flesh. This "cow complex" has meant that India supports an enormous number of cattle, 90 per cent of which are useless and nonproductive. The cost of maintaining the cow population is a tremendous drain on the Indian economy. As recently as 1966 there was serious rioting in New Delhi triggered by religious ascetics demanding that parliament pass legislation protecting cows.

Religious ritual controlled every aspect of life: offerings made to ancestors, caste regulations and ceremonies, and various domestic rites relating to such events as birth, marriage, and death. Every home had a shrine or prayer room for ritual and sacrifice. Religiosity and mysticism pervaded Hindu life probably more than in any other historic culture. Belief in astrology came to be widespread, frequent religious festivals had great mass appeal, and yearly great throngs made pilgrimages to sacred places such as the waters of the Ganges at Benares. And India has always supported a large number of holy men and mendicants who divorce themselves from the regimen of ordinary life.

India has been termed one of the greatest ethnographical museums in the world. A bewildering stream of invaders—Aryans, Greeks, Scythians, Huns, Iranians, Muslim Turks, Afghans, and Mughuls—has come through the mountain passes into the subcontinent. "India has been likened to a deep net into which various races and peoples of Asia have drifted and been caught."[3] All these intruders except the Muslims, however, found a place in Hinduism, which stresses conduct and ceremony rather than belief. God may be worshiped in many forms and by many names. As an Indian folk song says:

Into the bosom of the one great sea
Flow streams that come from hills on every side.
Their names are various as their springs,
And thus in every land do men bow down
To one great God, though known by many names.[4]

Hindu intellectuals are very proud of their faith's tolerance and all-embracing character. One has written:

Hinduism developed an attitude of comprehensive charity instead of a fanatic faith in an inflexible creed. It accepted the multiplicity of aboriginal Gods and others which originated . . . outside the Aryan tradition, and justified them all. It brought together into one whole all believers in God. Many sects professing many different beliefs live within the Hindu fold. Heresy-hunting, the favorite game of many religions, is singularly absent from Hinduism.[5]

The caste system. By the Gupta period the caste system was rapidly assuming its basic features. Each caste was usually related to a specific occupation. It was also endogamous, for a man was expected to select his bride from within his own group. Every caste had its own *dharma*—that is, the rules regulating the types of food eaten, the manner of consumption, and with what other castes there could be social contact. The untouchables, the lowest rung in the caste ladder, had a degraded status. Their contiguity, even sometimes their shadow, was deemed polluting to higher caste Hindus. In the light of modern democratic ideology, caste is a reprehensible system and indeed is so regarded by many of India's present leaders. Defenders of the institution, however, point out that a caste forms a kind of brotherhood in which all members are equal. Furthermore, within his caste the Hindu enjoys a sense of security that makes him feel part of a cosmic process in which no mistakes are made.

Gupta art. Indian art is difficult for westerners to understand or appreciate because it is entirely different from our own aesthetic traditions. It is nonnaturalistic; it seeks to represent feelings rather than things; it aims to convey aesthetic and religious emotions rather than to reproduce reality.

Although the Gupta period saw the decline of Buddhism's popularity and influence, Indian sculptors still continued to portray Gautama largely because the Buddha had provided the original source of inspiration for Indian sculptors in depicting the human form. But whereas Hellenized influences are readily apparent in Gandharan models (see p. 175), the Gupta artists created a different type of Buddhist image. The result of their efforts was to typify the essential elements of India's own cultural *ethos,* or character. The finest Gupta sculpture became the model for all later Indian art and also for that found in Indian colonies in the Malay peninsula, Java, and Cambodia.

Four centuries later than the Gupta period, the Kailasa Temple at Ellora is a marvel of human ingenuity and spiritual dedication. Rightly regarded as one of the most amazing accomplishments in religious architecture, it was carved out of a huge hill of solid rock. From the exterior one sees the original rock face of the hill pierced by several entrances. Once through these portals, the observer realizes that the entire inside of the hill of rock has been removed except for large sections that have been utilized to make a maze of statues, shrines, and galleries. The amount of human labor involved in stone cutting and carving is incredible (see illustration, p. 68).

The best examples of Gupta painting are found in the caves at Ajanta in the Deccan. Depicting the life of the Buddha as well as folk stories in Buddhist literature, some of these murals date from the second century B.C. The finest, however, were painted during the Gupta period. The murals in the dimly lit caves, where the artists worked by light reflected from the outside by metal mirrors, offer a brilliant kaleidoscope of contemporary life; princes, peasants, beggars, ascetics, women and children, beasts, birds, and flowers crowd one another in a vivid and exuberant panorama. After being long forgotten, the Ajanta caves were discovered accidentally early in the nineteenth century. Today a steady stream of Indians and visitors from abroad comes to marvel at the beauties of Ajanta and at the religious faith that inspired them (see illustration, p. 176).

Achievements in Sanskrit literature. The Gupta period has been called the golden age of Sanskrit, the classical language of India. Court poetry was zealously produced, and the kings were generous patrons of many writers.

The most famous writer was Kalidasa (c. 400-455), who excelled as both a lyric and an epic poet and who has been termed the Indian Shakespeare because of his superb dramas. Characterized by a lack of action unfamiliar to western audiences, his plays abound in splendid imagery; in this example, a young girl is given a fond send-off as she departs on a journey:

Thy journey be auspicious; may the breeze,
Gentle and soothing, fan thy cheek: may lakes,
All bright with lily-cups, delight thine eyes;
The sunbeam's heat be cooled by shady trees;
The dust beneath thy feet the pollen be
Of lotuses.[6]

India presented an unusually fertile soil for the creation of fables and folklore. Since its religion stressed the unity of all life and the cycle of transmigration, it was not difficult for storytellers to reverse the positions of the animal and human kingdoms and to conceive of beasts acting like men and vice versa. In addition, the country included then, as it does today, a multitude of races, languages, and customs and a wealth of birds, animals, fish, trees, and flowers.

Indian fairy tales and fables constitute the most original element in that country's literature. The variety of fascinating characters—thieves, courtesans, hypocritical monks, and strange beasts—still make for lively reading. Composed in Sanskrit between the years 300 and 500, the most famous story book—the *Panchatantra*—consists of a group of tales set within the pattern of a single narrative.

Many Indian stories were eventually carried to Europe by the Muslims. Perhaps the most famous is the story of Sindbad, which found its way into the *Arabian Nights*.

Boccaccio, Chaucer, La Fontaine, Grimm, and Kipling have all been indebted to Indian folklore.

Gupta science and technology. Scholars have not yet decided how much Indian science was influenced by Greek and Arabic contributions, especially in mathematics and medicine. But it is certain that scholarship and science were of a very high caliber during Gupta times. Students from all over Asia came to India's foremost university, at Nalanda. Founded in the fifth century, it had an enrollment of about ten thousand. Buddhist in tone, it was nevertheless quite tolerant of all creeds. The most famous scientist was the astronomer and mathematician Aryabhata, who lived in the fifth century. He discussed, in verse, quadratic equations, the value of π, solstices and equinoxes, the spherical shape of the earth, and the earth's rotation. Other Indian astronomers were able to predict eclipses accurately, to calculate the moon's diameter, and to expound on gravitation.

INDIA 400–650 A.D.

Gupta Empire, 413 A.D.

Area Under Gupta Influence

Harsha's Dominions, 606 A.D.

In astronomy and mathematics (except for geometry) the Hindus surpassed the achievements of any ancient western people. The Arabic numerals and the decimal system we use today appear to have come originally from India. Numerals can be found on the rock edicts of Ashoka, while Aryabhata and his successors were using decimals long before the Arabs, Syrians, and Chinese had a chance to borrow them. Even the zero may have come from Indian rather than from Arabic sources.

The Hindus were remarkably advanced in industrial chemistry; they discovered how to make soap and cement and were the finest temperers of steel in the world. Indian industry was also famous for its superior dyes and fine fabrics; the methods of production were taken over by the Arabs, and from them by Europeans. The Arabs named one Indian cloth *quittan*—hence the word *cotton.* *Calico* derives from Calicut in India and *cashmere* from the region of that name, Kashmir. *Chintz* and *bandanna* are also of Indian origin.

Indian medicine owes its development to various factors, including an interest in physiology which resulted from Yoga. Emphasizing the control of the body as a means of acquiring mental and spiritual discipline, the adherents of Yoga made a study of posture, breath control, and the regulation of the pulse. In short, Yoga sought to demonstrate the power of mind over body. The followers of Yoga developed certain forms of control of which western medical science is aware, yet which cannot altogether be explained.

Some Gupta physicians were surprisingly modern in their techniques; they prepared carefully for an operation and sterilized wounds by fumigation. Caesarean operations, bone setting, and plastic surgery were all attempted. The Indians also made use of many drugs then unknown in Europe; for treating leprosy they used the oil of the chaulmoogra tree—a drug which is still employed. Great advances were also made in discovering antidotes for snake bites. Indian medicine, however, made little progress after the Gupta period, except for borrowings from the Arabs.

A period of flux in northern India. By 413, when Chandragupta II died, the Gupta empire had reached the zenith of its power. In the last half of the fifth century, while their kinsmen were ravaging Europe under Attila, "The Scourge," Huns invaded the Punjab. They soon gained control of northwestern India but were prevented from advancing into eastern India by a confederacy of Hindu princes.

In the seventh century the various states in the Ganges valley fought constantly with one another until at last a strong man arose. In the short space of six years (606-612) Harsha, rajah of one of the northern kingdoms, mastered much of the territory formerly ruled by the Guptas. For a first-hand report about Harsha's reign, we are again indebted to a Chinese Buddhist pilgrim, the learned scholar Hsüan-tsang. Spending eight years in Harsha's dominions, Hsüan-tsang found the caste system well established, the taxes light, the standard of living high, learning held in esteem, and the government efficiently administered. An excellent example of a benevolent despot, the versatile Harsha was a soldier and an administrator, a patron of the arts, and a skillful poet and dramatist.

Unfortunately, Harsha left no heirs. After his death in 647, northern India characteristically reverted to political confusion and warfare which lasted for centuries. Particularly warlike were the descendants of Central Asian peoples who had followed the Huns into northwest India in the fifth century and intermarried with the local population. In time these people assumed the privileges of "blue-blooded" Hindus, haughtily called themselves Rajputs (Sons of Kings), and carved out kingdoms for themselves in parts of north India and especially what became known as Rajputana, a strategic area between the Indus and Ganges valleys. The Rajputs possessed a code of chivalry not unlike that which existed in medieval Europe. Youths were brought up with the privileges and obligations of the warrior caste (the Kshatriya) and taught to respect women, spare the fallen, and demand fair play.

Notwithstanding the political fragmentation, with various dynasties rising and falling, there was significant activity in culture and learning during this period. Hinduism especially expressed itself in magnificent temples such as at Khajuraho, Ellora, and Tanjore.

Impact of Indian culture. While not generally appreciated in the West until modern times, for nearly one thousand years India sent her art, religious ideas, literature, and traders to many parts of Asia. During this period *Mahayana* Buddhism spread into Central Asia, China, Korea, and finally Japan. The diffusion of this faith was the most striking sign of the dynamic power of Indian culture. The relationship between India and China was especially strong. Many Chinese scholars made pilgrimages to the former. One such was Fa-hsien who reached India in 405 A.D. after a tedious overland caravan journey of three years. Following a sojourn of nine years in the land of Buddha, the pilgrim returned to China by ship laden with Buddhist manuscripts. After Fa-hsien numerous Chinese scholars interested in Buddhism journeyed to India. The most celebrated was Hsüan-tang (or Yuan-chuang), who spent thirteen years (630-643) in Buddha's holy land. His journal is one of the most valuable sources of information on medieval India. Returning to his native land, Hsüan-tsang brought back 657 manuscripts, together with many Buddhist relics, and devoted the remainder of his life to translating his treasures (see Chapter 19 for further details).

THE MUSLIM CONQUEST OF INDIA

Decline of Hindu culture. What was the cause of the decline in Hindu vigor in India itself? In the political field, Harsha's death in 647 had left northern India in the grip of petty groups whose conflicts weakened and disorganized the land; effective resistance against outside aggression could not be marshaled consistently. But the existing weakness was more than political, for a decline was occurring throughout Hindu society. A sense of complacency and superiority grew up, partly connected with an increasing isolation from the outside world. By the tenth century the last great waves of cultural diffusion had subsided. As one contemporary observer recorded:

The Hindus believe that there is no country but theirs, no nation like theirs, no religion like theirs, no sciences like theirs. . . . If they travelled and mixed with other nations they would soon change their mind, for their ancestors were not so narrow-minded as the present generation.[7]

In short, Hindu India in the eleventh century no longer had the resilience to withstand the sustained attacks of a determined foe. And such a foe, implacably opposed to Hinduism and its culture, was already on the northwest frontier.

The Muslim invasions. Toward the end of the seventh century, the Muslim Arabs had their first encounter with the Indians. Some Muslim ships were attacked by Indian pirates, and the Muslims sent a retaliatory expedition along the Indian coast by the mouth of the Indus. In 711, the same year in which they invaded Spain, Arabs appeared in force. They made the southern valley of the Indus a province of the vast Umayyad empire, but the Rajput princes soon halted further Arab penetration of India.

At the very end of the tenth century more Muslim invaders swept through the northwest passes. The newcomers were Turks and Afghans, the most famous being the Muslim Turk Mahmud of Ghazni, ruler of a kingdom in Afghanistan. This fierce warrior regarded India as a land of infidels and unbelievers, fair prey for the followers of Allah. As a result of his campaign of 1022, he annexed the Punjab. Despite destructive forays by various Muslim sultans, the Rajput and other Hindu kingdoms of the interior remained independent. Not until the closing years of the twelfth century did the Muslims establish a large Indian dominion.

A new chapter in Muslim invasion began in 1191 when Muhammad Ghuri not only raided India but began to occupy the country. His overwhelming victories left all north India open to Muslim conquest. The ease of the Muslims' victory is explained by several factors. The Muslims were physically superior; they were driven by fierce fanaticism and the expectation of enormous booty; and Hindu military tactics—especially reliance upon elephants—were hopelessly outdated. Finally, the Hindus were divided by jealousies, and fighting was done only by the warrior caste.

The Delhi sultanate. After Muhammad of Ghur was assassinated in 1206, one of his generals set himself up as sultan at Delhi, ruling a strong Muslim kingdom covering much of north India. The Delhi sultanate existed until the early years of the fifteenth century, and during the period of its greatest power (1206-1388), it gave northern India political unity. The early Delhi sultans also pushed Muslim authority and religion southward into the Deccan and in the first

decades of the fourteenth century reached southernmost India. The Delhi sultanate, however, soon lost control in southern India to a rival sultanate in the Deccan and to other Muslim and Hindu states.

The Delhi sultans were a curious lot. While often patrons of the arts and builders of splendid architecture, they could also be fiercely cruel and tyrannical. Sultan Muhammad Tughluk (1325-1351) is a case in point. A complete mixture of opposites, he "acquired the throne by murdering his father, became a great scholar and an elegant writer, dabbled in mathematics, physics, and Greek philosophy, surpassed his predecessors in bloodshed and brutality, fed the flesh of a rebel nephew to the rebel's wife and children, ruined the country with reckless inflation, and laid it waste with pillage and murder. . . ."[8]

Tamerlane. The rapid decline of the Delhi sultanate threw the country into civil war and left it unprotected against a great inva-

MUSLIM EXPANSION IN INDIA

sion from the northwest. In 1398 there marched into the Punjab a Mongol who had already conquered Central Asia—Timur the Lame (Tamerlane). Defeating all armies sent against him, Timur looted wealthy Delhi, killing perhaps 100,000 prisoners. Afterwards, he departed westward for Samarkand, leaving Delhi's few surviving inhabitants to perish of famine and plague. It was said that for two whole months, not a bird moved a wing in the city.

After Timur's terrible visitation, all semblance of political unity was destroyed in north India. For half a century the authority of Delhi sultans hardly extended beyond the neighborhood of their capital, and in various parts of northern India, Muslim sultans maintained independent principalities in defiance of the ineffectual authority at Delhi.

Effects of Muslim rule. The initial Muslim raids and military conquest of India were unusually ruthless. To the Muslims, Hinduism with its many deities, elaborate ritual, powerful priestcraft, and fondness for images was the exact opposite of all Islam held sacred. Hindu forces desperately resisted their Muslim conquerors and, after defeat, often suffered wholesale massacre.

Following the conquest, however, the Muslim invaders had to organize and stabilize their governments and collect necessary revenues. While many rich Hindu nobles saw their property and land confiscated, the great masses of common folk were not so affected. Life in the villages went on undisturbed, the people treading the path of immemorial custom. Many clung tenaciously to their Hindu faith—the upper classes in particular—but a fairly large number were converted to Islam. In some cases it was a choice between Allah or the sword; in others it was a voluntary matter: poor men sought to avoid the heavier taxes levied on infidels, low-caste Hindus became Muslims to escape their degraded status, and ambitious administrators accepted Islam in order to succeed in the official service of the Muslim rulers.

There was, however, much give-and-take between the conquerors and conquered. Some Hindus imitated the Muslim practice of purdah (seclusion of women), and the new rulers' dress was widely copied. Some intermarriage also took place, mainly for political reasons in aristocratic circles. In the area of religion two diverse consequences may be noted. The conservatism of some orthodox Hindu circles hardened. But at the same time sects arose seeking a creed that could embrace both Hindus and Muslims. Another result of the Muslim intrusion was the emergence of a common spoken language—Urdu—during the Delhi sultanate. This language was a combination of Persian, Turkish, and Arabic words which utilized the grammatical constructions of the Hindu languages.

The injection of the Islamic way of life into the pattern of Hindu society was to have profound effects upon the history of the Indian subcontinent. The Muslims, unlike many previous invaders, were not assimilated into the socio-religious fold of Hinduism. They stood apart, fiercely monotheistic, disdainful of what appeared as Hinduism's voluptuous polytheism and its closed society of caste. "From the thirteenth century onwards, the life of India must be thought of as two distinct currents flowing side by side, mingling to a varying extent along the line of contact, but not uniting to form a single stream."[9] This division was to have momentous consequences in the twentieth century, when India, freed from British rule, split into two nations, India and Pakistan.

CHINA: THE MEN OF T'ANG

An age of political division. In India the transitional period between the fall of the Kushan empire and the rise of the Guptas was relatively short. But after the fall of the Han empire in 220 A.D., China was destined to suffer three and a half centuries of disorder and division before another great dynasty arose and reunited the country.

The internal collapse of the Han empire—as with the breakdown of the Mauryan and Gupta regimes in India and of Rome in the

West—allowed various nomadic peoples, mainly Turks and Huns, to penetrate the frontiers and raid and pillage. In North China these barbarians set up various petty states, especially after the opening of the fourth century.

The invaders were few in relation to their Chinese peasant subjects; their own political traditions were those of the nomadic war-band type that was common throughout the whole steppe zone across Eurasia. Thus their earliest form of rule was a privileged military elite. They made more fateful compromises than did the Franks on the northern Roman frontier; usually they ended up both depending on Chinese administrative assistants to produce revenues and adopting the Chinese way of life, even to the point of forgetting their native languages. Each petty king claimed to rule "all beneath Heaven," even though he held only a province or less.

The barbarian invaders usually became ardent patrons of Buddhism. They did so partly to use the literate and technical skills of Buddhist missionaries from India and Central Asian oases and thus to be less dependent on their Chinese subjects; but they were also deeply affected by the mystical and devotional aspects of Buddhism in its *Mahayana* or universalistic form. The first forms of a distinctive East Asian Buddhist art—including painting and sculpture—were developed under them in northern China.

Central and South China escaped these barbarian intrusions and were now more intensively developed than before, especially by émigrés from the confusion of the north. Hence the literate classical tradition was preserved in Chinese hands in the south; and a sequence of regimes, with capitals at Nanking on the Yangtze, kept alive the notion of a unified state under a "Son of Heaven." This very sequence strengthened belief in the "Mandate of Heaven" theory.

Buddhism adapts itself. Although Buddhism had been introduced into China during Han times, this religion made its most important gains from the third century A.D. on. In late Han times some Chinese intellectuals had found official Confucianism too devoid of speculative philosophic content and had developed an elaborate metaphysical system based on Taoism. It was an easy step from this to a fervent interest in the fully developed forms of *Mahayana* thought. Part of Buddhism's appeal also resembled that of the mystery religions and of Christianity in the decaying Roman world: the assurance of inner consolation through faith and of salvation in a glorious afterlife even for humble folk and for those without much learning. The monastic aspects of Buddhism appealed to those seeking seclusion and protection in the face of contemporary social chaos; many thousands of Chinese sought release from social obligation and political oppression.

As the sober, balanced social order inculcated by Confucianism came to make less sense in a world run by war lords, all classes of Chinese were touched by Buddhism. Even the popular cults derived from ancient Taoism paid Buddhism the compliment of imitation, developing a priesthood, a kind of monasticism, a large literature, and a service of spells and charms for the credulous.

The empire restored. After internal collapse and barbarian invasion, neither the Indian nor the Graeco-Roman world-state was ever able fully to regenerate itself politically. But in the late sixth and early seventh centuries the Chinese did just that, re-creating and improving on the Han model. The short-lived Sui dynasty (589-618) gave China new military and political unity and spent man power recklessly to inaugurate a vast canal system (to tie the new prime producing area of the Yangtze basin to the traditionally important north) and to wage an ill-planned, futile war in Korea. The Sui dynasty, however, finally foundered in its own extravagance and in the face of massive revolt.

The succeeding T'ang dynasty (618-907) built on these foundations a long period of stable growth and cultural flowering and gave China renewed preëminence in all East Asia. Direct control of Central Asia was restored, and the T'ang state served as the prime model for the first real high cultures that emerged in Korea, Japan, and Annam (Vietnam).

Political and economic conditions under the T'ang. As the Gupta empire represents the golden age of Hindu culture, the T'ang-dynasty represents the golden era of China. So vividly did the T'ang era impress itself upon China that even today many Chinese like to consider themselves not only "Sons of Han" but also "Men of T'ang."

The second emperor (and real founder) of the T'ang dynasty—T'ai Tsung—reigned from 627 to 650 and is considered one of China's greatest emperors. A successful warrior, T'ai Tsung attacked the Turkish empire which stretched across northern Asia. After defeating the Turks decisively in 630, T'ai Tsung took advantage of internal dissension in Turkestan to destroy the western Turks and to reëstablish Chinese dominance over the Tarim Basin. Under his son, a successful war was undertaken against Korea, which was made a tributary vassal state of the expanding Chinese empire. At this point China stood at the zenith of its power. The T'ang empire extended from Korea and Manchuria through Tibet and Central Asia to the borders of India and Persia (see map).

A statesman as well as a great soldier, T'ai Tsung was energetic in instituting reforms. One of his major reforms was to strengthen the administrative system of the country. The emperor governed the center of his empire by means of a bureaucracy recruited through a civil service program rooted in Han precedent but now more elaborated. In those areas inhabited by non-Chinese, the people were allowed to keep native princes, but they had to recognize Chinese suzerainty.

T'ang innovations also extended to land reform, because the government's chief source of revenue came from taxes on grain and other farm products. Laws were passed to curb the growth of large estates and to ensure equitable amounts of land for the peasants. The government also collected revenues on iron, copper, and salt monopolies as well as from taxes on rice, wine, and tea.

Economic prosperity resulted from these reforms as well as from the more efficient transportation system which the T'ang developed by completing the Sui canal system. A thriving foreign commerce also contributed to the economic boom. Caravans arrived frequently from West and Central Asia; and great quantities of silks, pottery, porcelain, and other luxury goods were exported to such far-distant points as Jerusalem and Cairo.

In their initial stage the reforms instituted by T'ai Tsung worked well: the government was efficiently and vigorously administered, the economy prospered, varieties of religious beliefs were tolerated, and the people as a whole were contented. Political expansion and economic prosperity in turn created new social habits and standards of living. A number of new foods, including pepper, sugar beets, almonds, and dates, made their appearance, and during the eighth century tea became available to all classes.

T'ang scholarship. The T'ang period was outstanding in scholarly achievements. Two encyclopedias were compiled to assist bureaucrats in their work, and Buddhist scholars translated sacred texts into Chinese. T'ai Tsung ordered the publication of an elaborate edition of the Thirteen Classics of Confucianism and also stressed the value of historical writings:

. . . by using a mirror of brass you may see to adjust your cap; by using antiquity as a mirror, you may learn to foresee the rise and fall of empires.[10]

Complete objectivity of the historical record was a basic value in T'ang scholarship, as this story from the official diary of the emperor's life indicates:

The year 839, Winter, 10th month. The Emperor Wen-tsung went to the Official in Charge of the Diaries of Action and Repose, Wei Mo, picked up his notes and began looking at them. Wei Mo objected, saying: "The Diaries of Action and Repose record both good and bad in order to warn and admonish the ruler of men. Your Majesty should only strive to do good. It is not necessary that Your Majesty see the records." The emperor said: "Once before I looked at them." "That,"

This smiling Bodhisattva, made of black stone, is a fine example of early Buddhist art, and represents the strong realism of T'ang sculpture.

replied Wei Mo, "was the fault of the official in charge of history at that time. If Your Majesty were to examine the records personally, the historiographers would be forced to distort or alter their accounts. Then how could we expect later ages to put any faith in them?" With this the emperor desisted.[11]

By the next dynasty, however, the emperors exerted greater control over the court's official daily records, and as a result, their value as historical source material diminished (see the Historical Critique, p. 308).

Li Po and Tu Fu, masters of T'ang poetry. An eighteenth-century anthology of T'ang poetry included dozens of volumes containing 48,900 poems by 2300 poets. The astonishing literary output of the T'ang era would almost appear to justify the remark: "[At this age,] whoever was a man was a poet."[12]

The two greatest poets of this era, Li Po (701?-762) and Tu Fu (712-770), were good friends who occasionally twitted each other in their works. Tu Fu summed up his fellow poet—a true Bohemian spirit who was notorious for his heavy drinking—in this fashion:

As for Li Po, give him a jugful of wine,
And he will write a hundred poems.[13]

And Li Po once addressed these witty lines to Tu Fu:

Here! is this you on the top of Fan-Ko
  Mountain,
Wearing a huge hat in the noon-day sun?
How thin, how wretchedly thin, you have
  grown!
You must have been suffering from poetry
  again.[14]

The poetry of Li Po exerted a great appeal for his countrymen; he was truly "a people's poet." But the majority of Chinese scholars and poets today consider Tu Fu the greater poet, perhaps China's greatest. A sample of his poetry appears later in this chapter (see p. 288).

T'ang artistic endeavors. The T'ang dynasty was the formative period of Chinese painting. The great Wu Tao-tzu furthered the development of a national school independent of foreign influences. The story is told that his last painting was a landscape to serve as a wall decoration for the emperor. As Wu and the emperor stood admiring the lifelike scene, the artist clapped his hands, a door in the painting opened, and Wu disappeared within, never to be seen again.

Sculptors used Buddhist subject matter, but their work bore the impress of indigenous artistic standards rather than those of India. In the head of the Bodhisattva at the left, for example, we see how a distinctively Chinese interpretation—with its strong humanistic and benevolent emphasis—was accorded the *Mahayana* religious figures. Aspects of court life were delightfully represented in terra-cotta figurines depicting court ladies, musicians, polo players, and cavalry.

The invention of printing. The T'ang period deserves credit for one of mankind's priceless inventions—printing. There was a growing demand for mass distribution of religious and educational materials. The Buddhist monks wished to duplicate passages from their scriptures, or *sutras*, for mass consumption, and the Taoists wanted prayer formulas and charms for warding off evil spirits and disease. In addition, there was an increasing market for such secular works as vocabularies and calendars and for textbooks to prepare those intending to take the civil service examinations. The need for written material could be met only if some method were devised faster than writing by hand with a brush, the method which had been in use since Shang times. In the first century A.D. the Chinese had discovered how to make paper, and in the fifth century they put ink stampings on documents by using seals fashioned from metal and stone. These technical discoveries paved the way for the culminating invention—printing.

Evidence would indicate that the process of block printing—printing from an image cut in a wooden block—was invented in China by about 600, although the earliest surviving examples come from Japan and date from 764 to 770. The first extant printed book is the *Diamond Sutra*, which was discovered in a cave in northwestern China. Printed in 868, the *Diamond Sutra* consists of six sheets of text pasted together to form a roll some sixteen feet long; the sheets are each two and a half feet by almost one foot in size and must have been printed from very large blocks.

Because the Chinese language is written not by means of an alphabet but by means of separate characters that represent entire words, the Chinese found block printing

The Chinese invented block printing in about 600, and the earliest existing book printed by this method is the *Diamond Sutra*, dating from about 868.

satisfactory. Nevertheless, they were the first to invent movable type, probably in the first half of the eleventh century.

T'ang decline: the end of an epoch. In the seventh century the T'ang dynasty still enjoyed a suzerainty that stretched from the Pamir Mountains in the west into Korea in the east, but the next century witnessed significant changes. Although the first half of the eighth century was marked by brilliant literary and artistic achievements and by imperial power and pomp, divisive political forces were at work.

From mid-century on, the imperial boundaries contracted, and within the empire, decadence and disorder held sway. Tu Fu contrasted the luxury and corruption of the royal court with the wretched condition of the masses:

The humble people have no share in the feastings.
But the silk distributed in the Imperial harem
Was woven by poor women. . . .
In the central halls [of the palace] there are fair
    goddesses;
An air of perfume moves with each charming
    figure.
They clothe their guests with warm furs of sable,
Entertain them with the finest music of pipe
    and string,
Feed them with the broth of the camel's pad,
With pungent tangerines, and oranges ripened
    in frost.
Behind the red-lacquered gates, wine is left to
    sour, meat to rot.
Outside these gates lie the bones of the frozen
    and the starved.
The flourishing and the withered are just a foot
    apart—
It rends my heart to ponder on it.[15]

In 755 a revolt broke out under the leadership of a military governor, and the emperor was forced to flee, abdicating in favor of his son. When the rebellion was finally put down, the weakened dynasty survived for a century and a half; but China turned markedly inward. The power and the prestige of Buddhism were irreparably shaken when the state expropriated Buddhist properties on a vast scale and coerced thousands of monks and nuns back into secular life. These persecutions were directed not against Buddhism as a religion but against the church as a wealthy institution whose revenues were needed to support the government's sagging finances. Despite such expropriations, however, state revenues declined, and trade diminished. The grievances of the common people mounted as taxes became heavier, and the ninth century witnessed many popular uprisings. As the dynasty grew financially and militarily weaker, the governors of various provinces declared their independence, and in 906 the T'ang dynasty came to an end.

The Sung dynasty. The fall of the T'ang dynasty left China vulnerable to external attack and in another of its eras of internal disorder. This upheaval was followed by the founding of the Sung dynasty (960-1279). By 979 the Sung had subdued the secessionist states in the south, but the Khitan Tatars still remained in the area north of the Huang Ho, where they had established the kingdom of Liao. Early in the next century the Sung emperors adopted the practice of "buying protection" by paying the northern barbarians an annual tribute of 100,000 ounces of silver and 200,000 pieces of silk. In time the Sung were forced to increase these amounts and to begin paying tribute to other border kingdoms. Even though they did not represent a large percentage of the total state revenues, such payments were a drain on the imperial finances.

The unprecedented development of large estates whose owners managed to evade paying their share of the taxes resulted in an increasingly heavy burden of taxation falling on the small farmers. The drop in state revenues, a succession of budget deficits, and widespread inflation caused the emperor to seek advice from one of China's most fascinating statesmen and economists, Wang An-shih (1021-1086).

Wang An-shih believed that the ruler was responsible for providing his subjects with the necessities of life. He expressed his social philosophy thus:

The state should take the entire management of commerce, industry, and agriculture into its own hands, with a view to succoring the working classes and preventing them from being ground into the dust by the rich.[16]

To this end, he initiated an agricultural loans measure to relieve the farming peasants of the intolerable burden of interest which callous moneylenders exacted from them in difficult times and to ensure that lack of capital would not hinder the work of agriculture. To destroy speculation and break the strangle hold of the monopolies, he initiated a system of fixed commodity prices; and he appointed boards to regulate wages and plan pensions for the aged and unemployed. In addition to these measures designed to improve the internal economy and alleviate social distress, Wang An-shih revamped the existing state examination system so that less emphasis was placed on literary style and memorization of the classics and more on practical knowledge.

In the next generation, opposition from vested interests, difficulties in maintaining reforming zeal and efficiency among officials, the impracticality of some reform projects, and renewed foreign crises—all these factors led to the permanent victory of the conservative opposition and to the rescinding of most of Wang's "new laws." It is remarkable, nonetheless, to see how modern were the theories of this statesman who lived nine hundred years ago. The concepts of the welfare state and a planned economy are apparently not quite so new as we may have supposed.

The Neo-Confucian scholastic synthesis. Under the impact of Buddhist thought, many of Wang's opponents were interested in finding a better philosophic basis for the Confucian ethical system; consequently there developed, from elements of the old classic literature and Buddhist scriptures, a metaphysics that did not depend on the Buddhist church for ultimate explanations. This conservative reinterpretation of tradition we call Neo-Confucianism.

The advocates of Neo-Confucianism included many outstanding scholars and officials. Most important was Chu Hsi (1130-1200), whose voluminous commentaries on the classics developed an elaborate synthesis that postulated a single universal principle—eternal law or reason—underlying all phenomena, which man could perceive by meditation and education. Chu Hsi and other Neo-Confucians succeeded in restoring Confucianism to its former place of preeminence in Chinese thought—a place of honor it held down to the twentieth century. His commentaries became the basis for the official examinations.

Buddhism, institutionally under strict state control, lost its old prestige and intellectual respectability among the upper classes and survived principally as one of several popular cults among the masses. Ch'an Buddhism alone was vital—perhaps because, like native Chinese Taoism, it emphasized individual, personal contemplative habits and subordination to nature. A Chinese gentleman who was a Confucian in his public life and in his view of society might indulge Ch'an or Taoist interests in the privacy of his study.

The empirical sciences. Chu Hsi contended that self-cultivation required the extension of knowledge, best achieved by the "investigation of things." As a consequence, Neo-Confucianism was accompanied by significant advances in experimental and applied sciences and their dissemination through the printed word. The Sung period witnessed the production of large numbers of works concerning chemistry, zoology, and botany. Algebra was developed until it was the most advanced in the world. In medicine, inoculation against smallpox was introduced. Progress was also notable in astronomy, geography, and cartography; at this time, the earliest relief maps were constructed. By the end of the eleventh century the magnetic compass was employed as an aid to navigation. Another major development in this era was the use of explosive powder—a mixture of sulfur, saltpeter, and other substances—first in fireworks and then in warfare.

Achievements and limitations of Chinese science. From this overview of Chinese science and technology, it becomes obvious that in the millennium ending in the fifteenth century, East Asian society was more inventive than its western counterpart in applying human knowledge of nature to useful purposes. How then can we account for the fact that science, as we know it today,

During the T'ang and Sung dynasties Chinese science and technology were far in advance of European science of the same era. The Chinese excelled in cartography at a time when westerners were producing crude sketches. The "Map of China and the Barbarian Countries" dates from about 1040. Places within China are drawn in detail and with considerable accuracy, while the "barbarian" countries are indicated by texts rather than by geographical markings. Chinese science frequently took a brilliantly utilitarian turn. The horsecollar was used in China as early as the fifth century, and the fishing reel, which is a type of windlass pulley, by at least the twelfth century. Even more remarkable was the development of the seismograph by the first century A.D. This reconstruction (top left) illustrates the basic pendulum mechanism by which the Chinese seismograph operated. An earthquake would jolt the machine so that a ball would drop into the mouth of one of eight toad figures, thus indicating from which direction the tremor had come. The Chinese may also have developed the magnetic compass as early as the first century, a millennium before the compass was used in Europe. This version of the compass (top right), a magnetized iron "fish" floating on water, pointed south, which the Chinese considered the primary pole. One of the most complicated Chinese mechanical and scientific creations, this astronomical observatory (bottom right) dating from about 1090, used a water-powered clock to rotate the instruments in time with the motion of the stars. Until very recently it was thought that the mechanical clock was a western achievement of the fourteenth century.

釣鱉

A seventeenth-century engraving demonstrates two methods of irrigation that were commonly used in Sung China: the Sung innovation of irrigation by a chain pump worked by treadmill operators (left) and the more traditional style of irrigation by a long suspended rod with a bucket at one end and a weight at the other.

their knowledge to do things. Thus the Taoists were responsible for the "beginnings of chemistry, mineralogy, zoology, botany, and pharmaceutics in East Asia."[18] However, because they distrusted reason and logic, the Taoists failed to define the experimental method with the necessary precision or to systematize their observations of the natural order. Hence their approach has been described as mystical-experimental rather than rational-systematic (as in the case of the Greeks). This cleavage between rational logic and experimental empiricism—reflecting a fundamental difference of outlook between the Confucians and Taoists—runs counter to the attitude of the Greeks and their successors and goes far to explain why science as we understand it originated in the West and not the East.

Yet we must not minimize the diversity and brilliance of the Chinese scientific contribution. For centuries scholars classified stellar phenomena and the diseases of men and animals; they worked out detailed pharmacopeias, devised complex instruments, including the seismograph and mechanical clock; they studied terrestrial magnetism; and they engaged in many forms of experimentation, obtaining results which they could repeat. Moreover, the Chinese scientific tradition was based upon the concept that change is a universal principle—a concept with which western science is in full agreement. In fact, present-day developments in biology and physics have much in common with the Chinese scientific tradition, with its emphasis upon an organic and relativistic concept of the order of nature. Indeed, according to one historian of science, "the gigantic historical paradox remains that although Chinese civilization could not spontaneously produce modern natural science, natural science could not perfect itself without the characteristic philosophy of Chinese civilization."[19]

Excellence in Sung art. Many critics assert that "at its best Chinese painting is one of the outstanding expressions of man's ability to create beauty."[20] The Chinese painter believed that only days spent in meditation of a vista would reveal to him the essential mood of the scene before him. When he had

developed only in western Europe? One scholar has listed three elements required for this development: (1) an empirical approach employing manual operations; (2) skepticism as part of the critical spirit needed for scientific thinking; and (3) "the formation of mature hypotheses couched in mathematical terms and experimentally verifiable." Although the first two elements existed in Chinese thought, it failed to produce those "mature hypotheses" which alone could supersede the primitive theories found in the "protoscientific" stage.[17] Let us see why.

Confucius and his followers, as we saw, were primarily interested in human relations and the development of social order through reason and logic. The Taoists, too, were concerned with order, but it was the order of *nature* that functioned organically in the mineral, plant, animal, and human kingdoms. Their attitude paralleled that of the pre-Socratic philosophers of Greece (see p. 109) inasmuch as both groups sought to understand the natural order and to use observed nature as long as he thought necessary, he would then paint the scene without looking at it.

Thus, to a Sung artist, landscape was primarily a state of mind. He was concerned above all with depicting the material attributes of forms in such a way that his painting would suggest the inner significance of the scene he had observed. This effect was achieved by simplifying line and shading, by utilizing the softening effects of mist and water, and by creating a feeling of the vastness of nature. The awe and love felt for nature by Chinese painters was the force behind much of their work (see Color Plate 13).

Chinese paintings were not publicly displayed but were mounted on heavy paper and kept hidden away. Only on special occasions were they taken out for a short period of concentrated aesthetic enjoyment. The painter was highly esteemed, for his techniques required years of intensive training. The use of ink on silk meant that he had to be sure of every line, for once the brush stroke had been made, no changes were possible. The use of the brush in writing the intricate Chinese word symbols gave the painters excellent training. In fact, calligraphy could be considered a branch of painting.

Sung pottery—especially porcelain—was also of unsurpassed excellence. The Chinese loved the delicacy and rare beauty of the elegant porcelain pieces produced in this period. Perhaps the best known of the Sung ware is the green celadon.

Foreign crisis. During the eleventh century a new factor was injected into the relations of the Sung with their northern neighbors—the appearance of a people from Manchuria, who took northern China, where they ruled for a century as the Chin dynasty (not related to the earlier Ch'in, p. 78). From 1127 on, the Sung had no control over territory north of the natural divide between the Yangtze and Huang Ho valleys. They established a capital in the south of China, first at Nanking and then at Hangchow, and for the next one hundred years China was thus divided into two empires, the Sung and the Chin.

Early modern China. The Southern Sung was militarily weak, but economically and socially it was one of the greatest periods in the history of China. Trends of change that had begun during the T'ang and increased in scope during the Northern Sung transformed Chinese society during the Southern Sung to such an extent that we may speak of this period as the beginning of the modern period in Chinese history. Most of the patterns of Chinese society with which the West became familiar in the nineteenth century were well established by the end of the Southern Sung period.

During the Northern Sung the population of China may have been more than 100 million and it probably never fell far below this again. This, together with marked improvements in production, led to a vastly increased internal and external trade. Commerce broke out of the controlled market places, and shops began to line the streets of the towns and cities. Cities became great commercial emporia, and more and more of the upper classes began to reside permanently in the urban centers rather than in the countryside. Wholesale firms and retail guilds developed.

As Chinese foreign trade grew, large communities of foreign merchants settled inside China. In 758, for instance, the Arab and Persian merchants at Canton took over that city, and in 760 thousands of foreigners were massacred in riots in Yangchow, a great commercial city near the Yangtze River. In 879, according to official figures, which are probably somewhat exaggerated, 120,000 foreigners were killed in Canton.

The growth of commerce, particularly inside China, required a more efficient money system. The production of copper cash increased markedly, and the government came to depend more and more on payment in cash rather than in goods. Chinese copper cash became an important medium of exchange in Japan and other countries in East Asia, and the export of cash together with the growth of internal commerce created a severe shortage of money. Consequently, as early as 811 the T'ang government was using paper money in the form of drafts for payment of goods purchased in distant regions. Private banking firms developed and issued deposit certificates that began to circulate as currency, and by 1024 the government itself started issuing paper currency. Unfortunately, monetary theory did not develop as rapidly as paper

currency, and the government constantly diminished the value of its currency by issuing new notes whenever it needed funds.

The Chinese commercial revolution strongly resembled the commercial revolution that was to take place several centuries later in Europe, but it did not change Chinese society as drastically as it was to change Europe. The European commercial revolution took place outside and apart from feudal society, since European feudalism was too rigid to accommodate commercial growth or to develop the new institutions that commerce required. In China, on the other hand, commerce grew and developed new institutions within the framework of a highly organized bureaucratic empire that could accommodate new institutions and new commercial activity, even benefiting financially from them, without challenging the basic social structure.

Other far-reaching social changes accompanied the commercial revolution but were not caused by it. The bureaucracy, recruited more and more by examination and from the Yangtze valley, began to replace the northern aristocracy as the main support of dynastic power. This professionalization of government service was an important factor in the early modernization of Chinese society. The power of the aristocracy and great landholders was further weakened by a change in the tax system that emphasized commercial tax revenues and permitted the appearance of small- and medium-sized landholdings. Landlordism

These richly detailed genre paintings, "Street Scenes in Times of Peace," date from the thirteenth century. In the first scene scribes and artisans work under umbrellas in a busy market, while an apothecary vends powders made from various bones and dried plants. At the far left a peasant (distinguished from a well-to-do merchant by his short shirt) gnaws a bone, while a dog begs for the remains. In the second scene two men are forcibly being prevented from fighting with one another. In the center, below the fighters, a father and mother have just located a lost son. The third scene depicts carpenters at work—sawing, hammering, planing, and measuring.

was still a problem, as is indicated by the fact that in the Northern Sung half the population was tenant farmers, but the new "gentry" class that emerged to full power by the Southern Sung eclipsed the northern aristocracy. Although still based largely on landownership, the gentry class exerted its power and influence through the government bureaucracy, which drew most of its members from this class.

City life. The Southern Sung capital of Hangchow is a good illustration of the development of urban institutions in early modern China. The city and its environs had a population of well over one million and was visited by many foreigners, including Marco Polo during the Mongol dynasty which followed the Sung. Marco Polo was so impressed with Hangchow that he said it was "the most noble city and the best that is in the world."[21] Its development required not only long years of growth but the sophisticated planning and administrative techniques which were characteristic of China's early modern period.

Since building land was in short supply, the city built up instead of out, and buildings with five to ten stories were not unknown. To alleviate overcrowding, the government built public housing projects for its employees and tried to institute a kind of rent control. Since fires were a constant problem, a network of observation towers was built, and fire-fighting crews were organized. The government took great care in keeping the lake reservoir and streets clean to avoid the outbreak of epidemics in the greatly overcrowded city.

Hangchow's large population and the vast number of visitors who came on business or for pleasure led to the development of a lively entertainment industry. Hotels, restaurants, tea houses, and brothels were established everywhere. On holidays and festivals the people flocked to the public parks and gardens outside the city walls and along the lake.

The concentration of wealth in the cities led to luxurious living for the upper classes, who lavished funds on their homes, on art, and even in the support of charitable institutions. Attracted by this wealth, impoverished peasants swelled the city's population further. Among the poor, however, life was often desperate, and the government established a dispensary with seventy branches to distribute cheap medicine to the populace, hospitals for the sick, homes for the aged and the poor, orphanages, funds for free funerals, and public cemeteries for the poor.

THE BARBARIAN CHALLENGE TO CIVILIZATION

China and the "barbarians." At the end of the twelfth century, with China split between the rule of the Chin and the Southern Sung, East Asian civilization faced a new threat from the north, greater than any in its previous history. By this time a recognizable pattern had emerged in China's relations with the nomadic and seminomadic peoples who surrounded her from the northeast to the southwest. Dynastic weakness encouraged "barbarian" invasions. The "barbarians" usually obtained the aid and advice of Chinese administrators and military specialists, and they had superior military power based on the cavalry of the Central Asian steppe and the stirrup, which enabled an archer to shoot from the back of his horse without falling off. The stirrup was the thirteenth-century equivalent of today's atomic bomb.

Recognizing that nomadic institutions would not work in ruling a village-dwelling people, the "barbarians" usually adopted Chinese government institutions and frequently employed the conquered Chinese in administration and tax collection. They also often employed other foreigners in their administration, feeling they could be trusted more than the Chinese.

All "barbarian" dynasties faced two great problems in their relationship with the Chinese. First, they sought to maintain their own identity by keeping their original homeland separate and by preserving their own language and customs. Always a small minority, they constantly faced the problem of losing their "barbarian" vigor by adopting the sedentary and "cultured" ways of the Chinese. Second, they had to control their new territories and alien population by military means. This meant stationing their forces at strategic locations throughout the country and defending major urban centers and economic regions from other "barbarians" and from internal revolt. Their resources were often not sufficient to accomplish this.

Genghis Khan and the Mongol onslaught. Up to the middle of the twelfth century the Mongol peoples had no national organization or identity but lived in scattered tribes and groups spread over large areas. Although some were hunters and fishermen, the majority lived as pure nomads, depending on animals instead of land for all their needs. The skin for their tents, the food for their table, and the wine for their pleasure all came from herds of horses, cattle, and sheep; the horse provided mounted transportation, and cattle pulled their carts. Because of the sparse rainfall, the nomads moved their animals seasonally in order to find the best grass. The "barbarian" nomads were never wholly independent from the sedentary civilizations like the Chinese, because they could not themselves produce the grains,

This silk painting of barbarian royalty worshiping Buddha gives some indication of the extent of Chinese interaction with the outside world during the T'ang and Sung periods. Notice the many different kinds of dress and facial expression among the foreigners and the quality of caricature in their depiction, as compared with the portrayal of the serene and very Chinese Buddha with his disciples and guardians.

metal goods, and luxury items they needed or desired. These they customarily obtained by trade or raid.

At the time of Genghis Khan's birth Mongol society was organized hierarchically. Families were united with their kin into clans which, in turn, formed tribes. Warfare over pasture lands and blood feuds were endemic, but no one leader had yet emerged to unite the Mongols as a whole. Genghis was born about 1162 into an impoverished aristocratic family. Legend has it that at birth he had a blood clot grasped in his hand, which symbolized his future power and greatness, so he was given the personal name Temüjin, or "man of iron." During his youth his father was killed in a blood feud, and Genghis and his mother were forced to hide from enemies. Brought up in a spirit of revenge, he slowly built up a personal following and overpowered his own overlord and other clans and tribes. At last, at a great meeting of the Mongol tribes on the Kerulen River in 1206, he was recognized as the ruler of all the Mongols and given the title by which he is known to history, Genghis Khan, which probably meant "ocean ruler" or "universal ruler."

Steadfast to his friends but ruthless toward his enemies, Genghis was a complex personality. One of his maxims was:

A man's greatest pleasure is to defeat his enemies, to drive them before him, to take from them that which they possess, to see those whom they cherish in tears, to ride their horses, to hold their wives and daughters in his arms.[22]

At the same time, Mongol historians described him as a visionary. He is supposed to have instructed his sons:

Be brotherly to one another and live in friendliness . . . making the whole great people walk on the road of the true state and of the law for the sake of attaining honor and glory.[23]

He was also one of the greatest organizational geniuses of all time. Out of a population of a little over a million Mongols, he fashioned a war machine based on units of ten and trained in the most sophisticated cavalry techniques. With this machine he and his people conquered most of the known world from the Pacific to the Danube and the Mediterranean, terrorized the rest, and established a *Pax Tatarica* in eastern Europe, the Middle East, Central Asia, and the Far East that permitted the greatest development of travel and trade between the continents that the world was to witness before the seventeenth century.

Leading his magnificent army, composed entirely of mounted horsemen who used the bow with deadly accuracy, Genghis campaigned against the Chin empire. In 1215 the Chin capital near Peking was sacked and its inhabitants massacred. Following this victory, the attack on the Chin slowed down because Genghis sent much of his army on a campaign through Central Asia and on into Russia (see Reference Map 7). But the conquest of northern China was later renewed, and city after city was subdued. The Great Khan himself was killed, probably by assassination, in 1227. A Mongol legend claims that he will return one day to lead the Mongols to world conquest once more.

Genghis' death did not slow down the Mongol war machine. By 1234 the last remnants of the Chin empire were extinguished by his son, who then embarked on the slow process of conquering the Sung in the south. After years of heroic resistance the Chinese were completely vanquished by the new Mongol dynasty, the Yüan, which was the first "barbarian" dynasty in history to rule all China. But, although China was now incorporated into an empire that stretched across the world, it did not lose its separate identity.

On the death of Genghis, portions of the empire had been administered by his sons and grandsons under the general leadership of one son elected as khan of all the Mongols. After 1260 the unity of an empire divided into a suzerain khanate and four vassal khanates was becoming a fiction, and Mongol China was a distinct state. The unity of the empire weakened after Kublai Khan, who from 1260 to 1294 held the suzerain khanate comprising China and Mongolia, moved his capital to Peking, which he rebuilt and beautified. Kublai fought a war with his own brother because of the move to China. His brother claimed

This medieval illumination of Marco Polo on an expedition in the Orient emphasizes the West's lack of knowledge of the East. The fanciful elephants look like a hybrid of a rhinoceros and a pachyderm, and the scenery and people are European rather than Asian in appearance.

that the Mongols could keep the empire together only if they retained their individual personality and "barbarian" vigor by keeping the center of the administration in their ancient homeland. Kublai, claiming that the Mongols had to learn from the superior civilization of the Chinese, won the battle, but his descendants lost the unity of the empire.

China under the Mongols. One of Genghis Khan's chief advisors, Yeh-lü Ch'u-ts'ai, born of a completely Sinified barbarian family, advised Genghis that "The empire has been conquered on horseback, but it cannot be governed on horseback."[24] As chief minister of the Mongol conquests in China, he is credited with preventing Genghis from turning all North China into one vast pasture land. Instead, he taught the khans the art of governing the sedentary Chinese and the advantages of maintaining a stable society in China from which the Mongols might obtain great benefits through taxation.

While separating themselves from the Chinese by custom and law, the Mongols adopted most of the T'ang and Sung administrative institutions and even instituted an examination system to recruit bureaucrats. They favored the North Chinese over the southerners because the latter, who had long resisted Mongol domination, were considered untrustworthy. For this same reason the Yüan employed many foreigners in high positions, including Marco Polo. They set up a hierarchical system of classes in which they themselves were at the top and the Southern Chinese, the most numerous group, were at the very bottom.

The arts flourished during this "barbarian" dynasty, particularly two new literary forms. The drama, which was probably influenced by Central Asian dance performances and which had become popular at the T'ang court, was popular during the Mongol period. What we now know as the "Chinese opera," a combination of singing, dancing, and acting accompanied by music, achieved its classical development during the Yüan. Growing out of the prompting books used by professional storytellers, the novel also developed rapidly under the Mongols. The earliest novel surviving to the present days, *The Romance of the Three Kingdoms,* is a long, involved, rambling romance laid in the third century. In its present form it evidently dates back to the fourteenth century.

The reign of Kublai Khan. For knowledge of Kublai Khan's reign, we are indebted to the famous Venetian traveler Marco Polo, author of probably the world's outstanding travelogue and what has been called the finest European account of Chinese civilization at this time. As a youth, Marco Polo accompanied his father and uncle, two Venetian merchants, eastward to Kublai Khan's court, arriving there around 1275. Received with honor and given posts in the imperial service, the Polos remained seventeen years in China.

In the following passage Marco Polo describes the impressive postal and courier system that Kublai Khan established:

. . . upon every great high road, at the distance of twenty-five or thirty miles . . . there are stations, with houses of accommodation for travelers . . . . At each station four hundred good horses are kept in constant readiness, in order that all messengers going and coming upon the business of the Grand Khan, and all ambassadors, may have relays, and leaving their jaded horses, be supplied with fresh ones . . . . In his dominions no fewer than two hundred thousand horses are thus employed in the department of the post, and ten thousand buildings . . . are kept up. It is indeed so wonderful a system, and so effective in its operation, as it is scarcely possible to describe.[25]

Marco Polo reported that the Great Khan maintained order throughout his dominions, improved the roads, constructed canals, revised the calendar, built granaries to store food surpluses against times of scarcity, and aided the sick, orphans, and old scholars by means of state care.

After Marco Polo returned to Italy, he wrote of his travels. But his fellow Venetians were so incredulous of the figures he used in describing the wealth and power of China, whose civilization was superior to that of thirteenth-century Europe, that they dubbed him "Messer Millions." His descriptions of the size and magnificence of Peking and of Hangchow with its "twelve thousand stone bridges," its palace, which he called "the greatest in the world, ten miles in compass," its "delectable gardens," and its women, who were "mostly dainty and angelical creatures," they considered pure fable. His account of black stones (coal) used for heating purposes and the people's habit of taking frequent baths also seemed fabulous to them, since coal was unknown in medieval Europe and Europeans in the Middle Ages seldom, if ever, took baths.

Pax Tatarica: relinking of East and West. In the first centuries of the Christian era the West had been linked with India and China by the spice and silk trades. The subsequent centuries of mutual isolation were broken during the T'ang dynasty when its court attracted such diverse groups as Muslims, Christians, and Persians. With the advent of the nomadic Mongols, East and West were again linked together along the ancient silk routes. The resumption of this trade had permanent consequences. By making the trade routes across Asia safe and by tolerating diverse religions, the Mongol dynasty attracted European traders and missionaries to China.

At the height of its power, the Mongol empire stretched from the Danube to the Pacific Ocean (see Reference Map 7). With the unification, however temporary, of almost all Asia and the restoration of roads, communication was restored to the point where the Polos were far from being the only travelers to cross the great spaces separating East and West. One monk, from a Christian community in Peking, traveled in the thirteenth century as an envoy of Mongol Persia to the pope and also met the kings of England and France. The papacy sent various missions to the Far East in the same century, with the result that in the early fourteenth century a Roman Catholic community with an archbishop and several thousand persons existed in China.

Cultural interchange between China and the West was also considerable during medieval times. One authority believes that the Mongols and other Central Asian peoples conveyed gunpowder to Europe, and we know that the Muslims transmitted westward such invaluable Chinese inventions as the arts of papermaking and printing and the magnetic compass. China itself was enriched by its imports. One of the most important was a new food, sorghum, which was brought to China by way of India in the thirteenth century. By that time the abacus, a familiar sight in Far Eastern shops today, had also made its appearance. Ceramics and bronzes were affected by influences from civilizations to the west, especially Persia, while the cloisonné technique was undoubtedly borrowed from the Byzantines.

These are but random examples of a cultural interchange which certainly enriched East and West alike. Yet the profound psychological effect created in Europe by the accounts of Marco Polo and other travelers was perhaps even more far-reaching in the evolution of world history. Travelers' accounts had revealed that the Far East not only equaled but exceeded Europe in population, wealth, and luxury. Europeans now realized that the Mediterranean was neither the central nor the most important area of the world. They began to develop new attitudes to fit this knowledge.

Decline of Mongol China. Actually, the prosperous appearances which Marco Polo described were largely deceptive. Kublai

Khan's ambitious foreign wars and domestic works necessitated heavy government spending. Tax rates rose, and many peasants were dispossessed of their land and forced to work for greedy landowners of vast estates. Large issues of paper money depreciated in value, while hard currency diminished. Kublai Khan's projected invasion of Japan was a disastrous failure (see p. 306).

Kublai Khan was succeeded by seven other Yüan emperors, all of whom proved to be inadequate rulers. Printing of paper money became so reckless that it had to be discontinued entirely; the Mongols allowed their armed strength to lapse until they could not even defend the coast against pirates; and the exclusion of Chinese from the imperial administration continued to fan the resentment of the people against the rule of foreigners. Although Kublai Khan had enacted legislation to safeguard the dominant position of the Mongols, who constituted only a minority of the population of his Chinese-Mongol state, legislation failed to prevent the resurgence of the native Chinese.

By 1368, less than a century after Kublai's final conquest of the Sung, the forces of Chinese popular rebellion, skillfully led by a one-time peasant and ex-Buddhist novice, had surged from South China to take Peking and exterminate or expel the Mongols and most foreigners associated with them. Thus was founded the Ming dynasty, which ruled until 1644 and successfully restored pre-Mongol ways within China.

Elsewhere in the Chinese cultural sphere in East Asia, as Mongol power disappeared new nativist regimes arose that usually accepted Chinese hegemony on the old tribute basis. This was true especially in Korea and Vietnam.

The nomad challenge of the Mongols was thus rebuffed in East Asia, but its scourge was longer felt elsewhere. Remnants of West Asian Mongols, converted to Islam, were part of continuing steppe-world invasions into India. Older Muslim centers in Mesopotamia never fully recovered. That segment of Mongols who had settled as overlords in southern Russia continued for more than two centuries to affect and condition Russian development.

THE EVOLUTION OF JAPAN

The geography of Japan. In the mountainous Japanese archipelago of over three thousand islands, only four are relatively large. On the principal island, Honshu, are located the historic capital of Kyoto and Tokyo, the modern capital. North of Honshu is Hokkaido and to the south are Shikoku and Kyushu (see map).

The oceanic sides of Kyushu and Honshu receive abundant rain and are warmed by the Japan Current (the Pacific's analog to the Gulf Stream); here have been the centers of Japanese life, past and present. Since more than three fourths of the land is forested and mountainous (including several active volcanoes), communication often is difficult among the many separate regions. Earthquakes, typhoons, and tidal waves are frequent catastrophes; yet the Japanese in all ages have expressed love for their native land and a sensitive appreciation of its scenic beauties.

Japan's distance from the major centers of older continental cultures has meant that while there have been crucial periods of close cultural borrowing (usually based on Japanese initiative), there have also been long periods of relatively isolated development. Japanese culture has been notably homogeneous, partly because in historic times there were no notable additions of new peoples—nothing equivalent to the British Isles' successive experience of Romans, Angles, Saxons, Danes, and Normans.

Origins of the Japanese people. In prehistoric times there must have been many strands of migration, particularly from Northeast Asia and the Asian mainland by way of Korea and from Southeast Asia and its adjacent islands by way of the island chain to the south of the Japanese home islands. No precise theories concerning the origins of the Japanese people are possible, but the evidence points to a mixed origin, even including some Polynesian strains. In time there developed a common ethnic community—predominantly Mongoloid, though darker and hairier than Mongoloid types on the Asian mainland—with a single basic language belonging to the same Altaic family as Korean. Remnants of another people, the Ainu, who resemble Caucasians in many physical features, still survive in a kind of "reservation life" on the northern island of Hokkaido. Their ancestors once lived on all the main islands but were driven northward, killed, or absorbed by the Japanese.

Early Japanese society. After a long early food-gathering cultural stage, agriculture (particularly wet-rice cultivation) appeared; shortly afterward came knowledge of both bronze and iron. These developments contributed to the consolidation of primitive clan groups into larger tribal units under hereditary chieftains, who claimed authority by descent from tribal deities. Archaeological and historical evidence indicates that there was a pronounced sense of hierarchy in this early Japanese society, with a prominent, if not dominant, role for the armored warrior on horseback, equipped with bow and sword.

Among many such groups, the people living on a small, fertile interior plain called Yamato, with easy access to the Inland Sea, coalesced into the strongest of these tribal states; their chief, claiming descent from the sun goddess, rose to paramountcy and ultimately gave rise to the historic Japanese state. The Yamato state conquered and maintained some authority all the way from the Kanto Plain, where today's Tokyo is located, to South Korea, but it was not a centralized state ruling over a society divided into distinctive classes, as was often the case in China. On the contrary, Japanese society was a highly complex system of social groups based variously on territory, descent, occupation, or a combination of these factors. Each group was apparently hereditary and had its own chief. By the fifth century A.D. the system had become exceedingly complex, and often the leaders of various clans or other groups overshadowed the imperial family in importance. The latter survived as the source of social and political legitimacy, but the emperors did not necessarily exercise real power (as was often to be the case throughout Japanese history).

The Yamato court successfully incorporated artisans, farmers, and scribes who had fled in small immigrant groups from disorders on the continent, especially from a triangular struggle among three petty kingdoms in Korea. Each of these Korean states had recently accepted forms of Buddhism from China, and some of them sought help from doughty Japanese warriors by sending intriguing examples of continental manufactures. In the mid-sixth century Buddhist statues and scriptures—recommended as a kind of superior magic—were also sent to Japan. This practice provoked sharp factionalism in the Yamato court between those hereditarily involved with the decaying clan society and its religious rituals, who wanted to have the foreign gods expelled, and, on the other hand, a group that saw value in both the material splendor and the intellectual values that might come from closer contact with the mainland. The latter group, which won out in the first part of the seventh century, sent formal missions to the warring Korean states and directly to the capital of the newly regenerated Chinese empire under the Sui. The earliest of these missions included carefully chosen young men who were to remain in the Sui capital in order to learn as much of the great world of China and its ways as possible. Shotoku Taishi, the prince regent of the Yamato court, became a devout Buddhist and an accomplished scholar in Chinese and by his personal prestige did much to foster the increasingly rapid adoption of Chinese ways and ideas.

The Taika reform: emulation of China. Within a few years of Prince Shotoku's death, however, a revival of clan struggles threatened the court. By a carefully planned coup d'état, a small group of able young men, aided by scholars who had returned from China, destroyed their competitors. In the name of the Yamato ruler they carried out drastic reforms based on the model of the strongly centralized T'ang state. During this Taika period—the "great change" period—the reformers attempted to establish and

assert the absolute authority of the Yamato ruler more effectively than the clan tradition alone allowed. Henceforth the ruler was given the new title, Tenno (Heaven sovereign). They sought to create a centralized bureaucracy, which would stretch from the court to the provincial administrative units set up to replace the old tribal territories, and to assign land and tax people directly.

It was a huge undertaking for a small, underdeveloped country, and from the first the Japanese made important adjustments in the model, necessitated by the great differences between Japanese and Chinese societies. For instance, most bureaucratic positions in the central and provincial governments quickly became hereditary, and recruitment through an examination system such as existed in China never developed in Japan, where membership in the aristocracy by birth was the major prerequisite for advancement. These modifications became increasingly important in later years and marked the borrowed institutions with a distinctive Japanese character.

The Yamato emperor had traditionally been the chief priest of the various animistic cults that made up the traditional religion of the Japanese people, Shinto, "the way of the gods." Under the new state created by the Taika reforms, the emperor retained this role, and a special government office was created to oversee the ancient religious ceremonies. Although they borrowed extensively from T'ang China, the Japanese did not accept the universal pretensions of the Chinese emperor, and Japanese missions were sent to China "from the Son of Heaven where the Sun rises to the Son of Heaven where the Sun sets," not as from a petitioning tributary to a suzerain power (though the Chinese court so interpreted them).

A new kind of court aristocracy and officialdom, nominally owing its position to imperial appointment or kinship with the imperial family, was in fact filled by persons from the old clan nobility and quickly became hereditary. Furthermore, the newly asserted power to tax all land and man power directly, based on Chinese practice, could not be carried out effectively, especially at any distance from the court itself. One reason for this was that the new class could be paid most easily, and the building of Buddhist temples could be subsidized most simply, by assigning them tax-exempt land holdings and manorial estates. Like court offices, these holdings quickly tended to become hereditary.

All these modifications reflected the persistence of old pre-Taika hierarchic traits. But the reforms had a great impact on Japanese society, not the least being the construction of a suitable capital where the new ways could flourish. Nara, the first such capital, built in the eighth century, was carefully planned as a miniature version of the Chinese city of Ch'ang-an, with broad streets laid out perpendicular to each other, imposing new palaces and mansions for the court and its retainers and officials, and many Buddhist temples and monasteries in and around the city. Scholars, priests, and artisans from the Asian mainland were welcomed there, because of their skills in technology, music, and the arts; and they found ready apprentices among the Japanese. Many examples of this culture survive in Nara to this day, though most of their continental prototypes have long since disappeared. One example is T'ang court music, perfectly preserved in the Japanese imperial court to this day, though it long ago disappeared in China.

The Heian period: Japanese innovations. At the end of the eighth century the capital was moved twice, finally to Heian-kyo, the city now called Kyoto. Here the emperor's court remained for more than a thousand years, until the 1860's. During its first three and a half centuries, usually called the Heian period, a curious kind of dualism developed that, in various ways, permanently marked Japanese culture.

At the center of government the sacred emperor went through his round of ritual and ceremonial duties, some Shinto, some Buddhist; but in secular matters of government he became a mere figurehead. The whole elaborate structure of governmental office continued to exist on paper and in name; but actual political and economic authority was gradually monopolized by the chief *kuge* (court nobility) family, the Fuji-wara (whose founding ancestor had conspired with an imperial prince to bring about the Taika coup d'état). Fujiwara ladies became consorts to emperors, and only their sons were deemed eligible for succession to the throne. Emperors were encouraged to abdicate as soon as such eligible sons could perform the ceremonial duties, often while they were still children. As maternal uncles or grandfathers of the boy sovereigns, Fujiwara nobles managed affairs as regents and continued to do so when the emperor matured. Thus a kind of unofficial but hereditary civil dictatorship wielded real power without setting aside the formal government.

Kyoto flourished uniquely as a cultural center. Private revenues from provincial estates supported a luxurious courtly life for a few at the capital, where alone there could be a proper dedication to Chinese literature, poetry, and history. But while men were expected to be skilled in this foreign written language, the gossip and intrigue of court life were conducted in Japanese. Early in the Heian period a purely phonetic system of writing was devised (with certain Chinese characters simplified to represent syllables of sound, not words or meanings). Fujiwara and imperial courtiers—and especially court ladies—used this script and the Japanese language for charming poems, love letters, and diaries. The finest example of this sophisticated classic Japanese literature is undoubtedly *The Tale of Genji,* a long novel by Lady Murasaki, who depicted this narrow courtly life with psychological and aesthetic sensitivity. There was also a spate of writing in the Chinese language and in all Chinese literary forms by Japanese scholars and courtiers, often not far inferior to mainland models.

Provincial developments: rise of the bushi. Japan was experiencing much growth and development as new lands came under cultivation in provinces distant from the capital. In frontierlike conditions, especially in eastern Japan, hardy provincials were winning some of Japan's ultimately richest farming land in wars with the aboriginal Ainu and with each other, and a new kind of society was coming into being to which Kyoto paid little attention. The civilian courtiers of Kyoto disdained actually going to distant provinces where they might hold governorships or private estates. Instead, such arduous and rustic life was left to deputies or stewards and bailiffs. Younger sons who could not expect to succeed to court office, men of the military families (the *buke* in contrast with the *kuge*) who ranked low in the court scale and had only ceremonial duty in Kyoto—these were thought particularly suitable for such demeaning provincial posts.

In the provinces, thus, there arose a local leadership group, of *buke* origin and usually called *bushi* (military men). For them, skill in the martial arts and in management of manorial estates was all important. Recurrent local wars, settled by their own skill and prowess with little reference to Kyoto, confirmed their need to build regional groupings of such men owing personal allegiance to one another in defense of common interests. They cultivated an outlook and a way of life quite at variance with the Kyoto style; but they were by no means the "country bumpkins" that courtiers might think them. Increasingly they, too, could command the services of artists, lawyers, and Buddhist prelates from the capital; and they were quite aware of the growing effeteness of the Kyoto system. Here, then, was the origin of the feudal military nobility that came to be predominant in Japanese affairs for the next seven centuries.

Origins of the shogunate. The day of opportunity for this provincial *bushi* class began when, in 1156, intriguing court factions in Kyoto, supporting rival claimants to succession in both imperial and Fujiwara houses, called up their military "retainers" from the country. When these disputes were settled by violence, the *bushi* leader of the winning group, Taira Kiyomori (1118-1181), decided that since real power was in his own hands, he would stay in Kyoto to enjoy it. By 1160 he had shattered the *bushi* coalition of the other side, sparing only Minamoto Yoritomo (1147-1199), the thirteen-year-old son of his chief opponent, and a handful of others. In Kyoto he simply used the old Fujiwara device of marrying his daughter to an imperial prince and raising his grandson

to the imperial throne. It was his turn, then, to control the entire system from behind the scenes. Not unnaturally he provoked acute resentment among all the old court groups, including the Buddhist monasteries.

By 1180 secret plotting had built a sound system of alliances among *bushi* in the east under the leadership of Yoritomo. Then, in five years of battles from one end of the country to the other, Yoritomo's forces totally destroyed Taira power. He did this less by leading his knightly warriors in the field than by concentrating on overall strategy from his own headquarters (or *bakufu*) at Kamakura in the east and closely controlling his lieutenants and vassals. The blood and thunder of this twelfth-century struggle between Taira and Minamoto have since provided Japanese with the stuff of history, romance, drama, and moralizing example, from the evolution of a kind of chivalric code of the warrior class, to the plots and characters of present-day movies, television series, and historical fiction.

The Kamakura shogunate. Once again, as in the seventh century and as later in the nineteenth, a highly conservative leadership gave new direction and form to Japanese life, preserving much of the old as a façade behind which new institutions held real sway. Yoritomo simply followed the Fujiwara pattern. To the fearful and hesitant court he paid outward respect and asked only that it grant him the ancient office of *shogun* (generalissimo) to use as he chose and the right to collect a tax even from tax-exempt estates to defray the costs of maintaining the peace.

Yoritomo used these powers to bring Japan under the control of his headquarters at Kamakura. Here all warriors swore personal loyalty to the shogun and received estates or stewardships and constableships that gave them rights to the produce of the land for the support of themselves and their own retainers. In addition to fiscal and political administrative functions, the government at Kamakura dispensed justice to petitioners who came to it from all over Japan. Strictly speaking, it was not a military dictatorship of the entire country but the Minamotos' clan government. Nevertheless, through its

This Japanese Buddhist temple guardian figure illustrates both the unusual nature of Japanese Buddhism and the more salient aspects of Kamakura sculpture. Kamakura sculpture, influenced by contemporaneous Chinese Sung art, abounded in vivid realism.

military and economic power it was able to control most of the country. The relatively powerless civil and religious center of Kyoto was undisturbed in either its imperial or its Fujiwara institutions, but actual power lay with the bakufu, or shogunate, the hereditary military government at Kamakura.

It mattered little that after the deaths of Yoritomo's sons there were no heirs to fill the shogunal office. Fujiwara and even imperial princes were brought out from Kyoto to fill this post, which quickly became a figurehead office like the Tenno's throne and the Fujiwara civil dictatorship. The system had evolved from the needs of the *bushi* as a whole and worked best through committees of chief vassals. Yet the hereditary principle continued to be invoked. The Hojo family in successive generations till 1333 monopolized a regency for the shogunate and maintained themselves and the system by sober, even-handed administration and justice.

Cultural changes. The Kamakura period witnessed changes in popular religious movements; renewal and then rupture of contacts with China; and the initial expressions of *bushido,* the emergent warrior's code.

The twelfth-century wars and disruptions contributed to a mood of anxiety, reminding clerics and courtiers that Buddhism's chief Law centered not on monastic discipline and learning, nor an ornate and aesthetically appealing ritual, but on the transcience of all things—even the Law itself. New Buddhist sects, many imported from China and emphasizing that faith alone could bring salvation, used the vernacular and street-corner preaching and singing and had wide response from commoner and high-born alike. Called the Amidist or Pure Land sects because they asked only for devout belief in a heavenly "Pure Land" after this life, where presided the Bodhisattva Amida, they denied the necessity for celibate monastic life. They remain the largest Buddhist groups in Japan to this day.

Renewed contacts with Sung China were largely unofficial, through traders and travelers from monastic centers. They resulted in new forms in architecture, painting, and literature, and in the introduction of tea into Japan. Many of these contacts involved the newly organized Zen (in Chinese, Ch'an) sects of Buddhism. As a religious system Zen discarded not only emphasis on ritual and learning, as did the Pure Land sects, but also the too-simple piety and devotionalism of the savioristic sects. Zen taught rigorous individual discipline and concentration, utter self-control and self-reliance as the only way to attain enlightenment. Enlightenment, according to Zen, is wholly personal. Such a creed appealed to the warrior, was supported at Kamakura, and was reflected in histories and popular tales about the rise of the *bushi.*

Breakdown of the Kamakura system. This first shogunate provided some unified control of the *bushi* through the underlying principle of personal loyalty of vassal to lord. The general tendency of such feudal-isms to disintegrate was fostered in Japan by the Mongol invasions attempted in 1274 and 1281, the only such external attacks the Japanese experienced until World War II. Both failed, partly because the Hojo ordered defense preparations on a large scale, but mainly because the ill-timed naval expe-ditions were shattered each time by foul weather along the Japanese coast. The second expedition was destroyed by a typhoon called in Japanese history the *kamikaze,* or divine wind, a name that in World War II was applied to Japanese suicide pilots. From such victories there were no spoils by which Kamakura could reward vassals who had stood in readiness for more than a decade. Moreover, the original *bushi* tradition of the shogunate had become diluted by Kyoto court effeteness. The Kamakura shoguns originally came from Kyoto, where their representatives often adopted the style of the court's life. As loyalty to the shogunate weakened, Kyoto intrigue heightened dis-affection.

The Ashikaga shogunate. By the 1330's an ambitious emperor, anxious to end the entire shogunal system, briefly won over one of the Hojo's chief generals, Ashikaga Takauji. In 1333 Kamakura, the seat of sho-gunate power, was destroyed.

When the emperor sent Ashikaga Takauji to quell the rebellion of a dissatisfied military group, the general placed himself at the head of the rebels, turned against his emperor, and after deposing him became virtual dic-tator of the central government. Thus, by a second act of treachery, Takauji in 1338 became the founder of a new shogunate, with headquarters at the imperial city of Kyoto. Known as the Ashikaga shogunate, the rule of this family lasted for some two hundred years. Seldom, however, did its authority extend far from its headquarters in Kyoto, where a curious cultural fusion of *kuge* and *bushi* ways occurred. Elsewhere in Japan, military men fought each other, creating large regional baronies that were virtually independent kingdoms. By 1500 Japanese society was almost completely feudalized in a fashion comparable to western Europe during the same period.

SUMMARY

At the very time when Europe was beset by the tribulations following the collapse of the Graeco-Roman world, Asia was being enriched by what were probably its most splendid centuries of cultural development. The first of these centuries saw the emergence of a golden age in India. With the Guptas, the zenith of Hindu culture was reached. Artists produced paintings of contemporary life and sculpture characterized by dignity and re-straint; the Gupta poet Kalidasa wrote dra-mas which have been compared favorably with those of Shakespeare. The art and poetry created in the Deccan and Tamil Land gave evidence of the artistic genius of southern India. In mathematics, the so-called Arabic numerals, the decimal system, and many of the basic elements of algebra came into use; and there were important discoveries in chemistry and medicine. So powerful was Gupta civilization that it diffused to many parts of Asia, thereby raising the cultural level of a large segment of mankind.

The Gupta age was followed in India by a period of internal dissolution and ex-ternal invasion, culminating in the subju-gation of the country by the forces of an uncompromisingly antagonistic religious culture, Islam. The consequences of that impact—which will be taken up more fully in Chapter 19—were in our own century to split the Indian subcontinent into two sep-arate states: India and Pakistan. But despite the political disunity and seeming chaos that marked Indian public life, the cultural amalgam we call Hinduism was an enduring and unifying phenomenon throughout the entire subcontinent.

China's outstanding achievement was the successful re-creation of a unitary cen-tralized state on classical lines that had no analogy in India or the West. Barbarians and their ways, such as Buddhism, were do-mesticated in the T'ang period, which also saw a rich flowering of poetry, painting, and sculpture, and the invention of printing.

The Sung period, despite its weakness in dealing with barbarian states, brought to perfection the bureaucratic civil service system, saw Buddhism lose ground to a secular Neo-Confucian philosophy among the upper classes, and refined many traditional arts and crafts, especially painting and ceramics. The invention of explosive powder for warfare, the magnetic compass, and paper money testify to the range of Chinese creative ability.

The short period of Mongol rule in China, through briefly uniting China with the West by trade routes, confirmed the growing Chinese tendency to be contemptuous of foreign ways and to accept despotic rule. Economic disorders and popular rebellion ended the Mongols' regime in China sooner than in other parts of their far-flung empire. The subsequent Ming dynasty, founded by a successful peasant rebel, strongly reasserted traditional claims to unique political and cultural superiority for the "Middle Kingdom."

Japan was brought within the world of civilized communities by impulses radiating from the T'ang. The Japanese blended continental forms of government, social organization, religion, and the arts with their own native traits. They preferred patterns of hereditary aristocratic privilege to the social mobility found in China. Embracing Buddhism, they also retained their native Shintoism in both public life and popular cult. While China was perfecting its centralized civilian administrative system, Japan was increasingly divided by the controls and ideals of an hereditary feudal military nobility.

Historical Critique

CHINESE AND INDIAN HISTORIOGRAPHY
by James T. C. Liu
and Ainslie T. Embree

James T. C. Liu, educated mainly in pre-World War II China, is Professor of History and Oriental Studies at Princeton University. His works include *Reform in Sung China* (1959), *Ou-yang Hsiu: An Eleventh-century Neo-Confucianist* (1967), and *Change in Sung China, Innovation or Renovation* (1968) which he coedited with Peter J. Golas. Ainslie T. Embree is the author of *Charles Grant and British Rule in India* (1962) and the editor of *The Hindu Tradition* (1966). He has spent ten years teaching in India and is currently Associate Professor of Indian History at Columbia University.

Compared to the European tradition of historical writing, in which there is a considerable time gap from its Greek and Roman origins to the Renaissance, Asian historiography, like Asian civilization as a whole, has had a more continuous development. But Indian and Chinese historical writing, while offering a sharp contrast to the western tradition, also differ markedly from each other. The Chinese produced the most voluminous body of written records among all ancient societies; while India, to all appearances, had no historical chronicles until the Muslim histories in the thirteenth century A.D.

Two major characteristics of Chinese historiography distinguish it clearly from both European and Indian historical writing. The first is an essentially linear concept of time, reflecting the Chinese self-conscious awareness of their homogeneous, long, and continuous civilization. The second is an overriding humanism.

How did the Chinese develop such a strong emphasis on history? The first records were kept by diviners and ritualists in the classic period (the millennium before imperial unification under the Ch'in). When the practice of noting secular matters in these archaic records gradually evolved, Chinese historiography was born. This process of secularization included an urge to establish what may be called in modern terms *group identity*. Aristocratic families, for example, kept genealogical records, and individual feudal states kept political chronicles; both conceived history

to be the record of human rather than divine activity, and both recognized its role in defining and preserving group character.

From these early beginnings, Chinese history became a more and more important part of the culture and philosophy that produced it. The Chinese cultivated this historical-mindedness even more assiduously after political unification. The Han dynasty (206 B.C.-222 A.D.) saw great progress in historical scholarship, chiefly made by Ssu-ma Ch'ien (see Chapter 6). His monumental work, *Shih chi* (sometimes translated as *Historical Memoirs*), covers the entire time span from antiquity to his own era and was for the Chinese their universal history. Integrating the information he gathered from written sources, oral legend, and his own travels, Ssu-ma Ch'ien established the technique of quoting earlier records whenever he considered them reliable and setting different accounts side by side whenever reliability was in doubt. His history presents an unfolding panorama of successive events, forming an unbroken thread linking past and present.

Since Ssu-ma is known as the "Chinese Herodotus," the essential differences between these two great historians are particularly revealing. While Herodotus was more informative on such concrete details as climates, soils, tides, rivers, architecture, and military logistics, Ssu-ma confined much of his attention to the imperial reigns, treating various government functions as separate topics and devoting individual chapters to the biographies of a few important men while grouping a large number of minor characters under various categories—such as imperial favorites, famous outlaws, poets, and many other classifications. For Herodotus, the emphasis was on man reacting to his environment, hopefully in the direction of the individual freedom and local autonomy found, most notably, in Athens. For Ssu-ma, the emphasis was on man's realization of his moral ideals through the improvement of the imperial rule and social well-being. In fact, one may characterize the entire body of Chinese historical writing as Confucian, human-centered, morally oriented, and institutionally weighted. This social concern (the second principal mark of Chinese history as a discipline) is illustrated by the fact that the most decisive role in the early development of history belonged to the rising philosophers. In their hands historical records took on a solemn ethical function: they were held as persuasive precedents in arguments, as a source of moral lessons, and as a standard for pronouncing lasting judgment of "praise and blame" on men. Later these records served as guidebooks for bureaucrats and elite elements in society.

History was further institutionalized during the T'ang period (618-907 A.D.). From this time on historical compilations were no longer left to individuals. Instead, a government agency called the History Office entrusted the writing of history to a corps of scholars, consisting of dozens of editors, and hundreds of copyists and clerks. Remarkably, the Chinese awareness of linear continuity manifested itself in this uninterrupted institution. Successive dynasties regarded it as their duty to produce with considerable fairness the history of preceding dynasties, while in turn leaving the definitive account of their own time to their successors (see p. 286). The scope and detail of these dynastic histories is suggested by the account of the Ming, which was begun in 1679, took fifty-three scholars some forty-six years to complete, and contained one hundred volumes. More than mere chronicles, these official histories contain treatises on law, economics, government administration, anthropological accounts of primitive tribes, and records of astronomical and other scientific phenomena, and each is accompanied by a variety of private works such as annotations, summaries, commentaries, interpretations, and the like. This enormous body of information is unrivaled in any civilization.

Following a few T'ang forerunners, the scholars of the Sung period (960-1279) pushed Chinese historiography to full maturity, developing critical methods, sophisticated techniques in writing, and a great variety of other genres quite apart from the dynastic histories. Unfortunately, the Sung growth in historiography was followed in later centuries by a rather rigid, unimaginative pedantry.

How accurate and objective were the traditional Chinese historians? They often suffered from blind conformity to convention, lack of independent verification, personal partiality, and sometimes outside pressure or fear of retaliation. These shortcomings, however, are much the common lot of historians in any land. On the whole, Chinese historiography had high professional standards and applied them with vigor. Although some modern critics have condemned the technique established by Ssu-ma Ch'ien as a primitive patchwork of paraphrased primary sources, the Chinese historians in their days thought they were reproducing authentic records faithfully. The neglect of ordinary peasant life has also been criticized, but Confucian scholars believed that in the final analysis it was the elite leadership that mattered.

Indian historiography presents a sharp contrast to that of China. Except for the *Rajatarangini* (a poetical chronicle of the history of Kashmir written during the thirteenth-century Muslim invasions) the Indian literary tradition is almost wholly lacking in the kinds of historical works in which Chinese culture is so rich. It is not very fruitful, however, to ask why India failed to produce such historical literature. The only general answer possible is that the needs of Indian civilization did not demand or foster this form of intellectual expression. Nor should the lack of historical narratives be taken as any indication that records were not kept, for like rulers everywhere, Indian kings sought to immortalize their greatness and to provide information for their administrative structures. But the ravages of climate and political change have prevented the preservation of royal archives, and all we have from Indian antiquity are inscriptions in stone and other durable materials. From these it has been possible to work out a rough chronology of Indian history from about 500 B.C. to 1200 A.D., when the Muslim histories begin, but there are many gaps. The normal method of transmitting the tradition was oral, not written; this worked well for the preservation of religious works, but dynastic chronicles were likely to disappear with a dynasty.

It should be emphasized that the intellectual classes in India were the guardians of the past, and in almost all periods the Brahmins were the intellectuals. They were profoundly interested in such questions as man's social role and kingship and the state as institutions; thus the assertion that their metaphysical concerns made them indifferent to the human situation is erroneous. But their concern must be seen in the context of the unquestioned assumptions of Indian society, and these are radically different from those of China or Greece.

Three such assumptions are especially relevant to the understanding of history in traditional Indian society. One is the concept of time, not as linear, but as moving in cycles without beginning or end, and including not just the terrestrial world but the whole cosmic universe of the gods. Within each cycle there is a movement of birth, growth, decay, and dissolution, but the cycles are endlessly renewed. These cycles, or *yugas*, are of varying length, but always, in normal human terms, of immense duration. The shortest one, the Kali-Yuga in which present human history is set, lasts for 432,000 years. Each cycle is characterized by increasing decline in virtue until its dissolution comes at the nadir of degradation, when the process is renewed. There are no unique events, no personalities that alter the process of devouring time; even the incarnations of great gods like Vishnu occur repeatedly. This concept of time, which makes life a process of eternal duration and repetition, has obvious implications for historiography, and the human story is placed in a perspective wholly different from that provided by Chinese or Greek conceptions. (Although some Greeks had a cyclical concept of time, its influence on the writers of history seems to have been minimal.)

Closely connected with the Indian understanding of time was the belief in rebirth, the most pervasive of all Indian ideas. Everything that has sentient life, including the divine order of beings, dies and is born again through *karma,* a working of cosmic law as impartial and as impersonal as the law of gravity. The Indian ideas of time and rebirth place men and gods in a continuum in which, strictly speaking, there is no dividing line between human and divine history.

A third assumption that colors Indian historical thinking is the elusive concept of *dharma,* perhaps best understood as duties and obligations which are imposed by life but which, when consciously accepted, define the good man. Through the working of *karma* men are born into the social order at a particular time and place, but virtue consists in their willingness to preserve this social order. Since society is part of the cosmic process, maintaining the social fabric is the ultimate concern of Indian social and political thought. The institutional expression of this concern is the system of caste and class that looms so large in Indian social history. In theory caste and class are parts of the eternal order, and their preservation represents the attempt to maintain man's harmonious place in the universe. Thus the concern with royal genealogy in Indian literature does not spring from a desire to show an exalted pedigree or links with a former dynasty but rather from a desire to legitimize a ruler, who was frequently either a usurper from a low caste or a foreigner. *Dharma* means, both in fact and theory, that society is stronger than the state. Two of the grand themes of western

history, the conflict between church and state and of the individual against society, are lacking in the Indian tradition. The individual and the state find their meaning in their recognition of the relation of the social order to the cosmos.

Given these assumptions it can be argued that traditional India did not lack a concern with history but that the understanding of what constituted the human story was vastly different from western—and Chinese—perceptions. The needs met in Greece and China by narrative historical works were filled in Indian culture by such literary productions as the *Mahabharata* and the *Puranas,* the class of literature referred to within the tradition as "history."

In summary, it is essential to recognize that the Indian concept of time is cyclical, whereas the Chinese concept is linear. That is, the Indian historian tends to perceive in human events a recurring pattern, whereas the Chinese historian has "straightened out" time to emphasize how one phenomenon *succeeds* another—an attitude that favors both classification and chronology in organizing temporal data. As regards the character and purpose of human society, the Indian saw man and his works integrated in a cosmic process. Consequently, societal relationships were always seen within a universal framework. The Chinese Confucians, however, emphasized the *social* order and correct relationships between the individual and his fellow beings. In effect, the Indian saw no fixed division between human and divine history, while the Confucian preferred to lower his sights and to depict the realization of virtue in human society.

SUGGESTED READINGS

For students interested in Chinese historiography, the following commentaries will be useful: W. G. Beasley and E. G. Pulleyblank, eds., *Historians of China and Japan,* Cambridge Univ. Press, 1961; or C. S. Gardner, *Chinese Traditional Historiography,* Harvard, 1961. Additional analysis of Indian historical writing may be found in C. H. Philips, ed., *Historians of India, Pakistan, and Ceylon,* Oxford, 1961; and a good brief summary is Robert Crane, *The History of India, Its Study and Interpretation,* Washington, D. C.: Service Center for Teachers of History, 1958.

Suggestions for Reading

POST-BIBLICAL JUDAISM AND CHRISTIANITY

J. A. Hexter, **The Judaeo-Christian Tradition,*** Harper & Row, 1966. Brief but highly valuable survey of the evolution of ancient Judaism and Christianity. Excellent on the late ancient history of the Jews are E. Bickermann, **From Ezra to the Last of the Maccabees: Foundations of Post-Biblical Judaism,*** Schocken, 1962; R. Herford, **The Pharisees,*** Beacon; C. Guignebert, **The Jewish World in the Time of Jesus,** Routledge & Kegan Paul, 1939.

Edmund Wilson, **The Scrolls from the Dead Sea,*** Meridian. The most readable introduction to a fascinating subject. More scholarly treatments are M. Burrows, **The Dead Sea Scrolls,** Viking, 1955, which includes extensive translations; R. K. Harrison, **The Dead Sea Scrolls: An Introduction,*** Torchbooks; A. P. Davies, **The Meaning of the Dead Sea Scrolls,*** Mentor; T. H. Gaster, **The Dead Sea Scriptures in English Translation,*** Anchor.

CHRISTIANITY

A vast number of books have been written about the origins and development of Christianity, and the works mentioned below represent only a few of the more important interpretations. The student should bear in mind that the author's viewpoint is bound to be affected by his own beliefs, whether positive or negative, Christian or non-Christian. Both T. R. Glover, **The Jesus of History,** Harper, 1916, and A. Edersheim, **The Life and Times of Jesus the Messiah,** 2 vols., Longmans, 1957, treat the life of Jesus and its implications from a conservative and devotional point of view. In **The Quest of the Historical Jesus,*** Macmillan, Albert Schweitzer describes various interpretations of Jesus' life and states his own eschatological point of view. Excellent on Jesus' teaching are M. Goguel, **The Life of Jesus,*** Torchbooks; R. Bultmann, **Jesus and the Word,*** Scribner; E. J. Goodspeed, **A Life of Jesus,*** Torchbooks.

H. Kee and F. Young, **Understanding the New Testament,** Prentice-Hall, 1957; R. Heard, **An Introduction to the New Testament,** Black, 1950. Valuable surveys. Current scholarship on the sources and writings of the New Testament is summarized in a brilliant introduction to primitive Christianity by M. Enslin, **Christian Beginnings,*** Torchbooks.

T. R. Glover, **The Conflict of Religions in the Early Roman Empire,*** Beacon; A. D. Nock, **Conversion: The Old and New in Religion from Alexander the Great to Augustine of Hippo,*** Oxford. Two classic studies.

E. R. Goodenough, **The Church in the Roman Empire,*** Holt (Berkshire Studies). A brief but excellent introduction. Important recent detailed histories of Christianity during its first two centuries are J. Klausner, **From Jesus to Paul,*** Beacon, by a Jewish scholar; H. Lietzmann, **A History of the Early Church,*** 2 vols., Meridian, the work of a great Protestant scholar; J. Lebreton and J. Zeiler, **A History of the Early Church,*** 2 vols., Collier, by two Roman Catholic experts. A. Alföldi, **The Conversion of Constantine and Pagan Rome,** Oxford, 1949, and A. H. M. Jones, **Constantine and the Conversion of Rome,*** Collier, are standard works on the subject.

On monasticism see C. Dawson, **Religion and the Rise of Western Culture,*** Image; H. B. Workman, **Evolution of the Monastic Ideal,*** Beacon.

E. Hatch, **The Influence of Greek Ideas on Christianity,*** Torchbooks. A scholarly account of early Christianity and its inheritance from the culture of ancient Greece. See also C. N. Cochrane, **Christianity and Classical Culture; A Study of Thought and Action from Augustus to Augustine,*** Galaxy.

A. D. Nock, **St. Paul,*** Torchbooks; and H. Marrou, **Augustine and His Influence,*** Torchbooks. Authoritative works on the great founders of Christian thought. See also the valuable survey by P. de Labriolle, **History and Literature of Christianity from Tertullian to Boethius,** Knopf, 1924.

ROME AND BYZANTIUM

F. Lot, **The End of the Ancient World and the Beginning of the Middle Ages,*** Torchbooks. An indispensable classic on this period of transition; attributes Rome's decline largely to economic causes. F. W. Walbank, **The Decline of the Roman Empire in the West,** Cobbett, 1953, is a brief survey which emphasizes economic interpretations and "lessons for today." For brief, clear accounts of this confused period, see R. F. Arragon, **The Transition from the Ancient to the Medieval World,*** Holt (Berkshire Studies); and S. Katz, **The Decline of Rome and the Rise of Medieval Europe,*** Cornell. R. M. Haywood, **The Myth of Rome's Fall,*** Apollo, and D. Kagan, ed., **Decline and Fall of the Roman Empire: Why Did It Collapse?,*** Heath (Problems in European Civilization), are brief surveys of scholarly opinion on this subject.

E. Gibbon, **The History of the Decline and Fall of the Roman Empire,** 7 vols., ed. by J. B. Bury, Methuen, 1901-1938. Probably the most famous work on the ancient world; Professor A. H. M. Jones' words about Gibbon are, however, worth quoting: "The reader . . . should be forewarned against Gibbon's great weakness, which is not so much anti-Christian bias as a temperamental incapacity to understand religion: to Gibbon's eighteenth-century rationalism a religious man was either a fool or a knave." Paperback editions of the more renowned sections of Gibbon's work are available. A. H. M. Jones, **The Later Roman Empire,** 2 vols., Univ. of Okla., 1965, is a recent major work on the period from Marcus Aurelius to the seventh century A.D.

The Age of Diocletian: A Symposium,* Metropolitan Museum of Art, 1953. Six excellent short papers on the various aspects of an age which presents "so many striking parallels with our own times." J. C. Burckhardt, **The Age of Constantine the Great,*** Anchor, views Constantine as an astute politician.

J. B. Bury, **The Invasion of Europe by the Barbarians,** Macmillan, 1928. The best general work on the nature and effect of the Germanic invasions. See also H. S. B. Moss, **The Birth of the Middle Ages,*** Galaxy; E. A. Thompson, **A History of Attila and the Huns,** Oxford, 1948; T. Hodgkin, **Theodoric the Goth: The Barbarian Champion of Civilization,** Putnam, 1891.

W. Bryher, **The Roman Wall,*** Vintage. A novel which gives a vivid picture of the last days of the Roman empire in the West.

C. Diehl, **Byzantium: Greatness and Decline,*** Rutgers. An excellent brief survey. For greater detail see A. Vasiliev, **History of the Byzantine Empire, 324-1453,*** 2 vols., Univ. of Wis.; and G. Ostrogorsky, **History of the Byzantine State,** Rutgers, 1957.

*Indicates an inexpensive paperbound edition.

D. A. Miller, **The Byzantine Tradition,*** Harper & Row, 1966. A brief perceptive survey of Byzantine civilization, with valuable annotated bibliography. See also S. Runciman, **Byzantine Civilization,*** Meridian. More detailed is N. H. Baynes and H. S. B. Moss, eds., **Byzantium, an Introduction to East Roman Civilization,*** Oxford.

P. N. Ure, **Justinian and His Age,*** Penguin. A first-rate study. See also C. Diehl, **Byzantine Portraits,** Knopf, 1927, which contains a particularly vivid account of the empress Theodora; and G. Downey, **Constantinople in the Age of Justinian,** Univ. of Okla., 1960.

E. Benz, **The Eastern Orthodox Church,*** Anchor; T. Ware, **The Orthodox Church,*** Penguin. Two sensitive surveys. S. Runciman, **The Eastern Schism,** Oxford, 1955, disentangles the history of the schism between eastern and western Christianity from the legends that have surrounded it.

D. Talbot Rice, **Byzantine Art,*** Penguin, and **Art of the Byzantine Era,*** Praeger. Complete coverage of all aspects of Byzantine art. For superb color reproductions of Byzantine mosaics, see A. Grabar, **Byzantine Painting,** Skira, 1953. See also T. G. Jackson, **Byzantine and Romanesque Architecture,** 2 vols., Macmillan, 1933, the standard authority on the architecture of the early Middle Ages.

RUSSIA

F. Dvornik, **The Slavs in European History and Civilization,** Rutgers, 1962. This premier account emphasizes Byzantine influences. G. Vernadsky, **Kievan Russia,** Yale, 1948, is detailed and authoritative. M. Florinsky, **Russia: A History and an Interpretation,** Vol. 1, Macmillan, 1954, is excellent on early Russia. On Byzantine aspects of early Russian culture see G. Fedotov, **The Russian Religious Mind: Kievan Christianity, the Tenth to the Thirteenth Centuries,*** Torchbooks, and G. Lazareff, **Russian Icons,*** Mentor.

ISLAM

P. K. Hitti, **The Arabs: A Short History,*** Gateway. An abridgment of the leading scholarly general history of the Arabs. Also highly recommended are B. Lewis, **The Arabs in History,*** Torchbooks, and C. Brockelmann, **History of the Islamic Peoples,*** Capricorn.

T. Andrae, **Mohammed: The Man and His Faith,*** Torchbooks. A sound assessment. For an interpretation and translation of the Koran, see M. M. Pickthall, **The Meaning of the Glorious Koran,*** Mentor. H. A. R. Gibb, **Mohammedanism: An Historical Survey,*** Mentor, traces the rise of Islamic teachings and delineates clearly the various sects of Islam. See also A. Guillaume, **Islam,*** Penguin.

H. Pirenne, **Mohammed and Charlemagne,*** Meridian. Propounds the controversial thesis that the expansion of Islam, and not the Germanic invasions, brought about the economic disintegration of the western Roman world. See also A. Havighurst, **The Pirenne Thesis: Analysis, Criticism, Revision,*** Heath (Problems in European Civilization).

P. Coles, **The Ottoman Impact on Europe,*** Harcourt, Brace & World, 1968. A lucid, profusely illustrated survey of Ottoman history to the end of the seventeenth century. See also H. A. Gibbons, **The Foundations of the Ottoman Empire, 1300-1403,** Century, 1916; S. Runciman, **The Fall of Constantinople, 1453,** Cambridge, 1965.

R. A. Nicholson, **A Literary History of the Arabs,** Cambridge, 1930. Traces the growth of Arab thought and culture through its literature. See also G. E. von Grunebaum, **Medieval Islam: A Study in Cultural Orientation,*** Phoenix; M. Mahdi, **Ibn Khaldun's Philosophy of History,*** Phoenix; D. Talbot Rice, **Islamic Art,*** Praeger; T. Arnold and A. Guillaume, eds., **The Legacy of Islam,** Oxford, 1931.

THE FAR EAST

H. G. Q. Wales, **The Making of Greater India,** B. Quaritch, 1951. A stimulating discussion of the expansion of Indian culture into Southeast Asia from the second to the tenth centuries A.D.

Sir Percival Spear, **India: A Modern History,** Univ. of Mich., 1961. Contains one of the best introductory accounts of Gupta India and the coming of the Muslims. See B. G. Gokhale, **Samudra Gupta,** Asia, 1962, for a brief study of one of the outstanding characters of ancient India. R. C. Majumdar and A. D. Pusalker, eds., **The Classical Age,** Paragon, 1954, Vol. III of **The History and Culture of the Indian Peoples,** is the most comprehensive study of the Gupta period.

For the expansion of Hindu culture see D. G. E. Hall, **History of South-East Asia,** Macmillan, 1964.

For the Islamic impact on India the following are authoritative: K. S. Lal, **Twilight of the Sultanate,** Asia, 1963; S. M. Ikram, **Muslim Civilization in India,** ed. by A. T. Embree, Columbia, 1964; R. C. Majumdar and A. D. Pusalker, eds., **The Delhi Sultanate,** Paragon, 1960, Vol. VII of **The History and Culture of the Indian Peoples;** Sir Wolseley Haig, ed., **Cambridge History of India,** Vol. III, 1928.

Marco Polo, **The Travels of Marco Polo,*** Penguin, L. Olschki, **Marco Polo's Precursors,** Johns Hopkins, 1943. Delightful accounts of thirteenth- and fourteenth-century travelers across Asia. See also M. Collis, **Marco Polo,*** New Direction.

Three excellent biographical studies of leading personalities under the T'ang are C. P. Fitzgerald, **Son of Heaven: A Biography of Li Shih-min, Founder of the T'ang Dynasty,** Cambridge, 1933; by the same author, **The Empress Wu,** Cresset, 1956; A. Waley, **The Red Tripitaka, and Other Pieces,** Macmillan, 1952.

The lives and works of the two greatest T'ang poets are treated authoritatively in A. Waley, **The Poetry and Career of Li Po: 701-762 A.D.,** Macmillan, 1950; and W. Hung, **Tu Fu, China's Greatest Poet,** 2 vols., Harvard, 1952.

John Meskill, ed., **Wang An-Shih: Practical Reformer?** Heath, 1963. An introduction, through readings and discussion, to the greatest premodern Chinese social theorist after the classical age.

H. D. Martin, **The Rise of Genghis Khan and His Conquest of North China,** Johns Hopkins, 1950. Relates the life-and-death struggle of the Chinese with their less civilized neighbors to the north and west, the Mongols.

For surveys of Indian, Chinese, and Japanese history and cultural development which contain sections pertinent to Chapter 10 text material, see *List of Readings,* p. 656. Special studies of more limited scope are included here.

Part Four

The Panorama of Medieval Europe

■ In the previous unit we were given a picture of the high level of civilization in the Near and Far East during the period called the Middle Ages in the history of the West. Throughout most of this era the East outshone the West even as Constantinople and Bagdad clearly outdazzled in material magnificence and intellectual and artistic triumphs any capital in western Europe. In the Far East, Indian culture reached its zenith under the illustrious Guptas, while China experienced a golden age during the overlordship of the T'ang. In this unit we shall trace the political, economic, social, and cultural currents of medieval Europe.

Traditionally, the millennium between 500 and 1500 A.D. in western Europe is viewed as the Middle Ages, although this term is an arbitrary and artificial one. Certainly the men of the Middle Ages did not think of themselves as ignorant barbarians living in an intermediate stage between the death of one civilization and the birth of another. This conception arose from the veneration which Renaissance scholars gave to the culture of the classical period—an excessive emphasis which blinded them to the many original contributions of their immediate predecessors. Such a warped perspective has been set right largely through the researches of modern scholars, but the term *Middle Ages* is still applied to the period. Why is history cut into such arbitrary time divisions? Because, by dividing the historical time stream into periods, historians are able to organize the study of the past into more convenient categories. The Middle Ages constitutes one such category; the medieval period can be viewed as a bridge between classical antiquity and the culture of modern times.

But the Middle Ages was not static—far from it. After the inundation of the Roman empire by Germanic tribes brought disorder and fragmentation, Europe began a painful search for stability. Centuries of confusion followed until Charlemagne established a new "Roman" empire. This ambitious and laudable experiment was premature, however, and after its collapse a new system had to be created—one which would offer at least a minimum of security, political organization, and law enforcement. This was feudalism. Under this system, the landed nobility acted as police force, judiciary, and army. Accompanying feudalism was the manorial system—an economic order which provided food and life's necessities and divided men into two great classes: the fighters or nobles and the workers or serfs.

Crude as it was, feudalism served to mitigate the chaos which followed the fall of Charlemagne's empire. Yet feudalism and the manorial system were inherently rural and rigid, and by the eleventh century new forces were at work. Shadowy outlines of new kingdoms began to emerge. Europe went on the offensive, ejecting the Muslims from the southern part of the Continent, breaking Muslim control of the Mediterranean, and launching crusades to capture Jerusalem from the infidel. The "closed-house" economy of the feudal countryside gave way before the revival of trade and communications, the growth of towns, the increased use of money as a medium of exchange, and the rise of a new class in society —the bourgeoisie.

The greatest stabilizing force in Europe during the medieval period was the Church. The Middle Ages has sometimes been characterized as the Age of Faith; to an extent greater than in classical or modern times, the attention of men living in those days was directed toward a religious goal—the salvation of the soul—and the Church was the great arbiter of human destiny. With the authority that stemmed from its vital spiritual service, the Church provided the nearest approach to effective and centralized supervision of European life. All men were born, lived, and died under its protection. In the thirteenth century, when popes such as Innocent III bent proud monarchs to their will, the Church reached the zenith of its influence as a kind of international government as well as the focus of medieval society, arts, and scholarship. The Church was the chief patron of poets and artists; its monasteries were repositories for precious manuscripts; and it fostered a new institution of learning—the university.

During the fourteenth and fifteenth centuries, despite opposition from popes and nobles alike, vigorous monarchs in England, France, and Spain succeeded in their attempts at nation-making—a process that fostered and was in turn supported by a growing national consciousness among the common people. (In Germany and Italy, however, unification was hampered by many obstacles, and in eastern Europe nation-making proceeded slowly, though Russia emerged as a powerful state after throwing off the Mongol yoke.) Thus by the end of the fifteenth century, the medieval ideal of universal political unity had been shattered by the emergence of separate national monarchies.

15. (preceding page) **Chi Rho page from Book of Kells** (c. 800). With the final dissolution of the Roman empire, the pendulum of European civilization swung to the north, where the barbarian peoples were gradually converted to Christianity. Among the most zealous missionaries were the Irish monks of the seventh and eighth centuries, who sustained and nourished Christian culture in their own monasteries. Applying traditional Celtic and Germanic barbarian motifs to their illuminations of the Holy Writ, they helped create a dynamically restless abstract style, largely detached from physical reality, which remained an indelible part of much subsequent medieval art. **16.** (above) **The French town of Conques, with the Church of Ste. Foy** (eleventh century). By the eleventh century a wave of religious fervor swept across the Continent. Hosts of pilgrims traveled set routes to sacred sites, and along these routes towns sprang up. The towns erected churches, which were grander than ever before, and whose complex floor plans could more readily accommodate the traffic of the pil-

grims. Christianity began to belong to the masses, and the flowering of the Middle Ages grew increasingly evident in the stately towers and arches of the monumental Romanesque style. **17.** (right) **Interior, Bourges Cathedral** (thirteenth century). The Gothic Age was the culmination of the Middle Ages, and the cathedral was the concrete synthesis of Gothic ideals. More than a house of worship, it was a summation of medieval man's knowledge and faith, craft and art. Structurally, it was based on a more thorough ordering of mass, space, and lighting than anything from previous Christian periods. A highly refined understanding of weights and thrusts permitted the Gothic architect to raise his building to unprecedented heights, thus endowing it with an almost dematerialized spirituality. He was able, moreover, to open the walls dramatically to light, which filtered through stained glass windows with a similarly mystical effect. The result is one of the most compelling unities of form and feeling in all of architecture.

18. The Unicorn at the Fountain (late fifteenth century). This French or Flemish tapestry, from the series called "The Hunt of the Unicorn," is an example of the courtly aspect of late Gothic art. The scene is a wood where a group of gentlemen-hunters and their attendants have confronted the unicorn, a fabulous animal whose symbolic meaning varies in history but which is here represented as a gentle, kindly beast. The unicorn dips his magical horn into a stream, thus cleansing the water of the impurities left there by the creatures of the night.

Chapter 11

Europe's Search for Stability

Early Medieval Politics (500-900), Feudalism and the Manorial System

INTRODUCTION. We last surveyed the fortunes of Europe at a crucial turning point in western civilization (see Chapter 7). The mighty Roman empire in the West was breaking apart under the pressure of incoming Germanic tribes. With the collapse of the old order and the triumph of the barbarians, unity and stability gave way to fragmentation and disorder. The only hope for the survival of western civilization lay with the rapidly growing Christian Church, which, by providing a spiritual authority to which diverse peoples could give loyalty and obedience, assumed something of the unifying role once performed by the Roman Caesars.

What was the future of western Europe to be? What parts would the old Graeco-Roman culture, the crude but dynamic Germanic tribes, and the young Christian Church play in the drama which was to unfold?

The first indication of the new forms that life and politics would take in the West came from the Germanic Franks in alliance with the Church. In the single century from 714 to 814, covering the reigns of the Frankish rulers from Charles Martel to Charlemagne, the Carolingian House of the Franks gave Europe an interim of stability and progress. A great empire was fashioned, civilization and Christianity were extended to many of the barbarian tribes, and law and order were maintained.

This accomplishment of the Carolingians was premature, however. Charlemagne's empire could not endure, partly because it lacked the economic basis that had supported the Romans. By the ninth century Muslim conquests had cut off what remained of European trade in the Mediterranean; inland trade shriveled up and urban life almost disappeared. In addition, the empire had no strong administrative machinery to compensate for the weak Carolingian rulers who followed the dominating figure of Charlemagne on the throne; the empire disintegrated amid invasions and civil wars.

Out of the ruins of the Carolingian empire emerged a new technique of government known as feudalism. Based on local authority, feudalism was a poor and primitive substitute for a powerful, comprehensive central government; but it was better than no authority at all, and it survived for several hundred years. The manorial system of economy, rural and self-sufficient, was another stopgap institution, appropriate to its time but inadequate in terms of human progress.

The mixed heritage of western man was clearly evident in many medieval institutions. The necessary harshness of existence during these years made his practice under the code of chivalry far different from the chivalric ideal, but the existence of that code proved that he had inherited the spiritual ideals of Christianity. In spite of its low ebb, civilization survived and retained within itself elements which germinated a new blossoming of city life, commerce, and culture by the end of the eleventh century.

NEW EMPIRE IN THE WEST

The Franks under the Merovingians. In the blending of the Roman and Germanic peoples and cultures, the Franks played an especially significant part. The kingdom of the Franks was not only the most enduring of all the Germanic states established in the West, but it became, with the active support of the Church, the center of the new Europe that arose upon the ruins of the western Roman empire.

Before the Germanic invasions the several tribes that made up the Franks lived along the east bank of the Rhine close to the North Sea. Late in the fourth century the Franks began a slow movement south and west across the Rhine into Gaul. By 481, they had occupied the northern part of Gaul as far as the old Roman city of Paris, and in this year Clovis I of the Merovingian House became ruler of one of the petty Frankish kingdoms. By the time of his death in 511, Clovis had united the Franks into a single powerful

kingdom that stretched southward to the Pyrenees.

Clovis achieved his goal with the aid of an arsenal of weapons that included marriage alliances, treachery, assassination, and religion. As a first step, Clovis allied himself with other petty Frankish kings to dispose of Syagrius, a Roman general in central Gaul, who represented the last foothold of Roman authority anywhere in that land. The victor then turned against his Frankish allies and subdued them.

Largely through the influence of his wife, a Christian Burgundian princess named Clotilda, Clovis became converted to Christianity. The sixth-century Gallo-Roman bishop and historian Gregory of Tours, whose *History of the Franks* is the fullest account of any Germanic people, mentions that the actual conversion came about as a result of a battle at Strasbourg against the Alemanni, also a pagan Germanic tribe. On the eve of the conflict Clovis looked up to heaven and declared:

If thou wilt give me victory over my enemies and I prove that power which thy followers say they have proved concerning this, I will believe in this and will be baptized in thy name.[1]

Clovis won the battle and was baptized together with his whole army. He became the only orthodox Christian ruler in the West, for the other Germanic tribes were either pagan or embraced the heretical form of Christianity known as Arianism (see pp. 203-204, 379).

The conversion of the Franks must be considered a decisive event in European history. Ultimately it led to an alliance of the Franks and the papacy, and immediately it brought local support to Clovis. Clovis had little interest in dogma or religion; what was important to him was the political significance of his faith. Clovis' conversion to orthodox Christianity assured him the loyalty of the native Christian population, who still greatly outnumbered all the German conquerors in old Roman Gaul. This was a political advantage not open to the heretical Christian rulers in Gaul—the Arian Visigothic and Burgundian kings. Reasoning that the native population in the rest of Gaul would welcome deliverance from their Arian rulers, Clovis expanded his realm in the name of Christian orthodoxy.

Clovis' southern neighbors were the Visigoths, who ruled France south of the Loire River and all of Spain (see map, p. 215). In 507 Clovis attacked this kingdom, declaring:

Verily it grieves my soul that these Arians should hold a part of Gaul; with God's help let us go and conquer them and take their territories.[2]

In the great battle that followed, the Visigothic king was killed, and his people abandoned their capital at Toulouse and most of their Gallic territory, crossed the Pyrenees, and set up a new capital in Spain at Toledo. Content with his conquests, Clovis spent the last years of his reign at Paris, which he made his capital.

Decline of the Merovingians. For the space of two hundred years the history of

This thirteenth-century statue of Clovis originally stood on one side of a French monastery. The Merovingian ruler once granted a charter exempting the monks of the abbey from secular liabilities and duties.

western Europe is largely the narrative of the rise, expansion, and decline of the Frankish kingdom. After Clovis' death in 511, his sons and grandsons overthrew the Burgundian king and extended the Frankish domain to include all modern France, Belgium, and much of Germany. Missionaries followed sharp on the heels of the Frankish invaders, for Clovis' conversion meant that the one active disseminator and preserver of civilization—the Church—was able to use Frankish expansion for its own purpose.

At the same time, however, the Merovingian House began to decay from inner weaknesses. The pernicious practice of treating the kingdom as personal property and dividing it among all the sons of the king resulted in constant and bitter civil war. The royal heirs plotted murders and became adept at intrigue and treachery. No wonder the Frankish monarchy at this time has been defined as "despotism tempered with assassination."[3] The Merovingian princes also engaged in all manner of debaucheries, the least unpleasant of which was excessive drinking. Gregory of Tours gives a vivid picture of the later Merovingians:

The court of the Merovingians was a brothel. . . . Drunkenness seems to have been the usual condition of all. Women got their lovers to murder their husbands. Everybody could be purchased for gold.[4]

The Merovingian kings became incompetent weaklings, and many died young. The Frankish state broke up into three separate kingdoms; in each, power was concentrated in the hands of the chief official of the royal household, the mayor of the palace. Their royal masters were mere puppets, the *rois fainéants* ("do-nothing kings"). The mayor of the palace soon became the instrument of the nobility in keeping the king weak and ineffectual.

A dark age. By the middle of the seventh century western Europe had lost most of the essential characteristics of Roman civilization. The Roman system of administration and taxation had completely collapsed, and the dukes and counts who represented the Merovingian king received no salary and usually acted on their own initiative in commanding the fighting men and presiding over the courts in their districts. International commerce had ceased except for a small-scale trade in luxury items carried on by adventurous Greek, Syrian, and Arab traders, and the old Roman cities served mainly to house the local bishop and his retinue. The virtual absence of a middle class meant that society was composed of the nobility, a fusion through intermarriage of aristocratic Gallo-Roman and German families who owned and exercised authority over vast estates, and, at the other end of the social scale, the semiservile *coloni,* who were bound to the land. These serfs included large numbers of formerly free German farmers. Only about 10 per cent of the peasant population of France maintained a free status.

The conditions of life in the seventh century have been summarized recently by a medieval historian:

KINGDOM OF CLOVIS I

NORTH SEA

Elbe R.

Cologne
Tournai
Rhine R.
Seine R.
Paris
Strasbourg
Danube R.
Loire R.
Tours
Bordeaux
Garonne R.
Rhone R.
ALPS
Po R.
Toulouse
PYRENEES
MEDITERRANEAN SEA

Urban life had almost entirely disappeared, and all leadership had passed to a very small group of royal princes and great aristocrats. These men were mainly interested in building up the wealth and power of their own families. Most of their life was spent in warfare, they were ignorant of the arts of government, they were blind to the ideals of justice and peace . . . Christianity for them was a system of magic, miracles, and hagiography. . . . the collapse of the western Roman empire was a political, economic, and cultural disaster of the greatest magnitude.[5]

More invaders. At the time of Merovingian decay, new waves of invaders threatened Europe. A great movement of Slavic people from the area that is now Russia had begun about 500 A.D. The original home of the Slavs is only vaguely suggested in ancient legend, but it seems that it was in the Pripet Marshes of western Russia (see map, p. 245). From this nucleus the Slavs fanned out in all directions, filling the vacuum left by the Germanic tribes when they pushed into the Roman empire. By 650 the western Slavs had established the Elbe River as their frontier. Many of them fell under the sway of the Avars, fierce Asiatic nomads like their forerunners the Huns, who invaded Europe in the latter half of the sixth century and penetrated to the region of the middle Danube. Impelled by the Avars, the Slavs raided German territory across the Elbe.

Another danger threatened western Europe from the south. In the late seventh century the Muslim Arabs, following their easy triumphs in Syria and Egypt, swept across North Africa and prepared to invade Spain.

Charles Martel and the rise of the Carolingians. During these perilous times of decaying Merovingian rule, those mayors of the palace who belonged to the Carolingian family defeated their rival Frankish mayors and seized control. A new period dawned with the accession to power of Charles Martel as mayor in 714. The Frankish realm was then in a critical condition. Charles beat down the rebellious nobles, restored unity among the often divided Franks, strengthened the eastern frontier against the inroads of the Slavs, and ruled the kingdom in all but name. For the time

being, however, the Merovingian kings were kept as harmless figureheads at the court.

Charles' greatest achievement was his victory over the Muslim invaders of Europe, which earned him the surname Martel, "The Hammer." We recall that when the Roman empire crumbled under the barbarian invasions in the fifth century, Visigothic tribes migrated to Spain and settled there, although they never succeeded in establishing a government supported by the entire population. While Roman Spain had been prosperous and highly civilized, economic life declined under the Visigoths, and their kings became progressively weaker. Such a state of affairs was an open invitation to conquest, and the Muslims took advantage of it. From North Africa an army of Moors invaded Spain in 711, and by 718 the weak kingdom of the Visigoths had collapsed. Only a few isolated Christian communities in the northern mountains survived the conquest. With the peninsula under control, the Muslims looked across the Pyrenees for new lands to conquer.

After a number of sorties in which various Frankish cities were raided, the Muslim host moved deep into the Frankish kingdom. In 732 Charles Martel met the Muslims near Tours. The Muslim losses were heavy, their commander was killed, and during the night the invaders deserted their tents and retreated toward Spain.

A major military reform coincided with the battle of Tours. For some time before this conflict, the effectiveness of mounted soldiers had been growing, aided by the introduction of the stirrup, which gave the mounted warrior a firm seat while wielding his weapons. To counteract the effectiveness of the quick-striking Muslim cavalry, Charles, like his immediate predecessors, needed a force of professional mounted soldiers. In order to support them, Charles distributed to each knight sufficient land to enable him to maintain himself, his equipment, and a number of war horses. This reform helped to encourage the growth of feudalism as a military system.

Historians once regarded Tours as one of the decisive battles in world history. The eighteenth-century historian Edward Gibbon, for example, saw the whole future of western Europe in the balance, with the possibility of mosques in London and Paris and the Koran substituted for the Bible. In reality, however, the battle of Tours meant little. The invaders had then advanced a thousand miles from the Strait of Gibraltar; by the time they reached Tours their strength had been spent. Although the Muslims continued their raids until their main base on the French coast was captured, they never again crossed the Pyrenees in force. The followers of Muhammad, however, retained their grip on Spain and continued to expand their influence in the Mediterranean.

Pepin the Short. Charles Martel's son, Pepin the Short, was a worthy successor to his father. Ruling from 741 to 768, he continued to strengthen the Frankish state. To legalize the regal power already being exercised by the mayors of the palace, he requested and received from the pope a ruling which stipulated that whoever had the actual power should be the legal ruler. In this maneuvering, St. Boniface (p. 379) was the intermediator, and in the winter of 751-752 Pepin was elected king by the Franks and crowned by St. Boniface. The last Merovingian was quietly shelved in a secluded monastery. A few years later, in 754, Pope Stephen reaffirmed St. Boniface's sanctioning of the usurpation by personally anointing Pepin as king.

Behind the pope's action lay his need for an ally in the face of threats to his independence. In this century Italy was a jumble of rival political units. On the northeast coast was the exarchate of Ravenna, the seat of Byzantine government in Italy. The Byzantine empire also controlled the island of Sicily and the heel and toe of the long Italian peninsula. The pope actually ruled the duchy of Rome even though he technically owed allegiance to the emperor at Constantinople. The remaining area in the peninsula was controlled by the Lombards. These Germanic people had two important duchies in the south and a vigorous, promising kingdom in the north, including much of the fertile Po valley. The Lombards gave promise of uniting all Italy under their rule, and in 751, after conquering the exarchate of Ravenna,

they demanded tribute from the pope. At this critical moment, Pope Stephen could not appeal to the eastern emperor for assistance, for the Byzantine ruler could not spare the resources for a campaign in Italy, and the iconoclastic controversy (see p. 236) had alienated the papacy from the eastern branch of the Church.

Pope Stephen's recognition of Pepin as king of the Franks placed the new ruler under obligation to the papacy. Following the coronation, the pope secured Pepin's promise of armed intervention in Italy and his pledge to give the papacy the exarchate of Ravenna, once it was conquered. In 756 a Frankish army forced the Lombard king to relinquish his conquests and pay an indemnity, and Pepin officially conferred the exarchate of Ravenna upon the pope. Known as the "Donation of Pepin," the gift made the pope a temporal ruler over the Papal States, a strip of territory that extended diagonally from coast to coast, cutting the peninsula in two (see map, p. 347).

The alliance between the Franks and the papacy, foreshadowed by the conversion of Clovis in 496 and thoroughly sealed by Pepin, not only influenced the direction of medieval history but also affected the course of politics and of religion for centuries. This alliance accelerated the separation of Latin from Greek Christendom by providing the papacy with a dependable western ally in place of the Byzantines; it created the Papal States which played a major role in Italian politics until the late nineteenth century; and, by providing western kingship with a religious sanction, it contributed to the rise of monarchs strong enough to pose a threat to the papacy.

Charlemagne's conquests. In 768 Pepin's son, Charlemagne (Charles the Great), inherited the Frankish kingdom. Under this ruler, the Frankish state and the Carolingian House reached the summit of their power. Einhard, a biographer of Charlemagne and a member of his court, pictured his king as a natural leader of men. Charlemagne was tall, physically strong, and a great horseman who was always in the van of the hunt. Although he was preëminently a successful warrior-king, leading his armies on

EUROPE WEST OF THE ODER

SHETLAND IS.

ORKNEY IS.

HEBRIDES

NORTH
SEA

GRAMPIAN MTS.

Edinburgh

BRITISH   ISLES

IRISH
CENTRAL
PLAIN

IRISH
SEA

PENNINE RANGE

Dublin

St. George's Channel

London
Thames R.

English   Channel

ATLANTIC

OCEAN

BRITTANY
PEN.

ARMORICAN
MASSIF

Seine R.
Paris
PARIS BASIN

Loire R.

BAY OF
BISCAY

MASSIF
CENTRAL

BASIN
OF
AQUITAINE

Garonne R.

PYRENEES

Ebro R.

CANTABRIAN   MTS.

Douro R.

SPANISH

SIERRA de
GUADARRAMA

Madrid

PLATEAU

Tagus R.

SIERRA de
GUADALUPE

Lisbon

Guadiana R.

SIERRA   MORENA

Guadalquivir R.

SIERRA   NEVADA

SIERRA

Str. of Gibralter

RIF   ATLAS

Christiania
(Oslo)

Stockholm

HIIUMAA

SCANDINAVIAN   PENINSULA

L. Vanern

SAAREMAA

GOTLAND

L. Vattern

BALTIC SEA

Skagerrak

Kattegat

ÖLAND

JUTLAND
PEN.

Copenhagen

NORTH GERMAN   PLAIN

Vistula R.

Zuider Zee

Amsterdam

Berlin

Weser R.

Oder R.

Elbe R.

SUDETEN   MTS.

Brussels

ARDENNES

Rhine R.

ORE
MTS.

BLACK FOREST

BOHEMIAN
FOREST

Moselle R.

Vienna

Danube R.

VOSGES

JURA MTS.

L. Constance

EAST ALPS

Bern

Drava R.

L. Geneva

Sava R.

DINARIC

CEVENNES

Rhône R.

WEST ALPS

Po R.

ALPS

APENNINES

ADRIATIC
SEA

Tiber R.

ITALIAN

CORSICA

Rome

PENINSULA

TYRRHENIAN
SEA

BALEARIC IS.

SARDINIA

MINORCA

MAJORCA

IBERIAN
PENINSULA

MEDITERRANEAN

SICILY

Tunis

Algiers
TELL   ATLAS

SEA

MALTA

TUNISIAN   ATLAS

yearly campaigns, he also sought to provide an effective administration for his realm. In addition, he had great respect for learning and was proud of the fact that he could read Latin.

In extending his territory by conquest and spreading Christian civilization by force when necessary, Charlemagne carried on the policies of the Merovingian king Clovis, but on a much grander scale. Taking advantage of feuds among the Muslims in Spain, he sought to extend Christendom southward into that land. In 778 Charlemagne and his army crossed the Pyrenees with indifferent success. As the Frankish army headed back north, it aroused the antagonism of the Christian Basques, who attacked its rear guard. In the melee, the Frankish leader, a gallant count named Roland, was killed. The memory of his heroism was later enshrined in the great medieval epic, the *Chanson de Roland* (*Song of Roland*). On later expeditions the Franks drove the Muslims back to the Ebro River and established a frontier area known as the Spanish March, or Mark, centered around Barcelona. French immigrants moved into the area, later called Catalonia, giving it a character distinguishable from the rest of Spain.

Charlemagne's greatest conquest was against the Saxons between the Rhine and the Elbe rivers. The Saxons were the last of the pagan, independent Germanic tribes, and it took thirty-two campaigns to conquer them. The Carolingians first beat down resistance and then established permanent garrisons. They divided the region into bishoprics and built monasteries and schools. Determined to destroy paganism, Charlemagne proclaimed harsh laws against any Saxon who refused to be baptized. Eating meat during Lent, cremating the dead (an old pagan practice), and pretending to be baptized were offenses punishable by death. The Church and its priests and monks were the main agents for pressing Charlemagne's rigorous program forward.

Like his father before him, Charlemagne intervened in Italian politics. Expansionist ambition drove the Lombard king to invade again the territories of the papacy. At the behest of the pope, Charlemagne defeated the Lombards in 774 and proclaimed himself their king. While in Italy, he cemented his father's alliance with the Church by celebrating Easter in Rome and by confirming the Donation of Pepin.

Saxony and northern Italy had been conquered, but the empire's eastern frontier was continually threatened by fierce tribes, the Avars and Slavs. In a series of six campaigns Charlemagne decimated the Avars and then set up his own military province in the valley of the Danube to guard against any possible future plundering by eastern nomads. Called the East Mark, this territory later became Austria.

Charlemagne's coronation in Rome. One of the most important single events in the momentous reign of Charlemagne took place on Christmas Day in the year 800. The previous year the unruly Roman nobility had revolted from the pope, charging him with moral laxity. Leo III rushed to the court of Charlemagne to seek assistance. After a conference with the Frankish king, the pope returned to Rome, followed by Charlemagne. The Frankish ruler examined the various charges brought against Leo and dismissed them as baseless, and the pope was restored to his office. At the Christmas service Charlemagne knelt before the altar at St. Peter's while the pope placed a crown on his head amid the cries of the assembled congregation: "To Charles Augustus crowned of God, great and pacific Emperor of the Romans, long life and victory!"[6]

This ceremony demonstrated that the memory of the Roman empire still survived as a vital tradition in Europe and that there was a strong desire to reëstablish political unity. Implicit also in this coronation was another great theme of medieval history, the struggle between the empire and the papacy. Charlemagne was crowned not only by, but presumably with the consent of, the pope. He was emperor by the grace of God, with heaven and its earthly agency, the Church, on his side. But it was not all gain for the ruler; the Church could claim its superiority over Charlemagne and other kings as well. "From this time on papal and imperial power stood side by side, each claiming supreme authority over all human affairs and relationships. The future was inevitably to witness a direct collision."[7]

Charlemagne's administration. The extent of Charlemagne's empire was impressive. His territories included all of the western area of the old Roman empire except Africa, Britain, southern Italy, and most of Spain. In the east the frontier stretched from the Baltic south to the Adriatic Sea, while in the west the line followed the coast from Denmark south to northern Spain (see map, p. 321). Seven defensive provinces, or marks, protected the empire against hostile neighbors.

The Carolingian territories were divided into some three hundred administrative divisions, each under a count (*graf*) or, in the marks along the border, a margrave (*mark graf*). In addition, there were local military officials, the dukes. In an effort to solve the problem of supervising the local officials, a problem that plagued all German rulers, Charlemagne issued an ordinance (capitulary) creating the *missi dominici,* the king's envoys. Pairs of these itinerant officials, usually a bishop and a lay noble, traveled throughout the realm to check on the local administration. To make the *missi* immune to bribes, they were chosen from men of high rank, were frequently transferred from one region to another, and no two of them were teamed for more than one year. The elaborate instructions laid down for the *missi* in this ordinance give us a clear picture of the emperor's philosophy and the objectives inspiring his government.

The most serene and most Christian lord emperor Charles has chosen from his nobles the wisest and most prudent men . . . and has sent them throughout his whole kingdom; through them he would have all the various classes of persons . . . live strictly in accordance with the law. . . .

And let the *missi* themselves make a diligent investigation whenever any man claims that an injustice has been done to him by any one. . . . And if there shall be anything of such a nature that they, together with the provincial counts, are not able of themselves to correct it and to do justice concerning it, they shall, without any reservations, refer this, together with their reports, to the judgment of the emperor. The

This picture of Charlemagne's coronation, from a fourteenth-century illuminated manuscript, reflects the Church's later view of this event. Earlier representations had shown Charlemagne and the pope as co-equals. In this picture, however, Charlemagne, kneeling at the pope's feet, seems to be little more than a vassal of the Church.

straight path of justice shall not be impeded by any one on account of flattery or gifts, or on account of any relationship, or from fear of the powerful.[8]

This ordinance illustrates notably how the Franks had taken over the Christian-Roman heritage. The wisest senators of old Rome would have applauded Charlemagne's concern for justice, and early Christians would have been amazed at a Germanic king who described himself in a letter to the pope as "the representative of God who has to protect and govern all the members of God."[9]

The Carolingian Renaissance. Charlemagne not only revived the Roman empire in the West, he also fostered a revival of learning and the arts. His efforts in this area were destined to be far more lasting than his restoration of the empire, and they have prompted historians to speak of this period as one of cultural rebirth.

In 789 Charlemagne decreed that every monastery must have a school for the education of boys in "singing, arithmetic, and grammar." As he stated in a letter to the abbot of Fulda, Charlemagne was greatly concerned over the illiteracy of the clergy:

ATLANTIC OCEAN

IRELAND

NORTHUMBRIA

WALES
MERCIA
EAST ANGLIA
WESSEX
ESSEX

CHARLEMAGNE'S EMPIRE

At His Accession, 768

At His Death, 814

Elbe R.

Magdeburg

Rhine

Aix-la-Chapelle (Aachen)

Fulda

Oder R.

0   200   400

Prague
Seine R.

Paris

Verdun

TRIBUTARY
SLAVIC
STATES

Loire R.

Tours

CAROLINGIAN

EMPIRE

St. Gall

Danube R.

EAST
MARCH

AVARS

Bordeaux

Rhone R.

Lyons

KINGDOM
OF
ASTURIAS

PYRENEES
SPANISH MARCH

Ebro R.

Po R.

KINGDOM

OF

Ravenna

PAPAL

KHANATE
OF
BULGARIA

Tagus R.

UMAYYAD
EMIRATE
OF
CORDOVA

Toledo

Barcelona

CORSICA

STATES

ITALY

Rome

DUCHY
OF
BENEVENTO

Constantinople

Cordova

SARDINIA

B Y Z A N T I N E   E M P I R E

Athens

M E D I T E R R A N E A N   S E A

SICILY

Carthage

Since in these years there were often sent to us from divers monasteries letters in which was set forth the zeal on our behalf in holy and pious prayers of the brethren dwelling there, we have observed in very many of the aforesaid writings of the same persons right sentiments and uncouth language, because that which pious devotion faithfully dictated inwardly, outwardly, owing to neglect of learning, the untutored tongue could not express without faultiness. Whence it came that we began to fear lest, as skill in writing was less, wisdom to understand the Sacred Scriptures might be far less than it ought rightly to be.[10]

At Aix-la-Chapelle, his capital, the emperor also sponsored a palace school for the education of the royal household and the stimulation of learning throughout the realm. Alcuin, an Anglo-Saxon scholar in charge of the school, began the arduous task of reviving learning by undertaking the first step of writing textbooks on grammar, spelling, rhetoric, and logic. "Ye lads," Alcuin exhorted his students, "whose age is fitted

for reading, learn! The years go by like running water. Waste not the teachable days in idleness!"[11]

The reform of handwriting and the preservation of classical manuscripts were significant achievements of the Carolingian revival. Encouraged by Charlemagne, copyists labored in monasteries to correct and copy the classics of pagan and Christian thought. The importance of this work is indicated by the fact that the oldest manuscripts of most of the Latin classics that have come down to us date from the age of Charlemagne. The corrupt and almost illegible script of the Merovingian period was replaced by a more legible style of writing, known as Carolingian minuscule, which employs small letters. (The Romans had used only capitals.) Alcuin made the monastery at Tours the center for diffusing the new writing. When, at the end of the Middle Ages, printing from movable type was introduced, this Carolingian minuscule became the foundation for the type face still used in present-day printing.

At Aix-la-Chapelle the Carolingian ruler also strove to recapture something of the grandeur of ancient Rome by building a stone palace church modeled after a sixth-century church in Ravenna. Its mosaics were probably the work of Byzantine artisans, and its marble columns were taken from ancient buildings in Rome and Ravenna. Thus the splendor of Aix was superficial: commerce—and with it flourishing urban life—had never revived sufficiently to permit the courts of western Europe to approach Roman imperial prosperity. Although trade and industry in northwestern Europe did show signs of revival during the Carolingian era—stimulated in part by the new silver coinage issued by Charlemagne, which was based upon the divisions of a pound of silver that are still used in England—the economy of Europe remained predominantly agrarian and rural. In fact, during much of his reign Charlemagne's court, like those of most early medieval rulers, was itinerant; with his retinue he moved about the land, remaining in one place only as long as the accumulated supplies of the particular district would support his followers.

Accomplishments of the Carolingians. In 814 Charlemagne died at Aix-la-Chapelle. This ruler, so remote in time from our own day, must be considered one of the great constructive statesmen of world history. He extended Christian civilization in Europe, set up barriers against incursions of the Slav and Avar, and created a new Europe whose center was in the north rather than on the Mediterranean and in which a measure of law and order was again enforced after three centuries of disorder. Furthermore, his patronage of learning left a cultural heritage that later generations would build upon.

Charlemagne's empire afforded no more than a breathing space, however, for its territories were too vast and its nobility too powerful to be held together under existing conditions after the dominating personality of its creator had passed from the scene. Charlemagne had no standing army; his foot soldiers were essentially the old Germanic war band summoned to fight by its war leader, and his mounted warriors served him, as they had Charles Martel, in return for grants of land. Nor did Charlemagne have a bureaucratic administrative machine comparable to that of Roman times. The Frankish economy was agricultural and localized, and there was no system of taxation adequate to maintain an effective and permanent administration.

The greatness of the Carolingian House was the achievement of three strong rulers—Charles Martel, Pepin the Short, and Charlemagne—during a single century. It took only one ruler and scarcely more than twenty-five years to undo the achievements of this great trio. The once mighty empire disintegrated amid the confusion of weak rulers, civil wars, and bloody feuds.

The division of the empire. Before Charlemagne's death he presided at the coronation of Louis the Pious, his surviving son. Louis the Pious subsequently partitioned his realm among his sons, and bitter rivalry broke out among the brothers and their father. In 840 Louis the Pious died, a well-meaning man who was loved by the clergy, ignored by the nobility, and mistreated by his sons.

After Louis' death, strife continued among the three surviving sons. Lothair, the elder, was opposed by the two younger—Louis the German and Charles the Bald. In 842 the younger brothers joined forces in the famous Strasbourg Oaths. The text of these oaths is significant in that one part was in an early form of French, the other in German. The first could be understood by Charles' followers, who lived mainly west of the Rhine; the other by Louis' followers, who lived east of the Rhine. These oaths are evidence that the Carolingian empire was splitting into two linguistic parts—East Frankland, the forerunner of Germany, and West Frankland, which ultimately became France.

In 843 the warring brothers called a halt to their fighting, came painfully to an agreement at Verdun, and split the Carolingian lands three ways. Charles the Bald obtained the western part and Louis the German the eastern; Lothair, who retained

NORTH SEA

THE DANELAW

ENGLISH KINGDOMS

ENGLISH CHANNEL

Aix-la-Chapelle (Aachen)

Paris

Verdun

WEST FRANKS

Loire

KINGDOM OF CHARLES

Strasbourg

EAST KINGDOM OF LOUIS FRANKS

Elbe

Vistula R.

TRIBUTARY

SLAVIC

Danube

STATES

KINGDOM OF LOTHAIR

Rhône

Rhine

UMAYYAD EMIRATE OF CORDOVA

Ebro

CORSICA

BYZANTINE EMPIRE

MEDITERRANEAN SEA

Charles the Fat, Charles the Simple, Louis the Child, and Louis the Sluggard. The last of the East Frankish rulers died in 911. In West Frankland the nobles, ignoring the eighteen-year-old Carolingian prince, chose Odo, the count of Paris, as king in 887.

The perspective of time enables us to see that the Carolingian empire was too grandiose and ambitious to last. Many of its inhabitants, particularly churchmen, looked back sentimentally to the traditions of the classical world, but the economic facts of a dominantly agricultural society made impossible the successful support of an imperial government.

The new invasions. During the ninth and tenth centuries the remnants of the Carolingian empire not only decayed from internal weakness but also were battered by new waves of invaders. Scandinavians attacked from the north, Muslims from the south, and a new wave of Asiatic nomads, the Magyars, struck from the east. Christian Europe had to fight for its life against these plundering and murdering raiders who did far more damage to life and property than the Germanic invaders of the fifth century.

From bases in North Africa, Muslim corsairs in full command of the sea plundered the coasts of Italy and France. In 827 they began the conquest of Byzantine Sicily, which they held until the eleventh century. Then they invaded southern Italy and harried coastal towns farther north; even the outskirts of Rome were pillaged. Along the Corniche coast in southern France, the Muslims erected forts from which swift raiding parties, like modern commando units, penetrated far inland to attack the caravans of merchants in the Alpine passes. What trade still existed between Byzantium and western Europe, except for that of Venice and one or two other Italian towns, was now almost totally cut off, and the great inland sea became a Muslim lake.

The most widespread and destructive raiders came from Scandinavia. During the ninth and tenth centuries Swedes, Danes, and Norwegians—collectively known as Vikings—stormed out of their remote forests and fiords. The reason for this expansion is not clear. Some historians stress overpopu-

the title of emperor, obtained an illogical middle kingdom which stretched a thousand miles from the North Sea to central Italy (see map).

The importance of the Treaty of Verdun is that it began the shaping of modern France and Germany and gave political recognition to the cultural and linguistic division shown in the Strasbourg Oaths. Lothair's middle kingdom soon collapsed into three major parts, Lorraine in the north and Burgundy and Italy in the south. Lorraine encompassed both Latin and Teutonic cultures, and although it was divided in 870 between Charles and Louis, the area was disputed for centuries. Lorraine remained one of the cockpits of Europe, a land drenched with the blood of countless French and German peoples.

After the Treaty of Verdun, the Carolingian rulers continued to decline. No strong leaders worthy of being called "Hammer" (Martel) or "Great" appeared; instead, we find kings with such revealing names as lation and a surplus of young men. Other scholars view these raiders as defeated war bands expelled from their homeland by the gradual emergence of strong royal power. Still others see a clue in the fact that the Vikings had developed seaworthy ships, long and narrow, capable of carrying a hundred men and powered by long oars or by sail when the wind was favorable. The ships had high prows usually carved in the form of some fearsome animal, often a dragon. Viking sailors also had developed expert sailing techniques; without benefit of the compass, they were able to navigate by means of the stars at night and the sun during the day.

The range of Viking expansion was amazing. The Vikings went as far as North America to the west, the Caspian Sea to the east, and the Mediterranean to the south. Few areas seemed immune from their lightning raids, which filled civilized Europeans with a fear that is reflected in a new prayer in the litany of the Church: "From the fury of the Northmen, O Lord deliver us."

Three main routes of Viking expansion can be identified. The outer path, which was followed principally by the Norwegians, swung westward to Ireland and the coast of Scotland. Between 800 and 850 Ireland was ravaged severely. Monasteries, the centers of the flourishing culture attained by the Irish Celts, were destroyed. By 875 the Norwegians were beginning to occupy remote Iceland, and it was here rather than in their homeland that the magnificent Norse sagas were preserved, little affected by either classical or Christian influences. During the tenth century the Icelandic Norsemen ventured on to Greenland and, later, to North America (see p. 609).

Another route, the eastern line, was followed chiefly by the Swedes, who went down the rivers of Russia as merchants and soldiers of fortune and, as has been described in Chapter 8, forged the nucleus of a Russian state.

The Danes took the middle passage, raiding England and the shores of Germany, France, and Spain. By the end of the eighth century the Danes had begun to raid England, and by the 870's they had oc-

cupied most of the country north of the Thames. Also in the middle of the ninth century their fury broke upon the Continent where their long boats sailed up the Rhine, Scheldt, Seine, and Loire. In particular the Danes devastated northwest France, destroying dozens of abbeys and towns. An eyewitness of these horrors declared:

The cities are depopulated, the monasteries ruined and burned, the country reduced to solitude. . . . As the first men lived without law or fear of God, abandoned to their passions, so now every man does what seems good in his own eyes, despising laws human and divine and the commands of the Church. The strong oppress the weak; the world is full of violence against the poor and of the plunder of ecclesiastical goods. . . . Men devour one another like the fishes in the sea.[12]

Unable to fend off the Viking attacks, the weak Carolingian king Charles the Simple arranged an epoch-making treaty with a Norse chieftain named Rollo in 911. This agreement recognized the Viking occupation of what became Normandy and Rollo as duke and vassal of the French king. Like

The people of Scandinavia first began to use sails during the Viking period. The huge, square-rigged sails, traditionally patterned with intersecting diagonals, were raised or furled by means of an intricate system of ropes. The Vikings in this stone carving, which dates from the tenth century, are under full sail and are ready for battle, dressed in pointed helmets, their round shields overlapping the side of the ship.

Viking settlers elsewhere, these Northmen, or Normans, soon adopted Christian civilization. By the eleventh century, as we shall see in the following chapter, Normandy was a powerful duchy, and the Viking spirit of the Normans was producing the most vigorous crusaders, conquerors, and administrators in Europe.

Europe in 900. Europe's response to the invasions of the ninth and tenth centuries was not uniform. In England by 900 Viking occupation initiated a strong national reaction which soon led to the creation of a united English kingdom. Similarly, Germany in 919 reacted to the Magyar danger by installing the first of a new and able line of kings who went on to create an empire and to become the most powerful European monarchs since Charlemagne. The response to the invasions in France, however, is a different story.

The Viking attacks on France had the effect of accelerating the trend toward political fragmentation that began under the Merovingians but was temporarily halted by the strong personal leadership provided by the Carolingians. But when Charlemagne's weak successors were unable to cope with the incessant Viking assaults, people increasingly surrendered both their lands and their persons to the many counts, dukes, and other local lords in return for protection.

In 847 Charles the Bald acknowledged his inability to protect his people by encouraging freemen to place themselves under the protection of lords. By this time, too, the king was forced to grant privileges of immunity to the great landowners, exempting them from the interference of royal officials. Domains in which the king could not intervene multiplied throughout the realm. The decline of trade further strengthened the aristocracy whose large estates, or manors, became economically self-sufficient. There was also the continuation of a trend already noted in connection with the military reforms of Charles Martel. The old Germanic levy of foot soldiers who provided their own arms when called to battle was dying out in favor of a professional force of heavily armed mounted knights, who received land

grants from the king in return for military service.

Out of all these elements—the disintegration of central power, the decrease in the class of freemen, the need for protection, the rise of a largely independent landed aristocracy, and the creation of the mounted knight—new patterns of society, feudalism and the manorial system, took shape. Reaching their height in France during the tenth and eleventh centuries, feudalism and manorialism were the culmination of earlier trends that had been accelerated by the Viking attacks.

FEUDALISM

Nature and origins of feudalism. Feudalism can be defined as a type of government in which political power is exercised locally by private individuals rather than by the agents of a centralized state. It is often a transitional stage which follows the collapse of a unified political system; it serves as a stopgap until conditions permit the emergence of a more effective centralized government. Feudalism has appeared in various areas and times in world history—in ancient Egypt and in modern Japan, for example—but the most famous of all feudal systems emerged in France following the collapse of Charlemagne's empire. Reaching its heyday there in the tenth and eleventh centuries, in time it spread elsewhere in Europe. The presence of strong rulers delayed its advent in Germany until the twelfth century. In 1066 the duke of Normandy, William the Conqueror, imposed feudalism on England, but in a highly centralized form which enhanced rather than weakened the power of the monarch.

The fully developed feudalism of western Europe was a fusion of three basic elements: (1) the personal element, called lordship or vassalage, by which one nobleman, the vassal, became the loyal follower of a stronger nobleman, the lord; (2) the property element, called the fief (usually land), which the vassal received from his lord in order to enable him to fulfill the obligations of vassalage; and (3) the governmental element, meaning the private exercise of governmental functions over vassals and fiefs. The roots of these three elements run back to late Roman and early Germanic times.

By the fifth century the ability of the Roman emperor to protect his subjects had disappeared, and citizens had to depend on the patronage system, by which a Roman noble organized a group of less fortunate citizens as a personal bodyguard and in return looked after their wants and interests. A similar arrangement existed among the Germanic tribes in the institution of *comitatus*. The German chiefs chose outstanding warriors as a personal retinue; the warriors swore to serve their chief loyally and in return were provided with food and military equipment. Vassalage, the personal element in feudalism, arose from the combination of patronage and *comitatus*.

The roots of the property element in feudalism, the fief, go back to Roman practices mainly. In the late Roman empire the owners of great estates (*latifundia*) were steadily adding to their already extensive holdings. Unable to manage their tracts, the nobles granted the temporary use of portions to other people in exchange for dues and services. Such land was called a *beneficium* or, when granted in answer to a humble man's prayerful request, a *precarium* ("prayer"). In late Merovingian times, when mounted warriors rather than old-style foot soldiers were needed to deal effectively with Muslim raiders from Spain, Charles Martel granted numerous benefices to compensate his mounted followers for this added expense. During the civil wars and foreign invasions of late Carolingian times, the competition among Charlemagne's successors for the available supply of mounted knights led not only to the wholesale granting of benefices but also to making the benefice hereditary. On the death of the vassal, the benefice now passed to his heir instead of reverting to the king. Hereditary benefices were commonly called fiefs.

The third basic element in feudalism, the exercise of governmental power by private individuals, also had antecedents in late Roman times. As the imperial government weakened, the powerful Roman landowners organized their own private armies to police their estates and fend off governmental agents, particularly tax collectors. The emperors also favored certain estates with grants of immunity from their authority, a practice which the Germanic kings often followed and which became the rule with Charlemagne's successors in their competitive efforts to fill their armies with mounted fief-holding vassals. And where immunity from the king's authority was not freely granted, it was often usurped.

With the coalescing of these three elements, feudalism can be said to have emerged as a definable—although highly complex and variable—governmental system in France by the end of the ninth century. To a greater or less degree the feudal system spread throughout most of western Europe, but our description of it applies particularly to the form it took in northern France.

It should always be kept in mind that feudalism was not a clear-cut, uniform system but varied from time to time and from place to place. As a famous scholar of medieval history has observed:

Any definition is either simple and wrong, or involved, approximately correct and unintelligible. . . . As the system in one form or another lasted from the ninth to the fourteenth centuries, as it changed materially during that time . . . what can be said about one place at one time may be wholly wrong about another place at another time.[13]

The feudal hierarchy. In theory feudalism was a vast hierarchy. At the top stood the king, and theoretically all the land in his kingdom belonged to him. He kept large areas for his personal use (royal or crown lands) and, in return for the military service of a specified number of mounted knights, invested the highest nobles—such as dukes and counts (in England, earls)—with the remainder. Those nobles holding lands directly from the king were called tenants-in-chief. They in turn, in order to obtain the services of the required number of mounted warriors (including themselves) owed to the king, parceled out large portions of their fiefs to lesser nobles. This process, called *subinfeudation,* was continued until, finally, the lowest in the scale of vassals was reached —the single knight whose fief was just sufficient to support one mounted warrior.

Subinfeudation became a problem when a conflict of loyalties arose. Since the Count of Champagne, for example, was vassal to nine different lords, on whose side would he fight should two of his lords go to war against one another? This dilemma was partially solved by the custom of liege homage. When a vassal received his first fief, he pledged liege homage to that lord. This meant that this obligation was to have top priority over services that he might later pledge to other lords.

Except for the knight with a single fief, a nobleman was usually both a vassal and a lord. Even a king might be a vassal; John of England was vassal to King Philip of France for certain French lands, yet he in no way thought himself inferior to Philip.

Relation of lord and vassal: the feudal contract. One of the principal elements of feudalism was a personal bond that was forged between a lord and a vassal. During the formative period of feudalism the vassal simply knelt before his lord, or suzerain, and promised to be his "man." But by the twelfth century this ceremony, the act of *homage,* took on all the solemnity which the Middle Ages could create. With the lord sitting and the man kneeling before him with head uncovered, the vassal placed both hands in those of the lord and said, "I become your man, to keep faith with you against all others." The lord then helped him to his feet, kissed him on the mouth, and promised to take him as his vassal. The latter then swore on the Bible or some other sacred object an oath of eternal fidelity to his lord, called the oath of fealty.

In the next part of the ceremony, known as *investiture,* the lord invested his new vassal with a fief, represented by a symbol. A lance, glove, stick, or even a bit of straw was handed the vassal to signify his jurisdiction (not ownership) over the fief.

The feudal contract thus entered into by lord and vassal was considered sacred and binding upon both parties. Breaking this tie of mutual obligations was considered a felony, because it was the basic agreement of feudalism and hence of early medieval society.

In the typical feudal contract the lord was obligated to protect the life, honor, family, and property of his vassal. Protection involved both military assistance and justice in the lord's feudal court. The nonfulfillment of these obligations broke the feudal contract and freed the vassal of his fealty and obligations.

The lord also had certain privileges, called *feudal incidents,* regarding the administration of the fief.

1) If the vassal failed to honor his feudal obligations, the lord might confiscate his estate. Such a practice was called *forfeiture.*

2) Whenever a vassal died without leaving any legitimate heirs, the fief reverted, or *escheated,* to the lord. The latter was then free to bestow it upon someone else.

3) When a vassal died leaving only a minor heir, the lord had the right of *wardship*—that is, administration of the estate until the boy came of age. Meanwhile the lord kept the annual revenues for himself as payment for his trouble. The right of wardship was also involved when a daughter was to inherit the fief. The lord then claimed the right to provide her with a suitable husband. He did this because it was essential that the fief be administered by a man who could fight and would be loyal to his suzerain. The right of wardship often brought misery to the women, for even girls of ten or less might be compelled to marry elderly men.

The vassal's obligations were more numerous and complex.

1) The primary duty was military service, and a vassal often owed not only his own service but also that of several other knights. He and his knights were expected to devote forty days of free military service to the lord each year. Beyond that, the vassal could demand payment for his services. (By the twelfth century a revived money economy allowed the king to commute this military service into a money payment called *scutage* [shield money], which enabled him to create a royal army of mercenary

soldiers. This development hastened the decline of feudalism by eliminating its military reason for being.) Another military duty was *castleward,* in which the vassal guarded the lord's castle.

2) Feudal law asserted the right of a noble to be judged only by his peers (social equals). Hence, the vassal, besides bringing his own disputes to the lord's court, devoted some time to judging cases involving other vassals.

3) The lord had the right to demand money payments, called *aids,* on at least three specific occasions: when the lord's eldest son was made a knight, when the lord's eldest daughter was to be married and a dowry had to be provided for her, and when the lord was captured and had to be ransomed. Other aids, such as defraying the expense of going on a crusade, could not be levied without the vassal's consent.

4) Another money payment, called *relief,* was exacted when either the lord or the vassal died and his heir succeeded. This "inheritance tax" accompanied the homage, which had to be renewed each time there was a new partner in the bond. Relief was often equivalent to the fief's revenues for the first year, another big expense for the vassal.

5) An obligation dreaded by the vassal was the right of hospitality. The lord and his retinue had to be provided with shelter, food, and entertainment when passing through the territory of his feudatory. Because a large retinue and a long stay might bankrupt the vassal, the duration of such hospitality in time came to be precisely limited.

Feudal warfare. The final authority in the feudal age was force, and the general atmosphere of the era was one of violence. Although some of the fighting was done for the king, private wars of feud or fortune and even warfare for its own sake were common. Recalcitrant vassals, particularly in France, frequently made war upon their suzerains.

War was considered a normal occupation by the ambitious nobles of the time, for success offered glory and rich rewards. First of all, land was the only real source of

wealth, and its supply was limited. Holdings could be increased by taking on another fief or, if the land was not available, by marriage or war. If marriage was not feasible, war was always an alternative. If successful, warfare enlarged a noble's territory; and, if they produced nothing else, forays and raids kept a man in good mettle. To die in battle was the only honorable end for a spirited gentleman; to die in bed was a "cow's death."

The Church's role in feudalism. Another unhappy result of feudalism was the inclusion of the Church in the system. The unsettled conditions caused by the Viking and Magyar invasions forced Church prelates to enter into close relations with the only power able to offer them protection—the feudal barons, that is, the more powerful lords who possessed one or more castles and a private army of their own vassals. Church officials thus became vassals of great lords, receiving fiefs for which they were obligated to perform the usual feudal services. Military service, involving the bloodshed which a clergyman was supposed to refrain from personally, was provided through his secular representative, the *advocatus.*

As the Church became increasingly immersed in feudalism, a fundamental conflict arose in that its officials, as churchmen, owed their loyalty to the pope but, as vassals holding land, had obligations to

Warfare was a normal occupation for gentlemen during the feudal age and even the more brutal aspects of combat were not considered ignoble subjects for art.

their feudal lords. This serious clash of loyalties was partially responsible for the bitter struggle between the heads of the feudal system, the kings, and the head of the Church, the pope (see p. 383).

On the positive side, however, the Church in time sought to influence for the better the behavior of the feudal warrior nobility. In addition to attempting to add Christian virtues to the code of knightly conduct called chivalry, which will be described later in this chapter, the Church sought to impose limitations on feudal warfare. In the eleventh century churchmen inaugurated the Peace of God and Truce of God movements. The Peace of God banned from the sacraments all persons who pillaged sacred places or refused to spare noncombatants. The Truce of God established "closed seasons" on fighting: from sunset on Wednesday to sunrise on Monday and certain longer periods, such as Lent.

While such peace movements were generally ineffective, we should be careful not to take an exaggerated view of the extent of lawlessness in the Middle Ages. Medieval chronicles were much like our modern newspapers in that they played up the sordid, unusual, and ruthless happenings. A vassal living on his fief, peacefully minding his own business, was not news.

An evaluation of feudalism. What shall be our general estimate of feudalism? Feudalism was crude and makeshift, but it brought some order out of the chaos into which part of Europe had fallen. It stabilized society and created a system of law and order. It even contributed to democracy, for its principle that feudal law was above the king (as witnessed in the Magna Carta—see p. 415) was later used by the middle class to curb royal absolutism. Despite its cruelty and high-handed methods, feudal society had instilled the ideals of personal honor and reciprocal obligations between individuals; and, however much these ideals were honored in the breach, they passed into the mores of our own society.

One historian states that feudalism "concealed in its bosom the weapons with which it would be itself one day smitten."[14] By maintaining a king at the head of the hier-

archy, feudalism was keeping intact the vestiges of monarchy, which would gradually reassert itself and restore centralized government.

Class structure. Though at times there was considerable social mobility, medieval society conventionally consisted of three classes: the nobles, the peasants, and the clergy. Each of these groups had its own task to perform. Since the vassals usually gave military service to their lord in return for their fiefs, the nobles were primarily fighters, belonging to an honored society distinct from the peasant people—freemen, villeins, and serfs. In an age of physical violence, society obviously would accord first place to the man with the sword rather than to the man with the hoe. The peasants were the workers; attached to the manors, they produced the crops and did all the menial labor. The Church drew on both the noble and the peasant classes for the clergy. Although the higher churchmen held land as vassals under the feudal system, the clergy formed a class which was considered separate from the nobility and peasantry.

Socially and politically the peasants were worlds apart from their "betters," yet the two groups often lived in close proximity. Not far from the manor house or the noble's castle was the village where the peasants lived. The contact between the nobles and the peasants was often the agent whom the lord sent to supervise the manor.

THE MANORIAL SYSTEM

The manor in relation to feudalism. Having discussed feudalism, the political system of medieval times, let us turn to the economic organization of medieval agrarian society, the manorial system. The feudal system was the means whereby protection was obtained for society; the manor was the agency which provided the necessary food for the members of both feudal and manorial groups. Feudalism and the manorial system evolved independently, but they were intimately connected.

The term manorial system refers to the type of economic and social system which centered around the manor. The manorial system governed the methods of agriculture, the lives of the serfs, and their relationships with each other and with the lord of the manor.

Like feudalism, the manor seems to have had its origins in both Roman and German institutions. The great Roman estates in Gaul, cultivated by tenants called *coloni* (see p. 207), survived the Germanic invasions. During the early Middle Ages they were held either by the descendants of their Roman owners or by Frankish kings, nobles, and the Church. The medieval serf was the direct descendant of the Roman *colonus* who worked the land, paid rent in kind, and could not leave the estate without the owner's permission.

The Germanic contribution is not so easily traced. Most scholars maintain that the Germans were originally tribes of freemen living in villages, though a servile class of cultivators always existed among them. During the disorders of the ninth and tenth centuries most of these villagers lost their freedom; either they voluntarily submitted to a mounted warrior whose protection they needed and who then gradually reduced them to serfdom, or they were forced to submit.

Agriculture, the chief function of the manor. The manor varied in size from one locality to another. A small one might contain only about a dozen households. Since the allotment to each family averaged about thirty acres, the small manors probably included about 350 acres of tillable land, not counting the meadows, woods, waste land, and the lord's demesne land. A large manor might contain fifty families and a total area of 5000 acres.

The center of the manor was the village, with the thatched cottages of the peasants grouped together along one street. Around each cottage was a space large enough for a vegetable patch, chicken yard, haystack, and stable. An important feature of the landscape was the village church, together with the priest's house and the burial ground. If the manor was large, the lord's dwelling might be a castle, with the village built up to its walls; if small, a manor house surmounted a knoll on the demesne. The fields stretched out from the village, and the peasants trudged to work along the roads.

Distribution of the land. As in the case of political feudalism, the manorial system was an institution which varied considerably depending upon the time and the locality. Every manor, however, contained two types of land, arable and nonarable. Part of the arable land, called the *demesne,* was reserved for the lord and was cultivated for him by his serfs. The remainder of the arable land was held by the villagers. The nonarable land, consisting of meadow, wood, and waste land, was used in common by the villagers and the lord.

From one third to two fifths of the arable land was given over to the lord's demesne. The demesne might be either sharply set off from the tenures of the villagers or distributed among the lands of the tenants. The land not held in demesne was allotted among the villagers under the open-field system, whereby the fields were subdivided into strips. The strips, each containing about an acre, were separated by narrow paths of uncultivated turf. The serf's holding was not all in one plot, for all soil throughout the manor was not equally fertile, and a serious attempt was made to give each of the villagers land of the same quality.

Each tenant was really a shareholder in the village community, not only in the open fields but also in the meadow, pasture, wood, and waste lands. His rights in these common lands were determined by the number of acres he held in the open fields: the meadow land where the hay was grown, for instance, was apportioned in strips to correspond with each villager's share of arable land, and the number of cattle which an individual might turn into the common pasture was again determined by the amount of land he held.

The hay produced in these times was neither plentiful nor of good quality, and this, coupled with ignorance of breeding principles, produced puny livestock. The winter diet of straw and tree loppings left the cattle so weak that in the spring the surviving animals sometimes had to be carried out to pasture. The supply of milk was small, and the peasants turned most of it into cheese. Often the peasants used oxen as draft animals instead of horses, because the former were cheaper to maintain.

The wooded land was valuable as a place to graze pigs, the most common animal on the manor. Again the tenant was limited in the number of pigs which he might turn loose there. The tenant could also gather dead wood in the forest, but cutting down green wood was prohibited unless authorized by the lord.

Medieval farming methods. Many medieval farming techniques were inefficient; other methods made good use of the available resources. The open-field system was cumbersome and wasteful; the intervening dividers occupied potentially fertile soil and cut down on the efficiency of the cultivating. On the other hand, the system represented a cooperative agricultural enterprise in which the resources of the manor were pooled. For example, the lord usually supplied the plow, and the villagers brought the oxen required to pull it.

It is dangerous to generalize too sweepingly about agricultural methods, because differences in locality, fertility of soil, crop production, and other factors resulted in a variety of farming methods (see the Historical Critique, p. 374). But if we study farming as practiced in northwestern Europe, we can discover some common factors. The implements which the peasants used were extremely crude; the plow was a cumbersome instrument with heavy wheels, often requiring as many as eight oxen to pull it. (By the twelfth century plow horses were common.) There were also crude harrows, sickles, beetles for breaking up clods, and flails for threshing. Inadequate methods of farming soon exhausted the soil. It has been estimated that the average yield per acre was only six to eight bushels of wheat, a fourth of the modern yield.

As far back as classical times farmers learned that soil planted continually with one crop rapidly deteriorated. To counteract this, the Romans and Germans employed a two-field system, whereby half of the arable land was planted while the other half lay fallow to recover its fertility.

Medieval farmers learned that wheat or rye could be planted in the autumn as well as in the spring. As a result, by the ninth century they were dividing the land into three fields, with one planted in the fall, another in the spring, and the third left lying fallow. Furthermore, they discovered that while the continual planting of the same crop soon exhausted the soil, the alternation of crops did not deplete the land so quickly.

The three-field system, of course, kept the land in more frequent production. Another advantage of this system over the two-field method was the fact that more crops could be produced with less plowing. Because fallow land was plowed twice, 300 acres cultivated on the three-field system would require 400 acres of plowing (100 acres of plowing for the fall planting, 100 acres of plowing for the spring crop, and 200 acres of plowing for the fallow land). The same land farmed on the two-field system would require 450 acres of plowing (150 acres for the crop, and 300 acres for the fallow land). The gain amounted to 50 acres less plowing and 50 acres more crops.

Administration of the manor. Though the lord might live on one of his manors, each manor was administered by such officials as the steward, the bailiff, and the reeve.

The steward, the highest ranking official, was general overseer for all his lord's manors, supervised the business of the manors, and presided over the manorial court. Through the steward, the lord had complete legal jurisdiction over the semifree inhabitants on the manor. A steward had the ultimate authority in the court, but he took into account the long-established customs of the manor. Justice was severe. Minor offenses brought in fines to the lord, while poaching, arson, murder, and robbery were punished by hanging. The severity of the sentences won respect and fear for the steward.

While the steward traveled from manor to manor, a bailiff was stationed permanently on each of the manors, where he acted as the lord's representative. The bailiff supervised the cultivation of the demesne, collected rents, dues, and fines,

Several aspects of peasant life on a self-sufficient medieval manor are depicted in these fourteenth-century illuminations. At the top, peasants reap grain under the direction of the reeve, or overseer, of the estate. Once the grain was harvested, it was ground in the mill belonging to the lord. A peasant (center), using a sack of grain for a saddle, rides to the mill. A medieval manor produced not only its own food, but also such necessities as cloth. In the last picture, the woman at the left turns her spinning wheel by means of a handle, while the woman at the right uses hand cards to comb the wool.

kept the manor's financial accounts, and inspected the work done by the peasants.

The reeve was the "foreman" of the villagers, chosen by them and representing their interests. He relayed to the lord the complaints of the peasants and cooperated with the bailiff in supervising cultivation. Responsible to the lord for the services of the tenants, he made sure that the serfs plowed, sowed, and reaped at the proper time.

Status and duties of people on the manor. It is difficult to distinguish the various social classes which made up the manor community. Furthermore, in status and function these classes differed not only from locality to locality but from period to period. However, they can be roughly divided into three major categories: the lord and his officials, the free element, and the semifree group. Originally there was a slave class, but most of these merged quite early with the lowest semifree group. All classes except the first belonged to the peasantry, for whether free or semifree they were not members of the feudal hierarchy.

There often were freemen on the manor, however small a proportion of its population they may have represented. They possessed personal freedom and were not subject to the same demands as the semifree people. The freeman did not have to work in the lord's fields himself but could send substitutes. He paid cash rent for his holding and, if he wanted to leave, could locate a new tenant for the land, provided the transfer took place in open court in the lord's presence and the new man was acceptable to the lord. Aside from these privileges, however, the freeman was little different from the semifree man. His strips in the open field adjoined those of the servile worker, and he lived in a cottage in the same village. The freeman class was very small in the twelfth century, but from then on it grew rapidly.

The semifree persons, the serfs, were bound to the manor and could not leave without the lord's consent. Serfdom was a hereditary status; the children of a serf were attached to the soil as their parents

were. In the event of a marriage between a serf and a freewoman, their children were generally considered serfs.

The lord of the manor was bound by the force of custom to respect certain rights of his serfs. So long as they paid their dues and services, serfs could not be evicted from their hereditary holdings. Although a serf could not appear in court against his lord or a freeman, he could appeal to the manor court against any of his fellows.

Among the semifree class, certain families enjoyed privileges not possessed by the majority. This upper crust was made up of the villeins. By paying a fee, the villein could usually obtain the lord's permission to leave the manor, marry his daughter to a freeman on the same manor or to a man on another manor, or send his son to learn a handicraft or to enter the Church. In time the classes of villein and serf tended to merge.

Whereas the peasants found in the manor their economic, political, legal, and social life, to the lord the manor was essentially a source of income. The earnings came from three obligations imposed on the peasantry: (1) services in the form of labor, (2) dues levied on the peasant, and (3) manorial monopolies.

The most important service was *week-work.* The peasant had to donate two or three days' work each week to the lord. The week-work included such jobs as repairing roads or bridges or carting manure to the fields. Because the lord's demesne "had always to be plowed first, sowed first, and reaped first," the peasant had to perform extra work, *boon-work,* at these times. He did not get paid for any labor, but during boon-days his meals were generally provided free by the lord.

Various dues or payments—usually in produce, in money if it was available— were made to the lord. The *taille* (or tallage), a tax on whatever property a peasant managed to accumulate, was the most common. It was levied on all peasants one or more times a year. The serf was taxable to the limit of the lord's mercy, although for freeman and villein the *taille* eventually became a fixed sum. Another burdensome tax was imposed when a peasant died; before a son could inherit his father's cottage and strips, the lord claimed the best beast or movable possession as inheritance tax.

In addition to services and dues, the lord profited from certain monopolies. On the manor the lord operated the grain mill, the oven for baking bread, and the wine and cider press. Since the peasant was prohibited from taking his grain, flour, and fruit elsewhere, the lord collected a toll each time these services were needed. Furthermore, since no peasant or group of peasants could have afforded, or would have been allowed, to set up competing equipment, the lord's control of these essential services was a monopoly of the most rigid kind.

Self-sufficiency of the manor. Economically the manor was almost self-sufficient. The food essential to sustain the local population was raised on the manor. Where rainfall was sufficient, flax for making linen was cultivated. Leather for boots was tanned on the manor, and yarn for clothing was spun at home. Specialized jobs were performed by the village miller, butcher, carpenter, and blacksmith. A few commodities, such as salt, iron, and millstones, had to be imported and were generally procured from one of the country fairs.

Because of bad roads and other dangers of travel, communication with the outside world was extremely limited. A rare journey beyond the manor, the arrival of a pilgrim who had visited faraway shrines or of a recent bride from another manor gave the inhabitants their only glimpses of the outside world. The manor remained the center of the peasants' lives; many of them never left its confines.

The weary round of peasant life. On the manors of the early Middle Ages the margin between starvation and survival was narrow, and the life of the peasant was not easy. Famines were common; warfare and wolves were a constant threat; grasshoppers, locusts, caterpillars, and rats repeatedly destroyed the crops. Men and women alike had to toil long hours in the fields. A medieval poem vividly describes the life of a peasant family:

Into this medieval print the artist has crowded the whole life of the manorial village. A hunting party is shown in the foreground, the ladies riding behind the knights. The castle, with its moat and drawbridge, dominates the countryside. In the midst of the village houses, which are surrounded by a fence, stands the church. Note also the mill and the millrace at the left and what appears to be a wine or cider press to the right of the mill. In the upper right corner a serf is using the heavy plow common to northwestern Europe (the artist has shown only two draft animals). The nets were apparently set to catch hares, and below them stands a wayside shrine. Visible on the horizon is a gibbet with buzzards wheeling over it.

I saw a poor man o'er the plough bending. . . .
All befouled with mud, as he the plough followed.
Two mittens had he, scanty, and made all of rags,
And the fingers were worn out and filled full of
mud.
This wight was bemired in the mud almost to the
ankle;
Four oxen were before him, that feeble had be-
come,
One might reckon rib, so rueful were they.
His wife walked by him with a long goad,
In a cutted skirt cutted full high,
Wrapped in a winnowing-sheet to keep her from
the weather,
Barefoot on the bare ice, so that the blood fol-
lowed.
And at the field's end lay a little bowl,
And therein lay a little child wrapped in rags,
And twain of two years old upon another side;
And all of them sang a song that sorrow was to
hear,
They cried all a cry, a sorrowful note,
And the poor man sighed sore, and said 'Children,
be still.'[15]

The difficulties of the peasant's life were reflected in his home, a cottage with mud walls, clay floor, and thatched roof. The fire burned on a flat hearthstone in the middle of the floor; and unless the peasant was rich enough to afford a chimney, the smoke escaped through a hole in the roof. The windows had no glass and were stuffed with straw in the winter. Furnishings were meager, consisting usually of a table, a kneading trough for dough, a cupboard, and a bed, often either a heap of straw or a box filled with straw, which served the entire family. Pigs and chickens wandered about the cottage continually, while the stable was frequently under the same roof, next to the family quarters.

The peasant's food was coarse and not overplentiful. He seldom obtained fresh meat, so he ate salt pork instead. Porridge, soups, and cheese, washed down with cheap wine, beer, or cider, were his usual fare. Sanitation was nonexistent in the crooked village streets, which were dotted with piles of refuse and manure. No medieval people were clean by our standards, but even by the standards of the feudal nobility the peasant was filthy.

There was no love lost between the peas-

antry and nobility. The latter believed that the peasants were inferior in every respect and, furthermore, that God had meant it to be so. Medieval literature is replete with scornful references to the stupidity, filthi- ness, and ugliness of the serfs:

Peasants are those who can be called cattle.
The devil did not want the peasants in hell because they smelled too badly.[16]

The peasant, despite his hard, monoto- nous life, was not without a few pleasures. Wrestling was exceedingly popular, as were cockfighting, a crude type of football, and fighting with quarterstaves, in which both the contestants stood an excellent chance of getting their heads bashed in. Everyone attended the pageants and entertainments put on by wandering actors and minstrels.

Around the porch of the parish church the peasants often congregated to dance and sing on the numerous holy days. The Church preached in vain against "ballads and danc- ings and evil and wanton songs and such- like lures of the Devil." The peasants re- fused to give up these amusements, a small enough compensation for the constant ex- ploitation they suffered.

It is unwise to generalize too broadly about the life of the peasants. Some nobles were kind and some were merciless, and their tenants prospered or suffered accord- ingly. Lords desired orderly and prosperous manors, and it was bad business to treat one's peasants so poorly that they could not work. Medieval serfs also possessed a large degree of economic security, and in this respect they were better off than the factory workers of the early nineteenth century.

THE AGE OF CHIVALRY

Chivalry in feudal society. One of the most interesting and significant legacies of the Middle Ages is its concept of chiv- alry, a code which, by the late Middle Ages, governed the behavior of all truly perfect and gentle knights. Such paragons are found in the accounts of Sir Lancelot and especially Sir Galahad—"the gentlest man that ever ate in hall among the ladies"—in Sir Thomas Malory's *Morte d'Arthur.* Early chivalry, however, which emerged during the heyday of feudalism in the eleventh century, was rough and masculine. It stressed the warrior virtues that were essential in a feudal society: prowess in combat, courage, and loyalty to one's lord and fellow warriors. The virtues of early chivalry are best expressed in early medieval epics, such as the eleventh-century *Song of Roland,* where they are summed up in the words of the hero who, surrounded by foes, cries: "Better be dead than a coward be called."

The later chivalry of the twelfth and thirteenth centuries contained new virtues which the Church and the ladies sought to impose upon the generally violent and uncouth behavior of feudal warriors. The chivalric romances that began to be written in the twelfth century mirror these new influences. In Chrétien de Troyes' *Perceval,* for example, the hero's mother sends him off to be dubbed a knight with these words of advice:

Serve ladies and maidens if you would be honored by all. If you capture a lady, do not annoy her. Do nothing to displease her. He has much from a maiden who kisses her if she agrees to give a kiss. You will avoid greater intimacy if you wish to be guided by me. . . . Above all I wish to beg you to go to churches and abbeys and pray to our Lord so that the world may do you honor and you may come to a good end.[17]

Churchmen advised knights that "they prostitute their knighthood who fight for profit. Those who take arms so that they may plunder are not knights but robbers and plunderers, not defenders but invaders."[18]

In sum, fully developed chivalry was a combination of three elements: warfare, religion, and reverence toward women. It required the knight to fight faithfully for his lord, champion the Church and aid the humble, and honor womankind. Unfortunately, the practice of chivalry was quite different from the theory. The pious Sir Galahad, whose strength was of the strength of ten because his heart was pure, remained an ideal. While he might cloak his motives under high-sounding words, the average knight was more superstitious than religious, and he continued to fight, plunder, and abuse women, especially those of the lower class.

Attitudes toward women. Divergent attitudes toward women existed during medieval times—one put forward by the Church and the other by the code of chivalry. Many moralists in the Church preached that Eve had caused Adam to lose the luxurious life in the Garden of Eden and that therefore women were not only inferior but offered the quickest way for a man to lose his soul. The medieval moralists constantly rebuked women for their extravagant dress. The use of stays to gain slimness, the plucking of eyebrows, the painting of cheeks, and the wearing of expensive clothes shocked the priests. Listen to Berthold of Ratisbon:

In order that ye may compass men's praise ye spend all your labour on your garments—on your veils and your kirtles. Many of you pay as much to the sempstress as the cost of the cloth itself; it must have shields on the shoulders, it must be flounced and tucked all round the hem; it is not enough for you to show your pride in your very buttonholes, but you must also send your feet to hell by special torments, ye trot this way and that with your fine stitchings. Ye busy yourselves with your veils, ye twitch them hither, ye twitch them thither; ye gild them here and there with gold thread; ye will spend a good six months' work on a single veil. . . . When thou shouldest be busy in the house with something needful for the goodman, or for thyself, or thy children, or thy guests, then art thou busy instead with thy hair, thou art careful whether thy sleeves sit well, or thy veil or thy headdress, wherewith thy whole time is filled.[19]

Despite the Church's attitude, the chivalric code specified that women should be glorified and adored, and that a knight should choose a fair lady on whom to shower his attention and his services. This placing of women on a pedestal was a by-product of romantic love, the main theme in the lyric poetry that first appeared in the second half of the eleventh century. In addition, the devotion which the Virgin Mary inspired in men's hearts may have been transferred to earthly women.

In reality the noblewoman's life was somewhat between these extremes. She was legally inferior to men. She had little real choice as to whom she might marry. A rich woman stood the chance of being kidnaped by an impulsive suitor. Such a predicament befell Eleanor of Aquitaine, who was pursued by no fewer than five men after she had been divorced from King Louis VII of France. The hazards notwithstanding, the lady was often a most influential person in the castle, aiding her husband in its administration and even defending it from attack when her lord was absent. Difficult as the role of the medieval wife might be, there was greater difficulty in finding a place in society except as a wife, and the loss of men to death on the battlefield or to the celibate life of the Church made it all the more likely that a medieval woman would face such a dilemma.

Women in general shared the characteristics of the menfolk. They lived in a crude and often brutal age devoid of many of our modern refinements. Like their husbands, medieval women were heavy drinkers and eaters. It is said that a common compliment to a member of the fair sex was that she was "the fairest woman who ever drained a bottle."[20]

Training for knighthood. From the time they were boys, men of the nobility underwent a rigid training for knighthood. A boy was kept in the care of his mother until the age of seven. Then his father sent him to the household of a relative, a friend, or the father's suzerain. There he became a page, attending the ladies, running their errands, and learning the rudiments of religion, manners, hawking, and hunting. During this segment of his training he was imbued with the virtue of obedience. When about fifteen or sixteen, he became a squire and prepared himself seriously for the art of war. He learned to keep a knight's equipment in good order, to ride a war horse with dexterity, and to handle the sword, the shield, and the lance correctly. To that end he practiced long hours in the tilting field against other squires or rode at full gallop against the quintain, a shieldlike object which revolved around a post. Unless the passing squire hit it squarely with his lance, the quintain struck him a crushing blow. The squire also waited on his lord and lady at the table and learned music and poetry and the popular medieval games of chess and backgammon.

If not already knighted on the battlefield for valor, the squire was usually considered eligible for knighthood at twenty-one. By the twelfth century the Church claimed a role in the ceremony on the grounds that the knight was privileged to serve God in the secular world. The knighting ceremony was invested with impressive symbolism. The candidate took a bath to symbolize purity and watched his weapons before the altar in an all-night vigil, confessing and making resolutions to be a worthy knight. During the solemn Mass which followed, his sword was blessed on the altar by the priest or bishop. The climax of the ceremony came when the candidate, kneeling before his lord, received a light blow on the neck or shoulder (the *accolade*), as the lord pronounced these words: "In the name of God, Saint Michael, and Saint George, I dub thee knight. Be valiant." The new knight was then armed ceremoniously. Particularly significant was the binding on of his golden spurs, for the horse was the knight's indispensable companion and the symbol of nobility. The knight then mounted his horse and tilted against the quintain to prove his dexterity at arms. The symbolic ceremony was designed to impress upon the knight that he must be virtuous and valiant, loyal to his suzerain and to God.

Heraldry. With its unique decorative designs, worn by each noble family on its armor and helmets, heraldry was one of the more colorful aspects of chivalry. The forerunners of this custom date back to early Mesopotamia and to China, where the five-clawed dragon was the heraldic device of the empire. The use of symbolic devices has long been a widespread custom; in Japan the emperor had his symbol of chrysanthemums, and the Aztec eagle is a well-known emblem. During the feudal period noble families took great pride in displaying on their armor an honored heraldic device, the badge of familial dignity.

The popularity of heraldry began to sweep through Europe in the twelfth century. The use of the closed helmet, which hid the face, required that some means of identification be developed. At first the distinguishing devices used were simple emblems, but in time complex forms and combinations of colors were designed. Ingenious feudal artists devised 285 variations of the cross and decorated the nobles' shields with such real and fictitious animals as the lion, leopard, griffin, dragon, unicorn, and a host of others in fanciful postures. A man's social position was evident in his coat of arms, for its quarterings, or divisions, showed to which noble families its owner was related.

Castles as fortresses and homes. The life of the nobles centered about the castle. The earliest of these structures, mere wooden blockhouses, were built in the ninth century. Stone was not used in northern Europe until the late eleventh century; and even then only the central tower, the donjon, was built of stone. Not until the twelfth and thirteenth centuries, when chivalry was in full bloom,

The text accompanying this illumination gives a detailed explanation of "How a man shall be armyd . . . when he shal fighte on foote." The squire in the picture has just begun to arm his master. When the job is finished, the knight will be wearing all the armor now resting on the pair of sawhorses at the left.

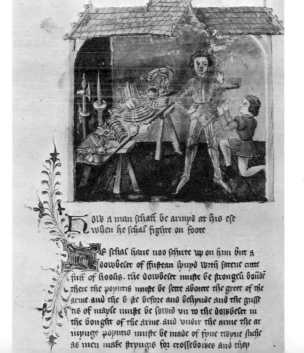

were massive castles constructed entirely of stone.

The donjon was the focal point of the castle; it was surrounded by an open space which contained storerooms, workshops, and a chapel. The outside walls of the castle were surmounted by turrets from which arrows, boiling oil, and various missiles might be showered upon the attackers. Beyond the wall was the moat, a steep-sided ditch filled with water to deter the enemy. The only entrance to the castle lay across the drawbridge. The portcullis, a heavy iron grating which could be lowered rapidly to protect the gate, was a further barrier against unwanted intrusion.

Life in the castle was anything but comfortable or romantic. The lord at first dwelt in the donjon, but by the thirteenth century he had built more spacious quarters. Because the castle was designed for defense, it possessed no large windows; and the rooms were dark and gloomy. The stone walls were bare except for occasional tapestries to allay the draft and dampness, and a huge fireplace provided the only warmth in the drafty room.

The furnishings were sparse. In the great hall, dining boards rested upon trestles; when not in use the boards were laid against the wall and the trestles cleared away. The principal table was set on a raised section called a dais, where the important persons sat. The seats were generally backless and uncomfortable. Carpets were an expensive oriental luxury which slowly won favor after the crusades. Earlier, the floor was covered with rushes, which were seldom replaced. They became dirty and evil-smelling from the bones and scraps of bread and meat which the diners threw over their shoulders to the dogs roaming about during the meal.

There was little variety in the bedroom furniture; each room contained a few chests and bureaus and an enormous bed. The bed was built upon a platform under a large canopy from which hung heavy curtains. The curtains kept away drafts and preserved modesty, for in feudal days nobody wore any night clothes. The lord's family had to share the bedrooms with falcons, hounds, and even barnyard creatures.

A French manuscript illumination of a knight entering the lists to fight in a tournament gives some idea of the splendor with which such contests were frequently invested. These often brutal battles were considered suitable entertainment for noble ladies and gentlemen.

The medieval family rose early and was served breakfast about six o'clock. The riser washed his face and hands with water brought in from the well or piped in through lead pipes; medieval civilization was not quite "a thousand years without a bath," as is sometimes said. Dinner was served at ten in the morning and the evening meal at five.

Our medieval ancestors were hearty eaters, but by today's standards their diet was rather limited. Although they devoured quantities of meat, fish, and fowl, often extravagantly spiced, many of the fruits and vegetables we enjoy were entirely unknown to them. They had no coffee or tea but plenty of other beverages. Beer and cider were commonplace drinks, while the noble prided himself upon his knowledge of wines.

Table manners were both interesting and startling. A dearth of silverware forced the gentleman to cut up his meat with a dagger. Since forks were unknown, food was carried to the mouth by the thumb and two fingers. Meat was served on thick slabs of bread, soaked in gravy. After the meat was eaten, the bread was thrown to the dogs or deposited in the alms basket for the poor. Poetic instructions in etiquette read:

Scratche not thy head with thy fyngers
    When thou arte at thy meate;
Nor spytte you over the table board;
    See thou doest not this forget.
Pick not thy teeth with thy knyfe
    Nor with thy fyngers ende,
But take a stick or some cleane thing,
    Then doe you not offende.[21]

Amusements of the nobles. The average noble derived his pleasures primarily from outdoor sports. Because the knight had been trained from birth in military matters, he considered warfare fine entertainment. In peacetime the joust and tournament substituted for actual battle. The joust was a conflict between two armed knights, each equipped with a blunted lance with which he attempted to unseat the other. The tournament was a general melee in which groups of knights attacked each other. Often fierce fighting ensued, with frequent casualties.

The nobles were very fond of hunting, and the constant demand for fresh meat afforded a legitimate excuse for galloping over the countryside. Most hunting was done in the nearby forests, but at times an unlucky peasant's crops might be ruined during the chase. Some great nobles had scores of horses and hounds trained to hunt stag and wild boar.

A similar outdoor pastime, which lords, ladies, and even high church dignitaries delighted in, was falconry, a method of hunting with predatory birds. The hawks were reared with the utmost care, and large companies of lords and ladies spent many afternoons eagerly wagering with one another as to whose falcon would bring down the first victim. The interest was so great that nobles often attended Mass with hooded falcons on their wrists.

Indoor amusements included the universally popular diversions of backgammon, dice, and chess. The long, monotonous nights were sometimes enlivened by the quips of jesters. At other times a wandering minstrel entertained his noble hosts in exchange for a bed and a place at the table.

The decline of chivalry. The development of national governments under strong kings who enforced tranquillity and order changed the whole basis of feudal society (see Chapter 14). Knights were no longer needed to fight for their lords, to rush to the succor of helpless maidens, or to take the law into their own hands in defense of personal honor. Yet chivalry continued on as an ideal, reaching its culmination in the fourteenth and fifteenth centuries. By the sixteenth century its code had become fantastic and even ridiculous, as is pointed out so cleverly in Cervantes' *Don Quixote.* Some knights continued to live in the past and obtained their excitement by becoming robbers, picking needless quarrels with their neighbors, or inventing imaginary females who had to be rescued from a fate worse than death. The ideals of chivalry, however, have affected manners in later eras. They carried over into modern life, and even today they color our concept of a gentleman.

SUMMARY

The political history in this chapter includes certain key events and institutions from the time of Clovis through the reign of Charlemagne to the invasions of the intrepid Vikings in the ninth century. The conversion of Clovis to Christianity and the subsequent Frankish alliance with the papacy meant that the most energetic of the Germanic tribes had united with the greatest existing force for civilization and refinement in western Europe. This was the Christian Church, which incorporated both the new religion and some of the best of the old Roman tradition.

As Charlemagne amassed a sizable empire in Europe, he spread the Roman-Christian tradition. Although his empire was unique in early medieval Europe for its well-organized government, it depended too heavily on the forceful personality of its founder and did not survive his inferior successors. After the Carolingian collapse, new political and economic patterns evolved to meet the turbulent conditions of the time.

Feudalism was a bridge between the all-embracing imperial governments of the Romans and Carolingians and the diversity of national states so characteristic of modern Europe. Like so many things in medieval civilization, feudalism was a blend of German and Roman customs, enriched and humanized by the ideals of Christianity. The people who held land under feudal tenure were a privileged caste of landed aristocrats whose main function was military service. Set apart from the feudal nobles but forming the backbone of economic life was the vast majority of the people—the peasants. On the manors, the economic units of early medieval life, the unfree peasants or serfs grew the food for all medieval people and performed the heavy labor needed. They were politically inarticulate, tied to the soil, and seldom masters of their own destinies.

One aspect of feudalism which has come down to the twentieth century as a highly romanticized tradition is chivalry. Chivalry continues to influence our code of manners and behavior. Although its practice in the Middle Ages fell far beneath its principles, its idealism became part of the medieval legacy to the twentieth century.

Chapter 12

The West Takes the Offensive

European Political History (900-1100), the Crusades, and the Rise of Trade and Towns

INTRODUCTION. Some periods in history seem haunted by disaster and decline. Following the collapse of Charlemagne's empire, Europeans probably felt that the future held little promise and that good times had passed. They had sound reason for their pessimism. No longer was there an effective central government to maintain peace and enforce laws over large territories, and with political fragmentation had come economic relapse. Trade had waned, and industry was stagnant.

In this chapter we shall trace the rise of a new Europe—a Europe which in the tenth and eleventh centuries was to emerge from what is sometimes called the "dark ages." Although the decentralized feudal system was still dominant in France, strong monarchs who would crush the power of unruly nobles, restore law and order, and inspire nationalistic fervor in their subjects began to appear in Germany and England. With the ejection of the Muslims from Sicily and the successful challenge to Muslim control of the Mediterranean, Christian Europe ceased to be on the defensive and took the offensive instead.

In northern Spain a few bands of Christians sparked a long struggle against the Muslims in a movement known as the *Reconquista,* meaning "reconquest"; but the most dramatic manifestation of Europe's new dynamism was the crusades. Spurred on by religious fervor, love of adventure, and, in some cases, selfish hopes of personal gain, the crusaders set out to drive the Muslims from the Holy Land and free Jerusalem from the infidel. These expansive movements helped the recovery of international trade and the rise of flourishing towns. New markets stimulated the growth of industry and crafts; and the development of banking and the use of money, which superseded the old exchange by barter, made everyday business transactions more efficient. At the same time, men cleared and drained forests and swamps, and new lands went under the plow. All these factors—particularly the revival of urban life—sounded the death knell for the manorial system in western Europe.

Above all, the forces transforming the western world led to the growth of a new class in society—townsmen, the bourgeoisie or middle class. The status of a member of the middle class was based not on ancestry or ownership of large estates, as was the case with the feudal aristocrat, but on possession of goods and money. Gradually the bourgeoisie gained influence as well as wealth and began to exert a growing influence on history.

UNIFIED GERMANY

German tribal duchies. The loyalty of Germans to their duchies has colored the history of Germany from the days of Charlemagne to those of Hitler. Until very recent times certain sections, such as Bavaria and Saxony, have tenaciously clung to old customs and traditions going back to tribal times. Following the collapse of the Carolingian empire, the tribal consciousness of its people kept Germany from falling into the extreme political fragmentation that characterized feudal France. When the successors of Louis the German, who received East Frankland in the Treaty of Verdun in 843, proved incapable of coping with the attacks of savage Magyar horsemen in the late ninth and early tenth centuries, the task was taken over by the tribal leaders of the Saxons, Bavarians, Swabians, and Franconians who assumed the title of duke. The dukes of the five German duchies—including Lorraine, which Louis the German had acquired on the breakup of Lothair's middle kingdom—usurped the royal power and crown lands in their duchies and also took control over the Church.

The independence of the duchies was somewhat tempered by the tradition of kingship, which, despite the fact that the Carolingian monarchs of the ninth century were weak and incompetent, carried over from the day of Charlemagne. When the last Carolingian, Louis the Child, died in 911, the dukes elected the weakest among them, Conrad of Franconia, to be their king. The new monarch ruled just eight years, long enough to prove himself completely incapable of reëstablishing a strong government, of meeting the menace of the Magyar raids, or of controlling the restless dukes. Conrad did accomplish one important act as he lay on his deathbed. He recommended that the most powerful of the dukes, Henry the Fowler, duke of Saxony, be chosen as his successor. Henry founded the illustrious line of Saxon kings who ruled for more than a hundred years, from 919 to 1024, and made Germany the most powerful state in western Europe.

Henry the Fowler. After some initial opposition, Henry I (919-936) obtained recognition of his kingship from the other dukes. He exercised little authority outside of his own duchy, however, and his kingdom was hardly more than a confederation of independent duchies.

Against Germany's border enemies, Henry was more successful. He pushed back the Danes, occupied the narrow neck of their peninsula, and established the Dane Mark as a protective buffer. Inroads were also made against the Slavs across the Elbe, where in 928 Brandenburg was set up as another defensive mark. Thus began the *Drang nach Osten* ("push to the East"), which became a permanent feature of German history. Henry protected the eastern frontier with a line of forts, called burgs, and began the slow process of colonizing the Slavic lands between the Elbe and the Oder. Further to the southeast, in Bohemia, the Saxon ruler forced the Slavic Czechs to recognize his overlordship.

More spectacular was Henry's great victory over the Magyars in 933, following his refusal to pay the annual tribute demanded by these marauders. By this victory Henry earned the gratitude of the German people, who remembered him as the defender of their country against the wild invaders. So great was the prestige of the Saxon house when Henry died that no one disputed the election of his son Otto to succeed him.

Otto the Great. Otto I, the Great (936-973), built upon the foundations laid down by his father. Resolutely intent upon exalting the status of German kingship and recalling the glory of Charlemagne, Otto went to Aix-la-Chapelle (Aachen) to be crowned. There at a great banquet he was served by the dukes of the realm, a ceremony that symbolized German unity. Yet soon thereafter Otto was busy putting down serious revolts engineered by these same dukes.

Realizing that the great hindrance to German unity was the truculence of the dukes, Otto initiated a policy of gaining control of the unruly duchies by setting up his own relatives and favorites as their rulers. As an extra precaution he appointed, as supervising officials, counts who were directly responsible to the king. This policy was only temporarily successful, however, for both the counts and Otto's relatives and favorites proved unreliable. Even Otto's son, who was made duke of Swabia, rebelled against his father.

In the long run it was by means of an alliance with the Church that Otto constructed a strong German monarchy. The king protected the bishops and abbots and granted them a free hand over their vast estates; in return the church prelates furnished him with the officials, the income, and the troops that he lacked. Otto appointed the bishops and abbots, and since their offices were not hereditary, he could be sure that their first obedience was to his royal person. These prelates replaced the counts as the chief agents of the king in the duchies and furnished as much as three quarters of his military forces.

This alliance of crown and Church was a natural one at the time. At his coronation at Aachen, Otto had insisted on being anointed *rex et sacerdos* ("king and priest") thus reviving the Carolingian concept of the theocratic ruler and the alliance between crown and Church. Furthermore, both partners feared the unruly and arrogant dukes whose usurpations included the right to appoint bishops and abbots in their duchies. "The strength of the bishops meant the weakness of the nobles and the break-up of tribal bonds. . . . The alternative was between a Church dominated and bullied by dukes and counts, and a Church controlled and utilized for the service of the nation by the king. As the Church required aid of the civil power, the civil power required aid of the Church."[1] Having once discarded much of the service and support of the nobility in favor of those of the Church, the German monarchs would have found it disastrous if they had lost the support of the bishops and abbots. Eventually, in the twelfth century, this did occur, and the strong monarchy created by Otto I collapsed and Germany soon became feudalized.

Otto also permanently put an end to the Magyar menace, thereby enhancing his claim that the king, and not the dukes, was the true defender of the German people. In 955 the Magyars, forgetting their defeat at the hands of Henry the Fowler, launched an invasion that threatened to engulf all of Germany. In the battle of Lechfeld near Augsburg (see map, p. 347), one of the decisive events of the Middle Ages, Otto was completely victorious; only a remnant of the Magyars escaped. The people of the time compared Lechfeld to the battle of Tours; and Otto the Great, like Charles Martel, was hailed as the savior of Europe. The remaining Magyars gave up invading Germany and settled quietly in Hungary. By the year 1000 they had accepted Christianity and the rule of an organized monarchy.

The eastward movement. In addition to frustrating the invasions of the dreaded Magyars, Otto continued German expansion eastward against the Slavs. Along the Elbe and Saale rivers, which constituted the Slavic line, he created five new defensive marks. These areas were protected by numerous burgs. Like Charlemagne earlier, Otto relied on the Church to Christianize the stubborn heathens, and several bishoprics were established in the conquered lands.

For hundreds of years the Germans continued this eastward movement, pushing from the Elbe to the Oder and eventually to the Vistula River. Impelled by a desire for land and adventure, this eastward surge of the German people can be compared to the American westward movement from the Alleghenies to the Pacific. In both cases the common people accomplished the colonization without much government initiative. In both cases the forests were cleared and land was cultivated.

This expansion was perhaps the greatest achievement of the medieval Germans. Had it not been for this move eastward, modern Germany would have been a narrow strip of land wedged in between the Rhine and the Elbe; it has been estimated that 60 per cent of German territory before the First World War had been taken from the Slavs.

On the other hand, the duel between the Slavs and the Germans continued to bring many serious problems to eastern Europe. Because the borders between the German colonists and the Slav natives were never clearly defined, pockets of Slavs and Germans intermingled. This ethnic admixture has caused serious disputes and conflicts in modern times.

The German empire. Like so many men of the Middle Ages, Otto the Great tended to revere the past. A devout believer in the imperial tradition, he regarded the Roman and Carolingian empires as the golden ages

of man. As one historian succinctly put it: "His objective was Empire, and his model was Charlemagne."[2] This pursuit of an empire became a characteristic pattern in the reigns of subsequent Saxon kings.

Italy in the tenth century was a tempting field for an invader. Lacking an outstanding leader to unify the peninsula after the decline of the Carolingian empire, Italy had split into warring fragments. In the north the old Lombard realm, which had been a part of Lothair's middle kingdom, became the object of various rival contenders. In central Italy were the Papal States, where the pope presided not only as head of the Christian Church but also as political ruler. During this century, however, the popes were appointed and controlled by the Roman nobility, and the power and prestige of the papacy was at its lowest ebb. Further south were two Lombard duchies; and, finally, at the extreme tip of the peninsula, the Byzantine empire retained a shaky foothold on the

GERMANY ABOUT 1000

☐ Holy Roman Empire

The crown of Otto I, probably made for his coronation in Rome, consists of eight gold plaques held together by hinges which open or close by means of pearl-headed pins. The crown was constructed in this portable fashion because Otto traveled a good deal and needed to have his crown with him for state occasions in various countries. Four of the plaques consist of pearls and gems held together by gold filigree. The other four plaques contain enamel panels showing God, David, Hezekiah with Isaiah, and (in the plaque visible here) Solomon. The upper part of the crown is an eleventh-century addition.

Italian mainland. Dotted here and there were cities which, unlike those in the north, had never become depopulated, and which eventually became strong and healthy miniature nations.

In deciding to invade Italy, Otto the Great's initial motive was defensive. The dukes of the south German duchies of Swabia and Bavaria were hopeful of seizing Burgundy and Lombardy, and Otto believed that his position as German king would be endangered if those large remnants of Lothair's old middle kingdom fell into the hands of his German rivals. He first placed Burgundy and its weak ruler under his "protection." Then he turned to Italy, where not only politics but, as chivalrous contemporary accounts explained it, romance also beckoned. A widower, Otto sought a queen; and it so happened that the widow of the former king of Lombardy had been ousted from her principality and imprisoned by a usurper. This was Queen Adelaide, whose beauty was renowned and whose lineage went back to Charlemagne. Her plight suited the political

ambitions of Otto. He crossed the Alps, met Adelaide, who had escaped, and married her. He then dethroned her captor and proclaimed himself ruler of the kingdom of Italy.

On his second expedition to Italy in 962, Otto was crowned emperor by the pope, whose Papal States were threatened by an Italian duke. No doubt Otto thought of himself as the successor of the imperial Caesars and Charlemagne; and, in fact, his empire later became known as the Holy Roman Empire (see Chapter 14). But Otto also needed the imperial title to legitimatize his claim to Lombardy, Burgundy, and Lorraine. These lands had belonged to the middle kingdom of Lothair, the last man to hold the imperial title. Otto's coronation was a momentous event that brought Italy and Germany, pope and emperor, into a forced and unnatural union.

Effects of Saxon involvement in Italy. The distracting, even malevolent, effect of the Saxon pursuit of an Italian empire is seen in the case of Otto II (973-983), who sought to annex southern Italy where the weak Byzantine foothold was threatened by the Arab Muslims of Sicily. His army was completely destroyed by the Muslims, and he died of fever before he could get reinforcements from home to recoup his loss. News of the defeat shocked Germany but produced jubilation among the Slavic peoples in the marks. The Slavs took advantage of the German disaster and rebelled, plundering Hamburg and destroying most of the German strongholds east of the Elbe. As a result German eastward expansion was halted for a century. Similarly, to the north the Danes overran the Dane Mark, which had been established by Henry the Fowler.

A still better example, perhaps, of the negative effect of the German pursuit of empire in Italy is demonstrated by the reign of the next king, Otto III (983-1002). Despite the disaster which overtook his father, Otto was eager to reëstablish the imperial glories of times past. Ignoring Germany, the real source of his power, he made Rome his capital, built a palace there, and styled himself "emperor of the Romans." As the "servant of Jesus Christ," another of his titles, Otto installed non-Italian popes in Rome and conceived of the papacy as a partner in ruling an empire of Germans, Italians, and Slavs. But notwithstanding Otto's love for Italy and his good intentions, the fickle Roman populace revolted and forced Otto to flee the city. He died a year later while preparing to besiege Rome, and with him died his grandiose scheme for what he and the churchmen at his court liked to call "the renewal of the Roman empire."

The outcome of Saxon policies. Despite the distractions in Italy, the Saxon rulers were the most powerful in Europe at that time. The early kings in particular had achieved notable successes within Germany. They had curbed the divisive tendencies toward feudalism, they had utilized the Church as an ally, and they had permanently halted Magyar pillaging in German provinces. Economically, too, there was progress. The Alpine passes had been freed of Muslim raiders and made safe for the Italian merchants who by the year 1000 were ready to act as middlemen linking western Europe with the eastern Mediterranean. In the wilderness of central and eastern Germany, a good start had been made in clearing the forests and draining the swamps. In comparison with most other European monarchs of the same period, the Saxon rulers stood out as giants.

On the other hand, the Saxon kings pursued policies which eventually led to the loss of Germany's position of preëminence among the states of Europe. Germany was to become the prime example of political localism and royal impotence. In the long run the domestic policies of these German kings were unsuccessful: (1) The ducal policy of Otto the Great ended in failure, for his appointees—relatives and favorites—made their holdings hereditary and attached themselves to local traditions in defiance of the crown. (2) They failed to develop new political institutions, such as a system of royal courts that would have given the king not only a source of revenue but also the loyalty of his subjects. (3) Ultimately the Saxon alliance with the Church miscarried, leading to a bitter struggle between the popes and the emperors. By bringing the German Church into their political system and by assuming emperorship, German monarchs had exercised their overlordship not only at home but also in Rome. They appointed the great bishops and abbots in their realm and also controlled the election of the popes. For a century this secular mastery functioned smoothly, but the rise of powerful popes in the last half of the eleventh century led to a bitter conflict between papacy and empire, centering on the king's right to appoint Church officials who were at the same time his most loyal supporters. This conflict is known as the Investiture Struggle (see p. 385).

All these factors impeded national unification in Germany, but the most decisive factor was the kings' dream of empire. Most historians maintain that, no matter what the original justification and occasional success, the union of Germany and Italy in the form of an empire was in the long run deeply inimical to the best interests of both countries.

The Saxons in a sense repeated the error of the Carolingians, whose empire was in large part the model for their own. They tried to do too much; they scattered their energies. "They were all Germans, but they had no German policy. All their strength lay to the north of the Alps, yet they were continually drawn to Italy. They were destined to wear themselves out in pursuit of their policy. Germany has been the victim of the Empire. . . ."[3] In Chapter 14 we shall have an opportunity to evaluate further the worth of this statement.

EARLY ENGLAND AND FRANCE

Britain after the Romans. In England, unlike France, a full-grown feudal system did not emerge from the havoc wrought by the Viking invasions of the ninth century. In response to the attacks of the Danes, and much like what happened in Germany, the small Anglo-Saxon kingdoms that had replaced Roman rule in Britain were formed into a single kingdom.

When the Roman legions withdrew from Britain to Italy at the beginning of the fifth century, they left the Celtic natives at the mercy of the German invaders—Angles, Saxons, Jutes, and Frisians. These savage tribes devastated Britain so thoroughly that little remained of Roman civilization other than a splendid system of roads. (Many highways in England today still follow the courses of the Roman roads.) Proof of the force with which the invaders struck is the fact that almost no traces of the Celtic language remain in modern English. Not only did the invaders wage war against the Celts, but the various Anglo-Saxon tribes fought among themselves. At one time there were more than a dozen little tribal kingdoms, all jealous and hostile, on the island of Britain. These chaotic conditions continued throughout the fifth and sixth centuries.

The Anglo-Saxon monarchy. Gradually peace and a semblance of order came to the distracted island as rivalries among the kingdoms diminished and the overlordship of the island was held in turn by the different rulers. In the ninth century the kingdom of Wessex in southern England held the dominant position. The Wessex king, Alfred the Great (871-899), one of England's better monarchs, was confronted with the task of turning back a new wave of invaders, the Danes, who overran all the other English kingdoms. After a series of disheartening reverses, Alfred defeated the Danes and forced them into a treaty whereby the Danes settled in the central part of England and accepted Christianity.

In addition to being a successful warrior, Alfred the Great made notable contributions in government in order, as he wrote, that he "might worthily and fittingly steer and rule the dominion that was entrusted to me."[4] He reorganized the militia of freemen (*fyrd*) so that part was always ready for battle while the rest tilled the soil, and the ships he built to repel future Viking attacks have won him the title of founder of the English navy. He also issued a set of laws, which reflect his desire to see the average man protected from wrongdoing and violence:

Injure ye not the widows and the step-children, nor hurt them anywhere: for if ye do otherwise, they will cry unto me, and I will hear them, and

I will then slay you with my sword; and I will so do that your wives shall be widows, and your children shall be step-children.[5]

Following the example of Charlemagne, Alfred also advanced the intellectual life of his country. He invited learned men from abroad and founded a palace school. He urged the bishops to promote the teaching of reading among freeborn youths and to have translated into English the books "which are most necessary for all men to know."[6] Alfred himself translated Pope Gregory the Great's *Pastoral Care,* Boethius' *Consolation of Philosophy,* and Bede's *Ecclesiastical History of the English Nation.* He encouraged monks to keep an account of current affairs, the *Anglo-Saxon Chronicle,* which continued to be written for hundreds of years afterward.

The descendants of Alfred through his great-grandson, who died in 975, were able rulers. They conquered the Danes in central England and created a unified English monarchy. Danes and Saxons intermarried, and soon all differences between the two people disappeared. After 975, however, a decline set in. The power of the central government lagged and with it the ability to keep order at home and repel outside attacks. The impotence of the kingdom is well illustrated in the unhappy reign of Ethelred the Unready (978-1016), who was unable to keep a firm hand on the great nobles or to cope with a new attack by the Danes. Ethelred imposed a heavy tax called the *Danegeld* on his subjects in order to raise money to buy off the invader.

In its political structure, the major defect of Anglo-Saxon England was the weakness of its central government: the inability of the king to control the great nobles, the earls, who were the king's deputies in their districts. But as a positive contribution to political history, the Anglo-Saxons developed local government to a strong degree. They left us a valuable legacy—the tradition of the people's participation in their government. In the local political divisions—the shires and their subdivisions, the hundreds—numerous assemblies or courts (moots) existed. Presided over by a royal official, the reeve, and composed of freemen of the area, the moots dispensed justice according to local custom and helped administer the realm. Here was one of the seeds of later democratic government. It is an interesting carry-over that American law students call their trial cases "moot court cases," and that our modern title of sheriff is derived from the name of the shire's most important official, the shire reeve.

Following the reign of Ethelred, the Anglo-Saxons were again overrun by the Vikings, and King Canute of Denmark ruled England as well as Norway. Canute proved to be a wise and civilized king and was well liked by his Anglo-Saxon subjects because he respected their rights and customs. Canute's empire fell apart after his death in 1035, and in 1042 the English crown was secured by Ethelred's son, Edward the Confessor. Although famed for his piety, Edward was a weak ruler who had little control over the powerful earls who had usurped most of the king's authority in their regions. This decline in government was reversed after the Normans invaded and conquered the island in 1066.

The Norman Conquest. The Norman Conquest of England really began in the reign of Edward the Confessor (1042-1066). Although he himself was English, Edward spent most of his early life in Normandy, where he received his education from Norman monks. When he returned to England and subsequently became king, Edward naturally showed a strong pro-Norman bias in all his actions. On his death in 1066 the *Witan*—the council of the kingdom—selected Harold Godwinson, a powerful English earl, as the new ruler. Immediately William, duke of Normandy, claimed the English throne, basing his demand on a flimsy hereditary right and on the assertion that Edward had promised him the crown.

One of the most outstanding statesmen and soldiers of his time, William became duke of Normandy at the age of eight. The nobility immediately rebelled, hoping to undo the vassalage and feudal obligations imposed on them by the strong Norman dukes who had preceded William. Three of the young duke's guardians were murdered, and for a few years he was kept under cover by his friends. When he was in his late teens, William came out of hiding and began to assert his power. He soon proved himself a man who showed little mercy to those who stood in his way. He subdued the rebellious nobles and from then on ruled a new kind of centralized feudal state. William effectively controlled his vassals, and his feudal army of one thousand knights made him the most powerful ruler west of Germany. The central authority of the duke of Normandy contrasted sharply with the situation in England, where the powerful earls were continually embarrassing the king.

By the clever use of propaganda, apparently an effective weapon as far back as the

The Bayeux tapestry, actually a woolen embroidery on linen, dates from the late eleventh century. Over 230 feet long and 20 inches wide, it both depicts and narrates (in Latin) the events of the Norman Conquest of England in 1066. The section at the left illustrates William's soldiers crossing the Channel in their Viking dragon boats; and the one at the right, the vanquished English fleeing and being stripped of their armor after the decisive battle.

eleventh century, William secured the sanction of the pope, which gave his invasion the flavor of a crusade. His well-equipped army of hard-fighting Norman knights and landless nobles from Brittany and Flanders looked upon the conquest of England as an investment which would pay them rich dividends in the form of lands and serfs.

Throughout the whole venture William had extraordinary luck. His neighbors around Normandy, often very quarrelsome, were obligingly tranquil. The cross-Channel maneuver was hazardous; five thousand knights, bowmen, and supporting infantry, as well as many horses, had to be transported in open boats. For several months the duke waited until a favorable breeze and a fairly calm sea finally enabled him to embark. Fortunately for William, at the critical moment Harold was forced to leave the south coast unguarded and hurry north to meet the invasion of the king of Norway who claimed the English throne as a descendant of Canute. After victory in the north, Harold rushed south to meet William's challenge.

On October 14, 1066, at Hastings, King Harold with his army of Saxons blocked the way of William on his march to London. An early twelfth-century description of the battle shows that the Norman victory was not a foregone conclusion:

They fought with ardour, neither giving ground, for great part of the day. Finding this, William gave a signal to his party, that, by a feigned flight, they should retreat. Through this device, the close body of the English, opening for the purpose of cutting down the straggling enemy, brought upon itself swift destruction; for the Normans, facing about, attacked them thus disordered, and compelled them to fly. In this manner, deceived by a strategem, they met an honourable death in avenging their country; nor indeed were they at all wanting to their own revenge, as, by frequently making a stand, they slaughtered their pursuers in heaps: for, getting possession of an eminence, they drove down the Normans, when roused with indignation and anxiously striving to gain the higher ground, into the valley beneath, where, easily hurling their javelins and rolling down stones on them as they stood below, they destroyed them to a man. . . . This vicissitude of first one party conquering, and then the other, prevailed as long as the life of Harold con-

tinued; but when he fell from having his brain pierced with an arrow, the flight of the English ceased not until night.[7]

The defeat ended Anglo-Saxon rule and brought a new pattern of government that would make England the strongest state in Europe.

France: political fragmentation. At the time William set sail, the monarchy in France barely existed. As we saw in Chapter 11, the later Carolingian rulers were generally weak and unable to defend the realm from Viking incursions. This task fell to the local counts and dukes, who built castles to protect the countryside and exercised the powers of the king in their territories. In France by the beginning of the tenth century there were more than thirty great feudal princes who were nominally vassals of the king but who gave him little or no support.

While the Carolingian kings tried to keep their precarious grasp on the throne, a new family sought to dislodge them. Founded by Robert the Strong, Count of Paris, this noble family gained renown when Robert's son Odo successfully defended Paris from Viking attacks between 885 and 887. In 887 the French nobility elected Odo king, but the Carolingians continued their efforts to obtain the throne. They were finally successful, for on Odo's death the French nobility gave the crown back to the Carolingians. The two rival houses contended for the throne for a century—until Louis v (Louis the Sluggard), the last Carolingian king, died in 987. As his successor, the nobles selected Hugh Capet, a descendant of the courageous Odo.

The "kingdom" which Hugh Capet theoretically ruled was roughly comparable to, but smaller than, modern France. The territory which Hugh actually controlled was a small feudal duchy extending from Paris to Orléans. It was almost encircled by rivers— hence, perhaps, its name: the Ile de France. The royal domain was surrounded by the great feudal holdings which made up more than three quarters of the country. These large independent dukedoms and counties, such as Flanders, Normandy, Anjou, and Champagne, were a law unto themselves. Their rulers paid little attention to the king and only tolerated him as a figurehead.

Ethnic and geographical differences added to the fragmentation of the kingdom. The population included such peoples as the Franks, Normans, Celts, Basques, and Provençals. In the north the Germanic element was very strong, and the climate was similar to that of England or Germany. In the south the sky was kinder, the climate warmer, and the people Mediterranean and Latin rather than Germanic. The most important areas in the south were the duchies of Gascony and Aquitaine and the county of Toulouse. One historian has contrasted the two cultures by saying that the north had a "beer and butter" economy while the south had one based on "oil and wine."[8] It was natural that the people of these two sections had trouble understanding each other and had little use for each other's customs. Under the last Carolingian monarchs and the first Capetians, the south was left pretty much alone and went its own way.

Early Capetians: groundwork for future greatness. The Capetian line of kings, founded by Hugh Capet in 987, ruled France until 1328. Starting with little power and limited territory under their direct rule, these monarchs inexorably extended their control over the great magnates. France was literally made by its kings, for ultimately the royal domain, in which the king's word was law, came to coincide with the boundaries of the entire country (see map, p. 425).

In the late tenth and eleventh centuries, however, there was little tangible evidence that the Capetian kings would fulfill their destiny. These kings of France were weaker than several of their own vassals, and they had no hand in the stirring events of their time. While they remained historical nonentities, one of their vassals, the duke of Normandy, seized the throne of England; another, the count of Flanders, became a leader of the First Crusade and ruler of the kingdom of Jerusalem; and another vassal became the founder of the kingdom of Portugal.

The major accomplishment of the first four Capetian kings was their success in keeping the French crown within their own family. The nobles who elected Hugh Capet to the kingship had no thought of giving the Capetian family a monopoly on the royal office. But the Capetian kings, with the support of the Church, cleverly arranged for the election and coronation of their heirs. Before the king died, the young prince was crowned by the Church and became "associated" with his father in his rule; after the king's death, his son was crowned again. For three hundred years the House of Capet never lacked a male heir, and by the end of the twelfth century the hereditary principle had become so ingrained that French kings no longer took the precaution of crowning their sons during their own lifetime.

In addition to maintaining their hold on the throne of France, the early Capetians carefully nurtured the tradition of kingship as a sacred office. Going back to the days of Pepin, the coronation ceremony as performed by a churchman gave the king a sacred character; he was allied with the Church and ruled by divine right. Thus, by virtue of being king, Hugh Capet was

FEUDAL FRANCE ABOUT 1000

Ile de France

unique, a man above all other men, the instrument of God. This "moral ascendancy" of the French king is expressed in the oath taken by young Philip I, the fourth Capetian, when he was crowned:

I Philip, by Grace of God soon to be king of France, on the day of my ordination promise, in the sight of God and his Saints, that I will maintain inviolate for every one of you and for all the churches under your charge their canonical privileges, their legal rights and their security in justice; that, with the help of God, I will defend you to the utmost as by right a king must defend every bishop and church in the kingdom committed to him. I promise furthermore to the people who are entrusted to me that I shall insure by my authority the enforcement of the laws which constitutes their right.[9]

It made no difference that the king's claim to be protector of both Church and people did not at all exist in fact. The important thing was that this claim kept alive the theory of anointed sovereignty along with that of feudal suzerainty. The opportunity would come for strong kings to make theory coincide with practice.

The first four Capetians did not antagonize the mighty vassals but were content to bide their time. Amid the feuds of the vassals, the kings maintained a precarious existence, nimbly hopping from one side to the other as the fortunes of war changed. The insignificant political power of the early Capetian kings, together with their primitive subsistence under the manorial system, is well described by a French historian:

Less powerful than certain of his great vassals, the king, like them, lived from the produce of his farms and tolls, from the dues of his peasants, from the labor of his serfs, from the contributions, disguised under the form of "voluntary" gifts, which he levied on the abbots and bishops of the country. His granaries . . . furnished him with wheat; his cellars . . . with wine; his forests . . . with venison. He passed his time in hunting, either for pleasure or to supply his table, and constantly traveled from manor to manor, from monastery to monastery, obliged to exploit his right of *droit de gîte* [right of hospitality], but frequently to change his abode lest he exhaust the resources of his subjects.[10]

In 1100, eight years before his death, the fourth Capetian, Philip I, turned over the reins of government to his son Louis the Fat. This event heralded the end of Capetian weakness and the beginning of a new period during which the potentialities of the royal title were realized.

EUROPE AGAINST THE MUSLIMS

Norman conquests in Italy and Sicily. About the year 1000, southern Italy was a battleground for rival Lombard dukes, the Byzantine empire, and the Muslims. The Lombards ruled several duchies; the eastern empire controlled the "heel and toe" of the peninsula, all that remained of Justinian's reconquest of Italy; and across the Strait of Messina a number of mutually hostile Muslim princes ruled the island of Sicily.

In 1016 Norman adventurers plunged into this maelstrom of continual warfare. A group of Norman knights, passing through southern Italy after a pilgrimage to Jerusalem, were urged to return home and bring back knights to help two of the Lombard dukes fight against their overlord, the Byzantine emperor. Soon the news spread among the land-hungry lesser nobles of Normandy that Italy was a land where a knight could easily acquire an estate, provided he had a sword and a strong right arm. At first the Norman knights fought for hire, looting their victims as they stormed through the land. Next they began to carve out large estates for themselves in southern Italy.

One obscure house, that of Tancred of Hauteville, was burdened with twelve husky sons, all of whom made their way to southern Italy. One blond giant of this family, Robert Guiscard, established his authority over his fellow Normans and by 1071 extinguished the last Byzantine foothold in southern Italy (see p. 230). Meanwhile, Robert had allied himself with the pope, and in return the papacy recognized him as the ruler of southern Italy and of Sicily, still in Muslim hands. Under the leadership of

Robert and his brother Roger, the Normans crossed the Strait of Messina in the face of a large Muslim fleet and gained a footing in Sicily just a few years before William the Conqueror crossed the Channel to invade England. In 1072 they captured Palermo, and twenty years later the entire island of Sicily had fallen to the Normans.

During the Sicilian campaign Robert Guiscard took time to launch an audacious attack on the Byzantine empire by invading the Adriatic coast, but his dream of becoming emperor of Constantinople did not become a reality. Despite the fact that he died in 1085 without conquering the eastern empire and before the conquest of Sicily was complete, he left his son a powerful military state.

In retrospect, the part the Normans played in early medieval history is nothing short of amazing. They left a deep impress upon the history of France, England, and Italy. In Sicily early in the next century Roger's son, Roger II, once again demonstrated Norman energy and genius by creating what was for a time the most advanced government, economy, and culture in Europe (see p. 430).

Venice, Genoa, and Pisa battle the Muslims. While the Normans had been ejecting the Muslims from Sicily, similar offensives had been going on elsewhere in the Mediterranean. The rapidly advancing city of Venice had cleared the Adriatic Sea and in 1002 had won a great naval victory over a Muslim fleet. This enhanced Venetian trade with Byzantium. During the eleventh century the coastal towns of western Italy also made rapid naval and commercial advances. Genoa and Pisa, in particular, began to fight the Muslims in the Tyrrhenian Sea, capturing Corsica and Sardinia. Finally, in 1087, the fleets of Genoa and Pisa attacked the Barbary Coast of North Africa and burned the main fleet of the Muslim rulers. The western Mediterranean had been cleared of Muslim pirates and traders; the crusades to the Holy Land would shortly do the same for the eastern Mediterranean.

Muslim civilization in Spain. Although the offensive of the West had cleared the Muslims from the waters of the western Mediterranean, Muslim power remained in Spain. We will recall that with the fall of Rome in the fifth century, Visigothic tribes had settled in Spain; but they in turn had fallen to the Muslim invasion (see p. 319). Muslim Spain was ruled from Damascus until 756, when it became an independent Muslim state under the last remaining member of the Umayyad dynasty.

From their center at Cordova, the ancient capital of Roman Spain, the Umayyad rulers (756-1031) inaugurated a brilliant era. The Caliphate of Cordova, as Muslim Spain was called after 929, made many economic and cultural advances. Water power was harnessed to drive mills, new crops such as rice and sugar cane were introduced, and grain cultivation flourished. Wine production and the making of olive oil were successful industries. Cordova itself far outshone contemporary cities and attained a pinnacle of luxury and beauty.

Cordova . . . at its highest point of prosperity, boasted of more than two hundred thousand houses, and more than a million of inhabitants. After sunset, a man might walk through it in a straight line for ten miles by the light of the public lamps. Seven hundred years after this time there was not so much as one public lamp in London. Its streets were solidly paved. In Paris, centuries subsequently, whoever stepped over his threshold on a rainy day stepped up to his ankles in mud. . . . The Spanish Mohammedans had brought with them all the luxuries and prodigalities of Asia. Their residences . . . had polished marble balconies, overhanging orange-gardens; courts with cascades of water; [and] shady retreats provocative of slumber in the heat of the day. . . . Great care was taken to make due provision for the cleanliness, occupation, and amusement of the inmates. Through pipes of metal, water, both warm and cold, to suit the season of the year, ran into baths of marble.[11]

Spain became famous throughout Europe for her industries and learning. Spanish linens were much sought after, and Cordova became noted for its leather goods. Spanish steel, silks, glass, and tapestries were unmatched in Europe. The Muslims of Spain were the most cultured people of the West. Literature and art became their glories, and learning flourished when the rulers, often men of letters themselves, invited some of

The Great Mosque at Cordova is a fine example of the Islamic art that flourished in Spain during the Muslim rule of that country.

the best scholars of the Muslim East to settle in Spain. By the twelfth century scholars from northern Europe were flocking to Spain to study, and through them much of the learning of the Arabs passed to Christian Europe.

The lot of the conquered Christians was not especially bad. Christian worship continued, and, generally speaking, tolerance was granted to all people—including Christians and Jews. The latter, who had been persecuted under the Visigoths, flourished in the professions and as officials of the state. Many Jews came .from Christian Europe and the East, and the Talmudic school at Cordova became a leading center of Hebrew learning. Christians were converted to Islam, there was much intermarriage, and many of the later Muslim leaders were of Gothic or Hispano-Roman descent.

Despite its accomplishments in the economic and intellectual fields, Muslim Spain was usually politically weak and disunited. Spain had been conquered by a medley of Arabs, Syrians, and Berbers, who were often in discord. The invaders themselves were outnumbered by the native population. The Caliphate reached the height of its power in the tenth century (912-1002) but thereafter declined. The caliphs after about 1000 were a mediocre lot, unable to withstand the pressures of factionalism. In 1031 the Umayyads were overthrown, and the Caliphate of Cordova was replaced by twenty-three small, warring states.

Early Christian victories in the Reconquista. During the seven years of the initial Muslim conquest of Spain, many Christians found a refuge in the north behind the Cantabrian Mountains (see Reference Map 8). Here, in 718, a Visigothic remnant defeated a small Muslim force; in later times this modest victory was looked upon as the beginning of the *Reconquista,* the reconquest of Spain from the Muslims. The *Reconquista* became the dominant theme of medieval Spanish history and did much to produce the religious ardor and military valor that ·characterized the Spaniard of early modern times.

Around this nucleus of opposition in the northeast the small kingdom of Asturias took shape, with a king and a capital at Oviedo. It was about this time that Charlemagne invaded Spain and established the Spanish March (see p. 322). When the Carolingian empire collapsed, the following Christian states survived in the north of Spain: the county of Barcelona, Charlemagne's Spanish March, in the east; Asturias in the west; and in between, Navarre, peopled by the fiercely independent Basques whom neither the Romans nor the Visigoths had wholly subdued.

Slowly gathering strength and resolution, these Christian states expanded south through the hills, with Asturias leading the way. Leon was reached by 866 and the Douro River by 900, when the Asturian king changed his title to King of Leon. An offshoot of Leon was the county of Castile, named after the many castles built to defend it. In the mid-tenth century Castile became strong enough to throw off the rule of the king of Leon and to develop into an independent Christian kingdom.

During the height of the Caliphate power in the tenth century, the Muslims halted and in some instances severely set back the expansion of the Christian kingdoms. However, the disintegration of the Caliphate of Cordova into small Muslim states after 1031 opened the way for further Christian advances: Castile captured a large part of what was to become Portugal, and the southern border of Castile was pushed from the Douro to the Tagus River. In 1063, a generation before the first crusade to the Holy Land, the pope proclaimed the *Reconquista* to be a holy crusade, and the first of many northern knights flocked to Spain to fight the Muslims. In 1085 the mighty bastion of Toledo fell to the king of Castile, and the end of the Muslim occupation seemed in sight. Yet the *Reconquista* continued for nearly five hundred years more, and militant expansion in the name of Christianity colored the formative years of the two modern nations of Spain and Portugal (see Chapter 14).

THE CRUSADES: "GOD WILLS IT!"

The call to a crusade. The most dramatic expression of Europe on the offensive was the crusades. For hundreds of years peaceful pilgrims had been traveling from Europe to the Holy Land to worship at the birthplace of Christ, in the Garden of Gethsemane, and at the Holy Sepulcher. By the tenth century bishops were organizing mass pilgrimages to the Holy Land. The largest of these, which set out from Germany in 1065, included about seven thousand pilgrims.

From the time of the first Muslim expansion in the Near East in the seventh century, these shrines, so venerated in Christian Europe, had lain under the domination of Islam. Until the eleventh century Christian pilgrims had met little trouble in the Holy Land; the Muslim governors had been enlightened rulers who were willing to permit the Christians to visit their shrines.

In the early eleventh century, however, Christian pilgrims began to be persecuted, and when the Seljuk Turks, new and fanatical converts to Islam, came sweeping and plundering into the Near East, the situation became especially aggravated. The Seljuks seized Jerusalem from their fellow Muslims and then swept north into Asia Minor. Byzantine forces desperately tried to bar the invader, but at the battle of Manzikert (1071) the eastern emperor was killed and his army scattered. Constantinople itself was threatened, and frantic appeals were sent to Europe and to the pope in particular for aid. Tales of alleged Turkish mistreatment of Christian pilgrims circulated throughout Europe, and though there is evidence that these stories were propaganda, men's minds became inflamed.

The journey to Jerusalem was one of the most popular Christian pilgrimages. This pilgrim's guide to Jerusalem, dating from about 1150, is a fairly accurate rendering of the important religious shrines in the city.

POLITICAL DIVISIONS OF EUROPE
IN THE EARLY 13TH CENTURY

English possessions in France
under Henry II, 1180

English possessions in France
at the death of Henry III, 1272

First Crusade, 1096
Second Crusade, 1147
Third Crusade, 1189
Fourth Crusade, 1204
First Crusade of Louis IX, 1248
Second Crusade of Louis IX, 1267

In 1095 Pope Urban II answered the pleas of the Byzantine emperor, Alexius Comnenus, and of the eastern Christians by calling the First Crusade to rescue both the Byzantine empire and the Holy Land. Preaching at the Council of Clermont in that year, he exhorted Christians to take up the cross and strive for a cause that promised not merely spiritual rewards but material gain as well, when Christians should possess the Holy Land that "flowed with milk and honey." At the end of his impassioned oration the crowd shouted "God wills it"—the expression which the crusaders later used in battle.

The primary impetus behind the crusades was undoubtedly religious; they constituted in effect a holy war, and following Pope Urban's appeal, there was a real and spontaneous outpouring of religious enthusiasm. The word *crusade* itself is derived from "taking the cross," after the example of Christ. (On the way to the Holy Land, the crusader wore the cross on his breast; on his journey home, he wore the cross on his back.) Urban also promised the crusaders that they would enjoy indulgence from purgatorial sufferings for their past sins. The pope, moreover, hoped that the religious enthusiasm following in the wake of the crusades would strengthen his claim to the moral leadership of Europe. Furthermore, the Church was eagerly promoting the Peace and Truce of God (see p. 332) in an effort to mitigate the evils of feudal warfare; and the pope saw in the crusades an outlet for the restless, pugnacious nobles—"aforetime robbers," to use Urban's own words. Their warring energies could be channeled for the glory of God.

Some crusaders were motivated by worldly considerations. When a crusader put the red cross on his tunic, he became a privileged person. Through the influence of the Church, he was exempt from taxes, and his debts were temporarily canceled; the Church assumed responsibility for his property and dependents while he was away from home. Also, some nobles saw a chance to seize valuable land in Syria, and merchants in the Italian city-states recognized a demand for Italian ships to carry the crusaders and their supplies to the Holy Land. Thus the crusades did clearly offer an opportunity for material as well as spiritual profit.

Like many historical movements, the crusades were compounded of undiluted idealism, enlightened self-interest, and downright skulduggery. Some of the crusaders were little more than riffraff—thieves trying to escape justice, debtors who could not satisfy their creditors, and outright ruffians and cutthroats. Strange paradoxes arose. The cynical and heretical German emperor Frederick II was more successful in his crusade than the saintly King Louis IX of France. Similarly, the grasping Italian merchants achieved more lasting benefits from the crusades than did the devout pilgrims, who were willing to give their lives that the Holy Sepulcher might be rescued from the infidel.

First Crusade gains a foothold in Jerusalem. From the end of the eleventh century to the end of the thirteenth, there were eight distinct crusades, as well as various small expeditions which from time to time tried their hands against the Saracen.

The First Crusade, led principally by princes and nobles from France, parts of Germany, and Norman Italy, proceeded overland to Constantinople. Having expected the help of European mercenaries against the Seljuks, Alexius Comnenus was taken aback when the crusaders arrived in Constantinople. He hastily directed the crusading zeal against the Turks, who were forced back in Asia Minor. The First Crusade was the most successful of the eight; with not more than five thousand knights and infantry, it overcame the resistance of the Turks, who were no longer united. Against terrible odds it won great victories at Dorylaeum and Antioch, and its crusaders fought with incredible valor. Above all, it captured the Holy City—Jerusalem. Unfortunately, with this religious exaltation went fanaticism and intolerance, as this contemporary account of the Christian entrance into Jerusalem shows:

But now that our men had possession of the walls and towers, wonderful sights were to be seen. Some of our men . . . cut off the heads of their enemies; others shot them with arrows, so that they fell from the towers; others tortured them longer by casting them into the flames. Piles of heads, hands, and feet were to be seen in the streets of the city. It was necessary to pick one's way over the bodies of men and horses. But these were small matters compared to what happened at the Temple of Solomon [where] . . . men rode in blood up to their knees and bridle reins. Indeed it was a just and splendid judgment of God that this place should be filled with the blood of the unbelievers, since it had suffered so long from their blasphemies.[12]

The First Crusade conquered a long strip of territory along the eastern coast of the Mediterranean and created the feudal Latin kingdom of Jerusalem, which lasted until its last remnant fell to the Muslims in 1291.

When the kingdom of Jerusalem became endangered, St. Bernard of Clairvaux organized a Second Crusade, and Louis VII of France and the German emperor Conrad III joined forces in 1147. They met with many misfortunes in getting to the Near East, and the Second Crusade ended when they failed to capture Damascus.

The "Crusade of Kings." The fall of Jerusalem in 1187 to the Muslims, reinvigorated under the leadership of Saladin (see p. 264), served to provoke the Third Crusade (1189). Europe's leading monarchs—Frederick Barbarossa of Germany, Richard I (the Lion-Hearted) of England, and Philip Augustus of France—set forth on their holy mission. Frederick was drowned; and, after a quarrel

with Richard, Philip returned home. Saladin and Richard remained the chief protagonists.

This crusade was distinguished by the dignity of Saladin and the valor of Richard. Saladin, "the merciful, chivalrous, and upright zealot," exhibited qualities of character duplicated by few of his Christian opponents. His common-sense approach to a settlement was evidenced when he proposed that Richard I should marry his sister and be given Palestine as a wedding present, a proposal which shocked the Europeans. One of the greatest warriors of his day, Richard amazed his foes by his outstanding deeds of heroism, and his feats became legendary in the Muslim as well as in the Christian world.

Richard and Saladin finally agreed to a three-year truce by which Christians were given control of a small strip of eastern Mediterranean coast, and pilgrims were allowed to visit Jerusalem. The truce scarcely compensated for the cost of such an expensive crusade.

Religious ideal missing from Fourth Crusade. The Fourth Crusade is an example of the degradation of a religious ideal. The few knights who answered Pope Innocent III's call were unable to meet the outrageous shipping charges demanded by the Venetians (see p. 231). The Venetians persuaded them to pay off the sum by capturing the Christian town of Zara on the Adriatic coast,

In this manuscript illumination Saladin wrests the cross, symbol of Christianity, from one of the leaders of the crusades.

which had long proved troublesome to Venetian trading interests. After Zara had been captured, the merchants of Venice next pressured the crusaders into attacking Constantinople. After conquering and sacking the capital of the eastern empire, the crusaders set up the Latin empire (1204-1261) to rule the area.

This attack on Constantinople utterly perverted the original purposes of the crusades. Although the First Crusade sought to preserve the independence of the eastern empire as well as to free the Holy Land of the Muslims, the Venetians used the Fourth Crusade to divest the Byzantine empire of its power and rich trade. The center of Mediterranean trade thereby shifted from the Near East to Venice and thence to western Europe. A religious movement had been corrupted to serve Venetian trading interests.

Later crusades fail. The thirteenth century saw other crusades. In the ill-fated Children's Crusade in 1212, thousands of youngsters were sold into slavery by Marseilles merchants. The Fifth Crusade captured Damietta in Egypt in 1219, only to lose it and fail altogether. The Sixth Crusade in 1228, organized by Frederick ii, differed from previous attempts in that it involved no slaughter, pillage, or robbery. Through Frederick's negotiating skill and tolerance, it gained privileges for Christian pilgrims far superior to any achieved previously. The Christians were granted Jerusalem and other shrines in the Holy Land, but this arrangement ended in 1244 with the Muslim conquest of the Holy City. As a result of this loss, Louis ix of France organized the Seventh Crusade, but despite the zeal and devotion of the leader, it proved a fiasco from beginning to end. In 1270 Louis attempted another crusade to Tunis but died at Carthage. Then, in swift succession, the feudal states created by the crusaders in the Near East were captured by the Turks, and in 1291, Acre, the last stronghold of the Christians, fell into the hands of the Muslims.

The crusader states. Altogether four crusader principalities, with the kingdom of Jerusalem dominant, had been established along the eastern Mediterranean coast (see map, p. 358). By the time Jerusalem fell to Saladin in 1187, however, only isolated pockets of Christians remained, surrounded by a vast hinterland of hostile Muslims. During their insecure existence the crusader states were able to survive only by reason of frequent transfusions of strength from Europe in the form of supplies and man power. In the crusader states the Europeans were only a small minority ruling over the native populations. The conquerors introduced a complex system of feudalism into these states. The "Assizes of Jerusalem," a body of customs drawn up by lawyers in the thirteenth century, constituted a frequently cited example of feudal law in the Middle Ages.

For two centuries the crusader states constituted a fertile point of cultural contact between the West and East, with little or no effect upon the latter but with important influences upon the Europeans. The European nobles who sought a permanent home in the Holy Land became orientalized. Amid the luxuries of the East and under the hot Palestinian sun, they found it difficult to live as they had in the damp and cold castles of northern Europe. It was natural for them to adopt the customs of their Muslim neighbors and dress in light, flowing robes and turbans. Their houses were like Moorish villas, decorated and furnished with divans of brocade, Persian rugs, mosaic floors, and silk hangings. These transplanted men of France or southern Germany became tolerant and easygoing, trading and even hunting with Muslims. Frequently there was bad blood between these domiciled crusaders and the visiting nobles who had merely come for a short visit and a dash against the infidel. The European settlers of the East had little sympathy for the fanaticism and impetuosity of the newcomers. They were ready to defend their lands and castles against Muslim attack but would much rather live and let live.

The military orders. The crusader states were protected by the semimonastic military orders: the Templars, or Knights of the Temple, so called because their first headquarters was on the site of the old temple of Jerusalem; the Hospitalers, or Knights of St. John of Jerusalem, who were founded originally to care for the sick and wounded; and the Teutonic Knights, exclusively a German order. Combining monasticism and militarism, these orders had as their aims the protection of all pilgrims and perpetual war against the Muslims. These men of the cross could put five hundred armed knights into the field; and their great castles guarded the roads and passes against Muslim attack. For two centuries the uniforms of these orders were a common sight in the crusader states; the Templars wore a white robe decorated with a red cross, the Hospitalers a black robe with a white cross, and the Teutonic Knights a white robe with a black cross.

Achievements of the crusades. After two centuries of struggling to push the infidel out of the Holy Land, of losing tens of thousands of lives, and of spending incalculable wealth, what was there to show for all this effort? No territorial gains remained for Christians on the Asian mainland after the Muslims won back the last Christian foothold in the Holy Land at Acre in 1291. Yet while they failed to achieve their specific objective, the crusades cannot be written off as mere adventures. On the contrary, their influence extended over a much wider geographical field than just the Holy Land. Much of the crusading fervor carried over to the fight against the Muslims in Spain and the pagan Slavs in eastern Europe. Politically the crusades weakened the Byzantine empire and accelerated its fall (see Chapter 8). Furthermore, by depleting the ranks of the nobles, they strengthened the rising power of the kings and national monarchies in western Europe. Although the early crusades strengthened the moral leadership of the papacy in Europe, the ill-success of the later crusades, together with the preaching of crusades against Christian heretics (see p. 388) and political opponents (see p. 432), lessened both the crusading ideal and respect for the papacy.

Contact with Muslim culture also led Europeans to adopt new foods and textiles. In architecture, Byzantine styles were borrowed, as shown by St. Mark's Cathedral in Venice. The crusades also influenced the style of castles, and heraldic emblems were copied from the Muslims.

The contact with the East widened the scope of the Europeans, ended their isolation, and exposed them to a vastly superior civilization. Although it is easy to exaggerate the economic effects of the crusades, they did complete the reopening of the eastern Mediterranean to western commerce; they also contributed to the growth of great ports and the rise of cities, the emergence of a money economy, and the increased contact between Europe and the unknown interior of Asia. The crusades as a movement were a manifestation of the dynamic vitality and expansive spirit of Europe, evident in many fields by the end of the eleventh century.

THE RISE OF TRADE AND TOWNS

Revitalized trade routes. Although scholars have long debated the extent of trade and urban life that existed during the early Middle Ages, there is general agreement that fresh trade activity was evident even before the crusades. With the ending of Viking and Magyar attacks in the tenth century, a northern trading area developed which extended from the British Isles to the Baltic Sea. Closely related to this northern trade area was the route established by the Vikings as early as the ninth century, when they settled in Russia and created the lucrative Varangian route from the eastern Baltic down the rivers of Russia to the Black Sea and Constantinople (see p. 244).

The center of this northern trade system was the county of Flanders. By 1050 Flemish artisans were producing a surplus of woolen cloth of such fine quality that it was in great demand. Baltic furs, honey and forest products, and British tin and raw wool were exchanged for Flemish cloth. From the south by way of Italy came oriental luxury goods—silks, sugar, and spices.

Equally important as a catalyst of the medieval commercial revolution—whose impact on the Middle Ages deserves to be compared to that of the Industrial Revolution on the modern world—was the opening up of the Mediterranean trading area. We recall that in the eleventh century the Normans and Italians broke the Muslim hold on the eastern Mediterranean and that the First Crusade inaugurated a flourishing trade with the Near East. Soon goods were being carried to the Far East and throughout Europe. Arab and Chinese vessels brought exports from India and China to ports on the Persian Gulf and Red Sea. From there they were shipped by caravan to Alexandria, Acre, and Joppa, and from those ports the merchants of Venice, Genoa, and Pisa transported the goods to Italy on their way to the markets of Europe. Other trade routes from Asia came overland, passing through Baghdad and Damascus and on to ports, such as Tyre and Sidon, in the crusader states. The recipients of this greatly expanded trade were the markets of Europe, which were supplied by way of inland trade routes. The easiest route from the Mediterranean to Flanders was via Marseilles, up the Rhone valley, then north to the Flemish towns.

Early in the fourteenth century two more major trade lanes developed within Europe. An all-sea route connected the central Mediterranean with England and northern Europe. Large fleets from such towns as Venice and Genoa defied the pirates still prevalent near the Strait of Gibraltar, and the galleys withstood the heavy storms of the Bay of Biscay. The old overland route from northern Italy through the Alpine passes to central Europe was also developed. From Venice and other north Italian cities, trade flowed through such passes as the Brenner to Augsburg, Nuremberg, Leipzig, and Lübeck, sharply reducing the business of the Rhone valley route and the fairs of Champagne which had functioned as a major clearing house for international trade.

Fairs, centers of European trade. In towns along the main European trade routes, astute lords set up fairs, where merchants from Italy and northern Europe congregated. During the twelfth and thirteenth centuries these fairs were the most important centers of international trade.

The fair differed from the market, which was a distinctly local affair held about once a week to allow the peasants to dispose of surplus goods from the manor and to obtain manufactured goods from the town. The fair was a much more important and elaborate event, held only seasonally or annually in specified areas of each European country. The laws of the region were set aside during a fair, and in their place was substituted a new commercial code called the "law merchant." Special courts, with merchants acting as judges, settled all disputes which arose. In England such courts were called "pie-powder courts," from the French *pied-poudré,* meaning "dusty foot."

The most famous fairs in all Europe were held in Champagne in northeastern France, but there were many others: in Leipzig and Frankfort in Germany, Venice and Genoa in Italy, Ypres and Lille in the Low Countries, Seville in Spain, and Boston in England. The word *tawdry* is derived from a corruption of the words *St. Audrey,* the name of a medieval English fair where cheap goods were often sold.

The fair was of great value in that it was a clearing house for both goods and ideas. From all over Europe, men congregated and exchanged information about new methods in industry, agriculture, and transportation. The fairs were largely responsible for the growing use of bills of exchange, letters of credit, and a money economy.

Factors in the rise of towns. The resurgence of trade in Europe was the prime cause of the revitalization of towns. To understand the importance of the revival of town life, we must remember that the urban civilization of the Romans had practically disappeared with the empire. During the early Middle Ages manufacturing languished, and city life became almost extinct; but from 1000 to 1200 the town became the invaluable agency in the growth of trade, the development of manufacturing, and the nurturing of art and thought. Trade and towns had an interacting effect on each other; the towns arose because of trade, but they also stimulated trade by providing greater markets and by producing goods for the merchants to sell.

In the revival of both commerce and cities, geography played an important role.

It determined the location of certain strategic towns and conditioned the type of commercial activities in which the towns engaged. Rivers, which were important in the evolution of ancient civilizations, played an equally important role in the development of medieval towns. They were natural highways on which articles of commerce could be easily transported. Many communities developed at the confluence of two important streams; others arose where a river might be easily crossed by a ford or bridge, "Oxford" or "Cam-bridge," for example. Locations near a mountain pass or on a good coastal harbor were also desirable.

Often at a strategic geographic location, a feudal noble had already erected a fortified castle, or *burg* (*bourg* in French, *borough* in English). The typical burg of the ninth and tenth centuries was just a fort; it had no real urban features. But later such a stronghold offered the merchants a good stopping place. The inhabitants of the burg were likely to buy some of the merchant's wares, and the castle offered him protection. In time a permanent merchant settlement, called a *faubourg,* grew up outside the walls of the burg. As an illustration, in the latter part of the tenth century Count Baldwin Iron-Arm of Flanders erected a castle in a loop of the river Lys; around this fortified center merchants and craftsmen settled permanently. Sometimes a merchant settlement adjoined an old Roman episcopal city like Cologne (Colonia Agrippina) or a fortified abbey or cathedral. Munich grew up around a monastery, and Durham was "half cathedral and half fortress against the Scot."

Other factors besides trade and geography contributed to the rise of towns. Perhaps the most striking social factor was the growth of population. In England, for example, the population more than tripled between 1066 and 1350. The reasons for this rapid increase in population are varied. The stabilization of feudal society with its furtherance of public safety and the ending of bloody foreign invasions were contributing factors. More important was an increase in food production brought about by the cultivation of waste lands, the clearing of forests, and the draining of marshes. Technological innovations such as the three-field system of crop rotation also increased production.

Another factor interacting with the growth of towns was the decline of serfdom. Many serfs escaped from the manors and made their way to the towns. After living a year and a day in the town, a serf was considered a freeman. A former serf could completely alter his old position and become a wealthy and influential craftsman or merchant in the town.

Italian, French, and Flemish towns. The factors encouraging the renewal of town life were first important in three areas: northern Italy, southern France, and Flanders. Stimulated by its ties with Constantinople (see p. 230), Venice by the eleventh century was trading regularly with the East. The coastal towns of Pisa and Genoa soon revived and followed the example set by Venice. Towns in the interior, such as Florence and Milan, became bustling trade centers, with Milan taking the lead in promoting trade over the Alps to Germany. Early in the twelfth century towns in southern France—Marseilles, Narbonne, and Montpellier—as well as Barcelona in nearby Catalonia, began to emulate the commercial success of the Italian towns.

Second only to the Italian towns were those in Flanders which grew up around the textile industry. Cambric from Cambrai, lisle from Lille, and gauntlets from Ghent (called "Gaunt" in England) became famous over all Europe. By the twelfth century the local supply of wool was inadequate, and it had to be imported on a large scale from England. Bruges was the leading commercial city in northern Europe until the late fifteenth century, when it was superseded by Antwerp. As the Flemish towns increased in population and wealth, trade and industry spread up the Rhine valley and stimulated the growth of towns like Cologne and Basel. Merchants from Cologne spurred the growth of such towns as Bremen, Hamburg, and Lübeck, which formed the nucleus of the great Hanseatic League.

The Hanseatic League. Originating in the thirteenth century, the Hanseatic League was a great trade association comprising the northern German cities. These cities joined forces for protection and to win economic privileges in foreign towns. The League built up a lucrative monopoly on Baltic and North Sea trade. Its wealth came primarily from its control of the Baltic herring fisheries, its corner on Russian trade, and its rich business with England and Flanders. It established permanent trading stations in such leading European centers as London and Bruges and in strategic locations like Novgorod, key town in the Russian trade. Until the fifteenth century, when it began to lose its privileges and monopolies, the Hanseatic League remained the great distributor of goods to northern Europe.

Because a strong German state had ceased to exist by the thirteenth century, the Hanseatic League formed its own organization to cope with political problems. A representative council dealt with trading problems common to all member cities, and a navy safeguarded its commerce from pirates and even waged a successful war with the king of Denmark.

Merchant guilds. When the merchants and artisans settled permanently in the towns, they organized themselves into guilds. These associations were useful not only from a business standpoint but also from a social and political viewpoint. The guild was designed to solve employer-worker problems, to regulate prices and wages, to govern production and distribution, to protect the individual member as a business associate, and to assure the social status of his family. There were two kinds of guilds: merchant and craft.

The merchant guild ensured monopoly of trade within a given locality. Membership usually included all merchants of a particular town, although merchants from other places were occasionally permitted to join. With a monopoly of the town's import and export trade, the guild could enforce its standards as it willed. All alien merchants were supervised closely and made to pay tolls. Disputes among merchants were settled at the guild court according to its own legal code. The guilds tried to make sure that the customers were not cheated: they checked

A guild master judges the work of a mason and a carpenter.

weights and measures and insisted upon a standard quality for goods. An example of punishment meted out to guild malefactors is given in the following contemporary account. For the sale of bad wine a court decided

that the said John Penrose shall drink a draught of the same wine which he sold to the common people; and the remainder of such wine shall then be poured on the head of the same John; and that he shall forswear the calling of a vintner in the city of London forever. . . .[13]

To allow only a legitimate profit, the guild fixed a "just price," which was fair to both the producer and consumer.

When guilds first appeared, there was no adequate central government to protect merchants as they carried on their trading activities throughout the land. As a result the guilds assumed some functions which would otherwise have been governmental. If a merchant was imprisoned in another town, the guild tried to secure his release at its own expense. If a merchant of a London guild refused to pay a debt owed to a merchant of a guild in Bristol, the merchant guild in the latter town would seize the goods of any London merchant coming to Bristol.

The guild's functions stretched beyond business and politics into charitable and social activities. If a guildsman fell into poverty, he was aided. The guild also provided financial assistance for the burial expenses of its members and looked after their dependents. Members attended social meetings in the guildhall, and each member was expected to attend the feast and "drink the guild" or be fined. The guilds also had a religious side and periodically held processions in honor of their patron saints. They performed such charitable duties as giving alms to friars and lepers, the poor and the sick.

Craft guilds. The increase of commerce brought a quickening of industrial life in the towns so that, as early as the eleventh century, the artisans began to organize. Craftsmen in each of the medieval trades—weaving, cobbling, tanning, and so on—joined forces. The result was the craft guild, which differed from the merchant guild in that membership was limited to artisans in one particular craft. Thus the goldsmiths were all together in one guild, the arrow makers in another, and so on with each trade. The system created much specialization; a guild might specialize in a single kind of hat, for example.

The general aims of the craft guilds were the same as those of the merchant guilds—the creation of a monopoly and the enforcement of a set of trade rules. Each guild had a monopoly of a certain article in a particular town, and every effort was made to prevent competition between members of the same guild. The guild restricted the number of its members, regulated the quantity and quality of the goods produced, and set prices. It also enforced regulations to protect the consumer from bad workmanship and inferior materials. Thus articles made at night or in private and out of sight were rightly regarded with suspicion. Even under close scrutiny, however, the customer could be robbed: "The subtle craft of the London bakers, who, while making up their customer's dough, stole a large portion of the dough under their customers' eyes by means of a little trap-door in the kneading-board and a boy sitting under the counter, was exceptional only in its ingenuity."[14] For the first offense, faulty workmen were fined, and old offenders were pilloried or banished.

The craft guild also differed from the merchant guild in its recognition of three distinct classes of workers—apprentices, journeymen, and master craftsmen. The relationship between the master and his workmen was very personal. The apprentice was a youth who lived at the master's house and was taught the trade thoroughly. Although he received no wages, all his physical needs were supplied. His apprenticeship commonly lasted seven years. When his schooling was finished, the youth became a journeyman (from the French *journée,* meaning "day's work"). He was then eligible to receive wages and to be hired by a master for varying periods of service. When about twenty-three, the journeyman sought admission into the guild as a master. To be accepted he had to prove his ability. Some crafts demanded the making of a "master piece"—for example, a pair of shoes that the master shoemakers would find acceptable in every way.

In the fourteenth century, when prosperity began to wane, the master craftsmen drastically restricted the number of journeymen who were allowed to become masters. The guilds either admitted only the relatives of masters or imposed excessively high entrance fees. When the journeymen then set up their own journeyman organizations, they were crushed by the wealthy guild masters, who usually controlled the town governments. By the fifteenth century most journeymen could not hope to become more than wage earners, and they bitterly resented the restrictions of the guild system.

Acquiring urban freedom. The guilds played an important role in local government. Both artisans and merchants, even though freemen, were subject to the lord upon whose domain the city stood. The citizens of the towns were not bound to the manor, and they resented the fact that the lord collected taxes as though they were

The horses pulling grain uphill in this illumination are wearing improved horseshoes which permit greater traction and collars which, by relieving pressure on their windpipes, greatly increase their pulling power.

serfs. In particular the tolls and dues imposed on the market rankled the merchants. Friction arose as the faubourg tried to declare its independence of the old burg. The townsmen demanded the privileges of governing themselves—of making their own laws, administering their own justice, levying their own taxes, and issuing their own coinage. Naturally the lord resented the impertinent upstarts who demanded self-government. But the towns won their independence in various ways.

One way was to become a commune, a self-governing town. The merchant guilds, in particular, forced the lord to agree to a charter which specifically granted the town certain rights to self-government. Often a charter had to be won by a revolt; in other circumstances it could be purchased, for the feudal lord was always in need of money. By 1200 the Lombard towns, as well as many French and Flemish towns, could boast of communal privileges.

Since the guilds had played such a large part in winning the concessions, they proceeded to run the commune, even though only a small portion of the town's inhabitants belonged to the guilds. Thus the guilds and the local government became closely allied, and a "businessman's government" often excluded from citizenship those who had not helped procure the charter.

Where royal authority was strong, we find "privileged" towns. In a charter granted to the town by the monarch, the inhabitants won extensive financial and legal powers. The town was given management of its own finances and paid its taxes in a lump sum to the king. It was also generally given the right to elect its own officials and organize its own guilds. The king was glad to grant such a charter, for it weakened the power of his nobles and at the same time won him the support of the townsmen.

Founding new towns was still another way in which feudal restrictions were broken down. Shrewd lords and kings, who recognized the economic value of having towns in their territories, founded carefully planned centers with well-laid-out streets and open squares. As a means of obtaining inhabitants, they offered many inducements in the form of personal privileges and tax limitations. Among such new towns were Newcastle, Freiburg, and Berlin.

Medieval technological advances. We will recall that the Greeks, by arriving at universal, underlying concepts, laid the foundations for a new philosophy and methodology of science (see p. 112) and that this new method virtually disappeared for a millennium prior to the sixteenth century (see p. 158). But the absence of a scientific method in the Middle Ages did not prevent the development of major technological advances. On the contrary, it can be argued that in this period "technology was the parent of science."[15]

During the Middle Ages a large number of important inventions and ideas spread from eastern Asia to western Europe. These included the wheelbarrow, deep-drilling machinery, iron-casting techniques, lock gates, paper, printing, gunpowder, the stern-post rudder, and the magnetic compass.

Another major area of technological advance occurred in the use of prime movers (natural agencies applied to the production of power). In Neolithic, fluvial, and classical societies men and animals were almost the only source of power. Our medieval ancestors succeeded to an unprecedented degree in maximizing the muscle power of draft animals by three major developments. First, for the traditional horse collar which fastened around the animal's neck and choked him when pulling a heavy load, they substituted a harness fitted so that the shoulders bore the weight. Second, they developed a tandem harness in order to utilize the strength of several horses; and finally, they improved traction with a new type of horseshoe. These inventions are said to have done for the eleventh and twelfth centuries what the steam engine did for the nineteenth. In addition, our medieval forebears increased the number of prime movers beyond sheer human and animal muscle power. They developed water-mills, both horizontal and vertical, as well as windmills with rotating turrets to catch the variable winds in the higher latitudes. Useful not only for grinding grains, these water- and windmills provided power for draining marshlands, for reclaiming areas from the sea (as in the Low Countries), for lumbering, and for new woolen mills, such as those in Flanders.

Technology and the new Europe. We have mentioned previously that during the early Middle Ages a new Europe emerged whose focus was no longer the shores of the Mediterranean but the plains north of the Loire River in the kingdom of the Franks. According to one eminent medievalist, this northward shift of Europe's center of gravity can be accounted for in the technological, and especially the agricultural, revolution of the early Middle Ages.

By the early ninth century all the major interlocking elements of this revolution had been developed: the heavy plough, the open fields, the modern harness, the triennial rotation. . . . The agricultural revolution . . . was limited to the northern plains where the heavy plough was appropriate to the rich soils, where the summer rains permitted a large spring planting, and where the oats of the summer crop supported the horses to pull the heavy plough. It was on those plains that the distinctive features both of the late medieval and of the modern worlds developed. The increased returns from the labour of the northern peasant raised his standard of living and consequently his ability to buy manufactured goods. It provided surplus food which, from the ninth century on, permitted rapid urbanization. . . . And in this new environment germinated the dominant feature of the modern world: power technology.[16]

Eotechnics—the dawn of a machine technology. At this point we come to a highly significant development in the history of western technology and society alike— the advent of the machine. Lewis Mumford coined the word *Eotechnic,* to describe what he considered to be the preparatory, or "dawn," stage required to initiate the Industrial Revolution. The Eotechnic phase, as we have just seen, initiated a shift from total reliance on human and animal muscles to a progressive exploitation of water and wind as prime movers. There was also an accompanying shift from complete dependence on tools to the production of crude machines. As Mumford points out, a tool lends itself to manipulation (such as by the hand) while a machine involves automation. In other words, whereas a tool permits flexibility and calls for human operation, the machine emphasizes specialization and repetition of function and does not necessarily require human manipulation or power. Machines have been in use since the potter's wheel, which is both specialized and repetitive in its function (although it uses human power). Thus although many earlier cultures had employed machines, it remained for western Europeans not only to invent machines in unprecedented numbers and for unique functions but also to develop a machine mentality—in other words, to gear the habits and goals of their civilization progressively to the capabilities and pace of the machine itself. Eventually, the acceptance of a machine technology was to result in the Industrial Revolution and the accelerating transformation of our contemporary environment.

Significance of a new emphasis on "measurement." The "Greek miracle" occurred not only because of the application of deductive reasoning but also because of the importance the Greeks attached to the concept of *metric,* namely, the use of precise techniques of measurement (such as those developed by Euclid or employed by Eratosthenes and Ptolemy). Reliance upon objective, impersonal forms of measurement is basic both to any truly scientific method and to a scientific attitude of mind. The Eotechnic phase in turn placed a new emphasis on measurement—which is essential both to the construction and the functioning of a machine.

In the Middle Ages the monastery led the way in developing agricultural technology. To avoid unnecessary labor, which reduced the time available for meditation and prayer, monasteries sought to mechanize all manufactures to the fullest extent of their resources. This helps explain why Cistercian regulations recommended that monasteries be built near rivers that could supply power.

The monasteries carried the process of mechanization still further, for they divided the day into a number of equal periods and needed some means of keeping count of the periods and ensuring their regular repetition. Mumford suggests that "the monasteries . . . helped to give human enterprise the regular collective beat and rhythm of the machine; for the clock is not merely a means of keeping track of the hours, but of synchronizing the actions of men."[17] Eventually, in both ecclesiastical and civil life, men came to reckon time in terms of equal hours, an attitude that coincided with the development of the mechanical clock.

The clock . . . is a piece of power-machinery whose 'product' is seconds and minutes; by its essential nature it dissociated time from human events and helped create the belief in an independent world of mathematically measurable sequences: the special world of science. . . . When one thinks of time, not as a sequence of experiences, but as a collection of hours, minutes, and seconds, the habits of adding time and saving time come into existence. Time took on the character of an enclosed space: it could be divided, it could be filled up, it could even be expanded by the invention of laborsaving instruments.[18]

This progressive measurement, or mechanization, of time in the Eotechnic phase illustrates again how the technological advances of our medieval ancestors helped create the basis of our contemporary machine-dominated society. Moreover, this technology was to help men understand again—as they had in classical times—that the phenomenal world can be objectively measured and analyzed.

Inventions in the late Middle Ages. The later Middle Ages was not lacking in ingenuity. In the twelfth century the mariner's compass was invented; this was followed about 1300 by the invention of the rudder and in the fourteenth and fifteenth centuries by changes in the design of ships. The West's acquaintance in the thirteenth century with gunpowder (invented by the Chinese) was followed in the fourteenth and fifteenth centuries by further developments in armor and fortifications and by the invention of firearms and artillery. The fourteenth century also witnessed the introduction of the blast furnace and progress in ironworking.

The use of money, banking, and credit. All the aspects of Europe's expansion—the crusades, the rapid revival of trade, the rise of cities, and the expansion of industry—had far-reaching effects on the financial structure. The first big change came with the reappearance of money as a medium of exchange. With the coming of the crusades, the participants had to raise money quickly to purchase equipment. Funds also had to be taken to the Holy Land for supplies.

To raise ready cash, the nobles in effect mortgaged their lands, usually to monasteries. Money also began to be used at the fairs. Coins were made from silver dug from new and improved mines throughout Europe, but during the whole of the Middle Ages silver bullion was in short supply. In

Representative of the burgeoning trade and commerce of the fourteenth century, this miniature depicts a Genoese moneylender bargaining with men who have come to pawn items similar to those hanging at the back of the shop, while a second moneylender enters accounts in a ledger.

the thirteenth century silver coins were superseded in international trade by gold, especially the florin of Florence, which became a monetary standard for Europe.

When the English king Henry III invaded France in 1242, he carried with him thirty barrels of money, each containing 160,000 coins, to defray the expenses of the expedition. This incident graphically illustrates the need for instruments of credit and other forms of banking. All important was the technique of "symbolic transfer." By this system a man deposited his money in a bank and received in return a receipt, which could later be cashed in any of the offices of the same bank. This method was very useful during the crusades, when the Templars arranged a system whereby crusaders could deposit money in the Paris office and withdraw it from the office in the Holy Land.

Banking also sprang from the activities of moneychangers at fairs and other trading centers. In addition to exchanging the coin of one region for another, these moneychangers would also accept money on deposit for safekeeping. The most important bankers, however, were Italian merchants from Florence and the Lombard cities, who by the middle of the thirteenth century were loaning their accumulated capital to kings and prelates. They found various ways of circumventing the Church's disapproval of all interest as usury. For example, if a sum was not repaid by a certain date, a penalty charge was levied.

THE EMERGENCE OF A NEW SOCIETY

Cities as centers of civilization. The growth of town life is synonymous with a quickening of the tempo of civilization. This was as true in medieval Europe as it was in ancient Egypt, India, Mesopotamia, Greece, Rome, and Byzantium. Cities have always been centers of new ideas, new inventions, new classes of people, new styles of dress, new tastes in food, new schemes in politics and economics, new ventures in trade, and new contacts in culture. Urban life has been one of man's chief aids in creating cultural changes. Similarly, new ideas were quickly transmitted in the medieval cities; in feudal and manorial Europe the same ideas would have been slow to spread.

The typical town. The medieval city was not large by modern standards. It has been estimated that Paris by 1450 had grown to a population of 300,000, which made it the largest city in Christian Europe. In 1400 London had merely 40,000 inhabitants. In spite of the relatively small populations, the towns were crowded. The inhabitants of the early towns had built walls around the faubourg, but the city usually outgrew these in a short time.

Since the area within the walls was at a premium, medieval towns were more crowded than the average modern city. Shops were even built on bridges (as on the Ponte Vecchio, which still stands in

Florence), and buildings were erected to a height of seven or more stories. The houses projected over the street with each additional story so that it was often possible for persons at the tops of houses opposite one another to touch hands.

The streets below were dark and narrow and almost invariably crooked, although they were often designed to be wide enough "to give passage to a horseman with his lance across his saddle-bows." The streets were full of discordant sounds—drivers yelled at pedestrians to get out of the way of the horses and oxen; dogs, pigs, and geese added their alarms; merchants bawled out their wares; people of every description jostled past one another, and unoiled signs above inns and shops creaked ominously in the wind, constantly threatening to crash down on some innocent passer-by.

The bourgeoisie. The triumph of the townsmen in their struggle for greater self-government meant that a new class had evolved in Europe, a powerful, independent, and self-assured group, whose interest in trade was to revolutionize social, economic, and political history. The members of this class were called burghers or the bourgeoisie.

The bourgeoisie emerged in the twelfth century to challenge the primacy of the landholding nobility. The haughty lords looked down on the bourgeoisie; they could not foresee that these self-made men would soon achieve a position of power in society. Kings came to rely more and more on them in combating the power of the feudal lords, and their economic interests gave rise to a nascent capitalism. With the rise of towns and the bourgeoisie was associated the decline of feudalism and manorialism, the waning of the Middle Ages, and the advent of modern society.

A medieval townsman's rank was based on money and goods, rather than birth and land. At the top of the social scale were the great merchant and banking families, the princes of trade, bearing such names as Medici, Fugger, and Coeur. Then came the moderately wealthy merchants and below them the artisans and small shopkeepers. In the lowest slot was the unskilled laborer.

His lot was miserable, and his poverty and discontent were destined to continue through the rest of the Middle Ages and most of modern history.

The townsman's pleasures. The townspeople did not lack for amusements. On the many holidays the apprentices and youths tilted, wrestled, and engaged in other sports in the neighboring countryside or in the city streets. In London wrestling had to be forbidden in St. Paul's churchyard, while sports of a raucous nature were prohibited in Westminster when Parliament was in session. Football was an exciting and irresponsible pastime in which huge numbers of ardent players, divided into two groups, competed in the narrow, congested streets, often with devastating results. "Bowls and quoits, played down the streets, doubtless relieved life of its monotony, but also occasionally relieved an unwary pedestrian of his life altogether, and were, therefore, not encouraged in towns. In the winter, when the marshes were covered with ice, the young men would fasten to their feet rough skates made of the leg-bones of animals, and, propelling themselves with ironshod poles, shoot across the ice, tilting at one another, to the breaking of many heads and limbs."[19] Drinking bouts were tremendously popular. In fact the city of Nuremberg kept a special wagon for picking up drunks.

Changes in the life of the feudal lord. The resurgence of cities and of the use of money transformed the mode of living of the feudal lords. Many of the peasants' obligations which had formerly been paid in produce could now be collected in money. Furthermore, produce could be sold to the townsmen. The result was that the feudal noble could buy what he needed; he was no longer forced to move from manor to manor but could settle on his favorite one. As a permanent resident, he built an imposing country house or castle which no longer needed to be primarily a fort. He moved from the dank donjon to quarters graced by the new luxuries of carpets, tapestries, china, and silver plate. His food was more toothsome because of the new imported spices and sugar.

The decay of serfdom. Even more dramatic were the changes for the serfs. Attracted by

In this representation of the Wat Tyler uprising, John Ball is shown at the head of a well-disciplined group of helmeted peasants bearing the banners of England and St. George.

the freedom of town life, many serfs simply ran away from their manors and established themselves in a town. As a result the serfs on the manors became unreliable. Sometimes the serfs secured enough money to buy their freedom by selling food surpluses in the towns, but often the lords freed their serfs and induced them to remain on the manor as tenants or hired laborers. As a first step in the emancipation of the serfs, the lords accepted a money payment from them as a substitute for their old obligations of labor and produce. The final step was for the lord to become a landlord in the modern sense, renting the arable land of the manor to free tenants. Thus former serfs became satisfied tenants or, on occasion, members of the yeoman class who owned their small farms.

As the manorial services were commuted to money, serfdom progressively decayed in western Europe. It had largely died out in England and France by 1500, although in the latter country many of the old and vexatious obligations, such as payment for the use of the lord's mill and oven, were retained. In eastern Europe serfdom persisted until the nineteenth century.

Peasant revolts. The improvement in the status of the serfs did not necessarily mean that life was pleasant and untroubled. The twelfth and thirteenth centuries were almost

a boom period; but economic depression, unrest, and tension followed in the period from 1350 to 1450. The Black Death, a bubonic plague carried by fleas on rats, struck western Europe in 1347, decimating and demoralizing society. It is estimated that about one third of the population was wiped out. Hardest hit were the towns; the population of Florence, for example, fell from 114,000 to about 50,000 in five years. Coupled with this blow was the destruction and death caused by the Hundred Years' War between France and England (1337-1453).

One of the symptoms of economic setback was the peasant revolts. In the northern part of France they occurred as early as 1251, in Flanders in 1323, and again in France in 1358. The last, called the *Jacquerie* (because the French peasant was known as *Jacques Bonhomme,* "James the Goodfellow"), was a protest against the increased hardships and exactions brought on by the depredations of the Hundred Years' War. Another revolt occurred as late as 1524 and 1525 in Germany. All of these insurrections were put down with unrestrained cruelty.

One famous revolt was the Wat Tyler uprising in England in 1381. The decimation of the peasant population by the Black Death caused a rise in the wages of the day laborers and an increased demand for the abolition of serfdom. Parliament tried to legislate against the pay raise but succeeded only in incurring the anger of the peasants. This resentment was fanned by the sermons of a priest, John Ball, known as the first English socialist:

Ah, ye good people, the matter goeth not well to pass in England, nor shall not do so till everything be common, and that there be no villains or gentlemen, but that we may be all united together and that the lords be no greater masters than we be. What have we deserved or why should we be thus kept in serfdom; we be all come from one father and one mother, Adam and Eve.[20]

As in the case of other revolts, this uprising was crushed amid a welter of blood and broken promises.

Depression and economic stagnation began to be eased by the end of the fifteenth century. The period for the appearance of strong and efficient monarchies was at hand; and Europe was on the verge of discovering another frontier, the Americas.

SUMMARY

Constructive forces fashioning a new Europe became apparent in the tenth century. One historian has seen the years around the critical date of 911 as a historical watershed separating earlier anarchy from the recovery that followed. He points out that in 911 the Norsemen were beginning to settle down peacefully in Normandy; that the Anglo-Saxon ruler in England won a much-needed victory over the Danes (an event which presaged a united England); and that the last Carolingian king of Germany died, opening the way for a stronger royal house. Four years later, the Muslims were ejected from the tip of the Italian peninsula. "So, while the history of Western Christendom in the ninth century [after Charlemagne] is mainly concerned with destruction and disintegration, in the tenth century there is a cessation of destruction and a revival of order: the construction of a new framework of government . . . and a renewal of civilization, which was not to be followed again by reaction. The year 911 marks the beginning of the change. . . ."[21]

If the great achievement of the tenth century was recovery, that of the eleventh was expansion and offensive action by the forces of western Europe. The Muslims lost naval supremacy in the Mediterranean, and a Christian reconquest was initiated in Spain. Above all, in 1095 a great movement, the crusades, was initiated. While the objective was to push the Muslims out of the Holy Land and particularly from Jerusalem, the crusades opened new doors for the narrow, ingrown Europeans.

In the eleventh century new forces were set in motion that brought about a transformed Europe. These currents were a revitalized trade, new towns, expansion of industry, and a money economy. A new society began to take shape; the bourgeoisie emerged and serfdom declined. The medieval economic way of life was passing, giving way to new institutions. In the political realm, the tradition of kingship persisted in spite of feudalism with its many local sovereignties. Ultimately, aided substantially by the new economic forces, the kings were to impose their will on the nobles and become masters of new nations.

Historical Critique

ADVANCES IN MEDIEVAL AGRICULTURE
by Archibald R. Lewis

A specialist in medieval social and economic history, Archibald R. Lewis presently teaches at the University of Texas. He is the author of several books, including Naval Power and Trade in the Mediterranean, A.D. 500-1100 *(1951),* The Development of Southern French and Catalan Society, 718-1050 *(1965), and* Emerging Medieval Europe, A.D. 400-1000 *(1967).*

As historians come to reject the idea of a "dark ages" during medieval times and instead find this a period of fruitful growth and change, their attention is more and more turning to a reëxamination of medieval agriculture. In part this interest is due to the realization that an adequate food supply forms the basic underpinning of a vigorous society. Progress on the farm must be deemed fully as important to history as events on the battlefield. But it is also due to the fact that in recent years new scholarly disciplines, such as archaeology, demography, the history of technology, and even the examination of air photos which show ancient field patterns, are making available a great deal of hitherto unknown information concerning this formative period in Europe's agricultural development. As a result we can now trace how western European agriculture changed during the six centuries that separate the age of Charlemagne from the coming of the Black Death in the mid-fourteenth century.

First of all, we need to note that the Europe that lay inside and outside the frontiers of the late Roman empire was extremely underpopulated by later standards. That portion inhabited by tribal barbarian peoples lacked population because its primitive technology could support only low densities on the land. Rural depopulation within the empire was due to more complex causes, including plagues, governmental regimentation and overtaxation, a shift of labor from the countryside to the towns, and a general fall in the birth rate.

Matters did not improve much between 400 and 750 A.D. True, there was a considerable movement of peoples into regions that were underpopulated: Germans into the western Roman world; Slavs into the Balkans and eastern Germany; Huns, Avars, and Bulgars into southern Russia and the Danube plains. But this movement not only disrupted local populations; it also took place during a period when bubonic plagues, spreading west from China and India, were decimating the population of Europe. By 750, however, the last of these great plagues ended. At the same time, in Muslim Spain, Anglo-Saxon Britain, the Carolingian empire, as well as the Slavic areas of central and eastern Europe, the emergence of greater political stability made possible agricultural progress. We can note this progress in a number of ways.

In the first place it was at about this time that technological advances, lacking in the late Roman period, again occurred. One was the spread of a heavy-wheeled plow beyond its original home in the vicinity of the Rhinelands. This plow allowed agriculturalists to break the sod in the fertile but damp clay bottom lands of western Europe, which, in general, the Romans had neglected. But use of this plow demanded a more efficient system of drawing it than the Romans had employed. Instead of using the yoke and teams of oxen, the people of the Carolingian world borrowed from the Avars the horse collar and a different system of rein attachments which enabled them to use the horse's power more effectively. To give their horses more traction, they invented the horseshoe, for use in damp, muddy ground. Finally, probably some time in the ninth century, they began to take advantage of the summer rains to initiate a three-field system of crop rotation to replace the older two-field system known to the Romans (see p. 334).

Partly because of these technological advances, the food supply increased, and with it the population. This larger market encouraged the cutting down of brush and forest, and a more intensive agriculture spread into areas where it had been relatively neglected.

Last of all, by the late eighth century manors began to appear in parts of the Carolingian empire. Unlike the Roman villas, these manors were essentially villages whose servile peasants managed the cropping of the village land under the supervision of a great proprietor's agents. We get a good idea of how this was done by reading Charlemagne's *Capitulary de villis*, which concerns his own manors, or the *Polyptype of Abbot Irminon*, which describes a great church estate in the Seine River valley. It was on such great estates, controlled by church abbeys or members of the aristocracy, that the improved agricultural techniques mentioned above could be most easily introduced and the labor of dependent cultivators most effectively used.

The progress made during the Carolingian period, which ended about 850, should not be overestimated, however. By and large most peasants still plowed with oxen instead of horses, and the two-field system was still the most common method used in the villages or on the manors. What progress there was came to an end after the mid-ninth century when the countryside bore the brunt of the invasions of the Vikings in the British Isles and the Carolingian empire, of the Hungarians in northern Italy and Germany, and of Muslim pirates in Provence and southern Italy. Only along the advancing frontiers of Christian Spain and in parts of south central France did agricultural progress continue.

By the late tenth century, however, the Vikings had ceased raiding, except briefly in England; the Hungarians had settled down; and the Muslims had been expelled from Provence and Italy. Consequently agricultural progress could begin again. At work were the same factors that we have noted in the Carolingian period. The first was peace, made possible by more effective government in a new Anglo-Saxon England of Alfred's successors, the Holy Roman Empire of the Ottos, the Christian Spanish kingdoms, the newly established monarchies of Scandinavia and central Europe, and even the feudal principalities of northern France.

But if political stability at this time again made for agricultural progress, so too did something else—the rise of new towns. These grew as the simple trading stations of the Carolingian period attracted sufficient merchants and artisans as a permanent population so that they became urban centers. Such towns grew earlier and more rapidly at the termini of major trade routes—about the North Sea and English Channel region of northern Europe and near the mouths of the Po, the Arno, and the Rhone in southern Europe. Wherever they arose, towns affected agriculture in a number of ways.

In the first place, they provided a new growing market for foodstuffs. This meant that it paid to drain marshes and fens and cut down the forest in the vicinity of new towns and to use the more effective heavy-wheeled plows, the new horse collar and rein attachments, and, where possible, the three-field system—all of which increased agricultural yields. In the second place, the towns provided a place to which peasants possessing skills could migrate to join the artisan population. Third, the towns encouraged more efficient agricultural specialization in certain regions— wine in the Garonne region of France, or the Moselle and Rhineland area of Germany, and wheat in Germany, Poland, and Sicily—all of which were produced for distant markets. Specialization also included animal products, such as the wool of western England and Yorkshire and Castile shipped to Flanders or the beef cattle sent north from Andalusia and other parts of the southern Spanish plains in great drives which foreshadowed the cattle kingdom of western America.

As these towns proliferated, western European French and German societies were expanding too, at the expense of Byzantium and Muslim lands or, again, the more primitive Celts of Britain's borderlands and the Slavs of eastern Germany. In all these areas there were vast expanses of territory which could be colonized. Germans, French, Flemings, Anglo-Saxons, and Spanish pushed forward into these lands and won new homes for themselves.

These developments, of course, made possible a great increase in western Europe's population. It is estimated that between 800 and 1300 the population reached a level of fifty million or perhaps even sixty million—a four- or fivefold increase, only matched in the world of this time by what was happening in the China of the T'ang and Sung.

Increased economic specialization, the exploitation of new lands inside and outside the borders of an expanding western Europe, the expansion of improved means of production, and the spectacular increase in the population level—all resulted finally in greater freedom for Europe's peasant population. By 1000 much of the peasantry had sunk to the level of serfs, bound to the soil on the great manors. Now the status of the peasants began to change for the better.

One reason for this change lay in the need to put into production the unused land along the expanded frontiers of Europe. In order to lure settlers to these regions, those nobles who controlled them had to give colonists better terms than prevailed in the old manors—freedom from serfdom and light money payments. As a result, free villages became the rule in such regions, and special model charters embodying this freedom were adopted far and wide, such as the "Laws of Bretail" in England, the "Customs of Lorris" in northern France, and special village charters throughout Spain, Germany, and the French Midi. Some religious orders, such as the Cistercians, further assisted this movement by allowing no serfdom on the lands they were putting into cultivation, relying instead on money rents.

Improvement in the peasants' status resulted also from the adoption of a money economy throughout the older manorial villages as the peasants took their surplus produce into the towns' markets and exchanged it for cash. This money enabled them to purchase their freedom from their manorial lords by commuting their labor services to money payments and even add to their land by renting the lord's demesne, since the latter no longer had the labor available for cultivation. Once money payments were introduced, village custom kept them fixed at the same rate—a great advantage for the peasant in an age of rising prices and inflation. Thus by 1250 most of Europe's peasants had left serfdom behind to become relatively prosperous free tenants, renting their lands from their secular or ecclesiastical landlords on a basis very advantageous to the cultivator.

But this economic, technological, and social progress had certain limitations which were apparent by 1300. First of all, by this date, the supply of frontier lands gave out and towns ceased to grow, so that dissatisfied peasants had no place to go if they found conditions unbearable. Second, though serfdom had disappeared, the village remained as the basic controller of agriculture. This meant that individual experimentation was impossible and yields could not be increased. Even selective breeding was impossible when all animals had to be pastured together on the village common. No further technological progress could be possible until the village pattern of life was drastically altered. Finally, two new changes of the late Middle Ages made matters even worse. One was the Black Death, arriving in the mid-fourteenth century; the second, a new capitalism which destroyed the structure of peasant village life. By 1350 the great days of medieval agriculture were over, and a period of peasant misery and revolt ensued that lasted until the new world overseas and the agricultural revolution of early modern times inaugurated a new period of freedom and prosperity for Europe's peasants.

SUGGESTED READINGS

For a comprehensive picture of the subject, students should consult *The Agrarian Life of the Middle Ages,* Vol. I of *The Cambridge Economic History of Europe,* rev. ed., Cambridge, 1966. Other interesting studies are Lynn T. White, *Medieval Technology and Social Change,* Oxford, 1963; Robert Latouche, *The Birth of Western Economy,* Harper Torchbooks, 1966; and Archibald R. Lewis, *Emerging Medieval Europe,* Knopf, 1967.

Chapter 13

To the Glory of God

Faith, Thought, and Art in Medieval Europe

INTRODUCTION. In Paris, on a small island in the Seine, stands an edifice of weather-beaten stone, the Cathedral of Notre Dame. Dedicated to the glory of God and the veneration of Our Lady, this cathedral offers a fascinating glimpse into the life and spirit of medieval Europe. Notre Dame de Paris was built between 1163 and 1235, during some of the most epoch-making years of the Middle Ages. While workmen were supporting the cathedral's vault with flying buttresses and carefully fitting the multicolored windows into place, churchmen and students lolled on the Petit Pont, a bridge that led to the Left Bank. The students wrangled over theology, accused one another of heresy, and occasionally composed blasphemous poems that parodied the sacred liturgy. Some of these same students were one day to occupy episcopal thrones as princes of the Church; one of the mightiest occupants of the papal throne, Innocent III, once studied in Paris.

The Middle Ages has with justification been called the Age of Faith. The basic drives and loyalties of medieval Christians centered around religion. The fundamental purpose of life was salvation of the soul, not the search for scientific fact or the control of nature or other goals which have preoccupied the lives of people in other eras. Whether or not he lived fully on this earth was of secondary concern to a medieval man as long as he achieved salvation in the next life. With rare exceptions, Europeans were born, lived, and died under the protection of the Church; this institution gave meaning and direction to their lives. Just as its monasteries dotted the countryside and its towering cathedrals dominated the towns, so the Church and its influence permeated the social fabric of western Christendom.

In an age abounding in physical affliction and social injustice, the Church provided consolation and brought warmth and color to monotonous lives. To our medieval ancestors, Christianity was as vivid and rich as the stained-glass windows in the churches where they worshiped. Sermons dwelled on lurid descriptions of hell and depicted heaven as "a splendor that is sevenfold brighter and clearer than the sun." Above all, the people received the sacraments to obtain the grace they needed to achieve their salvation.

The Church also molded the intellectual, the artistic, and, for several centuries, the political life of the West. The Church enlisted the greatest thinkers of the age to translate classical and Arabic treatises, to develop philosophical theories, and to make those educational advances that culminated in the establishment of universities. Poets and troubadours and such literary titans as Dante and Chaucer interwove spiritual and human themes in their works. Architects, sculptors, and other craftsmen pooled their talents to fashion Romanesque and Gothic buildings. Church administration, with authority stemming from the pope and passing through a hierarchy of archbishops to the parish priest, provided the nearest approach to a universal government during the Middle Ages.

The underlying difference between our medieval ancestors and ourselves would appear to be one of perspective. To them theology was the "science of sciences," whereas today there are those who say that we have made science our theology. Yet this difference is not due exclusively to the extension of knowledge during the intervening centuries. It also lies in the fundamental premise governing the lives of our medieval forefathers. They believed in a world order, divinely created and maintained. For them, the universe possessed an inner coherence and harmony, which it was the function of the theologian and the scientist alike to discover. Revelation and knowledge, faith and reason, Church and state, spirit and matter—these dualities could be reconciled in a great spiritual and social synthesis.

In this chapter we will examine the methods by which our ancestors sought to realize this synthesis and the measure of their success. As a first step, we shall trace the institutional growth of the one universal organization of medieval Europe, the Church. Next we shall watch its progressive assumption of secular powers, culminating in the triumphs of Innocent III. Finally, we shall see how, under the sponsorship of the Church, scholars and philosophers, scientists and inventors, and artists and artisans labored for the glory of God and the salvation of man.

THE SPIRIT AND STRUCTURE OF THE MEDIEVAL CHURCH

The Church in the early Middle Ages (500-1050). In our examination of medieval Christianity, we should think of its three distinct aspects: (1) as a religion—the personal faith in a divine Savior and the desire to enter into conscious affinity with God; (2) as a Church—an institution or ecclesiastical organization; and (3) as a theology—a methodical formulation of beliefs.

While Europe gradually recovered from the shock of the Roman empire's demise, the Church became the mainstay of European civilization. The Church's secular power grew as it developed its own hierarchy and landholdings. During the pontificate of Gregory the Great (590-604) the power of the pope in Italy increased sharply, and the medieval papacy began to take form. Gregory "ordered the police, regulated markets, coined money, maintained civil and criminal courts, repaired the walls and aqueducts, supported schools and hospitals, commanded the militia, and defended the city in the case of attack."[1]

Missionary activity of the Church. The Church made its influence more extensive and enduring in still other practical ways. This was a vital period of missionary activity, when Christianity was carried throughout Europe. Monasteries served as havens for those seeking a contemplative life, as repositories of learning for scholars, and often as progressive farming centers. The missionary activity of the Church not only spread Christianity but disseminated civilization among the barbarians and aided in the fusion of Germanic and classical cultures.

One of the earliest Christian missionaries to the Germans was Ulfilas (c. 311-383), who spent forty years among the Visigoths and translated most of the Bible into Gothic. Ulfilas and other early missionaries were followers of Arius, and thus the heretical creed of Arianism came to be adopted by all the Germanic tribes in the empire except the Franks and Anglo-Saxons. We have seen in Chapter 11 that the Franks' adoption of official Roman Catholic doctrines as espoused by the pope had momentous consequences for European statecraft.

Another great missionary, St. Patrick, was born in Britain about 389 and later fled to Ireland to escape the Anglo-Saxon invaders. As a result of his Irish missionary activities, monasteries were founded, and Christianity became dominant. From these monasteries in the late sixth and seventh centuries a stream of monks went to Scotland, northern England, the kingdom of the Franks, and even to Italy. The Irish monks eagerly pursued scholarship, and their monasteries were repositories for priceless manuscripts.

The Church at Rome was also very active in the missionary movement. One significant mission was that of St. Augustine (not the great Christian scholar), whom Pope Gregory the Great sent to the small kingdom of Kent in England in 596. St. Augustine converted its king, the first ruler in England officially to accept Christianity. Roman Christianity spread through England, and finally the Celtic Church founded by St. Patrick acknowledged the primacy of Rome.

The English Church in turn took an important part in the expansion of Christianity on the Continent. St. Boniface, the greatest missionary from England in the eighth century, spent thirty-five years among the Germanic tribes. Known as the "Apostle to the Germans," he established several important monasteries and bishoprics before he turned to the task of reforming the Church in France. There he revitalized the monasteries, organized a system of local parishes to bring Christianity to the countryside, and probably was instrumental in forming the alliance between the papacy and the Carolingian house. Roman Catholic missionaries also worked among the Scandinavians and the western Slavs.

The monks as custodians of knowledge. Perhaps the most significant contribution of the monasteries was the preservation of learning. Writing in the sixth century, the bishop of Tours lamented:

In these times . . . there has been found no scholar trained in the art of ordered composition to present in prose or verse a picture of the things that have befallen.[2]

While the bishop was being overly pessimistic, it was true that ability to write classical Latin had declined and knowledge of Greek was disappearing in western Europe.

Learning did not entirely die out in western Europe, of course. In the sixth century a Roman scholar, Boethius, who had entered the service of the Ostrogothic king Theodoric, hoped to preserve Greek learning by translating all of Plato and Aristotle into Latin. Only Aristotle's treatises on logic were translated, and these remained the sole works of that philosopher available in the West until the twelfth century. Unjustly accused of treachery by Theodoric, Boethius was thrown into prison, where he wrote *The*

Consolation of Philosophy while awaiting his execution. This work later became a medieval textbook on philosophy.

Cassiodorus, a contemporary of Boethius who had also served Theodoric, devoted most of his life to the collection and preservation of classical knowledge. By encouraging the monks to copy valuable manuscripts, he was instrumental in making the monasteries centers of learning. Following his example, many monasteries established *scriptoria,* departments concerned exclusively with copying manuscripts.

During the early Middle Ages most education took place in the monasteries, which sheltered the few teachers and scholars of the time. In the late sixth and seventh centuries, when the effects of the barbarian invasions were still being felt on the continent, Irish monasteries provided a safe haven for learning. There men studied Greek and Latin, copied and preserved manuscripts, and in illuminating them produced masterpieces of art. *The Book of Kells* is a surviving example of their skill (see Color Plate 15).

The outstanding scholar of the early Middle Ages, Venerable Bede (d. 735), was the product of an Irish-founded English monastery. Bede described himself as "ever taking delight in learning, teaching, and writing." His many writings, which included textbooks and commentaries on the Scriptures, summed up most knowledge available in his age. Through Alcuin later in the century, Bede's learning influenced the Carolingian Renaissance (see p. 323). Bede's best known work, the *Ecclesiastical History of the English People,* with its many original documents and vivid character sketches, is our chief source for early English history.

The Church's theological position. Although the Church was an institution, it was not an extraneous body imposed upon Christianity and consisting solely of a clerical hierachy and a liturgy. St. Paul's description of the Church as "the body of Christ" was interpreted to mean that the Church included all of Christian society. Every baptized child automatically began life within the Church and was subject to its authority. Obedience was enforced by all political as well as religious rulers in western Christendom.

The nature and process of salvation were set forth in theology, which deals with the nature of God and His relations to man and the universe. According to the theology of the Church, Adam had bequeathed the taint of original sin to his descendants, so that the human race was displeasing in the sight of God. But He did not leave man without hope. Jesus, the Son of God, had sacrificed Himself upon the cross to atone for mankind's sins, and through His sacrifice God gave man a chance to earn salvation. This opportunity was bestowed only on those who believed in redemption through Christ's atonement and who followed His precepts. But salvation itself was won only with the grace of God. Since man could perform no act worthy of salvation without divine grace, how was this to be earned? The theologians taught that God bestowed His grace on man by means of sacraments through the Church and its officials. Thus the Church was the necessary intermediary between God and man.

The problems of theology attracted the attention primarily of the intellectuals. The majority of the people, then, as today, accepted the current beliefs without much questioning. To the unlettered, the following points constituted the essentials of the Christian faith: (1) the creation and fall of Adam, (2) the Birth and Crucifixion of Christ, (3) the Last Judgment, (4) the horrors of hell, (5) the eternal bliss of heaven, and (6) the efficacy of the sacraments in helping man win salvation.

The sacraments. The sacraments have been defined as outward or visible signs instituted by Christ to signify and to give grace. By the twelfth century seven sacraments had been recognized, a number made official by a papal pronouncement in 1438. The seven sacraments were Baptism, Confirmation, Holy Eucharist, Penance, Extreme Unction, Holy Orders, and Matrimony.

In Baptism the taint of original sin was washed away, and the person was given a Christian name, hence "christening." Confirmation strengthened the character of the recipient and confirmed his membership in the Church. The sacrament of Matrimony was instituted to give the married couple spiritual help—although celibacy was prescribed for those who entered the Church as a career. Holy Orders, or ordination into the priesthood, was administered by a bishop. This sacrament conferred the power and grace to perform the sacred duties of the clergy; the ordained priest was capable of administering all sacraments except Confirmation and Holy Orders. Penance enabled sins committed after Baptism to be forgiven through the absolution of the priest. Extreme Unction was administered when death appeared imminent; it forgave remaining sins and bestowed grace and spiritual strength on the dying Christian.

The most important and impressive sacrament was the Holy Eucharist, defined as "both a sacrament and a sacrifice; in it Our Savior, Jesus Christ, body and blood, soul and divinity, under the appearance of bread and wine, is contained, offered, and received." The significance of this sacrament as the core of Christian worship can be fully appreciated only when the doctrine of transubstantiation is understood. According to this doctrine, when the priest performing the Mass pronounces over the bread and wine the words Christ used at the Last Supper, "This is My Body. . . . This is the chalice of My Blood . . . ," a miracle takes place. To all outward appearances, the bread and wine remain unchanged, but in "substance" they have been transformed into the very body and blood of the Savior.

Enforcing belief. The Church was ahead of secular states in emerging out of feudal decentralization and developing its own legal system of canon law and courts to enforce its teachings and commands. Canon law was based on the Scriptures, the writings of the Church Fathers, and the decrees of Church councils and popes. In the twelfth century the Church issued its official body of canon law, the ecclesiastical counterpart of the Justinian Code (see p. 227). Canon law guided the Church courts in judging perjury, blasphemy, sorcery, usury (the medieval Church denounced the taking of interest), and heresy. Heresy was the most horrible of all crimes in medieval eyes. A murder was a crime against society, but the heretic's disbelief in the teachings of Christ or His Church was considered a crime against God Himself.

Although the medieval Church sometimes resorted to physical punishment, the chief weapons to support clerical authority were spiritual penalties. The most powerful of these was excommunication, by which people became *anathema*, "set apart" from the Church and all the faithful. "They could not act as judge, juror, notary, witness, or attorney. They could not be guardians, executors, or parties to contracts. After death,

A monk copies a manuscript in the *scriptorium*, surrounded by other manuscripts and such tools of his trade as inkpots, pens, and brushes.

This detail from a fifteenth-century manuscript of Chaucer's *Canterbury Tales* shows the good parson.

they received no Christian burial, and if, by chance, they were buried in consecrated ground, their bodies were to be disinterred and cast away. If they entered a church during Mass, they were to be expelled, or the Mass discontinued. After the reading of a sentence of excommunication, a bell was rung as for a funeral, a book closed, and a candle extinguished, to symbolize the cutting off of the guilty man."[3]

Interdict, which has been termed "an ecclesiastical lockout," was likewise a powerful instrument. Whereas excommunication was directed against individuals, interdict suspended all public worship and withheld all sacraments other than Baptism and Extreme Unction in the realm of a disobedient ruler. Pope Innocent III successfully applied or threatened the interdict eighty-five times against refractory princes.

The papacy. The influence of the medieval Church was felt by every inhabitant of every hamlet throughout western Europe. The universality and power of the Church rested not only upon a systematized, uniform creed but also upon the most highly organized administrative system in the West.

At the head was the pope, or bishop of Rome (see Chapter 7). He was assisted by the Curia, the papal council or court, which in the twelfth and thirteenth centuries developed an intricate administrative system. Judicial and secretarial problems were handled by the papal Chancery, financial matters by the Camera, and disciplinary questions by the Penitentiary. Special emissaries called legates, whose powers were superior to those of local prelates, carried the pope's orders throughout Europe.

The higher clergy. Europe was divided into ecclesiastical provinces, each administered by an archbishop. A province comprised in turn several dioceses. The archbishop was a powerful prelate, who summoned provincial councils, occasionally visited dioceses and monastic houses, announced papal decrees of general import, and handled affairs in his own diocese.

While the archbishop was responsible for his own archdiocese, the other dioceses in each province were managed by bishops. A diocese included many parishes and religious houses. The bishop's court held wide jurisdiction over both clergy and laity. Because the claims of lay courts challenged the bishop's domain, especially on such matters as wills and dowries, which had both a spiritual and secular character, the scope of his administrative and disciplinary powers was a controversial issue.

The bishop had his headquarters in the city where his cathedral stood. (The word *cathedral* comes from *cathedra*, which means "bishop's throne.") Outside the city he had other houses and estates, where he occasionally resided. Often, though not necessarily, of high social origin, the bishop was an exalted person; whether haughty or humble, he had to maintain an elaborate household. As a rule the bishop did not come into close personal contact with the common people, even on his diocesan visits or on occasions when he confirmed the young, ordained deacons and priests, or dedicated churches. On the other hand, like the archbishop, he played a leading part in the council of the king.

The priest in his parish. The real foundation of the medieval Church was the ordinary people in the parishes. In the last analysis the Church's strength depended upon the parish priest. He administered the sacraments, attended the sick, heard confessions, supervised the morals of the parish, and held the respect of his parishioners. Although the priest was very likely of humble birth and little education, he was father confessor, social worker, policeman, and recreation director, all rolled into one. In most cases he was a credit to his Church. The "poor town Parson" in Chaucer's *Canterbury Tales* is a sympathetic portrayal.

He was a kind man, full of industry,
Many times tested by adversity
And always patient. . . .
Wide was his parish, with houses far asunder,
But he would not be kept by rain or thunder,
If any had suffered a sickness or a blow,
From visiting the farthest, high or low,
Plodding his way on foot, his staff in hand.
He was a model his flock could understand,
For first he did and afterward he taught.[4]

The parish priest instructed his charges mainly through sermons. He painted the terrors of hell—how the damned are thrust from the flames into icy water so they do not know which is worse and how

to increase their pains the loathsome hell-worms, toads, and frogs that eat out their eyes and nostrils, and adders and water-frogs, not like those here, but a hundred times more horrible, sneak in and out of the mouth, ears, eyes, navel, and at the hollow of the breast, as maggots in putrid flesh. . . .[5]

Heaven was pictured to be just as desirable as hell was hateful, and the Church assured the parishioner of heaven as the reward for his prayers and supplications. The priest would also upbraid his parishioners for their lax attendance at church, their addiction to the joys of the tavern, their squabbling and fighting, their laziness or gluttony. He made every person, high or low, supremely aware of the vividness, the omnipresence, and the reality of religion.

Although religion was indispensable to our ancestors, a glance at a medieval parish church would reveal a scene that would strike the modern mind as exceedingly informal: "the knight sauntered about with hawk on wrist, his dogs following, and perhaps fighting, behind; the women gathered together and talked (as women do) and laughed and took mental notes of each other's dresses for future imitation or disparagement."[6] Despite the apparent lack of reverence, the congregation regarded with awe the altar where the solemn mystery of transubstantiation took place.

Church revenues. The Church received its revenues from various sources. The tithe, which took one tenth of every man's income, and fees for performing religious services provided money for the parishes. A large source of revenue for the Church was the income from its lands. The tracts of land contributed to bishoprics and monasteries by kings and nobles were not held free of obligations, as we have seen in the discussion of feudalism in Chapter 11. Nevertheless, the Church eventually became the largest landholder in medieval Europe.

The wealth of this huge organization was a source of both strength and weakness. Its great riches enabled it to perform functions and support charities which the states neglected. But this wealth also encouraged abuses and worldliness among the clergy, conditions which caused increasing concern among the common people.

THE CHURCH MILITANT

The Church-state rivalry. Medieval political theory begins with the concept of a universal community divided into two spheres, the spiritual and the temporal—a view based upon Christ's injunction to "Render therefore to Caesar the things that are Caesar's, and to God the things that are God's" (Matthew 22:21). As Pope Gelasius I declared in the fifth century, God had entrusted spiritual and temporal powers to two authorities—the Church and the state—each supreme in its own sphere. At first the question of ultimate superiority between these authorities did not arise, although Gelasius had implied that the Church was superior to the state in the same way that the soul was superior to the body. The issue could not be permanently shelved, however; a fight for supremacy was in the long run inevitable.

When Pepin and later Charlemagne were crowned by the pope, the temporal prestige and authority of the head of the Church rose. From the ecclesiastical point of view these coronations could be interpreted to signify the supremacy of the pope over secular rulers. On the other hand, Charlemagne's imperial authority threatened the popes. There was always the danger that the pope would come under the domination of the western emperor, just as the patriarch of Constantinople had gradually fallen subservient to the Byzantine ruler.

When the German king Otto the Great revived the Roman empire in the West in 962 (see p. 348), his act reëmphasized the concept of the dual leadership of pope and emperor. Otto claimed to be the successor of Augustus, Constantine, and Charlemagne, although his actual power was confined to Germany and Italy. At first the papacy looked to the German king for protection against the unruly Italian nobles who for a century had been making a prize of the papacy. From the Church's viewpoint, however, this arrangement soon had its drawbacks, for the German kings continued to interfere in ecclesiastical affairs—even in the election of popes.

During the eleventh century the controversy between Church and state centered around the problem of lay investiture. Theoretically, on assuming office a bishop or abbot was subject to two investitures; his spiritual authority was bestowed by an ecclesiastical official and his feudal or civil authority by the king or a noble. In actual fact, however, almost everywhere in Europe feudal lords and kings came to control both the appointment and the installation of church prelates. In Germany, the strongest monarchy in western Europe, the practice of lay investiture was most pronounced.

The German king had granted many of the Church lands to the higher clergy, who became his vassals. The new bishop had to do homage for his fief and received from the king his ring and pastoral staff, symbols of his marriage to the Church and his obligations to his flock. Furthermore, the king controlled Church property during the vacancy between the death of one incumbent and the selection of his successor, which meant that he had an important stake in the election to Church offices. Thus "to all intents and purposes the German Church was a state Church."[7]

The king was anxious to have a faithful vassal on each bishop's throne or abbot's chair for a number of reasons. Most important, he needed to have the vast Church lands furnish loyal feudal troops for the royal armies. Many German bishops proved to be valiant warriors. Faithful prelates were also the most reliable and best-educated men to counsel a king and administer the royal government and finances.

The pope, therefore, had reason to complain about his bishops and abbots on both spiritual and temporal grounds. The papacy was rescued from its plight, however, by a great religious revival and the advent of Pope Gregory VII and his powerful successors.

The Cluniac reform. Beginning in the tenth century and reaching full force in the next two centuries, the religious revival—often called the medieval reformation—affected all classes. The first far-reaching force of the revival was the new monastic order of Cluny, founded in 910. From the original monastery in Burgundy and its many daughter houses all over western Europe, there radiated a powerful impulse for the reform of the feudalized Church. The Cluniac program began as a movement for monastic reform, but in time it called for the enforcement of clerical celibacy and the abolition of simony, whereby an ecclesiastical office was sold to the highest bidder or was acquired by bribery. (The term *simony* comes from Simon the magician, who tried to buy the gift of the Holy Spirit from the apostles.)

The ultimate goal of the Cluniac reformers was to free the entire Church from secular control and subject it to papal authority. Some three hundred Cluniac houses were freed from lay control, and in 1059 the papacy itself was removed from secular interference by the creation of the College of Cardinals, which elected the popes.

Gregory VII. The most ambitious proponent of the Cluniac reform was Gregory VII (1073-1085), who raised the papacy to unprecedented heights. Short-legged, fat, inclined to stammer, and having little formal learning, this seemingly unimpressive individual overshadowed monarchs with his zeal and magnetic power. Gregory held as his ideal the creation of an international government under papal control. Instead of conceding equality between the Church and the state, he drew from the Gelasian theory the logical conclusion that the spiritual power was supreme over the temporal. In the *Dictatus Papae* ("Dictate of the Pope") Gregory proclaimed his views on papal power:

That the Roman pontiff alone can with right be called universal.
That he alone may use the imperial insignia.
That of the pope alone all princes shall kiss the feet.
That it may be permitted to him to depose emperors.
That he himself may be judged by no one.
That he who is not at peace with the Roman church shall not be considered catholic.
That he may absolve subjects from their fealty to wicked men.[8]

Gregory devoted his extraordinary energy to breaking all resistance to the Church. Outstanding among his attempts at reforms—and certainly the most difficult to enforce—were his efforts to suppress simony and lay investiture.

The Investiture Struggle. In 1075 Gregory VII formally prohibited lay investiture and threatened to excommunicate any layman who performed it and any ecclesiastic who submitted to it. This drastic act virtually declared war against Europe's rulers, since most of them practiced lay investiture. The climax to the struggle occurred in Gregory's clash with the emperor Henry IV. The latter was accused of simony and lay investiture in appointing his own choice to the archbishopric of Milan and was summoned to Rome to explain his conduct. Henry's answer was to convene in 1076 a synod of German bishops which declared Gregory a usurper and unfit to occupy the Roman See:

Wherefore henceforth we renounce, now and for the future, all obedience unto thee—which indeed we never promised to thee. And since, as thou didst publicly proclaim, none of us has been to thee a bishop, so thou henceforth wilt be Pope to none of us.[9]

In retaliation Gregory excommunicated Henry and deposed him, absolving his subjects from their oaths of allegiance.

At last, driven to make peace with the pontiff by a revolt among the German nobles, Henry appeared before Gregory in January 1077 at Canossa, a castle in the Apennines. Garbed as a penitent, the emperor is said to have stood barefoot in the snow for three days and begged forgiveness until, in Gregory's words: "We loosed the chain of the anathema and at length received him into the favor of communion and into the lap of the Holy Mother Church."[10]

This dramatic humiliation of the emperor did not resolve the quarrel, nor do contemporary accounts attach much significance to the incident—public penance was not uncommon in those days even for kings. Yet the pope had made progress toward freeing the Church from interference by laymen and toward increasing the power and prestige of the papacy. The problem of lay investiture was settled in 1122 by the compromise known as the Concordat of Worms. The Church maintained the right to elect the holder of an ecclesiastical office, but only in the presence of the king or his representative. The candidate, such as a bishop, was invested by the king with the scepter, the symbol of his administrative jurisdiction, after which he performed the act of homage and swore allegiance as the king's vassal. Only after this ceremony had taken place was the candidate consecrated by the archbishop, who invested him with his spiritual functions, as symbolized by the ring and pastoral staff. Since the kings of England and France had earlier accepted this compromise, lay investiture waned.

Frederick Barbarossa's Italian ambitions. The struggle between Church and state continued for another century, sparked by the papacy's resentment at the emperors' continued interference in the affairs of the Italian kingdom. In 1152 Frederick I of the Hohenstaufen family—known as Frederick Barbarossa because of his red beard—crossed the Alps with the intention of restoring imperial control over the prosperous cities in northern Italy. He enjoyed temporary successes, but in 1167 these towns formed the Lombard League to maintain their political and economic independence. The League defeated Frederick and thus achieved the pope's aim of keeping the emperor out of Italy.

The papacy and the crusades. In the preceding chapter we saw that the First Crusade was proclaimed by Pope Urban II in 1095. As the ruler of a militant Church whose

The controversy over the relative powers of Church and state was exemplified by the struggle between Henry IV and Pope Gregory VII. This twelfth-century miniature, one of a series entitled "Scenes from the Life of Gregory VII," shows Henry (top left) with the bishop he chose to replace the pope (top right). Gregory died in exile in 1085 (bottom).

prestige, possessions, and influence penetrated every land in the West, the pope was uniquely able both to rouse religious fervor and to channel its expression in the form of military crusades. The spontaneous outpouring of religious enthusiasm which followed Urban's appeal undoubtedly strengthened the bonds of the Christian community under the prestige and power of the papacy. The First Crusade in particular represented an impressive display of European power organized to achieve objectives championed by the Church.

The papacy's zenith: Innocent III. Through the efforts of Gregory VII and the success of the First Crusade, the papacy emerged as potentially the most powerful office in Europe—a papal monarchy. In the hands of a strong leader, the papacy could reign supreme among the relatively weaker monarchies of Europe. Such a leader was Innocent III, a scholarly and brilliant pontiff (1198-1216), who, like Gregory VII, held an exalted view of his office:

The successor of Peter is the Vicar of Christ: he has been established as a mediator between God and man, below God but beyond man; less than God but more than man; who shall judge all and be judged by no one.[11]

Innocent III told the princes of Europe that the papacy was as the sun, whereas the kings were as the moon. As the moon derives its light from the sun, so the kings derived their powers from the pope. So influential was the pontiff's belief in his temporal as well as spiritual supremacy that many states, both large and small, formally acknowledged vassalage to the pope.

Innocent III was also sufficiently powerful to impose his will on all the major rulers, including the monarchs of England, France, and Germany. In the case of King John of England, a struggle developed over the election of the archbishop of Canterbury, and Innocent placed England under interdict and excommunicated John. Under pressure from his subjects, John capitulated to Innocent by becoming his vassal, receiving England back as a fief, and paying him an annual monetary tribute. Next the pope forced Philip Augustus of France to comply with the Church's moral code by taking back as his queen the woman he had divorced with the consent of the French bishops. As for the Holy Roman Empire, Innocent intervened in a civil war between rival candidates for the throne, supporting first one, then the other. In the end Innocent secured the election of his ward, the young Hohenstaufen heir Frederick II, who promised to respect papal rights and to go on a crusade.

The papacy had attained the zenith of its temporal power. Innocent's ideal of a papal theocracy seemed realized, for the nations of Europe acknowledged the power of Christ's vicar. Innocent III could and did "judge all and be judged by no one."

From the reign of Innocent III until the end of the thirteenth century, the Church radiated power and splendor. When Innocent's ward, Emperor Frederick II, turned out to be a clever and ambitious ruler, Innocent's successors frustrated Frederick's attempt to unite all of Italy under his rule and make it, rather than Germany, the core of his empire. The papacy declared Frederick a heretic, excommunicated him, and called for a crusade to overthrow him. After Frederick died a few years later (1250), the papacy and its allies crushed the last Hohenstaufen descendants and brought about the final collapse of central authority in Germany and Italy (see Chapter 14).

Yet cracks appeared in the foundation even while the medieval religious structure received its final embellishments. Weaknesses were evident in the lessening of religious zeal in the later crusades, in the need for renewed internal reform, and in the growth of heresy. Whereas the first three crusades had enhanced the papacy's prestige, the remainder exposed not only the mercenary motives of many of the participants but also the attempts by some popes to further their own temporal interests.

New monastic reforms. The medieval reformation gained momentum late in the eleventh century with a second movement of monastic reform brought on by the failure of the Cluniac reform to end laxity in monastic life. Among the new orders were the severely ascetic and hermit-like Carthusians and the very popular Cistercians.

During the fourteenth century the Church-state struggle produced a great amount of rival political theory, with the Church making much use of symbolism and allegory. In this illumination Christ hands the sword of temporal power to a worldly king, while St. Peter, as pope, receives the key to heaven, symbol of spiritual power. Christ's gaze is fixed on St. Peter, thus indicating that the Church was more important than the state.

The Cistercian movement received its greatest impetus from the zealous efforts of St. Bernard of Clairvaux in the twelfth century. The abbeys were situated in solitary places, and the monastic discipline emphasized austerity and manual labor. The order was so ascetic that sculptured figures were not allowed in any Cistercian abbey, and Bernard inveighed against the beautification of churches in general:

Oh! vanity of vanities! but not more vain than foolish. . . . What has all this imagery to do with monks, with professors of poverty, with men of spiritual minds? . . . In fact, such an endless variety of forms appears everywhere that it is more pleasant to read in the stonework than in books, and to spend the day in admiring these oddities than in meditating on the Law of God.[12]

Spurred on by this militant denouncer of wealth and luxury in any form, the Cistercian order had founded 343 abbeys in western Europe by the time of Bernard's death in 1153 and more than double that number by the end of the century. Yet in one important sense these austere new monastic orders were failures. Being exclusively agricultural and dwelling apart from society, these orders were unfit to cope with religious discontent in the towns and the consequent rise of heresy.

Heresies. Heresy, defined as "the formal denial or doubt by a baptized person of any revealed truth of the Catholic faith,"[13] flourished particularly in the towns, where an increasing consciousness of sin and a demand for greater piety went largely unheeded by old-style churchmen. This fertile ground produced many heresies, among which the Albigensian and Waldensian were major ones.

Harking back to Manicheism (p. 222), the Cathari ("Pure") or Albigensians—so called because Albi in southern France was an important center—went to extremes in thinking of the world as the battleground of the opposing forces of good and evil. The Albigensians condemned many activities of the state and the individual, even condemning marriage for perpetuating the human species in this sinful world. Because of their extreme antisocial views, the members of this group were punished by secular authorities as well as by the Church.

The Waldensians derived their name from Peter Waldo, a merchant of Lyons who gave up his possessions in 1176 to found a lay order called the Poor Men of Lyons. While the principal complaint of the Waldensians was the wealth and worldliness of the Church, their actual heresy came from their insistence that laymen were competent to preach and expound the Bible, parts of which

they had translated into French. As a historian has summed it up: "The Waldensians wanted above all to return to evangelical poverty, and they condemned everything in the Church which departed from this, the wealth of the clergy, their princedoms, and their temporal authority. In the ecclesiastical hierarchy they found no longer any sanctifying force; sanctity was in their eyes individual and could be acquired, not by sacraments or ritual practices, but by personal work."[14] Because the Waldensian church still exists today in northern Italy, it has been called the oldest Protestant sect.

For ten years Innocent III tried to reconvert these heretical groups. Failing, in 1208 he instigated a crusade against the prosperous and cultured French region of Toulouse, where the Albigensian heresy was widespread. The crusade began with horrible slaughter to the cry of "Kill them all, God will know His own."[15] Soon the original religious motive was lost in a selfish rush to seize the wealth of the accused. In time the Albigensian heresy was destroyed, along with the flourishing culture of southern France, and the Waldensians were scattered. The time was to come, however, when the popes could not suppress heresy so successfully.

The Inquisition. In 1233 a special papal court called the Inquisition was established to cope with the rising tide of heresy and to bring about religious conformity. The Inquisition was an elaborate system of inquiry into the beliefs of persons suspected of heresy. The accused was tried in secret without the aid of legal counsel. If he confessed and renounced his heresy, he was "reconciled" with the Church on performance of penance. If he did not voluntarily confess, he could be tortured. If this failed, the prisoner could be declared a heretic and turned over to the secular authorities, perhaps to be burned at the stake.

In any evaluation of the Inquisition, it should be remembered that the soul was considered incomparably more important than the body—therefore torturing a suspected heretic was justifiable if confession could save his soul from the greater torments of hell. Furthermore, the use of torture and the denial of legal counsel prevailed in civil as well as in ecclesiastical courts.

The Franciscans and Dominicans. As a more positive response to the spread of heresy and the conditions which spawned it, Innocent III approved the founding of the Franciscan and Dominican orders of friars ("brothers"). Instead of living a sequestered existence in a remote monastery, the friars moved among their brother men, ministering to their needs and preaching the Gospel.

The Franciscans were founded by St. Francis of Assisi (1182?-1226), who, like Waldo of Lyons, rejected riches and spread the gospel of poverty and Christian simplicity. Love of one's fellow men and all God's creatures, even "brother worm," were basic in the Rule of St. Francis, which was inspired by Christ's example in the Bible:

He called his twelve disciples together, and gave them power and authority over all devils, and to cure diseases. And he sent them to preach the kingdom of God, and to heal the sick. And he said unto them, Take nothing for your journey, neither staves, nor scrip, neither bread, neither money; neither have two coats apiece. . . . And they departed and went through the towns, preaching the gospel and healing everywhere.[16]

The second order of friars was founded by St. Dominic (1170-1221), a well-educated Spaniard whose early career had been spent fighting the Albigensian heresy in southern France. There he decided that to combat the strength and zeal of its opponents, the Church should have champions who could preach the gospel with apostolic fervor. Dominic's order of friar-preachers dedicated themselves to preaching as a means of maintaining and spreading the doctrines of the Church and of converting nonbelievers.

These two orders had much in common. Both took communal poverty and simplicity as their ideal, and each had as its objective to spread the gospel—the Dominicans by intellectual brilliance and fiery eloquence, the Franciscans by exemplifying the virtues of piety, humility, and good works. The enthusiasm and sincerity of the two orders in their early years made a profound impact upon an age which had grown increasingly critical of ecclesiastical worldliness. The Dominicans, quickly attaining prominence as philosophers and theologians, taught at such important universities as Paris, Bologna, and Oxford. Late in the thirteenth century the Franciscans became almost as prominent in education as the Dominican friars, particularly in the English universities.

The Franciscans and Dominicans vigorously fought heresy. While never formally vested in the friars, the Inquisition came to be placed chiefly in their hands, with the Dominicans playing the more prominent role. As they became investigators of heresy and active in papal affairs, the preaching orders increased in importance but lost

The simple piety preached by St. Francis is reflected in this altarpiece, painted only nine years after his death, which shows the characteristically austere saint surrounded by six scenes from his life. The marks on St. Francis' hands and feet are stigmata—symbolic wounds representing his identification with Christ—which he received after a period of prayer and meditation.

much of their original simplicity and freshness. Yet their message and zeal had done much to reform the Church and to provide it with moral and intellectual leadership at a time when such leadership was badly needed. In later centuries they also made outstanding contributions to the Church through their missionary efforts around the world.

Veneration of saints and relics. The Church's appeal to ordinary men did not lie in its theology or its claims to universal authority but in the extraordinary degree to which the Church affected their lives. They were born into it, and they died in its embrace; it was their moral guide and their spiritual sustenance; it brought them solace and assured them the means of salvation.

Chaucer's *Canterbury Tales* illustrates popular religious practices. The veneration of saints and particularly of martyrs, such as Thomas à Becket (see p. 414), loomed large among medieval worshipers. Every locale had its patron saint to whom appeals for heavenly aid in times of war, famine, pestilence, and personal trouble were directed. Frenchmen rode into battle invoking the aid of St. Denis; Englishmen shouted, "St. George for England!"; and Spaniards cried, "St. James and close in, Spain!" (*Santiago y cierra España!*).

The veneration of the Virgin Mary was one of the most potent forces in medieval religion. In an age when even the most educated persons believed that thunderstorms, plagues, and famines were the devil's work and that hell loomed perilously close, it seemed natural to pray to the Mother of Christ for protection and comfort. As an earthly mother supplicates for mercy on behalf of her erring child, so the Virgin Mary would supplicate her Son in heaven for her children on earth, particularly in answer to their prayers. Many magnificent Gothic cathedrals, such as Notre Dame (Our Lady) in Paris, were dedicated to Mary as symbols of the people's devotion.

Medieval people believed that relics of saints had miraculous powers. The bone of a saint, for example, supposedly would halt disease or create abundant harvests. The manner in which unscrupulous venders of fake relics sometimes duped Christians has

been vividly recounted by Chaucer in his description of the Pardoner:

No pardoner could beat him in the race,
For in his wallet he had a pillow case
Which he represented as Our Lady's veil;
He said he had a piece of the very sail
St. Peter, when he fished in Galilee
Before Christ caught him, used upon the sea.
He had a latten cross embossed with stones
And in a glass he carried some pig's bones,
And with these holy relics, when he found
Some village parson grubbing his poor ground,
He would get more money in a single day
Than in two months would come the parson's
  way.
Thus with his flattery and his trumped-up stock
He made dupes of the parson and his flock.[17]

Nevertheless, many relics were genuine. Furthermore, this reverence of relics stimulated artists to design elaborate caskets and reliquaries decorated with gold, silver, or enamel. Even churches were built as resting places for the remains of saints. One magnificent reliquary, erected by St. Louis to preserve what was believed to be Christ's crown of thorns, is Sainte Chapelle in Paris.

The omnipresent Church. The weary medieval traveler approaching any city was guided toward his destination by the towers of a church or perhaps a cathedral. Dominating the town and compelling the eyes of the visitor, the physical importance of the cathedral symbolized the importance of the Church in the lives of the people. Entering the city, the traveler found black- and yellow-cowled monks rubbing shoulders with soldiers of a bishop's retinue, nuns and their charges hurrying past tavern doors to escape coarse comments, pilgrims staring at unfamiliar objects while searching out the local shrine, and perhaps a cavalcade clattering through the narrow, twisting streets to announce the arrival of a papal legate from Rome. Besides the churches, the traveler saw other Church property—colleges, hospitals, almshouses, as well as the bishop's elegant palace. On leaving the city walls, he passed the massive buildings of a monastery. The roads led past wayside shrines, and the church steeples marked the neighboring villages.

THE INTELLECTUAL SYNTHESIS

The medieval renaissance. "The meeting of Roman decrepitude and German immaturity was not felicitous."[18] This concise commentary on the character of early medieval civilization is especially relevant to the intellectual side of the period, and it remains a moot question among modern scholars whether the seventh century or the tenth was "the darkest of the Dark Ages." By the close of the sixth century even the most influential of early medieval popes, Gregory the Great, was contributing to the growing intellectual murkiness by voicing strong disapproval of secular literature, insisting that "the same mouth cannot sing the praises of Jupiter and the praises of Christ." Gregory's views were echoed by his younger contemporary, Archbishop Isidore of Seville, who forbade his monks access to "the books of gentiles and heretics." In their place he substituted his own crude and error-filled encyclopedia (see p. 395), which has been characterized as "the fruits of the much decayed tree of ancient learning." So feeble had the light of learning become by the end of the eighth century that Charlemagne found it necessary to order the monasteries to revive their schools and resume instruction in the rudiments of "singing, arithmetic, and grammar" (see p. 323).

In sharp contrast to the fate of his political achievements, Charlemagne's modest educational revival survived his death. At least partly as a result of this stimulus, western Europe by the eleventh century was on the threshold of one of the most productive and energetic periods in the history of western thought—the medieval renaissance.

What was revived first of all during the medieval renaissance was intellectual curiosity, plainly evident from contemporary accounts, such as the following concerning an eleventh-century scholar from Liège:

Olbert was not able to satiate his thirst for study. When he would hear of some one distinguished in the arts he flew there at once, and the more he thirsted the more he absorbed something delightful from each master. At Paris he worked at Saint-Germain and studied the Holy Faith which glowed there. In Troyes he studied for three years, learning gratefully many things. . . . He felt obliged to listen to Fulbert of Chartres who was proclaimed in the liberal arts throughout France. Afterwards just like the bees among flowers, gorged with the nectar of learning, he returned to the hive and lived there studiously in a religious way, and religiously in a studious manner.[19]

Scholasticism. Living "religiously in a studious manner" aptly characterizes the scholars of the medieval renaissance and points up an essential difference between medieval thought on the one hand and early Greek philosophy and modern scientific thought on the other. With but few exceptions, medieval man did not think of truth as something to be discovered by himself; rather, he saw it as already existing in the authoritative Christian and pagan writings handed down from antiquity. Both literally and figuratively, medieval man was always "going to school," seeking to appropriate knowledge from the storehouse of the past. Spurred on by a new zest for employing reason (called logic or dialectic), medieval scholars of the twelfth and thirteenth centuries succeeded in understanding and re-expressing those elements in the Christian and pagan heritage that seemed significant to them. Since this task was carried out largely in the schools, these scholars are known as Schoolmen (or Scholastics), and the intellectual synthesis they produced is called Scholasticism.

The writings of Anselm (d. 1109)—teacher at the monastic school of Bec in France, later archbishop of Canterbury in England, and often called the first Scholastic—contain this early example of justifying the use of reason in religion:

Since the Apostles, the holy Fathers, and many of our teachers have said so much on the reason of our Faith, . . . we cannot hope to equal them today, or in the future, in this contemplation of Truth. But I do not think any one should be reprehended if, firm in his Faith, he wishes to exercise his reason. . . . Although I am a man of but little learning, who takes comfort in reasoning upon those things which we believe, as far as the Heavenly Grace deigns to allow it, I try to rise up at times and when I find what I did not behold before I proclaim this freely to others, so that what I myself believe I may teach to another's judgment.[20]

Even in his celebrated statement "I believe in order that I may understand," Anselm intended no slight on the importance of understanding, for he went on to add that "we should not neglect to study to understand what we believe."[21]

It should be clear from Anselm's longer statement quoted above that his humble attitude toward the ancients was clearly not his attitude toward his fellow scholars. Each formed his own judgments and earnestly sought to convince others. This led to much debate, often uncritical but always exuberant, on a wide range of subjects. Most famous was the argument over universals known as the nominalist-realist controversy.

Nominalists and realists battled over the problem of universal Ideas, basing their arguments on indirect evidence, transmitted by Boethius and others, that Plato and Aristotle did not agree on the subject. Plato had argued that Ideas had reality apart from their existence in men's minds. A specific object was *real* only insofar as it represented the nature of its Idea (see p. 110). Thus Plato himself, for example, was real inasmuch as he partook of the Idea of Man. Aristotle, taking an opposite view, maintained that individuals existed as individuals—a human being was a real entity, not just a reflection of the universal Idea of Man. To the realists in the Middle Ages, only universal Ideas could be real and exist independently. To the nominalists, abstract concepts such as universal Ideas were only names *(nomina)* and had no real existence.

Both realism and nominalism—if carried to their logical extremes—resulted in principles equally abhorrent to the Church. Realism became pantheism (the universe as a whole is God), and nominalism became materialism (the universe is composed solely of matter). In 1092 a Church council condemned the nominalist position as heretical.

The contribution of Abélard. The extreme views of nominalists and realists, along with other examples of the sterile use of logic ("whether the pig is led to market by the rope or by the driver"), outraged a brilliant young student named Pierre Abélard (1079-1142), later a popular teacher at the

cathedral school of Notre Dame in Paris. Like many bright students in all ages, Abélard succeeded in antagonizing his teachers, both realist and nominalist. "I brought him great grief," he wrote of one, "because I undertook to refute certain of his opinions." Another teacher was mercilessly ridiculed:

He had a miraculous flow of words, but they were contemptible in meaning and quite void of reason. When he kindled a fire, he filled his house with smoke and illumined it not at all. He was a tree which seemed noble to those who gazed upon its leaves from afar, but to those who came nearer and examined it more closely was revealed its barrenness.[22]

Abélard's great contribution to medieval thought was freeing logic from barrenness and rerouting it to become again a means to an end rather than an end in itself. Conceptualism, his common-sense solution to the nominalist-realist controversy, has satisfied most philosophers to this day. Abélard held that universals, while existing only in the mind as thoughts or concepts, are nevertheless valid (real) since they are the product of observing the similar qualities that exist in a particular class of things. Thus, by observing many chairs and sitting in them, we arrive at the universal concept "chair."

In addition to redefining the purpose of Scholastic thought, Abélard perfected the Scholastic method. Like Anselm before him, Abélard emphasized the importance of understanding, but whereas the former had begun with faith, the latter started with doubt. We must learn to doubt, Abélard insisted, for doubting leads us to inquire, and inquiry leads us to the truth. Abélard's intellectual skepticism was not that of modern experimental science, however; he never transcended superimposed authority. He aimed to arouse intellectual curiosity in his students and turn it into useful channels, bringing reason to bear on inherited truths in order to achieve understanding.

In an epoch-making work, *Sic et Non (Yes and No),* Abélard demonstrated his method. Listing 158 propositions on theology and ethics, he appended to each a number of statements pro and con taken from the authoritative writings of the Church. The following are typical propositions:

1. That faith is to be supported by human reason, *et contra.*
58. That Adam was saved, *et contra.*
106. That no one can be saved without baptism of water, *et contra.*
122. That marriage is lawful for all, *et contra.*
141. That words of mercy do not profit those without faith, *et contra.*
145. That we sin at times unwillingly, *et contra.*[23]

Abélard did not go on to reconcile these apparent contradictions, but he urged his students to do so by rational interpretation. Abélard's methodology was used by his successors to assimilate and reëxpress the pagan as well as the Christian heritage of the past. The resulting scholarly compilations, which bear such apt titles as *concordantia* (concordance), *speculum* (mirror), and *summa* (sum total), constitute the crowning achievement of the medieval intellectual synthesis.

Abélard is remembered as a great lover as well as a great scholar—a rather uncommon combination. His ill-starred romance with his pupil, the learned and beautiful Héloïse, niece of the canon of Notre Dame, cut short his promising career as a teacher. As related by Abélard in his autobiography, appropriately titled *The Story of My Misfortunes (Historia Calamitatum)*, Héloïse at first refused his offer of marriage:

What penalties, she said, would the world rightly demand of her if she should rob it of so shining a light! What curses would follow such a loss to the Church, what tears among the philosophers would result from such a marriage! How unfitting, how lamentable it would be for me, whom nature had made for the whole world, to devote myself to one woman solely, and to subject myself to such humiliation![24]

The two lovers were married in secret, but Héloïse's uncle, falsely believing that Abélard planned to abandon Héloïse, hired thugs who attacked and emasculated the scholar. Both Abélard and Héloïse then sought refuge in the Church—Pierre as a monk and Héloïse as the abbess of a nunnery.

The new material and the task of reconciliation. In the twelfth century the study of Greek learning with its Muslim additions was undertaken by western scholars who flocked to Spain and Sicily and there translated Muslim editions of ancient writings. As a result of these translations a host of new ideas, particularly in science and philosophy, were introduced to western scholars. Western knowledge was expanded to include not only Arabic learning but also such important classical works as Euclid's *Geometry,* Ptolemy's *Almagest,* Hippocrates' and Galen's treatises in medicine, and all of Aristotle's extant writings.

As his works became known, Aristotle became, in Dante's words, "the master of those who know," and his authority was generally accepted as second only to that of the Scriptures. But because the Church's teachings were considered infallible, Aristotle's ideas, as well as those of other great thinkers of antiquity, had to be reconciled with existing dogmas. By applying Abélard's methodology to the new sciences and philosophy and attempting to harmonize them with the Scriptures and Church dogmas, theologians hoped that the purpose of God's plan would then stand revealed. The intellectuals of today may not find the results convincing, but the magnitude of the Scholastics' task and their devotion and enthusiasm are admirable.

Scholasticism reached its zenith with St. Thomas Aquinas (1225?-1274). In his *Summa Theologica* this brilliant Italian Dominican dealt exhaustively with the great problems of theology, philosophy, politics, and economics. After collecting the arguments pro and con on a given problem—for example, "Whether it is lawful to sell a thing for more than its worth?"—he went on to draw conclusions. (His answer to the problem cited reflects the great influence of Christian ethics upon medieval economic thought: "I answer that, it is altogether sinful to have recourse to deceit in order to sell a thing for more than its just price, because this is to deceive one's neighbour so as to injure him."[25])

A major concern of St. Thomas was to reconcile Aristotle and Church dogma—in other words, the truths of natural reason and the truths of faith. There can be no real contradiction, he argued, since all truth comes from God. In case of an unresolved contradiction, however, faith won out, because of the possibility of human error in reasoning. St. Thomas was so convincing in settling this conflict—the first clash between science and religion in the history of our western civilization—that his philosophy still has its followers today.

The decline of Scholasticism. But Scholasticism, having reached its zenith, declined rapidly. The assumption that faith and reason were compatible was vigorously denied by two Franciscan thinkers, Duns Scotus (d. 1308) and William of Occam (d. c. 1349), who elaborated on Aquinas' belief that certain religious doctrines are beyond discovery by the use of reason. They argued that if the human intellect could not understand divinely revealed truth, it could hope to comprehend only the natural world and should not intrude upon the sphere of divine truth. Such a position tended to undermine the Thomistic synthesis of faith and reason. Realism and nominalism revived, the one promoting an increase in mystical, nonrational religion, the other contributing to the growing scientific spirit and to individualism and worldly concerns in general. For better or for worse, this trend toward the emancipation of human knowledge and action from the unifying authority of religion and the Church became a characteristic feature of western civilization.

After the thirteenth century Scholasticism increasingly became a term of reproach, for its adherents were obsessed with theological subtleties, discouraged independent thought, and in general lost touch with reality. But it should be remembered that the Scholastics sought to appropriate and make subjectively their own the store of Christian and pagan knowledge left to them by a more advanced civilization. In terms of their needs and objectives—an intelligible and all-embracing synthesis of faith, logic, and science—the Scholastics were eminently successful, and people of our own age should not look askance at their accomplishments. Ironically, we today increasingly recognize the importance of reconciling science and faith in an age which has so much of the former and so little of the latter.

Medieval science. As we saw in the previous chapter, our medieval ancestors made notable technological advances, thereby laying the foundations for a new power and machine technology described by the term *eotechnics*. This development, however, relied primarily upon an empirical, or trial-and-error, method, by which ingenious minds invented new forms of technology to cope with the challenge of local conditions. On the other hand, the method of abstracting universal principles from empirical data in order to investigate and understand the phenomenal world—which had been the major contribution of Greek thought to the history and philosophy of science—had to await rediscovery in early modern times. At this point, we shall examine the extent to which medieval science comprised part of the overall intellectual synthesis and the conditions under which it had to function.

Because of the emphasis upon authority and the all-pervasive influence of the Church, the early medieval atmosphere was not conducive to free scientific investigation. Those who studied science were churchmen, and their findings were supposed to illuminate rather than contradict the dogmas of the

This detail of a portrait of Saint Thomas Aquinas by Fra Angelico is in one of the Vatican chapels.

theologians. Perhaps the greatest obstacle facing science in the early Middle Ages was ignorance of Greek learning. Knowledge was limited to such compilations as the *Etymologies* of Isidore, bishop of Seville. Written in the seventh century, this fascinating encyclopedia included a jumble of odds and ends whose accuracy can be judged from a sample excerpt:

XI, 3, 23. The race of Sciopodes is said to live in Ethiopia. They have one leg apiece, and are of a marvellous swiftness, and the Greeks call them Sciopodes from this, that in summertime they lie on the ground on their backs and are shaded by the greatness of their feet.[26]

The *Etymologies* remained a standard reference work in the western world for three hundred years.

When Greek and Arabic works were translated in the twelfth century, the West inherited a magnificent legacy of scientific knowledge. Arabic numerals and the symbol *zero* made possible the decimal system of computation. Algebra came from the Arabs and trigonometry from the Muslims. Euclid's *Geometry* was also made available. Leonard of Pisa made a great original contribution to mathematics in the thirteenth century when he worked out a method to extract square roots and to solve quadratic and cubic equations. On the other hand, Ptolemy's belief that the earth was the center of the universe —a fallacious theory destined to handicap astronomy for centuries—was commonly accepted.

Early medieval geography, abounding in fabulous accounts of Arabian birds that could lift elephants and of sea serpents capable of devouring ships, was modified but not always improved by classical knowledge. The translation of Ptolemy's *Geography* in 1409 turned out to be a handicap in some respects because of its errors. On the other hand, the voyages of Christian pilgrims to the Holy Land and of European traders to China and India all added to geographical knowledge. It should be emphasized that educated men in the Middle Ages believed the earth to be round, not flat.

Physics was based on Aristotle's theory of four elements (water, earth, air, and fire) and on his theories of dynamics—doctrines which it took centuries to disprove. Various fourteenth-century thinkers, however, attacked the errors in Aristotle's works and advanced some worthwhile theories in regard to dynamics. Chemistry was based on Aristotelian concepts, mixed with magic and alchemy. Like the Chinese alchemist, his European counterpart tried in vain to transmute base metals into gold and silver and to obtain a magic elixir, but in both cases the attempts did much to advance experimental science.

Frederick II and Roger Bacon. Two notable exceptions to the medieval rule of subservience to authority were the emperor Frederick II (see p. 431) and the English Franciscan Roger Bacon. Frederick had a genuine scientific interest in animals and was famed for his large traveling menagerie, which included elephants, camels, panthers, lions, leopards, and a giraffe. He wrote a remarkable treatise, *The Art of Falconry*, which is still considered largely accurate in its observations of the life and habits of various kinds of hunting birds. "We discovered by hardwon experience," he wrote, "that the deductions of Aristotle, whom we followed when they appealed to our reason, were not entirely to be relied upon."[27] At his Sicilian court Frederick gathered about him many distinguished Greek, Muslim, and Latin scholars, and he wrote to others in distant lands seeking their views on such problems as why objects appear bent when partly covered by water. He indulged in many experiments; one was a test to determine what language children would speak if raised in absolute silence. The experiment was a failure because all the children died.

Roger Bacon (1214-1292) also employed the inductive scientific method—he coined the term "experimental science"—and boldly criticized the deductive syllogistic reasoning used by the Scholastic thinkers. His *Opus Maius* contains this attack on Scholasticism:

There are four principal stumbling blocks to comprehending truth, which hinder well-nigh every scholar: the example of frail and unworthy authority, long-established custom, the sense of the ignorant crowd, and the hiding of one's ignorance under the show of wisdom.[28]

RELIGIOUS AND INTELLECTUAL CENTERS OF MEDIEVAL EUROPE

■ French Centers of Gothic Architecture

△ Medieval Universities: Prior to 1200

✱ Medieval Universities: 1200 to 1300

→ Spread of Romantic Literature

→ Expansion of Roman Law

Today we are struck by some of Roger Bacon's startling predictions of the possible results of the application of science to man's needs:

Machines for navigating are possible without rowers, so that great ships suited to river or ocean, guided by one man, may be borne with greater speed than if they were full of men. Likewise cars may be made so that without a draught animal they may be moved *cum impetu inaesti-mabili* ["with inestimable speed"], as we deem the scythed chariots to have been from which antiquity fought. And flying machines are possible, so that a man may sit in the middle turning some device by which artificial wings may beat the air in the manner of a flying bird.[29]

In spite of the fact that Bacon never doubted the authority of the Bible or the Church—his interest lay only in natural science—his superiors considered him a dangerous thinker because of his criticism of Scholastic thought.

Medieval medicine. By the thirteenth century learned Muslim commentaries on Galen and Hippocrates and on Aristotle's biology were available in the West. This knowledge, coupled with their own discoveries and improved techniques, made medieval doctors more than just barbers who engaged in bloodletting. Surgeons systematically studied the dissection of bodies and became skilled in performing operations and autopsies. Many towns had municipal doctors, and public health received an important impetus when Venice began to combat contagious diseases with quarantines. In the fourteenth century leprosy was virtually stamped out in Europe.

On the other hand, the overall state of medical knowledge and practice was, by our standards at least, still primitive. This can be seen in the prevalence of superstitious beliefs and the resort to magical practices, the general lack of concern for public sanitation, the periodic decimation of entire populations by epidemics such as the Black Death, and that significant indicator of the state of public health—the infant mortality rate, which was staggeringly high.

Origin of universities. The old rhetoric schools of Rome had a curriculum of seven liberal arts, separated into two divisions: a *trivium* consisting of grammar, rhetoric, and dialectic; and a *quadrivium* of arithmetic, music, geometry, and astronomy. When the Roman empire in the West fell, the task of education went to the Church; and the classical liberal arts were adapted to prepare youths for the ministry. Through the work of Cassiodorus in the sixth century (see p. 380), monasteries became important centers of learning. By 1200, however, monastic schools were overshadowed by the more dynamic cathedral schools established by bishops in such important centers as Paris, Chartres, Canterbury, and Toledo.

The renaissance of the twelfth century brought back classical learning to the West, and unprecedented numbers of students flocked to the schools. The revival of learning and the development of professional studies in law, medicine, and theology led to the rise of organized centers of learning—the universities, which soon eclipsed the monastic and cathedral schools.

Originally the word *university* meant a group of persons possessing a common purpose. In this case it referred to a guild of learners, both teachers and students, analogous to the craft guilds with their masters and apprentices. In the thirteenth century the universities had no campuses and little property or money, and the masters taught in hired rooms or religious houses. If the university was dissatisfied with its treatment by the townspeople, it could migrate elsewhere. The earliest universities—Bologna, Paris, and Oxford—were not officially founded or created, but in time the popes and kings granted them and other universities charters of self-government. The charters gave legal status to the universities and rights to the students, such as freedom from military service and from the jurisdiction of town officials.

Two systems: Bologna and Paris. Two of the most famous medieval universities were at Bologna in northern Italy and at Paris. The former owed its growth to the fame of Irnerius (c. 1055-1130), who taught civil law. Because of his influence, Bologna acquired a reputation as the leading center for the study of law. The students soon organized a guild

In these pictures from a fifteenth-century manuscript, the students at the left are gambling in university rooms, a practice strictly forbidden by school authorities. At the right, they oppose one another in "disputation," the class debates which went on for hours.

for protection against the rapacious townspeople, who were demanding exorbitant sums for food and lodging. Because the guild went on to control the professors, Bologna became a student paradise. In the earliest statutes (1317) we read that a professor requiring leave of absence even for one day first had to obtain permission from his own students. He had to begin his lecture with the bell and end within one minute of the next bell. The material in the text had to be covered systematically, with all difficult passages fully explained. The powerful position of the students at Bologna developed as a result of a predominance of older students studying for the doctorate in law.

At the university in Paris conditions developed differently. This university, which had grown out of the cathedral school of Notre Dame, specialized in liberal arts and theology and became the most influential intellectual center in medieval Europe. Its administration was far different from Bologna's. The chancellor of Notre Dame, the bishop's officer who had long been accustomed to exercising authority over the cathedral school, refused to allow the students or the masters to obtain control of the burgeoning university. Charters issued by the French king in 1200 and by the pope in 1231 made the university an autonomous body controlled by the masters.

The collegiate system. Universities owned no dormitories, and students lived in rented rooms or pooled their resources to obtain housing on a cooperative basis. With masters' fees and living expenses to pay, the impoverished student labored under decided handicaps. A philanthropic patron, however, sometimes provided quarters where poor scholars could board free of charge. One such patron was Robert de Sorbon, the royal chaplain to the saintly Louis IX. About 1257 Robert endowed a hall for sixteen needy students working for their doctorates in theology, thus founding the College de Sorbonne; the University of Paris is still popularly known by the name of its great benefactor.

Similar bequests led to the establishment of the oldest colleges at Oxford. Balliol, for example, was started as a house for needy scholars and was supported by funds from John of Balliol as part of a penance imposed for his misdeeds. Oxford's origins are obscure; it may have been founded as a result of an academic migration from Paris. In any case, its organization and customs were influenced by the French university.

As more colleges were established, the large universities became collections of colleges in which the students lived and studied. Although organization by colleges finally disappeared in the University of Paris where the system originated, at both Oxford and Cambridge the collegiate system has remained an integral part of the university to this day.

A medieval student's day. As a rule the medieval student attended only one or two classes a day, but each might be three hours long. The first met at daybreak in a bleak unheated hall, very often without windows. The professor lectured from a platform while the students sat on low benches. Their only texts were manuscripts consisting of costly parchment leaves bound together; a manuscript text was not printed but copied, often inaccurately, by hand. The manuscripts were rented out to those students with sufficient funds; the less fortunate got along as best they could by copying the lectures on wax tablets.

After the initial lecture the scholars had their first meal at ten or eleven o'clock. Then came some free time, followed by a second lecture. Supper was at four or five o'clock. Many students did not study at night because they could not afford candles. The more exuberant youths sometimes spent their evening hours roistering or fighting the townsmen and scaling the college walls to get back to their rooms after the door was barred. To judge from letters written to their parents, students frequently were short of money:

This is to inform you that I am studying at Oxford with the greatest diligence, but the matter of money stands greatly in the way of my promotion, as it is now two months since I spent the last of what you sent me. The city is expensive and makes many demands; I have to rent lodgings, buy necessaries, and provide for many other things which I cannot now specify. Wherefore I respectfully beg your paternity that by the promptings of divine pity you may assist me, so that I may be able to complete what I have well begun. For you must know that without Ceres and Bacchus Apollo grows cold.[30]

Curriculum and degrees. The degrees available at medieval universities were similar to those offered today. The bachelor's degree, which could be obtained after studying from three to five years, was not considered very important. For a master of arts degree, which admitted the holder into the guild of masters and was a license to teach, particular emphasis was placed on the works of Aristotle. Scholars studied for a master's degree (commonly called a doctorate) in one of the three great professions —theology, law, and medicine—by reading texts relevant to their chosen field. It was no easy matter to get a master's degree (or doctorate) from a medieval university; many years of preparation were required, and at the final examination the candidate had to defend his thesis publicly for hours against the learned attacks of the dean and the masters. If successful in his defense, the candidate then stood the cost of a banquet for his examiners.

Legacy of the medieval university. Bologna and Paris influenced other universities. Bologna left her mark on Italy, southern France, and Spain. Paris became the model of universities founded in northern France, England, Germany, the Low Countries, and the rest of northern Europe. By the end of the fifteenth century there were about eighty universities in Europe.

The impact of the universities upon the Middle Ages was very great. They provided medieval society with doctors, scientists, scholars, and trained personnel for the Church and the state. Moreover, the medieval universities were conscious of the importance of their role in society. They believed their function was not only to train men capable of handling the most important spiritual and temporal offices of the day but also to foster learning, to discipline the intellect, and to stimulate a spirit of inquiry.

The modern university resembles its medieval alma mater in its primary purpose for existence: the organization of an institution for the advancement of human knowledge and the training of each new generation of students. In details, too, the similarities remain. Colleges still offer a stated curriculum, formal instruction, examinations, and degrees. The gowns and hoods seen at every commencement are the same kind of attire that medieval students wore. The voluminous sleeves originally functioned as carriers for books or food.

Latin language and literature. While local languages were generally spoken, among the educated people Latin served as an international means of communication. This common tongue provided much of the co-hesion of the Middle Ages, for virtually all the crucial communications of the Church, governments, and schools were in Latin. Religious and political documents, treatises on law and medicine, and essays on theology and dialectic were all written in this language. Undoubtedly the most splendid medieval Latin prose is found in the Church liturgy, which was chanted by the priest.

Latin poetry experienced periods of revival, the greatest of which came in the eleventh and twelfth centuries. After the twelfth century, however, literary expression in Latin could not compete successfully against the rising tide of literature in the vernacular tongues.

Any misconception that the Middle Ages were simply "other-worldly" and long-faced will be rudely shattered by glancing at the madcap literature of the students, who unhesitatingly proclaimed the pleasures of wine, women, and song. Known as goliardic poetry, this form of verse was written by wandering students. An example is the *Confession of Golias,* in which the poet asks a prelate to grant him absolution for his misdeeds:

'Tis most arduous to make
  Nature's self-surrender;
Seeing girls, to blush and be
  Purity's defender!
We young men our longings ne'er
  Shall to stern law render,
Or preserve our fancies from
  Bodies smooth and tender. . . .

In the public house to die
  Is my resolution;
Let wine to my lips be nigh
  At life's dissolution:
That will make the angels cry,
  With glad elocution,
"Grant this toper, God on high,
  Grace and absolution!"[31]

The goliardic poets were brilliant at parody and satire. Versed in classical mythology, they substituted Venus for the Virgin, wrote masses for drunkards, and were guilty of other blasphemies. Some of their sharpest satires bitingly scorned the clerics guilty of breaking their vows.

In contrast, the great Latin hymns such as the *Dies Irae* and the *Stabat Mater Dolorosa* show the genuineness of the religious spirit of the twelfth and thirteenth centuries. The latter hymn movingly describes the Virgin Mary standing beside the cross:

By the cross, sad vigil keeping,
Stood the mournful mother weeping,
While on it the saviour hung;
In that hour of deep distress
Pierced the sword of bitterness
Through her heart with sorrow wrung[32]

Vernacular literature. Even when their language was derived from Latin, the great majority of Europe's population neither spoke nor understood Latin, although they came in contact with it through the Church. Modifications of the spoken Latin of the provinces developed after the fall of the Roman empire. These different languages —known as the Romance languages—appeared in Italy, France, Spain, and Portugal during the early Middle Ages. In northern Europe—Germany, Scandinavia, and England—various Germanic tongues were used, and on the fringes of Catholic Europe, some Celtic and Slavic. Each of these languages was vernacular, which meant that it was commonly spoken in a specific country or locality. Any literature appealing to the common people had to be created in the language of their daily life. Vernacular literature had a dynamic flesh-and-blood quality, and thus it was natural that in the long run it would outstrip the Latin literature written by the scholars.

The types of medieval vernacular literature are varied. Down to the thirteenth century the most common manner of expression was poetry, of which the epic was the earliest form. The greatest of the French epics, or *chansons de geste* ("songs of great deeds"), is the eleventh-century *Song of Roland,* which recounts the heroic deeds and death of Count Roland in the Pyrenees while defending the rear of Charlemagne's army (see p. 322). The great Spanish epic, the *Poema del Cid* (see quoted selection, p. 427), is a product of the twelfth century. These stirring epic poems, with their accounts of prowess in battle, mirror the masculine warrior virtues of early chivalry (see p. 339).

By the twelfth century in the feudal courts of southern France, poets called troubadours were composing short, personal lyrics dealing mainly with romantic love. "The delicacy and romanticism of the troubadour lyrics betoken a more genteel and sophisticated nobility than that of the feudal north—a nobility that preferred songs of love to songs of war. Indeed, medieval southern France was the source of the entire romantic-love tradition of Western Civilization, with its idealization of women, its emphasis on male gallantry and courtesy, and its insistence on embroidering the sex drive with an elaborate ritual of palpitating hearts, moonlight, and sentimental ties."[33] Typical are these lines written in adoration of the lovely Eleanor of Aquitaine:

When the sweet breeze
Blows hither from your dwelling
Methinks I feel
A breath of paradise.[34]

Nothing comparable to these lines exists in the *chansons de geste,* but during the last half of the twelfth century this new interest in love fused with the purely heroic material of the early epics. The result was the medieval romance, an account of love and adventure, to which was often added a strong coloring of religious feeling. Thus, for example, there arose in England the cycle of romances concerning King Arthur and his Round Table of chivalrous knights who variously pursue adventure, charming ladies, and the Holy Grail. In Germany around the beginning of the thirteenth century, the old saga material dealing with Siegfried, Brunhild, and the wars against the Huns was recast into the *Nibelungenlied (Song of the Nibelungs).*

All of the foregoing types of poetry were designed primarily for the chivalric aristocracy. The self-made burgher preferred more practical and shrewd tales. His taste was gratified by the bawdy *fabliaux* and the animal stories about Reynard the Fox, the symbol of the sly bourgeois lawyer who easily outwits King Lion and his noble vassals. Still another class of literature, which

circulated for centuries by word of mouth before being written down, developed for the illiterate common people. The Robin Hood ballads of the fourteenth century are built around the theme of robbing the rich to give to the poor. In the same century was composed the *Vision of Piers Plowman* condemning the injustices of a social system that had brought on the peasant revolt in England (see p. 372 and quoted selection, p. 338).

The compelling interest which Dante's *Divine Comedy* has held for centuries of readers is aptly demonstrated by this engraving from an edition of the *Comedy* published and illustrated by William Blake, the English poet and artist of the late eighteenth and early nineteenth centuries. Shown is the marsh of the River Styx, the abode of the wrathful ("all naked and with brows in anger bent") and the sullen ("who gloom and blacken in the mire").

Dante Alighieri. The vernacular was also used by two of the greatest writers of the period—Dante and Chaucer. Combining a knowledge of Latin classics, a profound religious sense, and an understanding of great philosophers such as St. Thomas Aquinas, the Italian Dante (1265-1321) produced one of the world's greatest narrative poems. Written in the Tuscan dialect and entitled *Commedia* (later generations have called it the *Divine Comedy*), it is an allegory of medieval man (Dante) moving from bestial earthiness (hell) through conversion (purgatory) to the sublime spirituality of union with God (paradise). Dante describes how

Midway this way of life we're bound upon,
  I woke to find myself in a dark wood,
  Where the right road was wholly lost and gone.[35]

Dante then accepts the offer of Virgil, symbol of pagan learning, to be his "master, leader, and lord" to guide him through hell and purgatory. But it is Beatrice, the lady whom he had once loved from afar and who is now the symbol of divine love, who guides him through paradise. At last Dante stands before God, and words fail him as he finds peace in the presence of the highest form of love:

Oh, how fall short the words! . . .
The Love that moves the sun and every star.[36]

Concerning the *Divine Comedy*, which Dante said described his "full experience," Henry Wadsworth Longfellow has written:

Ah! from what agonies of heart and brain,
What exultations trampling on despair,
What tenderness, what tears, what hate of wrong,
What passionate outcry of a soul in pain,
Uprose this poem of the earth and air,
This mediaeval miracle of song![37]

The wit of Chaucer. In the *Canterbury Tales,* Geoffrey Chaucer (1340?-1400), one of the greatest figures in medieval literature, reveals a cross section of the contemporary English life, customs, and thought (see quoted selections, pp. 383, 390). The twenty-nine pilgrims who assembled in April 1387 at an inn before journeying to the shrine of St. Thomas à Becket at Canterbury were a motley group. The "truly perfect, gentle knight," just returned from warring against the "heathen in Turkey," was accompanied by his son, a young squire who loved so much by night that "he slept no more than does a nightingale." The clergy was represented by the coy prioress who "would weep if she but saw a mouse caught in a trap,"[38] the rotund monk who loved to eat fat swan and ride good horses, the friar who knew the best taverns and all the barmaids in town, and the poor parish priest who was a credit to his faith. Also included in the group were the merchant who could talk only of business, the threadbare Oxford student, the miller with a wart on his nose, and the worthy wife of Bath, who had married five times and was now visiting Christian shrines in search of a sixth husband.

Chaucer's fame rests securely upon his keen interest in human nature and his skill as a storyteller. The Midland dialect he used was the linguistic base for the language of future English literature, just as Dante's use of the Tuscan dialect fixed the Italian tongue.

Rebirth of drama. Dormant since classical times, drama was reborn in the Middle Ages under the supervision of the Church. Out of the choral singing of sacred stories developed the mystery plays, whose themes dealt with Biblical stories and the lives of the saints. At first the plays supplemented the regular service and were performed inside the church proper. As their popularity grew, they were presented either on the church steps or on a separate stage. The early mystery plays were in Latin, but later, phrases in the native language were added to the text, a practice which undoubtedly pleased the audience.

As the drama ceased to have a direct connection with the service, there developed another type, the morality play. Whereas the mystery plays were based on Biblical and saintly subjects, the morality plays had allegorical plots, sometimes of religious significance, sometimes not. The actors personified virtues and vices, and the plot of the drama usually centered on a conflict between them. *Everyman,* an excellent example of a morality play, is still occasionally produced.

THE AESTHETIC SYNTHESIS

Artistic correlation. The *Summa Theologica* of St. Thomas Aquinas and the *Divine Comedy* of Dante represent the best intellectual expressions of the medieval spirit. Similarly, the Gothic cathedral is the ultimate artistic expression of the age. Each of these masterpieces represents a different aspect of the attempt to organize everything into an overall pattern which would glorify God.

The order and form of Scholastic thought find their counterparts in the structure and style of the Gothic edifices. A Scholastic treatise was systematically arranged in logical parts; the cathedral was similarly articulated in space. The main sections, the nave, transept, and apse, were individually distinctive yet were integrated into a coherent structure.

Early Christian churches. In design, early Christian churches imitated the plan of the Roman basilicas. In this design a rectangle is divided into three aisles: a central aisle, or nave, ending in a semicircular apse, and a lower-ceilinged aisle on each side. Parallel rows of columns separated the nave from the side aisles. The roof over the nave was raised to provide a clerestory—a section pierced by windows to illuminate the interior (see illustration, p. 204). In the fourth century the basilica plan was modified by the addition of a transept across the aisles between the apse and the nave. This essentially "T" shape, altered by the Carolingians to form a cross by extending the apse beyond the transept, added Christian symbolism to the basic plan of the pagan-style building. Graceful bell-towers were erected separate from the church building; the "leaning tower" of Pisa is a famous later example.

Romanesque architecture. In the eleventh century occurred a tremendous architectural revival, marked by the recovery of the art of building in stone rather than in wood, as was common during the early Middle Ages. At a much later date the name *Romanesque* came to be applied to this new style, because, like early Christian architecture, it was based largely on Roman models. Although details of structure and ornamentation differed with locality, the round arch was a standard Romanesque feature (see Color Plate 16). Both barrel and cross vaults were used, particularly in northern Europe, where the need to build fireproof churches made it impractical to follow the common Italian practice of using wooden roofs. Thus, for example, the barrel vault was used over the nave, the cross vault over square areas of the aisles and transept. Thick outside walls and huge interior piers were necessary to support the heavy stone barrel and cross vaults. (In time, diagonal ribs were built along the groins of the cross vault, transforming it into the ribbed-groin vault; see diagram.) Because the walls would be weak-

The ribbed-groin vault developed by Romanesque architects derived from the Roman intersecting vaults The ribbed vault is made up of arches which span the sides of a square, with groin arches crossing diagonally from corner to corner. Ribbed-groin vaults with pointed arches formed the stone skeleton of Gothic cathedrals. Use of the pointed arch enabled Gothic builders to reach greater heights than had been possible with the semicircular arch because the pointed arch exerted less sideways thrust than the semicircular arch.

flying buttress
weighted pinnacle
vaults and arches
buttress

nave
transept
sanctuary
transept

By Ewing Galloway, N.Y.

The fusing of sculpture and architecture is apparent in this detail of one of the doorways of Amiens Cathedral. Medieval cathedrals were rich in sculptures of saints and great men of antiquity, episodes from history and the Old and New Testaments, and allegorical representations of science, philosophy, and theology. The unified effect of the fully developed Gothic style is one of awesome, but ordered, intricacy, as the photograph of the entire front of Amiens Cathedral demonstrates. At the far right is a drawing of the cross section and floor plan of the same cathedral. Vaults, arches, buttresses, and weighted pinnacles were important structural elements in the Gothic style of architecture.

ened by large window apertures, the clerestory windows were small or nonexistent. Thus the northern Romanesque interior was dark and gloomy, the exterior massive and monumental.

Gothic architecture. Actually, no clear-cut cleavage exists between Romanesque and Gothic. There was a gradual evolutionary process, which reached its culmination in the thirteenth and fourteenth centuries. The architects of the Gothic-style cathedral developed ribbed-groin vaults with pointed rather than round arches. This enabled them to solve the technical problem of cross-vaulting the nave, which, unlike the aisles, could only be divided into oblong areas (see diagram of floor plan, p. 405). Thus light ribbed-groin vaults, whose sides were of different length, replaced the heavy barrel vaults over the nave, and the roof of the nave could be raised to permit the use of large clerestory windows. The thrust of the vaults over both the nave and the aisles was concentrated on a few strong structural supports. Part of the weight was carried down to the ground by columns within the building, and part by flying buttresses at points along the walls. With such vaulting and buttresses, the weight of the roof was largely shifted off the walls (see diagram of cross section, p. 405).

The important principles of the concentration of thrusts and counterthrusts were worked out, so that the Gothic structure was supported by its essential frame. Large stained-glass windows were set into the walls between the buttresses. The dark, somber interior of the Romanesque churches gave way to the jeweled light of the Gothic interiors (see Color Plate 17).

Thirteenth-century architecture displays Gothic style at its best, with its finest examples in France. Splendid cathedrals like Notre Dame of Paris, Amiens, and Chartres are expressions of both the religious feeling and the engineering of the times. Soaring in strength and elasticity, their west façade crowned by two bell-towers, and their interiors softened by shadows and the colored tints of stained glass, these cathedrals epitomize an age of faith.

In England architects quickly adopted this style with enthusiasm and skill. The contribution of the English to Gothic architecture was the perpendicular style, with its vertical stonework in the windows and complicated fan vaulting, an exaggeration of a structural feature for decorative purposes. In many ways English Gothic is rather conservative. The low, spread-out plan, the lack of flying buttresses, and frequently, the single tower, instead of the pair of towers common to French Gothic, are all characteristics which carry over from Romanesque architecture.

The Romanesque churches had been built largely by monastic orders; the Gothic cathedral was the cooperative creation of townsmen and their clergy. They united in erecting a structure that would express the fervor of their devotion—and also eclipse the cathedral of a rival town. The enormous task of building these huge structures required decades or even centuries to complete. The heroic efforts of the entire population were described by a French archbishop thus:

Who has ever heard tell, in times past, that powerful princes of the world, that men brought up in honors and in wealth, that nobles, men and women, have bent their proud and haughty necks to the harness of carts, and that, like beasts of burden, they have dragged to the abode of Christ these wagons, loaded with . . . stone, timber, and all that is necessary for the construction of a church? When they have reached the church they arrange the wagons about it like a spiritual camp, and during the whole night they celebrate the watch by hymns and canticles. On each wagon they light tapers.[39]

Sculpture and stained glass. Thirteenth-century Gothic sculpture was carved to fit into the total composition of the cathedral. To use sculpture to the best architectural advantage, the subject was often distorted to achieve a particular effect. As long as sculpture remained strongly bound to its architectural setting, the individuality of the separate statues was suppressed. This was done to emphasize the "serial" character of the entire band of statues across the façade.

The making of stained-glass windows in medieval times was a fine art whose excellence has not since been duplicated. A stained-glass window is composed of small pieces of colored glass held together in a pattern by metal strips which both brace the glass and emphasize the design. By adding various minerals to molten glass, thirteenth-century craftsmen achieved brilliant hues. Details such as hair were painted on the glass. Unfortunately, the medieval method of making stained glass died out almost completely after the sixteenth century. The subsequent system of painting the color on the glass never resulted in the same luminous quality.

Secular architecture. What the cathedral was to religious life, the castle was to everyday living. Both were havens, and both were built to endure. The new weapons and techniques of siege warfare, which the crusaders brought back with them, necessitated more massive castles. By the thirteenth century castle building in Europe reached a high point of development. The towers were rounded, and bastions stood at strategic points along the walls. The castle as a whole was planned in such a skillful manner that if one section was taken by attackers, it could be sealed off from the remaining fortifications. Whole towns were fortified in the same way, with walls, watchtowers, moats, and drawbridges.

Toward the end of the Middle Ages, there was less need for fortified towns and castles. At the same time, the wealth accruing from the revived trade and increased industry encouraged the development of secular Gothic architecture. Town and guild halls, the residences of the rich, and the chateaux of the nobles all borrowed the delicate Gothic style from the cathedrals.

SUMMARY

The traditional division of history into "ancient," "medieval," and "modern" is fundamentally arbitrary and artificial in that history is a continuous process. Applying the same common denominator—"medieval"— to the thousand turbulent years between the fifth and fifteenth centuries obscures the

Considered the most perfect Benedictine abbey in existence, Westminster Abbey exemplifies the perpendicular Gothic architectural style. The worshipers' eyes are drawn toward the heavens by the fan-tracery vaulting, attesting to the success of the Gothic architects' design.

wide variations that existed during the period. For five centuries after the fall of Rome, western civilization was on the defensive against invading barbarians from the east and north. The Church took the lead in fusing classical, barbarian, and Christian elements and nurtured such intellectual activity as existed.

From the tenth century on, a very different kind of medieval West began to take shape. By the eleventh century Europe had shifted to the offensive, and its resurgence of strength was reflected in the Church's militant drive to political triumph in the thirteenth century.

Emerging out of feudal decentralization ahead of the state, the Church developed the first unified system of law and administration in medieval Europe and intimately affected the life of every person. It gave man a sense of security against the dangers on earth and those beyond. To perform its historical mission, the Church required a hierarchy of clergy and an elaborate doctrine, accompanied by methods for enforcing its will. We have followed the areas of reform, watched the Church's power reach its apex in the age of Innocent III, and noted signs of its eventual decline.

Within the Church, thinkers wrestled with philosophical issues, such as the realist-nominalist controversy. In the thirteenth century such famous Scholastics as St. Thomas Aquinas made herculean attempts to reconcile faith and reason, Church authority and classical thought.

Stimulated by the acquisition of Greek and Arabic knowledge, science and education established new frontiers. Practical inventions in navigation and public health produced some important progress. The earliest universities grew from unorganized groups of scholars and students to important centers of learning. Bologna and Paris, in particular, directly affected other universities. In literature, Latin, the international language of the educated, slowly gave way to the vernacular tongues. Chaucer and Dante, giants in the literary field, both wrote in their native languages and did much to develop modern English and Italian respectively.

Evolving from Romanesque patterns, the splendid Gothic cathedrals were the greatest artistic achievement of the medieval period. The rounded arches and massive walls of Romanesque architecture were replaced by pointed arches, ribbed-groin vaults, and the flying buttresses of the soaring Gothic cathedrals. This style carried over from churches to castles, town halls, and urban dwellings.

Chapter 14

Nations in the Making

Late Medieval Political History: 1100-1500

INTRODUCTION. At the end of the twelfth century political as well as economic change was manifest in Europe. Trade revived, cities grew, and kings developed their power at the expense of the feudal nobility. Inadequate to meet the demands of a new and progressive society in the making, feudalism was on the wane.

Perhaps the greatest weakness of feudalism was its inability to guarantee law and order. Too often feudalism meant anarchy in which robber barons, in the words of a twelfth-century writer, "levied taxes on the villages every so often, and called it 'protection money'" (see p. 412). Feudalism provided no effective agency to deal with such ruffians. While each feudal lord had his own court for settling the disputes of his vassals, no broad, uniform legal codes existed. As a result, confusion, inefficiency, and injustice prevailed.

The inefficiency inherent in the feudal system also hindered economic progress. Trade and commerce spread over ever larger areas, but the boundaries of many tiny feudal principalities acted as barriers to this expansion. Only by welding the confusing multiplicity of fiefs and principalities into a large territorial unit—the nation—could the irritating tolls and tariffs imposed by local barons be removed, trade advanced, the lack of a uniform currency be remedied, and justice established. In other words, the ills of feudalism could be cured only by the creation of unified and centralized national states. This chapter shows how various European monarchs—especially in England, France, and Spain—expanded their power, improved the machinery of government, and rallied their people around them, thus creating such states.

THE GENESIS OF MODERN ENGLAND

William the Conqueror's centralized feudal monarchy. With one stroke at the battle of Hastings (1066), William the Conqueror became king of England. From the outset, all of William's policies were aimed at a single goal—the increase of his own power within the context of political feudalism. And, sensibly, he utilized some of the institutions already familiar in England. He retained such administrative divisions as the Saxon shire and the hundred, along with the system of local courts and sheriffs. But the long arm of royal power also reached the local level through the king's commissioners, who occasionally toured the shires, and the sheriffs, who became the effective local agents of the king in collecting the feudal dues and in presiding over the shire courts.

William the Conqueror's determination to make his power supreme is also demonstrated by his introduction of the Norman system of centralized feudalism (see p. 351). As owner of all England by right of conquest, William retained some land as his royal domain and granted the remainder as fiefs to royal vassals called tenants-in-chief, among whom were bishops and abbots. In return for their fiefs, the tenants-in-chief provided William with a stipulated number of knights to serve in the royal army. To furnish the required knight service, the great vassals—most of whom were French-speaking Normans—subinfeudated parts of their fiefs among their own vassals. But from all the landholders in England, regardless of whether or not they were his immediate vassals, William exacted homage and an oath "that they would be faithful to him against all other men." Hence, both the tenants-in-chief holding fiefs directly from the king and the lesser tenants holding fiefs as vassals of the tenants-in-chief swore loyalty to the king, their feudal suzerain. This meant that a disgruntled noble could not call out his own vassals against the king, because every man owed his first allegiance to William.

Certain military modifications made the English version of feudalism distinctive. William did not depend solely upon feudal levies; he retained the old Anglo-Saxon militia in which every freeman was required to serve, and he hired mercenaries. Thus the king had in readiness an independent fighting force to crush a rebellious baron. Furthermore, private feudal warfare was forbidden, and no castle could be built without royal permission.

The Domesday Survey is another example of the energetic and methodical manner in which William took over full control of England. Because William, like all medieval kings, constantly needed money, he ordered an accurate census of the property and property holders in his realm as a basis for collecting all the feudal "aids" and "incidents" (see p. 330) owed to him. Royal commissioners gathered testimony from local groups of older men who were put under oath and questioned. The complaints and even riots which the inventory caused are reflected in the *Anglo-Saxon Chronicle:*

So very narrowly did he cause the survey to be made that there was not a single hide nor a rood of land, nor—it is shameful to relate that which he thought no shame to do—was there an ox or a cow or a pig passed by that was not set down in the accounts. . . .[1]

In line with his policy of controlling all aspects of the government, William revamped the old Anglo-Saxon *Witan*, which had elected and advised the kings. The new Norman ruler changed its title to the Great Council —also called *curia regis*, the king's council or court—and converted it into a feudal body composed of his tenants-in-chief. The Great Council met at least three times a year as a court of justice for the great barons and as an advisory body in important matters. At other times a small permanent council of barons advised the king.

William's determination to be master in his own house is also seen in his attitude toward the Church. Bishops and abbots were appointed by William and required to provide military service for their lands. Although he permitted the Church to retain its courts in which canon law was administered, he denied them the right to appeal cases to the high courts of Rome without his consent. Nor could the decrees of popes and Church councils circulate in England without royal approval.

Thus William, who has been called England's drillmaster, formed the conquered island into one of Europe's most advanced states. In his efforts to abolish civil strife and competing authorities, he ruthlessly oppressed any opposition to his will. The nobility and the Church were burdened with feudal services, and the Anglo-Saxon freemen, oppressed by the exactions of their Norman lords, were in time reduced to serfdom. William advanced political feudalism and the manorial system and fused the two into a highly centralized feudal structure. The *Anglo-Saxon Chronicle* contains this summation of William's character and kingship:

This King William was a very wise and a great man, and more honored and more powerful than any of his predecessors. He was mild to those good men who loved God, but severe beyond measure towards those who withstood his will. He founded a noble monastery on the spot where God permitted him to conquer England, and he established monks in it, and he made it very rich. In his days the great monastery at Canterbury was built, and many others also throughout England. . . . So also was he a very stern and a wrathful man, so that none durst do anything against his will, and he kept in prison those earls who acted against his pleasure. He removed bishops from their sees and abbots from their offices. . . .

Amongst other things the good order that William established is not to be forgotten; it was such that any man . . . might travel over the kingdom with a bosom full of gold, unmolested; and no man durst kill another, however great the injury he might have received from him . . . . The King also was of great sternness, and he took from his subjects many marks of gold and many hundred pounds of silver. . . . The rich complained and the poor murmured, but he was so sturdy that he recked naught of them; they must will all that the king willed, if they would live, or would keep their lands or would hold their possessions, or would be maintained in their rights. . . .[2]

William's sons. William ii, who followed his father, was a disappointing namesake. Utilizing his father's methods, but without

This seal was struck during the reign of William the Conqueror. The Latin inscription on the face (left) reads "Know by this sign William, chief of the Normans"; the counterseal reads "By this sign know the same William, king of the English."

his ability, William II stirred up several baronial revolts before being shot in the back—accidentally, it was said—while hunting. Succeeding him was his brother, Henry I (1100-1135), a more able and conciliatory monarch who met with only one baronial revolt.

While the Great Council, made up of the chief nobles, occasionally met to advise the king, the small permanent council grew in importance. From it now appeared the first vague outlines of a few specialized organs of government. The exchequer, or treasury, supervised the collection of royal revenue, including *scutage* or "shield money," a fee which the king encouraged his vassals to pay in lieu of personal military service (see p. 330). The well-trained "barons of the

These faces looking down from the capital of a medieval pillar, found today in the Cloisters Museum in New York City, are believed to represent Henry II (right) and his queen, Eleanor of Aquitaine. During their stormy married life, Henry was once forced to imprison Eleanor because she incited their sons to rebel against him. As Richard I and John I, two of these sons later ruled England; one daughter became queen of Sicily, and another became queen of Castile.

exchequer" also sat as a special court to try cases involving revenue. At times members of the small council were also sent throughout the realm to judge serious crimes which endangered what was called the King's Peace.

Henry I's achievements in strengthening the monarchy were largely undone by the nineteen years of chaos that followed his death. Ignoring their promise to recognize Henry's only surviving child, Matilda, wife of Geoffrey Plantagenet, count of Anjou in France, many barons supported Henry's weak nephew Stephen. During the resulting civil war the nobility became practically independent of the crown and, secure in their strong castles, freely pillaged the land. In the words of one of the authors of the *Anglo-Saxon Chronicle*:

They levied taxes on the villages every so often, and called it "protection money." When the wretched people had no more to give, they robbed and burned all the villages, so that you could easily go a whole day's journey and never find anyone occupying a village, nor land tilled. Then corn was dear, and meat and butter and cheese, because there was none in the country. Wretched people died of starvation; some lived by begging for alms, who had once been rich men; some fled the country.

There had never been till then greater misery in the country, nor had heathens ever done worse than then they did. . . . Neither did they respect bishops' land nor abbots' nor priests', but robbed monks and clerics, and everyone robbed somebody else if he had the greater power. If two or three men came riding to a village, all the villagers fled, because they expected they would be robbers. The bishops and learned men were always excommunicating them, but they thought nothing of it. . . .[3]

Henry II. Anarchy ceased with the accession of Matilda's son, Henry II (1154-1189), the founder of the Plantagenet, or Angevin, House in England. As a result of his inheritance (Normandy and Anjou) and his marriage to Eleanor of Aquitaine, the richest heiress in France, Henry II possessed a great empire stretching from Scotland to the Pyrenees. The English holdings in France far exceeded the land directly ruled by the French kings, who eyed their vassal rival with jealousy and fear. Henry's reign marks the outbreak of the strife between England and France, hostile since 1066, which runs like a red thread throughout the tapestry of medieval and modern history.

Historians have regarded Henry as one of England's greatest kings. He was unusually well educated and had a genius for the art of government. It is said that he found it very difficult to sit still during Mass and scandalized his subjects by scribbling notes and chatting with his cronies. Henry's reign was an expression of his restlessness. Ever improving, changing, and fighting, he squabbled with the feudal nobility, clashed with the Church, warred against the French Capetians, quarreled with his worthless sons, and had great difficulty managing his tempestuous queen.

Stephen, Henry's ineffectual predecessor, had left a sorry heritage. The judicial system was confused and corrupt. The royal courts administered by the king's justices faced strong competition from both the baronial courts, run independently by feudal lords, and the Church courts, which threatened to extend their supremacy over the whole realm.

In a series of decrees, called assizes, Henry extended the jurisdiction of the royal courts at the expense of the feudal courts. This was Henry's chief contribution to the development of the English monarchy, and it produced three major results: a permanent system of circuit courts presided over by itinerant justices, the jury system, and a body of law common to all England.

Itinerant justices on regular circuits were sent out once each year to try breaches of the King's Peace. To make this system of royal criminal justice more effective, Henry employed the method of inquest used by William the Conqueror in the Domesday Survey. In each shire a body of important men were sworn (*juré*) to report to the sheriff all crimes committed since the last session of the king's circuit court. This grand jury, as it was called, also gave information concerning the misbehavior of local officials. Thus originated the modern-day grand jury which presents information for an indictment.

Henry's courts also used the jury system as a means of settling private lawsuits. In-

THE DOMINIONS OF HENRY II

- Inheritance
- Suzerainty
- Acquisitions by Marriage to Eleanor of Aquitaine
- French Royal Domain

Ruling from 1154 to 1189, Henry II was king, feudal suzerain, and vassal—all in one. He was king of England, feudal overlord of Scotland, Wales, Ireland, and Brittany, and vassal to the French king for the English holdings in France (although he held more territory there than the French monarch).

stead of deciding such civil cases by means of oath-helpers or trial by ordeal (see p. 213), the circuit judges handed down decisions based upon evidence sworn to by a jury of men selected because they were acquainted with the facts of the case. This more attractive and efficient system caused litigants to flock to the royal courts, a procedure facilitated by the sale of "writs" by Henry's chancellor, which ordered a sheriff to bring the case to a royal court. Not only was the king's income greatly increased from fees, but the feudal courts of the nobility were greatly weakened.

This petit or trial jury eventually evolved into the modern trial jury whose members, no longer witnesses, determine guilt or innocence. Trial by jury became the most characteristic feature of the judicial system of all

English-speaking nations and was carried to the far corners of the earth as a hallmark of justice.*

Henry's judicial reforms promoted the growth of the common law—one of the most important factors in welding the English people into a nation. Unlike Roman law, English common law is not the result of legislation. Its beginnings lay in custom, but its full flowering resulted from Henry's judicial reforms. The decisions of the royal justices became the basis for future decisions made in the king's courts, superseded the many diverse systems of local justice in the shires, and became the law common to all Englishmen.

Thomas à Becket, victim of Church-state rivalry. While Henry skillfully diminished the activities of the baronial courts by making the royal courts more powerful, he was not so successful against his other legal rival —the Church courts. When he appointed Thomas à Becket archbishop of Canterbury, the king assumed that his former boon companion and royal chancellor could easily be persuaded to cooperate, but Becket proved to be stubbornly independent, stoutly up-holding the authority of the Church.

In 1164 Henry stipulated that clergymen accused of any crime should first be taken before a royal court, not an ecclesiastic court. Henry's idea was to prevent the abuses resulting from "benefit of clergy"—the principle that the Church alone had legal jurisdiction over its clergy. If the king's court thought a crime had been committed, the culprit was to be tried in a Church court. If pronounced guilty, he would then be turned over to the civil authorities for punishment. This arrangement seemed a fair remedy for the abuses of benefit of clergy, but Becket would have none of it.

When Becket received no support from the English clergy, he fled to France and appealed to the pope for aid. After a few years the pope patched up the quarrel, and the archbishop returned to England. His first act, however, was to excommunicate the bishops who, in his absence, had crowned the eldest prince heir to the throne. When this news reached Henry, in a fit of passion he roared: "What a pack of fools and cowards I have nourished in my house, that not one of them will avenge me of this turbulent priest."[5] Responding to this tirade, four knights went to Canterbury and, with swords drawn, entered the cathedral and seized Becket. An eyewitness wrote:

At the third blow he [Becket] fell on his knees and elbows, offering himself a living victim, and saying in a low voice, 'For the name of Jesus and the protection of the church I am ready to embrace death.' Then the third knight inflicted a terrible wound as he lay, by which the sword was broken against the pavement . . . the blood white with the brain, and the brain red with blood, dyed the surface of the virgin mother church . . . in the colors of the lily and the rose.[6]

A detail from a medieval illumination depicts the murder of Thomas à Becket.

*The workings of Roman law offer an interesting contrast. "Under Roman law, and systems derived from it, a trial in those turbulent centuries, and in some countries even today, is often an inquisition. The judge makes his own investigation into the civil wrong or the public crime, and such investigation is largely uncontrolled. The suspect can be interrogated in private. He must answer all questions put to him. His right to be represented by a legal adviser is restricted. The witnesses against him can testify in secret and in his absence. And only when these processes have been accomplished is the accusation or charge against him formulated and published. Thus often arise secret intimidation, enforced confessions, torture, and blackmailed pleas of guilty."[4]

The uproar that the murder caused destroyed all chance of reforming the Church courts. Becket became a martyr and, after miracles were reported to have occurred at his tomb, was canonized a saint. For the remainder of the Middle Ages, Church and state in England continued to differ on the matter of the court system. Benefit of clergy remained an obstacle to the royal ambitions for equal justice for all Englishmen.

Merging Norman and Anglo-Saxon traits. While England was being welded into a single whole by the judicial reforms and the governmental agencies of a strong monarchy, a comparable process was taking place culturally. Two distinct civilizations—the Norman-French and the Anglo-Saxon—had existed side by side after the Norman Conquest. For over two hundred years following William the Conqueror's invasion, the Norman-French civilization was dominant; in fact, England was only a cultural appendage of France. Gothic architecture and the university came from France, as did feudalism, chivalry, and the crusading spirit. The language of the ruling class in England was French; the common people, however, continued to speak their Old English, or Anglo-Saxon, dialects.

The assimilation of the two peoples proceeded fairly rapidly, and in time the conquerors and the conquered merged into a common stock—one in which English rather than French elements predominated. Out of the interaction of Norman-French and Anglo-Saxon emerged a distinctive language, Middle English, from which our Modern English developed.

Richard the Lion-Hearted, knight-errant. As was the case after William the Conqueror's reign, the good beginning made by Henry II was marred by the mistakes of his successors. Having no taste for the prosaic tasks of government, Richard the Lion-Hearted wasted his country's wealth on forays in Europe and military expeditions to the Holy Land. As we saw in Chapter 12, Richard earned fame in the Third Crusade as a peerless knight in his struggle against Saladin, the leader of the Saracens. Richard spent only five months of his ten-year reign (1189-1199) in England, which he regarded as a source of supplies for his overseas adventures. The royal bureaucracy worked so well, however, that the king's absence made little difference.

John's powers limited by Magna Carta. Richard's successor, his brother John (reigned 1199-1216), was an able ruler who worked hard to promote his father's governmental system but who lacked his brother's chivalrous qualities. His cruelty and unscrupulousness cost him the political support of his barons at the very time he needed them most in his struggles with the two ablest men of the age, Philip II of France and Pope Innocent III. As feudal overlord for John's possessions in France, Philip found the occasion to declare John an unfaithful vassal and his fiefs forfeit. John put up only feeble resistance, and after losing more than half his possessions in France he became involved in a struggle with Innocent III in which he was forced to make abject surrender (see p. 386). In the meantime, John had completely alienated the English barons by attempting to collect illegal feudal dues and committing other infractions of feudal law. The exasperated barons rebelled and in 1215 forced John to affix his seal to Magna Carta, which bound the king to observe all feudal rights and privileges. People in later centuries, however, looked back upon Magna Carta as one of the most important documents in the history of human freedom.

To Englishmen of the time this document did not appear to introduce any new constitutional principles. It was merely an agreement between the barons and the king, the aristocracy and the monarchy. But the seeds of political liberty were to be discovered in Magna Carta. Certain provisions were later used to support the movement toward constitutional monarchy and representative government:

Clause XII. [Taxation or feudal aids except those sanctioned by custom] . . . shall be levied in our kingdom only by the common consent of our kingdom [i.e., by the king's Great Council].

Clause XXXIX. No free man shall be taken or imprisoned or dispossessed, or outlawed, or banished, or in any way destroyed . . . except by the legal judgment of his peers or by the law of the land.

Clause XL. To no one will we sell, to no one will we deny, or delay right or justice.[7]

In 1215 these limitations upon the king's power applied only to freemen—that is, to the clergy, the barons, and a relatively small number of rural freeholders and burghers. Little or nothing was said in the charter about the rights of the majority of the population—the serfs living on the manors. As the feudal system gradually disappeared, however, the term *freeman* came to include every Englishman.

The importance of Magna Carta does not lie in its original purpose but rather in the subsequent use made of it. Two great principles were potential in the charter: (1) the law is above the king; and (2) the king can be compelled by force to obey the law of the land. This principle of the limited power of the crown was to play an important role in the seventeenth-century struggle against the despotism of the Stuart kings; Clause XII was interpreted to guarantee the principle of no taxation without representation and Clause XXXIX to guarantee trial by jury.

The origins of Parliament. The roots of what was to become perhaps the most significant institution in English government— Parliament—are buried deep in England's history. The beginnings of representative government can be traced to the *Witan* and the local assemblies of the Anglo-Saxon era. As we recall, William the Conqueror converted the *Witan* into a feudal body, the Great Council or *curia regis*, composed of the king's feudal tenants-in-chief. The French-speaking Normans commonly used the word *Parlement* (from *parler*, "to speak") for the Great Council; Anglicized as *Parliament*, the term was used interchangeably with Great Council and *curia regis*. Modern historians, however, generally apply the term to the Great Council only after 1265, when its membership was radically enlarged.

The first meeting of Parliament—the enlarged Great Council—took place in the midst of a baronial rebellion against Henry III, the son of King John. In an effort to gain the widest possible popular support, Simon de Montfort, the leader of the rebellion, convened the Great Council in 1265, summoning two knights from every shire and two burghers from every borough.

Parliament gains stature. Parliament first became important during the reign of Henry III's son, Edward I (1272-1307). Following the pattern set by Simon de Montfort, Edward continued the practice of summoning representatives of counties and towns to meetings of the Great Council. In 1295 he called the "model Parliament," the most representative group yet convened. Two years later the king agreed that certain taxes could not be levied without the assent of Parliament, a principle that assured that body of being summoned from time to time.

The first meetings of the English Parliament coincided with a general trend throughout Europe. In the thirteenth and fourteenth centuries there appeared representative assemblies such as the Estates-General in France and the Cortes in Spain. Except for the English Parliament, none of these assemblies fulfilled their early promise. They either ceased to exist or remained completely under the monarch's thumb.

From Edward's reign on, Parliament became more and more essential to English government. In calling Parliaments, the Eng-

A sixteenth-century engraving of the Tower of London, long used as a prison for those accused of crimes against English monarchs, shows the complex network of walls, towers, living quarters, and fortress which was continually added to and modified from the time of William the Conqueror until well into modern times.

lish kings had no idea of making any concession to popular government. Their main objective was revenue. As recognition of the growing wealth and influence of the bourgeoisie and as a means of obtaining another source of revenue, the English kings, along with other European monarchs, began the practice of including representatives of the bourgeoisie in their feudal councils. By the fourteenth century it became mandatory to consult Parliament, and the kings realized, too late, the threat that this new agency represented to their royal prerogatives.

During the fourteenth century the representatives of the knights and the burghers, called the "Commons," adopted the practice of consulting together separate from the lords spiritual and temporal. Thus arose the divisions of Parliament that came to be called the House of Commons and the House of Lords. The Commons soon discovered its power as the main source of money for the king. Using this "power of the purse" as a weapon, Parliament forced the king to agree that no tax could be levied without its consent. It gradually became the custom for Parliament to withhold its financial grants until the king had redressed grievances, made known by petitions. Later, taking advantage of the desperate financial straits of the English kings during the Hundred Years' War, Parliament acquired the important right to direct governmental expenditures.

Parliament made further important gains in lawmaking, which had originally been solely a royal function. The House of Commons presented petitions to the king with the request that they be promulgated as statutes, as the laws drawn up by the king and his council and confirmed in Parliament were called. Gradually the right to initiate legislation through petition was obtained. Again, Parliament's "power of the purse" turned the trick.

England was experiencing a formative period in political institutions. Two extraordinarily important concepts were slowly being incorporated into England's government: (1) the idea expressed in Magna Carta that consent of the barons was necessary to royal authority was being broadened to include the consent of the whole realm; and

Probably the earliest authentic view of Parliament in session, this picture shows a meeting called by Edward I. The dignitaries occupying the center benches are Church officials and secular lords. In the center are members of the judiciary seated on woolsacks to remind them that wool was vital to the English economy. Just below them are representatives from the towns and shires.

(2) Parliament was becoming the agency which both formulated and voiced the opinions of the citizens.

Edward I's statutes. Edward I, one of England's half-dozen outstanding monarchs, did more than augment the role of Parliament as a means of increasing royal authority. He issued a series of great statutes, many of which were aimed at curtailing the power of the nobility that had greatly increased during the baronial revolts of his father's reign. The statute known as *Quo Warranto,* which demanded of a lord that he prove "by what warrant" he exercised certain rights and privileges, led to the recovery of lost royal rights. Another statute established the entail system which enabled a landowner to will his entire estate to his eldest son on condition that the property remain forever undivided. The younger brothers were thus forced to shift for themselves in governmental service, in the professions, or in commerce. By contrast, estates on the Continent were usually divided among all the sons in a family, a practice which encouraged the growth of a large and parasitic class of landowners. Subinfeudation, whose complexities made it difficult to enforce feudal obligations owed to the king, was checked by another statute. Henceforth the buyer of land became the vassal not of the seller but of the seller's lord.

Furthermore, in the Statute of Mortmain, Edward restricted the power of the Church, which had grown rich through gifts of lands. Such lands were a direct loss to the crown in terms of feudal payments. Most important, these estates could never revert, or escheat, to the crown as could property held by land-owners who died without heirs. The Church never died; its lands fell into "mortmain," the "dead hand" of a perpetuating corporation. The Statute of Mortmain forbade the giving of any land to the Church without royal approval.

Widening the boundaries of the realm. Edward i was the first English king who was determined to be master of the whole island of Britain—Wales, Scotland, and England. He subdued Wales after a five-year struggle, and in 1284 English law and administration were imposed on that region. As a concession to the Welsh, who retained their separate character and language, Edward gave his oldest son the title of Prince of Wales.

A dispute over the succession to the Scottish throne in the 1290's gave Edward his opportunity to intervene in the land to the north. After calling upon Edward to settle the dispute, the Scots accepted him as their overlord. Then Edward unwisely demanded that the Scots furnish him with troops to fight in England's wars. Under the courageous William Wallace, rebellion quickly flared up. After winning several victories against the English, Wallace was defeated and hanged as a traitor.

Wallace had sparked the fires of Scottish nationalism, however, and these burned on despite numerous attempts to put out the flames. In 1307 Edward again invaded the north country, but he fell ill and died before he could engage the Scots in battle. Seven years later his successor, Edward ii, attempted to humble the Scots, but at the battle of Bannockburn (1314) the Scots, led by

Robert Bruce, were victorious and won their independence. Thus permanent union between England and Scotland was forestalled until 1707, and for centuries Bannockburn remained a symbol of Scottish pride and patriotism. Robert Burns perhaps best expressed this spirit in the words which he had Bruce utter before the battle:

Scots, wha hae wi' Wallace bled,
Scots, wham Bruce has aften led,
Welcome to your gory bed,
Or to victorie.

Now's the day, and now's the hour,
See the front o' battle lour!
See approach proud Edward's power—
Chains and slaverie![8]

Causes and campaigns of the Hundred Years' War. The great conflict that colored so much of fourteenth- and fifteenth-century history sprang from a fundamental clash between the aims of the English and the French monarchies. The English kings wanted to regain the large holdings in France that had been theirs in the days of Henry ii. The French kings, on the other hand, were determined not only to keep what had been taken from John of England but to expand further. Their ultimate goal was a unified France under the direct rule of the monarchy at Paris.

Another factor was the clash of French and English economic interests in Flanders, a region nominally under French feudal control. Flanders and England were economically dependent on each other through the wool trade, whereby English raw wool was shipped to the Flemish looms and the finished cloth was sold in England. The French king's attempts to gain complete control of Flanders led to local uprisings which were supported by the English king, whose income in great part came from duties on wool. Less basic but still important was the fact that the English barons and their king were thirsting for military glory.

The immediate excuse for the Anglo-French conflict was a dispute over the succession to the French throne. In 1328, after the direct line of the Capetians became extinct, Philip vi of the House of Valois assumed the throne. The English king, Edward III, maintained that he was the legitimate heir to the French throne because his mother was a sister of the late French king. The French nobility disputed this claim, which became a pretext for war.

Interrupted by several peace treaties and a number of truces, the so-called Hundred Years' War stretched from 1337 to 1453. At the naval battle of Sluys (1340) the English gained command of the Channel and thus were able to send their armies to France at will. Thereafter England won a series of great victories—at Crécy (1346), Poitiers (1356), and Agincourt (1415). In the process the English produced some of the greatest military figures of the Middle Ages. The most famous was Henry v, the hero of Agincourt, where the French lost some 7000 knights, including many great nobles, and the English only 500.

Militarily, the English armies were much more effective than those of the French, which were made up of knights full of dash and chivalry. With no thought of strategy, the French charged the enemy at a mad gallop and then engaged in hand-to-hand fighting. The English learned other methods. Their secret weapon was the longbow, apparently taken over from the Welsh. Six feet long and made of special wood, the longbow shot steel-tipped arrows which were dangerous at four hundred yards and deadly at one hundred. While the French knights would have no truck with ordinary folk, the English nobles fought side by side with the common bowmen. The usual English plan of battle called for the knights to fight dismounted. Protecting them was a forward wall of bowmen just behind a barricade of iron stakes planted in the ground to slow down the enemy's charge. By the time the enemy cavalry reached the dismounted knights, only a few remained to be taken care of; the "feathered death" had done its work.

English military triumphs stirred English pride and what we now think of as nationalism—love of country, identification with it, and a sense of difference from, and usually superiority to, other peoples. This patriotism is evident in an account of Henry v's reply to a knight who regretted that they did not have another ten thousand archers for the battle of Agincourt:

Then the king said: 'Thou speakest foolishly, for by the God in heaven, I would not, even if I could, increase my number by one, for those whom I have are the people of God, whom he thinks me worthy to have at this time. . . . Dost not thou believe the Almighty with these his humble few is able to conquer the haughty opposition of the French, who pride themselves on their numbers and their own strength?'[9]

After Agincourt, when Henry v dictated the Treaty of Troyes, which recognized the English sovereign as "heir of the kingdom of France," the English seemed irresistible, their hold on France unbreakable. Counternationalism, however, was stirring among the French, who were enraged at the treaty. The revival of French spirit is associated with Joan of Arc, who initiated a series of French victories (see p. 425). In the long run French ardor and tenacity more than made up for

This illumination depicts a scene of late medieval warfare typical of the Hundred Years' War. Note the suits of armor, crossbows, longbows, and the early form of cannon.

English superiority in arms. At the same time English strength was weakened by domestic feuds. By 1453 the English had been swept out of France, except for a precarious toe hold at Calais. After one hundred years of intermittent warfare they had learned the bitter lesson that it was wiser to concentrate on purely English affairs than to try to conquer France.

Wars of the Roses. Defeat in France brought in its train civil wars which had their beginnings in a turbulent domestic political struggle that coincided with the conflict across the Channel. England was exhausted by the Hundred Year's War, and discontent was rife in Parliament and among the peasants. (On the peasants' revolt of 1381, see p. 372.) Richard II, the last Plantagenet king, who reigned from 1377 to 1399, was unstable, cruel, and power hungry, and he foreshadowed modern absolute monarchs in believing that the king should control the lives and property of his subjects. His seizure of the properties of Henry, the duke of Lancaster, led to a revolt in which Henry was victorious. Richard was forced to abdicate and was later murdered.

Henry, a cousin of Richard II, became Henry IV, thereby establishing the House of Lancaster which ruled England from 1399 to 1461. Henry had the support of Parliament, which had deeply resented Richard's autocratic reign and was determined that its authority should not again be slighted. During the Lancastrian period the English kings became more and more financially dependent upon Parliament, a dependence which compelled them to grant one petition after another and to extend Parliament's powers so that during the first half of the fifteenth century Parliament became a dominant factor in England's government.

The most important gains made by Parliament during the Lancastrian period were the guarantee of freedom of debate, the right to approve the appointment of the king's chief officials and members of his council, the stipulation that money bills must originate in the House of Commons, and the rule that the king's statutes should duplicate exactly petitions presented by the Commons. Not until 1689, when England became a constitutional monarchy, would Parliament again exercise such powers.

The second Lancastrian king was Henry V, whose military valor in the Hundred Years' War has already been described. Worn out by his arduous campaigns, Henry died after ruling only nine years. His heir, Henry VI, was pious and well intentioned but unstable and given to attacks of insanity. His reign was marked by increased baronial rivalry to control Parliament and the crown.

When Henry VI went completely insane in 1453, the duke of York, the strongest man in the kingdom, became regent. Two years later full-scale civil war broke out between the House of York and the partisans of the Lancaster family. The struggle became known as the Wars of the Roses; the white rose was the badge of the House of York, and later tradition invented the red rose as the badge of the House of Lancaster. In 1461 the Yorkists managed to have their leader, Edward IV, crowned king. Ten years later Edward had succeeded in cowing the nobles and in winning the support of the middle class, who saw a strong monarchy as the only

In this painting by an unknown Flemish artist, Henry VII holds a red rose, symbolic of the House of Lancaster.

alternative to anarchy. Edward's power became practically absolute, foreshadowing the strong rule of the Tudors that soon followed.

The promise of the House of York ended in 1483 when Edward IV died, leaving two young sons as his heirs. Their uncle, Richard, induced Parliament to declare his nephews illegitimate and took the throne. The two boys were imprisoned in the Tower of London, where they were secretly murdered. The double murder was too much for the nation, and opposition to Richard III mounted. Support was thrown to the cause of Henry Tudor, who, in his lineage and later marriage to Edward IV's daughter, united the Houses of Lancaster and York. The armies of Richard and Henry met at Bosworth Field in 1485. Just as the battle began, some of Richard's lieutenants deserted his cause, but Richard refused to flee and died manfully on the field. According to tradition, his crown was found in a bush on the battlefield and placed on the head of Henry VII, the first of the Tudor line, which ruled England from 1485 to 1603. The nation was tired of aristocratic anarchy and civil war and stood ready for the masterful rule of the Tudors. A century later Shakespeare expressed the nation's relief at the ending of civil war with these words which he put in the mouth of Henry Tudor at Bosworth Field:

Abate the edge of traitors, gracious Lord,
That would reduce these bloody days again,
And make poor England weep in streams of blood;
Let them not live to taste this land's increase,
That would with treason wound this fair land's
　peace!
Now civil wounds are stopped, peace lives again;
That she may long live here, God say Amen.[10]

Beginning of Tudor rule. It was the shrewd and careful work of Henry VII (1485-1509) and his successor, Henry VIII (1509-1547) that laid the foundations for Tudor greatness. Strong, almost absolute government was reintroduced into England, but the people supported the monarchy because it held the nobility in check. The Court of Star Chamber, established by Edward IV, was the most effective royal instrument in suppressing the unruly barons; it by-passed the established common law courts, whose judges and juries were too often intimidated and bribed by powerful nobles, and operated secretly and swiftly without benefit of juries. Because the Tudor rulers restored order and promoted trade at home and abroad, they won the support of the people of middle rank—the burghers and landed gentry—and upon this support their power was primarily built. Though often high-handed, Tudor kings always worked through Parliament.

Under Tudor rule England achieved the full status of a national state. This royal house later also further stimulated English commercial and maritime enterprise, broke away from the papacy and established a new national church, and successfully defied the most vigorous power in sixteenth-century Europe—Spain.

THE BEGINNINGS OF THE FRENCH NATIONAL STATE

Nation-making in England and France: a comparison. Whereas England was united more or less at one time by the Normans, the Capetians (987-1328) had to build France up bit by bit, taking fiefs from the nobility and adding them to the royal domain. This explains why France was never so thoroughly unified in the Middle Ages as was England. Also, France had no common law, and until the Revolution in 1789 the provinces largely retained their own distinctive customs.

On the other hand, there were many parallels between England and France during this period of nation-making. In both lands the nobility, aware of how increases in royal authority diminished their own power, sought to impede the movement toward centralization and unification; and in both lands great monarchs, often with the support of the bourgeoisie, rose to curb the nobles. In time both monarchies faced a showdown with the Church. By 1300 the French kings were strong enough to defy and even abuse the pope. In England, largely as an aftermath of the martyrdom of Becket, the confrontation was deferred until the Reformation in the sixteenth century.

In the battle of Bouvines, Philip Augustus' greatest victory, the king was at one point unhorsed and saved only by the heroic defense of his personal bodyguard, as is depicted here. This battle decisively ended King John's hopes of regaining his French lands.

Following the reigns of the first four Capetians, who quietly established the principle of hereditary rule (see p. 353), a handful of capable French kings, worthy of being classed with such English monarchs as Henry II and Edward I, built up royal power with amazing success. The first of these remarkable rulers was Louis VI (1108-1137), also known as Louis the Fat, whose work paralleled on a smaller scale that of William the Conqueror in England.

Louis the Fat pacifies the Ile de France. By acquiring complete control over his royal domain, the Ile de France, Louis the Fat laid the foundations upon which subsequent monarchs built. He gave France, for the first time since the reign of Charlemagne, a responsible, conscientious monarch devoted to the task of governing the realm.

At the outset of his reign Louis, with the support of the Church (which supplied him with able advisers), determined to crush the lawless barons who were defying royal authority in the Ile de France. According to Abbot Suger, his chief adviser and biographer:

A king, when he takes the royal power, vows to put down with his strong right arm insolent tyrants whensoever he sees them vex the state with endless wars, rejoice in rapine, oppress the poor, destroy the churches, give themselves over to lawlessness which, and it be not checked, would flame out into ever greater madness. . . .[11]

The "war of the brigands," as the king's expeditions against the nobles were called, was a long, slow process, but in the end the castles of the defiant vassals were captured and in many cases torn down. "And this," writes Abbot Suger, "they deserved who had not feared to raise their hand against the Lord's anointed."[12] By asserting his authority, Louis made his word law in the Ile de France, established a solid base from which royal power could be extended, substantially raised royal revenues, and so increased the prestige of the monarchy throughout France that the great Duke of Aquitaine deigned to marry his daughter Eleanor to Louis' son. Unfortunately, Louis' pious son had the marriage annulled on grounds of infidelity, and Aquitaine passed to Eleanor's second husband, Henry II of England.

Philip Augustus extends royal rule. The first great expansion of royal control in France took place between 1180 (the year of the accession of Philip II) and 1314 (the date of Philip IV's death). By the end of this period France had replaced Germany as the strongest monarchy in continental Europe. The three most outstanding rulers during this period of unification and centralization were Philip II (known also as Philip Augustus), who increased his domain into a substantial kingdom; Louis IX, who ennobled and dignified the French crown; and Philip IV, who made the government a centralized, efficient bureaucracy.

Philip Augustus' greatest struggle was his effort to wrest from the English Plantagenets the territory they held in France. These vast holdings were ruled by Henry II, against whom Philip made little headway. He did, however, make Henry's life wretched by fomenting plots and by encouraging Henry's faithless sons, Richard the Lion-Hearted and John, to revolt. As we have seen, Philip took Normandy and Anjou from John, thereby tripling the size of the royal domain. John retaliated by allying himself with the counts of Flanders and Toulouse, who feared the growing power of their Capetian overlord, and with the German emperor. But the alliance broke up after Philip defeated John's allies at the decisive battle of Bouvines (1214). Not until the Hundred Years' War, more than a century later, did the English kings again attempt to regain the lost Plantagenet lands in France.

Philip not only greatly increased his domain but also strengthened the royal administrative system by devising new agencies for centralized government and tapping many new sources of revenue. New salaried officials, called bailiffs, performed duties similar to those carried out in England by itinerant justices and sheriffs. A corps of loyal officials, like the bailiffs recruited not from the feudal nobility but from the ranks of the bourgeoisie, was collected around the king. These professional civil servants—many of them lawyers acquainted with the workings of Roman law—soon developed into expert governmental advisers and administrators. As in England, special administrative departments were created: the *parlement*, a supreme court of justice (not to be confused with the English Parliament, which became primarily a legislative body); the chamber of accounts, or royal treasury; and the royal or privy council, a group of advisers who assisted the king in the conduct of the daily business of the state. The Capetian rulers, like the English monarchs, were creating an efficient central government.

In this early phase of consolidation of royal power, the Church, which was struggling with the German emperors, usually allied itself with the French monarchy. As in England and Germany, however, the kings sometimes collided with the Church. For example, Philip II flouted Church authority by annulling his marriage; Innocent III was determined that no secular monarch should defy the Church on such a matter. The upshot was that the pope imposed an interdict on France, Philip backed down, and his wife again became his queen. The first round between Church and state went to the Church.

On the other hand, the Church inadvertently helped to expand the royal domain. In southern France, particularly in Toulouse, the heretical Albigensian sect flourished. Determined to stamp out this sect, Innocent III in 1208 called the Albigensian crusade, discussed in Chapter 13. Philip, faced with the enmity of King John and the German emperor, did not take part, but he allowed his vassals to do so. Later he sent his son, the future Louis VIII, to assert his overlord-

The *Très Riches Heures du Duc de Berry* is a devotional book containing prayers for each day of the year. The months are illustrated by full-page miniatures. This one, of October, depicts peasants sowing grain in fields on one bank of the Seine, while on the far bank is the Louvre as it appeared in the time of Philip II, who built the fortress as a storage place for his records and money.

ship in troubled Toulouse, but Louis' attempt to do so failed. After Philip's death in 1223, however, Louis led a new crusade to exterminate the remnants of Albigensian resistance, and by the time he died, royal power had been established in much of southern France. Later, Toulouse escheated to the French crown when its count died without heirs. Thus, in less than fifty years after Philip's death, the royal domain in the south had doubled as a result of the Albigensian crusades. The French king's realm now stretched from the chilly coast of the English Channel to the warm shores of the Mediterranean.

Louis IX dignifies the throne. After the brief reign of Louis VIII, France came under the rule of Louis IX (1226-1270), better known as St. Louis because of his piety and noble character. In the rough-and-tumble melee of European rivalries, St. Louis' policies of government were exceptional. His ideal was to rule justly and in peace, and he made substantial sacrifices to that end. Exhibiting what more unscrupulous minds might call diplomatic naïveté, he signed a peace with the English king which gave back certain fiefs that had been annexed by Philip Augustus. Chided for giving away this territory, Louis replied: "The land I am giving him, I do not give because I am bound to him or his heirs, but for the sake of the great love existing between my children and his, who are first cousins."[13]

Louis' passion for justice and good government was reflected in significant developments in the machinery of government. Special officials, similar to the *missi dominici* of Charlemagne, were created to check on the bailiffs, holding them to a strict account of their activities and even forbidding them to encroach on the feudal rights of the nobility. Certain matters, such as treason and crimes on the highways, were declared to be the exclusive jurisdiction of the royal courts. Furthermore, Louis insisted on the right of appeal from the feudal courts of his vassals to the high royal court of *parlement* at Paris.

Louis' endeavor to hear personally his subjects' problems and complaints impressed his contemporaries. Joinville, his friend and biographer, whose *St. Louis, King of France* is a medieval masterpiece, has left us this sketch:

Many a time it happened that in summer time he would go and sit down in the wood at Vincennes, with his back to an oak, and make us take our seats around him. And all those who had complaints to make came to him without hindrance from ushers or other folk. Then he asked them with his own lips: "Is there any one here who has a cause?" Those who had a cause stood up when he would say to them: "Silence all, and you shall be dispatched [judged] one after another." Then he would call Monseigneur de Fontaines or Monseigneur Geoffrey de Villette and would say to one of them: "Dispose of this case for me." When he saw anything to amend in the words of those who spake for others, he would correct it with his own lips.[14]

Despite the fact that little territory was added to the royal domain during his reign, Louis IX imbued the monarchy with a quality perhaps more precious—moral dignity. Just, sympathetic, and peace-loving, St. Louis convinced his subjects that the monarchy was the most important agency for assuring their happiness and well-being.

Climax of Capetian rule under Philip IV. The reign of Philip IV, the Fair (1285-1314), climaxed three centuries of Capetian rule. The antithesis of his saintly grandfather, Philip was a man of craft, violence, and deceit. Taking advantage of the growing anti-Semitism that had appeared in Europe with the crusades, he expelled the Jews from France and confiscated their possessions. (Philip's English contemporary, Edward I, had done the same.) Heavily in debt to the Knights Templars, who had turned to banking after the crusades, Philip had the order suppressed on trumped-up charges of heresy.

Philip's need of money also caused him to clash with the last great medieval pope. As we shall see in Chapter 16, Pope Boniface VIII refused to allow Philip to tax the French clergy and made sweeping claims to supremacy over secular powers. He was speaking in the tones of Innocent III, but the national state had reached the point where such leaders as Philip IV would not brook interference with their authority no matter

1180
1223
English Possessions after 1223

THE GROWTH OF FRENCH ROYAL DOMAIN

1328   English Possessions

ENGLAND

1461
1589

what the source. The result of this controversy was the humiliation of Boniface, a blow from which the medieval papacy never recovered.

In domestic affairs the real importance of Philip's reign lies in the increased power and improved organization of the government, with its heart in Paris and its fingers extended over much of France. Philip's astute civil servants, recruited mainly from the middle class, concentrated their efforts on exalting the power of the monarch. Trained in Roman law, and inspired by its maxim that "whatever pleases the prince has the force of law," they sought to make the power of the monarch absolute.

Like Edward I in England, Philip enlarged his feudal council to include representatives of the third "estate" or class—the townsmen. This Estates-General of nobles, clergy, and burghers was used as a means of obtaining popular support for Philip's policies, including the announcement of new taxes. Significantly, Philip did not need to ask the Estates-General's consent for his tax measures, and it did not acquire the "power of the purse" that characterized the English Parliament. Philip had sown the seeds of absolutism in France, but their growth was to be interrupted by the Hundred Years' War.

France during the Hundred Years' War. Nation-making in both France and England was greatly affected by the long conflict that colored much of their history during the fourteenth and fifteenth centuries. In both lands the crisis of war led to a resurgence of feudalism. Another deterrent to the rise of royal power was the increase in the power of the representative assemblies, Parliament and the Estates-General. Nevertheless, in the long run the increasing anarchy and misery of the times stimulated nationalistic feelings and a demand for strong rulers who could guarantee law and order. Thus, by the late fifteenth century the French kings—like the Tudors in England—were able to resume the task of establishing the institutions of the modern nation-state.

Joan of Arc, a peasant girl from Domremy, symbolized the new nationalist spirit that emerged in France during the darkest days of the war following a long succession of English victories. Impelled by inner voices which she believed divine, she begged the timid French king to allow her to lead an army to relieve the besieged city of Orléans. Her request granted, Joan inspired confidence and a feeling of invincibility in her followers, and in 1429 Orléans was rescued from what had seemed certain collapse. But Joan met a tragic end. Captured by the enemy, she suffered a martyr's death at the stake, while the French king remained indifferent to her fate.

The salvation of Orléans was a turning point in the long struggle between France and England. The French made energetic plans to retain the offensive and expel their enemies from the land. The army was re-organized: a strong force of artillery was developed, and the soldiers were well paid and sternly disciplined. English resistance crumbled in the face of French victories. Military superiority had by now turned full circle; the English longbow was outmatched by French artillery. Of the vast territories they had once controlled in France, the English retained only Calais when the war ended in 1453.

The Hundred Years' War left France impoverished but with a new national consciousness. Royal power was stronger than ever before. During the war the Estates-General had acquired the right to assent to taxation but then had thrown away this right by making the *taille,* a new land tax levied to support a standing army, a permanent tax. Thus the purse strings, which the English Parliament used to gain concessions from the king, were kept firmly under royal control in France.

Louis XI, the "universal spider." After victory the process of consolidating royal power was continued by Louis XI, who reigned from 1461 to 1483. Physically unattractive, Louis had a spindly body and a cadaverous face with a long, sharp nose. He was completely lacking in scruples and loved intrigue; his intricate diplomatic webs earned him the epithet, the "universal spider." In his pursuit of power he used any weapon—violence, bribery, and treachery—to obtain his ends. When the French nobles rose in revolt, dignifying themselves as the League for the Public Welfare, Louis outfoxed them by agreeing to their Magna Carta-like demands and then ignoring his pledged word. Louis labored to restore prosperity, to extend the royal domain, and to wreck completely the few powerful feudal houses that still remained.

Louis XI's most powerful antagonist was the duke of Burgundy, Charles the Bold, whose possession of Flanders and the other Low Countries or Netherlands (modern Holland, Belgium, and Luxemburg) made him one of Europe's richest rulers. After Charles' death in 1477, Louis seized most of Burgundy, while the remainder of the duke's possessions passed to his daughter Mary. When she married the German emperor Maximilian I, the Netherlands came into the hands of the House of Hapsburg (see map, p. 520).

The French kings who succeeded Louis XI increased the royal domain until, by the middle of the sixteenth century, only the territory belonging to the Bourbons and a few other tiny pieces of land were outside the monarch's full control. When Louis' son Charles VIII ascended the throne in 1483, France's population was relatively large—sixteen million as compared with England's four million. Although industry was still undeveloped compared to that in the Netherlands and in Italy, France had rich soil and produced immense quantities of grain and wine. Economic prosperity and increasing political unity enabled France to play an important role in sixteenth-century politics.

THE POLITICAL UNIFICATION OF SPAIN AND PORTUGAL

The Reconquista. The unification of Spain was a more complex process than that of either France or England. The customary rivalry between the feudal aristocracy and the royal authority was complicated by another significant element—a religious crusade. Unification required the ejection or the Christianization of the Muslims, with their alien religion and civilization. Unity also called for the integration of several diminutive and distinct nations, each possessing its own way of life.

In Chapter 12 we noted the beginning of the *Reconquista,* or reconquest of Spain, up to the year 1085, when the Muslim stronghold of Toledo was captured. During this long struggle a mounting patriotism blended with a fanatical religious spirit. As early as the ninth century northern Spain became suffused with a religious zeal centering around Santiago de Compostela, reputed to be the burial site of the apostle St. James. His bones were enshrined in a great cathe-

THE RECONQUISTA 910

BAY OF BISCAY

Santiago de Compostela

KINGDOM OF LEON

K. OF NAVARRE

COUNTY OF BARCELONA

INDEPENDENT MOORISH STATES

EMIRATE OF

Toledo

CORDOVA

BALEARIC IS.

Seville

Cordova

Granada

MEDITERRANEAN SEA

IDRISID DOMINIONS

1150

BAY OF BISCAY

FRANCE

KINGDOM OF LEON AND CASTILE

K. OF NAVARRE

KINGDOM OF ARAGON

Oporto

KINGDOM OF PORTUGAL

Toledo

DOMINIONS

BALEARIC IS.

Seville

Cordova

OF

Granada

MEDITERRANEAN SEA

THE

ALMOHADS

1491

BAY OF BISCAY

FRANCE

K. OF NAVARRE

KINGDOM

KINGDOM OF ARAGON

Barcelona

KINGDOM OF PORTUGAL

Madrid

Toledo

Lisbon

OF

Valencia

BALEARIC IS.

CASTILE

×Las Navas de Tolosa

Seville

KINGDOM OF GRANADA

MEDITERRANEAN SEA

SULTANATE OF FEZ

dral which thousands of pilgrims visited. Banners were consecrated there, and the battle cry of the Christian soldiers became "Santiago" (a contraction of *Sante Iago*, St. James' name in Spanish).

Another symbol of national awakening was an eleventh-century soldier of fortune, El Cid Campeador. His exploits against the Muslims thrilled Europe, and he soon became the greatest hero in Spanish literature. Here is a portion of the most famous poem about him, *Poema del Cid:*

Before their breasts, the war-shields there have they buckled strong,

The lances with the pennons they laid them low along,

And they have bowed their faces over the saddle-bow,

And thereaway to strike them with brave hearts did they go.

He who in happy hour was born with great did call:

"For the love of the Creator, smite them, my gallants all.

I am Roy Diaz of Bivar, the Cid, the Campeador."

At the rank where was Per Vermudoz the mighty strokes they bore.

They are three hundred lances that each a pennon bear.

At one blow every man of them his Moor has slaughtered there,

And when they wheeled to charge anew as many more were slain.

You might see great clumps of lances lowered and raised again . . .

Cried the Moors "Mahound!" The Christians shouted on Saint James of Grace.

On the field Moors thirteen hundred were slain in little space.[15]

In the poem El Cid is characterized as the perfect Christian knight, although in reality he was an adventurer who, when exiled by the king of Castile, was not adverse to fighting under the standard of the Muslim Crescent.

In 1212, on the field of Las Navas de Tolosa, the Christians achieved one of the decisive victories of the Middle Ages. A few years later they captured first Cordova, whose great mosque was reconsecrated as a cathedral (see illustration, p. 356), and then Seville. By the end of the thirteenth century Moorish political control was confined to Granada. Following the reduction of Muslim power, the reconquest halted until the latter part of the fifteenth century.

The *Reconquista* has been discussed as an outburst of national feeling and as a religious crusade. But this generalization needs to be qualified somewhat. In the lands overrun by the Muslims, Christians had been tolerated in large measure. Conversely, it was quite usual for the Christian victors to treat their new Muslim subjects with respect, allowing them to enjoy their own religion and laws. Nor was it uncommon for the Christian kings to protect Muslim traders and businessmen because of their economic value. Muslim culture—art in particular—was often adapted by the Christians. It is said that on one occasion French crusaders left Spain in disgust when they saw how tolerantly the Muslims were treated.

Consolidation under Ferdinand and Isabella. In 1469 Isabella of Castile and Leon married Ferdinand, heir to the kingdom of Aragon, which had originated as a county attached to Navarre. Within a decade both rulers had succeeded to their respective thrones. By this personal union, the Iberian peninsula became politically united except for Granada, Navarre, and Portugal.

Although Spain was now a united land, many divisive factors existed. During the long struggle with the Muslims, the nobles had assumed extensive power, the military orders of crusading knights had developed into nearly independent organizations, and some of the important Church officials had become difficult for the sovereign to control. The independent spirit of the time is shown in the oath of allegiance which Aragon nobles took to the king:

We, who are as good as you, swear to you, who are no better than we, to accept you as our king and sovereign lord, provided you observe all our liberties and laws; but if not, not.[16]

The "Catholic Sovereigns," to use the title conferred on Ferdinand and Isabella by the Spanish Pope Alexander VI, set out to establish an effective royal despotism in Spain. The Holy Brotherhood, a league of cities which had long existed for mutual protection against unruly nobles, was taken over by the crown, and its militia was used as a standing army and police force. The powerful military orders were also brought under royal control. Although Ferdinand and Isabella were devout Catholics, they both believed that the Church should be subordinate to royal government—a belief they shared with the strong rulers of other rising European nation-states. By tactful negotiations, the Spanish sovereigns induced the pope to give them extensive rights in making Church appointments in Spain.

State control of the Church was increased when the pope permitted a separate Court

One of a chain of fortifications built by the kingdom of Castile during the *Reconquista,* this castle, known as Alcazar, was erected during the reign of Henry IV. Its design and name (which derives from the Arabic word for castle) show Moorish influence. Alcazar was constructed to serve both as the king's residence and the stronghold of the city of Segovia. Here Isabella, the stepsister and heiress of Henry IV, was crowned queen of Castile in 1474.

of Inquisition, largely free of papal control, to be set up in Castile. Ferdinand and his queen recognized the Inquisition as a means not only of wiping out heresy but also of increasing royal power. Under the dread leadership of Torquemada, the Inquisition confiscated the property of most Jews and Muslims and terrified the Christian clergy and laymen into accepting royal absolutism as well as religious orthodoxy. Thousands of persons were burned at the stake, and many more lost all their property. Although the Inquisition greatly enhanced the power of the Spanish crown, it also caused many talented people to flee the land of persecution.

Assemblies known as Cortes, representing nobles, clergy, and townsmen, had grown up in the Spanish kingdoms as early as the twelfth century. Although earlier in origin than the English Parliament, the Cortes did not fulfill its promise, because it was seldom summoned by the Catholic Sovereigns.

The most dramatic act of the Catholic Sovereigns was the conquest of Granada, inaugurated as a great Christian crusade. Ferdinand and Isabella went to the shrine of St. James to invoke divine blessing on the project, and their armies carried a silver cross sent by the pope. After ten years of hard fighting Muslim Granada fell in 1492, the same year that Columbus claimed the New World for Spain. Constantinople had fallen to the Muslim Turks in 1453, and Europe rejoiced at this squaring of accounts with the followers of the Crescent.

On the death of Queen Isabella in 1504, the territories of Castile came under Ferdinand's control. Before he died in 1516, the king seized that part of Navarre which lay south of the Pyrenees Mountains. This acquisition, together with the conquest of Granada, completed the national unification of Spain.

Results of Spanish unification. Royal absolutism and unification, coupled with the acquisition of territory in the New and Old Worlds, made Spain the strongest power in sixteenth-century Europe. But the process of unifying Spain had some unfortunate results: (1) In the early phase of the *Recon-*

quista, religious enthusiasm was whipped up as a means to an end, and when victory was achieved, the defeated Muslims were treated with respect. Under Ferdinand and Isabella, however, extermination rather than assimilation became the official policy, implemented by the Inquisition. The sequel was a heritage of religious bigotry and the death of that tolerance, intellectual curiosity, and sense of balance which had been characteristic of Muslim culture in Spain. (2) Centuries of fighting against the Muslims left a legacy of warlike spirit and inordinate national pride. (3) Among Spain's ruling classes, contempt for the Muslims created a scorn for those activities in which the unbelievers had engaged—trade, crafts, manual labor, and agriculture. This attitude hampered Spanish economic development in subsequent centuries.

Portugal. The nucleus of the area which eventually became Portugal was a part of Castile until 1095. In that year the king of Castile gave his daughter to Count Henry of Burgundy, one of many French knights who had helped take Toledo (see p. 357). Her dowry was the county of Portugal, named after its chief town Oporto ("The Port") at the mouth of the Duero River. The son of this marriage, Afonso Henriques, organized a revolt against his overlord, the king of Castile, and in 1139 proclaimed himself king of Portugal. By papal mediation in 1143, peace was made between the two, and Afonso's title was recognized. Four years later Lisbon was seized from the Muslims, and a century later the remaining land to the south was taken. Thus Portugal achieved territorial unification more than two centuries before Spain.

In the fourteenth century the rulers of Castile labored to reunite Portugal with their holdings, but the Portuguese ruler, King John, defeated the Castilians in 1385 and saved Portuguese independence. John also initiated Portuguese overseas expansion. Carried on by his son, Henry the Navigator, this policy eventually led to the momentous voyages of Vasco da Gama, the creation of a great empire in India and the Far East, and the establishment of the colony of Brazil (see Chapter 20).

FAILURES OF THE NATIONAL STATE: GERMANY AND ITALY

The Salian emperors vs. the Church. As we saw in Chapter 12, the foundation for strong government in Germany was laid by the House of Saxony (919-1024), which was also embroiled in Italian politics. Pioneers in nation-making, the Saxon kings were succeeded by a new royal line, the Salian House (1024-1125), whose members set about with increased vigor to establish a centralized monarchy. To the dismay of the nobility, a body of lowborn royal officials was recruited; and the power of the dukes was weakened further when the crown won the allegiance of the lesser nobles. Under Henry IV (1056-1106), the monarchy reached the height of its power, and there appeared to be hope for a strong, united Germany.

Yet it was also during Henry's reign that the first major reversal to unification occurred. The conflict between Henry IV and Pope Gregory VII, culminating in Gregory's humiliation of Henry at Canossa, resulted from the Investiture Struggle (see p. 385). In 1122, by the Concordat of Worms, a compromise on the subject of lay investiture was finally achieved. The main result of the struggle, however, was the loss of the monarchy's major sources of strength: the loyalty of the German Church, now transferred to the papacy; the support of the great nobles, now openly rebellious and insistent upon their "inborn rights"; and the chief material base of royal power, the king's lands, which were dissipated by grants to loyal nobles.

The real victors in the Investiture Struggle were the German nobles, who allied themselves with the papacy and continued to wage war against the monarchy long after the reign of Henry IV. From the time of Henry's death in 1106 until the accession of Frederick Barbarossa in 1152, the Welfs of Bavaria and the Hohenstaufens of Swabia, along with other noble factions, fought over the throne, which they made elective rather than hereditary. The outcome was that the structure of a strong national state was wrecked and Germany became extensively feudalized. The great nobles usurped royal rights, built strong castles, and forced lesser nobles to become their vassals. On the other hand, the great nobles acknowledged no feudal relationship to the king. Many free peasants, in turn, lost their freedom and became serfs. Despite some recovery of royal power later on, the evil effects of this period were never eradicated; the heritage of these decades hindered the development of a unified Germany until modern times.

Prosperity in divided Italy. Italy was even less unified than Germany. Jealous of one another and of their independence, the prosperous city-states in northern Italy joined the struggle between the German emperors and the papacy. The Welf-Hohenstaufen rivalry in Germany was reflected in Italy, where the rival factions were known as Guelphs and Ghibellines—the latter named derived from Waiblingen, the chief Hohenstaufen stronghold in Swabia. The former were usually propapal; the latter strongly favored the German monarchy's imperial claims in Italy. Yet, amidst the turmoil, the vitality, wealth, and culture of the northern Italian cities increased.

A brilliant civilization also flourished on the island of Sicily. By 1127 the Norman conquests resulted in the establishment of the kingdom of Naples and Sicily. Under the able rule of Roger II (1130-1154), this kingdom became one of the strongest and wealthiest states in Europe. During his reign busy merchant fleets nurtured the Mediterranean towns; the income of Palermo was said to exceed that of the English government. Scholars from all over the East and Europe traveled to Roger's court, which ranked next to Spain's in the translation of Arabic documents. Life and culture in the Sicilian kingdom, which included Norman, Byzantine, Italian, and Arabic elements, was diverse and colorful.

From the middle of the twelfth century to roughly the midpoint of the thirteenth, the history of Naples and Sicily and also the developments throughout the whole Italian peninsula were fatally entwined with the history of Germany and hinged on the rise and fall of the powerful German royal house of Hohenstaufen.

Frederick Barbarossa. Frederick Barbarossa of the House of Hohenstaufen, who reigned from 1152 to 1190, realistically accepted the fact that during the preceding half century Germany had become thoroughly feudalized; his goal was to make himself the apex of the feudal pyramid by forcing the great nobles to acknowledge his overlordship. Using force when necessary, he was largely successful, and Germany became a centralized feudal monarchy not unlike England in the days of William the Conqueror.

To maintain his hold over his German tenants-in-chief, Frederick needed the resources of Italy—particularly the income from taxes levied on the wealthy north Italian cities—and he resolved, as we saw in Chapter 13, to reëstablish his imperial power in Italy. He spent about twenty-five years fighting intermittently in Italy, but although some of the cities submitted to his authority, the final result was failure. The opposition from the popes and the Lombard League of cities was too strong. But Frederick did score a diplomatic triumph by marrying his son to the heiress of the throne of Naples and Sicily. The new threat of Hohenstaufen encirclement of northern and central Italy made it vital to the papacy that this royal house be destroyed.

Frederick Barbarossa died in Asia Minor while en route with the Third Crusade, and in time he became a folk hero in Germany. It was believed that he still lived, asleep in a cave in the mountains near Berchtesgaden in Bavaria. Some day, awakened by a flight of ravens, he would emerge and bring unity and strength back to Germany. "In the late nineteenth century, the artists of the Prussian court delighted to paint pictures of his last, and joyful, awakening in 1871, when the sky was full of ravens since a second German Empire had been called into existence. Statues of Frederick Barbarossa and Kaiser Wilhelm I were placed side by side to symbolize the 'fact' that where one had left off, the other had begun."[17]

Frederick II, a brilliant failure. It fell to the lot of Frederick Barbarossa's grandson,

The reign of Frederick Barbarossa as Holy Roman emperor was dominated by military expeditions. Frederick invaded Italy six times, intent on unifying the peninsula under his rule. His career ended in another military adventure, the Third Crusade, where he drowned in a river while leading his army through Asia Minor.

Frederick II (1194-1250), to meet the pope's challenge to the threat of Hohenstaufen encirclement. Orphaned at an early age, Frederick was brought up as the ward of the most powerful medieval pope, Innocent III. During Frederick's minority the empire fell on evil days; the Welf and Hohenstaufen factions resumed their struggle over the throne, and the strong feudal monarchy created by Frederick Barbarossa collapsed. In 1215, one year before Innocent died and with his support, Frederick was elected emperor. Faced by a resurgent nobility in Germany, he soon turned his attention to wealthy Italy.

Frederick did not quarrel with Innocent; he even turned control of the German Church over to the pope and promised to undertake a crusade. With Innocent's successors, however, the situation changed, for Frederick was determined to be a sovereign monarch in Italy, unchallenged by any other power.

The papacy and the north Italian cities successfully defied Frederick throughout his reign, and in the end he experienced the same failure as had Frederick Barbarossa. Frederick also clashed with the papacy in another sphere. Embarking on a crusade at the pope's insistence, he turned back because of illness. Later, however, although excommunicated by the pope, he negotiated with the Muslims and obtained important concessions, including the Holy City, Jerusalem. Ignoring this success, the pope excommunicated Frederick again, tried to dethrone him, called him "this scorpion spewing poison from the sting of his tail," and concluded a papal condemnation with the charge that "Frederick maintains that no man should believe aught but what may be proved by the power and reason of nature."[18] This latter charge was an attack upon the young emperor's philosophy of life, which was antireligious and—for his time—even revolutionary (see p. 395).

Frederick sacrificed Germany to pursue his interests in Italy. He transferred crown lands and royal rights to the German princes in order to keep them quiet and to win their support for his inconclusive Italian wars. Absorbed in his attempts to unite all Italy under his rule, Frederick permitted the German nobles to consolidate their power and to destroy the basis of any central authority. At heart he was a Mediterranean monarch; he shaped Sicily into a modern state, politically and economically. Administered by paid officials who were trained at the University of Naples, which he founded for that purpose, his kingdom was the most centralized and bureaucratic in Europe. Economically, too, it was far in advance of other states; Frederick minted a uniform currency and abolished interior tolls and tariffs, and his powerful fleet promoted and protected commerce.

As long as he lived, this brilliant Hohenstaufen held his empire together, but it quickly collapsed after his death in 1250. In Germany his son ruled ineffectively for four years before dying, and soon afterward Frederick's descendants in Sicily were killed by the count of Anjou, brother of St. Louis of France, who was invited by the pope to annihilate what remained of the "viper breed of the Hohenstaufen."

Significance of the fall of the Hohenstaufens. How important was the fall of the House of Hohenstaufen? In Italy the victory of the papacy was more apparent than real, for its struggle against the emperors lost it much of its integrity and prestige. Men had seen popes using spiritual means to achieve earthly ambitions—preaching a crusade against Frederick II and his descendants, for example. More and more, popes acted like Italian princes, playing the game of diplomacy amid shifting rivalries. This involvement in worldly concerns and the accompanying decay in ideals helps to explain the revolt against papal authority—one of the themes of Chapter 16.

Italy might have found the nucleus of a centralized government in the kingdom of Naples and Sicily. However, the count of Anjou's seizure of the kingdom after Frederick's death forestalled that possibility and initiated a long period of bitter rivalry between Spaniards of the House of Aragon, who had married into the Hohenstaufen family, and Frenchmen representing Anjou. Beset by this interference, southern Italy and Sicily precipitously declined amid alien rule, corruption, and, at times, horrible cruelty.

The Holy Roman Empire never again achieved the brilliance it had enjoyed during the reign of Frederick Barbarossa. The emperors usually did not try to interfere in Italian affairs, and they ceased going to Rome to receive the imperial crown from the pope. In German affairs the emperors no longer even attempted to assert their authority over the increasingly powerful noble families. After the fall of the Hohenstaufens, Germany lapsed more and more into the political disunity and ineffectual elective monarchy that remained characteristic of its history until the late nineteenth century.

The early Hapsburgs and the Golden Bull. Between 1254 and 1273 the German monarchy was made virtually nonexistent by the election of two rival foreign princes, neither of whom received wide recognition. Then in 1273 the imperial crown was bestowed upon the obscure Count Rudolf (1273-1291) of the House of Hapsburg. Rudolf's ancestors had gained control of a small domain in northern Switzerland. Toward the end of the eleventh century the family built a castle which was called Habichtsburg (Castle of the Hawk)—hence the word *Hapsburg*. During the remainder of the Middle Ages and in modern times, the Hapsburgs had amazing success in adding to their ancestral lands. Rudolf himself acquired Austria through marriage, and thereafter the Hapsburgs ruled their holdings from Vienna. In the sixteenth century they obtained Bohemia and much of Hungary (see p. 434).

For the time being, however, the Hapsburg hold on the imperial crown proved to be brief. After Rudolf's reign it was passed from one family to another. Then in 1356 the nobility won another significant victory. The Golden Bull, a document which served as the political constitution of Germany until early in the nineteenth century, laid down the procedure for election of the emperor by seven German dignitaries—three archbishops and four lay princes. The electors and other important princes were given rights that made them virtually independent rulers, and the emperor could take no important action without the consent of the imperial feudal assembly, the Diet, which met infrequently. It has been said that the Golden Bull "legalized anarchy and called it a constitution"; in reality it stabilized the political situation in Germany by recognizing the independence of the princes, thereby encouraging them to emulate the national monarchs and create stable governments in their principalities. It also ended disputed elections and civil wars over the succession. But with the emperor virtually powerless, people thereafter commonly referred to the welter of duchies, counties, bishoprics, and free cities as the Germanies, not Germany.

The imperial crown of Germany was returned to the Hapsburg family in 1438. From this time until 1806, when the Holy Roman Empire disappeared, the Hapsburgs held the imperial crown almost without a break. Maximilian I (1493-1519) helped make the Hapsburgs the most potent force in sixteenth-century Europe by taking as his wife Mary of Burgundy (see p. 427), heiress of the rich Low Countries, and by marrying his son to the heiress of Spain.

Inspired by the rise of new monarchies elsewhere, Maximilian attempted to strengthen his power. His program for a national court system, army, and taxation was frustrated by the German princes who insisted

on jealously guarding what they called "German freedom." The emperor continued to be limited in power; nor did the empire have an imperial treasury, an efficient central administration, or a standing army. And so the phantom Holy Roman Empire lived on as Voltaire characterized it: "Neither Holy, nor Roman, nor an Empire."

THE SLAVS IN EUROPE AND RUSSIA

German eastward expansion. Since the early tenth century German barons and churchmen had been pushing back the Slavs, founding bishoprics, and colonizing the land. East of the Elbe, however, the German settlements remained precariously isolated in the midst of large Slavic populations. Then, shortly after 1200, a new development occurred. The Teutonic Knights, a military-religious order founded at the time of the Third Crusade, transferred their operations to eastern Europe. Within fifty years the Knights had conquered the pagan Slavs in Prussia, and by 1350 they ruled the Baltic coastlands as far north as the Gulf of Finland. Assuming the role of a colonial aristocracy, the Knights built castles and towns, and a steady stream of German settlers moved into the conquered lands.

Poland and Lithuania at the height of their power. To the south of Prussia lay Poland. As a result of military pressure from the Germans to the west and the Prussians to the north, the Polish nation was welded into a strong military state in the middle of the tenth century. Also at this time, many Poles were converted to Roman Christianity, a factor which later linked Poland to western European culture.

After suffering severe setbacks in the twelfth and thirteenth centuries, Poland emerged as a strong power in the fourteenth century when its destiny was linked with that of the Lithuanians, who had risen from a very primitive background through a remarkable program of conquest, much of it well inside the western confines of modern

Russia. When Lithuania and Poland were united under a common sovereign in 1386, the expanded state became the largest in Europe.

The Poles and Lithuanians then waged war against their common enemy, the Teutonic Knights, and in 1410 defeated them overwhelmingly at Tannenberg. As a result, West Prussia was turned over to the Poles while East Prussia, under the Teutonic Knights, retained its autonomy but became a vassal state of Poland. This peace settlement was a great blow to German expansion, for the Poles obtained control of the Vistula River and a corridor north to the Baltic Sea, including the important port of Danzig. East Prussia was now cut off from the rest of Germany. In the history of modern Europe, the Polish corridor and Danzig have played an important role.

The early union of Poland and Lithuania was broken on several occasions, but the two countries were united under Poland's flag at the end of the fifteenth century. This huge state had the promise of a brilliant future, but the promise was never realized. The nobility succeeded in keeping the monarchy elective and weak, and the middle class, composed largely of German settlers and Jewish refugees from persecution in western Europe, remained small and powerless. Above all, Poland faced the hostility of Russia. The tsars' claims to certain Slavic groups in eastern Poland and their attempts to annex Polish territory provided grounds for the bitter enmity between Poles and Russians in modern times.

Bohemians and Magyars. Two other peoples appeared in the east European family in the Middle Ages. During the ninth and tenth centuries the Slavic Czechs established a kingdom on the Bohemian plain. German influence became strong in Bohemia, which was a part of the Holy Roman Empire, and the Golden Bull of 1356 made the Bohemian king one of the seven imperial electors.

Living southeast of Bohemia in the wide and fertile plain known as Hungary were the Magyars, an Asiatic people. Originally the terror of eastern Europe because of their brutal raids (see p. 346), they became civilized, adopted Christianity, and in the eleventh century expanded their state. But the promise of both their rising nation and that of the Bohemians (Czechs) was blighted by a common disaster. The king of both Hungary and Bohemia met his death fighting against the Turks in 1526. Terrified at the prospects of Muslim rule, both the Czechs and Hungarians elected the same man to their vacant thrones—Ferdinand, the Hapsburg archduke of neighboring Austria. The Turks, however, occupied most of Hungary (which they would hold until the end of the seventeenth century), leaving Ferdinand only a narrow strip along the western border (see map at left). This intertwining of national fortunes explains how the Hapsburgs at Vienna came to rule a polyglot empire of Bohemians, Hungarians, and German Austrians.

South Slavs and Turks in the Balkans. During the Middle Ages nation-making was not very successful in the Balkan peninsula. Confusion, racial diversity, and intermittent

CENTRAL AND EASTERN EUROPE 1526

■ Hungary

warfare existed as Bulgarians, Serbs, and Croats created ephemeral states.

The outstanding political development in southeastern Europe at the close of the Middle Ages was the disappearance of the Byzantine empire and the emergence of a threatening Muslim state which became heir not only to the lands formerly ruled by the Christian emperors at Constantinople but also to the whole Balkan area. Before the end of the fifteenth century the Ottoman Turks had extended their control over the Balkans and were pushing on toward Vienna. This huge new empire, with its center at Constantinople, was in no sense a national state but rather a bewildering mixture of Turks, Serbs, Hungarians, Bulgarians, Rumanians, Armenians, Greeks, and Jews.

The imposition of Turkish rule upon southeastern Europe delayed the rise of national states in the Balkan area until the nineteenth century. The multiplicity of small countries in the Balkans in modern times and the resultant tensions and conflicts have made the peninsula a European danger zone, a source of constant worry to diplomats, and, as in 1914, the direct or indirect cause of wars.

The Mongol conquest of Russia. In Chapter 10 we followed the amazing career of Genghis Khan, who united the unruly tribesmen of Mongolia and then launched them like a thunderbolt on a campaign of world conquest. By 1240 the Mongols had conquered the various Russian principalities, and in 1242 they penetrated to the outskirts of Vienna. Western Europe seemed theirs for the taking, but the death of the great Khan in far off Mongolia caused the Tatar, or Mongol, armies to return to the lower Volga pending the election of a new khan (see Reference Map 7).

Central Europe was not molested again, but the Mongols continued to dominate Russia from their capital at Sarai on the Volga not far from the modern city of Volgograd. The various Russian principalities were allowed to govern themselves as long as they paid tribute to the Golden Horde, as the Tatars in Russia were called. The khanate of the Golden Horde was only one of the Mongol states, however; the successors of Genghis Khan ruled an empire stretching from Korea on the east to Poland on the west. On the south their holdings included much of Asia Minor, Persia, and Afghanistan, as well as the area north of what is now India and Burma. Only since the Second World War has an empire arisen —that of Soviet Russia and its satellites —which could rival the vast expanse of contiguous territory controlled by the Mongols. In fact, the Russian empire with Communist China not only rivals but nearly duplicates that of the Mongol khanates.

Mongol domination changed the whole course of Russian history; it completed the break between Russia and western European civilization initiated by the decline of Kiev. Asian cultural influences were strong—the status of women was lowered as they accepted the veil and oriental seclusion. Mongols and Russians intermarried freely; hence the saying, "Scratch a Russian and you will find a Tatar." Many authorities believe that the Mongol conquest was a wholesale calamity. Russia was cut off from Europe, and a new Russia far to the east of Kiev began to develop. Its nucleus was the despotic state, the grand duchy of Moscow, where "civilization had been completely thrown back, learning was almost lost, and art in decline."[19]

Alexander Nevski: pioneer of Russian greatness. Following the Mongol conquest, the most important Russian leader was the prince of Novgorod, Alexander Nevski, who later became the ruler of Vladimir from 1252 to 1263. In the 1240's, before the Mongol onslaught, this staunch warrior had won great victories over the Swedes and the Teutonic Knights. To the Orthodox Church and most princes, the westerners seemed a greater threat to the Russian way of life than the Mongols. Indeed, Nevski obtained Mongol protection and assistance in fighting invaders from the west, who, hoping to profit from the Russian collapse under the Mongol impact, tried to annex territory. Meanwhile, Nevski may have looked forward to the day when his successors would be strong enough to challenge Tatar rule.

Moscow, challenge to Tatar rule. Daniel, the youngest son of Nevski, founded the

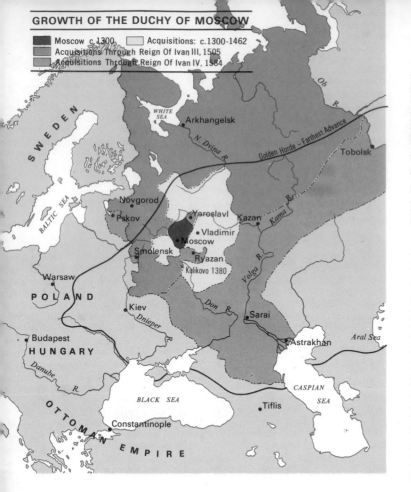

GROWTH OF THE DUCHY OF MOSCOW

■ Moscow c. 1300 □ Acquisitions: c.1300-1462
■ Acquisitions Through Reign Of Ivan III, 1505
■ Acquisitions Through Reign Of Ivan IV, 1584

yoke. In 1380, at Kulikovo on the Don, the khan was defeated, and although this hard-fought victory did not end Tatar rule of Russia, it did bring great fame to the Grand Prince. Thus in the latter part of the fourteenth century Moscow assumed a position of leadership in Russia. By the middle of the next century its territory had greatly expanded through purchase, war, and marriage (see map).

Ivan the Great. The Muscovite prince who laid the foundations for a Russian national state was Ivan III, the Great, a contemporary of the Tudors and other strong monarchs in western Europe. During his reign (1462-1505) he more than doubled his territories by placing most of north Russia under the rule of Moscow. He proclaimed his absolute sovereignty over all Russian princes and nobles by taking the title of "Great Prince and Autocrat of All Russia." Renouncing the last vestige of vassalage to the Tatars, Ivan in the 1490's initiated a series of attacks that opened the way for the complete defeat of the declining Golden Horde, now divided into several khanates.

Ivan married Sophia Palaeologus, the niece of the last Byzantine emperor, and she brought with her to Moscow a number of gifted Italians. Among them were architects who designed an enormous walled palace called the Kremlin. Ivan not only adopted the double-headed eagle and court ceremonies of the Byzantine emperors but also claimed to be their legitimate successor. Thus Ivan sometimes used the title of *tsar*, derived from "Caesar," and he viewed Moscow as the Third Rome, the successor of New Rome (Constantinople).

Ivan the Terrible. The next great ruler of Moscow was Ivan IV, known as "the Terrible." Under his rule (1547-1584) Russia became more despotic; all authority was centered in the tsar, and the nobility was ruthlessly subordinated to his will. With no consideration for human life, Ivan ordered the destruction of Novgorod, Russia's second city, on suspicion of treason. Another time, in a rage, he struck and killed his gifted eldest son. Yet Ivan was also a far-seeing statesman who promulgated a new code of laws, reformed the morals of the clergy, and

grand duchy of Moscow, which eventually expelled the Tatars from Russia. Well situated in the central river system of Russia and surrounded by protective forests and marshes, Moscow advanced rapidly in population and power. At first only a vassal of Vladimir, it soon absorbed its parent state. The rulers of Moscow continued to cooperate with their Mongol overlords; in time, each head of the state was given the title of Grand Prince and entrusted with the task of collecting the Mongol tribute from the various Russian cities and principalities.

Moscow's prestige was further enhanced when it became the center of the Russian Orthodox Church. Its head, the metropolitan, fled from Kiev to Vladimir in 1299 and a few years later established the permanent headquarters of the Church in Moscow.

In the middle of the fourteenth century it became evident that the power of the Tatars was declining, and the Grand Princes felt capable of openly opposing the Mongol built the fabulous St. Basil's Cathedral that still stands in Moscow's Red Square.

During Ivan's reign eastern Russia was conquered from the Tatars, and Cossack pioneers then crossed the Ural Mountains in their push to the Pacific—a movement which can be compared with the simultaneous expansion of western Europe across the Atlantic. Ivan's efforts to reach the Baltic and establish trade relations with western Europe were forcibly stopped by Sweden and Poland. Later, however, he was able to inaugurate direct trade with the West by granting English merchants trading privileges at the White Sea port of Archangel (Arkhangelsk) in the far north.

Ivan's death in 1584 was followed by the Time of Trouble, a period of civil wars over the succession and resurgence of the power of the nobility. Both Poland and Sweden intervened in Russian affairs, and their invasions across an indistinct frontier which contains no major natural barriers demonstrated again the danger from the West and contributed to Russia's growing tendency to withdraw into her own distinctive heritage. Order was restored in 1613 when Michael Romanov, the grandnephew of Ivan the Terrible, was elected to the throne by a national assembly that included representatives from fifty cities. The Romanov dynasty ruled Russia until 1917.

SUMMARY

During the period from 1100 to 1500, England, France, and Spain arose as pioneers in national unification and centralization. England was the first country to achieve an organized nationhood. English development is also noteworthy for its legal and constitutional achievements: the common law, the jury system, itinerant or circuit judges, early recognition of the need for popular consent to royal authority, and the first steps in the creation of representative government through Parliament.

The essential pattern of historical development was similar in these three nations, although each had its distinctive problems.

(1) At first, the kings were faced with serious competitors to their royal authority, the feudal nobility and the Church; (2) the kings became more powerful than their competitors, first by strengthening their power within the context of the feudal system, then by gradually establishing some of the military, judicial, and administrative agencies of a modern state; (3) the kings in effect made alliances with the rising middle class in the cities against their common enemy, the nobility. From the middle class came most of the money that the king needed to maintain a professional civil service, including a standing army with improved equipment, such as the longbow and artillery, which made the infantry superior in striking power to the time-honored, steel-clad, mounted knights.

In England the Normans secured a unified kingdom in 1066 as a result of the Conquest, and successive English kings managed to keep

Ivan the Terrible

their competitors under control and build up the machinery of royal administration. But in France the movement toward the consolidation of royal power started from a small area—from the minuscule Ile de France. Each noble had to be subordinated and brought within the framework of royal authority.

Nation-making in Spain was unique, since it was suffused with the religious fervor of a crusade. In the mid-eleventh century the Christian Spanish states began the *Reconquista* in earnest, and by the end of the fifteenth Ferdinand and Isabella had completed the task.

Although they had initial success in building a strong state at home, the German kings dissipated their energies by seeking the prize of empire over the Alps. For hundreds of years German rulers pursued this imperial phantom in Italy. In the face of resistance from the Italian cities, the treachery of the German nobles, and the opposition of the papacy, the German kings failed to achieve their goal. In both Germany and Italy after 1250, disunity and weakness prevailed; national unification was delayed until the nineteenth century.

Eastern and southern Europe were on the periphery of most of the dynamic currents of change that were transforming western Europe. There was much movement of peoples, and the rise and fall of states culminated in the emergence of Poland, Lithuania, Bohemia, and Hungary. In southeastern Europe and the Balkans the Byzantine empire, long the besieged buffer of the West, had disappeared before the onslaught of the victorious armies of the Ottoman Turks, now the custodians of Constantinople. And to the northeast was Russia, effectively sealed in and isolated on its frozen plains and, for years, languishing under the domination of the Mongols. The nucleus of a great national state to be was the tiny grand duchy of Moscow. Its dukes assumed leadership of the Russians by directing a long campaign against the alien Mongols and by founding the most autocratic state in Europe.

Truly, the later Middle Ages was a period of nation-making. The budding nation-states it produced—in particular England, France, and Spain—would assume new roles in the stirring international drama that is the story of Europe from about 1500 to 1650, a story which will be taken up in Chapter 17.

Suggestions for Reading

GENERAL ACCOUNTS

C. Warren Hollister, **Medieval Europe: A Short History,*** Wiley, 1964. Highly recommended as an introductory survey. H. Trevor-Roper, **The Rise of Christian Europe,** * Harcourt, Brace & World, 1965, is brief, unconventional, and richly illustrated. A more detailed fresh approach to the ebb and flow of medieval civilization is R. S. Lopez, **The Birth of Europe,** Evans, 1967.

The Cambridge Medieval History, 8 vols., 2nd ed., Cambridge, 1924-1936. Best used for reference, these volumes—a first-rank achievement of historical scholarship—include valuable bibliographies.

R. E. Sullivan, **Heirs of the Roman Empire,*** Cornell; S. Painter, **The Rise of the Feudal Monarchies,*** Cornell. Valuable interpretative essays on early medieval political history. The following are more detailed general surveys of the early Middle Ages: A. R. Lewis, **Emerging Medieval Europe, A.D. 400-1000,*** Knopf, 1967; H. Moss, **The Birth of the Middle Ages, 395-814,*** Oxford; J. Wallace-Hadrill, **The Barbarian West, 400-1100,*** Torchbooks; C. Dawson, **The Making of Europe,*** Meridian; R. H. C. Davis, **A History of Medieval Europe: From Constantine to St. Louis,** Longmans, Green, 1957, M. Deanesley, **History of Early Medieval Europe, 476-911,** Methuen, 1956; Z. N. Brooke, **A History of Europe from 911 to 1198,** Barnes and Noble, 1951.

The history of the late Middle Ages is authoritatively surveyed in C. Previte-Orton, **A History of Europe from 1198 to 1378,** Barnes and Noble, 1951; D. Hay, **Europe in the Fourteenth and Fifteenth Centuries,** Longmans, 1966; F. Heer, **The Medieval World: 1100-1350,*** Torchbooks; W. T. Waugh, **A History of Europe from 1378 to 1498,** Barnes and Noble, 1949.

H. Pirenne, **Economic and Social History of Medieval Europe,*** Harvest, and **Medieval Cities,*** Anchor (on town origins). Ground-breaking interpretations by a great scholar. See also P. Boissonade, **Life and Work in Medieval Europe,*** Torchbooks.

Recommended general accounts of the medieval Church are M. W. Baldwin, **The Medieval Church,*** Cornell; S. Baldwin, **The Organization of Medieval Christianity,** Holt, 1929; A. C. Flick, **The Rise of the Medieval Church and Its Influence on the Civilization of Western Europe from the First to the Thirteenth Century,** Putnam, 1909.

H. O. Taylor, **The Medieval Mind: A History of the Development of Thought and Emotion in the Middle Ages,** 2 vols., Harvard, 1949. Celebrated for the history of ideas. See also F. B. Artz, **The Mind of the Middle Ages, A.D. 200-1500: An Historical Survey,** Knopf, 1958, valuable for its excellent organization and useful annotated bibliographies; and W. T. Jackson, **Medieval Literature: A History and a Guide,*** Collier.

D. Knowles, **Evolution of Medieval Thought,*** Vintage; F. C. Copleston, **Medieval Philosophy,*** Torchbooks. Popular introductions. See also E. Gilson, **A History of Christian Philosophy in the Middle Ages,** Random House, 1955, and G. Leff, **Medieval Thought from St. Augustine to Ockham,*** Penguin. A. C. Crombie, **Medieval and Early Modern Science,*** 2 vols., Anchor, is detailed and scholarly. Lynn White, Jr., **Medieval Technology and Social Change,*** Galaxy, is a valuable unique survey.

C. R. Morey, **Medieval Art,** Norton, 1942; and, by the same author, **Christian Art,*** Norton. Authoritative surveys. Medieval architecture is described concisely in N. Pevsner, **An Outline of European Architecture,*** Penguin.

SPECIAL STUDIES

S. Dill, **Roman Society in Gaul in the Merovingian Age,** Macmillan, 1926. Excellent descriptions of the barbarized society governed by early Frankish kings in western Europe.

J. Bronsted, **The Vikings,*** Penguin. Outstanding on Viking activities. G. Turville-Petre, **The Heroic Age of Scandinavia,** Hutchinson Univ. Library, 1951, describes the Norse way of life as reflected in their heroic legends.

Carl Stephenson, **Mediaeval Feudalism,*** Cornell. A clear introduction to a complicated subject. See also F. L. Ganshof, **Feudalism,*** Torchbooks, and M. Bloch, **Feudal Society,*** 2 vols., Phoenix.

Valuable for an understanding of rural life and the manorial system are J. H. Clapham, *et al.*, eds., **The Agrarian Life of the Middle Ages,** Cambridge, 1941, Vol. I of **The Cambridge Economic History of Europe from the Decline of the Roman Empire;** G. G. Coulton, **Medieval Village, Manor, and Monastery,*** Torchbooks; H. S. Bennett, **Life on the English Manor,*** Cambridge.

S. Painter, **French Chivalry, Chivalric Ideas and Practices in Medieval France,** Cornell.* Deals skillfully and briefly with the feudal, religious, and courtly aspects of chivalry. A. Luchaire, **Social Life at the Time of Philip Augustus,** Ungar, 1957, shows that the age of feudal chivalry was also an age of violence, anarchy, and cruelty. See also J. Evans, **Life in Medieval France,** Phaidon, 1957. English castle architecture is interestingly described and superbly illustrated in W. D. Simpson, **Castles from the Air,** Scribner, 1949.

Z. Oldenbourg, **The Crusades,*** Ballantine. A vivid authentically detailed account of how the Crusades brought out both the noblest and the most despicable in feudal society. R. A. Newhall, **The Crusades,*** Holt (Berkshire Studies), is a brief and lucid introduction. For greater detail see S. Runciman, **A History of the Crusades,*** 3 vols., Torchbooks, R. C. Smail, **Crusading Warfare (1097-1193),** Cambridge, 1956, describes the weapons, organization, and tactics of both the Latin and Muslim armies together with the nature and function of the crusaders' castles. C. W. C. Oman, **The Art of War in the Middle Ages: A.D. 378-1515,*** Cornell, is the standard work on the subject.

R. Latouche, **The Birth of Western Economy: Economic Aspects of the Dark Ages,** Methuen, 1961. Throws new light on the economic history of Europe, particularly Gaul, from the fourth through the eleventh centuries. See also A. R. Lewis, **Naval Power and Trade in the Mediterranean, A.D. 500-1100,** Princeton, 1951, and **The Northern Seas: Shipping and Trade in Northern Europe, A.D. 300-1100,** Princeton, 1958.

H. Fichtenau, **The Carolingian Empire: The Age of Charlemagne,*** Torchbooks. The best work on the subject. R. Fawtier,

*Indicates an inexpensive paperbound edition.

The Capetian Kings of France,* St. Martin's, is an excellent survey of the period from 987 to 1328. For greater detail see the comparative study by C. Petit-Dutaillis, **The Feudal Monarchy in France and England from the Tenth to the Thirteenth Centuries,** Kegan Paul, 1936.

G. O. Sayles, **The Medieval Foundations of England,*** Perpetua. Considered the best work on the subject. Excellent brief surveys are H. Cam, **England Before Elizabeth,*** Torchbooks; D. M. Stenton, **English Society in the Early Middle Ages (1066-1307),*** Penguin; A. R. Myers, **England in the Late Middle Ages,*** Penguin; C. H. Williams, **The Making of Tudor Despotism,** Nelson, 1935. R. Furneaux, **Invasion: 1066,** Prentice-Hall, 1966, is one of several books reappraising the Norman Conquest on its 900th anniversary. T. Plucknett, **A Concise History of the Common Law,** 5th ed., Little, Brown, 1956, is a good introduction; and G. L. Haskins, **The Growth of English Representative Government,*** Perpetua, is excellent on the history of Parliament.

E. Perroy, **The Hundred Years' War,** Oxford, 1952. The standard work on the subject.

J. Mariéjol, **The Spain of Ferdinand and Isabella,** Rutgers, 1961. The classic history of the emergence of Spain; gracefully written.

J. Bryce, **The Holy Roman Empire,*** Schocken. An old masterpiece; should be supplemented by G. Barraclough, **The Origins of Modern Germany,*** Capricorn. The Investiture Struggle is treated authoritatively in G. Tellenbach, **Church, State and Christian Society at the Time of the Investiture Contest,** Oxford, 1940.

F. Dvornik, **The Making of Central and Eastern Europe,** Polish Research Center, 1949; and, by the same author, **The Slavs in European History and Civilization,** Rutgers, 1962. Good introductions to Slavic eastern Europe.

Medieval vernacular literature is surveyed in two works by W. Ker: **The Dark Ages,*** Mentor; and **Epic and Romance,*** Dover. See also E. Auerbach, **Introduction to Romance Languages and Literature,*** Capricorn. For Latin poetry see H. Waddell, **Mediaeval Latin Lyrics,*** Penguin, and **The Wandering Scholars,*** Anchor.

C. H. Haskins, **The Renaissance of the Twelfth Century,*** Meridian, and **The Rise of Universities,*** Cornell. Two important and attractive books on aspects of medieval thought and learning.

Stimulating interpretations of the interrelationship of medieval art, thought, and spirit are Henry Adams, **Mont-Saint-Michel and Chartres,*** Anchor; E. Mâle, **The Gothic Image: Religious Art in France of the Thirteenth Century,*** Torchbooks; E. Panofsky, **Gothic Architecture and Scholasticism,*** Meridian. See also J. Evans, **Art in Mediaeval France,** Oxford, 1948; K. J. Conant, **Early Medieval Church Architecture,** Johns Hopkins, 1942; O. Von Simpson, **The Gothic Cathedral,** Pantheon, 1956. A. Temko, **Notre-Dame of Paris,*** Compass, is an absorbing "biography" of a great cathedral.

H. C. Lea, **A History of the Inquisition of the Middle Ages,** 3 vols., S. A. Russell, 1955. A detailed discussion of medieval heresies and the methods employed by the Church in dealing with heretics. See also J. Guiraud, **The Medieval Inquisition,** Benziger, 1930; C. Roth, **The Spanish Inquisition,*** Norton; A. S. Turberville, **Medieval Heresy and the Inquisition,** Holt, 1920.

S. R. Packard, **Europe and the Church Under Innocent III,** Holt, 1927. Brief survey of the medieval papacy at its height. See also W. Ullmann, **The Growth of Papal Government in the Middle Ages,** Barnes and Noble, 1963, and D. Waley, **The Papal State** in the Thirteenth Century, St. Martins, 1961. The rival political theories supporting the Church-state conflict are judiciously set forth in C. H. McIlwain, **The Growth of Political Thought in the West,** Macmillan, 1932, and W. Ullmann, **A History of Political Thought: The Middle Ages,*** Penguin.

BIOGRAPHIES

Outstanding studies of medieval political figures include R. Winston, **Charlemagne: From the Hammer to the Cross,*** Vintage; E. S. Duckett, **Alcuin, Friend of Charlemagne, His World and His Work,** Macmillan, 1951 (the career of the foremost scholar at Charlemagne's court); E. S. Duckett, **Alfred the Great: The King and His England,*** Phoenix; F. M. Stenton, **William the Conqueror and the Rule of the Normans,** Putnam, 1908; Amy Kelly, **Eleanor of Aquitaine and the Four Kings,*** Vintage; J. T. Appleby, **Henry II, the Vanquished King,** Bell, 1962; F. Perry, **St. Louis, the Most Christian King,** Putnam, 1901; E. Kantorowicz, **Frederick the Second, 1194-1250,** Ungar, 1957; C. W. S. Williams, **Henry VII,** Barker, 1937; P. Champion, **Louis XI,** Dodd, Mead, 1929; G. Waas, **The Legendary Character of Kaiser Maximilian,** Columbia, 1945; J. Michelet, **Joan of Arc,*** Univ. of Mich.; L. Fabre, **Joan of Arc,** McGraw-Hill, 1954; J. Fennell, **Ivan the Great of Moscow,** Macmillan, 1961; I. Grey, **Ivan the Terrible,** Lippincott, 1964.

Excellent biographies of religious and cultural figures during this period include D. Knowles, **Saints and Scholars: Twenty-Five Medieval Portraits,*** Cambridge (from St. Benedict to John Wycliffe); E. Gilson, **Heloise and Abelard,*** Univ. of Mich.; R. Lloyd, **Peter Abelard: The Orthodox Rebel,** 2nd ed., McDonald, 1947; A. J. MacDonald, **Hildebrand, A Life of Gregory VII,** Methuen, 1932; J. Jorgensen, **St. Francis of Assisi,*** Image; B. Jarrett, **Life of Saint Dominic,*** Image; K. B. McFarlane, **John Wycliffe and the Beginnings of English Nonconformity,** Macmillan, 1952; T. Boase, **Boniface VIII,** Constable, 1933; A. Duggan, **My Life for a Sheep,*** Image (Church vs. state in the twelfth century mirrored in the life of Thomas à Becket); T. G. Bergin, **Dante,** Orion, 1965; M. Chute, **Geoffrey Chaucer of England,*** Dutton.

FICTION

E. Power, **Medieval People,*** Barnes and Noble. Fictionalized sketches of people of various social positions and occupations by a first-rate scholar and historian.

Z. Oldenbourg, **The World Is Not Enough,** Pantheon, 1948. A panorama of twelfth-century French society. **The Cornerstone,*** Ballantine, by the same author, is historically sound on the Crusades.

T. H. White, **The Once and Future King,*** Dell. The merry and melancholy doings in King Arthur's court.

H. Muntz, **The Golden Warrior,*** Scribner. A first-rate novel dealing with the Norman conquest of England.

J. Tey, **The Daughter of Time,*** Berkeley. A modern detective tries to vindicate Richard III of his nephew's murder.

C. Reade, **The Cloister and the Hearth,*** Washington Square. A famous panorama of life in the late Middle Ages.

Sir Walter Scott, **Quentin Durward,*** Signet. Set in the France of Louis XI.

T. Costain, **The Moneyman,*** Permabooks. The spectacular rise and fall of the fifteenth-century French capitalist, Jacques Coeur. Good reading also is I. Origo, **The Merchant of Prato, Francesco di Marco Datini, 1335-1410,** Knopf, 1957.

Part Five

The Quickening of the West

■ History—dealing as it does with events in time—may often be likened to a clock with a gigantic pendulum. At one end of its arc, this pendulum swings to societies which emphasize the group at the expense of the individual—such as we saw in ancient Egypt. At another time, it swings to the other extreme where individualism counts for more than collectivism—as in the case of the Greek city-states. In the Middle Ages the emphasis was once again upon the ideal of unity. Because the purpose of existence was believed to be essentially religious, the Church could claim supremacy over all aspects of life—social and political, as well as spiritual; and men believed that Church and State, and faith and reason, could be reconciled.

Despite the successful efforts of Scholastics such as St. Thomas Aquinas to integrate all human thought and action with religion, this medieval synthesis did not remain permanently satisfying. Why? To many scholars the explanation is that Europe had developed to the point where its political interests, economic life, social attitudes, and intellectual endeavors could no longer be contained within the confines of the medieval framework. The purpose of this unit is to follow the new directions taken by Europe's kings, merchants, and theologians—in short, to follow them into a new society where the pendulum of history has swung back to a strong emphasis upon the interests and rights of the individual. In the political sphere, this individualism resulted in the creation of separate national states; in the world of thought and art it produced the Renaissance; and in the area of religion it split Christendom through the Reformation.

This ever increasing emphasis upon individualism also transformed the economic structure of western Europe. The medieval economy had been collectivistic and under the control of the landed nobility. But the quickening of town life had been accompanied by the rise of a new and forceful middle class, which was to father the system of economic individualism known as capitalism.

Meanwhile, in the flourishing city-states of Italy, scholars known as humanists discovered in the manuscripts of ancient Greece and Rome the same emphasis on individual freedom which was rapidly gaining momentum in their own day, and with this spirit of individualism sprang up an unashamed delight in the beauties and joys of life. Heeding Protagoras' ancient maxim that "Man is the measure of all things" and revolting against medieval authority and asceticism, Renaissance man was impelled by a new spirit of independence, a new hunger for experience. The creative vigor of the Italian Renaissance in literature, thought, and the fine arts surged throughout Europe, resulting in one of the most fruitful epochs in the cultural history of mankind.

Carried into the religious sphere, the resurgence of individualism shattered the universal supremacy of the Church and gave rise to the religious diversity of the modern western world. The followers of Luther, Calvin, and Zwingli substituted the authority of the Scriptures for that of the Roman Church and interposed no priestly mediator between the individual and his God. The Roman Church, which launched a vigorous reform movement of its own, nevertheless continued to be a potent religious and historical force.

With the religious unity of Europe gone, the Church could no longer act as supreme arbiter in human affairs. In the field of power politics, where the papacy had played a dominant role, a vacuum now existed. The sovereigns of the new national states eagerly rushed in to fill it, and during the century and a half following 1500 they pursued power, wealth, prestige, and security, allowing few moral or religious scruples to interfere with these objectives. From the twisted motives and tragic human suffering which fill some of the most bloodstained pages in western history emerged the competitive state system that has survived into the second half of the twentieth century.

In regard to science we should think of the Renaissance not as a "rebirth" but as a "new birth." Present-day astronomy—and our breathtaking developments in rocketry—have their basis in the advances made in the sixteenth and seventeenth centuries by Copernicus, Kepler, and Galileo. Using mathematical reasoning and relatively crude instruments, these astronomical pioneers showed that the earth was not the center of the universe but revolved in a predictable orbit around the sun. The heliocentric concept and the equally revolutionary work performed in the fields of dynamics and magnetism were to bring about a profound change in men's thinking—namely, new ways of investigating nature and the idea that the universe was based on natural law. This change was stimulated in turn by philosophers such as Francis Bacon who argued for a new method of scientific inquiry that would make proper use of experimentation. The new developments produced a veritable intellectual revolution that was to reach its zenith in the eighteenth century, the so-called Age of Reason, when many men believed that the universe ran like a great clock—presumably "wound up" by God in the beginning—and could be explained in mathematical terms.

19. Andrea del Verrocchio: "Lorenzo de' Medici" (c. 1480). Among the Renaissance concepts which superseded the hierarchic medieval view of the world was the notion of man as a free individual, capable of fashioning his own destiny. A prime incarnation of this idea was the vibrant Florentine nobleman, statesman, and patron of the arts, Lorenzo de' Medici. The attributes of the Renaissance man of action are trenchantly conveyed in Verrocchio's polychrome portrait of Lorenzo.

20. Masaccio: "St. Peter Healing the Sick" (c. 1427). One of the most innovative contributors to the transformation of western culture during the Renaissance was the young Masaccio, whose painting reveals a profound new understanding of the natural world. The figures in this fresco have weight and conviction, and they move easily through deep space which is consistently illuminated by a single light source and organized rationally according to the laws of perspective. No trace remains of the decorative abstraction of Gothic painting. Masaccio's monumental realism did much to shape the painting of the next 450 years.

21. Sandro Botticelli: "Primavera" (c. 1478). Specifically, the term *Renaissance* refers to a rebirth of the ideals of classical antiquity, which the Italians of the fourteenth, fifteenth, and sixteenth centuries regarded as a time during which man had attained the apex of his creative powers. It is not surprising that the Renaissance emulation of Greece and Rome would finally extend to the large-scale treatment of pagan subjects in painting and sculpture. Perhaps the most moving Italian painter of classical allegories was the Florentine Sandro Botticelli, whose "Primavera" is a lyric celebration of spring and all its associations: youthfulness, love, fecundity, beauty. The pregnant figure of Venus in the center is flanked on the left by the god Mercury and the three Graces, and on the right by the bewitching goddess Flora and a nymph pursued by the North Wind.

22. (above) **Michelangelo Buonarroti:** "Pieta" (c. 1498). The High Renaissance, more than any other period, developed the idea of artistic genius—of great creative, even "divine" talent —in a single individual who, by its possession, stood above the rules of ordinary men. No one represented this concept more convincingly than Michelangelo—sculptor, painter, architect, and poet, who bestrode his time like a colossus. The nobility of sentiment and classic rectitude of the High Renaissance are clearly evident in this early work, executed when the sculptor was in his twenties. **23.** (right) **Jan van Eyck:** "Madonna of Chancellor Rolin" (c. 1434). Northern Europe's cultural pulse quickened at the same time as Italy's, but the northerners held to the ancient medieval vision more tenaciously, for, unlike the Mediterraneans, they possessed scarcely any memories of the classical past. Nonetheless, within a framework of transcendent Christian piety, Flemish artists like Van Eyck achieved an intimate, detailed realism which was as compelling as the grander scale of the Italians.

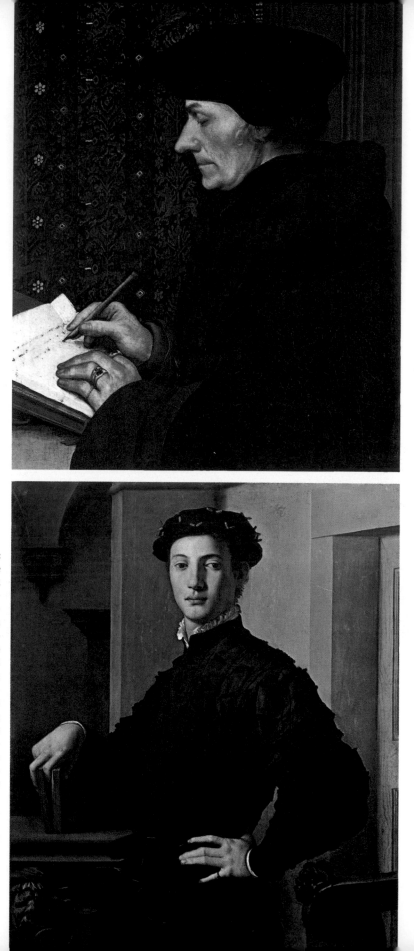

24. (above) **Hans Holbein the Younger: "Erasmus of Rotterdam"** (1523). The high level of European portraiture in the sixteenth century reflected the man-centered outlook of the time. The traditional meticulous realism of the north was employed with unforgettable lucidity by the German Holbein, who recorded the likenesses of numerous famous contemporaries—among them the Humanist Erasmus—with jewel-like accuracy and brilliance. **25.** (right) **Agnolo Bronzino: "Portrait of a Young Man"** (c. 1535-1537). Italy in the 1500's continued, meanwhile, to set the stylistic pace for the rest of Europe. By the middle of the century the High Renaissance and its serenely noble mood were over; the curious and consciously exaggerated style of the Mannerists had taken command of Italian art. Bronzino's secure place among the most polished and elegant Mannerist portraitists is clear from the hyper-refined countenance and delicately sinuous hands of the model in this painting.

Alte Pinakothek, Munich

26. Peter Paul Rubens: ''The Abduction of the Daughters of Leucippus'' (c. 1617).
Significant differences between northern and Italian art persisted into the seventeenth century but were then greatly resolved by the ascendancy of the Baroque style, a powerful form of dramatic realism which began, expectably enough, in Italy but quickly spread throughout Europe. Among the first painters to assimilate the Italian manner, and perhaps the most effective in popularizing it throughout northern Europe, was the great Flemish painter Peter Paul Rubens, whose surging compositions, dazzling color, and exuberantly sensual mood comprise an unsurpassed exemplar of the Baroque ideal.

27. (above) **Jan Steen: "Twelfth Night"** (1668) and **28.** (left) **Rembrandt van Rijn: "Self-Portrait"** (c. 1665). By the seventeenth century the split between Catholicism and Protestantism was a fact of European culture which was mirrored over and over again in the art of the time. Catholics continued to employ religious subjects freely in their painting and sculpture, as they had since the early days of the Church; meanwhile Protestants, ever fearful of idolatry, tended to favor the more modest themes which related to everyday life and everyday things. Despite the narrow restrictions which the latter viewpoint thus placed upon the artist, Protestant Dutch painters of the seventeenth century left an inspired legacy behind them. Only seldom looking beyond the life immediately around them, they built a great body of realist art which ranged from the down-to-earth delights Jan Steen took in bourgeois pastimes to the exactly introspective self-portraits of the aging Rembrandt.

Chapter 15

Man Is the Measure

The Renaissance: 1300-1600

INTRODUCTION. To the historians who viewed the Middle Ages as the "dark ages" —a time of stagnation and ignorance—the epoch of European history that followed seemed to spring to life suddenly like Minerva from the brow of Jove, resplendent in beauty and wisdom. They looked on the new age as an awakening from centuries of lethargy, and they labeled it *Renaissance,* meaning "rebirth."

Today most historians would deny that the Renaissance brought any distinct break in the development of European culture. As we have already noted, the Middle Ages made rich intellectual and artistic contributions to civilization. In what ways, then, can the Renaissance be said to signify a "rebirth"?

First of all, there was an intense renewal of interest in the literature of classical Greece and Rome—a development known as the Revival of Learning. No longer were scholars confined to medieval translations of the famous writers of ancient Greece; many began to read the works of Plato, Aristotle, and others in the original Greek. In addition,

they searched the monasteries for old manuscripts and translated hitherto unknown
works from Greek antiquity into Latin. Thus
the humanists, as these scholars were called,
reintroduced classical learning into the
mainstream of western thought. Second,
while the scholars rediscovered classical
thought, artists in Italy were stimulated and
inspired by their study and imitation of
classical architecture and sculpture.

But the spirit of the Renaissance was
not characterized by a mere cult of antiquity, a looking backward into the past. The
men of the Renaissance were the harbingers
of the modern world, energetically and
enthusiastically engaged in reshaping their
political, economic, and religious environment, in pushing back geographical boundaries and extending the limits of human
knowledge. Renaissance culture strikingly
exhibits belief in the worth of man and his
privileged place in the scheme of things and
the desire of man to think and act as a free
agent and a well-rounded individual. The
Renaissance spirit was admirably summed
up by a versatile genius of the fifteenth
century, Leon Battista Alberti, when he
declared, "Men can do all things if they
will."[1]

In some respects every age is an age of
transition, but it may be fair to state that the
Renaissance marks one of the turning points
in western civilization. The dominant institutions and social systems which had existed
in Europe for well-nigh a thousand years
were becoming devitalized; many were
being radically modified or even discarded.
Values were changing: medievalism with
its emphasis on Scholasticism, Church authority, and conformity was on the wane,
and a more modern culture which depended
on individualism, skepticism, and ultimately
on science was taking its place.

We must be cautious in our analysis,
however, because the period of the Renaissance does not fit into a neat chronological
or geographical pattern (see the Historical
Critique, p. 477). Some medieval habits and
institutions persisted for a long time;
throughout the Renaissance the vast majority
of illiterate common people clung to the
ways of their forefathers. And the Renaissance did not burst forth simultaneously
in all parts of Europe.

The Renaissance originated with a relatively small, educated group dwelling in the
cities of central and northern Italy. We shall
begin with the Revival of Learning and the
flowering of art in this locality and conclude
with a discussion of other facets of the Renaissance as its ideas crossed the Alps to
France, Germany, Spain, and England. It
was in England that the underlying optimism and dynamism of the entire Renaissance period were epitomized by Shakespeare when he said:

O, wonder!
How many goodly creatures are there here!
How beauteous mankind is! O brave new world,
That has such people in't![2]

THE ITALIAN RENAISSANCE: THE SETTING

The Italian city-states. The elimination
of German imperial influence by the middle
of the thirteenth century left the numerous
city-states of northern and central Italy free
to follow their own devices. Such cities as
Venice, Florence, Milan, Genoa, and Pisa
had grown wealthy from their thriving
industries and lucrative trade with the East,
and their banking houses handled papal
revenues and made loans to European monarchs. The Italian city-states bore some
similarity to those of ancient Greece in that
the Italian cities controlled the surrounding
countryside and in many cases even ruled
other towns. Also, as in Greece, each city-
state was extremely individualistic politically and intensely self-conscious, viewing
its neighbors with a hostility that often
flared into war.

Within each city there were intense rivalries and feuds. Unlike the situation in northern Europe, where the bourgeoisie inhabited
the towns and the nobles lived on country
manors, the Italian nobility had city houses

as well as country villas. In some Italian cities arcaded streets enabled the townsmen to go about their business safe from the arrows which from time to time flew between the towered houses of feuding nobles.

Civic patriotism and a desire for liberty advanced rapidly under the influence of the prosperous and newly powerful burghers, who finally succeeded in ousting the restless feudal aristocrats from positions of power. Ingenious city charters and civic constitutions were drafted, and there was much trial and error in the art of government. Single and plural executives, limited franchise and universal suffrage, long terms and short terms of office, together with rotation of officeholders in various civic positions —all these governmental techniques were tried with varying degrees of success. Until the end of the thirteenth century the prevailing political trend in the cities was toward republicanism and representative government.

Bitter factionalism did not die out, how-

ever, and rival cliques continued to spring up. As we saw in Chapter 14, in the fight against the German emperors the pro-imperial party in Italy was called Ghibelline, and the pro-papal and anti-imperial party the Guelph. These party names continued to be used by quarrelsome factions in the city-states long after the original conflict had become a dead issue.

Two city-state republics were of unusual interest. Venice, the "Pearl of the Adriatic," was one of the richest cities of its time, controlling an empire of ports and islands in the eastern Mediterranean and carrying much of Europe's maritime trade in its great fleets. Six fleets were kept in operation; the vessels were of a standard design so that spare parts could be stored at Venetian ports to prevent breakdowns in shipping schedules. The government of this rich republic had been in the hands of a doge (duke), together with a popular assembly, but beginning in the thirteenth century the rich merchants gradually took over the reins

RENAISSANCE EUROPE ABOUT 1500

→ Northward Spread of Renaissance

of power. They alone sat in the Great Council, which replaced the popular assembly. This oligarchic council appointed the doge and the members of smaller councils which administered the government. Most famous among the smaller councils was the secret Council of Ten, which dealt swiftly with suspected enemies of the government. The merchant oligarchy of Venice provided good government and, unlike other city-states, resolutely squashed internal strife.

Florence—the center of the flourishing wool, leather, and silk industries—boasted merchants and bankers who were among the most prosperous in Europe, and its gold florin circulated in many lands as a standard coin. With its many checks and counterchecks of power, the Florentine constitution was bewilderingly complex. For example, the head of the state held office for two months only, and all measures needed a two-thirds majority in five different committees or assemblies to become laws. In theory, Florence was a democracy but, as in Venice, real political power was wielded by wealthy businessmen.

Despotism replaces republicanism. In the fourteenth century a rapid decline in republicanism took place. Representative institutions had not worked well, and conspiracy, confusion, and incompetence caused many citizens to feel that a firm leader was needed to ensure internal stability and to lessen the danger from external enemies.

Actual power in the city-states gravitated more and more in the direction of one-man rule. Seizing power, the members of prominent families became political bosses or despots. Although Venice maintained the benevolent oligarchy of its merchants with the doge as a figurehead, Florence went under the thumb of the Medici family, and its republican institutions became largely empty forms. The Medici had no aristocratic antecedents; their status was based on commerce and finance. The significance of the family emblem—six red balls on a field of gold—is unknown, but we are all familiar with the later modification of this insigne —the three balls of the pawnbroker.

Nearly all the other Italian city-states came under the rule of despots—an amazing group of capable and ruthless men who loved power, luxury, and the fine arts. "They were brutal, unscrupulous, ambitious men, who were at the same time patrons of the arts and letters; men who murdered an enemy, applauded a poet or orator, or seduced a pretty woman with equal ease and pleasure. They hung pictures on their walls and enemies on their gibbets; wrote poetry and plotted treason; built churches and burned villages; excelled in courtly etiquette and inhuman tortures; lived lustily and died violently."[3]

The condottieri. In both the intracity rivalries and the struggles between city-states, mercenary soldiers under the command of leaders called *condottieri* were employed. Coming from all over Europe, these adventurers sold their swords to the highest bidder but carried on their fighting with a minimum of bloodshed. "They would try to win, because defeat would lower their market value, but they did not want to beat the enemy too much. He was in the same trade, and cut-throat competition was bad for everyone in the long run. Besides, a war ended too soon might mean unemployment for a long spell."[4] There were, therefore, always degrees of victory and limits to defeat. Far different from the twentieth-century wars of annihilation, the petty conflicts on the Italian peninsula hindered neither commercial progress nor the development of the arts and learning.

Renaissance patrons. In the Italian cities the newly wealthy class of traders, bankers, and manufacturers conspicuously displayed their wealth and bolstered their social importance by patronizing artists and scholars. While leading commissions for artists in the fifteenth century were still obtained from such communal bodies as guilds and churches, individual patronage began to play a more important role.

Among the most famous patrons were members of the Medici family who, by acting as champions of the lower classes, ruled Florence for sixty years (1434-1494) behind a façade of republican forms. Lorenzo de' Medici, who was first citizen of Florence from 1469 until his death in 1492, carried on his family's proud traditions and added so much luster to Florence that he became known as Lorenzo the Magnificent. His career signifies the zenith of Florentine leadership in the arts. A man of practical affairs, he also wrote poetry and songs and gave advice and money to scholars, sculptors, poets, and painters.

Other princes and despots of Italian city-states patronized the arts, and the popes were also eager to sponsor artists. In the sixteenth century the popes outdid secular rulers in the splendor of their court. Pope Alexander VI (1492-1503), the father of the unscrupulous poisoners Cesare and Lucrezia Borgia, was a target for criticism because he devoted more time and thought to furthering the fortunes of his family than he did to religious matters. Wealthy families actively sought to control the papacy, and the Medici succeeded in placing two of their members, Leo X (1513-1521), son of Lorenzo, and Clement VII (1523-1534), nephew of Leo, in this office. Leo's pontificate, in particular, was one of great activity in the arts and learning in Rome.

Although patrons allowed artists a great deal of freedom, a patron nevertheless had to be flattered occasionally and his wishes recognized. On the other hand, a Renaissance artist had the benefit of the security and protection offered by his patron and enjoyed a definite advantage from working exclusively on commission. The artist knew where his finished work would repose, in cathedral, villa, or city square; this situation contrasts with some later periods, when artists painted when and as they wished and then attempted to sell the work to anyone who would buy it.

Manners and morals. As might be expected, the dress of the most prosperous inhabitants of the Italian cities reflected the individualism of the period. Although Florence had regulations to prescribe dress and restrain extravagance, one official charged with administering them lamented that the women "met me with arguments such as are not found in any book of laws."

Both men and women took delight in wearing costly silks, furs, jewels, and brocaded materials; fashions in sleeves went through a bewildering number of changes;

In the early 1400's goods from many parts of the world flowed into Italy to be sold side by side in the market places, such as this drapers' market in Bologna.

and the individualism of the age was strikingly shown in such features of dress as parti-colored hose. Women made copious use of cosmetics, perfume, and false hair, blonde being the fashionable color.

To continue on a more constructive note, a distinct improvement was evident in cleanliness and the comforts of everyday existence. City streets were better paved than anywhere else in Europe, thus enabling people to take pleasure outings and to travel with ease. In educated circles, conversation with its "polished interchange of jest and earnest" became a highly cultivated art. In the higher strata of city society, women received the same education as men, became accomplished classicists, and took an active part in civic life. To those women who gave evidence of the energy and courage usually expected only of men, the term *virago* was applied.

During the Renaissance the newly wealthy citizens of the Italian cities sought refinement in every aspect of their culture. Believing that the mark of nobility was an elegance of manner as well as a cultivated mind, they eagerly read etiquette books to learn the rules of correct social behavior.

The most famous book on Renaissance manners, published in 1528, was *The Courtier* by Baldassare Castiglione (1478-1529), a scholar, poet, and courtier from Urbino. Because of its characterizations and witty conversation, this book became very popular; but its greatest significance lies in the fact that it established a model for the Renaissance courtier. To Castiglione, good manners and deportment were essential to the ideal courtier, but his central idea was that a courtier's true worth was more commensurate with his strength of character and excellence of intellect than with his hereditary social position. The courtier should be capable in the arts of war and peace and should be motivated by honesty and integrity in advising his ruler.

The *Autobiography* of Benvenuto Cellini (1500-1571) gives us a vivid insight into Renaissance manners and morals, but it is no book of etiquette. Cellini was a bold and worldly adventurer, constantly embroiled in excitement and adventure—duels, love affairs, and prison terms. But he was also a sculptor of repute (see p. 543) and the most skillful metalworker of his day. Vigorous and energetic, Cellini possessed *virtú*, a term used in the Renaissance to characterize a man of natural ability and abounding vitality. *Virtú* should not be confused with virtue; the words have no connection; in fact, a man possessing *virtú* often appeared to be singularly deficient in virtue, as Cellini's life story reveals. Possession of *virtú* enabled a man to be considered *l'uomo universale* ("the universal man" or "the complete man"), the Renaissance ideal of greatness. While Cellini approximated this ideal, it was left for others—geniuses like Leonardo da Vinci and Michelangelo—to achieve it completely.

THE REVIVAL OF LEARNING

The waning of the Middle Ages. By the fourteenth century there was a marked decline in medieval institutions and ideas. The feudal social structure was weakening before the growing power of the middle class, which sided with the new monarchs and thrived on the revival of trade and the growth of towns. The threat of armies using gunpowder was revolutionizing warfare at the expense of armor-clad knights. Heresy and schism racked the Church and its temporal power was increasingly being challenged by aggressive national monarchs.

An empty formalism replaced the creativeness that had given the twelfth and thirteenth centuries their unique forms of expression. Although asceticism remained a pious ideal, it gained few adherents among the acquisitive townspeople and was openly flouted by many of the clergy. Scholars still held learned disputations at the universities, but Scholasticism was unable to satisfy the growing interest in man and society.

In the religious life of the late Middle Ages, tendencies toward excess and materialism were evident. Reformers criticized the ever growing list of new saints, festivals, and special offices and Masses. The confusion of spiritual and temporal values is clearly seen in the excessive veneration of physical relics of the saints and in the tendency to invest favorite saints with fanciful and even grotesque characteristics. In previous centuries artists had skillfully used symbolism in their efforts to bridge the gap between the transient world and that of the spirit. But at this later stage, attempts to devise new symbols had become more or less mechanical, and the net result was an arid intellectual game. In architecture the Gothic style of the twelfth and thirteenth centuries, superb in its balance and restraint, had given place to exaggeration and flamboyance. Decoration and ornamentation became ends in themselves.

The traits of a once great cultural epoch in decline—formalism, sentimentality, flamboyance—were still manifest in the literature and art of northern Europe during the fifteenth century. Meanwhile, sophisticated Italian urban society no longer found medieval ideals of other-worldliness and asceticism satisfactory. Pious religious themes were not so engaging as satires directed against a sometimes corrupt clergy and the outworn conventions of chivalry. Searching for new modes of expression, thinkers and artists found what they wanted in the classical legacy of Greece and Rome.

Individualism and tradition in the Renaissance. In a sense, the Renaissance is the history of individual men expressing themselves brilliantly, and often tempestuously, in art, poetry, science, exploration, and religion. While the medieval way taught the unimportance of this life, stressed its snares and evils, and smothered the individual with a host of confining rules and prohibitions, the Renaissance beckoned man to enjoy beauty, to savor the opportunities of this world, and to be himself, regardless of restraints. Above all, the new spirit called upon its followers to adopt the concept of *l'uomo universale.* Life was best lived when the human personality showed its versatility by expression in many forms: advancement of the mind, perfection of the body, cultivation of the social graces, and appreciation and creativity in the arts.

Like any other movement, however, individualism had its negative aspects and its excesses. The lawlessness and political confusion of the Italian Renaissance and the strongly amoral character of its society were due in no small measure to the tendency of men to regard themselves as above the law.

In discussing the Renaissance as a new era, the historian must be careful to avoid oversimplification. Men continued to share in the corporate life of the Church and the guilds, and many medieval customs and habits of thought persisted for centuries. In the case of humanism, as we shall see, no sudden revolution of philosophical doctrines occurred to set the Renaissance apart from the Middle Ages. Similarly, the artists of the Renaissance, who found inspiration in antiquity and whose works reflected a renewed interest in classical mythology and in the beauties of the human body, did not break completely with the subject matter and artistic techniques of their medieval predecessors. Although their interest in rendering secular subjects increased, Renaissance artists still looked to the Church as their greatest single patron. Building churches, sculpturing saints and Madonnas, and painting religious murals continued to occupy the genius of hundreds of artists during this period.

Humanism and the classical revival. During the Middle Ages Virgil, Cicero, and Caesar were popular authors; Aristotle was venerated much as though he were a Church Father; and Roman law greatly influenced Church, or canon, law. But in medieval times the writers of antiquity had been interpreted within the framework of the Christian religion and often cited as authorities to bolster Church dogma. Although many aspects of antiquity were avoided because of their disturbingly pagan quality, churchmen did make use of pagan literature for allegorical narratives which were Christian in character. Consequently, the true nature of the classical world was often distorted or obscured.

In fourteenth-century Italy, however, a new perspective was attained. Here, in the early humanistic movement, a fresh appreciation of classical culture emerged. Such an approach was natural in a land where reminders of classical antiquity survived on every side. The ruins of Rome's imperial glory were to be seen in many parts of the Italian peninsula, and Greek remains existed in southern Italy and Sicily. The memory of the Italian cities' struggle against feudal, papal, and Hohenstaufen control recalled the efforts of ancient Rome to become a free republic. Humanism spread through the land, bringing with it a veneration of ancient civilization and a desire to make over the arts, literature, language, and modes of living to conform with models from Greek and Roman antiquity. Successors to a small group of medieval teachers of grammar and rhetoric, the representatives of this new intellectual movement called themselves humanists, a name derived from the *studia humanitatis,* or "humanities," which Roman authors had used in the sense of a liberal or literary education.

Leonardo da Vinci, who had a wide knowledge of many fields besides painting, typifies the Renaissance ideal of the "universal man." In his "Virgin of the Rocks" (National Gallery, London), from which the head of an angel (left) is a detail, Leonardo established himself as a master of the High Renaissance in form and style. Another version, now in the Louvre, was painted twenty-five years earlier and was originally intended for an altar panel. Throughout his life Leonardo carried a sketchbook which he would fill with drawings and notes in his unusual handwriting, written inverted from right to left and best deciphered with a mirror. Unfortunately, approximately two thirds of his original writings have been lost. He never organized his extensive work, and the *Treatise on Painting*, compiled after his death by one of his closest friends, and a few fragments are all that remain. Although he had a distinct ideal of beauty (as in the angel), Leonardo was also fascinated by ugliness, and he would often follow grotesque-looking people, making numerous caricatures and studies, like those in the sketch at bottom. His interest in nature and anatomy was more than a passing one. Sketches of flowers, such as the "Star of Bethlehem" (right), show an uncommonly keen botanical eye, and his drawings of embryos (far right) and other anatomical subjects are also amazingly accurate.

Medieval Scholastic education had emphasized the sciences and professional training in law, medicine, and theology at the expense of the "arts," or literary side of the curriculum. Hence the Scholastics had centered their attention on Aristotle's scientific writings and other ancient works on astronomy, medicine, and mathematics. Stimulated by a rebirth of men's interest in the problems and values of human living, the humanists reversed this medieval emphasis and called attention to the importance of an education in the humanities—history, grammar, rhetoric, poetry, and moral philosophy. The humanists disdained the sciences because, as Petrarch—the first of the Italian humanists —wrote:

. . . they help in no way toward a happy life, for what does it advantage us to be familiar with the nature of animals, birds, fishes, and reptiles, while we are ignorant of the nature of the race of man to which we belong, and do not know or care whence we come or whither we go?[5]

Thus, despite the fact that both the humanist and the Scholastic looked to the past and venerated its heritage, they differed widely in their choice of the ancient material to be revered.

Humanists and Scholastics also differed in the manner in which they saw themselves in relation to the writers of ancient times. While the Scholastic always felt himself inferior to the ancients and looked up to them as son to father or pupil to teacher, the typical humanist in his exultant individualism saw himself equal to the ancients and boldly hailed them as man to man and friend to friend. At the beginning of his *Divine Comedy* Dante described medieval man's reliance upon the authority of the ancients in allegorical terms. Dante (medieval man) is lost in the "dark wood" which is this life until he is rescued by Virgil (a favorite medieval symbol of ancient wisdom), who thereafter guides him along the right path. "Losing me," Virgil is made to say to Dante, "ye would remain astray." The noticeably different attitude of the humanists was well expressed by one of their few medieval forerunners, John of Salisbury (d. 1180): "Most delightful in many ways is the fruit of letters that, banishing the irksomeness of intervals of place and time, bring friends into each other's presence. . . ."[6] It was in this spirit that Petrarch wrote his *Letters to Ancient Authors,* addressing Homer, Plato, Cicero, and others in familiar terms and sharing with them his own thoughts and experiences. This feeling of equality with ancient authors was also behind the humanists' practice of stuffing their own writings with apt quotations from the classics. The humanists' purpose, however, differed from that of the Scholastics, who also quoted extensively from the ancients; as the humanist Montaigne explained in his essays (see p. 469), he quoted the ancients not because he agreed with them but because they agreed with him!

Petrarch, the "father of humanism." The "father of humanism" is a title that has been given to Francesco Petrarca, better known to us as Petrarch (1304-1374). Resentful as a youth of his father's desire to have him become a lawyer, he turned to reading Virgil and Cicero for consolation; and though he studied law at Bologna, he dreamed constantly of the glories of the classical age.

In 1327 he met the lady Laura and fell in love with her. Little is known of Laura or of the true nature of her relationship to Petrarch. But inspired by his love of her, Petrarch wrote sonnets which made him one of the greatest lyric poets of all time. In the love poetry of the age, his portrayal of Laura represents a fresh approach. Earlier poets had woven about their heroines an air of courtly love and religious idealization which made the characters quite unreal. Petrarch's Laura was a flesh-and-blood creature whom all readers could recognize as human.

The ancients wrote of the joys of this world, and their attitude toward living struck a sympathetic chord in Petrarch. In his *Secret* Petrarch has an imaginary conversation with St. Augustine, which forcibly brings out the conflict between new ideas and those of medieval times. Petrarch concluded that, despite the importance of the world to come, the world of here and now held many delights which should not be shunned.

A man of many diverse interests, Petrarch

liked travel, music, gardening, and the pleasures of nature. Others before him, such as Dante, had described the Italian landscape in the course of their works, but Petrarch shared with the writers of antiquity a love of nature for its own sake. In his famous *Ascent of Mont Ventoux* Petrarch tells of a day in April 1336 when he and a younger brother climbed a high and hazardous mountain. Such an outing, simply for the purpose of enjoying the view of the countryside from the summit, was unheard of in Petrarch's day. Opening the volume of Augustine's *Confessions* that he carried with him, Petrarch came upon a passage which disturbed him:

'And men go to admire the high mountains, the vast floods of the sea, the huge streams of the rivers, the circumference of the ocean, and the revolutions of the stars—and desert themselves.' I was stunned, I confess. I . . . closed the book, angry with myself that I still admired earthly things.[7]

This inner conflict between his love of earthly things and his loyalty to the traditional medieval ideal of self-denial and other-worldliness exemplifies the transitional position Petrarch occupied in western culture. A product of medieval beliefs and attitudes, he nevertheless could not accept a depreciation of man's importance in the scheme of things or a constriction of his mental horizons. And thus he condemned the rigidity and arid logic of Scholasticism and the extent to which medieval education was governed by dead tradition. He himself was not a careful scholar and never learned Greek, yet this versatile rebel had a profound influence upon his contemporaries and gave humanism its first great impetus.

Boccaccio and the Decameron. Another celebrated humanist, Giovanni Boccaccio (1313-1375), spent his childhood in Florence. Later, while working as a bank clerk in Naples, he witnessed the pleasures of the gay and brilliant Neapolitan court and in time abandoned commerce for a life of letters. When he was twenty-three, he caught sight in church of a beautiful young married woman, who later became his mistress. The love affair ended unhappily, but the ex-

Petrarch drew this sketch of a spring near Avignon, where he lived for several years, on a manuscript copy of Pliny in 1341. A staunch humanist, Petrarch combined a love for the classics with a love for nature.

perience inspired his writing of poetry and romances, gave his works a strongly personal character, and immortalized the lady, whom he called Fiammetta ("Little Flame").

In 1348, seven years after Boccaccio's return to Florence, the calamitous Black Death struck—a disaster which wiped out nearly two thirds of Florence's population. Boccaccio used this event to establish the setting of his masterpiece, the *Decameron*. To escape the pestilence, his characters—three young men and seven young women—sought seclusion in a country villa, where they whiled away the time by telling each other stories. Boccaccio suffused the hundred tales of the *Decameron*, based on the old *fabliaux* (see p. 401) and on chivalric accounts, with a new and different spirit. Recounted by sophisticated city dwellers, the tales satirize the follies of knights and other medieval types and express clearly the contempt which had developed for the old, and by then threadbare, ideals of feudalism. Many tales are bawdy and even scandalous—a charge which Boccaccio undertook to refute:

Some of you may say that in writing these tales I have taken too much license, bv making ladies sometimes say and often listen to matters which are not proper to be said or heard by virtuous ladies. This I deny, for there is nothing so unchaste but may be said chastely if modest words are used; and this I think I have done.[8]

Nevertheless, the *Decameron* offers a wealth of anecdotes, portraits of flesh-and-blood characters, and a vivid (although one-sided) picture of Renaissance life.

The *Decameron* closed Boccaccio's career as a creative artist. Largely through the influence of Petrarch, whom he met in 1350, Boccaccio gave up writing in the Italian vernacular and turned to the study of antiquity. He attempted to learn Greek, wrote an encyclopedia of classical mythology, and went off to monasteries in search of manuscripts. By the time Petrarch and Boccaccio died, the study of the literature and learning of antiquity was growing throughout Italy.

The search for manuscripts. Until Renaissance times knowledge of the ancient world had been limited because many manuscripts of classical works were not available to scholars. The Revival of Learning stimulated a search for manuscripts which became a mania, and before the middle of the fifteenth century works by most of the important Latin authors had been found. The degree of difference between humanist and Scholastic is indicated by the ease with which the early humanists recovered the "lost" Latin literary masterpieces: they were found close at hand in monastic libraries, covered by the undisturbed dust of centuries. The books had always been there; what had been largely lacking was a mature and appreciative audience of readers. In addition to these works, precious Greek manuscripts were later brought to Italy from Constantinople; by the beginning of the sixteenth century the most important Greek works in all fields of knowledge were obtainable in western Europe.

After the greater part of extant Greek literature had been transplanted to the West from the Byzantine world, the humanists facilitated the study of Greek by introducing it into the curriculums of the universities and the more advanced secondary schools. Greek was not widely known during the Renaissance, however, and many Europeans relied exclusively upon Latin versions of Greek classics for a knowledge of Greek literature.

Individual scholars had their favorite classical authors, both Greek and Roman, but the highest universal praise was reserved for Cicero. Compounded of moral philosophy and rhetoric, his work displayed a wide-ranging intellect which appealed to many humanists. Petrarch and many others copied Cicero's graceful, eloquent, and polished literary style. The revival of the art of writing classical Latin prose was due largely to the study and imitation of Cicero.

Revival of Platonism. As a result both of their rebellion against the Aristotelian emphasis upon natural science and of their search for a classical philosophy that stressed moral purpose and religious and mystical values, many humanists gravitated to Platonism. The revival of interest in Plato was accelerated by several factors. First of all, the widely admired Cicero had been influenced more by Plato than by Aristotle. Second, famous Byzantine scholars provided Italian audiences with a fresh understanding of Platonic teachings. "Florentines who had been fed the traditional pabulum of late medieval scholastic philosophers . . . turned eagerly from arid scholastic syllogisms to Platonic mysticism,"[9] and Florence became a center of Platonism. A third factor in the revival of Platonism was the study of Plato in the original Greek and the translation, in the first half of the fifteenth century, of the *Republic* and others of his major works. Still another stimulus to the growth of Platonism was provided when Cosimo de' Medici (1389-1464), one of the great patrons of the Renaissance, founded the informal club that came to be known as the Platonic Academy. Its leader, Marsilio Ficino (1433-1499), is credited with producing the first complete Latin version of Plato's works.

Ficino also developed a philosophy which attempted to synthesize Platonic and Christian doctrines. To the humanistic belief in man's ability to attain the highest good, Ficino added the conviction that the ultimate end of all human desire and activity must be "boundless truth and goodness"—namely, God. Basic to Ficino's teachings was the belief that philosophy and religion complemented each other; each required the other if ignorance was to be avoided and man's highest spiritual goals attained. In working out his synthesis of Platonism and Christianity, Ficino coined the expression "Platonic love" to describe an ideal, pure love. This concept found its way into much of Renaissance literature.

Aristotelianism. Despite its great attraction for many humanists, Platonism still had a formidable rival in Aristotelianism. Concerned chiefly with natural philosophy, logic, and metaphysics, Aristotelian commentators still dominated teaching in the Italian universities.

The most influential Aristotelians were the Latin Averroists, followers of the Muslim philosopher Averroës (see p. 269). Averroës brought to the study of Aristotle an original and even mystical approach. He taught that matter is eternal and that all men partake of a single Intellect. Inasmuch as their individual souls are absorbed in the larger reality of the universal Intellect, men cannot attain personal immortality. This concept was directly opposed to the teachings of the Church. In fact, to combat the widespread views of the Averroists, in 1512 Church leaders felt impelled to establish the dogma of the immortality of the soul.

The Averroists' denial of personal immortality and their emphasis upon the relative insignificance of individual man aroused the ire of Petrarch and other humanists. The extent of Petrarch's hostility is seen in an extract from a letter asking a friend to

set all your strength and all your nerves to the fight against that frantic dog Averroes, who is prompted by an undescribable fury to bark at his Lord and Master Jesus Christ and the Catholic Faith.[10]

By the fifteenth century Padua had become the center of Aristotelianism, and in the next century Italian Aristotelianism reached its peak. By championing a secular rationalism that kept philosophy separate from theology, its adherents helped create an en-

vironment necessary for the triumph of scientific thought in the seventeenth century. As we shall see in Chapter 18, the new developments that Aristotelianism encouraged were to overthrow Aristotle's own brilliant but outmoded theories in physics and other fields of science.

Humanism and Christianity. Because of the rationalistic and strongly anticlerical attitudes of the Aristotelian humanists, many historians in the past concluded that, as a group, humanists were pagan, antireligious, and even secretly atheistic. We have already seen, however, that Petrarch was a devout believer in the Christian faith and that Ficino and his friends were concerned with synthesizing Platonic and Christian doctrines. Actually, there were few if any atheists among the humanists, and while numbers of both Aristotelians and Platonists were indifferent or hostile to Church authority, they were in revolt not against Christianity itself but against the presentation of Christianity as manifested in medieval Scholasticism. The humanists turned eagerly to the Scriptures and, by comparing them with the works of the Church Fathers and classical sources, performed a valuable service in Biblical philology. New and careful translations were made of the Psalms from Hebrew into Latin and of the New Testament from Greek into Latin. This study of the Scriptures was to culminate in Martin Luther's German version of the Bible, completed in 1531; the revision by Catholic scholars of the Vulgate Bible during the second half of the sixteenth century; and the King James Version, completed in England in 1611.

Evaluation of humanism. We owe the humanists a debt of gratitude for reintroducing Greek literature into the mainstream of western thought and for making more exact translations of Greek and Latin classics. From their reading of the classics, humanists came to understand the classical world in a true historical perspective and corrected many misconceptions about ancient times which had existed in the Middle Ages. Medieval scholars, for example, had pictured Alexander the Great's soldiers as knights, but Renaissance historians no longer made such naïve mistakes.

The transitional period in painting and sculpture is illustrated here by "Madonna and Child Enthroned" by Giotto (above); "The Virgin with Child and St. Francis" by Cimabue (top right); "Corruption of Judas," a detail from a painting for the high altar of the Cathedral of Siena, by Duccio (center right); and "Adoration of the Magi" by Niccola Pisano (bottom right).

On the other hand, although the humanists condemned medieval restrictions, they themselves were often subservient to the authorities of antiquity. Indeed, theirs was a closed culture whose boundaries had been set by ancient Greece and Rome, so that the only course open to the humanists was to retravel the old ground, not to explore uncharted territory. "We must note that the idea of a progressive development taking place in the course of centuries—the world moving forward to an unimagined future, to wider horizons and opening vistas—is a modern one. The idea of history as an ascending process was not part of the equipment of a Renaissance mind."[11]

The cult of classical letters gave rise to other defects. Humanist scholars were so dominated by Roman and Greek forms that they tended to imitate rather than to create for themselves. Their passion for Ciceronian Latin became pernicious; too often their writings were rich in form but barren in content. Intent on returning to antiquity, so to speak, the humanists resented the centuries separating them from the golden days of Greece and Rome. Unfortunately, this viewpoint resulted in their disparagement of the best works produced in the Middle Ages. Worse still, their preoccupation with classical authors retarded the growth of a much more vital vernacular literature—as in the case of Boccaccio, who gave up writing prose and poetry in Italian to devote himself to Latin studies.

The humanists' contributions to philosophy were not extensive; they did little original thinking. Nevertheless, because of their intimate acquaintance with classical literature, the humanists acquired habits of thought and forms of expression associated with Greek and Roman culture: clarity and elegance of literary style and a discriminating sense of taste and balance. The spread of humanistic influence resulted in a renewed and valuable emphasis upon the freedom and dignity of man as an individual and the importance of his place in the cosmos. As a corollary, the humanities encouraged men to express their personal reactions to their environment as Petrarch did when he climbed Mount Ventoux. The realization of the propriety and value of exploring one's personality and of analyzing individual experiences was manifested not only in literature but also in the fine arts.

ITALIAN RENAISSANCE ART

Transitional period in sculpture and painting. As we have noted in Chapter 13, the techniques of sculpture had developed throughout the Romanesque and Gothic periods. In Italy the influence of numerous examples of classical Graeco-Roman art added to this rich legacy. The process of synthesizing these aesthetic traditions began in thirteenth-century Pisa, a wealthy mercantile center and seaport.

The first noteworthy sculptor of this transitional period was Niccola Pisano (c. 1220-1278). Commissioned to make a pulpit for the baptistery of the new cathedral at Pisa, he designed panels which display an interesting mixture of classical and Gothic influences. For example, the Virgin in the "Adoration of the Magi" (p. 456) looks like a Roman matron, while the crowded arrangement of figures in the panel has a medieval aspect. From Pisa the new developments in sculpture spread to other Italian cities, and during the fourteenth century the synthesis of Gothic and classical techniques, together with the creation of new forms, continued.

The transition from the Middle Ages to the Renaissance in painting can be seen in the works of Cimabue, Duccio, and Giotto. At first glance, the painting of Cimabue (1240?-1302) of Florence appears medieval (see p. 456). The stilted angle of the heads, the flat, round halos, and the Byzantine custom of scratching lines in the painted garments so that the gold background shows through are all techniques of medieval painters. But in his search for fresh modes of expression, Cimabue took a step toward the use of three-dimensional treatment by making the figures of the child and some of the angels look round and real.

The works of the Sienese painter Duccio (1260?-1320?) also exhibit the blending of medieval and Renaissance techniques. Like Cimabue, Duccio adhered to some Byzantine conventions but strove also for greater realism: in the "Corruption of Judas" (p. 456) the figures are individualized. As the illustration shows, Duccio was masterful in his composition.

The most accomplished of the transitional painters was Giotto (1266-1336). Reportedly a pupil of Cimabue and a friend of Dante, renowned as a sculptor and an architect and acclaimed as a wit and a poet, this versatile artist broke new ground. In spite of his limited knowledge of anatomy, Giotto gave a keener sense of reality to his works than any of his predecessors had done. Compare Cimabue's Madonna with Giotto's; unlike Cimabue, Giotto endowed his figures with a high degree of weight and volume and simplified his composition to make a unified impact on the viewer. Giotto observed from life and painted a three-dimensional world peopled with believable human beings dramatically moved by deep emotion.

Quattrocento painting. The lull in painting that followed Giotto, during which his technical innovations were retained but the spirit and compassion that make him one of the world's great painters were lost, lasted until the beginning of the *quattrocento* (Italian for "four hundred," an abbreviation for the 1400's). In his brief life-time the Florentine Masaccio (1401-1428) completed the revolution in technique begun by Cimabue, Duccio, and Giotto. As can be seen in "St. Peter Healing the Sick with His Shadow" (see Color Plate 20), Masaccio largely mastered the problems of perspective, anatomical naturalism of flesh and bone, and the modeling of figures in light and shade rather than by sharp line. Masaccio was also the first to paint nude figures whose counterparts can be found in classical, but not in medieval, art.

Inspired by Masaccio's achievement, most *quattrocento* painters constantly sought to improve technique. This search for greater realism culminated in such painters as Andrea Mantegna (1431-1506), whose "St. James on the Way to His Execution" (p. 459) well shows the results of his lifelong study of perspective.

While Masaccio and his successors were intent upon giving their figures a new solidity and resolving the problem of three-dimensional presentation, a later Florentine painter, Sandro Botticelli (1447-1510), proceeded in a different direction, abandoning the techniques of straightforward representation of people and objects. Botticelli used a highly sensitive, even quivering, line to stir the viewer's imagination and emotion and to create a mood in keeping with his subject matter, frankly pagan at first but later deeply religious. Movement and the

Secular themes began to replace religious themes during the *quattrocento*. Designed by Francesco Pesellino, this wooden panel depicting the "Seven Liberal Arts" and the men who founded them was originally the front of a "cassone," or wedding chest, used to hold bridal garments. Seated in front of the "liberal arts" are, from left to right: Pythagoras, Euclid, Tubalcain, Ptolemy, Aristotle, Cicero, and either Priscian or Donatus.

ARISMETRICA·   GEOMETRIA·   ·MVSICA·   ASTRO   LOGIA·   ·LOGICA·   ·RETHORICA·   GRAMMATICA·

"St. James on the Way to His Execution" (left), a fresco by Andrea Mantegna, is innovative in its perspective and use of classical models. St. James, at the left, is shown blessing a Roman soldier and healing a paralytic. Mantegna's interest in historical detail is obvious in both the classical buildings and the costumes of the soldiers. Although strongly influenced by Mantegna's sophisticated perspective and composition, Giovani Bellini's work always retained a softness and naturalism never found in his brother-in-law's sculpturally modeled paintings. The "Madonna" (right) is characteristic not only of Bellini's naturalism but also of his graceful and symmetrical grouping of figures.

patterning of hair and drapery in such allegorical and mythological works as the "Primavera" are particularly sensitive (see Color Plate 21). The emphasis upon line as a means of communicating movement and mood led the renowned art critic Bernard Berenson to remark that Botticelli was "the greatest artist of linear design that Europe has ever had."[12]

While the outstanding contribution of Florentine artists had been to solve problems of space and depth, the most striking achievement of the Venetian school was to integrate that development with a greater mastery of color. The initial impetus in this development came from Mantegna's brother-in-law, Giovanni Bellini (1430?-1516), the greatest painter in fifteenth-century Venice. In his earlier years he was influenced by Mantegna, yet Bellini managed even then to give his paintings a quality of softness and pathos unknown in the work of his austere brother-in-law. His Madonnas have a special tenderness and femininity (see above), while his landscapes are enveloped in warm colors. Two of Bellini's pupils were Giorgione and Titian; these painters were later to bring the Venetian school to new heights of achievement.

Quattrocento sculpture. In the meantime progress was being made in sculpture, and it, like painting, reached stylistic maturity at the beginning of the *quattrocento*. In his two sets of bronze doors for the baptistery in Florence, on which he labored for forty-four years, Lorenzo Ghiberti (1378-1455) achieved the goal he had set for himself: "I strove to imitate nature as closely as I could, and with all the perspective I could produce." These marvels of relief sculpture (p. 460), which drew from Michelangelo the declaration that they were worthy to be the gates of paradise, depict skillfully modeled human figures—including some classically inspired nudes—which stand out spatially against architectural and landscape backgrounds.

Although Ghiberti was a superb craftsman, he was less of an innovator than his younger contemporary in Florence, Donatello (1386-1466), who visited Rome to study the remains of antique statuary. Divorcing sculpture from its architectural background, Donatello produced truly free-standing statues based on the realization of the human body as a functional, coordinated mechanism of bones, muscles, and sinews, maintaining itself against the pull of gravity. His "David" is the first bronze nude made since antiquity and his equestrian statue of Gattamelata the *condottiere* is the first of its type done in the Renaissance. The latter clearly reveals the influence of classical models and was probably inspired by the equestrian statue of Marcus Aurelius in Rome.

More dramatic than either of these equestrian statues is that of the Venetian *condottiere* Bartolomeo Colleoni (see p. 461), the creation of Andrea del Verrocchio (1435-1488). A versatile Florentine artist noteworthy as a sculptor, painter, and the teacher of Leonardo da Vinci, Verrocchio designed the statue of Colleoni to permit one of the horse's forelegs to be unsupported—a considerable achievement. The posture and features of the *condottiere*—as well as the bust of Lorenzo de' Medici (see Color Plate 19)—convey dramatically a sense of the supreme self-confidence and arrogance usually associated with Renaissance public figures.

Quattrocento architecture. Renaissance architecture, which far more than sculpture reflects the influence of ancient Roman models, began with the work of Filippo Brunelleschi (1377-1446). As a youth Brunelleschi accompanied Donatello to Rome where he employed measuring stick and sketchbook to master the principles of classical architecture. Returning to Florence, Brunelleschi constructed the lofty dome of the cathedral, the first to be built since Roman times. Although strongly influenced by classical architecture, Brunelleschi's buildings in Florence, which include churches and palaces, were not just copies of Roman models. Employing arcades of Roman arches, Roman pediments above the windows, and engaged Roman columns and other decorative motifs, Brunelleschi re-created the Roman style in a fresh and original manner.

The High Renaissance, 1500-1530. In April 1492, Lorenzo the Magnificent, ruler of Florence, lay dying. The story goes that

This scene from the Old Testament story of Joseph is one of the panels from the bronze doors of the baptistery in Florence. Designed by Lorenzo Ghiberti, the two magnificently decorated doors well deserve the title given them by Michelangelo—the "Gates of Paradise."

"Monument to Colleoni" by Andrea del Verocchio.

he sent for the Dominican preacher Savonarola, whose preaching had taken Florence by storm. When he arrived, Savonarola told Lorenzo that he must have faith in the mercy of God, restore all ill-gotten gains to the city, and give back to Florence its freedom from the rule of the Medici. Lorenzo agreed to the first two commands but remained silent upon hearing the third. No true son of the Medici could consider giving up control of Florence!

Lorenzo died on the eve of an era of great change and confusion. A new day was at hand for Italy, though not exactly the kind Savonarola may have hoped for. Two years after Lorenzo's death, Charles VIII of France swooped down on Italy, and for about fifty years the Italian states were the pawns of foreign powers. French, Spanish, and German armies fought on Italian soil, and all Europe became involved in the struggle for supremacy between rival Hapsburg and French kings. In Chapter 17 a detailed discussion of these political events will be given, but we should be aware of the confusion and chaos in Italy during the early sixteenth century. In fact, the turbulence of

conditions might, in a sense, be considered an expression of Renaissance individuality. Strangely enough, in the midst of this turmoil, the artistic genius of the Italian Renaissance reached a new peak of achievement.

During the High Renaissance the center of artistic activity shifted from Florence to Rome and Venice, where wealthier patrons lived and where consequently greater opportunities were available to artists. The popes were lavish patrons, and the greatest artists of the period worked in the Vatican at one time or another. It did not seem inconsistent to popes and artists to include representations of pagan mythological figures in the decorations of the papal palace, and thus the Vatican was filled with secular as well as religious art.

The great architect of the High Renaissance was Donato Bramante (1444-1514) from Milan. Bramante's most important commission came in 1506 when Pope Julius II requested him to rebuild St. Peter's. Like some of the architects of the early Renaissance, Bramante designed a strictly centralized church in the form of a Greek cross instead of a longitudinal church such as tradition might have dictated. The inspiration to construct St. Peter's on symmetrical principles with the altar at the center was in keeping with current Platonic concepts that architectural forms should be expressed as mathematical harmonies. The desire for a building of this type also emphasized the extent to which humanistic thought influenced the papacy itself.[13]

Bramante's plan called for a structure surmounted by an immense dome. The exterior of St. Peter's exemplifies the spirit of High Renaissance architecture—to approach nearer to the monumentality and grandeur of Roman architecture. In Bramante's own words, he would place "the Pantheon on top of the Basilica of Maxentius." Bramante died when the cathedral was barely begun, and it was left to Michelangelo and others to complete the work (see illustrations, p. 462).

High Renaissance architects also produced magnificent palaces and other secular buildings. The decorative features of the Palazzo Farnese in Rome show how classical details

Bramante designed St. Peter's in the shape of a Greek cross with a dome similar to that of the Pantheon. After his death, however, his plan was modified. Michelangelo redesigned the dome, and later a long nave was added to the front of the church, giving it the form of a Latin cross rather than of a Greek cross. Michelangelo's greatness as an architect was first apparent in the vestibule of the Laurentian Library (below), built to house the Medici collection of books and manuscripts. Although his design was based on classical features, Michelangelo made several changes which broke tradition. A primary change was building the columns into the wall. The vestibule is much higher than it is wide or long, and the walls pushing in between the columns, the empty niches, and the fan-shaped, cascading stairs all add to this feeling of compression.

blended in a new fashion resulted in an impressive and refined structure. From the sixteenth century on, all Europe began to take to the new architecture.

The painters of the High Renaissance inherited the solutions to such technical problems as perspective space from the *quattrocento* artists. But whereas the artists of the earlier period had been concerned with movement, color, and narrative detail, painters in the High Renaissance strove to eliminate nonessentials and concentrated on the central theme of a picture and its basic human implications. By this process of elimination, many High Renaissance painters achieved a "classic" effect of seriousness and serenity and endowed their works with idealistic values.

Leonardo da Vinci. The great triad of High Renaissance painters consists of Leonardo da Vinci, Raphael, and Michelangelo. An extraordinary man, Leonardo da Vinci (1452-1519) was proficient in a variety of fields: engineering, mathematics, architecture, geology, botany, physiology, anatomy, sculpture, painting, music, and poetry. He was always experimenting, with the result that few of the projects he started were ever finished. As a fellow artist of the period wrote:

Leonardo . . . commenced various undertakings, many of which he never completed, because it appeared to him that the hand could never give its due perfection to the object or purpose which he had in his thoughts, or beheld in his imagination . . . .[14]

A superb draftsman, Leonardo was also a master of soft modeling in full light and shade and of creating groups of figures perfectly balanced in a given space. One of his most famous paintings is the "Mona Lisa," a portrait of a woman whose enigmatic smile has intrigued art lovers for centuries. Another is "The Last Supper," a study of the moment when Christ tells His twelve disciples that one will betray Him. When he painted this picture on the walls of the refectory of Santa Maria delle Grazie in Milan, Leonardo was experimenting with the use of an oil medium combined with plaster, and, unfortunately, the experiment was unsuccessful. The painting began quickly to disintegrate and has had to be repainted several times.

Last of the great Florentine painters, Leonardo developed the artistry of the *quattrocento* painters to its highest point. He combined an advanced knowledge of technique with deep psychological insight into many facets of human nature (see pp. 450-451).

Raphael. The second of the great triad of High Renaissance painters was Raffaello Santi, better known as Raphael (1483-1520). Summoned to Rome by Bramante to aid in the decoration of the Vatican, Raphael absorbed something of Leonardo's intellectuality and Michelangelo's "body dynamics" and grandeur while retaining his own incomparable style. Displaying a magnificent blending of classical and Christian subject matter, the Stanze frescoes in the Vatican are imbued with a clarity and breadth of vision expressive of the High Renaissance at its best. Considered by some critics as unrivaled in the mastery of space composition, Raphael was equally at home in handling a single figure or in grouping masses —in every case endowing his work with a maximum of spaciousness and freedom. (Examples of his paintings are on pp. 111 and 465.)

Michelangelo. The individualism and idealism of the High Renaissance have no greater representative than Michelangelo Buonarroti (1475-1564). Stories of this stormy and temperamental personality have helped to shape our ideas of what a genius is like. Indeed, there is something almost superhuman about both Michelangelo and his art. His great energy enabled him to complete in four years the entire work of painting the ceiling of the Vatican's Sistine Chapel, an area of several thousand square yards, and his art embodies a superhuman ideal of man. With his unrivaled genius for rendering the human form, he devised a wealth of expressive positions and attitudes for his figures in scenes from Genesis. Their physical splendor is pagan, but their spirit is Christian (see p. 465).

Michelangelo considered himself first and foremost a sculptor, and this *uomo universale,* who also excelled as poet, engineer, and architect, was undoubtedly the greatest

sculptor of the Renaissance. The glorification of the human body, particularly the male
nude, was Michelangelo's great achievement.
Fired by the grandeur of such newly discovered pieces of Hellenistic sculpture as
the Apollo Belvedere and the Laocoön group
and strongly influenced by Platonism, he
expressed in art his idealized view of man's
dignity and majesty (see Color Plate 22).

Writing as an old man, Michelangelo displayed ironic humor in describing himself:

I live alone confined like the pith in a tree. My
teeth rattle like the keys of a musical instrument;
my face is a scarecrow; in one ear a spider spins
its web; in the other a cricket chirps all night;
my catarrh rattles in my throat and will not let
me sleep. This is the end to which art, which
proves my glory, has brought me.[15]

His last years, however, were not inactive
ones. He became chief architect of St.
Peter's, designed the great dome (see p. 462),
and was in the midst of creative activities
when he died, almost in his ninetieth year,
in 1564. He had long outlived the High Renaissance.

The Venetian school. We have already
mentioned the flowering of Renaissance art
in Venice during the *quattrocento,* due largely
to the impetus given it by Giovanni Bellini.
Venice offered a congenial environment to
artists. A prosperous merchant-prince could
well afford to play the role of patron of the
arts; trade with the East provided Venetians
with luxuries and comforts which added
splendor and color to daily life; and the
beauty of the city itself would attract the eye
of any artist.

This wealthy, sophisticated milieu produced a secular rather than a devotional
school of painting. Most Venetian artists
were satisfied with the here and now; they
were not overly concerned with antiquity
or classical canons. While they sometimes
painted exquisite Madonnas, they more
often painted wealthy merchants and proud
doges, attired in rich brocades, jewels, and
precious metals and grouped with beautiful
young women who scarcely looked like
Madonnas. There is a sensuousness in the
Venetian painting of this period which is
evident in the artists' love of decoration,

rich costumes, and striking nude figures.

Giorgione (1478-1511), like Botticelli,
used classical themes and idyllic landscapes in his paintings. But unlike the Florentine master, who made his mythological
figures imaginative and idealized, Giorgione's muses and Venuses were lovely
Venetian models.

The pictures of Titian (1485?-1576) contain sensuous beauties of color and atmosphere. During his long working life he
proved himself a master of a wide variety
of subjects ranging from religion to pagan
mythology. His portraits, which earned him
the greatest fame among his contemporaries,
show the Venetian love of color and texture
of rich fabrics, although these elements
are subordinated to the portrayal of the
sitter's character (see the portrait of Pope
Paul III on p. 504 and illustration, p. 465).

High Renaissance music. In contrast to
the single-voiced or homophonic music
—called plain song or Gregorian chant—of
the early Middle Ages, the late medieval
composers wrote many-voiced, many-melo-
died, or polyphonic music. Polyphony often
involved a shuttling back and forth from one
melody to another—musical counterpoint.
By the fifteenth century as many as twenty-
four voice parts were combined into one
intricately woven musical pattern. The composers of the High Renaissance continued
to produce complicated polyphonic music,
but in a calmer and grander manner. Compared with the style of his predecessors,
that of Josquin des Près (d. 1521), the
founder of High Renaissance music, "is
both grander and more simple. All stark
intervals of early polyphony are ruled out;
few dissonances are used, and the rhythms
and forms used are based on strict symmetry
and mathematically regular proportions.
Josquin handled all technical problems of
complicated constructions with the same
ease and sureness one finds in the drawings
of Leonardo and Raphael."[16] During the
sixteenth century, also, instruments such
as the violin, spinet, and harpsichord developed from more rudimentary types.

The Renaissance in Italy stimulated many
new forms of secular music, especially the
madrigal, a love lyric set to music. The

Michelangelo's "Creation of Adam" (top), one of the major scenes on the ceiling of the Sistine Chapel, depicts God, with Eve protected under His left arm, instilling life in Adam by merely pointing His finger. The frescoed figures have a sculptural quality that creates an illusion of roundness and depth. While Michelangelo used the human figure as an expression of spirituality and sublime beauty, Raphael's works stressed the earthly qualities of natural human beauty. Although the subject matter is religious, his "Madonna of the Chair" (bottom right) is endowed with a warm, human quality. This painting also demonstrates Raphael's concern for form and equilibrium within a composition. Titian's paintings are marked by their sensuousness and intense, jewel-like colors. His "Young Woman at Her Toilet" (bottom left) typifies his favorite theme of warm feminine beauty.

madrigal found favor in England, while French *chansons* and German *lieder* added to the growing volume of secular music.

THE NORTHERN RENAISSANCE

The northward spread of the Renaissance. The Italian Renaissance had projected man once more into the center of life's stage and permeated the intellectual and artistic environment with humanistic values. In time the stimulating ideas current in Italy spread to other areas and combined with indigenous developments to produce a French Renaissance, an English Renaissance, and so on.

The increase in town life in northern Europe fostered a class of merchants and bankers and a more sophisticated cultural climate. The men of the northern cities were stimulated by the ideas which merchants carried with them over the Alps from Italy. But while the wealthy burghers patronized the work of artists and scholars, the prime sponsors of the Renaissance north of the Alps were often the kings of the new national states. By importing artists and learned men from Italy or supporting native geniuses, the rulers added brilliance to their courts.

The influence of printing. Perhaps even more important in the diffusion of the Renaissance and later in the success of the Reformation was the invention of printing in Europe. The essential elements—paper and movable type—had long been known in non-European cultures. As early as the second century the Chinese had made paper from rags and other materials. In the eighth century the Muslims had created a cotton paper which, along with its linen counterpart, entered Europe through Spain. By the eleventh century the enterprising Chinese had invented movable type, but the system was not put to use in Europe until 1448. In his printing shop at Mainz, Germany, John Gutenberg used movable type to print papal documents and the first published version of the Bible (1454).

Within fifty years after Gutenberg's Bible had been published, all the major countries of Europe possessed the means for printing books. It is said that the prices of books soon sank to one eighth of their former cost, thus placing books within the reach of a multitude of people who formerly had been unable to buy them. The availability of books encouraged more men to read, and learning was no longer the private domain of the Church or of those few laymen wealthy enough to own hand-copied volumes. At first the Church tried to use printing to further its own ends and attempted also to control what was printed, but such censorship was futile. It was now possible and profitable to cater to the tastes of the common people, and pamphlets and controversial tracts soon were widely circulated. As a result, knowledge and new ideas reached a thousand times more people in a relatively short span of time. In the quickening of Europe's intellectual life, it is difficult to overestimate the effects of the printing press.

Erasmus and northern Humanism. The intellectual life of the first half of the sixteenth century was dominated by Desiderius Erasmus (1466?-1536). Born in Rotterdam, he passed most of his long life elsewhere —in Germany, France, England, Italy, and especially Switzerland. The most influential and cosmopolitan of the northern humanists, he corresponded with nearly every prominent writer and thinker in Europe and knew personally popes, emperors, and kings. He was *the* scholar of Europe, and his writings were read eagerly everywhere.

Perhaps the most famous and influential work by Erasmus was *In Praise of Folly*, a satire written in 1511 at the house of the English humanist Sir Thomas More. The book concerns a female character called Folly, Erasmus' conception of human nature, who is represented as delivering a lecture to university students. A historian has described the work in these words: "At first the book makes kindly and approving fun of the ways of action and the foibles and weaknesses of mankind. It is not mordant, only amused. But gradually from fools innocent and natural and undebased, it passes to those whose illusions are vicious in their setting and results."[17] Among such are merchants ("they lie, swear, cheat, and practice all the intrigues of dishonesty"), lawyers ("they of all men have the greatest conceit of their own abilities"), Scholastic philosophers ("that talk as much by rote as a parrot"), and scientists ("who esteem themselves the only favourites of wisdom, and look upon the rest of mankind as the dirt and rubbish of the creation"). Most roughly handled are churchmen, in particular monks, who are "impudent pretenders to the profession of piety," and popes, cardinals, and bishops, "who in pomp and splendour have almost equalled if not outdone secular princes." While his satire is indeed harsh, Erasmus was himself balanced, moderate, and intolerant only of bigotry, ignorance, greed, and violence.

In Praise of Folly points up a significant difference between the northern humanists and their Italian predecessors. While both were repelled by much that seemed to them wrong in the life of their day, their reactions took different forms. The typical Italian humanist followed the course set by Petrarch: "In order to forget my own time I have constantly striven to place myself in spirit in other ages. . . ."[18] Disdaining such escapism, the great majority of northern humanists faced up to reality and became reformers of their society's ills. They also went further in broadening their interest in ancient literature to include early Christian writings—the Scriptures and the works of the Church Fathers. This led them to prepare new and more accurate editions of the Scriptures—Erasmus' Greek edition of the New Testament became famous and was used by Luther—and to compare unfavorably the complexities of the Church in their own day with the simplicity of primitive Christianity. Since the northern humanists held that the essence of religion was morality and rational piety—what Erasmus called the "philosophy of Christ"—rather than ceremony and dogma, it is not surprising that the Church became a major target of their reforming zeal.

Sir Thomas More's Utopia. The most significant figure in English humanism was Sir Thomas More (1478-1535), the famous friend of Erasmus. More is best known for his *Utopia*, the first important description of the ideal state since Plato's *Republic*. In his epoch-making work More criticized his age by using as his spokesman a fictitious sailor who contrasts the ideal life he has seen in Utopia (The Land of Nowhere) with the harsh conditions of life in England. More's denunciations centered on the new acquisitive capitalism, which he blamed for the widespread insecurity and misery of the lower classes. More felt that governments

Although printing was a far superior system of reproducing books than hand copying, it still was a slow, tedious, and expensive process. A copy of the Gutenberg Bible cost forty-two gulden, a price equivalent to that of fourteen oxen. Although large books were beyond the means of most common people, the presses turned out small books, pamphlets, and circulars in large quantities for common consumption.

are a conspiracy of the rich, who, in pretence of managing the public, only pursue their private ends, . . . first, that they may, without danger, preserve all that they have so ill acquired, and then, that they may engage the poor to toil and labor for them at as low rates as possible, and oppress them as much as they please.[19]

In Utopia, by contrast, no man is in want because the economy is planned and cooperative and because property is held in

Sir Thomas More, sketched by Hans Holbein the Younger as Lord Chancellor (left), is the author of what is considered England's first major contribution to Renaissance literature. His *Utopia,* technically classified as a romance, is really a humanist criticism of man and the society of his time. In the work More describes a fictional land called Utopia, supposedly located off the coast of South America. The frontispiece of the 1516 edition of *Utopia* (center) pictures an artist's conception of the island. At right is the alphabet which More devised for the citizens of his ideal state.

common. Utopia is the only true commonwealth, concludes More's imaginary sailor:

In all other places, it is visible that while people talk of a commonwealth, every man only seeks his own wealth: but there, where no man has any property, all men zealously pursue the good of the public. . . . in Utopia, where every man has a right to every thing, they all know that if care is taken to keep the public stores full, no private man can want any thing; for among them there is no unequal distribution, so that no man is poor, none in necessity; and though no man has any thing, yet they are all rich; for what can make a man so rich as to lead a serene and cheerful life, free from anxieties; neither apprehending want himself, nor vexed with the endless complaints of his wife?[20]

In writing *Utopia,* More was undoubtedly influenced by Plato's *Republic.* As a humanist, he read Plato avidly and must have been attracted to the idea of presenting the philosophical and sociological principles for an ideal state by means of fiction. In turn, More gave to Francis Bacon and many later writers the incentive to write about

ideal societies in fictional form. The word *utopia* has passed into the language, signifying an ideal society not likely to be achieved; and the adjective *utopian* has come to mean "visionary."

More was the first of the modern English socialists, but his philosophy should not be considered a forerunner of the socialism of our day. His economic outlook was a legacy from the Middle Ages, and his preference for medieval collectivism over modern individualism was of a piece with his preference for a Church headed—medieval style—by popes rather than by kings, a view that prompted Henry VIII to execute him for treason (see p. 498).

Rabelais. One of the best known of the French humanists was Francois Rabelais (1494-1553). A brilliant, if coarse, lover of all life from the sewers to the heavens, Rabelais is best remembered for his work *Gargantua and Pantagruel* (published 1533-1552). Centering on figures from French folklore, this work relates the adventures of Gargantua and his son Pantagruel, genial giants of tremendous stature and appetite, to whom were ascribed many marvelous feats.

In the course of his pungent narrative, Rabelais inserted his views on educational reform and his humanistic belief in man's inherent goodness and ability to solve his problems by reason. He made vitriolic attacks on the abuses of the Church and the shortcomings of Scholastics and monks, but he had little patience with overzealous Protestants either. What Rabelais could not stomach was hypocrisy and repression; and for those guilty of these tendencies, he reserved his choicest invective. In the following excerpt he bids his readers to flee from that

rabble of squint-minded fellows, dissembling and counterfeit saints, demure lookers, hypocrites, pretended zealots, tough friars, buskin-monks, and other such sects of men, who disguise themselves like masquers to deceive the world. . . . Fly from these men, abhor and hate them as much as I do, and upon my faith you will find yourself the better for it. And if you desire . . . . *to live in peace, joy, health, making yourselves always merry,* never trust those men that always peep out through a little hole.[21]

Von Hutten: German humanist and patriot. One of the outstanding German humanists was Ulrich von Hutten (1488-1523). In him was blended a hatred of ecclesiastical abuses with romantic nationalist feelings. This scion of an aristocratic family, who wanted to unite Germany under the emperor, led a tumultuous life as a wandering Greek scholar and satirist. He supported Luther as a rallying point for German unity against the papacy, to which Von Hutten attributed most of his compatriots' ills. Although he neither reconciled his humanistic philosophy with Luther's theology nor formulated a practical political program, Von Hutten reflected the tensions and aspirations of the German people in the early years of the sixteenth century.

Montaigne. The last notable northern humanist was the French skeptic Michel de Montaigne (1533-1592). The product of a splendid classical education, Montaigne had been taught Latin in his infancy by a German tutor who knew no French, so that the boy went off to school more fluent in Latin than in his mother tongue. Despite a career in law, he found his chief satisfaction in the well-stocked library at his country estate, where he studied and wrote.

Montaigne developed a new literary form and gave it its name—the essay. In ninety-four essays he set forth his personal views on many subjects: leisure, friendship, education, cannibalism, drunkenness, old age, and so forth. He did not pretend to have the final answer to the problems he discussed. Instead, he advocated open-mindedness and toleration—rare qualities in the sixteenth century, when France was racked by religious and civil strife.

Montaigne was soon considered the leading French humanist of his day. But at the time he began his literary career, the defects of humanism were revealing themselves, and he held these defects up to public view. He condemned the pedantry into which humanism had largely degenerated and sharply criticized the education offered his contemporaries, arguing that "To know by heart is not to know; it is to retain what we have given our memory to keep."[22] Even today's student may have cause to listen sympathetically to the following words:

Our tutors never stop bawling into our ears, as though they were pouring water into a funnel; and our task is only to repeat what has been told us. I should like the tutor to correct this practice . . . I want him to listen to his pupil speaking in his turn.[23]

Montaigne was not only the originator of the modern essay; he was also a thinker who realized that it is more important to solve the problems of life than the syntax of an obscure sentence from Horace. Montaigne's final essay, entitled "Of Experience," which developed the thought that "when reason fails us we resort to experience," is an acknowledgement of the bankruptcy of humanism and a foreshadowing of the coming triumph of science.

Cervantes, creator of Don Quixote. The transition from feudal knight to Renaissance courtier finds its greatest literary expression in a masterpiece of Spanish satire, *Don Quixote de la Mancha,* the work of Miguel de Cervantes (1547-1616). By Cervantes' day knighthood had become an anachronism, though its accompanying code of chivalry still retained its appeal in the new royal courts. It remained for a rationalist like Cervantes to show up the inadequacies of chivalric idealism in a world that had acquired new, and intensely practical, aims. He did so by creating a pathetic but infinitely appealing character to serve as the personification of an outmoded way of life.

Don Quixote, the "knight of the woeful countenance," mounted on his "lean, lank, meagre, drooping, sharp-backed, and rawboned" steed Rozinante, sets out in the Spanish countryside to right wrongs and uphold his lady's and his own honor. In his misadventures he is accompanied by his squire, the much less gallant but infinitely more realistic Sancho Panza, whose peasant adages and hard-grained common sense serve as a contrast to the unpractical nature of his master's chivalric code. Tilting at windmills, mistaking serving wenches for highborn ladies and inns for castles, and lamenting the invention of gunpowder as depriving ardent knights of a chance to win immortality, Don Quixote is, on the surface at least, a ridiculous old man whose nostalgia for the "good old days" is a constant source of grief to him. Thus the story represents a superb satire directed against the outworn ideology of the Middle Ages; in particular, it laughed the ideal of chivalric romance into the world of make-believe.

And yet *Don Quixote* is still more. Cervantes instilled in his main character a pathos born in large measure of the author's own career of frustrated hopes and ambitions. As a result, Don Quixote becomes more than a romantic lunatic; he serves to embody that set of ideals which each of us would like to see realized but which we must compromise in a world that has other interests to serve. Because of its universality and poignancy, Cervantes' novel ascended from the merely funny to the truly comic and gave to western thought the concept summed up in the adjective *quixotic*.

Humanist poets in France and England: Ronsard and Spenser. The impact of the Italian Renaissance and of classical letters led to the establishment in both France and England of new groups or schools of poetry, closely connected with court life. In Paris young poet-scholars attempted to elevate both the French language and French poetry by basing their work on classical models. But for the most part they produced slavish and arid copies—a chronic ailment among humanists at this time. Among their numbers, however, was one poet of genius, Pierre de Ronsard (1524-1585).

Ronsard's classical imitations greatly influenced later French poetry; yet today he is best known for his charming and sensitive lyrics. Here is one of his well-known sonnets:

When you are very old, at evening
You'll sit and spin beside the fire, and say,
Humming my songs, "Ah well, ah well-a-day!
When I was young, of me did Ronsard sing."
None of your maidens that doth hear the thing,
    Albeit with her weary task foredone,
    But wakens at my name, and calls you one
Blest, to be held in long remembering.
I shall be low beneath the earth, and laid
On sleep, a phantom in the myrtle shade,
    While you beside a fire, a grandame gray;
My love, your pride, remember and regret;
Ah, love me, love! we may be happy yet,
    And gather roses, while 'tis called to-day.[24]

The spring of lyric song that bubbled up in the England of Henry VIII formed a veritable stream of verse that sparkled through his daughter Elizabeth's countryside. Her reign (1558-1603) climaxed the English Renaissance and produced such a galaxy of talented writers that some scholars have felt it necessary to go back as far as Athens in the fifth century B.C. to find an age as prodigal of literary genius. Strongly influenced by the royal court, which served as the busy center of intellectual and artistic as well as of economic and political life, their writings were highly colored, richly romantic, and often wildly extravagant in spite of all their poetic allusions to classical times. Experimenting with the sonnet form, talented courtiers gave it a new rhyme scheme with the final two lines rhyming as a couplet. Known as the English sonnet, this form was to find its highest expression as a vehicle for Shakespeare.

The influence of classical studies, Italian Renaissance poets, and earlier English poets, chiefly Chaucer, is apparent in the work of the "poets' poet" Edmund Spenser (c. 1552-1599). His masterpiece, *The Faerie Queene* (1590-1596), is a lengthy narrative poem in which classical and humanist elements are interwoven with Arthurian romance and medieval allegory. The poem is, in large measure, a glorification of that chivalric ideal which Cervantes took such delight in satirizing. For that reason, perhaps, the modern reader finds it overfanciful, too remote and academic—even boring. Yet the work abounds in exquisite imagery, color, and verbal melody. Though there was a pseudo-archaic quality both in the vocabulary and in the very concept of the poem, *The Faerie Queene* markedly influenced Spenser's fellow poets and still remains the most significant narrative poem of the Elizabethan Age.

Secular drama appears. Like Greek drama, medieval drama developed out of religious ceremonies; it was used by the Church primarily for purposes of visual instruction. Miracle and morality plays drew townsmen to the church or to an adjacent temporary stage to witness the enactment of Biblical scenes. Although naïve secular elements were introduced, a complete divorce of the Church and stage did not occur until the middle of the fifteenth century when the Renaissance era of drama began in Italian cities with the performance of ancient Roman comedies. In the following century appeared the *commedia dell'arte*, reflections of everyday life in vulgar and slapstick fashion usually improvised by the players from a plot outline.

As secular dramas grew in popularity, theaters were built as permanent settings for their presentations. Great ingenuity was shown in the design of elaborate, realistic stage scenery as well as in lighting and sound effects. Theaters embodying these innovations only gradually appeared outside Italy. Not until 1576 was the first public theater erected in London; three years later, a similar theater was constructed in Madrid.

Imitating the ancient models they admired, French and Italian writers followed what they believed were the rigid conventions of the classical drama and, to a large extent, catered to the aristocracy. By contrast, the medieval folk plays in Spain and England had created in both these countries a theatrical environment that was at once more socially democratic, more hospitable to national themes, and less concerned with classical models.

Lope de Vega, the prolific Spanish dramatist. Free of classical restraints are the plays of Shakespeare's contemporary Lope de Vega (1562-1635), the prodigious Spanish playwright who claimed to have written some fifteen hundred plays. Although only a third of this number survive, he must be considered history's champion mass producer of plays. A rapid worker, he did not portray his characters with the psychological depth that Shakespeare did; most of them are conventional types: the wise monarch, the cruel feudal noble, the young lovers, the proud peasant, and the witty clown, whose outrageous but shrewd comments inject both comedy and realism into the play.

Lope de Vega's genius was for plot construction. His comedies, melodramas, histories, and sacred plays offer intriguing variations on three basic themes—religious, nationalist, and romantic—attesting to his countrymen's devotion to *Dios, el rey, y mi dama* (God, the king, and my lady). Celebrated during his lifetime, Lope de Vega was the most important influence in the development of native Spanish drama.

Christopher Marlowe, author of Dr. Faustus. As in Spain, playwrights in England were familiar with classical drama yet could draw upon a popular dramatic tradition sufficiently vigorous to enable them to assert their independence of classical models. This significant trait is seen clearly in the plays of Christopher Marlowe (1564-1593), the most brilliant English dramatist prior to Shakespeare.

After graduating from Cambridge, young Marlowe became a member of the Earl of Nottingham's company of players and subsequently began to write dramas. Little is known about the last years of his all-too-brief life, but it is recorded that he was killed in a tavern brawl in 1593. Marlowe wrote several tragedies of tremendous vitality and force. His themes concerned power and its tragic implications for those who would wield it.

Marlowe's most famous play is *Doctor Faustus* (c. 1589-1592). The story is based on a German legend about a magician who, being dissatisfied with the limits set by God upon human knowledge, sells his soul to Lucifer in return for superhuman power. Marlowe converts the old tale into an agonizing conflict between Faustus' conscience and the Archfiend for the doctor's soul. Over two centuries later the great German writer Goethe was to build his masterpiece upon this universal theme.

William Shakespeare. The supreme figure in Elizabethan literature and perhaps in all literature is William Shakespeare (1564-1616). Our knowledge of his life is limited, but the scanty records show that he was born in Stratford-on-Avon and as a young man with little formal schooling went to London, where he was employed as an actor and wrote his plays. Eventually he acquired sufficient means to retire to Stratford, where he died.

We can only touch briefly upon a few facets of this versatile genius. His rich vocabulary and poetic imagery were matched only by his turbulent imagination. He was a superb lyric poet, and numerous critics have judged him the foremost sonnet writer in the English language. Below is one of his most beautiful sonnets:

Shall I compare thee to a summer's day?
Thou art more lovely and more temperate:
Rough winds do shake the darling buds of May,
And summer's lease hath all too short a date:
Sometime too hot the eye of heaven shines,
And often is his gold complexion dimm'd;
And every fair from fair sometime declines,
By chance or nature's changing course un-
    trimm'd;
But thy eternal summer shall not fade
Nor lose possession of that fair thou owest;
Nor shall Death brag thou wander'st in his shade,
When in eternal lines to time thou growest:
    So long as men can breathe or eyes can see,
    So long lives this and this gives life to thee.[25]

Shakespeare wrote thirty-eight plays—histories, comedies, and tragedies. His historical plays reflected the patriotic upsurge experienced by Englishmen as their country grew stronger and more prosperous. For his comedies and tragedies, Shakespeare was content in a great majority of cases to borrow plots from earlier works. His forte lay in his creation of characters—perhaps the richest and most diversified collection conceived by the mind of one man—and in his ability to translate his knowledge of human nature into dramatic speech and action. Today his comedies are played to enthusiastic audiences: *The Taming of the Shrew, As You Like It, The Merchant of Venice, Merry Wives of Windsor,* to mention but a few. But it is in his tragedies that the poet-dramatist runs the gamut of human emotions and experience. Shakespeare possessed in abundance the Renaissance concern for man and the world about him. Hence his plays deal first and foremost with man's personality, passions, and problems. In such works as *Romeo and Juliet, Measure for Measure,* and *Troilus and Cressida,* the problems of love and sex are studied from many angles. Jealousy is analyzed in *Othello,* ambition in *Macbeth* and *Julius Caesar,* family relationships in *King Lear,* and man's struggle with his own soul in *Hamlet.* Shakespeare's extraordinary ability to build every concrete fact and action upon a universal truth makes his observations as applicable today as they were when first presented in the Globe Theater. Small wonder that next to the Bible, Shakespeare is the most quoted of all literary sources in the language.

Developments in painting: Van Eyck, Dürer, Holbein, Brueghel. Before the Italian Renaissance permeated the artistic circles of northern Europe, the painters of the Low Countries had been making significant advances on their own. Outstanding among the painters were the brothers Van Eyck, especially Jan van Eyck (1385?-1440). His work has been called "the full flowering of the spirit of the late Middle Ages,"[26] but in fact it was just as revolutionary in its own way as that of the great Florentines. In a detailed, realistic manner, his paintings depict many different sorts of Flemish people

Sir John Falstaff Knight

Drawn by William Shakspere. *Etched by Geo. Cruikshank.*

The Tragicall History
of the Life and Death
of *Doctor Faustus*.

Written by *Ch. Mar*

LONDON,
Printed for *Iohn Wright*, and are to be fold at his fhop
without Newgate, at the figne of the
Bi* 1636.

The late sixteenth century witnessed considerable literary brilliance. The three authors whose works are represented here all created characters so vivid and so important that they are recognized by everyone today, almost four hundred years later. The intensity of the images these writers created is illustrated by the engraving of Sir John Falstaff by the famed nineteenth-century caricaturist, George Cruikshank, who credits his work as "drawn by William Shakespere, etched by Geo. Cruikshank." Second only to Shakespeare in English drama is Christopher Marlowe. Dr. Faustus, the main character of Marlowe's most famous play, is depicted on the title page of the 1636 edition of *Dr. Faustus*. So powerful is the character of Dr. Faustus that he has reappeared frequently, sometimes under a different name, in the novels, operas, and short stories of later times. A third great character of this era, created by the Spanish writer Miguel de Cervantes, is Don Quixote, shown on an adventure with his squire, Sancho Panza, in a print from an early German edition of *Don Quixote de la Mancha*.

Northern Renaissance painting, with its original Gothic realism (see Color Plate 23), began to be affected by the Italian tendency toward naturalism and secularism at the end of the fifteenth century. One of the first German painters influenced by the Italian style was Albrecht Dürer. His copper engraving "Melancholia I" (left) is typical of his combination of the new style with medieval subject matter. Personified in female form, Melancholy broods in frustration, surrounded by the symbols of intellect and activity but unable to create. Italian influences derived from Mantegna's work are evident in Dürer's treatment of space, texture, line, and detail. In the "Legend of Sts. Elegius and Godeberta" by the Flemish painter Petrus Christus (Lehman collection, New York), St. Elegius is weighing the wedding rings of a betrothed couple. Realism and an emphasis on materialism are evident in the detail and numerous physical objects in the painting. In "Landscape with the Fall of Icarus" (detail, right) Pieter Brueghel the Elder has depicted an ancient myth as though it occurred in contemporary Flanders. Icarus (lower right) plunges into the water unnoticed by the herdsman and farmer, who continue their work.

and costumes (see Color Plate 23). In his portraits Van Eyck achieved a new level of individuality.

The first talented German painter to be influenced deeply by Italian art was Albrecht Dürer (1471-1528) of Nuremberg. Dürer made more than one journey to Italy, where he was impressed both with the painting of the Renaissance Italians and with the artists' high social status—a contrast with northern Europe, where artists were still treated as craftsmen. Because he did not entirely lose many of the medieval qualities

of the milieu in which he worked, his own work is a blend of the old and the new; but among German artists he did the most to break away from medieval standards and to incorporate ideas from Italy. In the long run Dürer became better known for his numerous engravings and woodcuts than for his paintings.

Another German painter, Hans Holbein the Younger (1497-1543), was less imaginative than Dürer; but whereas the latter lived principally in Germany and interpreted its spirit, the younger artist worked abroad, especially in England, and as a result his painting acquired a more cosmopolitan character. It has been said that "Holbein was the first painter north of the Alps to belong entirely to the Renaissance."[27] In his portraits of such figures as Sir Thomas More, Henry VIII, and Erasmus, Holbein demonstrated the Renaissance emphasis on the individual man (see also Color Plate 24).

While many Flemish painters lost their northern individuality in the rush to adopt Italian techniques, Pieter Brueghel the Elder (1525?-1569) retained a strong Flemish flavor in his portrayal of the faces and scenes of his native land. Possessing a strong affection for life in the country towns, Brueghel painted village squares, skating scenes, peasant weddings, and dances. He also took Biblical or mythological themes and depicted them as if the events were taking place in the Flanders of his own day. The depiction of everyday scenes in realistic fashion is known as *genre* painting; and in this medium, Pieter Brueghel and the Flemish school as a whole remained unexcelled.

SUMMARY

In the Middle Ages man had thought and acted primarily as a member of a community —a manor, a guild, or, above all, the universal Christian community represented by the Church and the Holy Roman Empire. But gradually, for a variety of reasons, he began to attach importance to himself as an individual and to develop an interest in worldly things for their own sake without relation to the divine. This new individualistic and secular spirit, the period in which it became prominent, and the ways in which it manifested itself in art, literature, and learning we call the Renaissance.

The change took place earliest in Italy and first expressed itself in the great intellectual movement known as humanism. In its early stages humanism was a revival of classical learning. Wealthy patrons sponsored the search for ancient manuscripts, and scholars eagerly introduced the literature of Greece and Rome into schools and universities. This reverence for antiquity led to the copying of classical literary and artistic forms, and many humanists wasted on such imitation talents which might better have been employed in creating original literature in their native language.

But humanism was much more than sterile imitation. It provided the West not only with a comprehensive knowledge of classical literature and thought but also with a more accurate historical perspective. In philosophy the humanists revived interest in Platonism and modified the medieval concept of Aristotelianism. They absorbed classical ways of thinking, as well as classical modes of expression, and fostered an appreciation of the studies we know today as the "humanities." Above all, humanism reintroduced into western culture a much-needed emphasis on the dignity of man as an individual and on his place in the cosmos.

In its broader ramifications humanism stimulated a vital concern for the problems and challenges of the contemporary world. As we saw in this chapter and the one preceding, there was a progressive quickening of social life, resulting in sweeping changes in politics and economics and in men's minds. The common denominator of these changes was the emergence of individualism, manifested in the society of the *quattrocento*—in the structure of the city-state, the role of patrons, and the manners, dress, and amusements of the people. Individualism manifested itself no less in the way in which the artist related his aesthetic canons to the new man-centered view of the world. The extent to which the *quattrocento* sculptor, architect, and painter succeeded remains one of the glories of western civilization. Theirs were the accomplishments upon which the creative geniuses of the High Renaissance later built.

In the sixteenth century the stimulating ideas current in Italy began to spread beyond the Alps and to combine with local developments to produce renaissances in France, England, and elsewhere. While influenced profoundly by Italian antecedents, thought and art in each country developed in distinctive ways. These developments included the invention of printing, the impact of humanism on society and literature, and further achievements in painting.

Historical Critique

THE RENAISSANCE: A HISTORICAL CONTROVERSY
by Lewis W. Spitz

Lewis W. Spitz, Professor of History at Stanford University, is the author of *Conrad Celtis, the German Arch-Humanist* (1957), *The Religious Renaissance of the German Humanists* (1963), *Life in Two Worlds—William Sihler* (1968), and the editor of *Luther's Works*, Vol. 34 (1960), *The Reformation—Material or Spiritual?* (1962), and *The Protestant Reformation* (1966).

The historian confronts the problem of setting limits and divisions in history in order to have a conceptual framework upon which to construct his narrative. Whether these periods are merely a verbal convention, reflect the reality of history as past actuality, or do violence to the continuity of the "seamless web" of history are questions sufficiently difficult to challenge the most active mind. Wallace K. Ferguson has called the Renaissance "the most intractable problem child of historiography." As an extremely complex cultural and socio-political phenomenon, the Renaissance has defied easy categorization and remains today the subject of heated debate.

The very terms *Renaissance, renovatio,* and *restitutio* applied to the age by men of that time suggest rebirth, renewal, and restoration as the beginning of a new and different age reminiscent of the golden age of classical antiquity. The Renaissance humanists believed that they were living at the dawn of a new era, and what men believe subjectively about their own times can be as significant as what the objective realities would suggest to be true. Petrarch felt a sense of distance from classical antiquity and spoke of the ancient times and the modern times, by which he really meant the "dark ages" during the centuries just preceding his own days. Boccaccio in his *Life of Dante* said that the great poet was the first to open the door to the muses since the Romans. This sense of living in a new age grew and became a formal convention in the course of the fifteenth and early sixteenth centuries.

The Italian humanists' conviction that they were living in a new age was shared by the humanists and reformers in northern Europe. Erasmus wrote: "I anticipate the near approach of a golden age." Ulrich von Hutten, the German humanist, exclaimed: "What a century! What

scholarship! It is a sheer joy to be alive. . . . Learning flourishes, men are spiritually quickened. O Barbarism, take a rope and prepare for extinction!" And the German reformer Martin Luther declared that he was living at the dawn of a new golden age.

The Protestants, in fact, adopted the view that Renaissance humanism, like John the Baptist, heralded an evangelical reawakening. This reading of history was formalized in the work of Cellarius (Keller), a Lutheran minister who used the term *medium aevum* to classify the centuries between Roman antiquity and modern times as the Middle Ages. The idea that the Renaissance and the Reformation were the twin sources of modernity became a fixed conception in subsequent historiography.

During the eighteenth century the leading intellectuals were in the rationalist tradition, very unsympathetic to the ecclesiastical Middle Ages and convinced that the Renaissance had been a harbinger of their own age of light. Voltaire pointed up four great ages of the world which had been of supreme worth: the ages of Pericles, of Augustus, of the Italian Renaissance, and of Voltaire. Gibbon, Robertson, and other historians of the Enlightenment subscribed to the view of the Renaissance's central role in history.

By the first decades of the nineteenth century a romantic reaction had set in against both the Enlightenment and its conception of the Renaissance. Such romanticists as Herder and Schlegel developed a new appreciation for the Middle Ages. Gothic architecture, as a spontaneous expression of medieval spirituality, was held to be as authentic and praiseworthy as the neoclassicism of the Renaissance, which for its part was denigrated as an artificial imitation of another age and culture!

It was the Swiss historian Jacob Burckhardt who created the dominant conception of the Renaissance as the cradle of modern culture and of Italy as the first born among the sons of Europe. He sketched the Italian Renaissance as the period which marked Europe's emergence from the medieval centuries of collectivism, ecclesiastical culture, and other-worldliness. Taking his cue from Jules Michelet's characterization of the Renaissance as the rediscovery of the world and of man, Burckhardt described the political life of the Italian city-states. His central thesis was that the character of the Italian states, whether republics or despotisms, was the chief reason for the early development of the new individualism in Italy, which he characterized as follows: "In the Middle Ages . . . human consciousness . . . lay dreaming or half awake beneath a common veil. . . . Man was conscious of himself only as a member of a race, people, party, family, or corporation—only through some general category. In Italy this veil first melted into air; an *objective* treatment and consideration of the State and of all the things of this world became possible. The *subjective* side at the same time asserted itself with corresponding emphasis; man became a spiritual individual, and recognized himself as such.''[1]

Burckhardt's interpretation of the Renaissance dominated historical theory for decades. In England John Addington Symonds wrote his massive *Renaissance in Italy,* which remains the only comprehensive history of the whole Renaissance era. Though his passages were at times gross caricatures of Burckhardt's views, Symonds made a great impact upon the popular mind, especially with his volume entitled ''The Age of the Despots.'' He depicted the Renaissance man as the *uomo universale,* the genial aesthete and all-around man.

In Germany leading scholars undertook the writing of learned works on Renaissance humanism, worked out detailed accounts of the rediscovery of ancient classics, and described the northern Renaissance as related generically to the Italian. At the very time when Burckhardt was writing his famous work, a young scholar named Georg Voigt published *The Revival of Classical Antiquity, or The First Century of Humanism,* which gave a detailed account of the finding of classical manuscripts, analyzed the literary production of the humanists, and was very critical of their limitations in style and originality. Voigt's work provided a great storehouse of scholarly information about Renaissance humanism which was exploited by other writers in later years.

The Berlin philosopher Wilhelm Dilthey, a neo-Kantian idealist and the founder of a new approach to the ''intellectual or spiritual sciences,'' proved to be a powerful influence upon the interpretation of the Renaissance. He saw the Reformation as the religious expression of the Renaissance, a renewal in theology parallel to that revival which had taken place in art and letters. The Reformation took its place with the Renaissance as ''the hinge upon which all of modern history turned'' (James Froude).

Other German historians adhered basically to Burckhardt's view of the Renaissance, although they were ready to concede that the Burckhardtians had exaggerated the contrast between the Renaissance and the Middle Ages. In the Burck-

hardtian tradition, Hans Baron studied the relation of humanism to civic life in Florence. He developed the concept of civic humanism as a special emphasis, distinct from the literary humanism of the fourteenth century and the metaphysical phase of humanism in the second half of the fifteenth century, when Neo-platonic philosophers such as Marsiglio Ficino became the most prominent thinkers. A number of Italian scholars embraced a Burckhardtian point of view in turn, combining with it an interpretation of the Renaissance based upon idealistic philosophy.

It is not necessarily true in history, as in physics, that to every action there is an equal and opposite reaction. But in the historical writing on the Renaissance a very marked reaction against the Burckhardtian interpretation gradually set in. Revisionism took three different forms. First, some historians saw many antecedents for the Renaissance in the Middle Ages and spoke of the twelfth-century Renaissance, the Ottonian Renaissance of the tenth century, the Carolingian Renaissance of the ninth century, and the Iro-Celtic Renaissance before that. Second, some revisionists found the Renaissance to be more religious and culturally more medieval than the Burckhardtians supposed. Third, a few historians came to view the Renaissance as a period of decline from the heights of thirteenth century culture.

The revolt of the medievalists produced a variety of fascinating studies. Heinrich Thode, an art historian, traced the beginnings of naturalism and a realistic portrayal of man back to the influence of St. Francis, Giotto's inspiration. Charles Homer Haskins emphasized the extensive knowledge of the classics and the revival of learning in the twelfth century. Giuseppe Toffanin depicted classical Renaissance humanism as orthodox and basically more Christian than the high rationalism of late Scholasticism. Jan Huizinga saw the very century of the Renaissance in Italy as one of waning and medieval disintegration in Burgundy and France.

Perhaps the historians of science have been the most critical of the concept of the Renaissance. Of these, Lynn Thorndike was one of the keenest and most contemptuous, referring as a matter of course to the ''so-called Renaissance.'' He compared the humanist rhetoricians unfavorably to the medieval Scholastic metaphysicians and logicians and saw in the Renaissance a period of decline in the natural sciences. He wrote: ''Was not humanism in part an easier way for princes and their sons who found the existing university requirements too harsh, and for those in general who preferred to write poems, letters, and orations, instead of following intricate arguments and arranging their own thought in a systematic orderly manner? To escape this stern necessity, the humanists glorified what had been a grammar-school subject, Latin, into the sum and substance of culture. . . . Indeed, leisure and cultured ease were the ideal of many humanists, as against either great literary productivity or sustained reasoning."[2]

The efforts of the revisionists have not succeeded in destroying the concept of the Renaissance as a unique and extremely important age in the development of western culture and in the introduction of modern times. The scholarship of recent years has led to further refinement and consolidation. Although history is in constant change, at certain times lines of development merge so that in reinforcing one another they accelerate the rate of overall change. The Renaissance was such an age of accelerated change and transition which had characteristic features setting it apart from the centuries which preceded and from those which followed it.

The Renaissance began in Italy and received its most intense and characteristic cultural expression in the city-state of Florence. Its cultural achievements were most striking in the fine arts and literature, pioneered most dramatically by Giotto and Petrarch. Its cultural self-consciousness included a sense of distance from the ancient past, breaking the deceptive feeling of continuity with the ancient world so characteristic of the medieval mind. Whereas in earlier cultural renascences the educational revival was largely restricted to the clerical class, the advance in the Italian Renaissance of lay culture and learning through humanistic education, especially of the aristocracy and bourgeoisie, broadened the cultural base in a marked way. Classical values were increasingly accepted as norm, not just classical style as form. For the first time the triple linguistic tiara of Latin, Greek, and Hebrew became a real cultural possession of a growing number of learned men, in the north as well as in the south.

This brilliant golden age of culture was also characterized by economic change and by the unique city-state political context of Italy. Whereas capitalism had its origins in earlier centuries, the Italian city-states developed the instruments and institutions of capitalism and a merchant-banker bourgeoisie more active and dominant than had any society for centuries. Before the intervention of the great powers at the end of the fifteenth century, the city-state structure with political units of manageable size, and blessed with an inordinate amount of civic pride, served as a matrix congenial to cultural development, whether the city was ruled as a republic or dominated by a tyrant. The residency of the papacy in Rome contributed an ecclesiastical context favorable to culture and aligned with Italian interests. This period of European history, then, stands out like a cameo against its medieval background and differs in equally specific and obvious ways from the age of the Reformation which followed.

The Renaissance as a special period in European history, characterized in particular by certain common cultural aspects, is a perfectly reasonable and useful conception. Periodization in history is an aid to the historian's finite mind in grappling with what the philosopher Schopenhauer referred to as "the infinite subject matter of history." Periods are useful and meaningful to the extent to which the historian moves beyond empty and arbitrary chronological divisions to analyze the content of periods in terms of their unique characteristics and inner cohesion. Historians are bound to vary in their judgments somewhat from person to person and from time to time. History is truly, as Cicero observed, a "witness of the times"—of the times in which it is written as well as of the times about which it is written.

FOOTNOTES

1 Jacob Burckhardt, *The Civilization of the Renaissance in Italy*, Modern Library, 1954, p. 100.
2 Lynn Thorndike, *Science and Thought in the Fifteenth Century*, Columbia, 1929, p. 10.

SUGGESTED READINGS

A number of scholarly works are available to the student who wishes to explore further the challenging question of historical periodization and the historians' interpretation of the Renaissance. A great scholarly survey of the changing historical currents is Wallace K. Ferguson's *The Renaissance in Historical Thought: Five Centuries of Interpretation*, Houghton Mifflin, 1948. Tinsley Helton, ed., *The Renaissance: A Reconsideration of the Theories and Interpretations of the Age*, Univ. of Wisconsin Press, 1961, offers learned essays on various aspects of the problem by leading scholars. Karl H. Dannenfeldt, ed., *The Renaissance: Medieval or Modern?* Heath, 1959, provides substantial selections from the analytical essays of historians of very different schools of thought.

Chapter 16

Here
I Take
My Stand

**The Decline of the Medieval Church
and the Protestant and Catholic Reformations**

INTRODUCTION. When the humanistic ideas of the Renaissance moved northward over the Alps, they carried with them seeds of discontent with the Roman Church. Besides encouraging interest in the classics, bolstering scholarship, and placing new emphasis on individualism, the northern humanists criticized the abuses of the clergy and urged Church reform. Taken up by others, these complaints spread and grew until a veritable explosion shattered the religious unity of Europe.

On all sides the medieval ideal of unity was falling before the onslaught of Renaissance individualism. In the last chapter we saw how the humanists rebelled against the Scholasticism of the Middle Ages and the orientation of medieval thinkers toward other-worldliness and asceticism. In the next chapter we shall see the medieval ideal of a universal empire fall victim to the aims of aggressive national states. In the sixteenth century even the strongest of medieval institutions, the Church, was stripped of preeminence. Henceforth, the Roman Church was to share its influence, both spiritual and political, with other churches, built on re-formed doctrines.

On October 31, 1517, a professor of theology named Martin Luther nailed some papers on the door of the castle church in Wittenberg, Germany. It was the custom of the day for a man who wanted to engage in a Scholastic debate with another to post his propositions publicly. In this respect Luther's action was not unusual, yet the forces he set in operation altered the entire religious and intellectual pattern of the western world. A religious revolt was launched that split Christendom into numerous factions and sects.

Until his death in 1546, Luther believed that it might be possible to reform Catholicism to the practices existing in early Christian times. From this standpoint the religious upheaval which he did so much to set in motion can be logically designated as the Reformation. On the other hand, because the struggle shattered western Christendom permanently, it might be described from a broader historical viewpoint as a revolution or, alternatively, as the Protestant Revolt. The sixteenth century also witnessed a significant revival of Catholicism itself. This renewal of the traditional faith was not solely a Counter Reformation in the sense

that it represented a belated response to the challenge of Protestantism. As modern scholars have demonstrated, a strong Catholic Reformation had been gathering momentum even before Luther posted his theses.

The Reformation had both its negative and its positive aspects. In the name of God, men persecuted and killed their fellow men. Rulers anxious for absolute power used the conflicts engendered by the religious upheaval to serve their own political ends. Yet, much as in the early centuries of Christianity, when the blood of the martyrs became the seed of the Church, so the struggles of the sixteenth century, led by men afire with conviction and ready to sacrifice their lives for what they believed, renewed and stimulated the religious consciousness of western Europe. Luther declared: "Here I take my stand"; and in a broad sense this affirmation was echoed by Zwingli in the Swiss cantons, by Calvin at Geneva, and by the Catholic Church at the Council of Trent. Such staunch and uncompromising assertions of honest differences of doctrine gave institutionalized Christianity the new religious vitality and intellectual diversity that were to leave their mark on almost every phase of life in the West and bequeath us a rich legacy of values.

THE DECLINE OF THE MEDIEVAL CHURCH

Dangers facing the papacy. The history of the medieval Church divides roughly into three periods—dissemination, domination, and disintegration. In the initial period, which lasted from about the fifth through the eleventh centuries, Roman Christianity spread throughout the West—even into Slavic and Scandinavian lands. The Church's administrative apparatus was disrupted by feudalism, but by the end of the eleventh century the Church had become the most powerful propertied and political institution in the West. The period of domination—the twelfth and thirteenth centuries—reached its zenith in the pontificate of Innocent III, who made and deposed temporal princes at will.

The Church then seemed unassailable in its prestige, dignity, and power. Yet that strength had already begun to wane, and during the next two centuries the processes of disintegration were to run their course.

Papal centralization was harassed by the growth of nation-states, which were challenging the power of the weakened Holy Roman Empire as well as the Church's temporal pretensions. Joined by some of the local clergy, princes opposed papal interference in state matters and favored the establishment of general Church councils to curb papal power. In addition, the papacy was criticized by reformers, who had seen the medieval reformation and the crusades transformed from their original high-minded purposes to suit the ambitions of the pontiffs, and by the bourgeoisie, whose contact with new ideas was fostering growing skepticism, national patriotism, and religious self-reliance. During the fourteenth and fifteenth centuries these factors took their toll, and papal influence rapidly declined.

Boniface VIII. A century after the papacy's zenith under Innocent III, Boniface VIII (1294-1303) was forced to withdraw his fierce opposition to taxes levied on the great wealth of the Church by Edward I in England and Philip IV in France. Emulating Innocent, Boniface threatened to depose the "impious king," as he termed Philip, but he gave way when Philip with the support of the Estates-General prohibited the export of precious metals to Rome.

A final and more humiliating clash with the French king had long-range implications for the papacy. When Boniface boldly declared, in the famous papal bull *Unam Sanctam* (1302), that "subjection to the Roman pontiff is absolutely necessary to salvation for every human creature," Philip summoned a Church council and had the pope deposed for his "sins." In 1303 Philip's henchmen broke into Boniface's summer home at Anagni to arrest him and take him to France to stand trial. Their kidnaping plot was foiled when the pope was rescued by his friends. Shocked and humiliated, Boniface died a month later.

The Avignon papacy. The success of the French monarchy was as complete as if Boniface had been dragged before Philip. Two years after Boniface's death, a French archbishop was chosen pope. Taking the title of Clement V, he acted according to the wishes of Philip IV. Clement even moved the papal headquarters from Rome to Avignon in France, where the papacy remained under French influence from 1305 to 1377. During this period, the so-called "Babylonian Captivity" of the Church, papal prestige suffered enormously. All Christendom believed that Rome was the only rightful capital for the Church. Moreover, the citizens of Rome missed the papal court and its revenues; the English justifiably accused the popes of favoring the French kings; and the

Germans resented the pope's claims to temporal power over the Holy Roman emperor.

The Avignon papacy added fuel to the fires of those critics who were attacking Church corruption, papal temporal claims, and the apparent lack of spiritual enthusiasm. Deprived of much of their income and living in splendor in a newly built fortress-palace, the Avignon popes expanded their bureaucracy, added new Church taxes, and collected the old taxes more efficiently. This produced a cry for reformation by Church councils and stimulated questioning, especially by John Wycliffe in England (see p. 483), about such basic beliefs as the divinity of the papal office.

The Great Schism. When Gregory XI took heed of popular opinion and returned the papal headquarters to Rome in 1377, it seemed for a time that the fortunes of the Roman Church would improve. But the reverse proved true. Upon the death of Gregory in 1378, the demand of the Roman multitude for an Italian pope led to the election of Urban VI; but the French cardinals maintained that the election was invalid because of outside pressure on the voters, and they elected a Frenchman, Clement VII, who reigned from Avignon.

The Church was now in an even worse state than it had been during the Babylonian Captivity. During the Great Schism, as the split of the Church into two allegiances was called, there were two popes, each with his college of cardinals and capital city, each claiming universal sovereignty, each sending forth papal administrators and taxing Christendom, and each excommunicating the other as the anti-pope. The nations of Europe gave allegiance as their individual political interests prompted them. France supported Clement, as did Scotland, Navarre, Castile, and Aragon. Urban found his strength in Italy, Portugal, Flanders, England, and most of eastern Europe. In order to keep the allegiance of the various countries, the rival popes had to make concessions to their political supporters and largely abandoned the practice of interfering in national politics.

Religious life suffered. The Great Schism had become an international disgrace. "Christendom looked upon the scandal helpless and depressed, and yet impotent to remove it. With two sections of Christendom each declaring the other lost, each cursing and denouncing the other, men soberly asked who was saved. The longer the schism lasted, the more difficult did it seem to heal it, and yet people generally felt that for that very reason positive action was all the more necessary. The very sublimity of Papal pretensions made earthly jurisdiction and compulsory abdication seem very difficult. Still the fact stared Europe in the face that the schism itself, with the cupidity, selfishness, and meanness accompanying it, had shattered the sanctity of Papal claims . . . .''[1]

The Conciliar Movement. Positive action came in the form of the Conciliar Movement, a return to the early Christian practice of solving Church problems by means of a general council of prelates. In 1395 the learned doctors of the University of Paris suggested that if the two claimants to the papal throne would not abdicate, a general council of all the Church should be held. Neither pope would abdicate, nor would they arbitrate their differences. In 1409, therefore, a majority of the cardinals of both camps met at the Council of Pisa, deposed both pontiffs, and elected a third man. But neither of the two deposed popes would give up his office, and the papal throne now had three claimants.

Such an intolerable situation necessitated another Church council. In 1414 the Holy Roman emperor assembled at Constance the most impressive Church gathering of the period. For the first time voting took place on a purely national basis. Instead of the traditional assembly of bishops, the Council included lay representatives and was organized as a convention of "nations" (German, Italian, French, and English, the Spanish entering later). Each nation had one vote. The nationalistic structure of the Council was highly significant as an indication that the new tendency toward such alignments was being recognized by some members of the Church's hierarchy. Finally, through the deposition of the various papal claimants and the election of Martin v in 1417, the Great Schism was ended, and a single papacy

was restored. In addition, the papal court was returned to Rome.

Failure of internal reform. The Church had demonstrated at Constance that in the Conciliar Movement it possessed the means of reforming itself. But the movement was not to endure. At that time the Conciliar Movement represented a reforming - and democratizing influence in the Church, aimed at transforming the papacy into something like a limited monarchy. The success of the Council of Constance strengthened the theory that councils were above popes. Such a notion would have destroyed the supremacy of the pope, and a fundamental conflict arose between the Church councils and the popes, both claiming supreme power. Taking steps to preserve his position, one pope announced that to appeal to a Church council without having first obtained papal consent was heretical. The restoration of a single head of the Church, together with the inability of later councils to bring about much-needed reform, enabled the popes to discredit the Conciliar Movement for the most part by 1450. It was almost a century before the great Council of Trent met in 1545 to reform a Church which had already irreparably lost many countries to Protestantism.

Unfortunately, while the popes hesitated to call councils to effect reform, they refused to bring about reform themselves. The popes busied themselves not with internal problems but with Italian politics and patronage of the arts. Thus, "the papacy emerged as something between an Italian city-state and a European power, without forgetting at the same time the claim to be the vice-regent of Christ. The pope often could not make up his own mind whether he was the successor of Peter or of Caesar. Such vacillation had much to do with the rise and success . . . of the Reformation.''[2]

Heresy: Wycliffe and Huss. Throughout the fourteenth century the cries against Church corruption became louder at the same time that heretical thoughts were being voiced. *The Vision of Piers Plowman,* (see p. 401), an allegorical English poem attributed to William Langland (d. 1400?), mercilessly upbraided the corruption, ignorance, and worldliness of the clergy.

During the Avignon papacy a master of Oxford named John Wycliffe (1320?-1384) assailed not only Church abuses but Church doctrines. Because of his beliefs that the Church should be subordinate to the state, that salvation was primarily an individual matter between man and God, that transubstantiation as taught by the Church was false, and that outward rituals and veneration of relics were idolatrous, Wycliffe may be considered the dawn-star of the Protestant Revolt. He formed bands of "poor priests," called Lollards, who taught his views; and he provided the people with an English translation of the Bible, which he considered the final authority in matters of religion. Although Wycliffe's demands for reform did not succeed, the Lollards, including the famous John Ball (see p. 372), spread a more radical version of Wycliffe's ideas until the movement was driven underground early in the next century.

In Bohemia, where a strong reform movement was under way, Wycliffe's doctrines were propagated by Czech students who had heard him at Oxford. In particular, his beliefs influenced John Huss (1369?-1415), an impassioned preacher in Prague and later rector of the university there. Although he borrowed many of his doctrinal views from Wycliffe, Huss did not adopt the latter's denial of the validity of transubstantiation. His chief literary work, *Concerning the Church,* included Wycliffe's views that the Church was composed of a universal priesthood of believers and that Christ alone was its head.

Huss' doctrines became so popular and his influence so great that the Church decided to silence him. Huss was excommunicated for his attacks on the doctrine of indulgences, but he found refuge outside Prague and kept on writing. Later he was given a safe-conduct to the Council of Constance, which had as its purpose not only to heal the schism but also to stamp out heresy. Because Huss did not recant his teachings, the Council condemned him, and he was burned at the stake in spite of his safe-conduct. This action did not stamp out heresy; on the contrary, it made Huss a martyr and strengthened the resolve of those who believed in his doctrines. In the sixteenth century the remaining Hussites merged with the Lutherans.

Humanist scholarship and criticism of the Church. In Chapter 15 we saw how the worth of the individual was reaffirmed during the Renaissance, particularly in the areas of art and learning. As the new ideas spread to northern Europe, the humanists turned their attention to the Church and religion. Bringing a mistrust of authority to their evaluation of the Church, the humanists undertook a twofold investigation. First, they applied critical scholarship to Christian documents and literature. Second, they raised the problem of the individual's relationship to the Church. These activities helped set off the chain of events which eventually led to the Protestant Revolt.

The scholarly interest of the humanists was directed to the recovery of a Christianity based upon the New Testament and the doctrines of the early Church. Occasionally their findings conflicted sharply with the teachings of the medieval Church. In at least one instance, humanist scholarship was responsible for deflating the historical basis on which the pope claimed control over central Italy. It had long been believed that the emperor Constantine, when he left Rome and took up residence in Constantinople, had assigned extensive temporal powers to the bishop of Rome and that this grant had been confirmed in a document. In 1440, however, the Italian humanist Lorenzo Valla proved beyond doubt that the document, called the Donation of Constantine, was an eighth-century forgery and that the papal claims to suzerainty constituted usurpation.

In the whole area of the individual's relation to the Church, the humanists' views may be summed up by saying that they wished to remain in the Church but to reform it. They compared—not always favorably—the highly complex Church of their day with early Christianity. These Renaissance scholars were acutely aware that all was not as it should be. Erasmus, for example, was a rationalist, and yet he saw about him only passions; he was tolerant, and yet Europe was bleeding from bigotry. He saw no conflict between secular and religious truth, and he liked to refer to Christianity as the "philosophy of Christ":

Truly the yoke of Christ would be sweet and his burden light, if petty human institutions added nothing to what he himself imposed. He commanded us nothing save love one for another, and there is nothing so bitter that charity does not soften and sweeten it. Everything according to nature is easily borne, and nothing accords better with the nature of man than the philosophy of Christ, of which almost the sole end is to give back to fallen nature its innocence and integrity. . . . How pure, how simple is the faith that Christ delivered to us! How close to it is the creed transmitted to us by the apostles, or apostolic men. . . . Would that men were content to let Christ rule by the laws of the gospel and that they would no longer seek to strengthen their obscurant tyranny by human decrees![3]

This rational attribute of the humanist position was also a weakness. Since it was primarily an intellectual movement, humanism could not create the dynamic drive necessary to inspire widespread reform. Having laid the intellectual groundwork for the pending religious revolt, the humanists left to other men—the militant and the martyrs alike—the task of arousing action. They preferred the pen of the scholar to the cross of the martyr.

Reasons for Church decline. A noted Church historian has divided the reasons for the Church's decline during the fourteenth and fifteenth centuries into those that existed within the Church itself and those that were weakening it from the outside. The internal factors go far to explain the Church's loss of prestige, while the second group of factors was largely responsible for its loss of universal power and authority. All of the factors blended together to bring about the Reformation.

As we have seen, trenchant criticisms of the clergy had come from such a variety of sources as Erasmus, Wycliffe, and the author of *The Vision of Piers Plowman*. The Conciliar Movement had gone so far as to challenge the supreme power of the pope himself. And while criticisms increased, the Church continued to decline in spiritual leadership. The worldly concerns of the Renaissance

In this contemporary sketch of John Huss being led to execution, the reformer wears the headgear which branded him as a heretic condemned by the Council of Constance in 1415.

popes—including their deep involvement in Italian politics—pushed the Church further in the direction of secularization. The growing formality of much of the worship and the failure of the Church to keep pace with intellectual developments taking place in the outside world also weakened the Church's position.

Among the outside pressures that led to the Church's decline, the new spirit of inquiry encouraged by the Renaissance in general and the northern humanists in particular resulted in a new critical attitude toward religious institutions. In the revival of intellectual activity, the printing press provided the means for the rapid dissemination of the new secular ideas. In the socio-economic field, the medieval Church was slow in adapting itself to the new environment of the towns. The problems arising from town life too often went unanswered by the Church, which failed to provide enough parish priests to keep pace with the growth of urban population. It is no accident that the towns became centers of heresy. Finally, the development of nationalism and the growing reluctance of kings to obey any opposing institution, including the Church, were evident in the encounters between Boniface VIII and the French ruler Philip IV.

Church domination depended on the continuance of the medieval world order, and forces were slowly modifying every aspect of that order. The spirit of the Middle Ages was fundamentally one of faith, devotion to institutions—the feudal order, the guild, and the Church—and the subordination of the individual's interests to those of the group. It was this spirit which fed the power of the Church. When the Renaissance changed this spirit, the universalities of the Middle Ages were shattered into a multitude of fragments. Man became assertive. He began to rebel against all institutions which prevented him from acting as he wished.

Broadly speaking, the ideal of the Middle Ages was other-worldliness; the ideal of the Renaissance was present-worldliness. The Church represented the older ideal. Thus it was not simply that the Church's financial and moral abuses stood in need of correction; the Church had long tended to lose contact with the people, and its ideals no longer commanded the same respect and allegiance. The European townsman, for example, found himself increasingly out of sympathy with the Church's economic concepts of the "just price" and anti-usury statutes, for they conflicted with the new capitalism.

The Church itself embodied a dangerous contradiction at this time. In dogma it was medieval, yet its highest officials, including the popes, were patrons of a Renaissance culture deriving its inspiration from pagan

The deterioration of monasticism was responsible for much disenchantment with the Church. Monks were accused of every possible vice, from drunkenness and adultery to the frequenting of brothels. Such charges fostered the contempt vividly illustrated in this early sixteenth-century woodcut.

Greece and Rome. The Church might denounce usury, but at the same time it utilized the services of powerful moneylending families.

The time was ripe for the rise of some leader with a religious message more compatible with the spirit of the age. When he appeared, it was likely that he would employ as his weapon not the conflict of Renaissance ideology with that of the Church, for that was a philosophical problem of which few were conscious, but rather the financial and moral abuses of the Church, which were common knowledge. Furthermore, it is not surprising that this figure arose in Germany, a country newly touched by the Renaissance, geographically removed from Rome, and the home of an earnest and pious people.

THE RELIGIOUS REVOLT

The revolt in Germany. The religious struggle first came to a head in Germany. Stimulated by the invention of printing, educated Germans had been studying the Scriptures carefully and censuring the ignorance of many of the German clergy. Whereas in Italy familiarity bred a tolerance and rationalization of papal corruption, the Germans fiercely resented papal abuses and expected practice and theory to coincide.

The political situation also had a bearing on the religious question. Divided into hundreds of states, Germany lacked unity except for the nominal rule of the elected emperor of the Holy Roman Empire. The failure of administrative reform (see p. 433) encouraged the many German states to imitate the new nationalism of countries to the west. This political trend proved highly significant; because the religious affairs of each principality came under the control of its ruler, a greater diversity of religious opinion and organization could exist in Germany than in a state ruled by a centralized authority.

Nor must economic factors be overlooked. Trade and banking flourished, and the German burgher found no conflict between

Under Julius II the secular interests of the Renaissance popes reached their highest point. A patron of the arts, Julius was also known as the "Pope in Armor" because he waged four wars between 1506 and 1512 and concluded many alliances with the major powers of his day in an effort to free Italy from foreign influence.

piety and profits. On the other hand, his piety and profits were both affected by the draining of German revenues by the Roman Church, especially when unscrupulous means were used to gather them. In short, Germany was ripe for religious change.

Martin Luther. The son of a poor German peasant couple, Martin Luther was born on November 10, 1483. Young Martin received a sound education which included university studies, but he accepted as a matter of course the prevalent beliefs in witchcraft and other superstitions. To the end of his life Luther believed vividly in the existence of devils and witches. The story goes that he once threw an inkpot at a devil whom he thought he saw leering at him. In 1505 he became a member of the mendicant order of Augustinian monks, a move which met with scant favor from his practical father, who by virtue of thrift and hard work had become a petty capitalist. In 1508 Luther received a temporary appointment as a lecturer at the new University of Wittenberg, and a few years later he became professor of theology.

In the meantime Luther had struggled with and solved for himself the spiritual problem that confronted many people in his time: In view of God's absolute power and man's powerlessness, how can man be certain of salvation for his soul? For many years Luther probed deeply this problem of eternal salvation. Finally, in 1515, while contemplating St. Paul's Epistle to the Romans, he came upon these words: "For therein is the righteousness of God revealed from faith to faith: as it is written, The just shall live by faith."[4] Luther believed that his quest for spiritual certainty had been solved:

Night and day I pondered until I saw the connection between the justice of God and the statement that "the just shall live by his faith." Then I grasped that the justice of God is that righteousness by which through grace and sheer mercy God justifies us through faith. Thereupon I felt myself to be reborn and to have gone through open doors into paradise.[5]

Man was saved only by his faith in the validity of Christ's sacrifice, which alone could wash away sin and save him from the grasp of the devil. Luther had come to his famous doctrine of justification by faith, as opposed to the Roman Church's doctrine of justification by faith and good works—the demonstration of faith through virtuous acts, acceptance of Church dogma, and participation in Church ritual. Later, in a hymn that reflects his vigorous style of expression, Luther described his spiritual journey from anxiety to conviction:

In devil's dungeon chained I lay
    The pangs of death swept o'er me.
My sin devoured me night and day
    In which my mother bore me.
My anguish ever grew more rife,
I took no pleasure in my life
    And sin had made me crazy.
                . . .
Thus spoke the Son, "Hold thou to me,
    From now on thou wilt make it.
I gave my very life for thee
    And for thee I will stake it.
For I am thine and thou art mine,
And where I am our lives entwine,
    The Old Fiend cannot shake it."[6]

The implications of Luther's doctrine were enormous. If salvation could come only through a personal belief in Christ's sacrifice, then an interceding priesthood became superfluous, for each man would then be his own priest. But Luther himself had no idea as yet where his views would eventually lead him and half of Christendom. It required a financial abuse by the Church to bring on the religious revolt.

Tetzel and the indulgences. Leo x, a cultured scion of the Medici family, "who would have made an excellent Pope if he had only been a little religious,"[7] wanted to complete the magnificent new St. Peter's in Rome, but he lacked money for the costly enterprise. Several papal agents were sent out to sell indulgences as a means of raising money. One of these agents, named Tetzel, discharged his mission "in the German archbishopric of Mainz in a manner which would be recognized in America to-day as high-pressure salesmanship."[8]

An anonymous caricature of Johann Tetzel, the German hawker of indulgences, entitled "Johann Tetzel and His Indulgence-Junk." The last two lines of the notorious jingle here ascribed to Tetzel read: "As soon as coin in the coffer rings, Right then the soul to Heaven springs."

Johann Tezel mit seinen Ablaß-Kram.

LEO DECIMUS

BULLÆ INDULGENT

O Ihr Teutschen, merkt mich recht,
Des heiligen Vater Pabsts Knecht
Bin ich, und bring euch itzt allen
Zehntausend und Neunhundert Karnen
Gnad und Ablaß eurer Sünd,

Vor euch, eure Aeltern, Weib und Kind,
Soll, ein jeder, gewähret seyn,
Sa viel er legt ins Kästel ein.
So bald der Gülden im Becken klingt,
Im Huy d.e S.el in Himmel sich schwingt.

The Church's position in regard to indulgences has often been misunderstood. Although the sacrament of Penance absolved the sinner from guilt and eternal punishment, some temporal punishment remained. An indulgence remitted part or all of this remaining penalty but in return presupposed that the sinner repented of his misdeeds and did some form of penance, such as praying, visiting shrines, or contributing to worthy causes. Theologically, the concept of indulgences rested on the theory of a "treasury of merits," which held that Christ and the saints had won merit far in excess of their own needs and had thereby created a vast storehouse of merits. By means of indulgences the Church was able to draw upon and distribute this surplus to help those who felt they had not rendered sufficient penance to extinguish the punishment which they deserved. Contrary to a popular misconception, an indulgence did not permit a person to buy forgiveness.

It was the abuse attending the sale of indulgences to raise money that was chiefly responsible for the growing tide of resentment. The common folk did not understand theology and thought that a payment of money was all that was required to escape all the penalties of sin and, in fact, to purchase their salvation. Tetzel did nothing to enlighten the populace as to the true nature of indulgences but rather exhorted them to give liberally for themselves and for their dead relatives in purgatory who were "crying to them for help." Luther's case against indulgences rested on both moral and theological grounds.

Development of Luther's ideas. On October 31, 1517, Luther, following a university custom, posted ninety-five propositions (theses) on the subject of indulgences on the church door at Wittenberg, at the same time challenging anyone to debate them with him. Here are some of the more important of Luther's theses:

11. The erroneous opinion that canonical penance [earthly penance, specified by the Church] and punishment in purgatory are the same assuredly seems to be a tare sown while the bishops were asleep.

21. Therefore those preachers of indulgences err who say that a papal pardon frees a man from all penalty and assures his salvation.

28. It is certain that avarice is fostered by the money clinking in the chest, but to answer the prayers of the Church is in the power of God alone.

43. Christians are to be taught that he who gives to the poor or lends to one in need does better than he who buys indulgences.[9]

Luther wrote the ninety-five theses in Latin for the edification of his fellow theologians, but they were soon translated into the common tongue and six months later were well known throughout Germany. At first the Church at Rome did not seriously trouble itself. Heresy was anything but new, as the history of the Waldensians, Albigensians, and the followers of Wycliffe and Huss showed. But this particular "squabble among monks," as Leo X dismissed the matter, did not subside.

In 1519 Luther debated with the eminent Catholic theologian John Eck at Leipzig. Luther maintained that the pope ruled by virtue of human rather than divine authority and was not infallible; that Church councils did not exist by divine right either and could also err; and that Scripture constituted the sole authority in matters of faith and doctrine. When Eck pointed out that such views were similar to those of Wycliffe and Huss, Luther boldly declared that "among the opinions of John Huss and the Bohemians many are certainly most Christian and evangelic, and cannot be condemned by the universal church."[10] Yet in spite of these wide theological divergences, Luther continued to speak with affection of his "mother Church," which he hoped could be reformed and remain unified. By basing his position squarely on the doctrine of justification by faith alone, however, Luther found himself propelled by its implications—and by external circumstances—to a position far removed from that of the Church.

Following the Leipzig debate, Eck initiated proceedings at Rome to have Luther declared a heretic. Luther in turn decided to put his case before the German people by publishing a series of pamphlets. In his *Address to the Nobility of the German Nation,*

At top left is the title page of Leo x's bull condemning Luther and threatening him with excommunication. Forced to seek refuge in the Wartburg castle under the protection of the elector of Saxony after being excommunicated by the pope and outlawed by the German Diet, Luther masqueraded as Knight George (top right) while he continued to write sermons, letters, and treatises expounding his theological views. At the right is his workroom in the Wartburg castle where he completed his translation of the New Testament into German.

Luther called on rulers to reform ecclesiastical abuses, to strip the Church of its wealth and worldly power, and to create, in effect, a national German Church. Among numerous other proposals contained in this influential treatise, Luther urged a union with the Hussites, claiming that Huss had been unjustly burned at the stake.

The Babylonian Captivity of the Church summarized Luther's theological views. He attacked the papacy for having deprived the individual Christian of his freedom to approach God directly by faith and without the intermediation of priesthood, and he set forth his views on the sacramental system. To be valid, a sacrament must have been instituted by Christ and be exclusively Christian. On this basis Luther could find no justification for making a sacrament of matrimony, which was also observed by non-Christians, or for any of the other sacraments except Baptism and the Lord's Supper (his term for the sacrament known to Roman Catholics as the Holy Eucharist). Luther rejected the doctrine of transubstantiation on the grounds that a priest could not perform the miracle of transforming bread and wine into the Body and Blood of the Lord. Nevertheless, he believed in the real presence of Christ in the bread and wine of the sacrament. In Luther's view (known as consubstantiation), the bread and wine coexist with the Body and Blood without a change of substance.

Luther's third pamphlet, *The Freedom of a Christian Man,* which was dedicated to the pope in the slight hope that reconciliation was still possible, set forth in conciliatory but firm tones Luther's views on Christian behavior and salvation. He did not discourage good works but argued that the inner spiritual freedom which comes from the certainty found in faith leads to the performance of good works. "Good works do not make a man good, but a good man does good works."[11]

The breach made complete. In June 1520, Pope Leo x issued the bull *Exsurge Domine:*

Arise, O Lord, and judge Thy cause. A wild boar has invaded Thy vineyard. Arise, O Peter, and consider the case of the Holy Roman Church, the mother of all churches, consecrated by thy blood. Arise, O Paul, who by thy teaching and death hast illumined and dost illumine the Church. Arise all ye saints, and the whole universal Church, whose interpretation of Scripture has been assailed.[12]

The bull gave Luther sixty days to turn from his heretical course. If at the end of that time he had not confessed his errors, he was to be cut off from the Church and handed over to secular authorities for punishment. The time limit expired without any immediate action, and in December Luther publicly burned the bull amid the applause of students and townsmen. This act propelled him into the center of German politics and brought about a showdown with Rome. In January 1521 Leo x excommunicated Luther.

Meanwhile, Charles v, who had recently been crowned emperor, found himself in a difficult situation. On the one hand, he was aware of popular German feelings and was not anxious to see papal power reconsolidated in his domains. On the other hand, he was bound by his oath to defend the Church and extirpate heresy and, moreover, was orthodox in his own religious beliefs. It was decided that Luther should be heard at the emperor's first Diet, which was held at Worms. Summoned under an imperial safe-conduct, Luther was asked whether he intended to stand by everything he had written. He stood before the assembly and replied firmly:

Your Imperial Majesty and Your Lordships demand a simple answer. Here it is, plain and unvarnished. Unless I am convicted of error by the testimony of Scripture or (since I put no trust in the unsupported authority of Pope or of councils, since it is plain that they have often erred and often contradicted themselves) by manifest reasoning I stand convicted by the Scriptures to which I have appealed, . . . I cannot and will not recant anything, for to act against our conscience is neither safe for us, nor open to us.

On this I take my stand [*Hier stehe Ich*]. I can do no other. God help me. Amen.[13]

In May 1521 the Diet declared Luther a heretic and outlaw. He was, however, given protection by the elector of Saxony, in whose castle he lived for almost a year under the disguise of "Knight George."

Some of the giants of the Protestant Reformation are shown in this picture painted about 1530 by Lucas Cranach the Elder. At the far left is Luther, and at the far right his associate Melanchthon, who wrote the Augsburg Confession. Next to Melanchthon is Zwingli. In the center of the picture is John Frederick the Magnanimous, elector of Saxony, whose family supported Luther, John Frederick's uncle, Frederick III, once sheltered Luther in his Wartburg castle.

During this period Luther began the construction of an evangelical church distinct from Rome. He wrote incessantly, setting forth his theological views in a collection of forceful sermons for use by preachers, in correspondence with friends and public figures, and in a treatise condemning monasticism. (In 1525 Luther married an ex-nun who had left the cloister after reading this treatise.) An outstanding feat was his translation of the New Testament into German, a monumental job accomplished in only eleven weeks. This translation was largely responsible for creating a standard language for all Germany. Later Luther also translated the Old Testament into German.

Luther and the Peasants' War. Luther's teachings spread quickly through central and northern Germany. Pious persons who wanted the Church reformed embraced the new cause. Worldly individuals who believed that it would afford an opportunity to appropriate Church property also aided the movement, as did men like Von Hutten (see p. 469), who saw in it a means of uniting Germany. The emperor, meanwhile, was too deeply involved in a struggle with Francis I of France to stamp out the new heresy (see p. 520).

Encouraged by Luther's concept of the freedom of a Christian man, which they applied to economic and social matters, the German peasants revolted in 1524. Long ground down by the nobles, the peasants included in their twelve demands the abolition of serfdom "unless it should be shown us from the Gospel that we are serfs"; a reduction of "the excessive services demanded of us, which are increased from day to day"; the fixing of rents "in accordance with justice"; and an end to "the appropriation by individuals of meadows and fields which at one time belonged to a community."[14] Their grievances were legitimate and their demands reasonable, and Luther, of peasant origin himself, showed sympathy for these demands. On the other hand, he consistently opposed armed rebellion and held that social and political reforms should be instituted by authorities, such as the princes. As the revolt grew in intensity, Luther became increasingly impatient with the revolutionaries until, in a virulent pamphlet, *Against the Thievish and Murderous Hordes of Peasants,* he called on the princes to act as "both judge and executioner" and

[to] knock down, strangle, and stab . . . and think nothing so venomous, pernicious, or Satanic as an insurgent. . . . Such wonderful times are these that a prince can merit heaven better with bloodshed than another with prayer.[15]

The revolt was stamped out in 1525 at a cost of about fifty thousand lives, and the lot of the German peasant for the next two centuries was probably the worst in Europe. Luther had become a false prophet to the serfs, and his cause received a serious check. Politically and economically conservative, Luther believed that the equality of all men before God applied in spiritual but not in secular matters. This philosophy alienated the peasants, who either returned to Catholicism or turned to more radical forms of Protestantism. On the other hand, it made allies of the princes, many of whom became Lutheran in part because it placed them in control of the church in their territories, thereby enhancing their power and wealth.

Local religious autonomy in Germany. The Diet of the Holy Roman Empire was composed of the seven electors, the lesser princes, and representatives of the free cities. The emperor was not supposed to do anything affecting the various states in the empire without the approval of this body. At its meeting in 1526 the princes of Germany were divided into two parties, one Lutheran and the other Catholic. Without specifying the legal status of the Lutherans, the Diet agreed that until a Church council could settle the religious issues, "each prince should so conduct himself as he could answer for his behavior to God and to the emperor."[16] Three years later the Catholic princes, with the emperor's support, pushed through a decree that the Mass must not be interfered with anywhere. This meant that while Lutheran activities were restricted in Catholic regions, those of the Catholics could be carried on even in Lutheran areas. In answer, the Lutheran leaders drew up a protest, and from this incident the word *Protestant* derives.

The Diet which met at Augsburg in 1530 was presented with a statement of Christian doctrine from the Lutheran viewpoint designed to conciliate the two parties. The Diet did not accept this statement, but the Augsburg Confession became the creed of the new faith.

The emperor now made public his intention to crush the growing heresy. In defense, the Lutheran princes banded together in 1531 in the Schmalkaldic League, and between 1546 and 1555 a sporadic civil war was fought. A compromise was finally reached in the Peace of Augsburg (1555), which allowed each prince to decide the religion of his subjects, gave Protestants the right to keep all Church property confiscated prior to 1552, forbade all sects of Protestantism other than Lutheranism, and ordered all Catholic bishops to give up their property if they turned Lutheran.

The implications of the provisions were profound. The Peace of Augsburg confirmed Lutheranism as a state religion in large portions of Germany. For the first time in Christian history, religious opinions became the private property of princes, thus giving strong impetus to the theories of political absolutism and the divine right of rulers. Furthermore, the new Protestantism did not bestow political or religious liberty on the individual, who had to believe what his prince wanted him to believe, be it Lutheranism or Catholicism. By formally sanctioning state religion and thus enhancing a ruler's power, the Peace of Augsburg added to Germany's political disintegration.

The reference to Catholic property in the settlement was important, for it had been the cause of much bitterness. After Luther's religious revolt, many nobles accepted his doctrine not because they necessarily believed it but because it gave them an excuse to seize Church property. Wholesale plundering of Church lands enriched many princes, and there was little prospect of peace until a compromise could be worked out. This was reached in the agreement of 1555: the Protestant princes retained the lands they had already confiscated, while the Church was assured that the seizures would be discontinued.

The death of Luther. In 1546, during the Schmalkaldic Wars, the founder of the new faith died. Martin Luther had been a born leader, genius, and zealot. His life had been molded by an absolute conviction of the rightness of his beliefs, which goes far to explain both his driving power and his limitations. "His weaknesses were manifest: intransigency in theological views, proneness to vehemence, narrowness of social concepts. . . . But Luther also had qualities to offset these: sincere desire for the truth, courage, determination, power of organization, an outstanding gift for identifying himself with the language and thought of the simple man. These were the qualities that permitted him to carry through what he had begun."[17]

In closing this account of Luther and the momentous movement which he set rolling, we might append an ironic footnote. The same sale of indulgences which furnished the money to build a fitting capital for a universal Church (St. Peter's in Rome) at the same time provided the occasion for destroying the Church's unchallenged position.

Lutheranism in Scandinavia. While its birthplace was the Holy Roman Empire, outside Germany Lutheranism permanently established itself as a state religion only in the Scandinavian countries. By 1560 Denmark established a national Lutheran Church. The Augsburg Confession was adopted, the Bible was translated into Danish, and other sects, Protestant or Catholic, were suppressed. Norway was at this time part of Denmark, and Lutheranism also triumphed there. Sweden, which had belonged to the union of the Scandinavian countries, made itself an independent state with Gustavus Vasa as its king (1523-1560). During his rule Protestantism was introduced, and the rise of this faith was closely interwoven with the nationalistic movement. More than once during the sixteenth century it appeared possible that Catholicism might win back its lost power in Sweden, but in the end Lutheranism triumphed. In 1593 the Swedish Church officially adopted the Confession of Augsburg, and in 1604 Catholics lost their property and offices.

Zwingli in Switzerland. Meanwhile, Protestantism had taken firm root in Switzerland. In the German-speaking area of that country —particularly in Zurich—the Reformation was led by Ulrich Zwingli (1484-1531). The same age as Luther and, like him, an earnest student of theology, Zwingli shared a number of beliefs with the German reformer. Both repudiated papal in favor of scriptural authority, preached justification by faith, attacked monasticism and clerical celibacy, and drastically revised the sacramental system. But the differences between the two leaders proved irreconcilable when they met in 1529 at the University of Marburg, founded two years earlier as the first Protestant university in Europe. Whereas Luther looked on Baptism as a means of helping to regenerate the individual, Zwingli considered it only a means of initiating a child into society, much as circumcision did in the Jewish community. Nor did he believe with Luther that the real presence of Christ was found in the Lord's Supper. To Zwingli, who had been trained as a humanist and was therefore more of a rationalist than Luther, it was simply a service commemorating the Last Supper. He acknowledged the spiritual, but not the physical, presence of Christ.

Zwingli was an ardent Swiss patriot who had once served as chaplain with Swiss mercenaries in Italy. The Swiss Confederation, comprising thirteen cantons, was almost autonomous even though it was part of the Holy Roman Empire. At the same time, it was subject to internal rivalries and to external pressures from more powerful neighbors. From Zurich, which he ruled as a theocracy, Zwingli sought to strengthen the political position of the Swiss cantons, especially those in the north that were Protestant. The southern cantons, however, remained firm in their allegiance to the Roman Catholic Church.

In the civil war that broke out in 1531, Zwingli and many of his followers were slain in battle. After the war, which ended in that same year, the cantons agreed to retain their respective religious doctrines. This settlement was largely responsible for keeping Switzerland from taking sides in the great religious wars that subsequently

ATLANTIC
OCEAN

NORTH
SEA

NORWAY
1536/1607

Bergen
• Oslo
Stockholm

Helsinki

BALTIC
SEA

ESTONIA

LIVONIA
Riga

Dvina R.

LITHUANIA

SCOTLAND
Edinburgh
John Knox,
1505-1572
Penetration of Calvinisim
into England after 1558

DENMARK Copenhagen

Danzig

Vilna

PRUSSIA

IRELAND
Dublin

ENGLAND
Oxford
John Wycliffe
1320-1384
Plymouth
London
Amsterdam

Hamburg
BRANDENBURG
Posen

Vistula R.
Warsaw
• Brest

Münster

Elbe R.

Wittenberg
Martin Luther, 1483-1546
Oct. 31, 1517 The 95 Theses
Philipp Melanchthon, 1497-1560

POLAND

NETHERLANDS
Brussels

Marburg
Leipzig

Noyon
Birthplace of
John Calvin, 1509
Paris

Rhine R.

GERMANY

Prague
John Huss 1369-1415

BOHEMIA

MORAVIA

Rennes

Orléans

Worms
Edict of Worms
1521

Basel

Danube R.

BAVARIA

Vienna

AUSTRIA

TRANSYLVANIA

Nantes
Edict of Nantes,
1598
La Rochelle

Augsburg
Constance Munich

Zurich
Ulrich Zwingli, 1484-1531

Pest
Buda
HUNGARY

BAY OF
BISCAY
Bordeaux

FRANCE
Religious Wars, 1562-1598

Lyons

Geneva
John Calvin,
1509-1564

Drava R.

Sava R.

Milan
Trent
Council of Trent,
1545-1563

Po R.

Venice

Belgrade

OTTOMAN
EMPIRE

Loyola
Birthplace of Ignatius Loyola, 1491
Founder of the Jesuit Order

Toulouse

Avignon

Genoa

Marseilles

Florence
Savonarola
1452-1498
Pisa

ADRIATIC SEA

Durazzo

Bari

Salonika

PORTUGAL

Douro R.

SPAIN

Ebro R.

Barcelona

CORSICA

ITALY

Rome
Roman Inquisition,
Established 1542

Lisbon

Madrid
Tagus R.
Toledo

Guadiana R.

Valencia

BALEARIC IS.

SARDINIA

Naples

Seville

Granada

MEDITERRANEAN

Palermo
SICILY

Tangier

Oran

Algiers

Bona

Tunis

MALTA

SEA

MUSLIM

STATES

Tripoli

Benghazi

REFORMATION AND
COUNTER-REFORMATION

Lutheran
Reformed (Calvinist)
Church of England
Roman Catholic
○ Huguenot Centers

engulfed Europe. Furthermore, it helped set the policy of neutrality which the Swiss have followed to our own day.

Calvin's beliefs in theory and practice. The most famous sixteenth-century Protestant leader after Luther was John Calvin (1509-1564). A Frenchman of the middle class, Calvin studied theology and law at Paris, where he became interested in Luther's teachings. About 1533 he had what he called a "conversion," whereby he abandoned Catholicism. When Francis I began to persecute heretics, Calvin fled to Switzerland and settled at Basel, a Protestant city. In 1536 he published the first edition of his great work, the *Institutes of the Christian Religion,* unquestionably one of the most influential books of systematic theology ever written. His capacity for creative thinking was overshadowed by his ability as an organizer and synthesist. Influenced by his legal training as well as by humanistic scholarship and the doctrines of Luther, Calvin set forth a system that was a masterpiece of logical reasoning.

Whereas Luther's central doctrine was justification by faith, Calvin's was the sovereignty of God. "The great text for Luther was 'Thy sins are forgiven,' but for Calvin it was 'If God is for us who can be against us?' Both Calvin and Luther had an overwhelming sense of the majesty of God, but whereas for Luther this served to point up the miracle of forgiveness, for Calvin it gave rather the assurance of the impregnability of God's purpose."[18] God was omnipotent and for His own purposes had created the world and also man in His image. Since Adam and Eve had fallen from a state of sinlessness, man was utterly depraved and lost.

Carrying these doctrines to their logical conclusions, Calvin defined man's relation to God in his famous doctrine of predestination. Since God is omniscient, He knows the past, present, and future. Consequently, He must always know which men are to be saved and which men are to be damned eternally. Man's purpose in life, then, is not to try to work out his salvation—for this has already been determined—but to honor God. While Calvin did not profess to know absolutely who were to be God's chosen—the elect—he believed that the following three tests constituted a good yardstick by which to judge who might be saved: participation in the two sacraments, Baptism and the Lord's Supper; an upright moral life; and a public profession of the faith.

Calvin's emphasis upon the sovereignty of God led him to differ with Luther on the relationship of church and state. To Luther, the state was supreme, but to Calvin, the church and its ministers, as representatives of the sovereignty of God, must dominate. Calvinist church government in turn was democratically oriented in that it was based on the authority not of bishops but of synods or presbyteries, elected bodies composed of ministers and elders. Although Calvin upheld lawful political authority, he also approved of rebellion against a tyranny "which overrides private conscience." Thus,

Enamel paintings such as this one were used to illustrate the teachings of John Calvin. A Calvinist is shown deep in prayer despite the temptations arrayed before him.

wherever Calvinism spread it carried with it the seeds of representative government and of defiance against despotism.

In 1536 the Protestants of Geneva invited Calvin to become their leader, and there he put his ideas on government into effect. Calvin believed it was the duty of the elect to glorify God by establishing a theocracy that would be governed according to scriptural precept. Although the Bible was the supreme authority, the chief instrument of government was the Consistory, or Presbytery, a council of ministers and elders which made and enforced the laws. Calvin in turn dominated the Consistory, which showed great zeal in disciplining the community and punishing or removing any person found guilty of unseemly behavior. Pains were taken to provide instruction in the fundamentals of faith, to prepare the young for useful Christian citizenship, to safeguard the purity of the faith, and to extirpate any remnant of Catholicism. Although the regime was high-minded, it carried its zeal to ridiculous lengths. Penalties were inflicted for being absent from sermons or laughing during the church service, for wearing bright colors, for swearing or dancing, for not reciting prayers, for playing cards, or for having one's fortune told by gypsies. Such puritanical regulations had also existed in medieval times, but in Calvin's Geneva they were energetically enforced.

In regard to more serious offenses, especially in the religious sphere, Calvin and his associates acted with a severity common to the Reformation age. They used torture to obtain confessions and banished citizens for heresy, blasphemy, witchcraft, and adultery. When the Spanish physician Servetus sought refuge in Geneva, having fled from Catholic persecution because he denied the doctrine of the Trinity, Calvin had him burned for heresy. "Because the Papist persecute the truth," Calvin explained, "should we on that account refrain from repressing error?"

The spread of Calvinism. From Geneva, Calvinism spread far and wide, imbued with its founder's spirit of austerity and a self-righteousness born of confidence

These pen and ink sketches of John Calvin in his later years were drawn by one of his students.

in being among the elect of God. Many of its leaders studied at the Academy (today the University of Geneva), which trained students from other countries in Calvin's theology. In France, Calvinism made influential converts among both the bourgeoisie and the nobility. Known as Huguenots, the French Calvinists were only a fraction of the population, but their importance far outweighed their numbers. In Chapter 17 we shall see how the Huguenots became involved in the religious wars of France.

Spreading into Germany and the northern Netherlands, Calvin's teachings formed the basis for the German and Dutch Reformed churches. In the latter half of the sixteenth century and the first half of the seventeenth, the Dutch struggle for independence against Spain strengthened Protestantism in their country. And in Scotland the authority of the Roman Church was successfully challenged by John Knox (see p. 500).

The quarrel between Henry VIII and Rome. In Germany the revolt against the Church was primarily religious in nature, although it possessed political implications; in England the situation was reversed. True, there was an ecclesiastical revolt, but the leader was a monarch, Henry VIII (1509-1547), not a priest. Henry broke with Rome not for theological reasons but because the pope would not annul his marriage.

Henry was the second son of Henry VII; his older brother Arthur was the heir apparent. The crafty and miserly Henry VII had engaged Arthur to Catherine, the daughter of Ferdinand and Isabella of Spain. The Tudors were to receive a large dowry, but Arthur died shortly after his marriage to Catherine and before all the dowry had been paid. Eager for both the dowry and the alliance with Spain, Henry VII then arranged the marriage of the young Henry to Catherine, which took place shortly after Henry VIII ascended the throne. Henry and Catherine had six children, of whom only one, Mary, survived.

Henry VIII became convinced that a male heir was necessary if the newly established Tudors were to endure as a dynasty and England kept from reverting to anarchy. Catherine was the widow of his brother, and Church law forbade a man to marry his brother's widow. A special papal dispensation had been granted for Henry's marriage, but Henry may have feared that God in His displeasure had denied him a son. At any rate, Henry claimed that he had never been validly married to Catherine, who was now past childbearing, and in 1527 he asked Pope Clement VII to revoke the dispensation which had allowed him to marry Catherine.

Normally the pope might have acquiesced to Henry's wishes, for other popes had granted similar favors to monarchs and Henry had been loyal to the Church. In answer to Luther's *The Babylonian Captivity of the Church,* he had written a *Defense of the Seven Sacraments* (1521), in which he castigated Luther as a "poisonous serpent," the "wolf of hell," and the "limb of Satan." The pope gratefully bestowed on Henry the title "Defender of the Faith"—a title which English monarchs still possess. Confronted now with Henry's request for an annulment, the pope went so far as to send a commission to England to investigate the case and even

to appoint a favorite of Henry's to the commission. But much as he might have wished, the pope could not support Henry in his desires. There were two good reasons. First, the pope felt it would be dangerous for one pontiff to reverse the judgments of a predecessor. Second, the emperor Charles V, the most powerful monarch in Europe, was a nephew of Catherine and threatened the pope if he declared the marriage null and void. Clement decided to wait before giving his answer, hoping that in the meantime events would resolve themselves.

But Henry would not wait. His chief adviser, Thomas Cardinal Wolsey, who had served his king well for years, failed to obtain the all-important consent of the pope, and in a rage Henry deprived Wolsey of his office. Disgraced, Wolsey died in 1530, barely escaping the headsman's ax. One year later Henry fined the English clergy a large sum of money and compelled them to acknowledge the king as "their singular protector, only and supreme lord, and, as the law of Christ allows, even Supreme Head." Next he obtained from Parliament the power to appoint bishops in England without papal permission, designating Thomas Cranmer as archbishop of Canterbury—a willing tool who was sure to do his master's bidding. In 1533 Cranmer pronounced the king's marriage to Catherine invalid and legalized Henry's marriage to Anne Boleyn, whom he had secretly married three months earlier. At last goaded into action, Clement VII excommunicated Henry and maintained that Catherine alone was the king's true wife.

Establishment of the Anglican Church. In 1534 Henry severed all connections with Rome. A compliant Parliament passed the famous Act of Supremacy, which stated that the king "justly and rightfully is and ought to be supreme head of the Church of England, called *Anglicana Ecclesia.*" It also enacted the Treason Act, which declared liable to the death penalty anyone who called the king a "heretic, schismatic, tyrant, infidel, or usurper." Turning on his old friend, Henry had Sir Thomas More beheaded because he would not acknowledge the sovereign as head of the English Church. In

Both Catholics and Protestants were guilty of incredible atrocities in their respective attempts to achieve religious uniformity. The print at top showing the persecution of English Catholics by the Protestants was originally printed in a French book that the English ambassador demanded be suppressed because of its inflammatory nature. The print at bottom, which first appeared in Foxe's *Acts and Monuments* (1632), depicts a group of Protestants being led to London for trial. During Queen Mary's five-year reign three hundred people were burned for heresy.

Ye shall be led before Princes and Rulers for my names sake.
Matthew 10.

recent years More has been canonized by the Catholic Church not only for his saintly life but also for his martyrdom in opposing Henry VIII's divorce and break with the Church.

To replenish the royal coffers and to gain popular approval, Henry took possession of the rich monasteries, giving much of the land to cooperative landowners for their sheep raising and thus making them, in a sense, accomplices in the conflict with Rome. It must be remembered that Henry and Parliament could not perhaps have effected such sweeping changes if many Englishmen—particularly the members of the prosperous and increasingly powerful middle class—had not been anticlerical. By 1539 all monastic houses were dissolved. But in the same year Parliament passed the Six Articles, which reaffirmed the main points of Catholic theology. By this act, both the Catholic who denied the supremacy of the king and the Protestant who denied the validity of transubstantiation were to be punished severely.

It is idle to discuss whether the Tudor king deliberately planned the break from the Church. In the early phases of the revolt in England it seems likely that Henry had no thought of breaking from the Church if he could have his way on the annulment question. Unlike the revolt in Germany, that in England involved at its inception no quarrel with the doctrines of the Church. In fact, Henry took great pride in his theological orthodoxy, and the Six Articles reinforced the basic tenets of Catholicism while denying papal supremacy over the monarch. Thus England threw off the supremacy of the pope without at that time adopting the Protestant faith; the elements of Protestantism in the English Church crept in after the break with Rome.

After Henry's death in 1547, his frail ten-year-old son mounted the throne as Edward VI. During his reign the growing Protestant party in England became ascendant. The Six Articles were repealed; priests were no longer held to their vows of celibacy; and the old Latin service was replaced by Cranmer's Book of Common Prayer, written in English, which brought the service much closer to the people and exerted a powerful influence on the development of the language. In 1553 the Forty-Two Articles defined the faith of the Church of England along Protestant lines.

Under the devoutly Catholic Mary (1553-1558), the unfortunate daughter of the still less fortunate Catherine of Aragon, Catholicism was reinstated, and hundreds of heretics, including Archbishop Cranmer, were put to death. But with the accession to the throne of Anne Boleyn's red-headed and fiery-tempered daughter, Elizabeth I (1558-1603), the Anglican Church took on a strong Protestant character. Realizing the political necessity for religious peace, Elizabeth worked hard to achieve a compromise settlement. Although the Church of England remained a state church under the control of the monarch, Elizabeth astutely changed her title from "Supreme Head" to the more modest "Supreme Governor." In accepting the Bible as the final authority, and in recognizing only Baptism and Holy Eucharist as Christ-instituted sacraments, Elizabeth's Thirty-Nine Articles (1563) were essentially Protestant, although many articles were ambiguously phrased in an effort to satisfy both parties. Much Catholic ritual was preserved, along with the ecclesiastical government of bishops in apostolic succession.

Presbyterianism in Scotland. The religious revolt in Scotland was largely the work of the zealous reformer John Knox (1505?-1572), who had become a disciple of Calvin in Geneva, which he called "the most perfect school of Christ that ever was on earth since the days of the Apostles." After returning to his native Scotland in about 1559, Knox became the leader of a group of Protestant nobles who wished to overthrow both the jurisdiction of the Roman Catholic Church and the monarch—Queen Mary Stuart, who was residing in France (see p. 527). In 1560 Knox drew up the Articles of the Presbyterian Church, modeled after Calvin's views on theology and church government.

One year later, the beautiful but ill-fated Mary Stuart returned from France to find her bleak kingdom alienated from her own Catholic views. From his pulpit and in his debates with Mary, Knox defied the queen's authority and thundered against her religious principles. The fiery reformer gained the support of the Scottish Lowlanders in his denunciation of the queen. By the time Mary had been executed by Elizabeth in 1587 (see p. 528), much of Scotland had been won over to Calvinistic Presbyterianism.

The Anabaptists. The picture of religious developments in sixteenth-century Europe would not be complete without an account of the multitude of other Protestant sects which sprang up during this period. Many of these sects opposed infant baptism on the grounds that an infant could not possibly understand the significance of this sacrament. Historians often lump them together under the term *Anabaptists,* meaning "those baptized again," since individuals were sometimes rebaptized as adults when they joined any of these groups. Although there were important differences among the various sects, the Anabaptists, broadly speaking, believed firmly in their own interpretation of Biblical authority and rejected the necessity for a body of clergymen, maintaining that a person should follow the guidance of his "inner light." Because they questioned many doctrines fundamental to other forms of Protestantism and to Catholicism, the Anabaptists suffered religious persecution and social ostracism.

The Anabaptists, often referred to as the "left wing" of Protestantism, displayed the most radical social tendencies of the time. Many of the peasants whose hopes for economic and social reform had been crushed by the Peasants' War turned from Luther to the Anabaptists. In communities of their own, they shared their worldly goods with one another and lived as they thought the primitive Christians had lived, working and praying together. The Anabaptists believed in the separation of church and state, condemned military service and the taking of oaths, and often refused to pay taxes to governments engaged in warfare. For these reasons they were persecuted intermittently by secular authorities and even forced to flee from their homes. Today their spirit lives on among such groups as the Mennonites, the Amish, and the Quakers.

In this contemporary illustration John Knox sounds his trumpet of reform in the ears of Mary, Queen of Scots. The text accompanying the picture reads, "No Queen in her kingdom can or ought to sit fast, if Knox's . . . books blow any true blast."

THE CATHOLIC REFORMATION

Catholic reformers and reform movements. The Catholic Reformation should not be viewed as only a retaliatory movement or a series of measures taken to stem the rising tide of Protestantism. The Roman Church had always retained latent forces of recuperation and strength which it could draw upon in challenging times. Before Luther had posted his ninety-five theses, renewed vitality and internal reform were apparent in the Roman Church.

One of the prime examples of this resurgence occurred in Spain under Ferdinand and Isabella, ardent Catholics as well as autocrats. To deal with Moors, Jews, and heretics, the "Catholic Sovereigns" requested and got papal permission for a separate Spanish Inquisition under their control (see p. 428). The Inquisition soon came to dominate the Spanish Church, making it virtually a state church, and moved on to the problem of religious reform. Under the able Grand Inquisitor, Cardinal Ximenes (d. 1517), both the secular clergy and the monastic orders were invigorated by a renewal of spirit, discipline, and education —the latter including the scientific study of the Bible at the University of Alcala, founded by Ximenes as a means of training able bishops. Thus Spain became a model Catholic state, where Protestantism would make few converts.

In a category of his own was the Dominican friar Savonarola (1452-1498), an ardent puritan, mystic, and reformer of Church and society. In 1496, when the Medici were expelled from Florence, Savonarola emerged as master of the city. For four years he ruled the Kingdom of God, as he called Florence, invoking the wrath of God upon worldly living and sinful luxuries. Bands of children were organized to go about the city collecting and burning "vanities"—fashionable clothes, wigs, ornaments, and secular books and paintings. Savonarola also bitterly denounced the iniquities of the Borgia pope, Alexander VI, and called for a general council to reform the Church. But he lacked the power to reform the papacy and the Church, or even to maintain his hold on the fickle Florentines. Publicly humiliated by having his Dominican garb torn from him in the great square of Florence, Savonarola was hanged and burned, a victim of political intrigue. He was later hailed by Luther and the Protestants as a forerunner of their movement.

After many abortive attempts at establishing a "Christian council" to review Catholic dogma and discipline, the Council of Trent was finally convened in December 1545. The Council reaffirmed the Church's basic tenets, but it did order reforms in Church discipline and administration.

By the middle of the sixteenth century the inroads of Protestantism were apparent, and in retaliation the Church rallied its forces and prepared a powerful offensive. This renewal of strength, known as the Catholic Reformation—or, as some prefer, Counter Reformation—penetrated all areas of the Church. New monastic orders adapted monastic life to the needs of the time, the papacy headed a program of vigorous reform, and the Church regained much ground lost to the Protestants. Climaxing the whole movement was the Council of Trent, where the Church boldly reaffirmed its traditional doctrines and flatly refused to compromise in any way with the Protestants.

Reformist monasticism. In response to the same forces that had produced monastic reform during the earlier medieval reformation, a number of new monastic orders sprang up in the first half of the sixteenth century. In the same year that Luther issued his ninety-five theses, a group of clerics and laymen in Rome founded the Oratory of Divine Love. Its purpose was to use prayer, sermons, and good works to create a strong personal religious consciousness but at the same time to retain the traditional Catholic framework and the leadership of the papacy.

Other prominent new orders were the Theatines, a body of devoted priests who undertook to check the spread of heresy by concentrating upon the regeneration of the clergy; the Capuchins, an offshoot of the Franciscan order inspired by the original spirit of St. Francis, who became notable for their preaching and for the care of the poor and the sick; and the Ursulines, whose special task was the education of girls. Reflecting both the reforming zeal of the new orders and the mystical reaffirmation of faith that characterized most reformers, Protestant as well as Catholic, was the order of barefoot Carmelites and their founder, the Spanish nun St. Theresa. These devout sisters slept on straw, ate no meat, and lived on alms. Quietistic mysticism, which teaches that spiritual peace can be attained by losing the sense of self in passive contemplation of God and His works, is well reflected in St. Theresa's written accounts of her ecstasies and visions.

Loyola and the Jesuits. The Society of Jesus, better known as the Jesuits, founded by the Spanish nobleman and ex-soldier Ignatius Loyola (1491-1556), played a vital role in the Catholic Reformation. While recovering from a severe battle wound, Loyola experienced a mystical religious conversion and vowed to become a soldier of Christ and "serve only God and the Roman pontiff, His vicar on earth." His "Company [*Societas*] of Jesus," founded in 1534 and given papal authorization in 1540, was organized along military lines with Loyola as "general." Members were carefully selected, rigorously trained, and subjected to an iron discipline. One of the classics in the field of religious literature, Loyola's *Spiritual Exercises,* a work of great psychological penetration based on his own mystical religious experience, was used to inculcate disciplined asceticism and absolute obedience to superior authority. In addition to the usual monastic vows of chastity, obedience, and poverty, the Jesuits took a special vow of allegiance to the pope. As preachers, confessors to monarchs and princes, and educators, the Jesuits had remarkable success in stemming and even reversing the tide of Protestantism, particularly in Poland, Bohemia, Hungary, Germany, France, and the Spanish Netherlands (modern Belgium). In addition, the Jesuits performed excellent missionary work in America and Asia.

Papal reform: Paul III. A new era was at hand for the Church when Paul III, who reigned from 1534 to 1549, ascended the papal throne. He chose outstanding men as cardinals and appointed a commission to look into the need for reform. Their report listed the evils requiring correction, including the appointment of worldly bishops and priests, the traffic in benefices and indulgences and other financial abuses, the venality of some cardinals, and the absence of others from the papal court. Paul's decision to begin acting upon this report aroused considerable opposition from various quarters. But he persisted, and among other reforms improved the papal administrative machinery. Again ignoring the opposition of high churchmen who feared for their positions and incomes, Paul made plans to reform the entire Church organization at a general council.

The Council of Trent: climax of the Catholic Reformation. Reviving the device of a Church council, so useful at the time of the Great Schism, the Catholic Reformation came to a climax in the Council of Trent, which met in three sessions between 1545 and 1563. Rejecting all compromise with Protestantism, the Council restated the basic tenets of Catholic doctrine. It declared salvation to be a matter of both faith and good works, and it affirmed the source of doctrine to be not only the Bible, as interpreted by the Church, but also the "unwritten traditions, which were received by the Apostles from the lips of Christ himself, or, by the same Apostles, at the dictation of the Holy Spirit, and were handed on and have come down to us. . . ."[19] The Council also reaffirmed the seven sacraments, with special emphasis on transubstantiation, decreed that only Latin be used in the Mass, and approved the spiritual usefulness of indulgences, pilgrimages, veneration of saints and relics, and the cult of the Virgin.

At the same time, the Council sought to eliminate abuses by ordering reforms in Church discipline and administration. Such evils as simony, absenteeism, the abuse of indulgences, and secular pursuits on the part of the clergy were strictly forbidden. Bishops were ordered to supervise closely both the regular and the secular clergy, appoint reputable and competent men to ecclesiastical positions, and establish seminaries to provide a well-educated clergy. The clergy, in turn, were requested to preach frequently to the people.

In addition to freeing the Church of its worst abuses and formulating its doctrines clearly and rigidly, the Council of Trent strengthened the authority of the papacy. The pope's party in the Council, ably led by Jesuit theologians, defeated all attempts to revive the theory that a general council was supreme in the Church. And when the final session of the Council voted that none of its decrees were valid without the consent of the Holy See, the Church became more than ever an absolute monarchy ruled by the pope.

EFFECTS OF THE RELIGIOUS UPHEAVAL

Religious division but renewed faith. Prior to 1517 there had been two religious divisions of Christendom—Greek Orthodox and Roman Catholic. By 1550 Christendom was composed of three divisions—Orthodox, Catholic, and Protestant. Protestantism predominated in northern Europe, while Catholicism prevailed in the south. This great religious division had struck a mortal blow at the medieval unity of Europe. The Catholics placed their faith in the authority of the pope and the need for a mediatory priesthood. The Protestants placed their faith in the authority of the Bible and held that every Christian could win salvation without priestly mediation. The Protestants differed among themselves in their interpretation of the Bible and the methods of church organization; and in time hundreds of Protestant sects arose, many claiming to

"Pope Paul III and His Two Nephews" by Titian.

possess the one and only true interpretation and logical administration.

Although the religious upheaval irreparably split the unity of Christendom, and in so doing fostered the religious diversity of modern times, it also represented in some aspects a return to medievalism. It was a great religious revival, a renewal of faith. After the Renaissance era of free and secular thought, of individualism and humanism, men's thoughts were turned again to salvation and the life hereafter. Free thought gave way again to authority—for Protestants it was the Bible; for Catholics, the Church. The Renaissance movement, having fostered doubt and criticism of medieval values, was now engulfed in a return to some of those values. Freethinkers were persecuted by both sides, and talented writers and thinkers who in Renaissance times might have followed the prevailing pattern of individualism and secularism now devoted their abilities to arguing one side or another of the burning conflict of the day. Thus, temporarily at least, the Renaissance spirit was stifled. But it was to prove stronger than this intense religious revival and in time was to profit from the passing of the single religious authority of the universal Church.

Along with a renewal of faith, the religious upheaval brought about a great deal of genuine religious reform. The Protestant service of worship was simplified in an effort to return to the purity of early Christian times. Strict attention was given to conduct and morals. In answer to the Protestant challenge, a reform movement also took place within the Catholic Church, beginning, as we have seen, with the accession of Pope Paul III and culminating in the decrees of the Council of Trent. This movement changed neither doctrine nor organization but attempted to clarify and reaffirm doctrine and purify and strengthen discipline among the clergy and laity alike.

A by-product of the religious upheaval was a new interest in education. Each faith wanted its youth to be properly trained in its teachings. As part of its campaign to win Protestants back to the fold, the Jesuits in particular developed a school system so superior and so attractive that many Protestant as well as Catholic youths attended. Protestant churches of the period developed few schools to challenge the Jesuit colleges and universities, but one feature of Protestantism eventually stimulated education a great deal. Its tenet that the one source of religious truth is the Bible encouraged its members to read the Scriptures. As a result, training in reading became a basic feature of education.

On the debit side the Reformation era witnessed an intensification of religious intolerance. There seems little choice between Catholics and Protestants in the degree of their detestation for one another and for religious liberty in general. Each religious sect assumed that salvation came through it alone, and all were equally intolerant when they had the power to be so. In the words of Sebastian Castellio (d. 1563), a one-time follower of Calvin who wrote a protest against the execution of Servetus:

Although opinions are almost as numerous as men, nevertheless there is hardly any sect which does not condemn all others and desire to reign alone. Hence arise banishments, chains, imprisonments, stakes, and gallows and this miserable rage to visit daily penalties upon those who differ from the mighty about matters hitherto unknown, for so many centuries disputed, and not yet cleared up.[20]

How can we call ourselves Christians, Castellio asked in effect, if we do not imitate Christ's clemency and mercy?

O Creator and King of the world, dost Thou see these things? Art Thou become so changed, so cruel, so contrary to Thyself? When Thou wast on earth none was more mild, more clement, more patient of injury. . . . O blasphemies and shameful audacity of men, who dare to attribute to Christ that which they do by the command and at the instigation of Satan![21]

Unfortunate, too, was the break between the humanists and the Protestants, which began when Luther broke with the Church. Although both groups wanted to reform the Church by removing its abuses and returning to the practices and faith of early Christianity, Erasmus could say of Luther's revolt: "I laid a hen's egg: Luther hatched a bird of quite different breed."[22] The humanists, in

The blind John Milton dictates to his daughters in this painting by George Romney.

other words, desired reform, not revolution. Furthermore, because they exalted the rationality and innate goodness of man, the humanists disagreed with the strong Protestant emphasis on man's depravity and the necessity of salvation by superhuman means. As Luther saw it, "The human avails more with Erasmus than the divine."[23]

The Reformation affects literature. Soon after James I ascended the throne of England in 1603 (see Chapter 2, Volume II), the new monarch assembled a conference of scholars from Oxford, Cambridge, and elsewhere who in 1611 brought out a new translation of the Bible known as the King James Version. Powerful, sonorous, majestic—these adjectives describe what is still considered by many the most successful of all vernacular translations of the Old and New Testaments. Like Luther's translation of the Bible into German, the King James Version constitutes one of the strongest single influences upon the course of English thought and literature.

But the effect of the Reformation on literature was by no means restricted to Bible translation. For decades the forces set in motion by the Protestant Revolt had been exerting a growing influence on European thought, and this influence was reflected in the works of contemporary writers. England during the period of Puritan ascendancy offers a number of examples. After the establishment of the Commonwealth, the Puritans repressed the theater as immoral and stifled any incentive for dramatists to continue their creative efforts. Yet the Puritan environment stimulated the creation of outstanding religiously motivated poetry and prose.

Often ranked second only to Shakespeare among English poets is John Milton (1608-1674). The son of a prosperous lawyer, young Milton received an excellent classical education, as the many allusions to antiquity in his verse attest. He became familiar with humanistic concepts while visiting Italy during a tour of the Continent and later served in Cromwell's administration. When the monarchy was restored in 1660, Milton retired to a life of writing.

During his later years, despite total blindness, Milton composed the epic *Paradise Lost,* which he dictated to members of his family and published in 1667. Here the story of man's fall makes the universe a battleground between the forces of good and evil. The poem is magnificent in its cosmic sweep, and the portrait of Lucifer as a majestic figure of power is easily Milton's finest.

In Milton were blended the strains of Renaissance humanism and Puritanism. His reverence for antiquity and his belief in human dignity and freedom are attributable to the former; his moral earnestness, to the latter. Although inclined by nature to quiet study, he devoted twenty years of his life to public service in a period of great turmoil and was a fearless pamphleteer for Puritan causes.

John Bunyan (1628-1688), another Puritan spokesman, lacked both the family background and the education of Milton but became one of the great masters of vernacular prose. Strongly imaginative and filled with religious zeal, Bunyan wrestled for years with agonizing fears that he was doomed to damnation. He even renounced such favorite "vices" as dancing and ringing the bells of the parish church. Bunyan became an eloquent Puritan preacher, but after the restoration of the monarchy in 1660 he was thrown into jail for continuing to preach Puritan doctrine. During his twelve years in prison he wrote *Pilgrim's Progress,* one of the most widely read books in literature. In this allegory of a journey that typifies the Christian life, the hero, named Christian, leaves the City of Destruction and traverses the Slough of Despond, the Valley of the Shadow of Death, Vanity Fair, and other places of temptation until at length he comes to the Celestial City,

... and, behold, the City shone like the sun; the streets also were paved with gold, and in them walked many men, with crowns on their heads, palms in their hands, and golden harps to sing praises withal.[24]

Protestantism and capitalism. While the Reformation fostered a return to medieval attitudes in many ways, in the economic sphere the opposite was true. The Renaissance encouraged a new individualism in economic matters, which contributed to a breakdown of the guild system and to the rise of the individual entrepreneur. Protestantism moved away from the old concept of the "just price" and the ban against usury (receiving interest on money loaned). Investment of capital and loaning of money became respectable. Calvinism especially encouraged enterprise; some Calvinists regarded prosperity as a sign of election to grace and poverty as evidence of damnation. Indeed, it has been asserted that:

Calvin did for the bourgeoisie of the sixteenth century what Marx did for the proletariat of the nineteenth, ... the doctrine of predestination satisfied the same hunger for an assurance that the forces of the universe are on the side of the elect as was to be assuaged in a different age by the theory of historical materialism. He set their virtues at their best in sharp antithesis with the vices of the established order at its worst, taught them to feel that they were a chosen people, made them conscious of their great destiny in the Providential plan and resolute to realize it.[25]

The confiscation of monastic lands in Protestant countries also stimulated economic development. England in particular benefited from the use of former monastic lands. We noted earlier that the business classes were among those that encouraged the revolt from Rome; we can now see that they were also among those that gained most by it.

Union of religion and politics. In many cases the religious division of Europe followed political lines. Just as the English king bound the national church and the national state together under his own leadership, so in Germany the Peace of Augsburg gave the ruler of each state the right to decide the faith of his subjects, thus controlling the church in his realm. Similarly, rulers of other countries, both Catholic and Protestant, developed national churches, so that Europe was divided religiously into an Anglican Church, a Dutch Church, a Swedish Church, and so on.

In many countries one effect of such division was to strengthen the hand of the king in building a unified state. The authority and prestige of the Protestant monarch was increased as he became the spiritual as well

This portrait of John Bunyan dreaming the story of *Pilgrim's Progress* appeared in an early edition of the book; burdened with his load of sin and carrying the Bible, the pilgrim Christian is shown in the background, journeying from the City of Destruction to the Celestial City.

as the political ruler of his subjects. Even in Catholic countries, though the pope remained the spiritual ruler, the Church became national in sentiment, and it was the king rather than the pope who enforced religious conformity among his subjects. Conversely, where the split between Protestants and Catholics was deep, as in the Holy Roman Empire, the power of the central ruler was limited and national unity impeded.

Freedom of religion, as we have noted, was still far from a reality. Persecution flourished, partly because the clash between faiths engendered intolerance but even more because religious uniformity was the ideal of the rulers of the rising national states. Just as he sought to create a uniform system of law and justice throughout his realm, so the strong monarch endeavored to establish a single faith to which his subjects owed complete obedience. An incidental result of this policy was the emigration of religious minorities to areas where they could worship freely, as in the New World.

Political and religious developments continued to be closely related throughout the sixteenth and early seventeenth centuries. In the Religious Wars political duels were superimposed on religious quarrels, resulting in some of the bloodiest and most prolonged warfare in human history. The founder of the Christian religion had given as a primary command, "Thou shalt love thy neighbor as thyself." But there was no brotherhood between Catholic and Protestant nor between political rivals who played on religious antagonisms to serve their own ends. The story of this politico-religious warfare will be told in the next chapter.

SUMMARY

The Renaissance represented a new emphasis on man's individuality, an outlook which could not fail eventually to have its impact on religion. An appeal for religious reform came from such outstanding human-

ists such as Erasmus, who criticized ecclesiastical abuses and called for a Christianity based closely upon the New Testament. By means of the printing press, which vastly increased the number of books available, the new ideas spread rapidly throughout Europe. Already beginning to revolt against all institutions which hampered them in their new economic freedom, many men of the middle class were sympathetic to the cry for Church reform. The new spirit also found an ally in the new nationalism and in the growing power of the kings, who were reluctant to be thwarted by any force, even the Church. When a leader appeared with a religious message in keeping with the spirit of the age, the long bottled-up forces of reform exploded.

In the meantime, the Church itself was badly weakened as a result of the Babylonian Captivity and the Great Schism. While the Conciliar Movement healed the Great Schism, reformers within the Church made little headway until after the religious unity of Europe was irretrievably torn.

Luther's open breach with the Church encouraged such Protestant leaders as Zwingli, Calvin, and other reformers to form their own churches. The essence of the new movements was an emphasis on Biblical authority, a denial of the need for priestly mediation for salvation, and a repudiation of the pope as head of organized religion. After the Protestant Revolt, churches were firmly tied to the political administration of the states. Thus Calvin and Zwingli established theocracies in Geneva and Zurich in Switzerland. In Germany each prince chose between Lutheranism and Catholicism for the religion of his subjects. In the Scandinavian countries the national churches were Lutheran. Without repudiating the basic elements of Catholicism, the English king broke with Rome and assumed the headship of the Anglican Church. As religious issues became inextricably entangled with politics, Protestants and Catholics clashed bitterly.

The challenge flung at the Church did not remain unanswered. On the contrary, in such countries as Italy, Spain, and France, the forces of religious reform achieved noticeable results. As the medieval Church had arrested decline by new zealous orders of monks, so once again the Church was invigorated by various new brotherhoods and a resurgence of mysticism. Meanwhile, Pope Paul III instigated an energetic program to excise the abuses which had plagued the Church for centuries. Without any compromise with the Protestants, the Council of Trent reaffirmed the fundamental doctrines of the Church. But there was no possibility of the Church reuniting Europe.

Europe was plunged into an epoch of intolerance and bigotry from which it slowly emerged when, after prolonged and bloody struggles, it became apparent that no one faith could exterminate the others. But if the clock was set back in some ways, in other ways the religious upheaval furthered the transition from a medieval to a modern pattern of life. The revolt from the universal Church shattered the medieval ideal of unity and gave us the religious diversity of the modern world.

Chapter 17

The Strife of States and Kings

**Power Politics and the New Diplomacy:
1500-1650**

INTRODUCTION. All of us are deeply concerned about the quest for peace and order in the world. Constantly aware of the strife in the crisis-ridden areas of the world, the clash of rival ideologies, and the threat of world conflagration, we follow the debates and tactical maneuvers in the UN General Assembly and the Security Council with keen interest and do our best to keep abreast of the constant shifts and countershifts in international politics. By acquiring a historical perspective, by studying the pattern of European politics in early modern times, we can do much to illuminate today's events and problems and bring them into focus. The period from 1500 to 1650 is particularly significant; it can serve as a laboratory in which we can watch the genesis and development of the statecraft of modern times.

The crucial factor in this troubled period was the rise of the competitive state system, involving independent and sovereign nations, each controlled by a single, all-powerful government. As early as the eleventh century such nation-states as England, France,

Portugal, and Spain had begun their respective journeys toward greatness. By the beginning of the sixteenth century these budding nations exhibited three fundamental features that contrasted sharply with the characteristics the same territories had possessed in earlier, feudal times: they had strong and effective central governments, their citizens displayed increased national consciousness, and their rulers claimed sovereignty—that is, supreme power within the boundaries of their own states. As we shall see in this chapter, these states were expansionist and aggressive, taking every opportunity to grow more powerful at the expense of weaker nations.

As a few strong sovereign states replaced the multitude of comparatively small and weak feudal units, they were forced to work out a power relationship among themselves. Would one state be able to dominate all the rest? Would there be varying degrees of power among states without any one becoming supreme? Would these independent and sovereign nations be able to establish a pattern of cooperation, ensuring thereby a measure of peace and political amity in the western world? Furthermore, we saw in Chapter 16 that the decline of the medieval Church and the religious revolt in the sixteenth century ended the Church's role as the arbiter of right and justice in disputes between secular rulers. The rulers of the sovereign states were thus completely free and untrammeled in the arena of international politics. Would they exercise restraint? Would they develop among themselves some moral basis for the conduct of statecraft? All these fundamental questions were answered in Europe between 1500 and 1650. And the way in which they were answered set the pattern of international relations from that day to this.

The one hundred fifty years following 1500 are among the bloodiest and most complex in European history. The story of these years is chiefly one of battles, alliances, and treaties—in a word, drum-and-trumpet history. Yet running through the wars and complexities of this period two major threads can be discerned: the emergence of the modern diplomatic technique of the "balance of power" as a means of providing some degree of equilibrium to the new European state system, and the rise and fall of Spain as the dominant power in Europe.

THE COMPETITIVE STATE SYSTEM EMERGES

Medieval political ideals and realities. The medieval ideal was unity—a Europe united as a Christian commonwealth and ruled by dual powers, the universal Church and an all-embracing Holy Roman Empire. To Dante, the basis of human welfare was a system of politics consisting of "divine governance, universal empire, perpetual peace, eternal justice and the general reign of law."[1]

In theory the emperor would rule in the temporal or earthly realm, and the pope in the affairs of the spirit. But the Church claimed, and was given, primacy. All governments and men were expected to support and obey the universal Church. As vicars of Christ, popes crowned rulers, restrained warfare by the Truce of God, acted as arbiters in royal disputes, and on occasion forced recalcitrant kings to their knees as Pope Gregory did the emperor Henry IV at Canossa.

Because papal authority was not constricted by national boundaries, the Church was nearly all-embracing. By contrast, the emperor's authority was limited for the most part to Germany and Italy, and even there imperial power was intermittent and shadowy. Therefore, the imperial ideal was never realized.

Effective political power was found in the feudal pyramid—the political structure of each "nation," which was presided over by the suzerain, or king. In this pyramid every-

Indicative of the monarchs' quest for complete sovereignty was Henry VIII's establishment of the Church of England, answerable ultimately only to the king. This new arrangement was made quite clear by the title page of the Church of England's first Bible which shows Henry dominating the scene as he presents copies to Thomas Cromwell and Archbishop Cranmer for public distribution.

one from the lowliest vassal up to the king shared degrees of power; authority was not concentrated or monopolized at the top.

Sovereignty replaces suzerainty. The medieval conception of universal empire and Church was undermined by the rise of strong monarchs who defied popes and churchmen and put down rebellious nobles. Proud of their dynasties and imbued with the secular spirit of the Renaissance, these kings sought glory, wealth, and power.

At the close of the fifteenth century the power of the national monarchies was rapidly increasing. The past century had witnessed much disorder, civil conflict, and war; more and more, people looked to their kings to provide the state with a measure of stability and security. Because rulers took an active part in stimulating the economy of their nations, in return they obtained from the bourgeoisie larger revenues than had for-

merly been available, and the administrative bureaus and government services were expanded. Of great importance was the fact that kings could now afford to hire soldiers for standing armies—monarchs were no longer dependent upon the irregularly available feudal forces. Moreover, the king's army could easily squelch the retainers of a rebellious noble.

As kings built up their power, they began to seek legal and philosophical justification to buttress their claims to increased royal authority. From the Italian universities, the study of Roman law spread throughout Europe, and middle-class lawyers cited Justinian's Code, "What the emperor has determined has the force of law since . . . the people has transferred to him all its power and authority,"[2] and claimed that the king was an emperor in his own kingdom. As the Middle Ages drew to a close, the power once distributed throughout the feudal pyramid was gradually being concentrated in the hands of the ruler.

The fact of national sovereignty existed before the theory of centralized unchallenged authority—that is, sovereignty—was given its first comprehensive expression by a French lawyer and university professor, Jean Bodin (1530-1596). Dismayed by the disorders of the religious wars in France (see p. 530), Bodin attacked both the feudal idea of contract and the universalism of empire and Church in his work *Concerning Public Affairs.* He supported the power of the monarch and his right of sovereignty, which he defined as "unlimited power over citizens and subjects, unrestrained by law."[3] According to Bodin, the king was free of all restraint save some rather shadowy limitation exercised by God and divine law. Although Bodin implied that other limitations existed, later political theorists were to favor complete royal absolutism.

The advent of power politics. Equipped with a standing army, royal courts, and new sources of revenue and backed by the growing support of the bourgeoisie, a European monarch was master in his own nation by the beginning of the sixteenth century. And, equally significant, he was his own master in foreign affairs. The Church was no longer an international arbiter, and the factionalism of the Protestant Reformation was soon to reduce appreciably the Church's claim to universal influence. The international arena now consisted of a number of free agents who could keep what they could defend and take what they wanted if they had sufficient force. A nation-state depended for survival on the exercise of its power, and war was the chief instrument at hand. Thus statecraft became the politics of power, and the competitive state system emerged.

As permanent forces, subject to effective discipline and commanded by career officers, armies and navies grew more efficient. The heavily armored medieval knight was outmoded; the victories of the English longbow had marked the first step in his passing, and the introduction of artillery and muskets swept him from the battlefield. Fired from a wooden fork and requiring laborious reloading, muskets were still primitive, however. To protect the musketeer from cavalry charges while reloading, pikemen with long pikes or lances were employed to present a

The introduction of artillery and muskets revolutionized the character of warfare. The drawing shows cannons of about the year 1550 bristling hedgehog defense against mounted men. Later the bayonet was invented, providing the foot soldier with a means of defense or attack between shots. The use of gunpowder opened a new chapter in the history of warfare; ''. . . war passed into its technological phase . . . he who could wield the superior weapon was the more formidable foe. . . .''[4] Thus war began its ''scientific stage,'' moving toward a day of contests between machines.

The rise of modern diplomacy. The development of the competitive state system gave rise to the practice of modern diplomacy. Rulers needed to be informed about the plans and policies of their rivals; states fearful of attack from stronger foes had to seek out allies; and, after wars had been fought, agreements between victor and vanquished required negotiations.

Medieval popes customarily sent envoys to reside at royal courts, but modern diplomatic practice had its real birth among the fiercely independent, prosperous, and antagonistic city-states of northern Italy. The republic of Venice—''the school and touchstone of ambassadors''—was particularly active; its authorities registered treaties, maintained diplomatic archives, and sent their representatives throughout Europe with elaborate instructions. To act as a safeguard against poisoning, trusted cooks were part of a diplomat's retinue, but ambassadors' wives were forbidden to accompany their husbands on diplomatic missions for fear they might divulge state secrets. About 1455 the first permanent embassy in history was sent to Genoa by the duke of Milan. Within a short time most of the important nations of the day followed suit and posted representatives in European capitals.

On many occasions the new diplomacy encouraged negotiation and prevented war. Diplomatic methods so often involved deceit and treachery, however, that negotiations often fanned rather than diminished the fires of international hostility. A seventeenth-century Englishman defined an ambassador as ''an honest man sent to lie abroad for the commonwealth.''[5] Diplomacy during the past three hundred years often has done little to refute this definition.

Balance-of-power politics. One of the most important achievements of the new diplomacy was the technique known as the ''balance of power,'' whereby a coalition of states could checkmate the swollen power of one or more rival states and thereby restore equilibrium. Balance-of-power politics then and later aimed not so much at preventing war as at preserving the sovereignty and independence of individual states from threatened or actual aggression. Yet as international relations more and more took the form of alignments aimed at preserving the balance of power, a sense of the interdependence of the European state system developed. The strong movement toward European unity in our day is the latest manifestation of this sense of interdependence.

The sixteenth century was the formative period for the behavior pattern of modern nations in international affairs. Unrestrained by religious or ethical scruples, the sovereign governments were about to begin an era of international strife with the quest for power as their only guide to success. With disunited Italy as a pawn in the game, the counters on the chessboard began to move.

ITALY: CASE STUDY IN POWER POLITICS

Italy: wealthy but divided. Italy was the home of one of the most remarkable cultural developments in the history of the western world: the Renaissance. A lively urban culture supported by flourishing commerce and industry provided the material basis for the cultivation of learning and the fine arts. At the close of the fifteenth century, Italy, with about thirteen million people, had one of the largest populations in Europe. But while nation-states were developing in other parts of Europe, the Italian peninsula north of the backward Kingdom of Naples remained divided into Papal States and numerous fiercely independent city-states, which, as a result of the new diplomacy, maintained their own small-scale political equilibrium.

Actually, Italy owed its freedom from foreign intervention less to statesmanship than to good luck—the rulers of western Europe were preoccupied with consolidating their own dominions. With this task completed, they were ready to pluck the Italian plum, and in 1494 Charles VIII of France became the first to reach for the fruit.

Charles VIII and the Italian Wars. Because of Louis XI's success as a statemaker (see p. 426), his son Charles VIII (1483-1498) entertained grandiose notions of imitating the exploits of Hannibal and Charlemagne upon ascending the French throne in 1483. To the south of France lay Italy, rich and divided; the prospect of little fighting and much loot tempted Charles sorely. He claimed to be the heir of the duke of Anjou who had taken Naples from the Hohenstaufens in the thirteenth century (see p. 432), and to make his designs look even more respectable, he posed as the opponent of the ruling despots in the Italian city-states and talked of restoring liberty to Italy. To the role of self-chosen liberator he added hints of a plan to lead a great crusade against the Ottoman Turks in Constantinople.

Employing bribes of money or small cessions of territory, Charles first mended his diplomatic fences by ensuring the neutrality of Henry VII of England, Maximilian I of the Holy Roman Empire, and Ferdinand of Spain. Then, in 1494, Charles crossed the Alps at the head of thirty thousand well-trained troops and initiated the Italian Wars that were to last intermittently until 1559. At first the expedition was little more than a holiday for the French. Charles' mounted knights, pikemen, and light, quick-firing cannon won easy victories, and he soon took possession of Naples.

This quick conquest alarmed the rulers who had previously acquiesced to Charles' plan. Ferdinand of Spain suspected that Charles might next try to conquer the Spanish possession of Sicily, and the Holy Roman emperor became uneasy at the prospect of French dominance in Italy. In addition, Venice feared for its independence and took the lead in forming a league which also included the Papal States, the Holy Roman Empire, and Spain. Called the Holy League,

it was the first important example of a coalition of states formed to preserve the balance of power in Europe. Its armies drove Charles out of Italy in 1495, thus halting French designs on the peninsula for the moment.

End of the first phase of the Italian Wars. Following the death of Charles VIII in 1498, his successor, Louis XII, invaded Italy. The counters again moved on the chessboard according to the maxims of power politics: alliances were made and then broken, pledges went unhonored, and allies were deserted. The net result was the ejection of the French from Italy in 1513. Thus the first phase of the Italian Wars came to an end, though peace for Italy was not to last for long.

By the time Louis XII was finally defeated, it was apparent that the new sovereign states reveled in unscrupulous diplomacy. Ferdinand of Spain offers a particularly good example of duplicity and treachery. He betrayed Charles and joined Charles' enemies. Later he helped Louis XII conquer Naples, then tricked him out of the spoils of war. He again betrayed Louis by deserting him and allying himself with a coalition of powers against France. No wonder that Louis XII accused Ferdinand of cheating him on at least two occasions. Hearing this, Ferdinand scoffed: "He lies, the drunkard; I have deceived him more than ten times."[6]

In the first phase of the Italian Wars, one can see the new power politics at work, without benefit of rules and indeed without benefit of any moral or religious scruples. The only important objectives were glory, power, and wealth. In attaining these objectives "necessity knows no law," as Renaissance lawyers liked to observe. Clearly prophesying the mode of future relations among the rising sovereign states, the conflict in Italy demonstrated that dynastic rivalries unfettered by any concept of European unity would set the keynote for subsequent international relations.

Machiavelli and Machiavellian politics. The primer for diplomacy and power politics was written by Niccolò Machiavelli (1469-1527), a Florentine who ranks as one of the most important men in the development of political theory. After the Medici had been

Machiavelli's works had tremendous impact all over Europe. His books were translated into several different languages and became very popular. Above is the title page of the English translation of *The Art of War* in which Machiavelli outlined his suggestions for successful military strategy.

ousted as a by-product of Charles VIII's invasion, Machiavelli served as secretary to the Council of Ten in Charge of War in the Florentine republic. A rather frail man, with a thin, delicate face and penetrating dark eyes, he was sent on numerous missions and gained wide knowledge about the politics of his day. In 1512, after the republic was overthrown and the Medici restored, Machiavelli lost his position. He retired to a small farm, where he whiled away his time writing stories, poems, plays, and, most important, several books on politics.

Outraged at the cavalier manner in which invaders had smashed their way into his beloved Italy, Machiavelli mourned his native land as being

more a slave than the Hebrews, more a servant than the Persians, more scattered than the Athenians; without head, without government; defeated, plundered, torn asunder, overrun; subject to every sort of disaster.[7]

Detesting the course of politics that had toppled him from power, he began to write *The Prince*. Machiavelli's wide acquaintance with the unprincipled politics of the early Italian Wars and his own bitter personal frustration combined to produce his cynical and ruthless attitude toward men and politics. *The Prince*—one of a half-dozen volumes that have helped form western political thought—was written as a guide for an audacious leader who would use any means to win and hold power, free Italy from invaders, and end Italian disunity. A realist who wanted his leader-statesman to understand the political facts of life as they had been operating in Europe, Machiavelli wrote:

A prudent ruler . . . cannot and should not observe faith when such observance is to his disadvantage and the causes that made him give his promise have vanished. If men were all good, this advice would not be good, but since men are wicked and do not keep their promises to you, you likewise do not have to keep yours to them. Lawful reasons to excuse his failure to keep them will never be lacking to a prince.[8]

Machiavelli did not, of course, invent the precepts of ruthlessness in politics.

Rulers had dishonored treaties and used force to attain their ends before *The Prince* was written. What Machiavelli did was to accept the politics of his day without any false illusions. He gave his Prince many suggestions for survival and conquest in the brutal world of unrestrained power:

In the actions of all men, and especially those of princes, where there is no court to which to appeal, people think of the outcome. A prince needs only to conquer and to maintain his position. The means he has used will always be judged honorable and will be praised by everybody, because the crowd is always caught by appearance and by the outcome of events, and the crowd is all there is in the world. . . .[9]

Though Machiavelli set down maxims intended only to instruct an Italian ruler, others studied his ideas carefully, and Machiavellian methods became an indispensable part of European politics. Napoleon read Machiavelli, and King Victor Emmanuel, under whose rule Italy was united in the nineteenth century, slept with Machiavelli's *Prince* beneath his pillow. But while "Machiavellian politics" is generally a term of condemnation, it should be noted that Machiavelli had an idealistic end in view: to "bring good to the mass of the people of the land" of Italy.[10]

EUROPEAN EMPIRE OR SOVEREIGN STATES?

Charles v. The manner in which the rulers of Europe practiced power politics is shown clearly by the events in Europe during the first half of the sixteenth century, a period often referred to as the Age of Charles v. Charles dreamed of restoring royal authority in Germany and reviving the medieval ideal of a Christian empire. While recognizing the need for some reforms in the Church, as a sincere Catholic he also desired to maintain the religious unity of Christendom. We shall see, however, that just as French hopes of conquest in Italy had been destroyed by the employment of the new diplomatic tech-

nique of the balance of power, so Charles' dream of a dominant European empire founded on religious unity was destined to be thwarted.

Charles' grandfather, Maximilian I, Archduke of Austria and Holy Roman emperor (1493-1519), had added the Netherlands and Franche Comté to his realm by marrying Mary of Burgundy. (Franche Comté was that part of Burgundy not seized by Louis XI; see p. 426.) Maximilian's son (Charles' father) had married a daughter of Ferdinand and Isabella of Spain. Thus, by a calculated policy of dynastic marriages, the Austrian Hapsburgs had extended their interests and given rise to a popular Austrian saying: "Where others have to fight wars, you, fortunate Austria, marry!" Born in 1500, Charles, as scion of the House of Hapsburg, thus enjoyed a position no ruler since Charlemagne had held. Following his father's death in 1506, Charles became ruler of the Netherlands; in 1516 his maternal grandfather, Ferdinand, bequeathed him Spain and the southern half of Italy. The death of his other grandfather, Maximilian, gave him Austria and left vacant the throne of the Holy Roman Empire, to which Charles was elected in 1519 as Emperor Charles v.

The Hapsburg lands in both the Old and the New Worlds were vast. Charles ruled the Netherlands; he was emperor of the Holy Roman Empire and possessor of the hereditary Hapsburg states in eastern Europe; he wore the crowns of Castile and Aragon, and with them came Naples, Sicily, and Sardinia; and he was master of a vast colonial empire as well. To be sure, his empire was not cohesive and compact; he constantly found himself with too many irons in the fire even though his younger brother Ferdinand administered the Austrian territory for him. Intelligent, conscientious, and industrious, Charles was forced to divide his attention among his several dominions, frustrating plots, crushing rebellions, and repelling invasions.

Charles' problems were inextricably connected with the activities of Francis I of France, Henry VIII of England, and Suleiman, ruler of the Ottoman empire. Out of the interplay of their rivalries unfolded the

Two kings on the European chessboard, Francis I (top left, portrait by Jean Clouet) of France and Henry VIII of England (top right, portrait by Hans Holbein), met on the Field of the Cloth of Gold in France to discuss matters of state. A huge palace was built for Henry, hundreds of tents were put up for visitors, and numerous banquets, pageants, and tournaments were held. In spite of this lavish display of ceremony and good will, Henry soon allied himself with Francis' enemy, Charles V of Germany.

bloody drama of the first half of the sixteenth century.

New moves on the chessboard. The basic cause of Franco-Hapsburg rivalry was the fact that Charles' empire threatened the independence of France. To the north, east, and south, Hapsburg lands encircled the realm of Francis I (1515-1547). Just before Charles V came into his inheritance, Francis made a move that set the stage for the great struggle between these powers.

Despite the sorry conclusion of his predecessors' Italian adventures, Francis too sought glory in Italy, invaded the peninsula in 1515, and occupied Milan. Across the English Channel, Henry VIII followed the events closely, aiming to use his state, with its small population of 2,500,000, as a counterweight in the Franco-Hapsburg rivalry. He was wooed by both Francis and Charles, and in 1520 the French and English kings met on the famous Field of the Cloth of Gold near Calais, France. Hundreds of ornately decorated tents were set up, graceful ceremonies were conducted, and knights pitted their skill against each other in tournaments. Henry and Francis were friendly as they discussed matters of state; however, it "was rubbing noses, but rubbing noses very politely, with a pane of glass between."[11] Believing Francis to be militarily stronger than Charles, Henry shortly thereafter allied himself with the Hapsburg emperor in order to check French power.

The test of strength began as Charles' forces drove the French from Milan. Francis soon recaptured it. At the battle of Pavia (1525) the Hapsburgs finally crushed the French, and Francis was taken prisoner. He was released the following year after making promises which he had no intention of keeping. Milan and Naples were destined to remain Spanish, and Spain was to dominate most of Italy for nearly two hundred years.

By backing the stronger of the two rivals on the Continent, Henry VIII had miscalculated. Executing a sudden about-face after the battle of Pavia, he deserted Charles and supported France and a coalition of lesser powers against the Hapsburgs. This use of England's power to equalize the strength of Continental rivals is a spectacular example of what now became the cornerstone of English foreign policy. Time and again in modern history, when a single country or dynasty has grown too powerful, England has employed balance-of-power diplomacy to checkmate it and restore equilibrium.

Suleiman, ruler of the Turks. Early in the sixteenth century the impotence of eastern European governments offered the vigorous Ottoman Turks an invitation to conquest (see p. 265). Led by the aggressive Sultan Selim the Grim, who ruled from 1512 to 1520, the Turks had secured the eastern frontiers of their empire by conquering Syria and Egypt. Then, in 1520, just a year after Charles became Holy Roman emperor, Suleiman the Magnificent ascended the Turkish throne. No one could have predicted that Suleiman would soon be a party to the struggle between Charles and Francis and also a threat to Christian Europe. In fact, western Europe rejoiced when the youthful Suleiman succeeded his father, the fearful Selim the Grim, who had once considered massacring all the Christians in his empire. As an observer of the day expressed it:

It seemed to all men that a gentle lamb had succeeded a fierce lion . . . since Suleiman himself was but young and of no experience . . . and altogether given to rest and quietness.[12]

Equanimity gave way to alarm when in 1521 a Turkish army captured Belgrade, long the key fortress of the Hungarian frontier. In 1526 the sultan met the army of the weak Hungarian king on the plain of Mohacs. Only one hour and a half later, the Hungarians were completely routed and their king drowned while fleeing the field. Mohacs has been aptly termed "the tomb of the Hungarian nation," for most of the country fell under direct or indirect Turkish rule.

The king who perished at Mohacs had ruled both Hungary and Bohemia. Bereft of their king and terrified by the prospect of new Turkish attacks, both the Bohemians (Czechs) and the Hungarians offered their vacant thrones to Ferdinand, brother-in-law of the dead king and brother of Charles V. Since most of Hungary had been occupied by the Turks, Ferdinand's rule extended only over the northwest portion of that country. Thus a Turkish victory placed the destiny of both Hungary and Bohemia in the hands of the Hapsburgs and established the Turks as a threat on Charles' Austrian borders.

Religion and politics on the chessboard. Following his release from captivity in 1526, Francis I decided upon an alliance with Suleiman. The enemies of the French king protested loudly against this "unholy alliance," but Francis' subjects apparently had little trouble squaring the compact with their pliable consciences. One bluntly declared:

Princes on the other side made much ado about our master calling in the Turk to his aid. For my part, I would call up all the devils of Hell to break my enemy's head when he is trying to break mine.[13]

As for the Turk, Suleiman sent messages of encouragement to Francis I. Power politics took precedence over religion in both Paris and Constantinople.

Francis I and Charles V continued their conflict. Throughout the struggle Charles was seriously embarrassed by the Protestant Revolt in the Holy Roman Empire. War with the French and the menace of the Turks prevented him from making a serious attempt to crush the heresy until it had reached formidable proportions. In 1531 the Lutheran princes formed the Schmalkaldic League for mutual defense. Though open civil war between the League and the Catholics led by Charles did not develop for fifteen years, the constant controversy diverted Charles' attention from his quarrels with the French king.

Indirectly, the Turks aided the Protestant cause in Germany. In 1529 Suleiman's armies besieged Vienna, but the attackers were thrown back by the valiant garrison. Three years later Suleiman returned with a huge army, larger than before. To deal with the Turkish threat, Charles, who had been planning measures against the Lutherans, was forced to arrange a truce with the Protestant

EUROPE IN THE EARLY 16TH CENTURY

- Holdings of Charles V, 1520
- Acquired by Ferdinand, Brother of Charles, 1526
- Holdings of Henry VIII of England
- Holdings of French Kings
- Suleiman's Empire
- Holy Roman Empire

princes to gain their support against the Turks. A large army was collected, the Turkish danger was foiled, and Lutheranism was strengthened by the breathing space.

After Suleiman's unsuccessful thrusts against Vienna, the Turks turned to the Mediterranean, and French and Turkish fleets attacked Italian towns. The strength that Charles might have amassed to crush the French monarchy was diverted to his besieged lands bordering on the Mediterranean. During Charles' entire reign most of the North African coast was controlled by Turkish pirates, known as corsairs, who preyed upon Christian shipping and harried the coasts of Sicily and Italy. After an unsuccessful expedition against the Turkish stronghold of Algiers in 1541, Charles ceased active warfare against the Mediterranean corsairs. By the mid-sixteenth century Turkish sea power was at its height; corsairs even ventured into the Atlantic to harass Portuguese and Spanish ships.

Charles recognizes Lutheranism. A truce in 1544 called a halt to the French-Hapsburg struggle. The Franco-Turkish alliance was now inoperative since the French king was mortally ill. Charles again concentrated his efforts on the German states, where in 1546 the Lutheran struggle flared into civil war. With France aiding the Lutherans and the Catholic princes giving only half-hearted support to Charles lest he become powerful enough to dominate them, the Schmalkaldic Wars ended in 1555 with the compromise Peace of Augsburg (see p. 493). The Lutheran faith received official sanction, and Charles was thwarted in his cherished aim of restoring religious unity to Germany. Politically the Augsburg settlement entrenched the power of the German princes still further and frustrated the revival of a strong imperial government.

Charles' abdication. Francis I died in 1547, and his heir, Henry II, renewed the war against Charles. In the same year Charles signed a five-year truce with Suleiman, temporarily postponing a showdown with the Turks. Between 1554 and 1556 the exhausted Hapsburg emperor turned over the imperial authority in the Holy Roman Empire to his younger brother, Ferdinand, and gave Spain,

This allegorical portrait of Charles V was painted after his campaign against Suleiman in 1532 by Cornelis Cornelisz, a Dutch artist. Charles is depicted as the "Protector of Christiandom," riding triumphant over the prostrate body of the vanquished Turkish sultan.

the Netherlands, and his Italian possessions to his own son, Philip. Thereafter two Hapsburg dynasties, one Spanish and the other Austrian, ruled in Europe.

After dividing his lands, Charles retired to a monastery to spend his remaining years. A legend has it that he spent his time trying to make several clocks keep exactly the same time—apparently an allegory suggesting that he was faced with so many problems that he could never settle all of them. In 1558 Charles died, his dreams unrealized. French resistance to the House of Hapsburg was stronger than ever, religious unity had not been secured in Germany, and Suleiman the Turk still menaced Christian Europe.

Significance for modern times. The complex narrative that revolves around the ambitions of four monarchs—Charles v, Henry VIII, Francis I, and Suleiman the Magnificent—is significant because the events which transpired during the first half of the sixteenth century laid down much of the political and religious foundation for modern Europe:

1) During the reign of Charles v it was decided by force of arms that no single state was to dominate all of Europe. The growth of nations had advanced too far to permit the revival of a single European empire. The balance of power was maintained.

2) The general course of events during the Age of Charles v further stunted German and Italian national growth. Italy had been a battlefield for the French and the Hapsburgs; and when peace was finally arranged between them in 1559, much of Italy was left to the Spanish Hapsburgs. The Schmalkaldic Wars and the Peace of Augsburg accentuated the political and religious division of the German states and destroyed Charles' hopes of restoring imperial authority in the empire. The Peace of Augsburg also confirmed France's hold on the bishoprics of Metz, Toul, and Verdun in Lorraine, which the French had occupied during the Schmalkaldic Wars. French expansion toward the Rhine had begun, with momentous consequences for the future.

3) Charles' rivalry with Francis I and the French king's alliance with Suleiman played an important part in reducing the pressure that Charles might have applied against the Lutherans. Although a Catholic, Francis sent aid to the German Protestants in order to embarrass their ruler. As a result of this aid, the Protestant movement gained such a firm foothold that the religious unity of Europe was destroyed.

4) The advance of Ottoman power in Europe meant that Turkish control over the Balkans was handed down to later European statesmen as an explosive legacy. The alliance of France with Turkey became an enduring though irregular factor in European diplomacy.

5) The history of the first half of the sixteenth century made it quite clear that diplomacy a la Machiavelli was to be the order of the day. Deceit, treachery, surprise attacks, and broken promises were written into the record.

In our study of later modern history we will see that the question of political unity versus diversity is a recurring problem. Ambitious conquerors such as Louis XIV, Napoleon, and Hitler threatened to destroy the balance of power in Europe and also the independence of various nation-states. There is much to be said for eliminating the rather artificial political boundaries dividing Europe in order to bring the entire area under centralized management. But national diversity has been treasured because it ensures the enjoyment of national customs and ways of life; and it also has been a protection against the creation of a tyrannical super-government. Today Europeans are seeking a united Europe not by the creation of a single, all-powerful government but by the establishment of common cooperative agencies in defense, trade, and atomic energy.

FAITH AND NATIONALITY IN WESTERN EUROPE

Era of the Religious Wars. While the danger of a single empire controlling Europe had been lessened after Charles v divided his lands, the Continent was still to witness convulsive rivalries and a century more of warfare. The period from roughly the middle of the sixteenth century to the middle of the seventeenth century is often referred to as the Era of the Religious Wars, for the religious issues which flamed forth from the Protestant upheaval colored every political conflict. Sometimes the alliance between religious and political factions was genuine and well intentioned. Often, however, ambitious rulers employed religious causes to cloak their designs for dynastic glory, more territory, or the defeat of rivals.

Nevertheless, the Religious Wars were not without religious significance; many men fought and died for their faiths. In addition, religious beliefs and loyalties sometimes conflicted with political interests. A zealous Catholic or Calvinist might put loyalty to religion above loyalty to a dynastic state. The Huguenots in France often had more in common with Dutch Calvinists and English Presbyterians than they had with the majority of their countrymen, who were Catholics.

Zenith of the Spanish state. The Era of the Religious Wars began in 1556 when Philip II, the son of Charles V, became king of Spain. Philip continued the policies of his father with even greater zeal, and dread of Spanish power caused people to say, as they had under Charles V, that "When Spain moves, the whole world trembles."

Several factors made it seem that Philip's future would be impressive and successful. Most important, when his uncle Ferdinand received the Hapsburg Austrian lands together with the imperial crown of the Holy Roman Empire, Philip was freed of the political and religious complexities in middle Europe; that is, he had no "German problem." Second, Philip inherited a new empire overseas which was more lucrative and more easily administered than his father's empire in the Germanies had been. During the reign of Charles V Cortés had conquered Mexico, Pizarro had vanquished the Incas of Peru, and various other conquests had been made from the Straits of Magellan to Mexico (see Chapter 20). From the New World came untold treasure to enrich the Hapsburg coffers at Madrid.

In addition to the riches of the Americas and the Spanish possessions in Europe—the Netherlands, Franche-Comté, Naples, Sicily, and Milan—Philip had the best army of the time. Only the Turkish Janissaries could rival the training and discipline of the Spanish infantry. The Spanish soldier's code was

to obey orders, to aid a comrade even when he is a personal enemy, to keep one's place unshaken, to step into the place of a dead soldier, to stand firm and to charge home.[14]

During his long reign (1556-1598) Philip sought three basic goals: to make his royal power absolute, to combat heresy and strengthen Catholicism, and to extend Spain's influence. Under Charles V the traditional parliaments, or Cortes, of Castile and Aragon had been largely superseded by a number of royal councils staffed by a well-trained civil service. Building on this foundation, Philip erected a centralized system of government in which every decision rested with the king and in which all agencies of government were subordinate to his will. Philip read all official documents and burdened himself with a vast amount of paper work. In fact, he was overly fastidious in this regard. One letter from the king's ambassador in London described a new kind of insect he had seen crawling on his windowpanes; Philip solemnly scribbled on the manuscript, "Probably fleas."

Philip's devotion to the Catholic Church has led some historians to declare that he subordinated the interests of Spain to those of Catholicism. As we shall see in this chapter, however, religious scruples did not interfere with the interests of the Spanish state. It was convenient for Philip that his duties to the Church appeared to coincide with his designs as the ruler of Spain. The Spanish Inquisition ferreted out heretics, and at the same time Philip used it to strengthen royal power. In addition, by championing Catholicism he was able to justify his interference in the political and religious conflicts of other European nations.

One of Philip's great achievements was the uniting of the Iberian peninsula under the Spanish crown. In 1580 the direct line of the Portuguese royal family died out, and Philip claimed the throne through his mother, a Portuguese princess. When the Portuguese refused to accept him as their ruler, Philip invaded the country and seized the throne. The annexation of Portugal and its vast colonial empire brought new riches to Madrid from Brazil, Africa, and the East Indies.

Crusade in the Mediterranean. After Suleiman's death in 1566 the Turkish sultans continued his policy of conquest, but Europe was now better prepared to meet the Ottoman threat. France and Spain made peace in

The 1566 rebellion in the Netherlands was instigated by mobs of Calvinists who invaded Catholic churches, toppling images, smashing windows and looting valuable articles (top). The Spanish reaction to such riots was alarming in its ferocity. Spanish raids on Dutch towns gave Pieter Brueghel the Younger the motivation for this allegorical painting (bottom) copied from his father's famous painting "The Massacre of the Innocents." In depicting the slaughter of the children of Bethlehem by Herod's soldiers, Brueghel used the scenes and costumes of his own day. Thus, he drew a parallel between the cruelty of Herod's soldiers and that of the Spanish troops who raided Dutch villages, killing the Protestant inhabitants.

1559, and the alliance between Paris and Constantinople was broken. In 1570 the Venetian island of Cyprus, the last Christian outpost in the eastern Mediterranean, fell to the Turks. At the pope's urging, Christian Europe turned to Philip, the champion of the Catholic faith, to block Turkish expansion. Philip gained tremendous prestige by his contribution to a great victory over the Turks.

A Holy League was formed to raise a great fleet and destroy Ottoman naval power in the Mediterranean. Spanish and Venetian warships, together with the smaller squadrons of Genoa and the Papal States, made up a fleet of over two hundred vessels which was joined by volunteers from all over Europe. Cervantes, the great Spanish author of *Don Quixote,* laid down his pen to fight against the Turk and lost an arm in the fray. In 1571 the League's fleet and the Turkish navy clashed at Lepanto, on the western side of Greece. The outcome was a decisive victory for Christian Europe; Ottoman sea power was crushed, never to be restored as a major threat to Christendom. Lepanto, which Cervantes called "the noblest occasion that past or present ages have seen or future ones may hope to see," is often considered the last crusade. It can also be considered an extension of the *Reconquista.*

Unrest in the Netherlands. The conquest of Portugal and the defeat of the Turks were signal victories for Philip, but the specter of failure stalked him in the Netherlands. The seventeen provinces of the Low Countries (which included today's Holland, Belgium, and Luxemburg) had been restive during the reign of Philip's father. Charles v had imposed heavy taxes to help finance his wars and had made the people support large contingents of Spanish troops. But in spite of these unpopular acts, he had continued to enjoy the confidence of the Netherlanders, who regarded him as one of themselves because he had been born in the city of Ghent. But the Netherlanders did not feel the same about Philip, whom they distrusted as a foreigner. Seeking to make his rule absolute in the Netherlands, Philip excluded the local nobility from the administration, maintained an army of occupation, and introduced the Inquisition.

In spite of the Inquisition, Calvinism spread in the Netherlands, and in 1566 a series of violent anti-Catholic and anti-Spanish riots broke out. Philip sent more troops and his best general, the Duke of Alva, to restore order. On his arrival in the Netherlands, Alva purportedly announced: "I have tamed men of iron and I shall soon have done with these men of butter."[15] "The Council of Troubles"—soon dubbed "The Council of Blood"—was set up to stamp out treason and heresy. It has been estimated that during Alva's reign of terror fifty to seventy victims were executed on an average day. A total of 8,000 were slain, 30,000 were deprived of their lands and property, and 100,000 fled the country.

The Duke of Alva continued to antagonize most Netherlanders, Catholic as well as Protestant, who were fighting for the freedom to maintain their own institutions and their own local self-government. Philip also alienated the wealthy burghers by burdening them with heavy taxes and restricting their commercial activity in order to benefit Spanish merchants. In 1568, under Dutch leadership, discontent flared into open revolt against Spain.

Birth of the Dutch nation. From the perspective of the twentieth century, the Netherlands revolt has sometimes been seen as an early chapter in the story of the march of democracy, but the Dutch of the sixteenth century, with their rather aristocratic society dominated by nobles and rich burghers, had only the vaguest notion of what we today think of as democratic government. Nevertheless, there were certain modern democratic principles embodied in the Dutch revolt, and when the war began, the Dutch leader, William the Silent of the House of Orange, declared:

The privileges are not free grants of the sovereign to his subjects, but form contracts binding both prince and people.[16]

In the first years of the war the Duke of Alva and his successors were victorious, and the puny forces commanded by the tenacious William the Silent were dispersed again and again. The Netherlands turned to the sea to outfit privateers to prey on Spanish shipping and continued to fight on land as best they could, but the famed Spanish armies held the upper hand. In 1576, however, the incident of the Spanish Fury electrified the Netherlands. Usually well-disciplined, the badly fed and unpaid Spanish soldiers mutinied and marched on Antwerp. Setting upon the hapless city, they burned public buildings and murdered seven thousand citizens. This calamity settled the local differences between the seventeen provinces that had prevented them from making a concerted effort against Spanish tyranny. The Pacification of Ghent, which the provincial representatives signed in 1576, declared that all Spanish soldiers must be expelled from the land, after which the representative body, the Estates-General, would govern the country. While Philip was to be the nominal overlord of the provinces, the actual ruler was to be William the Silent.

Unfortunately for the rebels' cause, the seventeen provinces did not long maintain the unity manifested in the Pacification of Ghent. The Spaniards were able to take advantage of the differences between the Protestant provinces in the north and the predominantly Catholic provinces in the south. Employing a combination of diplomacy and force, the Spanish succeeded in reuniting the ten southern provinces with Spain in 1579. The Dutch leaders in the north, however, declared that they would not rest until Spanish tyranny had been crushed and complete freedom achieved. In 1581 the Estates-General of the United Provinces, as the northern provinces came to be known, formally repudiated the Spanish sovereign in an announcement that can be regarded as the Dutch Declaration of Independence. One of its provisions stated:

The people were not created by God for the sake of the Prince . . . but, on the contrary, the Prince was made for the good of the people.[17]

The declaration of 1581 set the model for later declarations justifying revolution in England, France, and the English colonies in America. It also established another landmark in modern history by decreeing freedom of worship for the large Catholic minority in the new nation. The stability of the state had become a greater concern than the concept of heresy as an offense to be punished.

Three years after the declaration the cause of Dutch freedom was placed in serious jeopardy when William the Silent was assassinated by a young Catholic fanatic and the Spanish stepped up their efforts to destroy the Dutch Republic. At this critical moment Elizabeth I of England, fearing that Philip planned to use the Netherlands as a base for an invasion of England, rushed troops to the aid of the Dutch. The destruction of Philip's Armada by England in 1588 (see p. 530) further weakened Spanish ability to crush the Dutch.

With English assistance, the Dutch held out until Philip's death in 1598, after which peace negotiations began. In 1609 a twelve years' truce was signed, which recognized the partition of the Netherlands along the line where the fighting had stopped. Although the United Provinces (commonly called Holland because of the preëminence of that province with its flourishing city of Amsterdam) had in fact constituted a sovereign nation since 1609, not until the end of the Thirty Years' War in 1648 did the Dutch gain from the Spanish formal recognition of their independence.

For more than two hundred years the southern provinces remained in the hands of the Hapsburgs, first as the Spanish Netherlands and then as the Austrian Netherlands (see Reference Map 10). Early in the nineteenth century, following a brief and unsatisfactory union with Holland, the Austrian Netherlands obtained their independence as the nation of Belgium.

Reasons for Dutch success. There are several reasons why the Dutch ultimately foiled Philip's attempts to crush them. The patient and cautious William the Silent refused to fight decisive battles when the Spanish armies were too strong, choosing instead to play a waiting game that wore out his adversaries. Also, on several occasions the Dutch opened the dikes and flooded the land to block the advance of Spanish troops. As important as any factor was Dutch prowess on the water; time and again the Dutch navy brought help to the beleaguered armies. Privateering activities and growing commerce gave the Dutch funds to hire mercenary soldiers, and the rebels were aided by the friends of Protestantism, especially England. Finally, the people of the northern provinces displayed a resolute courage and steadfastness without which victory could never have been achieved. The Dutch people are justly proud of their royal coat of arms with its motto *Je maintiendrai* ("I shall persist").

The English throne: Protestant or Catholic? On more than one occasion during the reign of Philip II, it seemed that England would come under Spanish domination. In 1554, two years before he ascended the throne of Spain, Philip had married Mary Tudor, the older daughter of Henry VIII. Mary adored her husband, and as queen she was strongly influenced by him, although he had no official status in the governing of England. After a brief reign Mary died, and in 1558 her half-sister, Elizabeth I, assumed the throne.

Elizabeth's disputed succession provided the next occasion for possible Spanish domination of England. The daughter of Henry by his second wife, Anne Boleyn, Elizabeth was considered illegitimate by English Catholics, who recognized only Henry's first marriage as valid. Furthermore, in the eyes of Catholic Europe, the rightful heir to the throne was the great-granddaughter of Henry VII, Mary Stuart, Queen of Scotland.

Brought up in France as a Catholic, Mary had wed the heir to the French throne and reigned for two years as queen of France. After the death of her husband, she returned to her native Scotland, where her French mother had been ruling as regent with the aid of French troops. Mary found Scotland in the hands of rebellious nobles and vigorous Protestant preachers under the leadership of the Calvinist patriot John Knox (see

EUROPE IN THE LATE 16TH CENTURY

Holdings of Philip II (Spanish Hapsburgs)
Holdings of Elizabeth I
Ottoman Empire
Holy Roman Empire

Chapter 16). A widow of eighteen, famous for her charm, beauty, and grace, Mary proceeded to alienate her subjects by a series of blunders: she was too frivolous for her strait-laced Calvinistic subjects, she was unsuccessful in concealing her pro-Catholic sympathies, and, finally, she was accused of being involved in the sordid murder of her weakling husband, Lord Darnley. The Scottish Presbyterians revolted, and in 1568 Mary was forced to seek refuge with her cousin Elizabeth in England. There, her Catholicism and her good claim to Elizabeth's throne made her an unwelcome guest, potentially dangerous to the Tudor monarch and to English Protestantism.

For his part, Philip had no compunctions about plotting to place Mary on the throne of England. Philip's ambassador in London became the center of a web of intrigue against Elizabeth.

The island fortress: obstacle to Spanish hegemony. As Philip became the chief enemy of Protestant England, Elizabeth gradually emerged as the foremost obstacle to Spanish expansion. Unlike the impetuous Mary Stuart, who was often the blind instrument of her emotions, Elizabeth was realistic, calculating, and thoroughly Machiavellian. As the Spanish ambassador wrote to Philip:

> . . . what a pretty business it is to treat with this woman who I think must have a hundred thousand devils in her body, notwithstanding that she is forever telling me that she yearns to be a nun and to pass her life in prayer.[18]

Elizabeth resorted to every subterfuge and trick available to her in the duel with Philip of Spain. Using her sex as a diplomatic weapon, she carried on long flirtations with the brothers of the French king, thereby helping to prevent an alliance between France and Spain. In addition she sent covert assistance to the Dutch, aware that their rebellion was sapping Spanish strength.

While nominally at peace with Philip, Elizabeth secretly encouraged her sea captains to prey upon Spanish shipping and to attack the rich Spanish settlements in the New World. The most famous of the Elizabethan Sea Dogs, Sir Francis Drake, sailed into the Pacific, plundered the western coast of Spanish America, and, after circumnavigating the globe, arrived in England with a hold full of gold and silver. Elizabeth disclaimed any responsibility for these acts of piracy, and her sea captains knew full well that their queen would not lift a hand to save them if they were captured by the Spanish.

Although aware of Elizabeth's duplicity, Philip planned to gain control over England by employing a minimum of resources rather than by expending Spanish energies in preparation for a maximum effort—war. He hoped to place Mary Stuart on the English throne following the assassination of Elizabeth. But a plot against Elizabeth's life, in which Mary was obliquely implicated, was discovered. Parliament was convinced that as long as Mary lived, Elizabeth's life would be endangered, and therefore, in 1587, Elizabeth signed Mary's death warrant. "Mary had arrayed herself superbly for the final scene. As she disrobed for the headsman's act, her garments of black satin, removed by the weeping handmaids, revealed a bodice and petticoat of crimson velvet. One of her ladies handed her a pair of crimson sleeves, which she put on. Thus the unhappy Queen halted, for one last moment, standing blood-red from head to foot against the black background of the scaffold. There was a deathly hush throughout the hall. She knelt, and at the second stroke the final blow was delivered."[19]

But in a sense Mary had not failed. She had left behind in Scotland a son, James, who was destined to become the common monarch of England and Scotland, not by conspiracy or force but by common consent.

Philip and Elizabeth at war. After the discovery of the plot against her life, Elizabeth realized that the time had come for a decisive test of arms. She sought to hinder Philip's plans by openly sending arms and soldiers to the Netherlands, by aiding the Protestant cause during the French religious wars, and by authorizing Drake to destroy Spanish shipping—exploits described as "singeing the King of Spain's beard." By 1587—the year in which Mary Stuart went to the scaffold—Philip decided to invade England.

The lives of Europe's monarchs were often interwoven through ties of marriage and kinship; these bonds were emphasized or ignored according to the monarchs' nationalistic aims. During the period when Philip II of Spain was married to Queen Mary of England (top left), it seemed that England might pass under Spanish domination. After Mary's death, Philip tried to regain his influence over the English monarchy by courting Mary's successor, her shrewd and fiery half-sister Elizabeth (above). Unsuccessful in his attempt, Philip transferred his support to Elizabeth's cousin Mary, Queen of Scots. Until she was widowed at eighteen, Mary had also ruled France as the queen of the youthful Francis II (lower left). Subsequently driven from Scotland by her rebellious subjects, this queen without a country took refuge with Elizabeth, who had her beheaded on charges of conspiracy against the throne.

Just as Spanish oppression had stimulated Dutch nationalism, so the threat of invasion raised English patriotism to a high pitch. Elizabeth gave her people an example of courage and resolution. An eminent biographer has written: "The fierce old hen sat still, brooding over the English nation, whose pullulating energies were coming swiftly to ripeness and unity under her wings. She sat still; but every feather bristled; she was tremendously alive."[20]

England defeats the Spanish Armada. Philip's strategy was to have a fleet of 130 ships, called by contemporaries the "Invincible Armada," join a large Spanish army in the Netherlands and then land this force on the coast of England. Blocking the main ports in the Low Countries, the Dutch prevented the rendezvous, and Philip's designs were ruined completely when the Elizabethan Sea Dogs trounced the Armada in the English Channel. The small, swift English ships outmaneuvered the bulky Spanish galleons, savage fighting ensued, and a severe storm, the famed "Protestant wind," completed the debacle.

Here is a contemporary account of the defeat of the Armada, which limped home after losing a third of its ships:

They being in this disorder, wee made ready to follow them, where began a cruell fight, and wee had such advantage both of wind and tide as wee had a glorious day of them; continuing fight from foure o'clocke in the morning, till almost five or six at night, where they lost a douzen or fourteene of their best shippes. . . . After God had given us this great victory, they made all the hast they could away, and wee followed them Tuesday and Wednesday. . . . That night wee parted with them, wee had a mighty storme. Our fleet cast anchor, and endured it; but the Spanish fleet, wanting their anchors, were many of them cast ashore on the west of Ireland, where they had all their throates cutt by the Kernes [Irish]; and some of them on Scotland, where they were no better used; and the rest . . . gott into Spaine againe. Thus did God blesse us, and gave victory over this invincible navy. . . .[21]

The defeat of the Armada meant that England would remain Protestant, that it would soon emerge as a dominant sea power, and that the rebellion in Holland against Spanish tyranny would eventually succeed. By building new ships, Spain quickly recovered from the material effects of the defeat of the Armada, but it never overcame the psychological effects of that disaster. The Spanish people had been told that the Armada was "the most important [enterprise] undertaken by God's Church for many hundreds of years. . . . we are defending the high reputation of our King and lord, and of our nation; . . . and simultaneously our peace, tranquillity and repose."[22] The optimism engendered by Spain's great past achievements soon vanished; in the words of a modern scholar, "If any one year marks the division between the triumphant Spain of the first two Hapsburgs and the defeatist, disillusioned Spain of their successors, that year is 1588."[23]

The Wars of Religion in France. While the Dutch were valiantly fighting for their independence and Elizabeth and Philip were

The belief that Spain was the greatest power in Europe is illustrated by this contemporary map showing Spain as the head and crown of Europe.

In July 1588, after three days of maneuvering, the English dispersed the Invincible Armada by launching flaming ships into the Spanish fleet. The Armada fell into complete disorder and retreated, pursued by the English.

sparring for power, France was undergoing one of the most terrible civil conflicts in its history. The Valois kings were stout Catholics, and under their rule the Huguenots in France were persecuted severely. But in spite of governmental measures, by 1560 the Huguenots numbered about one million out of a population of sixteen million. Although Protestantism was strong in the cities, the most influential element was the 40 to 50 per cent of the nobility that had been attracted to Calvinism.

Because the weakling sons of Henry II, grandsons of the vigorous Francis I, left no heirs, the French believed that the Valois line, which had ruled France since 1328 (see p. 418), would soon become extinct. This situation led to ruthless factional rivalry between two noble houses in France, both of which aspired to the throne. The Bourbons, who espoused Protestantism, had the better claim because they traced their descent from St. Louis, a revered Capetian king of the thirteenth century. Champions of Catholicism were the powerful Guises, who claimed descent from Charlemagne. This was the setting for the civil war that broke out in 1562. The conflict was partly religious as Catholics and Huguenots reviled one another, partly political as the Guises and Bourbons plotted to gain control of the state. Eight bitterly fought wars followed.

During this period and until her death in 1589, the most powerful individual in France was Catherine de' Medici, the queen mother. Like her contemporary in London, Queen Elizabeth, Catherine was completely cynical and ruthless in statecraft. Even her youngest son referred to her as "Madame la Serpente." No matter how cruel or base, no technique was beneath her use; one of Catherine's political weapons was "'a flying squadron' of twenty-four maids of honor of high rank and low principles to help her seduce the refractory nobles on both sides."[24]

Determined to maintain the power of her sons, Catherine attempted to steer a middle course between the Protestant and Catholic factions and to play one party off against the other. But as the Huguenots grew stronger, she resolved to crush them. Thus, Catherine is blamed for the terrible Massacre of St. Bartholomew's Day. At dawn on August 24, 1572, with a signal from the bell of the Palace of Justice in Paris, the Catholics fell upon their Protestant rivals, and ten thousand Huguenots were slain. On hearing of the massacre, Philip II of Spain wrote that it "was indeed of such value and prudence and of such service, glory and honour to God and universal benefit to all Christendom that to hear of it was for me the best and the most cheerful news which at present could come to me."[25]

The massacre did not destroy Huguenot power, however, and civil conflict continued. A new phase began in 1585, when Philip II entered the war on the side of the Catholics. He hoped first to extirpate Protestantism in France and then to control French policy, thereby gaining valuable support in crushing the Dutch revolt and in conquering England.

In 1589, after assassins had eliminated both the Guise pretender and the last weakling Valois ruler, the Protestant Bourbon prince Henry of Navarre became King Henry IV of France by right of succession. Philip determined to crush the new king before he could consolidate his power. At this critical moment Queen Elizabeth intervened by sending Henry five thousand troops which turned the tide in his favor. Realizing that most Frenchmen were Catholic and sensing that all were weary of civil war, Spanish intervention, and anarchy, Henry decided to place the welfare of France ahead of his own conscience and accepted the faith of Rome. "Paris is well worth a mass," he is supposed to have said, and soon Paris and other cities opened their gates to him.

A major tool utilized by Philip II in his attempt to increase his influence in France was the Holy League, financed by Philip and controlled by the duke of Guise. Processions such as this became common in French cities as members of the League paraded through the streets seeking out Huguenots to execute for heresy.

By 1595 the civil war was over and Philip was forced to withdraw his troops and sign a treaty of peace. This failure in France was the last of Philip's many setbacks. His final opponent, Henry IV, provided some fitting last words on Philip's hopes for Spanish dominance in Europe: while witnessing the departure of Spanish troops from Paris, Henry called out, "Gentlemen, commend me to your master, but do not come back."

The Edict of Nantes. Although Henry IV changed his own faith, he sought to protect the liberties of the Huguenot minority in the Edict of Nantes (1598). When both Catholic and Protestant extremists denounced the measure as unsatisfactory, Henry refused to be intimidated: "I insist upon being obeyed. It is time that we all, having had our fill of war, should learn wisdom by what we have suffered."

The Edict of Nantes followed the example first set by the Dutch Republic of recognizing that more than one religion could be maintained within a state. The Peace of Augsburg had given each ruler in the Holy Roman Empire the right to choose the religion of his subjects, but the Edict of Nantes differed from the earlier agreement in that the monarch gave the choice of religion to his subjects. Thus the Edict ensured freedom of religion to the Huguenots and saved Protestantism in France. It should be added that in order to guarantee this religious freedom, Henry allowed the Protestants to fortify about a hundred French towns and garrison them with their own troops. As a result, the Huguenots in France constituted virtually a state within a state (see map, p. 495).

The failure of Philip II. Before the close of the sixteenth century his disasters in France, Holland, and England had ended Philip's chances of establishing Spanish domination in western Europe. While in the eyes of his Spanish subjects Philip was a wise, moderate, pious, and hardworking monarch, his enemies singled him out as a detestable example of trickery, cruelty, and religious intolerance. As we have seen, Philip was not equal to Elizabeth in duplicity and diplomatic cunning. And, in answer to the charge of bigotry, it must be remembered that nearly all sixteenth-century

Henry IV of France is shown here accepting Catholocism, after supposedly remarking: "Paris is well worth a Mass."

European monarchs believed that the relentless persecution of nonconformists was essential to the welfare of the state. Therefore, Philip's failures cannot be attributed to defects ingrained in his nature but to the fact that, in general, he was less skillful than his opponents in the game of power politics.

Most important, perhaps, is that Philip unwittingly pitted himself against the growing feelings of nationalism. Just as the love of native land had contributed to England's failure in the Hundred Years' War, so had patriotism thwarted Philip's ambitions in the Netherlands and in the waters around the British Isles. Nationalism also contributed to the failure of Philip's intervention in the French religious wars.

Despite Philip's failures, Spain still enjoyed the reputation of being the first power in Europe. Spanish soldiers were the best trained on the Continent, and Spain's wealth from its vast overseas possessions seemed inexhaustible. Moreover, Spanish writers, scholars, and painters were outstanding; in fact, the last half of the sixteenth century and the first half of the seventeenth are usually regarded as the zenith of Spanish culture.

In the seventeenth century, however, Spanish power began to decline. Bad economic policies (see Chapter 20) coupled with continued overexertion in the game of power politics proved too great a burden for a nation of only eight or nine million people. The last of the so-called religious conflicts, the Thirty Years' War (1618-1648), accelerated the decline of Spain and left France the dominant state in Europe.

A brief interlude of peace. Early in the seventeenth century Europe enjoyed a respite from war. Elizabeth's successor, King James I (who as Mary Stuart's son was also king of Scotland), was a sincere lover of peace and also pro-Spanish, even though he had been reared a Protestant. Internal troubles prevented France from renewing the quarrel with Spain: the assassination of Henry IV by a Catholic extremist in 1610 was followed by a sharp resurgence of the nobility during the regency of Henry's widow and the minority of his son, the future Louis XIII. (Not until 1624, when Cardinal Richelieu became Louis XIII's chief minister and actual ruler of France, was the work of strengthening the monarchy at home and humbling the Hapsburgs in Spain and Germany resumed.) In 1609 the long war between Spain and Holland, which had begun over forty years before, was halted by the signing of a truce. Prospects for a long period of peace were illusory, however, for the most terrible of all the Religious Wars—and, because most of Europe became involved, the greatest European war until the age of the French Revolution—broke out in 1618.

THE THIRTY YEARS' WAR

The issues of the Thirty Years' War. The Peace of Augsburg failed to bring about a satisfactory religious settlement in the Germanies, and friction continued after 1555. Many of the higher clergy who accepted Protestantism secularized and

retained for themselves the land they had held as Catholic prelates. The Protestant princes claimed the right to take over former Church lands within their states, while Catholics maintained that the Peace of Augsburg had stipulated that no further secularization of Church property might take place. Another cause of dispute was the fact that the Peace of Augsburg had recognized only the Lutheran and Catholic religions. There was no toleration of Calvinism, a faith that had spread rapidly in the latter part of the sixteenth century. But while the religious differences between Catholic, Lutheran, and Calvinist sharpened local rivalries among the German princes, the basic issues of the Thirty Years' War were at least as much political as religious.

The Jesuit-educated Holy Roman emperor, Ferdinand II of the Austrian Hapsburgs, had a deep antipathy toward heretics and aimed at eradicating them wherever he ruled. He also wanted a united and subservient empire to strengthen his position in Europe. Ferdinand's desire to reassert imperial authority was opposed by the princes whose own power would remain strong with Germany divided and the emperor weak. Even the Catholic princes, who willingly supported Ferdinand as a Catholic leader against Protestants, were opposed to any strengthening of imperial power. The papacy, too, was often lukewarm in its support, regarding a strong emperor as a threat to the freedom of the Church in Germany and fearing that a too-close association with the Hapsburgs would alienate the rulers of other states. Ferdinand could hope for unquestioned support only from his cousin, the Hapsburg king of Spain, who was still considered the most powerful ruler in Europe.

The varied issues in the Holy Roman Empire created an atmosphere of tension in which one slight incident might upset the precarious peace. A prelude to the contest of arms was the formation of a Protestant League of German princes in 1608 and a similar Catholic League in 1609. The rival parties began to muster their strength.

Phases of the Thirty Years' War. The complexities of the Thirty Years' War may be simplified by dividing the events into four phases: (1) Bohemian, (2) Danish, (3) Swedish, and (4) French.

The first battleground was Bohemia, preponderantly Protestant and strongly nationalistic, which had enjoyed a large measure of toleration under its Catholic Hapsburg kings. When Ferdinand withdrew that tolerance on mounting the throne of Bohemia in 1617, he precipitated the "defenestration" incident of 1618. In Prague, the capital of Bohemia, a number of Czech nobles entered the castle where the king's officials were quartered, dragged them to an open window, and hurled them into space. The two officials and their secretary dropped fifty feet but, seemingly by a miracle, escaped unharmed. The Catholics declared their escape was divine providence; the Czechs retorted that the officials had landed on a soft dunghill.

The Bohemian rebellion became a general religious war in 1619 when, to gain Protestant support, the Bohemians invited the Calvinist head of the Protestant League to rule them. By the end of the following year Ferdinand had crushed the Bohemians, and his kinsmen, the Spanish Hapsburgs, had defeated the German Protestants supporting the Bohemian insurrection. Protestantism was stamped out in Bohemia, and

the Protestant League in Germany was dissolved.

The second phase of the conflict began when the Danes invaded Germany in 1625. The Danish king, who was also Duke of Holstein, a state within the Holy Roman Empire (see Reference Map 10), sought not only to champion hard-pressed Protestantism but also to gain additional territory along the North Sea and to thwart Hapsburg ambitions. However, the Hapsburg armies crushed the Danes and invaded the Danish peninsula.

This second defeat of the Protestants threatened to undo the work of the Protestant Reformation and to create a unified, Hapsburg-ruled Germany. This prospect drew the leading Lutheran power, Sweden, into the fight. The third phase of the war started in 1630 when King Gustavus Adolphus invaded Germany, having announced to his people that "As one wave follows another in the sea, so the papal deluge is approaching our shores." The Swedish monarch was motivated not only by religious considerations but also by his desire to dominate the Baltic; he had earlier pushed back the Russians, defeated the Poles and Danes, and now hoped to acquire territories along Germany's Baltic coast as "guarantees against the emperor." Gustavus Adolphus was the

During the Thirty Years' War the German city of Munich was captured by the Swedish monarch Gustavus Adolphus, whose invading army was strengthened by German allies. In this old drawing, the warrior-king rides in from the left, while the officials of Munich kneel in homage at lower right, ready to present their conqueror with the keys to the city.

founder of a new technique of warfare which stressed discipline, mobility, and morale; in Germany his well-drilled, hymn-singing veterans and mobile cannon quickly scored a series of brilliant victories. But in the midst of a successful battle, Gustavus Adolphus was killed. The anti-Hapsburg forces then began to weaken, and in 1635 a compromise peace was arranged. Gustavus Adolphus had checked the emperor's drive to impose political and religious unity on Germany, and this is the substance of his reply when enemy soldiers purportedly found him mortally wounded on the battlefield and asked his name: "I am the King of Sweden, who do seal the religion and liberty of the German nation with my blood."[26]

The compromise peace never went into effect, however, for Cardinal Richelieu, the chief adviser of the French king and the actual head of the government, decided that France would be secure only when the Hapsburgs of Austria and Spain, whose lands ringed France on three sides, had been defeated. Though he himself was a prince of the Catholic Church and France a Catholic state, Richelieu had been giving secret aid to the German Protestants, Denmark, and Sweden in their struggle against the Catholics. Now, in 1635, he came out in the open.

Although the various parties in Germany were tired of bloodshed, Richelieu's game of power politics was to lengthen the conflict by thirteen years. Religious issues by now were distinctly secondary considerations. The struggle was primarily a dynastic contest between Bourbons and Hapsburgs, while smaller powers sought what gains they could. France was in a strong position because the Swedes and German Protestants could keep the Austrian Hapsburg armies busy in Germany while French arms were concentrated against the Spanish Hapsburgs.

At the end of the twelve years' truce in 1621 (see p. 526), Philip IV of Spain had renewed the war against the Dutch. But with France's entry into the fray, he was obliged to abandon his notions of reconquering Holland, since French attacks in Franche-Comté, the Spanish Netherlands, Italy, and even in Spain itself were forcing him to concentrate all his efforts in these areas.

The French army soon developed into an effective, battle-hardened force under the command of two skillful generals, Condé and Turenne. In 1643 Condé, at the battle of Rocroi in the Spanish Netherlands, ended the legend of the invincibility of the Spanish infantry. An English historian has described this defeat vividly. "The Spanish masses stood with all the strength of a mediaeval fortress. There was no manoeuvering power in them. The French artillery ploughed its way through the ranks, and the dashing charges of the infantry drove the disaster home. . . . Yet if victory was lost to Spain, the cherished honour of the Spanish arms was safe. Man by man the warriors fell in the ranks in which they stood, like the English defenders of the banner of Harold at . . . [Hastings]. Their leader, the Count of Fuentes, an old man worn with years and gout, and unable to stand, was seated in an arm-chair to direct the battle within a square composed of his veteran troops. Death found him at his post. . . . The last of a long heroic race of statesmen and soldiers had bowed his head before the rising genius of France."[27]

By 1643 the power of the Spanish Hapsburgs had been broken, and the French turned to the Germanies. Turenne scored victories against the Austrian Hapsburgs and their allies, the Catholic princes. Then a combined Swedish and French force pillaged Bavaria until this important Catholic principality was prostrate. Before warfare ceased in 1648, Richelieu's objective had been secured. The French architect of Bourbon supremacy on the Continent had died in 1642, but his successor, Cardinal Mazarin, continued to carry on Richelieu's designs for weakening the power of the Hapsburgs.

The Peace of Westphalia. Peace negotiations began in 1644 without a cease-fire agreement, but they proceeded slowly. The delegates wrangled endlessly over such questions of protocol as who was to enter the conference room first and where they were to sit, and the fortunes of war frequently altered the bargaining power of the rival diplomats. Finally, in 1648, the longest peace negotiation on record ended in a series of treaties collectively known as the Peace of Westphalia.

A recapitulation of the various provisions of the peace would be very complex; suffice it to say that France moved closer to the Rhine with the acquisition of much of Alsace; Sweden and the Protestant state of Brandenburg made important territorial gains; and Holland and Switzerland—the latter having successfully resisted its Hapsburg overlords since 1291—were granted independence. The Calvinists were given recognition in Germany, and the land issue that had been an important factor at the beginning of the war was settled in an agreement whereby Church property was to be retained by the group—either Protestant or Catholic—that had held the land in the year 1624. Only the pope refused to accept the peace settlement, condemning it as "null, void, invalid, iniquitous, unjust, damnable, reprobate, inane, empty of meaning and effect for all time."[28] The fact that the pope's condemnation was ignored is a measure of the waning power of the papacy within the European state system.

The Peace of Westphalia also permanently ended Hapsburg dreams of reviving the authority of the emperor in Germany. The sovereignty of the more than three hundred German states was recognized, with each state having the right to coin money, make war, maintain armies, and send diplomatic representatives to foreign courts. In the words of a seventeenth-century German historian, "the imperial office had become a mummy; the constitution a monstrosity."[29] Henceforth the Hapsburg emperors worked to form a strong Danubian monarchy out of their varied Austrian, Bohemian, and Hungarian possessions.

The great significance of the Peace of Westphalia was that it symbolized the emergence and victory of the sovereign state which acknowledged no authority higher than its own interests and was prone to assume what Thomas Hobbes three years later called "the position of gladiators." More specifically, the conference established the basic principle underlying the modern state system—the essential equality of all independent sovereign states. It also instituted the diplomatic procedure of convening international congresses in order to settle the problems of war and peace by negotiation.

The settlement brought no peace to harried Spain, however. Both the French and the Spanish stubbornly refused to end hostilities, which continued for another eleven years until France's military superiority was again made clear. In the ensuing peace treaty, signed in 1659, Philip IV not only agreed to French demands for frontier provinces in the Spanish Netherlands and along the Pyrenees but also humbly consented to the marriage of his daughter to Louis XIV, the Bourbon king of France.

Thus the struggle against the Hapsburg encirclement of France begun by Francis I against Charles V early in the sixteenth century ended more than a century later. Changes had been wrought in the relative power of nations. Both England and Holland had become great sea powers, and their commercial prosperity was increasing rapidly. France emerged as the greatest power in Europe, the potential master of the Continent. The golden age of Spain was over; never again would this nation or Portugal be considered first-class powers. Although reports of devastation, population decline, and cultural retrogression in the Germanies have perhaps been exaggerated, the Thirty Years' War left a grievous legacy and thwarted German progress for a century. But by demonstrating that Protestants and Catholics were unable to exterminate each other, the Thirty Years' War—indeed, the entire Era of the Religious Wars—greatly promoted the cause of religious toleration in Europe.

THE CONTINUING SENSE OF EUROPEAN INTERDEPENDENCE

Proposals for keeping the peace. The irresponsible use of power was the outstanding feature of international politics in the late sixteenth and early seventeenth centuries. But gradually powerful rulers and diplomats realized that frequent wars threatened the growth of European trade and commerce and menaced even the existence of civilized society in the West. We have seen some of the early steps taken to improve international relations—the establishment of consular and diplomatic services, the formation of alignments to preserve the balance of power, and the first use of a general European peace congress to adjust conflicting interests after a great war. In addition, trade agreements and treaties formed the crude beginnings of a system of international law. Although these varied measures all too often had a negligible effect on the continued use of war as the means of settling disputes among nations, they reflect a continuing sense of the interdependence of the European state system —the Concert of Europe, as it would later be called.

To some visionaries, the ideal of religious and political unity of the Middle Ages, although imperfect, was preferable to international anarchy among sovereign states. The increased destructiveness of modern warfare had aroused the protests of many sixteenth-century humanists. Erasmus wrote that "war is sweet only to the inexperienced" and asserted that the most unjust peace was preferable to the justest war. Sir Thomas More denounced the folly of most wars; to him only defensive wars or wars against tyranny were justifiable. In the seventeenth century other students of international affairs made more specific recommendations.

In 1623, Emeric Crucé, an obscure French monk, published a plan to eliminate war by means of an international organization which, he claimed, would be "useful to all nations, and agreeable to those who have some light of reason and the sentiment of humanity." The central idea in his work was that all wars were harmful and their abolition would allow governments to devote themselves to the arts of peace. To this end he proposed that a permanent corps of ambassadors from all over the world be maintained at Venice as an international assembly for the settlement of all disputes through negotiation and arbitration. Crucé acknowledged that his plan for a seventeenth-century "United Nations" was in advance of his time, but added:

I have wished, nevertheless, to leave this testimony to posterity. If it serves nothing, patience. It is a small matter to lose paper and words. I have said and done what was possible for the public good, and some few who read this little book will be grateful to me for it, and will honor me, as I hope, with their remembrance.[30]

Either the first Bourbon monarch, Henry IV, or his chief minister, the Duke of Sully, devised the plan known as the Grand Design, which called for the establishment of a European federal union headed by a council of representatives from all states. The council was to secure disarmament and to control an international police force which would back its decisions by force. Each state was to contribute troops and money according to its strength.

Despite its theoretical and utopian character, the Grand Design "shows that at the very moment when the modern national state, centralized within and dividing Europe into mutually hostile camps, emerged from the ruins of medieval unity, the ablest minds realized that eventually a new unity would have to be built out of these distinct entities, a United States of Europe. . . ."[31]

Grotius and international law. By the beginning of the seventeenth century a number of European scholars were also at work laying the foundation for a science of international law by developing the principle that the nations formed a community based upon natural law. The first to obtain a hearing outside scholarly circles was Hugo Grotius (1583-1645), a gifted Dutch historian, theologian, practicing lawyer, and diplomat. In 1625 appeared *De Jure Belli ac Pacis (On the Law of War and Peace)*, the work which gained Grotius instant fame and lasting recognition as the founder of international law. "Such a work," he declared, "is all the more necessary because in our day, as in former times, there is no lack of men who view this branch of law with contempt as having no reality outside of an empty name." And he continued:

I have had many and weighty reasons for undertaking to write upon this subject. Throughout the Christian world I observed a lack of restraint in relation to war, such as even barbarous races should be ashamed of; I observed that men rush to arms for slight causes, or no cause at all, and that when arms have once been taken up there is no longer any respect for law, divine or human; it is as if, in accordance with a general decree, frenzy had openly been let loose for the committing of all crimes.[32]

Grotius endeavored to set forth a new code of international conduct based not upon the authority of the Church but on what he termed the fundamental idea of the law of nature. The law of nature was in turn founded on the dictates of reason, morality, and justice. If civilization was to endure, Grotius argued, relations among nations should be guided by reason, and humane considerations should prevail in the councils of the mighty.

War and Peace are reconciled in the allegorical title page from the 1689 edition of Grotius' *De Jure Belli ac Pacis*. Four years before he wrote this great work, Grotius had escaped from a Dutch prison, where he had been sentenced to life imprisonment as a result of his campaign for religious toleration between Protestant and Catholic and for a more liberal regime in his own country, Holland.

More realistic than his contemporaries Crucé and Sully, Grotius did not propose to eliminate war entirely. He sought instead to outlaw "unjust" wars and limit the effects of "just" wars. According to Grotius, wars were justified only to repel invasion or to punish an insult to God. His appeal, however intelligent, fell largely upon deaf ears. Machiavelli's *The Prince* enjoyed more popularity in European palaces than *On the Law of War and Peace.*

SUMMARY

By the middle of the seventeenth century the pattern of politics in western Europe had changed significantly. Gone was the ideal of unity, whether based on empire or on universal Church; sovereignty had replaced suzerainty. The new monarchies were largely absolute in authority within their own frontiers and free agents in the domain of international affairs. Following the dictates of diplomacy systematized by Machiavelli, these sovereign states pursued power, prestige, wealth, and security. No moral or religious scruples were allowed to interfere with these objectives. It was considered axiomatic that a nation had no permanent enemies or friends—only permanent interests. This maxim was illustrated by the manner in which alliances based on the new diplomatic technique of the balance of power were formed on the European chessboard. We shall see in our study of later eras how the great powers have continued to alter their alliances in deference to the exigencies of the balance of power. For example, the foes of the United States in World War II became our allies against the Soviet Union— one of our chief supporters in that conflict. Only by studying past political history can these situations be understood. It is also noteworthy that since balance-of-power diplomacy was the product of a felt need to preserve the security and independence of the new sovereign states, it reflected an early recognition of the interdependence of the European state system. The present-day movement toward European unity can be viewed as the latest expression of this recognition.

Power politics between 1500 and 1650 developed amid complex happenings, especially the so-called Religious Wars. Just what was religion and what politics was often difficult to determine, especially since religion was often used as a cover for political intrigue. Elizabeth fought the Spanish Armada and aided the Dutch in the name of Protestantism, but she was concerned chiefly with preventing Spanish domination of Europe and interference with English maritime expansion. With Philip II of Spain, Catholic conviction appropriately coincided with Spanish national interests; to champion the Catholic Church was, in Philip's mind, to build a strong Spain. Expediency, not religious principles, governed international politics: witness Francis I's alliance with the Turks and Richelieu's support of the German Protestants.

The revolt of the Dutch from Spain was the first large-scale example before 1650 of a successful countertrend to the increasing centralization of the monarch's power. The establishment of the Dutch Republic in the name of people's rights foreshadows the later and more famous revolts against absolutism which would establish constitutional government in England during the last half of the seventeenth century and in North America and France by the end of the eighteenth.

In the survey of European affairs in this chapter, two opposing principles were discussed: one, the right of a state to conduct its foreign affairs—even to waging war—without hindrance; the other, the concept that nations should accept some limitation to their freedom of action in international affairs. Ever since the sixteenth century, when scholars began to think of limiting wars and the need for international law, national sovereignty and internationalism have been in competition. Sovereignty has gotten the best of it by far. But we will see that since Grotius' time, much effort has been devoted to a study of averting conflicts and subordinating disputes to the rule of law.

Chapter 18

New Dimensions of the Mind

**The Fine Arts, Science, and Thought:
1530-1650**

INTRODUCTION. The approximately one hundred years covered in this chapter witnessed a reaction to Renaissance art and thought in western Europe. During this restless, inventive age artists and scientists were in the forefront in extending the dimensions of the mind. The transitional character of the period is reflected in these lines written in 1611 by John Donne:

And new philosophy calls all in doubt
'Tis all in pieces, all coherence gone.[1]

The reaction to Renaissance art began about 1530 in Italy. Growing weary of High Renaissance serenity and poise and moved by the impact of new religious and political tensions, Mannerist painters began experimenting with new stylistic devices in composition, drawing, and color. By the end of the sixteenth century Mannerist exploration and invention gave way to a dramatic and radiant new style of expression—the Baroque—which affected all the fine arts and spread beyond the Alps.

Meanwhile, the intelligent curiosity of a few men had led to startling discoveries in scientific knowledge which fostered a radically new understanding of the relationship between man and the universe. The medieval notion that the earth must be the center of the universe was proved false, and a new theory was established in which the sun replaced the earth as the center of all things— only to give way in turn to the concept of a vast and perhaps infinite universe populated by endless suns all moving in space and fixed only in their relations to each other. Near the end of the sixteenth century the Italian philosopher Giordano Bruno exultantly proclaimed the effects which the new thinking in astronomy had upon the minds of Renaissance men:

Thus the excellence of God is magnified, and the grandeur of his Empire made manifest. He is not glorified in one but in numberless Suns, not in one Earth or in one World, but in ten hundred thousand, in infinite Globes. . . . By this science we are loosened from the chains of a most narrow dungeon and set at liberty to rove in a most august empire.[2]

As men surpassed the ancients in the understanding of nature and in the acquisition of new scientific tools, scientific horizons were broadened. While some scientists were learning about the macrocosm, or universe, others were making equally significant discoveries about the microcosm, or man himself, as they investigated the structure and mechanics of the human body. Philosophers in turn sought to construct a new world order which could be reconciled with man's fresh insights into the physical universe. In France Descartes employed the deductive method to construct in the abstract a unified, mathematically ordered universe that operated as a perfect mechanism. In England Francis Bacon championed the use of the experimental and inductive method as a systematic approach to the investigation of natural phenomena. The inductive method, in particular, has remained an indispensable tool to the present day and has intimately conditioned the thought processes of everyone reading this page.

The scientific revolution was a part of an overall intellectual revolution, the significance of which can hardly be exaggerated. When Charles Darwin in the nineteenth century wrote that "science and her methods gave me a resting place independent of authority and tradition," he was describing what has been called the fundamental faith of modern western man. The foundation for this outlook was laid in the seventeenth century.

THE WORLD OF EL GRECO AND REMBRANDT

The "anti-Renaissance" style: Mannerism. In Chapter 15 we studied the Italian Renaissance at its zenith, when Leonardo da Vinci, Raphael, and Michelangelo created their masterpieces. The Italian Renaissance was a period of splendid sweep and vision in which art, literature, and music reflected the calm assurance that an excellence equal to that of the ancients had been achieved. Yet, just at the very peak of the High Renaissance, in about 1520, during the pontificate of the cultivated Medici pope Leo X, the traditional unity of Christendom was shattered by Luther's challenge. In the decades that followed, new religious and political tensions developed, schism rent Europe, and for a century or more persecutions, hangings, burnings, and massacres were justified— even glorified—in the name of the Prince of Peace.

It was in Italy, where the Renaissance initially came forth, that a countermovement first made its appearance. There artists— who so often act as barometers to register sensitive changes in the cultural atmosphere —responded swiftly to the new tensions. They rejected the classical serenity and poise of the High Renaissance and began restlessly searching for new modes of expression. The result was the development in Italian painting from about 1530 to 1600 of a new, "anti-Renaissance" style called Mannerism.

The Mannerist style had two aspects: psychological and technical. No longer was the artist working in that spirit of calm and balance, of harmony and proportion, which had prevailed in Renaissance art at its finest. The typical Mannerist artist lived instead in a state of doubt and indecision; he was inwardly troubled and uncomfortable, and his work reflected those tensions. Technically speaking, Renaissance painters had mastered the problems of space and perspective, so that the artist placed his figures in balanced relationships enriched by vigorous and harmonious colors. By contrast, Mannerist painters such as Tintoretto (1518-1594) often defied the rules of perspective in order to obtain an oblique and even twisted point of view; their lines might be agitated, their colors weird and clashing, their designs asymmetric. They did not hesitate to distort the human figure in order to achieve emotional intensity and create new psychological effects (see illustrations, p. 545).

Among the sculptors of the Mannerist period was the boastful and conceited Benvenuto Cellini (see p. 448), whose overelaborate compositions—called "snuff-box ornaments" and "whoreson gewgaws" by his contemporaries—are typical of the extreme individualism and experimentation of the period. Mannerist architects—like some early Mannerist painters (see Color Plate 25)—sought to surpass the work of earlier Renaissance masters by adhering to a more lavish classical style. The exaggerated magnificence of the Villa Rotunda near Venice, designed by Andrea Palladio (1518-1580), was achieved by grouping four identical temple façades on the sides of a square domed building. The Palladian style so impressed later generations that Thomas Jefferson used the Villa Rotunda as a prototype for his own Monticello.

El Greco, the Mannerist master. The Mannerist style found its final and finest flowering in the paintings of El Greco ("the Greek"). Born in Crete as Domenico Theotocopuli, El Greco (1541?-1614) studied under Titian and Tintoretto and later settled in Toledo in Spain, where he spent the rest of his life.

In his canvases he captured the religious intensity of his adopted land, which was the leading Catholic power of the time and the most ardent center of the Catholic Reformation and the Inquisition.

El Greco employed *chiaroscuro* (strong contrasts of light and shade) and abrupt transitions in color to achieve dramatic effects; he was not concerned with depicting nature realistically but distorted space and perspective to create an often eerie world of the imagination. From his Byzantine background and his study of the Italian Mannerists, he had learned how to distort the human body for emotional effect. El Greco's paintings are easily recognizable for their elongated figures (see illustration, p. 545)—an exaggeration ascribed by many of his contemporaries to madness and by others, more recently, to astigmatism! To us he appears surprisingly "modern," and his works have had an influence upon twentieth-century painting.

Triumph of the Baroque style. While El Greco was still at work in Toledo, in Italy another artist, Caravaggio (1565-1609), was

During the Renaissance renewed interest in classical antiquity resulted in the frequent use of subjects from Greek and Roman mythology. Benvenuto Cellini's saltcellar represents Neptune, god of the sea, and Tellus, goddess of the earth. A virtuoso study in the technique of the goldsmith, it is less a utilitarian object than a piece of fine art. The boat in the foreground served as a salt receptacle, while an arch of triumph on the opposite side was designed to hold pepper.

busily reacting against the eccentricities of Mannerism. Caravaggio also painted religious themes but with a realism and solidity totally different from that of the Mannerists. By using common laborers as his models and painting their weathered faces in sharp light against a dark background, he substituted a down-to-earth naturalism for the artifices of Mannerism.

Meanwhile, other developments had been pushing aside the confusion and uncertainty characteristic of Mannerism and were helping to create a style expressing the character of the seventeenth century. The Catholic Church indirectly exerted one of the most powerful of these influences. Confronted with the challenge of the Reformation, the leaders of the Church convened at the Council of Trent (1545-1563) in an atmosphere of tension and defensiveness. But in a sweeping movement of reform, the Church recovered its sense of mission and restated its religious values. By announcing its regeneration with majestic voice, the Church of the Catholic Reformation stimulated the drive toward a new style of artistic expression—one that would proclaim the message of the revived Church with pomp and circumstance. The new style was the Baroque.

The High Renaissance had been characterized by simplicity, restraint, and balance; Mannerism, by unresolved doubts and attenuated, unearthly figures. The Baroque style reconciles the emotion, tension, and color of Mannerism with Renaissance harmony and grandeur. It revels unashamedly in the grandiose and grandiloquent; it glories in color, size, height, space, and the flesh. The Baroque is decorative, robust, splendid, and even theatrical. With none of the restraint of the High Renaissance or the doubts of Mannerism, the Baroque seeks to overawe and to convince by the plenitude of its grandeur. It reflects joy in this life and confidence in the hereafter.

Masters of the Baroque: Rubens and Velasquez. One of the creators of the new style in painting whose influence permeated western Europe was the Flemish artist Peter Paul Rubens (1577-1640). As a young man Rubens spent ten years in Italy where he came under the influence of Caravaggio's naturalism. A painter of prodigal gifts and incredible energy, Rubens delighted in ambitious undertakings. As he wrote:

The large size of a picture gives us painters more courage to represent our ideas with the utmost freedom and semblance of reality. . . . I confess myself to be, by a natural instinct, better fitted to execute works of the largest size.[3]

He liked to choose dramatic themes from either pagan or Christian literature, crowding his canvases with an exuberant and typically Baroque mass of forms (see Color Plate 26). Also truly Baroque is his sensuous use of rich textures, as exhibited in his painting of flesh, satin, armor, and the hides of horses.

The cool and objective point of view displayed by the canvases of the Spanish court painter Diego Velásquez (1599-1660) seem static alongside the sensuous exuberance of Rubens and the mannerisms of El Greco. Velásquez, too, had been impressed by Caravaggio's style, and he painted exactly what he saw in a style essentially his own, an unaffected and unadorned naturalism. Velásquez did not paint forms or surfaces so much as the movement of light over those surfaces, which produced an effect of the utmost reality. This preoccupation with light explains his "modernity" and especially his influence upon the French Impressionists of the nineteenth century.

Trio of Dutch masters: Hals, Vermeer, Rembrandt. The first half of the seventeenth century was a golden age for Holland. Prosperous and comfortable, the burghers often acted as patrons of the arts. Their tastes in paintings differed greatly from those of kings, prelates, and aristocrats; the stolid Dutchmen favored "endless 'views,' pictures of cows in meadows, boats on the canals, ruddy girls and self-satisfied grocers, household interiors and family incidents, taverns and drinking"[4] (see Color Plate 27). A horde of competent Dutch painters arose in response to the demands of this republican art, and their overproduction soon depressed prices and created the image of the starving artist. Among the Dutch painters, the names of Hals, Vermeer, and Rembrandt stand out.

The robust Frans Hals (1580-1666) possessed a vigorous style that enabled him to

The works of the three painters represented here demonstrate the transition of art from the Renaissance to the Baroque style. Tintoretto, an early apprentice of Titian, soon fell out with his master and developed his own style. In his "Abduction of the Body of St. Mark" (left), his taste for intensive drama is expressed in the lighting, and the tension is compounded by the asymmetrical design. This is in sharp contrast to the balanced and classical mood of High Renaissance paintings. El Greco, the master of the Mannerist style, was deeply influenced by Tintoretto. Carrying the revolt against Renaissance style even further, El Greco distorted his figures in order to obtain the desired emotional intensity. In "St. Martin and the Beggar" (bottom left) the elongation gives the beggar's body a suggestion of weightlessness. The mannered and artificial idiom of these post-Renaissance artists inspired yet another revolt in style. Caravaggio began painting with a natural realism, using real people caught in natural circumstances as his subjects. In "The Fortune Teller" (bottom right), for example, a gypsy slips the ring off a young man's finger while pretending to tell his fortune.

catch with particular success the spontaneous, fleeting expressions of his portrait subjects (see illustration, p. 547). His canvases provide us with a wonderful gallery of types —from cavaliers to fishwives and tavern denizens. As for Jan Vermeer (1632-1675), the subtle delicacy with which he handled the fall of subdued sunlight upon interior scenes has never been equaled (see illustration, p. 547). His few canvases raised *genre* painting to perfection, and today each commands a king's ransom.

The finest of the Dutch painters—and one who indeed ranks with the outstanding artists of all time—was Rembrandt van Rijn (1606-1669). Rembrandt achieved fame at an early age and for the rest of his life had a large following among other painters. But though fashionable in the 1630's, his work became less popular in later decades as his style evolved away from the more straightforward and realistic presentation of his earlier days, which had been very much to the liking of the down-to-earth and uncomplicated burghers. Instead, he concentrated progressively in his portraits on psychological and emotional qualities (see Color Plate 28). His mastery of the use of light and shadow reached its zenith in his later paintings. Although Rembrandt stood outside the religious conflicts of his day, his inner concern for spiritual values is attested by the deep sincerity of his canvases devoted to themes from the life of Christ. Some of them have a strong touch of the dramatic, and this links Rembrandt to the mainstream of the Baroque style.

Baroque architecture. The Baroque style endowed architecture with a new emotional significance, dynamism, and fluidity. Where the architecture of the High Renaissance is severe and self-contained and emphasizes symmetry and "squareness," the Baroque sweeps us off our feet by subjecting us to an almost physical "pull." It is a magnificent stage set, full of visual illusions intended to arouse an emotional response.

Rome was the capital of the new Baroque architecture. Giovanni Lorenzo Bernini (1598-1680), the most renowned seventeenth-century architect of the Baroque school, designed the great colonnades in front of the

Basilica of St. Peter's. They symbolize the embracing arms of the Church, and their curving lines and colossal size are typical of the Baroque style. Besides being an accomplished architect and painter, Bernini was also a magnificent sculptor (see illustration, p. 548), as were many other artists of the Baroque. In fact, the architect also acted as a sculptor, painter, and interior decorator, for the integration of Baroque art reached the point where it was difficult to see where one art left off and another began.

After 1600 the Baroque style spread over much of Europe, being favored both by the Catholic Church and by rulers whose palaces were designed to serve as symbols of power and magnificence. More than merely a new decorative style or the exercise of ingenious techniques for theatrical effects, Baroque displayed—even as medieval Gothic had in its day—the value of blending architectural, sculptural, and ornamental elements in the creation of an artistic unity (see illustration, p. 549).

Beginning of modern music. As we saw in Chapter 15, late medieval religious music was polyphonic, not homophonic, in form. By the sixteenth century many-voiced polyphonic music had become so excessively complicated that some Church reformers at the Council of Trent demanded an end to polyphonic music and a return to the homophonic Gregorian chant of the early Middle Ages. The results of the Council's compromise decision were best expressed in the sacred music of Giovanni da Palestrina (1526?-1594), a choirmaster at the Vatican, who greatly simplified the prevailing style by uniting homophony with polyphony. The restrained yet powerful effect of Palestrina's music has earned him the honor of being called the "first Catholic Church musician."

Protestantism also stimulated new forms of musical expression. Luther encouraged his followers to participate in the church service by singing hymns. He himself wrote a number of hymns, including the stirring "A Mighty Fortress Is Our God." Sung in the vernacular languages instead of in Latin, a remarkable body of religious song called the chorale developed. These compositions

Seventeenth-century Dutch artists preferred portraits of the citizens themselves and scenes of daily life to religious subjects and grandiose display. Within these confines, however, they used various techniques and created different effects, as evident in these paintings: "Malle Babbe" by Franz Hals (left), "The Lacemaker" by Jan Vermeer (bottom left), and "Jan Six," Burgomaster of Amsterdam, by Rembrandt van Rijn (bottom right).

Bernini's Baroque sculpture for a side altar in a small Roman church depicts a vision of St. Theresa. Describing her mystical experiences, St. Theresa once told of a moment of ecstasy and pain in which an angel pierced her heart with a flaming arrow. As the saint ascends to heaven on a cloud, the angel approaches her and she swoons.

had a plain melody, strong harmony, and stately rhythms.

In the seventeenth century the Baroque spirit was manifested in music by the development of new forms of expression and by experiments in harmony which moved away from the calm and exalted manner of Palestrina. For the first time instrumental music—in particular that of the organ and the violin family—became of equal importance with vocal music.

Outstanding among Baroque innovations was opera. The Venetian composer Claudio Monteverdi (1567-1643) is regarded as the first master of tragic opera and the foremost musical figure of his day. He wrote many operas, the most famous being *Orfeo* (1607). Italian opera quickly conquered Europe, and in the second half of the seventeenth century French and German composers began to make their own contributions to the new art form.

Opera was almost the perfect musical expression of the Baroque style. Here again we find an integration of the arts: dramatic literature, music, and acting, with the skills of the painter employed for elaborate stage settings. The opulence of opera and its highly charged emotional content and sweep of expression could not fail to appeal to an age that rejoiced in the obviously theatrical.

THE SCIENTIFIC REVOLUTION

Hindrances to science. In Chapter 15 we saw how the Italian humanists in such centers as Padua emphasized a rationalistic philosophy separate from theology. This approach helped create an intellectual environment suitable for the development of new scientific theories. On the other hand, the humanists' quite understandable reverence for classical authorities, such as Aristotle, tended to inhibit criticism of works from antiquity. Aristotelian theories dominated physics; medicine was studied from the works of Hippocrates and Galen (as well as from the Muslim scientist Avicenna); and astronomers continued to accept Aristotle's concept that the earth was the center of the universe. So firmly entrenched were scholars in their veneration of ancient authority that the occasional innovator who sought to observe and experiment found himself discredited if his conclusions ran counter to those of Greek science. Although Renaissance artists were experimenting with new techniques and poets with new modes of expression, scientists were still striving to master Greek scientific texts. However, in their endeavor "to see in nature what Greek writers had declared to be there, European scientists slowly came to see what really was there."[5]

Science takes to the heavens. Science made its first spectacular advance in astronomy. Western Europe had accepted the cosmological speculations of Greek scientists, backed by the authority of Aristotle, that the earth and not the sun was stationary. Rotating around the earth were nine concentric, impenetrable, crystalline spheres to which were attached the moon, the sun, the five known planets, and the fixed stars. Beyond the fixed stars was the ninth sphere, the *primum mobile* or "first mover," whose function was to spin the entire celestial system around the earth from east to west once every twenty-four hours. Surrounding this finite universe was the Empyrean, where God dwelt. During the Hellenistic Age this scheme had been modified in order to explain the irregular movements of the planets. As viewed from the earth, the planets do not move continuously eastward; at times they stop and then move backward for a while. The logical explanation for this shuttling movement was that the planets move in orbits of their own while encircling the earth. By assuming the existence of these epicycles—circles moving upon circles—all irregular movements in the heavens were accounted for. This version of the geocentric (earth-centered) theory was handed down to the Middle Ages in the *Almagest* of Ptolemy and incorporated into the Scholastic thought of the Church.

By the sixteenth century the Ptolemaic system had become exceedingly cumbersome, since a complicated arrangement of cycles and epicycles had to be postulated to explain all the observed movements of the celestial bodies. One must remember, however, that the details of planetary motions were of interest only to mathematical astronomers. Those interested in physics and cosmology drew their background from Aristotle's writings rather than Ptolemy's. The astronomers did not claim that their mathematical theories were physically true but only that they expressed planetary motions in mathematically satisfying ways.

There was hence no grounds for conflict until two changes occurred: first, a claim by the mathematicians that the Creator was a mathematician, so that *mathematical* theories about the universe would have *physical* meaning; second, an alteration in those mathematical theories that would bring them in conflict with the Aristotelian cosmology and physics. These changes were brought about chiefly through the labors of a Pole, Copernicus; a Dane, Tycho Brahe; a German, Kepler; and an Italian, Galileo.

Copernicus and the heliocentric theory. Born in Poland in 1473, Copernicus was a contemporary of Martin Luther and Michelangelo. Since his uncle and guardian, a priest who later became a bishop, had decided that his nephew should enter the Church, at nineteen Copernicus was sent to the University of Cracow and then went on to northern Italy to continue his studies at the universities at Bologna, Padua, and Ferrara. In preparation for a career as a Church official, he studied Church law and medicine. Following the completion of his priestly studies, he served at a cathedral

An example of early Baroque architecture, the Church of Jesus in Rome was the first church built by the newly founded Jesuit order.

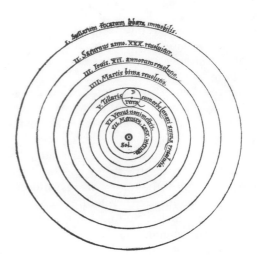

The 1559 engraving at left illustrates Ptolemy's system of the universe. Surrounding the earth are spheres containing the moon, sun, planets, and fixed stars. An additional sphere provides the system's motion. Beyond that is the Empyrean. The diagram above, illustrating the helio-centric theory of the universe, appeared in the first edition of Copernicus' *Concerning the Revolutions of the Heavenly Bodies* (1543). It places the sun in the center, surrounded by the first six planets in their correct order. The outer sphere was thought to be the home of all fixed stars.

in his homeland. Copernicus' educational experiences in Italy profoundly altered his outlook. At Bologna he came into contact with Dominico da Novarra, a Florentine Platonist. The Platonistic philosophy taught that beauty was supreme and that mathematics was the ideal science.

Copernicus was not so much concerned with the physical nature of the universe as with the mathematics of planetary motion. He found parts of the Ptolemaic theory "not sufficiently pleasing to the mind" and hence began to seek a more pleasing combination of circles to express the motions of the planets. His Platonistic commitment to beauty led him to write:

[I] began to chafe that philosophers could by no means agree on any one certain theory of the mechanism of the Universe, wrought for us by a supremely good and orderly Creator, though in other respects they investigated with meticulous care the minutest points relating to its circles. . . . I therefore took pains to read again the works of all the philosophers on whom I could lay hand. . . . I found first in Cicero that Hicetas had realized that the earth moved. Afterwards I found in

Plutarch that certain others had held the like opinion. . . .

Taking advantage of this I too began to think of the mobility of the Earth; and though the opinion seemed absurd, yet knowing now that others before me had been granted freedom to imagine such circles as they chose to explain the phenomena of the stars, I considered that I also might easily be allowed to try whether, by assuming some motion of the Earth, sounder explanations than theirs for the revolution of the celestial spheres might so be discovered.[6]

Copernicus found that he could obtain a more intellectually pleasing model of planetary motions by assuming that the earth moves "like any other planet," while the sun stands still in the middle of the planetary orbits. In a brief, popular account circulated in 1530, he proposed his new theory, but he was in no hurry to publish it. Near the end of his life, his friends persuaded him to allow the publication of a complete exposition of his views. Written in Latin and entitled *Concerning the Revolutions of the Heavenly Spheres*, it was addressed to mathematicians who would appreciate the ordered simplicity of his system. The theory postulated that the earth rotates every twenty-four hours upon its axis from west to east and that it and the other planets revolve around the sun in circular orbits. "Why will we not recognize," he wrote,

that the appearance of a daily revolution belongs to the heavens, but the actuality to the earth; and that the relation is similar to that of which one says: 'We run out of the harbor, the lands and cities retreat from us.' Because if a ship sails along quietly, everything outside of it appears to those on board as if it moved with the motion of the boat, and the boatman thinks that the boat with all on board is standing still, this same thing may hold without doubt of the motion of the earth, and it may seem as if the whole universe revolved.[7]

Copernicus' application of the heliocentric theory diminished the degree of dependence upon epicycles found in the Ptolemaic system, and he could claim that his hypothesis reduced the total number of such devices from eighty to thirty-four.

The Copernican theory and Copernicus' book, published in 1543, caused little stir.

A number of mathematicians found it pleasing; physicists found it irrelevant, for mathematics was not yet a standard tool in physics. The Copernican theory was just one more mode of expressing planetary motions mathematically.

Tycho Brahe. Precision of astronomical observation was introduced by the Danish scientist Tycho Brahe (1546-1601). After many years of travel and study Brahe had decided to settle in Basel, when, in 1576, the Danish king made him an extraordinary offer. Brahe could have the Danish island of Hveen (including its inhabitants!) for his own, as well as essentially carte blanche on the royal treasury. Brahe accepted and built himself a magnificent home named Uraniborg ("Castle of Urania," goddess of the heavens) and an observatory, Sterneborg ("Castle of the Stars").

For twenty-one years Brahe carried on accurate observations and carefully plotted the positions of hundreds of celestial bodies. Thus he tracked the planets through the whole of their courses instead of contenting himself with picking them out at different

The diagram above shows the exterior of Tycho Brahe's main observatory and the surrounding auxiliary buildings which housed specialized sextants, quadrants, and other astronomical instruments. In the print on the left Brahe and his assistants are plotting the position of the planets by means of the precision instruments he designed.

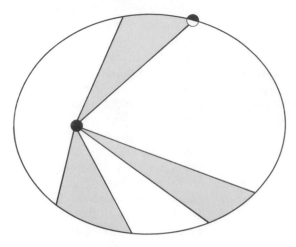

This chart illustrates Kepler's second law of planetary motion. The planet takes an equal amount of time to traverse each shaded area, because it moves slower the farther it gets from the sun. Kepler proved that the radius vector of a planet sweeps over equal areas in equal intervals of time.

points in their orbits. Brahe even attempted to work out a compromise between the Ptolemaic and Copernican systems by having all of the planets except earth move around the sun, with the latter in turn orbiting around the earth, which was motionless in this theory.

Curiously this system, which combined elements of both the older theories never attracted much interest. This was perhaps because the heliocentric theory attracted two ardent and capable propagandists, the mathematicians Kepler and Galileo.

Johann Kepler. The most acute mind ever born is how the philosopher Immanuel Kant described the German mathematician Johann Kepler (1571-1630). A devout Christian, the young Kepler was upset and disturbed over the religious wars that dominated his era. The slaughter and repression of Christians by one another seemed to violate the precepts of that religion. It is thus not surprising that he embarked on the career of theologian. While studying for the ministry at the University at Wittenberg, he became the pupil and friend of a professor of mathematics named Michael Mästlin. Kepler found that he had a talent for mathematics and that, further, he could serve God as well by studying His work, the universe, as by being a theologian. As a mathematician with a strong leaning toward Platonic idealism, Kepler quickly adopted the Copernican

theory. His first efforts went to "cleaning up" certain irregularities in that theory, but he quickly moved on to alter it significantly. While adopting its heliocentric character, he abandoned the idea that planetary motions must be expressed as combinations of circular motions. He found that he could satisfactorily account for the known planetary motions by assuming that each planet moves in an ellipse around the sun, a postulate that came to be called Kepler's first law of planetary motion. In testing this idea, as well as his later ones, he had available Brahe's extraordinarily precise observations of planetary positions.

Knowing that the planets move around the sun with a variable speed, Kepler's preconceptions caused him to search for a mathematical regularity in this variation. He decided that each planet changes speed so that "the line from the planet to the sun sweeps across equal areas in equal times," a statement called Kepler's second law of planetary motion. This law destroyed another assumption held by both Copernicus and the Greeks, that the planets move at a uniform speed. After reading William Gilbert's book on magnetism (see p. 555), Kepler concluded that the sun emitted a magnetic force that moved the planets in their courses. Kepler's ideas on this subject formed a valuable basis for Isaac Newton's theory of gravitation.

Finally, after discovering a third law of planetary motion—that the time it takes for a planet to orbit the sun is related mathematically to its distance from the sun—Kepler became an elated missionary for a new view of the universe as a "celestial machine." He felt a religious fervor in his increased understanding of God's creation and wrote to his former teacher, Mästlin:

. . . the die is cast, the book is written, to be read either now or by posterity, I care not which; it may well wait a century for a reader, as God has waited six thousand years for an observer![8]

The daring of Galileo. The most ardent supporter of the Copernican theory was Galileo Galilei (1564-1642). Although a contemporary and friend of Kepler, Galileo never accepted Kepler's idea of elliptical planet orbits, adhering instead to Copernicus' epicyclic system. But he did join Kepler in fighting for the heliocentric conception of the universe.

Born at Pisa in the Grand Duchy of Tuscany, Galileo spent most of his life in the capital city, Florence, and was proud of his Tuscan origin. His father, Vincenzo Galilei, was a musician whose *Dialogue on Ancient and Modern Music* led to the invention of opera. His son, Galileo, was raised a Platonist, in that hotbed of Platonism, Florence. The boy learned to paint, to play the lute, to value mathematics, and to write poetry. He associated throughout his life with poets, artists, and musicians. Such a background led him naturally to mathematics as a profession and to the Copernican theory.

Galileo early began to propound the idea that had been building up for almost a century: God the Creator created the universe mathematically and hence mathematicians understood physics better than the physicists. It is not astonishing that he got into difficulties with the physicists—then known as "natural philosophers"—at the University of Pisa which he attended (and left without a degree). Obtaining a job at the University of Padua as a mathematician, he became more restrained and confined himself to research in mathematics, including astronomy.

In 1609, having heard of a Dutch invention which arranged lenses in a tube to magnify objects, Galileo made a telescope for himself. With it he discovered mountains on the moon, sunspots, the rings of Saturn, and the four satellites of Jupiter—the latter he interpreted as a visible small-scale model of the solar system. Thrilled by these discoveries, Galileo put aside his previous caution and began to publicize his findings and beliefs.

In a book published in 1610 he named the four satellites of Jupiter after the grand duke of Tuscany and, as he had hoped, was put on the grand duke's staff and payroll and returned to Florence. From this seemingly safe base he began to propagandize for the Copernican theory. The Aristotelian philosophers and physicists became alarmed at his undermining of the geocentric theory and began to form a solid front against Galileo. Unfortunately for the new view, the Catholic Church had frozen education as part of the fight against Protestantism and had naturally chosen the geocentric theory as the best available theory of the universe. Galileo forced the issue, and in 1616 a Church decision was made against the heliocentric theory as anything but a "plausible conjecture" of planetary motions. Thus the Aristotelian theory of a geocentric universe was confirmed as the most suitable theory. Galileo agreed to suppress his arguments on this subject.

In 1623 a Florentine cardinal and friend of Galileo's became Pope Urban VIII, and with Urban's permission Galileo wrote the *Dialogue on the Two Great Systems of the World,* published in 1632. This work was cast in the form of a Platonic dialogue, and in it Galileo brought to bear his vast literary ability to force a belief in the Copernican theory. Pope Urban had not expected this result and felt, with considerable justice, that he had been misled by Galileo. The Church found itself in the odd position of having to suppress a

At left are Galileo's drawings showing the course of sunspots across the face of the sun. These observations were the basis for Galileo's discovery that the sun rotates on its axis just as the earth does.

book that had the approval of the reigning pope. Galileo was tried by a Church court and found guilty of disobeying the injunction of 1616 and of only pretending to present the heliocentric theory "as an hypothesis." He was forced to recant any belief in the physical reality of the Copernican theory, to swear he would not teach or defend it, and to spend most of the rest of his life under technical arrest.

A legend has it that Galileo, upon rising from his knees after renouncing the idea that the earth moved, stamped the ground and exclaimed, *"Eppur si muove!"* ("But it does move!"). Although this tale is now dismissed as apocryphal, it epitomizes Galileo's conviction in the correctness of his views.

Opposition to the heliocentric theory. The discoveries of Copernicus and his successors set off a struggle in European thought in which traditionalists sought to prevent acceptance of the new, disturbing ideas. After 1616, when it became clear that the Copernican theory was more than a matter for speculation among mathematicians, the Roman Catholic Church assumed the leading role in this controversy primarily because it was the strongest and most widespread

This illustration from Gilbert's *De Magnete* (1600), demonstrates the technique of forming a magnet by beating a hot iron bar while it is aligned parallel to the direction of the earth's magnetic field. This orients the electrons in the iron bar to produce magnetic polarity.

religious organization. Furthermore, it had for centuries acted as the traditional arbiter in conflicts of ideas and as the relentless foe of anything considered to be capricious change. The best available scientific opinions also were almost unanimously against the Copernican theory, viewing it as a speculative idea held by a few mathematicians who were not qualified to discuss the physical nature of the universe. By and large the universities continued to teach the geocentric cosmology.

In the geocentric system the earth was conceived to be the center of the universe, and with man occupying the center of the world's stage (according to the theologians), this view of the universe had strong religious and moral implications. Opponents of the heliocentric theory felt that these implications were obscured in the search for the natural laws governing the planet earth and determining its relation to other celestial bodies.

Protestants were, like Catholics, disturbed by what seemed to be both a contradiction of, and an attack upon, Holy Scripture. Shocked by Copernicus, Luther said:

People give ear to an upstart astrologer who strove to show that the earth revolves, not the heavens or the firmament, the sun and the moon. . . . but sacred Scripture tells us that Joshua commanded the sun to stand still, and not the earth.[9]

Calvin entered the fray with the Biblical text "the world also is established, that it cannot be moved"[10] and exclaimed: "Who will venture to place the authority of Copernicus above that of the Holy Spirit?"[11] Nor was opposition confined to theologians. Such intellectuals as Francis Bacon refused to accept the Copernican theory.

Yet each succeeding generation felt less aversion to the discoveries, which were gradually fitted into a system of thought in which religion and science were integrated. By 1650 European science had largely accepted the Copernican system, although religious groups were slower in being convinced. Not until 1757 was all reference to the ban heretofore imposed on works containing Copernican thought omitted from the Roman Catholic *Index of Prohibited Books*.

This seventeenth-century trade card advertises many of the fashionable scientific objects being made in London at that time.

Discoveries in magnetism and motion: Gilbert and Galileo. The year 1600 marked the publication of *De Magnete*, a remarkable book on magnetism by William Gilbert (1544-1603). This English scientist had constructed a spherical magnet called a *terrella* ("small earth"), with which he examined the action of the magnetic compass and similar phenomena. Gilbert concluded that the earth itself possesses the same properties as the magnet, such as attractional polarity and the tendency to revolve. He held that the earth acts as a huge magnet, with its poles nearly coincident with the geographical poles. For the earth or any other loadstone, the strength of its magnetism is directly proportional to its quantity or mass. In other words, the greater the mass of the loadstone, the greater the pull which it exerts on related objects. Gilbert paved the way for the work of later scientists, such as Newton, who applied many of Gilbert's ideas in working out his theory of gravitation.

At this time, too, discoveries were being made in kinematics, the branch of mechanics which deals with the motion of bodies.

Kepler had undermined Ptolemaic astronomy by proposing laws of planetary motion that were only valid for the heliocentric system; now Galileo undermined Aristotelian mechanics by insisting that the mathematical study of motion was the only profitable path. Aristotle had contended that bodies fall to the earth at speeds proportional to their weight. About 1590 a Flemish scientist had experimented with dropping lead balls of different weights from a height of some thirty feet and had found that they reached the ground simultaneously. But it remained for Galileo, who may have repeated the same experiment—according to legend from the leaning tower of Pisa—to make a scientific study of motion.

Galileo was the first to establish the law of falling bodies, proving that, irrespective of weight or size, their acceleration is constant (the increase of velocity being thirty-two feet per second). He proved this law by conducting an experiment with a piece of wooden molding some twelve cubits long, in which was cut a channel "a little more than one finger in breadth." The board having been placed in a sloping position, a smooth bronze ball was rolled the length of the channel; the time required to make the descent was carefully measured more than once to ensure that, in Galileo's own words,

... the deviation between two observations never exceeded one-tenth of a pulse-beat . . . we now rolled the ball only one-quarter the length of the channel; and having measured the time of its descent, we found it precisely one-half of the former. Next we tried other distances, comparing the time for the whole length with that for the half, or with that for two-thirds, or three-fourths, or indeed for any fraction; in such experiments, repeated a full hundred times, we always found that the spaces traversed were to each other as the squares of the times, and this was true for all inclinations of the plane, *i.e.*, of the channel, along which we rolled the ball.[12]

Galileo's continued researches led him to the discovery of the law of inertia: a body at rest or in motion will remain at rest or in motion (and in a straight line at constant speed) unless acted upon by an external force. Thus he refuted another entrenched belief inherited from the ancients: Aristotle's contention that a body in motion requires a continuously acting force to keep it in motion. Galileo also demonstrated that the motion of a fired projectile describes a parabola. In terms of the law of inertia, such movement away from a straight line meant that the projectile was being influenced by some external force. Twenty-five years after Galileo's death, Newton would discover the nature of this force.

With good reason Galileo used the term "new science" for his method of scientific investigation and its results. He had rejected the philosophical speculations that characterized much of ancient and medieval science and had concentrated upon investigating natural phenomena and expressing the results in mathematical terms. This combination of experiment and mathematical analysis became the foundation upon which modern science was built.

Advances in mathematics and scientific instruments. Meanwhile, mathematicians had been keeping abreast of the work of the astronomers and physicists and providing them with new tools. About 1600 the most important mathematical need was for quicker methods of calculation. Tables to help shorten the process of computation had been devised, but they were cumbersome and inadequate. Then in 1614 a Scotsman, John Napier, published *A Description of the Marvellous Rule of Logarithms*. It has been said that by halving the time involved in solving intricate problems, Napier doubled the lives of his fellow mathematicians. Still other timesaving devices were invented: the slide rule in 1622 and the first adding machine in 1645.

Algebra and geometry had first developed among the Babylonians and Egyptians; it remained for the famous French mathematician and philosopher René Descartes (see p. 564) to mate them by applying algebraic methods to the geometric field. The result, analytic geometry, permitted relationships in space to be translated into algebraic equations—a development of obvious value to astronomers, for example, since it helped them to represent astronomical phenomena in mathematical symbols and formulas.

In Galileo's thermometer the fluid rose or fell in the glass tube depending on the temperature of the air in the bulb.

Shown here is Otto von Guericke's famous experiment in which sixteen horses were needed to separate two hemispheres after the air had been pumped from them. The demonstration provided dramatic evidence of the force of air pressure.

The work of science was no less dependent upon the development of more precise instruments. At the beginning of the seventeenth century appeared two by-products of the glassmaking industry of Holland— the telescope and microscope. We have already seen the invaluable use to which the first of these instruments was put by Galileo. The first microscopes, on the other hand, were apparently of little use because the lens gave a distorted image at high magnification. But simple lenses were greatly improved about 1650, and within a few years microscopic examinations of the lungs and other organs of the body were yielding vital information regarding their structure and functions.

At this time too, Galileo and others were constructing crude thermometers; Galileo's consisted of a glass bulb containing air, with the end of its open tube dipping in water. Although a really accurate thermometer using mercury was not invented until the eighteenth century, an Italian constructed a mercury barometer in 1643. This instrument, along with Otto von Guericke's in-

vention of the air pump about 1650, gave strong evidence that, contrary to Aristotle, a vacuum could exist in nature. Von Guericke astounded observers with an experiment in which sixteen horses were needed to pull apart two hollow iron hemispheres from which the air had been pumped.

Crude mechanical clocks made their appearance during the Middle Ages (see p. 369), and the first watches are ascribed to a Nuremberg clockmaker near the beginning of the sixteenth century. Being spherical, they were nicknamed Nuremberg eggs. Chronometry received another impetus as the result of Galileo's research work on the theory of pendulums. It remained for a Dutchman, Christian Huygens (1629-1695), to use the pendulum for regulating the movement of clocks, an invention dating from 1656. Huygens also determined the relation between the length of a pendulum and the time of its oscillation, while his theorems on centrifugal force—worked out in connection with his work on the pendulum clock— were to help Newton formulate his law of gravitation.

Newton and the law of gravitation. Great as the contributions of Brahe, Kepler, and Galileo had been, their individual discoveries had yet to be united into an embracing principle or law which would explain the motion of all bodies in the heavens and on earth and present the universe as one great unity operating according to unalterable principles. This goal was realized by Isaac Newton (1642-1727), the most illustrious scientist in the age of the scientific revolution.

Newton was born the same year Galileo died and nearly a century after the death of Copernicus. While still in his early twenties Newton had formulated three supremely important scientific discoveries: the law of gravitation, the principles of calculus, and the compound nature of light.

The notion of gravitation occurred to him in 1666. Much later, in 1727, he described his discovery to an acquaintance who wrote this account:

In 1668, fifty-nine years after Galileo first constructed his telescope, Newton developed a new type, utilizing a concave mirror at the bottom of a tube to collect and magnify light images and reflect them into an eyepiece.

. . . [Newton's discovery] was occasion'd by the fall of an apple, as he sat in contemplative mood. Why should that apple always descend perpendicularly to the ground, thought he to himself. Why should it not go sideways or upwards, but constantly to the earth's center? Assuredly, the reason is, that the earth draws it. There must be a drawing power in matter: and the sum of the drawing power must be in the earth's center, not in any side of the earth. Therefore does this apple fall perpendicularly, or towards the center. If matter thus draws matter, it must be in proportion of its quantity. Therefore the apple draws the earth, as well as the earth draws the apple. That there is a power, like that we here call gravity, which extends itself thro the universe.[13]

At twenty-seven the youthful genius was given a professorship in mathematics at Cambridge University. Even though he had formulated his ideas on gravitation several years earlier, Newton was reticent to publish them. It was not until 1687 that his momentous work was published in Latin under the title *Philosophiae Naturalis Principia Mathematica (Mathematical Principles of Natural Philosophy)*. By this work Kepler's laws of celestial motion and Galileo's laws of terrestrial motion were synthesized in a master principle for the universe, the law of gravitation, which was expressed in mathematical terms:

Every particle in the universe attracts every other particle with a force varying inversely as the square of the distance between them and directly proportional to the product of their masses.

Not only had Newton explained Kepler's elliptical orbits and Galileo's parabolic trajectories, but he had confirmed the mathematical-experimental method of modern science. Much concerned with establishing a sound method of scientific analysis, Newton in his *Principia* and other writings stressed not only the formulation of mathematical principles but also the need for observation and experiment:

. . . Analysis consists in making Experiments and Observations, and in drawing general Conclusions from them by Induction, and admitting of no Objections against the Conclusions, but such as are taken from Experiments, or other certain Truths.[14]

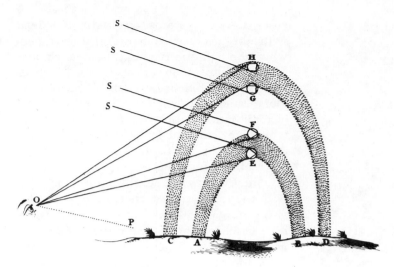

Through the use of prisms, Newton discovered the compound nature of light. This is Newton's diagram of how the eye sees a rainbow.

Newton also had confirmed the premise of modern science that all nature is governed by orderly laws which are discoverable by man. This view was contagious, and the poet Alexander Pope expressed the sentiments of Newton's contemporaries:

Nature and Nature's laws lay hid in night:
God said, Let Newton be! and all was light.[15]

The publication of the *Principia* completed the scientific revolution that had begun with Copernicus nearly a century and a half earlier. As Newton himself observed, "If I have seen farther . . . it is by standing on the shoulders of giants."[16]

THE DAWN OF MODERN MEDICINE

Medicine in the Middle Ages. Although medieval medicine has been ridiculed as ridden with superstition and practiced by either charlatans or ignoramuses, modern scholarship has done much to explode these traditional derogatory notions. However, in the Middle Ages and the early Renaissance medicine did suffer from an excessive reliance upon the books of Galen and Avicenna; professors often placed more confidence in these texts than in the dissected body. "The story is told of a professor who, being confronted with a discrepancy between the text and the dissection, preferred to throw the blame upon the miserable body rather than upon Galen."[17]

Thus medicine still had to be placed upon a firmer foundation, a development which was mainly the result of the work of three outstanding sixteenth-century men, all of whom led colorful and even stormy lives. Paracelsus inaugurated a new era in internal medicine; Vesalius created the modern science of anatomy; and Paré evolved operating techniques so important that he has been called the father of modern surgery.

Paracelsus, rebel against medical tradition. Paracelsus (1493-1541) was an egotistical, opinionated German-Swiss physician who was so annoyed with the tyranny of tradition in his field that he traveled through most of Europe to learn by direct experience and observation instead of trusting solely to the deductive scholarship prevalent in the universities. His life was one long journey also because he was never permitted to stay long in one place. For a time he taught at the University of Basel, where he burned publicly the works of Galen, Hippocrates, and Avicenna. He also shocked his faculty colleagues by lecturing in German instead of Latin, ridiculing the reliance upon classical authorities, and continuing to advocate the value of his own observations and experiences. Opposition to his views forced him to take up his journey again. In spite of his quarrels, his fame as a healer became wide-

This weird figure, a cadaver with its jawbone split and its muscles cut away, appears in an illustration from Vesalius' book on anatomy.

spread. Of this Paracelsus bitingly remarked, "I pleased no one except the sick whom I healed."

Prior to Paracelsus, medical teaching had been based upon anatomy and botany; Paracelsus' principal contribution was the addition of chemistry. Although such chemical drugs as mercury had been employed before his time, Paracelsus was the first to insist upon the role of chemistry in preparing medicines. The gist of his teachings was that since the human body was basically chemical in its construction, the prescription of chemicals was in turn required to cure disease. He appears to have been the first to use such drugs as silver nitrate, copper vitriol, and arsenic and antimony compounds, and he introduced the zinc oxide ointment commonly used today for treatment of skin dis-

eases. One of his most original books dealt with the peculiar ailments of the miners whom he had observed and treated. He discussed the poisonous effects of metallic dusts that penetrated their skin, lungs, and mucous membranes, as well as the environmental factors that contributed to the diseases from which they suffered. His was the first treatise devoted to an occupational disease.

Vesalius, founder of modern anatomy. Still another scientist to find himself at odds with the followers of Galen and Hippocrates was Andreas Vesalius (1514-1564), a native of Brussels. Although he did not deny the merits of the Greek authorities, Vesalius contended that in medical schools attention should first be given to the actual dissection of human bodies. Existing laws, however, limited the number of such bodies to which a school was entitled, and often dogs had to serve the needs of the class. Vesalius complained that a medical student might just as well try to learn human anatomy by working in a butcher shop.

At the age of twenty-three Vesalius became a lecturer at the famous University of Padua, where he found conditions much more suited to his anatomical investigations. Cadavers—generally those of executed criminals—were supplied by the city authorities, and an effective working relationship existed between the school and the prison. When a number of criminals were sentenced to be executed, the medical school would arrange with the civil authorities to space out the executions in order to fit in best with the dissecting needs of the school.

As a popular lecturer and inveterate dissector, Vesalius contributed to the fame of Padua as a medical center. In 1543, within a few weeks of the appearance of Copernicus' masterpiece, Vesalius published his treatise *The Fabric of the Human Body*. This enormous book, with its splendid drawings of cadavers and skeletons prepared by a pupil of Titian, is a landmark in the history of medicine. Although not the first illustrated work on anatomy to correct errors found in Galen, it went far beyond its predecessors in the number of such corrections, in its descriptions of new discoveries, and in becoming a replacement for Galen.

Paré, father of modern surgery. Vesalius' discoveries in anatomy proved of immediate value to surgery, which was transformed by the new techniques evolved by a French surgeon, Ambroise Paré (1510-1590). Apprenticed at an early age to a barber, Paré later became a military surgeon. While serving in the army, he gained much practical knowledge concerning the extraction of bullets, the treatment of sword wounds, and the amputation of limbs. Since gunshot wounds were considered poisonous, it was customary to cauterize them with boiling oil, a treatment which resulted in terrible suffering and often led to dangerous complications. After one bloody battle, the oil supply was used up, and Paré prepared as a substitute a salve of egg yolk, attar of roses, and turpentine to treat the wounds of those not cauterized with the boiling oil. To his surprise, he found that those treated with his salve recuperated much faster than those who had been tortured with the oil. Soothing salves were thus shown to be superior to hot oil for healing, but could anything take the place of the painful searing by oil as a cautery for stopping the flow of blood especially when limbs had to be amputated? Paré solved one of surgery's most basic problems when he employed ligatures to arrest hemorrhage.

Harvey's discoveries in physiology and embryology. The anatomical discoveries of Vesalius and the surgical innovations of Paré were not matched at first by commensurate advances in physiology (without which there could be no science of internal medicine). This situation changed, however, in the late sixteenth century and the early years of the seventeenth. The school at Padua continued to lead the medical world as its professors made important studies of the vasomotor system and various organs. It was here that the Englishman William Harvey (1578-1657), one of the pioneers of early modern medicine, carried on his studies.

After four years of study at Padua, Harvey returned to England, where he quickly gained recognition as an outstanding doctor. Becoming interested in the problem of how blood travels, Harvey plunged into painstaking research. Aristotle had declared that the blood was carried from the liver to the heart and thence sent by veins to the various parts of the body, and Galen believed that the arteries also contained blood. In Harvey's time doctors thought that the blood moved in the body; but they knew nothing of the functions of the heart, nor did they know that the blood travels in a continuous stream, returning to its source. In 1628 Harvey published a treatise entitled *Anatomical Exercise on the Motion of the Heart and Blood*. In this epoch-making work he tells that he determined the quantity of blood driven forward by each heartbeat and from this ascertained that the heart pumps as much blood in half an hour as is contained in the whole body. He concluded that the blood must somehow have to find its way back to the heart.

I began to think whether there might not be *a motion, as it were, in a circle.* Now this I afterwards found to be true; and I finally saw that the blood, forced by the action of the left ventricle into the arteries, was distributed to the body at large and its several parts, in the same manner as it is sent through the lungs impelled by the right ventricle into the right pulmonary artery, and that it then passed through the veins and along the *vena cava*, and so round to the left ventricle in the manner already indicated, which motion we may be allowed to call circular.[18]

Harvey's description of the circulation of the blood was a kind of master key that unlocked the many doors leading to an understanding of how the human body functions. His work was of obvious value in surgery for excess bleeding would be difficult to control without knowledge of the blood's circulation.

Harvey's fame does not rest solely on his work on circulation. His second work, *Exercise on Generation in Animals* (1651), represents the most notable advance in embryology since Aristotle. In fact, Harvey has been credited with being the founder of that science in its modern form. The traditional view held by many of Harvey's contemporaries was known as "preformation": at the time of conception an animal was a tiny but exact copy of the adult form which would finally develop. Only after meticulous experimentation and observation did Harvey put forward the theory of "epigenesis," which maintains that the embryo goes through definite, successive stages of development, its form progressively changing until the time of birth.

While much of Harvey's data on embryology was superseded by later scientists equipped with microscopes, his work on circulation and the embryo demonstrated that the human body, no less than the earth and other celestial bodies, functioned on the basis of physical mechanics. It is this emphasis upon natural, mechanical causes which stamps the work of men like Galileo and Harvey as basically "modern," in contrast to the earlier, often supernatural, explanations of natural phenomena.

This engraving of William Harvey, the English physician who discovered the circulation of blood, contains one of Harvey's diagrams of the human heart and its connections to the veins and arteries.

SCIENCE AND THE NEW PHILOSOPHY

The necessity for a new philosophy. As we have seen earlier, philosophers in the Middle Ages constructed an intricate theological philosophy whose basic purpose was to reconcile all knowledge with the doctrines of the Church. For over a thousand years, in fact, philosophy was the handmaiden of theology. But under the impact of new attitudes resulting from the discoveries in science, damaging blows were struck against both the restrictions and prestige of traditional authority. Part of this changing attitude was due to Protestantism, for Luther and other early reformers attacked the Church's Scholasticism and the attachment of its theologians to "the damned heathen" Aristotle. The change was also due to a growing skepticism, already discernible in the late Middle Ages and strengthened in the sixteenth century by religious conflicts and the proliferation of sects, many claiming to have a monopoly of truth. Thus the tendency for philosophy to become independent of theology, which had begun in the fourteenth century (see p. 394), was accelerated.

As a direct result of the changed conditions and new insights, Michel de Montaigne (see p. 469) was led to conclude that a man's religious faith was determined more by the chance of birth than by reason. His studies at length made him an amiable agnostic, content to shrug off any discussion with his favorite phrase, *"Que sçais-je?"* ("What do I know?"). Montaigne was witnessing the end of one great world view which could no longer contain man's increasing knowledge within its special, unified framework. Although the French skeptic had nothing to put in its place, other thinkers, inspired by science, began to build a new intellectual structure, based not on Aristotle or Genesis, but on experiment or mathematical reasoning.

Bruno's infinite universe. The impact of the new science upon philosophy is eloquently demonstrated in the life and thinking of Giordano Bruno (1548-1600), a Dominican friar who was perhaps the first to make a philosophical adjustment to the heliocentric theory of Copernicus. We have already quoted in the introduction to this chapter the words of this spirited champion of the new truth, intoxicated as he was by the immensity of the universe which he saw revealed by the new cosmology.

Copernicus had placed the sun in the center of the universe. Bruno, however, conceived the idea that the stars were also suns —less bright and smaller in appearance only because of their remote distance from us— and that the universe was infinite, filled with worlds like our own which might also be inhabited by living beings. To Bruno, God was not only the Father of man on this planet but was also present in the entire universe—which "is a great organism, whose dwelling-place is the infinite reaches of space." Everything in the universe is alive; God is the single unifying soul of this infinite universe—"Nature is God in things."

Bruno's pantheism was anathema to Catholics and Protestants alike as he bravely proclaimed it throughout Europe. Homesickness and poverty finally caused him to return to Italy, where he was arrested by order of the Inquisition, imprisoned for seven years, excommunicated, and in 1600 burned at the stake in Rome as a heretic. His martyrdom has ever since been considered a memorial to the spirit of intellectual liberty.

New ideas on scientific method. The sixteenth and seventeenth centuries were a time of vast changes in scientific knowledge. The new astronomical thought changed not only man's conception of the universe but also many of his most fundamental ideas concerning the nature of science itself. Aristotle had declared mathematics of no value in describing change; mathematicians from Copernicus to Newton invaded physics precisely in that area concerned with change— the study of motion. The Aristotelian universe centered upon man, who now found himself on an off-center planet whirling about the sun. It is understandable that, with this crumbling of Aristotelian scientific theories, philosophers began to doubt Aristotle's philosophical ideas, particularly those concerned with scientific inquiry. And, in so doing, they tended to look to their modern world for ideas on new procedures. Among

the leaders in this movement were two philosophers, Bacon in England, whose contribution comes within the first quarter of the seventeenth century, and Descartes in France, whose principal work falls within the second quarter.

Bacon's attack on unscientific thinking. Sir Francis Bacon's approach to philosophy was entirely practical. He is said to have originated the saying "Knowledge is power," and he advocated keeping philosophy divorced from theology. Bacon attacked humanism and Scholasticism and derided Plato and Aristotle, maintaining that the latter had managed to survive for centuries only because of their shallowness, which had given them the necessary buoyancy to ride down the stream of time.

In his *Novum Organum (The New Instrument),* published in 1620, Bacon described the course which science and a scientifically oriented philosophy should take. First, men must cope with four major prejudices (in Bacon's famous term, *Idols*) which had so far obstructed human progress. The Idols of the Tribe are the prejudices inherent in human nature itself; in particular, they represent the tendency to see only those facts which support an opinion one wishes to entertain. The Idols of the Cave are prejudices fostered in the individual by his particular environment—the circumstances of his birth, childhood, education, and so forth. Or, in Bacon's words:

For every one . . . has a cave or den of his own, which refracts and discolours the light of nature. . . .[19]

There are also Idols of the Market Place, false opinions in fashion when men consort together. Last, there are the Idols of the Theater, resulting from men's tendency to become attached to particular theories, schools of thought, and philosophies and to hold on to them long after the logical basis for their continuance has disappeared. Bacon named the latter fallacies as he did

because in my judgment all the received systems are but so many stage-plays, representing worlds of their own creation after an unreal and scenic fashion.[20]

If better results were to be obtained, new ways of thinking and of approaching the world of nature had to be devised. On the one hand, Bacon said, scientists were engaged in haphazard experimentation, while on the other, philosophers were guilty of speculating on insufficient evidence about the ultimate principles of the universe:

The men of experiment are like the ant; they only collect and use: the reasoners resemble spiders, who make cobwebs out of their own substance. But the bee takes a middle course; it gathers its material from the flowers . . . but transforms and digests it by a power of its own.[21]

This "middle course" should be "the true business of philosophy."

Bacon champions the inductive method. Bacon advocated a systematic directing and recording of experiments, believing that from the resulting accumulation of facts universal principles and scientific laws could readily be induced. In his enthusiasm for experimentation, Bacon undervalued the importance of hypotheses and the role of

Portrait of Sir Francis Bacon by an unknown artist.

mathematics in deducing from hypotheses. Bacon was not a scientist but a philosopher. While attacking the past, he drew most of what he had to say from Aristotle and while praising change he utterly failed to recognize the importance of the achievements of such scientists as Copernicus, Galileo, and Gilbert.

The significance of Bacon's work lies in his insistence on the importance of the experimental method. He set forth a program—or, as it has been described, a "manifesto" —to direct the course of scientific and philosophical inquiry at the time when the old world order as conceived by Aristotle and his school was crumbling and a new system was still in the blueprint stage. In his own words, he called for a "total reconstruction of the sciences, arts, and all human knowledge."

René Descartes, champion of the deductive method. Advocate as he was of experimentation and the inductive method, Bacon undervalued the role of mathematics. He did not properly appreciate the ability of Kepler and Galileo to resolve the problems of celestial bodies and motion in mathematical terms. But experimentation is not the only approach to scientific knowledge, as the mathematical approach attests. The mathematical approach is to begin with a simple hypothesis and then, by logical reasoning, to deduce various inferences. Applied to scientific investigations as a whole, this type of approach—known as the deductive method—advances by logical steps from simple self-evident truths to more complex truths. Aristotle had employed the syllogism to point out fallacies in human reasoning (see p. 112). It was the achievement of René Descartes (1596-1650) to make brilliant use of this method of reasoning in his attempt to extend the mathematical method to all fields of human knowledge. His methodology is the outstanding aspect of his philosophy.

Man of science, mathematical genius, and one-time soldier of fortune, Descartes has been called the founder of modern philosophy. As such, he is famous for his system of dualism, which will be discussed in Chapter 1, Volume II. Here we are concerned only with his development of a new method for inquiring after knowledge. Like Bacon, Descartes maintained that the first step was for men to get rid of preconceived notions and to take nothing for granted. In fact, Descartes went even farther. While Bacon called for "minds washed clean of opinions," the French philosopher began by doubting everything except the self-evident truth of his own existence. For if he doubted, he must in fact exist—hence his famous expression "*Cogito, ergo sum*" ("I think, therefore I am").

For Bacon, experiment was the next step in the quest for truth. Although Descartes by no means rejected the value of experimentation, he relied above all on the attainment of knowledge through reason. By logical deduction from self-evident truths, which he defined as "presented to my mind so clearly and distinctly that I could have no occasion to doubt [them],"[22] Descartes built up a concept of a unified, mathematically ordered universe which operated mechanically like a clock. In this universe supernatural phenomena were impossible and everything could be explained rationally, preferably in mathematical terms.

Some scientists criticized Descartes for not having made sufficient use of experiment, even as he had criticized Bacon for weakness in mathematics. The experimental and mathematical methods are complementary, and during the lifetime of Bacon and Descartes the two methods had been successfully combined by Galileo. Thus, by the time of Descartes' death in 1650 the foundation of modern science and modern philosophy had been laid. "The new philosophy enabled men to reduce the whole universe to matter and motion. It made possible the explanation of the whole of nature in mechanistic terms. . . . The ideal of a clockwork universe was the great contribution of seventeenth-century science to the eighteenth-century age of reason."[23]

Science looks to the future. Like Roger Bacon before him (see p. 395), Sir Francis Bacon made amazing predictions of flying machines, submarines, and many future improvements in medicine, meteorology, and mechanical contrivances. More important, this thinker of the early seventeenth century forecast with clarity the vast im-

Through deductive logic, René Descartes attempted to explain scientifically the phenomenon of sight. His diagram above shows the image of an arrow being transmitted to the brain's pineal gland, which Descartes thought contained man's soul.

portance of the new science in enabling man to control nature and thereby increase his material welfare. In the *New Atlantis*—Bacon's description of a utopian society—interest is centered on a research institute called "Solomon's house," where experimentation and invention were subsidized and directed toward the goal of "the enlarging of the bounds of Human Empire, to the effecting of all things possible."[24] Bacon's vision of an organization in which scholars and scientists would labor at the tasks of gathering knowledge survived his death in 1626 and became a reality soon afterwards, for to the impetus of his writings has been ascribed the establishment in 1662 of the oldest and most illustrious of British scientific organizations: the Royal Society for Improving Natural Knowledge. By the midpoint of the seventeenth century, it was becoming apparent that respect for science and scientific attitudes was to be the keynote of the culture of the next era.

SUMMARY

We have now briefly examined a period in European thought and expression which in the short span of little more than a century (1530-1650) laid much of the foundation for modern science and contributed outstanding achievements in the arts.

The tensions of the Reformation era are reflected in a new style of painting known as Mannerism. The best example of this troubled, distorted style is the work of El Greco in Spain. At the beginning of the seventeenth century Mannerism gave way to a new integration of forces—religious, cultural, and aesthetic—which by its very exuberance and grandiloquence captured the imagination and allegiance of all Europe. This was the Baroque style. Although the Baroque developed in Italy, its most representative painter was the Flemish artist Rubens. Also representing the Baroque but manifesting strong individual tendencies of their own were Velasquez, the Spanish court painter, and that Dutch master of psychological penetration, Rembrandt. The Baroque spirit also triumphed in architecture and music, thanks in large measure to the genius and technical creativeness of the architect and sculptor Bernini, and of the first master of opera, Monteverdi.

At this time science—which is the hallmark above all else of modern civilization—underwent a veritable revolution. The most immediate and striking development was in the field of astronomy. Here five men in particular—Copernicus, Brahe, Kepler, Galileo, and Newton—were responsible for the rapid alteration of man's conception of the universe. The overall result was not only to dethrone the geocentric theory but also to invite intellectual and theological consequences of the first magnitude.

Scientific horizons were also being pushed back by brilliant efforts in other directions. At the same time that the English scientist William Gilbert was hypothesizing that our planet has the same properties as a magnet and that the strength of its magnetism is directly proportional to its mass, Galileo was establishing the laws of terrestrial motion. For the mathematician no less than the astronomer and physicist, this was an eventful era; Napier provided him with logarithms, and Descartes with analytic geometry. The formulation of these tools of the mind are paralleled by the invention of new instruments: the telescope and microscope, the barometer and the thermometer, the pendulum clock, the air pump, and the slide rule.

Doctors in turn have reason to hail this era as one of outstanding achievement in their profession. Four men in particular exemplify the rapid changes occurring in medical technology. Paracelsus taught the value of applying chemical drugs to cure disease and wrote the first treatise on occupational diseases. Vesalius put anatomy on a firm footing, while Paré transformed surgery by new techniques, including methods of arresting hemorrhages. And Harvey, as a result of superb reasoning and meticulous experimentation, proved that the blood circulates in the body—thereby providing those who came after him with a fundamentally new understanding of the manner in which the human body functions.

The discoveries and inventions of a science-starred age could not fail to make their impact upon the philosophy of the time. Two philosophers, especially, investigated the problem of making use of appropriate methods of scientific inquiry in order to harness science still more effectively to the service of mankind. Francis Bacon placed chief reliance upon the inductive method, in which facts drawn from experimentation are used to formulate universal principles and scientific laws. A younger contemporary in France, Descartes, was more interested in deduction and used the mathematical method to reason his way to the concept of a mechanically run universe. Actually, the mathematical and experimental methods were complementary, as the work of Galileo clearly demonstrated. Their combination served to develop an overarching scientific method that was to prove universally applicable not only to their day but to our own as well.

Suggestions for Reading

GENERAL ACCOUNTS

W. K. Ferguson, **Europe in Transition, 1300 to 1520,** Houghton Mifflin, 1962. A comprehensive work of synthesis. Also comprehensive and up to date is S. H. Thomson, **Europe in Renaissance and Reformation,** Harcourt, Brace & World, 1963. Highly recommended also are E. P. Cheyney, **The Dawn of a New Era, 1250-1453,*** Torchbooks; M. P. Gilmore, **The World of Humanism, 1453-1517,*** Torchbooks; C. J. Friedrich, **The Age of the Baroque, 1610-1660,*** Torchbooks. Sir George Clark, **Early Modern Europe: From About 1450 to About 1720,*** is very brief but perceptive.

The classic study of the Italian Renaissance is J. C. Burckhardt, **The Civilization of the Renaissance in Italy,*** Mentor. Should be read in conjunction with W. K. Ferguson, **The Renaissance in Historical Thought: Five Centuries of Interpretation,** Houghton Mifflin, 1948.

W. K. Ferguson, **The Renaissance,*** Holt. The best brief survey. G. Sellery, **The Renaissance: Its Nature and Origins,*** Univ. of Wis., concentrates on leading personalities and movements. W. Durant, **The Renaissance: A History of Civilization in Italy from 1304 to 1576 A.D.,** Simon and Schuster, 1953, Vol. V of **The Story of Civilization,** is a popular survey. T. Aston, ed., **Crisis in Europe, 1560-1660,** Anchor,* is a stimulating interpretation of such topics as the Puritan Revolution, the rise of capitalism, and the wars of the seventeenth century.

A. G. Dickens, **Reformation and Society in Sixteenth-Century Europe,*** Harcourt, Brace & World, 1966. Vivid, concise, and richly illustrated. Other good short surveys are G. Mosse, **The Reformation,*** rev. ed., Holt, and Philip Hughes, **A Popular History of the Reformation,*** Image. Detailed and authoritative is H. Grimm, **The Reformation Era, 1500-1650,** Macmillan, 1965. H. R. Trevor-Roper, **The Crisis of the Seventeenth Century; Religion, the Reformation and Social Change,** Harper & Row, 1968, describes the impact of the Reformation on Europe.

Standard political histories of the period are V. H. H. Green, **Renaissance and Reformation: A Survey of European History Between 1450 and 1660,** Arnold, 1952; A. J. Grant, **A History of Europe from 1494 to 1610,** Barnes and Noble, 1951; Sir Charles Oman, **The Sixteenth Century,** Dutton, 1937; D. Ogg, **Europe in the Seventeenth Century,*** Collier. See also the topical survey by G. N. Clark, **The Seventeenth Century,*** Galaxy.

J. Bronowski and B. Mazlish, **The Western Intellectual Tradition from Leonardo to Hegel,*** Torchbooks. A highly readable survey of intellectual history. See also J. H. Randall, **The Making of the Modern Mind,** Houghton Mifflin, 1940; and Vol. I of Preserved Smith, **A History of Modern Culture, 1543-1776,*** 2 vols., Collier.

H. Butterfield, **The Origins of Modern Science, 1300-1800,*** Free Press; A. R. Hall, **The Scientific Revolution, 1500-1800,*** Beacon. Two highly recommended works on the formation of the modern scientific attitude.

Marie Boas, **The Scientific Renaissance: 1450-1630,** Harper & Row, 1962; A. R. Hall, **From Galileo to Newton: 1630-1720,** Harper & Row, 1963. Two well-written volumes in the Rise of Modern Science series. For a condensed account see A. R. Hall and Marie Boas Hall, **A Brief History of Science,*** Signet.

L. Marsak, ed., **The Rise of Science in Relation to Society,*** Macmillan; Thomas P. Hughes, ed., **The Development of Western Technology Since 1500,*** Macmillan. Reprints of important articles reflecting the latest scholarship.

F. B. Artz, **From the Renaissance to Romanticism: Trends in Style in Art, Literature, and Music, 1300-1830,*** Phoenix. Highly valuable overall view of the arts through six centuries, with a comprehensive bibliography.

SPECIAL STUDIES

J. Huizinga, **The Waning of the Middle Ages,*** Anchor. An influential study of "fading and decay" in the culture of the fourteenth and fifteenth centuries.

D. Hay, **The Italian Renaissance in Its Historical Background,*** Cambridge. A recent general survey. A. W. O. von Martin, **Sociology of the Renaissance,*** Torchbooks, discusses the changes in the Renaissance milieu which explain the dynamism of the period.

P. O. Kristeller, **Renaissance Thought: The Classic, Scholastic, and Humanist Strains,*** Torchbooks. An excellent analysis of Italian humanism. See also, by the same author, **The Classics and Renaissance Thought,** Harvard, 1955, and J. H. Whitfield, **Petrarch and the Renascence,** Oxford, 1943.

R. Roeder, **The Man of the Renaissance,*** Meridian. An analysis of four key figures of the Italian Renaissance: Savonarola, Machiavelli, Castiglione, and Aretino. Each is viewed as a prototype of one aspect of Renaissance man.

F. Schevill, **Medieval and Renaissance Florence,** Vol. II: **The Coming of Humanism and the Age of the Medici,*** Torchbooks. An absorbing history.

J. Huizinga, **Erasmus and the Age of the Reformation,*** Torchbooks. Excellent on the northern humanists' criticisms of the Church. See also E. H. Harbison, **The Christian Scholar in the Age of the Reformation,*** Scribner, and J. H. Hexter, **More's Utopia: The Biography of an Idea,*** Torchbooks.

V. H. H. Green, **Luther and the Reformation,*** Capricorn. A good introduction. See also R. Fife, **The Revolt of Martin Luther,** Columbia, 1957.

G. Harkness, **John Calvin: The Man and His Ethics,*** Abingdon. A sympathetic treatment. See also J. T. McNeill, **The History and Character of Calvinism,** Oxford, 1954.

On the "left wing" of Protestantism, see N. Cohn, **The Pursuit of the Millennium,*** Torchbooks, and R. Bainton, **The Travail of Religious Liberty,*** Torchbooks.

F. M. Powicke, **The Reformation in England,*** Oxford. An excellent summary which stresses political developments. See also T. M. Parker, **The English Reformation to 1558,** Oxford, 1950.

*Indicates an inexpensive paperbound edition.

P. Janelle, **The Catholic Reformation**, Bruce, 1949. The best sympathetic study of the subject. J. Brodrick, **The Origin of the Jesuits,*** Image, is an inspired account by a Jesuit scholar.

K. Holl, **The Cultural Significance of the Reformation,*** Meridian. A brief account. More detailed and controversial are R. H. Tawney, **Religion and the Rise of Capitalism,*** Mentor, and E. Troeltsch, **Protestantism and Progress: A Historical Study of the Relation of Protestantism to the Modern World,*** Beacon.

T. Kuhn, **The Copernican Revolution,*** Vintage. A skillful recapitulation of the climate of opinion in which the heliocentric theory emerged. A. Armitage, **The World of Copernicus,*** Mentor, is a popular account. See Also A. Koyré, **From the Closed World to the Infinite Universe,*** Torchbooks. G. de Santillana, **The Crime of Galileo,*** Phoenix, is an exciting account of Galileo's struggle against censorship.

H. Sigerist, **Great Doctors,*** Anchor. A notable biographical history of medicine by a distinguished authority on medical history. Also recommended are two books by C. Singer: **From Magic to Science,*** Dover; and **A Short History of Anatomy and Physiology from the Greeks to Harvey,*** Dover.

G. Mattingly, **Renaissance Diplomacy,*** Penguin. The classic study of the growth of diplomatic practices and the interplay of political forces in early modern times.

J. H. Whitfield, **Machiavelli,** Blackwell, 1947. A sympathetic account of Machiavelli and his significance in the history of political thought. The older, unfavorable view is well presented in H. Butterfield, **The Statecraft of Machiavelli,*** Collier.

E. Salmon, **Imperial Spain,** Holt, 1931. A good brief introduction to the Spain of Charles V and Philip II. Valuable for their greater detail are R. Trevor Davies, **The Golden Age of Spain, 1501-1621,*** Torchbooks, and especially J. H. Elliott, **Imperial Spain, 1469-1716,*** Mentor.

H. Holborn, **A History of Modern Germany,** Vol. I: **The Reformation,** Knopf, 1959. A reappraisal of the period in which Germany exercised its greatest influence on Europe, by the foremost authority on German history in the United States. The best study on Charles V and his age is K. Brandi, **The Emperor Charles V: The Growth and Destiny of a Man and of a World Empire,*** Humanities.

G. Mattingly, **The Armada,*** Sentry. A fascinating account of Philip II's most spectacular defeat.

P. Geyl, **The Revolt of the Netherlands, 1555-1609,** Williams and Norgate, 1945. Acknowledged to be the best short account of the Dutch rebellion.

S. Bindorff, **Tudor England,*** Penguin. Well written and highly recommended. See also G. W. O. Woodward, **A Short History of Sixteenth-Century England,*** Mentor, and A. L. Rowse, **The England of Elizabeth,*** Collier.

J. Neale, **The Age of Catherine de' Medici,*** Torchbooks. The religious and political troubles of sixteenth-century France. For a briefer account, see F. Palm, **Calvinism and the Religious Wars,** Holt, 1932.

C. V. Wedgwood, **The Thirty Years' War,*** Anchor. A vigorous account.

E. Newton, **European Painting and Sculpture,*** Penguin. Brief and particularly valuable for the period under study. Recommended for greater detail are A. Hauser, **A Social History of Art,** Vol. II: **Renaissance to Baroque,*** Vintage; B. Berenson, **Italian Painters of the Renaissance,*** Meridian; F. M. Simpson, **History of Architectural Development,** Vol. 4: **Renaissance Architecture,** rev. ed. by O. Hughes and N. Lynton, McKay, 1961; W. Sypher, **Four Stages of Renaissance Style: Transformations in Art and Literature, 1400-1700,*** Anchor; O. Benesch, **The Art of the Renaissance in Northern Europe: Its Relation to the Contemporary Spiritual and Intellectual Movements,** Harvard, 1945; R. Wilenski, **Introduction to Dutch Art,** Faber, 1929; V. Tapié, **The Age of Grandeur: Baroque Art and Architecture,*** Praeger.

On music see A. Einstein, **A Short History of Music,*** Vintage; G. Reese, **Music in the Renaissance,** Norton, 1954; M. Bukofzer, **Music in the Baroque Era,** Norton, 1947.

BIOGRAPHY

Outstanding studies of Renaissance figures include E. H. Wilkings, **Life of Petrarch,*** Phoenix, F. Schevill, **The Medici,*** Torchbooks; C. Ady, **Lorenzo de' Medici and Renaissance Italy,*** Collier; E. McCurdy, **The Mind of Leonardo da Vinci,** Dodd, 1939; R. W. Chambers, **Thomas More,*** Univ. of Mich.; D. B. W. Lewis, **Doctor Rabelais,** Sheed and Ward, 1957; M. Chute, **Shakespeare of London,*** Everyman.

R. H. Bainton, **Here I Stand: A Life of Martin Luther,*** Mentor. An excellent presentation of Luther's personality and of the theological complexities of his time. The best Catholic biography of Luther is H. Grisar, **Martin Luther, His Life and Work,*** Newman. For works about other religious leaders, see J. Brodrick, **St. Ignatius Loyola; The Pilgrim Years, 1491-1538,** Farrar, Straus, 1956; R. Ridolfi, **The Life of Girolamo Savonarola,** Knopf, 1959.

R. B. Merriman, **Suleiman the Magnificent, 1520-1566,** Harvard, 1944. An admirable study of the career of Charles V's formidable foe.

F. Hackett, **The Personal History of Henry the Eighth,*** Bantam. The life and loves of the lusty Tudor monarch. J. J. Scarisbrick, **Henry VIII,** Univ. of Calif., 1968, is probably the best biography. See also G. Mattingly, **Catherine of Aragon,*** Vintage.

The first biography of Elizabeth I mentioned below focuses on her childhood, the second of her mature years: E. Sitwell, **Fanfare for Elizabeth,*** Macmillan; and G. I. Strachey, **Elizabeth and Essex,** Harcourt, 1939. A first-rate complete biography is J. Neale, **Queen Elizabeth I,*** Anchor.

C. V. Wedgwood, **William the Silent,*** Norton. A beautifully written biography of the great Dutch leader.

FICTION

D. Merejkowski, **The Romance of Leonardo da Vinci,*** Washington Square. An outstanding historical novel.

I. Stone, **The Agony and the Ecstasy,*** Signet. A highly successful fictional biography of Michelangelo.

L. Zara, **Against This Rock,** Creative Age, 1943. A noteworthy fictionalized biography of Charles V.

Z. de Harsanyi, **The Star-Gazer,*** Universal. A biographical novel about Galileo and his times.

H. von Grimmelshausen, **Simplicius Simplicissimus,*** Liberal Arts. This famous satirical novel, published in 1668, depicts the carnage and brutality of the Thirty Years' War.

Part Six

One
Wide
Expanse

Then felt I like some watcher of the skies
When a new planet swims into his ken;
Or like stout Cortez when with eagle eyes
He stared at the Pacific—and all his men
Looked at each other with a wild surmise—
*Silent, upon a peak in Darien.**

■ Actually, it was Balboa, not Cortés, who was the first European to gaze on the Pacific; but no matter, for the poet Keats caught in the lines above man's sense of wonder, of discovery, and of exaltation when he succeeded in making "one wide expanse" of the whole world and the heavens above. With these dual triumphs, he ushered in our modern age. The period in world history which now begins was characterized by amazing economic, political, and intellectual advances in Europe that were ultimately to make this, the smallest of the continents, the arbiter and master of much of the world.

While scientists and philosophers were eagerly pursuing their quest for new truths, other men were driven by an equally intense curiosity to explore the unmapped portions of the earth. Led by mariners in the service of Portugal and Spain and quickly followed by soldiers, missionaries, and merchants, this movement in all directions of the compass developed into a mighty expansion of European civilization and power. Portugal staked out a lucrative commercial domain in Asia and Africa; Spain sent its hardy subjects into the steaming jungles of Central America, across the deserts of southwest North America, and over the freezing passes of the Andes to carve out a magnificent empire. France, Holland, and England soon joined in the search for glory and gold in Africa, Asia, and the Americas.

This outward European thrust encountered the long-isolated peoples of sub-Saharan Africa. While they had achieved little in technology and exercised minimal control over nature, their cultures manifested unique achievements in art and religion and well-organized political forms. In India, Europeans were impressed with the Mughul dynasty, comparing it in wealth and power with any of its contemporaries in the West. At this time Chinese civilization under Ming rule and Japan under its shogunate were enjoying a kind of "Indian summer" of their classical history. In Southeast Asia notable kingdoms, influenced by Chinese and Indian contacts, had risen and fallen. This area in general presented a complex picture of ethnic and political flux resulting from diverse migrations and unstable governments. In the Western Hemisphere high civilizations, comparable to any in the Old World, had developed at the hands of the Mayan, Inca, and Aztec Indians.

After 1500 all of these non-European peoples were to feel increasingly the impact of western intrusion. For some the consequences were catastrophic. Europeans overwhelmed the indigenous civilizations of the New World, and, in Africa, carried on a lucrative slave trade profiting from human misery and servitude. Whatever the results, and they were mixed, for the next four hundred years, European civilization—the most creative, expansive, and acquisitive on earth—was to be the dominant and pervasive influence in world history.

*John Keats, "On First Looking into Chapman's Homer," in *The Literature of England*, 5th ed., Vol. II (Glenview: Scott, Foresman and Co., 1966), p. 363, ll. 9-14.

29. (preceding page) **Moronobu: "Gay Life in Early Edo"** (seventeenth century). The impact of the commercial class was felt in Japanese art of the late seventeenth century. At that time the country's merchants were gaining rapidly in power and influence, and cities like Edo (today's Tokyo) were growing at a brisk rate. Edo in fact was the center of an unprecedented new art which found its subject matter in the activities of everyday life. This screen painting shows local merchants providing a variety of pleasures to feudal lords who had lately moved to the city and were enjoying its delights with great relish. **30.** (above) **Chinese jade carving** (c. 1660). Some sense of the gulf between the East and the West can be had by remembering that the grandiloquent Baroque style was at its crest in Europe at the same time that Chinese artisans were turning out exquisitely crafted objects like this carving, the reticence of which is characteristic of the art of the Manchu period. **31.** (left) **Chimu knife** (1000-1400). The pre-Columbian Chimu culture flourished along the northern coast of Peru and was distinguished more by its technological accomplishments (large cities, vast irrigation projects) than by the quality of its art. Chimu metalwork, however, was an exception, as this sacrificial knife attests. The elaborately worked gold handle inlaid with turquoise represents a god.

32. Angkor Wat, Cambodia (early twelfth century). Indian art styles spread far beyond the borders of India and in many cases not only retained vitality but gained in it. Many critics consider Angkor Wat, the immense temple city of the Khmers in Cambodia, to be the most perfectly realized example of Indian architectural technique. The gigantic size of the complex (its moat is two and one half miles long and one of its courtyards contains a half mile of sculptured reliefs) is matched by the brilliant spatial ordering of its profusion of galleries, sanctuaries, pavilions, and towers.

33. Mural painting at Bonampak (c. sixth century). This fresco from the classic period of Mayan culture represents Central American antiquity at its most sophisticated. Although no historical link has been established, Mayan painting looks curiously like that of ancient Egypt, in that it deals with the facts of daily life and is rendered in flat color, linear contour, and horizontal registers. Here a group of captives, surrounded by victorious Mayas, are shown waiting in fear to learn the role they will play in a sacrificial ceremony.

Chapter 19

Old Worlds Beyond the Horizon

India, China, Japan (1500-1650), Southeast
Asia (100-1650), Africa (1000 B.C.-1650 A.D.),
and Native Cultures in the Americas
(1000 B.C.-1500 A.D.)

INTRODUCTION. Europe's isolation from
Asia and its ignorance of sub-Saharan Africa
and the Americas ended in the fifteenth century. A multitude of European explorers,
traders, conquerors, and missionaries secured footholds in territories far from their
homelands, reaching out to trade, to conquer, and to spread the gospel of Christianity.
In the process they encountered civilizations
and ways of life which dramatically revealed
the limitations of their own knowledge and
experience. The story of their explorations
and discoveries will be taken up in Chapter
20; this chapter is concerned with the civilizations in the Far East, Africa, and the
Americas prior to the arrival of the Europeans.

In recounting the histories of India, China,
and Japan up to the middle of the seventeenth century, we shall be continuing a
story we began much earlier. But in describing early times in Southeast Asia, sub-
Saharan Africa, and the Americas, we shall
be introducing to the stage of world history

peoples we have not previously encountered. In a number of instances we shall be taking a giant step backward to the dawn of civilization, for both Africa and the Americas had inhabitants who, in 1650, were not so advanced as some of their European and Asian brothers had been two thousand years before. Yet both continents had fascinating cultures, some of which were to make important contributions to the civilization we know today. The variety of these contributions—from cotton, coffee, and Indian corn to the rhythms upon which jazz is based and sculpture which strongly influenced the development of modern art—reflects the remarkable diversity of the peoples of these lands, peoples who hunted, farmed, built cities, worshiped gods, and waged wars for centuries while Europeans remained totally ignorant of their existence.

Today a significant aspect of our world is the reawakening of old centers of civilization in the Americas, Africa, and the Far East. Nationalistic fervor and brave hopes for the future have been built on pride in the past. Even in Communist China, where many Confucian traditions are being superseded by Marxist practices, inspiration is still drawn from past days of glory. The people of present-day India and Pakistan also seek inspiration from bygone years, particularly from the era of power, grandeur, and wealth enjoyed under the Guptas and the Mughuls. African nationalist leaders look back to their native roots; for example, the former British colony known as the Gold Coast adopted the name of a long-dead African empire, Ghana, when it was granted independence in 1956. In the New World, Mexican artists take their themes and motifs not from their Spanish colonial heritage but from the pre-Spanish Indian cultures.

Thus, if we are to understand the new dynamic spirit that now moves many Afro-Asian regions, we must know something of the sources of inspiration upon which their people draw. Such sources are outlined in the history of the non-European world in the centuries covered by this chapter and the next.

THE GLORY OF THE MUGHULS IN INDIA

Babur, founder of the Mughul empire. By the end of the twelfth century Hindu power in India had been eclipsed by Muslim armies from the north which were penetrating the mountain passes and raiding the countryside at will. As we saw in Chapter 10, a strong alien force established the Delhi sultanate and ruled a powerful Muslim kingdom covering much of northern India. Between 1200 and 1300 the sultans at Delhi enjoyed considerable power and prestige. But by 1500 there stood at the gates of India a new Muslim force which was to conquer India and raise it to new heights.

Two years after Columbus sailed westward toward what he hoped would be India, a descendant of Genghis Khan and Timur the Lame mounted the throne of a little principality in Turkestan (see map, p. 285). The youthful ruler was Babur (the Tiger), an able general with the strength of a giant, who was to be the founder of the Mughul empire in India. In his memoirs Babur says that he used to think ceaselessly of the capture of Hindustan. At length he set out with an army of no more than twelve thousand men to achieve his goal. Defeating the large forces belonging to the sultan of Delhi, who then ruled all Hindustan, Babur made himself sultan in 1526. A year later he subdued the Rajputs, who were trying to restore Hindu supremacy in northern India. The submission of the Rajputs placed the Mughul dynasty securely on the Delhi throne. Babur himself did not live long to enjoy the fruits of his victory; worn out by his campaigns and adventures, he died in 1530.

The name *Mughul* is a corruption of *Mongol,* a word much dreaded in India because of its association with Tamerlane, the ruthless destroyer of Delhi. It has been suggested that *Mongol* was converted into *Mughul* either through a common mispronunciation or through a wish on the part of the Indians to conceal the fact that the Mughuls were in truth Mongols.

Akbar, conqueror and administrator. Babur's grandson was Akbar, meaning "Very Great." In 1560 Akbar's empire consisted of a strip of territory some three hundred miles wide, extending from the northwest frontier eastward to Bengal. Sixteen years later Akbar had extended his rule over all of India north of the Vindhya Mountains, the natural boundary between Hindustan and the Deccan. Continuing southward, Akbar invaded part of the Deccan. When he died in 1605, his dominions ran from Kashmir in the far north well into the Deccan in the south, and his heirs were to extend them even farther. But in following his policy of expansion into the Deccan, they proved it to be overly ambitious. Only 150 years after Akbar's death, revolts in the Deccan brought on the downfall of the Mughul empire.

Akbar's greatness should not be measured by his military conquests alone, however. He instituted innovations and reforms in the government and fostered cultural growth and religious toleration. As an administrator he had few equals. He divided his empire into twelve provinces (later increased to fifteen), ruled by governors whom he appointed and who were paid monthly salaries from the imperial treasury. Each province was divided into districts, and each district into smaller units. Akbar kept a strict check on bribery and embezzlement and left a rich surplus in the treasury when he died.

Law was similarly well administered. In each village the headman was responsible for keeping law and order, while in the larger cities special officials were in charge of the administration of justice. Akbar himself often acted as a judge, for everyone in his domain had the right to appeal to him personally. The practice of *suttee* (burning a wife on her husband's funeral pyre), which had come into use during the Gupta age, was forbidden, and widows were permitted to remarry. Akbar prohibited child marriages and trial by ordeal, although he permitted

such tortures as impalement, amputation, and death by elephant dragging. Nevertheless, in contrast to the barbaric punishments permitted in Europe at this time, the Mughul emperor probably had the most enlightened criminal code in the sixteenth century.

As a boy, Akbar had refused to do his lessons, and until his dying day he could neither read nor write. But he possessed an insatiable love of learning and constantly had all types of literature read to him. He patronized poets, musicians, painters, and architects liberally and collected a valuable library of 24,000 volumes, many of them illustrated with brilliant, jewel-like illuminations.

Despite the allegiance of the Mughul dynasty to the Muslim faith, Akbar allowed complete freedom of religious belief in his empire. For centuries India had suffered from the intolerance of the Hindus toward the Buddhists, and we noted in Chapter 10 how the Muslims had been savagely intolerant of the Hindus. Because Akbar realized that religious strife made for political and social disintegration, he favored complete tolerance of belief.

Akbar's views were not based simply on political expediency, however; his own temperament was the chief reason for his enlightened policy. He felt that every faith had something of truth to offer but that all were untrue when they denied each other's sincerity of purpose. Every Thursday, Muslims, Brahmins, and members of smaller sects congregated in his Hall of Worship for religious debates which often lasted far into the night. When the Jesuits arrived in India, Akbar had them stay at his court for periods of several years and treated them with every courtesy. But the sultan never accepted any one religion completely, and the Jesuits had to admit ruefully that

the Emperor is not a Muhammadan, but is doubtful as to all forms of faith and holds firmly that there is no divinely accredited form of faith, because he finds in all something to offend his reason and intelligence, for he thinks everything can be grasped by reason.[1]

Instead Akbar created his own religion, called *Din Ilahi*, the "Divine Faith," which

In this contemporary painting the great Mughul ruler, Akbar, is depicted superintending the construction of his new capital at Fathpur Sikri.

incorporated what he considered the best features of the other existing religions. By promulgating this new faith, he hoped to bring all India into common agreement on religious matters. But the older faiths were too strongly entrenched, and Akbar's religious theories died with him.

Monuments of Mughul architecture. At the crest of their power in the reigns of Akbar and his immediate successors, the Mughuls displayed one of the most magnificent civilizations of their time. In military strength, government efficiency, and patronage of the arts, they had few equals. And, above all, they were great builders.

The Indo-Islamic style of architecture which the Mughuls developed for tombs,

mosques, forts, and palaces was a blend of Indian and Persian elements characterized by a lavish use of mosaics, bulbous domes, cupolas, and lofty vaulted gateways. The Mughuls were also fond of formal gardens in which pools and fountains, architecture and greenery were carefully harmonized.

The Mughul style began with Akbar, an avid builder. Not far from the modern city of Agra, he erected a new capital, Fathpur Sikri, which he occupied for only fourteen years before abandoning it for Lahore. Fathpur Sikri is still preserved intact today, and a tourist strolling through its splendid buildings can feel the power of the great empire that made this city possible.

Nothing sadder or more beautiful exists in India than this deserted city—the silent witness of a vanished dream. It still stands with its circuit of seven miles, its seven bastioned gates, its wonderful palaces, peerless in all India for noble design and delicate adornment; its splendid mosque and pure marble shrine . . . its carvings and paintings—stands as it stood in Akbar's time, but now a body without a soul.[2]

During the reign of Shah Jahan, Akbar's grandson, Mughul architecture reached its zenith. Shah Jahan had the red sandstone buildings of Akbar at Delhi demolished and erected a huge capital of marble containing fifty-two palaces. The famous Hall of Private Audience had ceilings of solid silver and gold and a Peacock Throne encrusted with costly gems. On the walls can still be seen the inscription by a Muslim poet: "If anywhere on earth there is a Paradise, it is here, it is here, it is here."

Besides making Delhi a site of unrivaled splendor, Shah Jahan erected at Agra the famous Pearl Mosque and the Taj Mahal, the marble mausoleum built as a final resting place for himself and his favorite wife. Twenty-two thousand men worked twenty-two years to complete this costly structure.

Signs of Mughul decline. The blend of Hindu-Islamic cultural elements which was achieved under the Mughuls brought civilization in India to the highest point yet achieved there. It is unfortunate for world culture that the union of Muslim and Hindu genius could not continue to flower. But

Akbar's tolerance and wisdom were lost in the fanaticism of his successors.

Shah Jahan, who came to the throne in 1628, held none of Akbar's views on religious toleration. He officially promoted the Muslim faith, destroyed Hindu temples, and forcibly opposed the spread of Christianity. In 1630 Shah Jahan began the conquest of the Deccan; eventually it was subjugated and divided into four provinces. After Shah Jahan's health began to fail in 1657, a ruinous civil war broke out among his four sons, each of whom became an almost independent ruler. The last eight years of Shah Jahan's life (d. 1666) were spent as a prisoner of his son and successor, Aurangzeb. Despite his ignominious end, the reign of Shah Jahan marked the summit of the Mughul empire.

During the reign of Aurangzeb (1658-1707) the forces which eventually destroyed the Mughul empire began to manifest themselves. Aurangzeb's intolerance toward the Hindus was extreme, and from time to time he was bothered by dangerous revolts in the Deccan and by the laxity of the army stationed there. The Marathas, a Hindu people living in the western Deccan, were particularly troublesome. In 1761 they would deal the final blow to the Mughul empire.

CHINA CLOSES ITS DOORS

Establishment of the Ming dynasty. As we recall from Chapter 10, the T'ang rulers were succeeded by the Sung, who were not equal to the task of protecting China from the onslaughts of neighboring barbarian tribes. Taking advantage of China's weakness, the Mongols finally overran the entire country and early in the thirteenth century established the Yüan dynasty. Under the rule of Kublai Khan (1260-1294), the Mongols were strongly influenced by Chinese civilization.

A succession of weak rulers following Kublai and the inroads of Chinese culture on Mongol life led to the overthrow of the Yüan dynasty. Humiliated by alien rule, the Chinese detested the Mongol garrisons in their cities and the control of a military clique which had superseded the age-old scholarly civil service. During the last years of Mongol rule secret societies, often with their roots in Buddhism and conspiring to revolt, became widespread. Serious rebellions broke out in the 1350's and 1360's. Finally, under the leadership of a poor orphan turned Buddhist monk who had left the monastery and organized his own band of rebels, the Chinese captured Peking, established the Ming dynasty (1368-1644), and drove the Mongols back into Central Asia.

Under the first emperor, Hung-wu, and his able successor, Yung-lo (1403-1424), the Ming sought to reëstablish such Chinese traditions as the examination system and rule by scholar-bureaucrats. They aided education, compiled a great law code based on T'ang and Sung precedents, rebuilt the country's defenses, and repaired the irrigation systems. While officially espousing Sung Neo-Confucianism as the philosophy of the state (the government issued an edition of the classics with Chu Hsi's commentaries to serve as the text for education and examination), the Ming dynasty was far more despotic than any of its Chinese predecessors. The emperor's personal rule was strengthened by the abolition of the office of prime minister and by the improvement of such institutions as the censorate and the growth of the palace eunuchs, both personally loyal to the emperor himself. Moreover, harsh punishments for both the people and the bureaucracy became a major characteristic of Ming rule, despite Confucian teachings that the emperor should rely on the virtuous to rule the empire.

China in isolation. Political stability and economic prosperity in Ming China encouraged the growth of antiforeignism, which had originally developed in reaction to Mongol rule. Chinese antagonism to foreign influence and concentration on the unique qualities and superiorities of Chinese civilization eventually grew into an attitude of indifference to all things foreign. In philosophy this was accompanied and encouraged by the emergence of a new Confucian school of thought which taught that knowledge was intuitive and should be sought through meditation.

Antiforeignism and the intellectual introspection of Ming China did not, however, lead to the physical isolation of China. Contacts with the outside world, particularly with Japan, and foreign trade increased considerably. Yung-lo strenuously tried to extend China's influence beyond her borders by encouraging other rulers to send ambassadors to China to present tribute. The most remarkable venture was the dispatch of seven spectacular naval expeditions abroad during the reigns of Yung-lo and his successors. The first fleet sailed in 1405, and the last returned to China in 1433. Ranging far and wide through the Indian Ocean and the Southeast Asian archipelago, the Chinese fleets visited Java in the east and Aden and the east coast of Africa in the west. The first expedition consisted of 62 ships and 28,000 men, the largest naval expedition and greatest feat in seamanship the world had witnessed to that date. The expeditions proved costly, however, and while they brought China knowledge and items of material culture from exotic lands, they did not contribute to the economic well-being of the state and were stopped after the seventh venture. By the next century imperial edicts forbade Chinese ships to sail beyond China's own coastal waters. Thus after an initial adventure into international maritime activity, China shut itself off from the era of expansion that began at approximately the same time to spread European influence across the globe.

As we shall see in Chapter 20, the ruthless activities of the Portuguese traders who arrived in China in the sixteenth century hampered the development of cordial East-West trade relations. In fact, the Chinese restricted European trade to a few closely watched cities. Unpleasant experience with outsiders encouraged China to isolate itself, a development which in the long run had stultifying effects on its civilization.

Ming decay. Although the most powerful dynasty in China since the T'ang, the Ming did not fulfill its promise. Its naval and trade activity, its early contacts with the outside world, and its territorial expansion seemed to promise a dynamic and expansive period; but the energy of the dynasty dried up and the empire shrank. Ming sea power became so restricted that pirates from the offshore islands preyed on passing ships and raided mainland ports.

In 1592 the Japanese attempted to conquer Korea, a vassal of the Ming empire, and through it, China. Following a successful landing in Korea, the Japanese won victories over both Chinese and Korean armies, but Korean sailors thwarted Japanese hopes by defeating the invading fleets. Cut off from supplies from their island home, the Japanese were forced to withdraw, leaving the Ming dynasty still on the Chinese throne.

This victory did not halt Ming decay, however. More and more, the Chinese became convinced of the superiority of their culture, and their experiences with outsiders intensified their desire to isolate themselves. Chinese citizens were forbidden to travel abroad, and the country was almost completely sealed tight against foreign influences. Complacent and static, the empire rapidly lost its strength. By the early part of the seventeenth century China was in a state of dissolution: the court was a center of corruption, taxes had become exorbitant,

The Chinese belief in the superiority of their culture is reflected in this map of the world which appeared in the *Chinese Encyclopaedia* by Chang Huang in the late sixteenth century. China dominates the entire map, while other nations are represented as peripheral islands.

and the plight of the peasants was pitiable. Peasant uprisings broke out throughout the land.

At the same time that rebellions began to break out against the Ming regime, new invaders—the Manchus—were launching assaults in the north. In 1644 they captured the Ming capital at Peking and a few weeks later proclaimed their rule; China once again was under an alien emperor.

Ming art and scholarship. Whether the Ming dynasty deserved its name, which means "brilliant," depends on how one would evaluate its achievements. Many excellent works of art were produced, but few were as original as those from earlier periods. Ming artisans tried to duplicate the standards of the classic Sung pottery, but instead of emphasizing the beauty of the form of the vessel, they concentrated on brilliant coloring and elegant decoration.

The Forbidden City, the imperial family's area of palaces and temples at Peking, was constructed in the early years (1403-1424) of the Ming dynasty. With its series of courtyards, brilliant lacquer work, and tile, marble, and alabaster decorations, it is typical of a period of richly ornamented architecture.

When the Ming reëstablished the traditional competitive examination system, scholarship was stimulated and histories, encyclopedias, dictionaries, and other important scholarly works appeared. Civil service examinations, based upon a thorough knowledge of the classics, were given every three years. In use until 1904, the examination system preserved Chinese traditions remarkably well but kept China excessively conservative and intellectually sterile.

JAPAN'S SELF-IMPOSED ISOLATION

Ashikaga state and culture. The decline of the Kamakura shogunate resembled the end of a dynasty in China. It was accompanied by economic difficulties, political and military strife, and the erosion of the bonds of feudal loyalty. Although the successors to the Kamakura shogunate, the Ashikaga, retained the shogunal office from 1338 to 1573, their government was so different from the Kamakura bakufu that it represented a new stage in the history of Japanese feudalism. The local lords called *daimyo* ("great names"), not the shoguns, were the key figures during this period, and effective Ashikaga rule did not extend far from the capital. The warriors were no longer considered the personal vassals of the shogun; instead, the warrior class had broken up into separate groups of lords and retainers, and Japan, like feudal Europe, was almost constantly involved in warfare between various feudal lords.

Despite warfare and political decentralization, the Ashikaga period was one of important economic growth. The feudal lords encouraged trade and commerce in their own domains, and as the money economy grew, various merchants and even some Buddhist monasteries began to play the role of bankers. Merchants organized themselves into a kind of guild system to protect their interests and encourage trade across feudal boundaries, and towns began to develop at important geographical points and around castles and monasteries. Early Ashikaga shoguns, often with Zen monks as their agents, traded profitably with China and for a time even accepted investiture as Ming vassals. This trade was not infrequently mixed with piracy, which became a serious problem for the Ming.

The Ashikaga period was also a period of great cultural developments. With ancient Kyoto as their capital, the shoguns promoted a distinctive new culture, fusing the once separate courtier and warrior cultures. Zen Buddhism dominated both the imperial and the shogunal courts, and Japanese culture came to be pervaded by an urbane taste for things elegantly simple: the restrained and quiet contemplation of the tea ceremony, new architectural styles, monochrome painting, and landscape gardening, which eventually influenced western gardening. The *No* drama, which combined stately mimetic dancing, music, and song, was the most important literary development of the Ashikaga period.

With the arrival of the Portuguese in Japan in 1542, western influence began to make itself felt. Francis Xavier, a Jesuit missionary, began to preach Christianity in western Japan and Kyoto in 1549, and by the end of the century Japan may have had as many as 300,000 Christians, including some of the feudal lords in Kyushu, who converted in order to gain commercial advantages and advanced military technology from their relations with the westerners.

Changes toward unification. Warfare among Japanese feudal lords sharpened as they adopted improved European firearms. This led to the fall of some feudal houses and the rise of new ones and a general blurring of class lines towards the end of the Ashikaga period. It also meant increasing economic burdens on the peasants and townfolk, so that riots and local uprisings became frequent. Between 1560 and 1600, however, three able leaders in sequence progressively established a single military power over all the daimyo. At first this drive for unification was conducted in the name of the last Ashikaga shogun, but he was driven out of Kyoto by his own supporter, Nobunga,

in 1573 and no successor was chosen, bringing the line to an end.

The second of these leaders, Hideyoshi, son of a peasant soldier, created a dictatorial power unique in Japanese history. Although theoretically the chief minister of the emperor, Hideyoshi ruled Japan through the feudal institution of vassalage. In attempting to create stability by halting social change, he tried to define more sharply than before the differences and functions of the various social classes and to prevent people from changing their class status. He also disarmed the populace and banned foreign missionaries and began persecuting Japanese Christians. Hideyoshi regarded both foreign and Japanese Christians as possible agents for change in Japanese society. His large-scale invasion of Korea in 1592 may have been in response to his increasing megalomania as well as to dispose of some of Japan's surplus of professional soldiery, always a danger to internal peace and stability. Korea appealed to China as suzerain; Chinese armies were slowly thrown into the peninsular war, which reached such a stalemate that, on Hideyoshi's death in 1598, his field commanders completely withdrew.

The Tokugawa shogunate. Now was the moment of opportunity for the third leader, Tokugawa Ieyasu, who, as Hideyoshi's agent, had been lord of eastern Japan. By cautious maneuvering and a minimum of fighting, he brought all the barons and their fighting men under his allegiance. Without purporting to establish a national government, he revived the devices of ancient feudalism. He required the emperor to bestow upon him the title of shogun, took the best lands for himself and his family, and assigned the rest to lesser lords in accordance with his conception of their loyalty to him. From his personal headquarters at Edo (the city now known as Tokyo), not far from Kamakura, where the first shogunate had stood, he set up a rigid system of laws and institutions designed to perpetuate his family's position indefinitely. Fear of developments that might threaten the status quo led the regime to question European missionary activity and ultimately to ban Christianity altogether; to expel European missionaries and

As a defense measure, the Tokugawa shogunate banned the building of bridges across major rivers where they intersected important roads. The people were thus forced to cross the rivers by palanquin or on the backs of coolies, as shown in this contemporary painting.

traders; to execute large numbers of native Christians; and finally to exclude all foreigners except the nonproselyting Dutch, who were allowed limited and rigidly controlled trade at the single port of Nagasaki. At the same time, all Japanese were forbidden to go abroad or even to build ships capable of navigating beyond coastal waters. This was the beginning of Japan's "centuries of isolation."

SOUTHEAST ASIA: BACKGROUND OF CONFLICT

The geographical foundations of disunity. At the southern tip of the Asian mainland, wedged between India and China and including a multitude of islands in both the Indian and Pacific oceans, lies Southeast Asia. Stretching over a combination of land and sea far greater in size than the United States, Southeast Asia is geographically, culturally, and politically one of the most complex regions in the world.

The Irrawaddy, Salween, and Mekong rivers, all flowing from north to south, and the Yangtze River, which flows from west to east, rise in close proximity to each other in the Tibet-Burma-China border region. But they enter the ocean through deltas located far apart, from Rangoon in Burma in the southwest to Shanghai in Central China in the northeast. The Irrawaddy, Salween, and Mekong, with their valley systems, provided avenues for the southward migration of distinctive ethnic groups from South China (see Reference Map 7). North-south mountain chains, which divide Burma from Thailand and Thailand from Vietnam, provided barriers to communication that further emphasized the cultural and political differentiation between the peoples occupying the river valleys. Moreover, later migrants pushed earlier inhabitants out of the valleys and into the mountainous regions, making for further ethnic complexities. Unlike China, where some form of political unity and cultural homogeneity developed, Southeast Asia has always been characterized by polit-

ical and cultural balkanization. The thousands of islands that make up the Philippine and Indonesian archipelagoes were also subject to natural division rather than unity. Continued migrations into late historical times and pervasive influences exerted by the great civilizations of India and China added to the confusion.

Expansion of Indian culture into Southeast Asia. The spread of Indian culture throughout Southeast Asia provides an outstanding example of the process of culture diffusion and modification that recurs time and again in world history. Resulting mostly from peaceful trading activities, Indian cultural expansion in what has been called "Greater India" began about the second century A.D. and continued until the ninth or tenth century. The people of southern India may have represented the strongest single outside influence in Malaya, Sumatra, Java, and Borneo, while traces of Gupta influences found in Burma and Siam suggest that the Asia mainland east of India may have been primarily affected by Indians from further north.

The impact of Indian culture was not, of course, equally strong or enduring over all sections. One scholar has divided Greater India into two segments: the western zone—including Ceylon, Burma, the central part of Siam, and the Malay peninsula—received the full force of Indian colonizing activity and consequently developed a culture that was largely a colonial imitation of the original; the eastern zone—comprising mainly Java, Cambodia, and Champa in Indochina—experienced Indianization that was very definite but not strong enough to prevent the indigenous peoples from developing their own distinctive cultures and ways of life.

From the second century A.D. on, the kingdoms established in Greater India were ruled by monarchs with Indian names. Some of these kingdoms endured more than a thousand years, persisting, in fact, after India itself had been overwhelmed by foreign invaders.

The kingdoms of Champa and Cambodia. Two powerful kingdoms existed in Southeast Asia. Champa, in what is now South

Vietnam, lasted until it was finally overrun by Vietnamese invaders in the fifteenth century. More important was the kingdom of Cambodia, which at one time consisted of modern Cambodia and parts of Laos, Thailand, Burma, Malaya, and Vietnam. This kingdom was ruled by various Hindu dynasties until the middle of the fourteenth century, when *Hinayana* Buddhism became ascendant throughout the country.

About 1100 one of the greatest architectural edifices in history was erected in Cambodia—Angkor Wat (see Color Plate 32). Of central political, economic, and religious importance, this vast complex was long forgotten and swallowed up by the jungle, until it was accidentally discovered by a French naturalist in 1861. It is surrounded by a stone enclosure measuring half a mile from north to south and two thirds of a mile from east to west. Nearby lay the Cambodian capital city, which may have had a population of close to one million. The splendor of the city is shown by the ruins of its gate and towers, the great avenues running to its center, and its royal terrace, some twelve hundred feet long, sculptured with reliefs of great beauty. As one scholar has pointed out:

A building operation of the magnitude of Angkor Wat required . . . a high degree of economic and social integration, plus a government strong enough to command the labor and talents of vast numbers of trained participants. It reflected also the presence of an abundant food supply, a prosperous commerce, and a widely shared sensitivity to aesthetic values.[3]

The maritime empires of Malaysia. Meanwhile, another great empire—Srivijaya—had risen further south, with its center in the island of Sumatra. Extending over much of the Malay peninsula and most of the Indonesian archipelago, Srivijaya was ruled by the Sailendra kings from the eighth century until its fall in the fourteenth.

In central Java one of the most imposing Buddhist shrines in the world is located: the immense monument of Borobudur, representing the cosmic mountain which, according to Hindu and Buddhist mythology, is the center of the world. Erected on the top of a hill in nine successive terraces, Borobudur is covered with images of the Buddha, sculptures illustrating Buddhist texts, and carved scenes of everyday life. The art of Southeast Asia was unmistakably influenced by Indian styles and techniques, but in Angkor Wat and Borobudur the works created were larger than anything found in India itself.

In the thirteenth century a Javanese dynasty began to supplant Sailendra rule. By 1365 the Javanese kingdom of Madjapahit comprised almost all of the Malay peninsula and the Indonesian archipelago. Hinduism dominated Madjapahit until its rulers were driven from their thrones in the fifteenth century, and Islam became the dominant faith throughout the archipelago, with the exception of the island of Bali.

China and Southeast Asia. India was not, however, the sole civilizing influence in Southeast Asia. Chinese influence spread to this region when, in 111 B.C., the great Han emperor, Wu Ti, completed his conquest of the kingdom of Nam Viet, which included the present Chinese provinces of Kwantung and Kwangsi as well as Tonkin and Annam in Vietnam. By the end of the first century A.D. Chinese administration was extended to these regions, which remained part of the Chinese empire for a thousand years, until the end of the T'ang dynasty.

Although far less influenced by Chinese culture, the Burmans and the Thais, the two other major ethnic groups of modern mainland Southeast Asia, also migrated into the area because of developments inside China. The Burmans entered Burma from Southwest China during the ninth or tenth centuries, probably as refugees from wars between the kingdom of Nan Chao, a Thai state in modern China's Yünnan province, and the Tibetans. The Thai peoples originally lived in an area bounded by the headwaters of the Red River in the east, the Yangtze in the north, and the Mekong in the west. Han Wu Ti conquered most of this area, but independent Thai states survived in Southwest China, particularly in Yünnan. The most powerful kingdom, Nan Chao, established control over the others as a vassal of the T'ang dynasty, in the face of the rising power of the Tibetans in the eighth century A.D. Although already in decline, Nan Chao was finally destroyed by the Mongols in 1253, as part of their conquest of China, and the Thai people migrated to the south, settling in an area extending from Assam in India's northeast through the Shan States of Burma, northern Thailand, and Laos. Today's Shans, Thais, and Laos are all ethnic Thais, who continued their southward migrations in succeeding centuries (see Chapter 11, Volume II).

King Rama the Brave (1275-1317) established the first Thai empire in Southeast Asia on the foundations laid by his father and elder brother. The territories to which he laid claim sometimes tenuously included large parts of Thailand, Laos, Cambodia, and Malaya. While accepting the suzerainty of the Mongols in China, and even importing Chinese artisans into Siam, he patterned his government on the Cambodian Indianized model, built Cambodian style temples and fortresses, adapted the Cambodian script to the Thai language, and adopted *Hinayana* Buddhism as the official state religion. The chief influence on the Thais, therefore, was Cambodian, not Chinese, and through Cambodia, Indian religion, art, and culture.

Following the Mongol dynasty Chinese influence remained weak in Southeast Asia, partly due to the isolationism of the Ming. While some of the seven great Ming naval expeditions (see p. 576) touched Southeast Asian ports, they did not exert any important cultural impact. And although Chinese merchants traded at Malayan and Indonesian ports, it was not until the arrival of the Europeans in Southeast Asia that Chinese began to enter the area as settlers in significant numbers. Following the well-established trade routes, Chinese merchants, artisans, and coolies emigrated in increasing numbers in the late fifteenth and especially in the sixteenth centuries and later. The Chinese became a major component of urban population centers. In some countries they spread from the cities into the small towns and villages. Almost everywhere the Chinese formed a merchant middle class, dominating not only foreign commerce but domestic trade as well. Almost nowhere did they become peasants or assimilate into the local population, as did the Indian merchants. Today, throughout Southeast Asia, they remain foreigners in lands where they have lived for centuries, owing their primary allegiance to China and to Chinese culture.

Crescent and Cross in the Indies. In addition to India and China, two other major cultural forces, both from the west, contributed to the complexity of Southeast Asia: Islam and Christianity.

Muslim merchants from Persia and the Arab lands had long traded with the Indies and the East and, indeed, were prominent in China's foreign trade during the T'ang dynasty; but they were apparently unconcerned with the propagation of their faith among the peoples with whom they traded. The spread of Islam to the Far East started only after the conquest of India by Turkish Muslims during the eleventh and twelfth centuries. Several factors contributed to the growth of missionary activity. Islam found many converts in India among those classes engaged in foreign trade, particularly in regions like Gujarat and Bengal that had long traded with Southeast Asia and the Far East. These new Muslims had the morale and enthusiasm often characteristic of converts. Moreover, the form of Islam that developed in India was a mystical and syncretic faith which was not tied to any particular national grouping and could challenge Hindu and Buddhist mysticism on their own terms. Requiring no priests or professionals, the Islamic faith stressed brotherhood while making only minimal demands on its adherents. Consequently individual groups of Muslims were self-sufficient in their faith and could settle abroad without maintaining ritual ties with their homelands. For these same reasons, Islam strongly appealed to the inhabitants of the Indies as a form of release from the rigid and hierarchical Hindu faith.

Commercial interests required safe and secure trade routes in Southeast Asia, but the collapse of the Madjapahit empire was followed by a rise in piracy and general disorder. Consequently, Muslim political and military power began to fill the social vacuum in the area, and many local rulers found it to their political and commercial advantage to become Muslims. During the fifteenth century, as Hindu rulers were driven from their thrones, Java was completely converted to Islam, which also spread to Sumatra, the Malay peninsula, and the other islands of the Indonesian archipelago. The one exception was the fabled island of Bali, which became the refuge of the former ruling family and has retained its basically Hindu culture into modern times.

Malayan and Indonesian merchants and settlers carried Islam into the Philippines in the fifteenth and sixteenth centuries, particularly to the large southern island of Mindanao. But its influence was too late and too weak to spread further north, where Christianity was beginning to make significant inroads.

Spain began a concerted attempt to occupy the Philippines in the middle of the sixteenth century and established its colonial capital at Manila in 1571. By 1581, when Manila was made a bishopric, no fewer than four Catholic orders were active in the islands, and the Catholic university of Santo Tomàs was founded in 1611. By 1622 there were half a million Catholic converts in the Philippines, and this number increased to almost a million within a century. With the exception of Mindanao and some minor peripheral islands, the Philippines was destined to become the only Christian country in Southeast Asia.

The birth of nationhood. The heritage of geographical and ethnic complexity, of conflict between lowland immigrants and older settlers in the hills, and the waves of distinctive cultural influences from outside Southeast Asia, all made for uneven political development throughout the area in the centuries before the arrival of the West, and it is almost impossible to make any generalizations that are valid for the entire region.

What is now Burma was occupied in successive waves and regions by the Burmans, the Shan (who are related to the Thais), and various other ethnic groups. Constantly at war with each other and with the neighboring Thais, and often in conflict with the Chinese to the north, the Burmese never succeeded in developing a unified kingdom

with a centralized bureaucracy. There was often little continuity in succession from king to king, and though often successful in war, the Burmese kings were more given to raids and brief occupations than to the painstaking business of nation building and statecraft.

The Thai, or Siamese, on the other hand, early developed a sense of nationhood and a durable administrative system. This may have been the product of a national self-consciousness that resulted from constant warfare with the Burmese. Furthermore, the Thais were culturally more homogeneous than the Burmese. By the early seventeenth century the Thai monarchs were already in active contact with the West, sending embassies to Holland and the court of Louis xiv. With a rice surplus available for export, they were also in early and active contact with China, whose merchants purchased rice in Thailand and transported it by sea to the markets of China's southeast coastal region. Chinese merchants and their families settled in Thailand early and in such numbers that they became a significant part of Thai society and were not even considered foreigners. Because the Chinese community was an important source of attractive women for the royal harem, many Thai monarchs were at least half Chinese, and the present Chakkri dynasty and its capital, Bangkok, were founded by Taksin, a half-Chinese general, in the latter part of the eighteenth century.

Laos, lying in the northwestern part of the Indochinese peninsula, was a congeries of petty princedoms fought over by the Thais, Vietnamese, and Cambodians. The modern Cambodians are largely descended from the Khmer builders of the great empire that flourished before the fifteenth century, which centered on Angkor Wat. Indonesia and Malaya remained the realm of petty Muslim princes and European empires, who fought to control the rich resources of these lands and the trade routes between eastern and southern Asia.

In the islands of the Indonesian archipelago, one kingdom and empire succeeded another on the great islands of Sumatra and Java. The sea was their thoroughfare, and the important Strait of Malacca, which controlled the trade routes between the Indian Ocean and the Far East, was a major prize of war. But the successive waves of cultural influence that traveled along the trade routes were not a sufficient basis for unification when faced with the geographical and ethnic divisions that plagued both continental and island Southeast Asia. The religious and political thought and institutions of *Hinayana* Buddhism, superimposed on early Brahminic Hindu influence, dominated, and continue to dominate today, Burma, Thailand, Laos, and Cambodia. Islam today dominates Indonesia, the southern Philippines, and the Malay peninsula, as it did in the sixteenth and seventeenth centuries.

The only region in Southeast Asia to come under Chinese cultural and political domination was what today constitutes North and South Vietnam. The Vietnamese people are the product of the integration of early migrants from South China with local populations, and their language, closely resembling Chinese, has marked Khmer and Thai elements. Spending over a thousand years of their history, beginning with the Han dynasty, under Chinese rule, and even longer under Chinese influence, Vietnam so closely resembled China culturally and politically that it has been called "The Lesser Dragon." Adopting *Mahayana* Buddhism, Confucian political thought, Chinese institutions, and the Chinese written language, the Vietnamese constructed a Confucian state on the Chinese model, complete with an emperor (who called himself a king in communications with the Chinese), a civil service bureaucracy recruited through the traditional Confucian examination system, a mandarin class, and court records and a literature in the Chinese style. Even the imperial palace at the capital at Hue in central Vietnam was built on the Chinese model. Sometimes more conservative than the Chinese themselves, the Vietnamese held onto tradition longer. For instance, Confucian examinations were abolished in China in 1905, but they remained in force in Vietnam until the mid-1920's. But despite the amazingly strong Chinese influence on

Vietnam and its culture, the Vietnamese throughout their history remained strongly conscious of themselves as Vietnamese. They constantly struggled for independence from China and, once independence was achieved, for the continuity and integrity of their own state.

AFRICA: THE NEGLECTED CONTINENT

Reconstructing Africa's past. Extending from the fringes of the Sahara Desert south to the Cape of Good Hope is sub-Saharan Africa. The terms *Africa* and *Africans* are often used to refer solely to this part of the African continent and its native inhabitants. While the Nile valley was one of the original cradles of civilization and North Africa was an integral part of the Graeco-Roman classical world, it is one of history's ironic touches that sub-Saharan Africa, despite its proximity to both regions, was one of the last areas to come to the attention of the outside world. Only after 1500 A.D. did European traders, missionaries, and explorers progressively penetrate the so-called Dark Continent. Finally, in the nineteenth century most parts of Africa were parceled out among the various European powers.

This outside impact came at a time when the West was experiencing remarkable advances in technology and the arts stemming from the Renaissance, geographical exploration, and the scientific and the industrial revolutions. From the vantage point of these advances, Africa south of the Sahara appeared static, and its people primitive. Above all the absence of writing in African societies colored western stereotypes. Preliterates were considered barbaric, a people without records of their past and therefore without history. Since 1945, however, a new school of African studies has become established, dedicated to demonstrating that there is "a recoverable African past," notwithstanding the paucity of written materials. Its advent as an integral part of world history is one of the most exciting and rewarding happenings in contemporary historical studies.

The progressive rediscovery of the African past has been aided by the newly independent sub-Saharan states' interest in archaeological and historical research. Greatly expanded archaeological and anthropological activity has led to the discovery of many new prehistoric sites and to the possibility that manlike creatures may actually have originated in Africa (see Chapter 1). Mainly, however, the rediscovery of Africa's past has been made possible by the development of new research techniques.

In the new types of research methods now being utilized, specialists from other fields collaborate with historians. Botanists' study of the introduction and diffusion of food crops has illuminated significant features of Africa's pre-European past. The utilization of oral tradition is promising to be a significant technique where no records are available. Another research approach, called glotto-chronology, involves the use of linguistics to trace the routes and times of migrations as well as the diffusion of various culture items. These new methods used in recovering the African past are collectively known as ethnohistory. With them, the badly needed chronology of African history is slowly being pieced together.

Peoples of Africa. Between the Sahara and the Mediterranean, North Africa has been peopled for at least five thousand years by the Hamitic-speaking Berbers. In addition, this area has a prominent Semitic element, introduced through the immigration of both Jews and Arabs during the period of the Roman empire and the later era of Muslim expansion. Southward, a wide variety of physical types are found: the so-called true Negro living along the west coast; the tall, slender Nilo-Sudanic people in the northeast; the congeries of Bantu-speaking peoples dominant in the center and south of the continent; the Pygmies living in the deep rain forest of central Africa; and the Bushmen and Hottentots of southern Africa.[4]

Continent in isolation. The key to an understanding of the history of sub-Saharan Africa has been its geographic isolation. To the north stretches the huge barrier of the Sahara. For centuries this wide expanse of sand prevented easy contact with the dynamic civilizations fringing the Mediterranean. The African coastline is forbidding, with few bays or inlets to serve as harbors. Great breakers roll in and dash against the shore, making it hazardous for ships to approach land. Most of the rivers are blocked by rapids and sandbanks and are useless as highways into the interior. The coastal area is often narrow, ending abruptly in high plateaus; the miasmal swamps and dense jungles in some areas are other obvious obstacles to communication. Added to these barriers is the threat of tropical disease.

But the geographical picture is not completely negative. Sub-Saharan Africa also has cool highlands, broad grassy plains, fertile valleys, valuable mineral reserves, and abundant animal resources—ivory, ostrich feathers, hides. The coast of western Africa has been successfully farmed since early times, supporting a comparatively dense population. The largest rivers of western Africa have been useful for communication—the Niger for most of its 2600 miles, the Senegal for 560 miles, and the Gambia for 350 miles.

Even so, the isolation of much of sub-Saharan Africa must be considered a major factor in its history. It not only helps explain the remarkable continuity and distinctiveness of the African way of life; but it is also a key to sub-Saharan retardation, especially in technology.

Africa: the formative period. It is now believed that during the long, primitive period of the Old Stone Age, Africa was the most advanced area in the world, a leader in the slow march toward civilization. In addition to developing the hand-ax, Africa had produced the first true weapon of attack, the bolas, and its tool-making techniques may have been diffused to other continents by streams of migration.

In contrast to some other areas in the world, Africa suffered a culture lag after 8000 B.C. The Neolithic revolution had dawned in the Middle East, and the technique of plant domestication spread from western Asia to North Africa. Under the pharaohs, farming flourished in the lower Nile valley at least by the fifth millenium B.C. Unfortunately, farming and other adjuncts of civilization did not diffuse rapidly southward into the African continent, and it is now generally held that there was no independent invention of agriculture in sub-Saharan Africa. The people of the savanna region of the Sudan, directly south of the Sahara and north of the forests, probably did not begin to cultivate crops until after 2000 B.C. In fact, the earliest important Neolithic farm culture yet identified dates from 800 B.C. to 200 A.D. Known as the Nok culture, it originated in northern Nigeria. Its people had begun to work iron and tin, and their most distinctive accomplishment was the production of strikingly beautiful terra-cotta sculpture.

During the first millennium B.C. the tempo of movement in Africa began to quicken. Iron was introduced, and its use spread over much of Africa between 300 B.C. and 900 A.D. In West Africa (in the area of Nigeria) Bantu-speaking peoples who farmed and worked iron began to increase in numbers. This "population explosion" led to an historic migration southward into the rain forest regions. At the outset, the Bantu migrants needed crops that could thrive in the wet and excessively hot forests. Such new crops as bananas and varieties of yams became available when Asian immigrants brought them to East Africa in the early centuries A.D. These Indonesian peoples colonized the island of Madagascar, and their knowledge of new crops diffused into the African interior. The Bantus increased rapidly, and as they pushed southward, they absorbed most of the Pygmy and Bushmen types they encountered. By the eighth century A.D. they had reached the area of present-day Rhodesia and by the sixteenth century were nearing the tip of South Africa.

Africa's contacts with the earliest civilizations. The vast coastline of sub-Saharan Africa was touched only here and there by sailors and traders in ancient times. In general the contacts were spasmodic and not very important. By about 300 B.C. merchants from southern Arabia began trading with

the peoples on the east coast of Africa. In their search for ivory and slaves, merchants from India may have ventured inland as far as the Great Lakes in central Africa. Certainly the ancient Egyptians sailed far up the Nile and sent their mariners down the east coast. The most famous expedition was sent by Queen Hatshepsut in about 1470 B.C. to the legendary land of Punt, which probably was located in what is now Somaliland (see illustration, p. 41).

Of all the ancient peoples who approached sub-Saharan Africa, the most successful were the Phoenicians. According to the Bible, King Solomon in the tenth century B.C. hired some of these intrepid sailors to bring him ivory, silver, and gold from the land of Ophir—represented today perhaps by the modern seaport of Sofala in Mozambique. About 600 B.C. the Egyptian pharaoh Necho organized an expedition of Phoenician sailors to sail around the entire continent of Africa, an almost unbelievable feat of circumnavigation. Of more certain authenticity is the voyage in 520 B.C. of a fleet of sixty ships sent by the Phoenician colony at Carthage to explore northwestern Africa and to establish trading posts there. The expedition sailed as far south as the modern British colony of Sierra Leone, some three thousand miles from its home port in the Mediterranean.

Along the valley of the Nile, the pharoahs had extended their civilization and control well into Upper Egypt by 2000 B.C., and five hundred years later they gained mastery of the area known as Kush in the northern part of the modern state of the Sudan. The Kushites became thoroughly Egyptianized, but about 1000 B.C., when Egyptian power had begun to wane, they set up an independent kingdom.

Waxing strong and prosperous, the Kushites soon conquered Egypt, which they ruled from about 725 B.C. to 600 B.C., when they were pushed out of Egypt back into the Sudan. Not far from the modern city of Khartoum the Kushites founded their capital of Meroë. From 250 B.C. to the beginning of the Christian era Meroë enjoyed its golden age. The Kushite dynasty, ruling over a mixed white and black population, encour-

Near the junction of the White and Blue Nile in the Sudan, the Kushites built their fabulous capital, Meroë. Today its remains give a vivid impression of the city's former grandeur.

aged trade, accumulated wealth, and produced great architecture—Egyptian-inspired. Massive monuments, palaces, and sculptured gods were built; their remains still attest to the glory of Meroë. The Meroitic kingdom was undoubtedly an active center for iron smelting and manufacturing, as proved by the many slag heaps that still can be identified. In fact Meroë can be called the Pittsburgh of ancient Africa. While scholars do not all agree, Meroë may have been an important channel of culture diffusion, mainly Egyptian, into central Africa. Knowledge of iron working may also have spread from this center to other parts of the continent. Although generally not appreciated, Meroë can be considered, along with Carthage and Egypt, as one of the great civilizations of ancient Africa.

Africa and the classical world. While the Greeks and Romans were setting the pattern for western culture and the Han in China and the Guptas in India were support-

ing highly civilized societies, little was known about Africa south of the Sahara, and its advancement was definitely hindered by its relative isolation. The Phoenicians and Greeks had dotted the African Mediterranean coast with colonies and trading posts, and, with the rise of the Roman empire, the entire region had become part of the realm of the Caesars. Imperial North Africa flourished and great cities gradually developed. After about 100 A.D. the Romans made a few Sahara crossings, and the great classical geographer Ptolemy, in the second century A.D., apparently learned of the junction of the Blue and the White Nile and their source in the great inland lakes. But after the decline of Rome, what little knowledge had been gained about the great continent was forgotten or lay hidden in unread manuscripts.

At the time of the Roman empire the kingdom of Axum (in present-day Ethiopia) became prominent. We have only fragmentary knowledge of this kingdom, which flourished from the first to the seventh centuries A.D. Its people were a mixture of Hamitic stock and Semitic-speaking immigrants who came from Arabia about 1000 B.C. Their kings traced their lineage from Menelik, (the son, according to Ethiopian tradition, of King Solomon and the Queen of Sheba). Christianity, which had spread down into most of northeastern Africa during the time that the Roman empire was becoming Byzantine, became the official religion in Axum in the fourth century A.D. Led by powerful kings, Axum armies subdued surrounding territory as far as the valley of the Nile, but their expansion was eventually halted by the equally victorious force of Islam in Egypt and the entire Red Sea area. Thereafter the Ethiopians remained isolated and stagnant in their highlands, and this part of Africa was cut off from the rest of Christendom (and, in fact, from any contact with Europe) until 1500.

Afro-Muslim empires in the Sudan. Between the fourth and sixteenth centuries A.D. a series of large empires rose, flourished, and disappeared in the western Sudan. Their history is gradually being reconstructed from the Arabic writings of Muslim traders together with oral traditions and archaeological discoveries. The first such imperial state was Ghana, located in the upper areas of the Niger and Senegal rivers (see Reference Map 6). In the fourth century a group of immigrants from North Africa, probably Hamitic Berbers, established their control over the indigenous peoples. Gradually the more numerous Negroes absorbed their conquerors and, in the late eighth century, seized control and created a Negro dynasty.

After the amazingly rapid spread of the Islamic Arabs across North Africa in the eighth century, a new and more potent alien influence traversed the Sahara. Muslim Berber tribes, together with Arab adherents of the Prophet, began to filter into the Sudan—a huge grassy plain stretching from the Atlantic to the Nile valley. The Sudan became an area of racial mixture, where Negroid peoples came under the influence of Muslim culture.

Many of these North African Muslims settled in the capital city of Ghana, as merchants and officials, making it the first great commercial center of the Sudan. Arabic became the official language of the empire, and the Islamic way of life and religion made numerous converts. Ghana attained a remarkable degree of control of the western trans-Saharan trade route. Great camel caravans plied back and forth across the Sahara. Gold and slaves from the south were traded for salt from northern desert areas and for goods from Morocco.

From the revenues from this trans-Saharan trade, the Ghanian rulers were able to maintain a sumptuous royal court, and their empire enjoyed stable government for more than two hundred years. This wealth, however, attracted the cupidity of Muslim neighbors, desert Berbers who had embraced a form of militant Islam. Ostensibly crusaders pledged to extirpate the paganism of the Ghanian rulers, these invaders captured Ghana in 1076 (just ten years after the Norman victory at Hastings in England), forcing many of its inhabitants to accept Islam. Thus the conquerors conveniently mixed religious zeal with a desire to enjoy the profits of the trans-Saharan trade.

Several centuries later Ghana became part of a new empire—that of Mali. This most famous Afro-Muslim kingdom stretched for fifteen hundred miles in the western Sudan. Ruled by Mandingos, a Negro people whose chiefs had been converted to Islam in the eleventh century, Mali attained greatness in the thirteenth century. Its major commercial city, Timbuktu, succeeded Ghana as the main point of convergence for the north south caravan routes (see Reference Map 6) and became a great metropolis.

Under Mandingo rule, Timbuktu boasted a great mosque and a nearby university for Koranic studies. The noted fourteenth-century traveler ibn-Batuta (see p. 267) reported an amazing degree of order and justice in the Mali empire:

. . . [The people of Mali] possess some admirable qualities. They are seldom unjust, and have a greater abhorrence of injustice than any other people. Their sultan shows no mercy to anyone who is guilty of the least act of it. There is complete security in their country. Neither traveller nor inhabitant in it has anything to fear from robbers or men of violence. . . . Another of their good qualities is their habit of wearing clean white garments on Fridays. Even if a man has nothing but an old worn shirt, he washes it and cleans it, and wears it to the Friday service. Yet another is their zeal for learning the Koran by heart. . . . I visited the Qádí in his house on the day of the festival. His children were chained up, so I said to him "Will you not let them loose?" He replied "I shall not do so until they learn the Koran by heart."[5]

Mali at its height controlled an area as large as western Europe, but it enjoyed only a century of greatness and after 1350 rapidly dwindled in extent and power. It was replaced by another great empire—Songhai—which reached its height in the fifteenth and sixteenth centuries. Its capital was Gao, a commercial center on the Niger. At the end of the sixteenth century the Songhai empire was destroyed by a Moroccan army made up largely of Spanish and Portuguese mercenaries whose superior firearms were new to the Sudan. The period of greatness of the Sudanese kingdoms was over.

No European ever saw Timbuktu until 1828, when René Caillé, disguised as a Muslim pilgrim, made the journey. The mixture of Muslim and native architecture is apparent in his drawing of the city. Caillé was most impressed by the difficulties the builders must have encountered in setting up a great city "in the midst of the sands."

These Sudanic empires had a number of common features, which made each of them relatively short-lived. Their boundaries were ill defined and embraced a variety of ethnically and culturally diverse peoples. Often established by conquest, these empires depended upon military force and personal leadership for their perpetuation, and they lacked stable systems of succession to the throne. But despite their built-in forces of disunity, these empires are rightly regarded as important political achievements in sub-Saharan history.

Some historians deny the importance of external influences in West African political development. There is, however, evidence that Islamic traders and settlers from North Africa played a significant role in the rise of the Sudanic empires. As Muslim schools were founded in the Sudan, a class of educated and literate scholars was produced whose services were indispensable in setting up and running imperial administrations. Arabic was also the lingua franca of diplomacy and trade. It has been said that "Without losing their distinctive 'Sudanic' character, the great states and cities of the western Sudan became definitely part of the Islamic world."[6]

Impact of Islam in East Africa. The impact of Islam was also strongly felt along the East African coast. From the seventh century A.D. Arab traders came in growing numbers for gold, ivory, and slaves. Permanent settlements sprang up until the entire east coast was dotted with small Muslim states. These urban trading centers, such as Lamu, Kilwa, Mombassa, and Zanzibar, were never effectively united and controlled from any one point, and there was continuous rivalry among them.

One of the results of this active coastal trade was the emergence of an important, prosperous African state in what is now Rhodesia. The rulers of this kingdom built the great stone city of Zimbabwe over a long time period from as early as the fifth to the eighth century until the early eighteenth. Constructed of granite blocks without mortar or cement, the massive walls of its temple ruins measure from ten to fifteen feet thick and from twenty to thirty feet high. The

In this 1375 map from the Catalan Atlas, Mansa Musa, the wealthy king of Mali, awaits the arrival of a Muslim trader. Although both are West Africans, the Arab is from the Sahara Desert, while the Negro king is from the western Sudan. The system of trade within the African continent was highly organized in the precolonial era.

remains of the acropolis—built to be an impregnable fortress—can be seen on a nearby hill. Close by is the Valley of the Ruins, probably the site of a flourishing tribal administrative center.

The various Arab settlements along the eastern coast made up the Zenj empire, and the entire coastal strip was called Zenjibar, meaning "black coast." Made wealthy by trade, the Zenj empire attracted merchants from as far east as Malaya and China, and numerous Chinese coins and many fragments of Chinese porcelain have been found along the coast. The empire endured for nearly five hundred years, until the arrival of the Portuguese in 1497. In the last half of the seventeenth century Arabs from Oman ejected the Portuguese from the East African coast north of Mozambique, but Mozambique is still under Lisbon's control.

European contact and the slave trade. For some eight hundred years, beginning about 700 A.D., Islam had been the most important outside influence in Africa and the main agency of communication with the outside world. This Islamic contact had been mainly by land across the Sahara Desert and by sea along the east coast. With the coming of the Europeans in the fifteenth century, the pattern of outside contact was revolutionized, for now it was to come mainly from the west and by sea to both the east and west coasts. Trans-Saharan trade dwindled as European ships came to the coasts to trade for gold, ivory, and especially slaves. Their arrival marked the beginning of the European period of African history which lasted for about five hundred years.

Domestic slavery had been practiced in Africa since ancient times, but the slave trade was first organized by the Arabs mainly along the east coast. The Arabs used East African slaves themselves and exported thousands across the Indian Ocean. After the European trade began, West African slaves, possibly more than thirty million in all, were brought to the Americas. Furthermore, it is said that for every slave sold to a colonial plantation, another lost his life in the cruel roundup in Africa or on the crowded slave ships.

The African slave trade has been called the greatest crime in history; and some Negro leaders blame this nefarious trade for Africa's failure to keep up with European progress in early modern times. While not attempting to exculpate Europeans, it should be understood that both Europeans and Africans accepted the trade and cooperated with it. Slaves were captured in the hinterland by Africans who then delivered the victims to the slave ships on the coast. It was a very lucrative enterprise. On the basis of this traffic in human beings, new West African states, such as Benin, Dahomey, Oyo, and Ashanti, rose to power and wealth. Although

they compared in artistic development and territorial influence with the earlier empires of the western Sudan, these states of the Guinea forest quickly declined as a result of tyrannical, greedy rulers and wars with their African trade rivals.

Historians continue to study and debate the long-term effects of the slave traffic. There is a consensus on the unmitigated evils of the slavers in East Africa, but authorities are reluctant to make sweeping generalizations about its effects in West Africa. Granting the stimulus to intertribal wars, the depopulation of raided areas, and its ultimate inhumanity and cruelty, the slave traffic did result in a new type of contact with the outside world that was not completely evil. New medicines and tools became known. Above all the introduction of new crops, such as maize, cassava, and the sweet potato, made a revolutionary difference to food supplies. Depopulation caused by the slave trade was in some instances more than offset by an increase in population made possible by these more productive crops.

Indigenous culture of Black Africa. What can be said of the collective achievement of the African before the European impact? Certainly Africans lagged behind Europe and America in their control over nature. There was no science, mathematics, or technology worthy of the name; no sails for ships, no animal-drawn plows, no use of the wheel, and above all no alphabet or forms of writing. But aside from these aspects of material culture, African society in its law, government, education, and codes of social conduct was as complex and efficiently regulated as our own. Rules and conventions regarding the role of parents, worship of the gods, education of children and customs relating to eating, recreation, and the like were carefully worked out, and effective methods were at hand to compel the individual to conform.

In political organization the basic unit was the tribe. In Africa there are still hundreds of these tribal units, microscopic or large. And while Africans did not develop the highly centralized and bureaucratically organized nations that emerged in late medieval Europe, they did establish a number of important kingdom states. Moreover, African

The ruins in the valley of Zimbabwe, meaning "the sacred graves of the chiefs," are dominated by the massive stone wall of the temple.

rulers were not usually despots; they had to govern within the framework of accepted custom and seek the advice of their council of elders.

Religion touched every phase of African life—births, marriage, death, war, rainmaking, and harvest. While religious practices varied from tribe to tribe, three basic essentials could usually be recognized: "spiritism," which includes ancestor worship and the propitiation of such spirits of nature as lightning and rain; belief in some kind of supreme being or highest power; and the practice of magic.[7] This last element may be defined as a technique directed at obtaining the aid of supernatural powers and forces. On its positive side it is definitely protective. But there is also "black magic" and witchcraft, the magic that has been most feared by Africans.

The most distinctive African art form has been music, which plays an integral part in everyday life. "The African sings about work, about hunting, about money, about women, about canoeing, about planting, about war—in short about all the things that men dwell naturally upon in their minds."[8] Unlike music in the western world where there are usually two parties—the artist and the audience—all Africans participate in the rendering of music. Their music is communal, not individual.

African visual art par excellence is sculpture. While it is sometimes called "primitive," it follows complex traditions. The sculpture is usually carved of wood, but ivory, terra cotta, and bronze have also been used. Some bronze work has been compared to the best produced by Renaissance artists. An amazingly naturalistic bronze head found at the site of the ancient city-state of Ife in Nigeria has been pronounced the finest surviving example of African art.

Indigenous African culture cannot be summarily dismissed as uncivilized. To be sure, the term *civilization* has traditionally referred to a stage of human culture characterized by writing and an urban base in which there is considerable use of technology, the operation of economic specialization, and a complex infrastructure of law

This bronze relief was fashioned by artisans of the ancient city-state of Benin in present-day Nigeria. The king in the center, wearing coral necklaces up to his jowl, is flanked by pages and guards. Plaques like these decorated the walls and square pillars of the Royal Palace of Benin.

and government. In recent years, however, there has been substantial rethinking on this matter as social scientists, particularly anthropologists, have learned more about the culture of people usually referred to as primitive. A spokesman for this new viewpoint has written:

The term civilization refers literally to a city state, at the least to a state that encourages urbanization and industrialization. But in its more general usage it implies a system of living where law and order are maintained with justice and equality, human conflicts both inside and outside the group are resolved with a minimum of violence, and where there is a moral code which people keep, more because they believe in it than because they are afraid of the consequences of breaking it.[9]

Seen in this light, Africa has indeed a long tradition of civilization. In fact, while African culture was certainly deficient in technology and writing, it could boast outstanding sculpture, complicated and vital music, functional and well-organized political forms, and significant religious systems. Some tribes paid careful attention to family planning and population control. Capital punishment was rare; only the habitual murderer or thief was put to death. The rights of a wife—in relation to property, custody of children, and protection from abuse from the husband—were often more carefully spelled out than in western societies until very recent times. One of the most admirable traits of African society was "the prevalence of the idea of community." A built-in system of social security took care of the needy, the old, the orphan, or the widow. Unlike the westerner with his emphasis on individual advance (often at the expense of the group), the African always had to think of group and family interests rather than his own.

The new image of Africa. The advent of European explorers marked the beginning of a new era in Africa, one which, while it created new problems, also removed age-old handicaps. With the end of its isolation, a more accurate knowledge of African cultures spread to the outside world; and increasingly, a new value was placed upon some of the qualities of pre-European African societies. Shortly after 1900 the artistic worth of African sculpture was discovered by the Paris school of avant-garde painters, among them Picasso and Matisse. This so-called primitive art, long considered grotesque and infantile, provided artists with a sought-for channel to revolt against the naturalistic conventions that had dominated western art for two thousand years. African sculpture soon came to be recognized as one of the world's major art forms and was a source of inspiration for the rise of Cubism, Post-Impressionism, and the general vogue of abstract art in the western world. African music also made an important contribution. It has been the major ultimate source of American spirituals and of jazz. Similarly, the popular music of Latin America, such as the rumba of Cuba, the calypso of Trinidad, the samba of Brazil, reveal their debt to the rhythmic figures of African music.

During the past two decades—building on the growing appreciation of Negro artistic gifts, the widening vista of African history, and the amazing postwar emergence of more than thirty independent nations—a new ideology has developed among African intellectuals. Known as *Négritude,* it asserts the Negro's distinctiveness from other races and proudly champions his unique qualities, including blackness. It has been tersely defined as the "positive affirmation of the values in African culture."[10]

Négritude seeks to rediscover the long-forgotten African past and to make it the foundation for group dignity and aspirations. It endeavors to find cultural antecedents which have been forgotten or minimized. Believing that Europeans have downgraded African achievements, it passionately denies the still dominant idea of the long history of barbarism in Africa before the advent of European colonial rule. It calls attention to early African achievements in art, folk literature, music, and dance forms and to the virtues in African religious and social systems. Undoubtedly there is an element of idealization in these claims, but on the whole they are a long-needed corrective.

OLD CIVILIZATIONS IN THE NEW WORLD

The earliest American immigrants. The questions of how and when the Western Hemisphere was first settled remain uncertain. It is generally agreed that man did not originate in the Americas, for no bones of anthropoids or of humans earlier than *Homo sapiens* have been found there. Most scholars believe that man arrived in America from Asia, fully developed as *Homo sapiens,* by way of Alaska as early as 10,000 B.C. and perhaps as much as twenty thousand years or so earlier. The number of early migrations to the New World is uncertain—there may have been only one or several—but, in any event, these nomadic groups spread out in all directions on the American continents so that eventually there were areas of human habitation extending from the arctic through the temperate plains and lush jungles to the southern tip of South America (see Reference Map 1).

The cultural levels achieved by different groups of American Indians before the arrival of the Europeans varied. Most of the Indians of North America and those in the Amazon region never attained civilization as traditionally defined. They built no great cities, nor did they progress further than the Neolithic stage, with its dependence upon hunting, primitive agriculture, and village life. By contrast, the Mayas and the Aztecs in Mexico and Central America and the Incas in the Andes of Peru created advanced civilizations on a par with those which arose in Asia and the Near East. Perhaps one of the major reasons for the more advanced cultures of the Incas, Mayas, and Aztecs was the domestication of the potato and the all-important maize, or Indian corn, known as the "food of the gods." This former wild grass, skillfully bred into a basic crop grain, was capable of supporting large populations. The achievements of these advanced American civilizations were prodigious. Tenochtitlán, the great Aztec city on the present site of Mexico City, which was destroyed by the Spanish *conquistadores* under Cortés, was a finer and better organized urban center than any that existed in sixteenth-century Europe from which the Spaniards came.

Social and political institutions of the advanced Indian areas were by no means so static as was once believed. In the Mexican-Central American area and in Peru, changing types of social organization can be traced. The introduction of agriculture, the arts, and village life was followed by the appearance of religious centers like small cities, where priestly rule maintained the sacred ceremonies of nature and the fertility cycle. Centuries later the warrior element predominated in states centered around real cities. Warfare among city-states often led to leagues of cities and finally to the military empires which the Europeans, with their advanced technology including the gun and the wheel and their remarkable horses, encountered and destroyed.

North American Indians. Among the North American Indians were many differ-

Theodor de Bry's engraving (adapted from a watercolor by John White) shows a sixteenth-century Secoton Indian village, located in what is now North Carolina. The lower quarter of the engraving depicts the religious activities of the Secotons. Near their major shrine (A) is "the place of solemne prayer" (B) and a circle of posts carved with men's faces, around which the Secotons performed their religious dances (C). Pictures such as this were used to depict native life in the New World to the Europeans.

ent types. The Eskimo, perhaps the last to emigrate from Asia, adapted remarkably well to a harsh environment. In the arctic and subarctic regions food was so difficult to come by and shelter so hard to maintain that simply staying alive taxed man's ingenuity and self-reliance and left him little energy for cultivating the arts. The Eskimo was a born inventor, however. Among the aids to living he devised were a lance for hunting seals, snow goggles, and excellent sledges. He also made a remarkable waterproof canoe, the kayak, out of walrus skins and developed moccasinlike footgear called mukluks, which were suited to his needs. His traps were especially ingenious.

The northeast woodlands of North America presented less challenge to inhabitants. Among the farming and hunting Indians of this area, the Iroquois were especially important. Five politically astute tribes formed the League of the Iroquois, probably in the last half of the fifteenth century. The decisions of the League in matters of war and peace were binding on the members; their joint military prowess was almost invincible; and, as the neighboring tribes were defeated, the Great Peace of the Iroquois was extended over most of the northeastern United States. The terms of the Peace read as follows:

When peace shall have been established by the termination of the war . . . then the war captain shall cause all weapons of war to be taken from the nation. Then shall the Great Peace be established and the nation shall observe all the rules of the Great Peace for all time to come.

Whenever a foreign nation is conquered or has by their [*sic*] own free will accepted the Great Peace, their own system of internal government may continue so far as consistent but they must cease all strife with other nations.[11]

The Great Peace of the Iroquois was not a compact between equals, however. Instead, it served as the instrument of Iroquois imperialism. Iroquois territorial ambitions received an impetus after the coming of the Europeans; among the first large tribes to secure firearms, the Iroquois extended their raids through the forest lands to the edge of the western plains. Remnants of the League of the Iroquois still exist in both Canada and the United States.

The Plains Indians of the West owed what prosperity they achieved to the advent of the Europeans. The Spaniards brought the first horses to the Americas, and from Spanish settlements in Mexico and the Southwest the animals spread to the central plains. By the early seventeenth century bands of wild horses roamed the plains, and in time the Indians learned to tame and ride them. Hunting the buffalo was transformed from a weary pursuit on foot to an exciting chase on horseback, which rewarded the Indians with abundant meat and hides. Tribes that had barely survived by hunting alone, and those that had eked out a meager existence by hunting and by raising a little corn in favored valleys, suddenly achieved prosperity and power. The usual cultural development was reversed: prosperity was achieved by the development of hunting rather than an agricultural economy. Ironically, both the rise to power and the later decline of the Plains Indians were the white man's doing. First he made it possible for them to hunt buffalo successfully; later he wiped the buffalo off the face of the prairies.

In what is now the southwestern United States, there developed between the birth of Christ and 1300 one of the highest cultures north of the Rio Grande, that of the Pueblo Indians. Deriving their name from their style of architecture, these peoples built communal villages which the Spanish called *pueblos* ("villages"). Unique among the Indians of North America, the Pueblo Indians used masonry for permanent buildings in contrast to the relatively temporary structures of the other tribes.

In Colorado the Mesa Verde people—true cliff dwellers—constructed their pueblos in large natural niches on the face of a canyon wall beneath an overhanging rim to protect themselves against assault from above or below. Other Indians built their pueblos on the flat tops of defensible mesas or on the floors of canyons. At Chaco Canyon, New Mexico, forty or more such settlements have been excavated. These villages consisted of single-room houses or cubicles stacked one on top of another in terraced levels.

The people of the pueblos were farmers who intensively cultivated small plots of ground ranging from a few square feet to a few acres. Corn, squash, beans, and other crops were staples of their diet; they cultivated cotton and domesticated the turkey. Through such ceremonials as corn dances and snake dances, the Pueblo Indians tried to solicit good weather for their crops.

In the Pueblo culture the governing body was a council presided over by a chief chosen by the people. Some anthropologists assert

PUEBLO, AZTEC, AND
MAYA CIVILIZATIONS

that Pueblo government is one of the oldest republican governments in world history.

The high civilizations of the Americas. In sharp contrast with the Indians of the United States and Canada, the peoples we call Maya, Aztec, and Inca created high civilizations that were comparable with the great cultures of Asia and the ancient Near East. But we probably know less about these South and Central American peoples than about any great civilization of the Old World. Most of our knowledge comes from archaeological research, recorded oral tradition, descriptions by early Spanish soldiers and priests, and the extraordinarily few surviving native records, such as three Mayan books of pictures and partially deciphered hieroglyphs. In their fanatical missionary zeal, many of the early Spanish *conquistadores* and missionaries sought to obliterate all traces of these remarkable civilizations; they destroyed libraries, dismantled cities, and suppressed as much of the native tradition as possible. This perhaps most extreme

example of the destructive consequences of contact between the West and non-European peoples damaged the historical record of the Americas beyond repair.

The American civilizations have much to tell us about the development of civilization in general. For instance, they demonstrate that there is no direct relationship between the level of technology and the development of a high and sophisticated social and political organization. The history of civilization in Mexico and Central and South America covers a time span almost equal to that of China from the Chou to the Ming dynasties. The first Spanish soldiers to see the Aztec capital of Tenochtitlán thought they were looking at a dream city from some romantic enchantment, "a city finer and greater than any in sixteenth-century Europe." Peruvian architectural remains, ceramic and gold work, remain wonders of the world even today (see Color Plate 31). And yet these early Americans had no implements of iron, a metal unknown before the Spanish conquest.

They had no animals capable of carrying burdens other than the dog in Mexico and the Peruvian llama, which would rather die on the spot than carry anything but the lightest load. Most of the population in Mexico were Neolithic small farmers who used a slash-and-burn technique on their lands. In the Andes the peasants terraced the hills and knew the use of fertilizer, but in neither place was the plow known, only the primitive digging stick. Peoples who produced some of the most exquisite weaving in history killed their enemies with stone-edged clubs. In Mexico, "where good manners and elegant behaviour were even more highly regarded than in the punctilious court of Spain,"[12] human sacrifice was widely practiced.

How are we to explain the rise of these remarkable civilizations? The historical record is so meager that we can only engage in the vaguest conjecture. The domestication of maize, or Indian corn, and the potato permitted the development of settled agricultural communities. The Mayas, Aztecs, and Incas all lived in areas where water was scarce and precious, or was available only in unsuitable form, and villagers needed water for themselves and their crops. This necessitated a social organization capable of planning and controlling the development and use of water resources. Calendars were required for the designation of planting and harvest times and the performance of those rituals that would ensure a bountiful harvest; and the development and refinement of calendars and the performance of complex rituals required a class of technicians, usually priests, who were supported by the rest of society. But all this is only suggestive. We shall now examine each of these three remarkable American civilizations more closely.

The splendid culture of the Mayas. Some scholars have characterized the Mayas as the "intellectuals of the New World." Their cities, now only ruins scattered through the jungles of Yucatán, Guatemala, and Honduras, were filled with gracefully ornamented buildings. The Mayas developed a remarkably accurate calendar and a sophisticated writing system based on hieroglyphics, but aside from dates almost nothing has been deciphered.

The earliest known Mayan stone buildings, dating from about 300 B.C., have been found in what is now northern Guatemala. Living in city-states composed primarily of ritual and administrative centers surrounded by agricultural lands, the Mayas shared a common language and a great culture, but apparently they never considered themselves a "nation" and never developed an imperial system as did the Chinese or the Incas. After about 900 A.D. the Mayas of northern Guatemala appear to have abandoned their stately temple centers or cities—for reasons as yet unknown. Perhaps they were overrun by Toltec invaders from central Mexico. In any event, the evidences of the Toltec militarists are clearly seen in the northern Yucatecan Mayan city of Chichén Itzá, from where it is believed that these conquerors dominated most of the Mayan lowlands until about 1200 A.D. After that date political and military leadership passed to the neighboring city of Mayapán, the capital of the so-called "League of the Mayapán." Presumably the cities of the league were by this time ruled by Mayan families, but they had been strongly influenced by the Mexican Toltecs. Mayapán was finally destroyed in civil wars among the various member cities of the league in 1441, a half century before Columbus discovered America.

The land of the Mayas was rich in flora and fauna, and the people were fishermen as well as farmers. Heavy rainfall saturated the jungles, but there are no significant rivers on the Yucatán peninsula, and drinking water was not easily available. Consequently the Mayan cities were constructed near natural wells or "cenotes," and in some instances the Mayas made artificial cisterns and reservoirs. Disastrous droughts appear to have punctuated Mayan history, but by and large the climate and soil of Yucatán permitted them to grow maize in such abundance that a surplus supported a leisure class which could develop the civilization and preserve its cultural achievements.

Mayan society within the city-states was highly stratified, and almost inflexible social barriers existed between classes. The priests, charged with management of the calendar and the performance of rituals, were at the top. There were also nobles, who governed the civil aspects of society, such as land distribution and the collection of taxes. The priests taught the skills of government—rituals, reading, and administrative practices—to their own children and the children of the nobility. The high priests also developed a primitive examination system; according to an early Spanish observer:

They [the high priests] provided priests for the towns when they were needed, examining them in the sciences and ceremonies and committed to them the duties of their office, and set good examples to people and provided them with books and sent them forth.[13]

The priests and the nobility lived luxurious lives, supported by the populace at large. Each city and its environs was governed by a chieftain or lord known as the "true man," who was assisted by local administrators, town councilors, tax collectors, and the like.

The peasants lived in small stucco and thatch huts of a type that is still characteristic of Yucatán today. They were closely bound to a rigorous cycle of taxes and religious dues. It has been estimated that no less than two thirds of each harvest was collected by the priests and nobles for their own support. In addition, the peasants had to work the nobles' lands free and make special presentations of gifts and tribute on stated occasions. There was no private property in land, and the "true man" was responsible for the redistribution of land to maximize production. All classes bathed daily. The dress of the lower classes was simple, but the nobility and priests wore richly ornamented costumes decked with feathers and jade jewelry. Tattooing was also common, as was the custom of dyeing the body; class distinctions could be told at a glance from the color that an individual was dyed. Trade was widespread, but it meant arduous labor for the peasant, who was the primary beast of burden in a land that lacked other animals for transportation.

Strict obedience to elders and to the demands of the ruling hierarchy were fundamentals of any child's upbringing. The Mayas also had highly developed concepts

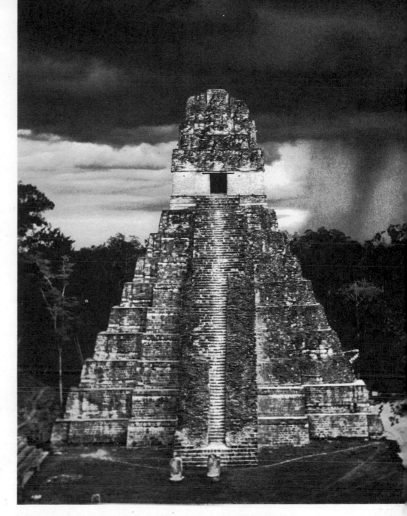

Tikal, located in what is now northern Guatemala, is the oldest and one of the largest of the Mayan temple centers. The Mayas lived close to their fields and only came to their cities for religious ceremonies and to work on necessary construction.

of human beauty. New-born infants' heads were pressed between boards to flatten and elongate the forehead. This was not only considered beautiful but had practical uses as well, since it made carrying by headstrap easier. Crossed eyes were also thought beautiful, and mothers placed beads of resin before the child's eyes, attached by a string to his forelock, in order to encourage crossed eyes.

Religion permeated all aspects of Mayan life, and the government of priests and nobles was a form of theocracy. The Mayan cosmos resembled that of other Middle American groups. It had thirteen heavens and nine hells. The earth, which rested on the back of a crocodile, had been destroyed four times. The Mayas were living, they thought, in its fifth existence. Like the peoples of both the Near and the Far East, the Mayas too had legends of world destruction by flood. The numerous gods were divided into three groups according to where they lived: the sky, the earth, and the underworld. The Mayan gods had many different aspects and personalities and were often ambiguous in their relations to man. The god Chac, for example, sent rain to make the crops grow, but he also inflicted long damp spells which rotted the grain. Moreover, he made the rain fall equally on both the just and the unjust. Because of the lack of rivers and the dependence of agriculture on natural rainfall, Chac was one of the most important Mayan gods. This is in contrast to societies where irrigation was highly developed, as in China and Peru, where rain gods were relatively unimportant. The Mayan gods were living beings who, like all living beings, had to be fed. They were particularly fond of blood and throbbing human hearts.

The religious rituals were closely connected to the calendar, and modern scientists have been amazed by the Mayas' remarkably accurate measurement of time. The Mayas built observatories, run by the priests, to assist them in observing the movement of the heavenly bodies on which the calendar was based. Accuracy in astronomical and calendrical calculations was possible because of the excellent Mayan numerical system which, unlike our system, was based on twenty instead of ten. A dot was equal to one unit and a bar to five, and numbers from one to nineteen were written in varying combinations of these two elements. Of the American Indians, only the Mayas used the concept of zero.

In architecture and sculpture the Mayas produced work of the highest quality. The principal buildings of a city enclosed a central square, or plaza, which was a sort of civic center. In the plaza was a terraced mound, or pyramid, topped by a temple. Mayan architectural composition emphasized horizontal lines and exhibited an excellent sense of proportion. Decorating the terraces of the temple pyramids were pieces of highly stylized sculpture, regarded by some experts as among the world's best.

This artistic achievement appears even more extraordinary since Mayan sculptors did their intricate carving without the aid of anything better than stone tools. Almost completely religious in inspiration, Mayan art depicted the deities and the animals connected with them—snakes, frogs, jaguars, and hummingbirds. Walls as well as sculptured figures and limestone monoliths called stelae were profusely decorated and painted in brilliant hues. Minor arts such as weaving, jade sculpture, ceramics, and gold and silver work were also highly developed and showed an extremely sophisticated sense of design which compares favorably with the best of Egyptian art.

Despite the high achievements of Mayan culture, increasing warfare among their cities brought their collapse and the final decline of the culture. When the *conquistadores* came upon the scene, the country was in chaos; the Spaniards found it a simple matter to subdue the Mayan peoples.

The warlike Aztecs. In the early centuries A.D., while the Mayas were building their cities in the jungles of Yucatán and Guatemala, the peoples of the Mexican plateau were themselves advancing toward high civilization. The temple ruins at the Toltec city of Tula north of Mexico City and the huge pyramids and temples at Teotihuacán near the Mexican capital are the remains of early plateau cultures. Successive waves of nomadic, warlike tribes came out of the deserts of northern Mexico and the southwestern United States to found new cultures and build their own monuments. The last and perhaps the greatest were the Aztecs.

According to their tribal legends, the Aztecs were to found a city on a site where they would see an eagle on a rock with a serpent in its mouth. After a century and a half of wandering and fighting, they reached central Mexico and, in 1325, founded a lake settlement called Tenochtitlán (where Mexico City is today) at a place where the prophecy was fulfilled. The eagle on a rock with a serpent in its mouth is remembered on the Mexican flag. The Aztecs, gradually conquering some of their neighbors and allying themselves with others, created a confederacy with two other major cities in central

Mexico by the end of the fifteenth century. Their rule extended from the Gulf of Mexico to the Pacific and from the Mayan jungles and mountains into the northern deserts (see map, p. 595).

Although the Aztecs were imperialists, conquering new lands and peoples by force of arms, theirs was not an empire in the true sense of the word. Nor was the emperor a true emperor. He was head of the confederacy and of the empire's civil authority, but he was elected by a council of high nobles and priests from among the closest relations of his immediate predecessor. The council usually chose the warrior most brave in battle and noble in speech. The emperor was thus both hereditary and elective at the same time. His two major personal attributes were indicated by his titles: *tlatoani,* "he who speaks," and *tlacatecuhtli,* "chief of the warriors." He was, in fact, commander in chief of the confederated cities' armies.

The emperor was assisted by a fairly sophisticated bureaucracy, consisting of a vice-emperor, who handled much of the day-to-day business; governors, tax collectors, and of course an entrenched military organization that dominated the entire civil society. As with the emperor himself, the civil bureaucracy and army attained position, rank, and advancement through a combination of heredity and merit. As time went on, more and more positions, including district chiefs, were hereditary, but all appointments, whether purely hereditary or by nomination by a local council (a pre-empire tribal form), had to be approved by the emperor himself.

Paralleling the civil bureaucracy and army was the church, materially wealthy and politically powerful. At its head was, again, the emperor, and under him two high priests who ruled an entire priestly bureaucracy governing the temples throughout the land. The priests were distinguished for their learning, poverty, and piety. Father Bernardino de Sahagun, a Catholic priest and accurate early chronicler of the Aztecs, has left a remarkable testimony to the quality of the priesthood. Priests, he wrote, were chosen only with attention

to morals and observance of religion, knowledge of doctrine and purity of life. Those were chosen who were humble, righteous and peaceable, earnest and reasonable, not given to levity, but sober, severe and scrupulous in morals, full of love and charity, compassion and friendship for all, god-fearing and devout.[14]

Unlike their Spanish conquerors, whose Christian religion excluded all but the One God, the Aztecs welcomed all the gods of the lands over which they ruled. The two high priests ruled over an elaborate religious establishment in Tenochtitlán, which was centered on a great dual temple that stood approximately where the national cathedral in Mexico City stands today. The gods walked closely with the Aztecs, and each priest and sacrifical victim was considered an incarnation of the god whom he served. One of the two priests and central temples was dedicated to Uitzilopochtli, the sun god and the god of war, a close relation of the gods of the hunt, the archetypal soldier. His victims were reborn as birds into a carefree immortality. The other priest and temple were dedicated to Tlaloc, the ancient rain god, the god of the peasant, the fruits of whose labors made civilization and the empire possible. Uitzilopochtli was probably an unconscious representation of the Aztec past, when the people were wandering in the desert before they reached their promised land on the lake. Tlaloc represented the sedentary peasant society, the empire, that developed after the end of their desert trek.

In every city of their domain the Aztecs built great pyramids topped by temples to the sun god and the rain god. Stone altars were set up in front of the temples, and human beings were sacrificed to Uitzilopochtli by the priests, who tore the heart out of the victim's living body. The Aztecs feared the future and the void which they considered the future to be, and human sacrifices were an essential means of keeping the gods, and therefore the world, alive. The primary objective of war among the Aztecs was to capture prisoners for sacrifice to Uitzilopochtli, and when the growth of the Aztecs' power diminished the frequency of war in Mexico, an institution known as the "war of flowers" developed, a symbolic war whereby prisoners could continue to be taken.

Latter-day historians and moralists have vigorously condemned the Aztecs for conducting human sacrifices on such a grand scale, but the Aztecs were themselves horrified at the individual tortures to which the Spaniards subjected their enemies and the wholesale slaughter to which they condemned the conquered Aztecs. There are some indications that the Aztecs' sacrificial victims may have considered their fate not only inevitable but even an honor, for by the sacrifice they became the god himself. As cruel and barbaric as this practice may seem to us, we should keep in mind that our own century has seen some of the most "civilized" nations of the world massacre millions of people for purely racial or political reasons, and that we have developed weapons capable of wiping out instantly more people than the Aztecs sacrificed in their entire history.

The Aztec capital of Tenochtitlán was a thriving metropolis with well-regulated great market places, immaculately clean streets, running water, great gardens, and magnificent buildings, all constructed without the aid of the wheel or any beast of burden other than man. It was a young city: not quite two hundred years passed between its foundation in 1325 and its destruction at the hands of the Spaniards.

At the time of the Spanish conquest this young Aztec society was in the process of rapid social change. The upper civil classes—the emperor, nobility, bureaucracy, and military officers—were increasingly wealthy and ostentatious. At the beginning of the sixteenth century, during the reign of the famed Montezuma II, an aristocratic reaction apparently set in against those of common birth who were rising in society, and measures were taken to exclude them from high office and social position. Had Aztec society not been destroyed by the *conquistadores*,

Dominating the one-quarter-square-mile Great Temple precinct in the Aztec's capital city of Tenochtitlán was the huge double pyramid sacred to Uitzilopochtli, sun god and god of war, and Tlaloc, the rain god. The precinct was separated by a "serpent wall" and a moat from the rest of the city.

it is possible that a purely hereditary nobility would have developed. Moreover, a new merchant class, economically powerful and wealthy but unostentatious in its style of life, was rising rapidly, and it may have eventually challenged the power of the nobility and even of the emperor himself. Their power was such that the emperor was granting them more and more special privileges. Private property in land was also beginning to make its appearance, leading to wealth, rather than merit, as a basis for social status. All these developments were cut short by the Spanish conquest, however, and the only group to survive were the masses of peasants, who figure so little in the writing of history.

A fair analogy may be drawn between the Mayas and Aztecs in the New World and the ancient Greeks and Romans. Generally speaking the Mayas were more artistic and intellectual than the Aztecs and remind us somewhat of the Greeks. The characteristics of the Aztecs in turn are sometimes very Roman. Like the Romans, the Aztecs borrowed many aspects of their culture from their predecessors or from those they held in thrall. An important cultural acquisition was the Mayan calendar, which the Aztecs modified with different names for days and dates and a differing numbering system, and they also gave new names to old Mayan and Toltec gods.

For all that historians have written about them, however, the Aztecs were civilized in every sense of the word. As one great modern specialist on Aztec history has written, "At the height of their career the Romans shed more blood in their circuses and for their amusement than ever the Aztecs did before their idols."[15]

The Inca empire. The origins of the cultures and high civilizations established by the Indians who dwelled along the Pacific coast of South America and in the Andes mountain range are as obscure as those of Mexico and Central America. By the first millennium B.C., however, the inhabitants of the coastal communities had progressed to the point where they were building homes and pyramids of adobe, fashioning superb and highly imaginative pottery, and irri-

The face in the center of this reproduction of the Aztec calendar represents the sun, while the various figures around the sun depict events in Aztec history.

gating the river valleys. Up in the highlands, in the region of the world's highest lake, Titicaca, flourished a more developed group of Indians, the Aymaras, who built a great stone city, Tiahuanaco, thirteen thousand feet above sea level. The city was a marvel of palaces and huge, perfectly carved monoliths. Between 400 and 1000 A.D. it dominated a large empire, including most of Peru, but little is known of its inhabitants or how or why their advanced culture declined. Their direct descendants still form an important part of the population of Bolivia and Peru.

The most spectacular achievement of the Indians of South America, however, was the great empire of the Incas, who settled in the heartland of the Andes, in the valley of Cuzco, about the eleventh century. Like the Aztecs in Mexico, they were the final heirs of the Peruvian cultures of the plateaus and the coastal plains. From Cuzco, they began to extend their dominion over the mountain and coastal peoples. From 1438 until the arrival of the *conquistador* Pizarro in 1532, a vast Inca empire flourished, extending for about 2700 miles along the western coast of the continent, including a population estimated at some ten million at the time of the Spanish conquest. The bulk of the Peruvian and Bolivian population today is descended from Inca stock.

Unlike the Aztecs, the Incas—which is what the emperors were called—established a true empire in every sense of the word. The Incas ruled absolutely and despotically. The monarchy, which was hereditary, created an imperial administration, exercised the power of life and death over its subjects, and issued laws and administered justice. Like the Chinese across the Pacific, the Incas considered themselves the possessors of the only true civilization; all the peoples living outside the empire were considered barbarians dwelling in outer darkness.

The Incas conquered their empire with a peasant army organized in units of multiples of tens. New regions and peoples were thoroughly incorporated into the imperial system. A census of all people, animals, and

crops was taken; a relief model in clay or stone was made of the new territory; the vast Inca road system, one of the engineering marvels of the Americas before Columbus, was extended to the new territory. The bureaucracy of the empire took over the tasks of imperial government, and the defeated chieftains and their people were taught the Quechua language of the empire. Defeated chieftains were required to visit Cuzco—which means "navel [of the world]" in Quechua—at regular intervals and were often tied by marriage to the imperial dynasty. The conquerors taught the peasants advanced agricultural methods, built fortresses at strategic points, and repaired war damage. Local culture was integrated with imperial culture rather than destroyed. Integration even took place in religion. The gods of the newly conquered people were incorporated into the Inca pantheon or left undisturbed, while the new territories were obliged to take up the worship of the sun, one of the chief deities of the Incas, whose emperor was considered to be a direct descendant and an incarnation of the sun.

Perhaps the most remarkable aspect of the Inca empire was the totalitarian quality of its social organization and life style. It has even been called, incorrectly, the first "socialist state." In addition to military control and cultural integration, statistics were a mainstay of the imperial structure. At least every five years a regular census was taken of every inhabitant, domesticated animal, land unit, harvest, building, and tool in the empire. Beginning in each locale, the statistics were passed up the bureaucratic ladder to Cuzco where they were compiled for the entire empire by a central statistical bureau. This made possible a kind of empire-wide economic planning. The country was dotted with storehouses, where supplies and food were kept in case of famine, making it possible to organize economic relief for areas suffering from drought or other misfortunes. When Pizarro and his men entered the empire in the sixteenth century, they had no difficulty whatsoever in maintaining themselves from these "granaries." In order to facilitate the passage of information along the roads to Cuzco and

THE INCA EMPIRE

Inca Empire
Royal Road

A natural fortress, Machu Picchu was built by the Incas probably after 1440 on a narrow ridge between two mountain peaks. It appears to have been the residence and stronghold of the last Incan ruler after the Spanish conquest had begun. When the ruler died, the city was abandoned and lost until it was rediscovered in 1911.

the distribution of orders to the provinces from the emperor, a system of inns was established for messengers and travelers. Often these were in association with the granaries. Information, both statistical and historical, was recorded by an ingenious system of knotted strings, known as *quipu;* learning to read these required a great deal of education and a superb memory. The Incas had no writing system.

The Inca rulers impressed a vast uniformity over their entire society as a means of maximizing authoritarian social control. The ruling class was made up of three categories of people. First, there was the emperor and his relatives and associates. Second, there were the chiefs of the conquered peoples, and third were those individual Indians who through the performance of feats of valor or acts of merit had gained admission into the ruling class. Under these three groups were the mass of people, who lived in relative poverty compared to the nobility but not in a state of deprivation. Except for those

very few individuals who made their way up the social ladder by their own efforts, the nobility and the masses were completely separated from each other.

In addition to differences in dress and standard of living, the nobility and the masses differed intellectually. At the end of each emperor's reign, an official history of the reign was established by the highest court officials for dissemination among the masses of peasants. This was a carefully calculated story intended to glorify the deceased emperor. Only the nobility were permitted to learn the more general history of the reign. The nobility perpetuated itself through mastery of the arts of war and government in schools in Cuzco; they were completely at the service of the Inca, and their range of interests covered the entire empire. The masses, on the other hand, were required to live and die where they were born, unless given explicit permission by the state to move. Consequently, a kind of social and psychological individualism flourished among the nobility, while the peasants lived in a uniform and highly controlled environment.

The life of the people was organized and controlled down to the most minute activities. The entire society was based on the principle of dualism, or division into two parts. All the people were members of an *ayllu,* an organization of people related socially or by descent. Each *ayllu* had its own section of town or village in which it had to live, and in every town or village square, areas were marked off where each *ayllu* had to stand on public occasions. This encouraged the development of communal solidarity and cooperation which remains to this day an outstanding characteristic of the Peruvian Indians. Family life was also closely regulated. Men and women were required to marry by the ages of twenty-four and eighteen respectively, and annual marriage rites were conducted throughout the empire when those who had not yet chosen their marriage partners were assigned husbands or wives.

The hierarchical uniformity of Inca society found expression in religion too. While the masses worshiped their multitude of gods and spirits, the Incas and the nobility gradually developed a belief in a new and unique deity, who was both abstract and inexpressible. This supreme god eclipsed the sun as the major object of Inca worship. He was above all and encompassed the entire universe. The Incas built only two temples to this new deity, one at Cuzco and one at another spot in the empire. Well-informed early Spanish observers believed that the Incas had discovered the one true God in which they themselves believed.

The Incas and the peoples of the western coast of South America may not have been without knowledge of or influence from peoples living across the Pacific. Archaeological evidence indicates that as early as 3000-1500 B.C. coastal Indians began making pottery similar to pottery being produced in Japan at about the same time; this has given rise to speculation concerning the possibility of stray Japanese fishermen being carried to Ecuador or Peru by winds and currents across the Pacific.[16] There is also an Inca legend about a voyage made into the Pacific as far as Polynesia in the fifteenth century. According to the story, some twenty thousand men on a fleet of rafts made a year's voyage out into the Pacific and brought back objects of great fascination to the Incas. Other evidence of early contact is abundant. Some words in Quechua and Maori, the language of the Polynesian inhabitants of New Zealand, are almost identical. The American sweet potato was found in Polynesia, and American cotton has been interpreted by some botanists as the result of a cross between Peruvian and Asiatic cotton. Even architectural similarities have been noted in some regions. While this evidence is not positive proof of such contact, it cannot be completely ignored.

The ease of the conquest. Many explanations can be offered for the ease with which the Spaniards conquered the high civilizations of Mexico and Peru. Internal social and political disruption is certainly one. In the course of building their confederation, the Aztecs alienated many local tribes who willingly became allies of the Spanish invaders. In Peru the vastness of the empire led the emperor to divide it between his two sons, who rapidly became rivals and enemies; a civil war between them weakened the imperial system shortly before Pizarro's arrival. In Mexico Aztec legends apparently foretold the arrival of strangers resembling the Spaniards, and the *conquistadores* were welcomed into Mexico before the Aztecs realized what they were about. In Peru the long unchallenged authority of the Inca emperors gave them a sense of security and superiority; consequently, they did not destroy the first *conquistador* band of Pizarro and his men, as they easily could have. Nor did the rigid uniformity of the Inca imperial system permit the development of a flexible response to the Spaniards. Like the Chinese in the nineteenth century, the Incas in the sixteenth had become so culturally and psychologically self-centered, because of their mastery of the only world known to them, that they did not recognize their own weakness in the face of new and more advanced European weapons; nor did they understand the historical significance of the European challenge. As in China, so in Mexico and Peru: the high culture was destroyed, but the masses survived, together with some facets of their traditional culture, to become a part of world civilization.

SUMMARY

Most of the Indians of North America never achieved what can be called "civilization," but in Mexico and Central and South America, however, a number of brilliant civilizations emerged—those of the Aztecs, Mayas, and Incas, each with unique characteristics. The Aztecs have been compared to the Romans: they were practical, martial people, skillful at conquest and at governing subject peoples. By contrast, the Mayas have been likened to the Greeks: they were great builders and artists, and they were also scholars and scientists who invented a remarkable calendar, studied astronomy, and pursued mathematics. Of all the American Indians, the Incas should be remembered for developing one of the first totalitarian states in history.

During the many centuries covered by this volume, little has been seen of Africa south of the Sahara. This vast region lay on the periphery of great world movements; and the key to its past has been the factor of isolation. Much of African history, therefore, was unknown, and the achievements of its people usually dismissed as inconsequential. A more accurate evaluation, however, has developed in recent decades. Scholars, while recognizing that Africans did not attain the achievements of Europeans and Asians in the mechanical arts and in the sciences, point out the Africans' significant advances in social organization and in the arts.

Far more advanced than societies in the Americas or in Africa were the civilizations of India, China, Japan, and Southeast Asia. They seemed to reach their height in the period corresponding to Europe's Middle Ages; then they began to decline. The alien Mughuls gave India its most brilliant period, surpassing the glories of the Guptas. The Mughul ruler Akbar is regarded as one of the greatest statesmen of all time. All facets of culture flourished under Mughul rule, but the noblest legacy was in architecture; the Taj Mahal and the buildings of Fathpur Sikri are ample evidence of the genius of Mughul builders.

Conditions in India were reversed in China, for here the alien Mongol rulers were ousted and a native dynasty set about developing the country. A bright period of prosperity, expansion, and cultural activity followed. But the Ming suffered from a serious psychological handicap. The essence of their rule was restoration of the old and suspicion of the strange and new. China became self-satisfied and impervious to new ideas. The inevitable result was decline and, ironically, conquest by another foreign dynasty, the Manchu.

Under the Tokugawa shoguns, the Japanese were even more determined to cut themselves off from the outside world. Like the Ming, they had no use for foreign ways. But new forces, mainly economic, were at work, which would end isolation and abolish forever the institution of the shogunate.

Although strongly influenced by Indian and Chinese cultures, the incredible political and ethnic complexities that characterized Southeast Asia inhibited the growth of the kind of cultural and national self-consciousness that marked China and Japan. Moreover, geographical considerations contributed to the inability of the peoples of this region to develop political unity and stability. These factors were to make Southeast Asia a relatively easy prey for Europe's expanding empires.

In following the detailed accounts of events in Europe and in European colonies, we must not lose sight of these peoples of the other continents, who far outnumbered Europeans and who, in the centuries ahead, would move ever closer to the center of the stage of world history.

Chapter 20

Seek Out, Discover, and Find

**Exploration, Colonization, and
the Commercial Revolution: 1450-1650**

INTRODUCTION. "Be it known that we have given and granted . . . to our well-beloved John Cabot . . . full and free authority, leave, and power to sail to all parts, countries, and seas of the East, of the West, and of the North, under our banners and ensigns . . . to seek out, discover, and find whatsoever islands, countries, regions or provinces of the heathen and infidels whatsoever they be, and in what part of the world soever they be, which before this time have been unknown to all Christians. . . ."[1] So began the letter patent from Henry VII of England authorizing John Cabot in 1497 to make a voyage which was one day to constitute England's claim to vast stretches of the New World. While these instructions were addressed to Cabot, Columbus and other mariners received similar instructions from the sovereigns who authorized their voyages to "seek out, discover, and find" what lay beyond the horizon. Braving vast, uncharted oceans, these mariners persisted in their quest until the earth had been girdled and the "banners and ensigns" of Europe had been planted on every continent.

Before 1500 the people of Europe inhabited an area of four million square miles and existed largely on their own resources, supplemented by a slender trade with Africa and Asia. But within the next 150 years the picture was dramatically altered through the discoveries of new continents and trade routes. The riches of the entire world were funneled into Europe's economy, and the horizons of Europe's people were immensely widened—socially and intellectually as well as geographically.

Who wrought this miracle? First, there were the sea captains—da Gama, who made the first ocean voyage from Europe to India; Columbus, who introduced Europe to a New World; and Magellan, whose expedition ventured ever westward until its weary survivors had sailed completely around the world and dropped anchor once more in their home port. Close on the heels of such captains came the *conquistadores*—the "conquerors"—resourceful and ruthless soldiers like Cortés and Pizarro, who laid the foundations for a vast European empire by overwhelming flourishing native cultures in the New World.

Then came the task of exploiting what had been found and won. The European powers took advantage of the claims of their discoverers and explorers in one of two basic ways—through trade or by colonization. In Africa and Asia the emphasis was on trade; Europeans carried on their business from forts, acting as foreign merchants rather than as settlers. While in Africa their dealings were mostly with primitive tribesmen, in the Far East they faced venerable civilizations and urban cultures. There, they were the barbarians, and when their activities proved offensive by native standards, reprisals could be swift and severe. Because of the bad behavior of the Portuguese, for example, all Europeans found their trade with China, India, and Japan sharply restricted.

The story of European expansion in the New World, on the other hand, is largely that of colonization, of the transplanting of European civilization to a new and exotic environment. Politically, the territories in the Americas were treated as extensions of the mother countries. The Spanish colonies, for example, were ruled directly by the king of Spain; the colonial economy was geared to supplement that of the homeland; and the Spanish priests set out to bring the Indians into the spiritual fold with their Spanish masters. Similarly, the English and French who settled in North America brought with them the economic, political, and social institutions they had known at home.

For the native peoples of the New World, the arrival of the Europeans was cataclysmic. And the impact of the New World on the Old, while obviously quite different, was no less significant. As new stores of wealth were tapped by the immensely lucrative transatlantic trade, Europe's economic center of gravity shifted from the Mediterranean to the Atlantic seaboard; and the rapid influx of gold and silver made possible an unprecedented expansion of the economy. Nor was the revolution confined to economics: new medicines, foods, and beverages became available to Europeans, and even styles of dress were altered. Thus a handful of adventurers, ranging beyond the horizon in quest of El Dorado, the legendary city of gold which symbolized their hopes and dreams, set in motion a train of events which brought significant changes to European society and which ultimately influenced the very history of civilization.

CAPTAINS AND CONQUISTADORES

Ptolemy, the classical geographer. In Roman times the farther a traveler ventured from the Mediterranean basin, the less accurate was the available geographical data. Western Europe, the eastern Mediterranean countries, North Africa, the Red Sea region, Persia, and that part of Central Asia reaching to western India were fairly well known, but the rest of the world stretched north, south, east, and west in uncharted regions about

This map, designed by Ptolemy in the second century, represents the first attempt to project the curved surface of the earth on a flat surface. The outline of the European continent (upper left) is fairly accurate.

which the most extraordinary legends were told. To consolidate all the available information about these mysterious lands was the self-assigned job of the most influential of all classical geographers, Ptolemy (see p. 157).

Forced to rely often on sailors' legends and the tales of travelers, Ptolemy in the second century A.D. constructed a map of the world that was inaccurate in many respects. Yet two of his mistakes encouraged later generations of explorers to sail boldly across the uncharted oceans. Ptolemy's poor calculations resulted in his exaggeration of the width of the known continents so that the ocean between western Europe and eastern Asia looked much smaller than it really is. Furthermore, he underestimated the circumference of the world by five thousand miles. Because men of the fifteenth century still accepted Ptolemy as the chief geographical authority, Columbus was encouraged to sail west from Spain in search of the Asian coast. Had he been aware of the exact distance between Europe and Asia,

he probably would never have attempted such a journey.

Another important error in Ptolemy's map was the inclusion of a strip of land which extended from Africa to Asia, making the Indian Ocean an inland sea. Explorers searched the southern seas for the fictitious territory, known as *terra australis incognita,* and eventually, in 1606, a Dutch captain stumbled on Australia. But other errors in Ptolemy's theorizing had less fortunate results, and some sharply hindered the progress of exploration. One of them was his belief that the habitable world of the North Temperate Zone was separated from the South Temperate Zone by a belt of heat so torrid that it was impenetrable.

Medieval maps, adventurers, and traders. During the Middle Ages devout cartographers made geography a handmaiden of theology. In *Christian Topography,* written about 547, the earth was made flat, with paradise in the east, the Pillars of Hercules in the west, and Jerusalem in the center. Such early medieval maps were curiosities rather than documents of fact. They included lands which no man had ever seen; the oceans were shown abounding in sea dragons, while drawings of elephants and more fanciful animals were used to fill up empty land spaces, thereby adding to the picturesqueness of the map as well as conveniently concealing the ignorance of the map maker. However, by the end of the Middle Ages men were learning more about geography. Books on astronomy taught that the earth was a sphere; and by the middle of the fourteenth century a number of European travelers were venturing beyond their own continent.

Prime examples of the medieval adventurers were the Norsemen, who crossed the Atlantic as early as the tenth century. In about 982 Eric the Red, son of a Norwegian noble, was banished from the Norse settlements in Iceland and sailed west to Greenland, which may have been discovered earlier in the century by Celtic refugees from Ireland, fleeing Viking raids on their homeland. Eric founded two settlements on the western coast of Greenland, which existed until about 1500 when they mysteriously vanished. It now appears that the first European to set foot on the North American coast was Bjarni Herjolfson. In 985 Bjarni was blown off course while sailing from Iceland to Greenland and made a landfall in Newfoundland. About fifteen years later Leif, son of Eric the Red, retraced Bjarni's route and named the country *Vinland* (Wineland) because of its wooded, vine-covered shore. A number of other voyages were made to Vinland, whose lumber was highly prized in treeless Greenland. Apparently no permanent settlement was made in Vinland, although archaeologists have recently discovered what appears to be the remains of a Viking camp in Newfoundland at L'Anse au Meadow.[2]

Thus, the Norse sailed the arctic waters in open boats with neither chart nor compass five hundred years before Columbus dared the crossing in warmer waters. But monumental as these voyages were, their implications were lost on contemporary Europeans, and they added little or nothing to European knowledge of geography.

In the thirteenth and fourteenth centuries a number of Europeans, many of them Christian missionaries, journeyed overland to the Far East. The most famous of the travelers was Marco Polo (see p. 298). But the exploits of the fourteenth century had little permanent effect because of political changes in Asia in the last decades of that century. The Mongol dynasty in China, which had been friendly to European missionaries and merchants, was overthrown, and the succeeding Ming rulers proved anti-Christian. Meanwhile, the Turks with their fanatic conversion to Islam had overrun western Asia. These two developments put an end to further European penetration into the Orient. Although trade continued at certain terminals controlled by the Muslims, travel was stopped.

The search for new routes. The three major routes by which trade flowed from the Far East to Europe had existed since Roman times (see map, p. 166). The northern one cut across Central Asia and the Caspian and Black seas to Constantinople (Byzantium); the middle route went by sea along the coasts of India and Persia through the Persian Gulf and the Euphrates valley to Antioch; and the southern route utilized the monsoon winds to strike across the Indian Ocean and up the Red Sea to Alexandria in Egypt.

During the fifteenth century the commerce that flowed westward to Europe was rich indeed, even though the expansion of the Turks greatly reduced the importance of the northern route across Asia. The most important imports into Europe were spices—pepper, cinnamon, nutmeg, ginger, and cloves—highly valued as condiments and preservatives for food. Also in great demand were Chinese silk, Indian cotton cloth, and various precious stones.

The Mediterranean carrying trade in oriental goods was in the hands of Venice and other Italian city-states, which wielded an extensive and lucrative monopoly. Since the Arabs held a similar monopoly east of the Mediterranean, oriental goods were sold in the West at many times their price in India. As the demand for the products of the East increased during the latter half of the fifteenth century, the rulers of the

The tremendous feats of exploration accomplished during this era never would have been possible without the introduction of technological innovations. In a romanticized seventeenth-century print (left) entitled the "Light of Navigation," Dutch sailors are taught the use of the globe, hourglass, cross-stave, astrolabe, and dividers. The first printed star chart (below), another invaluable tool of navigation, was engraved in 1515 by Albrecht Dürer with the help of two astronomers. The chart helped the navigator identify a constellation and then locate his position relative to it by the use of an astrolabe. Improvements in shipbuilding also aided in discovery. John Hawkins, treasurer of the British navy in the late sixteenth century, designed the hull of his ships like the body of a fish, making them the most efficient ships at sea.

new nations of western Europe became aware that an adverse balance of trade was draining their coined money away to Italy and the East. They determined to find new trade routes of their own, and, as rulers of powerful nation-states, they had the resources to support the stupendous feats of discovery and conquest that were needed.

It was the Portuguese who spearheaded the drive to find oceanic routes that would provide cheaper and easier access to oriental products. By the time the monarchs of Aragon and Castile had ousted the last of the Muslims from the Iberian peninsula in 1492, the Portuguese had rounded the southern tip of Africa and the Orient was clearly within their reach. The Spaniards in turn embarked on their own career of exploration and discovery. The combined results explain the preëminence of the peoples of the Iberian peninsula prior to 1600 in carving out rich commercial empires to the east and opening up a New World to the west.

Prince Henry the Navigator. The driving force behind the brilliant Portuguese achievements in exploration and discovery was Prince Henry the Navigator (1394-1460). Born the third son of King John I of Portugal, Henry devoted his life to scientific exploration and the extension of Portugal's empire and commerce.

We will recall that because of Ptolemy's mistaken views on the distance between Europe and Asia, many mariners believed that contact could be made directly between the two continents by sailing west. Still other sailors maintained that if Africa could be circumnavigated, a route could be opened to India and China. For more than forty years Prince Henry pored over maps and sent forth expedition after expedition to unravel the secrets of the African coastline.

He saw to it that his sailors were the best-equipped mariners of their time. To do this he employed skilled cartographers and navigators to construct accurate maps, and under his direction the caravel, the finest vessel afloat for long voyages, was developed. By utilizing the lanteen rig, the triangular sail developed by the Arabs, the caravel revolutionized sailing by enabling ships to tack into the wind. Augmenting Henry's

innovations were other navigation aids. In the twelfth century the Europeans set their course with the aid of a magnetic needle floating on a straw in a bowl of water. By the time Henry's sailors were setting sail, the compass consisted of a needle which pivoted·on a card showing the points of the compass. During the fifteenth century another great aid to navigation came into general use—the astrolabe, a graduated brass circle by which the altitude of stars could be estimated and latitudes more accurately measured.

The African voyages. Although Henry died before any of the numerous expeditions he sent forth had explored the entire length of Africa, his mariners did not fail him. In 1488 Bartholomew Diaz rounded the southern tip of Africa which he dubbed "Cape of Storms," from which point he noticed that the coast swung northeast. But his disgruntled crew forced him to turn back without investigating the eastern shoreline. Diaz' ships sailed back to Lisbon with the good news that a sea passage south of Africa did exist. Pleased with the prospect of soon finding a direct sea route to India, King John II of Portugal renamed the Cape of Storms with a less forbidding title, "Cape of Good Hope."

The final stage in the African voyages was reached by Vasco da Gama, who commanded the African expedition of 1497. His daring was demonstrated after his four ships had arrived at the Cape Verde Islands. Instead of hugging the coastline as his predecessors had done, da Gama fearlessly struck out into the Atlantic and sailed for ninety-three days in a direct course toward the Cape of Good Hope. Rounding the Cape, he pushed northward into Arab waters. Finally he procured an Arab pilot who brought him, after a sail of twenty-three days across the Indian Ocean, to Calicut on the west coast of India. It is amusing to read that the Portuguese mistook the Hindus for Christians (because they were not Muslims) and even reverently attended a religious ceremony. "They took us to a large church," states the journal of the voyage. "Many saints were painted on the walls of the church, wearing crowns. They were painted variously, with teeth protruding an inch from the mouth, and four or five arms."[3]

The Portuguese expedition incurred the enmity of the Arabs, whose Indian trading monopoly had been broken by da Gama. They delayed the return voyage, and not until July 1499 did da Gama drop anchor in Lisbon. He had lost half his ships and one third of his men through scurvy and other misfortunes. But his cargo of pepper and cinnamon was worth sixty times the cost of the expedition.

Lured by such fantastic profits another expedition set sail the following year and established a permanent base south of Calicut at Cochin. The Portuguese soon acquired a monopoly over trade in the Indian Ocean, and by 1516 their ships had reached Canton in China. The king of Portugal assumed the impressive title "Lord of the Conquest, Navigation, and Commerce of Ethiopia, Arabia, Persia, and China."

Columbus discovers the New World. Meanwhile, Spanish ambitions for riches and prestige were realized through the exploits of a Genoese sailor named Christopher Columbus (1451?-1506). His son described him as

a well built man of more than medium stature . . . but neither fat nor thin. He had an aquiline nose and his eyes were light in color; his complexion too was light, but kindling to a vivid red. In youth his hair was blond, but when he came to his thirtieth year it all turned white. In . . . the adornment of his person he was always . . . modest.[4]

Columbus believed that Japan was less than 3000 nautical miles from Europe (the actual distance is 10,600 nautical miles) and that it could be reached in one or two months by sailing westward. To finance a voyage, he sought the support of Ferdinand and Isabella, who agreed to sponsor him. In August 1492 Columbus set sail from Spain with three small ships. On October 12 he landed on a small island in the West Indies. After he returned to Spain, Columbus announced that he had found the route to Asia, and the Spanish monarchs proclaimed him "Admiral of the Ocean Sea, Viceroy and Governor of the Islands that he has discovered in the Indies." Even after da Gama's voyage had

opened up the eastward route to India, Columbus steadfastly refused to acknowledge that what he himself had discovered was in fact a massive obstacle on the route to the Far East. Although he made three more voyages to the New World in a vain attempt to find a direct opening to the Asian mainland, Columbus had already changed the course of history, though he did not know it. A New World had been revealed; old geographical views had been shattered; and the entire history of Europe was soon to be affected by the discovery of the new lands.

Spain and Portugal divide the new lands. An immediate repercussion of Columbus' first voyage was the destruction of Portugal's monopoly over discovery. Some sort of compromise had to be worked out between the two countries, and the Spanish monarchs invited the pope to define the pagan areas which Spain and Portugal might claim. In 1493 the Spanish pope, Alexander VI, issued the Bull of Demarcation, which drew a line from north to south running one hundred leagues west of the Azores and proclaimed that all heathen lands west of this line as far as the Indies were reserved for Spain. The Portuguese protested, claiming that this arrangement would confine their operations too closely to the African coast. By the Treaty of Tordesillas (1494) Spain agreed to have the line moved farther west. This new demarcation later enabled Portugal to claim Brazil after Cabral's sighting of South America. In 1529 another treaty fixed a similar demarcation line in the Eastern Hemisphere (see map, p. 613).

Pedro Cabral was a Portuguese commander who, in 1500, while sailing along the African coast on his way to the Indies, bore so far west to avoid the treacherous calms off the Gulf of Guinea that he came in sight of the South American continent. It was apparently unpromising territory, and Portugal was already overextended; thus for fifty years little was done to settle Brazil other than to dump criminals there.

The search for riches drove the Spaniards to organize many expeditions to chart the coastlines and to penetrate the interior of the New World. One such enterprise was particularly successful. Having heard from

GREENLAND

NORTH AMERICA

ATLANTIC

Cabot

EUROPE

ASIA

CANARY IS.

Columbus

WEST INDIES

CANARY IS.

CAPE VERDE IS.

Diaz

AFRICA

CHINA

JAPAN

Xavier

PACIFIC

OCEAN

Magellan

INDIA

ST. LAZARD
(PHILIPPINES)

PANAMA

SOUTH AMERICA

OCEAN

da Gama

da Gama

ZANZIBAR

SUMATRA

BORNEO

INDIAN

OCEAN

MADAGASCAR

"Magellan"

PACIFIC

OCEAN

Cape of Good Hope

Magellan's Crew

TO SPAIN

TO PORTUGAL

Str. of Magellan

Treaty of Tordesillas – 1494 →

← Pope's Line of Demarcation – 1493

Treaty of Saragossa – 1529 →

Indians of a vast ocean only a short distance to the west, Vasco de Balboa led a band of 190 Spaniards across the Isthmus of Panama. On September 25, 1513, Balboa climbed to the summit of a hill from which he beheld the Pacific Ocean—and in that act paved the way for European exploration of the largest single portion of the world's surface.

Magellan sails around the world. Ferdinand Magellan, a Portuguese navigator in the service of Spain, found a sea route into the Pacific. Encouraged by Balboa's discovery of the short distance between the two oceans, Magellan believed it was possible to sail around South America just as Diaz had rounded Africa. After outfitting Magellan with a fleet of five small ships which were "very old and patched up," the Spanish king ordered him to make straightway for the East Indies. In August 1520 Magellan made his memorable discovery of the strait which bears his name. Between huge ice-clad mountains and through tortuous passages the small ships

made their way, taking thirty-eight days to journey 320 miles. Finally they sailed out upon the western ocean, which looked so calm after the stormy straits that Magellan termed it "Pacific." After hugging the coast northward for some time, Magellan set off northwest to cross the unknown expanse of the Pacific.

The hardships that Magellan and his men suffered have been vividly portrayed for us by the chronicler on the expedition:

We were three months and twenty days without getting any kind of fresh food. We ate biscuit, which was no longer biscuit, but powder of biscuits swarming with worms .... We drank yellow water that had been putrid for many days. We also ate some ox hides that covered the top of the mainyard to prevent the yard from chafing the shrouds ... and often we ate sawdust from boards. Rats were sold for one-half ducado apiece. ... But above all the other misfortunes the following was the worst: The gums of both the lower and upper teeth of some of our men swelled, so that they could not eat under any circumstances and therefore died. . . . We sailed about four thousand leagues during those three months and twenty days through an open stretch in that Pacific Sea. In truth it was very pacific, for during that time we did not suffer any storm. . . . Had not God and His blessed Mother given us so good weather we would all have died of hunger in that exceeding vast sea. Of a verity I believe no such voyage will ever be made [again].[5]

Early in the spring of 1521 Magellan came to the Philippine Islands, where he was slain during a skirmish with the natives. One of his ships, the *Victoria,* proceeded to the East Indies, crossed the Indian Ocean, rounded the Cape of Good Hope, and dropped anchor in a Spanish harbor in 1522. The *Victoria*'s cargo from the East Indies paid for the cost of the entire expedition.

The remarkable achievement of Magellan entitles him to rank with da Gama and Columbus. Magellan's tiny vessel had taken three years to circumnavigate the world, but henceforth no one could doubt that the

The Spanish troops, aided by Indian allies, storm the main gate of Tenochtitlán in this illustration from a sixteenth-century Aztec manuscript.

earth was round and that the Americas constituted a New World.

Cortés conquers Mexico. Thus far we have concentrated chiefly on the herculean labors of the great sea captains and the discoveries they made. While the Portuguese soon profited from their hold on the rich oriental trade, the Spaniards found that the islands and coasts of the New World did not immediately produce the harvest of riches which they had eagerly sought. Such wealth was not to be found along the seashore but in the unknown hinterland, where rich indigenous cultures flourished. Penetration of inland areas was the work of the *conquistadores,* the courageous but independent-minded and often brutal conquerors who looted whole native empires and planted the Spanish flag from California to the tip of South America.

In the same year that Magellan set forth (1519), the Spanish governor of Cuba dispatched Hernando Cortés on an expedition to Mexico, from which had come rumors of a great Aztec empire, flowing with gold. Montezuma, ruler of the Aztecs, had thousands of warriors, while Cortés had about six hundred men. But the Spaniards were equipped with horses, armor, and gunpowder, all unknown to the Aztecs. Two other factors aided the Europeans: the discontent of many subject tribes, which looked for a chance to break the Aztec rule; and an ancient Mexican legend which prophesied that the Aztecs would one day be conquered by the white-skinned descendants of an ancient god-king who had been repudiated by their ancestors.

Having made the fateful decision to march inland on the capital, Tenochtitlán, Cortés destroyed his ships to prevent his men from turning back. Montezuma sent embassies with lavish gifts to Cortés along with orders to leave the country, but the gifts only excited the gold-hungry adventurers to push on to the capital. In time they climbed out of the mosquito-infested coast lands and across spectacular mountains to enter the valley of Mexico, which contained cities of startling magnificence. Awaiting them in splendor was Montezuma, who warily welcomed them to his capital. Cortés treacherously made a virtual prisoner of Montezuma and through his cooperation ruled peacefully until a popular uprising drove the Spaniards from the capital—and gave them an excuse to plunder and destroy it.

Yet Cortés was more than a plunderer; he built a new City of Mexico on the site of Montezuma's capital and demonstrated administrative skills in adapting the former Aztec confederacy to Spanish rule. He and his men explored the new domain thoroughly, brought the Indian tribes under control, introduced European seeds and plants into Mexican soil, and substituted Christianity for the Aztec religion.

Pizarro in Peru. The conquest of the Incas in Peru was carried out with less skill and more enduring ill effects than Cortés' exploit in Mexico. Obsessed by tales of a rich and mighty empire in South America, a tough, illiterate peasant's son named Francisco Pizarro determined to explore and conquer it. In 1531 Pizarro sailed from Panama with 180 men and 27 horses. Landing on the Peruvian coast, the small band made its way across the barren mountains into the interior, where they seized the Incan monarch Atahualpa.

Attempting to buy his freedom by paying a huge ransom, Atahualpa offered to have a room measuring seventeen by twelve feet filled to a height of some seven feet with plates and vessels of gold and to have it filled twice over with silver. Magnificent treasures—"fountains designed to emit sparkling jets of gold" and golden trees, plants, animals, and birds—were melted down into solid bullion. Despite this ransom, the Spaniards did not release the emperor but instead sentenced him on trumped-up charges to be burned to death. In the end, because Atahualpa accepted Christian Baptism, he was merely strangled. The imprisonment and death of its ruler rendered the highly centralized Incan government incapable of effective, organized resistance; and Pizarro soon captured the capital.

Pizarro's effort to rule through Incan puppets failed; the Incas fled to the mountains and sought to resist the newcomers. But European military advantages overcame all armed opposition. The natives died at fantastic rates from European diseases and from the forced labor and cruel punishment inflicted by the conquerors.

For forty years after the conquest, anarchy prevailed in Peru. Within a decade civil war broke out among the conquerors, and Pizarro was murdered. When the Spanish royal government sought to protect the oppressed Indians from their colonial masters, Gonzalo Pizarro, a brother of Francisco, set up a government independent of Spain. But Madrid dispatched officials and soldiers to arrest the unruly *conquistadores* and to pacify the area so that silver could be mined for Spain and conversion of the natives to Christianity could proceed. Not until near the end of the sixteenth century was Spanish authority securely established over Peru.

The conquistadores fan out from Peru. The sixteenth century also saw the exploration and conquest of the remaining part of South America, largely through Spanish efforts. Gonzalo Pizarro led a large band into the valley of the Amazon, so called by the Europeans because of the fierce female warriors encountered there. The jungles which bordered the river were so forbidding that the Spanish allowed the area to slip into the hands of the Portuguese, who eventually took possession of the vast hinterland of Brazil. Another expedition founded Bogotá in what is now Colombia; still other Spaniards established the city of Buenos Aires along the banks of the Rio de la Plata. In time Spanish dominions in South America formed a huge, uninterrupted semicircle (see Reference Map 11).

Spanish penetration into North America. Using Mexico and the West Indies as bases, the Spanish explorers searched what is now the southern part of the United States for the treasures which rumors planted there. That the expeditions failed to find gold or other riches does not detract from the tremendous progress they made in opening up new and potentially wealthy areas. Not only mythical treasure but an equally mythical Fountain of Youth attracted Spanish *conquistadores*. In 1521 Juan Ponce de León, whose gold and slaves had already made him wealthy in Puerto Rico, lost his life trying to find the Fountain of Youth in Florida.

Explorers' journals were very popular in Europe during the age of discovery. Top left is an illustration from Magellan's journal showing his men fighting off Indians on the coast of what is today Ecuador and on the island of Puna just off the coast. In 1597 the Dutch explorer Willem Barents, while searching for a Northeast Passage to China above Russia, was trapped in the arctic. These engravings from his journal depict his men leaving their icebound ship (bottom left) and show the shelter in which he and his men were forced to spend the winter (top). James Cook, an eighteenth-century English explorer, laid the foundation for two of Britain's greatest colonies, Australia and New Zealand. His journal describing his expeditions to the South Pacific contained these prints showing a traditional native dance on Hapaee (center) and the domestic life of the Indians of Tierra del Fuego, an island at the southernmost tip of South America (bottom).

Eighteen years later Hernando de Soto, whose participation in the conquest of Peru had gained him a fortune, landed in Florida with a company of some six hundred adventurers. His search for treasure took him through the southern United States, and De Soto was possibly the first white man to sight the Mississippi River. He died without finding any treasure, and his followers buried him in the Mississippi.

Another ambitious expedition also failed to locate the riches it sought but in the process investigated much of southwestern United States. Tales had persisted of a fabled land north of Mexico containing seven cities with golden towers, and in 1540 Francisco de Coronado set out from Mexico with a large band to find them. But the fabled cities turned out to be only adobe pueblos. In his vain search Coronado appears to have penetrated as far as Kansas, becoming the first European to behold the vast herds of buffalo roaming the American plains. The adventurer returned embittered by failure, and the Spanish authorities concluded that there was little to be gained in occupying the area north of the silver mines of Mexico.

Drawn by Sir Humphrey Gilbert in 1582, this polar map shows a clear northwest route to the East. The mistaken belief in such a route helped stimulate the exploration and colonization of Canada.

English search for the Northwest Passage. Both in exploration and conquest in the New World and in the economic and political changes that resulted in Europe, the period from 1492 to 1650 was one of Iberian preeminence. As we shall see later in the chapter, the riches from the Americas made Spain a wealthy nation but at the same time contributed to its eventual decline. It was largely after 1650 that the nation-states along the northern Atlantic seaboard—Holland, France, and England—really came into their own in the New World. Yet before 1650 these northern nations had not been completely idle. The division of the overseas world between Spain and Portugal, as set forth by the Bull of Demarcation and the Treaty of Tordesillas, aroused little enthusiasm among other European powers, and it was not long before France, England, and Holland encroached on the private preserves of both Portugal and Spain.

In 1497—the same year in which da Gama embarked for India—John Cabot, an Italian mariner financed by the merchants of Bristol in England, sailed across the North Atlantic in a small ship manned by only eighteen men. Although the close-fisted Henry VII had contributed no money to defray the expenses, we have seen the liberal authority which the king bestowed on Cabot (p. 606). Manned by English sailors, Cabot's ship headed off across the Atlantic, supposedly in the direction of China. After a turbulent six weeks' voyage, the expedition dropped anchor off the northern coast of the New World. When Cabot returned to England, Henry VII rewarded him with ten pounds, the title of Grand Admiral, and the right to make another voyage. Cabot made his second voyage in 1498, coasting along the eastern shore of America in a vain attempt to find a passage to the Orient.

Cabot was the first European after the hardy Norse sailors to land on the mainland of North America; and, what was most important, his discovery laid the foundation for England's claim to the whole rich continent. Thus for ten pounds and a title England eventually acquired all of Canada and the territory along the Atlantic coast which constituted the thirteen American colonies—

Pictured above is New Amsterdam (New York) as it appeared around 1640. In the center foreground are the gallows, to the right the West India Company stores (G), and to the left the governor's house (D), a church (B), the jail (C), and the fort (A).

certainly an excellent business transaction.

For the next hundred years English seamen tried to reach China through the illusive Northwest Passage, a sea route believed to exist north of Canada. Since it was possible to sail south around Africa and South America, it was felt that there must be a similar route around North America. Many explorers lost their lives in vain attempts to discover the Northwest Passage. Although similar expeditions trying to reach China by way of the Northeast Passage above Russia also failed, one of them reached Archangel and was granted trading privileges by Tsar Ivan the Terrible (see p. 437).

French explorations of inland America. France also joined in the search for the Northwest Passage. In 1523 Francis I commissioned the Florentine mariner Giovanni da Verazzano to investigate the coast from North Carolina to Newfoundland. Eleven years later Jacques Cartier was sent on the first of two voyages that explored the St. Lawrence River as far as the present city of Montreal. These expeditions gave France its claim to sovereignty over eastern North America, a claim which duplicated England's.

Not until after its Wars of Religion did France resume its activities in the St. Lawrence region. Sponsored by the energetic first Bourbon ruler, Henry IV, Samuel de Champlain not only founded the first successful French overseas colony at Quebec (1608) but also journeyed over the lake which bears his name and westward to the Great Lakes. In 1673 Louis Joliet, a fur trader, and Father Marquette, a Jesuit missionary, reached the Mississippi River and followed it as far south as Arkansas in the hope of finding a short route to the Pacific. Nine years later René de La Salle explored the Mississippi to its mouth, taking possession of the entire territory and naming it *Louisiana* in honor of Louis XIV.

The Dutch in America. Appearing somewhat later on the scene than the English and French were the Dutch. Their interest in the New World coincided with the rise of the United Provinces (Holland) to a position of political independence and great economic strength during the first half of the seventeenth century. Dutch ambitions to find a shorter route to the Far East caused them to hire the English explorer Henry Hudson, who in 1609 sailed up the river that now bears his name. Reports that the land was fertile and that furs could be obtained from the Indians led to the founding of trading posts on Manhattan Island and near present-day Albany. In 1621 the Dutch West India Company was founded for the purpose of trading in western Africa and the Americas. As part of its work, the company founded New Amsterdam on Manhattan Island and permanently colonized Guiana, Curaçao, and Aruba in the Caribbean area.

The gigantic strides which had been made in exploring the unknown parts of the world excited Europeans even more than have the results of space exploration in our own day. They had discovered not only new sea routes to familiar lands but also entirely strange areas. The Portuguese had explored the whole mysterious coast of Africa, and Columbus had opened two entirely unfamiliar continents to exploration and exploitation. The original explorers were followed by a host of adventurers looking for riches and lucrative trade. In the process, the rough outlines of the whole world were charted.

EUROPE INVADES THE EAST

Portugal's eastern empire. Before the exciting era of exploration began to wane, the Europeans were faced with the problem of exploiting their newly found territories. Depending on the area, the newcomers concentrated their efforts on mining, trapping, trading, or colonizing—or, in some cases, on a combination of these activities. In virtually every case, the natives suffered. Only in a few instances, notably in the Far East, were the indigenous people able to enforce their own policies. In most extreme contrast was Africa, where the natives were captured and sold as slaves.

In the late fifteenth century, as we have seen, Portuguese mariners had pushed their way south along the African coast. To ensure their toe hold in Africa, the Portuguese built fortified posts along the coast and on rivers such as the Congo and the Gambia. In 1497 the Portuguese began to develop a colony in Angola. On the east side of the continent the newcomers forced the Arabs to acknowledge their supremacy, and Portuguese traders settled along the coast and on the island of Zanzibar.

Early in the sixteenth century Afonso de Albuquerque, the greatest of all Portuguese viceroys (1509-1515), resolved to consolidate his country's position in Africa and in the East. As a realist, he saw that Portugal could wrest commercial supremacy from the Arabs

only by force, and he therefore devised a plan to establish forts at strategic sites which would dominate the trade routes and also protect Portuguese interests on land. The western end of the Arab trade routes was partially sealed off: Ormuz at the mouth of the Persian Gulf (see Reference Map 11) was captured, but the Portuguese attempt to close the entrance to the Red Sea at Aden was only temporarily successful. To obtain a major base for a permanent fleet in the Indian Ocean, Albuquerque in 1510 seized Goa on the coast of India, which the Portuguese held until 1961. From Goa the Portuguese dominated the Indian ports that had supplied the Arab traders.

Albuquerque next set about securing control of the trade with the East Indies and China. His first objective was Malacca, a large trading center on the Malay peninsula. The capture of Malacca in 1511 was of inestimable value; it controlled the narrow strait through which most Far Eastern trade moved, and it became the springboard for further eastward penetration. The first Portuguese ship reached Canton on the south coast of China in 1516, but it was not until 1557 that the Portuguese gained a permanent base in China at Macao, which they still hold. About 1516, also, the first trading post was established in the rich Moluccas, or Spice Islands, source of the finest spices.

Thus did Portugal in the sixteenth century develop the first European commercial empire through its control of most of the traffic between India and Europe as well as the trade between India and the Far East. Arab traders were largely cut off from Indian commerce, while Venice and Genoa suffered serious losses. Portugal's greatest poet, Luis de Camoëns (1524-1580), in 1572 celebrated his compatriots' overseas achievements in a memorable epic poem, *The Lusiads* ("The Portuguese"):

In golden treasures rich, distant Cathay,
And all the farthest Islands of the East,
And all the seas, to them shall homage pay.[6]

An already lucrative trade was vastly augmented when the Portuguese began to export slaves from Africa in 1541. Envying the rich profits, other nations—England, Holland, France, and Sweden—began to send in rival expeditions, and Portugal was forced on the defensive. In 1642 the Dutch drove the Portuguese out of the Gold Coast, and this rich trade and slaving area was left to the other Europeans, especially the Dutch and English. Built by rival slavers, some of the mighty forts with their drawbridges, auction rooms, dungeons, and massive stone walls can still be seen along the African coast.

Portugal's star was destined to set for many reasons, not the least of which was that the country was too small to defend its many interests abroad. In a land of a million and a half people, it became difficult to recruit the quota of men necessary to maintain such a vast trading empire; and as the man-power shortage increased, the quality of recruits went down. The morale in the colonies deteriorated with the influx of banished criminals, the easy but illegal acquisition of riches, the debilitating climate, and the inefficiency and corruption of the colonial governments. Portugal was not only dislodged from the Gold Coast; in the latter part of the seventeenth century the Arabs succeeded in reclaiming many of their trading centers on the east side of Africa. However, the Portuguese still hold Angola and Mozambique.

The religious intolerance of the Portuguese hastened their decline in the East. When first in India, they harassed only the Muslims, asking no mercy and giving none. After 1540 the respect which had been accorded the Hindus was destroyed by a Church injunction against the Hindu rites and temples. The situation worsened as the Inquisition appeared in India. Refusing to dwell in Portuguese territory under such conditions, the Hindu merchants left in huge numbers. The loss of their trade seriously impaired the economic life in Goa and other cities.

Dutch inroads in the East. Portuguese decline was further accelerated by attacks on their commercial empire launched by the Dutch and the English—the beginning of a world-wide struggle over empire that would last until 1763.

Two events facilitated Dutch encroachment on the Portuguese monopoly of oriental trade. One was the Netherlands revolt against Spanish rule, and the other was the Spanish acquisition of Portugal. After the Dutch had declared themselves independent of Spain in 1581, they looked on Spain's trade and colonies as fair game. A year later, when the two crowns of the Iberian peninsula were joined, the Dutch felt free to attack Portuguese territory in eastern waters. Furthermore, the Dutch had previously enjoyed a rich trade carrying oriental goods from Lisbon to the ports of northern Europe; this traffic ceased when Spain took control of Portuguese ports. If Dutch trade was to survive, the Hollanders had to capture its source in the East.

In the 1590's a number of Dutch companies were formed to finance trading expeditions to the Far East. They concentrated their efforts on the Malay archipelago, preferring that region to India, where the Portuguese were in greater force. Because competition lowered their profits, in 1602 the Dutch companies amalgamated into the Dutch East India Company. The government gave this powerful body the right to trade and rule in the area stretching from the Cape of Good Hope eastward to the Strait of Magellan. It was the Dutch East India Company that broke the power of the Portuguese in the islands of the Malay archipelago.

The governor-general of the East Indies who was appointed in 1618 might be called the Albuquerque of the Dutch. This administrator, Jan Pieterszoon Coen, laid the foundations for the Dutch empire in the East Indies. Whereas Albuquerque had felt that it was sufficient to occupy strategic points along the sea routes, Coen believed that the Dutch had to control the actual areas of production as well. He built a fortified trading station at Batavia on Java, a site which eventually became the capital of the Dutch East Indies, including Sumatra and the Moluccas. Dutch monopoly of the spice trade became complete after they drove the Portuguese from Malacca (1641) and Ceylon (1658), the latter the main source of cinnamon. As a port of call on the long journey to the Far East, the Dutch in 1652 established a colony at Cape Town on the southern tip of Africa.

The English gain a foothold in India. While the Dutch East India Company was exploiting the Malay archipelago, its English counterpart was staking out claims in India at the expense of the Portuguese. In 1600 Queen Elizabeth incorporated the British East India Company, granting it a monopoly of trade from the Cape of Good Hope eastward to the Strait of Magellan. The company soon established numerous outposts in India, on the islands of the Malay archipelago, and even in Japan. By 1622 the company had put the Portuguese posts on the Persian Gulf out of business, and in 1639 it acquired Madras. Through political stratagems, bribes, diplomacy, and exploitation of weak native rulers, the company prospered in India, where it was at times the most powerful political force in the subcontinent. Although the company failed to obtain a permanent foothold either in the East Indies, where the Dutch were too powerful, or in Japan, it found India and the Red Sea area rich enough.

Europeans unwelcome in China. When the Portuguese first arrived in Canton in 1516, they were given the same privileges that Persian and Arab merchants had enjoyed for centuries. In response, the Portuguese behaved very badly, scorning the customs of the sophisticated inhabitants, and treating the "heathen" with arrogance and cruelty.

A typical case of violence was one Portuguese captain's actions at Canton. This braggart sailor built a small fort, erected a gallows, and scandalized the Chinese by hanging one of his own men. Later he was discovered buying Chinese boys and girls who had been kidnaped. To climax his violent acts, he refused to leave port when

Portuguese ships are shown anchored at the port of Macao on the Chinese coast in this sixteenth-century engraving.

AMACAO.

ordered, waging a bloody skirmish in the city streets. Tales which Chinese officials had heard from merchants returning from India, the Persian coast, and the East Indies were now confirmed: the Portuguese first came to a new land in the guise of peaceful traders, but as soon as they gained a foothold, they used violence to establish their own authority. The upshot of the incidents was the banning of the foreigners from Chinese waters in 1522.

Twenty years later the Portuguese reappeared at a coastal town whose officials either had forgotten previous events or else risked safety for the sake of profitable trading. At first all went well, and hundreds of Portuguese flocked to the city. But when the foreigners felt themselves powerful enough, they reverted to their old practices and began to pillage and murder. Their anger aroused, the embittered city officials attacked the Portuguese fort and slew all who could not escape. It is little wonder that westerners earned the nickname "ocean devils." However, because trade was mutually profitable to both Chinese and foreign merchants, in 1557 the Portuguese were granted the right to trade at Macao. There, under close surveillance and subject to many strict regulations, the "ocean devils" conducted business. Stemming from this period is the mutual suspicion and hostility which characterized Sino-European relations in the nineteenth and early twentieth centuries.

A somewhat friendlier contact occurred when Jesuit missionaries arrived in China during the second half of the sixteenth century. St. Francis Xavier, who had made converts in Goa, Malacca, and Japan, died before reaching the Chinese mainland; but his followers carried on the work, converting many important persons at the imperial court and in the provinces and thereby gaining protection for Christians generally.

Japan rejects European contacts. About 1542 three Portuguese ships from Macao were driven far off their course and landed at one of the southern Japanese islands. Before long, others visited the islands and began trading. Hearing about Japan after he had sailed from Lisbon for the Far East, St. Francis Xavier went there and started to convert the inhabitants. After Xavier's death, his work was carried on by other Jesuit missionaries. Within thirty years Japanese converts to Christianity numbered about 150,000.

Suspicion on the part of the Japanese rulers that Christianity was merely a cloak for political usurpation was reinforced by the bigotry of many Christians and by economic exploitation on the part of various unscrupulous Portuguese merchants. The regent Hideyoshi (d. 1598) instituted a policy of persecuting the Jesuits and their converts. Some priests were killed, but many others continued their activities in secret. However, later rulers continued and strengthened Hideyoshi's anti-Christian policy. In 1614 priests and churches, as well as the acceptance of Christianity by any Japanese subject, were outlawed. In desperation the remaining Christians unsuccessfully revolted in 1637, and a year later the final expulsion edict was proclaimed:

For the future, let none, so long as the Sun illuminates the world, presume to sail to Japan, not even in the quality of ambassadors, and this declaration is never to be revoked on pain of death.[7]

Except for a small, closely watched Dutch post at Nagasaki, the islands were closed to western contact until 1853.

The Philippines, Spanish trading stop. In the Far East, Spanish energies were concentrated primarily on the Philippine Islands. Despite Magellan's fatal visit there, the Spanish did not occupy the islands until 1565. After that, cargoes of Chinese goods were transported from the Philippines to Mexico and from there to Spain. By this complicated route, Spain enjoyed some of the oriental commerce about which Columbus had dreamed. Spanish officials and missionaries brought Christianity and a degree of European civilization to the islands, which were henceforth a corner of the Far East fundamentally oriented toward the West, in contrast to Japan and China.

Renewal of East-West contact. The remarkable series of geographical discoveries which began in the fifteenth century and carried intrepid European explorers, soldiers, traders, and missionaries to the ends of the earth recalls a similar movement in the second and third centuries A.D. when rich contacts in commerce and culture existed among three intercommunicating empires—the Graeco-Roman, the Indian, and the Chinese. But the fourth century witnessed the decline of Rome and depredations along the trade routes. Other factors (discussed in Chapter 6) weakened and ultimately destroyed the lines of contact. For nearly a thousand years there was little exchange or communication between East and West.

Until the fifteenth century civilizations in the Near East, India, and China had been fully as advanced as those in Europe; and in some eras and in some aspects of culture they had surpassed the West. In the late Middle Ages, however, western Europe began to experience an astonishing resurgence—a ''rebirth'' which was reflected in the rise of powerful and well-administered nation-states, the increase of wealth and trade, the growing importance of the bourgeoisie, and the intellectual and artistic achievements of humanist scholars and artists. While the West was pulsating with this insatiable energy, the empires of India and China (as we saw in Chapter 18) were becoming decadent culturally and impotent politically. And in Japan, isolation was the keynote of the Tokugawa shogunate—a regime no longer dynamic. Therefore, when the contact between East and West was renewed in the fifteenth century, it was not a meeting of equals. The discrepancies in effective political organizations, in disciplined armies, in energy and ambition prevented the resumption of East-West contacts on the same equal footing as had prevailed a thousand years earlier.

Europe's increasing strength. The same imbalance was readily apparent in both Africa and the Americas, areas which had not previously been breached by the Europeans. In the Western Hemisphere promising civilizations among the Incas, the Aztecs, and the Mayas were no match for armed invaders. African potentialities had been severely restricted by isolation and harsh environmental forces, so that the natives fell an easy prey to the Europeans. Any progress

the Negroes might have made was probably cut short by the effects of the slave trade.

The natural result of the impact of the strong upon the weak was that Europe took advantage of the other continents; the wider world became the servant of the West. The expansion of Europe and its mastery of much of the world and its people, particularly those in Africa and Asia, is generally referred to as imperialism. Many of the conflicts and tensions in modern world politics find their source to a large degree in the imperial systems created by the West.

VICEROYS AND COLONISTS IN THE NEW WORLD

Obstacles to colonizing America. More than in Africa and far more than in the Far East, Europeans in the Americas used colonization as the means for exploiting the riches of the territory. But colonization proved to be a difficult and costly project. The conquerors quickly learned that the natives of the New World were no match for their superior arms and organization; but while the invaders ruthlessly took advantage of Indian weaknesses, they paid a price for settling their new empires.

The trials and tribulations which the Europeans had to endure underscored two basic obstacles to their occupation of the New World: the consuming problem of simply staying alive in completely undeveloped regions; and the chronic shortage of man power skilled enough to harness and develop an area many times the size of Europe. Thus the Portuguese had to contend with the almost impenetrable jungles of Brazil and the Spaniards with the virtually unassailable Andes and the vast arid stretches in Mexico. For their part, the French and English had to endure the rigorous winters in North America. All of them had the never ending task of maintaining communications between small and widely separated communities; of keeping in check the resentment of the natives, who equipped themselves whenever possible with the conqueror's own weapons;

Among the greatest threats to Spain's American treasure were the warships of rival nations, particularly the English under Sir Francis Drake. Commissioned by Queen Elizabeth as a privateer, Drake spent many years raiding and plundering Spanish possessions in America. This print from a contemporary journal of his exploits diagrams the strategy used to sack and burn the city of St. Augustine in Florida. Drake first razed the fort (upper center) and then made an amphibious landing at the town itself (upper left), which was garrisoned by 150 Spanish troops.

and of standing off the depredations of ambitious European rivals.

Spain consolidates its empire in the Americas. The *conquistadores* who carved out a mighty Spanish empire in the New World had been allowed to embark on their expeditions only after having secured royal permission. The Spanish king received one fifth of all treasure discovered, together with title to all new territory taken. The crown's ultimate purpose was to replace these brilliant but erratic men of action with staid but reliable civil servants who would consolidate the territorial gains into a centralized colonial regime.

In theory, all overseas dominions were the personal property of the king, who made the major administrative decisions aided by one of his advisory councils, the Council of the Indies. Holding almost unrestricted power during the reigns of weak monarchs, the Council of the Indies formulated legislation, appointed colonial officials, and heard important colonial law cases. Before the end of the sixteenth century Spain possessed an American empire twenty times its own size, comprising in 1574 some 200 towns and about 160,000 Spanish settlers. For most of the colonial period the Spanish empire in the Americas was divided into two kingdoms: New Spain, which was made up of the West Indies, Venezuela, and the lands north of the Isthmus of Panama; and Peru, which consisted of all Spanish territory south of those lands.

Each kingdom had a viceroy who lived in splendor in Mexico City or Lima. Although the viceroys were the kings' representatives in America, they enjoyed only the appearance of great power. The Council of the Indies kept a tight rein on imperial affairs, judging the viceroys chiefly by their effectiveness in sending back treasure to Madrid. Under orders from the Spanish crown, the colonial regimes sharply restricted self-government. In the ten largest cities of the empire lawyers sent from Spain were in charge of courts called *audiencias,* which not only heard appeals against the decisions of viceroys and governors but also advised them in administrative matters. The crown levied head taxes, customs on imports, and excise charges on goods exchanged within the colonies, as well as demanding one fifth of all the gold and silver mined. The colonists were left no voice in the taxation. Membership in town councils was the only regular political outlet for the Spanish settlers, and there only the richest could participate. The Spaniards born in the Americas (Creoles) were regarded as potential rebels against the mother country, as indeed they proved to be in the nineteenth century.

According to one balanced analysis, the political system was "not intolerably bad, but . . . was also never vigorously good."[8] Its cumbrous system of checks and balances often delayed essential action for years, yet the fact that Spain could so quickly cast a governmental apparatus over such a vast area far from Spain itself was an impressive display of administrative acumen. Furthermore, without maintaining itself by naked force, the Spanish colonial system endured for three centuries with few important changes, permitting the transfer of Spanish culture and preserving internal peace.

Mercantilism guides economic life. The economic theory current in the nation-states of Europe during this period was mercantilism, a doctrine which stressed the need of governmental intervention to increase the wealth and power of the state. Mercantilism had ramifications for the colonies as well as for the mother country. Put briefly, mercantilism postulated that a nation should be as economically self-sufficient as possible and that the colonies should be exploited for the gain of the ruling country. (See Chapter 3, Volume II, for a more complete discussion of mercantilism.) Each European nation wanted to export more than it imported, and the colonies provided ready-made markets for the finished products of the homeland. Thus Spain sent wines and finished goods to the New World but forbade the colonists to supply products such as olives which would compete with those produced in Spain. From its colonies, Spain imported raw materials for processing and manufacture.

Under the mercantile system a nation's wealth was measured by the amount of precious metal it had accumulated. The New World was a source of fantastic riches for Spain in this respect. In 1803 the scientist Alexander von Humboldt estimated that between his day and that of Columbus the New World had provided the Old with a greater amount of precious metal than the whole world had seen since the days of Solomon. Mexico and Peru were famous for their silver mines, which became the basis for many private fortunes and the principal source of royal revenue.

Transporting the silver and gold back to Spain was a perilous business. Each spring two well-guarded fleets left Seville or Cádiz, one heading for Mexico and the other for Panama. Laden with silver from the Andes and Mexico, the convoys returned to Spain in the autumn at great risk. After a rendezvous at Havana the combined fleets ran the gantlet back to Spain. Pirates and buccaneers were ever ready to swoop down on stragglers, as were warships of rival powers. Yet most of the treasure usually reached Spain, where the crown received its royal fifth together with revenues from various taxes and monopolies.

In return for exploiting the virgin wealth of the New World, the Spanish introduced new products and methods which revolutionized agriculture, the mainstay of the American economy. To obtain farms, settlers often banded together to found a town in exchange for a royal grant of land, which was apportioned among the citizens. On the large estates of the aristocrats and the clergy, the forced labor of Indians or Negro slaves was employed in the cultivation of cotton, vanilla, indigo, cacao, and other crops for export. The Spanish brought with them wheat, barley, rye, and rice, as well as coffee, sugar cane, and a variety of fruits. The importation of cattle and other livestock not only drastically modified the native diet but also stimulated such valuable new industries as breeding animals and exporting their hides. Originally the Indians had been their own pack animals, for the New World lacked beasts of burden except for the llamas domesticated by the Incas. The *conquistadores* introduced horses and mules and further revolutionized transportation by the introduction of the wheel. Through these imports and many more, the cultural state of certain areas in the Americas was abruptly jerked from a Neolithic level to a position approaching that of the Old World.

Indian plight eased by the Church. In the search for a new way to the Indies, Queen Isabella had to no small degree been motivated by the desire to extend Christianity among the heathen. This missionary task had also been one of the avowed objectives of every *conquistador*; but it was almost invariably overlooked in the mad scramble to acquire gold and silver, jewels and slaves.

In the islands of the Caribbean the forced labor and even enslavement of natives on the plantations proved so injurious that most of them died off. They were replaced by Negro slaves, who were imported to the islands about 1503 and to the American mainland a few years later. From the middle of the sixteenth century to the middle of the eighteenth century, some three thousand Negro slaves were imported annually, eventually transforming the racial composition of the Caribbean islands.

The work of the Church in establishing missions and persuading the crown to enact safeguards enabled the natives to survive in other areas of Spanish America rather than be wiped out as they were in some islands in the Caribbean. Early in the sixteenth century some clerics began to upbraid the Spaniards for their cruelties in exploiting the labor of the Indians. The most famous of these reformers was a Dominican friar, Bartolomé de Las Casas (1474-1566), who insisted that the Indians, as subjects of the Spanish king, enjoyed the same rights as the Spaniards. He obtained royal permission to establish missions and settlements where the Indians and Spaniards could live on civilized terms. Las Casas' efforts also led to the promulgation of the New Laws of the Indies, directed at the greed of the plantation owners. But the attempt to improve the lot of the Indians was a losing battle, since the reforms ran counter to the economic interests of the settlers. As a member of the Council of the Indies wrote:

All these instructions have been thought out by prudent and humane jurisconsults and sanctioned by religious men. But what of that? When our compatriots reach that remote world, so far away and so removed from us, beyond the ocean whose courses imitate the changing heavens, they find themselves distant from any judge. Carried away by love of gold, they become ravenous wolves instead of gentle lambs, and heedless of royal instructions.[9]

In order both to convert and to protect the Indians, a number of religious orders established mission towns. There, a few friars shielded the natives from white exploitation and taught them Christianity along with European habits and skills. The missionaries followed Las Casas in believing that the Indians should be converted not by force but by patient persuasion, "as rain and snow falls from heaven, not impetuously, not violently, not suddenly like a heavy shower, but gradually, with suavity and gentleness, saturating the earth as it falls."[10] Large mission organizations in Brazil, Paraguay, Venezuela, and Mexico converted and at least superficially Europeanized hundreds of thousands of Indians. Later, missions were established in Upper California, where the monks taught their charges improved farming methods as well as irrigation and a variety of crafts. However, the Indians, denied the freedom of their natural environment and forced to live an alien life in the missionary settlements, rapidly died off. The "rim of Christendom" was pushed farther into the wilderness, but not without a serious toll in human life.

The work of the Catholic Church was so extensive that it constituted the chief unifying force in the Spanish and Portuguese possessions. In both empires the ecclesiastical establishment supported the interests of the government, just as the crown protected the Church and enforced conformity in religious matters.

An early drawing shows the arrival of the first French colonists, led by Cartier, against a map of the St. Lawrence estuary.

Spanish culture imported to the New World. For three hundred years Spain was a potent agent in transmitting European culture and institutions to the New World. First and foremost of its contributions in this field was its language and literature. Each convoy of ships to the colonies carried hundreds of books, ranging from religious tracts and the works of Cicero and Virgil to those of Cervantes and other popular Spanish authors. By 1536 printing presses had been set up in Mexico City.

A memorable year in the cultural history of the Americas was 1551; for it was then, eighty-five years before the founding of Harvard College, that the first two universities in the New World were established— one at Lima, the other at Mexico City. By the end of the seventeenth century no less than seven universities had been founded in Spanish America.

Portuguese activity in South America. Already burdened by its sprawling African and Asian interests, Portugal managed to establish a local administration in Brazil by the middle of the sixteenth century. In the 1570's Brazil's surge forward began as great numbers of African slaves were imported to cultivate sugar. This forced immigration continued for almost three centuries. In time the settlers fanned out to explore nearly half of the South American continent. Spain acquiesced in the expansion of Brazil beyond the demarcation line of Tordesillas because, from 1580 to 1640, the Spanish monarch was also king of Portugal and Brazil. During this period the crown imposed a highly centralized control on Brazil through its own officials, and a mercantilist policy was pursued in economic affairs.

After the Spanish king acquired control over Portugal, the Dutch and English regarded Portuguese possessions as lawful prizes to be won from their Spanish enemies. The Dutch took over land north of the mouth of the Amazon and founded Dutch Guiana. Subsequently, the English and French gained control over other parts of Guiana.

French colonization of North America. Earlier we followed the explorations of the French in the New World. That chapter in history opened with Cartier's voyages between 1534 and 1541, when he sailed up the St. Lawrence as far as the modern metropolis of Montreal. A small settlement which he established above the spot where Quebec now stands ended in quick failure. For more than a half a century afterwards France neglected Canada.

The next major impetus came in 1608 when the city of Quebec was founded as a permanent settlement by Samuel de Champlain. To exploit the infant colony, a joint-stock company headed by Cardinal Richelieu was formed about twenty years later. In return for a perpetual monopoly on the fur trade and the title to certain lands, this company was supposed to bring several thousand settlers to Canada. But the company was unable to attract colonists. Stories of the severe Canadian winters frightened away most potential settlers; and the Huguenots, who would have been glad to escape religious restrictions, were not allowed to leave France. When Champlain died in 1635, New France had a population of only a few hundred European inhabitants; but his colony at Quebec was destined to be the center and capital of New France for nearly two centuries.

By the middle of the seventeenth century New France had survived the initial, dangerous stages of an infancy marked by parental neglect. After La Salle in 1682 had explored the Mississippi River to its mouth, France also claimed the entire Mississippi valley. The tempo of development and growth was about to pick up—the French were at last firmly established in North America, ready to do battle with the English for the northern half of the continent and the Mississippi basin and prepared to resist any encroachment by the Spaniards from the Gulf of Mexico.

English colonies on the Atlantic seaboard. Like France, England was slow in following up the valuable work of its explorers. Cabot had given it the means of claiming an entire continent, yet it was not until the days of such Elizabethan seamen as Sir Francis Drake that Englishmen began to interest themselves in the potentialities of the New World. This interest was encouraged by an active propagandist, Richard

Hakluyt (1552?-1616), who urged his countrymen to build new Englands overseas. Several unsuccessful attempts to establish colonies on the eastern coast of North America were made, and the sixteenth century ended without any permanent English settlement there.

New factors were to bring about a decisive change, however. The defeat of the Spanish Armada in 1588 and the building of a strong English navy ensured safer passage from the Old World to the New. Reports of the wealth garnered by the Spaniards whetted the appetites of Englishmen to look for El Dorado. More important, the economic difficulties accompanying the spread of the enclosure movement—the diverting of land from food growing to sheep raising—brought unemployment and with it the desire by many to try their luck overseas. Added to these factors was the religious question. Although the Spanish and French governments forbade nonconforming religious elements to move to the New World, the English government saw emigration as an excellent means of getting rid of minority sects which were difficult to handle. For their part, these strong-willed, God-fearing dissidents were eager to migrate to a new land where they could worship freely.

Various methods were used to induce Europeans to make their home in the New World. This playing card, promoting the virtues of settling in North America, was distributed by the Pennsylvania Company.

Actually, the first successful English settlement was founded by a chartered trading company known as the London Company. Its members—merchants, government officials, and other gentlemen of means—bought shares to finance colonies. On the basis of a charter issued by the English crown, the company was permitted to act as a miniature government, even to the extent of coining money, levying taxes, and annexing territory.

In 1607 a small fleet outfitted by the London Company landed an exploration party which established the colony of Jamestown in Virginia. For a number of years the colonists suffered from lack of food and other privations, but they were tided over this initial period by the dauntless Captain John Smith, whose motto was "It is less perilous to go forward than to go backward," and whose romantic rescue by the beautiful Pocahontas is one of the legends most cherished by Americans. Recent scholarship suggests that this story, like other of Smith's improbable tales, may have a basis in fact.

The first example of the transplantation to the New World of English common law and representative government is found in the royal charter to the London Company:

All and every the Persons, being our Subjects, which shall dwell and inhabit within every and any of the said several Colonies and Plantations, and every of their children . . . shall have and enjoy all Liberties, Franchises and Immunities within any of our Dominions . . . as if they had been abiding and born within this our Realm of England.[11]

In 1619 the governor of the Jamestown colony called a representative assembly to assist in the tasks of government. This body, which later became the legislature of the state of Virginia, is one of the oldest representative assemblies in existence.

Another great landmark in American history was the landing of the Pilgrims at Plymouth in 1620, after James I had granted them permission. This momentous royal decision in effect opened English North America to settlement by religious dissenters. Ten years later another Puritan group, organized as the Massachusetts Bay Company, settled around Boston. The members of this group, like those at Plymouth, had secured a royal charter which allowed them a virtually self-governing colony.

Between 1629 and 1642, as a result of increased hostility toward religious dissenters in England, some 25,000 Puritans emigrated to New England. This movement, called the Great Migration, had important consequences for the future. It brought to the New World a number of educated and responsible people whose courage and intellectual attainments greatly stimulated the process of colonization. By the middle of the seventeenth century the English language and law and the religious and cultural institutions of England had become firmly rooted in North American soil.

THE COMMERCIAL REVOLUTION

The transformation of Europe's economic life. In the period between 1450 and 1650 an economic and social revolution—sometimes termed the Commercial Revolution—wrought significant changes on the European scene. The geographical discoveries, the new colonial markets, the access to new sources of raw materials, the influx of wealth, the improvement of business techniques—all these factors had the cumulative effect of refining and enriching the life of Europe. It was during the Commercial Revolution that the principal modern European economic powers, especially those along the Atlantic seaboard, experienced their major growth and development.

During the Middle Ages the central agency of European trade was the city-state. Trade in northern Europe had been dominated by the wealthy trading confederacy of towns in the Baltic area known as the Hanseatic League. After the fifteenth century, however, the League rapidly declined, a victim of mercantile rivalry from rising nation-states and the ravages of warfare. The absence of a strong central government in Germany left the League without adequate protection.

In southern Europe the merchants of the Italian city-states, with Venice in the lead, had for centuries acted as the great middlemen of Europe because they controlled the lucrative Asiatic trade. But the Portuguese smashed the Italian monopoly by discovering a new sea route to India and by obstructing the Red Sea and Persian Gulf routes that led to the Mediterranean ports. In addition, the Italian Wars of the sixteenth century (see Chapter 17) had a disastrous effect upon the prosperity of the Italian city-states.

Portugal, temporarily paramount. With its diminishing population, Portugal could not permanently administer and protect an empire scattered over three continents. During the sixteenth century, emigration, plague, and famine reduced the country's population from one and a half million to less than one. The commercial empire of the Portuguese depended upon their command of the sea, and they were unable to man their ships and fortresses adequately. In 1580 Portugal came under the Spanish crown, and when it regained its independence in the following century, it retained only a few small possessions in the Far East, some islands in the mid-Atlantic, Brazil, and Mozambique and Angola in Africa. The economic power of Portugal ebbed away, not from lack of initiative so much as from lack of resources to support so great a task.

The economic decay of Spain. The decline of Spain's commercial might cannot be explained so simply. This nation apparently had everything—and failed. During the sixteenth century Spain had far more gold and silver than any of its rivals; and to this wealth was added that of Portugal and its possessions. Yet the wealth and power lavishly displayed during the reign of Philip II (1556-1598) were only surface deep. Farming was neglected, and the industrial guilds were overburdened with governmental regulations. Religious persecution and the expulsion of the Jews and Moors had deprived Spain of many of its skilled financiers and craftsmen. Since the Church and the upper classes were exempt from certain forms of taxation, the tax burden fell disproportionately on the classes engaged in trade, commerce, and industry.

An outward symbol of wealth, the rich flood of bullion from the Americas wreaked havoc in the Spanish economy by causing inflation. The rise in prices was higher in Spain than anywhere else in Europe, a condition which attracted a stream of lower-priced products from Holland, France, and England, to the detriment of Spanish manufacturers. Spain not only lost out in manufacturing but also paid its gold and silver to foreign merchants for goods which in many cases it ought to have been making at home. In the decades after 1600 Spain's industry and commerce steadily diminished, and its population likewise decreased.

Antwerp's period of glory. As Spain and Portugal declined, the commercial center of Europe moved northward to Antwerp. To this great Flemish port came prominent European bankers, merchants, and manufacturers. Antwerp was made a toll-free port, and the city fathers set up a perpetual trade fair. "Soon it was said that Antwerp did as much business in one month as Venice in two years. In the town there were about a thousand business houses, while every week fifty vessels sailed into port, not to speak of eight or nine hundred fishing-boats."[12] Various institutions of modern capitalism developed there. In 1531 the first stock exchange, or Bourse, was founded. Life and property insurance came into extensive use. But the spectacular prosperity of Antwerp was short-lived, for in 1576, during the wars of the Netherlands against Spain, the city was sacked. Henceforth Antwerp's trade and finances were largely appropriated by the Dutch city of Amsterdam.

Holland's golden age. By 1650 Holland was the principal commercial, financial, and manufacturing country in Europe. Both the Dutch East India Company and the West India Company were markedly successful. The Dutch built better ships than their rivals and operated them more efficiently; their lower freight rates gained for them a monopoly on the carrying trade of Europe. The Dutch policy of religious toleration attracted artisans from abroad, and Holland became the leading industrial nation of

Europe. Dutch exports included textiles, salted herring, glazed pottery, fine jewelry, and printed books. Trade, in turn, made Amsterdam the center of banking and credit (see p. 635).

Nevertheless, like Portugal, Holland was a comparatively small nation, and larger neighbors were presently to overtake it. Rivalry with England resulted in three wars in the latter half of the seventeenth century. Yet Dutch skill, together with the retention of the East Indies, enabled Holland to remain a significant factor in world commerce.

We have seen important shifts in Europe's economic center of gravity. Using the effect which the commercial expansion had on various European areas as a yardstick, one historian has divided early modern Europe into four economic categories.[13] Certain

During Holland's Golden Age trade brought a strong eastern influence to that country. This Delftware tulip vase fashioned like a pagoda is one example of the Chinese accent in Dutch craftsmanship.

countries—Russia, Prussia, Austria, Poland, and the Balkan states—remained little affected by the growth of commerce and continued at this time to be overwhelmingly rural. Two regions—the Hanseatic towns and the Italian city-states—which had enjoyed a lucrative trading position in the Middle Ages were now outstripped by areas which they had once supplied. Two countries —Portugal and Spain—built up the first magnificent empires, only to fall behind when their more aggressive neighbors challenged them. After 1600 Holland, England, and France took the ascendancy and carved out powerful colonial empires. Thus, in a period covering two centuries, the commercial life of western Europe changed completely from what it had been in the days of Prince Henry the Navigator.

More imports in Europe's markets. The discovery of sea routes to both Asia and the Americas provided an unparalleled impetus to the expansion of Europe and its commerce by allowing a greater volume of goods to be carried at a much smaller cost. Part of this saving was due to the increased efficiency and carrying capacity of ships. Beyond that, maritime transportation in general was much cheaper than overland caravans. One continuous sea journey profitably replaced the countless handlings and loadings that accompanied caravans from the Orient to Europe. As a result of these factors, the volume of trade increased enormously during early modern times.

For the first time large quantities of such luxuries as aromatic woods, silks, precious stones, and spices were imported from the East. The spice trade was especially profitable because there was no refrigeration for foods at this time, and slightly spoiled food could be made palatable by cooking it with cloves, cinnamon, or pepper. Cloths from the East—calicoes, chintzes, and ginghams—became popular. The textile workers of England became so incensed at the foreign competition that they demanded a prohibition on the import of these inexpensive fabrics, which they maintained were "tawdry, pie-spotted, flabby, ragged, low priced, made by a parcel of heathens and pagans that worship the Devil and work for ½*d.* a day."[14] Among other imports from Asia were carpets, rugs, porcelain, brassware, and the all-important beverages tea and coffee.

From the New World came a variety of products which revolutionized the eating and drinking habits of the Europeans. The food supply of Europe was greatly improved by the addition of potatoes, maize (Indian corn), and tomatoes. From the Caribbean came sugar, which soon became so popular that it supplanted honey. An abundant supply of fish, primarily cod, came from Newfoundland's Grand Banks; and warm furs were obtained by trappers penetrating the interior of North America. The sacred beverage of the Aztecs, cocoa, found its way to Spain and thence throughout Europe in the seventeenth century.

The Indians were responsible for introducing a still popular habit—smoking. Cigars, cigarettes, pipe and chewing tobacco, and snuff were adopted by the Spaniards. A sixteenth-century French diplomat named Jean Nicot brought tobacco home from Portugal and thereby gave his name to its nicotine products.

Gold and ivory came to Europe from Africa, but the most important African export enriched the European powers indirectly. This export was that most misery-ridden produce—slaves. To obtain slaves to labor in the mines and on the plantations of the New World, slavers sailed to the Guinea coast, where they bought or stole their human freight.

A woman slave might change hands for a gallon of brandy, six bars of iron, two small guns, one keg of powder, and two strings of beads; a man slave might cost eight guns, one wicker-covered bottle, two cases of spirits, and twenty-eight sheets.[15]

The voyage across the Atlantic to America cost the lives of from 10 to 25 per cent of the Africans—inhumanly packed as they were in evil-smelling, suffocating quarters below deck—but the remainder were profitably disposed of at their destination. One authority estimates that in three centuries some twenty million Negroes were brought to the Americas.

Expansion of industry. New products stimulated the creation of completely new industries in the homelands. Thus, England and France now engaged in sugar refining as well as the manufacture of molasses and rum, and various countries produced snuff and clay pipes for smoking tobacco. The fur trade made possible the manufacture of that smart new accessory to one's wardrobe—beaver hats.

A further impetus to Europe's industry came from the demands of overseas settlers for finished products not manufactured in the colonies. For many years settlements in the New World had to rely on the homeland to supply necessities such as textiles, hardware, firearms, and glassware. The English colonies required so many nails that new processes were developed in the English Midlands to satisfy the market. In addition, handsome profits were realized from the construction and outfitting of innumerable ships and from supplying provisions for the long sea voyages. Because losses were often heavy on the high seas, the shipbuilding industry was even more lucrative than it might have been.

The influx of precious metals. The gold and silver brought into the European market from the colonies in enormous quantities may have had a more direct effect on Europe's economy than any of the other products of Africa, Asia, or the Americas. By the middle of the fifteenth century Europe had been confronted with a severe shortage of gold and silver, caused both by the depletion of European mines and by increasing demands for currency to finance the new standing armies and navies and to pay for spices and other luxury commodities. But the critical situation was partially relieved by the development of new European mines, by imports of gold from West Africa, and, above all, by the unprecedented quantities of precious metals from the mines of Spanish America. It has been estimated that the amount of precious metals in Europe tripled—a development that completed the changeover from a barter to a money economy. By the seventeenth century it had become customary to carry on one's business and to pay rent, wages, and taxes in currency.

The New World provided Europe with many valuable raw materials. From Potosí, in the Andes mountains, came enough silver to triple Europe's silver supply. A 1584 painting (top left) shows relays of llamas carrying ore down from the "mountain of silver" to the primitive Spanish refinery. From Virginia came tobacco. The slaves in the contemporary engraving (bottom) are packing tobacco in barrels for shipment to England. Farther north fur was the major export. An early seventeenth-century engraving (top right) shows Iroquois Indians driving animals into traps by striking bones together. The animals were then killed and skinned and their pelts shipped to Europe.

The bonanza of precious metals had still other effects. It upset the old price level, so that between 1500 and 1650 the prices of goods doubled or tripled in western Europe. Also, large sums of money were now available for investment, thereby facilitating trade with all parts of the world.

Banking becomes big business. One indicator of the resurgence of active commercial life was the growth of banking and related business practices. Banking had arisen in the late Middle Ages. The word *bank* derives from the Italian *banca,* meaning "bench," on which medieval Italian moneylenders sat in the market place to carry on their business. When a man failed, the people broke his bench, and from this custom came the word *bankrupt,* or "broken bench." During the late Middle Ages moneylending became indispensable to the administration of both national monarchies and the Church, so that the traditional prohibition on usury was largely ignored.

Large-scale banking was first developed in Italian cities, where merchant bankers arranged bills of exchange and negotiated loans. By 1350 some eighty banking houses were in business in Florence alone, and certain families grew wealthy as a result. The most illustrious of these families was the Medici, whose clever members established branch offices all over western Europe and acted as financial agents for the popes. In the fifteenth century the Medici represented a new capitalist class which treated money as a commodity. Whereas in medieval economic theory money was only a means of exchange and was justified only to the extent that it reflected both honest labor and a "just price" concept, early capitalist speculators like the Medici valued and traded in currencies and bullion for their own sake. Furthermore, money could be used to dictate political policies—a technique which the astute Medici in Florence employed for their own advantage.

Following the Medici policy of using money not only to earn interest but also to gain political power were the Fuggers, a family of German bankers in the sixteenth century. The Fuggers set up counting houses and merchandise depots in a number of cities and in time gained virtual control of the silver, copper, and iron markets of central Europe and the silver and mercury mining in Spain. They also engaged in international finance and politics. For decades the Fuggers realized an average yearly profit of over 30 per cent, but they went bankrupt in 1607 when several governments defaulted on their loans.

Soon after this, however, numerous other banking concerns came into existence. Most important was the Bank of Amsterdam, founded by local merchants in 1609. Its main purpose was to facilitate trade by the conversion of various currencies into credits called bank money, which because of its standard value came to be preferred to coins. It also accepted deposits and paid interest on them.

With banking there naturally evolved new financial techniques. Despite the increase in precious metals after 1500, the supply could not keep pace with the increase in trade, and the Bank of Amsterdam began the practice of issuing loans against its deposits. Because it found that it could safely loan larger sums than had been deposited, the Bank of Amsterdam thus initiated a new and effective means of expanding credit. Likewise, bank notes came to replace bulky, heavy metal for large sums. To overcome the dangers of losing money through theft or accident, bills of exchange, which had originated during the crusades, came into more widespread use.

Progress was also made in commercial arithmetic and in bookkeeping. Simple single-entry bookkeeping had been developed as early as the thirteenth century. Soon afterwards, double-entry bookkeeping came into use; it was well known in Italy by 1500 and in western Europe a century later. By listing a transaction either as a *debit* (meaning, "he owes") or a *credit* ("he believes" a promiser will carry out his promise), a businessman could readily determine his status in terms of profit and loss.

New methods of financing companies. Not only banks but also modern corporations were developed in response to needs arising from the expanded commerce of early modern times. Unprecedented difficulties resulted from trading at long distances overseas in strange lands. In *The Merchant of Venice* (1596), Shakespeare spoke of the dangers which merchants faced:

. . . ships are but boards, sailors but men: there be land-rats and water-rats, water-thieves and land-thieves, I mean pirates, and then there is the peril of waters, winds and rocks.[16]

It was natural that those engaged in overseas trade should seek to combine their efforts both to provide mutual protection and to share losses as well as profits.

The companies were of two main types—regulated and joint-stock—and both were chartered, regulated, and granted monopolies by the state. In the regulated company individuals financed their own businesses and abided by the rules the group had accepted to protect the trade in which the members had a mutual interest. The majority of earlier companies were of this nature.

Later companies were of the joint-stock variety, which involves an association of capital as well as of men. The members put their money into a common fund and gave over the management to a board of directors. Because of its advantages, the joint-stock company became almost universal. As many people as wanted could contribute capital. This type of company had a permanent legal personality that did not expire, whereas the regulated company was not a legal entity, and in case of damages each member had to sue or be sued individually. Stock in a joint-stock company might be transferred as the owner saw fit, and at the same time, the company's policy underwent no serious change. The British and Dutch East India companies both started as regulated companies but were later reorganized as joint-stock entities.

The vast corporations of today grew out of this early type of business organization. Some historians also hold that the principle of voting rights for stockholders in joint-stock companies carried over into some of the governmental units of colonial America, establishing the right of the citizen to vote.

Stock exchanges and insurance. The creation of joint-stock companies gave impetus to the growth of stock exchanges, because the shares could be easily transferred from one person to another like any other commodity. A stock exchange made possible the purchase and sale of stocks, bonds, and debentures. It performed valuable functions for capitalism, including the easy amalgamation of capital from many different sources, thereby enabling large commercial companies to be formed. Not only stock but also produce exchanges arose, fulfilling much the same need as their present-day descendants. The produce exchange is a market for dealing in such products as wheat, wool, cotton, and metals. Following the lead of the first exchange in Antwerp, the Bourse, the early exchanges acted as both produce and stock exchanges. Later the two functions were separated.

Besides joint-stock companies, other methods of sharing losses evolved, including insurance. Since the loss of his vessel might well ruin an individual merchant, it came to be the practice to distribute losses among a group of traders by means of insurance. Interested merchants drew up an agreement by which each was responsible for a percentage of any possible loss. Because they signed their names at the bottom of this document, the practice came to be known as underwriting.

SUMMARY

Braving the terrors of uncharted seas and the dreadful hardships of long voyages, a few daring sea captains, such as da Gama, Columbus, and Magellan, opened up rich trade routes to the East and discovered new lands in the Western Hemisphere. In the New World the feats of the explorers were followed by the bold, and often cruel, exploits of the *conquistadores,* who carved out vast empires for their homelands. Thus, for Spain, Cortés captured Mexico and Pizarro humbled the Incas in Peru, while Cabral claimed the magnificent territory of Brazil for Portugal.

In vain Ponce de León sought the magic elixir of youth and Coronado the fabled cities beyond Mexico, but in the process the Spanish flag was planted in Florida and in what is now the southwestern region of the United States. In the northeastern part of North America Cartier and Champlain took possession of the rich St. Lawrence valley for France, and the French explorer La Salle investigated the Mississippi basin. Soon after Columbus' first voyage, John Cabot provided England with a claim to North America, and Henry Hudson's exploration opened the way for Dutch traders and colonists.

Meanwhile, various European countries, including Portugal, Holland, England, and France, had erected forts on the African coast for the purpose of exploiting the slave trade. In the teeming lands of Asia, European penetration was secured only by the establishment of strongly fortified trading settlements at strategic sites. Using this system, the Portuguese controlled trade in the East during the 1500's but gradually lost out to the English and Dutch, who garnered most of the profits in the next century. While the Dutch concentrated more and more on the East Indies, the British East India Company built up a commercial stronghold in India. In China and Japan the unwarranted violence of the Portuguese caused native officials to restrict the westerners to a narrow theater of operations. In the East, European standards were successfully and permanently imposed only in the Philippines.

In sharp contrast to their failures in Japan and China, the western European powers were able to transplant not only their authority but also their institutions and culture to the sparsely populated lands of the Americas. The government and economics of the Spanish and Portuguese colonies were directly—and minutely—controlled by royal decrees and officials, whereas the development of the French, English, and Dutch colonies was left largely to private companies.

The impact of the New World upon the Old was in turn so far-reaching as to create the Commercial Revolution. With the outburst of geographical discoveries and the creation of new trade routes, the areas which had thrived on the Mediterranean trade lost their leading roles to those along the Atlantic seaboard. The first great colonial empires were built up by Portugal and Spain, only to be superseded through the dynamism of Holland and later of France and England. New products poured into Europe to augment diet, clothing, and the general standard of living, while the influx of gold and silver completed the change from a barter to a money economy and raised the level of prices.

This era also saw the development of large-scale banking and commercial practices. By the seventeenth century important banking institutions had been founded throughout western Europe. Because overseas trading ventures required large amounts of capital and entailed great risks, merchants pooled their resources by forming companies, the earlier ones of the regulated type, the later and more successful ones joint-stock companies—forerunners of present-day corporations. To serve as market places for stock that could change hands readily, stock exchanges developed.

The geographical, political, and commercial expansion of Europe between the years 1450 and 1650 was so immense that it transformed the basic pattern of global existence. With it we enter the formative period of modern times. For the next three centuries the civilization of western Europe—carried to the four corners of the earth and stimulated by new and dynamic forces—was to dominate world culture.

Historical Critique

THE QUESTION OF PARALLEL INVENTION IN THE OLD AND NEW WORLDS
by Robert McC. Adams

Robert McC. Adams, Professor in the Oriental Institute and Department of Anthropology of the University of Chicago and formerly the director of the Oriental Institute, has conducted archaeological fieldwork both in the Near East and in Mexico. His published works include *Land Behind Baghdad: A History of Settlement on the Diyala Plains* (1965) and *The Evolution of Urban Society: Early Mesopotamia and Prehispanic Mexico* (1966).

In ordinary American parlance the word *invention* calls to mind consciously created technical devices or improvements. We regard the inventor as a prime contributor to the tide of material progress. But we generally fail to place his achievement in its technical and social context, seeing it instead only as a solitary, inexplicable act.

In these terms, the idea of "parallel" inventions merely compounds the enigma. We can invoke the principle of limited possibilities to explain the independent recurrence of simple design elements, processes of manufacture, or mechanical devices. But how do we determine objectively what the limits to the possibilities are in any particular cultural setting? Especially for the early stages of civilization, before the flood of documents associated with European conquest and colonization, how often can we find evidence to make a definitive choice between some unrecorded process of diffusion from a single center and genuine parallelism?

A less narrow definition of invention is probably more useful. For example, we can extend the term to include lengthy sequences of technical development in which many contributors significantly enlarged man's command of energy or the range of resources he is able to utilize. We can also include innovations in the social, aesthetic, and moral order that quickened communication, centralized control, or deepened the integrative ties on which growth in social scale and complexity must always have depended. Above all, we can stress the importance of studying inventions in their context—the uses to which they were put, by whom, and for what purposes, both immediately and in the long run.

Comparisons between early civilizations in the Old and New Worlds furnish an important avenue of approach to this problem. Certain general similarities in the initial growth of urban societies in Mesopotamia, Egypt, the Indus valley, China, Mesoamerica, and Peru have long been noted. Summarized by V. Gordon Childe under the general designation of the "Urban Revolution," these include the emergence of priests and kings, the appearance of full-time craft specialists, the division of homogeneous societies into social classes, the elaboration of exact and predictive sciences, long-distance trade in luxury products, the invention of writing, the introduction of representational art and monumental architecture, and, of course, the growth of cities.

To be sure, not all of these features appeared to the same degree or at the same time in each of the civilizations mentioned. Moreover, some of them may have been carried or diffused from one area to another rather than independently invented. This seems to have been the case with the spread of writing from Mesopotamia to Egypt (see p. 32). A case has also been made for the diffusion of certain formal religious themes (and hence perhaps of organized priesthoods) between Mesoamerica and Peru, and a few authorities argue for the transmission across the Pacific of some elements in the aboriginal civilizations of the New World. But whatever their sources and variations in particular instances, Childe's characteristics do roughly define a major organizational level or stage in the evolution of human society, characteristics which to a significant degree are shared by early civilizations but are not found among their precivilized antecedents. Hence these individual characteristics deserve empirical scrutiny as possible examples of parallelism, while in combination they help us to study other examples of invention by holding variations in the social and cultural context within reasonable limits.

Let us take first a specialized craft that played a particularly crucial role according to Childe's analysis—the development of copper and bronze metallurgy. Childe felt that the demand for superior metal tools and weapons, and the smiths' demand in turn for ores from distant regions and for their subsistence to be furnished by their host communities, contributed strongly to the growth of expansionistic, diversified, truly urban societies. However, this model applies only imperfectly to any of the early civilizations, and it is entirely at odds with some of them. The most precocious phases of metallurgical development in Mesopotamia, the "type" case on which Childe relied, came about the middle of the fourth millennium B.C. from the hands of tiny numbers of craftsmen whose main efforts seem to have been devoted not to utilitarian products at all but to ritual objects for temples. For all of the heuristic value of Childe's distinction between full- and part-time specialists, it is also worth noting that many Mesopotamian coppersmiths depended for part of their subsistence on the produce of the little plots of agricultural land they occupied.

In Egypt, as the text notes, the introduction of bronze metallurgy proceeded much more slowly than in western Asia, and in both Egypt and the Indus valley the design of metal utensils in general seems to have been little influenced by the utilitarian considerations that promoted the rapid growth of the industry during its later phases in Mesopotamia. Moreover, the acquisition of copper in Egypt remained for a long time an exclusively royal enterprise. Vast quantities of the metal that were brought back from Sinai at the time of the first dynasties never entered mundane circulation but were set aside as provisions to accompany the dead pharaoh into the afterlife.

Turning further afield, China and Peru tended to follow the Mesopotamian model, both in the rapidity of metallurgical progress and in the variety of uses, both ritual and mundane, to which copper and bronze were put. On the other hand, the Aztecs, for all of their warlike reputation as the "Assyrians" of the New World, failed completely to integrate their knowledge of copper into their all-consuming militarism. And the classic flowering of Mayan civilization came and went in virtually total ignorance of metals.

Copper or bronze metallurgy, we may conclude, is at best a gross description of a complex, highly variable series of achievements. The inherent advantages of the new materials over stone or wood must have contributed to their acceptance and spread over the very long run, but these advantages almost certainly were perceived only very imperfectly when the craft originated, and they provide little help in understanding the uses to which metals and metalworking were put at any given place and time. Still less does the development of metallurgy provide a valid index of overall cultural complexity, or even of the extent of craft specialization as a single component of that complexity. The narrowly focused study of a particular industry or invention is no substitute, in other words, for a more comprehensive analysis of the whole context in which it arose.

Similar conclusions emerge if we turn to a seemingly crucial mechanical device like the wheel. Comparisons emphasizing differences rather than similarities between early civilizations in the Old and New Worlds frequently stress the absence of wheeled vehicles in the latter, but this cannot be accepted without several important qualifications. To begin with, the absence was not quite complete: pre-Hispanic examples of such vehicles are known from Mesoamerica—as toys! In other words, the principle was indeed discovered; what was lacking was the opportunity to place it into effective use. Domesticable transport animals were not available in aboriginal Mesoamerica; in fact, they were restricted in the New World to the high Andes. Wheeled vehicles were lacking in that region also, but this may reflect only the limited tractive power of the llama and the extremely rugged, unsuitable terrain. Moreover, systematic use of transport trains of pack animals provided Andean society with an obviously effective substitute. Probably no society in the world at a comparable stage of development has ever succeeded in amassing the immense, centralized stores of foodstuffs, textiles, and other supplies for which the Inca empire was noted.

Effective substitution is also a factor if we consider not wheeled transport but the potter's wheel. In the New World civilizations the employment of molds for fabricating pottery played a roughly similar role to that of the potter's wheel in the Old World. In other words, the industries evolved with different emphases and directions, so that no comparison on the basis of the presence or absence of a particular device is very meaningful.

And finally, the emphasis attached to the use of the wheel in the ancient Near East is itself often distorted. Representations of wheeled vehicles, as well as some archaeological examples, extend back into the fourth millennium B.C. But on closer inspection most of the evidence turns out to reflect ritual and military use, not the employment of wheeled carts for ordinary economic transport. Widespread, decisive use of the latter, upon which the notion of a sharp contrast with the New World partly depends, is attested to by written records only at about the beginning of the second millennium or even later.

Monumental architecture is another useful case to consider. Massive pyramids, temples, and similar structures are often the most impressive surviving vestiges of early civilizations, but the archaeological handbooks which exhaustively describe features of their construction usually deal less adequately with their significance and function. By what combination of coerced and voluntary labor, on behalf of an acknowledged deity who was also a temporal ruler, was the great pyramid of Cheops built? Need we think of masses of highly organized laborers working continuously or only of smaller crews mobilized under the somewhat autonomous authority of their village headmen during a long succession of slack agricultural seasons? Such questions continue to be debated not only for the ancient necropolises of Egypt but for Mayan temples in Yucatán rain forests, and for pyramids on the Peruvian coast and in central Mexico.

What makes these questions relevant for us is that monumental architecture, at least by any ordinary definition, was not associated exclusively with civilized societies in which highly organized controls over labor can be taken for granted. An earth mound like Poverty Point, constructed in Louisiana early in the first millennium B.C., must be described as monumental in scale although its builders had not even approached the threshold of civilization. This and similar cases suggest that monumental architecture may signify different things, or arise in response to entirely different sets of circumstances, in societies that have entered upon Childe's "Urban Revolution" and in those that have not. If so, the idea or invention of monumentality not only has arisen independently in different parts of the world (as detailed studies of the evolution of architectural forms in different regions clearly indicate) but represents a different type of parallelism than we have considered previously—a formal feature whose separate occurrences do not reflect underlying similarities of context.

Difficulties like the foregoing underline the disadvantages of focusing on isolated traits or discoveries. Instead it is the broadest, most inclusive "inventions" for which it is most rewarding to speak of parallelisms. The achievement of civilization or "Urban Revolution" was an invention in this sense, as was the preceding "Neolithic Revolution" leading to the independent origins of agriculture in different regions of the Old and New Worlds. In speaking of parallelisms among these great transformations, however, it is not sufficient to trace similarities and differences in the separate forms that were finally achieved in different regions. What is crucial instead is to emphasize and compare the central processes of change involved.

In these terms, the underlying parallelisms in the "Urban Revolution" are not found in the presence or absence of specific features such as

metallurgy—or even writing or cities themselves. The Inca managed their elaborate storage economy very nicely with records kept in knotted string. The sophistication of classic Maya astronomy and art came with a dispersed settlement pattern to which some authorities decline to apply the term "urban" at all, and for Egypt, too, it has been seriously questioned whether there were true cities before the time of the New Kingdom. But certain closely linked trends of development can be found at the heart of all the relatively independent sequences leading to the stage of "civilization." These trends include increasing social stratification; an increasingly important and elaborate division of labor; the initial binding together of communities by highly symbolic, theocratic forms of organization and then the emergence alongside, and ultimately over, the temples and their priesthoods of political authorities largely preoccupied with warfare and territorial expansion.

Of course we must expect considerable local variability in the forms that these trends took under different environmental and historic circumstances—and the available evidence, fragmentary as it is, does not disappoint us. But parallelisms do not imply identities, and in any case the human experience is too richly variable to be reduced to complete regularity by some iron law. The underlying similarities remain, and frequently they can be traced not only at the generalized level to which we are limited in this brief space but in small and significant details as well. Here, at this integrative level, which treats societies as dynamic wholes, lies the greatest promise for studies of the widening ripples of change that radiate outward from the dropping of small pebbles of innovation.

SUGGESTED READINGS

The classic formulation of the problem is contained in V. Gordon Childe's provocative article, "The Urban Revolution," *Town Planning Review*, 1950. The author has attempted a systematic comparison of two civilizations that touches more fully on some of these questions in *The Evolution of Urban Society: Early Mesopotamia and Prehispanic Mexico*, Aldine, 1966. For a general statement of the framework of such studies, see Julian H. Steward, *Theory of Culture Change*, U. of Ill. Press, 1955. An interesting and still important early statement (first published in 1895), which deals primarily with parallelisms in primitive technology, is Otis T. Mason, *The Origins of Invention*, M.I.T. Press, 1966.

Suggestions for Reading

THE FAR EAST

G. A. Lensen, **The World Beyond Europe,*** 2nd ed., Houghton Mifflin, 1966. The best brief introduction. The best large-scale general survey of the Far East from antiquity to the nineteenth century is E. O. Reischauer, J. K. Fairbank, and A. Craig, **History of East Asian Civilization,** Vol. I, **East Asia: The Great Tradition,** Houghton Mifflin, 1960. See also Woodbridge Bingham et al., **A History of Asia,** 2 vols., Allyn and Bacon, 1964-1965, and K. S. Latourette, **A Short History of the Far East,** 3rd ed., Macmillan, 1957. For further study consult Phillips Talbot, ed., **A Select Bibliography. Asia, Africa, Eastern Europe, Latin America,** American Field Staff Inc., 1960; supplement, 1961; and A. T. Embree et al., eds., **A Guide to Paperbacks on Asia,** Asia, 1964; supplement, 1966.

M. Biardeau, **India,** Viking, 1960. A well-illustrated introduction to Indian history and tradition (See "List of Readings," p. 656, for standard histories of India.*) V. Smith, **Akbar the Great Mogol,** Chand, 1958, and L. Binyon, **Akbar,** Peter Davies, 1932, are two important biographies of Akbar. See also W. E. Moreland, **India at the Death of Akbar,** Macmillan, 1920; **The Cambridge History of India,** Vol. IV, 1937; S. M. Ikram, **Muslim Civilization in India,** Columbia, 1964.

Dun J. Li, **The Ageless Chinese: A History,*** Scribner, 1965. A well-written full account. (For other histories of China see p. 656.) On Sino-European contacts see G. F. Hudson, **Europe and China: A Survey of Their Relations from Earliest Times to 1800,*** Beacon, and K. Panikkar, **Asia and Western Dominance, 1498-1945,** Allen & Unwin, 1959.

E. O. Reischauer, **Japan, Past and Present,** 3rd ed., Knopf, 1964. Lucid and authoritative. G. B. Sansom, **A History of Japan,** 3 vols., Stanford Univ., 1958-1963, is the best detailed account. Pertinent special studies include G. B. Sansom, **The Western World and Japan: A Study of the Interaction of European and Asiatic Cultures,** Knopf, 1950; and C. R. Boxer, **The Christian Century in Japan, 1549-1650,** Univ. of Calif., 1951.

The following are excellent general surveys on Southeast Asia with valuable material on the Hindu and Buddhist impact: D. G. E. Hall, **A History of South-East Asia,** 2nd ed., St. Martins, 1964; J. F. Cady, **Southeast Asia: Its Historical Development,** McGraw-Hill, 1964; and B. Harrison, **Southeast Asia: A Short History,** St. Martins, 1954. For further study consult **Southeast Asia: An Annotated Bibliography of Selected Reference Sources in Western Languages,** Government Printing Office, 1965, and **Southeast Asian History: A Bibliographic Guide,** ed. by S. N. Hay and M. H. Case, Praeger, 1965.

AFRICA

W. Fitzgerald, **Africa: A Social, Economic and Political Geography of Its Major Regions,** Methuen, 1955. The best treatment of the African geographical background.

Basil Davidson, **Africa: History of a Continent,** Macmillan, 1966. A superbly illustrated survey of African culture from the earliest times. R. Oliver and J. D. Fage, **A Short History of Africa,*** Penguin, is the best introductory general history. Two brief, useful studies are Z. A. Marsh and G. Kingsnorth, **An Intro-**duction to the History of East Africa, Cambridge, 1957; and J. D. Fage, **An Introduction to the History of West Africa,*** Cambridge.

For additional facets of African history see D. P. Mannix and M. Cowley, **Black Cargoes,** Viking, 1962, the history of the slave trade in the Atlantic; A. P. Kup, **A History of Sierra Leone,** Cambridge, 1961; R. Hallett, **The Penetration of Africa,** Vol. I, Routledge & Kegan Paul, 1965, a thorough study of the European intrusion; Roland and Caroline Oliver, eds., **Africa in the Days of Exploration,** Prentice-Hall, 1965, a collection of documentary readings; J. S. Trimingham, **A History of Islam in West Africa,** Oxford, 1962; Ruth Slade, **King Leopold's Congo,** Oxford, 1962, a background of early history; Genesta Hamilton, **In the Wake of Da Gama,** Skeffington, 1965, a readable, popular account of the Portuguese pioneers in East Africa.

E. Elisofan and W. Fagg, **The Sculpture of Africa,** Praeger, 1958. Some 300 photos, with ample text, of the masterpieces of African art. See also P. Wingert, **The Sculpture of Negro Africa,** Columbia Univ., 1950.

R. A. Lystad, ed., **The African World,** Praeger, 1965. An invaluable survey and evaluation of the new African studies. For an analysis of **Negritude** consult Colin Legum, **Pan-Africanism,** Praeger, 1962. Although T. Walter Wallbank, ed., **Documents on Modern Africa,** Van Nostrand,* covers primarily the nineteenth and twentieth centuries, a section on "The African Renaissance and the African Past" evaluates **Negritude** and past African cultures.

AMERICAN INDIANS

J. Collier, **Indians of the Americas,*** Mentor. A former U.S. Commissioner of Indian Affairs discusses sympathetically the past and present of the American Indians. See also H. S. Driver, **Indians of North America,** Univ. of Chicago, 1961.

R. Benedict, **Patterns of Culture,*** Mentor. A pioneer study in the field of social anthropology. Includes case studies of Pueblos of New Mexico and the Indians of the Pacific Northwest.

M. Astrov, ed., **American Indian Prose and Poetry (The Winged Serpent),*** Capricorn. An outstanding anthology. See also E. E. Clark, **Indian Legends of the Pacific Northwest,*** Univ. of Calif.

S. G. Morley, **The Ancient Maya,** Stanford Univ., 1956. Written by a distinguished archaeologist, this is the best general survey of the twelve centuries of Mayan life. V. W. von Hagen, **The World of the Maya,*** Mentor, is a rapid survey.

Frederick Peterson, **Ancient Mexico,*** Capricorn. A valuable survey. A. Caso, **The Aztecs: People of the Sun,** Univ. of Okla., 1958, is a lavishly illustrated work. Recommended for brief, lucid surveys of Aztec civilization are V. W. von Hagen, **The Aztec: Man and Tribe,*** Mentor; G. C. Vaillant, **The Aztecs of Mexico,*** Penguin.

J. A. Mason, **The Ancient Civilizations of Peru,*** Penguin. An anthropological history of the culture and peoples of pre-

*Indicates an inexpensive paperbound edition.

Columbian Peru. A popular and vivid account of Inca life by an American explorer is V. W. von Hagen, **Realm of the Incas,*** Mentor. For a scholarly account of the Inca civilization at its height, including the story of the Spanish invasions, see B. Flornoy, **The World of the Inca.*** Anchor.

DISCOVERY AND CONQUEST

J. H. Parry, **The Age of Reconnaissance,*** Mentor. An excellent history of the Europeans who streamed across the oceans to trade, plunder, or settle between 1450 and 1650. Good reading also are B. Penrose, **Travel and Discovery in the Renaissance, 1420-1620,*** Atheneum; E. Prestage, **The Portuguese Pioneers,** Black, 1933.

J. H. Parry, **The Establishment of the European Hegemony: 1415-1715,*** Torchbooks; C. E. Nowell, **The Great Discoveries and the First Colonial Empires,*** Cornell. Two excellent surveys of European expansion. More detailed is P. Sykes, **A History of Explorations,*** Torchbooks. On geographic knowledge before Columbus see G. H. T. Kimble, **Geography in the Middle Ages,** Methuen, 1935.

J. B. Brebner, **The Explorers of North America, 1492-1806,*** Mentor. Engrossing survey of the explorations which revealed the character of the New World to Europe, and the men who undertook them. See also J. Bakeless, **The Eyes of Discovery: America as Seen by the First Explorers,*** Dover. On the Norse adventurers see F. Mowat, **Westviking: The Ancient Norse in Greenland and North America,** Little, Brown, 1965; R. A. Skelton, *et al.,* **The Vinland Map and the Tartar Relation,** Yale, 1965.

F. A. Kirkpatrick, **The Spanish Conquistadores,*** Meridian. A colorful treatment. See also P. Horgan, **Conquistadores in North American History,*** Premier; C. O. Sauer, **The Early Spanish Main,** Univ. of Calif., 1966; J. Bannon, ed., **The Spanish Conquistadores: Men or Devils?*** Holt, Rinehart and Winston (European Problem Series). Two classic accounts by W. H. Prescott, the famous American historian, of the Spanish conquests in the New World are **History of the Conquest of Mexico and History of the Conquest of Peru,** 1 vol. ed., Modern Lib., 1936.

Excellent biographies which deal with figures discussed in Chapter 20 include E. Bradford, **A Wind from the North: The Life of Henry the Navigator,** Harcourt, Brace, 1960; H. Hart, **Sea Road to the Indies** (Vasco da Gama), Macmillan, 1952; S. E. Morison, **Christopher Columbus, Mariner,*** Mentor; C. M. Parr, **Ferdinand Magellan: Circumnavigator,** Crowell, 1964.

S. Shellabarger, **Captain from Castile,*** Bantam. A fascinating novel which provides a vivid portrayal of sixteenth-century Spain and of Cortés' conquest of Mexico.

C. H. Haring, **The Spanish Empire in America,*** Harbinger. The best introduction to the colonial period in Spanish America.

See also J. H. Parry, **The Spanish Seaborne Empire,** Knopf, 1966, and **The Spanish Theory of Empire,** Macmillan, 1940.

C. Boxer, **Four Centuries of Portuguese Expansion, 1415-1825,** Dufour, 1961. See also A. Toussaint, **History of the Indian Ocean,** Univ. of Chicago, 1966.

C. Boxer, **The Dutch Seaborne Empire, 1600-1800,** Knopf, 1965. The rise and fall of the principal seafaring nation. C. Masselman, **The Cradle of Colonization,** Yale, 1963, deals with the Dutch in Southeast Asia, with emphasis on the work of Jan Pieterszoon Coen.

THE COMMERCIAL REVOLUTION

L. B. Packard, **The Commercial Revolution, 1400-1776,** Holt, 1927. A reliable brief survey; especially good on the theory and practice of mercantilism. Also good on governmental economic policies during this period is J. U. Nef, **Industry and Government in France and England, 1540-1650,*** Cornell. Robert L. Reynolds, **Europe Emerges: Transition Toward an Industrial World-Wide Society, 600-1750,** Univ. of Wis., 1961, is a clarifying account of the emergence of Europe as an economic and social force.

H. E. Sée, **Modern Capitalism, Its Origin and Evolution,** Adelphi, 1928. A valuable account of capitalism's growth during the Age of Discovery. The author stresses the importance of trade in the evolution of capitalism.

Donald F. Lach, **Asia in the Making of Europe,** Vol. I: **The Century of Discovery,** Univ. of Chicago, 1965. A monumental study of the impact of the Orient on the West. See also J. E. Gillespie, **The Influence of Oversea Expansion on England to 1700,** Columbia Univ., 1920; G. N. Clark, **The Wealth of England from 1490 to 1760,** Oxford, 1946. Carl Bridenbaugh, **Vexed and Troubled Englishmen, 1590-1642,** Oxford, 1968, is a fascinating account of the factors influencing English migration to America. On the effects in Spain and Europe of the influx of precious metals, see Earl J. Hamilton, **American Treasure and the Price Revolution in Spain, 1501-1650,** Harvard, 1934.

R. Ehrenberg, **Capitalism and Finance in the Age of the Renaissance; A Study of the Fuggers and their Connections,** Harcourt, 1928. Excellent portrayal of the Fuggers and of other great financier families of the sixteenth century. Also recommended are R. De Roover, **The Rise and Decline of the Medici Bank, 1397-1494,*** Norton; V. Barbour, **Capitalism in Amsterdam in the Seventeenth Century,*** Univ. of Mich.; B. N. Nelson, **The Idea of Usury: From Tribal Brotherhood to Universal Otherhood,** Princeton, 1949, which discusses the reasons for the prohibition against the charging of interest.

R. H. Tawney, **The Agrarian Problem in the Sixteenth Century,*** Torchbooks. Lucid account of the transition to capitalistic agriculture and the economic and social results.

Chronological Tables

Table 1

NEAR EAST	EGYPT
B.C. 5000 Ubaid culture in Sumer—agricultural village economy, land and crops held in common; priests a dominant group	**Predynastic period** (5000-3100)—agricultural village economy; clan warfare
4000 Uruk period in Sumer (4000-3500): the first "civilization"—city life, pictographic writing, vocational specialization	
	Kingdoms of Lower Egypt and Upper Egypt, each divided into *nomes*
First appearance of wheeled carts in Sumer and Assyria (3500-3000)	Sailboat developed; trade contacts with Sumer
Potter's wheel first used, in Sumer c. 3250	Menes unites Upper and Lower Egypt 3100—city life; vocational specialization; role of pharaoh as god and king
3000 Bronze replaces stone for tools and weapons; plows drawn by oxen c. 3000	
Early Dynastic period in Sumer c. 2800-2370—cuneiform records become numerous; frequent wars of theocratic, independent city-states; economy largely collectivized	**Old Kingdom** (c. 2700-2200)—heyday of pyramid building; trade with Near East and Crete; hieroglyphic writing; Pyramid Texts; improved lunar calendar; rigid stylization in art
Akkadian empire founded by Sargon c. 2370—first empire in history; state-assisted capitalism flourishes	Plows in use c. 3000; potter's wheel introduced c. 2750
	First Intermediate Period (2200-2050)—*nomes* autonomous; civil strife: "people in terror, panic, fear"
Period of Sumerian revival: Third Dynasty of Ur c. 2113-2006—bureaucratic state; deified rulers; social legislation	**Middle Kingdom** (2050-1800)—general welfare promoted; "democratization of the hereafter"
2000	Bronze supersedes copper for tools and weapons c. 2000
	Second Intermediate Period (1800-1570)
Babylonian empire founded by Hammurabi 1792-1750 Hammurabi's code—"to further the welfare of the people" Babylonian culture—mathematics, astronomy, literature Hittites sack Babylon 1595	Hyksos conquer northern Egypt, introduce horses and wheeled vehicles; Hebrews enter Egypt c. 1700
Hittite empire c. 1600-1200—iron tools and weapons; Babylonian influences on culture; transmitter to the West	**New Kingdom or Empire** (1570-1080) Thutmose III (1490-1436)—the "Napoleon of Egypt" Queen Hatshepsut's African expedition 1470 Amenhotep III (1398-1361)—empire at its height Akhenaton (1369-1353)—introduces monotheistic concept in religion; naturalism in art; empire neglected
Era of small states (1200-700) Period of exploration and colonization by Phoenicians (1200-850); Carthage founded c. 800; Phoenicians develop alphabet of 22 consonant symbols	Ramses II (1290-1224)—conflict with Hittites; Hebrew Exodus
	Period of Decadence (1090-332)—Egypt divided (Upper and Lower Egypt)
1000 The Hebrews—kingdom established (c. 1300) rules of David (1000-961) and Solomon (961-922); the divided kingdom: Israel and Judah 922	
Hebrew prophets begin religious reform (eighth century)	
Lydians invent coined money c. 675	
Later empires (c. 700-331) Assyria is master of Fertile Crescent 700 Zoroaster, 6th century Destruction of Nineveh by Medes and Chaldeans 612 Nebuchadnezzar, king of Chaldeans, rules Fertile Crescent; Chaldean advances in astronomy and mathematics Destruction of Jerusalem by Nebuchadnezzar 586	Assyrians invade Egypt 671 Unsuccessful attempt to revive Egypt's greatness (663-525) Necho (609-593) commissions African expedition
500 Persian empire—Cyrus conquers Near East; efficient imperial system established, great highways built	**Persians conquer Egypt 525**

INDIA	CHINA	
		5000 B.C.
		4000
Prehistoric inhabitants in Quetta valley c. 3000—herdsmen with bone and stone tools; worship of mother goddess		3000
Indus valley civilization (2500-1500)—capitals at Mohenjo-Daro and Harappa; well-organized government and economy; excellent city planning; trade relations with Sumer		
	Neolithic cultures: Yang Shao (c. 2200) and Lung Shan (c. 2000)	
		2000
	Shang dynasty (1766?-1122 or 1027): China's "first civilization"—ruler functions as military commander and high priest; religious practices (fertility rites, divination); agrarian economy (silk raising); writing (partly pictorial, partly ideographic); magnificent bronzes; two-wheeled chariot	
Invasion of Indus valley by Aryans from Black and Caspian seas c. 1500		
Early Vedic Age (c. 1500-900)—beginning of three pillars of Indian society: autonomous village, caste system, joint-family		
Vedas—oldest Sanskrit literature, pantheistic concepts		
	Chou dynasty (1122 or 1027-256): China's "classical age"—"Decree of Heaven" promulgated; capital city (near modern Sian); creation of many feudal states; increased emphasis on ancestor worship; writing (ideograms); money economy; iron supersedes bronze for tools and weapons; advances in agriculture and crafts	1000
Later Vedic Age (c. 900-500)—sovereign city-states headed by rajahs rise in Ganges valley; trade with Mesopotamia; caste system becomes more complex. Brahman (priest), Kshatriya (warrior), Vaisya (merchant), Sudra (serf), Pariah ("untouchable")		
Upanishads—foundation of Hinduism, composed (800-600)	Rebellion by nobles 771; Chou capital moved to Lo-yang	
Gautama Buddha (563-483)—founder of Buddhism		
	Confucius (551-479)—empirical approach to knowledge; emphasis on humanistic values; political and social conservatism	
	Poetry collected in *Shih Ching*, or *Book of Odes*	500
Two greatest Sanskrit epics composed: *Mahabharata* (including the *Bhagavad-Gita*) and *Ramayana*		
	Lao-tzu and Taoism—intuitive approach to knowledge, metaphysical values; *Tao Te Ching*	
	Mencius (372?-289?)—democratic concept of the will of the people in government	
	Period of Warring States (403-221)—Ch'in victorious over Chou; China reunited under First Emperor, Shih Huang Ti 221	
	Civil service examination system established	100

Table 2

GREECE	ROME

B.C. 2000

Indo-European tribes invade Peloponnesus 1900
Zenith of Cretan culture (1750-1500)—sophisticated, pleasure-seeking society; great palaces and villas; flourishing Mediterranean trade; worship of Earth Mother

Indo-Europeans invade Italian peninsula (2000-1000); first settlers in Po valley; Latins settle in lower Tiber valley (Latium)

1500 Mycenaeans capture Knossos c. 1500
Mycenae—master of the Aegean world (1400-1200)

Dorians invade Greek mainland c. 1100; destruction of city of Mycenae c. 1120; Mycenaeans flee to Attica and Ionia
Greek Dark Ages (1150-750)—tribal government, animistic religion;
1000 Mycenaeans ancestors of Athenians; Dorians, of Spartans

Etruscans settle on Italy's west coast, dominate northern Italy (c. 900-c. 400); employ arches and vaults in buildings; acquire Hellenic culture from Great Greece

750 **Hellenic Age** or "classical Greece" (c. 750-338)—rise of independent city-states
Age of Nobles (750-500)—nobility gains supreme political power; land ownership shifts from tribe to noble families; extensive Greek colonization, notably Great Greece
Growth of Athenian democracy: Solon (594) establishes Council of Four Hundred and court of appeals, broadens franchise; Pisistratus (560) banishes nobles, increases power of popular assembly; Cleisthenes (508) reclassifies citizens, introduces *ostracism*
Sparta controls Peloponnesus (sixth century)

Rome founded; elective monarchy, *imperium* conferred by popular assembly; king's council (Senate); class divisions (patrician, plebeian)

500 Persian Wars: Miletus destroyed by Persians 494; Athenians defeat Persians at Marathon 490; Persians defeat Spartans at Thermopylae 480; Persian navy crushed at Salamis 480; Persian army defeated at Plataea 479
Delian League, established in 478, becomes agency for Athenian imperialism
Athens' Golden Age under Pericles (461-429)
Peloponnesian War (431-404)—Athens vs. Sparta and Corinth

Nobles revolt against Etruscan king, establish **Roman republic** headed by two patrician consuls 509
Plebeians on the rise (509-300)—Laws of the Twelve Tables drafted; powers of Senate and rights of patricians decrease
Latin League allied with Rome 493

400

Philip II of Macedonia conquers Greece 338
Alexander the Great defeats Persia 331; spreads Greek culture through the East; establishes network of Greek cities in Near East; institutes theory of divine kingship
Tripartite division of Alexander's empire (331-323): Ptolemy, Seleucus, and Antigonus Gonatas
300 **Hellenistic Age** (323-30)
Alexandria becomes commercial and intellectual capital of Hellenistic world

Rebellion of Latin League quelled by Rome, League dissolved 338

Internal problems in Rome—large-scale farming ruins small landowner; corruption in government; Senate retains power
Great Greece conquered; Rome master of all Italy south of Rubicon 270; Roman conquest facilitated by efficient military organization and consolidated by wise government of subject peoples

Roster of Greek geniuses in Hellenic period—philosophers and scientists: Thales, Pythagoras, Heraclitus, Democritus, Hippocrates, Socrates, Plato, Aristotle; historians: Herodotus, Thucydides; poets and dramatists: Sappho, Aeschylus, Sophocles, Euripides, Aristophanes; sculptors: Myron, Phidias, Praxiteles

First Punic War (264-241)—Carthage beaten; Rome gains naval supremacy in western Mediterranean
Second Punic War (c. 218-201)—"colossal contest between the nation Rome and the man Hannibal"; Romans victorious at battle of Zama

200 Roster of Greek geniuses in Hellenistic period: Epicurus, Zeno, Euclid, Archimedes, Aristarchus, Eratosthenes

Rome defeats Macedonia 197; Rome defeats Seleucids; Egypt forms alliance with Rome 168

Third Punic War—Rome demolishes Carthage 146
Civil War (133-31)—Tiberius and Gaius Gracchus attempt unsuccessful reform movement (133-121); Sulla vs. Marius, Sulla and Senate victorious (88-79); Pompey vs. Caesar, Caesar becomes dictator (49-44); Octavian vs. Antony, Octavian defeats Antony and Cleopatra at battle of Actium 31

Golden Age of literature: Cicero, Catullus, Lucretius, Virgil, Horace, Ovid, Livy

100

Octavian becomes Augustus; establishes **principate;** improves governmental administration and economy; initiates **Pax Romana** (30 B.C.-235 A.D.)
Julio-Claudian line (14-68)—Tiberius, Claudius, Caligula, Nero
Flavian emperors (69-96)

A.D. 100

Silver Age of literature: Juvenal, Martial, Tacitus, Plutarch, Seneca; scientists—Pliny the Elder, Ptolemy, Galen
Antonines, "five good emperors" (96-180)—Hadrian, Marcus Aurelius

INDIA	CHINA	
Prehistoric inhabitants in Quetta valley c. 3000 Indus valley civilization (2500-1500)—capitals at Mohenjo-Daro and Harappa	Neolithic cultures: Yang Shao (c. 2200) and Lung Shan (c. 2000)	**2000** B.C.
Invasion of Indus valley by Aryans from Black and Caspian seas c. 1350 Early Vedic Age (c. 1500-900)	Shang dynasty (1766?-1122 or 1027)—China's "first civilization"	**1500**
	Chou dynasty (1122 or 1027-256)—China's "classical age"	**1000**
Later Vedic Age (c. 900-500)		**750**
Gautama Buddha (563-483) Magadha state, nucleus for India's first empire, expands c. 540	Confucius (551-479)	**500**
		400
Alexander the Great reaches Indus valley 326 Chandragupta Maurya seizes Magadhan state, founds **Maurya dynasty** 322; capital city (Pataliputra); efficient government; extensive trade relations		**300**
Ashoka (273-232)—"the first great royal patron of Buddhism"; erects pillar edicts and *stupas*; practices religious toleration and nonviolence; propagates Buddhism outside India	Ch'in ruler, the First Emperor, Shih Huang Ti (221-210)—establishes absolutist military state; persecutes Confucian scholars; builds highways and Great Wall	
Tamil kingdoms—Hindu states, chief trading area with the West	**Han dynasty** (202 B.C.-220 A.D.)—Imperial expansion and establishment of *Pax Sinica*; flowering of Confucianism; revision of calendar; invention of paper	**200**
Mauryan empire falls 185; Bactrian rule extends over northern India (185-30)—Graeco-Bactrian cultural influences; bilingual coinage		
	Han emperor Wu Ti sends ambassador west to seek allies, silk trade begins 138	
Andhra dynasty flourishes in Deccan (100 B.C.-225 A.D.)		**100**
Kanishka, Kushan ruler (c. 78-128)—sponsors *Mahayana* or "Great Vehicle," new form of Buddhism, which spreads north and east; *Hinayana* or "Lesser Vehicle" spreads south and east Kushan empire declines 220		**100** A.D.

Table 3

ROME AND BYZANTIUM	NEAR EAST
	Jews under Judas Maccabaeus rebel against Seleucid ruler of Palestine 168; independence won, Maccabean dynasty founded 142

B.C. 100

ROME AND BYZANTIUM	NEAR EAST
Julius Caesar, dictator of Rome (46-44)	Pompey annexes Palestine 63 Herod, king of Judea (37-4)

A.D. 1 Octavian becomes Augustus, initiates principate 29

Birth of Jesus c. 4 B.C.
Crucifixion of Jesus c. 30 A.D.
Paul (d. c. 65), greatest of early Christian missionaries
Jewish rebellion (66-70) climaxed by destruction of Jerusalem

200
Marcus Aurelius (161-180)—Germanic tribes endanger Roman frontiers
Accession of Septimius Severus (193) signals end of principate, increased control of government by army cliques
Persecution of Christians by Decius 250, by Diocletian 303

Persian king overthrows Parthians, establishes Sassanid rule 226

Diocletian (285-305)—stops imperial decline by autocratic rule; splits civil-military administration; controls prices
Christianity made legal religion in eastern empire by Edict of Toleration 311; legalized throughout empire by Edict of Milan 313; made sole and official state religion 395
Ulfilas (311-383), Arian Christian missionary among Visigoths; St. Patrick (c. 389-c. 461) founds Celtic Church in Ireland
Church Fathers—Clement of Alexandria (East); St. Jerome, St. Ambrose, St. Augustine, author of *The City of God* (West)
Constantine sole emperor of Rome (324-337)—enforces rigid economic measures, dedicates "New Rome" 330
Arianism branded heretical at Council of Nicaea 325
Battle of Adrianople 378—Roman legions defeated by Visigoths
Theodosius splits empire into eastern and western branches 395

Persian religions: revival of Zoroastrianism under Sassanids; growth of Manicheism and Mithraism, rivals to Christianity

400 Rome sacked by Visigoths 410, by Vandals 455
Battle of Troyes 451; German-Roman alliance repels Huns
Council of Chalcedon begins schism between eastern and western Churches 451
Odovacar deposes Romulus Augustus 476—event symbolizes fall of Roman empire in the West
Theodoric (c. 454-526)—defeats Odovacar, establishes Ostrogothic kingdom in Italy with Ravenna as capital
Justinian (527-565)—crushes *Nike* rebellion 532; extends domain into Italy, Spain, North Africa; supervises *Corpus Juris Civilis* (528-535); dedicates Hagia Sophia 537
Lombards establish kingdom in Italy 568

Chosroes I, "the Great King" (531-579)—defeats Turks and Romans; reorganizes government; encourages scholarship
Muhammad (570-632)—the Hijra, migration of Muhammad from Mecca to Medina 622; triumphal return to Mecca 630

600 Heraclius (610-641) defeats Sassanid Persia (622-628)
Eastern Roman empire becomes "Byzantine" (seventh century)—Greek becomes official language; styles in art combine Hellenic and Near Eastern traditions; Greek scholarship preserved
St. Boniface (680?-755), "the apostle to the Germans"

Sassanids crushed by Byzantine empire 628, by Muslims c. 642
Reign of First Four Caliphs (632-661)—caliphate elective office; expansion of Islam in Near East and Egypt; Koran prepared 652

Umayyad dynasty (661-750)—caliphate dynastic, not elective; capital city, Damascus; expansion in North Africa, Turkestan, India; invasion of Visigothic Spain (711-718); defeat by Franks at battle of Tours 732
Abbasid rule begins 750; city of Baghdad, capital built in 762
Breakup of Abbasid hegemony—independent Muslim states set up in Spain 756, Morocco 788, Tunisia 800

Leo III (717-741)—centralizes government; edict forbidding use of images in worship leads to iconoclastic controversy (725-843)

800
Novgorod and Kiev joined 882; Byzantine-Russian trade begins c. 900
Basil II (976-1025), Byzantine emperor, defeats Bulgars
Conversion of Kievan Russia to Orthodox Christianity c. 990

Zenith of Islamic power and civilization (900-1100)—end of Arab predominance of Islam; flowering of arts and learning

1000 Reign of Yaroslav the Wise (1019-1054)—peak of Kievan Russia; Byzantine influences in art and literature
Battle of Manzikert (Byzantine defeat by Seljuk Turks) and fall of Bari to Normans (last Byzantine stronghold in Italy)—1071
Alexius Comnenus (1081-1118) deflects First Crusade (1095-1096) from Constantinople

Seljuk Turks seize Persia and Iraq, conquer Baghdad 1055
Fatimids rule North Africa, Egypt, Syria, western Arabia (eleventh century); capital at Cairo
First Crusade (1095-1096) weakens Muslim power in Near East

Saladin crushes Fatimids 1171
Roster of Muslim geniuses: Al-Razi, Avicenna, Alhazen, Al-Khwarizmi, Omar Khayyám, Al-Idrisi, ibn-Batuta, Averroës, ibn-Khaldun

1200 **Fourth Crusade** (1202-1204)—Constantinople sacked; schism between eastern and western Churches final
Latin empire in Constantinople (1204-1261)
Rule of the Palaeologi (1261-1453)—decline of Byzantine empire; final collapse when Constantinople captured by Ottoman Turks 1453

Fall of Abbasid dynasty, conquest by Mongols 1258

1400

Ottomans capture Constantinople 1453; extend rule in Egypt, North Africa, and Near East (sixteenth century)

INDIA	CHINA	JAPAN	
		Rule by Yamato clan	
			100 B.C.
			1 A.D.
Kanishka (78-128) Expansion of Indian culture into Southeast Asia begins (second century)			
	Fall of Han dynasty 220 Buddhism gains popularity in China (third century)		**200**
Panchatantra composed (300-500) Chandragupta I founds **Gupta dynasty** 320			
Chandragupta II (c. 380-c. 413)—zenith of Gupta power; dominance of Hinduism Kalidasa (c. 400-455), lyric poet, the "Indian Shakespeare"			**400**
		Buddhism enters Japan (sixth century)	
Harsha (606-647) rules northern India	Sui dynasty (581-618) ends civil strife; era of canal building **T'ang dynasty** founded 618 T'ai Tsung (627-650)—first great T'ang ruler; expands empire (Turkestan, Korea); initiates political and economic reforms, publishes *Thirteen Classics* T'ang poets: Li Po and Tu Fu	Taika Reform 646; Yamato ruler becomes "The Supreme Monarch" Nara period (710-784)	**600**
Shankara (c. 788-828) synthesizes Hindu doctrines Expansion of Indian culture into Southeast Asia ends (tenth century) Mahmud of Ghazni annexes Punjab 1022	China loses Turkestan to Arabs 751 *Diamond Sutra* printed 868 T'ang dynasty falls 907 **Sung dynasty** founded 960 Gunpowder used by Sung c. 1000 Wang An-shih (1021-1086), socialistic reformer	Fujiwara period (794-1192); capital at Kyoto	**800** **1000**
Angkor Wat built c. 1100 Muhammad of Ghuri conquers northern India 1191 **Delhi sultanate** established 1206; Indian culture divided into Hindu and Muslim	China divided between empires of Sung (south) and Chin (north) 1127 **Genghis Khan** (1162-1227) unites Mongols Mongols conquer Chin 1234, Sung 1279; *Pax Tatarica* links East and West via trade routes Kublai Khan (1260-1294), Yüan emperor	Yoritomo (1147-1199)—*shogun* ruling from Kamakura; establishes *Bakufu* Hojo period (1199-1333)	**1200**
Tamerlane destroys Delhi 1398	Ming dynasty established 1368	"The Great Wind" 1281 Kamakura destroyed 1333; Ashikaga shogunate founded 1338	**1400**

Table 4

THE STATE

Theodoric (c. 454-526) establishes Ostrogothic kingdom in Italy with Ravenna as capital; Justinian drives Ostrogoths from Italy 554

Odovacar deposes Romulus Augustus 476—fall of the Roman empire in the West

Clovis I, Merovingian ruler of the Franks (481-511)—becomes Christian convert; expands realm (Burgundy, Rhineland, southern France)

500 Invasion of Europe by Slavs (500-900; Slavs establish Elbe as western frontier c. 650

Lombards establish kingdom in Italy 568

600 Merovingian decline—civil war divides Frankish state into three parts; kings become puppet rulers

700 Muslim conquest of Visigothic Spain (711-718)
Charles Martel, Mayor of the Palace, rules Franks (714-741)—restores Frankish unity; defeats Muslims at battle of Tours 732

Pepin the Short (741-768)—ends rule of Merovingian kings; crowned king of the Franks by St. Boniface 751, title reconfirmed by Pope Stephen 754; conquers Lombard-controlled exarchate of Ravenna and makes "Donation of Pepin" 756

800 **Charlemagne** (768-814)—extends empire against Saxons in Germany, Avars in Danube valley, Lombards in north Italy, Muslims in Spain; establishes *missi dominici* system of royal envoys; crowned Emperor of the Romans by pope 800; fosters Carolingian Renaissance
Division of Carolingian empire foreshadowed in Strasbourg Oaths 842; confirmed in Treaty of Verdun 843—tripartite split among Charles the Bald (West Frankland), Louis the German (East Frankland), Lothair (Lotharingia or Lorraine); Lotharingia divided between Charles and Louis 870
Alfred the Great (871-899)—establishes strong Anglo-Saxon kingdom in England; improves local government and schooling
Muslim and Viking invasions threaten Europe (ninth-tenth centuries); Muslim control of Mediterranean diminishes European trade and towns

900 Feudalism and manorial system, based on Roman and German customs, create makeshift system of law and order; stabilize class structure and land ownership

Treaty between Rollo and king of France awards Normandy to Vikings 911
Henry I (the Fowler), king of Germany (919-936)—founder of Saxon dynasty; defeats Danes, Magyars, Slavs
Otto I (the Great) (936-973)—promotes centralized government in Germany; builds alliance with Church; routs Magyars at battle of Lechfeld 955; crowned emperor by pope 962
Edgar the Peaceful (959-975)—height of Anglo-Saxon monarchy
Otto II (973-983)—defeated by Muslims in southern Italy; Slav uprising and Danish invasion halt German eastward expansion for over a century
Ethelred the Unready (978-1016)—levies *Danegeld* to buy off invaders; invasion by Canute, ruler of Denmark and Norway; Anglo-Saxon monarchy reëstablished 1042
Hugh Capet (987-996) founds Capetian dynasty in France; practice of king's double coronation (crowning heir apparent during king's lifetime, crowning again after king's death) ensures survival of dynasty

1000

Normans arrive in Italy 1016

Overthrow of Umayyad rule in Caliphate of Cordova, small Muslim states overthrown by expansive Christian kingdoms, **Reconquista gains strength** 1031

William, Duke of Normandy, defeats Harold at battle of Hastings 1066
Norman conquests in Mediterranean area: Bari, last Byzantine stronghold in Italy 1071; Palermo 1072; Sicily 1092

1100 Mediterranean open to European commerce (c. 1100) after destruction of Muslim fleets by Italian navies; rebirth of town life, rise of bourgeoisie
Louis the Fat (1108-1137)—first strong Capetian ruler in France

1200

1300 *Jacquerie* revolt in France 1358; Wat Tyler uprising in England 1381

THE CHURCH

Council of Chalcedon 451; first schism between eastern and western Churches

Boethius (475?-525?) and *Consolations of Philosophy*

St. Benedict (c. 480-543) founds Benedictine order

Clovis and Franks converted to Christianity 496

500

Gregory the Great (590-604)—sharp increase in temporal powers of papacy

600

St. Augustine (d. 604) converts Anglo-Saxon king to Christianity 596
Venerable Bede (673-735) and the *Ecclesiastical History of the English Nation*
St. Boniface (680?-755), "the apostle of Germany"

700

Iconoclastic controversy between eastern and western Churches (725-843)

Pope Stephen becomes temporal ruler over Papal States through the "Donation of Pepin" 756

800

900

Monastic order of Cluny founded in Burgundy 910; impetus for widespread religious revival and reform

Russians converted to Greek Orthodox Christianity c. 990
Truce of God inaugurates "closed seasons" to curb warfare (eleventh century)

1000

Final separation of eastern and western churches 1054
College of Cardinals formed to elect pope 1059

Gregory VII (1073-1085)—proponent of religious reform; abolishes lay investiture and simony; humiliates Henry IV at Canossa 1077
Pierre Abélard (1079-1142) proposes theory of Conceptualism as compromise between Realism and Nominalism
Nominalism condemned as heretical at Council of Soissons 1092
First Crusade (1095-1096)—Jerusalem conquered; Latin kingdom of Jerusalem established (1099-1187)
Cistercian order founded 1098

Renaissance of the twelfth century—return of classical learning to the West, translations of Greek and Arabic works; rise of universities (Bologna, Paris,   **1100**
Oxford), development of professional curriculums in law, medicine, theology; revival of Latin poetry, development of vernacular literature (epics, *chansons de geste, fabliaux*, morality plays); Romanesque and Gothic styles in architecture
Concordat of Worms mitigates problem of lay investiture 1122; Church maintains right to approve clerical offices
Second Crusade (1147-1149)—Christians fail to capture Damascus
Cathedral of Notre Dame in Paris built (1163-1235)
St. Dominic (1170-1221) forms Dominican order
St. Francis of Assisi (1182-1226) founds Franciscan order
Third Crusade (1189-1192)—the "Crusade of Kings" (Frederick Barbarossa, Richard the Lion-Hearted, Philip Augustus)
Innocent III (1198-1216)—zenith of temporal power of the papacy
The Inquisition established 1233
Fourth Crusade (1202-1204)—fall of Constantinople; schism between eastern and western Churches final; Latin empire (1204-1261) rules Constantinople   **1200**
St. Thomas Aquinas (1225?-1274) reconciles faith and reason in *Summa Theologica*
Dante Alighieri (1265-1321) and the *Divine Comedy*, allegorical poem tracing imaginary journey through hell, purgatory, and paradise
Acre, last Christian foothold in Holy Land, conquered by Muslims 1291

Geoffrey Chaucer (1340?-1400) and the *Canterbury Tales*, poetic panorama of medieval life in England   **1300**

Table 5

POLITICS

1000

Salian House rules Germany (1024-1125)

William the Conqueror rules England (1066-1087)—centralizes government, initiates well-knit feudal system, establishes Great Council (*curia regis*), supervises Domesday Survey

1100

Reconquista—fall of Toledo 1085

Welf-Hohenstaufen rivalry (1106-1152) destroys hope for unified Germany

Louis the Fat (1108-1137)—rules lle de France; builds prestige of French monarchy

Kingdom of Naples and Sicily established 1127

Afonso recognized as king of independent Portugal 1143

Frederick Barbarossa (1152-1190)—Germany a centralized feudal monarchy; attempts to win Italy

Henry II (1154-1189)—founds Plantagenet (Angevin) House; reforms English judicial system by Assize of Clarendon 1166

Philip II (Augustus) of France (1180-1223)—gains control of Angevin lands in France; establishes *parlement*, Chamber of Accounts, Royal Council

Frederick II (1194-1250)—brilliant, erratic Hohenstaufen ruler; holds court at Palermo, neglects Germany

1200

Reconquista—Muslims defeated at Las Navas de Tolosa 1212

Magna Carta limits power of English monarch 1215

Louis IX (1226-1270) brings moral dignity to throne of France; known as St. Louis

Conquest of Russia by Mongols 1237

Alexander Nevski defeats Teutonic Knights at Lake Peipus 1242; rules Vladimir (1252-1263); son Daniel founds grand duchy of Moscow

Edward I (1272-1307)—Parliament gains stature; royal statutes; conquest of Wales; wars with Scotland

Philip IV (the Fair) of France (1285-1314)

1300

Battle of Bannockburn 1314—Scotland wins independence from England

Hundred Years' War between France and England begins 1337

Golden Bull establishes constitution of Holy Roman Empire and, in effect, crystallizes German disunity 1356

Grand Prince of Moscow defeats Mongols at Kulikovo 1380

Poland and Lithuania united 1386

1400

The **quattrocento** in northern Italy (1400-1500)—political turmoil, economic prosperity, flowering of the arts; Venice under merchant oligarchy, Florence ruled by Medici

Poles and Lithuanians crush Teutonic Knights at Tannenberg 1410

Hapsburg rule of Holy Roman Empire begins 1452

Hundred Years' War ends 1453; Joan of Arc spurs French to victory

Fall of the Byzantine empire 1453

Wars of the Roses (1455-1486)—rivalry between Houses of York and Lancaster ends with accession of Henry VII (1485-1509), founder of Tudor dynasty

Louis XI of France, the "universal spider" (1461-1483), seizes Burgundy

Ivan the Great of Russia (1462-1505)

Spain united under Catholic Sovereigns Ferdinand and Isabella 1469

Reconquista ends with conquest of Granada 1492

Charles VIII of France invades Italy 1494; repulsed by Venice, Papal States, Holy Roman Empire, and Spain

1500

Henry VIII of England (1509-1547)

Charles V elected Holy Roman emperor 1519

Suleiman ascends Turkish throne 1520

Gustavus Vasa elected king of Sweden 1523

Battle of Pavia 1525—French under Francis I crushed by Hapsburgs

King of Bohemia and Hungary slain fighting Turks 1526; Czechs offer throne to Hapsburgs; Hungary divided between Turks and Hapsburgs

Ivan IV (the Terrible) of Russia (1547-1584)

Charles V divides his empire (1554-1556)—central Europe to brother Ferdinand; Spain, Netherlands, New World to son Philip

Philip of Spain (1556-1598) seizes Portugal 1580

Elizabeth of England (1558-1603)—condemns Mary Stuart to death 1587; defeats Spanish Armada 1588

Civil war in France (1562-1589)—Guises (Catholic) vs. Bourbons (Protestant); conflict ends with accession of Henry IV (1589-1610)

Eighty Years' War between Dutch and Spanish begins 1568, Netherlands split between northern and southern provinces 1579; United Provinces declared independent 1581

Battle of Lepanto, the "last great crusade" 1571—Holy League crushes Ottoman sea power

Time of Trouble (1584-1613)—civil war in Russia, ends with accession of Romanovs

1600

Thirty Years' War (1618-1648)—Spanish and Austrian Hapsburgs vs. German Protestant states, Denmark, Sweden, France; Austria surrenders in Peace of Westphalia 1644; Spain recognizes Dutch independence 1648; Spain vs. France (1648-1659)

RELIGION   **THOUGHT & ART**

1000

Gregory VII (1073-1085)—humiliates Henry IV at Canossa 1077

The First Crusade (1095-1096)   1100

Concordat of Worms 1122
The Second Crusade (1147-1149)
Henry II of England attempts to limit "benefit of clergy", foiled by murder
of Thomas à Becket, Archbishop of Canterbury 1170
The Third Crusade (1189-1192)
Innocent III (1198-1216)
The Fourth Crusade (1202-1204); fall of Constantinople 1204   1200

St. Thomas Aquinas (1225?-1274)

                                                Transitional period in Italian art (c. 1250-c. 1400)—Cimabue, Duccio,
                                                Giotto (painters) and Pisano (sculptor) synthesize medieval and classical
                                                techniques and subject matter
                                                Dante (1265-1321) and the *Divine Comedy*
Center of Russian Orthodox Church moved from Kiev to Moscow c. 1299
Philip IV of France humiliates Boniface VIII 1303   **Humanism and the Revival of Learning in Italy**   1300
Avignon papacy (1305-1377)—the Babylonian Captivity of the Church   Petrarch, the "father of humanism" (1304-1374)
Wycliffe (1320?-1384)—dawn star of the Protestant revolt   Chaucer (1340?-1400) and the *Canterbury Tales*
Great Schism (1378-1417)—two papal claimants, Clement VII and Urban VI   Boccaccio's *Decameron* 1348
(1378-1409); Conciliar Movement: Council of Pisa deposes two popes and
elects a third 1409; Council of Constance elects Martin V, heals schism   Platonism centers in Florence; Platonic Academy established by Cosimo   1400
(1414-1417), burns Huss for heresy   de Medici; Ficino synthesizes Platonism and Christianity
                                                Aristotelianism centers in Padua; Averroists deny immortality of the soul
                                                Florence center for Early Renaissance art—Brunelleschi (architect); Ghiberti,
                                                Donatello, Verrocchio (sculptors); Masaccio, Botticelli (painters). Other
Cardinal Ximenes (1436?-1517) reforms Spanish Church   painters—from Padua, Mantegna; from Venice, Bellini
                                                Painters of the Northern Renaissance—Van Eyck, Dürer, Holbein, Brueghel

Savonarola, puritanical reformer, burned as heretic 1498

                                                The High Renaissance in Italy (1500-1530)—Rome center of the arts;   1500
                                                Bramante (architect); Michelangelo (sculptor-painter); Da Vinci, Raphael,
                                                Giorgione, Titian (painters); Palestrina (composer)
                                                Benvenuto Cellini (1500-1571)
Luther posts his ninety-five theses 1517; Pope Leo X issues *Exsurge Domine*   *In Praise of Folly* (1511) by Erasmus
1520; Luther excommunicated by pope, declared heretic and outlaw at   *Utopia* (1516) by Thomas More
Diet of Worms 1521
Peasants revolt in Germany (1524-1525)
Augsburg Confession 1530—creed of Lutheran faith; Schmalkaldic Wars
(1546-1555)—Lutheran vs. Catholic princes in Germany; **Peace of Augsburg**
1555—each prince decides religion of his subjects   Castiglione's *The Courtier* 1528
Henry VIII establishes Anglican Church 1534; Six Articles reaffirm Catholic   *The Prince* (1532) by Machiavelli—objective exposé of ruthless statecraft
theology, deny papal supremacy 1539; Mary reinstates Catholicism (1553-   Rabelais' *Gargantua and Pantagruel* (1532-1564)
1558); Elizabethan compromise (1558-1603)
Loyola establishes the Society of Jesus (Jesuit order) 1534
Papal reform under Pope Paul III (1534-1549)
Calvin's *Institutes of the Christian Religion* 1536
Council of Trent (1545-1563): climax of Catholic Reformation—reaffirms
Church doctrines, reforms Church administration
Knox draws up Articles of Presbyterian Church 1560
Lutheranism becomes state religion in Denmark 1560, in Sweden 1593
St. Bartholomew's Day Massacre in France 1572

Edict of Nantes ensures religious toleration in France 1598

                                                                                        1600

King James Version of the Bible 1611

                                                Grotius' *De Jure Belli ac Pacis* 1625—foundation for international law

Table 6

THOUGHT & ART IN EUROPE	EUROPEAN EXPLORATION

1000

Eric the Red discovers Greenland c. 982
Leif Ericson sails to Labrador and Nova Scotia 1002

Pierre Abélard (1079-1142) proposes theory of Conceptualism
Renaissance of the twelfth century—revival of classical learning; rise of universities (Bologna, Paris, Oxford)

1200

Roger Bacon (1214-1292)
St. Thomas Aquinas (1225?-1274) and *Summa Theologica;* Dante (1265-1321) and the *Divine Comedy*

Marco Polo arrives at Kublai Khan's court c. 1275; visits southern India 1292-1293

Petrarch, the "father of humanism" (1304-1374)

Boccaccio's *Decameron* 1348; Chaucer's *Canterbury Tales* c. 1387

Prince Henry the Navigator (1394-1460) stimulates exploration

1400 The *quattrocento* in Italy (1400-1500)

Commercial Revolution in Europe (1450-1650)—Atlantic seaboard nations dominate trade; inflation; influx of gold and silver, new products; growth of banking, stock companies, insurance
Diaz rounds Cape of Good Hope 1486
Columbus discovers New World 1492
Spain and Portugal divide New World—Bull of Demarcation 1493, Treaty of Tordesillas 1494
Da Gama rounds Cape of Good Hope, reaches India, returns to Lisbon (1497-1499)
Cabot claims eastern North America for England 1497
Angola founded by Portuguese 1497
Cabral discovers Brazil 1500
Balboa sights the Pacific Ocean 1513
Portuguese traders arrive in China 1516

1500 The High Renaissance in Italy (1500-1530)
Erasmus' *In Praise of Folly* 1511; More's *Utopia* 1516
Castiglione's *The Courtier* 1528; Machiavelli's *The Prince* 1532
Revolution in astronomy: Copernicus refutes geocentric theory of the universe 1530, publishes *Concerning the Revolutions of the Heavenly Bodies* 1543; Brahe attempts compromise between geocentric and heliocentric theories; Kepler coordinates Brahe's data; Galileo confirms Copernican theory; Copernicus' masterwork placed on *Index* 1617; Galileo recants heliocentric views 1633
Montaigne (1533-1592) develops informal essay form
El Greco (1541?-1614), master of Mannerist style in painting
Pioneers in medicine: Paracelsus—experiments with new drugs; Vesalius—founder of modern anatomy, writes *The Fabric of the Human Body* 1543; Paré—father of modern surgery; Harvey—describes circulation of blood 1628, advances theory of epigenesis 1651
Francis Bacon (1561-1626)—champions inductive method in philosophy; *Novum Organum* 1620; *New Atlantis* 1627
Shakespeare (1564-1616); Lope de Vega (1562-1635)
Court poets: Ronsard; Spenser (*The Faerie Queene* 1590-1596)
Descartes (1596-1650) champions deductive method of philosophical inquiry; develops analytical geometry

Round-the-world voyage: Magellan sails around South America 1520, killed in Philippines 1521; crew returns to Spain via India and Cape of Good Hope 1522
Conquistadores: Cortés (Mexico); Ponce de León (Florida); Pizarro (Peru); De Soto (southern U.S.); Coronado (southwest U.S.)
Further exploration and conquest of South America by Spain (sixteenth century)
Portuguese trade monopoly in Far East (sixteenth century)
Universities founded at Lima and Mexico City 1551
French explorers in North America: Cartier (St. Lawrence); Champlain (Great Lakes); Marquette, Joliet, La Salle (Mississippi)
Chinese restrict European trade to Macao 1557

Philippines occupied by Spanish 1565

1600 Bruno burned at the stake for heresy 1600
Gilbert's *De Magnete* 1600; Galileo's study of dynamics; Napier's treatise on logarithms 1614
Cervantes' *Don Quixote de la Mancha* (1605-1615)
Baroque style: Rubens, Velasquez, Vermeer, Hals, Rembrandt (painters); Bernini (architect); Monteverdi (composer)
Inventions: astrolabe, telescope, microscope, thermometer, barometer, pendulum clock, air pump

Royal Society founded in England 1662
Milton's *Paradise Lost* 1667; Bunyan's *Pilgrim's Progress* 1678

Queen Elizabeth incorporates East India Company 1600
Dutch East India Company formed to break Portuguese trade monopoly in East 1602
Jamestown founded 1607; Quebec 1608; Plymouth 1620
Bank of Amsterdam established 1609; Bank of England 1694
Dutch West India Company set up 1621; Manhattan settled 1624

AMERICAS	AFRICA, NEAR EAST	FAR EAST	
	Ghana empire (c. 300-c. 1200)	Sailendra empire of Srivijaya (c. 700-c. 1300)	**1000**
Mayan city-states in Yucatán peninsula (980-1200)—theocratic government; rigid social stratification; advances in mathematics and astronomy; splendid art	Fatimids rule North Africa, Egypt, Syria, Arabia (eleventh century); capital, Cairo		
	Mali empire (c. 1000-c. 1400)—ruled by Mandingos; chief city, Timbuktu		
	Zenj empire (c. 1000-c. 1500)—trade with Near East and Orient; Swahili language		
Incas settle Cuzco valley (eleventh century)	Capital of Ghana empire plundered by Berbers 1076		
		Angkor Wat built c. 1100	
Toltecs dominate Mexican plateau (twelfth century)		China divided between empires of Sung (south) and Chin (north) 1160	
		End of Fujiwara period in Japan 1192	
		Hojo period in Japan (1199-1333)	
		Madjapahit Kingdom (c. 1200-c. 1400)	**1200**
		Delhi sultanate established 1206; Indian culture divided into Hindu and Muslim	
	Fall of Ghana state 1240	Nan Chao destroyed 1253	
	Abbasids conquered by Mongols 1258	First Thai empire established; King Rama the Brave 1275-1317	
		Mongols conquer Chin 1234, Sung 1279; *Pax Tatarica* links East and West via trade	
Tenóchtitlan built by Aztecs c. 1325		Ashikaga shogunate founded in Japan 1338	
Aztec confederacy extends across Mexico (fourteenth century)—strong army; fluid social structure; barbaric religious rites; culture borrowing from Mayas	Atlantic slave trade begins 15th century	Fall of Mongol China; Ming dynasty founded 1368—scholar rule restored, Code of the Great Ming compiled	**1400**
	Songhai empire (c. 1400-c. 1600)—capital, Gao	Forbidden City in Peking built (1403-1424)	
	Ottomans capture Constantinople 1453; extend rule in Egypt, North Africa, Near East (sixteenth century)	Chinese naval expeditions to India, Near East, Africa begin (fifteenth century)	
Zenith of Inca empire (1438-1532)—totalitarian government; worship of sun; skillful engineering projects			
Great Peace of the Iroquois extends over northeast U.S. (fifteenth century)			
			1500
Aztec empire falls to Cortés 1519		Babur (the Tiger)—defeats Delhi sultanate and Rajputs (1526-1527); founds Mughul dynasty in India	
Plains Indians of southwest U.S. exchange farm life for buffalo hunting (sixteenth century)		Edict forbids Chinese naval expeditions (sixteenth century); China in isolation	
		Akbar (1556-1605)—expands Mughul empire; reforms government; promotes religious tolerance; builds Fathpur Sikri	
		Manila established by the Spanish 1571	
		Japanese attempt invasion of China and Korea 1592	
		Hideyoshi (d. 1598) persecutes Christians in Japan	
		Tokugawa period begins in Japan 1603	**1600**
		Shah Jahan (1628-1658)—promotes Muslim faith; conquers Deccan; builds Taj Mahal	
		Europeans forbidden entry to Japan, Japanese forbidden exit 1639	
		Manchu invade Ming China; establish Manchu dynasty 1644	
		Aurangzeb (1658-1707)—decline of Mughul power; intolerance and civil disorder	

List of Readings

The titles listed below are recommended to supplement the study of various aspects of world history. This list, along with the six lists of suggested readings within the text, provides a wide assortment of works for assigned outside reading and for leisure-time reading. Paperbound editions are indicated by an asterisk.

TOOLS OF THE TRADE

The historian, like all craftsmen, has his basic tools and methods. In order to obtain the information he needs, he learns quickly to use special tools. Some of his most important tools are the bibliographies which provide compilations of the literature available in many areas of history. The **American Historical Association's Guide to Historical Literature,** rev. ed., Macmillan, 1961, is indispensable for world history. For medieval study the basic guide is L. J. Paetow, **Guide to the Study of Medieval History,** Appleton, 1931; supplementing this work is C. P. Farrar and A. P. Evans, **Bibliography of English Translations from Medieval Sources,** Columbia, 1946. For the general student the inexpensive pamphlets published by the Service Center for Teachers of History, sponsored by the American Historical Association, cannot be recommended too highly. Some seventy have been published thus far. Each pamphlet covers a specific subject or area, such as Greek and Roman history, India, Japan, or Renaissance humanism. Trends in historical research, the status of scholarship, important archives, and schools of interpretation—all are touched upon; each pamphlet also includes many bibliographical references.

Invaluable for reference purposes are a number of well-known multivolume works written by specialists: **The Cambridge Ancient History,** 12 vols., 1923-1939 (Vols. I-II are being revised); **The Cambridge Medieval History,** 8 vols., 1911-1936; **The Cambridge Modern History,** 14 vols., 1902-1912. A **New Cambridge Modern History** is now appearing, and the following volumes are available and pertinent: Vol. I, **The Renaissance,** G. R. Potter, ed., 1957; Vol. II, **The Reformation,** G. R. Elton, ed., 1958. One of the most valuable series in European history, profusely illustrated and strong in intellectual and cultural history, is **The Rise of Modern Europe,** W. L. Langer, ed., 13 vols., Harper, 1935-1953 (also Torchbooks*). **The University of Michigan History of the Modern World,** Allan Nevins and Howard Ehrmann, eds., is a series which will interest not only the scholar of history but the amateur and beginning student as well. Sixteen volumes have been published.

General reference works include **An Encyclopedia of World History,** W. L. Langer, ed., Houghton Mifflin, 1952; **The Worldmark Encyclopedia of the Nations,** Harper, 1960; **The Columbia Encyclopedia,** W. Bridgwater and E. J. Sherwood, eds., Columbia, 1963; Van Nostrand's **Scientific Encyclopedia,** 1958. **The Encyclopedia of the Social Sciences,** 15 vols., 1937, Macmillan, while somewhat dated, contains many scholarly articles of great value. For biographies, the **Dictionary of National Biography,** a multivolume series, is indispensable for information concerning British personalities; for American notables, see the **Dictionary of American Biography.**

One cannot fully understand the course of human affairs without reference to good maps. The following atlases are most helpful in this regard: **Muir's Historical Atlas—Ancient, Medieval and Modern,** G. Goodall and R. F. Treharne, eds., Barnes and Noble, 1956; C. McEvedy, **The Penguin Atlas of Ancient History,*** and **The Penguin Atlas of Medieval History,*** W. R. Shepherd, **Historical Atlas,** Barnes and Noble, 1956; E. W. Fox and H. S. Deighton, eds., **Atlas of European History,*** Oxford, 1957; **Atlas of World History,** R. R. Palmer, ed., Rand McNally, 1957 (also available as **Abridged Historical Atlas***); J. D. Fage, **An Outline Atlas of African History,** Arnold, 1958.

MEANING AND METHOD IN HISTORY

To obtain a general idea of what history is all about, one could not do better than to read the handy small volume by A. L. Rowse, **The Use of History,*** Collier, in which a British historian examines the content, use, and pleasures of history and its relation to life and culture. Other helpful studies on the philosophy and meaning of history are R. Aron, **Introduction to the Philosophy of History,*** Beacon; Nicolas Berdyaev, **The Meaning of History,*** Meridian; Herbert Butterfield, **Man on His Past,*** Beacon; E. H. Carr, **What Is History?*** Vintage; R. G. Collingwood, **The Idea of History,*** Oxford. Different approaches to the writing of history are described in H. E. Barnes, **A History of Historical Writing,*** Dover; Fritz Stern, ed., **The Varieties of History,*** Meridian.

Such topics on the meaning of method in history, the training of a historian, principles of historical criticism, finding material, and the process of writing can be found in J. Barzun and H. Graff, **The Modern Researcher,*** Harbinger; L. R. Gottschalk, **Understanding History,** Knopf, 1950; H. C. Hockett, **The Critical Method in Historical Research and Writing,** Macmillan, 1955; Sherman Kent, **Writing History,*** Appleton; C. V. Langlois and C. Seignobos, **Introduction to the Study of History,** Holt, 1912 (a pioneer text); G. J. Renier, **History, Its Purpose and Method,*** Torchbooks. See also N. Cantor and R. Schneider, **How to Study History,*** Crowell, 1967, and Robert V. Daniels, **Studying History: How and Why,*** Prentice-Hall, 1966.

GENERAL HISTORIES

Sir Ernest Barker, *et al.,* eds., **The European Inheritance,** 3 vols., Oxford, 1954; S. Barr, **The Pilgrimage of Western Man,*** Preceptor; W. Durant, **The Story of Civilization,** Simon and Schuster, 1935-1968, 10 vols.; J. F. C. Fuller, **A Military History of the Western World,** Funk and Wagnalls, 1956; W. H. McNeill, **The Rise of the West: A History of the Human Community,*** New American Library, and **A World History,** Oxford, 1967; H. J. Muller, **The Uses of the Past,*** Galaxy.

PREHISTORY

Ruth Benedict, **Patterns of Culture,*** Sentry; M. Burkitt, **The Old Stone Age,*** Atheneum; R. J. Braidwood, **The Near East and the Foundations for Civilization,** Univ. of Oregon, 1952; Bernard Campbell, **Human Evolution: An Introduction to Man's Adaptations,** Aldine, 1966; V. G. Childe, **Man Makes Himself,*** Mentor; V. G. Childe, **The Prehistory of European Society,*** Penguin; Y. Cohen, ed., **Man in Adaptation,*** 2 vols., Aldine, 1968; S. Cole, **The Prehistory of East Africa,*** Penguin; W. A. Fairservis, Jr., **The Origins of Oriental Civilization,*** Mentor; G. Rachel Levy, **The Gate of Horn: A Study of the Religious**

Conceptions of the Stone Age and Their Influence upon European Thought, Faber, 1948; B. Malinowski, Crime and Custom in Primitive Society,* Littlefield; R. Redfield, The Primitive World and Its Transformations,* Cornell; O. Struve, The Universe,* M.I.T. Press; Sol Tax, ed., Evolution After Darwin, 3 vols., Univ. of Chicago, 1960; F. Zeuner, Dating the Past: An Introduction to Geochronology, 4th ed., Methuen, 1962.

THE ANCIENT WORLD

F. Adcock, The Greek and Macedonian Art of War,* Univ. of Calif.; N. Bailkey, Readings in Ancient History: From Gilgamesh to Diocletian,* Heath, 1969; A. E. R. Roak and W. Sinnigen, A History of Rome to 565 A.D., Macmillan, 1965; F. Bourne, A History of the Romans, Heath, 1966; J. H. Breasted, A History of Egypt,* Bantam; W. E. Caldwell and Mary F. Giles, The Ancient World, Holt, Rinehart and Winston, 1966; M. Cary, A History of Rome Down to the Time of Constantine, St. Martin's, 1954; V. G. Childe, What Happened in History,* Penguin; M. Grant, ed., The Birth of Western Civilization: Greece and Rome, McGraw-Hill, 1964 (contains over 700 illustrations); M. I. Finley, ed., Slavery in Classical Antiquity, Heffer, 1960; K. Freeman, Greek City-States,* Norton; E. N. Gardiner, Athletics in the Ancient World, Oxford, 1955; R. M. Haywood, Ancient Greece and the Near East, McKay, 1964, and Ancient Rome, McKay, 1967; F. Heichelheim and C. Yeo, A History of the Roman People, Prentice-Hall, 1962; Tom B. Jones, Ancient Civilization, Rand McNally, 1964; H. Marrou, A History of Education in Antiquity,* Mentor; S. Mazzarino, The End of the Ancient World, Knopf, 1966; H. J. Muller, Freedom in the Ancient World,* Bantam; T. R. Glover, The Ancient World,* Pelican; C. Roebuck, The World of Ancient Times, Scribner, 1966; M. Rostovtzeff, Greece,* and Rome,* Galaxy; C. Seltman, Women in Antiquity,* Collier; C. Starr, A History of the Ancient World, Oxford, 1965 (includes India and China); J. W. Swain, The Ancient World, 2 vols., Harper, 1950.

Highly recommended as handy reference books of ancient history are M. Cary, et al., The Oxford Classical Dictionary, Oxford (Clarendon Press), 1949, and Smaller Classical Dictionary,* Everyman.

For works which offer coverage of the ancient East, see the listings for India, China, and Japan on these pages. See also *Suggestions for Reading,* pp. 87-88.

THE MIDDLE AGES

C. Brooke, Europe in the Central Middle Ages, 962-1154, Holt, Rinehart and Winston, 1964; N. F. Cantor, Medieval History: The Life and Death of a Civilization, Macmillan, 1963; D. Geanakoplos, Byzantine East and Latin West: Two Worlds of Christendom in Middle Ages and Renaissance,* Torchbooks; R. Guerdan, Byzantium,* Torchbooks; George Holmes, The Later Middle Ages, 1272-1488,* Norton; B. Lyon, Medieval History, Harper & Row, 1962; Romilly Jenkins, Byzantium: The Imperial Centuries, A.D. 610-1071, Random House, 1967; J. L. LaMonte, The World of the Middle Ages: A Reorientation of Medieval History, Appleton, 1949; S. Painter, A History of the Middle Ages, 284-1500, Knopf, 1953; H. Pirenne, A History of Europe from the Invasions to the XVI Century,* 2 vols., Anchor; R. Southern, The Making of the Middle Ages,* Yale; J. R. Strayer and D. C. Munro, The Middle Ages, 395-1500, Appleton-Century-Crofts, 1959; P. Vinogradoff, Roman Law in Medieval Europe, Oxford, 1929.

ENGLAND

E. H. Carter and R. A. F. Mears, A History of Britain, Oxford, 1937; W. S. Churchill, The Birth of Britain and The New World,

Vols. I and II of A History of the English-Speaking Peoples,* Bantam; A. B. Erickson and M. J. Havran, England: Prehistory to the Present,* Anchor, 1968; F. Marcham, A Constitutional History of Modern England, 1485 to the Present, Harper & Row, 1960; G. M. Trevelyan, A Shortened History of England,* Penguin; E. L. Woodward, History of England from Roman Times to the End of World War I,* Colophon.

FRANCE

A. Guérard, France, Univ. of Mich., 1959; A. Maurois, A History of France,* Minerva; R. Sedillot, Outline of French History, Knopf, 1953; C. M. Seignobos, The Evolution of the French People, Knopf, 1932.

GERMANY

E. F. Henderson, A Short History of Germany, Macmillan, 1916; K. F. Reinhardt, Germany: 2000 Years,* 2 vols., Ungar; J. Rodes, Germany: A History, Holt, Rinehart and Winston, 1964; W. M. Simon, Germany: A Brief History, Knopf, 1966; S. H. Steinberg, A Short History of Germany, Macmillan, 1945.

ITALY

L. Salvatorelli, A Concise History of Italy from Prehistoric Times to Our Own Day, Oxford, 1939; J. P. Trevelyan, A History of the Italian People, Pitman, 1956.

SPAIN AND PORTUGAL

William C. Atkinson, A History of Spain and Portugal,* Penguin; A. Castro, The Structure of Spanish History, Princeton, 1954; Charles E. Chapman, A History of Spain,* Free Press; R. L. Davies, Spain in Decline, 1621-1700, Macmillan, 1957; J. Descola, A History of Spain, Knopf, 1963; C. E. Nowell, A History of Portugal, Van Nostrand, 1952; W. Montgomery Watt, History of Islamic Spain,* Anchor.

CENTRAL AND EASTERN EUROPE

J. Billington, The Icon and the Axe: An Interpretive History of Russian Culture, Knopf, 1966; R. D. Charques, A Short History of Russia,* Everyman; M. T. Florinsky, Russia: A Short History, Macmillan, 1964; C. Gulick, Austria from Habsburg to Hitler, 2 vols., Univ. of Calif., 1948; O. Halecki, Borderlands of Western Civilization: A History of East Central Europe, Ronald, 1952, and A History of Poland, Roy, 1956; W. Medlin, Moscow and East Rome, Droz, 1952; B. Pares, A History of Russia,* Vintage; N. Pounds, Poland Between East and West,* Searchlight; N. V. Riasanovsky, A History of Russia, Oxford, 1963; D. Sinor, History of Hungary, Praeger, 1959; S. H. Thompson, The Czechs in European History, Princeton, 1943; G. Vernadsky, A History of Russia,* Bantam, The Mongols and Russia, Yale, 1953, and The Origins of Russia, Oxford, 1959; M. C. Wren, The Course of Russian History, Macmillan, 1968.

INDIA

The Cambridge History of India, 6 vols., Cambridge, 1922-1937, supplementary vol., 1953; R. C. Majumdar, et al., An Advanced History of India, Macmillan, 1946; W. H. Moreland and A. C. Chatterjee, A Short History of India, Longmans, 1957; J. Nehru, The Discovery of India,* Anchor; J. C. Powell-Price, A History of India, Nelson, 1955; H. G. Rawlinson, India: A Short Cultural History, Praeger, 1953; V. A. Smith, The Oxford History of India, Oxford (Clarendon Press), 1923; T. W. Wallbank, A Short History of India and Pakistan from Ancient Times to the Present,* Mentor.

CHINA

W. Eberhard, **A History of China,** Univ. of Calif., 1950; J. K. Fairbank, **The United States and China,** Viking, 1962; C. P. Fitzgerald, **China, A Short Cultural History,** Praeger, 1950; E. Balazs, **Chinese Civilization and Bureaucracy: Variations on a Theme,** Yale, 1964; M. Granet, **Chinese Civilization,*** Meridian; R. Grousset, **The Rise and Splendour of the Chinese Empire,*** Univ. of Calif.; A. de Riencourt, **The Soul of China,** Coward-McCann, 1958.

JAPAN

W. T. de Bary *et al.,* eds., **Sources of Japanese Tradition,** 2 vols., Columbia, 1964; J. W. Hall, **Japanese History; New Dimensions of Approach and Understanding,** American Historical Association, 1966; M. D. Kennedy, **A Short History of Japan,*** Mentor; E. O. Reischauer, **The United States and Japan,** Viking, 1962; R. K. Reischauer, **Japan: Government—Politics,** Ronald, 1939; G. B. Sansom, **Japan: A Short Cultural History,** Century, 1931; G. B. Sansom, **The Western World and Japan,** Cresset, 1950.

AFRICA

R. I. Rotberg, **A Political History of Tropical Africa,** Harcourt, Brace, and World, 1965; J. F. Ajayi and Ian Espie, eds., **A Thousand Years of West African History,** Nelson, 1965; D. L. Wiedner, **A History of Africa,** Random House, 1962; R. Oliver and G. Mathew, **History of East Africa,** Oxford, 1963; V. Harlow and E. M. Chilver, eds., **History of East Africa,** Vol. II, Oxford, 1965.

THE NEAR EAST

S. N. Fisher, **The Middle East: A History,** Knopf, 1968; R. Ghirshman, **Iran: From the Earliest Times to the Islamic Conquest,*** Penguin; P. K. Hitti, **History of the Arabs: From Earliest Times to the Present,** St. Martin's, 1956; P. K. Hitti, **Syria: A Short History,*** Collier; G. E. Kirk, **A Short History of the Middle East,*** Praeger; G. Le Strange, **Baghdad During the Abbasid Caliphate,** Allen & Unwin, 1954; Sir Percy Sykes, **A History of Persia,** 2 vols., St. Martin's, 1952; P. Wittek, **The Rise of the Ottoman Empire,** Royal Asiatic Society, 1957.

RELIGION—GENERAL

A. C. Bouquet, **Comparative Religion,*** Penguin, and **Sacred Books of the World,*** Penguin; P. Colum, **Myths of the World,*** Universal; Jack Finegan, **The Archaeology of World Religions,*** 3 vols., Princeton; Sir James G. Frazer, **The Golden Bough,** 1 vol. ed., Macmillan; J. Hastings, ed., **Encyclopedia of Religion and Ethics,** Scribner, 1908-1927; Adolph E. Jensen, **Myth and Cult Among Primitive Peoples,** Univ. of Chicago, 1963; J. Noss, **Man's Religions,** 3rd ed., Macmillan, 1963; H. B. Parkes, **Gods and Men: The Origins of Western Culture,*** Vintage; Paul Radin, **Primitive Religion,*** Dover; W. H. D. Rouse, **Gods, Heroes and Men,*** Signet; Huston Smith, **The Religions of Man,*** Mentor; A. Waley, **Three Ways of Thought in Ancient China,*** Anchor.

RELIGION—CHRISTIANITY

Archibald Baker, ed., **A Short History of Christianity,*** Phoenix; E. Benz, **The Eastern Orthodox Church: Its Thought and Life,*** Anchor; H. Bettenson, ed., **Documents of the Christian Church,*** Oxford; S. Bullough, **Roman Catholicism,*** Penguin; H. Butterfield, **Christianity and History,*** Scribner; F. L. Cross, ed., **The Oxford Dictionary of the Christian Church,** Oxford, 1957; C. Guignebert, **Christianity Past and Present,** Macmillan, 1927; K. Latourette, **Christianity Through the Ages,*** Harper & Row; M. Marty, **A Short History of Christianity,*** Meridian.

RELIGION—ISLAM

A. J. Arberry, trans., **The Holy Koran,** Allen & Unwin, 1953; Sir Muhammed Zafrulla Khan, **Islam, Its Meaning for Modern Man,** Routledge & Kegan Paul, 1962; Duncan Macdonald, **Development of Muslim Theology, Jurisprudence and Constitutional Theory,** Russell and Russell, 1966; K. W. Morgan, ed., **Islam,** Ronald, 1958; J. Trimingham, **Islam in East Africa,** Oxford, 1964; A. S. Tritton, **Islam: Belief and Practices,** Hutchinson Univ. Lib., 1951.

RELIGION—JUDAISM

I. Epstein, **Judaism,*** Penguin; E. Flannery, **The Anguish of the Jews: 2000 Years of Anti-Semitism,*** Macmillan; P. Goodman, **History of the Jews,*** Everyman; M. Margolis and A. Marx, **History of the Jewish People,*** Meridian; L. Sachar, **A History of the Jews,** 5th ed., Knopf, 1967; G. Ernest Wright, **Biblical Archaeology,** Westminster, 1957.

PHILOSOPHY AND POLITICAL THEORY

Crane Brinton, **Ideas and Men: The Story of Western Thought,** Prentice-Hall, 1963; G. Catlin, **The Story of the Political Philosophers,** McGraw-Hill, 1939; H. G. Creel, **Chinese Thought from Confucius to Mao Tsè-Tung,*** Mentor; J. Declareuil, **Rome, the Lawgiver,** Knopf, 1927; W. T. DuBarry, *et al.,* **Introduction to Oriental Civilizations: Sources of the Japanese Tradition,** Columbia, 1958; Will Durant, **The Story of Philosophy,*** Pocket Books; M. Hammond, **City-State and World State in Greek and Roman Political Theory Until Augustus,** Harvard, 1951; F. Heer, **Intellectual History of Europe,*** 2 vols., Anchor; E. Lewis, **Medieval Political Ideas,** Knopf, 1954; Mou-shêng Lin, **Men and Ideas; An Informal History of Chinese Political Thought,** Day, 1942; C. H. McIlwain, **The Growth of Political Thought in the West: From the Greeks to the End of the Middle Ages,** Macmillan, 1932; C. A. Moore, ed., **Philosophy—East and West,** Princeton, 1944; B. Russell, **A History of Western Philosophy,*** Simon and Schuster; W. Montgomery Watt, **Islamic Philosophy and Theology,** Aldine, 1962; W. Windelband, **A History of Philosophy,*** Torchbooks; W. H. Zimmer, **Philosophies of India,*** Meridian.

LITERATURE AND THE ARTS

W. J. Anderson, *et al.,* **The Architecture of Ancient Rome; An Account of Its Historic Development,** Scribner, 1927; A. Badawy, **Architecture in Ancient Egypt and the Near East,** M. I. T. Press, 1966; G. Bazin, **A History of Art,** Houghton Mifflin, 1958; F. Boas, **Primitive Art,*** Dover; G. Brenan, **The Literature of the Spanish People,*** Meridian; S. Cheney, **The Theatre; Three Thousand Years of Drama, Acting, and Stagecraft,** Tudor, 1941; O. M. Dalton, **East Christian Art,** Oxford, 1925; M. S. Dimand, **A Handbook of Muhammedan Art,** Metropolitan Museum of Art, 1944; H. Goetz, **India: Five Thousand Years of Indian Art,** Methuen, 1960; G. Highet, **The Classical Tradition; Greek and Roman Influences on Western Literature,*** Galaxy; E. G. Holt, **The Middle Ages and the Renaissance,*** Anchor, Vol. I of **A Documentary History of Art;** H. W. Janson, **History of Art,** Prentice-Hall, 1962; D. Keene, **Japanese Literature: An Introduction for Western Readers,*** Evergreen; S. Kramrisch, **The Art of India Through the Ages,** Doubleday, 1954; P. H. Lang, **Music in Western Civilization,** Norton, 1941; E. Leuzinger, **Africa: The Art of the Negro Peoples,** Methuen, 1962; E. Mâle, **Religious Art,*** Noonday; Lai Ming, **History of Chinese Literature,*** Capricorn; R. T. Paine and A. Soper, **The Art and Architecture of Japan,** Penguin, 1955; A. Parrot, **Sumer: The Dawn of Art,** Golden Press, 1961; T. E. Peet, **A Comparative Study of the Literature of Egypt, Palestine and Mesopotamia,** Oxford, 1931; Arthur U. Pope, **A Survey of Persian Art,** Oxford, 1958; G. Reese,

Music in the Middle Ages, Norton, 1940; D. M. Robb, *et al.*, **Art in the Western World,** Harper, 1953; D. S. Robertson, **A Handbook of Greek and Roman Architecture,** Macmillan, 1944; B. Rowland, **The Art and Architecture of India,*** Penguin, 1959; L. Sickman and A. Soper, **The Art and Architecture of China,** Penguin, 1956; W. Volbach, **Early Christian Art,** Abrams, 1962; E. M. Upjohn, *et al.*, **History of World Art,** Oxford, 1958; R. Warnock and G. K. Anderson, **The World in Literature,** 2 vols., Scott, Foresman, 1967; W. Willetts, **Chinese Art,** 2 vols., Penguin, 1958-1959; G. B. Woods, *et al.*, **The Literature of England,** 2 vols., Scott, Foresman, 1968; J. Yohannan, ed., **A Treasury of Asian Literature,** Day, 1956; H. Zimmer, **Myths and Symbols in Indian Art and Civilization,*** Torchbooks.

SCIENCE AND TECHNOLOGY

R. Calder, **Medicine and Man,*** Mentor; L. Casson, **The Ancient Mariners,** Macmillan, 1959; C. Cipolla, **Guns, Sails and Empire: Technological Innovations and the Early Phases of European Expansion,** Pantheon, 1966; H. J. Cowan, **Time and Its Measurement: From the Stone Age to the Nuclear Age,** World, 1958; W. C. Dampier, **A Shorter History of Science,*** Meridian; T. Dantzig, **Number: The Language of Science,*** Anchor; R. J. Forbes, **Man the Maker: A History of Technology and Engineering,** Abelard-Schuman, 1958; B. Jaffe, **Crucibles: The Story of Chemistry,*** Premier; R. S. Kirby, *et al.*, **Engineering in History,** McGraw-Hill, 1956; M. Kranzberg and C. Pursell, **Technology in Western Civilization,** Vol. I: **The Emergence of Modern Industrial Society, Earliest Times to 1900,** Oxford, 1967; W. T. Sedgwick, *et al.*, **A Short History of Science,** Macmillan, 1939; C. A. Singer, ed., **Studies in the History and Method of Science,** 2 vols., Oxford, 1921; C. J. Singer, *et al.*, **A History of Technology,** Oxford, 1957; W. H. Stahl, **Roman Science,** Univ. of Wis., 1962; A. Vagts, **A History of Militarism,*** Free Press; A. D. White, **A History of the Warfare of Science with Theology in Christendom,*** Free Press; H. J. J. Winter, **Eastern Science; An Outline of Its Scope and Contribution,** Transatlantic Press, 1952.

ECONOMICS

M. Beard, **A History of Business,*** 2 vols., Univ. of Mich.; M. P. Charlesworth, **Trade-Routes and Commerce of the Roman Empire,** Cambridge, 1926; S. B. Clough and C. W. Cole, **Economic History of Europe,** Heath, 1952; T. Frank, **An Economic History of Rome,** Johns Hopkins, 1927; G. Glotz, **Ancient Greece at Work,** Knopf, 1926; H. Heaton, **Economic History of Europe,** Harper, 1948; P. Hohenberg, **A Primer on the Economic History of Europe,*** Random House, 1968; E. S. Kirby, **Introduction to the Economic History of China,** Macmillan, 1954; W. F. Leemans, **The Old-Babylonian Merchant: His Business and Social Position,** Brill, 1950; H. Michel, **The Economics of Ancient Greece,** Heffer, 1958; W. F. Oakeshott, **Commerce and Society, A Short History of Trade and Its Effects on Civilization,** Oxford, 1936; M. Rostovtzev, **The Social and Economic History of the Roman Empire,** 2 vols., Oxford, 1957; W. P. Webb, **The Great Frontier,** Houghton Mifflin, 1952.

EXPLORATION

J. N. L. Baker, **A History of Geographical Discovery and Exploration,** Harrep, 1937; C. R. Beazley, **The Dawn of Modern Geography,** 3 vols., J. Murray, 1897-1906; M. Cary and E. H. Warmington, **The Ancient Explorers,*** Penguin; R. E. Dickinson and O. J. R. Howarth, **The Making of Geography,** Oxford, 1933; A. P. Newton, ed., **The Great Age of Discovery,** Univ. of London, 1932; R. and C. Oliver, eds., **Africa in the Days of Exploration,*** Spectrum; A. Grenfell Price, **The Western Invasions of the Pacific and Its Continents: A Study of Moving Frontiers and Changing Landscapes, 1513-1958,** Oxford, 1963.

Footnotes

PROLOGUE: PERSPECTIVE ON MAN

1. P. Gardiner, *The Nature of Historical Explanation* (London: Oxford University Press, 1952), p. 98.
2. H. Butterfield, *Christianity and History* (London: G. Bell & Sons, Ltd., 1949), p. 132.
3. See A. J. Toynbee, *Civilization on Trial* (New York: Oxford University Press, 1948).
4. H. A. L. Fisher, *A History of Europe*, I (Boston: Houghton Mifflin Co., 1935), p. vii.
5. Toynbee, p. 11.
6. W. D. Howells, *Mankind So Far* (New York: Doubleday & Co., Inc., 1952), p. 312.

CHAPTER 1: OUT OF DARKNESS

1. See Jane Goodall, "Chimpanzees on the Gombe Stream Reserve," *Primate Behavior*, ed. by Irven DeVore *et al.* (New York: Holt, Rinehart and Winston, Inc., 1965), pp. 425-473.
2. Ernst Cassirer, *An Essay on Man: An Introduction to a Philosophy of Human Culture* (New Haven, Conn.: Yale University Press, 1965), pp. 24-25.
3. Kenneth P. Oakley, "Skill As a Human Possession," *A History of Technology*, I (Oxford: Clarendon Press, 1958), p. 33. Reprinted by permission of the Clarendon Press, Oxford.
4. This chronology is based upon James Mellaart, "Tentative Interpretation of Cultural Progress in the Near East," *The Dawn of Civilization*, ed. by Stuart Piggett (London: Thames and Hudson Ltd., 1961), p. 42.

CHAPTER 2: ALONG THE BANKS OF RIVERS

1. See R. J. Forbes, "Extracting, Smelting, and Alloying," in *A History of Technology*, I (Oxford: Clarendon Press, 1956), pp. 572-599. Reprinted by permission of the Clarendon Press, Oxford.
2. V. Gordon Childe, *What Happened in History* (New York: Pelican Books, 1946), p. 74.
3. V. Gordon Childe, *New Light on the Most Ancient East* (London: Routledge & Kegan Paul Ltd., 1954), p. 114.
4. Tom B. Jones, *Ancient Civilization* (Chicago: Rand McNally & Co., 1960), p. 10.
5. H. Frankfort, *The Birth of Civilization in the Near East* (Bloomington: Indiana University Press, 1951), p. 60.
6. For greater detail, see Nels Bailkey, "Early Mesopotamian Constitutional Development," *The American Historical Review*, LXXII (July 1967), 1211-1236.
7. "Les reformes d'Urukagina," trans. by M. Lambert in *Revue d'Assyriologie,* L (Paris, 1956), p. 183.
8. James B. Pritchard, ed., *Ancient Near Eastern Texts Relating to the Old Testament*, 2nd ed., trans. by E. A. Speiser (Princeton: Princeton University Press, 1955), p. 119.
9. *Sumerische und Akkadische Hymnen und Gebete,* trans. by A. Falkenstein and W. von Soden (Zurich: Artemis-Verlag, 1953), p. 188. For a partial translation and full discussion of this text, see S. N. Kramer, *From the Tablets of Sumer* (Indian Hills, Colorado: The Falcon's Wing Press, 1956), pp. 267-271.
10. H. de Genouillac, trans., in *Revue d'Assyriologie*, XXV (Paris, 1928), p. 148.
11. Quoted in S. N. Kramer, "The Oldest Laws," *Scientific American*, Vol. 188, No. 1 (January 1953), p. 28. Copyright © 1953 by Scientific American, Inc. All rights reserved.
12. C. H. Gordon, *Hammurabi's Code: Quaint or Forward-Looking?* (New York: Rinehart and Co., 1957), p. 8.
13. R. F. Harper, *The Code of Hammurabi* (Chicago: University of Chicago Press, 1904), p. 3. Copyright 1904 by the University of Chicago Press.
14. *Ibid.*, p. 49.
15. *Ibid.*, p. 101.
16. A. Leo Oppenheim, *Ancient Mesopotamia: Portrait of a Dead Civilization* (Chicago: University of Chicago Press, 1964), p. 306. Copyright 1964 by the University of Chicago Press.
17. Otto Neugebauer, "Ancient Mathematics and Astronomy," *A History of Technology*, I (Oxford: Clarendon Press), p. 791. Reprinted by permission of the Clarendon Press, Oxford. See also his work, *The Exact Sciences in Antiquity*, 2nd ed.
18. From *Epic of Gilamesh*, trans. by Thorkild Jacobsen, in H. A. Frankfort *et al.*, *The Intellectual Adventure of Ancient Man* (Chicago: University of Chicago Press, 1946), pp. 210-211. Copyright 1946 by the University of Chicago Press.
19. Quoted in Sabatino Moscati, *The Face of the Ancient Orient* (Chicago: Quadrangle Books, Inc., 1960), p. 84. Reprinted by permission of Quadrangle Books, Inc. Copyright © 1960 by Vallentine, Mitchell & Co., Ltd.
20. Quoted in *City Invincible: A Symposium on Urbanization and Cultural Development in the Ancient Near East*, ed. by Carl H. Kraeling and Robert McC. Adams (Chicago: University of Chicago Press, 1960), p. 163.
21. Quoted in M. A. Murray, *The Splendour That Was Egypt* (London: Sidgwick & Jackson, Ltd., 1949), p. 67.
22. Trans. by John A. Wilson, *The Burden of Egypt* (Chicago: University of Chicago Press, 1951), p. 117. Copyright 1951 by the University of Chicago Press.
23. *Ibid.*, p. 164.

24. Adolf Erman, *The Literature of the Ancient Egyptians*, trans. by Aylward M. Blackman (London: Methuen & Co., Ltd., 1927), pp. 190, 196, 197.

25. Murray, p. 122.

26. A. A. Trever, *History of Ancient Civilization*, I (New York: Harcourt, Brace & Co., 1936), p. 50.

27. From "The Instruction of Meri-ka-Re," trans. by John A. Wilson, *The Burden of Egypt*, p. 120.

28. *Ibid.*, p. 119.

29. Quoted in George Steindorff and George Hoyningen-Huene, *Egypt* (Locust Valley, N.Y.: J. J. Augustin Inc., 1943), p. 23.

30. Trans. by George Steindorff and Keith E. Seele, *When Egypt Ruled the East* (Chicago: University of Chicago Press, 1942), p. 125. Copyright 1942 by the University of Chicago Press.

31. Quoted in J. H. Breasted, *The Development of Religion and Thought in Ancient Egypt* (New York: Charles Scribner's Sons, 1924), pp. 324, 326. Reprinted by permission.

32. Quoted in O. R. Gurney, *The Hittites* (Harmondsworth: Penguin Books, Ltd., 1954), p. 83.

33. Ezekiel 27:33-34. Revised Standard Version of the Bible.

34. I Samuel 8:6, 20. Revised Standard Version of the Bible.

35. I Kings 4:20 ff.; 10:14 ff. Revised Standard Version of the Bible.

36. II Kings 25:14. Revised Standard Version of the Bible.

37. Micah 6:8. Revised Standard Version of the Bible.

38. Quoted in G. A. Dorsey, *Man's Own Show: Civilization*, Blue Ribbon Books (New York: Halcyon House, 1937), p. 333. Reprinted by permission of Harper & Row, Publishers.

39. Thorkild Jacobsen, "Early Political Development in Mesopotamia," *Zeitschrift für Assyriologie*, XVIII (Berlin, 1957), pp. 139-140.

40. Nahum 3:8. Revised Standard Version of the Bible.

CHAPTER 3: THE ASIAN WAY OF LIFE

1. W. A. Fairservis, *Excavations in the Quetta Valley, West Pakistan*, Anthropological Papers of the American Museum of Natural History, Vol. 45, Pt. 2 (New York: American Museum of Natural History, 1956), p. 357.

2. R. C. Majumdar *et al.*, *An Advanced History of India* (London: Macmillan & Co. Ltd., 1946), p. 21.

3. L. S. S. O'Malley, ed., *Modern India and the West* (London: Oxford University Press, 1941), p. 3.

4. Quoted in H. G. Rawlinson, *India: A Short Cultural History* (New York: D. Appleton-Century Co., Inc., 1938), pp. 36-37. Reprinted by permission of The Meredith Publishing Company.

5. Herbert H. Gowen, *A History of Indian Literature* (New York: D. Appleton-Century Co., Inc., 1931), p. 251.

6. "Rig-Veda," in *Chips from a German Workshop*, 1, trans. by F. M. Müller (New York: Scribner, Armstrong and Co., 1873), pp. 76-77.

7. W. S. Taylor, "Basic Personality in Orthodox Hindu Culture Patterns," *The Journal of Abnormal and Social Psychology*, XLIII (January 1948), p. 7.

8. W. T. De Bary, Jr., *et al.*, eds., *Sources of Indian Tradition* (New York: Columbia University Press, 1958), pp. 284-285.

9. W. H. Moreland and A. C. Chatterjee, *A Short History of India*, 4th ed. (London: Longmans, Green & Co., Ltd., 1957), p. 16.

10. S. Radhakrishnan, *The Hindu View of Life* (New York: The Macmillan Company, 1927), p. 46. Reprinted by permission of The Macmillan Company and George Allen & Unwin Ltd.

11. F. M. Müller, ed., *The Sacred Books of the East*, XI (Oxford: Clarendon Press, 1881), pp. 96, 114.

12. R. K. Mookerji, *Hindu Civilization* (London: Longmans, Green & Co., Ltd., 1936), p. 249.

13. J. Takakusu, "Buddhism As a Philosophy of 'Thusness,'" in *Philosophy—East and West*, ed. by C. A. Moore (Princeton: Princeton University Press, 1944), p. 73.

14. N. Dutt, "Religion and Philosophy," in *The Age of Imperial Unity*, Vol. II of *The History and Culture of the Indian People*, ed. by R. C. Majumdar and A. D. Pusalker (Bombay: Bharatiya Vidya Bhavan, 1951), p. 371. Reprinted by permission of The Macmillan Company and George Allen & Unwin Ltd.

15. Cited in Rawlinson, pp. 51-52.

16. See Li Chi, *The Beginnings of Chinese Civilization* (Seattle: University of Washington Press, 1957), p. 17.

17. See Ch'ao ting Chi, *Key Economic Areas in Chinese History* (London: George Allen & Unwin Ltd., 1936), p. 62.

18. See M. C. Yang, *A Chinese Village—Taitou, Shantung Province* (New York: Columbia University Press, 1945), p. 240.

19. R. Grousset, *The Rise and Splendour of the Chinese Empire* (Berkeley and Los Angeles: University of California Press, 1953), p. 26.

20. W. T. de Bary, Jr., *et al.*, eds., *Sources of Chinese Tradition* (New York: Columbia University Press, 1960), p. 24.

21. *Ibid.*, p. 31.

22. Quoted in E. O. Reischauer and J. K. Fairbank, *East Asia: The Great Tradition* (Boston: Houghton Mifflin Co., 1950), p. 70.

23. De Bary, *Sources of Chinese Tradition*, p. 31.

24. *Ibid.*, p. 79.

25. *Ibid.*, pp. 63-64.

26. H. Waddell, *Lyrics from the Chinese* (Boston: Houghton Mifflin Co., 1913), p. 5. Reprinted by permission of Constable & Co. Ltd., London.

27. Quoted in Hu Shih, *Development of the Logical Method in Ancient China* (Shanghai: The Oriental Book Company, 1928), p. 4.

CHAPTER 4: THE GLORY THAT WAS GREECE

1. Plutarch's *Lives*, II, trans. by Sir T. North (London: J. M. Dent & Sons Ltd., 1898), p. 144. Reprinted by permission of E. P. Dutton & Co., Inc. and J. M. Dent & Sons Ltd.

2. Chester G. Starr, *The Origins of Greek Civilization, 1100-650 B.C.* (New York: Alfred A. Knopf, Inc., 1961), p. 55.

3. See Leonard R. Palmer, *Mycenaeans and Minoans: Aegean Prehistory in the Light of the Linear B Tablets* (New York: Alfred A. Knopf, Inc. and London: Faber and Faber, Ltd., 1961), Chapter 5, "The Last Days of Pylos."

4. Starr, p. 74.

5. Homer, *Iliad,* Book XXII, trans. by Richard Lattimore (Chicago: University of Chicago Press, 1951), pp. 445-446, lines 396-403. Copyright 1951 by the University of Chicago Press.

6. Aristotle, *Politics*, Book I, Chapter 2, trans. by H. Rackham in The Loeb Classical Library (Cambridge: Harvard University Press, 1932), pp. 9, 11.

7. Quoted in Werner Jaeger, *Paideia: The Ideals of Greek Culture*, I (New York: Oxford University Press, 1939), p. 70.

8. "Laws," in *The Dialogues of Plato*, I, trans. by B. Jowett (New York: Random House, 1937), p. 503.

9. Plutarch's *Lives,* trans. by J. Dryden, rev. by A. H. Clough (New York: Modern Library, 1932), p. 107.

10. E. H. Blakeney, ed., Herodotus' *History*, II, trans. by H. G. Rawlinson, Everyman's Library Edition (New York: E. P. Dutton & Co., Inc., 1910), pp. 102-103. Reprinted by permission of E. P. Dutton & Co., Inc.

11. Trans. by A. R. Burn, *The Pelican History of Greece* (Baltimore: Penguin Books, 1966), p. 186.

12. C. E. Robinson, *Hellas: A Short History of Ancient Greece* (New York: Pantheon Books, 1948), p. 68.

13. Thucydides, *The History of the Peloponnesian War*, II, 65, ed. in trans. by Sir R. W. Livingstone, The World's Classics (New York: Oxford University Press, 1963), p. 130.

14. *Ibid.*, II, 37, 40, pp. 111, 113.

15. Thucydides, *The History of the Peloponnesian War*, II, 45, trans. by B. Jowett (Oxford: Clarendon Press, 1900). Reprinted by permission of the Clarendon Press, Oxford.

16. Aristotle, Book I, Chapter 5, p. 59.

17. Thucydides, II, 40, trans. by B. Jowett.

18. Thucydides, II, 40-41, trans. by Sir R. W. Livingstone.

19. *Ibid.*, I, 23, p. 46.

20. *Ibid.*, II, 65, p. 130.

21. *Ibid.*, V, 105, p. 270.

22. *Ibid.*, VI, 90, p. 325.

23. Quoted in Gustave Glotz, *The Greek City and Its Institutions* (New York: Alfred A. Knopf, Inc., 1930), p. 319.

24. Trans. J. H. Freese, *The Orations of Isocrates,* I (London: G. Bell & Sons, Ltd., 1894), pp. 105-106.

25. Archilochus, quoted in Sir R. W. Livingstone, *The Greek Genius and Its Meaning to Us* (Oxford: Clarendon Press, 1949), p. 93. Reprinted by permission of the Clarendon Press, Oxford.

26. Quoted in M. Cary and T. J. Haarhoff, *Life and Thought in the Greek and Roman World* (London: Methuen & Co., Ltd., 1951), p. 200.

27. "Apology," in *The Four Socratic Dialogues of Plato,* trans. by B. Jowett (Oxford: Clarendon Press, 1924), pp. 91-92. Reprinted by permission of the Clarendon Press, Oxford.

28. "Phaedrus," 247; quoted in *The Greek World*, ed. by Hugh Lloyd-Jones (Baltimore: Penguin Books, 1965), pp. 137-138.

29. "Republic," 473, in *Plato: Selected Passages,* ed. by Sir R. W. Livingstone, The World's Classics (New York: Oxford University Press, 1940), p. 87.

30. Marshall Clagett, *Greek Science in Antiquity* (New York: Collier Books, 1963), pp. 34-35.

31. Derek J. deSolla Price, *Science Since Babylon* (New Haven, Conn.: Yale University Press, 1961).

32. Quoted in *Encyclopaedia Britannica*, XV, 1957 ed., pp. 197-198.

33. Thucydides, I, 22, trans. by Sir R. W. Livingstone, pp. 44-45.

34. Trans. by Andrew Robert Burn, *The Lyric Age of Greece* (London: Edward Arnold Ltd. and New York: St. Martin's Press, 1960), p. 166.

35. *Ibid.*, p. 236.

36. From *Agamemnon*, trans. by Gilbert Murray in *Ten Greek Plays*, ed. by Lane Cooper (New York: Oxford University Press, 1929), p. 96.

37. Moschus, *Idyl IX*, trans. by Ernest Myers in A. Lang, *Theocritus, Bion and Moschus* (London: Macmillan & Co. Ltd., 1911), p. 210. Reprinted by permission of the publisher.

38. G. Murray, *Hellenism and the Modern World* (Boston: Beacon Press, 1953), pp. 56-57. Reprinted by permission of the Beacon Press and George Allen & Unwin Ltd. Copyright 1954 by the Beacon Press.

CHAPTER 5: THE GRANDEUR THAT WAS ROME

1. M. Cary, *The Geographic Background of Greek and Roman History* (Oxford: Clarendon Press, 1949), p. 133. Reprinted by permission of the Clarendon Press, Oxford.

2. Plutarch's *Lives*, "Pyrrhus," XX, 3-4, trans. by Bernadotte Perrin in The Loeb Classical Library (Cambridge: Harvard University Press, 1920), Volume IX, p. 409. Reprinted by permission of the publishers.

3. Polybius, *Histories*, I, 10, trans. by Evelyn S. Shuckburgh (Bloomington: Indiana University Press, 1962), Volume I, p. 10.

4. J. H. Breasted, *Ancient Times* (Boston: Ginn and Co., 1935), p. 611. Used with the permission of Ginn and Company.

5. Quoted in C. A. Robinson, Jr., *Ancient History* (New York: The Macmillan Company, 1951), p. 477. Reprinted by permission of the publisher.

6. Quoted in Moses Hadas, *A History of Rome* (New York: Doubleday & Co., Inc., 1956), p. 75. Copyright © 1956 by Moses Hadas. Reprinted by permission of Doubleday & Co., Inc. and G. Bell & Sons, Ltd.

7. Livy, *Roman History,* XXXIII, 33, trans. by E. T. Sage in The Loeb Classical Library (Cambridge: Harvard University Press, 1945), Volume IX, p. 367.

8. *The Roman History of Appian of Alexandria*, II, trans. by Horace White (New York: The Macmillan

Company, 1899), p. 6. Reprinted by permission of the publisher.

9. Plutarch's *Lives,* "Tiberius Gracchus," IX, 5, trans. by Bernadotte Perrin in The Loeb Classical Library (Cambridge: Harvard University Press, 1945), Volume X, pp. 165, 167. Reprinted by permission of the publishers, Harvard University Press and The Loeb Classical Library.

10. M. Cary and T. J. Haarhoff, *Life and Thought in the Greek and Roman World,* 5th ed. (London: Methuen & Co., Ltd., 1951), p. 75.

11. M. Hammond, *City-State and World State in Greek and Roman Political Theory Until Augustus* (Cambridge: Harvard University Press, 1951), p. 153. Reprinted by permission of the publishers, Harvard University Press. Copyright 1951 by the President and Fellows of Harvard College.

12. Quoted in M. Hadas, p. 112.

13. *Ibid.,* p. 113.

14. Tertullian, *Concerning the Soul,* quoted in S. Katz, *The Decline of Rome and the Rise of Medieval Europe* (Ithaca, N.Y.: Cornell University Press, 1955), p. 7. Copyright 1955 by Cornell University. Used by permission of Cornell University Press.

15. Virgil, *Aeneid,* trans. by J. W. MacKail, Modern Library (New York: Random House, 1934), p. 126.

16. Aristides, *To Rome* (Oration XXVI), trans. by S. Levin (Glencoe, Ill.: The Free Press, 1950), p. 16.

17. R. C. Trevelyan, *Translations from Horace, Juvenal and Montaigne* (New York: Cambridge University Press, 1941), p. 129. Reprinted by permission of the publisher.

18. *Ibid.,* pp. 130-131.

19. Quoted in Grant Showerman, *Century Readings in Ancient Classical Literature* (New York: The Century Co., 1925), p. 386.

20. Lucretius, *On the Nature of the Universe,* Book III, line 70, trans. by Ronald Latham (Baltimore: Penguin Books, Inc., 1951), p. 98.

21. Horace, "Ad Leuconoen," in *Tobogganing on Parnassus,* trans. by Franklin P. Adams (New York: Doubleday & Co., Inc., 1911), p. 7. Copyright 1911 by Doubleday & Co., Inc. Reprinted by permission of the publisher.

22. *Juvenal's Satires,* trans. by William Gifford, rev. by John Warrington, Everyman's Library Edition (New York: E. P. Dutton & Co., Inc., 1954), p. 5. Reprinted by permission of E. P. Dutton & Co., Inc. and J. M. Dent & Sons Ltd.

23. Martial, "Galla's Hair," in *The Epigrams of Martial,* trans. by Sir J. Harington (London: G. Bell & Sons, Ltd., 1904), p. 268.

24. Martial, "Union Labor," in *A Roman Wit,* trans. by P. Nixon (New York: Houghton Mifflin Co., 1911), p. 98.

25. Livy, *History of Rome,* I, 10, trans. by B. O. Foster in The Loeb Classical Library (Cambridge: Harvard University Press, 1919), Volume I, p. 7. Reprinted by permission of the publishers, Harvard University Press and The Loeb Classical Library.

26. Lucretius, *On the Nature of Things,* Book III, lines 830 ff., trans. by John Dryden.

27. Quoted in W. Durant, *Caesar and Christ* (New York: Simon & Schuster, Inc., 1944), p. 506.

28. Benjamin Farmington, *Greek Science* (Baltimore: Penguin Books, Inc., 1944), p. 303. Reprinted by permission.

29. Ptolemy, *Anthologia Palatina,* IX, 577, trans. by W. R. Paton.

CHAPTER 6: THE MEETING OF EAST AND WEST

1. Quoted in M. P. Charlesworth, *Trade-Routes and Commerce of the Roman Empire* (New York: Cambridge University Press, 1926), p. 224.

2. Quoted in F. Hirth, *China and the Roman Orient* (Leipzig: G. Hirth, 1885), p. 42.

3. Vincent Smith, *The Oxford History of India* (Oxford: Oxford University Press, 1958), p. 115.

4. Quoted in H. G. Rawlinson, *Intercourse Between India and the Western World from the Earliest Times to the Fall of Rome* (New York: Cambridge University Press, 1926), p. 39.

5. J. Bloch, *Les Inscriptions d'Asoka* (Paris, 1950), quoted in A. L. Basham, *The Wonder That Was India* (London: Sidgwick & Jackson, Ltd., 1954), pp. 53-54. Reprinted by permission of Sidgwick & Jackson, Ltd.

6. Smith, p. 129.

7. *Ibid.,* p. 131.

8. H. G. Wells, *The Outline of History,* I (New York: The Macmillan Company, 1920), pp. 432-433.

9. R. K. Mookerji, "Asoka the Great," in *The Age of Imperial Unity,* Vol. II of *The History and Culture of the Indian People,* ed. by R. C. Majumdar and A. D. Pusalker (Bombay: Bharatiya Vidya Bhavan, 1951), p. 92. Reprinted by permission of The Macmillan Company and George Allen & Unwin Ltd.

10. W. W. Tarn, *The Greeks in Bactria and India* (New York: Cambridge University Press, 1951), p. 181.

11. Quoted in Basham, p. 465.

12. *Ibid.,* p. 467.

13. Rawlinson, p. 109.

14. Compare M. Wheeler, *Rome Beyond the Imperial Frontiers* (New York: Philosophical Library, Inc., 1955).

15. E. O. Reischauer and J. K. Fairbank, *East Asia: The Great Tradition* (Boston: Houghton Mifflin Co., 1958), p. 86.

16. *Ibid.,* p. 87.

17. See Hu Shih, "The Establishment of Confucianism As a State Religion During the Han Dynasty," *Journal of the North China Branch of the Royal Asiatic Society,* LX (Shanghai, 1929), pp. 34-35. See also J. K. Shryock, *The Origin and Development of the State Cult of Confucius* (New York: D. Appleton-Century Co., Inc., 1932).

18. See J. Needham, *History of Scientific Thought,* Vol. II of *Science and Civilization in China* (New York: Cambridge University Press, 1956), p. 34.

19. Pliny, *Natural History,* trans. by H. Rackham (London: William Heinemann, Ltd., 1945), Book VI, I, 101, and Book XII, I, 84.

20. R. C. Majumdar, "India and the Western World," in *The History and Culture of the Indian People*, II, ed. by R. C. Majumdar and A. D. Pusalker (Paragon Book Reprint Corp., 1951), p. 631. Reprinted by permission of George Allen & Unwin Ltd. and The Macmillan Company.
21. J. Needham, *Introductory Orientations*, Vol. I of *Science and Civilization in China* (New York: Cambridge University Press, 1954), p. 239.
22. Rudyard Kipling, "The Ballad of East and West." From *Rudyard Kipling's Verse*: Definitive Edition. Reprinted by permission of Mrs. George Bambridge and Doubleday & Company, Inc.

CHAPTER 7: THE CITY OF GOD

1. St. Jerome's *Commentary of Ezekiel*, I, Prologue.
2. Flavius Josephus, *War of the Jews*, Book IV, Ch. 5, trans. by W. Whiston.
3. *Ibid.*, Book II, Ch. 8.
4. E. Wilson, *The Scrolls from the Dead Sea* (New York: Oxford University Press, 1955), p. 60.
5. John 18:33-38. *Good News for Modern Man: The New Testament in Today's English Version* (New York: American Bible Society, 1966), p. 258. Copyright American Bible Society 1966. Used by permission.
6. Acts 22:6-10. *Good News for Modern Man*, p. 324.
7. Tertullian, *Apology*, Ch. 50, trans. by A. Souter (Cambridge: Cambridge University Press, 1917), p. 145.
8. Quoted in Moses Hadas, *A History of Rome* (New York: Doubleday & Co., Inc., 1956), p. 184. Copyright 1956 by Moses Hadas. Reprinted by permission of Doubleday & Co., Inc. and G. Bell & Sons, Ltd.
9. Quoted in Henry Bettenson, ed., *Documents of the Christian Church* (London: Oxford University Press, 1943), p. 28.
10. *Ibid.*, p. 9.
11. Naphtali Lewis and Meyer Reinhold, *Roman Civilization: Selected Readings*, II (New York: Columbia University Press, 1955), pp. 464-465.
12. See Frank C. Bourne, *A History of the Romans* (Boston: D. C. Heath & Co., 1966), p. 536.
13. Tacitus, *Germania*, Chs. 23-24, trans. by H. Mattingly, *Tacitus on Britain and Germany* (Harmondsworth: Penguin Books, Ltd., 1948), pp. 120-121.
14. *Ibid.*, Ch. 14, p. 112.
15. Quoted in Hadas, pp. 203-205.
16. S. Katz, *The Decline of Rome and the Rise of Medieval Europe* (Ithaca, N.Y.: Cornell University Press, 1955), p. 7. Copyright 1955 by Cornell University. Used by permission of Cornell University Press.
17. E. Gibbon, *The History of the Decline and Fall of the Roman Empire*, Ch. XXXVIII, "General Observations on the Fall of the Roman Empire in the West" (London: Methuen & Co., Ltd., 1896).
18. A. E. R. Boak, *Manpower Shortage and the Fall of the Roman Empire in the West* (Ann Arbor: University of Michigan Press, 1955), p. 115.
19. Katz, p. 98.
20. Richard N. Frye, *The Heritage of Persia* (Cleveland: The World Publishing Co., 1963), p. 244.

CHAPTER 8: NEW ROME AND THE THIRD ROME

1. E. Gibbon, *The History of the Decline and Fall of the Roman Empire*, II (London: Methuen & Co., Ltd., 1896), p. 148.
2. Procopius, *History of the Wars*, Book I, trans. by H. B. Dewing (London: William Heinemann, Ltd., 1914), pp. 231, 233.
3. Quoted in A. A. Vasiliev, *History of the Byzantine Empire*, I, Studies in the Social Sciences and History, No. 13 (Madison: University of Wisconsin Press, 1928), p. 198.
4. Geoffrey de Villehardouin, *Villehardouin's Chronicle of the Fourth Crusade and the Conquest of Constantinople*, quoted in Sir Frank T. Marzials, *Memoirs of the Crusades*, Dutton Paperback Edition (New York: E. P. Dutton & Co., 1958), pp. 25-26. Reprinted by permission of E. P. Dutton & Co., Inc. and J. M. Dent & Sons Ltd.
5. S. Runciman, *A History of the Crusades*, III (Cambridge: Cambridge University Press, 1954), p. 130.
6. Quoted in J. F. C. Fuller, *A Military History of the Western World*, I (New York: Funk & Wagnalls, 1954), p. 522. By permission of the publishers, Funk & Wagnalls, A Division of Reader's Digest Books, Inc.
7. Quoted in G. Ostrogorsky, *History of the Byzantine State* (New Brunswick, N.J.: Rutgers University Press, 1957), p. 505.
8. Runciman, p. 131.
9. *The Itinerary of Benjamin of Tudela*, trans. by M. N. Adler (London: Oxford University Press, 1907), p. 13.
10. N. H. Baynes, *The Byzantine Empire* (London: Oxford University Press, 1926), p. 31.
11. H. E. Barnes, *The History of Western Civilization*, I (New York: Harcourt, Brace & Co., 1935), p. 508.
12. See C. P. Baker, *Justinian* (New York: Dodd, Mead & Co., 1931).
13. Quoted by C. Diehl, "Byzantine Art," in *Byzantium: Introduction to East Roman Civilization*, ed. by N. H. Baynes and H. St. L. B. Moss (New York: Oxford University Press, 1948), p. 166.
14. Procopius, *Buildings*, I, i, 33-34, trans. by H. B. Dewing (Cambridge: Harvard University Press, 1940), p. 17.
15. D. Talbot Rice, *Byzantine Art* (Harmondsworth: Penguin Books, Ltd., 1954), pp. 150-151.
16. Quoted in M. Cherniavsky, "'Holy Russia': A Study in the History of an Idea," *The American Historical Review*, LXIII, No. 3 (April 1958), p. 619.
17. *Ibid.*, p. 625.
18. *Ibid.*, p. 619.
19. G. Barraclough, *History in a Changing World* (Oxford: Basil Blackwell, 1955), p. 134.

CHAPTER 9: THE ASCENDANCY OF ISLAM

1. Quoted in R. A. Nicholson, *A Literary History of the Arabs* (Cambridge: Cambridge University Press, 1953), p. 136.
2. Quoted in Alfred Guillaume, *Islam* (Harmondsworth: Penguin Books, Ltd., 1954), p. 26.

3. *Ibid.*, pp. 28-29.

4. *Ibid.*, p. 74.

5. See T. P. Hughes, *A Dictionary of Islam* (London: W. H. Allen and Co., 1885).

6. The Koran, trans. by M. M. Pickthall in *The Meaning of the Glorious Koran* (New York: Mentor Books, 1956), p. 431. Reprinted by permission of George Allen & Unwin Ltd., London.

7. Quoted in P. K. Hitti, *The Arabs: A Short History*, 5th rev. (Princeton: Princeton University Press, 1949), p. 32.

8. Gustave von Grunebaum, *Medieval Islam: A Study in Cultural Orientation*, 2nd ed. (Chicago: University of Chicago Press, Phoenix Books, 1962), p. 161. Copyright 1962 by the University of Chicago Press.

9. Quoted in B. Lewis, *The Arabs in History* (London: Hutchinson & Co., Ltd., 1950), p. 90.

10. Quoted in E. H. Palmer, *Haroun Alraschid, Caliph of Bagdad* (London: Marcus Ward and Company, 1881), p. 76.

11. See Von Grunebaum, p. 177.

12. H. A. R. Gibb, ed. and trans., *Ibn Batuta. Travels in Asia and Africa, 1325-1354* (London: Routledge & Kegan Paul Ltd., 1953), p. 30.

13. Quoted in S. Lane-Poole, *A History of Egypt in the Middle Ages* (London: Methuen & Co., Ltd., 1901), p. 145.

14. Hitti, pp. 182-183.

15. Quoted in L. S. Stavrianos, ed., *The Ottoman Empire: Was It the Sick Man of Europe?* (New York: Rinehart and Co., 1957), p. 1.

16. Usāmah Ibn Murshid, *An Arab-Syrian Gentleman and Warrior in the Period of the Crusades*, trans. by P. K. Hitti (New York: Columbia University Press, 1929), p. 162.

17. H. A. R. Gibb, "Literature," in *The Legacy of Islam*, ed. by T. W. Arnold and A. Guillaume (Oxford: Clarendon Press, 1931), p. 182. Reprinted by permission of the Clarendon Press, Oxford.

18. *Rubáiyát of Omar Khayyám*, trans. by E. Fitzgerald (Boston: Thomas B. Mosher, 1899), pp. 26-27.

19. A. Guillaume, "Philosophy and Theology," in *The Legacy of Islam*, p. 281.

20. R. Flint, *The Philosophy of History in France* (New York: Charles Scribner's Sons, 1894), p. 158.

21. Ibn Khaldun, *The Mugaddimah: An Introduction to History*, trans. by Franz Rosenthal, Vol. I (London: Routledge & Kegan Paul Ltd., 1958), p. 71.

22. Von Grunebaum, p. 343.

CHAPTER 10: THE GUPTAS AND THE T'ANG: TWO GOLDEN AGES

1. J. Legge, "The Travels of Fa-hsien," in *Chinese Literature* (London: The Cooperative Publishing Company, 1900), p. 230.

2. A. D. Bouquet, *Hinduism* (London: Hutchinson & Co., Ltd., 1948), p. 98.

3. J. H. Hutton, *Castle in India* (London: Cambridge University Press, 1946), p. 1.

4. C. E. Gover, *The Folk-Songs of Southern India* (London: Trübner and Co., 1872), p. 165.

5. Radhakrishnan, *The Hindu View of Life* (London: George Allen & Unwin Ltd., 1927), p. 37. Reprinted by permission of George Allen & Unwin Ltd. and The Macmillan Company.

6. Quoted in H. G. Rawlinson, *India; A Short Cultural History* (New York: D. Appleton-Century Co., Inc., 1938), p. 138. Reprinted by permission of The Meredith Publishing Company.

7. Quoted in K. M. Panikkar, *A Survey of Indian History* (London: Meridian Books, Ltd., 1948), p. 130.

8. W. Durant, *Story of Civilization*, I (New York: Simon & Schuster, Inc., 1935), p. 461.

9. W. H. Moreland and Atal Chandra Chatterjee, *A Short History of India* (London: Longmans, Green & Co., Ltd., 1936), p. 185.

10. Quoted in H. H. Gowen and J. W. Hall, *An Outline History of China* (New York: D. Appleton & Co., 1926), p. 117.

11. W. T. De Bary *et al.*, eds., *Sources of Chinese Tradition* (New York: Columbia University Press, 1960) p. 496.

12. *The Works of Li Po*, trans. by Shigeyoshi Obata (London: J. M. Dent & Sons, Ltd., and New York: E. P. Dutton & Co., Inc., 1950), p. 1. Copyright, 1922, renewal, 1950, by E. P. Dutton & Co., Inc. Reprinted by permission of the publishers.

13. Quoted in Gowen and Hall, p. 127.

14. Obata, p. 39.

15. Quoted in W. Hung, *Tu Fu, China's Greatest Poet* (Cambridge: Harvard University Press, 1952), p. 88.

16. Quoted in Gowen and Hall, p. 142.

17. J. Needham, *Science and Civilization in China*, II (New York: Cambridge University Press, 1959), p. 346.

18. *Ibid.*, p. 161.

19. *Ibid.*, p. 340.

20. K. S. Latourette, *The Chinese: Their History and Culture*, II (New York: The Macmillan Company, 1934), p. 264. Copyright The Macmillan Company 1946. Reprinted by permission of the publisher.

21. Quoted in Jacques Gernet, *Daily Life in China on the Eve of the Mongol Invasion, 1250-1276* (New York: The Macmillan Company, 1962).

22. Quoted in H. D. Martin, *The Rise of Chingis Khan and His Conquest of North China* (Baltimore: Johns Hopkins Press, 1950), p. 5.

23. Quoted in E. O. Reischauer and J. K. Fairbank, *East Asia: The Great Tradition* (Boston: Houghton Mifflin Co., 1958), p. 267.

24. *Ibid.*, p. 273.

25. See Latourette, II, pp. 301-306.

CHAPTER 11: EUROPE'S SEARCH FOR STABILITY

1. Compare M. Fessier, *Clovis* (New York: Dial Press, 1948).

2. Quoted in C. Dawson, *The Making of Europe* (London: Sheed & Ward Ltd., 1932), p. 94. Reprinted by permission of the Society of Authors and Mr. Christopher Dawson.

3. Quoted in J. L. LaMonte, *The World of the Middle*

Ages (New York: Appleton-Century-Crofts, Inc., 1949), p. 47.

4. Quoted in H. Pirenne, *Mohammed and Charlemagne* (New York: Barnes & Noble, Inc., and London: George Allen & Unwin Ltd., 1955), p. 47.

5. Norman F. Cantor, *Medieval History: The Life and Death of a Civilization* (New York: The Macmillan Company, 1963), pp. 153-154. Reprinted by permission of the publisher.

6. Quoted in H. St. L. B. Moss, *The Birth of the Middle Ages, 395-814* (Oxford: Clarendon Press, 1935), p. 222. Reprinted by permission of the Clarendon Press, Oxford.

7. E. M. Hulme, *The Middle Ages* (New York: Henry Holt & Co., 1938), pp. 272-273.

8. Quoted in J. H. Robinson, *Readings in European History*, I (Boston: Ginn and Co., 1904), pp. 139-140. Used with permission of Ginn and Co.

9. Quoted in Dawson, p. 219.

10. Quoted in M. L. W. Laistner, *Thought and Letters in Western Europe, A.D. 500 to 900* (Ithaca, N.Y.: Cornell University Press, 1931), pp. 196-197.

11. *Ibid.*, p. 390.

12. Quoted in Dawson, pp. 266-267.

13. LaMonte, p. 206.

14. Quoted in G. B. Adams, *Civilization During the Middle Ages* (New York: Charles Scribner's Sons, 1914), p. 222.

15. Quoted in E. M. Hulme, *History of the British People* (New York: Century Co., 1929), pp. 121-122.

16. Quoted in J. W. Thompson and E. N. Johnson, *An Introduction to Medieval Europe, 300-1500* (New York: W. W. Norton & Co., Inc., 1937), p. 343. Copyright 1937 by W. W. Norton & Co., Inc. Copyright renewed 1964 by Edgar Nathaniel Johnson. With the permission of the publisher.

17. Quoted in Sidney Painter, *French Chivalry: Chivalric Ideas and Practices in Medieval France* (Baltimore: Johns Hopkins Press, 1940), p. 169.

18. *Ibid.*, pp. 75-76.

19. Quoted in L. F. Salzman, *English Life in the Middle Ages* (Oxford: Clarendon Press, 1927), p. 261. Reprinted by permission of the Clarendon Press, Oxford.

20. Quoted in S. Painter, *A History of the Middle Ages, 284-1500* (New York: Alfred A. Knopf, Inc., 1954), p. 121.

21. Quoted in Salzman, p. 139.

CHAPTER 12: THE WEST TAKES THE OFFENSIVE

1. Quoted in J. W. Thompson, *The Middle Ages* (New York: Alfred A. Knopf, Inc., 1931), p. 377.

2. Z. N. Brooke, *A History of Europe from 911 to 1198* (London: Methuen & Co., Ltd., 1951), p. 28. Reprinted by permission.

3. H. Pirenne, *A History of Europe* (London: George Allen & Unwin Ltd., 1939), p. 140.

4. Quoted in Dorothy Whitelock, *The Beginnings of English Society* (Baltimore: Penguin Books, Inc., 1952), p. 66.

5. B. Thorpe, *Ancient Laws and Institutes of England*, I (London: Eyre and Spottiswoode, Ltd., 1840), p. 53.

6. Quoted in Whitelock, p. 215.

7. William of Malmesbury, *Chronicle of the Kings of England*, Book III, trans. by J. Sharpe (London: G. Bell & Sons, Ltd., 1876), p. 277.

8. See W. O. Ault, *Europe in the Middle Ages*, rev. ed. (Boston: D. C. Heath & Co., 1937), p. 261.

9. Quoted in C. Petit-Dutaillis, *La Monarchie Féodale en France et en Angleterre, X-XIII Siècle* (Paris: La Renaissance du Livre, 1933), p. 23.

10. E. Lavisse, *Histoire de France*, II, pt. 2, (Paris: Librairie Hachette, 1901), pp. 176-177.

11. J. W. Draper, *History of the Intellectual Development of Europe*, 5th ed. (New York: Harper & Bros., 1872), pp. 347-349.

12. Quoted in A. C. Krey, *The First Crusade* (Princeton: Princeton University Press, 1921), p. 261.

13. Quoted in G. G. Coulton, *Medieval Panorama* (Cambridge: Cambridge University Press, 1938), p. 303.

14. L. F. Salzman, *English Industries of the Middle Ages* (Oxford: Clarendon Press, 1923), p. 309.

15. Charles Singer, "East and West in Retrospect," *A History of Technology*, II (Oxford: Clarendon Press, 1956), p. 774.

16. Lynn White, Jr., *Medieval Technology and Social Change* (Oxford: Clarendon Press, 1962), p. 78. Reprinted by permission of the Clarendon Press, Oxford.

17. Lewis Mumford, *Technics and Civilization* (New York: Harcourt, Brace & World, Inc., 1934), pp. 9-12. Reprinted by permission of Harcourt, Brace & World, Inc. and Routledge & Kegan Paul Ltd.

18. *Ibid.*, pp. 12-18.

19. L. F. Salzman, *English Life in the Middle Ages* (Oxford: Clarendon Press, 1926), p. 83.

20. Edward P. Cheyney, *The Dawn of a New Era, 1250-1453* (New York: Harper & Bros., 1936), p. 132.

21. Brooke, p. 14.

CHAPTER 13: TO THE GLORY OF GOD

1. J. W. Thompson, *Economic and Social History of the Middle Ages* (New York: Century Co., 1928), p. 132. Copyright 1928 by the Century Company. Reprinted by permission of Appleton-Century-Crofts, Division of Meredith Corporation.

2. Quoted in S. M. Brown, *Medieval Europe* (New York: Harcourt, Brace & Co., 1935), pp. 382-383.

3. Summerfield Baldwin, *The Organization of Medieval Christianity* (New York: Henry Holt & Co., 1929), p. 35.

4. T. Morrison, ed. and trans., *The Portable Chaucer* (New York: Viking Press, 1949), p. 74. Copyright 1949 by Theodore Morrison. Reprinted by permission of The Viking Press, Inc.

5. Quoted in Brown, pp. 382-383.

6. *Ibid.*, pp. 386-387.

7. J. W. Thompson and E. N. Johnson, *An Introduction to Medieval Europe, 300-1500* (New York: W. W. Norton & Co., Inc., 1937), pp. 359-360.

8. Harry J. Carroll, Jr., *et al.*, *The Development of Civilization: A Documentary History of Politics, Society, and Thought*, I (Chicago: Scott, Foresman and Co., 1961), p. 304.

9. Henry Bettenson, ed., *Documents of the Christian Church* (London: Oxford University Press, 1943), p. 144.

10. Quoted in J. H. Robinson, *Readings in European History*, I (Boston: Ginn and Co., 1904), p. 283.

11. Quoted in S. R. Packard, *Europe and the Church Under Innocent III* (New York: Henry Holt & Co., 1927), p. 15.

12. Quoted in J. Evans, *Life in Medieval France* (New York: Oxford University Press, 1925), p. 87.

13. *A Catholic Dictionary*, ed. by Donald Attwater (New York: The Macmillan Company, 1949), p. 227. Reprinted by permission of the publisher.

14. J. Guiraud, *The Medieval Inquisition*, trans. by E. C. Messenger (London: Burns Oates and Washbourne, 1929), p. 133.

15. Packard, p. 79.

16. Luke 9:1-6. Authorized King James Version of the Bible.

17. Morrison, pp. 80-81.

18. Robert S. Lopez, *The Tenth Century: How Dark the Dark Ages?* (New York: Rinehart and Co., 1959), p. 1.

19. Quoted in Urban T. Holmes, Jr., "Transitions in European Education," in *Twelfth-Century Europe and the Foundations of Modern Society*, ed. by Marshall Clagett, Gaines Post, and Robert Reynolds (Madison: University of Wisconsin Press, 1961), p. 17. Reprinted by permission of the copyright owners, the Regents of the University of Wisconsin.

20. *Ibid.*, p. 20.

21. Quoted in Charles Homer Haskins, *The Renaissance of the Twelfth Century* (Cambridge: Harvard University Press, 1927), p. 350. Copyright, 1927, by the President and Fellows of Harvard College, 1955 by Clare Allen Haskins. Reprinted by permission of the publishers.

22. *The Story of My Misfortunes: The Autobiography of Peter Abélard*, trans. by Henry Adams Bellows (Glencoe, Ill.: The Free Press, 1958), pp. 3, 10.

23. Quoted in Haskins, pp. 354-355.

24. *Ibid.*, p. 23.

25. Quoted in *Introduction to Contemporary Civilization in the West: A Source Book*, I (New York: Columbia University Press, 1946), p. 85.

26. *An Encyclopedist of the Dark Ages*, trans. by E. Brehaut (New York: Columbia University Press, 1912), p. 220.

27. *The Art of Falconry . . . of Frederick II of Hohenstaufen*, trans. by Casey A. Wood and F. Marjorie Fyfe (Boston: Charles T. Branford Co., 1943), pp. 3-4.

28. Quoted in H. O. Taylor, *The Mediaeval Mind*, II (London: Macmillan & Co. Ltd., 1938), p. 524.

29. *Ibid.*, p. 538.

30. Quoted in Haskins, p. 395.

31. J. A. Symonds, *Wine, Women and Song* (New York: Oxford University Press and London: Chatto & Windus Ltd., 1931), pp. 67-69.

32. Quoted in Frederick B. Artz, *The Mind of the Middle Ages, A.D. 300-1500*, 2nd ed. (New York: Alfred A. Knopf, Inc., 1954), p. 332.

33. C. Warren Hollister, *Medieval Europe: A Short History* (New York: John Wiley & Sons, Inc., 1964), p. 230.

34. Amy Kelly, *Eleanor of Aquitaine and the Four Kings* (Cambridge: Harvard University Press, 1952), p. 86. Copyright, 1952, by the President and Fellows of Harvard College. Reprinted by permission of the publishers, Harvard University Press.

35. *L'Inferno*, Canto I, lines 1-3, trans. by Dorothy L. Sayers, *Dante, The Divine Comedy, I: Hell* (Harmondsworth: Penguin Books, Ltd. 1949), p. 71. Reprinted by permission of the publisher.

36. *Paradise*, Canto XXXIII, lines 121, 144, trans. by J. B. Fletcher.

37. Henry Wadsworth Longfellow, quoted in Artz, p. 383.

38. Geoffrey Chaucer, *Canterbury Tales*, trans. by J. U. Nicolson (New York: Crown Publishers, Inc., 1936), pp. 3-5.

39. Quoted in Thompson, *Economic and Social History of the Middle Ages*, p. 672.

CHAPTER 14: NATIONS IN THE MAKING

1. Quoted in E. P. Cheyney, *Readings in English History Drawn from the Original Sources* (Boston: Ginn and Co., 1908), p. 112.

2. *Ibid.*, pp. 107-108.

3. D. C. Douglas and G. Greenaway, *English Historical Documents, 1042-1189* (New York: Oxford University Press, 1953), p. 200.

4. W. S. Churchill, *The Birth of Britain*, Vol. I of *A History of the English-Speaking Peoples* (New York: Dodd, Mead & Co., 1965), pp. 222-223.

5. Quoted in Churchill, I, p. 210.

6. Quoted in Cheyney, pp. 157-158.

7. Compare Cheyney, pp. 183-185.

8. Robert Burns, "Scots, Wha Hae."

9. Quoted in Cheyney, p. 286.

10. William Shakespeare, *King Richard III*, Act V, Scene iv.

11. Quoted in J. H. Robinson, *Readings in European History*, I (Boston: Ginn and Co., 1904), p. 202.

12. *Ibid.*, p. 204.

13. Quoted in R. W. Collins, *A History of Medieval Civilization* (Boston: Ginn and Co., 1936), p. 350.

14. Jonathon F. Scott *et al.*, *Readings in Medieval History* (New York: F. S. Crofts and Company, 1933), pp. 464-465.

15. *The Lay of the Cid*, trans. by R. S. Rose and L. Bacon (Berkeley: University of California Press, 1919), pp. 25-26. Reprinted by permission.

16. Quoted in A. J. Grant, *A History of Europe from 1494 to 1610* (London: Methuen & Co., Ltd., 1938), p. 28.

17. R. H. C. Davis, *A History of Medieval Europe from Constantine to Saint Louis* (New York: Longmans, Green & Co., Ltd., 1957), p. 315.

18. Quoted in J. W. Thompson and E. N. Johnson, *An Introduction to Medieval Europe, 300-1500* (New York: W. W. Norton & Co., Inc., 1937), p. 424.

19. B. Pares, *A History of Russia* (New York: Alfred A. Knopf, Inc., 1956), p. 78.

CHAPTER 15: MAN IS THE MEASURE

1. Quoted in J. Burckhardt, *The Civilization of the Renaissance in Italy*, trans. by S. G. C. Middlemore (London: George Allen & Unwin Ltd., 1921), p. 138.
2. William Shakespeare, *The Tempest*, Act V, Scene i.
3. J. L. LaMonte, *The World of the Middle Ages* (New York: Appleton-Century-Crofts, Inc., 1949), p. 710. Copyright 1949 by Appleton-Century-Crofts, Inc.
4. W. T. Waugh, *History of Europe from 1378 to 1494* (New York: G. P. Putnam's Sons, 1932), p. 448.
5. Quoted in J. H. Randall, Jr., *The Making of the Modern Mind* (Boston: Houghton Mifflin Co., 1940), p. 213.
6. Quoted in F. B. Artz, *The Mind of the Middle Ages* (New York: Alfred A. Knopf, Inc., 1954), p. 307.
7. Petrarch, "The Ascent of Mont Ventoux," trans. by H. Nachod and quoted in *The Renaissance Philosophy of Man*, ed. by E. Cassirer, P. Kristeller, and J. Randall, Jr. (Chicago: University of Chicago Press, 1948), p. 44. Copyright 1948 by the University of Chicago Press.
8. *The Decameron of Giovanni Boccaccio*, trans. by Richard Aldington (New York: Garden City Publishing Co., 1949), p. 559.
9. H. S. Lucas, *The Renaissance and the Reformation* (New York: Harper & Bros., 1934), p. 216.
10. Quoted in *The Renaissance Philosophy of Man*, p. 143.
11. H. Butterfield, *The Statecraft of Machiavelli* (London: G. Bell & Sons, Ltd., 1940), p. 46.
12. B. Berenson, *The Italian Painters of the Renaissance* (New York: Oxford University Press, 1953), p. 69.
13. See R. Wittkower, *Architectural Principles of the Age of Humanism* (London: Warburg Institute, University of London, 1949), pp. 1-28.
14. G. Vasari, *Lives of Seventy of the Most Eminent Painters, Sculptors, and Architects*, II (New York: Charles Scribner's Sons, 1901), p. 376.
15. Quoted in T. Craven, *Men of Art* (New York: Simon & Schuster, Inc., 1931), p. 158.
16. F. B. Artz, *From the Renaissance to Romanticism: Trends in Style in Art, Literature, and Music, 1300-1830* (Chicago: University of Chicago Press, 1962), p. 102. Copyright 1962 by the University of Chicago Press.
17. H. O. Taylor, *Thought and Expression in the Sixteenth Century*, I (New York: The Macmillan Company, 1920), p. 175. Reprinted by permission of the Estate of Henry O. Taylor.
18. Quoted in Randall, p. 118.
19. From the 1684 translation by Gilbert Burnet, in *Introduction to Contemporary Civilization in the West: A Source Book*, I (New York: Columbia University Press, 1946), p. 461.
20. *Ibid.*, p. 460.
21. Quoted in Taylor, pp. 328-329.
22. Montaigne, "Of the Education of Children," in *The Complete Works of Montaigne*, trans. by D. M. Frame (Stanford: Stanford University Press, 1957), p. 112.

23. *Ibid.*, p. 110.
24. "Of His Lady's Old Age," trans. by Andrew Lang. From *The Poetical Works of Andrew Lang*. Reprinted by permission of Longmans, Green & Co., Ltd. and the representatives of the late Andrew Lang.
25. William Shakespeare, Sonnet 18.
26. J. van der Elst, *The Last Flowering of the Middle Ages* (New York: Doubleday & Co., Inc., 1946), p. 59.
27. Compare H. W. Van Loon, *The Arts* (New York: Simon & Schuster, Inc., 1937), pp. 329-344.

CHAPTER 16: HERE I TAKE MY STAND

1. A. C. Flick, *Decline of the Medieval Church*, I (London: Kegan Paul, Trench, Trübner and Co., Ltd., 1930), p. 293.
2. R. H. Bainton, *The Reformation of the Sixteenth Century* (Boston: Beacon Press, 1952), p. 15. Reprinted by permission of the Beacon Press. Copyright © 1962 by Beacon Press.
3. Quoted in P. Smith, *The Age of the Reformation* (New York: Henry Holt & Co., 1920), pp. 58-59. Reprinted by permission.
4. Romans 1:17. Authorized King James Version of the Bible.
5. Quoted in R. H. Bainton, *Here I Stand: A Life of Martin Luther* (New York and Nashville: Abingdon-Cokesbury Press, 1950), p. 65.
6. *Ibid.*, pp. 66-67.
7. Compare Bainton, *The Reformation of the Sixteenth Century*, p. 27.
8. Quoted in C. Hayes, *A Political and Cultural History of Modern Europe*, I (New York: The Macmillan Company, 1933), p. 154. Reprinted by the permission of the publisher.
9. Quoted in P. Smith, *The Life and Letters of Martin Luther* (New York: Houghton Mifflin Co., 1911), p. 41.
10. Quoted in Smith, *The Age of the Reformation*, p. 69.
11. Quoted in George L. Mosse, *The Reformation*, 3rd ed. (New York: Holt, Rinehart and Winston, Inc., 1963), p. 31.
12. Quoted in Bainton, *The Reformation of the Sixteenth Century*, p. 58.
13. Quoted in H. Bettenson, *Documents of the Christian Church* (London: Oxford University Press, 1943), pp. 282-283.
14. From *The Twelve Articles*, in A. Schrier *et al.*, *Modern European Civilization: A Documentary History of Politics, Society, and Thought from the Renaissance to the Present* (Chicago: Scott, Foresman and Co., 1963), pp. 105-106.
15. Quoted in H. J. Grimm, *The Reformation Era, 1500-1650* (New York: The Macmillan Company, 1956), p. 175. Reprinted by permission of the publisher.
16. Quoted in Hayes, I, p. 158.
17. R. Fife, *The Revolt of Martin Luther* (New York: Columbia University Press, 1957), p. 693. Reprinted by permission.
18. Bainton, *The Reformation of the Sixteenth Century*, p. 114.

19. Bettenson, p. 365.
20. *Concerning Heretics . . . . An anonymous work attributed to Sebastian Castellio,* ed. by R. H. Bainton (New York: Columbia University Press, 1935), pp. 122-123.
21. *Ibid.,* pp. 134-135.
22. Quoted in V. H. H. Green, *Luther and the Reformation* (New York: Capricorn Books, 1964), p. 141.
23. *Ibid.,* p. 142.
24. John Bunyan, *Pilgrim's Progress,* in *The Literature of England,* I, 5th ed., ed. by G. K. Anderson and William E. Buckler (Chicago: Scott, Foresman and Co., 1966), p. 1198.
25. R. H. Tawney, *Religion and the Rise of Capitalism* (Baltimore: Penguin Books, Inc., 1947), p. 99. Reprinted by permission.

CHAPTER 17: THE STRIFE OF STATES AND KINGS

1. E. R. A. Seligman, ed., *Encyclopaedia of the Social Sciences,* I (New York: The Macmillan Company, 1930), p. 90. Reprinted by permission of the publisher.
2. Justinian, *Digest* I, iv, 1; *Institutes* I, ii, 6.
3. Compare B. Reynolds, *Proponents of Limited Monarchy in Sixteenth Century France: Francis Holman and Jean Bodin* (New York: Columbia University Press, 1931), p. 182.
4. J. F. C. Fuller, *A Military History of the Western World,* I (New York: Funk & Wagnalls, 1954), p. 470.
5. Sir Henry Wotton, *Reliquiae Woltonianae* (1651).
6. Quoted in M. Guizot, *The History of France from the Earliest Times to 1848,* II (New York: Thomas Y. Crowell & Co., n. d.), p. 428.
7. *Machiavelli: The Prince and Other Works,* trans. by A. H. Gilbert (Chicago: Packard and Co., 1941), p. 177 (Ch. 26).
8. *Ibid.,* p. 148 (Ch. 18).
9. *Ibid.,* p. 150 (Ch. 18).
10. *Ibid.,* p. 177 (Ch. 26).
11. Compare H. G. Wells, *The Outline of History* (New York: Garden City Publishing Co., 1931), p. 794.
12. Quoted in R. B. Merriman, *Suleiman the Magnificent* (Cambridge: Harvard University Press, 1944), p. 37.
13. Quoted in Sir C. Oman, *The Sixteenth Century* (New York: E. P. Dutton & Co., Inc., 1937), pp. 64-65.
14. Quoted in A. J. Grant, *A History of Europe from 1494 to 1610* (New York: G. P. Putnam's Sons, 1932), p. 374.
15. *Ibid.,* p. 389.
16. *Ibid.*
17. Quoted in R. Ergang, *Europe from the Renaissance to Waterloo* (Boston: D. C. Heath & Co., 1954), p. 296.
18. *Ibid.,* p. 246.
19. W. S. Churchill, *The New World,* Vol. II of *A History of the English-Speaking Peoples* (New York: Dodd, Mead & Co., 1956), p. 119.
20. L. Strachey, *Elizabeth and Essex* (New York: Harcourt, Brace & Co., 1928), p. 16.
21. Quoted in E. P. Cheyney, *Readings in English History Drawn from the Original Sources* (Boston: Ginn and Co., 1935), pp. 407-408.

22. Quoted in J. H. Elliott, *Imperial Spain, 1469-1716* (New York: St. Martin's Press, 1964), p. 282.
23. *Ibid.,* p. 283.
24. Quoted in P. Smith, *The Age of the Reformation* (New York: Henry Holt & Co., 1920), p. 215.
25. Quoted in V. H. H. Green, *Renaissance and Reformation: A Survey of European History Between 1450 and 1660* (London: Edward Arnold, Ltd., 1952), p. 272.
26. Quoted in C. R. L. Fletcher, *Gustavus Adolphus and the Struggle of Protestantism for Existence* (London and New York: G. P. Putnam's Sons, 1923), p. 284.
27. S. R. Gardiner, *The Thirty Years' War* (New York: Charles Scribner's Sons, 1892), p. 207.
28. Quoted in L. Gottschalk and D. Lach, *Europe and the Modern World,* Vol. I of *The Rise of Modern Europe* (Chicago: Scott, Foresman and Co., 1951), p. 306.
29. Quoted in *Encyclopedia of the Social Sciences,* III, p. 426.
30. Quoted in Carl L. Becker, *Modern History* (Chicago: Silver Burdett Co., 1942), pp. 204, 205.
31. Carl J. Friedrich, *The Age of the Baroque, 1610-1660* (New York: Harper & Bros., 1952), p. 129.
32. See "Grotius: *Law of War and Peace, Prolegomena,*" in *The American Journal of International Law,* XXXV, No. 2 (April 1941), pp. 206, 217.

CHAPTER 18: NEW DIMENSIONS OF THE MIND

1. Quoted in F. Artz, *From the Renaissance to Romanticism: Trends in Style in Art, Literature, and Music, 1300-1830* (Chicago: University of Chicago Press, 1962), p. 113. Copyright 1962 by the University of Chicago Press.
2. Giordano Bruno, "Of the Infinite Universe and Innumerable Worlds," quoted in *World in Literature,* I, ed. by R. Warnock and G. K. Anderson (Chicago: Scott, Foresman and Co., 1950, 1967), p. 505.
3. Quoted in *Encyclopaedia Britannica,* XIX, 1957 ed., p. 612.
4. S. Cheney, *A World History of Art* (New York: Viking Press, 1944), p. 687.
5. Marie Boas, *The Scientific Renaissance, 1450-1630* (London: Collins, 1962), p. 49.
6. Nicolas Copernicus, "Dedication of *The Revolutions of the Heavenly Spheres,*" quoted in Thomas S. Kuhn, *The Copernican Revolution* (Cambridge: Harvard University Press, 1957), pp. 140-141.
7. "De Revolutionibus Orbium Celestium," quoted in *World in Literature,* I, pp. 501-502.
8. Quoted by E. Nagel, "The Development of Modern Science," in *Chapters in Western Civilization,* I, 3rd ed. (New York: Columbia University Press, 1961), p. 505.
9. Quoted in B. Russell, *A History of Western Philosophy* (New York: Simon & Schuster, Inc., 1945), p. 528.
10. Psalms XCIII:1. Authorized King James Version of the Bible.
11. Quoted in Russell, p. 528.
12. Quoted in T. V. Smith and Marjorie Grene, *From Descartes to Kant* (Chicago: University of Chicago Press, 1950), pp. 28-29.

13. Quoted in A. R. Hall, *The Scientific Revolution* (London: Longmans, Green & Co., Ltd., 1954), pp. 248-249.

14. Sir Isaac Newton, *Opticks: or a Treatise of the Reflections, Refractions, Inflections and Colours of Light* (New York: Dover Publications, 1952), p. 404.

15. A. Pope, *The Poetical Works of Alexander Pope* (London: John James Chidley, 1846), p. 434.

16. Quoted in H. Shapley *et al.*, eds., *A Treasury of Science* (New York: Harper & Bros., 1958), p. 147.

17. G. Sarton, *Six Wings: Men of Science in the Renaissance* (Bloomington: Indiana University Press, 1957), p. 174.

18. Quoted in Sir W. D. D. Dampier-Whetham, *A History of Science and Its Relations with Philosophy* (Cambridge: Cambridge University Press, 1929), p. 130.

19. F. Bacon, *The Works of Francis Bacon*, VI, ed. by J. Spedding (London: Longman and Co., 1861), pp. 497-498.

20. *Ibid.*, p. 55.

21. *Ibid.*, pp. 92-93.

22. "Discourse on Method," quoted in A. Schrier, *et al.*, eds., *Modern European Civilization: A Documentary History of Politics, Society, and Thought from the Renaissance to the Present* (Chicago: Scott, Foresman and Co., 1963), p. 62.

23. H. Butterfield, *The Origins of Modern Science* (London: G. Bell & Sons, Ltd., 1949), pp. 104, 108.

24. Bacon, III, p. 156.

CHAPTER 19: OLD WORLDS BEYOND THE HORIZON

1. Quoted in H. G. Rawlinson, *India: A Short Cultural History* (New York: D. Appleton-Century Co., Inc., 1938), p. 313.

2. S. Lane-Poole, *Medieval India* (New York: G. P. Putnam's Sons, 1903), p. 271.

3. John F. Cady, *Southeast Asia: Its Historical Development* (New York: McGraw-Hill Book Company, 1964), pp. 98-99. Reprinted by permission.

4. This classification follows that of Melville Herskovits, *The Human Factor in Changing Africa* (New York: Alfred A. Knopf, Inc., 1962).

5. H. A. R. Gibb, ed. and trans., *Ibn Batuta: Travels in Asia and Africa, 1325-1354* (London: George Routledge and Sons, Ltd., 1929), pp. 329-330.

6. Cited from Roland Oliver and J. D. Fage, *A Short History of Africa* (Baltimore: Penguin Books, Inc., 1962), p. 90.

7. This classification is from George H. Kimble, *Tropical Africa*, II (New York: Twentieth Century Fund, 1960), p. 19.

8. Lord Hailey, *An African Survey* (New York: Oxford University Press, 1957), p. 68.

9. Colin M. Turnbull, *The Peoples of Africa* (Leicester, England: Brockhampton Press, 1963), pp. 29-30.

10. Cited in Herskovits, p. 469.

11. A. C. Parker, *The Constitution of the Five Nations,*

New York State Museum Bulletin, No. 184 (Albany: April 1916), p. 10.

12. C. A. Burland, *The Gods of Mexico* (New York: G. P. Putnam's Sons, 1967), p. 185.

13. Quoted in Charles Gallenkamp, *Maya: The Riddle and Rediscovery of a Lost Civilization* (New York: Pyramid Publications, 1965), p. 93.

14. Quoted in Jacques Soustelle, *The Daily Life of the Aztecs on the Eve of the Spanish Conquest* (New York: The Macmillan Company, 1962), p. 52. Reprinted by permission of the publisher.

15. *Ibid.*, p. 99.

16. Betty J. Meggers and Clifford Evans, "A Transpacific Contact in 3000 B.C.," *Scientific American*, 214 (January 1966), pp. 28-35.

CHAPTER 20: SEEK OUT, DISCOVER, AND FIND

1. "The letters patents of King Henry the seuenth granted vnto Iohn Cabot and his three sonnes, Lewis, Sebastian, and Sancius for the discouerie of new and vnknowen lands," from *The Voyages of the English Nation to America Before the Year 1600, from Hakluyt's Collection of Voyages*, I (Edinburgh: E. and G. Goldsmid, 1889), p. 21.

2. See H. Ingstad, "Vinland Ruins Prove Vikings Found the New World," *National Geographic Magazine*, Vol. 126, No. 5 (November 1964), pp. 708-734.

3. Quoted in Sir Percy Sykes, *A History of Exploration*, Harper Torchbooks (New York: Harper & Row Publishers, 1961), p. 111.

4. Quoted in S. E. Morison, *Admiral of the Ocean Sea, A Life of Christopher Columbus* (Boston: Little, Brown and Co., 1942), p. 62.

5. Quoted in J. E. Gillespie, *A History of Geographical Discovery, 1400-1800* (New York: Henry Holt & Co., 1933), pp. 36-37.

6. Quoted in Sykes, p. 108.

7. Quoted in H. H. Gowen, *An Outline History of Japan* (New York: D. Appleton Co., 1927), p. 255.

8. C. H. Haring, *The Spanish Empire in America* (New York: Oxford University Press, 1947), p. 122.

9. Quoted in L. Hanke, *The Spanish Struggle for Justice in the Conquest of America* (Philadelphia: University of Pennsylvania Press, 1949), p. 17.

10. Quoted in H. Herring, *A History of Latin America*, 3rd ed. (New York: Alfred A. Knopf, Inc., 1968), p. 173. Reprinted by permission.

11. Quoted in H. Robinson, *The Development of the British Empire* (Boston: Houghton Mifflin Co., 1922), p. 38.

12. G. F. Renard and G. Weulersse, *Life and Work in Modern Europe* (New York: Alfred A. Knopf, Inc., 1926), p. 43. Reprinted by permission.

13. H. Heaton, *Economic History of Europe* (New York: Harper & Bros., 1936), p. 255.

14. Quoted in Heaton, p. 238.

15. Heaton, p. 239.

16. William Shakespeare, *The Merchant of Venice*, Act I, Scene iii.

List of Illustrations

Index

Abbreviations for special features—Reference Maps *(Ref. M.)*, spot maps *(m.)*, and illustrations *(ill.)*—are indicated in italics. Suggested pronunciations for difficult or unusual words are respelled according to the table below, which is repeated in simplified form at the bottom of each right-hand page of the INDEX. The local pronunciations of many foreign words are too unusual for persons untrained in linguistics, and pronunciations given here are those commonly acceptable in unaffected, educated American speech.

a	hat, cap	j	jam, enjoy	u	cup, son	**FOREIGN SOUNDS**
ā	age, face	k	kind, seek	ù	put, book	
ã	care, air	l	land, coal	ü	rule, move	Y as in French *lune*. Pro-
ä	father, far	m̧	me, am	ū	use, music	nounce ē with the lips
		n	no, in			rounded as for Eng-
b	bad, rob	ng	long, bring			lish ü in *rule*.
ch	child, much			v	very, save	
d	did, red	o	hot, rock	w	will, woman	Œ as in French *deux*. Pro-
		ō	open, go	y	you, yet	nounce ā with the lips
		ô	order, all	z	zero, breeze	rounded as for ō.
e	let, best	oi	oil, toy	zh	measure, seizure	
ē	equal, see	ou	out, now			N as in French *bon*. The
ėr	term, learn					N is not pronounced,
		p	pet, cup			but shows that the
f	fat, if	r	run, try	ə	represents:	vowel before it is nasal.
g	go, bag	s	say, yes	*a*	in *a*bout	
h	he, how	sh	she, rush	*e*	in tak*e*n	H as in German *ach*. Pro-
		t	tell, it	*i*	in penc*i*l	nounce k without clos-
i	it, pin	th	thin, both	*o*	in lem*o*n	ing the breath pas-
ı	ice, five	ᵮH	then, smooth	*u*	in circ*u*s	sage.

Aachen (ä′kən) *m. 347, 396. See also* Aix-la-Chapelle.

Abbasid dynasty (a bas′id), 259-264, 265, *m. 324*

Abelard (ab′ə lärd), Pierre, 392-393

Absolutism: in Byzantine empire, 235, in China, 178, 188-189; in Hellenistic Age, 119; of Inca kings, 602-603; in Italian city-states, 446; in Mauryan empire, 188; among Muslims, 260; in Roman empire, 140, 148, 189, 206-207, 208-210; in Spain, 428-429. *See also* National monarchies, Power politics.

Abu Bakr (ə bü′ bak′ėr) 253, 254, 256-257

Abyssinia. *See* Ethiopia.

Achaeans, 94, 95

Achilles, 97, 124

Acre, 361, 362, 363, *Ref. M. 7*

Acropolis, 97: of Athens, 91; of Mycenae, 94; at Zimbabwe, 589

Actium, battle of, 140, *m. 143*

Act of Supremacy, 498

Adelaide of Lombardy, 348

Aden, 166, *m. 173, Ref. M. 7, 11*

Adrianople, *m. 215:* battle of, 214

Adriatic Sea, *m. 105, 132, Ref. M. 3, 4, 10*

Aegean (ē jē′ən) civilizations, 93, *m. 92:* Crete, 93-95; Dorian invasion of, 96; Mycenae, 94, 95; Troy, 95-96

Aegean Sea, *m. 92, 105, Ref. M. 2, 3, 4, 10*

Aeneas (i nē′əs), 127, 154

Aeneid, 127, 154

Aeschylus (es′kə ləs), 125

Afghanistan, 167, 281, 435

Afghans, in India, 281

Afonso Henriques, king of Portugal, 429

Africa, *Ref. M. 6:* arts of, 591; exploration of, 611-612; Graeco-Roman trade in, 164-167, *m. 166;* history of, 584-590; new nations of, 592; Portuguese in, 620; primitive cultures of, 20, 584; rediscovery of, 583-584; slave trade in, 589-590, 620-621, 633; sub-Saharan, 588-592, Sudan, 587-588. *See also* North Africa.

Agincourt (aj′in kōrt′), 419, *m. 413, Ref. M. 8*

Agra (a′grə), 574

Agriculture: beginning of, 21-22, 26, 28; in China, 76, 78; in Egypt, 37; in Greece, 98; of Incas, 602-603; in India, 62, 171; under manorial system, 332-338; Mayan, 597; in Muslim empire, 261; plow in, 28; in Roman empire, 135, 144; advances in medieval Europe, 374-376; in Sassanid empire, 221; Spanish innovations in New World, 626-627

Ahimsa, 172

Ahriman (ä′ri mən), 55

Ahura Mazda (ä′hù rə maz′də), 55, 222

Ainu (ī′nü), 301

Aix-la-Chapelle (āks′ lä shä pel′), 324, 325, 347, *m. 324. See also* Aachen.

Ajanta caves (ùj un′tù), 278, *m. 279*

Akbar (ak′bär), 573-575

Akhenaton (ä′ke nä′tən), 39, 43, 46

Akhetaton, 39, *m. 39, Ref. M. 2*

hat, āge, cāre, fär; let, ēqual, tėrm; it, īce; hot, ōpen, ôrder, oil, out; cup, pút, rüle, ūse; ch, child; ng, long; th, thin; ᴛʜ, then; zh, measure; ə represents *a* in *a*bout, *e* in tak*e*n, *i* in penc*i*l, *o* in lem*o*n, *u* in circ*u*s.

hat, āge, cāre, fär; let, ēqual, tėrm; it, īce; hot, ōpen, ôrder, oil, out; cup, pút, rüle, ūse; ch, child; ng, long; th, thin; ᴛʜ, then; zh, measure; ə represents *a* in *a*bout, *e* in tak*e*n, *i* in penc*i*l, *o* in lem*o*n, *u* in circ*u*s.

hat, āge, cāre, fär; let, ēqual, tèrm; it, īce; hot, ōpen, ôrder, oil, out; cup, put, rüle, ūse; ch, child; ng, long; th, thin; тн, then; zh, measure; ə represents *a* in about, *e* in taken, *i* in pencil, *o* in lemon, *u* in circus.

hat, āge, cãre, fär; let, ēqual, tèrm; it, īce; hot, ōpen, ôrder, oil, out; cup, pút, rüle, ūse; ch, child; ng, long; th, thin; ᵺ, then; zh, measure; ə represents *a* in *a*bout, *e* in tak*e*n, *i* in penc*i*l, *o* in lem*o*n, *u* in circ*u*s.

hat, āge, cãre, fär; let, ēqual, tèrm; it, īce; hot, ōpen, ôrder, oil, out; cup, pùt, rüle, ūse; ch, child; ng, long; th, thin; ᴛʜ, then; zh, measure; ə represents *a* in *a*bout, *e* in tak*e*n, *i* in penc*i*l, *o* in lem*o*n, *u* in circ*u*s.

hat, āge, cãre, fär; let, ēqual, tėrm; it, īce; hot, ōpen, ôrder, oil, out; cup, pút, rüle, ūse; ch, child; ng, long; th, thin; ᴛʜ, then; zh, measure; ə represents *a* in about, *e* in taken, *i* in pencil, *o* in lemon, *u* in circus.

hat, āge, cāre, fär; let, ēqual, tèrm; it, īce; hot, ōpen, ôrder, oil, out; cup, pút, rüle, ūse; ch, child; ng, long; th, thin; ᴛʜ, then; zh, measure; ə represents *a* in *a*bout, *e* in tak*e*n, *i* in penc*i*l, *o* in lem*o*n, *u* in circ*u*s.

hat, āge, cãre, fär; let, ēqual, tèrm; it, īce; hot, ōpen, ôrder, oil, out; cup, pu̇t, rüle, ūse; ch, child; ng, long; th, thin; ᴛʜ, then; zh, measure; ə represents *a* in *a*bout, *e* in tak*e*n, *i* in penc*i*l, *o* in lem*o*n, *u* in circ*u*s.

---

hat, āge, cāre, fär; let, equal, tèrm; it, īce; hot, ōpen, ôrder, oil, out; cup, pùt, rüle, ūse; ch, child; ng, long; th, thin; ᴛʜ, then; zh, measure; ə represents *a* in *a*bout, *e* in tak*e*n, *i* in penc*i*l, *o* in lem*o*n, *u* in circ*u*s.

The Reference Maps

To understand man's experiences, knowledge of his planetary environment is essential—his activities must be viewed in space-time relationships. These reference maps, showing key areas at significant periods, include basic physical features because these affect man's attempts to control his environment and his fellow man.

Map 1: Stone Age Environments. Some 99 per cent of mankind's history was lived in Stone Age environments depicted in this map. Major prehuman and human fossil sites are located in Africa, whence *Homo* migrated into Europe as well as across Eurasia. For millennia the fourth glaciation set severe boundaries on the movements of Paleolithic man in Europe, but its retreat enabled him to extend his hunting grounds gradually into the higher latitudes. The transition from food-gathering to farming occurred in well-watered sites such as Jericho in the Great Rift Valley of the Jordan, and again at Jarmo in uplands to the east of the Tigris. Food-gatherers also migrated across what is now the Bering Strait and penetrated the length of the Western Hemisphere.

Map 2: The Ancient Near East and Greece. The breakthrough from Neolithic barbarism to civilization, i.e., to societies sufficiently complex to permit the emergence of urban centers, occurred in two important river basins, the Tigris-Euphrates and the Nile, linked by a Fertile Crescent with minimal natural obstacles to impede the movement of peoples and goods. Meanwhile, improvements in maritime technology permitted the emergence of a splendid Aegean civilization with centers at Knossos in Crete, Mycenae and Pylos on the Greek mainland, and Troy in northwest Asia Minor. Civilization's center of gravity shifted progressively northward across the eastern basin of the Mediterranean, culminating in Hellas with its sea-oriented city-states: Corinth, Thebes, and, above all, Athens.

Map 3: Greek and Phoenician Colonization. Continued advances in maritime technology enabled the Greek city-states to master the eastern Mediterranean and Black seas and establish colonies over a wide area. Meanwhile, the Phoenicians carried their mercantile ventures along the North African coast, founding settlements that included Carthage in the western basin of the Mediterranean, a city which ultimately waged a fight to the death with Rome (see Map 4). The Romans also had to come to terms with the Greek colonies in southern Italy and Sicily, and with the Etruscans, whose culture dominated central and northern Italy. As we examine this map, we can better understand the importance of the Mediterranean. What the Tigris-Euphrates had been to the Babylonians, and the Nile to the Egyptians, the Mediterranean became to the Greeks, the Phoenicians, and eventually to the Romans—namely, the "middle of the earth."

Map 4: The Roman Empire c. 117 A.D. Here we see the importance of physical features in the creation of the Roman world-state. From its east-west maritime axis, it stretched into the hinterland. Roman expansion followed a logical sequence. Beginning with the conquest of Italy and Sicily, Rome then annexed the Mediterranean's western basin as a result of the Punic Wars with Carthage. Subsequent intrusion into the eastern basin made Rome mistress of the Hellenistic world. In the first century B.C. Rome consolidated control in Asia Minor, conquered transalpine Gaul, annexed Egypt, Numidia, and Cyrenaica. The territorial domain was completed later by the acquisition of Mauretania, Dacia, Armenia, and Mesopotamia. Note the role played by rivers, mountains, and deserts in providing natural frontiers for the Roman imperium, linked by the greatest communications network then devised. When the empire declined, it polarized into two segments, administered by Rome and New Rome (built on the site of former Byzantium).

Map 5: The Ancient East. Here we encounter two other major fluvial societies, centering on the Indus-Gangetic and Huang Ho drainage basins. The remarkable longevity of Indian and Chinese societies owed much to physical factors inhibiting alien intrusion. The Indian triangle was protected by the Indian Ocean and the Himalayas—though invasion did occur through western passes. As for China, the obstacles posed by the Pacific Ocean, the Taklamakan and Gobi deserts, and a series of mountain ranges effectively limited entrance into the Huang Ho valley. During the era under examination, we find three great empires: the Han in China, the Mauryan in India, and the Parthian in western Asia. They were contemporary with Rome at its zenith, and this is the period when East met West, with commercial and cultural ties spanning the far-flung Eurasian land mass and the sea lanes of the Indian Ocean.

Map 6: Africa 700-1500 A.D. The cultural evolution of Africa owes much to two physical features—the Sahara Desert and the Great Rift Valley. Northwest Africa is largely oriented to the Mediterranean, while peoples east of the Great Rift Valley—which extends from Palestine's Jordan Valley south to Lake Nyasa—trade along the Red Sea and Indian Ocean. Sub-Saharan Africa is drained by the Niger, Congo, Zambesi, and Limpopo rivers. The map depicts the major cultures of the area and the various empires that arose during the millennium under review, as well as trade routes across the Sahara, over which caravans carried Islamic proselytizers, ivory, slaves, and the wares of the market place and mind alike.

Map 7: The Mongol Empire 1200-1350. One of the most spectacular phenomena of medieval history is the emergence of the Mongols and their rapid conquest of vast areas of Eurasia. A nomadic people eking out subsistence in drought-stricken steppe country, they united under brilliant warriors to pillage Baghdad in 1258 and to create empires in India and China. The map demarcates the Khanates and other political divisions of the Mongol empire, as well as the routes taken by Marco Polo.

Map 8: Medieval France, Spain, and the British Isles 1328. Here we can see the emerging outlines of the national state system in western Europe. Thus, in 1328, Scotland was recognized as independent. Meanwhile, ambitious French kings enlarged their domain from the Ile de France southward to the Mediterranean. The Holy Roman Empire and the Iberian peninsula were both fragmented, but in the latter the Christian kingdoms were girding to clear the peninsula of Moors still entrenched in Granada. Important economic areas include the Lowland countries with their textile-manufacturing towns; Champagne, renowned for its fairs; and the thriving commercial centers of Narbonne and Marseilles in southern France.

Map 9: The New World. Columbus made landfall first on a small West Indian island; before long, the Spaniards had fanned out in the Caribbean. In 1519 Cortés led an expedition to Mexico, thereby inaugurating European settlement that was to spread the length and breadth of two continents. Spanish conquistadors carved out a great empire extending from the middle latitudes of North America to Tierra del Fuego. Meanwhile, Portugal acquired Brazil, and the English, French, and Dutch proved no less ambitious. Thanks to Cabot, Cartier, Champlain, and Hudson, they obtained possessions in the higher latitudes of eastern North America and islands in the Caribbean. In both North and South America a number of major cities were established before 1650.

Map 10: Europe 1648. The Thirty Years' War ended in 1648 with the triumph of the national state which acknowledged no authority higher than itself. This map shows the further territorial consolidation of the national state system (as compared with Map 8). Scotland and England are now one; the Iberian peninsula is delimited between Spain and Portugal; France has acquired bishoprics in Lorraine and a foothold in Alsace. Switzerland, the three Scandinavian countries, Poland, and Russia have also emerged, but Germany and Italy still remain fragmented.

Map 11: European Empires c. 1700. This map has much to tell us. Maritime European powers tended to acquire lands in the New World in a spatial relationship similar to their own in Europe. Thus Denmark obtained Iceland and Greenland; England, Holland, and France competed for possessions north of the Rio Grande; while Spain and Portugal staked their respective claims in more southerly latitudes. We can clearly see the contrasting depths of European penetration of the New and Old Worlds. In North and South America the conquest was so complete that European civilization was transplanted *in toto*. But in sub-Saharan Africa as well as South and East Asia, where the Europeans remained outnumbered, they never replaced indigenous culture patterns.

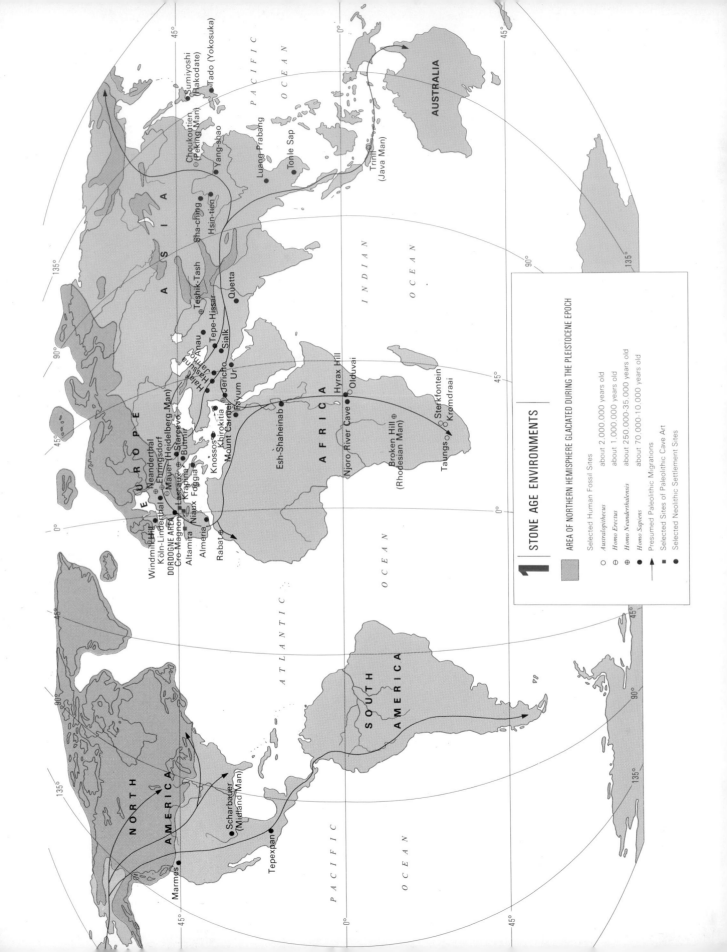

STONE AGE ENVIRONMENTS

AREA OF NORTHERN HEMISPHERE GLACIATED DURING THE PLEISTOCENE EPOCH

Selected Human Fossil Sites

○ *Australopithecus*   about 2,000,000 years old
⊖ *Homo Erectus*   about 1,000,000 years old
⊕ *Homo Neanderthalensis*   about 250,000–35,000 years old
● *Homo Sapiens*   about 70,000–10,000 years old

▲ Presumed Paleolithic Migrations

▪▪ Selected Sites of Paleolithic Cave Art

● Selected Neolithic Settlement Sites

AUSTRALIA

PACIFIC OCEAN

INDIAN OCEAN

ATLANTIC OCEAN

NORTH AMERICA

SOUTH AMERICA

EUROPE

ASIA

AFRICA

Choukoutien (Peking Man)
Sumiyoshi (Hakodate)
Tado (Yokosuka)
Yang-shao
Luang-Prabang
Tonle Sap
Trinil (Java Man)
Sha-ching
Hsin-tien
Teshik-Tash
Quetta
Tepe-Hissar
Anau
Sialk
Ur
Jericho
Fayum
Mount Carmel
Khirokitia
Knossos
Haua
Hassuna
Jarmo
Altamira
Niaux Font-de-Gaume
Lascaux
Starcevo
Krapina
La Ferrassie
Bruniquel
Cro-Magnon
DORDOGNE AREA
Neanderthal
Mauer (Heidelberg-Man)
Ehringsdorf
Köln-Lindenthal
Windmill Hill
Almeria
Rabat
Esh-Shaheinab
Njoro River Cave
Olduvai
Hyrax Hill
Broken Hill (Rhodesian Man)
Sterkfontein
Kromdraai
Taungs

Marmes
Scharbauer (Midland Man)
Tepexpan

BLACK SEA

CASPIAN SEA

BALKAN MTS.

Danube River

CAUCASUS MOUNTAINS

Kura River

Lake Sevan

PONTIC MOUNTAINS

Troy

PHRYGIA
Pergamum

AEGEAN SEA

Delphi
Chaeronea
Thebes
Corinth
Athens
Mycenae

Pylos

Hermus R.

Sardis
LYDIA

Hattusas

Halys River

Lake Tuz

Tyana

TAURUS MTS.

Lake Van

Lake Urmia

Nineveh

Jarmo

Ecbatana

ZAGROS MTS.

Aleppo

Euphrates River

Tigris River

Ialysus

RHODES

Knossos

CRETE

Salamis

CYPRUS

Orontes R.

Hamath

Kadesh

Sidon
Tyre

Damascus

SYRIAN DESERT

MESOPOTAMIA

Babylon
Nippur
Erech
Ur

Lagash
Larsa
Eridu

Susa

MEDITERRANEAN SEA

Jericho

Jerusalem

Dead Sea

Present day River
Present day Coast Line

PERSIAN GULF

LIBYAN DESERT

LOWER EGYPT
Gizeh

Memphis

SAHARA

Akhetaton

Nile River

Thebes

UPPER

EGYPT

Syene
(Aswan)

1st Cataract

ARABIAN PENINSULA

RED SEA

2nd Cataract

3rd Cataract

NUBIA

4th Cataract

Napata

5th Cataract

6th Cataract

White Nile River

Blue Nile River

2 THE ANCIENT NEAR EAST AND GREECE

- Hammurabi's Empire c.1750 B.C.
- Egyptian Empire c.1450 B.C.
- Mycenaean Greece c.1300 B.C.
- Hittite Empire c. 1300 B.C.

0   100   200
Scale in Miles

Prepared by
Rand McNally & Co., Chicago

ATLANTIC

OCEAN

BAY

OF

BISCAY

CASSITERIDES
(SCILLY IS.)

ISLE OF
WIGHT

ENGLISH

CHANNEL

Meuse R.

Rhine R.

Elbe R.

Seine R.

Loire R.

G
R
A
U
L

Saône R.

Danube

CANTABRIAN MTS.

PYRENEES

Dordogne R.

MASSIF
CENTRAL

Garonne R.

Rhone R.

ALPS

Po R.

Mantua

Felsina

ETRUSCANS

A
P
E
N
N
I

Douro R.

Ebro R.

Tagus R.

I
B
E
R
I
A

Agathe

Rhode

Emporium

Massilia
(Marseilles)

Athenopolis

Olbia

Nicaea

Antipolis

Arretium

Tarquinii

Rome

Cumae

Neap
(Nap

Guadiana R.

SIERRA MORENA

Guadalquivir R.

Saguntum

Hemerscopium

Alonae

BALEARIC IS.

Mago

CORSICA

Almeria

Olbia

SARDINIA

Carales

TYRRHENIAN

SEA

SIERRA NEVADA

Gades
(Cádiz)

Malaca

Abdera

M
E
D
I
T
E
R
R
A
N

Panormus

Him

Lilybaeum

SICILY

Selinus

Acragas

Gel

Camar

Tingis

Zilis

Strait of Gibraltar

Melilla

Icosium

Hippo Regius

NUMIDIA

Medjerda R.

Hippo
Diarrhytus

Utica

Carthage

Hadrumetum

Thapsus

Moulouya R.

ATLAS

Chelif R.

MOUNTAINS

A
N

E

MAI

Tacape

Sabrata

Lepti

SAHARA

| 3 | GREEK AND PHOENICIAN SETTLEMENT IN THE MEDITERRANEAN 700-550 B.C. |

Greece and Primary Greek Settlements

Greek Colonies

Phoenicia

Phoenician Colonies

– – – Principal Trade Routes

0   100   200
Scale in Miles

ATLANTIC

OCEAN

50°

30°

20°

10°

0°

10°

IRELAND

IRISH
SEA

NORTH
SEA

BALTIC

Antoninus' Wall
(C. 140 A.D.)

Hadrian's Wall
(C. 122 A.D.)

PENNINES

York

Chester

Lincoln

BRITAIN

Colchester

Thames R.

Bath

London

ENGLISH CHANNEL

GERMANIA

Elbe

Oder

River

River

SUDETES

Cologne

Rhine

BELGICA

Seine

River

Mainz

River

Meuse

Paris

River

River

GAUL

Loire

Saône R.

Danube

River

Rhône

Lyons

ALPS

CISALPINE GAUL

Po

River

BAY OF
BISCAY

Bordeaux

Garonne R.

CENTRAL
MASSIF

Genoa

Ravenna

ADRIATIC

CANTABRIAN MTS.

PYRENEES

Marseilles

Pisa

APENNINES

Salonae

SEA

Douro

River

Ebro

Segovia

River

SPAIN

CORSICA

ITALY

Rome

Tagus

River

Toledo

Saguntum

Naples

Guadiana

River

Valencia

SARDINIA

Pompeii

SIERRA   MORENA

Cordova

BALEARIC
ISLANDS

TYRRHENIAN
SEA

Guadalquivir   R.

Cádiz

Strait of Gibraltar

SIERRA NEVADA

New
Carthage

M E D I T E R R

Messina

Tangier

Pillars of Hercules

SICILY

Syracuse

MADEIRA
ISLANDS

MAURETANIA

ATLAS

MOUNTAINS

Medjerda R.

Utica

Carthage

A N E A N

MALTA

Moulouya

R.

Chélif R.

30°

CANARY
ISLANDS

ATLAS

Chott
Djerid

NUMIDIA

Oea

Leptis
Magna

GRAND ERG   OCCIDENTAL

40°

20°

30°

4 | THE ROMAN EMPIRE
C. 117 A.D.

GRAND ERG   ORIENTAL

0   100   200   300

Scale in Miles

20°

AHAGGAR

MOUNTAINS

SAHARA

10°

SEA

Lake
Ladoga

HUNS

Western Dvina River

GOTHS

Volga   River   Kama   River

Bug   River

Vistula   R.

Dnieper   River

Dniester   River

SARMATIA

URAL   MOUNTAINS

Tobol R.

Ural   River

Volga   River

CARPATHIANS

Olbia

SEA OF
AZOV

ARAL
SEA

Apulum

TRANSYLVANIAN ALPS

River

DACIA

BALKAN MTS.

BLACK   SEA

CAUCASUS   MOUNTAINS

Kura   River

CASPIAN   SEA

Naissus

Sinope

Trapezus

Aras   River

Lake
Sevan

Artaxata

ELBURZ   MTS.

THRACE

PONTIC MOUNTAINS

ARMENIA

MACEDONIA

Byzantium

PONTUS

Lake
Van

Lake
Urmia

Daryācheh-ye
Namak

Sea of
Marmara

River

Kizil

ASSYRIA

PLATEAU

PINDUS MTS.

Pergamum

ASIA

Lake
Tuz

MESOPOTAMIA

Tigris

ZAGROS

PARTHIAN EMPIRE

OF   IRAN

EPIRUS

AEGEAN SEA

Ephesus

Ecbatana

Thebes

Tarsus

Euphrates

River

Ctesiphon

MTS.

Corinth

Athens

CILICIA

Sparta

RHODES

CYPRUS

Palmyra

Dura
Europos

River

PERSIAN GULF

Knossos

SYRIA

CRETE

Sidon

Damascus

Tyre

S   E   A

PALESTINE

Jerusalem

Dead
Sea

Cyrene

Alexandria

CYRENAICA

Memphis

ARABIA

EGYPT

LIBYAN

Nile

DESERT

Thebes

River

RED

Berenice

Syene

SEA

Prepared by
Rand McNally & Co., Chicago

OCEAN

PACIFIC

SEA OF JAPAN

EAST CHINA SEA

PHILIPPINE SEA

SOUTH CHINA SEA

SIKHOTE ALIN RANGE

KHINGAN MTS.

Amur River

YABLONOVY RANGE

Great KHINGAN MTS.

Lena River

GOBI DESERT

Great Wall

ORDOS DESERT

Yen

Taiyuan

Chinan

Tai Mtn.

LUNG SHAN

Lo-yang

YANG SHAO

Yellow (Huang) R.

Wu

Yangtze River

Han R.

NAN LING

Hsi River (West R.)

Yuan

Panyu

Wei R. Ch'ang-an

Pa

Shu

Mekong River

Angara River

Lake Baikal

SAYAN MOUNTAINS

Yenisey River

River

ALTAI MOUNTAINS

TIEN SHAN

Tarim River

Loulan

TAKLAMAKAN DESERT

Kokonor

ALTYN TAGH

PLATEAU OF TIBET

Salween River

Irrawaddy River

BAY OF BENGAL

Ob River

Irtysh River

Ishim River

Lake Balkash

Kashgar

Yarkand

Khotan

KUNLUN MOUNTAINS

Brahmaputra River

Mt. Everest

Champa

H I M A L A Y A S

URAL MTS.

KIRGIZ STEPPE

ARAL SEA

Syr Darya (Jaxartes R.)

PAMIRS

Samarkand

Tashkurgan

HINDU KUSH

GANDHARA

Taxila

Indus River

Harappa

Indraprastha

Ganges R.

Mathura

KOSALA

Pataliputra

MAGADHA

Narbada R.

ANDHRA

KALINGA

EASTERN GHATS

Godavari R.

Kistna R.

WESTERN GHATS

THAR DESERT

Mohenjo-Daro

Amu Darya (Oxus R.)

Bactria

BACTRIA

Helmund R.

SEISTAN DEPRESSION

PARTHIA

Caspian Sea

ELBURZ MTS.

PERSIA

Persepolis

Ecbatana

Susa

Persian Gulf

ARABIAN SEA

INDIAN OCEAN

Volga River

Don R.

Ural River

CAUCASUS MTS.

BLACK SEA

Aras River

Tigris River

Khorsabad

Ctesiphon

Seleucia

Babylon

MESOPOTAMIA

Euphrates R.

Present-day Coast Line

ARABIAN PENINSULA

Antioch

Damascus

Jerusalem

MEDITERRANEAN SEA

RED SEA

Prepared by
Rand McNally & Co., Chicago

5 THE ANCIENT EAST

Maurya Empire 320 B.C.–190 B.C.

Han Empire 200 B.C.–200 A.D.

Parthian Empire 200 B.C.–226 A.D.

Scale in Miles

0   200   400   600

ATLANTIC
OCEAN

30°   20°   10°   0°   10°   20°   30°   40°   50°   60°   70°

London

Paris

EUROPE

Vienna

Belgrade

Rhine R.

Danube R.

Dnieper R.

Don R.

Volga R.

Caucasus Mts.

BLACK SEA

ALPS

Madrid

Rome

Constantinople

Athens

CRETE

CYPRUS

Damascus

Baghdad

Baku

CASPIAN SEA

Aral Sea

Syr Darya (Jaxartes R.)

Amu Darya (Oxus R.)

Lisbon

CORSICA

SARDINIA

SICILY

MEDITERRANEAN   SEA

ASIA

ATLAS   MTS

Tigris R.

Euphrates R.

Persian Gulf

ARABIAN

MADEIRA IS.

Ceuta

Fez

Algiers

Tunis

Tripoli

Barqa

Cairo

MAMLUK EMPIRE 1260–1340

AGADIR

Sijilmasa

Ghadames

CANARY IS.

Adrar

SAHARA

Gat

Aujila

LIBYAN DESERT

KUFRA OASES

Kharga

RED SEA

Mecca

PENINSULA

Sebka D'idjil

GHANA 4th–11th Centuries

Taudeni

Tamanrasset

Bilma

DONGOLA

NUBIA

FUNG

Nile R.

Atbara R.

Axum

Tichitt

SONGHAI 15th–16th Centuries

Timbuctu

Agadès

KANEM

Sennar

ETHIOPIA

L. Tana

TEKRUR

Walata

Gao

S   U   D   A   N

L. Chad

N'djimi

DARFUR

White Nile R.

Blue Nile R.

AMHARA

PLATEAU

ADAL

Senegal R.

Ghana

YATENGA

Sokoto

BORNU

Abeshèr

El Fasher

Gambia R.

Mali

Kano

HAUSA BOKWOI STATES

Gulf of Aden

MALI 13th–Mid 15th Centuries

MOSSI

Niger R.

DAGOMBA

NUPE

Benue R.

KWARARAFA

NILOTES

L. Rudolf

BUNYORO-KITARA 13th–17th Centuries

Mogadishu

YORUBA

Ife

BENIN

TERNANDO POO

GULF OF GUINEA

PRINCIPE

SÃO TOMÉ

Bomu R.

CONGO BASIN

Uell R.

L. Albert

MT. KENYA

Lake Victoria

MT. KILIMANJARO

Ubangi R.

Malindi

Mombasa

ZANZIBAR

ANNOBON

Congo R.

Kasai R.

Kwango R.

MT. KILIMANJARO

L. Tanganyika

6 | AFRICA 700-1500 A.D.

→ Caravan Routes

0   200   400   600   800

Scale in Miles

KONGO 15th–16th Centuries

LUNDA 16th–17th Centuries

LUBA 15th–16th Centuries

Ruvuma R.

L. Nyasa

COMORO IS.

Mozambique

Zambezi R.

MONOMOTAPA

Zimbabwe

Sofala

MOZAMBIQUE CHANNEL

MADAGASCAR

ATLANTIC

OCEAN

NAMIB DESERT

KALAHARI DESERT

Orange R.

DRAKENSBERG MTS

CAPE OF GOOD HOPE

INDIAN

OCEAN

40°   30°   20°   10°   0°   10°   20°   30°

BERING
SEA

CENTRAL

SIBERIA

SIBERIAN

UPLANDS

KAMCHATKA

PENINSULA

SAYAN MTS.

Lake Baikal

EMPIRE OF

THE GREAT

SEA OF
OKHOTSK

KOLYMA MTS.

STANOVOY MTS.

GREATER KHINGAN MTS.

SIKHOTE-ALIN RANGE

SAKHALIN

KURIL IS.

Karakorum

THE G R E A T

GOBI DESERT

(KUBLAI)

SEA OF
JAPAN

J A P A N

Kamakura

Kyoto

Suchow

Great Wall

Taiyuan

Shangtu

Khanbaligh
(Peking)

Kaosong

KOREA

Kamakura

CHIN EMPIRE

Sian

Huang Ho

Kaifeng

(CATHAY)

YELLOW
SEA

Chingkiang

Wuchang

Kinsay

KHAN

Chengtu

Yangtze

SOUTHERN SUNG

EAST CHINA SEA

RYUZYU IS.

ASSAM

Tali

EMPIRE

Hsi R.

Foochow

NAN CHAO

Salween

Zaitun

Canton

FORMOSA

Ava
Pagan

BURMA

TONKIN

Hanoi

ANNAM

HAINAN

SOUTH
CHINA

LUZON

PHILIPPINE

CHIANGMAI

Mekong

CHAMPA

SEA

THAI EMPIRE

Angkor

KHMER EMPIRE
(CAMBODIA)

To Java and Sumatra

MINDANAO

ISLANDS

7 THE MONGOL EMPIRE 1200-1350

Empire of the Great (Kublai) Khan

Jagatai Empire

Ilkhan (Hulagu) Empire

Batu (Kipchak) Empire of the Golden Horde

Areas Under Mongol Suzerainty

Primary Mongol Invasion Routes

Mongol Raids Not Resulting in Complete Conquest

Route of Marco Polo

0   100   200   300   400   500
Scale in Miles

8 — MEDIEVAL FRANCE, SPAIN, AND THE BRITISH ISLES 1328

Legend:
- England and possessions
- France
- Kingdom of Navarre
- Kingdom of Castile and Leon and dependencies
- Kingdom of Aragon and dependencies
- Kingdom of Granada
- Portugal

Scale in Miles: 0 — 100 — 200

Atlantic Ocean

SCOTLAND — Aberdeen, Glasgow, Edinburgh, Durham

IRELAND — Galway, Dublin, Limerick, *Shannon R.*, Wexford, Cork, St. David's

ENGLAND — York, Lincoln, Chester, *Severn R.*, London, *Thames River*, Bath, Winchester, Hastings

WALES

North Sea

NORWAY, SWEDEN, DENMARK — Copenhagen

Brandenburg, *Elbe River*, *Weser River*, Haarlem, Amsterdam, Rotterdam

Rhine River

FLANDERS — Bruges, Ghent, Louvain, Ypres, Brussels, Lille, Cateau-Cambrésis, Agincourt, Crécy, Cambrai, *Meuse R.*, ARDENNES, LUXEMBOURG, Rocroy, Vervins, Soissons, Verdun

HOLY ROMAN EMPIRE

Amiens, Rouen, Compiègne, Paris, *Seine R.*, CHAMPAGNE, LORRAINE, Toul, ALSACE, *Danube River*

NORMANDY, Chartres, Clairvaux, Luxeuil, *Rhine River*

BRITTANY — Brest, Mont St. Michel, Champeaux, Orléans, Molesme, Vézelay, *Saône R.*

ANJOU, Carnac, *Loire R.*, Tours, BURGUNDY, Cluny, SWITZERLAND, ALPS

POITOU, FRANCE, Poitiers, Lyons, VENICE, *Po River*

English Channel

Bay of Biscay

Cognac, AQUITAINE, *CENTRAL MASSIF*, *Rhône R.*, PAPAL STATES

Bordeaux, *Dordogne*, *Garonne River*, THE CORNICHE

GASCONY, Nîmes, Toulouse, Marseilles, Toulon, CORSICA

Carcassonne, Narbonne, Perpignan, SARDINIA, Cagliari

Santiago de Compostela, ASTURIAS, Oviedo, Cave of Covadonga, Roncesvalles Pass, KINGDOM OF NAVARRE, PYRENEES

Miño R., CANTABRIAN MTS., *Ebro R.*, León, Saragossa, KINGDOM OF ARAGON, Barcelona

Porto, *Douro River*, Salamanca, Segovia, KINGDOM OF ARAGON

PORTUGAL, KINGDOM OF, Madrid, Toledo, Palma, BALEARIC ISLANDS

Lisbon, *Tagus River*, CASTILE AND, Valencia

Guadiana River, LEON, *Segura R.*

Cordova, *Guadalquivir River*, Granada, Seville, KINGDOM OF GRANADA

Cádiz, Las Navas de Tolosa

Strait of Gibraltar, Pillars of Hercules, Tangier

MEDITERRANEAN SEA

MUSLIM STATES

Prepared by Rand McNally & Co., Chicago

GREENLAND

ICELAND

Baffin
Bay

E S K I M O

Hudson
Bay

N O R T H

A M E R I C A

R O C K Y   M O U N T A I N

Missouri R.

Mississippi R.

Colorado R.

NEWFOUNDLAND

Cartier 1534–1535

Quebec
1608

Montreal
1642

St. Lawrence R.

IROQUOIS

Port Royal *1604*

Plymouth *1620*

New Amsterdam
1614/1623

Jamestown
1607

A T L A N T I C

O C E A N

Santa Fe *1609*
Acoma Pueblo

PUEBLO

Arkansas R.

Rio Grande

De Soto 1539–1542

St. Augustine
1565

1540–1542

Colorado R.

Culican

Monteroy
1600

Gulf of
Mexico

1519

de Leon 1513

Havana
1615/1619

CUBA

Compostela

AZTEC

Mexico City
(Tenochtitlan)
1521

Cortes
1525

MAYA

JAMAICA

HISPANIOLA

PORTO RICO

Guatemala
1524

Leon
1523

Caribbean   Sea

Caracas *1667*

Panama
1540

Balboa
1913

Orinoco R.

Paramaribo *1613*

Cayenne
1626

P A C I F I C

Bogotá
1539

Pizarro

GALAPAGOS IS.

Quito
1534

Orellana 1541–1543

Amazon R.

Belém (Para)
1616

O C E A N

A N D E S

1531–1535

S O U T H

Recife
1563

Lima
1535

INCA

Cuzco
1534

La Paz
1548

São Salvador
(Bahia)
1549

A M E R I C A

Paraná

Valdivia 1540–1552

Rio de Janeiro
1666

Asunción
1537

São Paulo
1532

Santiago
1541

Buenos Aires
1536

Rio de la Plata

M O U N T A I N S

Valdivia
1552

MALVINAS IS.
(FALKLAND IS.)

Strait of Magellan
CAPE HORN

TIERRA del FUEGO

Drake   Passage

9 THE NEW WORLD

0   500   1000
Scale in Miles

EUROPE 1648

URAL MOUNTAINS

Tura R.
Tura R.

Vychegda River

Sukhona River

Northern Dvina R.

KAZAKH

Ural River

Kuma River

Volga River

R U S S I A

Lake Onega

Lake Ladoga

• Moscow

• Novgorod

• Pskov

INGRIA

FINLAND

Gulf of Finland

Gulf of Bothnia

S W E D E N

Stockholm

GOTLAND

Ö L.
Vättern

L. Vänern

N O R W A Y

Oslo

FAEROE IS. (Den.)

SHETLAND IS. (Scot.)

ORKNEY IS.

SCOTLAND

Edinburgh

PENNINES

ENGLAND

London

Bristol

Southampton

Thames R.

English Channel

ULSTER

Dublin

IRELAND

ATLANTIC OCEAN

NORTH SEA

BALTIC SEA

Copenhagen

DENMARK

HOLSTEIN

Hamburg

Bremen

Oldenburg

Osnabrück

Münster

HOLLAND

Amsterdam

Antwerp

Brussels

Spanish NETHERLANDS

Cologne

Rhine

Elbe R.

Weser R.

ESTONIA

LIVONIA

Riga

COURLAND

EAST PRUSSIA

Königsberg

BRANDENBURG

Berlin

Wittenberg

SAXONY

BOHEMIA

Prague

Oder R.

Vistula River

Bug R.

Warsaw

Vilna

LITHUANIA

P O L A N D

Dniester River

Dnieper River

Kiev

Don River

Sea of Azov

BLACK SEA

CASPIAN SEA

CAUCASUS MTS.

Mt. Elbrus

PONTIC MOUNTAINS

Kura R.

Kizil River

PERSIA

L. Urmia

L. Van

L. Sevan

TAURUS MTS.

Tigris River

Euphrates River

A R A B I A

S Y R I A

CYPRUS

Nile Delta

EGYPT

Alexandria

CYRENAICA

Bengasi

MEDITERRANEAN SEA

TRIPOLITANIA

Tripoli

TUNIS

Tunis

Bona (It.)

ALGIERS

ALGIERS

Oran (Sp.)

Melilla (Sp.)

FEZ AND MOROCCO

Fez

Tangier (Sp.)

Strait of Gibraltar

Gibraltar

Cádiz

Seville

Córdoba

Granada

SIERRA MORENA MTS.

Guadalquivir R.

Guadiana R.

Madrid

S P A I N

P O R T U G A L

Lisbon

Oviedo

Douro R.

Tagus R.

Ebro River

Saragossa

PYRENEES

BALEARIC ISLANDS

Barcelona

Toulouse

Marseilles

Garonne R.

Bordeaux

BAY OF BISCAY

Nantes

Brest

F R A N C E

Paris

Orléans

Seine

Loire R.

Rhône River

Saône

CENTRAL MASSIF

Lyon

AVIGNON

ORANGE

Mont Blanc

SWITZERLAND

Basel

Zürich

Geneva

METZ

TOUL

VERDUN

Nancy

Strasbourg

Worms

Stuttgart

Augsburg

BAVARIA

Munich

PALATINATE

FRANCHE COMTE

G E R M A N   S T A T E S

Milan

Turin

Genoa

Venice

Po R.

I T A L I A N   S T A T E S

CORSICA

SARDINIA

TYRRHENIAN SEA

Rome

PAPAL STATES

Tiber

APENNINES

Naples

NAPLES

Messina

SICILY

Palermo

MALTA

ADRIATIC SEA

Ragusa

IONIAN SEA

Naval Battle of Lepanto 1571

Venetia

AUSTRIA

Buda

HUNGARY

TRANSYLVANIA

Danube

Bucharest

CARPATHIAN MTS.

BALKAN MTS.

PINDUS MTS.

Salonica

Athens

CRETE (Venice)

RHODES

AEGEAN SEA

Constantinople

Sea of Marmara

Dardanelles

Bosporus

O T T O M A N   E M P I R E

Kattegat

Skagerrak

10 | EUROPE 1648

Austrian Hapsburgs	(dotted pattern)
Spanish Hapsburgs	(dotted pattern)
Holy Roman Empire	—

Anglican	Calvinist	Greek Orthodox
Islamic	Lutheran	Roman Catholic

Scale in Miles
0   100   200   300   400

Prepared by Rand McNally & Co., Chicago

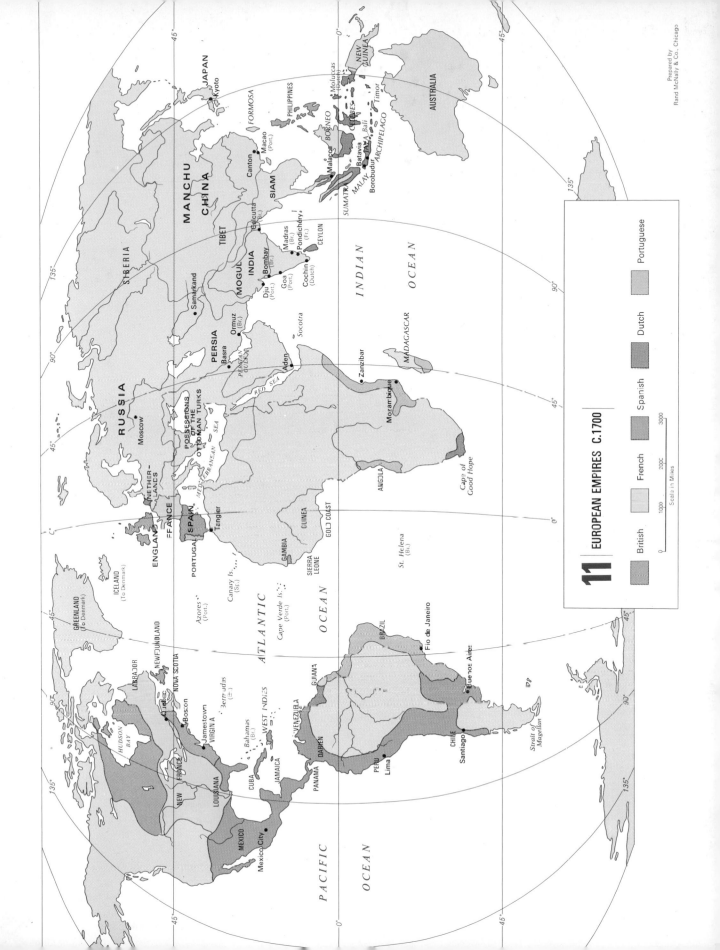

Prepared by
Rand McNally & Co., Chicago

11 | **EUROPEAN EMPIRES C.1700**

British   French   Spanish

Portuguese   Dutch

Scale in Miles
0   1000   2000   3000

JAPAN
Kyoto

MANCHU
CHINA

SIBERIA

RUSSIA
Moscow

Macao
(Port.)
Canton

FORMOSA

SIAM

PHILIPPINES

Moluccas
(Dutch)

NEW
GUINEA

AUSTRALIA

BORNEO

CELEBES

Malacca
MALAY
Batavia
Borobudur
JAVA   Bali
ARCHIPELAGO
Timor

SUMATRA

Calcutta
(Br.)

TIBET

MOGUL
INDIA

Madras
(Br.)
Pondichéry
(Fr.)
Bombay
(Br.)
Goa
(Port.)
Cochin
(Dutch)

CEYLON

Diu
(Port.)

Samarkand

PERSIA
Ormuz
(Br.)
Basra

PERSIAN
GULF

INDIAN   OCEAN

Socotra

Aden

RED SEA

MADAGASCAR

Zanzibar

Mozambique

POSSESSIONS
OF THE
OTTOMAN TURKS

CASPIAN
SEA

MEDITERRANEAN SEA

NETHER-
LANDS

ENGLAND

FRANCE
SPAIN
PORTUGAL

Tangier

Canary Is.
(Sp.)

Azores
(Port.)

Cape Verde Is.
(Port.)

GUINEA

GAMBIA

SIERRA
LEONE

GOLD COAST

ANGOLA

Cap of
Good Hope

St. Helena
(Br.)

ATLANTIC

OCEAN

ICELAND
(To Denmark)

GREENLAND
(To Denmark)

LABRADOR

NEWFOUNDLAND

NOVA SCOTIA
Quebec
Boston
Jamestown
VIRGINIA

HUDSON
BAY

NEW
FRANCE

LOUISIANA

MEXICO
Mexico City

Bermudas
(Br.)

Bahamas

WEST INDIES

CUBA

JAMAICA

PANAMA

VENEZUELA

GUIANA

DARIEN

PERU
Lima

CHILE
Santiago

BRAZIL

Rio de Janeiro

Buenos Aires

Strait of
Magellan

PACIFIC

OCEAN

PACIFIC
OCEAN

2 3 4 5 6 7 8 9 10 11 12 13 14 15 16 17 18 19 20 21 22 23 24 25 RM 74 73 72 71 70